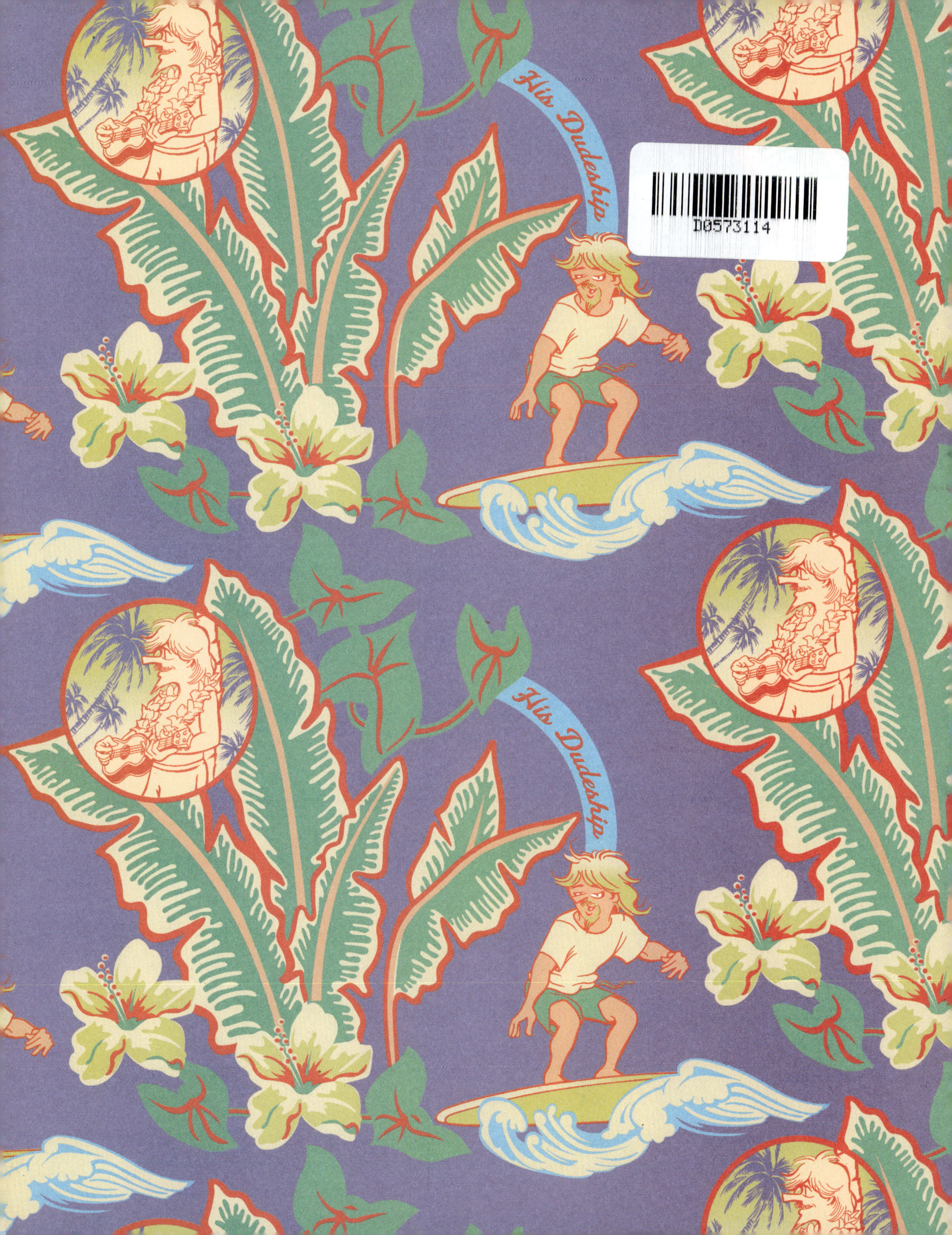
His Dudeship
His Dudeship

DUDE

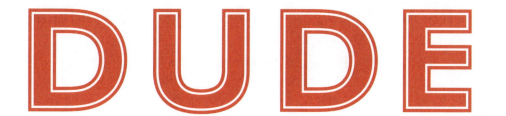

Recent *Doonesbury* Books by G. B. Trudeau

Read My Lips, Make My Day, Eat Quiche and Die!
Give Those Nymphs Some Hooters!
You're Smokin' Now, Mr. Butts!
I'd Go With the Helmet, Ray
Welcome to Club Scud!
What Is It, Tink, Is Pan in Trouble?
Quality Time on Highway 1
Washed Out Bridges and Other Disasters
In Search of Cigarette Holder Man
Doonesbury Nation
Virtual Doonesbury
Planet Doonesbury
Buck Wild Doonesbury
Duke 2000: Whatever It Takes
The Revolt of the English Majors
Peace Out, Dawg!
Got War?
Talk to the Hand

Special Collections

The Doonesbury Chronicles
Doonesbury's Greatest Hits
The People's Doonesbury
Doonesbury Dossier: The Reagan Years
Doonesbury Deluxe: Selected Glances Askance
Recycled Doonesbury: Second Thoughts on a Gilded Age
Action Figure!: The Life and Times of Doonesbury's Uncle Duke
The Portable Doonesbury
Flashbacks: Twenty-Five Years of Doonesbury
The Bundled Doonesbury
The Long Road Home: One Step at a Time

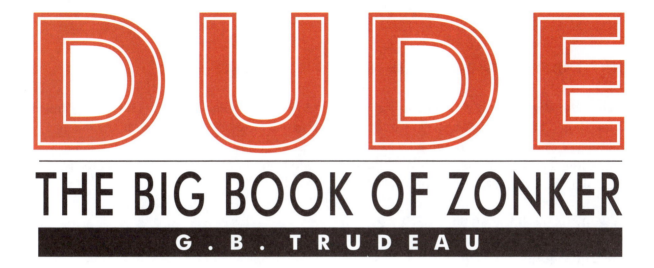

DUDE

THE BIG BOOK OF ZONKER

G.B. TRUDEAU

Andrews McMeel
Publishing

Kansas City

DOONESBURY is distributed internationally by Universal Press Syndicate.

*Dude: **The Big Book of Zonker*** copyright © 2005 by G. B. Trudeau. All rights reserved. Printed in the United States of America. No part of this book may be used or reproduced in any manner whatsoever without written permission except in the case of reprints in the context of reviews. For information, write Andrews McMeel Publishing, an Andrews McMeel Universal company, 4520 Main Street, Kansas City, Missouri 64111.

05 06 07 08 09 BAM 10 9 8 7 6 5 4 3 2 1

ISBN-13: 978-0-7407-5536-1
ISBN-10: 0-7407-5536-6

Library of Congress Control Number: 2005929143

www.andrewsmcmeel.com

DOONESBURY may be viewed on the Internet at www.doonesbury.com and www.ucomics.com.

Give me the splendid silent sun with all his beams full-dazzling.

—Walt Whitman

1

THE PHENOM

Far Freakin' Out, Cap'n!

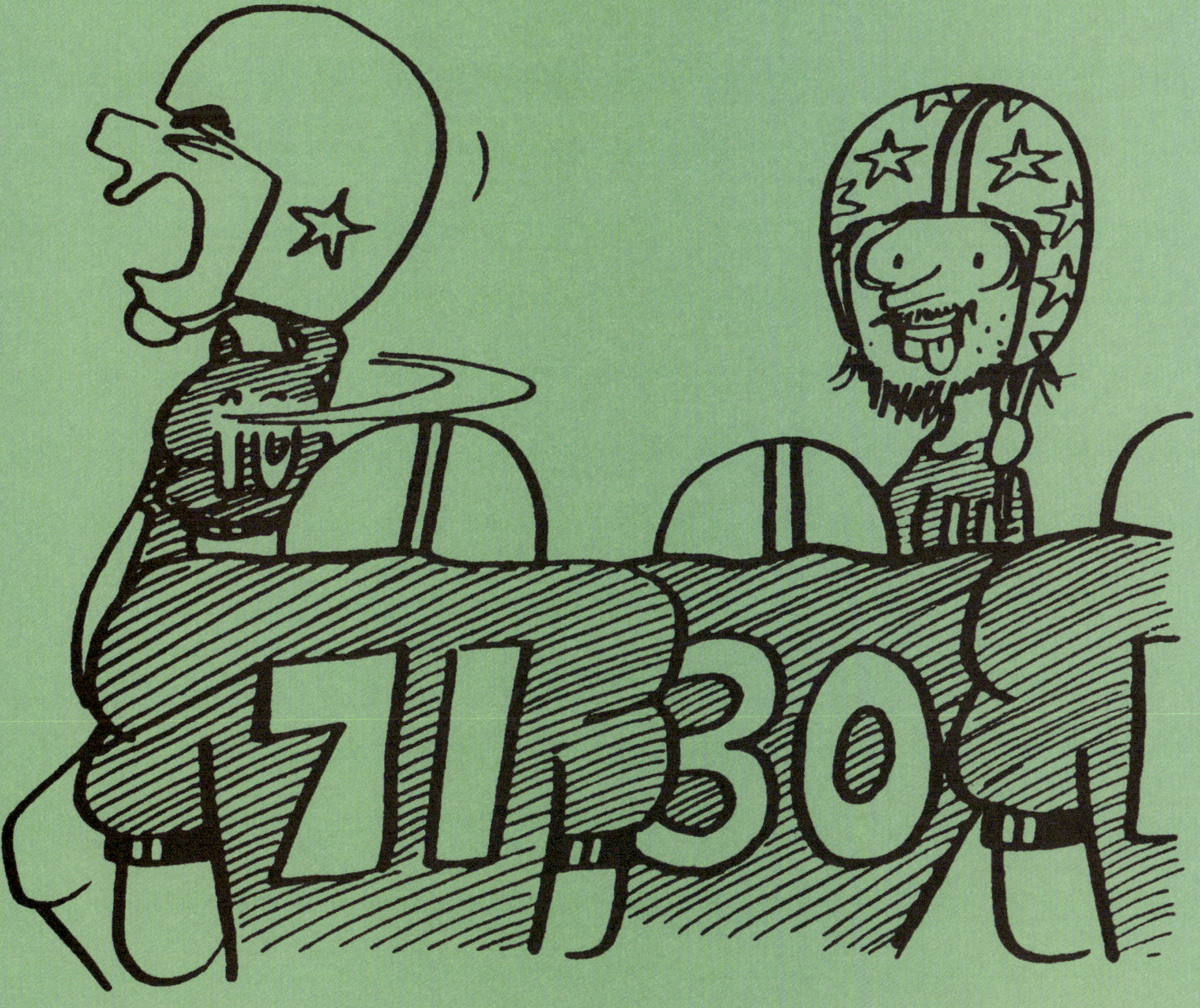

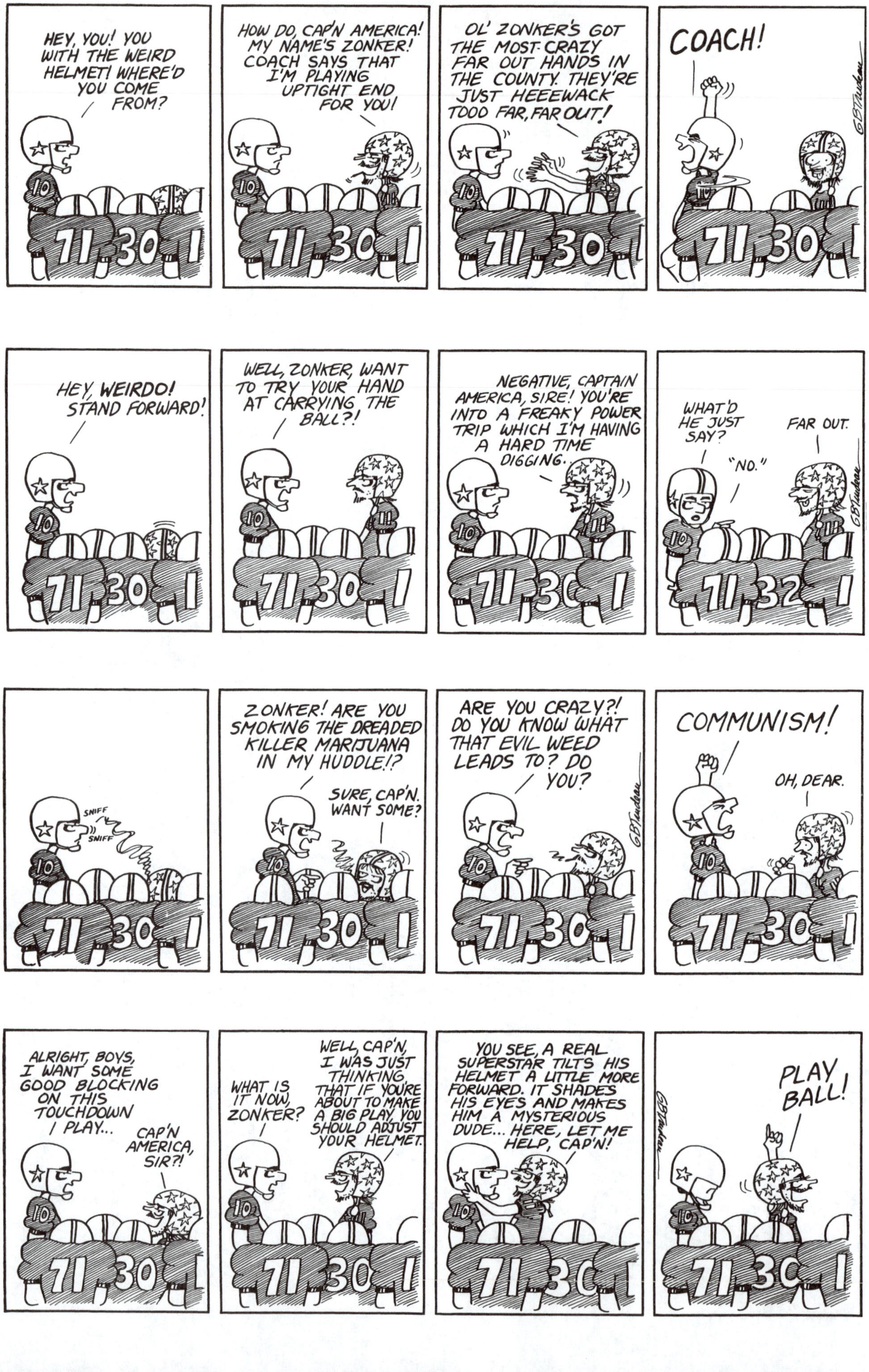
HEY, YOU! YOU WITH THE WEIRD HELMET! WHERE'D YOU COME FROM?
HOW DO, CAP'N AMERICA! MY NAME'S ZONKER! COACH SAYS THAT I'M PLAYING UPTIGHT END FOR YOU!
OL' ZONKER'S GOT THE MOST CRAZY FAR OUT HANDS IN THE COUNTY. THEY'RE JUST HEEEWACK TOOD FAR, FAR OUT!
COACH!
HEY, WEIRDO! STAND FORWARD!
WELL, ZONKER, WANT TO TRY YOUR HAND AT CARRYING THE BALL?!
NEGATIVE, CAPTAIN AMERICA, SIRE! YOU'RE INTO A FREAKY POWER TRIP WHICH I'M HAVING A HARD TIME DIGGING.
WHAT'D HE JUST SAY?
"NO."
FAR OUT.
SNIFF
SNIFF
ZONKER! ARE YOU SMOKING THE DREADED KILLER MARIJUANA IN MY HUDDLE!?
SURE, CAP'N. WANT SOME?
ARE YOU CRAZY?! DO YOU KNOW WHAT THAT EVIL WEED LEADS TO? DO YOU?
COMMUNISM!
OH, DEAR.
ALRIGHT, BOYS, I WANT SOME GOOD BLOCKING ON THIS TOUCHDOWN PLAY...
CAP'N AMERICA, SIR?!
WHAT IS IT NOW, ZONKER?
WELL, CAP'N, I WAS JUST THINKING THAT IF YOU'RE ABOUT TO MAKE A BIG PLAY, YOU SHOULD ADJUST YOUR HELMET.
YOU SEE, A REAL SUPERSTAR TILTS HIS HELMET A LITTLE MORE FORWARD. IT SHADES HIS EYES AND MAKES HIM A MYSTERIOUS DUDE... HERE, LET ME HELP, CAP'N!
PLAY BALL!

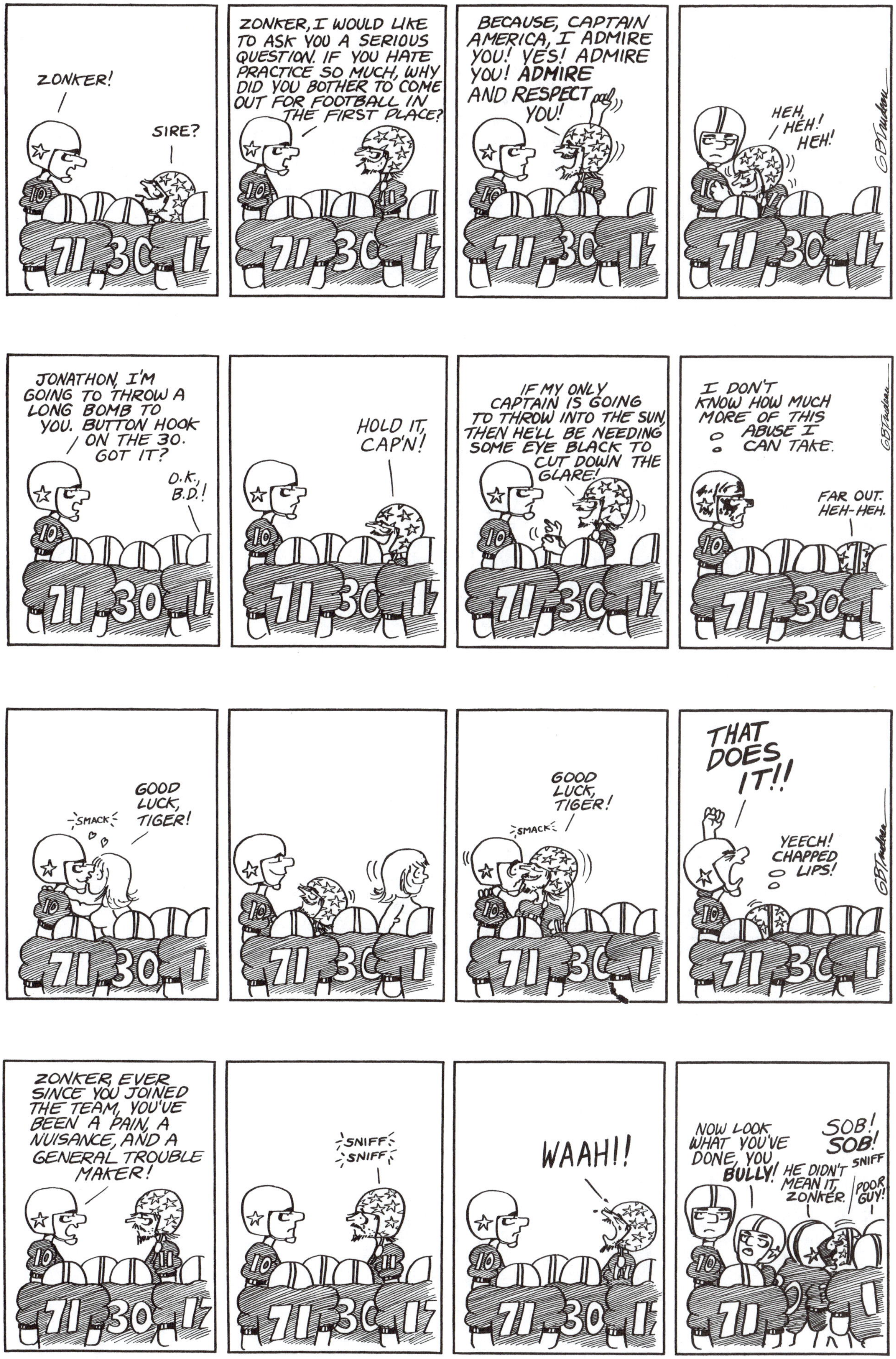
ZONKER!
SIRE?
ZONKER, I WOULD LIKE TO ASK YOU A SERIOUS QUESTION. IF YOU HATE PRACTICE SO MUCH, WHY DID YOU BOTHER TO COME OUT FOR FOOTBALL IN THE FIRST PLACE?
BECAUSE, CAPTAIN AMERICA, I ADMIRE YOU! YES! ADMIRE YOU! ADMIRE AND RESPECT YOU!
HEH, HEH! HEH!
JONATHON, I'M GOING TO THROW A LONG BOMB TO YOU. BUTTON HOOK ON THE 30. GOT IT?
O.K., B.D.!
HOLD IT, CAP'N!
IF MY ONLY CAPTAIN IS GOING TO THROW INTO THE SUN, THEN HE'LL BE NEEDING SOME EYE BLACK TO CUT DOWN THE GLARE!
I DON'T KNOW HOW MUCH MORE OF THIS ABUSE I CAN TAKE.
FAR OUT. HEH-HEH.
SMACK
GOOD LUCK, TIGER!
SMACK
GOOD LUCK, TIGER!
THAT DOES IT!!
YEECH! CHAPPED LIPS!
ZONKER, EVER SINCE YOU JOINED THE TEAM, YOU'VE BEEN A PAIN, A NUISANCE, AND A GENERAL TROUBLE MAKER!
SNIFF SNIFF
WAAH!!
NOW LOOK WHAT YOU'VE DONE, YOU BULLY!
HE DIDN'T MEAN IT, ZONKER.
SOB! SOB!
SNIFF
POOR GUY!

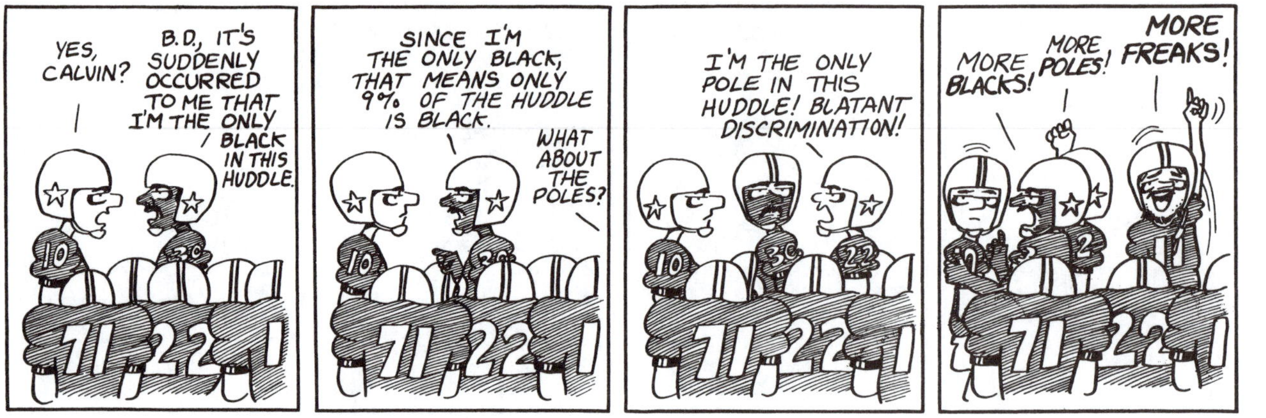
YES, CALVIN?
B.D., IT'S SUDDENLY OCCURRED TO ME THAT I'M THE ONLY BLACK IN THIS HUDDLE.
SINCE I'M THE ONLY BLACK, THAT MEANS ONLY 9% OF THE HUDDLE IS BLACK.
WHAT ABOUT THE POLES?
I'M THE ONLY POLE IN THIS HUDDLE! BLATANT DISCRIMINATION!
MORE BLACKS!
MORE POLES!
MORE FREAKS!

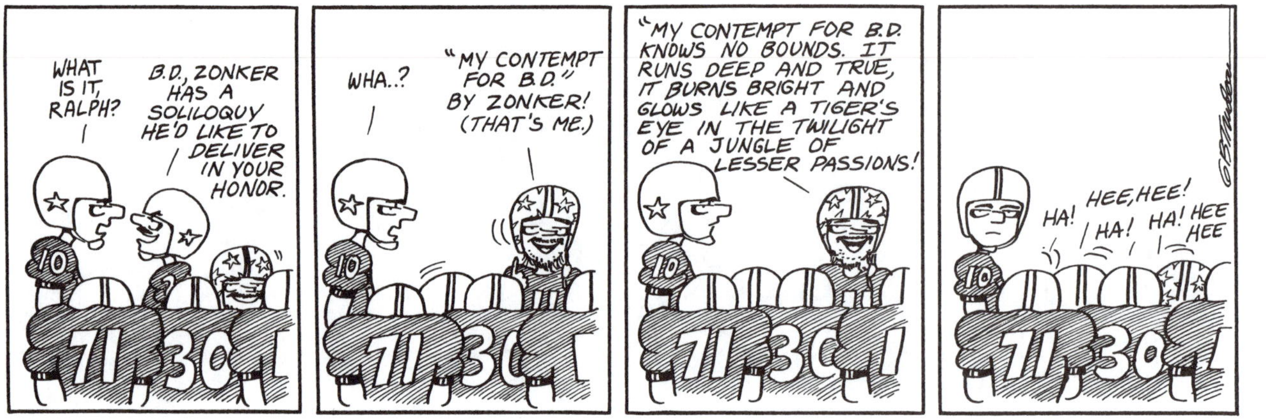
WHAT IS IT, RALPH?
B.D., ZONKER HAS A SOLILOQUY HE'D LIKE TO DELIVER IN YOUR HONOR.
WHA..?
"MY CONTEMPT FOR B.D." BY ZONKER! (THAT'S ME.)
"MY CONTEMPT FOR B.D. KNOWS NO BOUNDS. IT RUNS DEEP AND TRUE, IT BURNS BRIGHT AND GLOWS LIKE A TIGER'S EYE IN THE TWILIGHT OF A JUNGLE OF LESSER PASSIONS!
HA! HEE, HEE! HA! HA! HEE HEE

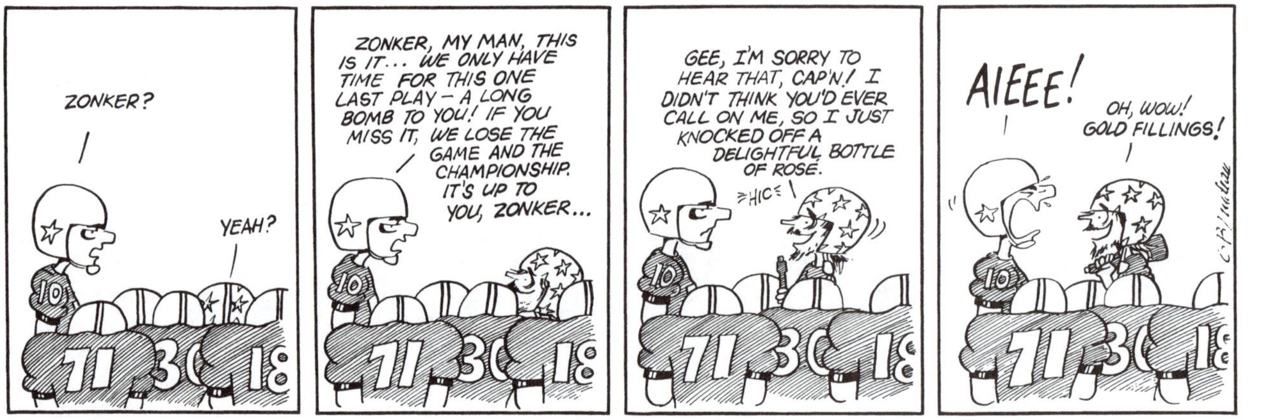
ZONKER?
YEAH?
ZONKER, MY MAN, THIS IS IT... WE ONLY HAVE TIME FOR THIS ONE LAST PLAY — A LONG BOMB TO YOU! IF YOU MISS IT, WE LOSE THE GAME AND THE CHAMPIONSHIP. IT'S UP TO YOU, ZONKER...
GEE, I'M SORRY TO HEAR THAT, CAP'N.! I DIDN'T THINK YOU'D EVER CALL ON ME, SO I JUST KNOCKED OFF A DELIGHTFUL BOTTLE OF ROSE.
HIC
AIEEE!
OH, WOW! GOLD FILLINGS!

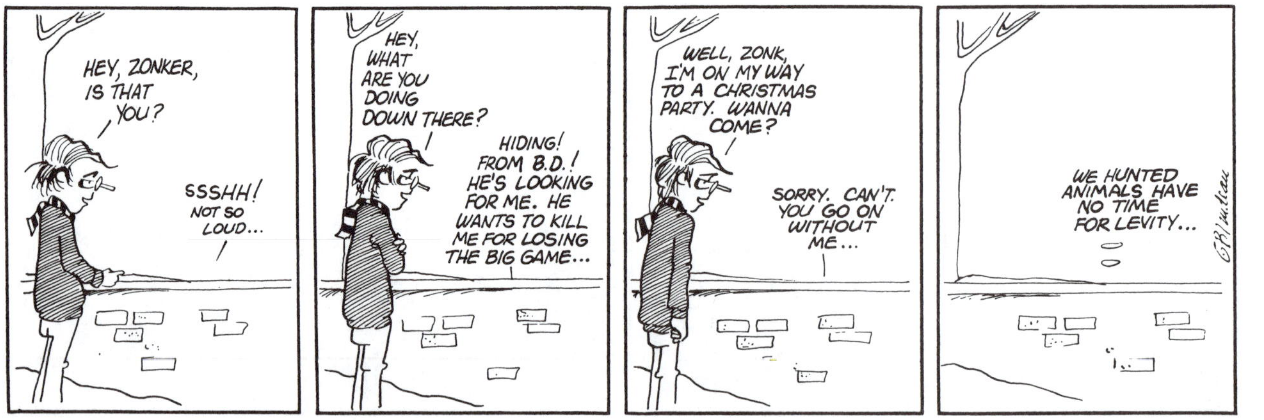
HEY, ZONKER, IS THAT YOU?
SSSHH! NOT SO LOUD...
HEY, WHAT ARE YOU DOING DOWN THERE?
HIDING! FROM B.D.! HE'S LOOKING FOR ME. HE WANTS TO KILL ME FOR LOSING THE BIG GAME...
WELL, ZONK, I'M ON MY WAY TO A CHRISTMAS PARTY. WANNA COME?
SORRY. CAN'T. YOU GO ON WITHOUT ME...
WE HUNTED ANIMALS HAVE NO TIME FOR LEVITY...

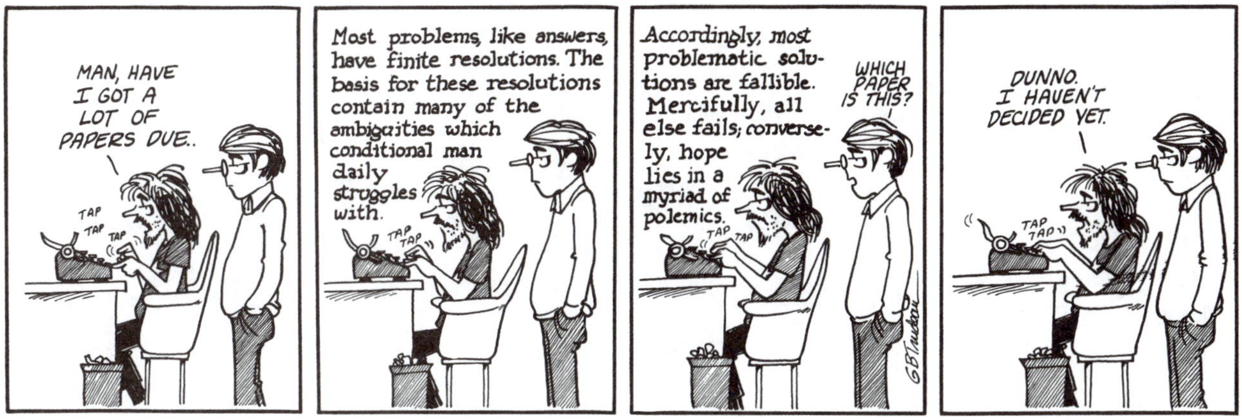
MAN, HAVE I GOT A LOT OF PAPERS DUE..
TAP TAP TAP
Most problems, like answers, have finite resolutions. The basis for these resolutions contain many of the ambiguities which conditional man daily struggles with.
TAP TAP
Accordingly, most problematic solutions are fallible. Mercifully, all else fails; conversely, hope lies in a myriad of polemics.
TAP TAP
WHICH PAPER IS THIS?
DUNNO. I HAVEN'T DECIDED YET.
TAP TAP

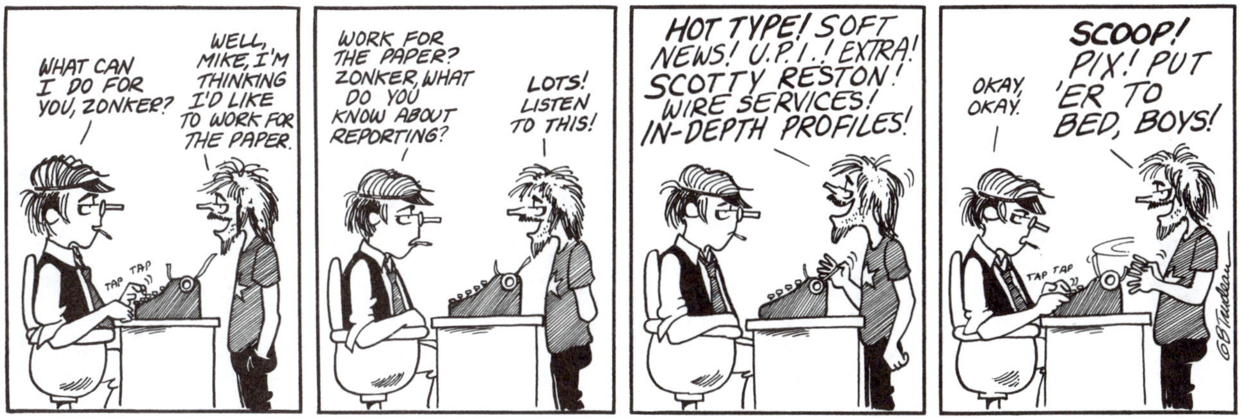
WHAT CAN I DO FOR YOU, ZONKER?
WELL, MIKE, I'M THINKING I'D LIKE TO WORK FOR THE PAPER.
TAP TAP
WORK FOR THE PAPER? ZONKER, WHAT DO YOU KNOW ABOUT REPORTING?
LOTS! LISTEN TO THIS!
HOT TYPE! SOFT NEWS! U.P.I..! EXTRA! SCOTTY RESTON! WIRE SERVICES! IN-DEPTH PROFILES!
OKAY, OKAY.
SCOOP! PIX! PUT 'ER TO BED, BOYS!
TAP TAP

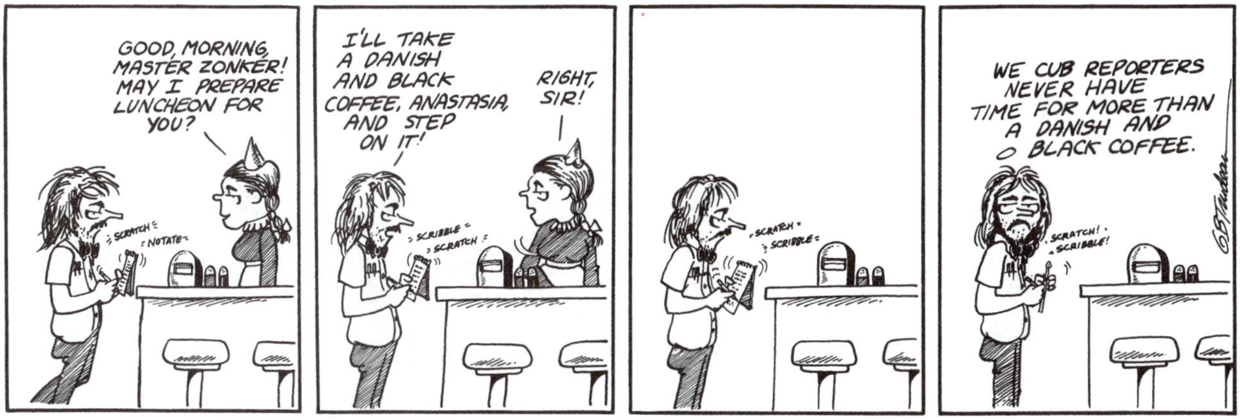
GOOD, MORNING, MASTER ZONKER! MAY I PREPARE LUNCHEON FOR YOU?
SCRATCH
NOTATE
I'LL TAKE A DANISH AND BLACK COFFEE, ANASTASIA, AND STEP ON IT!
RIGHT, SIR!
SCRIBBLE
SCRATCH
SCRATCH
SCRIBBLE
WE CUB REPORTERS NEVER HAVE TIME FOR MORE THAN A DANISH AND BLACK COFFEE.
SCRATCH!
SCRIBBLE!

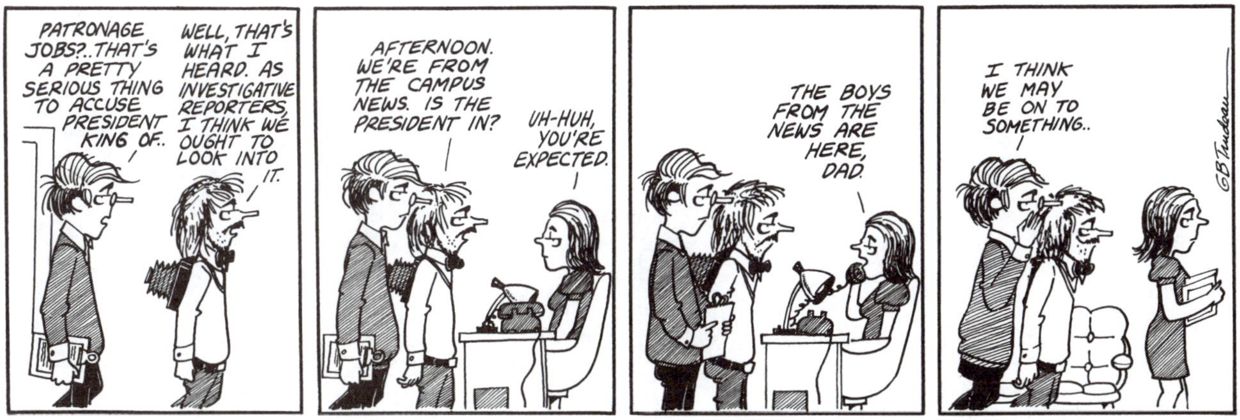
PATRONAGE JOBS?..THAT'S A PRETTY SERIOUS THING TO ACCUSE PRESIDENT KING OF..
WELL, THAT'S WHAT I HEARD. AS INVESTIGATIVE REPORTERS, I THINK WE OUGHT TO LOOK INTO IT.
AFTERNOON. WE'RE FROM THE CAMPUS NEWS. IS THE PRESIDENT IN?
UH-HUH, YOU'RE EXPECTED.
THE BOYS FROM THE NEWS ARE HERE, DAD.
I THINK WE MAY BE ON TO SOMETHING..

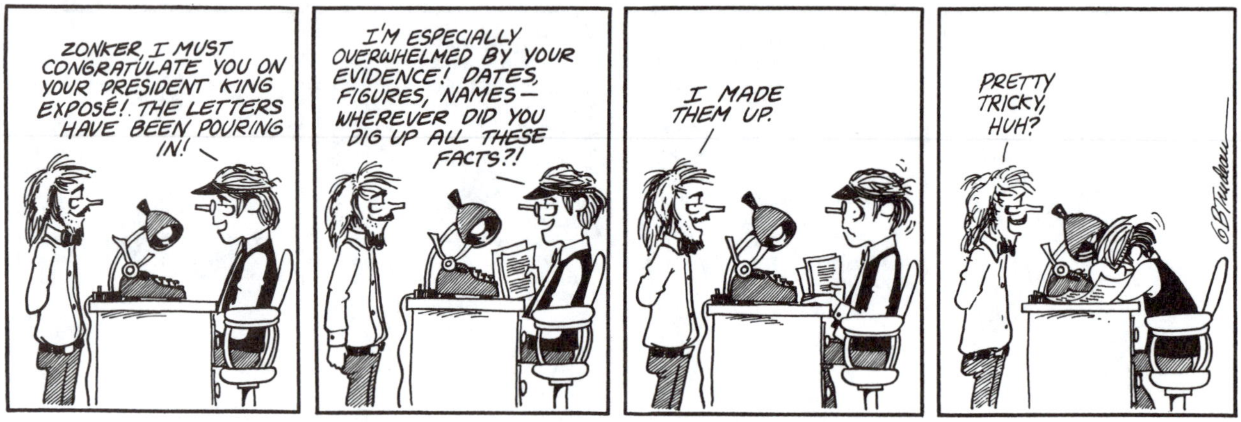
ZONKER, I MUST CONGRATULATE YOU ON YOUR PRESIDENT KING EXPOSÉ! THE LETTERS HAVE BEEN POURING IN!
I'M ESPECIALLY OVERWHELMED BY YOUR EVIDENCE! DATES, FIGURES, NAMES— WHEREVER DID YOU DIG UP ALL THESE FACTS?!
I MADE THEM UP.
PRETTY TRICKY, HUH?

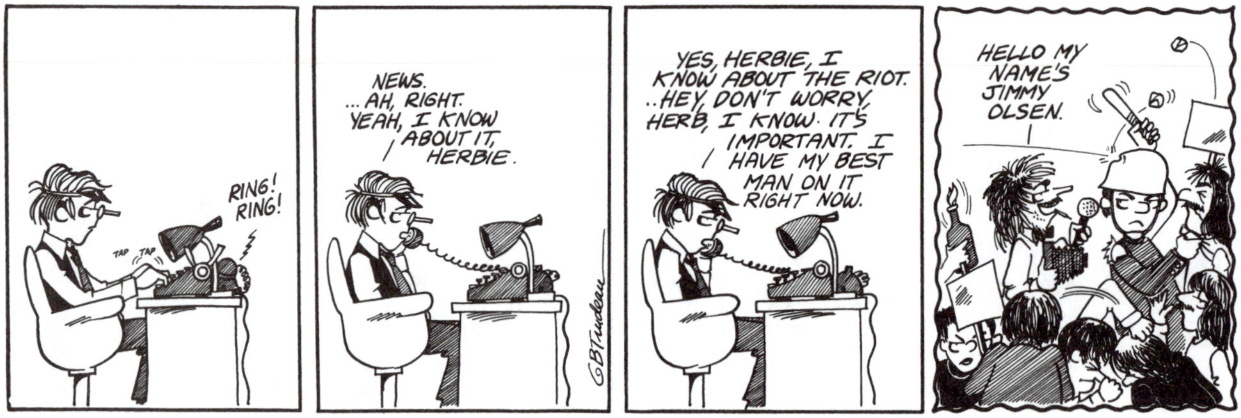
TAP TAP
RING! RING!
NEWS. ...AH, RIGHT. YEAH, I KNOW ABOUT IT, HERBIE.
YES, HERBIE, I KNOW ABOUT THE RIOT. ..HEY, DON'T WORRY, HERB, I KNOW. IT'S IMPORTANT. I HAVE MY BEST MAN ON IT RIGHT NOW.
HELLO MY NAME'S JIMMY OLSEN.

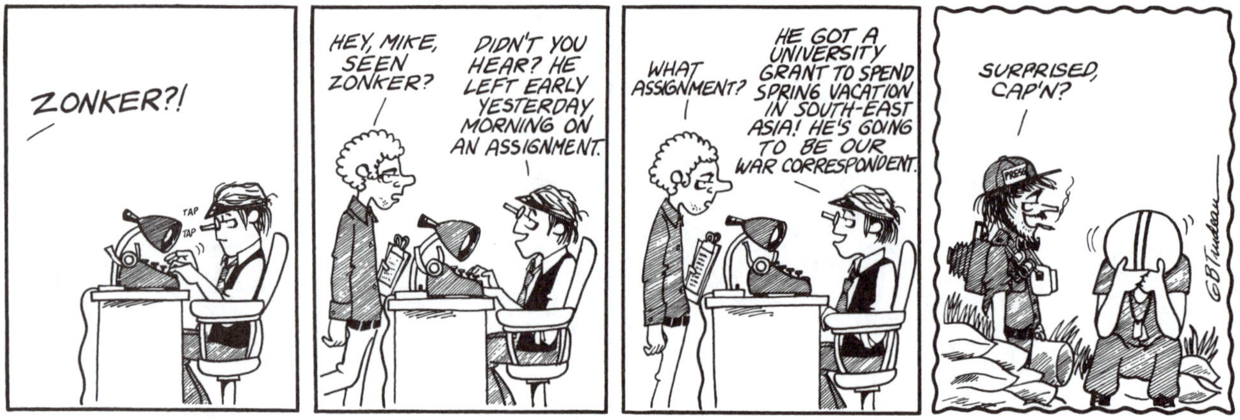
ZONKER?!
TAP TAP
HEY, MIKE, SEEN ZONKER?
DIDN'T YOU HEAR? HE LEFT EARLY YESTERDAY MORNING ON AN ASSIGNMENT.
WHAT ASSIGNMENT?
HE GOT A UNIVERSITY GRANT TO SPEND SPRING VACATION IN SOUTH-EAST ASIA! HE'S GOING TO BE OUR WAR CORRESPONDENT.
SURPRISED, CAP'N?

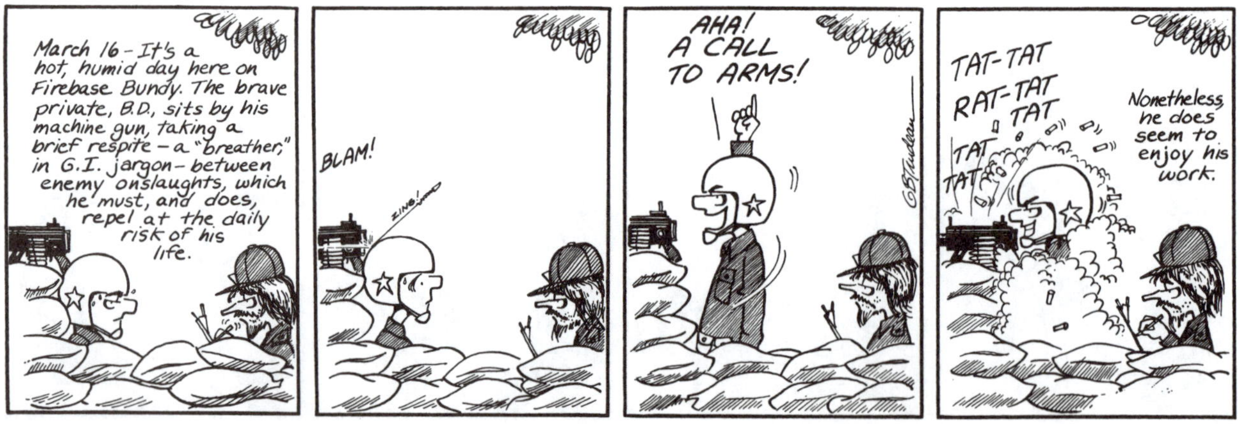
March 16 - It's a hot, humid day here on Firebase Bundy. The brave private, B.D., sits by his machine gun, taking a brief respite – a "breather," in G.I. jargon – between enemy onslaughts, which he must, and does, repel at the daily risk of his life.
BLAM!
AHA! A CALL TO ARMS!
TAT-TAT
RAT-TAT TAT
TAT TAT
Nonetheless, he does seem to enjoy his work.

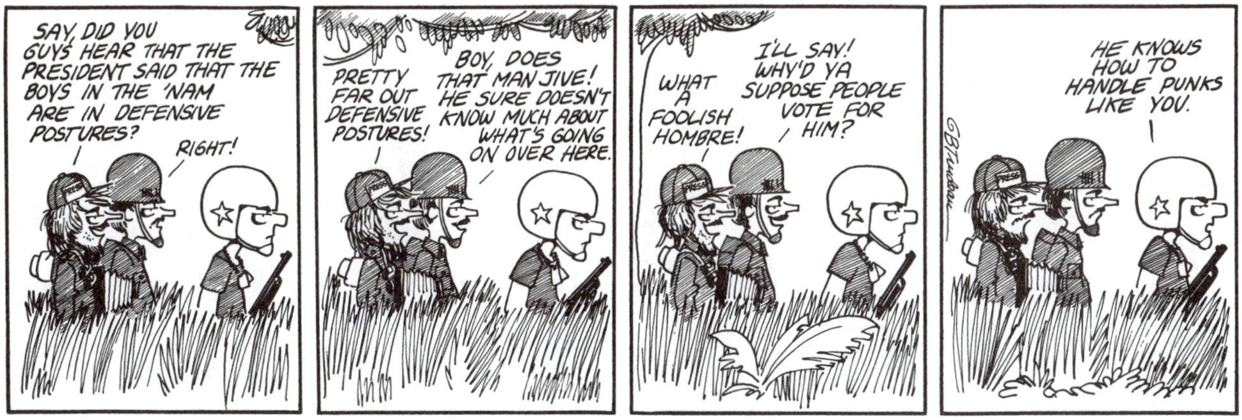
SAY, DID YOU GUYS HEAR THAT THE PRESIDENT SAID THAT THE BOYS IN THE 'NAM ARE IN DEFENSIVE POSTURES?
RIGHT!
PRETTY FAR OUT DEFENSIVE POSTURES!
BOY, DOES THAT MAN JIVE! HE SURE DOESN'T KNOW MUCH ABOUT WHAT'S GOING ON OVER HERE.
WHAT A FOOLISH HOMBRE!
I'LL SAY! WHY'D YA SUPPOSE PEOPLE VOTE FOR HIM?
HE KNOWS HOW TO HANDLE PUNKS LIKE YOU.

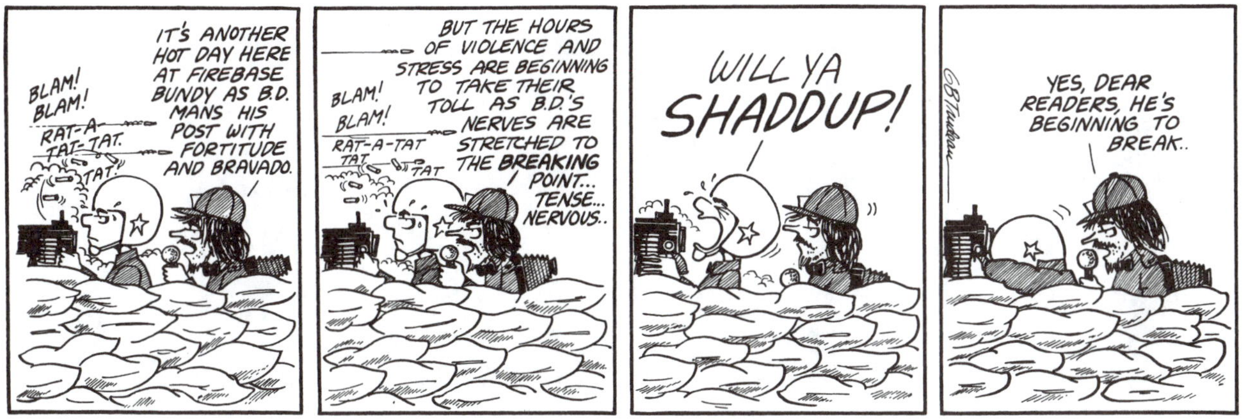
BLAM! BLAM!
RAT-A-TAT-TAT! TAT!
IT'S ANOTHER HOT DAY HERE AT FIREBASE BUNDY AS B.D. MANS HIS POST WITH FORTITUDE AND BRAVADO.
BLAM! BLAM!
RAT-A-TAT TAT TAT
BUT THE HOURS OF VIOLENCE AND STRESS ARE BEGINNING TO TAKE THEIR TOLL AS B.D.'S NERVES ARE STRETCHED TO THE **BREAKING** POINT... TENSE... NERVOUS..
WILL YA SHADDUP!
YES, DEAR READERS, HE'S BEGINNING TO BREAK..

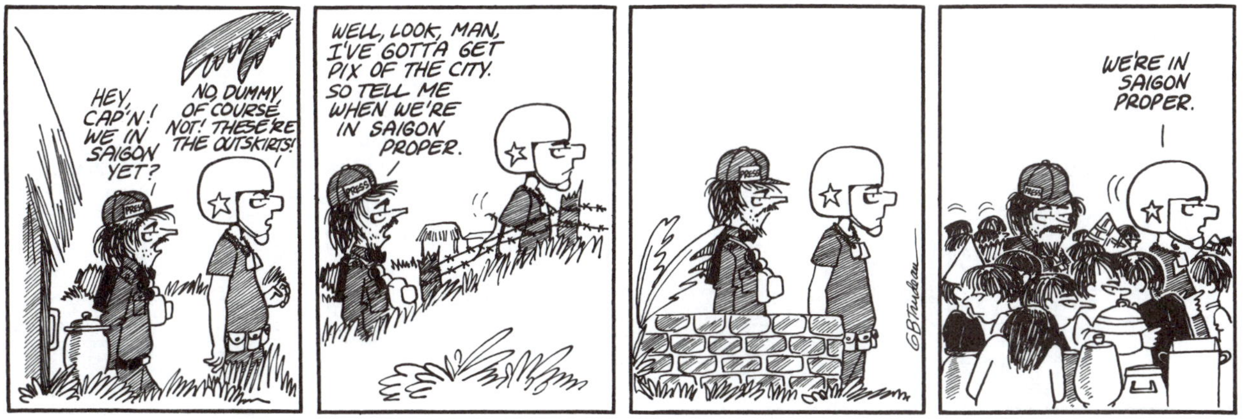
HEY, CAP'N! WE IN SAIGON YET?
NO, DUMMY, OF COURSE NOT! THESE'RE THE OUTSKIRTS!
WELL, LOOK, MAN, I'VE GOTTA GET PIX OF THE CITY. SO TELL ME WHEN WE'RE IN SAIGON PROPER.
WE'RE IN SAIGON PROPER.

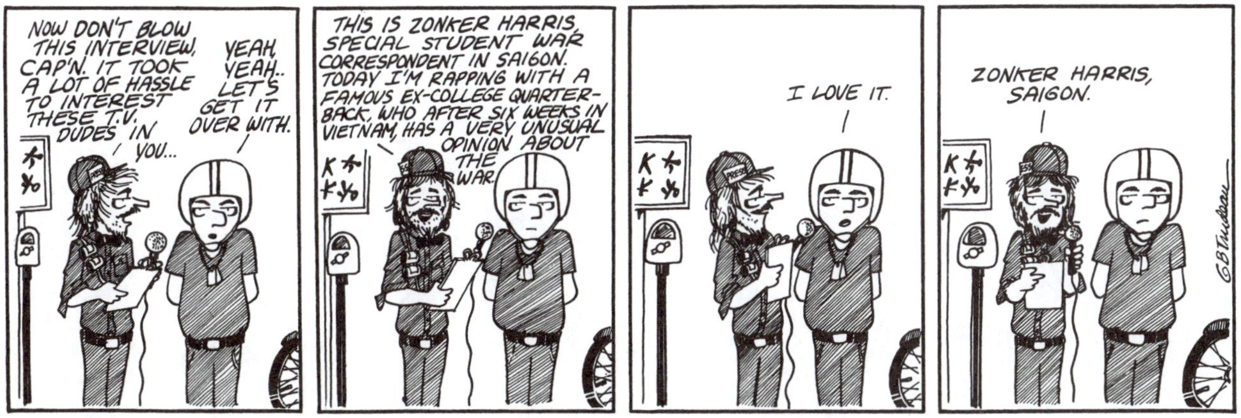
NOW DON'T BLOW THIS INTERVIEW, CAP'N. IT TOOK A LOT OF HASSLE TO INTEREST THESE T.V. DUDES IN YOU...
YEAH, YEAH.. LET'S GET IT OVER WITH.
THIS IS ZONKER HARRIS, SPECIAL STUDENT WAR CORRESPONDENT IN SAIGON. TODAY I'M RAPPING WITH A FAMOUS EX-COLLEGE QUARTER-BACK, WHO AFTER SIX WEEKS IN VIETNAM, HAS A VERY UNUSUAL OPINION ABOUT THE WAR.
I LOVE IT.
ZONKER HARRIS, SAIGON.

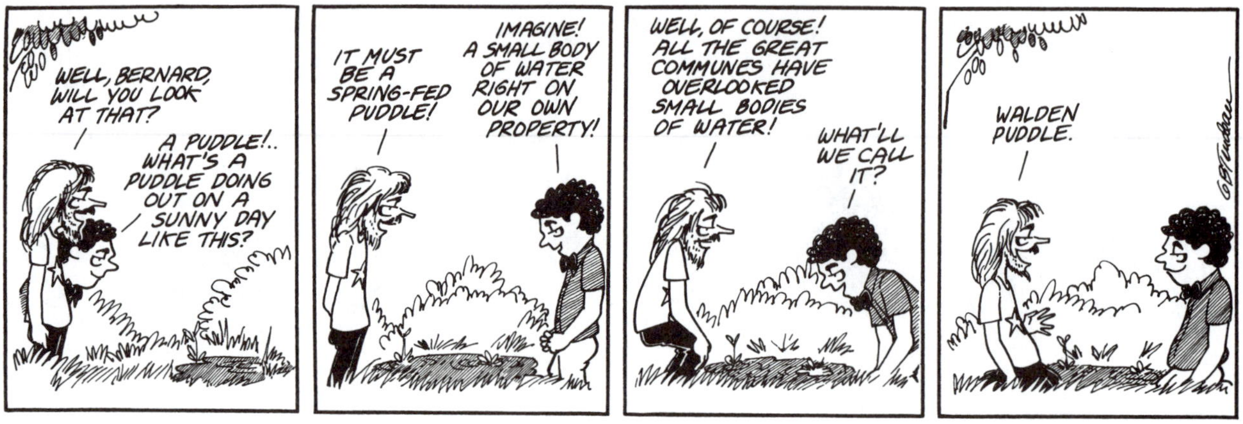
WELL, BERNARD, WILL YOU LOOK AT THAT?
A PUDDLE!.. WHAT'S A PUDDLE DOING OUT ON A SUNNY DAY LIKE THIS?
IT MUST BE A SPRING-FED PUDDLE!
IMAGINE! A SMALL BODY OF WATER RIGHT ON OUR OWN PROPERTY!
WELL, OF COURSE! ALL THE GREAT COMMUNES HAVE OVERLOOKED SMALL BODIES OF WATER!
WHAT'LL WE CALL IT?
WALDEN PUDDLE.

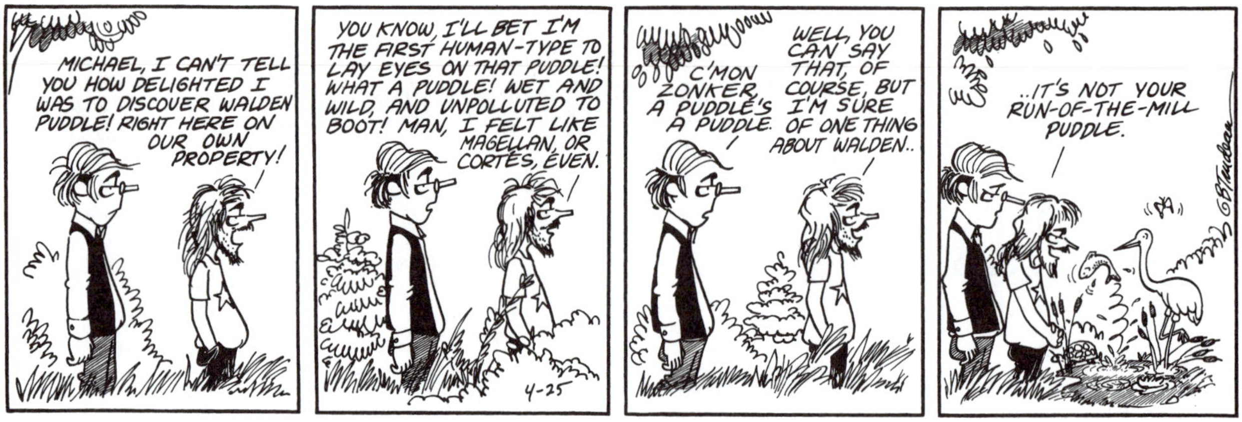
MICHAEL, I CAN'T TELL YOU HOW DELIGHTED I WAS TO DISCOVER WALDEN PUDDLE! RIGHT HERE ON OUR OWN PROPERTY!
YOU KNOW, I'LL BET I'M THE FIRST HUMAN-TYPE TO LAY EYES ON THAT PUDDLE! WHAT A PUDDLE! WET AND WILD, AND UNPOLLUTED TO BOOT! MAN, I FELT LIKE MAGELLAN, OR CORTÉS, EVEN.
4-25
C'MON ZONKER, A PUDDLE'S A PUDDLE.
WELL, YOU CAN SAY THAT, OF COURSE, BUT I'M SURE OF ONE THING ABOUT WALDEN..
..IT'S NOT YOUR RUN-OF-THE-MILL PUDDLE.

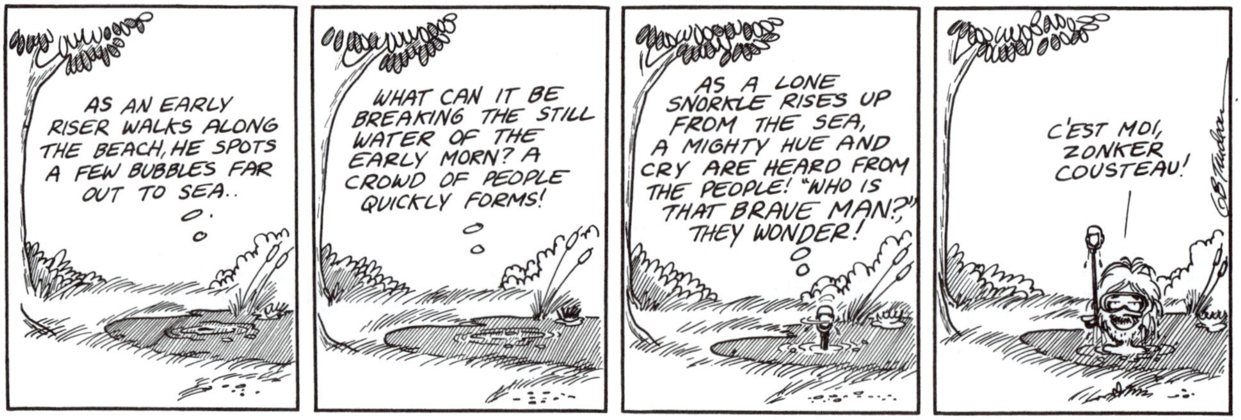
AS AN EARLY RISER WALKS ALONG THE BEACH, HE SPOTS A FEW BUBBLES FAR OUT TO SEA..
WHAT CAN IT BE BREAKING THE STILL WATER OF THE EARLY MORN? A CROWD OF PEOPLE QUICKLY FORMS!
AS A LONE SNORKLE RISES UP FROM THE SEA, A MIGHTY HUE AND CRY ARE HEARD FROM THE PEOPLE! "WHO IS THAT BRAVE MAN?," THEY WONDER!
C'EST MOI, ZONKER COUSTEAU!

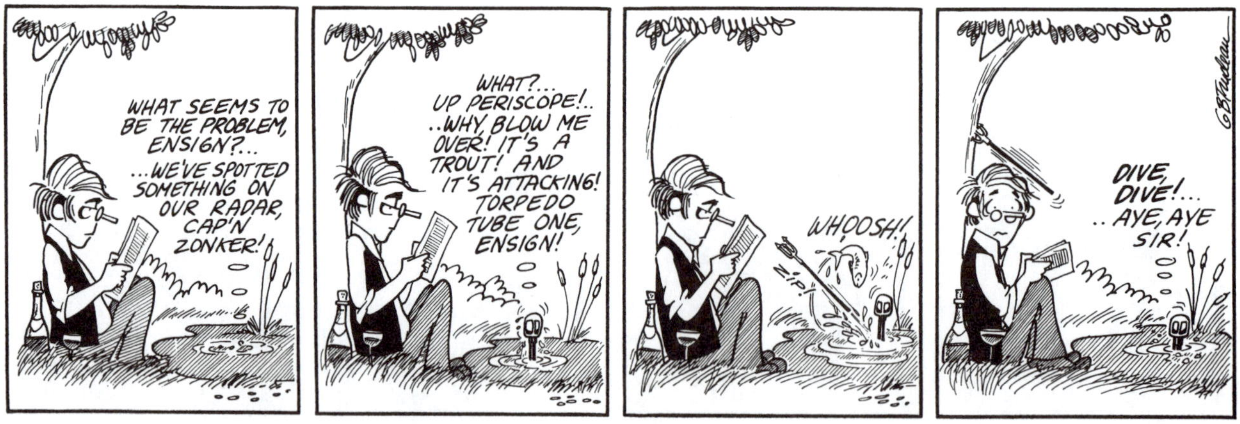
WHAT SEEMS TO BE THE PROBLEM, ENSIGN?... ...WE'VE SPOTTED SOMETHING ON OUR RADAR, CAP'N ZONKER!
WHAT?... UP PERISCOPE!.. ..WHY, BLOW ME OVER! IT'S A TROUT! AND IT'S ATTACKING! TORPEDO TUBE ONE, ENSIGN!
WHOOSH!
ZIP!
DIVE, DIVE!... ..AYE, AYE SIR!

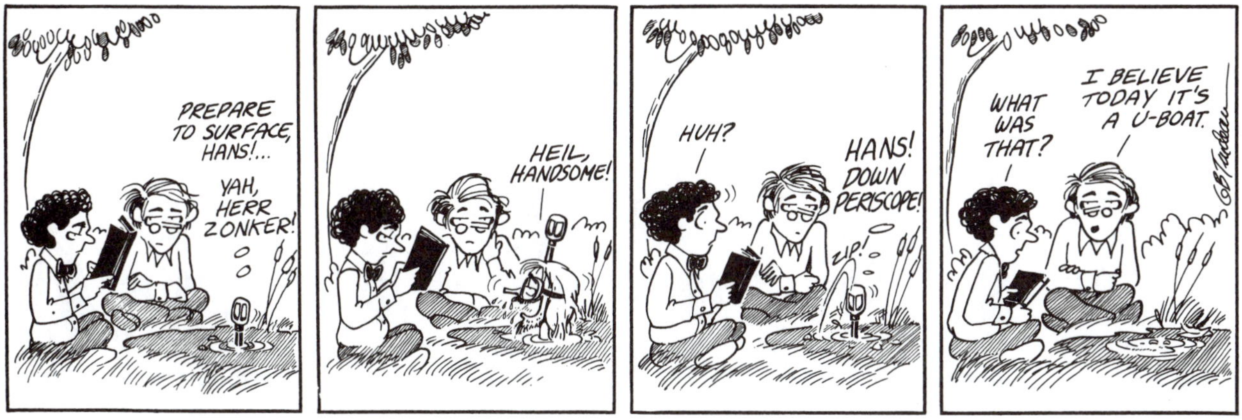
PREPARE TO SURFACE, HANS!...
YAH, HERR ZONKER!
HEIL, HANDSOME!
HUH?
HANS! DOWN PERISCOPE!
ZIP!
WHAT WAS THAT?
I BELIEVE TODAY IT'S A U-BOAT.

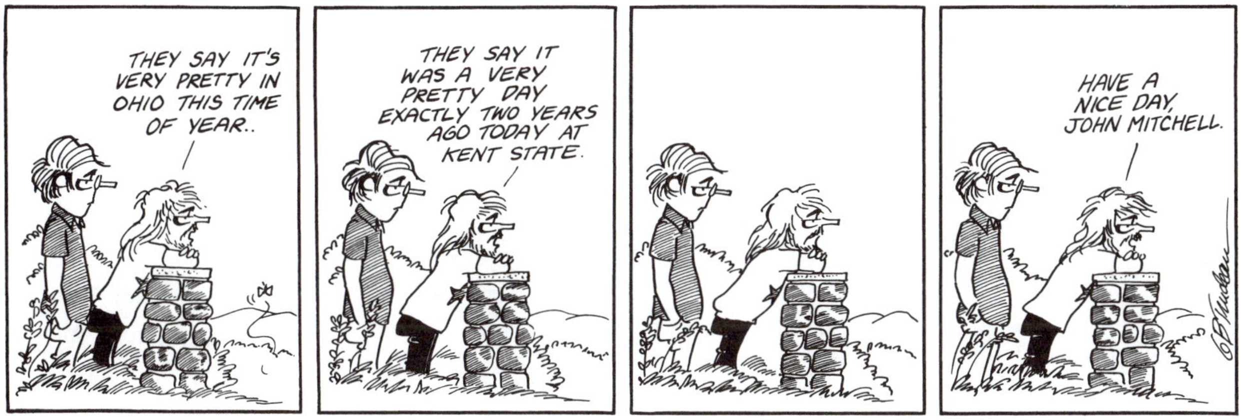
THEY SAY IT'S VERY PRETTY IN OHIO THIS TIME OF YEAR..
THEY SAY IT WAS A VERY PRETTY DAY EXACTLY TWO YEARS AGO TODAY AT KENT STATE.
HAVE A NICE DAY, JOHN MITCHELL.

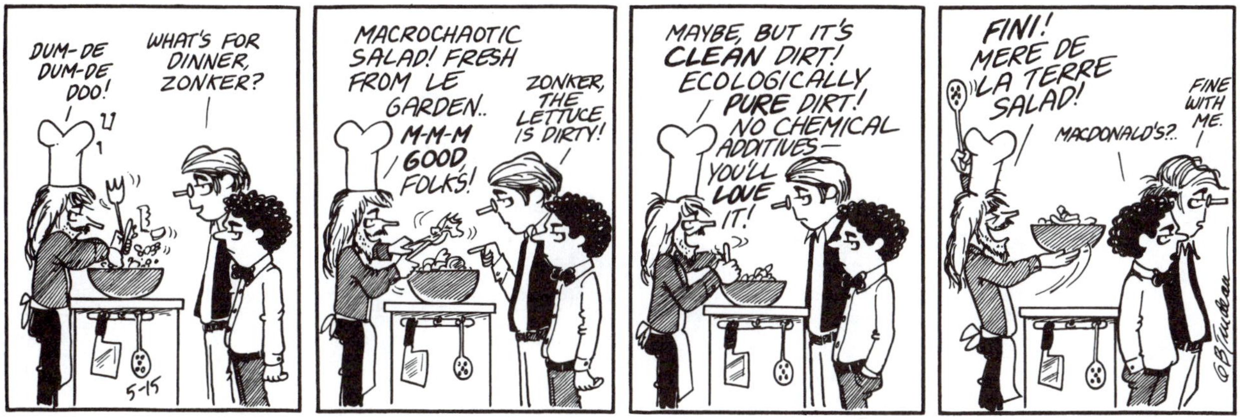
DUM-DE DUM-DE DOO!
WHAT'S FOR DINNER, ZONKER?
5-15
MACROCHAOTIC SALAD! FRESH FROM LE GARDEN..
M-M-M GOOD FOLKS!
ZONKER, THE LETTUCE IS DIRTY!
MAYBE, BUT IT'S CLEAN DIRT! ECOLOGICALLY PURE DIRT! NO CHEMICAL ADDITIVES— YOU'LL LOVE IT!
FINI! MERE DE LA TERRE SALAD!
MACDONALD'S?.
FINE WITH ME.

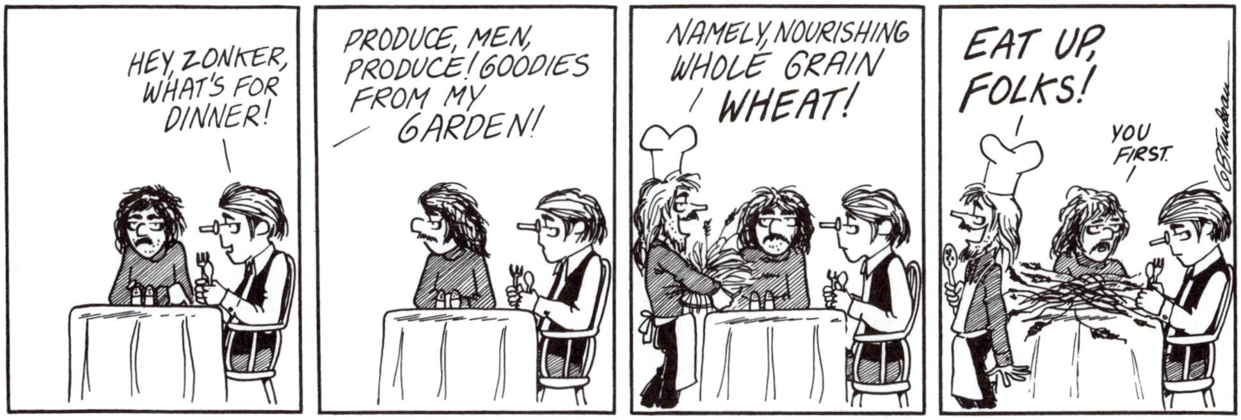
HEY, ZONKER, WHAT'S FOR DINNER!
PRODUCE, MEN, PRODUCE! GOODIES FROM MY GARDEN!
NAMELY, NOURISHING WHOLE GRAIN WHEAT!
EAT UP, FOLKS!
YOU FIRST.

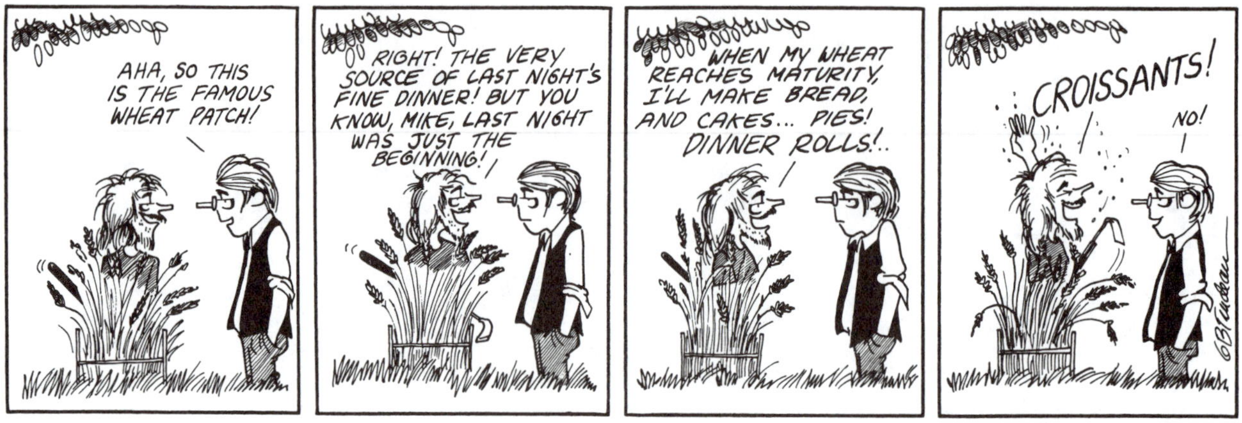
AHA, SO THIS IS THE FAMOUS WHEAT PATCH!
RIGHT! THE VERY SOURCE OF LAST NIGHT'S FINE DINNER! BUT YOU KNOW, MIKE, LAST NIGHT WAS JUST THE BEGINNING!
WHEN MY WHEAT REACHES MATURITY, I'LL MAKE BREAD, AND CAKES... PIES! DINNER ROLLS!..
CROISSANTS!
NO!

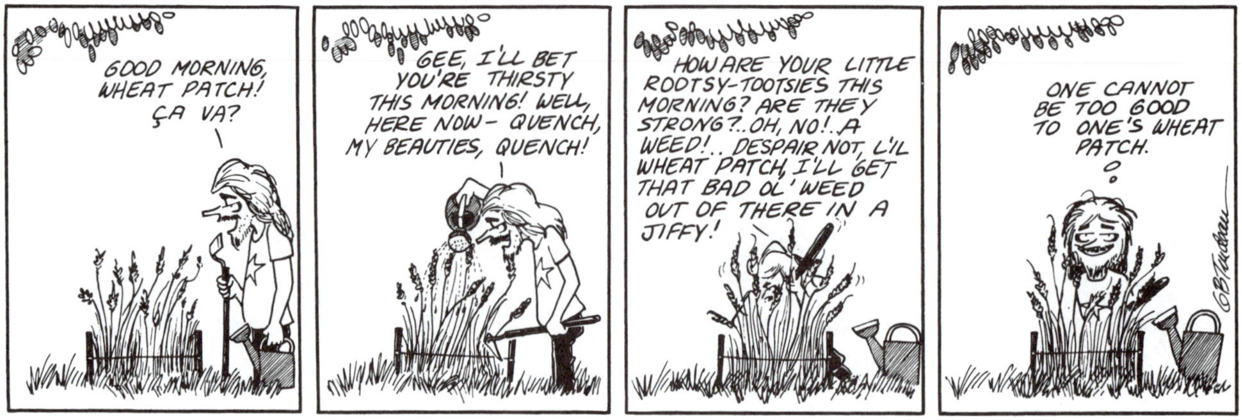
GOOD MORNING, WHEAT PATCH! ÇA VA?
GEE, I'LL BET YOU'RE THIRSTY THIS MORNING! WELL, HERE NOW– QUENCH, MY BEAUTIES, QUENCH!
HOW ARE YOUR LITTLE ROOTSY-TOOTSIES THIS MORNING? ARE THEY STRONG?..OH, NO!..A WEED!.. DESPAIR NOT, L'IL WHEAT PATCH, I'LL GET THAT BAD OL' WEED OUT OF THERE IN A JIFFY!
ONE CANNOT BE TOO GOOD TO ONE'S WHEAT PATCH.

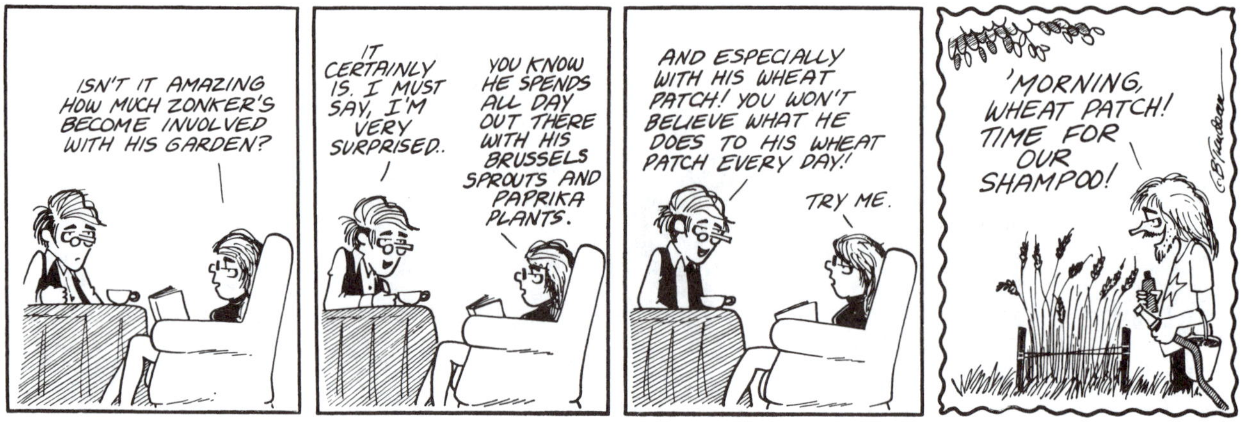
ISN'T IT AMAZING HOW MUCH ZONKER'S BECOME INVOLVED WITH HIS GARDEN?
IT CERTAINLY IS. I MUST SAY, I'M VERY SURPRISED..
YOU KNOW HE SPENDS ALL DAY OUT THERE WITH HIS BRUSSELS SPROUTS AND PAPRIKA PLANTS.
AND ESPECIALLY WITH HIS WHEAT PATCH! YOU WON'T BELIEVE WHAT HE DOES TO HIS WHEAT PATCH EVERY DAY!
TRY ME.
'MORNING, WHEAT PATCH! TIME FOR OUR SHAMPOO!

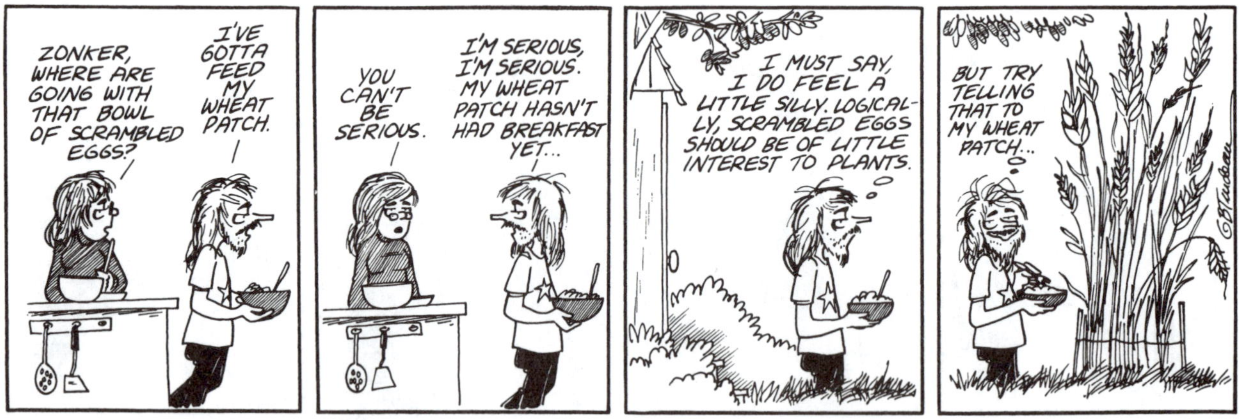
ZONKER, WHERE ARE GOING WITH THAT BOWL OF SCRAMBLED EGGS?
I'VE GOTTA FEED MY WHEAT PATCH.
YOU CAN'T BE SERIOUS.
I'M SERIOUS, I'M SERIOUS. MY WHEAT PATCH HASN'T HAD BREAKFAST YET...
I MUST SAY, I DO FEEL A LITTLE SILLY. LOGICALLY, SCRAMBLED EGGS SHOULD BE OF LITTLE INTEREST TO PLANTS.
BUT TRY TELLING THAT TO MY WHEAT PATCH...

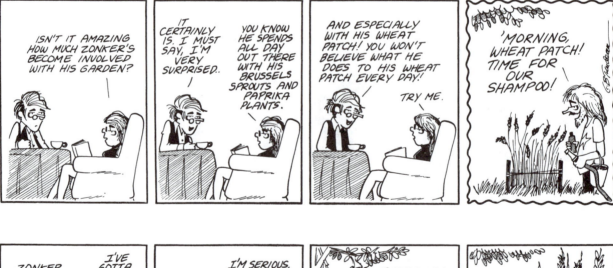

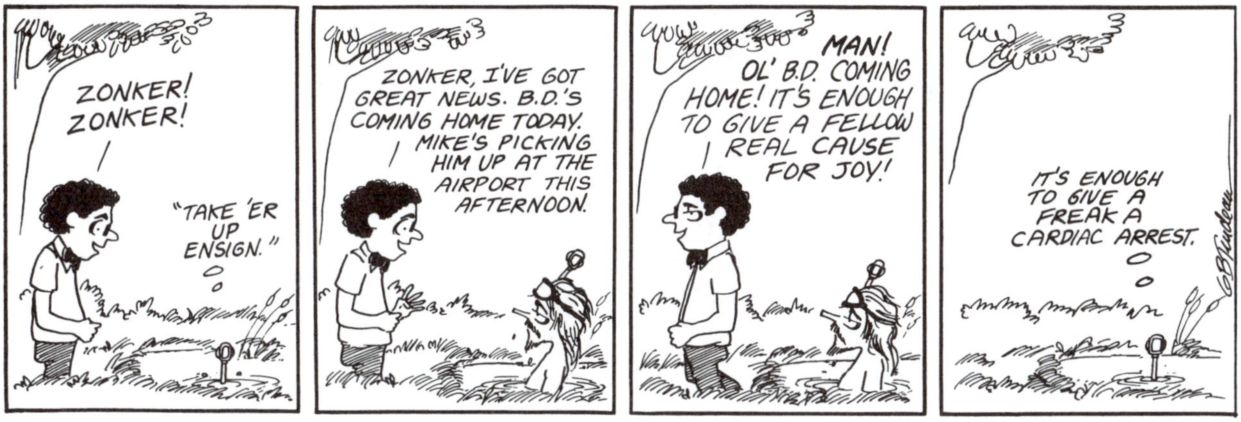
ZONKER! ZONKER!
"TAKE 'ER UP ENSIGN."
ZONKER, I'VE GOT GREAT NEWS. B.D.'S COMING HOME TODAY.
MIKE'S PICKING HIM UP AT THE AIRPORT THIS AFTERNOON.
MAN! OL' B.D. COMING HOME! IT'S ENOUGH TO GIVE A FELLOW REAL CAUSE FOR JOY!
IT'S ENOUGH TO GIVE A FREAK A CARDIAC ARREST.

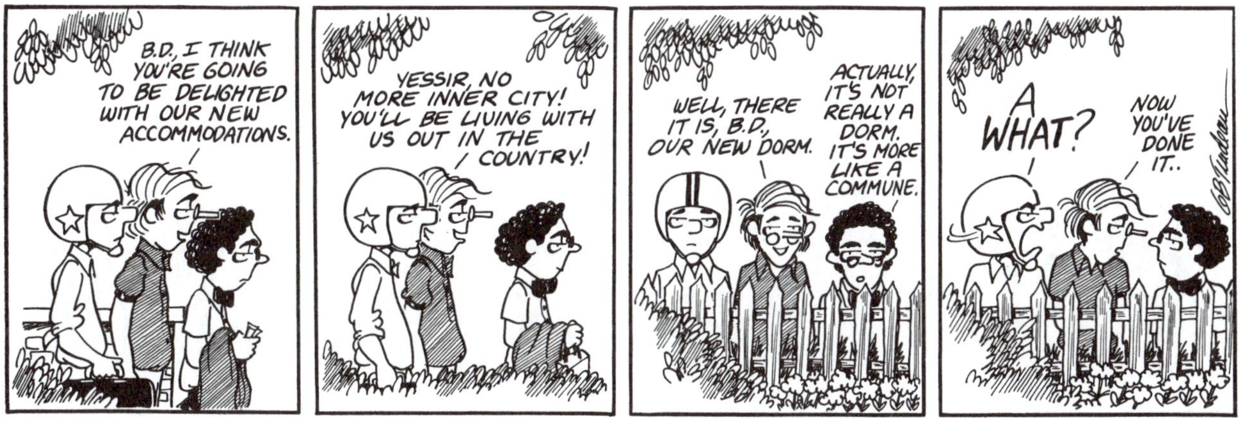
B.D., I THINK YOU'RE GOING TO BE DELIGHTED WITH OUR NEW ACCOMMODATIONS.
YESSIR, NO MORE INNER CITY! YOU'LL BE LIVING WITH US OUT IN THE COUNTRY!
WELL, THERE IT IS, B.D., OUR NEW DORM.
ACTUALLY, IT'S NOT REALLY A DORM. IT'S MORE LIKE A COMMUNE.
A WHAT?
NOW YOU'VE DONE IT..

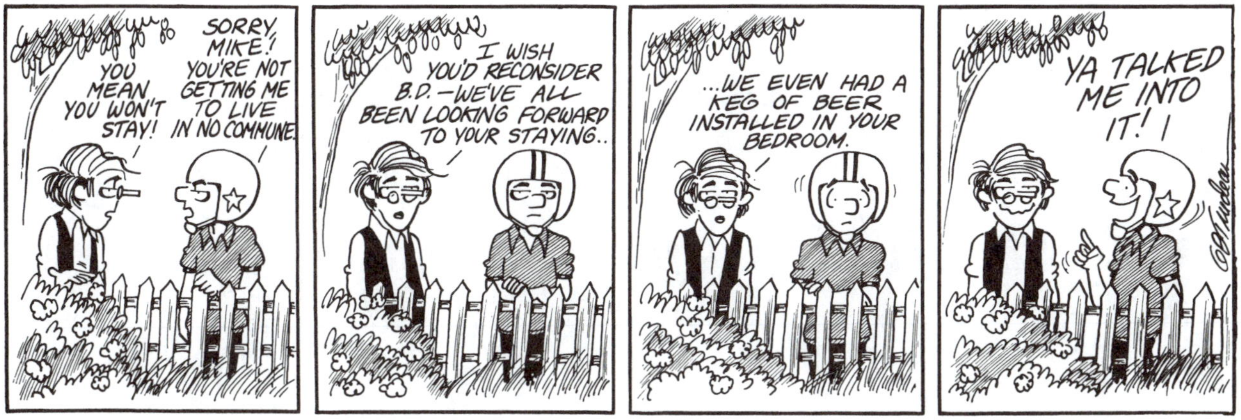
YOU MEAN YOU WON'T STAY!
SORRY, MIKE! YOU'RE NOT GETTING ME TO LIVE IN NO COMMUNE.
I WISH YOU'D RECONSIDER B.D.—WE'VE ALL BEEN LOOKING FORWARD TO YOUR STAYING..
...WE EVEN HAD A KEG OF BEER INSTALLED IN YOUR BEDROOM.
YA TALKED ME INTO IT!

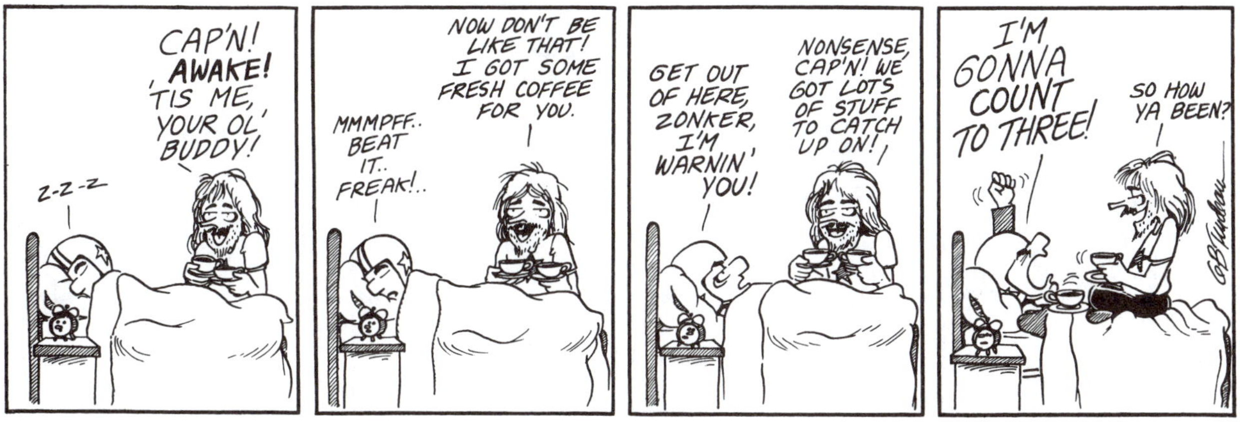
Z-Z-Z
CAP'N! AWAKE! 'TIS ME, YOUR OL' BUDDY!
MMMPFF.. BEAT IT.. FREAK!..
NOW DON'T BE LIKE THAT! I GOT SOME FRESH COFFEE FOR YOU.
GET OUT OF HERE, ZONKER, I'M WARNIN' YOU!
NONSENSE, CAP'N! WE GOT LOTS OF STUFF TO CATCH UP ON!
I'M GONNA COUNT TO THREE!
SO HOW YA BEEN?

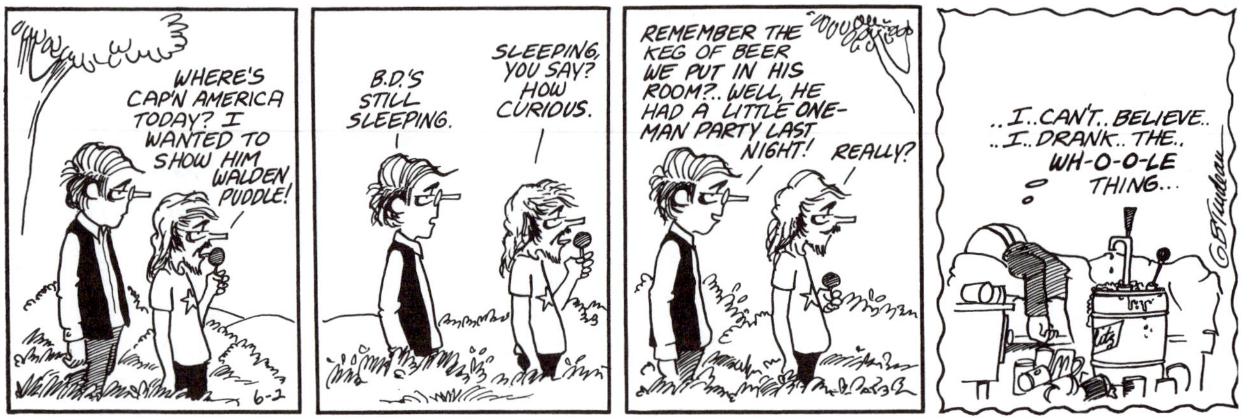
WHERE'S CAP'N AMERICA TODAY? I WANTED TO SHOW HIM WALDEN PUDDLE!
B.D.'S STILL SLEEPING.
SLEEPING, YOU SAY? HOW CURIOUS.
REMEMBER THE KEG OF BEER WE PUT IN HIS ROOM?.. WELL, HE HAD A LITTLE ONE-MAN PARTY LAST NIGHT!
REALLY?
..I..CAN'T..BELIEVE.. ..I..DRANK..THE.. WH-O-O-LE THING...

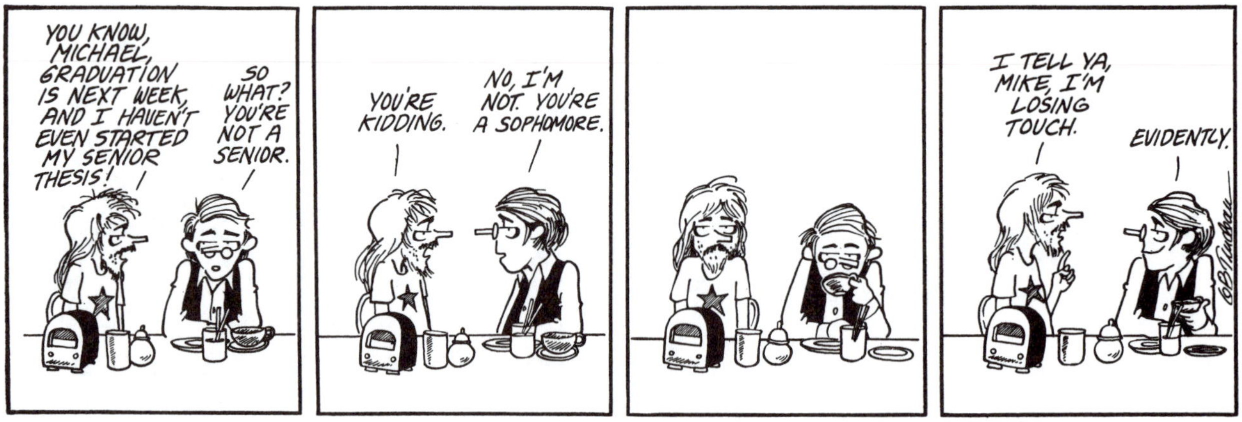
YOU KNOW, MICHAEL, GRADUATION IS NEXT WEEK, AND I HAVEN'T EVEN STARTED MY SENIOR THESIS!
SO WHAT? YOU'RE NOT A SENIOR.
YOU'RE KIDDING.
NO, I'M NOT. YOU'RE A SOPHOMORE.
I TELL YA, MIKE, I'M LOSING TOUCH.
EVIDENTLY.

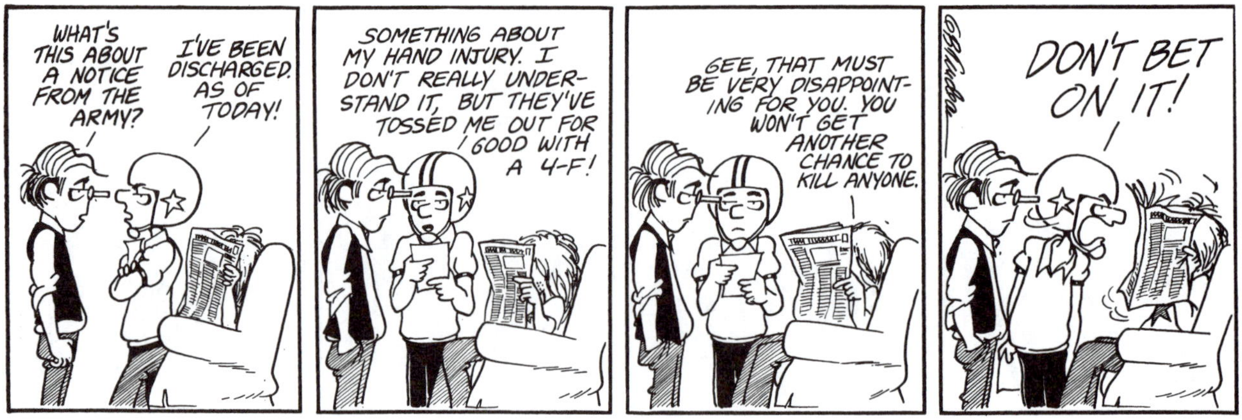
WHAT'S THIS ABOUT A NOTICE FROM THE ARMY?
I'VE BEEN DISCHARGED. AS OF TODAY!
SOMETHING ABOUT MY HAND INJURY. I DON'T REALLY UNDERSTAND IT, BUT THEY'VE TOSSED ME OUT FOR GOOD WITH A 4-F!
GEE, THAT MUST BE VERY DISAPPOINTING FOR YOU. YOU WON'T GET ANOTHER CHANCE TO KILL ANYONE.
DON'T BET ON IT!

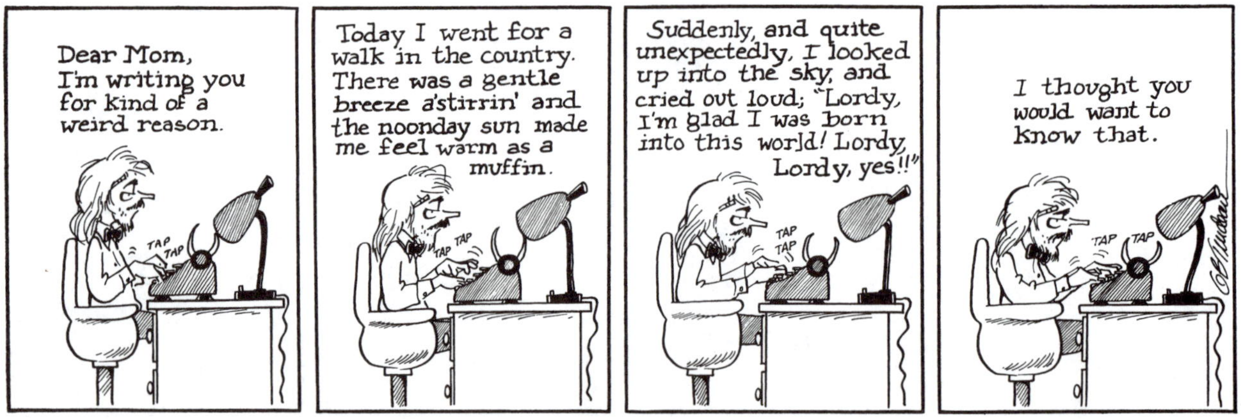
Dear Mom, I'm writing you for kind of a weird reason.
TAP TAP
Today I went for a walk in the country. There was a gentle breeze a'stirrin' and the noonday sun made me feel warm as a muffin.
TAP TAP
Suddenly, and quite unexpectedly, I looked up into the sky, and cried out loud; "Lordy, I'm glad I was born into this world! Lordy, Lordy, yes!!"
TAP TAP
I thought you would want to know that.
TAP TAP

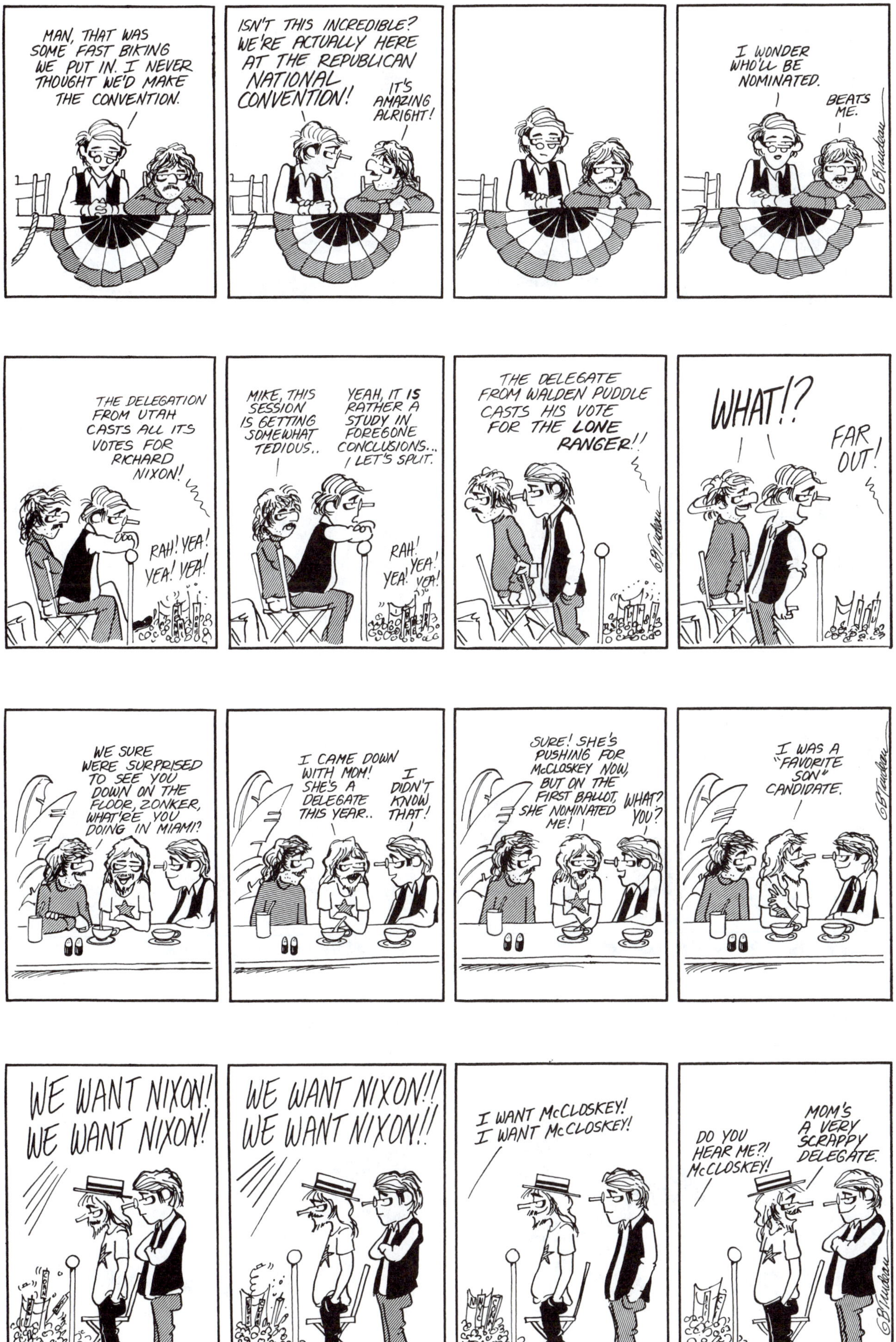

MAN, THAT WAS SOME FAST BIKING WE PUT IN. I NEVER THOUGHT WE'D MAKE THE CONVENTION.
ISN'T THIS INCREDIBLE? WE'RE ACTUALLY HERE AT THE REPUBLICAN NATIONAL CONVENTION!
IT'S AMAZING ALRIGHT!
I WONDER WHO'LL BE NOMINATED.
BEATS ME.
THE DELEGATION FROM UTAH CASTS ALL ITS VOTES FOR RICHARD NIXON!
RAH! YEA! YEA! YEA!
MIKE, THIS SESSION IS GETTING SOMEWHAT TEDIOUS..
YEAH, IT IS RATHER A STUDY IN FOREGONE CONCLUSIONS... LET'S SPLIT.
RAH! YEA! YEA! YEA!
THE DELEGATE FROM WALDEN PUDDLE CASTS HIS VOTE FOR THE LONE RANGER!!
WHAT!?
FAR OUT!
WE SURE WERE SURPRISED TO SEE YOU DOWN ON THE FLOOR, ZONKER. WHAT'RE YOU DOING IN MIAMI?
I CAME DOWN WITH MOM! SHE'S A DELEGATE THIS YEAR..
I DIDN'T KNOW THAT!
SURE! SHE'S PUSHING FOR McCLOSKEY NOW, BUT ON THE FIRST BALLOT, SHE NOMINATED ME!
WHAT? YOU?
I WAS A "FAVORITE SON" CANDIDATE.
WE WANT NIXON! WE WANT NIXON!
WE WANT NIXON!! WE WANT NIXON!!
I WANT McCLOSKEY! I WANT McCLOSKEY!
DO YOU HEAR ME?! McCLOSKEY!
MOM'S A VERY SCRAPPY DELEGATE.

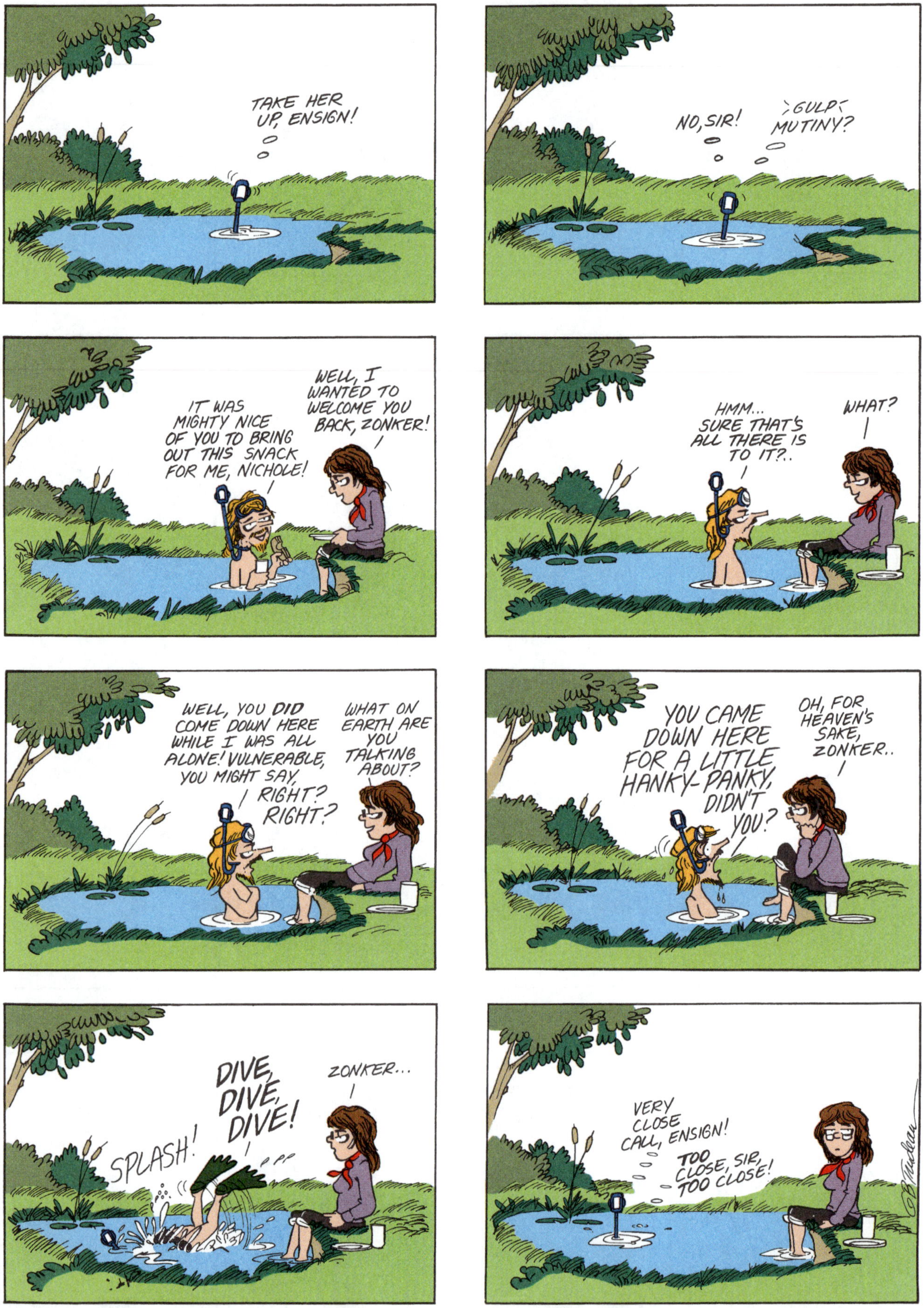
TAKE HER UP, ENSIGN!
NO, SIR!
GULP MUTINY?
IT WAS MIGHTY NICE OF YOU TO BRING OUT THIS SNACK FOR ME, NICHOLE!
WELL, I WANTED TO WELCOME YOU BACK, ZONKER!
HMM... SURE THAT'S ALL THERE IS TO IT?..
WHAT?
WELL, YOU DID COME DOWN HERE WHILE I WAS ALL ALONE! VULNERABLE, YOU MIGHT SAY, RIGHT? RIGHT?
WHAT ON EARTH ARE YOU TALKING ABOUT?
YOU CAME DOWN HERE FOR A LITTLE HANKY-PANKY, DIDN'T YOU?
OH, FOR HEAVEN'S SAKE, ZONKER..
SPLASH!
DIVE, DIVE, DIVE!
ZONKER...
VERY CLOSE CALL, ENSIGN!
TOO CLOSE, SIR, TOO CLOSE!

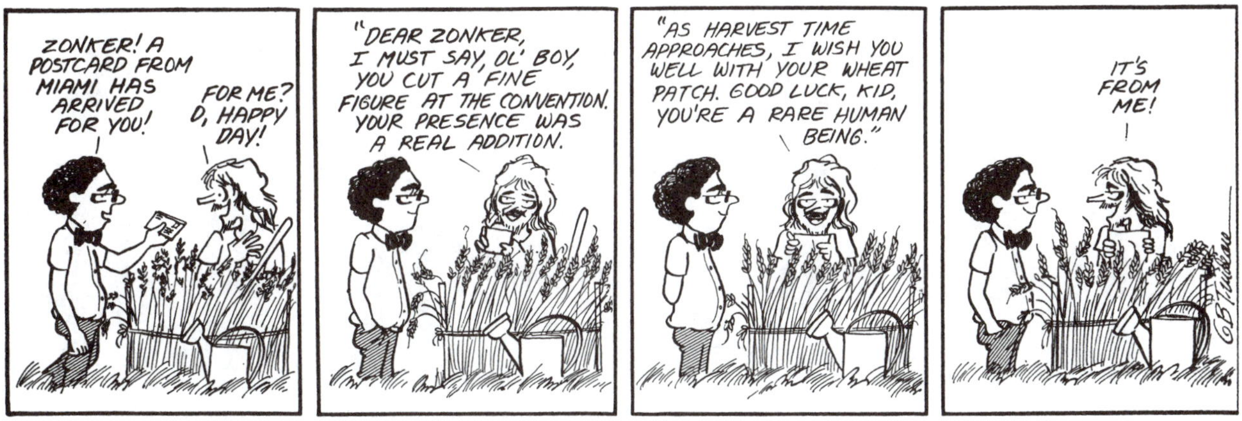
ZONKER! A POSTCARD FROM MIAMI HAS ARRIVED FOR YOU!
FOR ME? O, HAPPY DAY!
"DEAR ZONKER, I MUST SAY, OL' BOY, YOU CUT A FINE FIGURE AT THE CONVENTION. YOUR PRESENCE WAS A REAL ADDITION.
"AS HARVEST TIME APPROACHES, I WISH YOU WELL WITH YOUR WHEAT PATCH. GOOD LUCK, KID, YOU'RE A RARE HUMAN BEING."
IT'S FROM ME!

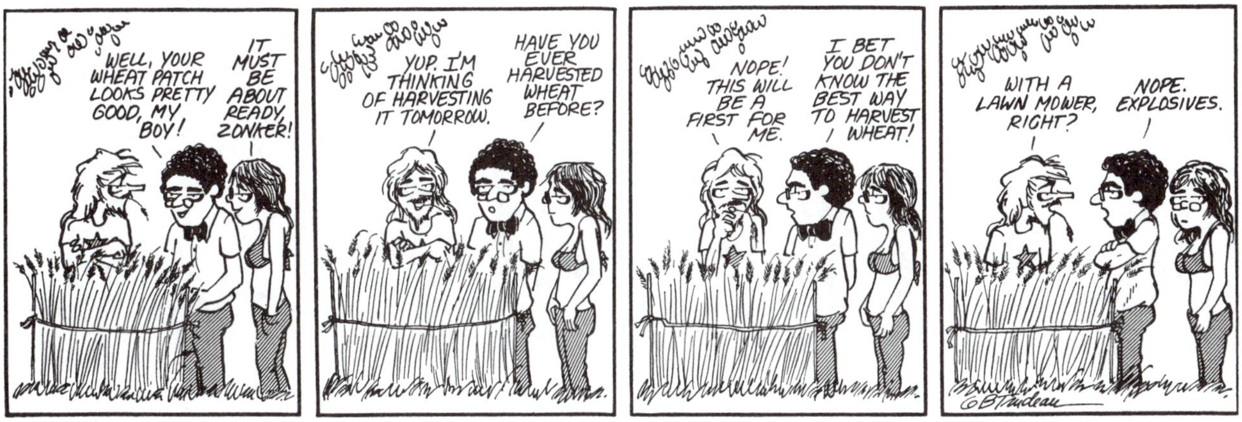
WELL, YOUR WHEAT PATCH LOOKS PRETTY GOOD, MY BOY!
IT MUST BE ABOUT READY, ZONKER!
YUP. I'M THINKING OF HARVESTING IT TOMORROW.
HAVE YOU EVER HARVESTED WHEAT BEFORE?
NOPE! THIS WILL BE A FIRST FOR ME.
I BET YOU DON'T KNOW THE BEST WAY TO HARVEST WHEAT!
WITH A LAWN MOWER, RIGHT?
NOPE. EXPLOSIVES.

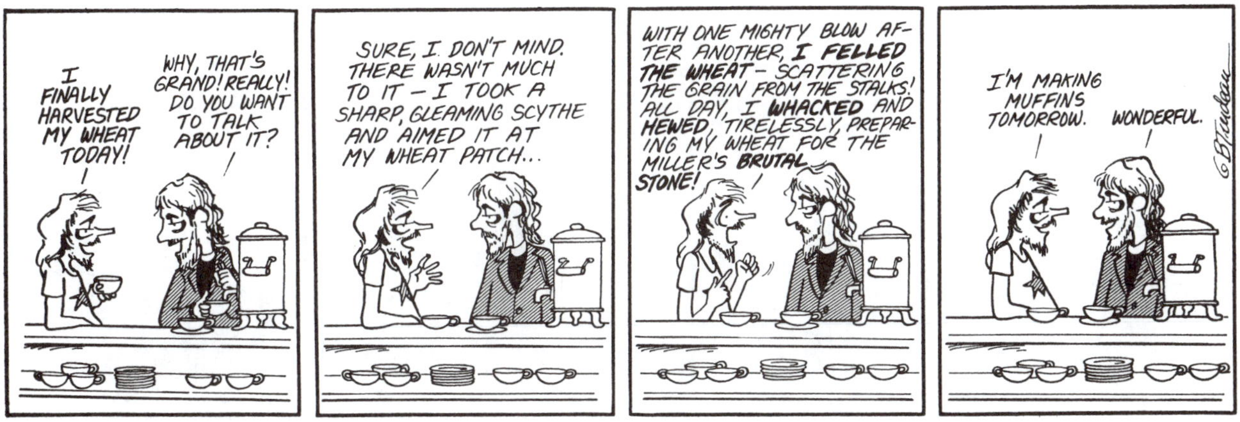
I FINALLY HARVESTED MY WHEAT TODAY!
WHY, THAT'S GRAND! REALLY! DO YOU WANT TO TALK ABOUT IT?
SURE, I DON'T MIND. THERE WASN'T MUCH TO IT – I TOOK A SHARP, GLEAMING SCYTHE AND AIMED IT AT MY WHEAT PATCH...
WITH ONE MIGHTY BLOW AFTER ANOTHER, I FELLED THE WHEAT – SCATTERING THE GRAIN FROM THE STALKS! ALL DAY, I WHACKED AND HEWED, TIRELESSLY, PREPARING MY WHEAT FOR THE MILLER'S BRUTAL STONE!
I'M MAKING MUFFINS TOMORROW.
WONDERFUL.

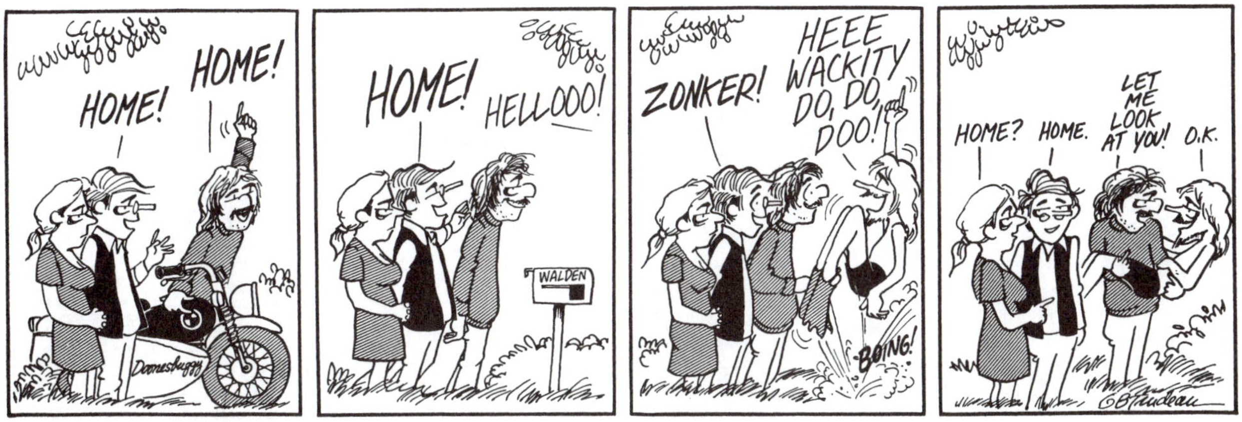
HOME!
HOME!
HOME!
HELLOOO!
WALDEN
ZONKER!
HEEE WACKITY DO, DO, DOO!
BOING!
HOME?
HOME.
LET ME LOOK AT YOU!
O.K.

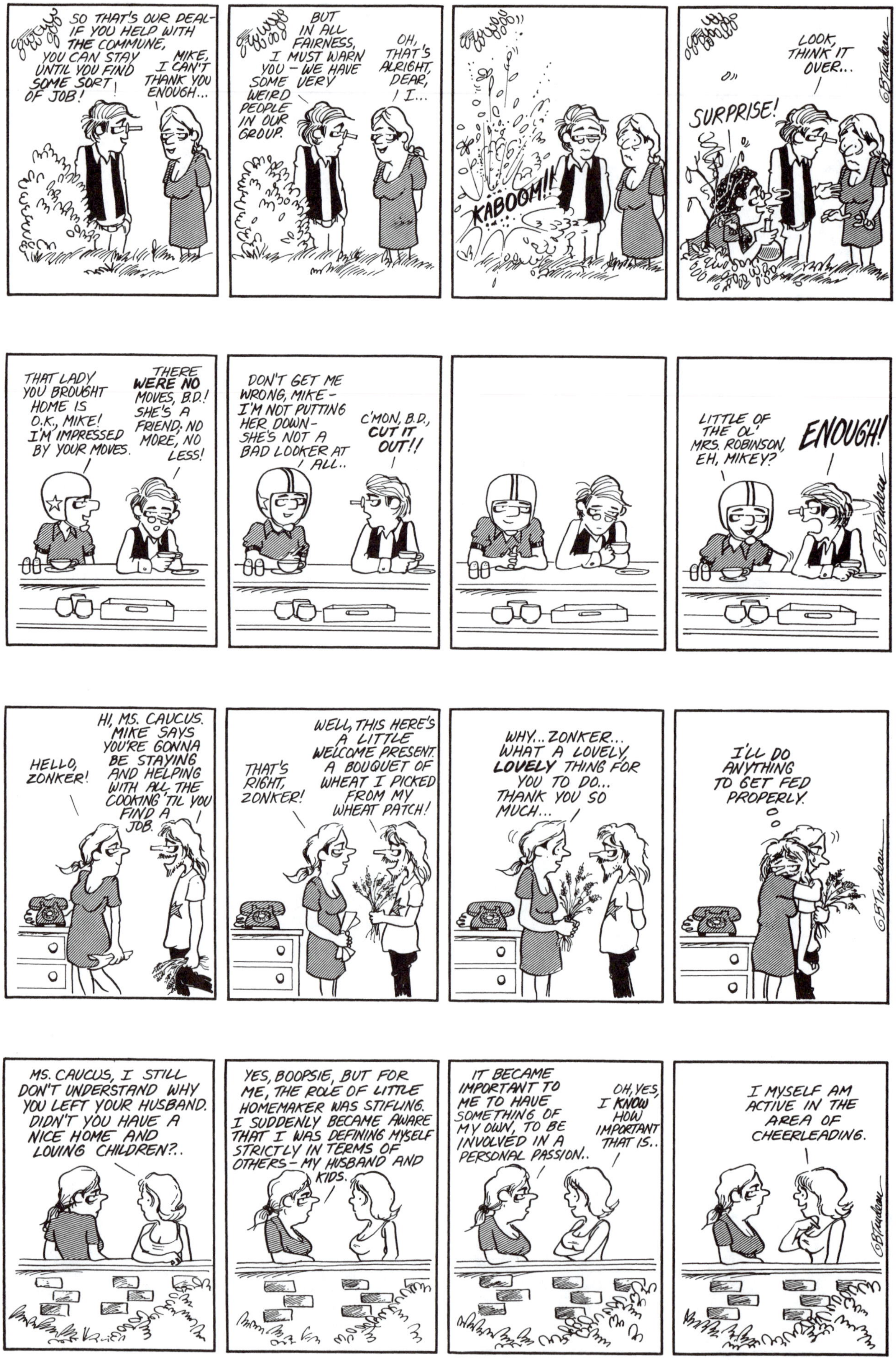
SO THAT'S OUR DEAL— IF YOU HELP WITH **THE** COMMUNE, YOU CAN STAY UNTIL YOU FIND **SOME** SORT OF JOB!
MIKE, I CAN'T THANK YOU ENOUGH...
BUT IN ALL FAIRNESS, I MUST WARN YOU — WE HAVE SOME VERY WEIRD PEOPLE IN OUR GROUP.
OH, THAT'S ALRIGHT, DEAR, I...
KABOOM!!
SURPRISE!
LOOK, THINK IT OVER...
THAT LADY YOU BROUGHT HOME IS O.K., MIKE! **I'M** IMPRESSED BY YOUR MOVES.
THERE **WERE NO** MOVES, B.D.! SHE'S A FRIEND, NO MORE, NO LESS!
DON'T GET ME WRONG, MIKE— **I'M** NOT PUTTING HER DOWN— SHE'S NOT A BAD LOOKER AT ALL..
C'MON, B.D., **CUT IT OUT!!**
LITTLE OF THE OL' MRS. ROBINSON, EH, MIKEY?
ENOUGH!
HELLO, ZONKER!
HI, MS. CAUCUS. **MIKE** SAYS YOU'RE GONNA **BE** STAYING AND HELPING WITH **ALL** THE COOKING 'TIL YOU FIND A JOB.
THAT'S RIGHT, ZONKER!
WELL, THIS HERE'S A LITTLE **WELCOME** PRESENT. A BOUQUET OF WHEAT I PICKED FROM MY WHEAT PATCH!
WHY... ZONKER... WHAT A LOVELY, **LOVELY** THING FOR YOU TO DO... THANK YOU SO MUCH...
I'LL DO ANYTHING TO GET FED PROPERLY.
MS. CAUCUS, I STILL DON'T UNDERSTAND WHY YOU LEFT YOUR HUSBAND. DIDN'T YOU HAVE A NICE HOME AND LOVING CHILDREN?..
YES, BOOPSIE, BUT FOR ME, THE ROLE OF LITTLE HOMEMAKER WAS STIFLING. I SUDDENLY BECAME AWARE THAT I WAS DEFINING MYSELF STRICTLY IN TERMS OF OTHERS— MY HUSBAND AND KIDS.
IT BECAME IMPORTANT TO ME TO HAVE SOMETHING OF MY OWN, TO BE INVOLVED IN A PERSONAL PASSION..
OH, YES, I **KNOW** HOW IMPORTANT THAT IS..
I MYSELF AM ACTIVE IN THE AREA OF CHEERLEADING.

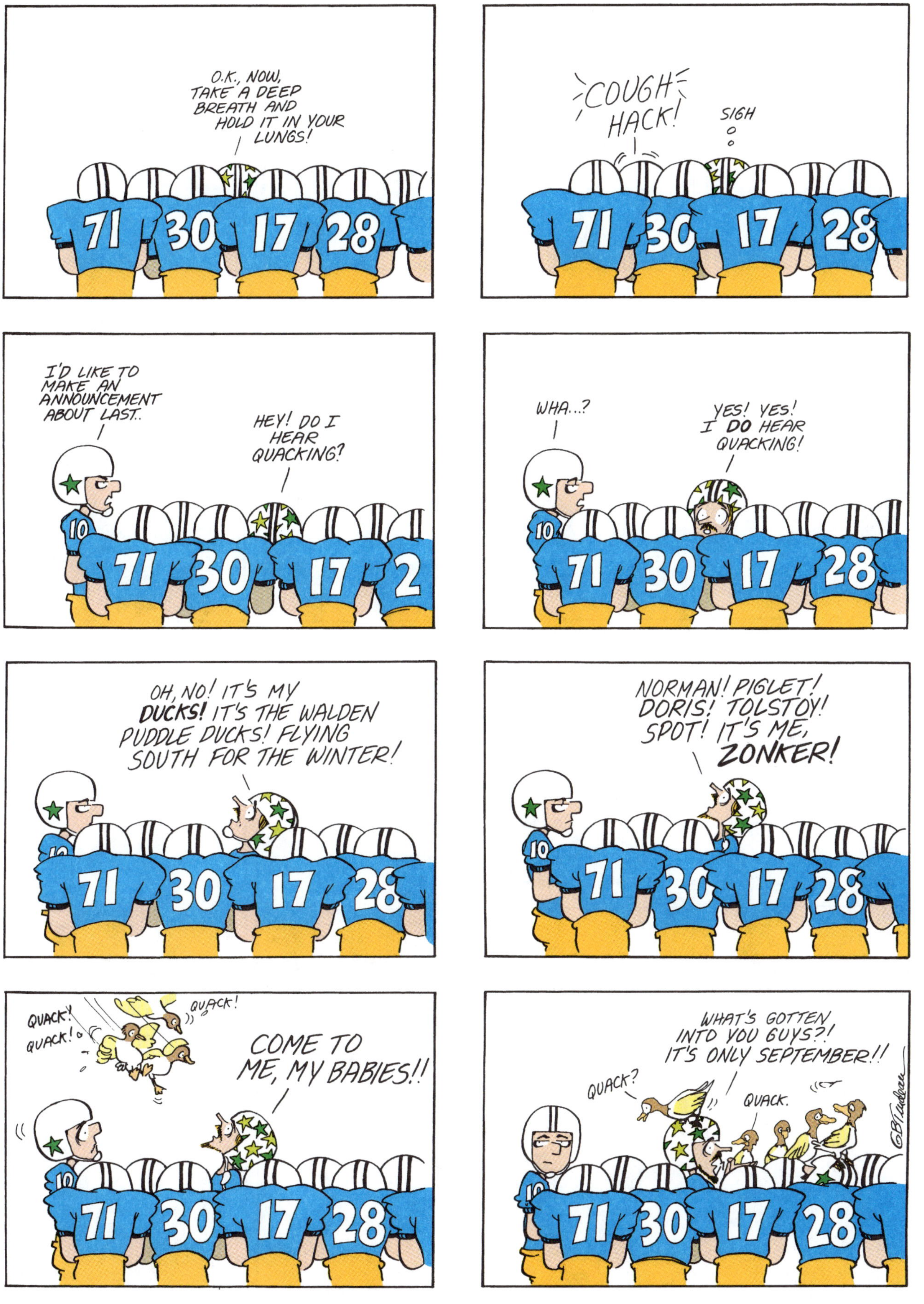
O.K., NOW, TAKE A DEEP BREATH AND HOLD IT IN YOUR LUNGS!
COUGH HACK!
SIGH
I'D LIKE TO MAKE AN ANNOUNCEMENT ABOUT LAST..
HEY! DO I HEAR QUACKING?
WHA...?
YES! YES! I **DO** HEAR QUACKING!
OH, NO! IT'S MY **DUCKS!** IT'S THE WALDEN PUDDLE DUCKS! FLYING SOUTH FOR THE WINTER!
NORMAN! PIGLET! DORIS! TOLSTOY! SPOT! IT'S ME, **ZONKER!**
QUACK!
QUACK!
QUACK!
COME TO ME, MY BABIES!!
WHAT'S GOTTEN INTO YOU GUYS?! IT'S ONLY SEPTEMBER!!
QUACK?
QUACK.

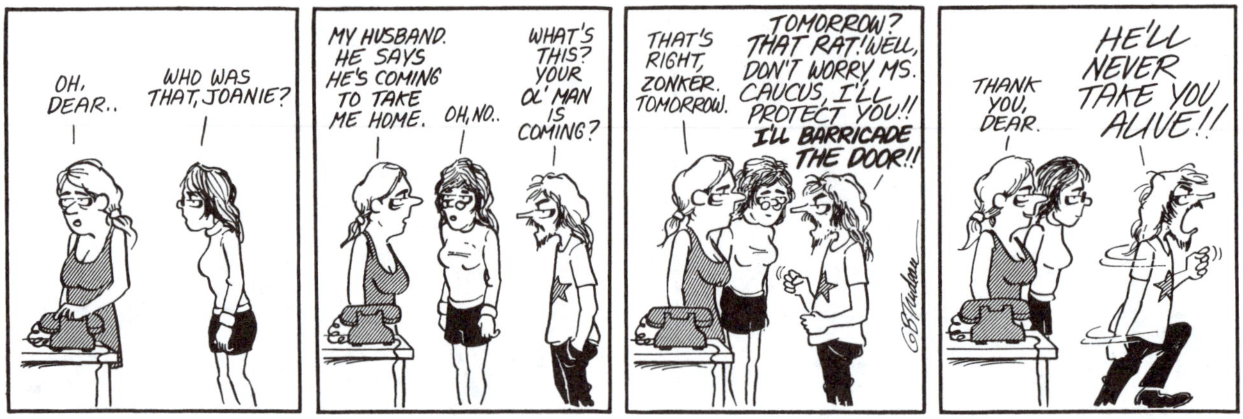
OH, DEAR..
WHO WAS THAT, JOANIE?
MY HUSBAND. HE SAYS HE'S COMING TO TAKE ME HOME.
OH, NO..
WHAT'S THIS? YOUR OL' MAN IS COMING?
THAT'S RIGHT, ZONKER. TOMORROW.
TOMORROW? THAT RAT! WELL, DON'T WORRY MS. CAUCUS, I'LL PROTECT YOU!! I'LL BARRICADE THE DOOR!!
THANK YOU, DEAR.
HE'LL NEVER TAKE YOU ALIVE!!

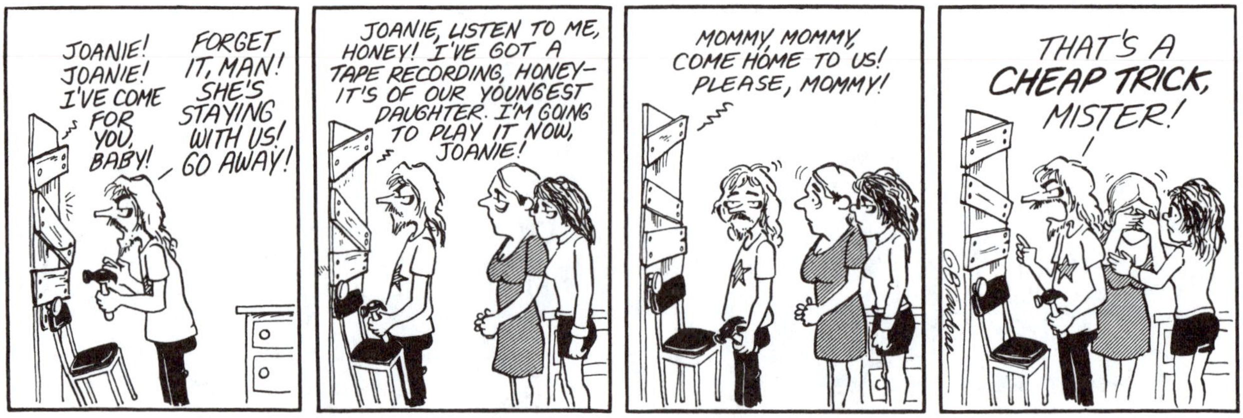
JOANIE! JOANIE! I'VE COME FOR YOU, BABY!
FORGET IT, MAN! SHE'S STAYING WITH US! GO AWAY!
JOANIE, LISTEN TO ME, HONEY! I'VE GOT A TAPE RECORDING, HONEY— IT'S OF OUR YOUNGEST DAUGHTER. I'M GOING TO PLAY IT NOW, JOANIE!
MOMMY, MOMMY, COME HOME TO US! PLEASE, MOMMY!
THAT'S A CHEAP TRICK, MISTER!

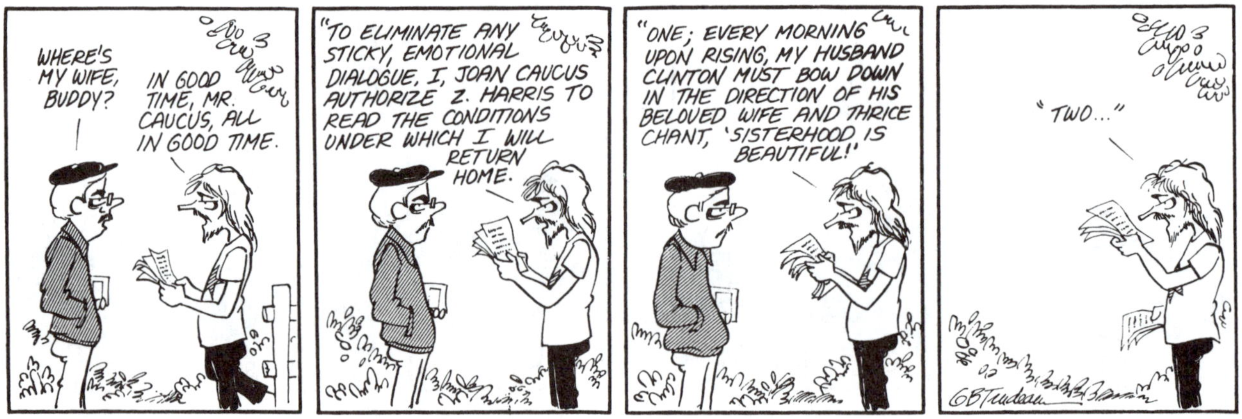
WHERE'S MY WIFE, BUDDY?
IN GOOD TIME, MR. CAUCUS, ALL IN GOOD TIME.
"TO ELIMINATE ANY STICKY, EMOTIONAL DIALOGUE, I, JOAN CAUCUS AUTHORIZE Z. HARRIS TO READ THE CONDITIONS UNDER WHICH I WILL RETURN HOME.
"ONE; EVERY MORNING UPON RISING, MY HUSBAND CLINTON MUST BOW DOWN IN THE DIRECTION OF HIS BELOVED WIFE AND THRICE CHANT, 'SISTERHOOD IS BEAUTIFUL!'
"TWO..."

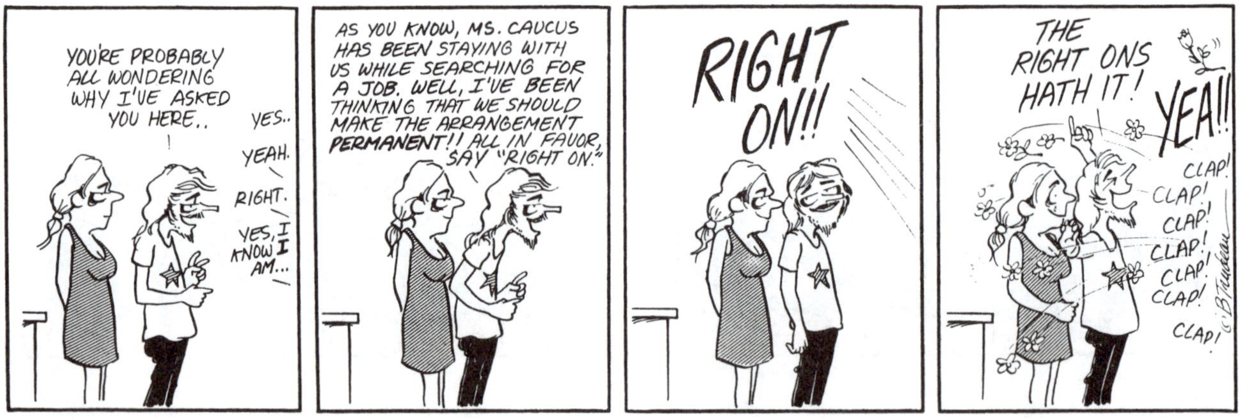
YOU'RE PROBABLY ALL WONDERING WHY I'VE ASKED YOU HERE..
YES..
YEAH.
RIGHT.
YES, I KNOW I AM...
AS YOU KNOW, MS. CAUCUS HAS BEEN STAYING WITH US WHILE SEARCHING FOR A JOB. WELL, I'VE BEEN THINKING THAT WE SHOULD MAKE THE ARRANGEMENT PERMANENT!! ALL IN FAVOR, SAY "RIGHT ON."
RIGHT ON!!
THE RIGHT ONS HATH IT!
YEA!!
CLAP! CLAP! CLAP! CLAP! CLAP! CLAP! CLAP!

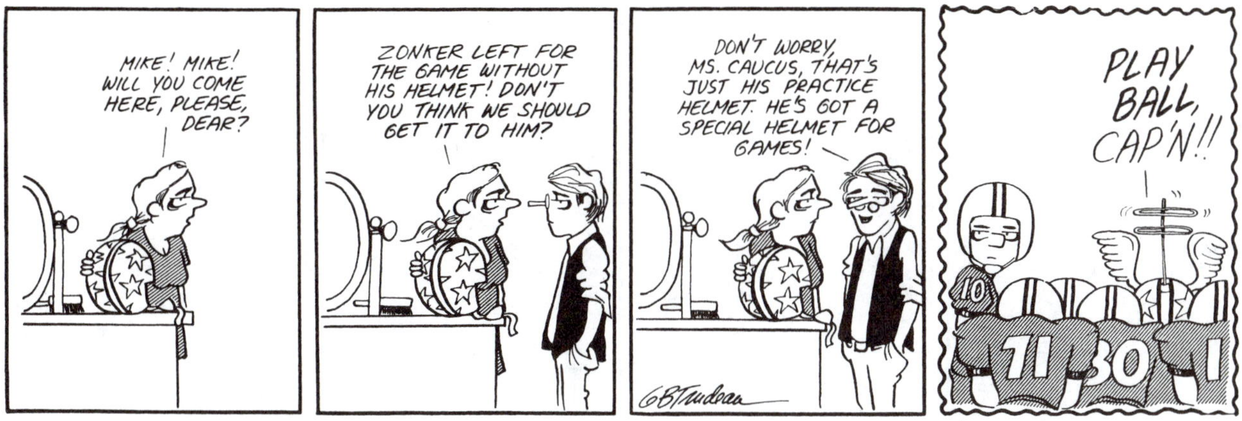
MIKE! MIKE! WILL YOU COME HERE, PLEASE, DEAR?
ZONKER LEFT FOR THE GAME WITHOUT HIS HELMET! DON'T YOU THINK WE SHOULD GET IT TO HIM?
DON'T WORRY, MS. CAUCUS, THAT'S JUST HIS PRACTICE HELMET. HE'S GOT A SPECIAL HELMET FOR GAMES!
PLAY BALL, CAP'N!!
10
11
30
1

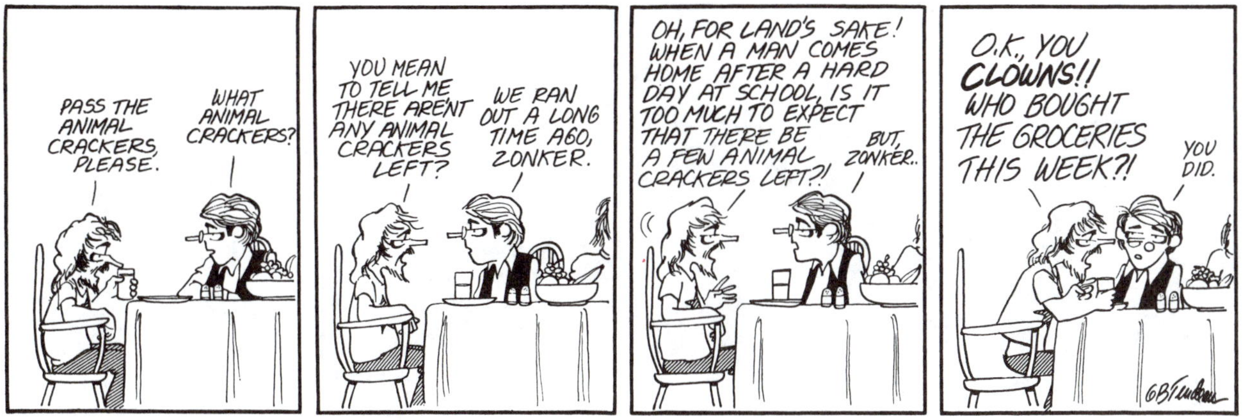
PASS THE ANIMAL CRACKERS, PLEASE.
WHAT ANIMAL CRACKERS?
YOU MEAN TO TELL ME THERE AREN'T ANY ANIMAL CRACKERS LEFT?
WE RAN OUT A LONG TIME AGO, ZONKER.
OH, FOR LAND'S SAKE! WHEN A MAN COMES HOME AFTER A HARD DAY AT SCHOOL, IS IT TOO MUCH TO EXPECT THAT THERE BE A FEW ANIMAL CRACKERS LEFT?!
BUT, ZONKER..
O.K., YOU CLOWNS!! WHO BOUGHT THE GROCERIES THIS WEEK?!
YOU DID.

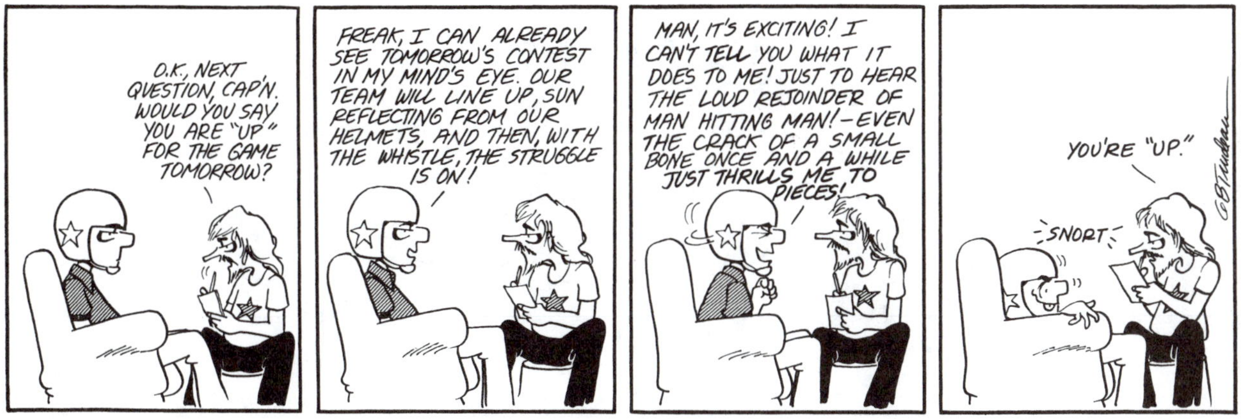
O.K., NEXT QUESTION, CAP'N. WOULD YOU SAY YOU ARE "UP" FOR THE GAME TOMORROW?
FREAK, I CAN ALREADY SEE TOMORROW'S CONTEST IN MY MIND'S EYE. OUR TEAM WILL LINE UP, SUN REFLECTING FROM OUR HELMETS, AND THEN, WITH THE WHISTLE, THE STRUGGLE IS ON!
MAN, IT'S EXCITING! I CAN'T TELL YOU WHAT IT DOES TO ME! JUST TO HEAR THE LOUD REJOINDER OF MAN HITTING MAN! – EVEN THE CRACK OF A SMALL BONE ONCE AND A WHILE JUST THRILLS ME TO PIECES!
SNORT
YOU'RE "UP."

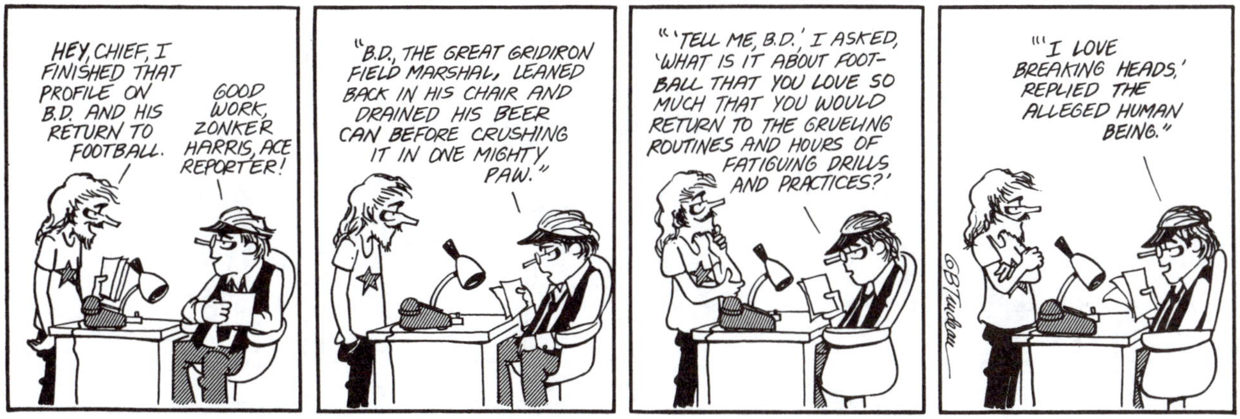
HEY, CHIEF, I FINISHED THAT PROFILE ON B.D. AND HIS RETURN TO FOOTBALL.
GOOD WORK, ZONKER HARRIS, ACE REPORTER!
"B.D., THE GREAT GRIDIRON FIELD MARSHAL, LEANED BACK IN HIS CHAIR AND DRAINED HIS BEER CAN BEFORE CRUSHING IT IN ONE MIGHTY PAW."
"'TELL ME, B.D.,' I ASKED, 'WHAT IS IT ABOUT FOOTBALL THAT YOU LOVE SO MUCH THAT YOU WOULD RETURN TO THE GRUELING ROUTINES AND HOURS OF FATIGUING DRILLS AND PRACTICES?'
"'I LOVE BREAKING HEADS,' REPLIED THE ALLEGED HUMAN BEING."

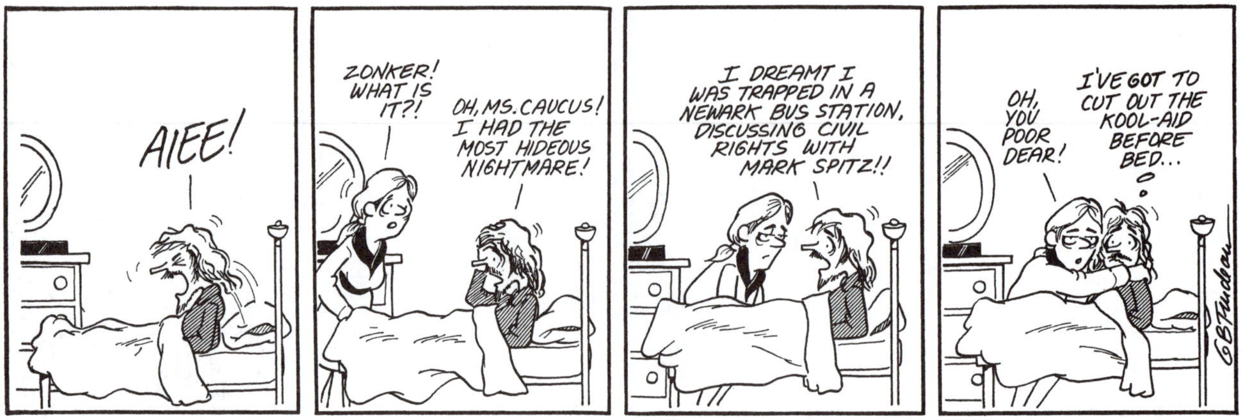
AIEE!
ZONKER! WHAT IS IT?!
OH, MS. CAUCUS! I HAD THE MOST HIDEOUS NIGHTMARE!
I DREAMT I WAS TRAPPED IN A NEWARK BUS STATION, DISCUSSING CIVIL RIGHTS WITH MARK SPITZ!!
OH, YOU POOR DEAR!
I'VE GOT TO CUT OUT THE KOOL-AID BEFORE BED...

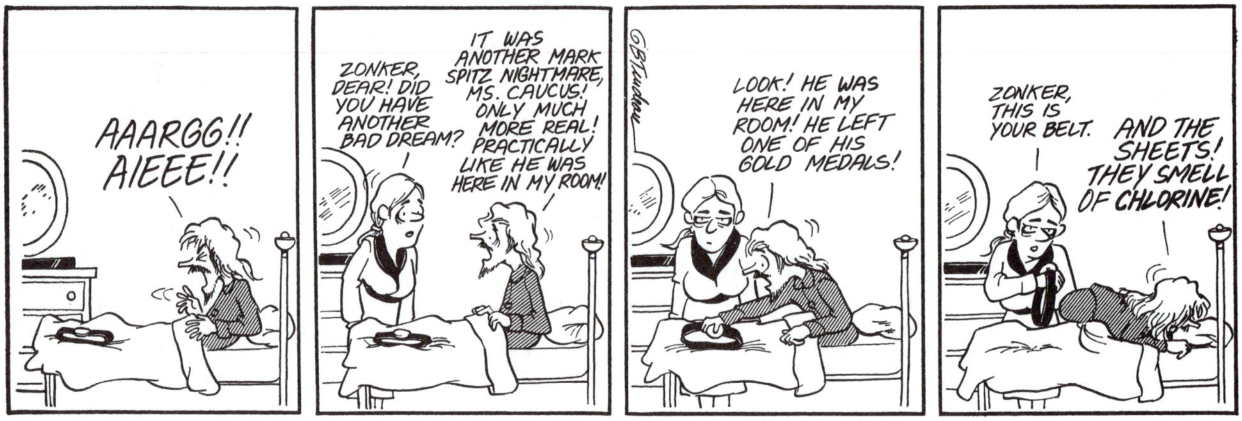
AAARGG!! AIEEE!!
ZONKER, DEAR! DID YOU HAVE ANOTHER BAD DREAM?
IT WAS ANOTHER MARK SPITZ NIGHTMARE, MS. CAUCUS! ONLY MUCH MORE REAL! PRACTICALLY LIKE HE WAS HERE IN MY ROOM!
LOOK! HE WAS HERE IN MY ROOM! HE LEFT ONE OF HIS GOLD MEDALS!
ZONKER, THIS IS YOUR BELT.
AND THE SHEETS! THEY SMELL OF CHLORINE!

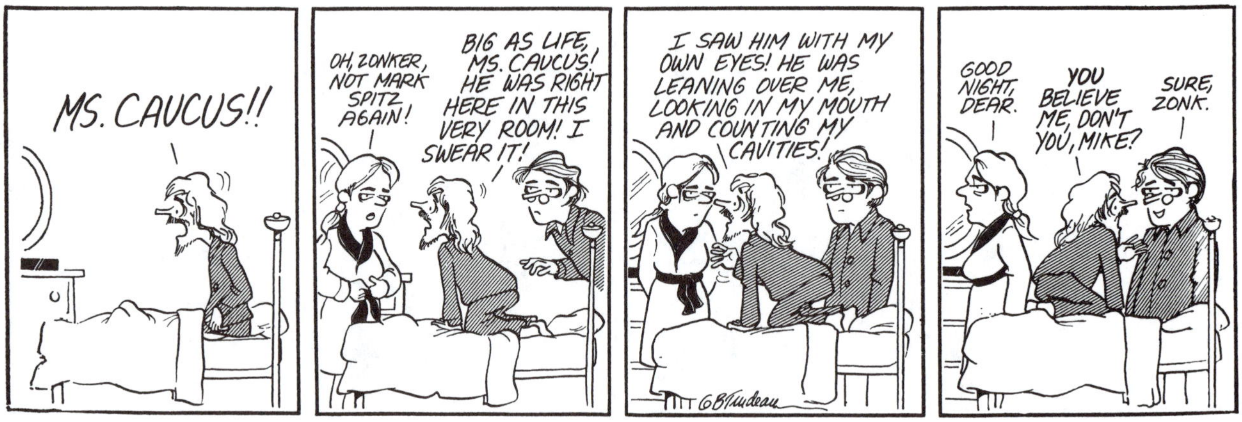
MS. CAUCUS!!
OH, ZONKER, NOT MARK SPITZ AGAIN!
BIG AS LIFE, MS. CAUCUS! HE WAS RIGHT HERE IN THIS VERY ROOM! I SWEAR IT!
I SAW HIM WITH MY OWN EYES! HE WAS LEANING OVER ME, LOOKING IN MY MOUTH AND COUNTING MY CAVITIES!
GOOD NIGHT, DEAR.
YOU BELIEVE ME, DON'T YOU, MIKE?
SURE, ZONK.

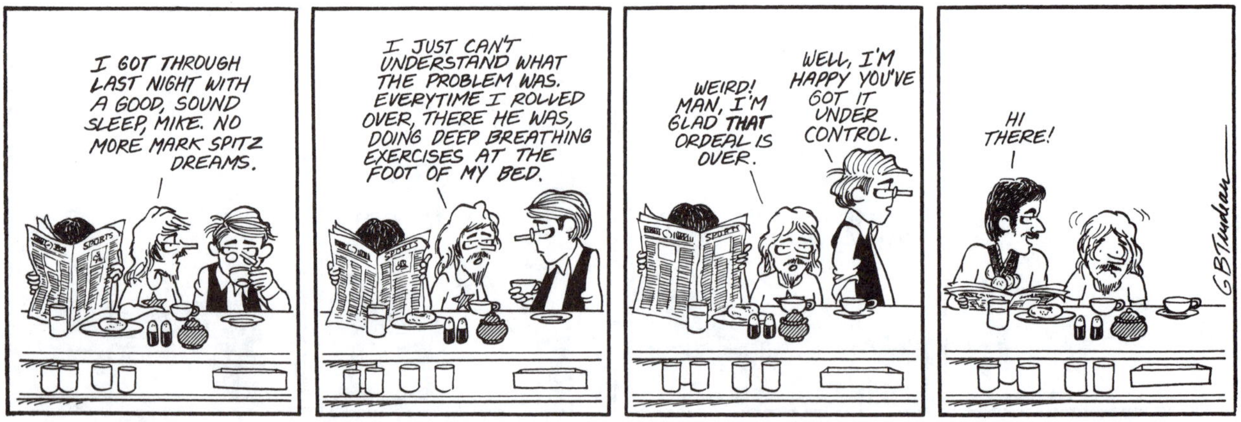
I GOT THROUGH LAST NIGHT WITH A GOOD, SOUND SLEEP, MIKE. NO MORE MARK SPITZ DREAMS.
I JUST CAN'T UNDERSTAND WHAT THE PROBLEM WAS. EVERYTIME I ROLLED OVER, THERE HE WAS, DOING DEEP BREATHING EXERCISES AT THE FOOT OF MY BED.
WEIRD! MAN, I'M GLAD THAT ORDEAL IS OVER.
WELL, I'M HAPPY YOU'VE GOT IT UNDER CONTROL.
HI THERE!

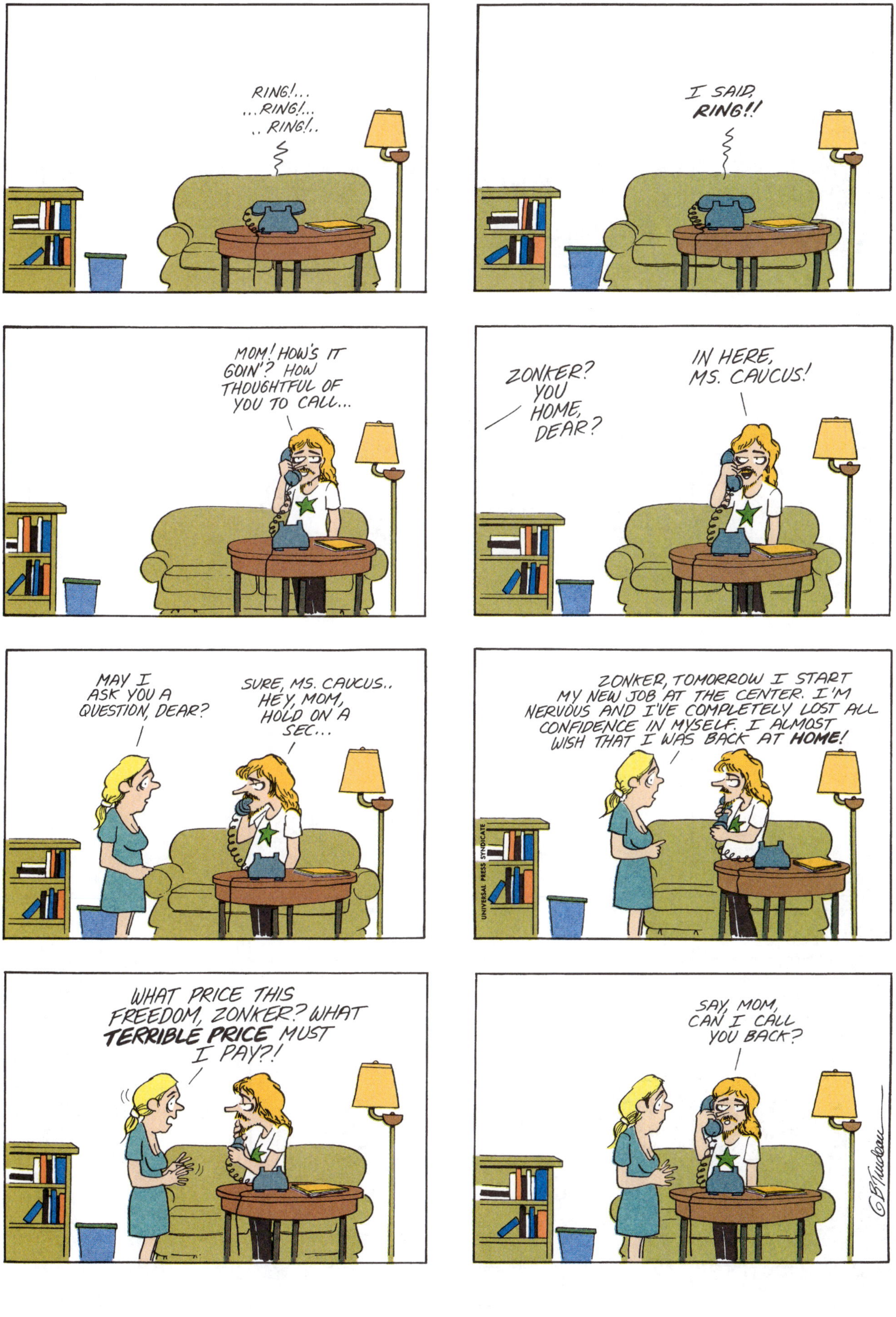
RING!... ...RING!... .. RING!..
I SAID, RING!!
MOM! HOW'S IT GOIN'? HOW THOUGHTFUL OF YOU TO CALL...
ZONKER? YOU HOME, DEAR?
IN HERE, MS. CAUCUS!
MAY I ASK YOU A QUESTION, DEAR?
SURE, MS. CAUCUS.. HEY, MOM, HOLD ON A SEC...
ZONKER, TOMORROW I START MY NEW JOB AT THE CENTER. I'M NERVOUS AND I'VE COMPLETELY LOST ALL CONFIDENCE IN MYSELF. I ALMOST WISH THAT I WAS BACK AT HOME!
UNIVERSAL PRESS SYNDICATE
WHAT PRICE THIS FREEDOM, ZONKER? WHAT TERRIBLE PRICE MUST I PAY?!
SAY, MOM, CAN I CALL YOU BACK?

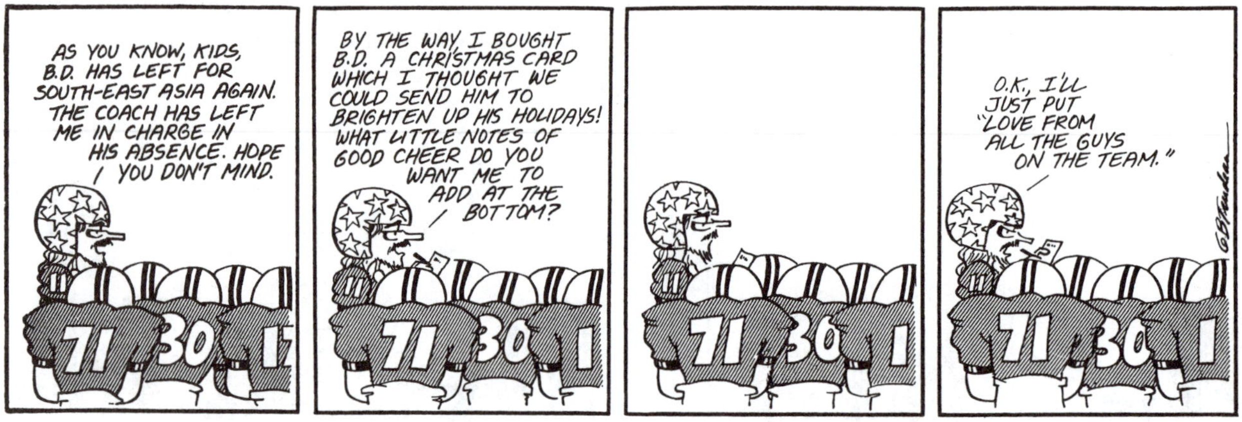
AS YOU KNOW, KIDS, B.D. HAS LEFT FOR SOUTH-EAST ASIA AGAIN. THE COACH HAS LEFT ME IN CHARGE IN HIS ABSENCE. HOPE YOU DON'T MIND.
BY THE WAY I BOUGHT B.D. A CHRISTMAS CARD WHICH I THOUGHT WE COULD SEND HIM TO BRIGHTEN UP HIS HOLIDAYS! WHAT LITTLE NOTES OF GOOD CHEER DO YOU WANT ME TO ADD AT THE BOTTOM?
O.K., I'LL JUST PUT "LOVE FROM ALL THE GUYS ON THE TEAM."

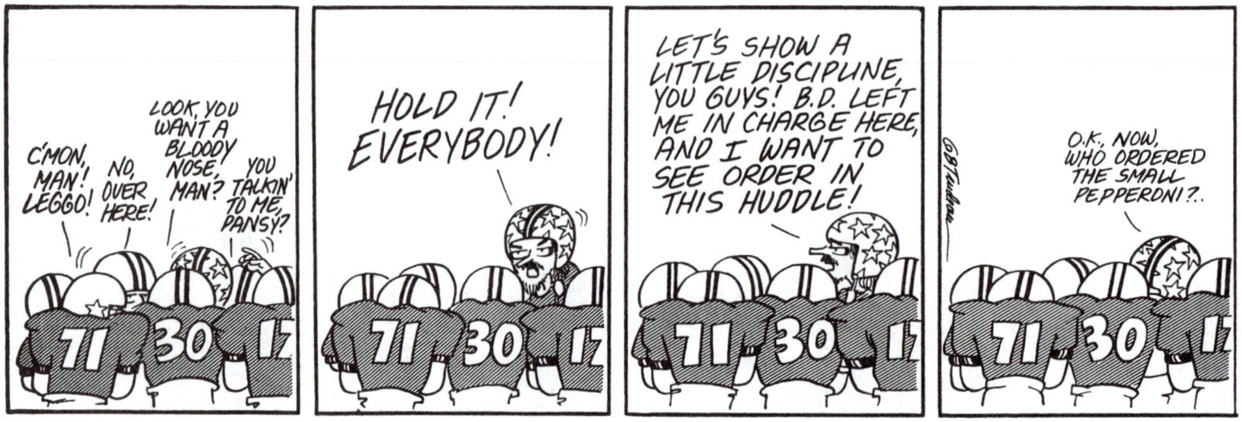
C'MON, MAN! LEGGO!
NO, OVER HERE!
LOOK, YOU WANT A BLOODY NOSE, MAN?
YOU TALKIN' TO ME, PANSY?
HOLD IT! EVERYBODY!
LET'S SHOW A LITTLE DISCIPLINE, YOU GUYS! B.D. LEFT ME IN CHARGE HERE, AND I WANT TO SEE ORDER IN THIS HUDDLE!
O.K., NOW, WHO ORDERED THE SMALL PEPPERONI?..

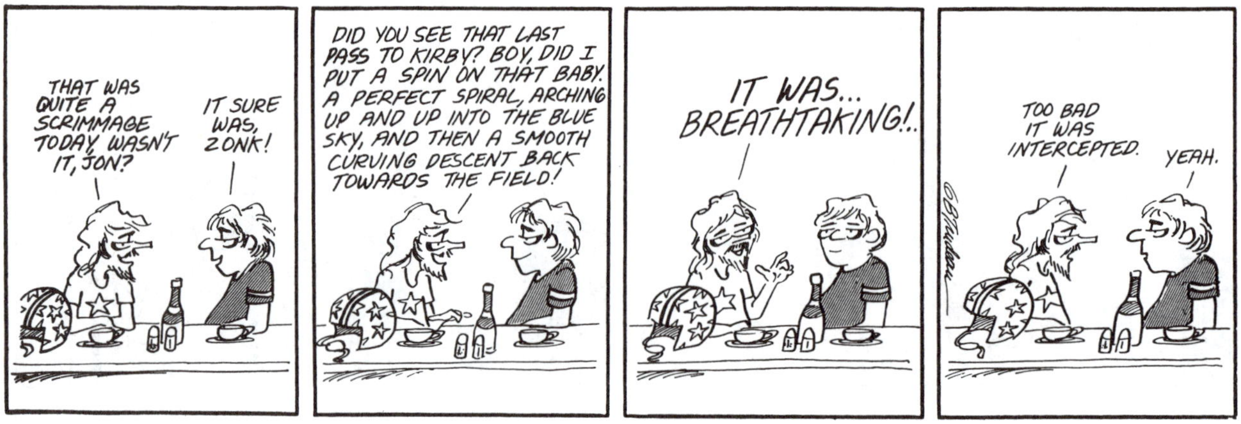
THAT WAS QUITE A SCRIMMAGE TODAY, WASN'T IT, JON?
IT SURE WAS, ZONK!
DID YOU SEE THAT LAST PASS TO KIRBY? BOY, DID I PUT A SPIN ON THAT BABY. A PERFECT SPIRAL, ARCHING UP AND UP INTO THE BLUE SKY, AND THEN A SMOOTH CURVING DESCENT BACK TOWARDS THE FIELD!
IT WAS... BREATHTAKING!..
TOO BAD IT WAS INTERCEPTED.
YEAH.

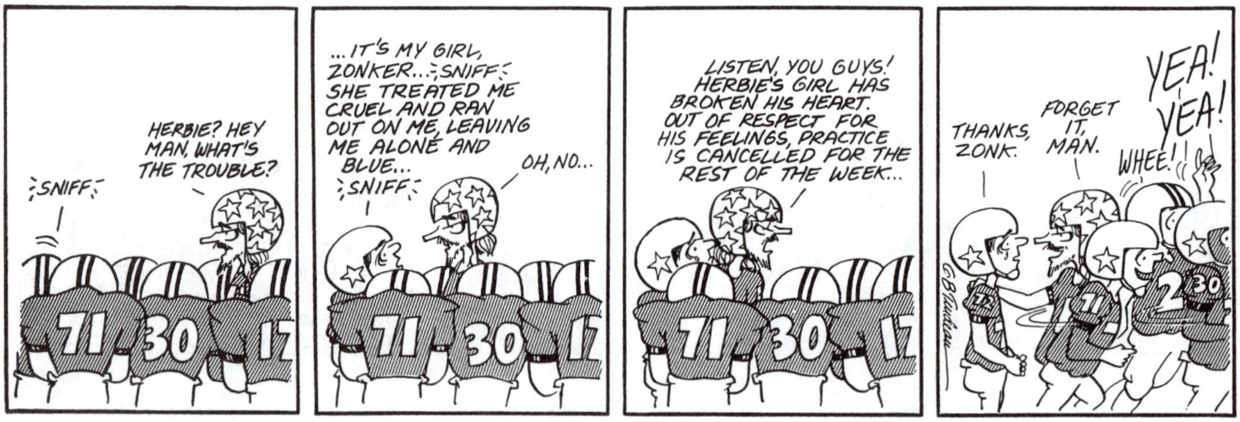
SNIFF
HERBIE? HEY MAN, WHAT'S THE TROUBLE?
...IT'S MY GIRL, ZONKER... SNIFF SHE TREATED ME CRUEL AND RAN OUT ON ME, LEAVING ME ALONE AND BLUE...
SNIFF
OH, NO...
LISTEN, YOU GUYS! HERBIE'S GIRL HAS BROKEN HIS HEART. OUT OF RESPECT FOR HIS FEELINGS, PRACTICE IS CANCELLED FOR THE REST OF THE WEEK...
THANKS, ZONK.
FORGET IT, MAN.
YEA! YEA!
WHEE!

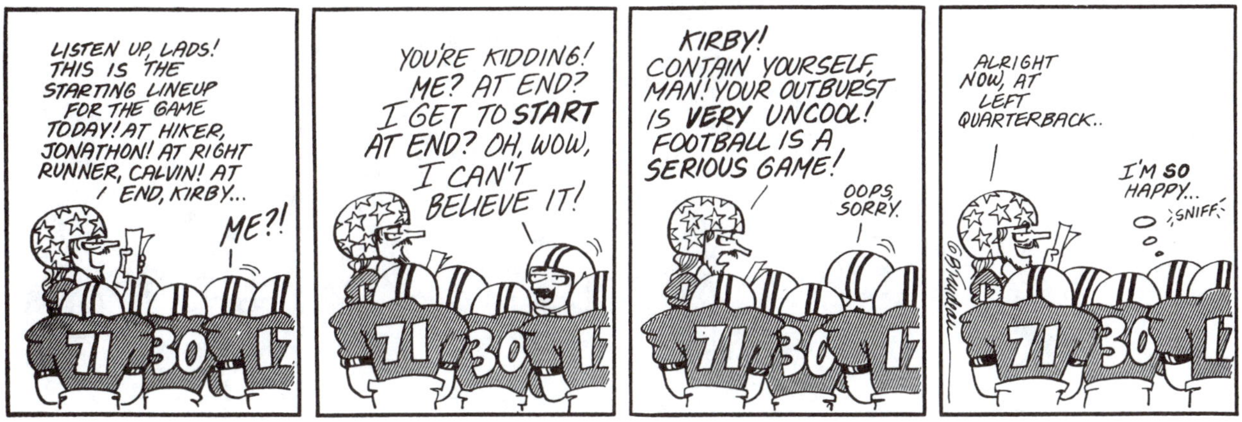
LISTEN UP, LADS! THIS IS THE STARTING LINEUP FOR THE GAME TODAY! AT HIKER, JONATHON! AT RIGHT RUNNER, CALVIN! AT END, KIRBY...
ME?!
YOU'RE KIDDING! ME? AT END? I GET TO START AT END? OH, WOW, I CAN'T BELIEVE IT!
KIRBY! CONTAIN YOURSELF, MAN! YOUR OUTBURST IS VERY UNCOOL! FOOTBALL IS A SERIOUS GAME!
OOPS, SORRY.
ALRIGHT NOW, AT LEFT QUARTERBACK..
I'M SO HAPPY...
SNIFF

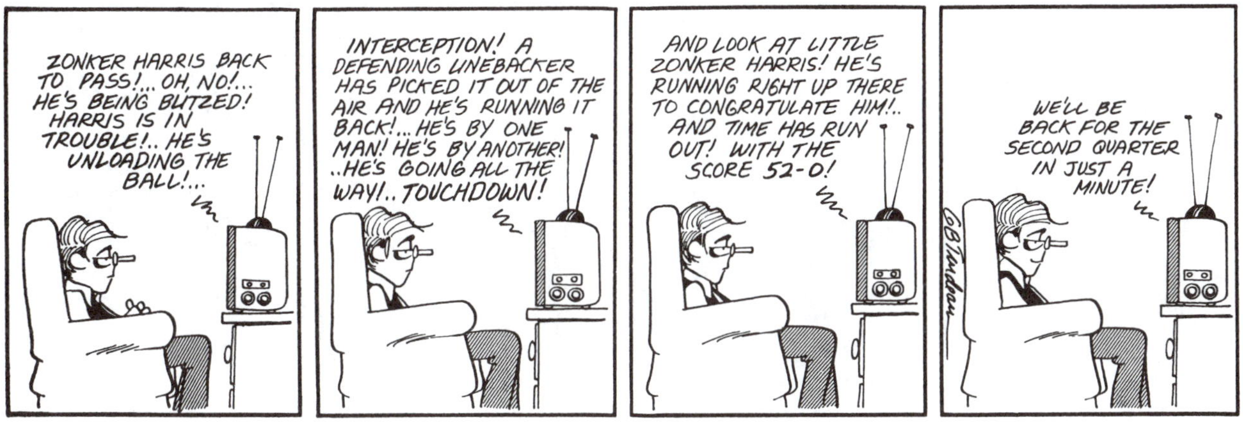
ZONKER HARRIS BACK TO PASS!... OH, NO!... HE'S BEING BLITZED! HARRIS IS IN TROUBLE!.. HE'S UNLOADING THE BALL!...
INTERCEPTION! A DEFENDING LINEBACKER HAS PICKED IT OUT OF THE AIR AND HE'S RUNNING IT BACK!... HE'S BY ONE MAN! HE'S BY ANOTHER! ..HE'S GOING ALL THE WAY!.. TOUCHDOWN!
AND LOOK AT LITTLE ZONKER HARRIS! HE'S RUNNING RIGHT UP THERE TO CONGRATULATE HIM!.. AND TIME HAS RUN OUT! WITH THE SCORE 52-0!
WE'LL BE BACK FOR THE SECOND QUARTER IN JUST A MINUTE!

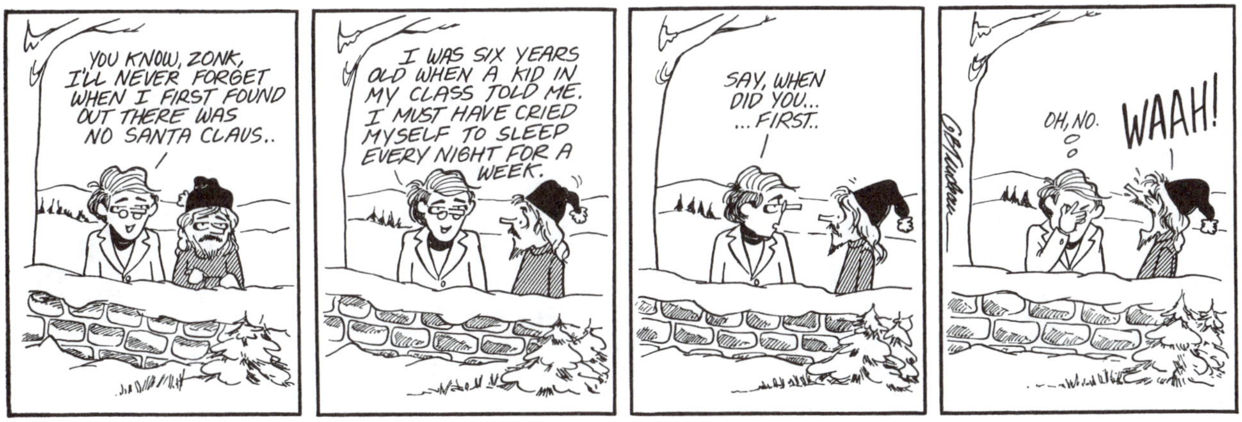
YOU KNOW, ZONK, I'LL NEVER FORGET WHEN I FIRST FOUND OUT THERE WAS NO SANTA CLAUS..
I WAS SIX YEARS OLD WHEN A KID IN MY CLASS TOLD ME. I MUST HAVE CRIED MYSELF TO SLEEP EVERY NIGHT FOR A WEEK.
SAY, WHEN DID YOU... ...FIRST..
OH, NO.
WAAH!

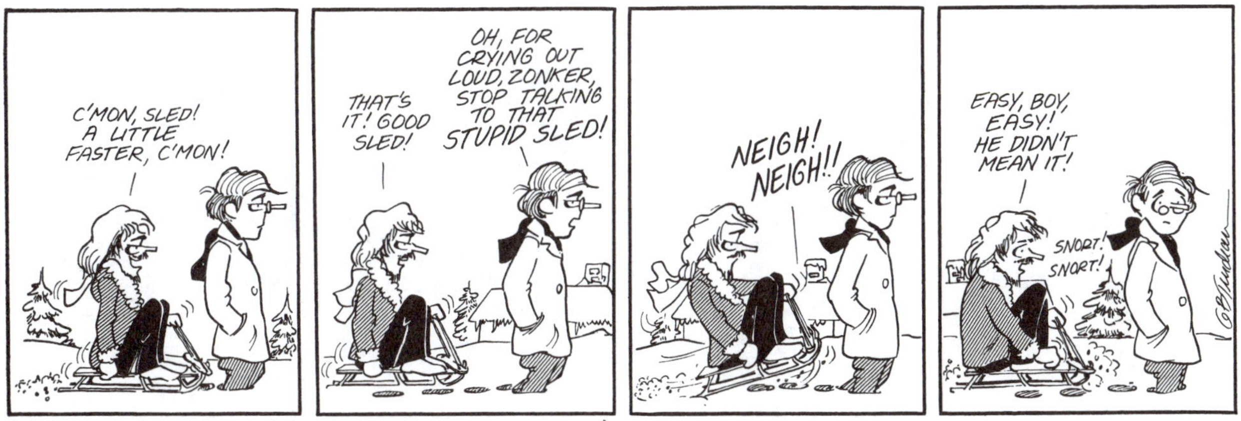
C'MON, SLED! A LITTLE FASTER, C'MON!
THAT'S IT! GOOD SLED!
OH, FOR CRYING OUT LOUD, ZONKER, STOP TALKING TO THAT STUPID SLED!
NEIGH! NEIGH!!
EASY, BOY, EASY! HE DIDN'T MEAN IT!
SNORT! SNORT!

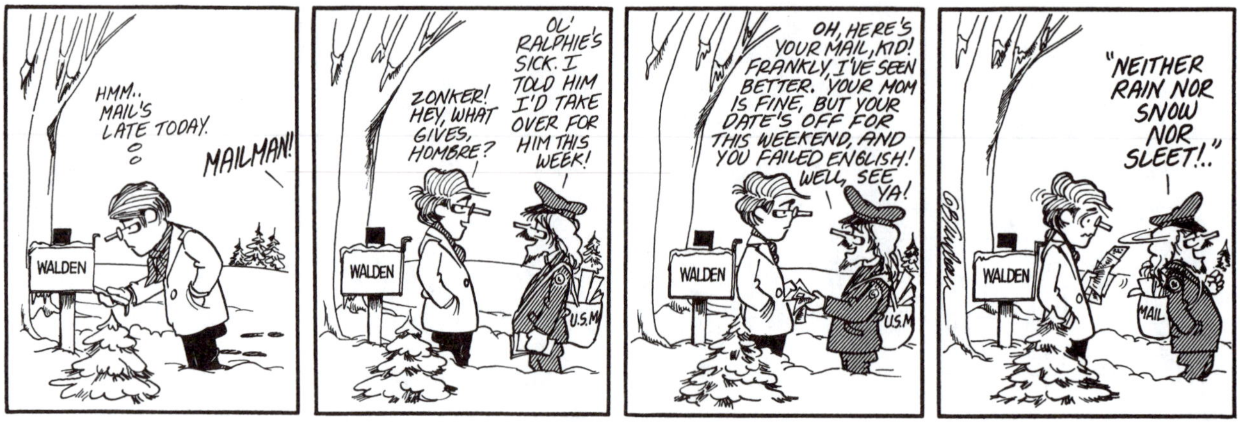
HMM.. MAIL'S LATE TODAY.
MAILMAN!
ZONKER! HEY, WHAT GIVES, HOMBRE?
OL' RALPHIE'S SICK. I TOLD HIM I'D TAKE OVER FOR HIM THIS WEEK!
WALDEN
U.S.M
OH, HERE'S YOUR MAIL, KID! FRANKLY, I'VE SEEN BETTER. YOUR MOM IS FINE, BUT YOUR DATE'S OFF FOR THIS WEEKEND, AND YOU FAILED ENGLISH!
WELL, SEE YA!
"NEITHER RAIN NOR SNOW NOR SLEET!.."
MAIL

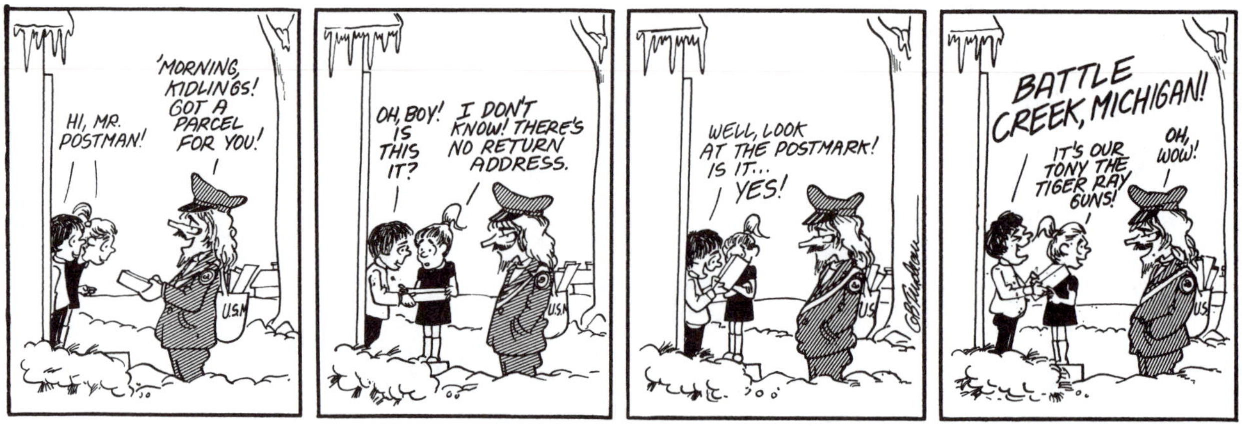
HI, MR. POSTMAN!
'MORNING, KIDLINGS! GOT A PARCEL FOR YOU!
U.S.M
OH, BOY! IS THIS IT?
I DON'T KNOW! THERE'S NO RETURN ADDRESS.
WELL, LOOK AT THE POSTMARK! IS IT...
YES!
BATTLE CREEK, MICHIGAN!
IT'S OUR TONY THE TIGER RAY GUNS!
OH, WOW!

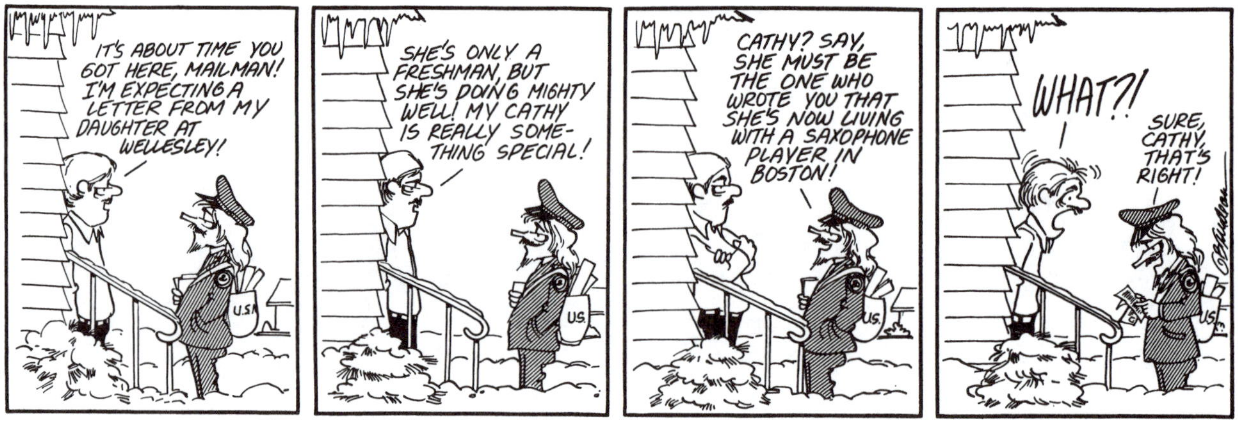
IT'S ABOUT TIME YOU GOT HERE, MAILMAN! I'M EXPECTING A LETTER FROM MY DAUGHTER AT WELLESLEY!
SHE'S ONLY A FRESHMAN, BUT SHE'S DOING MIGHTY WELL! MY CATHY IS REALLY SOMETHING SPECIAL!
CATHY? SAY, SHE MUST BE THE ONE WHO WROTE YOU THAT SHE'S NOW LIVING WITH A SAXOPHONE PLAYER IN BOSTON!
WHAT?!
SURE, CATHY, THAT'S RIGHT!

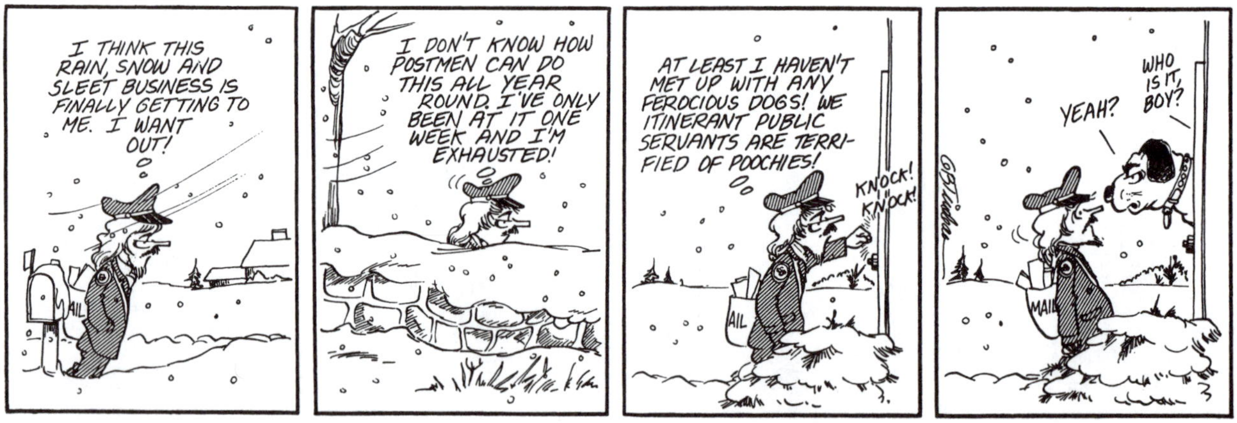
I THINK THIS RAIN, SNOW AND SLEET BUSINESS IS FINALLY GETTING TO ME. I WANT OUT!
I DON'T KNOW HOW POSTMEN CAN DO THIS ALL YEAR ROUND. I'VE ONLY BEEN AT IT ONE WEEK AND I'M EXHAUSTED!
AT LEAST I HAVEN'T MET UP WITH ANY FEROCIOUS DOGS! WE ITINERANT PUBLIC SERVANTS ARE TERRIFIED OF POOCHIES!
KNOCK! KNOCK!
YEAH?
WHO IS IT, BOY?

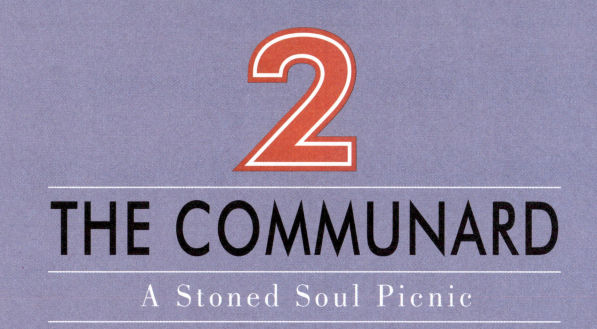

2

THE COMMUNARD

A Stoned Soul Picnic

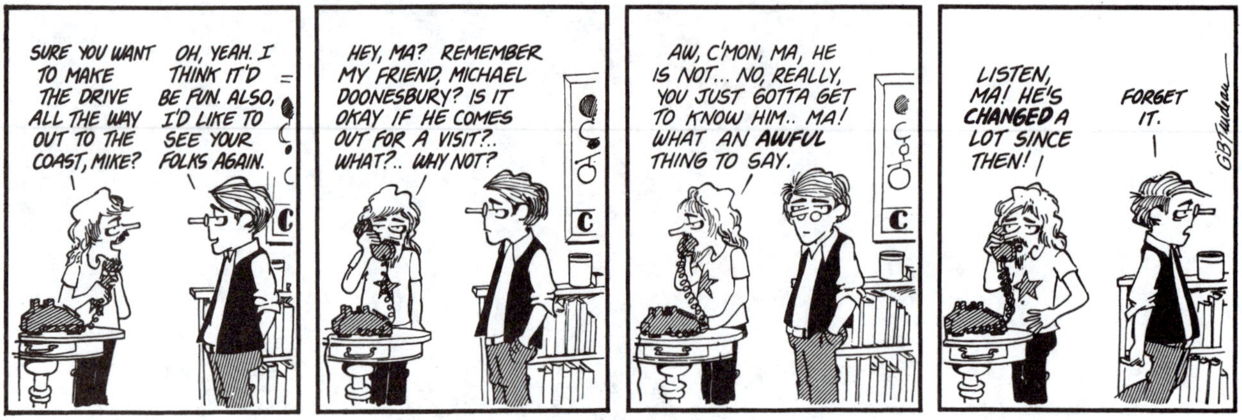
SURE YOU WANT TO MAKE THE DRIVE ALL THE WAY OUT TO THE COAST, MIKE?
OH, YEAH. I THINK IT'D BE FUN. ALSO, I'D LIKE TO SEE YOUR FOLKS AGAIN.
HEY, MA? REMEMBER MY FRIEND, MICHAEL DOONESBURY? IS IT OKAY IF HE COMES OUT FOR A VISIT?.. WHAT?.. WHY NOT?
AW, C'MON, MA, HE IS NOT... NO, REALLY, YOU JUST GOTTA GET TO KNOW HIM.. MA! WHAT AN AWFUL THING TO SAY.
LISTEN, MA! HE'S CHANGED A LOT SINCE THEN!
FORGET IT.

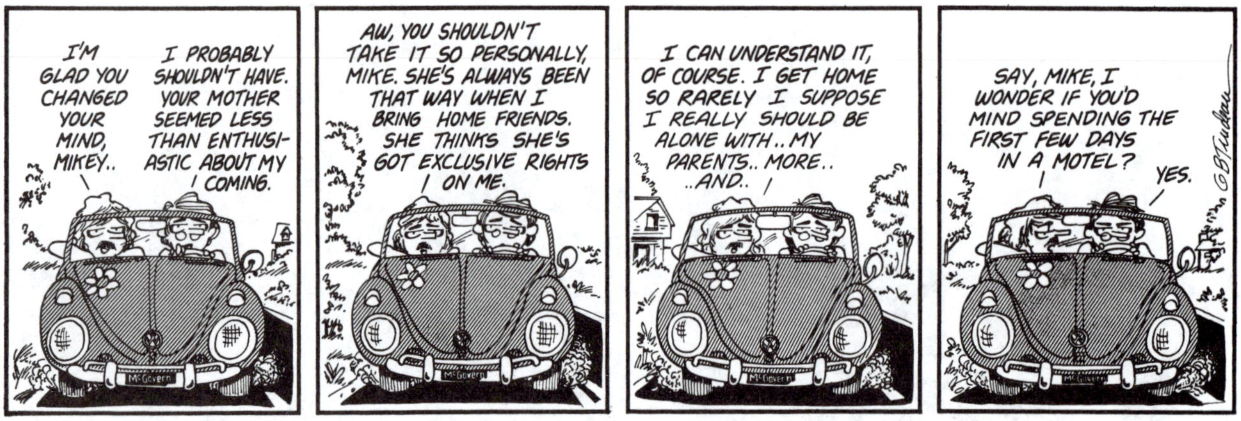
I'M GLAD YOU CHANGED YOUR MIND, MIKEY..
I PROBABLY SHOULDN'T HAVE. YOUR MOTHER SEEMED LESS THAN ENTHUSIASTIC ABOUT MY COMING.
AW, YOU SHOULDN'T TAKE IT SO PERSONALLY, MIKE. SHE'S ALWAYS BEEN THAT WAY WHEN I BRING HOME FRIENDS. SHE THINKS SHE'S GOT EXCLUSIVE RIGHTS ON ME.
I CAN UNDERSTAND IT, OF COURSE. I GET HOME SO RARELY I SUPPOSE I REALLY SHOULD BE ALONE WITH.. MY PARENTS.. MORE.. ..AND..
SAY, MIKE, I WONDER IF YOU'D MIND SPENDING THE FIRST FEW DAYS IN A MOTEL?
YES.

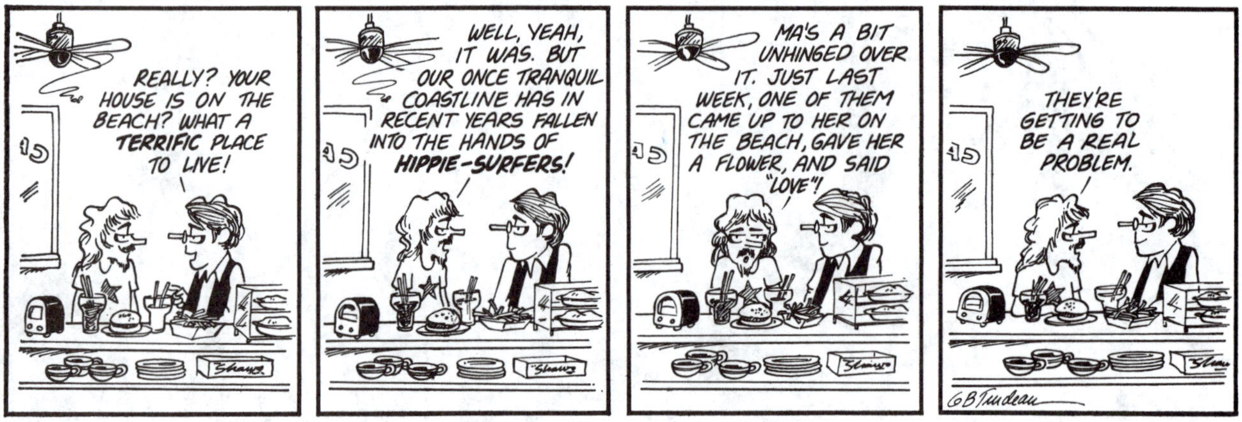
REALLY? YOUR HOUSE IS ON THE BEACH? WHAT A TERRIFIC PLACE TO LIVE!
WELL, YEAH, IT WAS. BUT OUR ONCE TRANQUIL COASTLINE HAS IN RECENT YEARS FALLEN INTO THE HANDS OF HIPPIE-SURFERS!
MA'S A BIT UNHINGED OVER IT. JUST LAST WEEK, ONE OF THEM CAME UP TO HER ON THE BEACH, GAVE HER A FLOWER, AND SAID "LOVE"!
THEY'RE GETTING TO BE A REAL PROBLEM.

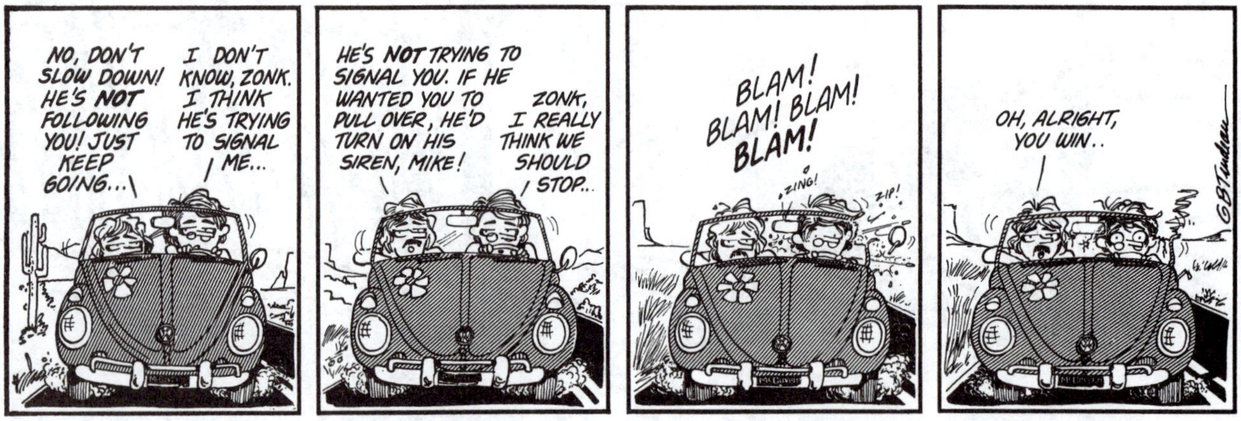
NO, DON'T SLOW DOWN! HE'S NOT FOLLOWING YOU! JUST KEEP GOING...
I DON'T KNOW, ZONK. I THINK HE'S TRYING TO SIGNAL ME...
HE'S NOT TRYING TO SIGNAL YOU. IF HE WANTED YOU TO PULL OVER, HE'D TURN ON HIS SIREN, MIKE!
ZONK, I REALLY THINK WE SHOULD STOP..
BLAM! BLAM! BLAM! BLAM!
ZING!
ZIP!
OH, ALRIGHT, YOU WIN..

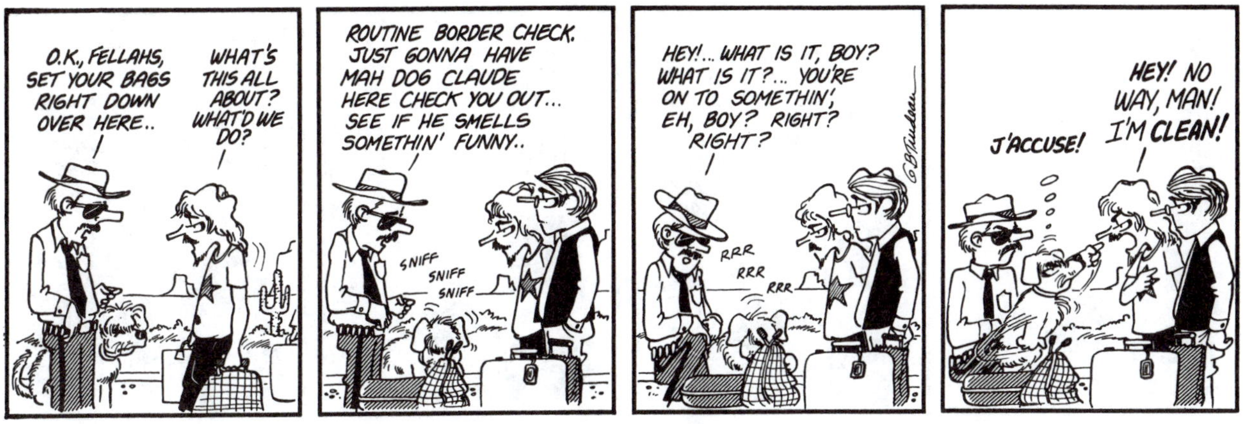
O.K., FELLAHS, SET YOUR BAGS RIGHT DOWN OVER HERE..
WHAT'S THIS ALL ABOUT? WHAT'D WE DO?
ROUTINE BORDER CHECK. JUST GONNA HAVE MAH DOG CLAUDE HERE CHECK YOU OUT... SEE IF HE SMELLS SOMETHIN' FUNNY..
SNIFF SNIFF SNIFF
HEY!... WHAT IS IT, BOY? WHAT IS IT?... YOU'RE ON TO SOMETHIN', EH, BOY? RIGHT? RIGHT?
RRR RRR RRR
J'ACCUSE!
HEY! NO WAY, MAN! I'M CLEAN!

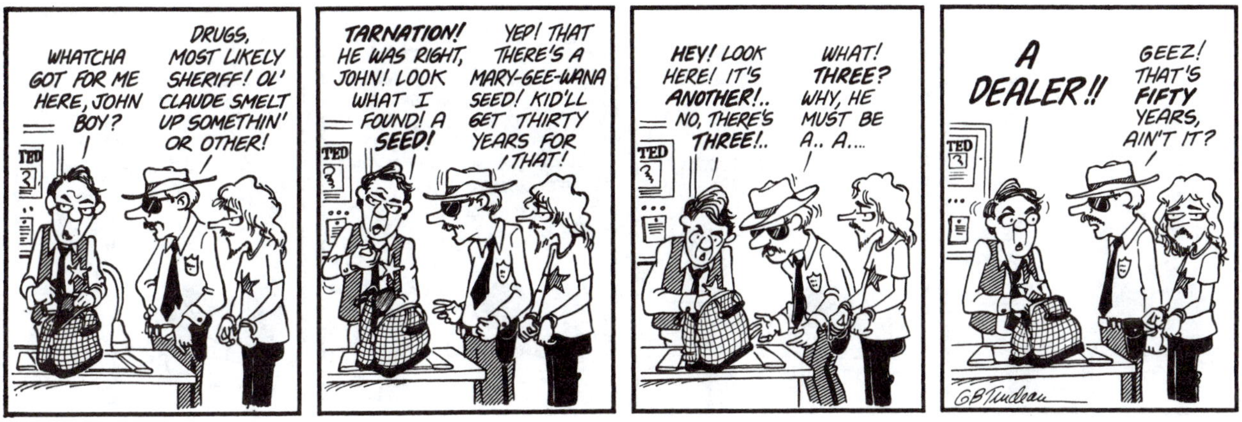
WHATCHA GOT FOR ME HERE, JOHN BOY?
DRUGS, MOST LIKELY SHERIFF! OL' CLAUDE SMELT UP SOMETHIN' OR OTHER!
TARNATION! HE WAS RIGHT, JOHN! LOOK WHAT I FOUND! A SEED!
YEP! THAT THERE'S A MARY-GEE-WANA SEED! KID'LL GET THIRTY YEARS FOR THAT!
HEY! LOOK HERE! IT'S ANOTHER!.. NO, THERE'S THREE!..
WHAT! THREE? WHY, HE MUST BE A.. A....
A DEALER!!
GEEZ! THAT'S FIFTY YEARS, AIN'T IT?

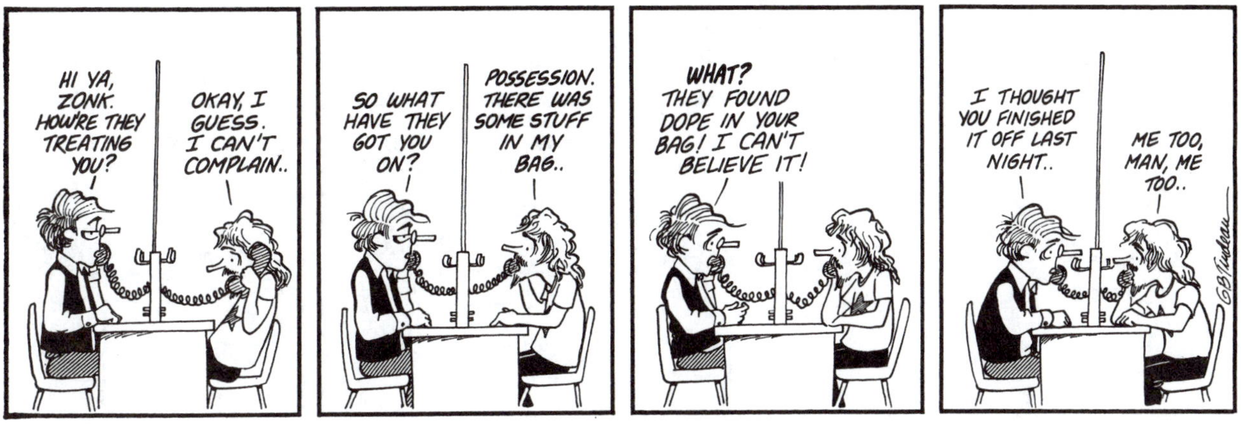
HI YA, ZONK. HOW'RE THEY TREATING YOU?
OKAY, I GUESS. I CAN'T COMPLAIN..
SO WHAT HAVE THEY GOT YOU ON?
POSSESSION. THERE WAS SOME STUFF IN MY BAG..
WHAT? THEY FOUND DOPE IN YOUR BAG! I CAN'T BELIEVE IT!
I THOUGHT YOU FINISHED IT OFF LAST NIGHT..
ME TOO, MAN, ME TOO..

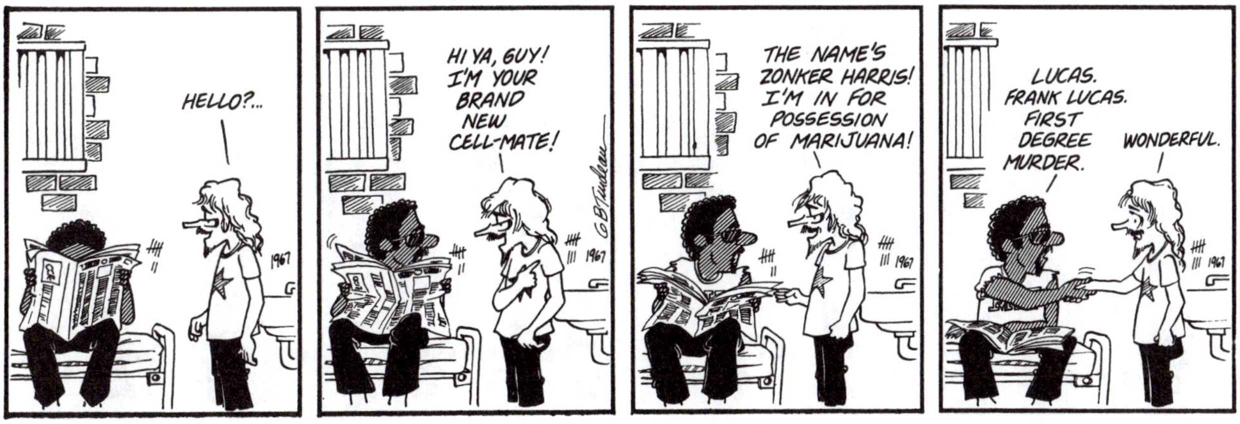
HELLO?...
HI YA, GUY! I'M YOUR BRAND NEW CELL-MATE!
THE NAME'S ZONKER HARRIS! I'M IN FOR POSSESSION OF MARIJUANA!
LUCAS. FRANK LUCAS. FIRST DEGREE MURDER.
WONDERFUL.

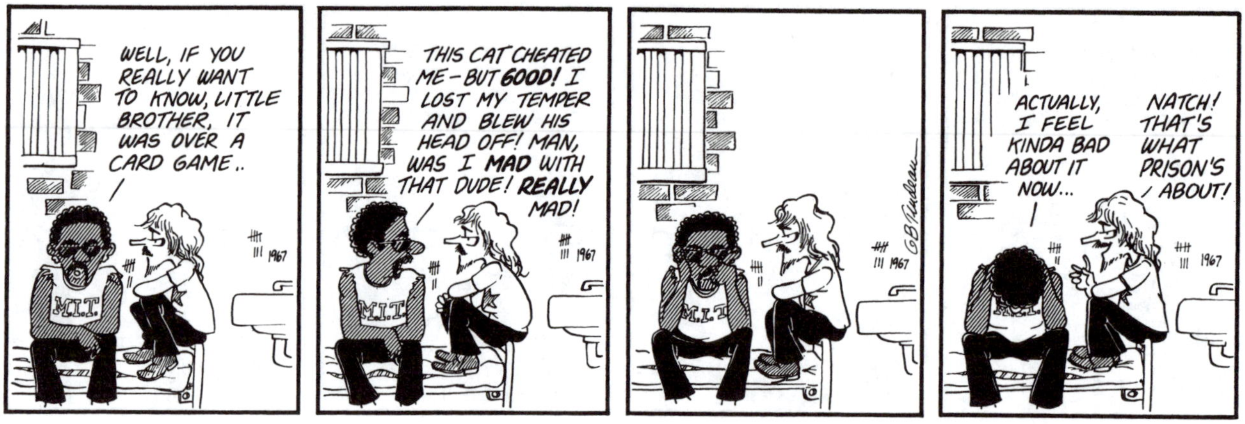
WELL, IF YOU REALLY WANT TO KNOW, LITTLE BROTHER, IT WAS OVER A CARD GAME..
THIS CAT CHEATED ME–BUT **GOOD!** I LOST MY TEMPER AND BLEW HIS HEAD OFF! MAN, WAS I **MAD** WITH THAT DUDE! **REALLY** MAD!
ACTUALLY, I FEEL KINDA BAD ABOUT IT NOW...
NATCH! THAT'S WHAT PRISON'S ABOUT!

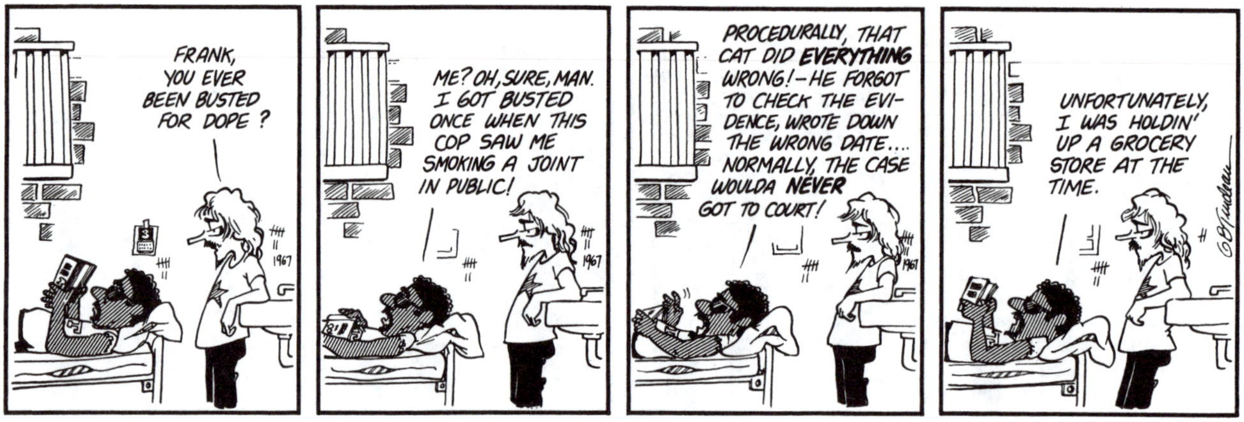
FRANK, YOU EVER BEEN BUSTED FOR DOPE ?
ME? OH, SURE, MAN. I GOT BUSTED ONCE WHEN THIS COP SAW ME SMOKING A JOINT IN PUBLIC!
PROCEDURALLY, THAT CAT DID **EVERYTHING** WRONG!–HE FORGOT TO CHECK THE EVIDENCE, WROTE DOWN THE WRONG DATE.... NORMALLY, THE CASE WOULDA **NEVER** GOT TO COURT!
UNFORTUNATELY, I WAS HOLDIN' UP A GROCERY STORE AT THE TIME.

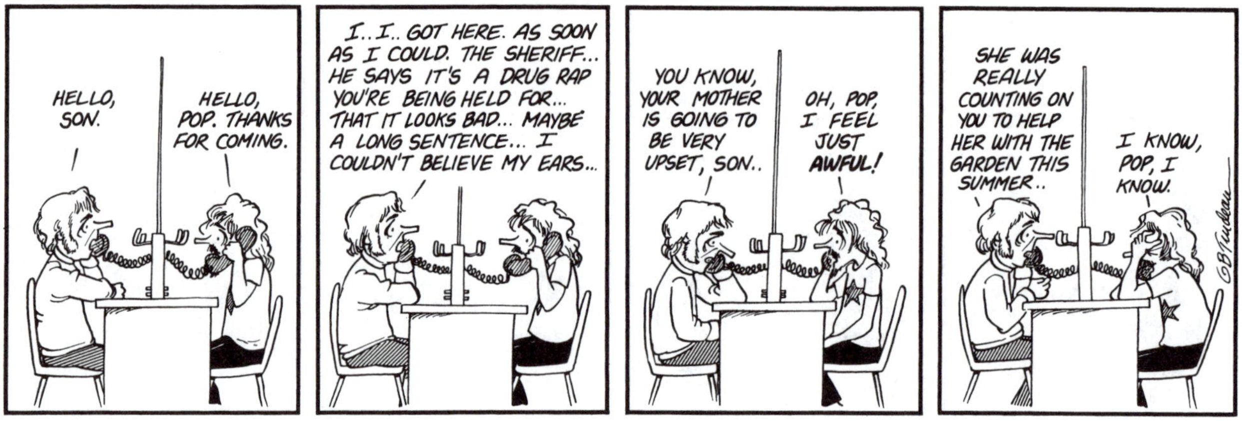
HELLO, SON.
HELLO, POP. THANKS FOR COMING.
I.. I.. GOT HERE. AS SOON AS I COULD. THE SHERIFF... HE SAYS IT'S A DRUG RAP YOU'RE BEING HELD FOR... THAT IT LOOKS BAD... MAYBE A LONG SENTENCE... I COULDN'T BELIEVE MY EARS...
YOU KNOW, YOUR MOTHER IS GOING TO BE VERY UPSET, SON..
OH, POP, I FEEL JUST **AWFUL!**
SHE WAS REALLY COUNTING ON YOU TO HELP HER WITH THE GARDEN THIS SUMMER..
I KNOW, POP, I KNOW.

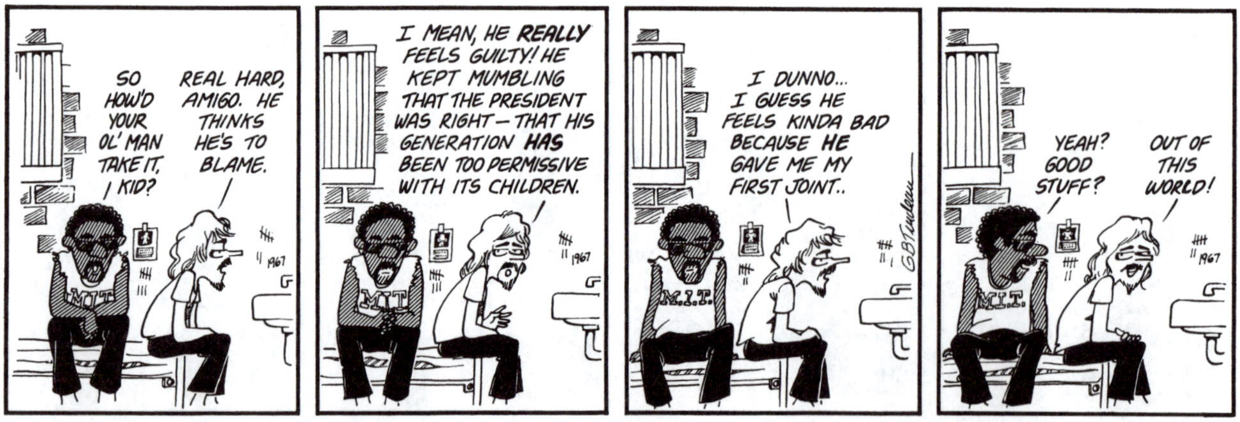
SO HOW'D YOUR OL' MAN TAKE IT, KID?
REAL HARD, AMIGO. HE THINKS HE'S TO BLAME.
I MEAN, HE **REALLY** FEELS GUILTY! HE KEPT MUMBLING THAT THE PRESIDENT WAS RIGHT–THAT HIS GENERATION **HAS** BEEN TOO PERMISSIVE WITH ITS CHILDREN.
I DUNNO... I GUESS HE FEELS KINDA BAD BECAUSE **HE** GAVE ME MY FIRST JOINT..
YEAH? GOOD STUFF?
OUT OF THIS WORLD!

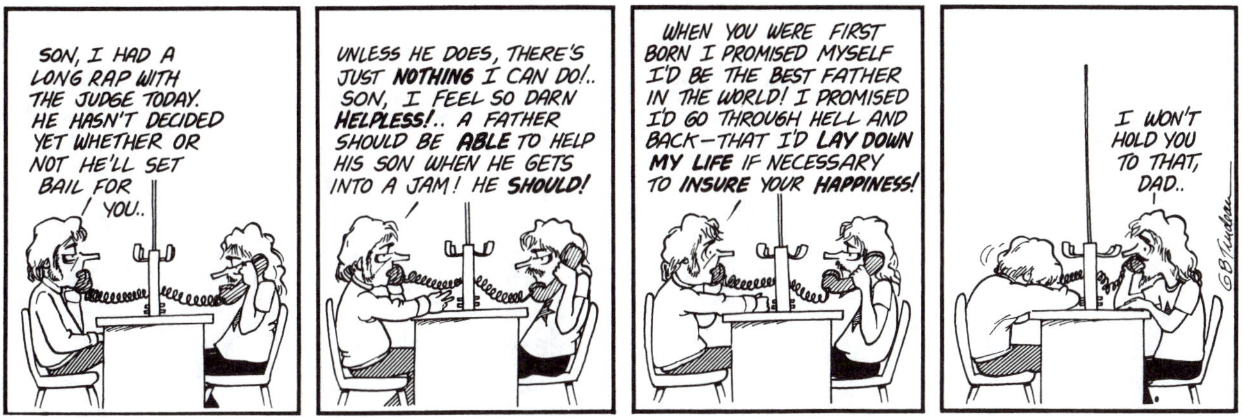
SON, I HAD A LONG RAP WITH THE JUDGE TODAY. HE HASN'T DECIDED YET WHETHER OR NOT HE'LL SET BAIL FOR YOU..
UNLESS HE DOES, THERE'S JUST NOTHING I CAN DO!.. SON, I FEEL SO DARN HELPLESS!.. A FATHER SHOULD BE ABLE TO HELP HIS SON WHEN HE GETS INTO A JAM! HE SHOULD!
WHEN YOU WERE FIRST BORN I PROMISED MYSELF I'D BE THE BEST FATHER IN THE WORLD! I PROMISED I'D GO THROUGH HELL AND BACK—THAT I'D LAY DOWN MY LIFE IF NECESSARY TO INSURE YOUR HAPPINESS!
I WON'T HOLD YOU TO THAT, DAD..

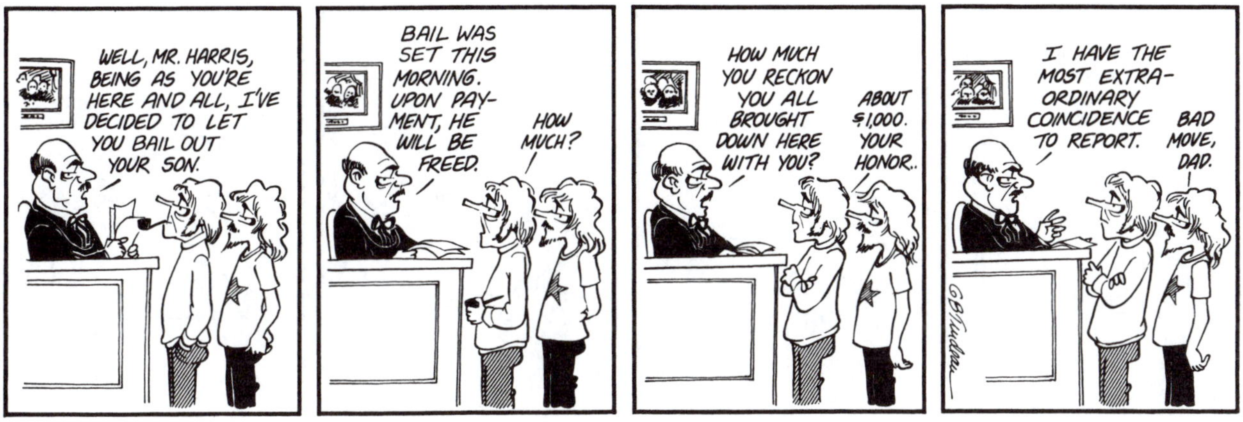
WELL, MR. HARRIS, BEING AS YOU'RE HERE AND ALL, I'VE DECIDED TO LET YOU BAIL OUT YOUR SON.
BAIL WAS SET THIS MORNING. UPON PAYMENT, HE WILL BE FREED.
HOW MUCH?
HOW MUCH YOU RECKON YOU ALL BROUGHT DOWN HERE WITH YOU?
ABOUT $1,000. YOUR HONOR..
I HAVE THE MOST EXTRAORDINARY COINCIDENCE TO REPORT.
BAD MOVE, DAD.

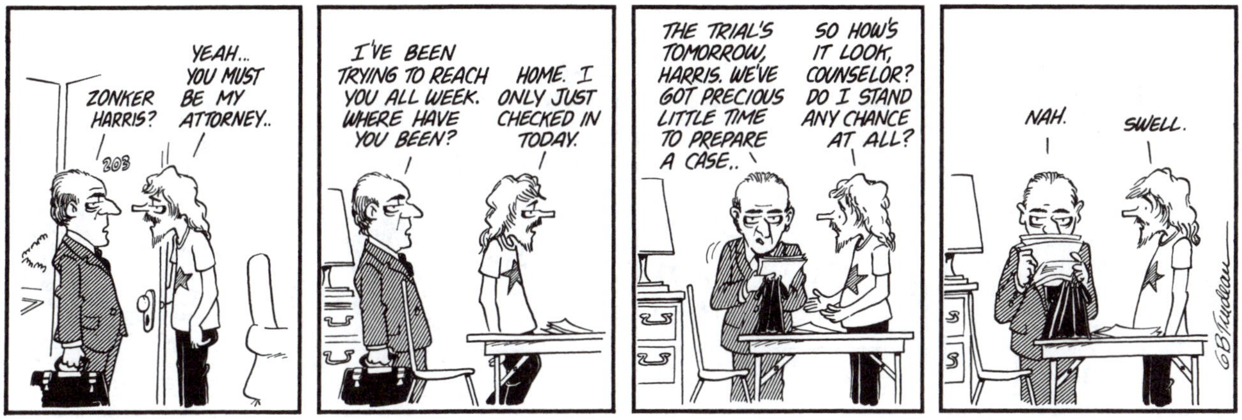
ZONKER HARRIS?
203
YEAH... YOU MUST BE MY ATTORNEY..
I'VE BEEN TRYING TO REACH YOU ALL WEEK. WHERE HAVE YOU BEEN?
HOME. I ONLY JUST CHECKED IN TODAY.
THE TRIAL'S TOMORROW, HARRIS. WE'VE GOT PRECIOUS LITTLE TIME TO PREPARE A CASE..
SO HOW'S IT LOOK, COUNSELOR? DO I STAND ANY CHANCE AT ALL?
NAH.
SWELL.

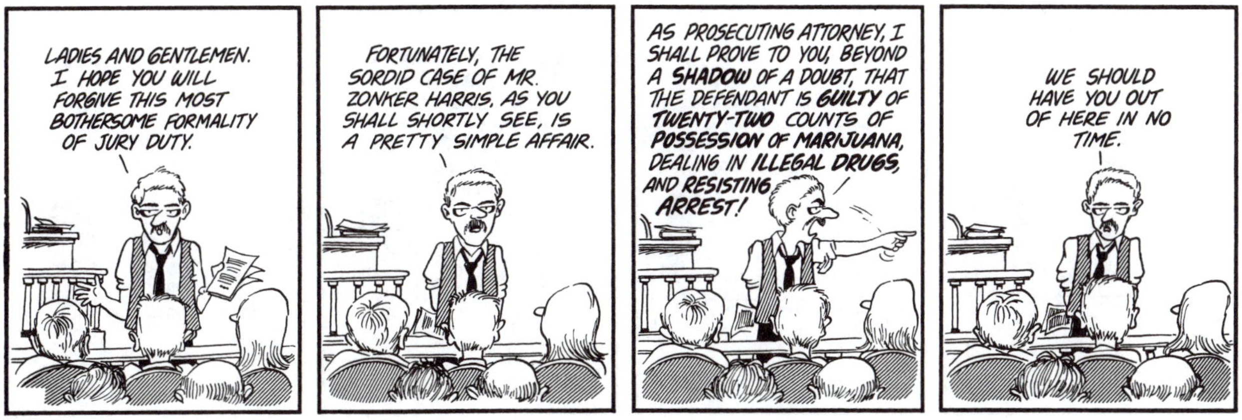
LADIES AND GENTLEMEN. I HOPE YOU WILL FORGIVE THIS MOST BOTHERSOME FORMALITY OF JURY DUTY.
FORTUNATELY, THE SORDID CASE OF MR. ZONKER HARRIS, AS YOU SHALL SHORTLY SEE, IS A PRETTY SIMPLE AFFAIR.
AS PROSECUTING ATTORNEY, I SHALL PROVE TO YOU, BEYOND A SHADOW OF A DOUBT, THAT THE DEFENDANT IS GUILTY OF TWENTY-TWO COUNTS OF POSSESSION OF MARIJUANA, DEALING IN ILLEGAL DRUGS, AND RESISTING ARREST!
WE SHOULD HAVE YOU OUT OF HERE IN NO TIME.

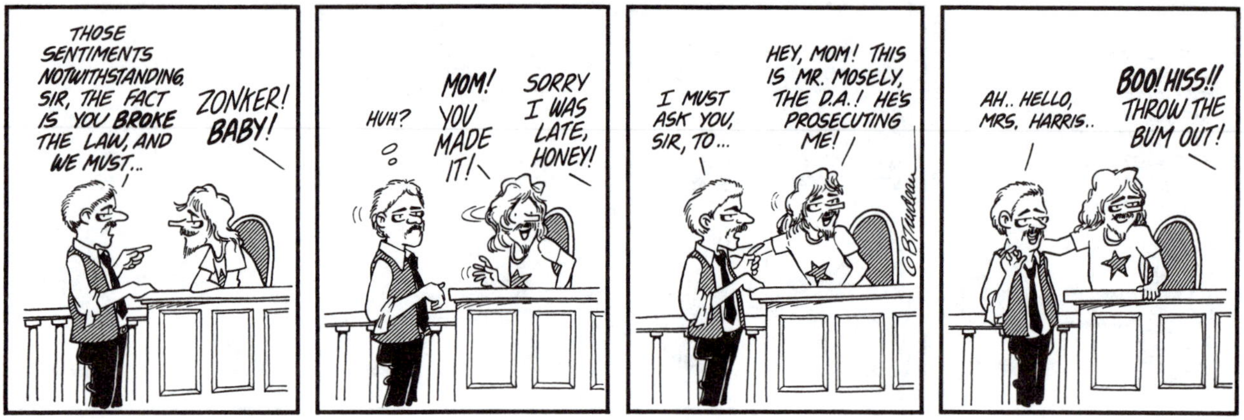
THOSE SENTIMENTS NOTWITHSTANDING, SIR, THE FACT IS YOU **BROKE** THE LAW, AND **WE MUST**...
ZONKER! **BABY!**
HUH?
MOM! YOU MADE IT!
SORRY I WAS LATE, HONEY!
I MUST ASK YOU, SIR, TO...
HEY, MOM! THIS IS MR. MOSELY, THE D.A.! HE'S PROSECUTING ME!
AH.. HELLO, MRS. HARRIS..
BOO! HISS!! THROW THE BUM OUT!

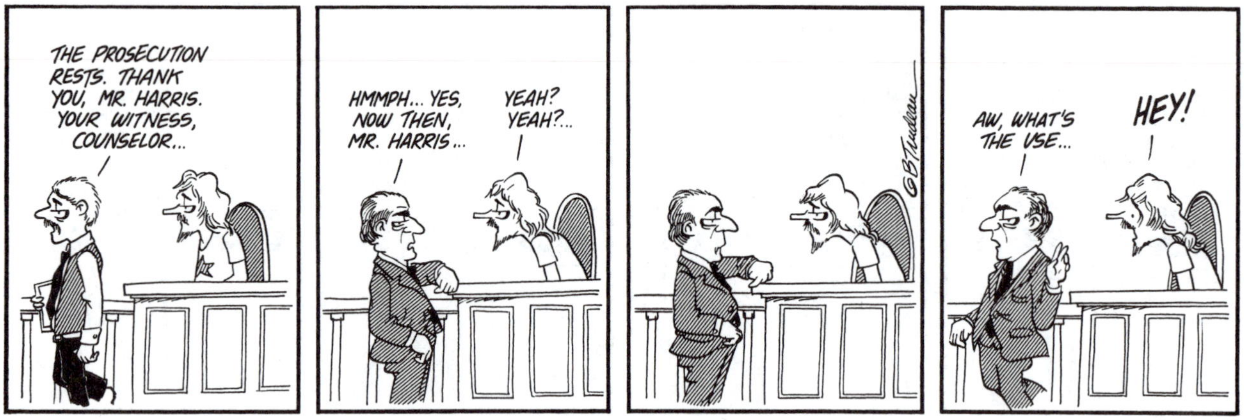
THE PROSECUTION RESTS. THANK YOU, MR. HARRIS. YOUR WITNESS, COUNSELOR...
HMMPH... YES, NOW THEN, MR. HARRIS...
YEAH? YEAH?...
AW, WHAT'S THE USE...
HEY!

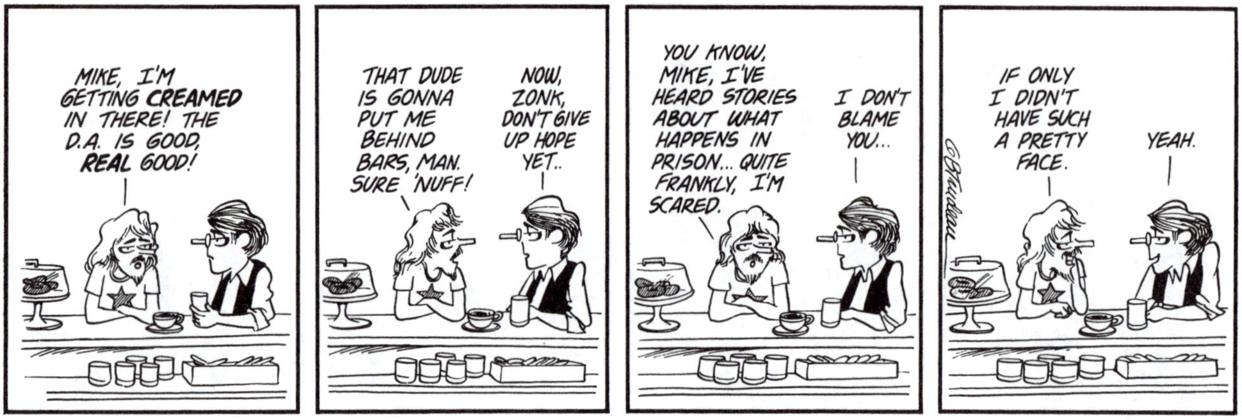
MIKE, I'M GETTING **CREAMED** IN THERE! THE D.A. IS GOOD, **REAL** GOOD!
THAT DUDE IS GONNA PUT ME BEHIND BARS, MAN. SURE 'NUFF!
NOW, ZONK, DON'T GIVE UP HOPE YET..
YOU KNOW, MIKE, I'VE HEARD STORIES ABOUT WHAT HAPPENS IN PRISON... QUITE FRANKLY, I'M SCARED.
I DON'T BLAME YOU...
IF ONLY I DIDN'T HAVE SUCH A PRETTY FACE.
YEAH.

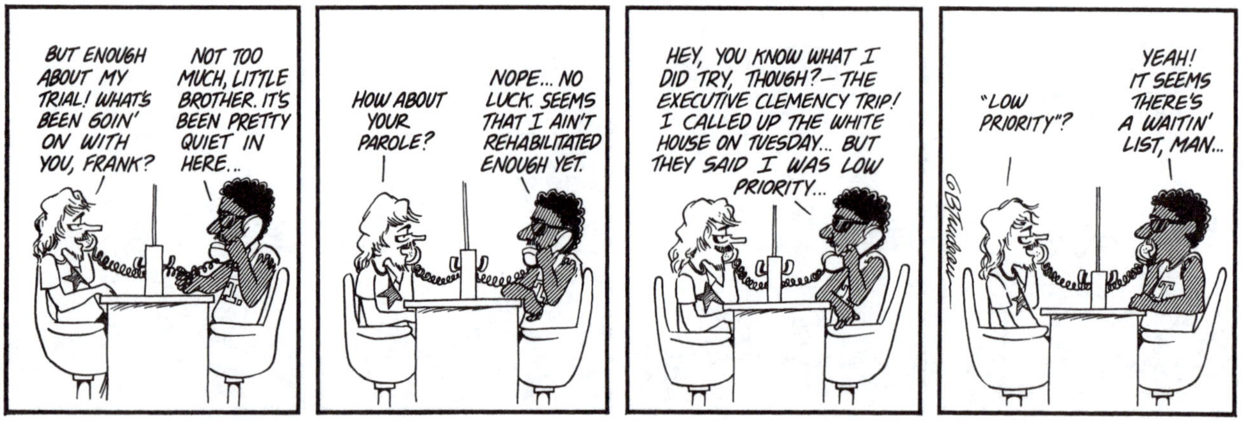
BUT ENOUGH ABOUT MY TRIAL! WHAT'S BEEN GOIN' ON WITH YOU, FRANK?
NOT TOO MUCH, LITTLE BROTHER. IT'S BEEN PRETTY QUIET IN HERE...
HOW ABOUT YOUR PAROLE?
NOPE... NO LUCK. SEEMS THAT I AIN'T REHABILITATED ENOUGH YET.
HEY, YOU KNOW WHAT I DID TRY, THOUGH?— THE EXECUTIVE CLEMENCY TRIP! I CALLED UP THE WHITE HOUSE ON TUESDAY... BUT THEY SAID I WAS LOW PRIORITY...
"LOW PRIORITY"?
YEAH! IT SEEMS THERE'S A WAITIN' LIST, MAN...

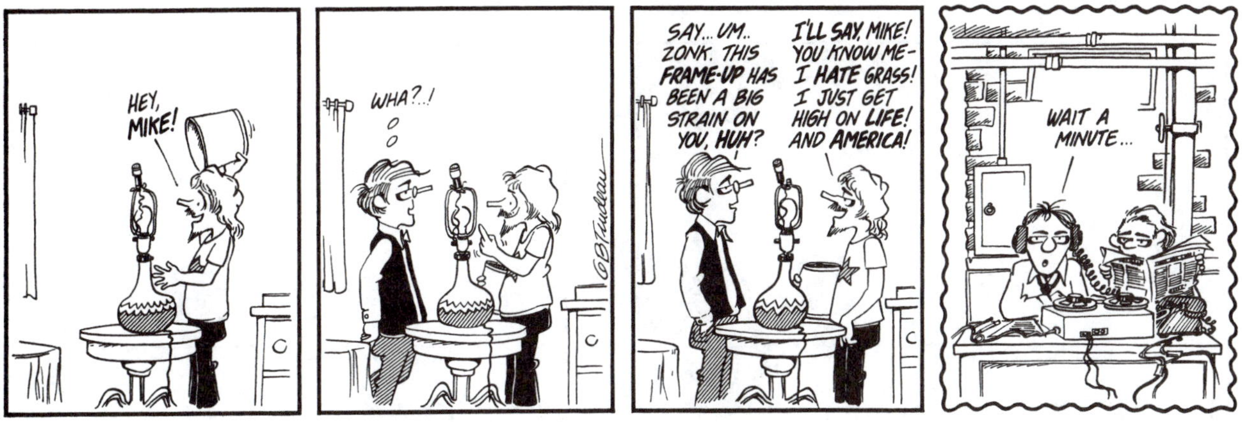
HEY, MIKE!
WHA?..!
SAY... UM.. ZONK.. THIS FRAME-UP HAS BEEN A BIG STRAIN ON YOU, HUH?
I'LL SAY, MIKE! YOU KNOW ME- I HATE GRASS! I JUST GET HIGH ON LIFE! AND AMERICA!
WAIT A MINUTE...

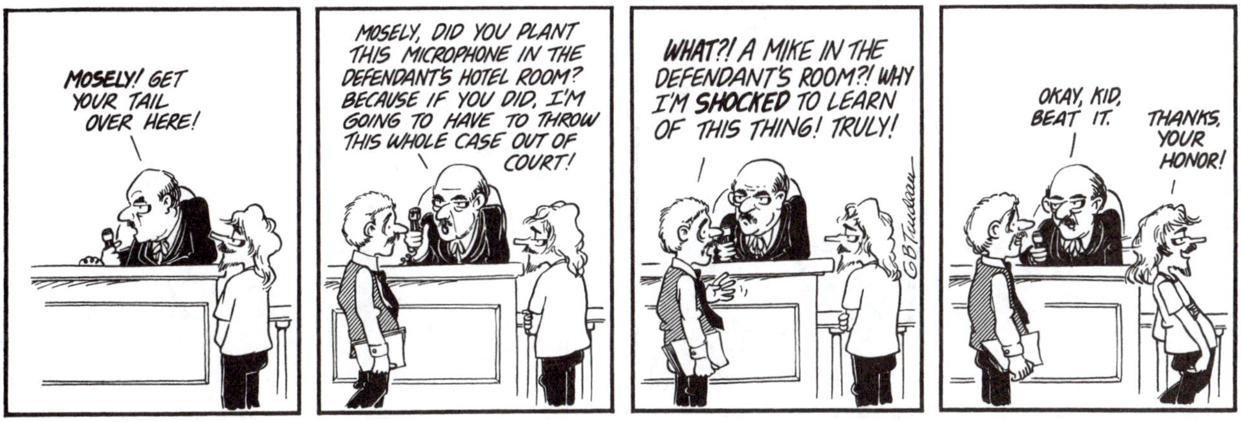
MOSELY! GET YOUR TAIL OVER HERE!
MOSELY, DID YOU PLANT THIS MICROPHONE IN THE DEFENDANT'S HOTEL ROOM? BECAUSE IF YOU DID, I'M GOING TO HAVE TO THROW THIS WHOLE CASE OUT OF COURT!
WHAT?! A MIKE IN THE DEFENDANT'S ROOM?! WHY I'M SHOCKED TO LEARN OF THIS THING! TRULY!
OKAY, KID, BEAT IT.
THANKS, YOUR HONOR!

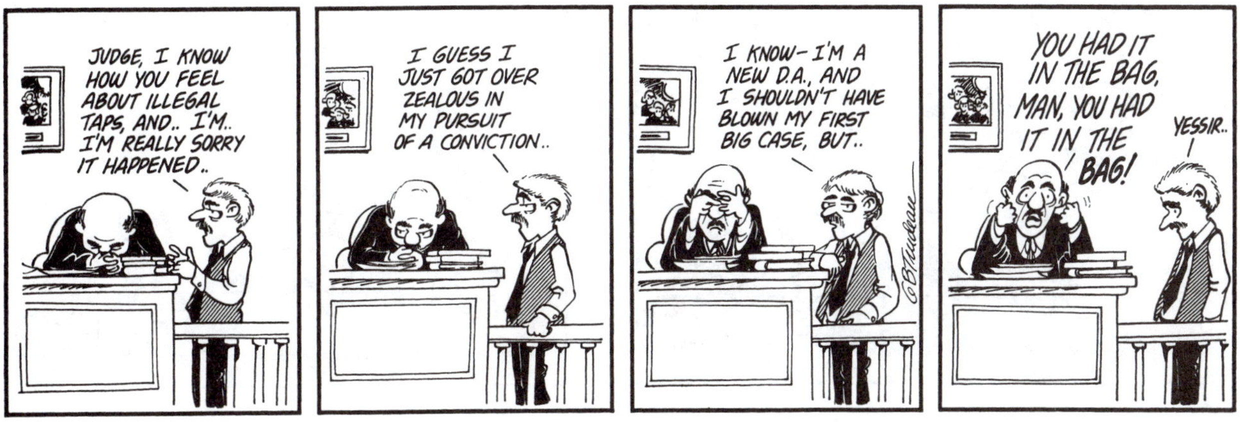
JUDGE, I KNOW HOW YOU FEEL ABOUT ILLEGAL TAPS, AND.. I'M.. I'M REALLY SORRY IT HAPPENED..
I GUESS I JUST GOT OVER ZEALOUS IN MY PURSUIT OF A CONVICTION..
I KNOW- I'M A NEW D.A., AND I SHOULDN'T HAVE BLOWN MY FIRST BIG CASE, BUT..
YOU HAD IT IN THE BAG, MAN, YOU HAD IT IN THE BAG!
YESSIR..

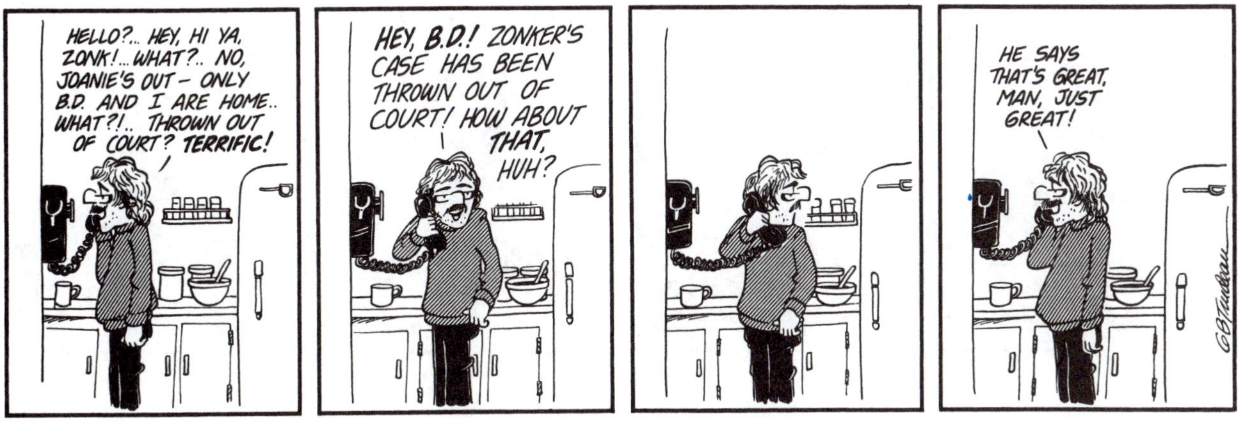
HELLO?.. HEY, HI YA, ZONK!... WHAT?.. NO, JOANIE'S OUT - ONLY B.D. AND I ARE HOME.. WHAT?!.. THROWN OUT OF COURT? TERRIFIC!
HEY, B.D.! ZONKER'S CASE HAS BEEN THROWN OUT OF COURT! HOW ABOUT THAT, HUH?
HE SAYS THAT'S GREAT, MAN, JUST GREAT!

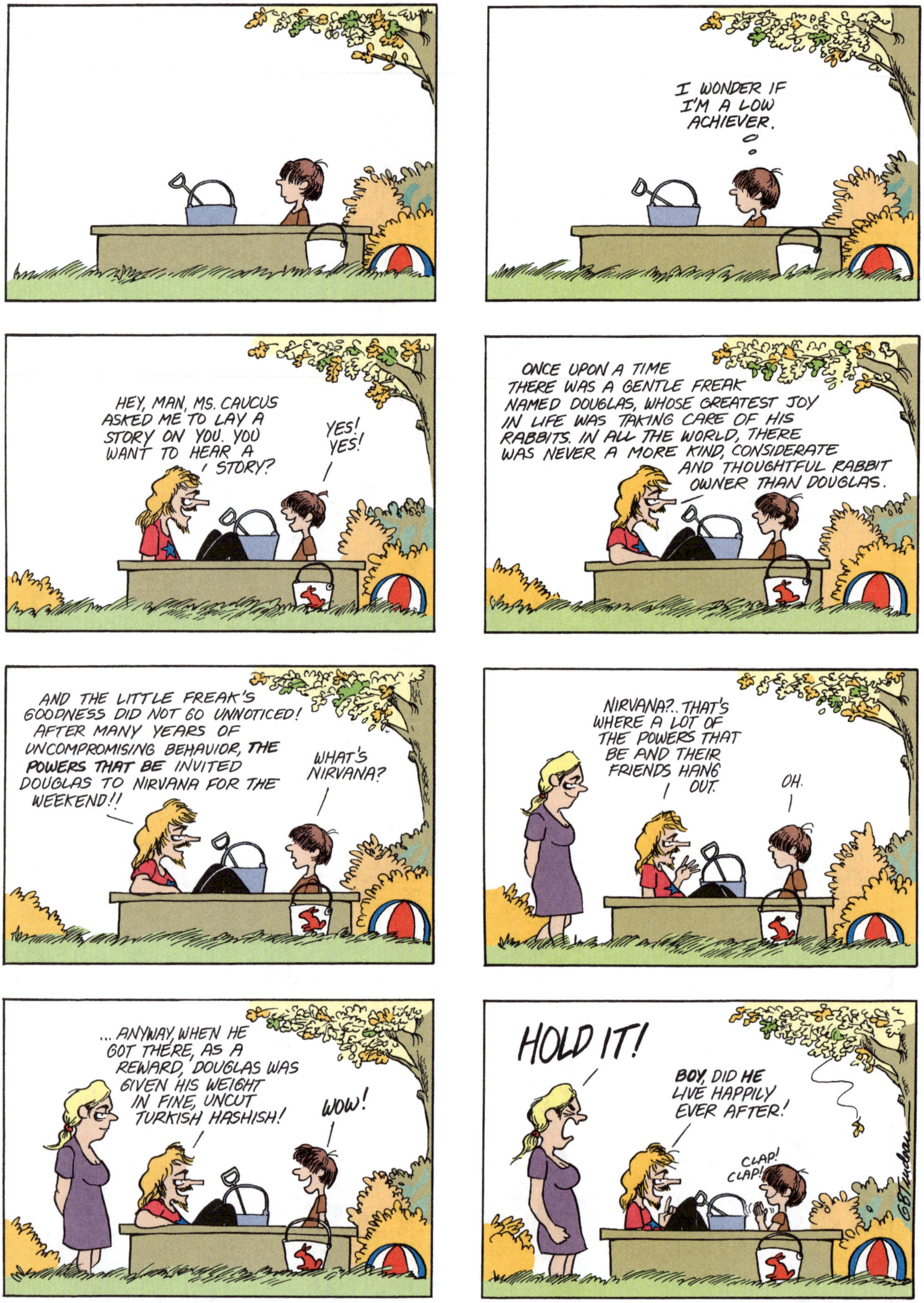
I WONDER IF I'M A LOW ACHIEVER.
HEY, MAN, MS. CAUCUS ASKED ME TO LAY A STORY ON YOU. YOU WANT TO HEAR A STORY?
YES! YES!
ONCE UPON A TIME THERE WAS A GENTLE FREAK NAMED DOUGLAS, WHOSE GREATEST JOY IN LIFE WAS TAKING CARE OF HIS RABBITS. IN ALL THE WORLD, THERE WAS NEVER A MORE KIND, CONSIDERATE AND THOUGHTFUL RABBIT OWNER THAN DOUGLAS.
AND THE LITTLE FREAK'S GOODNESS DID NOT GO UNNOTICED! AFTER MANY YEARS OF UNCOMPROMISING BEHAVIOR, **THE POWERS THAT BE** INVITED DOUGLAS TO NIRVANA FOR THE WEEKEND!!
WHAT'S NIRVANA?
NIRVANA?.. THAT'S WHERE A LOT OF THE POWERS THAT BE AND THEIR FRIENDS HANG OUT.
OH.
...ANYWAY, WHEN HE GOT THERE, AS A REWARD, DOUGLAS WAS GIVEN HIS WEIGHT IN FINE, UNCUT TURKISH HASHISH!
WOW!
HOLD IT!
BOY, DID **HE** LIVE HAPPILY EVER AFTER!
CLAP! CLAP!

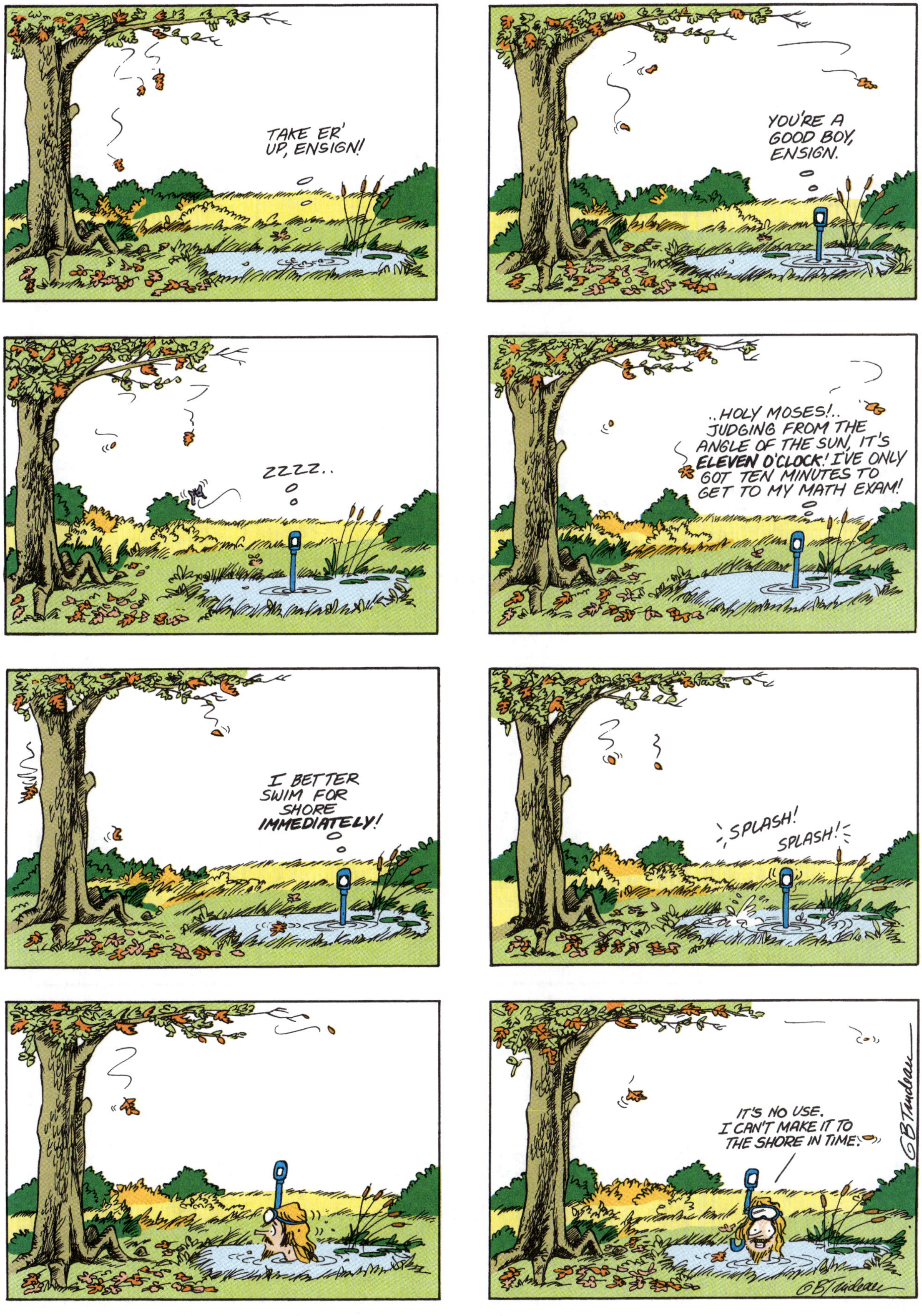
TAKE ER' UP, ENSIGN!
YOU'RE A GOOD BOY, ENSIGN.
ZZZZ..
..HOLY MOSES!.. JUDGING FROM THE ANGLE OF THE SUN, IT'S ELEVEN O'CLOCK! I'VE ONLY GOT TEN MINUTES TO GET TO MY MATH EXAM!
I BETTER SWIM FOR SHORE IMMEDIATELY!
SPLASH!
SPLASH!
IT'S NO USE. I CAN'T MAKE IT TO THE SHORE IN TIME.
GBTrudeau

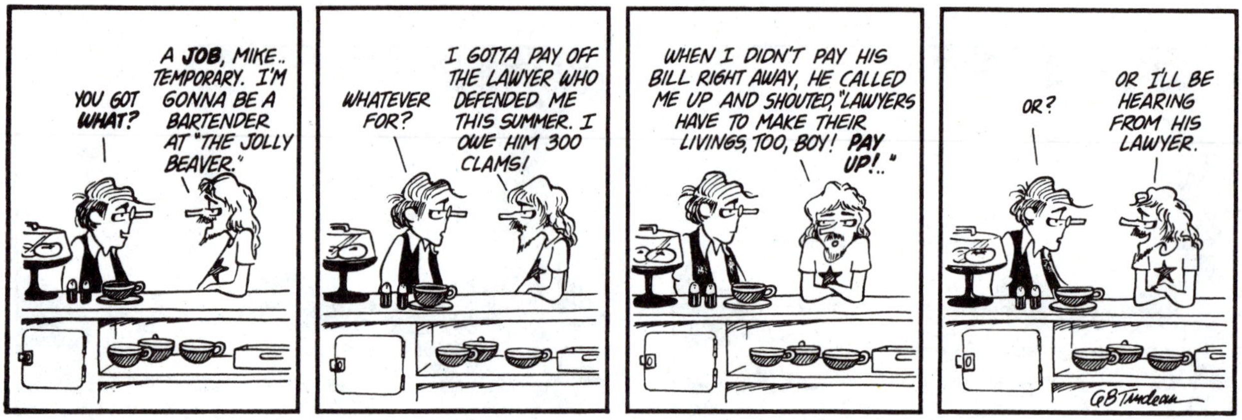
YOU GOT WHAT?
A JOB, MIKE.. TEMPORARY. I'M GONNA BE A BARTENDER AT "THE JOLLY BEAVER."
WHATEVER FOR?
I GOTTA PAY OFF THE LAWYER WHO DEFENDED ME THIS SUMMER. I OWE HIM 300 CLAMS!
WHEN I DIDN'T PAY HIS BILL RIGHT AWAY, HE CALLED ME UP AND SHOUTED, "LAWYERS HAVE TO MAKE THEIR LIVINGS, TOO, BOY! PAY UP!.."
OR?
OR I'LL BE HEARING FROM HIS LAWYER.

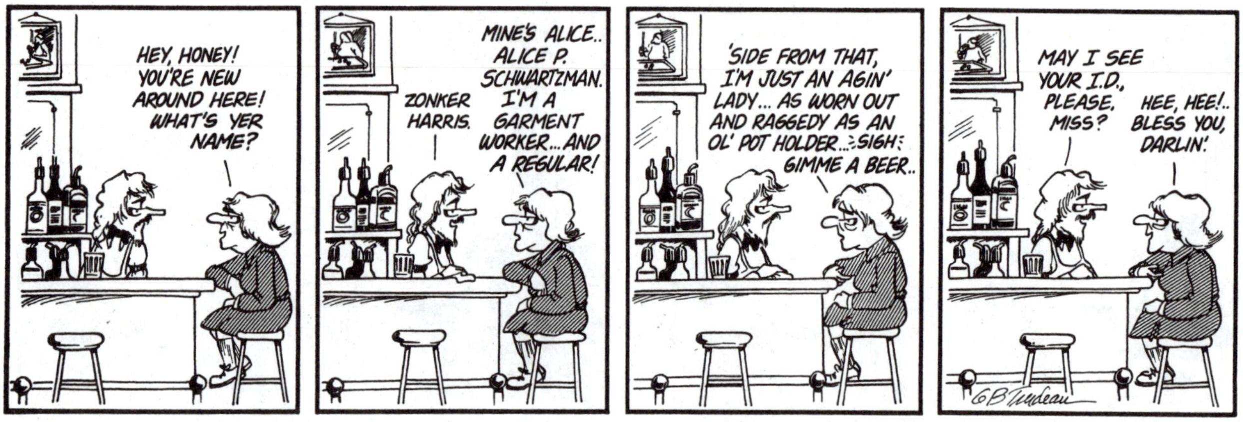
HEY, HONEY! YOU'RE NEW AROUND HERE! WHAT'S YER NAME?
ZONKER HARRIS.
MINE'S ALICE.. ALICE P. SCHWARTZMAN. I'M A GARMENT WORKER... AND A REGULAR!
'SIDE FROM THAT, I'M JUST AN AGIN' LADY... AS WORN OUT AND RAGGEDY AS AN OL' POT HOLDER... :SIGH: GIMME A BEER..
MAY I SEE YOUR I.D., PLEASE, MISS?
HEE, HEE!.. BLESS YOU, DARLIN'.

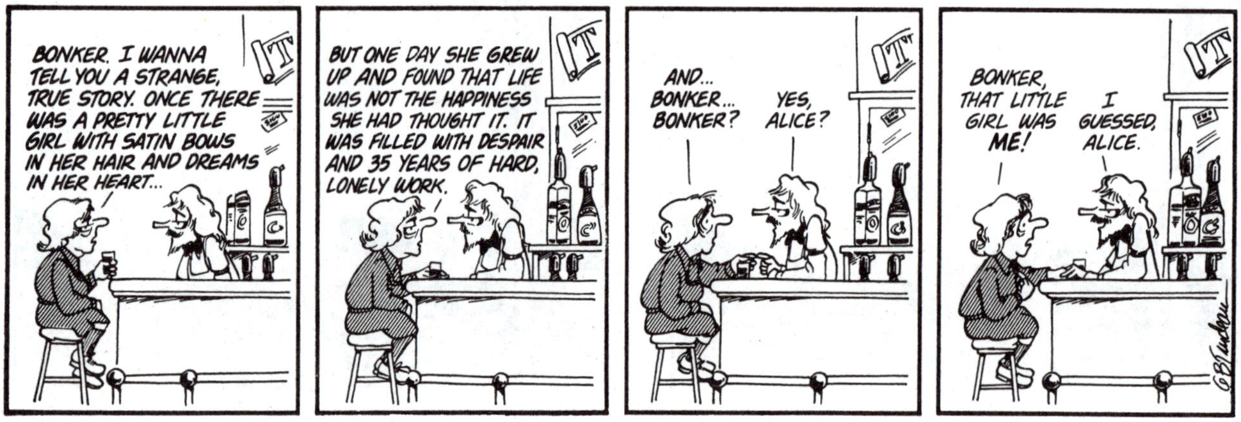
BONKER. I WANNA TELL YOU A STRANGE, TRUE STORY. ONCE THERE WAS A PRETTY LITTLE GIRL WITH SATIN BOWS IN HER HAIR AND DREAMS IN HER HEART...
BUT ONE DAY SHE GREW UP AND FOUND THAT LIFE WAS NOT THE HAPPINESS SHE HAD THOUGHT IT. IT WAS FILLED WITH DESPAIR AND 35 YEARS OF HARD, LONELY WORK.
AND... BONKER... BONKER?
YES, ALICE?
BONKER, THAT LITTLE GIRL WAS ME!
I GUESSED, ALICE.

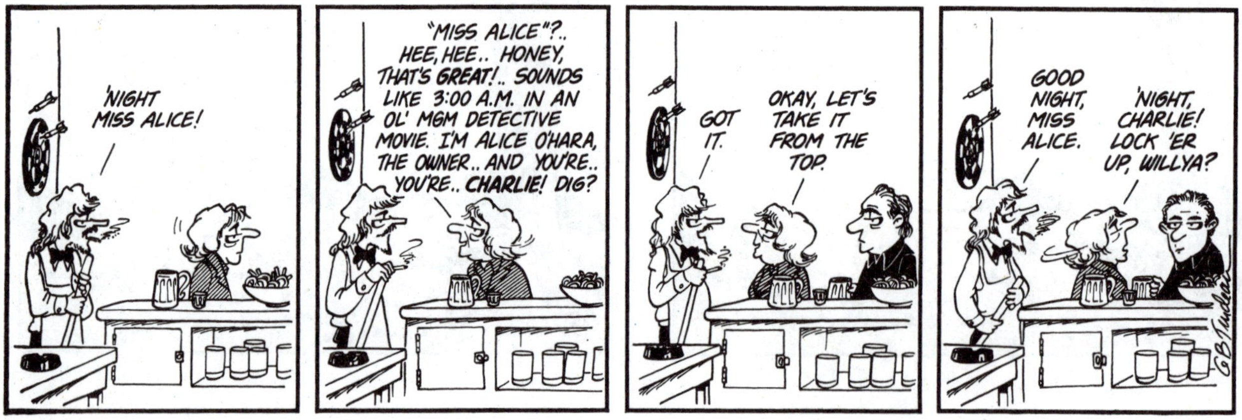
'NIGHT MISS ALICE!
"MISS ALICE"?.. HEE, HEE.. HONEY, THAT'S GREAT!.. SOUNDS LIKE 3:00 A.M. IN AN OL' MGM DETECTIVE MOVIE. I'M ALICE O'HARA, THE OWNER.. AND YOU'RE.. YOU'RE.. CHARLIE! DIG?
GOT IT.
OKAY, LET'S TAKE IT FROM THE TOP.
GOOD NIGHT, MISS ALICE.
'NIGHT, CHARLIE! LOCK 'ER UP, WILLYA?

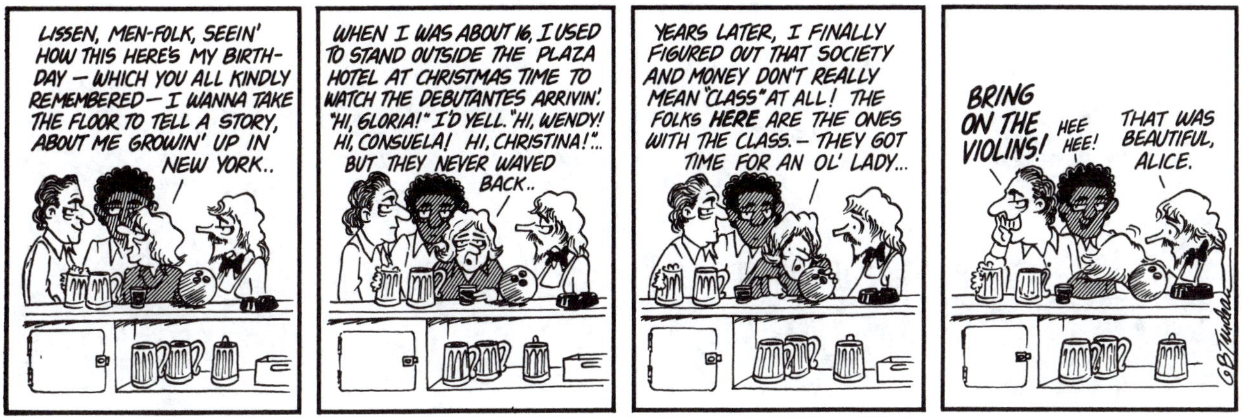
LISSEN, MEN-FOLK, SEEIN' HOW THIS HERE'S MY BIRTH-DAY — WHICH YOU ALL KINDLY REMEMBERED — I WANNA TAKE THE FLOOR TO TELL A STORY, ABOUT ME GROWIN' UP IN NEW YORK..
WHEN I WAS ABOUT 16, I USED TO STAND OUTSIDE THE PLAZA HOTEL AT CHRISTMAS TIME TO WATCH THE DEBUTANTES ARRIVIN'. "HI, GLORIA!" I'D YELL. "HI, WENDY! HI, CONSUELA! HI, CHRISTINA!"... BUT THEY NEVER WAVED BACK..
YEARS LATER, I FINALLY FIGURED OUT THAT SOCIETY AND MONEY DON'T REALLY MEAN "CLASS" AT ALL! THE FOLKS HERE ARE THE ONES WITH THE CLASS. — THEY GOT TIME FOR AN OL' LADY...
BRING ON THE VIOLINS!
HEE HEE!
THAT WAS BEAUTIFUL, ALICE.
GB Trudeau

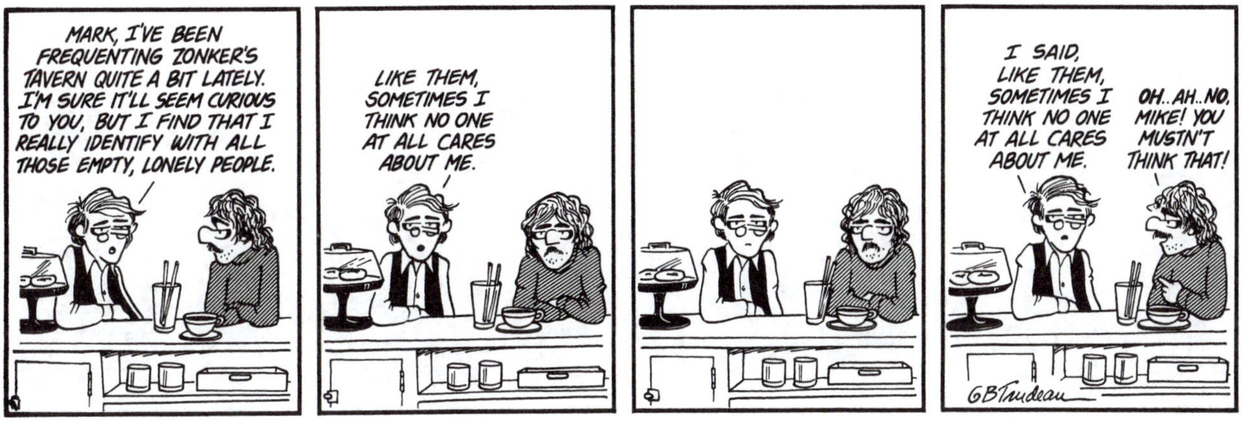
MARK, I'VE BEEN FREQUENTING ZONKER'S TAVERN QUITE A BIT LATELY. I'M SURE IT'LL SEEM CURIOUS TO YOU, BUT I FIND THAT I REALLY IDENTIFY WITH ALL THOSE EMPTY, LONELY PEOPLE.
LIKE THEM, SOMETIMES I THINK NO ONE AT ALL CARES ABOUT ME.
I SAID, LIKE THEM, SOMETIMES I THINK NO ONE AT ALL CARES ABOUT ME.
OH.. AH.. NO, MIKE! YOU MUSTN'T THINK THAT!
GBTrudeau

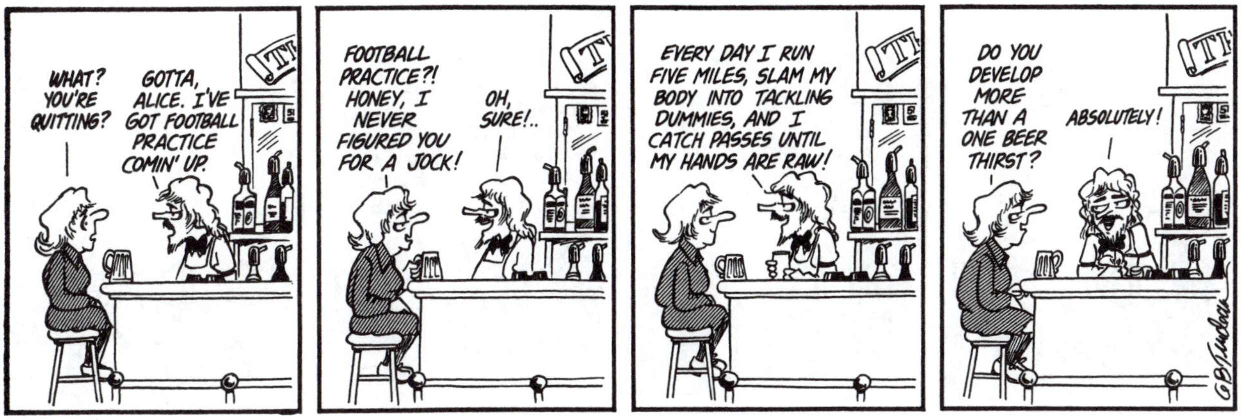
WHAT? YOU'RE QUITTING?
GOTTA, ALICE. I'VE GOT FOOTBALL PRACTICE COMIN' UP.
FOOTBALL PRACTICE?! HONEY, I NEVER FIGURED YOU FOR A JOCK!
OH, SURE!..
EVERY DAY I RUN FIVE MILES, SLAM MY BODY INTO TACKLING DUMMIES, AND I CATCH PASSES UNTIL MY HANDS ARE RAW!
DO YOU DEVELOP MORE THAN A ONE BEER THIRST?
ABSOLUTELY!
GBTrudeau

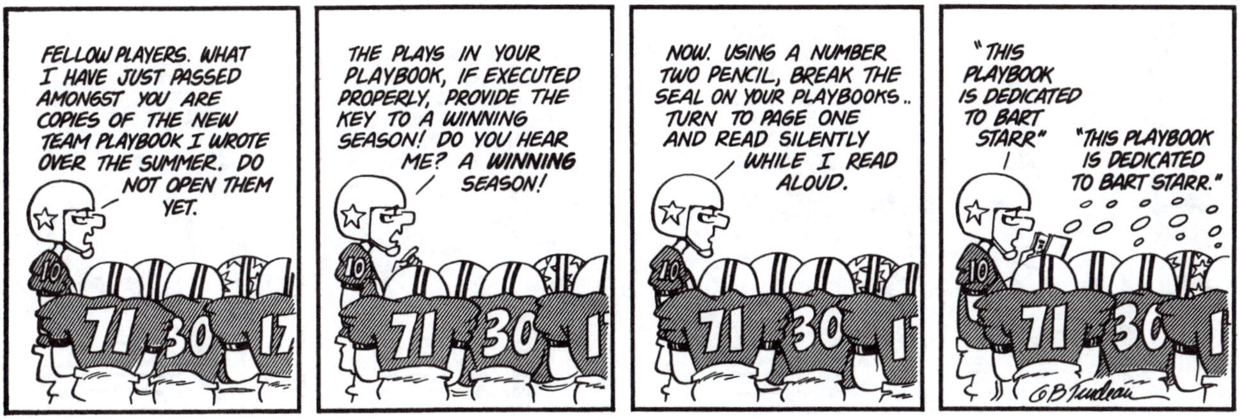
FELLOW PLAYERS. WHAT I HAVE JUST PASSED AMONGST YOU ARE COPIES OF THE NEW TEAM PLAYBOOK I WROTE OVER THE SUMMER.. DO NOT OPEN THEM YET.
THE PLAYS IN YOUR PLAYBOOK, IF EXECUTED PROPERLY, PROVIDE THE KEY TO A WINNING SEASON! DO YOU HEAR ME? A WINNING SEASON!
NOW. USING A NUMBER TWO PENCIL, BREAK THE SEAL ON YOUR PLAYBOOKS.. TURN TO PAGE ONE AND READ SILENTLY WHILE I READ ALOUD.
"THIS PLAYBOOK IS DEDICATED TO BART STARR"
"THIS PLAYBOOK IS DEDICATED TO BART STARR."
GBTrudeau

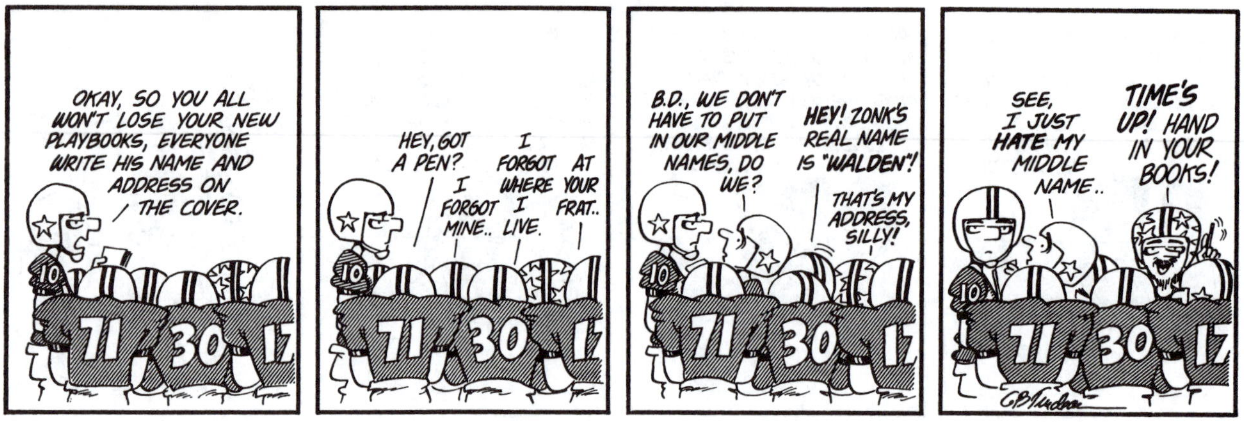
OKAY, SO YOU ALL WON'T LOSE YOUR NEW PLAYBOOKS, EVERYONE WRITE HIS NAME AND ADDRESS ON THE COVER.
HEY, GOT A PEN?
I FORGOT MINE..
I FORGOT WHERE I LIVE.
AT YOUR FRAT..
B.D., WE DON'T HAVE TO PUT IN OUR MIDDLE NAMES, DO WE?
HEY! ZONK'S REAL NAME IS "WALDEN"!
THAT'S MY ADDRESS, SILLY!
SEE, I JUST HATE MY MIDDLE NAME..
TIME'S UP! HAND IN YOUR BOOKS!

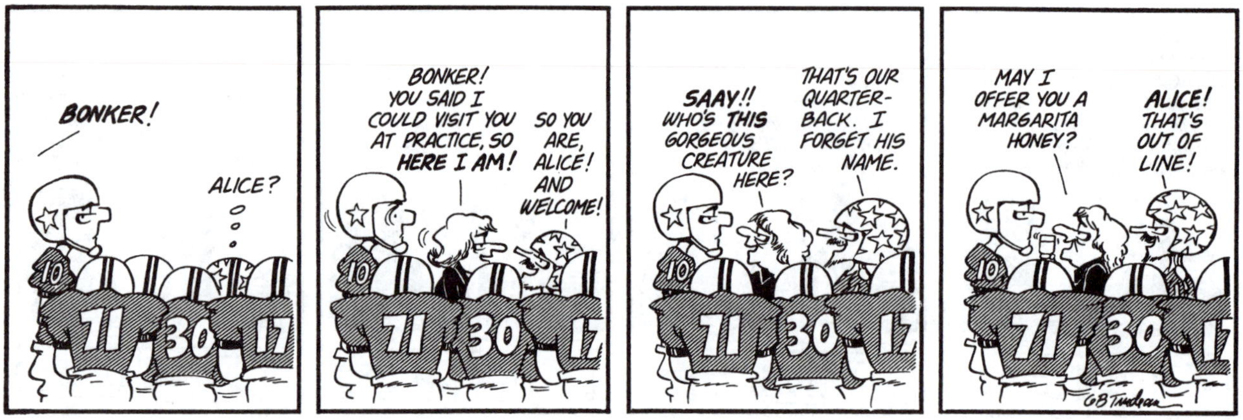
BONKER!
ALICE?
BONKER! YOU SAID I COULD VISIT YOU AT PRACTICE, SO HERE I AM!
SO YOU ARE, ALICE! AND WELCOME!
SAAY!! WHO'S THIS GORGEOUS CREATURE HERE?
THAT'S OUR QUARTER-BACK. I FORGET HIS NAME.
MAY I OFFER YOU A MARGARITA HONEY?
ALICE! THAT'S OUT OF LINE!

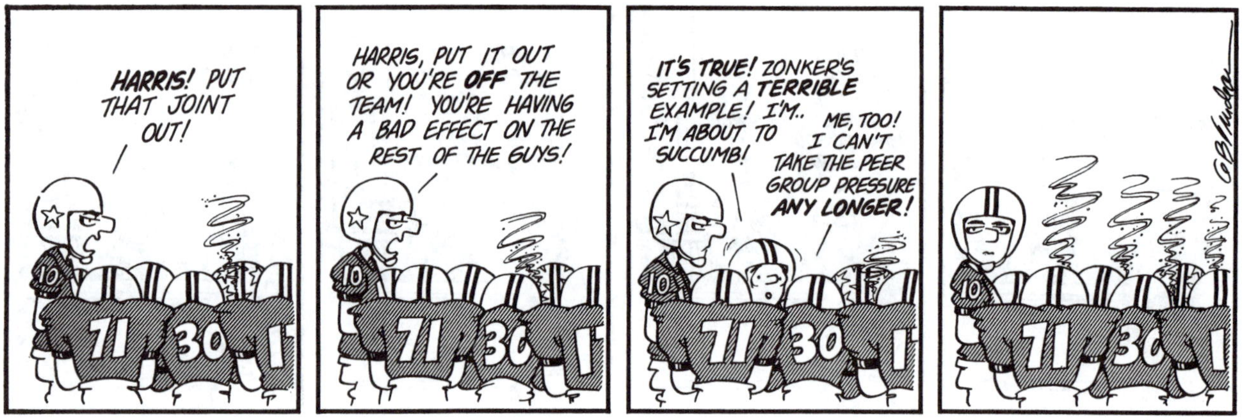
HARRIS! PUT THAT JOINT OUT!
HARRIS, PUT IT OUT OR YOU'RE OFF THE TEAM! YOU'RE HAVING A BAD EFFECT ON THE REST OF THE GUYS!
IT'S TRUE! ZONKER'S SETTING A TERRIBLE EXAMPLE! I'M.. I'M ABOUT TO SUCCUMB!
ME, TOO! I CAN'T TAKE THE PEER GROUP PRESSURE ANY LONGER!

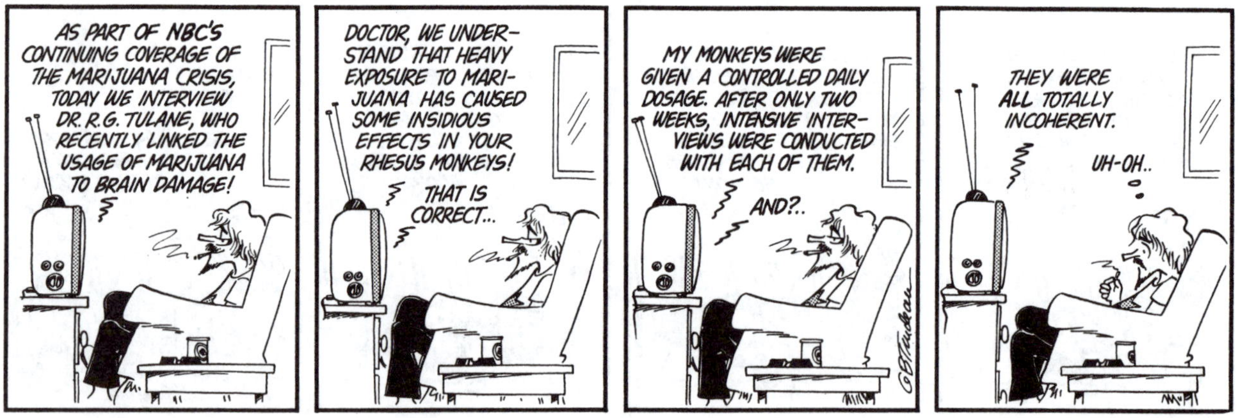
AS PART OF NBC'S CONTINUING COVERAGE OF THE MARIJUANA CRISIS, TODAY WE INTERVIEW DR. R.G. TULANE, WHO RECENTLY LINKED THE USAGE OF MARIJUANA TO BRAIN DAMAGE!
DOCTOR, WE UNDER-STAND THAT HEAVY EXPOSURE TO MARI-JUANA HAS CAUSED SOME INSIDIOUS EFFECTS IN YOUR RHESUS MONKEYS!
THAT IS CORRECT...
MY MONKEYS WERE GIVEN A CONTROLLED DAILY DOSAGE. AFTER ONLY TWO WEEKS, INTENSIVE INTER-VIEWS WERE CONDUCTED WITH EACH OF THEM.
AND?..
THEY WERE ALL TOTALLY INCOHERENT.
UH-OH..

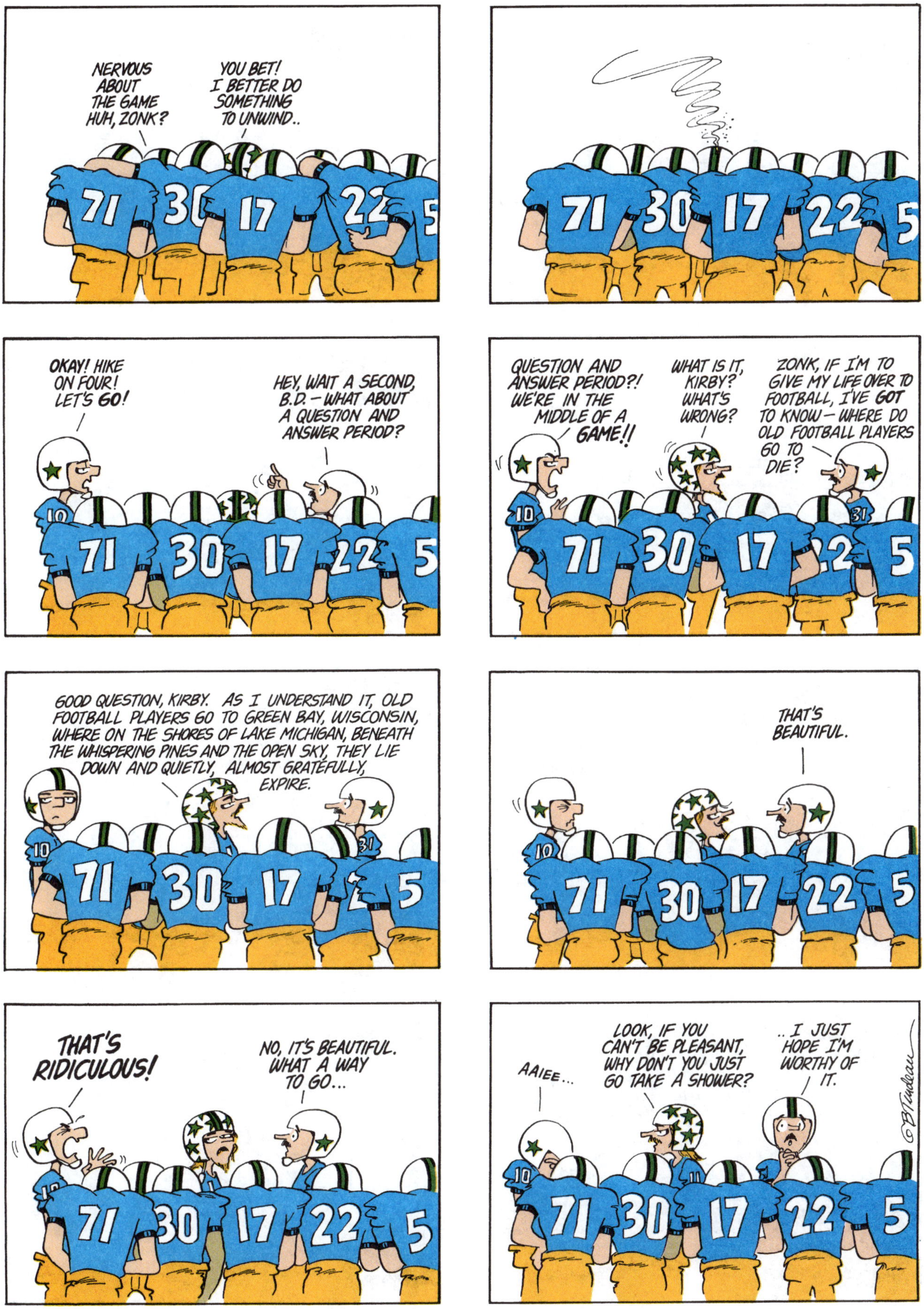
NERVOUS ABOUT THE GAME HUH, ZONK?
YOU BET! I BETTER DO SOMETHING TO UNWIND..
OKAY! HIKE ON FOUR! LET'S GO!
HEY, WAIT A SECOND, B.D. – WHAT ABOUT A QUESTION AND ANSWER PERIOD?
QUESTION AND ANSWER PERIOD?! WE'RE IN THE MIDDLE OF A GAME!!
WHAT IS IT, KIRBY? WHAT'S WRONG?
ZONK, IF I'M TO GIVE MY LIFE OVER TO FOOTBALL, I'VE GOT TO KNOW – WHERE DO OLD FOOTBALL PLAYERS GO TO DIE?
GOOD QUESTION, KIRBY. AS I UNDERSTAND IT, OLD FOOTBALL PLAYERS GO TO GREEN BAY, WISCONSIN, WHERE ON THE SHORES OF LAKE MICHIGAN, BENEATH THE WHISPERING PINES AND THE OPEN SKY, THEY LIE DOWN AND QUIETLY, ALMOST GRATEFULLY, EXPIRE.
THAT'S BEAUTIFUL.
THAT'S RIDICULOUS!
NO, IT'S BEAUTIFUL. WHAT A WAY TO GO...
AAIEE...
LOOK, IF YOU CAN'T BE PLEASANT, WHY DON'T YOU JUST GO TAKE A SHOWER?
..I JUST HOPE I'M WORTHY OF IT.
© GBTrudeau

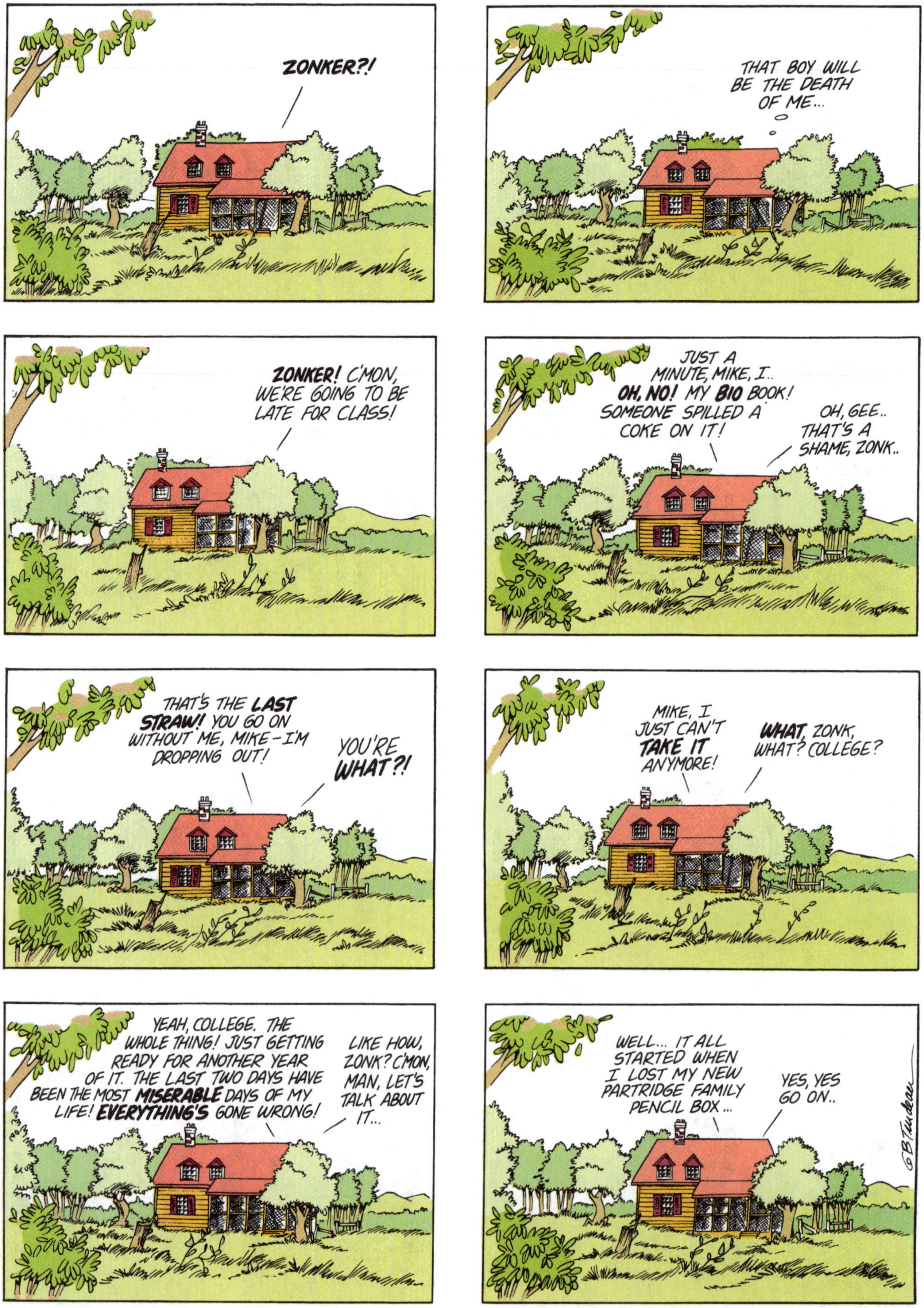

ZONKER?!
THAT BOY WILL BE THE DEATH OF ME...
ZONKER! C'MON, WE'RE GOING TO BE LATE FOR CLASS!
JUST A MINUTE, MIKE, I.. OH, NO! MY BIO BOOK! SOMEONE SPILLED A COKE ON IT!
OH, GEE.. THAT'S A SHAME, ZONK..
THAT'S THE LAST STRAW! YOU GO ON WITHOUT ME, MIKE–I'M DROPPING OUT!
YOU'RE WHAT?!
MIKE, I JUST CAN'T TAKE IT ANYMORE!
WHAT, ZONK, WHAT? COLLEGE?
YEAH, COLLEGE. THE WHOLE THING! JUST GETTING READY FOR ANOTHER YEAR OF IT. THE LAST TWO DAYS HAVE BEEN THE MOST MISERABLE DAYS OF MY LIFE! EVERYTHING'S GONE WRONG!
LIKE HOW, ZONK? C'MON, MAN, LET'S TALK ABOUT IT...
WELL... IT ALL STARTED WHEN I LOST MY NEW PARTRIDGE FAMILY PENCIL BOX...
YES, YES GO ON..

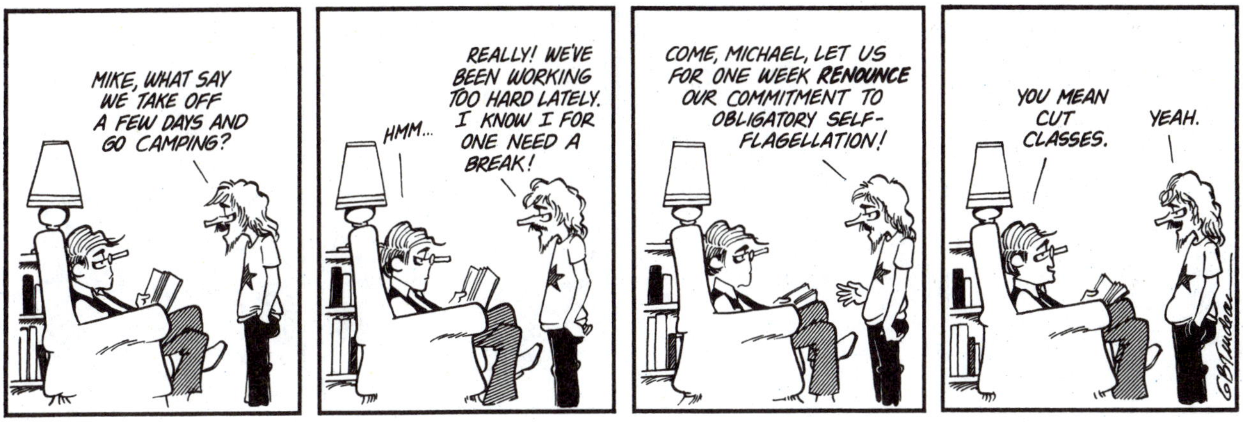
MIKE, WHAT SAY WE TAKE OFF A FEW DAYS AND GO CAMPING?
HMM...
REALLY! WE'VE BEEN WORKING TOO HARD LATELY. I KNOW I FOR ONE NEED A BREAK!
COME, MICHAEL, LET US FOR ONE WEEK RENOUNCE OUR COMMITMENT TO OBLIGATORY SELF-FLAGELLATION!
YOU MEAN CUT CLASSES.
YEAH.
GBTrudeau

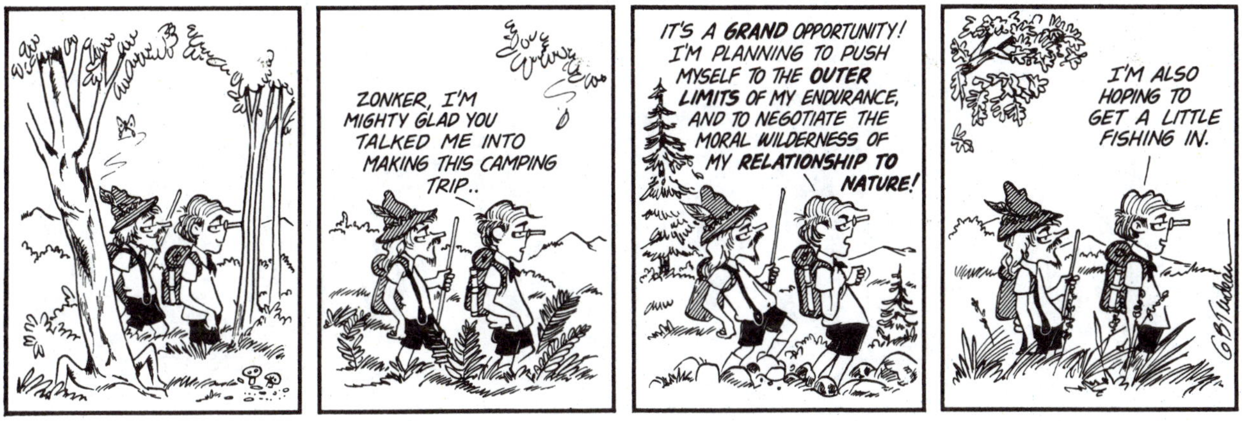
ZONKER, I'M MIGHTY GLAD YOU TALKED ME INTO MAKING THIS CAMPING TRIP..
IT'S A GRAND OPPORTUNITY! I'M PLANNING TO PUSH MYSELF TO THE OUTER LIMITS OF MY ENDURANCE, AND TO NEGOTIATE THE MORAL WILDERNESS OF MY RELATIONSHIP TO NATURE!
I'M ALSO HOPING TO GET A LITTLE FISHING IN.
GBTrudeau

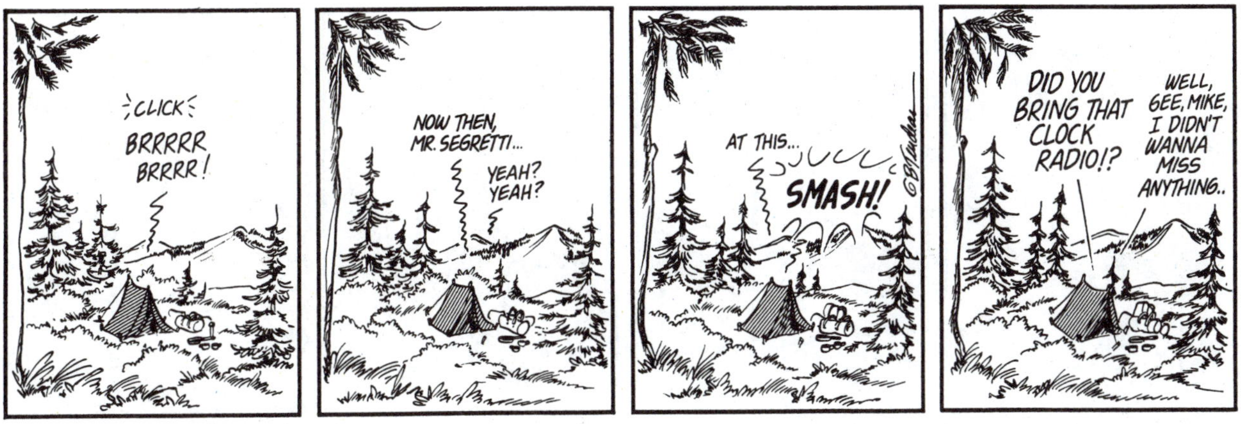
CLICK
BRRRRR BRRRR!
NOW THEN, MR. SEGRETTI...
YEAH? YEAH?
AT THIS...
SMASH!
GBTrudeau
DID YOU BRING THAT CLOCK RADIO!?
WELL, GEE, MIKE, I DIDN'T WANNA MISS ANYTHING..

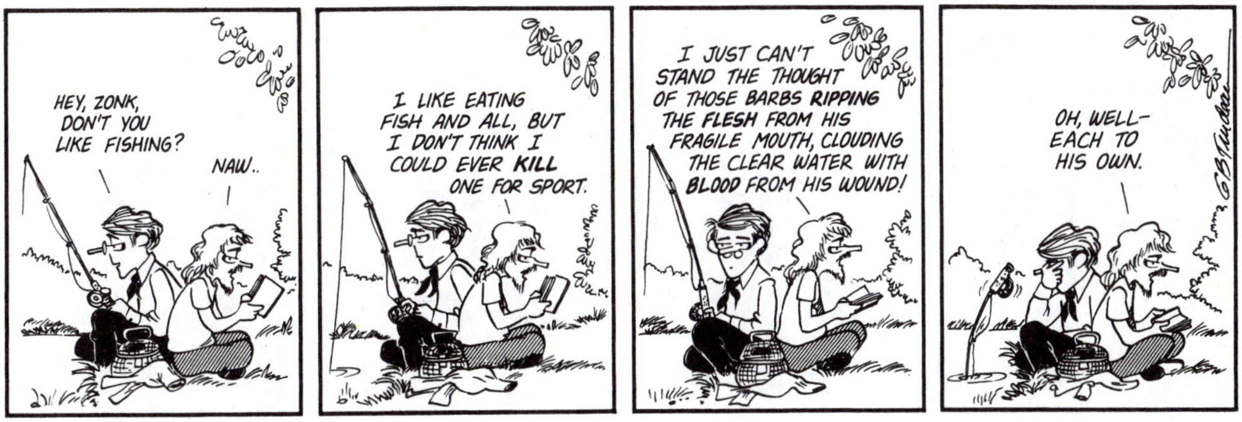
HEY, ZONK, DON'T YOU LIKE FISHING?
NAW..
I LIKE EATING FISH AND ALL, BUT I DON'T THINK I COULD EVER KILL ONE FOR SPORT.
I JUST CAN'T STAND THE THOUGHT OF THOSE BARBS RIPPING THE FLESH FROM HIS FRAGILE MOUTH, CLOUDING THE CLEAR WATER WITH BLOOD FROM HIS WOUND!
OH, WELL- EACH TO HIS OWN.
GBTrudeau

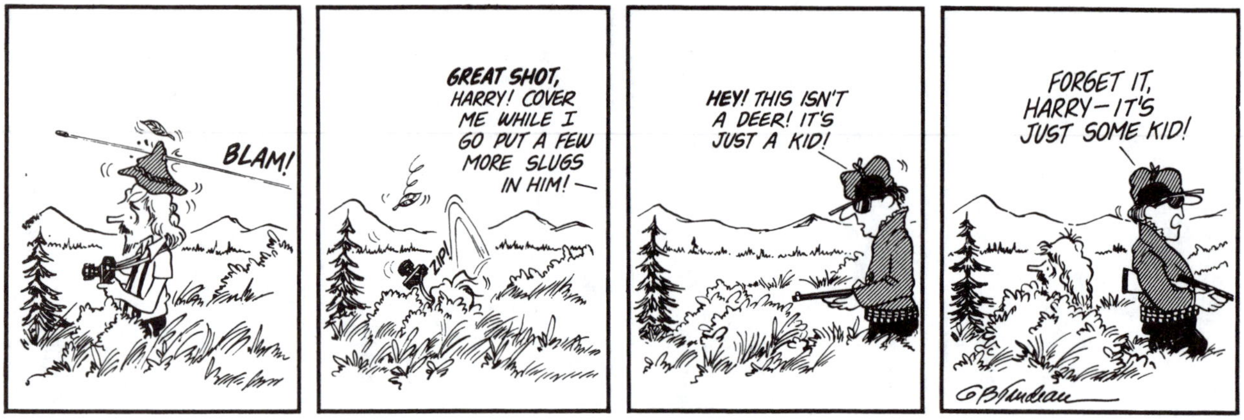
BLAM!
GREAT SHOT, HARRY! COVER ME WHILE I GO PUT A FEW MORE SLUGS IN HIM!
ZIP!
HEY! THIS ISN'T A DEER! IT'S JUST A KID!
FORGET IT, HARRY—IT'S JUST SOME KID!

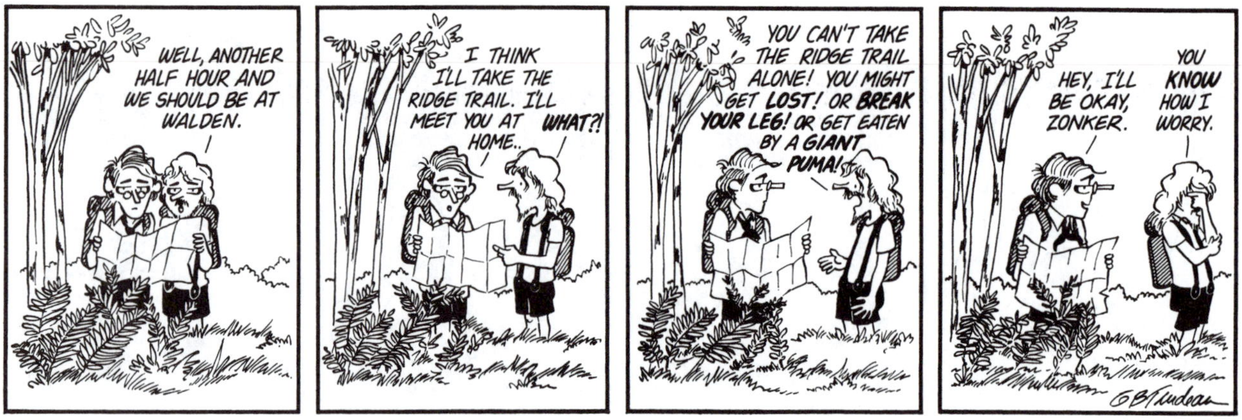
WELL, ANOTHER HALF HOUR AND WE SHOULD BE AT WALDEN.
I THINK I'LL TAKE THE RIDGE TRAIL. I'LL MEET YOU AT HOME..
WHAT?!
YOU CAN'T TAKE THE RIDGE TRAIL ALONE! YOU MIGHT GET LOST! OR BREAK YOUR LEG! OR GET EATEN BY A GIANT PUMA!
HEY, I'LL BE OKAY, ZONKER.
YOU KNOW HOW I WORRY.

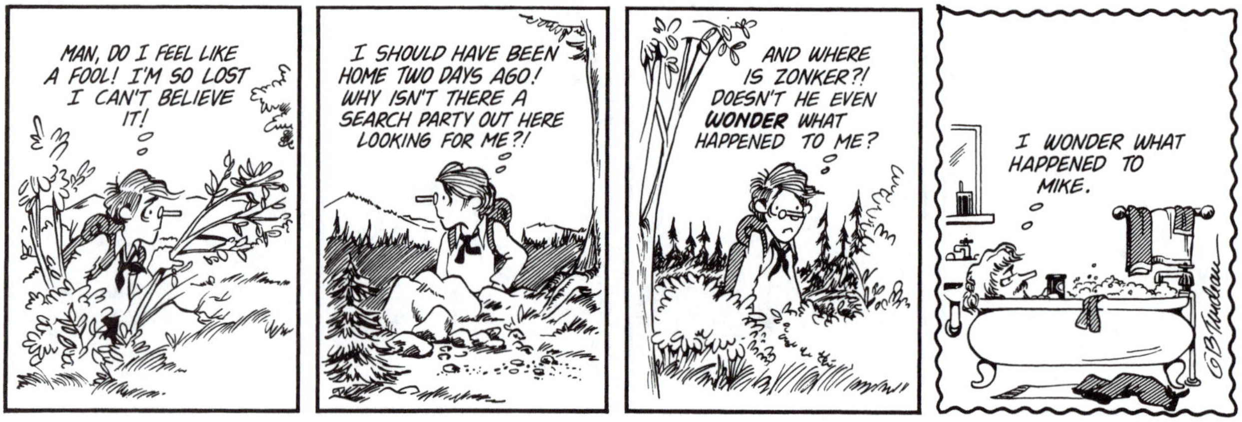
MAN, DO I FEEL LIKE A FOOL! I'M SO LOST I CAN'T BELIEVE IT!
I SHOULD HAVE BEEN HOME TWO DAYS AGO! WHY ISN'T THERE A SEARCH PARTY OUT HERE LOOKING FOR ME?!
AND WHERE IS ZONKER?! DOESN'T HE EVEN WONDER WHAT HAPPENED TO ME?
I WONDER WHAT HAPPENED TO MIKE.

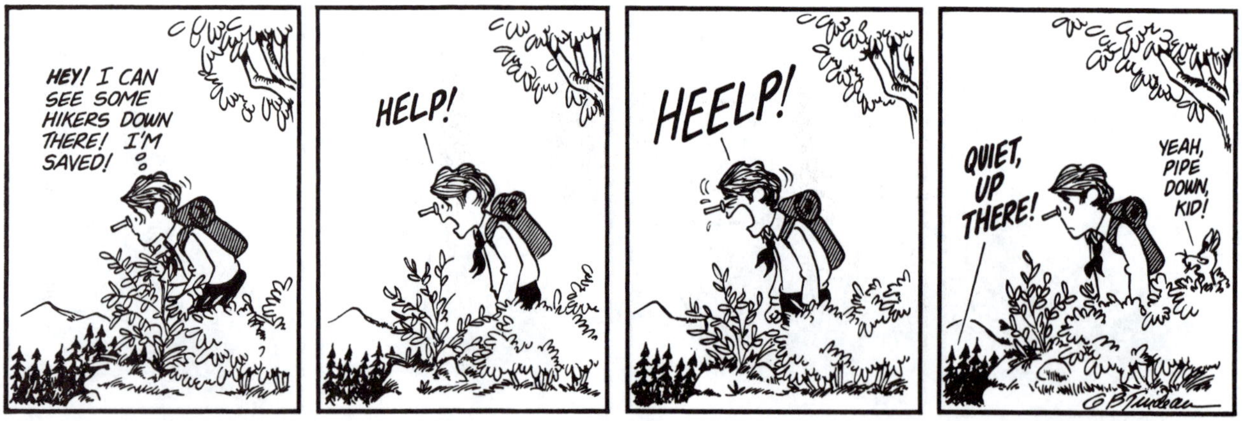
HEY! I CAN SEE SOME HIKERS DOWN THERE! I'M SAVED!
HELP!
HEELP!
QUIET, UP THERE!
YEAH, PIPE DOWN, KID!

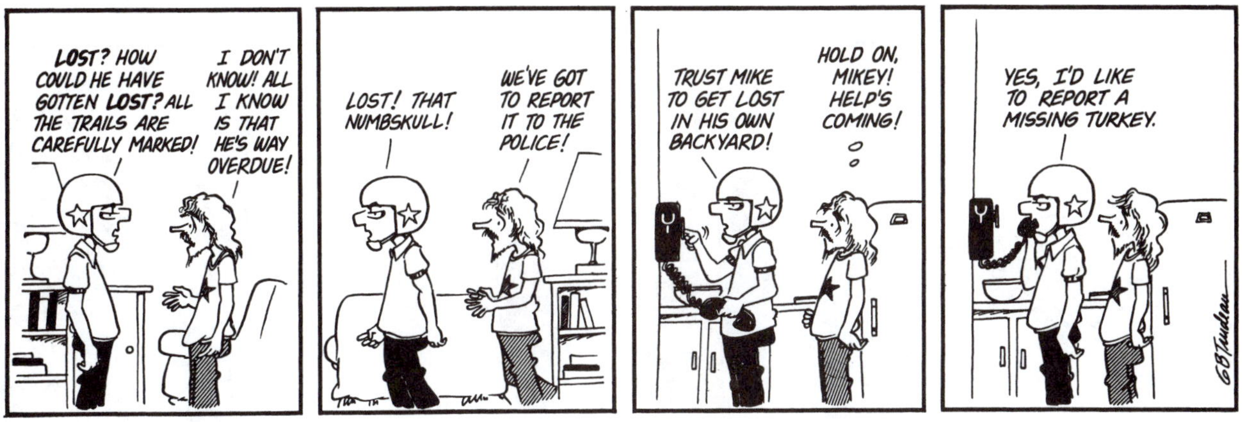
LOST? HOW COULD HE HAVE GOTTEN LOST? ALL THE TRAILS ARE CAREFULLY MARKED!
I DON'T KNOW! ALL I KNOW IS THAT HE'S WAY OVERDUE!
LOST! THAT NUMBSKULL!
WE'VE GOT TO REPORT IT TO THE POLICE!
TRUST MIKE TO GET LOST IN HIS OWN BACKYARD!
HOLD ON, MIKEY! HELP'S COMING!
YES, I'D LIKE TO REPORT A MISSING TURKEY.

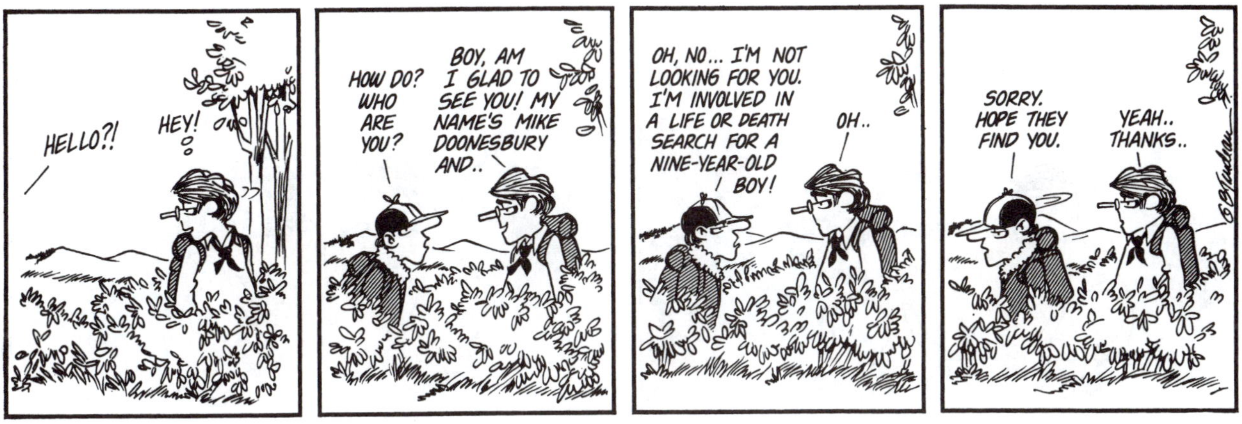
HELLO?!
HEY!
HOW DO? WHO ARE YOU?
BOY, AM I GLAD TO SEE YOU! MY NAME'S MIKE DOONESBURY AND..
OH, NO... I'M NOT LOOKING FOR YOU. I'M INVOLVED IN A LIFE OR DEATH SEARCH FOR A NINE-YEAR-OLD BOY!
OH..
SORRY. HOPE THEY FIND YOU.
YEAH.. THANKS..

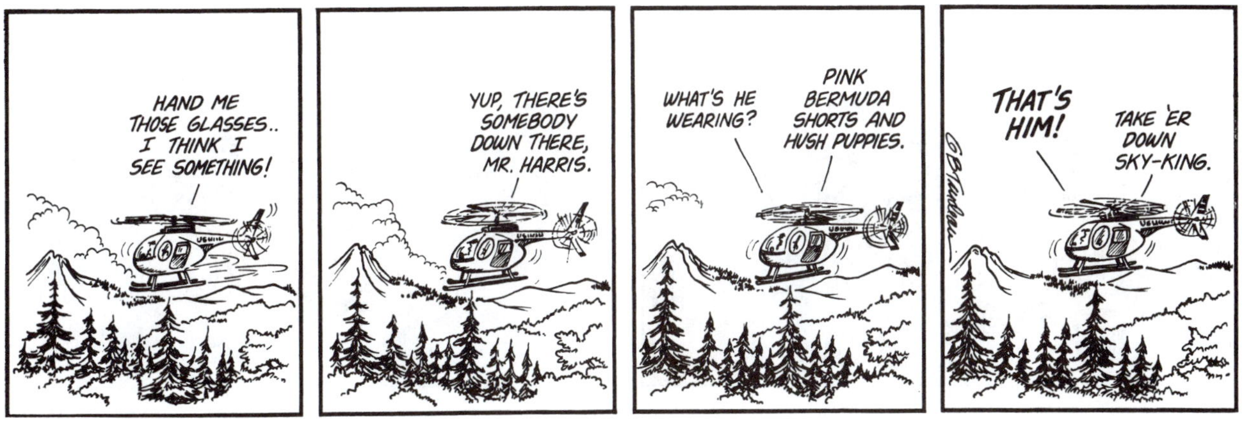
HAND ME THOSE GLASSES.. I THINK I SEE SOMETHING!
YUP, THERE'S SOMEBODY DOWN THERE, MR. HARRIS.
WHAT'S HE WEARING?
PINK BERMUDA SHORTS AND HUSH PUPPIES.
THAT'S HIM!
TAKE 'ER DOWN SKY-KING.

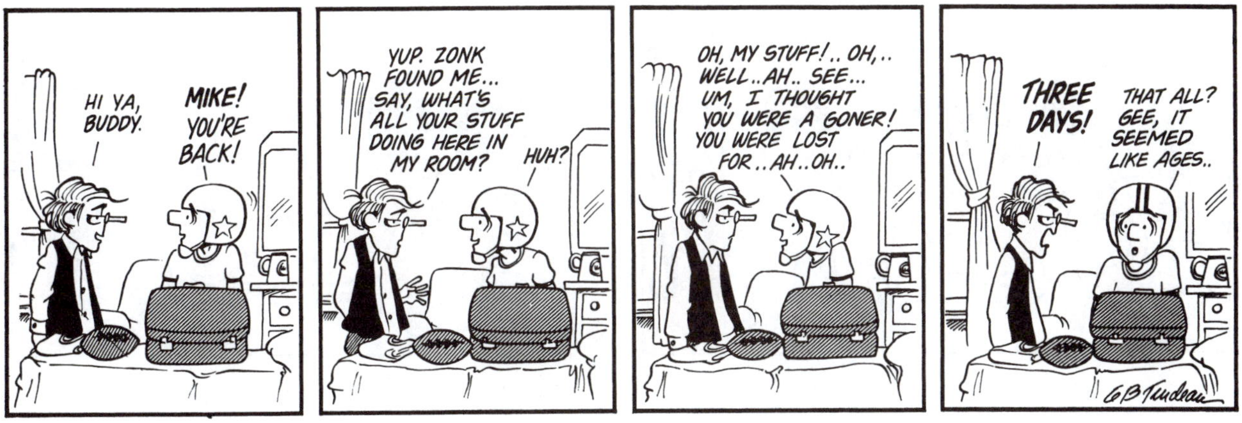
HI YA, BUDDY.
MIKE! YOU'RE BACK!
YUP. ZONK FOUND ME... SAY, WHAT'S ALL YOUR STUFF DOING HERE IN MY ROOM?
HUH?
OH, MY STUFF!.. OH,.. WELL..AH.. SEE... UM, I THOUGHT YOU WERE A GONER! YOU WERE LOST FOR..AH..OH..
THREE DAYS!
THAT ALL? GEE, IT SEEMED LIKE AGES..

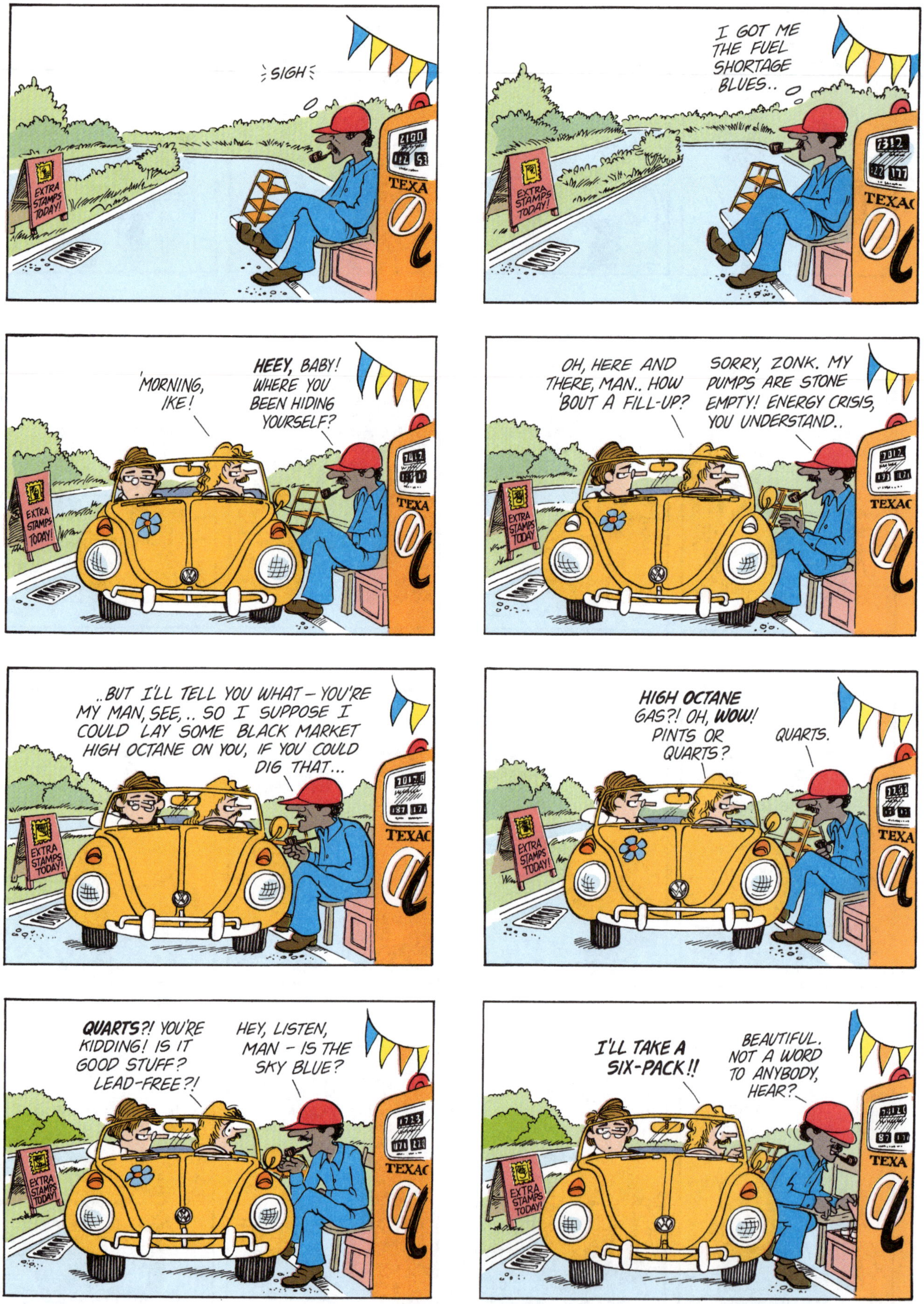

SIGH
EXTRA STAMPS TODAY!
TEXA
I GOT ME THE FUEL SHORTAGE BLUES..
'MORNING, IKE!
HEEY, BABY! WHERE YOU BEEN HIDING YOURSELF?
OH, HERE AND THERE, MAN.. HOW 'BOUT A FILL-UP?
SORRY, ZONK. MY PUMPS ARE STONE EMPTY! ENERGY CRISIS, YOU UNDERSTAND..
..BUT I'LL TELL YOU WHAT – YOU'RE MY MAN, SEE,.. SO I SUPPOSE I COULD LAY SOME BLACK MARKET HIGH OCTANE ON YOU, IF YOU COULD DIG THAT...
HIGH OCTANE GAS?! OH, WOW! PINTS OR QUARTS?
QUARTS.
QUARTS?! YOU'RE KIDDING! IS IT GOOD STUFF? LEAD-FREE?!
HEY, LISTEN, MAN – IS THE SKY BLUE?
I'LL TAKE A SIX-PACK!!
BEAUTIFUL. NOT A WORD TO ANYBODY, HEAR?

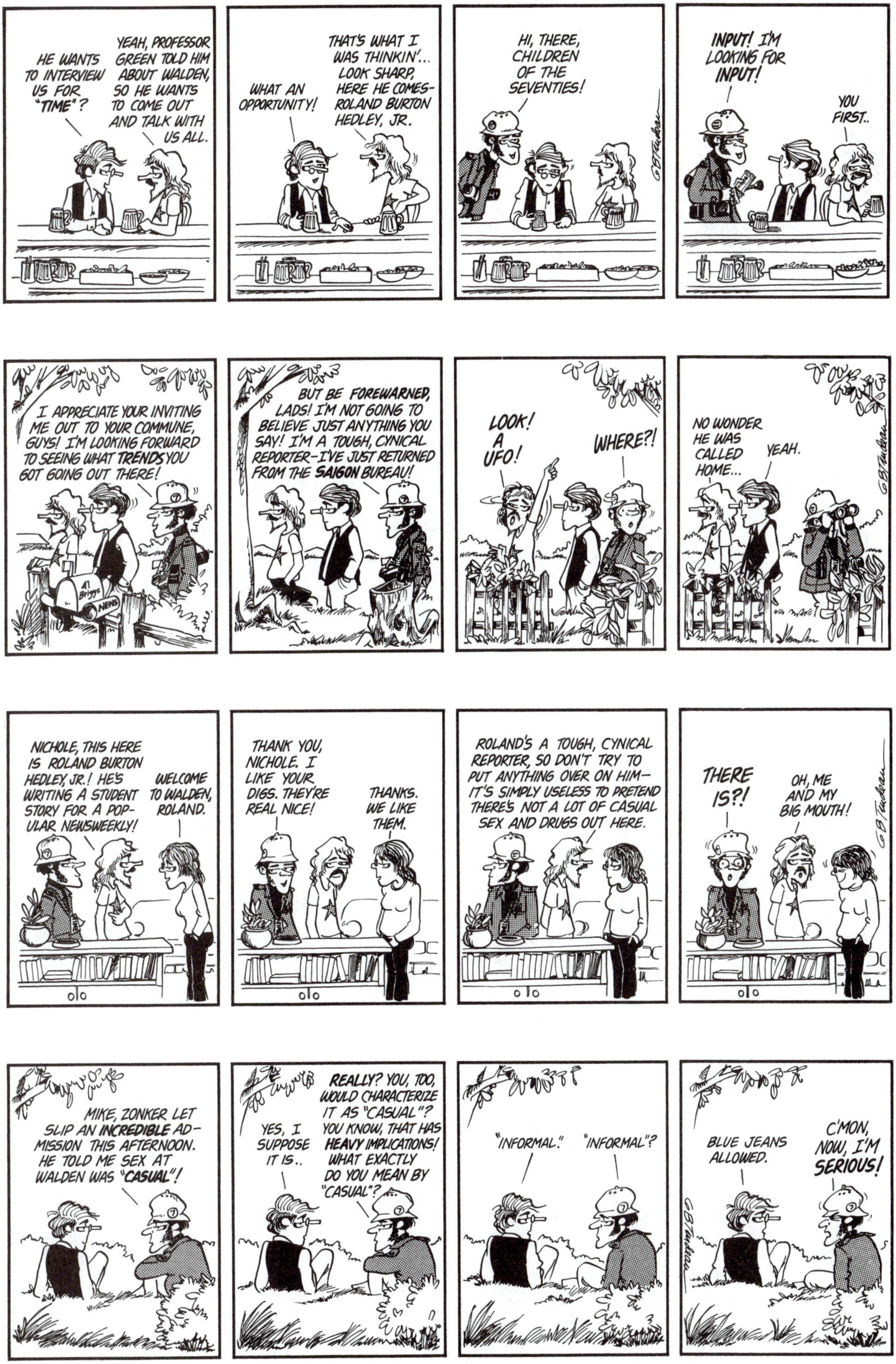
HE WANTS TO INTERVIEW US FOR "TIME"?
YEAH, PROFESSOR GREEN TOLD HIM ABOUT WALDEN, SO HE WANTS TO COME OUT AND TALK WITH US ALL.
WHAT AN OPPORTUNITY!
THAT'S WHAT I WAS THINKIN'... LOOK SHARP, HERE HE COMES- ROLAND BURTON HEDLEY, JR.
HI, THERE, CHILDREN OF THE SEVENTIES!
INPUT! I'M LOOKING FOR INPUT!
YOU FIRST..
I APPRECIATE YOUR INVITING ME OUT TO YOUR COMMUNE, GUYS! I'M LOOKING FORWARD TO SEEING WHAT TRENDS YOU GOT GOING OUT THERE!
41 Briggs
NEWS
BUT BE FOREWARNED, LADS! I'M NOT GOING TO BELIEVE JUST ANYTHING YOU SAY! I'M A TOUGH, CYNICAL REPORTER-I'VE JUST RETURNED FROM THE SAIGON BUREAU!
LOOK! A UFO!
WHERE?!
NO WONDER HE WAS CALLED HOME...
YEAH.
NICHOLE, THIS HERE IS ROLAND BURTON HEDLEY, JR.! HE'S WRITING A STUDENT STORY FOR A POPULAR NEWSWEEKLY!
WELCOME TO WALDEN, ROLAND.
THANK YOU, NICHOLE. I LIKE YOUR DIGS. THEY'RE REAL NICE!
THANKS. WE LIKE THEM.
ROLAND'S A TOUGH, CYNICAL REPORTER, SO DON'T TRY TO PUT ANYTHING OVER ON HIM- IT'S SIMPLY USELESS TO PRETEND THERE'S NOT A LOT OF CASUAL SEX AND DRUGS OUT HERE.
THERE IS?!
OH, ME AND MY BIG MOUTH!
MIKE, ZONKER LET SLIP AN INCREDIBLE ADMISSION THIS AFTERNOON. HE TOLD ME SEX AT WALDEN WAS "CASUAL"!
YES, I SUPPOSE IT IS..
REALLY? YOU, TOO, WOULD CHARACTERIZE IT AS "CASUAL"? YOU KNOW, THAT HAS HEAVY IMPLICATIONS! WHAT EXACTLY DO YOU MEAN BY "CASUAL"?
"INFORMAL."
"INFORMAL"?
BLUE JEANS ALLOWED.
C'MON, NOW, I'M SERIOUS!

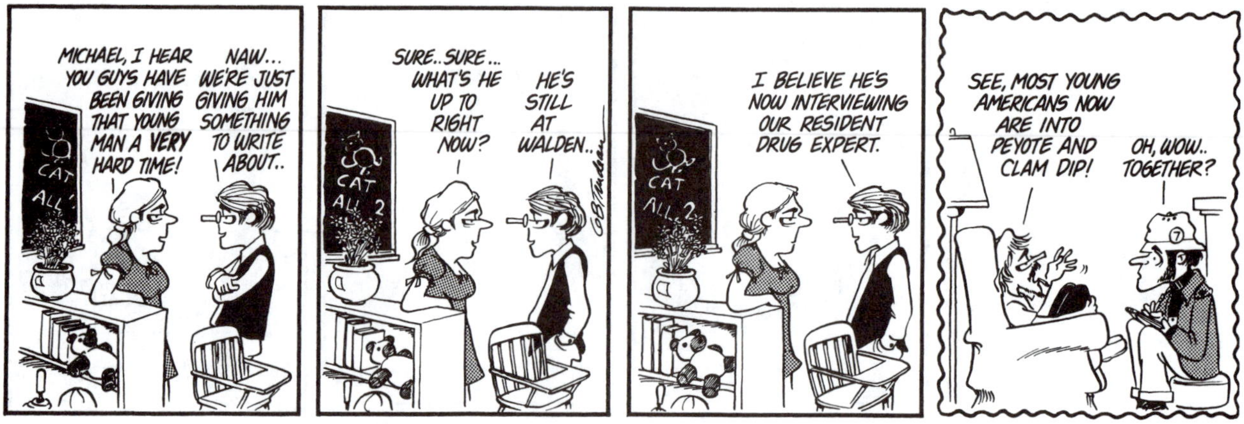
MICHAEL, I HEAR YOU GUYS HAVE BEEN GIVING THAT YOUNG MAN A VERY HARD TIME!
NAW... WE'RE JUST GIVING HIM SOMETHING TO WRITE ABOUT..
SURE..SURE... WHAT'S HE UP TO RIGHT NOW?
HE'S STILL AT WALDEN..
I BELIEVE HE'S NOW INTERVIEWING OUR RESIDENT DRUG EXPERT.
SEE, MOST YOUNG AMERICANS NOW ARE INTO PEYOTE AND CLAM DIP!
OH, WOW.. TOGETHER?

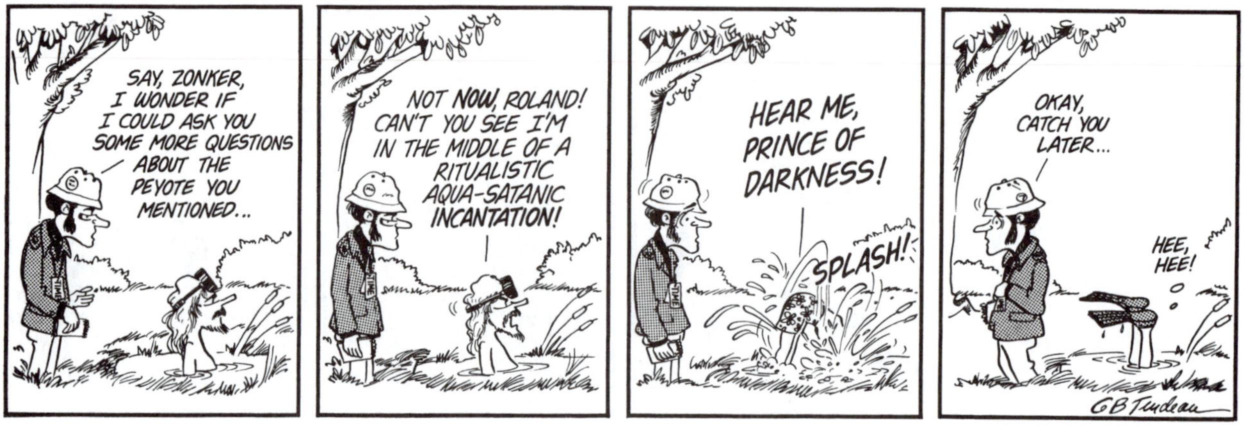
SAY, ZONKER, I WONDER IF I COULD ASK YOU SOME MORE QUESTIONS ABOUT THE PEYOTE YOU MENTIONED...
NOT NOW, ROLAND! CAN'T YOU SEE I'M IN THE MIDDLE OF A RITUALISTIC AQUA-SATANIC INCANTATION!
HEAR ME, PRINCE OF DARKNESS!
SPLASH!
OKAY, CATCH YOU LATER...
HEE, HEE!

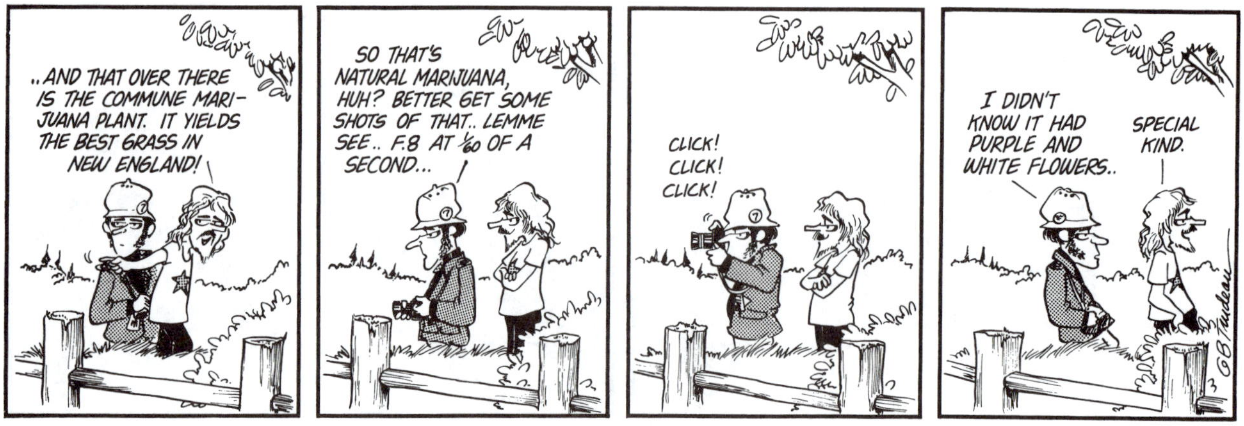
..AND THAT OVER THERE IS THE COMMUNE MARIJUANA PLANT. IT YIELDS THE BEST GRASS IN NEW ENGLAND!
SO THAT'S NATURAL MARIJUANA, HUH? BETTER GET SOME SHOTS OF THAT.. LEMME SEE.. F.8 AT 1/60 OF A SECOND...
CLICK! CLICK! CLICK!
I DIDN'T KNOW IT HAD PURPLE AND WHITE FLOWERS..
SPECIAL KIND.

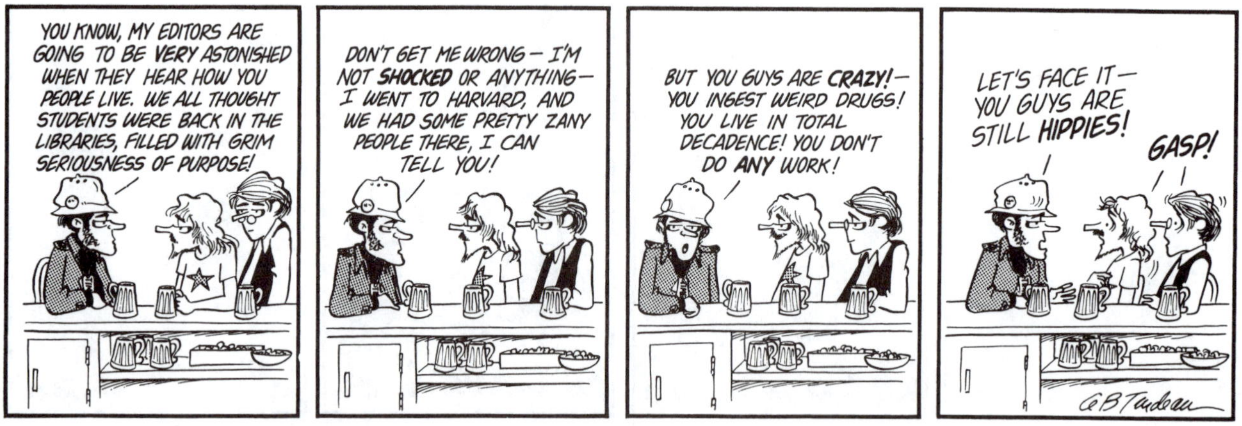
YOU KNOW, MY EDITORS ARE GOING TO BE VERY ASTONISHED WHEN THEY HEAR HOW YOU PEOPLE LIVE. WE ALL THOUGHT STUDENTS WERE BACK IN THE LIBRARIES, FILLED WITH GRIM SERIOUSNESS OF PURPOSE!
DON'T GET ME WRONG — I'M NOT SHOCKED OR ANYTHING — I WENT TO HARVARD, AND WE HAD SOME PRETTY ZANY PEOPLE THERE, I CAN TELL YOU!
BUT YOU GUYS ARE CRAZY! — YOU INGEST WEIRD DRUGS! YOU LIVE IN TOTAL DECADENCE! YOU DON'T DO ANY WORK!
LET'S FACE IT — YOU GUYS ARE STILL HIPPIES!
GASP!

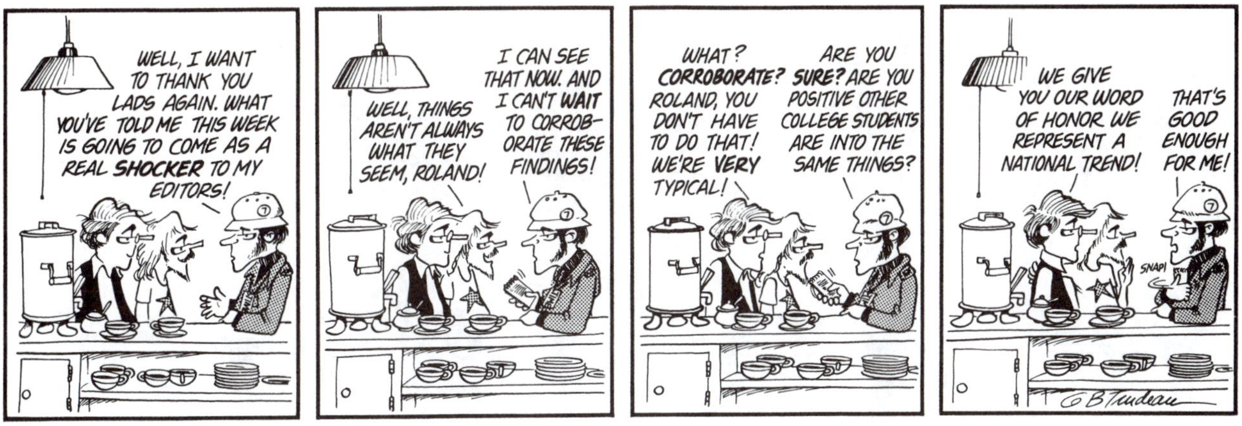
WELL, I WANT TO THANK YOU LADS AGAIN. WHAT YOU'VE TOLD ME THIS WEEK IS GOING TO COME AS A REAL SHOCKER TO MY EDITORS!
WELL, THINGS AREN'T ALWAYS WHAT THEY SEEM, ROLAND!
I CAN SEE THAT NOW. AND I CAN'T WAIT TO CORROBORATE THESE FINDINGS!
WHAT? CORROBORATE? ROLAND, YOU DON'T HAVE TO DO THAT! WE'RE VERY TYPICAL!
ARE YOU SURE? ARE YOU POSITIVE OTHER COLLEGE STUDENTS ARE INTO THE SAME THINGS?
WE GIVE YOU OUR WORD OF HONOR WE REPRESENT A NATIONAL TREND!
THAT'S GOOD ENOUGH FOR ME!
SNAP!
GBTrudeau

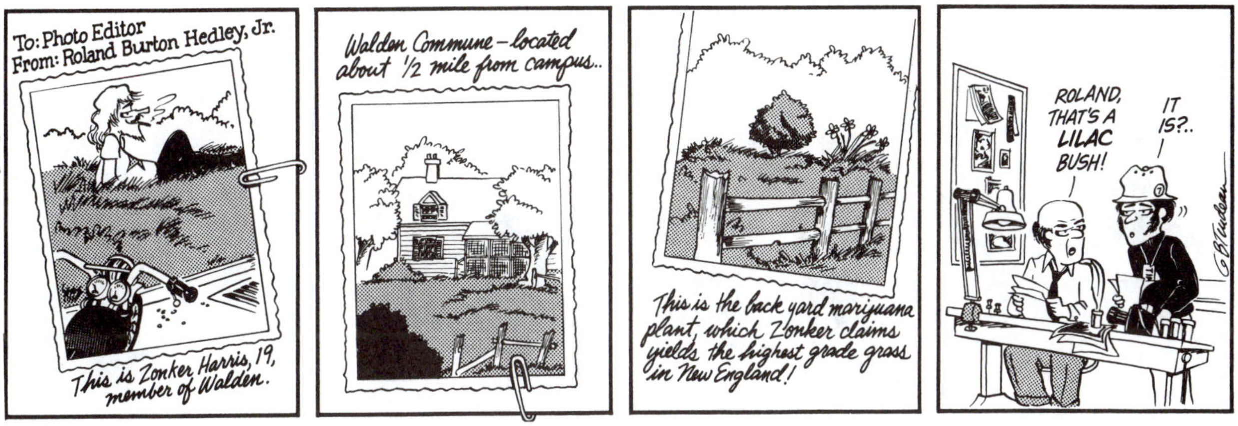
To: Photo Editor
From: Roland Burton Hedley, Jr.
This is Zonker Harris, 19, member of Walden.
Walden Commune—located about ½ mile from campus..
This is the back yard marijuana plant, which Zonker claims yields the highest grade grass in New England!
ROLAND, THAT'S A LILAC BUSH!
IT IS?..
GBTrudeau

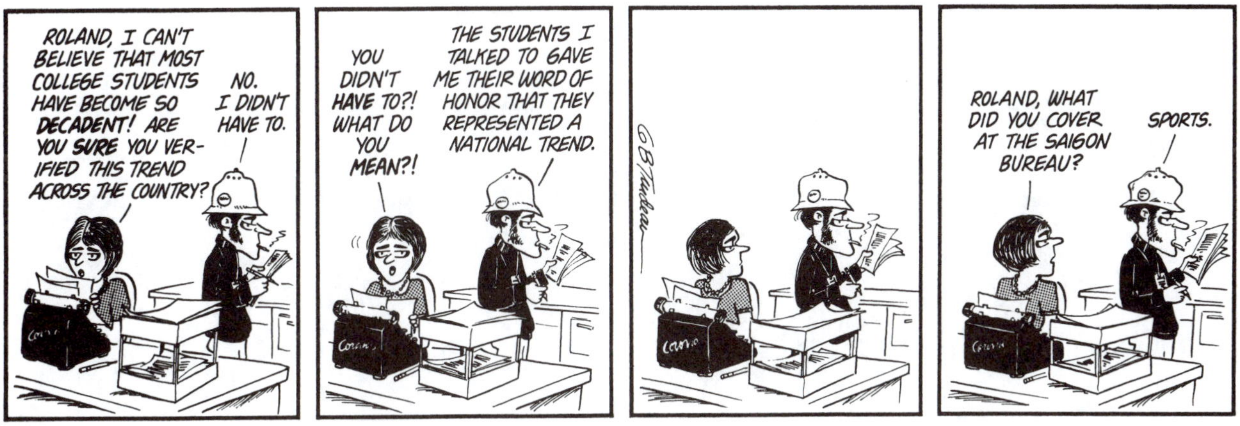
ROLAND, I CAN'T BELIEVE THAT MOST COLLEGE STUDENTS HAVE BECOME SO DECADENT! ARE YOU SURE YOU VERIFIED THIS TREND ACROSS THE COUNTRY?
NO. I DIDN'T HAVE TO.
YOU DIDN'T HAVE TO?! WHAT DO YOU MEAN?!
THE STUDENTS I TALKED TO GAVE ME THEIR WORD OF HONOR THAT THEY REPRESENTED A NATIONAL TREND.
GBTrudeau
ROLAND, WHAT DID YOU COVER AT THE SAIGON BUREAU?
SPORTS.

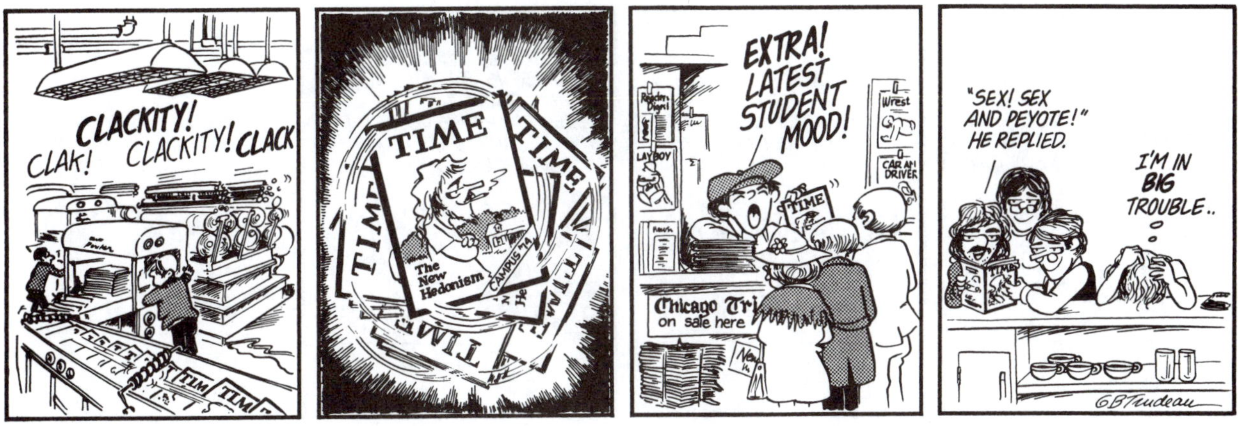
CLACKITY! CLAK! CLACKITY! CLACK
TIME
The New Hedonism
EXTRA! LATEST STUDENT MOOD!
TIME
Chicago Tri
on sale here
"SEX! SEX AND PEYOTE!" HE REPLIED.
I'M IN BIG TROUBLE..
GBTrudeau

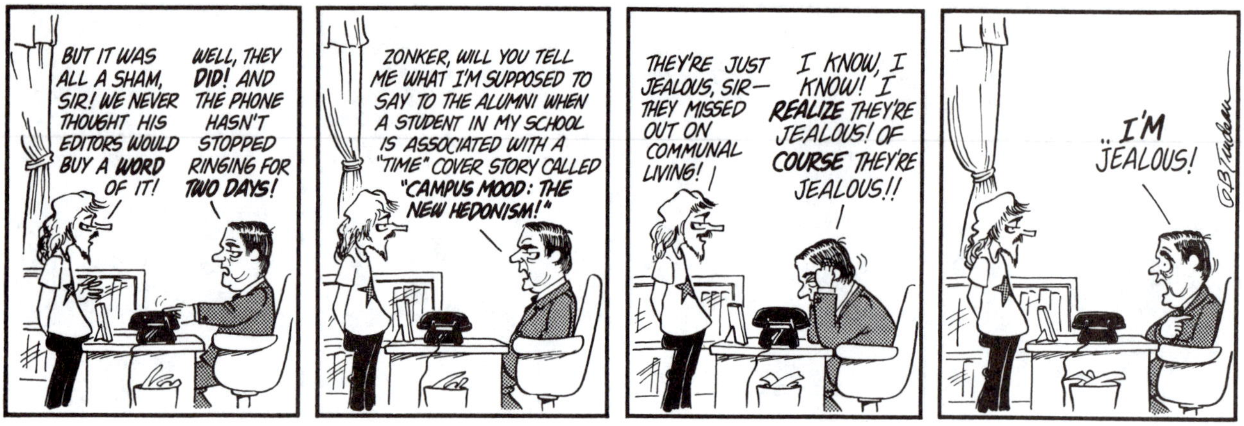
BUT IT WAS ALL A SHAM, SIR! WE NEVER THOUGHT HIS EDITORS WOULD BUY A WORD OF IT!
WELL, THEY DID! AND THE PHONE HASN'T STOPPED RINGING FOR TWO DAYS!
ZONKER, WILL YOU TELL ME WHAT I'M SUPPOSED TO SAY TO THE ALUMNI WHEN A STUDENT IN MY SCHOOL IS ASSOCIATED WITH A "TIME" COVER STORY CALLED "CAMPUS MOOD: THE NEW HEDONISM!"
THEY'RE JUST JEALOUS, SIR— THEY MISSED OUT ON COMMUNAL LIVING!
I KNOW, I KNOW! I REALIZE THEY'RE JEALOUS! OF COURSE THEY'RE JEALOUS!!
..I'M JEALOUS!

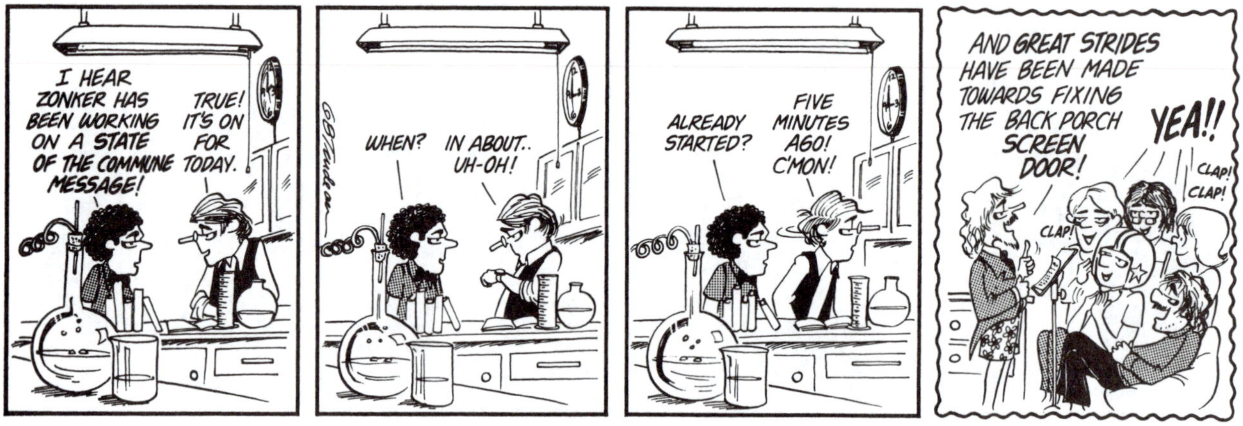
I HEAR ZONKER HAS BEEN WORKING ON A STATE OF THE COMMUNE MESSAGE!
TRUE! IT'S ON FOR TODAY.
WHEN?
IN ABOUT.. UH-OH!
ALREADY STARTED?
FIVE MINUTES AGO! C'MON!
AND GREAT STRIDES HAVE BEEN MADE TOWARDS FIXING THE BACK PORCH SCREEN DOOR!
YEA!!
CLAP! CLAP!
CLAP!

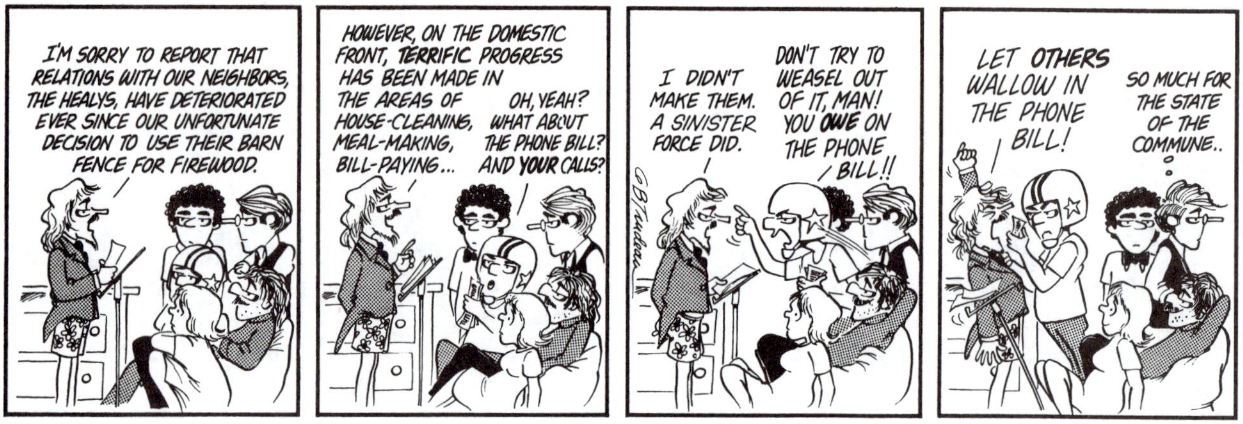
I'M SORRY TO REPORT THAT RELATIONS WITH OUR NEIGHBORS, THE HEALYS, HAVE DETERIORATED EVER SINCE OUR UNFORTUNATE DECISION TO USE THEIR BARN FENCE FOR FIREWOOD.
HOWEVER, ON THE DOMESTIC FRONT, TERRIFIC PROGRESS HAS BEEN MADE IN THE AREAS OF HOUSE-CLEANING, MEAL-MAKING, BILL-PAYING...
OH, YEAH? WHAT ABOUT THE PHONE BILL? AND YOUR CALLS?
I DIDN'T MAKE THEM. A SINISTER FORCE DID.
DON'T TRY TO WEASEL OUT OF IT, MAN! YOU OWE ON THE PHONE BILL!!
LET OTHERS WALLOW IN THE PHONE BILL!
SO MUCH FOR THE STATE OF THE COMMUNE..

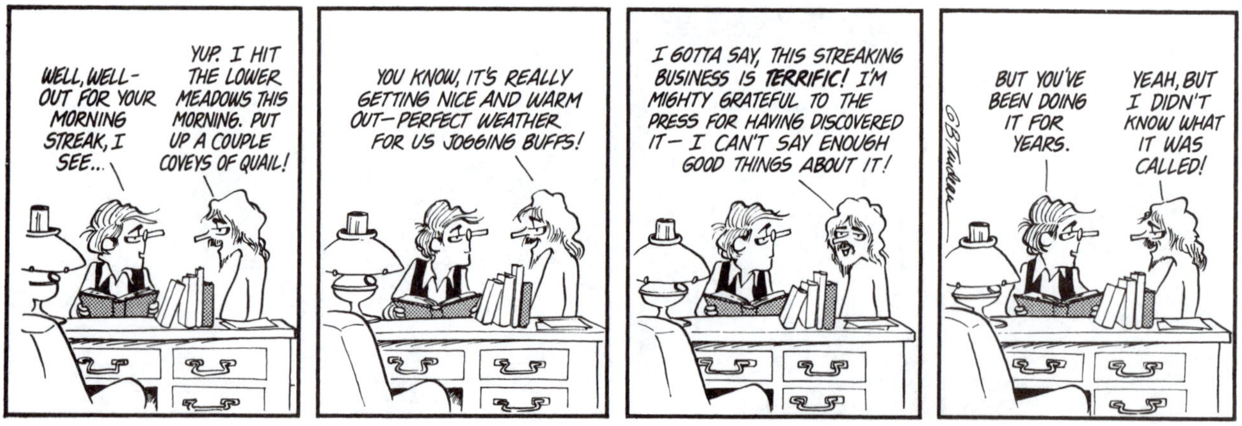
WELL, WELL- OUT FOR YOUR MORNING STREAK, I SEE...
YUP. I HIT THE LOWER MEADOWS THIS MORNING. PUT UP A COUPLE COVEYS OF QUAIL!
YOU KNOW, IT'S REALLY GETTING NICE AND WARM OUT— PERFECT WEATHER FOR US JOGGING BUFFS!
I GOTTA SAY, THIS STREAKING BUSINESS IS TERRIFIC! I'M MIGHTY GRATEFUL TO THE PRESS FOR HAVING DISCOVERED IT— I CAN'T SAY ENOUGH GOOD THINGS ABOUT IT!
BUT YOU'VE BEEN DOING IT FOR YEARS.
YEAH, BUT I DIDN'T KNOW WHAT IT WAS CALLED!

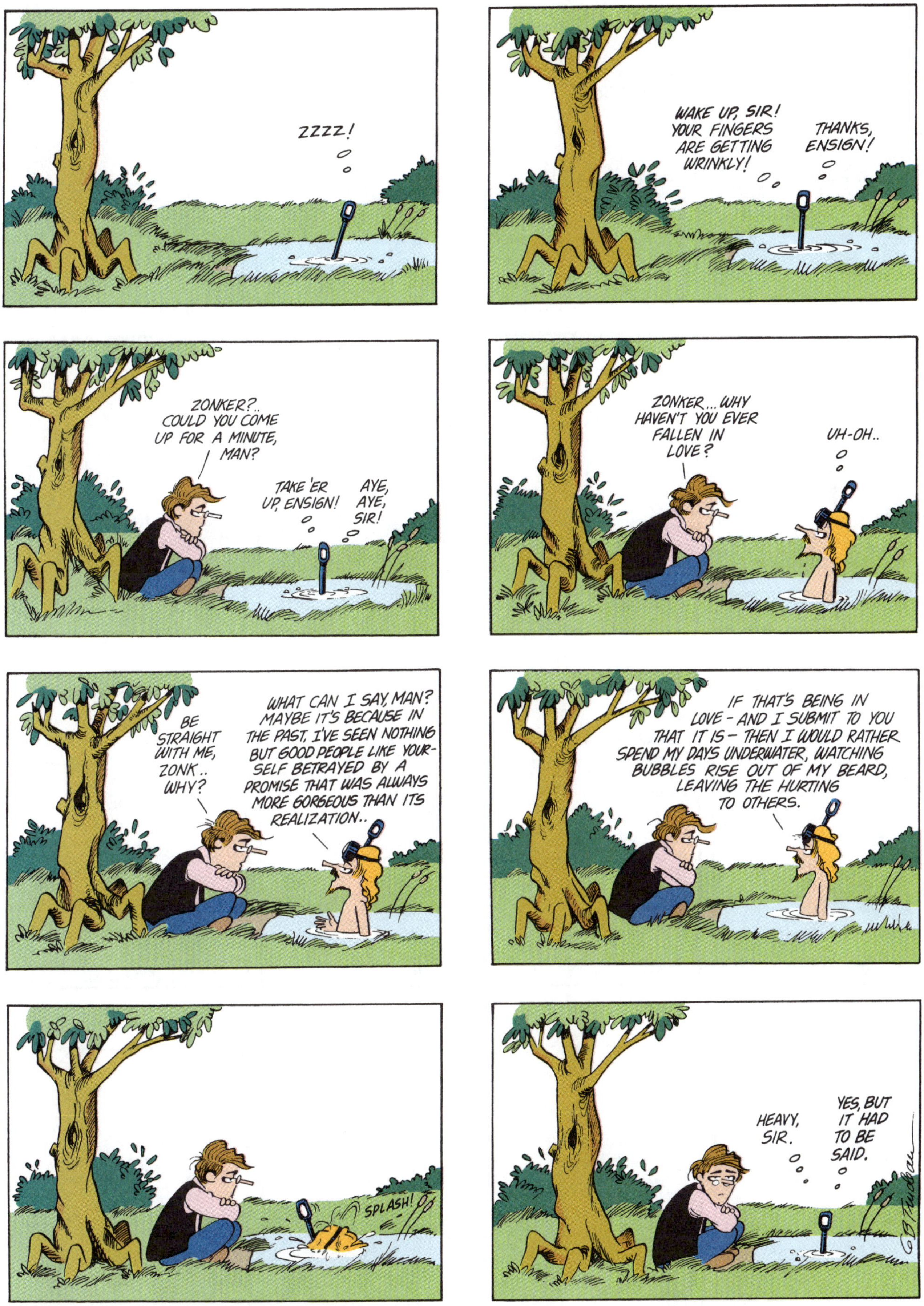
ZZZZ!
WAKE UP, SIR! YOUR FINGERS ARE GETTING WRINKLY!
THANKS, ENSIGN!
ZONKER?.. COULD YOU COME UP FOR A MINUTE, MAN?
TAKE 'ER UP, ENSIGN!
AYE, AYE, SIR!
ZONKER... WHY HAVEN'T YOU EVER FALLEN IN LOVE?
UH-OH..
BE STRAIGHT WITH ME, ZONK.. WHY?
WHAT CAN I SAY, MAN? MAYBE IT'S BECAUSE IN THE PAST, I'VE SEEN NOTHING BUT GOOD PEOPLE LIKE YOURSELF BETRAYED BY A PROMISE THAT WAS ALWAYS MORE GORGEOUS THAN ITS REALIZATION..
IF THAT'S BEING IN LOVE - AND I SUBMIT TO YOU THAT IT IS - THEN I WOULD RATHER SPEND MY DAYS UNDERWATER, WATCHING BUBBLES RISE OUT OF MY BEARD, LEAVING THE HURTING TO OTHERS.
SPLASH!
HEAVY, SIR.
YES, BUT IT HAD TO BE SAID.

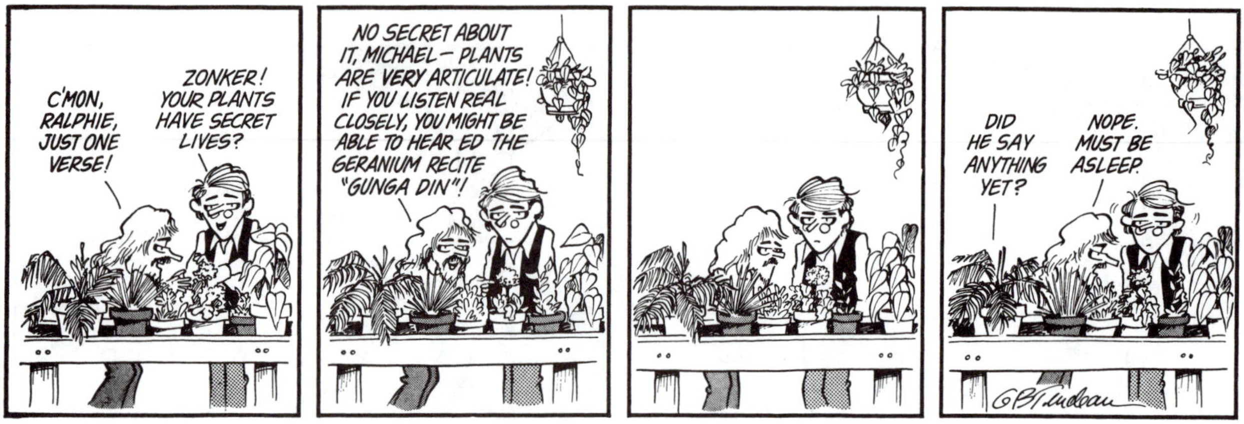
C'MON, RALPHIE, JUST ONE VERSE!
ZONKER! YOUR PLANTS HAVE SECRET LIVES?
NO SECRET ABOUT IT, MICHAEL— PLANTS ARE VERY ARTICULATE! IF YOU LISTEN REAL CLOSELY, YOU MIGHT BE ABLE TO HEAR ED THE GERANIUM RECITE "GUNGA DIN"!
DID HE SAY ANYTHING YET?
NOPE. MUST BE ASLEEP.
GBTrudeau

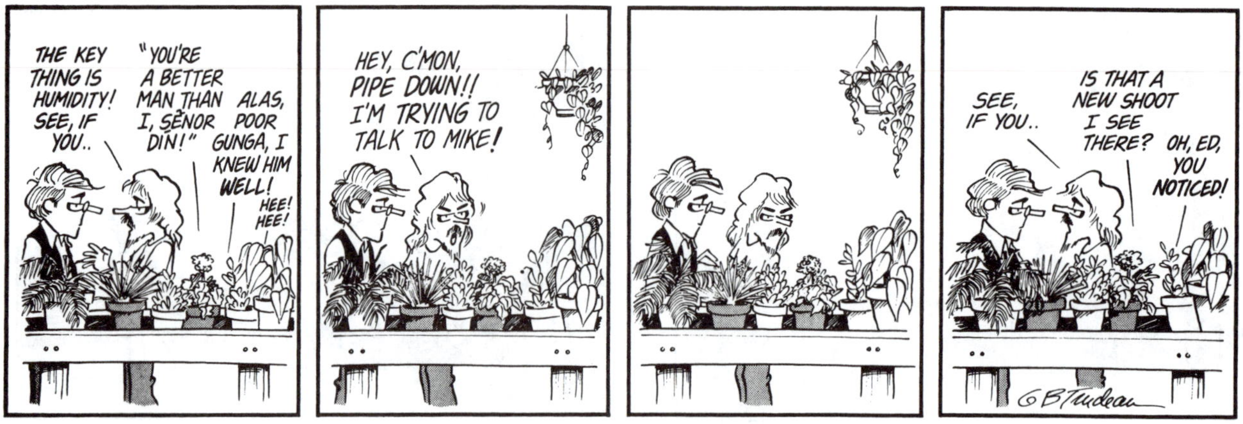
THE KEY THING IS HUMIDITY! SEE, IF YOU..
"YOU'RE A BETTER MAN THAN I, SEÑOR DIN!"
ALAS, POOR GUNGA, I KNEW HIM WELL!
HEE! HEE!
HEY, C'MON, PIPE DOWN!! I'M TRYING TO TALK TO MIKE!
SEE, IF YOU..
IS THAT A NEW SHOOT I SEE THERE?
OH, ED, YOU NOTICED!
GBTrudeau

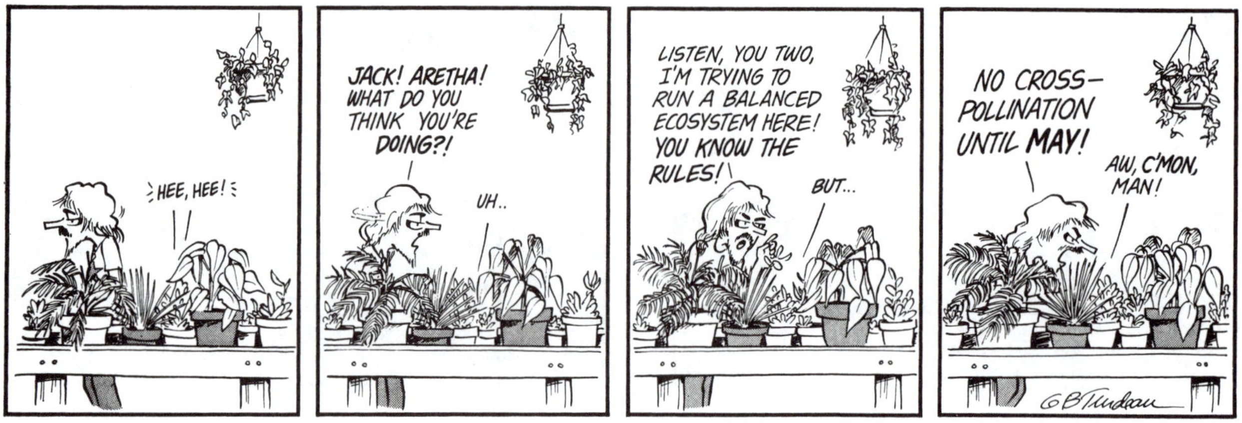
HEE, HEE!
JACK! ARETHA! WHAT DO YOU THINK YOU'RE DOING?!
UH..
LISTEN, YOU TWO, I'M TRYING TO RUN A BALANCED ECOSYSTEM HERE! YOU KNOW THE RULES!
BUT...
NO CROSS-POLLINATION UNTIL MAY!
AW, C'MON, MAN!
GBTrudeau

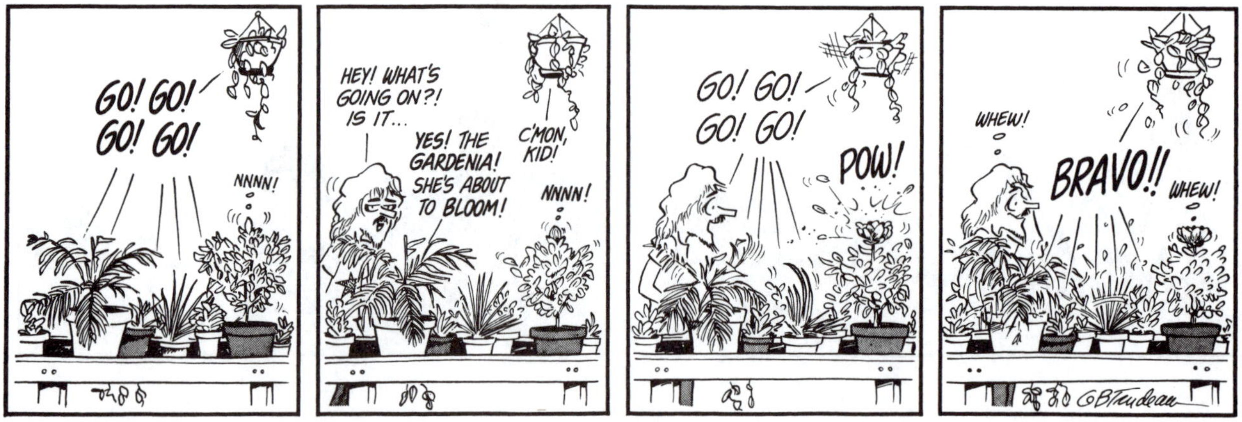
GO! GO! GO! GO!
NNNN!
HEY! WHAT'S GOING ON?! IS IT...
YES! THE GARDENIA! SHE'S ABOUT TO BLOOM!
C'MON, KID!
NNNN!
GO! GO! GO! GO!
POW!
WHEW!
BRAVO!!
WHEW!
GBTrudeau

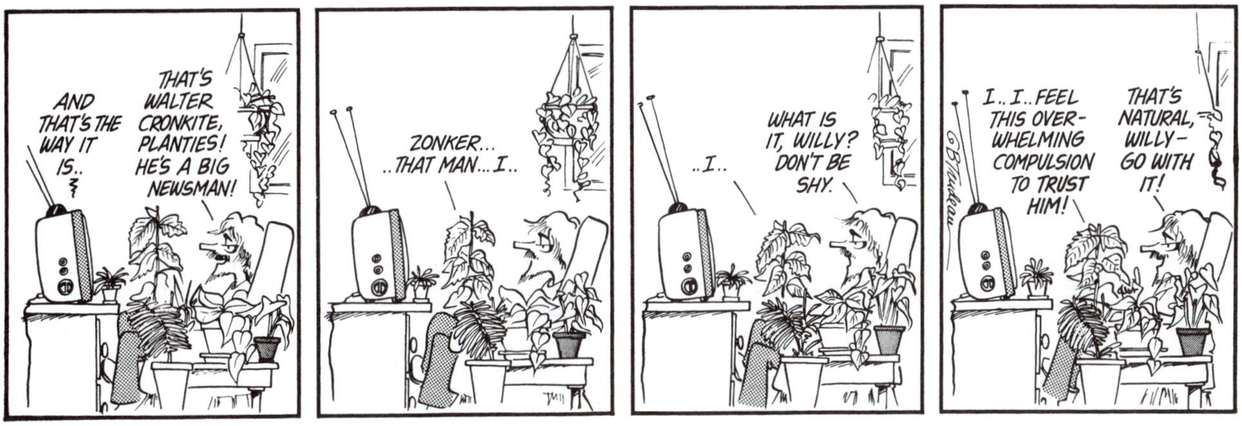
AND THAT'S THE WAY IT IS..
THAT'S WALTER CRONKITE, PLANTIES! HE'S A BIG NEWSMAN!
ZONKER... ..THAT MAN... I..
..I..
WHAT IS IT, WILLY? DON'T BE SHY.
I.. I.. FEEL THIS OVER-WHELMING COMPULSION TO TRUST HIM!
THAT'S NATURAL, WILLY— GO WITH IT!

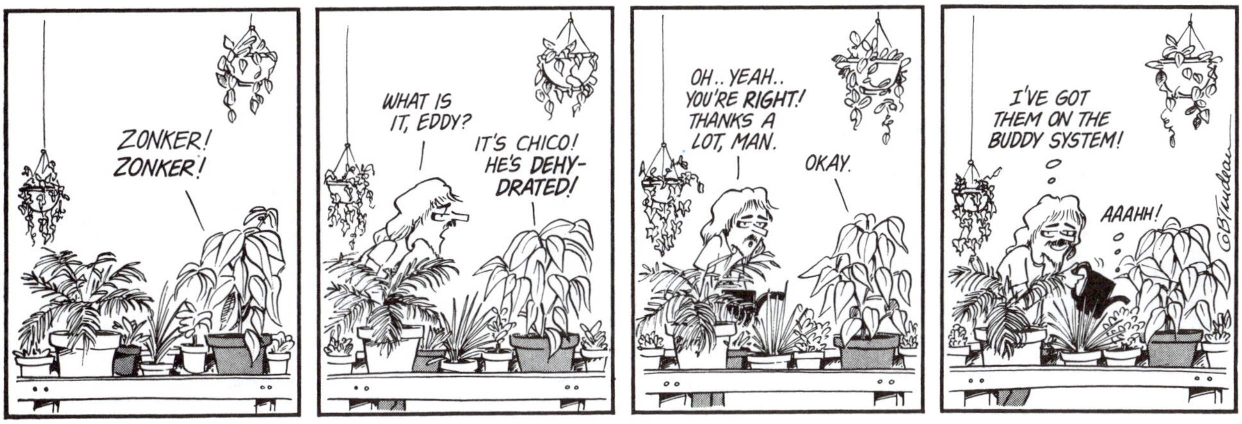
ZONKER! ZONKER!
WHAT IS IT, EDDY?
IT'S CHICO! HE'S DEHY-DRATED!
OH.. YEAH.. YOU'RE RIGHT! THANKS A LOT, MAN.
OKAY.
I'VE GOT THEM ON THE BUDDY SYSTEM!
AAAHH!

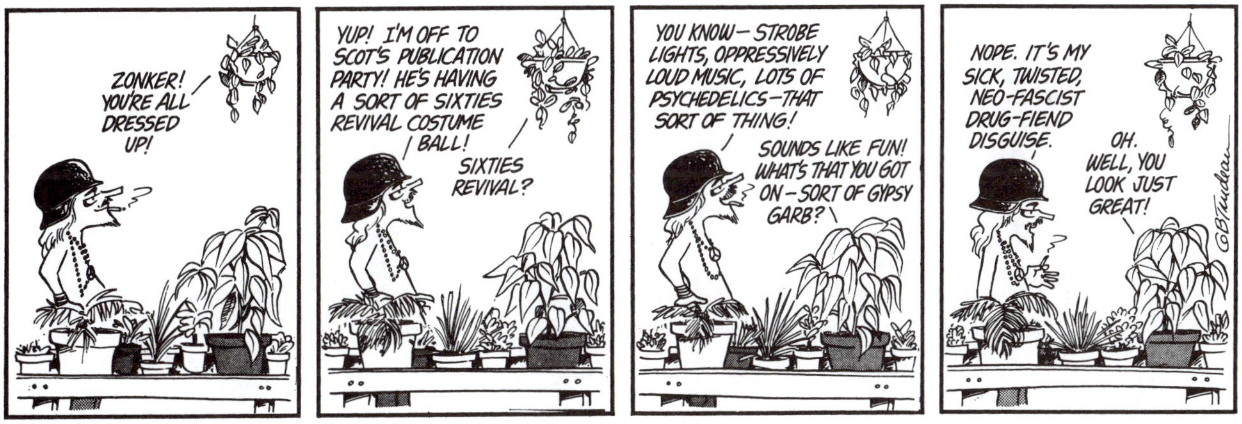
ZONKER! YOU'RE ALL DRESSED UP!
YUP! I'M OFF TO SCOT'S PUBLICATION PARTY! HE'S HAVING A SORT OF SIXTIES REVIVAL COSTUME BALL!
SIXTIES REVIVAL?
YOU KNOW— STROBE LIGHTS, OPPRESSIVELY LOUD MUSIC, LOTS OF PSYCHEDELICS—THAT SORT OF THING!
SOUNDS LIKE FUN! WHAT'S THAT YOU GOT ON— SORT OF GYPSY GARB?
NOPE. IT'S MY SICK, TWISTED, NEO-FASCIST DRUG-FIEND DISGUISE.
OH. WELL, YOU LOOK JUST GREAT!

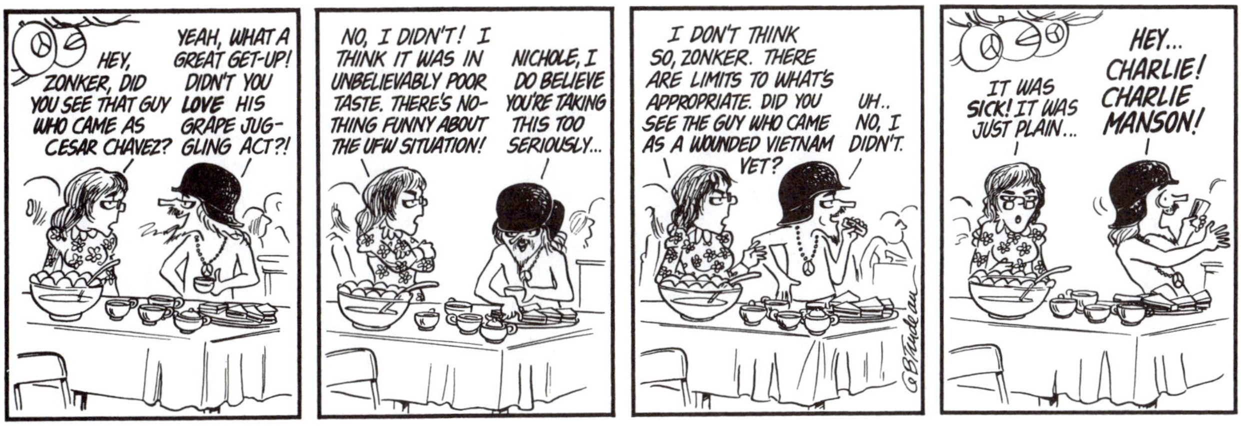
HEY, ZONKER, DID YOU SEE THAT GUY WHO CAME AS CESAR CHAVEZ?
YEAH, WHAT A GREAT GET-UP! DIDN'T YOU LOVE HIS GRAPE JUG-GLING ACT?!
NO, I DIDN'T! I THINK IT WAS IN UNBELIEVABLY POOR TASTE. THERE'S NO-THING FUNNY ABOUT THE UFW SITUATION!
NICHOLE, I DO BELIEVE YOU'RE TAKING THIS TOO SERIOUSLY...
I DON'T THINK SO, ZONKER. THERE ARE LIMITS TO WHAT'S APPROPRIATE. DID YOU SEE THE GUY WHO CAME AS A WOUNDED VIETNAM VET?
UH.. NO, I DIDN'T.
IT WAS SICK! IT WAS JUST PLAIN...
HEY... CHARLIE! CHARLIE MANSON!

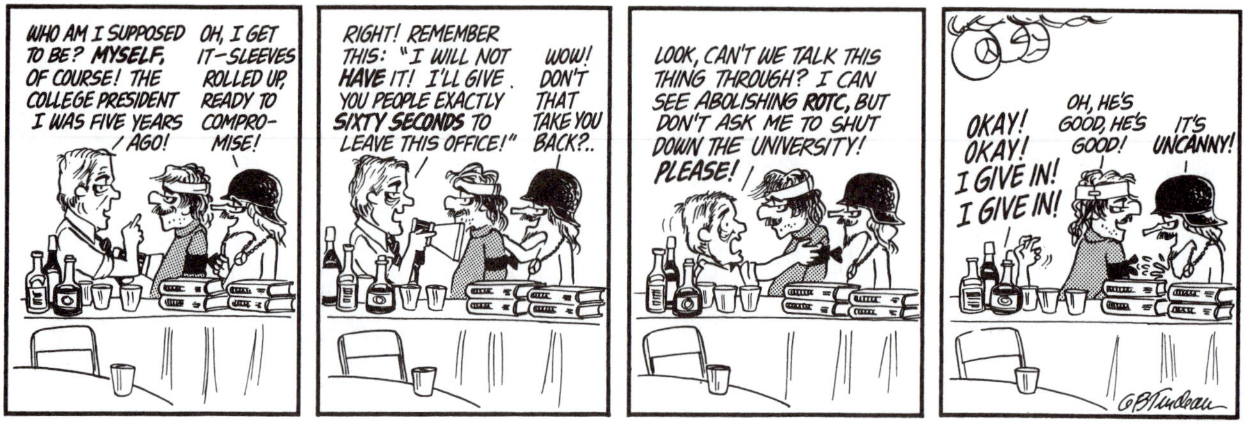
WHO AM I SUPPOSED TO BE? MYSELF, OF COURSE! THE COLLEGE PRESIDENT I WAS FIVE YEARS AGO!
OH, I GET IT—SLEEVES ROLLED UP, READY TO COMPROMISE!
RIGHT! REMEMBER THIS: "I WILL NOT HAVE IT! I'LL GIVE YOU PEOPLE EXACTLY SIXTY SECONDS TO LEAVE THIS OFFICE!"
WOW! DON'T THAT TAKE YOU BACK?..
LOOK, CAN'T WE TALK THIS THING THROUGH? I CAN SEE ABOLISHING ROTC, BUT DON'T ASK ME TO SHUT DOWN THE UNIVERSITY! PLEASE!
OKAY! OKAY! I GIVE IN! I GIVE IN!
OH, HE'S GOOD, HE'S GOOD!
IT'S UNCANNY!
G B Trudeau

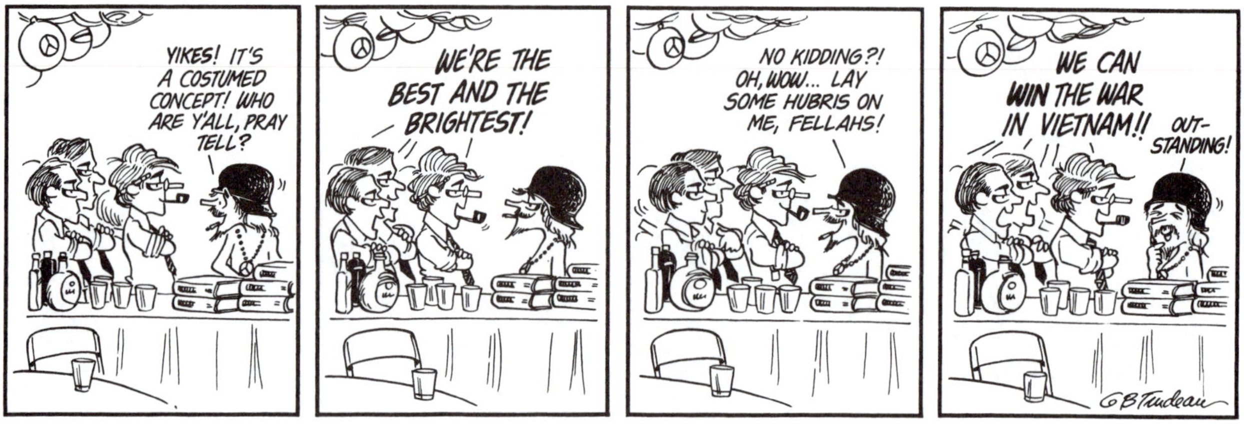
YIKES! IT'S A COSTUMED CONCEPT! WHO ARE Y'ALL, PRAY TELL?
WE'RE THE BEST AND THE BRIGHTEST!
NO KIDDING?! OH, WOW... LAY SOME HUBRIS ON ME, FELLAHS!
WE CAN WIN THE WAR IN VIETNAM!!
OUT-STANDING!
G B Trudeau

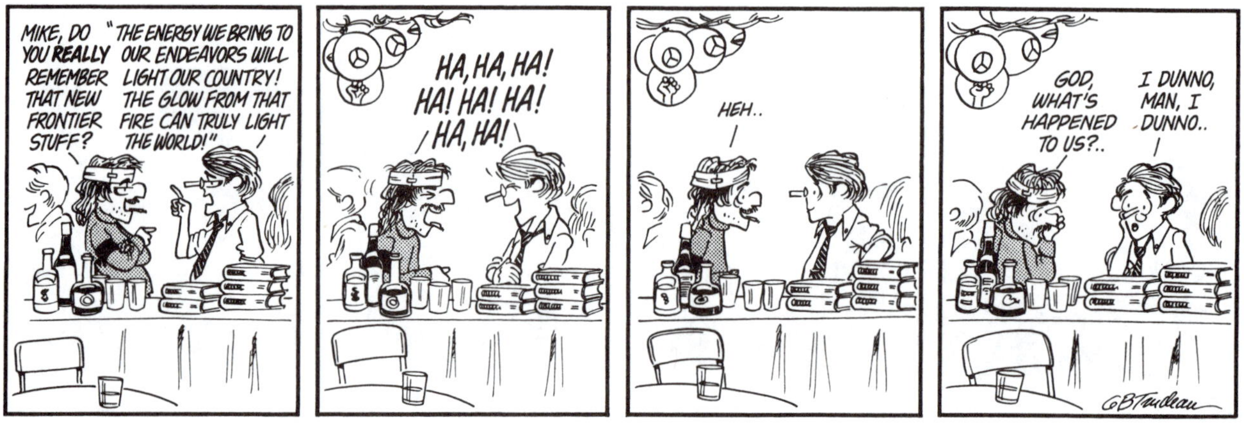
MIKE, DO YOU REALLY REMEMBER THAT NEW FRONTIER STUFF?
"THE ENERGY WE BRING TO OUR ENDEAVORS WILL LIGHT OUR COUNTRY! THE GLOW FROM THAT FIRE CAN TRULY LIGHT THE WORLD!"
HA, HA, HA! HA! HA! HA! HA, HA!
HEH..
GOD, WHAT'S HAPPENED TO US?..
I DUNNO, MAN, I DUNNO..
G B Trudeau

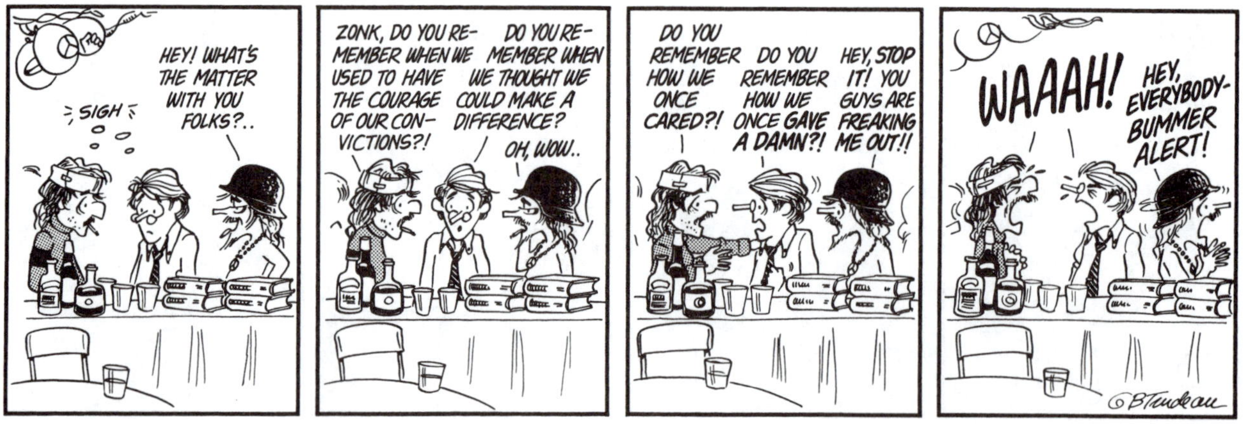
HEY! WHAT'S THE MATTER WITH YOU FOLKS?..
SIGH
ZONK, DO YOU REMEMBER WHEN WE USED TO HAVE THE COURAGE OF OUR CONVICTIONS?!
DO YOU REMEMBER WHEN WE THOUGHT WE COULD MAKE A DIFFERENCE?
OH, WOW..
DO YOU REMEMBER HOW WE ONCE CARED?!
DO YOU REMEMBER HOW WE ONCE GAVE A DAMN?!
HEY, STOP IT! YOU GUYS ARE FREAKING ME OUT!!
WAAAH!
HEY, EVERYBODY-BUMMER ALERT!
G B Trudeau

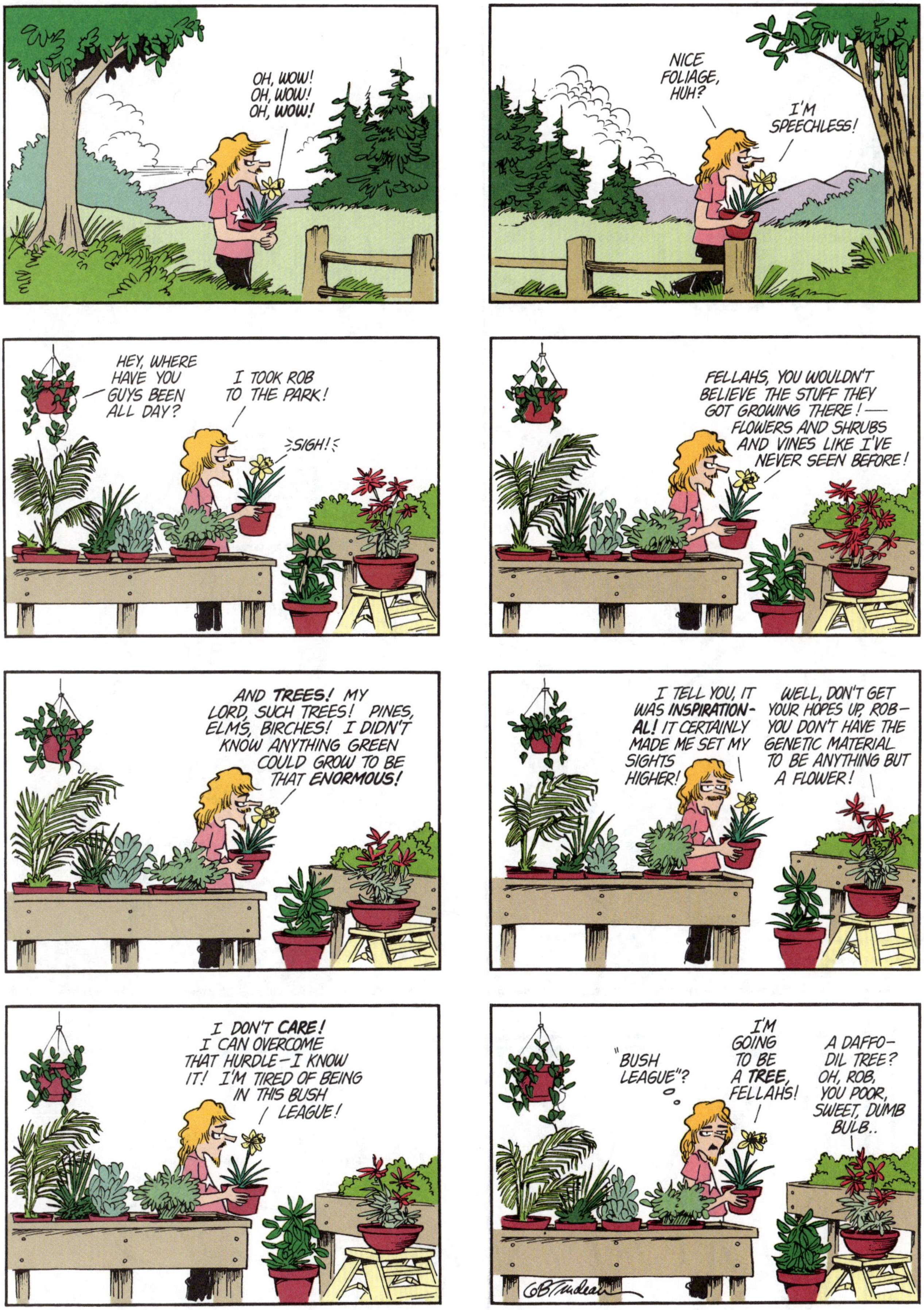
OH, WOW! OH, WOW! OH, WOW!
NICE FOLIAGE, HUH?
I'M SPEECHLESS!
HEY, WHERE HAVE YOU GUYS BEEN ALL DAY?
I TOOK ROB TO THE PARK!
SIGH!
FELLAHS, YOU WOULDN'T BELIEVE THE STUFF THEY GOT GROWING THERE!— FLOWERS AND SHRUBS AND VINES LIKE I'VE NEVER SEEN BEFORE!
AND TREES! MY LORD, SUCH TREES! PINES, ELMS, BIRCHES! I DIDN'T KNOW ANYTHING GREEN COULD GROW TO BE THAT ENORMOUS!
I TELL YOU, IT WAS INSPIRATIONAL! IT CERTAINLY MADE ME SET MY SIGHTS HIGHER!
WELL, DON'T GET YOUR HOPES UP, ROB—YOU DON'T HAVE THE GENETIC MATERIAL TO BE ANYTHING BUT A FLOWER!
I DON'T CARE! I CAN OVERCOME THAT HURDLE—I KNOW IT! I'M TIRED OF BEING IN THIS BUSH LEAGUE!
"BUSH LEAGUE"?
I'M GOING TO BE A TREE, FELLAHS!
A DAFFODIL TREE? OH, ROB, YOU POOR, SWEET, DUMB BULB..
GBTrudeau

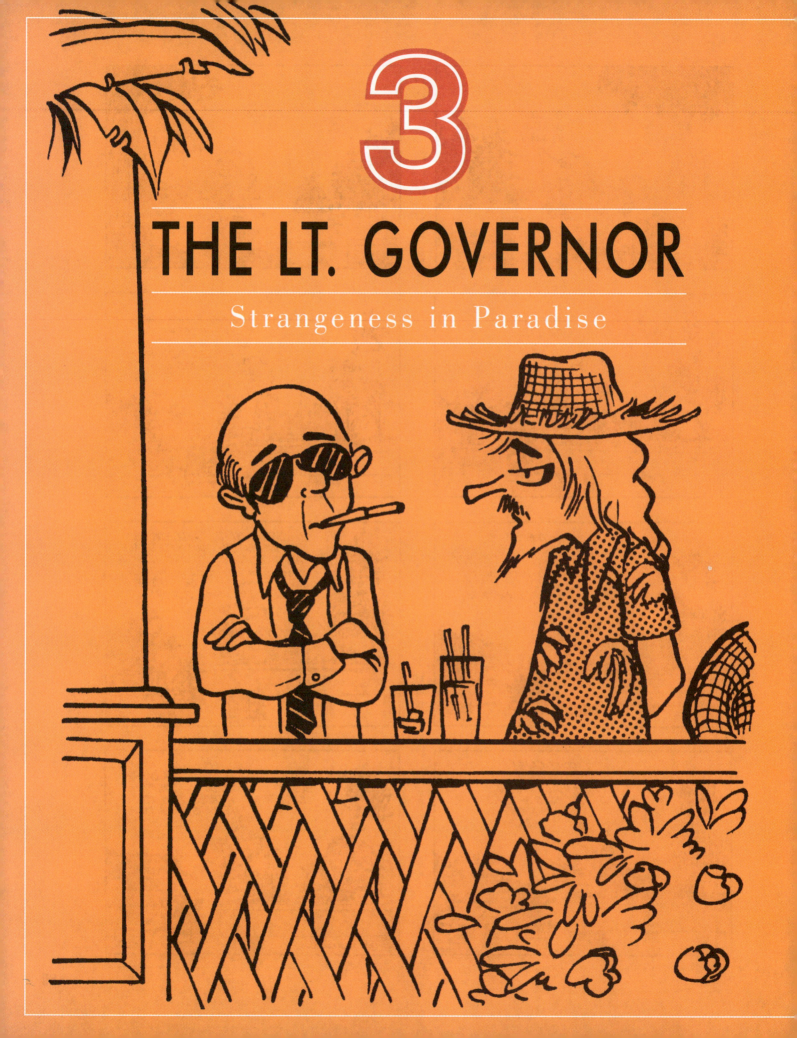

3

THE LT. GOVERNOR

Strangeness in Paradise

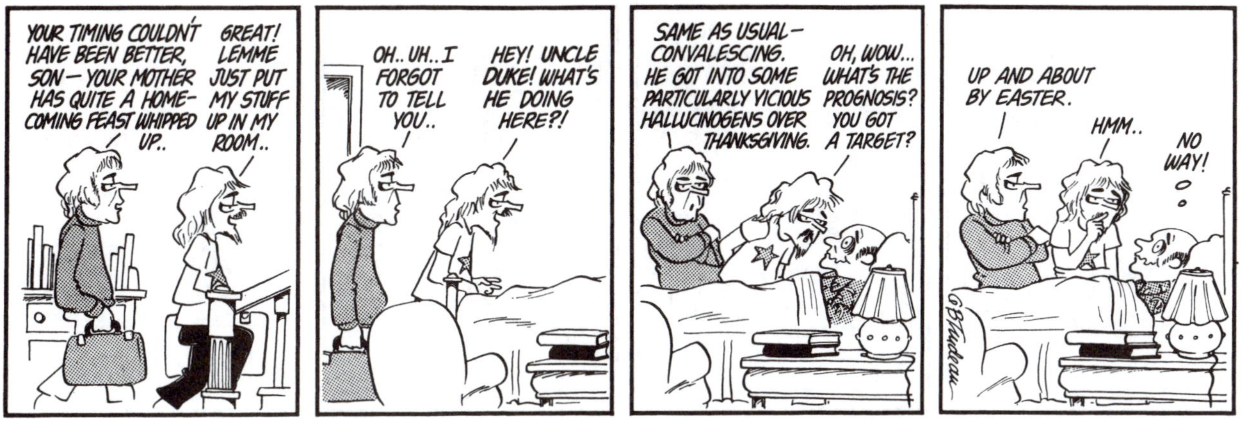
YOUR TIMING COULDN'T HAVE BEEN BETTER, SON — YOUR MOTHER HAS QUITE A HOME-COMING FEAST WHIPPED UP..
GREAT! LEMME JUST PUT MY STUFF UP IN MY ROOM..
OH.. UH.. I FORGOT TO TELL YOU..
HEY! UNCLE DUKE! WHAT'S HE DOING HERE?!
SAME AS USUAL — CONVALESCING. HE GOT INTO SOME PARTICULARLY VICIOUS HALLUCINOGENS OVER THANKSGIVING.
OH, WOW... WHAT'S THE PROGNOSIS? YOU GOT A TARGET?
UP AND ABOUT BY EASTER.
HMM..
NO WAY!
©GBTrudeau

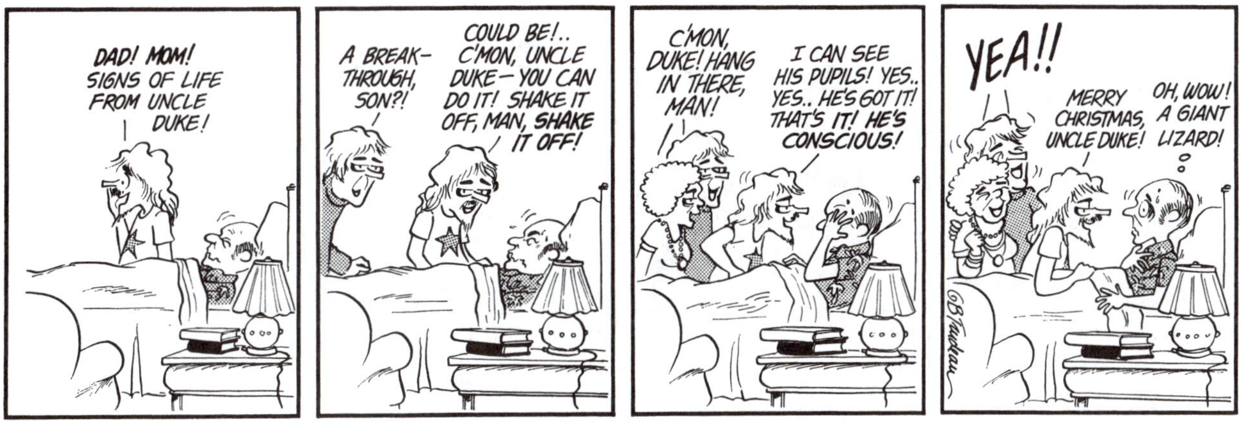
DAD! MOM! SIGNS OF LIFE FROM UNCLE DUKE!
A BREAK-THROUGH, SON?!
COULD BE!.. C'MON, UNCLE DUKE — YOU CAN DO IT! SHAKE IT OFF, MAN, SHAKE IT OFF!
C'MON, DUKE! HANG IN THERE, MAN!
I CAN SEE HIS PUPILS! YES.. YES.. HE'S GOT IT! THAT'S IT! HE'S CONSCIOUS!
YEA!!
MERRY CHRISTMAS, UNCLE DUKE!
OH, WOW! A GIANT LIZARD!
©GBTrudeau

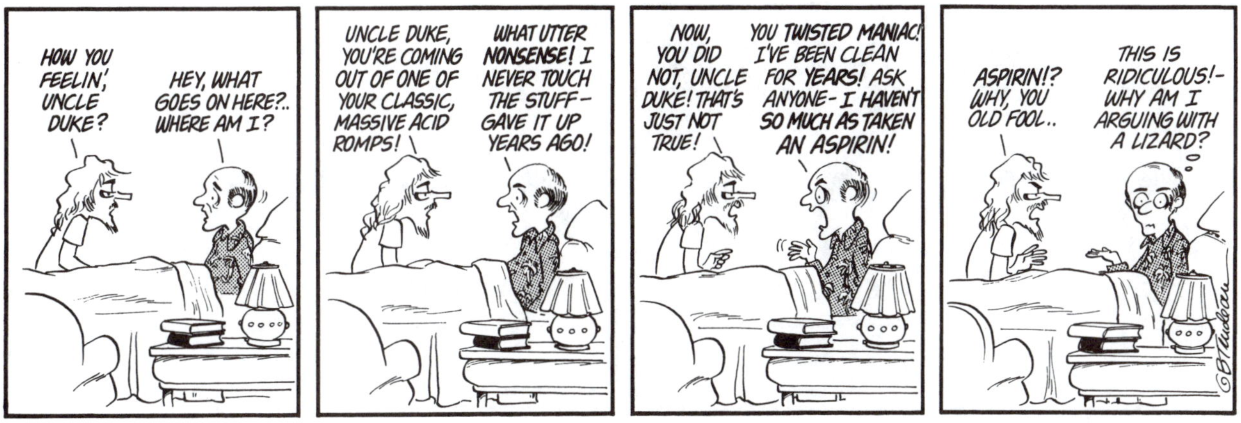
HOW YOU FEELIN', UNCLE DUKE?
HEY, WHAT GOES ON HERE?.. WHERE AM I?
UNCLE DUKE, YOU'RE COMING OUT OF ONE OF YOUR CLASSIC, MASSIVE ACID ROMPS!
WHAT UTTER NONSENSE! I NEVER TOUCH THE STUFF — GAVE IT UP YEARS AGO!
NOW, YOU DID NOT, UNCLE DUKE! THAT'S JUST NOT TRUE!
YOU TWISTED MANIAC! I'VE BEEN CLEAN FOR YEARS! ASK ANYONE - I HAVEN'T SO MUCH AS TAKEN AN ASPIRIN!
ASPIRIN!? WHY, YOU OLD FOOL..
THIS IS RIDICULOUS! - WHY AM I ARGUING WITH A LIZARD?
©GBTrudeau

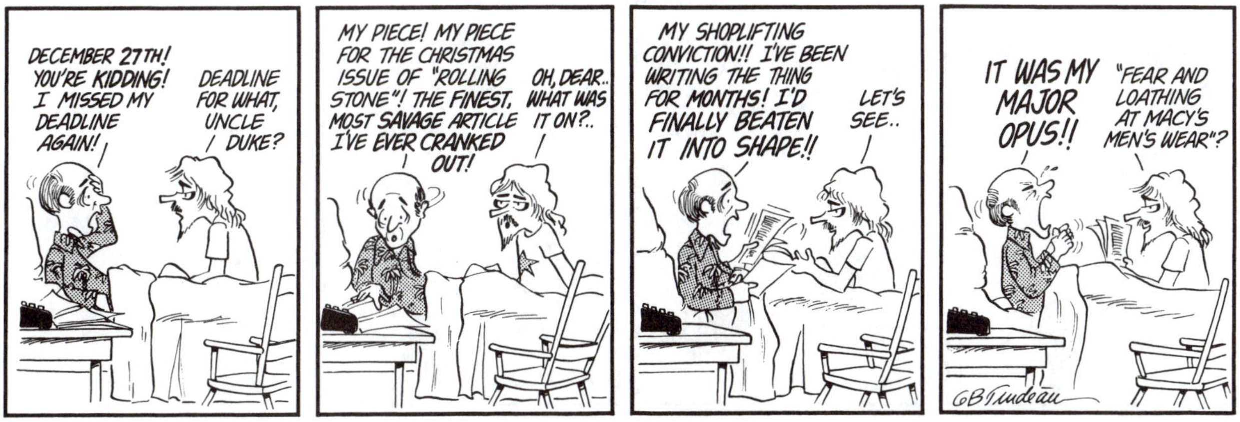
DECEMBER 27TH! YOU'RE KIDDING! I MISSED MY DEADLINE AGAIN!
DEADLINE FOR WHAT, UNCLE DUKE?
MY PIECE! MY PIECE FOR THE CHRISTMAS ISSUE OF "ROLLING STONE"! THE FINEST, MOST SAVAGE ARTICLE I'VE EVER CRANKED OUT!
OH, DEAR.. WHAT WAS IT ON?..
MY SHOPLIFTING CONVICTION!! I'VE BEEN WRITING THE THING FOR MONTHS! I'D FINALLY BEATEN IT INTO SHAPE!!
LET'S SEE..
IT WAS MY MAJOR OPUS!!
"FEAR AND LOATHING AT MACY'S MEN'S WEAR"?
GBTrudeau

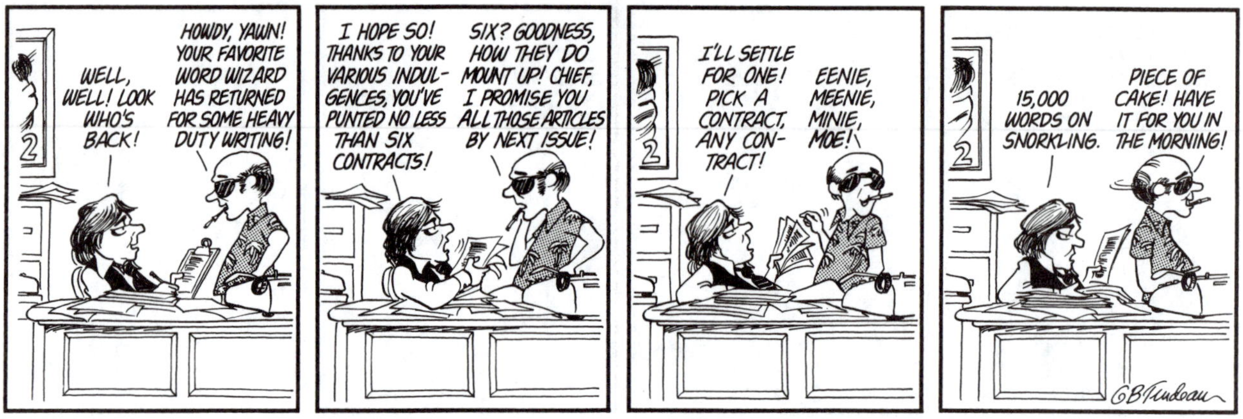
WELL, WELL! LOOK WHO'S BACK!
HOWDY, YAWN! YOUR FAVORITE WORD WIZARD HAS RETURNED FOR SOME HEAVY DUTY WRITING!
I HOPE SO! THANKS TO YOUR VARIOUS INDULGENCES, YOU'VE PUNTED NO LESS THAN SIX CONTRACTS!
SIX? GOODNESS, HOW THEY DO MOUNT UP! CHIEF, I PROMISE YOU ALL THOSE ARTICLES BY NEXT ISSUE!
I'LL SETTLE FOR ONE! PICK A CONTRACT, ANY CONTRACT!
EENIE, MEENIE, MINIE, MOE!
15,000 WORDS ON SNORKLING.
PIECE OF CAKE! HAVE IT FOR YOU IN THE MORNING!
GBTrudeau

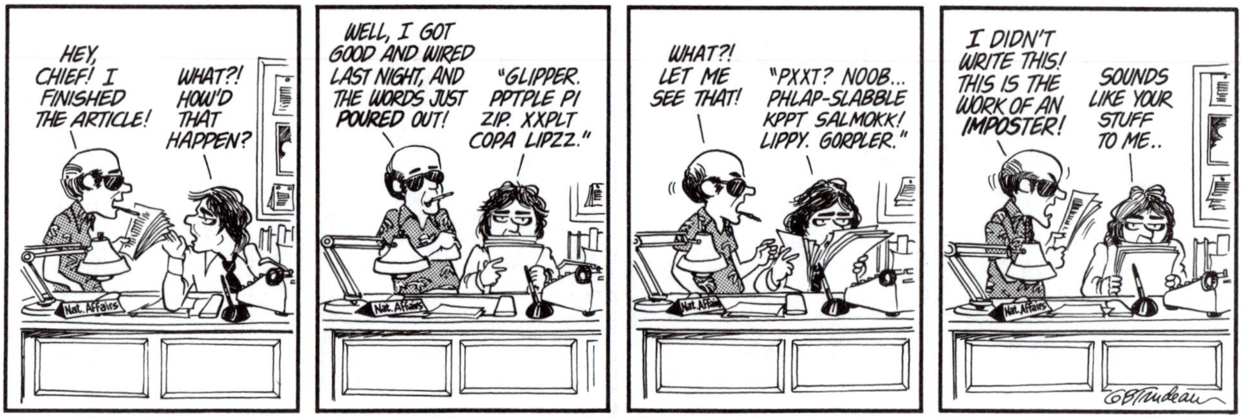
HEY, CHIEF! I FINISHED THE ARTICLE!
WHAT?! HOW'D THAT HAPPEN?
Nat. Affairs
WELL, I GOT GOOD AND WIRED LAST NIGHT, AND THE WORDS JUST POURED OUT!
"GLIPPER. PPTPLE PI ZIP. XXPLT COPA LIPZZ."
WHAT?! LET ME SEE THAT!
"PXXT? NOOB... PHLAP-SLABBLE KPPT SALMOKK! LIPPY. GORPLER."
I DIDN'T WRITE THIS! THIS IS THE WORK OF AN IMPOSTER!
SOUNDS LIKE YOUR STUFF TO ME..
GBTrudeau

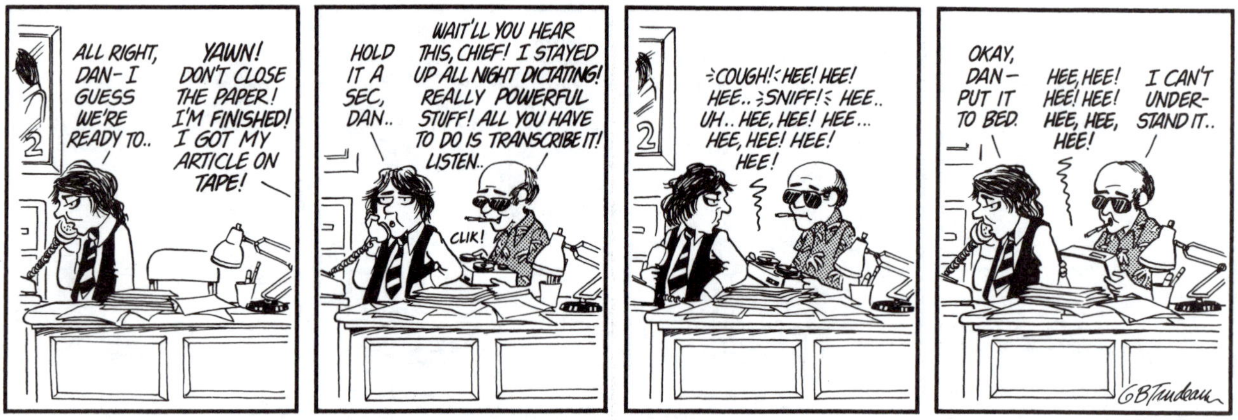
ALL RIGHT, DAN- I GUESS WE'RE READY TO..
YAWN! DON'T CLOSE THE PAPER! I'M FINISHED! I GOT MY ARTICLE ON TAPE!
HOLD IT A SEC, DAN..
WAIT'LL YOU HEAR THIS, CHIEF! I STAYED UP ALL NIGHT DICTATING! REALLY POWERFUL STUFF! ALL YOU HAVE TO DO IS TRANSCRIBE IT! LISTEN..
CLIK!
COUGH! HEE! HEE! HEE.. SNIFF! HEE.. UH.. HEE, HEE! HEE... HEE, HEE! HEE! HEE!
OKAY, DAN- PUT IT TO BED.
HEE, HEE! HEE! HEE! HEE, HEE, HEE!
I CAN'T UNDERSTAND IT..
GBTrudeau

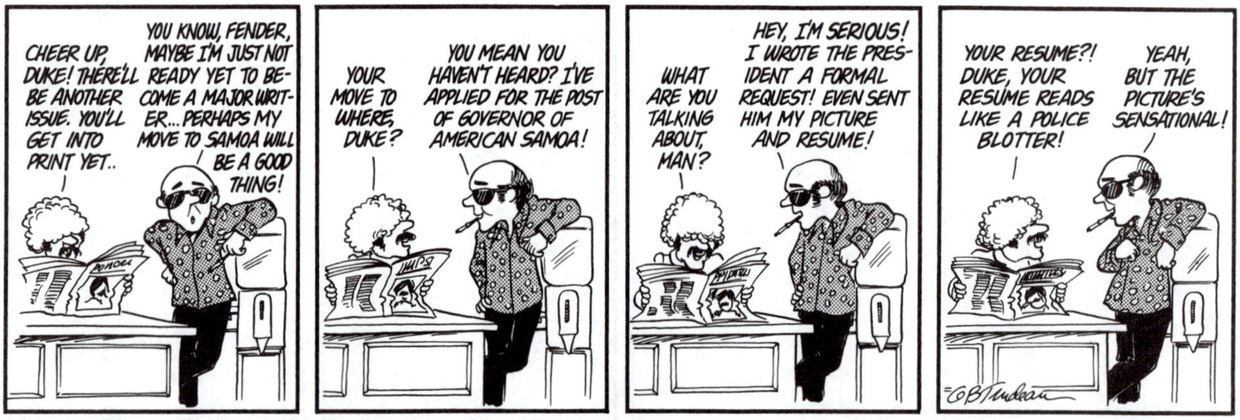
CHEER UP, DUKE! THERE'LL BE ANOTHER ISSUE. YOU'LL GET INTO PRINT YET..
YOU KNOW, FENDER, MAYBE I'M JUST NOT READY YET TO BECOME A MAJOR WRITER... PERHAPS MY MOVE TO SAMOA WILL BE A GOOD THING!
YOUR MOVE TO WHERE, DUKE?
YOU MEAN YOU HAVEN'T HEARD? I'VE APPLIED FOR THE POST OF GOVERNOR OF AMERICAN SAMOA!
WHAT ARE YOU TALKING ABOUT, MAN?
HEY, I'M SERIOUS! I WROTE THE PRESIDENT A FORMAL REQUEST! EVEN SENT HIM MY PICTURE AND RESUME!
YOUR RESUME?! DUKE, YOUR RESUME READS LIKE A POLICE BLOTTER!
YEAH, BUT THE PICTURE'S SENSATIONAL!
GBTrudeau

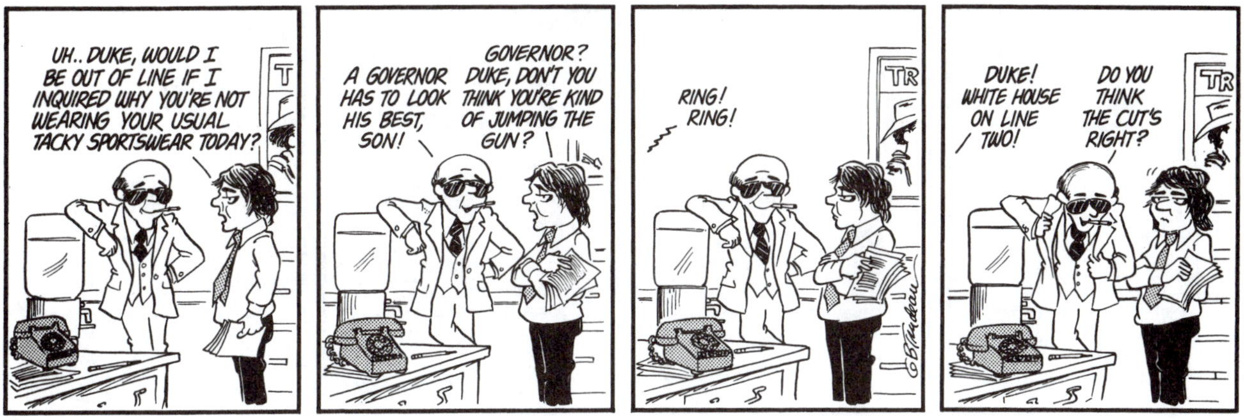
UH.. DUKE, WOULD I BE OUT OF LINE IF I INQUIRED WHY YOU'RE NOT WEARING YOUR USUAL TACKY SPORTSWEAR TODAY?
A GOVERNOR HAS TO LOOK HIS BEST, SON!
GOVERNOR? DUKE, DON'T YOU THINK YOU'RE KIND OF JUMPING THE GUN?
RING! RING!
DUKE! WHITE HOUSE ON LINE TWO!
DO YOU THINK THE CUT'S RIGHT?

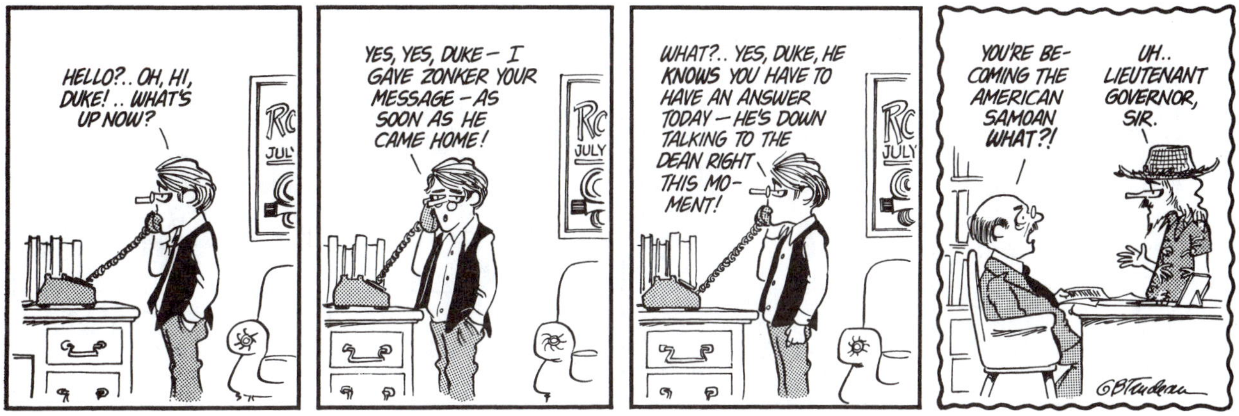
HELLO?.. OH, HI, DUKE! .. WHAT'S UP NOW?
YES, YES, DUKE — I GAVE ZONKER YOUR MESSAGE — AS SOON AS HE CAME HOME!
WHAT?.. YES, DUKE, HE KNOWS YOU HAVE TO HAVE AN ANSWER TODAY — HE'S DOWN TALKING TO THE DEAN RIGHT THIS MOMENT!
YOU'RE BECOMING THE AMERICAN SAMOAN WHAT?!
UH.. LIEUTENANT GOVERNOR, SIR.

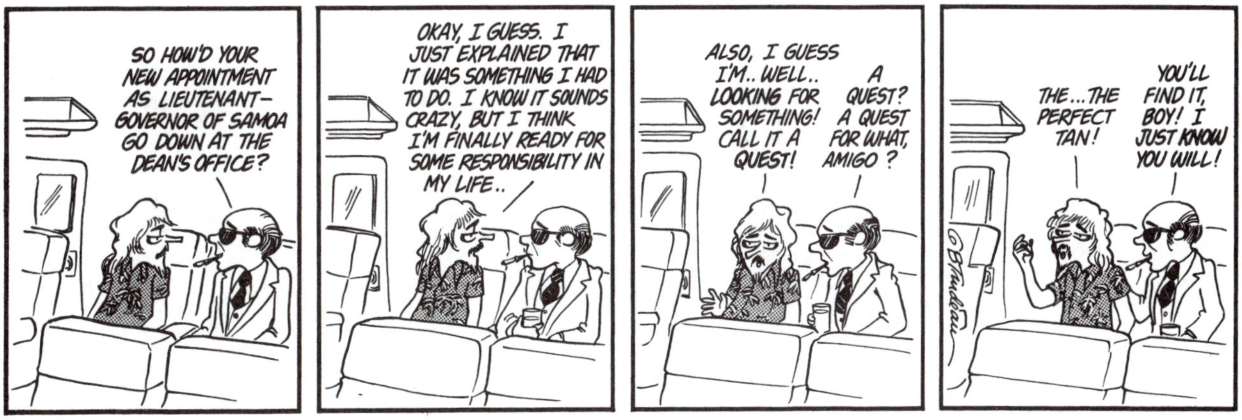
SO HOW'D YOUR NEW APPOINTMENT AS LIEUTENANT-GOVERNOR OF SAMOA GO DOWN AT THE DEAN'S OFFICE?
OKAY, I GUESS. I JUST EXPLAINED THAT IT WAS SOMETHING I HAD TO DO. I KNOW IT SOUNDS CRAZY, BUT I THINK I'M FINALLY READY FOR SOME RESPONSIBILITY IN MY LIFE..
ALSO, I GUESS I'M.. WELL.. LOOKING FOR SOMETHING! CALL IT A QUEST!
A QUEST? A QUEST FOR WHAT, AMIGO?
THE... THE PERFECT TAN!
YOU'LL FIND IT, BOY! I JUST KNOW YOU WILL!

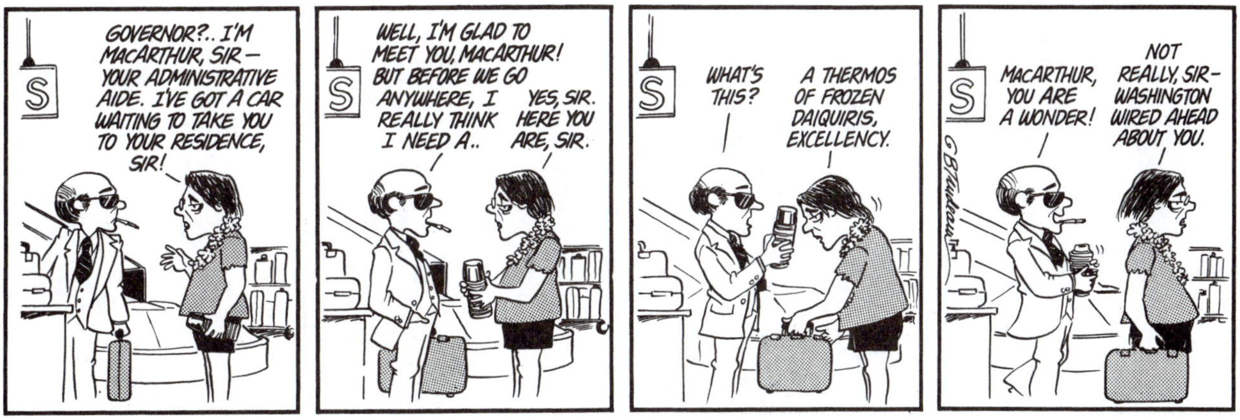
GOVERNOR?.. I'M MACARTHUR, SIR — YOUR ADMINISTRATIVE AIDE. I'VE GOT A CAR WAITING TO TAKE YOU TO YOUR RESIDENCE, SIR!
WELL, I'M GLAD TO MEET YOU, MACARTHUR! BUT BEFORE WE GO ANYWHERE, I REALLY THINK I NEED A..
YES, SIR. HERE YOU ARE, SIR.
WHAT'S THIS?
A THERMOS OF FROZEN DAIQUIRIS, EXCELLENCY.
MACARTHUR, YOU ARE A WONDER!
NOT REALLY, SIR — WASHINGTON WIRED AHEAD ABOUT YOU.

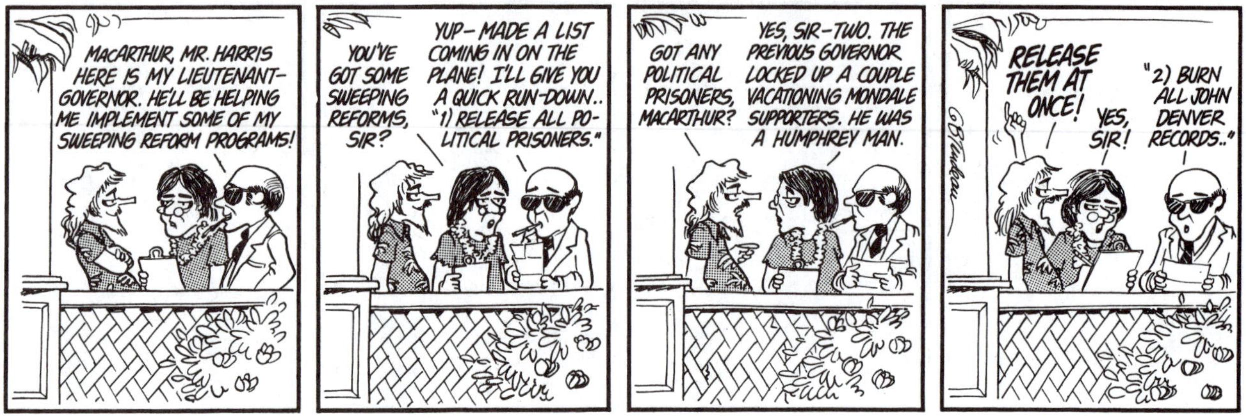
MacARTHUR, MR. HARRIS HERE IS MY LIEUTENANT-GOVERNOR. HE'LL BE HELPING ME IMPLEMENT SOME OF MY SWEEPING REFORM PROGRAMS!
YOU'VE GOT SOME SWEEPING REFORMS, SIR?
YUP–MADE A LIST COMING IN ON THE PLANE! I'LL GIVE YOU A QUICK RUN-DOWN.. "1) RELEASE ALL POLITICAL PRISONERS."
GOT ANY POLITICAL PRISONERS, MacARTHUR?
YES, SIR–TWO. THE PREVIOUS GOVERNOR LOCKED UP A COUPLE VACATIONING MONDALE SUPPORTERS. HE WAS A HUMPHREY MAN.
RELEASE THEM AT ONCE!
YES, SIR!
"2) BURN ALL JOHN DENVER RECORDS.."

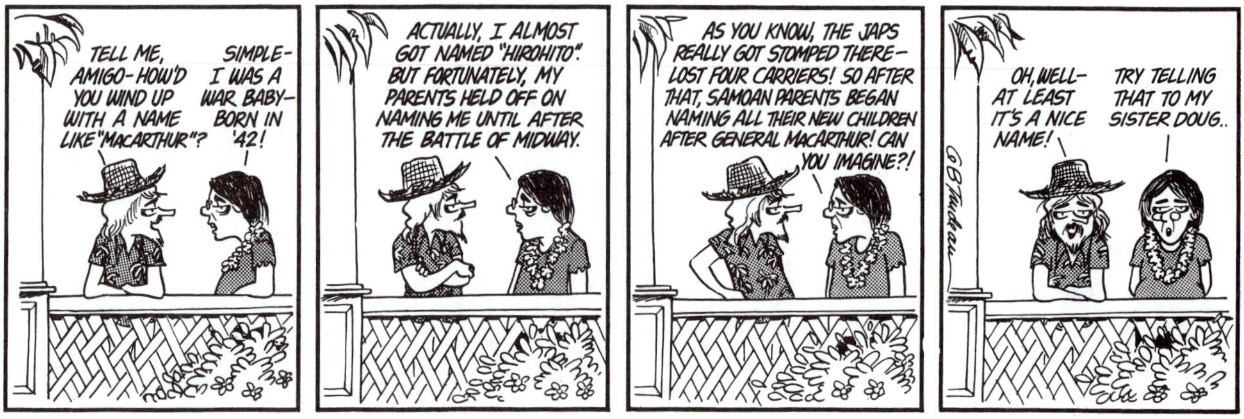
TELL ME, AMIGO–HOW'D YOU WIND UP WITH A NAME LIKE "MacARTHUR"?
SIMPLE–I WAS A WAR BABY–BORN IN '42!
ACTUALLY, I ALMOST GOT NAMED "HIROHITO". BUT FORTUNATELY, MY PARENTS HELD OFF ON NAMING ME UNTIL AFTER THE BATTLE OF MIDWAY.
AS YOU KNOW, THE JAPS REALLY GOT STOMPED THERE–LOST FOUR CARRIERS! SO AFTER THAT, SAMOAN PARENTS BEGAN NAMING ALL THEIR NEW CHILDREN AFTER GENERAL MacARTHUR! CAN YOU IMAGINE?!
OH, WELL–AT LEAST IT'S A NICE NAME!
TRY TELLING THAT TO MY SISTER DOUG..

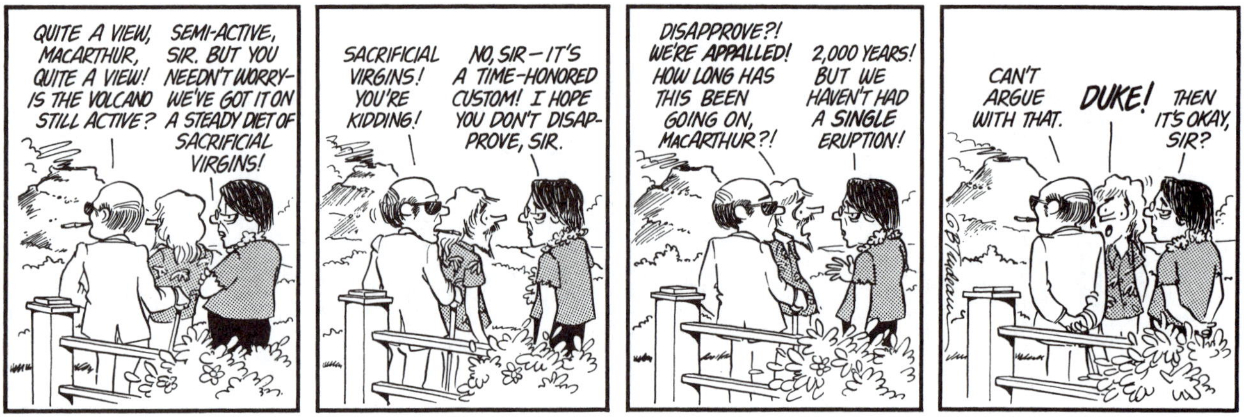
QUITE A VIEW, MacARTHUR, QUITE A VIEW! IS THE VOLCANO STILL ACTIVE?
SEMI-ACTIVE, SIR. BUT YOU NEEDN'T WORRY–WE'VE GOT IT ON A STEADY DIET OF SACRIFICIAL VIRGINS!
SACRIFICIAL VIRGINS! YOU'RE KIDDING!
NO, SIR–IT'S A TIME-HONORED CUSTOM! I HOPE YOU DON'T DISAPPROVE, SIR.
DISAPPROVE?! WE'RE APPALLED! HOW LONG HAS THIS BEEN GOING ON, MacARTHUR?!
2,000 YEARS! BUT WE HAVEN'T HAD A SINGLE ERUPTION!
CAN'T ARGUE WITH THAT.
DUKE!
THEN IT'S OKAY, SIR?

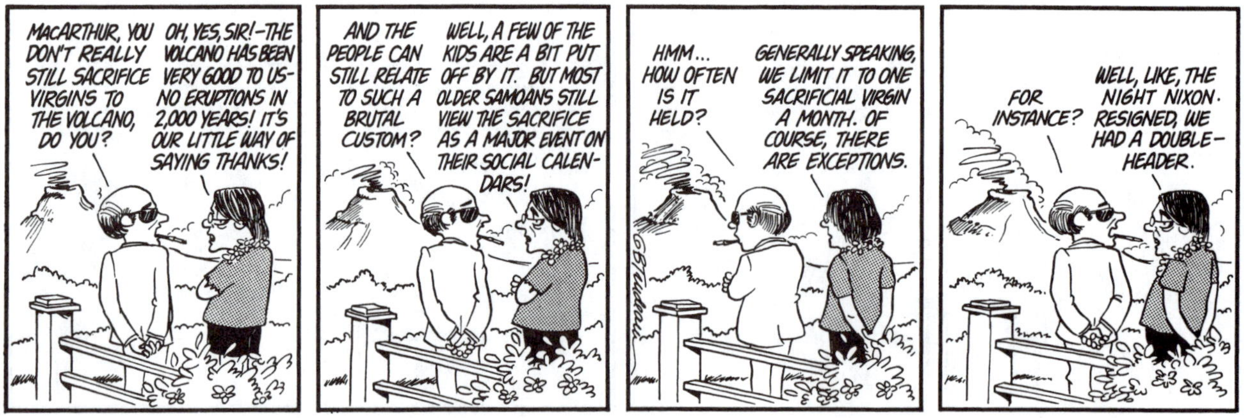
MacARTHUR, YOU DON'T REALLY STILL SACRIFICE VIRGINS TO THE VOLCANO, DO YOU?
OH, YES, SIR!–THE VOLCANO HAS BEEN VERY GOOD TO US–NO ERUPTIONS IN 2,000 YEARS! IT'S OUR LITTLE WAY OF SAYING THANKS!
AND THE PEOPLE CAN STILL RELATE TO SUCH A BRUTAL CUSTOM?
WELL, A FEW OF THE KIDS ARE A BIT PUT OFF BY IT. BUT MOST OLDER SAMOANS STILL VIEW THE SACRIFICE AS A MAJOR EVENT ON THEIR SOCIAL CALENDARS!
HMM... HOW OFTEN IS IT HELD?
GENERALLY SPEAKING, WE LIMIT IT TO ONE SACRIFICIAL VIRGIN A MONTH. OF COURSE, THERE ARE EXCEPTIONS.
FOR INSTANCE?
WELL, LIKE, THE NIGHT NIXON RESIGNED, WE HAD A DOUBLE-HEADER.

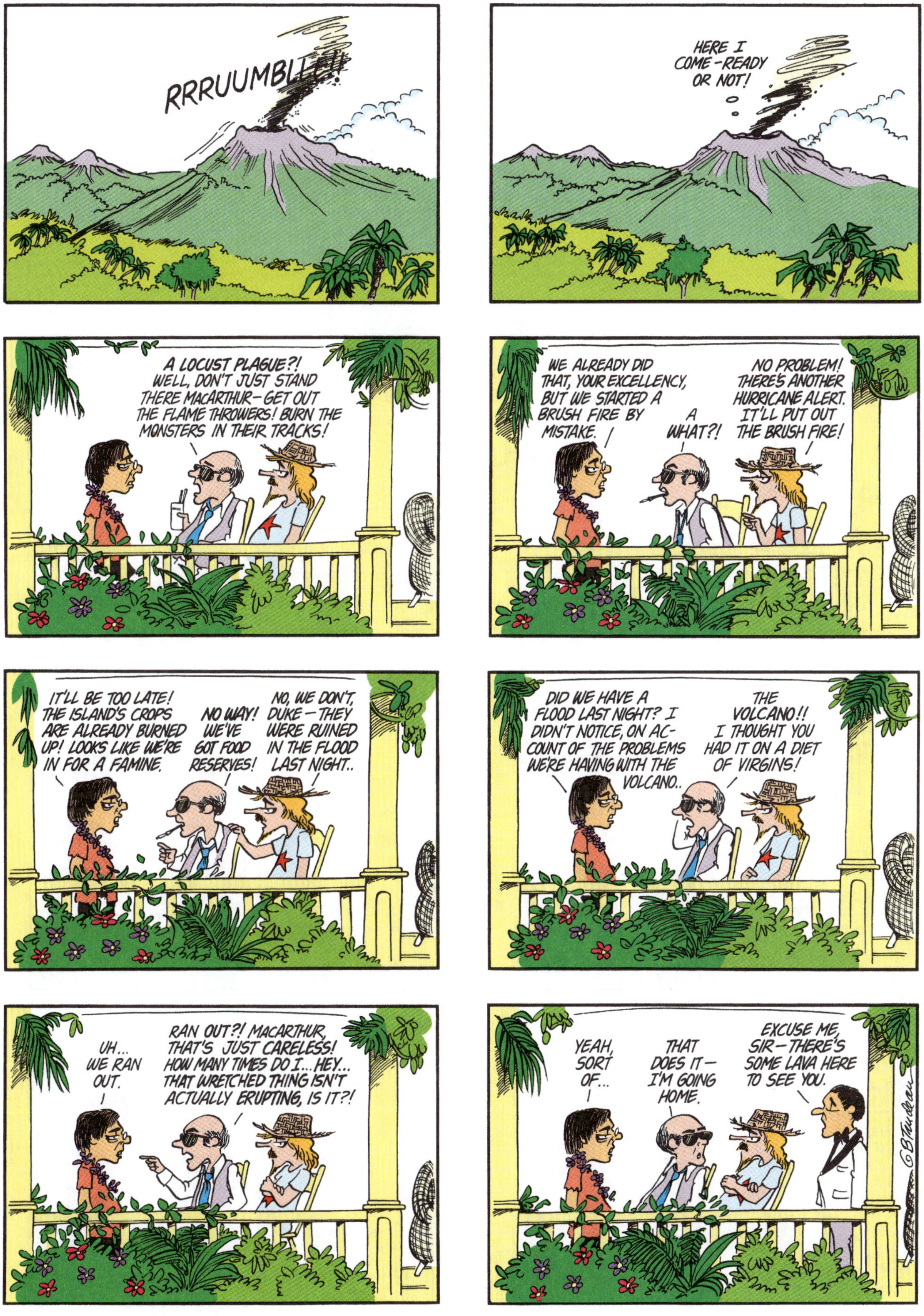
RRRUUMBLLE!!
HERE I COME–READY OR NOT!
A LOCUST PLAGUE?! WELL, DON'T JUST STAND THERE MacARTHUR–GET OUT THE FLAME THROWERS! BURN THE MONSTERS IN THEIR TRACKS!
WE ALREADY DID THAT, YOUR EXCELLENCY, BUT WE STARTED A BRUSH FIRE BY MISTAKE.
A WHAT?!
NO PROBLEM! THERE'S ANOTHER HURRICANE ALERT. IT'LL PUT OUT THE BRUSH FIRE!
IT'LL BE TOO LATE! THE ISLAND'S CROPS ARE ALREADY BURNED UP! LOOKS LIKE WE'RE IN FOR A FAMINE.
NO WAY! WE'VE GOT FOOD RESERVES!
NO, WE DON'T, DUKE–THEY WERE RUINED IN THE FLOOD LAST NIGHT..
DID WE HAVE A FLOOD LAST NIGHT? I DIDN'T NOTICE, ON ACCOUNT OF THE PROBLEMS WE'RE HAVING WITH THE VOLCANO..
THE VOLCANO!! I THOUGHT YOU HAD IT ON A DIET OF VIRGINS!
UH... WE RAN OUT.
RAN OUT?! MacARTHUR, THAT'S JUST CARELESS! HOW MANY TIMES DO I... HEY... THAT WRETCHED THING ISN'T ACTUALLY ERUPTING, IS IT?!
YEAH, SORT OF...
THAT DOES IT– I'M GOING HOME.
EXCUSE ME, SIR–THERE'S SOME LAVA HERE TO SEE YOU.
©BTrudeau

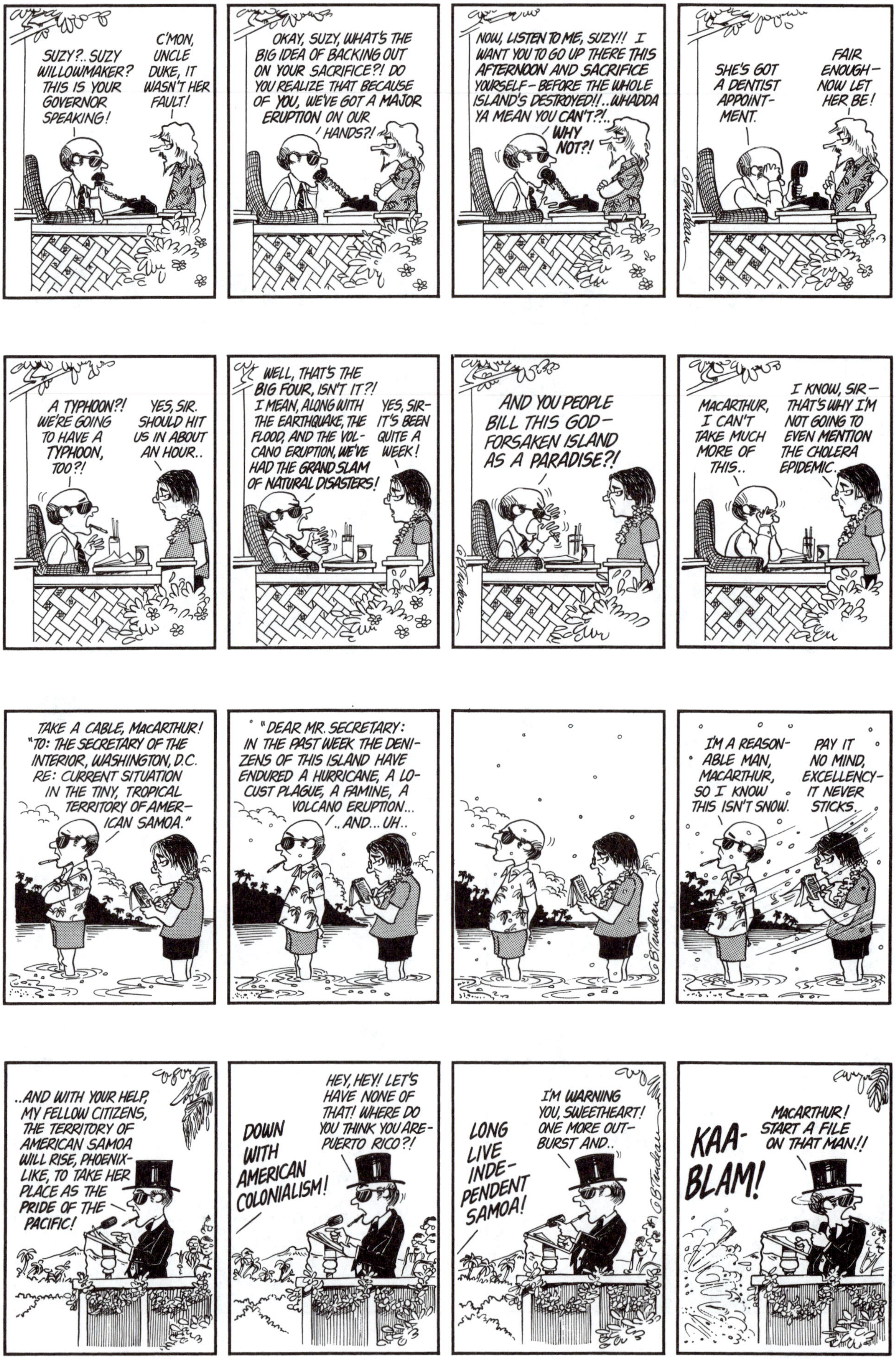
SUZY?.. SUZY WILLOWMAKER? THIS IS YOUR GOVERNOR SPEAKING!
C'MON, UNCLE DUKE, IT WASN'T HER FAULT!
OKAY, SUZY, WHAT'S THE BIG IDEA OF BACKING OUT ON YOUR SACRIFICE?! DO YOU REALIZE THAT BECAUSE OF YOU, WE'VE GOT A MAJOR ERUPTION ON OUR HANDS?!
NOW, LISTEN TO ME, SUZY!! I WANT YOU TO GO UP THERE THIS AFTERNOON AND SACRIFICE YOURSELF—BEFORE THE WHOLE ISLAND'S DESTROYED!!..WHADDA YA MEAN YOU CAN'T?!.. WHY NOT?!
SHE'S GOT A DENTIST APPOINT-MENT.
FAIR ENOUGH—NOW LET HER BE!
A TYPHOON?! WE'RE GOING TO HAVE A TYPHOON, TOO?!
YES, SIR. SHOULD HIT US IN ABOUT AN HOUR..
WELL, THAT'S THE BIG FOUR, ISN'T IT?! I MEAN, ALONG WITH THE EARTHQUAKE, THE FLOOD, AND THE VOL-CANO ERUPTION, WE'VE HAD THE GRAND SLAM OF NATURAL DISASTERS!
YES, SIR-IT'S BEEN QUITE A WEEK!
AND YOU PEOPLE BILL THIS GOD-FORSAKEN ISLAND AS A PARADISE?!
MacARTHUR, I CAN'T TAKE MUCH MORE OF THIS..
I KNOW, SIR—THAT'S WHY I'M NOT GOING TO EVEN MENTION THE CHOLERA EPIDEMIC.
TAKE A CABLE, MacARTHUR! "TO: THE SECRETARY OF THE INTERIOR, WASHINGTON, D.C. RE: CURRENT SITUATION IN THE TINY, TROPICAL TERRITORY OF AMER-ICAN SAMOA."
"DEAR MR. SECRETARY: IN THE PAST WEEK THE DENI-ZENS OF THIS ISLAND HAVE ENDURED A HURRICANE, A LO-CUST PLAGUE, A FAMINE, A VOLCANO ERUPTION... ..AND...UH..
I'M A REASON-ABLE MAN, MacARTHUR, SO I KNOW THIS ISN'T SNOW.
PAY IT NO MIND, EXCELLENCY-IT NEVER STICKS.
..AND WITH YOUR HELP, MY FELLOW CITIZENS, THE TERRITORY OF AMERICAN SAMOA WILL RISE, PHOENIX-LIKE, TO TAKE HER PLACE AS THE PRIDE OF THE PACIFIC!
DOWN WITH AMERICAN COLONIALISM!
HEY, HEY! LET'S HAVE NONE OF THAT! WHERE DO YOU THINK YOU ARE-PUERTO RICO?!
LONG LIVE INDE-PENDENT SAMOA!
I'M WARNING YOU, SWEETHEART! ONE MORE OUT-BURST AND..
KAA-BLAM!
MacARTHUR! START A FILE ON THAT MAN!!

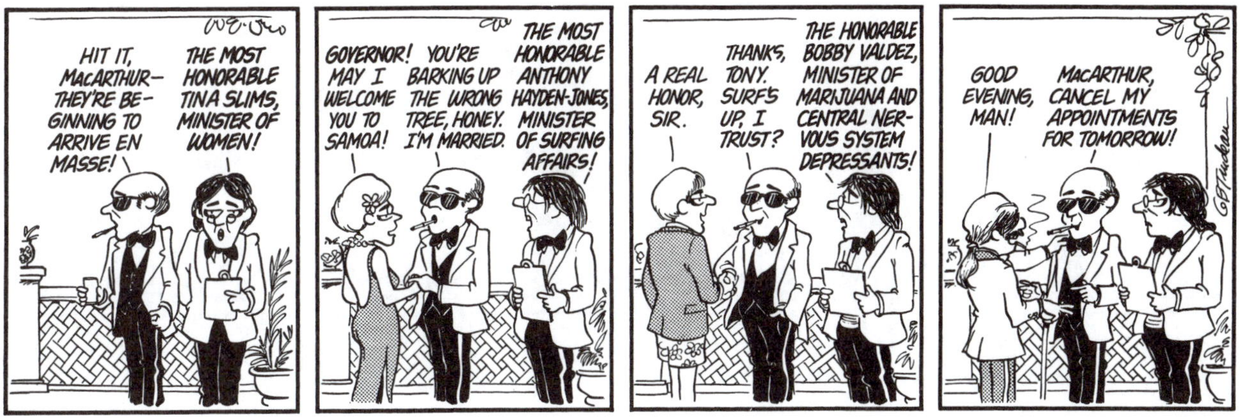
HIT IT, MacARTHUR— THEY'RE BE-GINNING TO ARRIVE EN MASSE!
THE MOST HONORABLE TINA SLIMS, MINISTER OF WOMEN!
GOVERNOR! MAY I WELCOME YOU TO SAMOA!
YOU'RE BARKING UP THE WRONG TREE, HONEY. I'M MARRIED.
THE MOST HONORABLE ANTHONY HAYDEN-JONES, MINISTER OF SURFING AFFAIRS!
A REAL HONOR, SIR.
THANKS, TONY. SURF'S UP, I TRUST?
THE HONORABLE BOBBY VALDEZ, MINISTER OF MARIJUANA AND CENTRAL NER-VOUS SYSTEM DEPRESSANTS!
GOOD EVENING, MAN!
MacARTHUR, CANCEL MY APPOINTMENTS FOR TOMORROW!

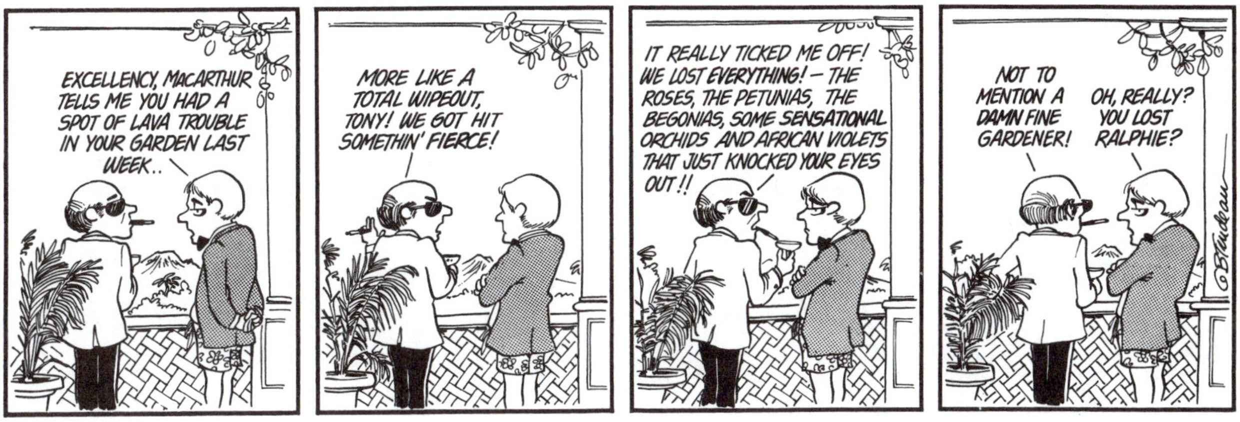
EXCELLENCY, MacARTHUR TELLS ME YOU HAD A SPOT OF LAVA TROUBLE IN YOUR GARDEN LAST WEEK..
MORE LIKE A TOTAL WIPEOUT, TONY! WE GOT HIT SOMETHIN' FIERCE!
IT REALLY TICKED ME OFF! WE LOST EVERYTHING! — THE ROSES, THE PETUNIAS, THE BEGONIAS, SOME SENSATIONAL ORCHIDS AND AFRICAN VIOLETS THAT JUST KNOCKED YOUR EYES OUT!!
NOT TO MENTION A DAMN FINE GARDENER!
OH, REALLY? YOU LOST RALPHIE?

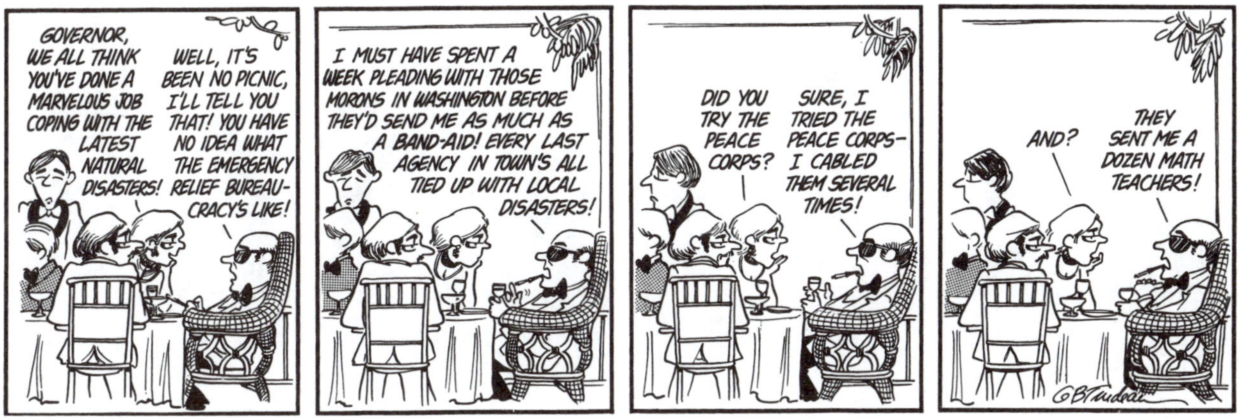
GOVERNOR, WE ALL THINK YOU'VE DONE A MARVELOUS JOB COPING WITH THE LATEST NATURAL DISASTERS!
WELL, IT'S BEEN NO PICNIC, I'LL TELL YOU THAT! YOU HAVE NO IDEA WHAT THE EMERGENCY RELIEF BUREAU-CRACY'S LIKE!
I MUST HAVE SPENT A WEEK PLEADING WITH THOSE MORONS IN WASHINGTON BEFORE THEY'D SEND ME AS MUCH AS A BAND-AID! EVERY LAST AGENCY IN TOWN'S ALL TIED UP WITH LOCAL DISASTERS!
DID YOU TRY THE PEACE CORPS?
SURE, I TRIED THE PEACE CORPS— I CABLED THEM SEVERAL TIMES!
AND?
THEY SENT ME A DOZEN MATH TEACHERS!

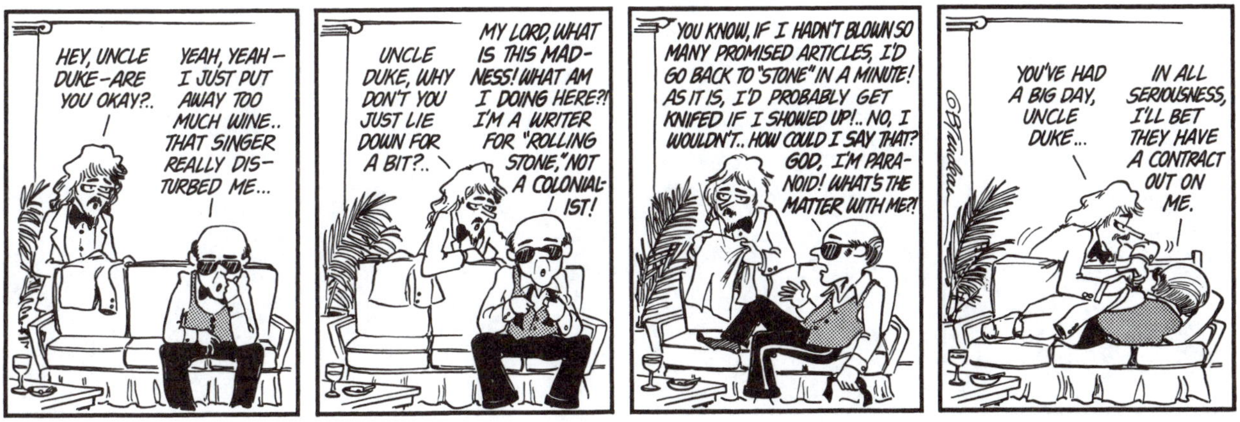
HEY, UNCLE DUKE—ARE YOU OKAY?..
YEAH, YEAH— I JUST PUT AWAY TOO MUCH WINE.. THAT SINGER REALLY DIS-TURBED ME...
UNCLE DUKE, WHY DON'T YOU JUST LIE DOWN FOR A BIT?..
MY LORD, WHAT IS THIS MAD-NESS! WHAT AM I DOING HERE?! I'M A WRITER FOR "ROLLING STONE," NOT A COLONIAL-IST!
YOU KNOW, IF I HADN'T BLOWN SO MANY PROMISED ARTICLES, I'D GO BACK TO "STONE" IN A MINUTE! AS IT IS, I'D PROBABLY GET KNIFED IF I SHOWED UP!.. NO, I WOULDN'T.. HOW COULD I SAY THAT? GOD, I'M PARA-NOID! WHAT'S THE MATTER WITH ME?!
YOU'VE HAD A BIG DAY, UNCLE DUKE...
IN ALL SERIOUSNESS, I'LL BET THEY HAVE A CONTRACT OUT ON ME.

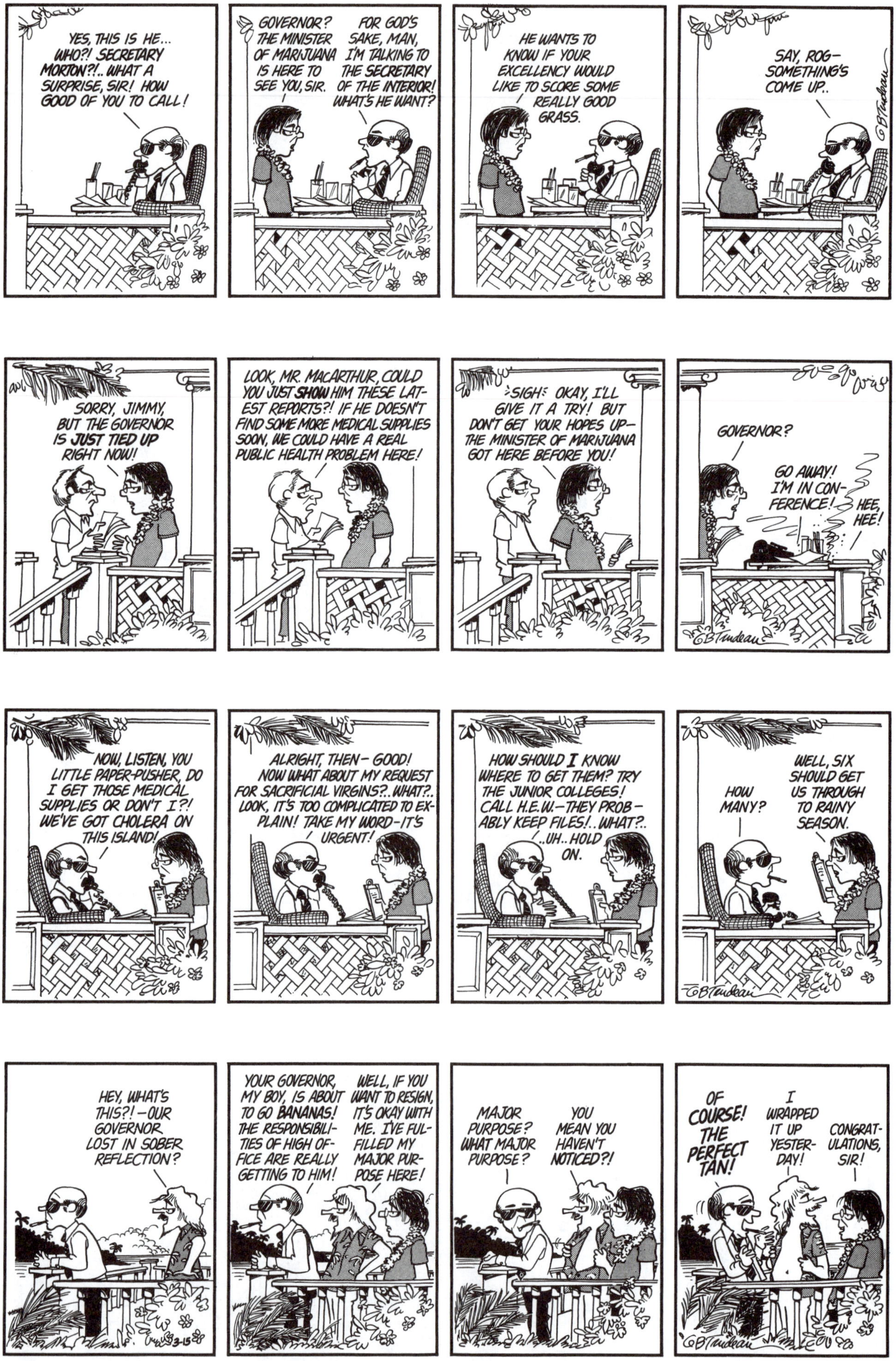
YES, THIS IS HE... WHO?! SECRETARY MORTON?!.. WHAT A SURPRISE, SIR! HOW GOOD OF YOU TO CALL!
GOVERNOR? THE MINISTER OF MARIJUANA IS HERE TO SEE YOU, SIR.
FOR GOD'S SAKE, MAN, I'M TALKING TO THE SECRETARY OF THE INTERIOR! WHAT'S HE WANT?
HE WANTS TO KNOW IF YOUR EXCELLENCY WOULD LIKE TO SCORE SOME REALLY GOOD GRASS.
SAY, ROG– SOMETHING'S COME UP..
SORRY, JIMMY, BUT THE GOVERNOR IS JUST TIED UP RIGHT NOW!
LOOK, MR. MACARTHUR, COULD YOU JUST SHOW HIM THESE LATEST REPORTS?! IF HE DOESN'T FIND SOME MORE MEDICAL SUPPLIES SOON, WE COULD HAVE A REAL PUBLIC HEALTH PROBLEM HERE!
SIGH OKAY, I'LL GIVE IT A TRY! BUT DON'T GET YOUR HOPES UP– THE MINISTER OF MARIJUANA GOT HERE BEFORE YOU!
GOVERNOR?
GO AWAY! I'M IN CONFERENCE!
HEE, HEE!
NOW, LISTEN, YOU LITTLE PAPER-PUSHER, DO I GET THOSE MEDICAL SUPPLIES OR DON'T I?! WE'VE GOT CHOLERA ON THIS ISLAND!
ALRIGHT, THEN– GOOD! NOW WHAT ABOUT MY REQUEST FOR SACRIFICIAL VIRGINS?..WHAT?.. LOOK, IT'S TOO COMPLICATED TO EXPLAIN! TAKE MY WORD–IT'S URGENT!
HOW SHOULD I KNOW WHERE TO GET THEM? TRY THE JUNIOR COLLEGES! CALL H.E.W.–THEY PROBABLY KEEP FILES!..WHAT?.. ..UH.. HOLD ON.
HOW MANY?
WELL, SIX SHOULD GET US THROUGH TO RAINY SEASON.
HEY, WHAT'S THIS?! –OUR GOVERNOR LOST IN SOBER REFLECTION?
YOUR GOVERNOR, MY BOY, IS ABOUT TO GO BANANAS! THE RESPONSIBILITIES OF HIGH OFFICE ARE REALLY GETTING TO HIM!
WELL, IF YOU WANT TO RESIGN, IT'S OKAY WITH ME. I'VE FULFILLED MY MAJOR PURPOSE HERE!
MAJOR PURPOSE? WHAT MAJOR PURPOSE?
YOU MEAN YOU HAVEN'T NOTICED?!
OF COURSE! THE PERFECT TAN!
I WRAPPED IT UP YESTERDAY!
CONGRATULATIONS, SIR!

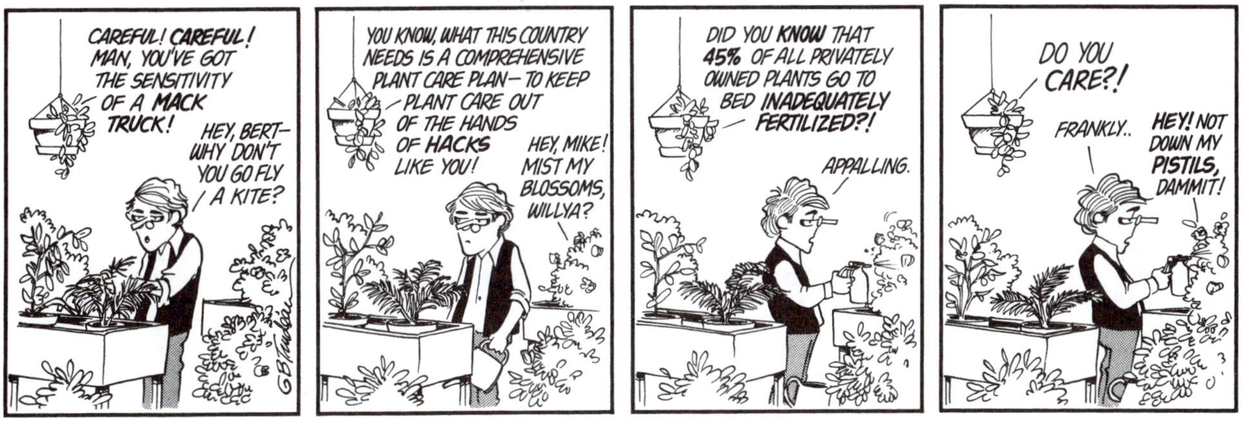
CAREFUL! **CAREFUL!** MAN, YOU'VE GOT THE SENSITIVITY OF A **MACK TRUCK!**
HEY, BERT—WHY DON'T YOU GO FLY A KITE?
YOU KNOW, WHAT THIS COUNTRY NEEDS IS A COMPREHENSIVE PLANT CARE PLAN— TO KEEP PLANT CARE OUT OF THE HANDS OF **HACKS** LIKE YOU!
HEY, MIKE! MIST MY BLOSSOMS, WILLYA?
DID YOU **KNOW** THAT **45%** OF ALL PRIVATELY OWNED PLANTS GO TO BED **INADEQUATELY FERTILIZED?!**
APPALLING.
DO YOU **CARE?!**
FRANKLY..
HEY! NOT DOWN MY **PISTILS,** DAMMIT!

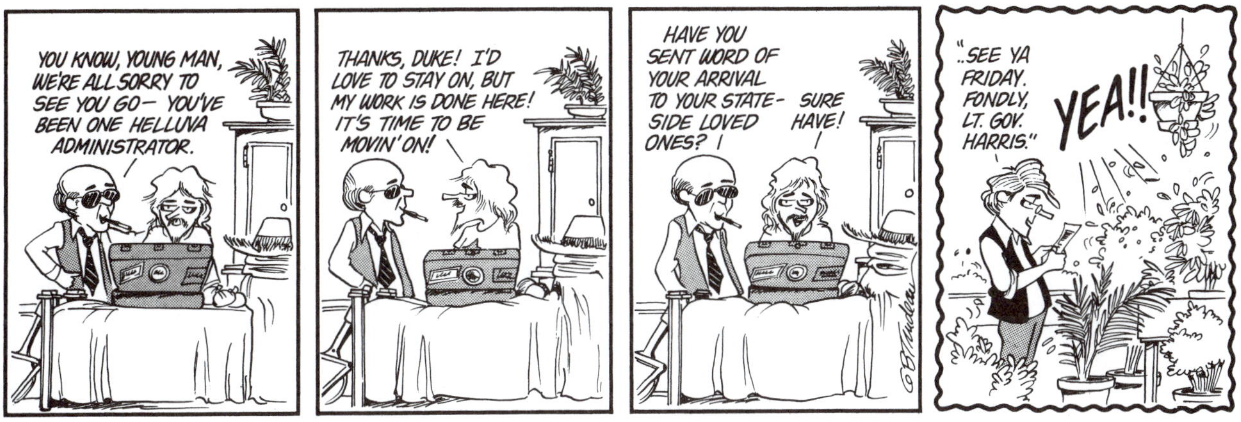
YOU KNOW, YOUNG MAN, WE'RE ALL SORRY TO SEE YOU GO— YOU'VE BEEN ONE HELLUVA ADMINISTRATOR.
THANKS, DUKE! I'D LOVE TO STAY ON, BUT MY WORK IS DONE HERE! IT'S TIME TO BE MOVIN' ON!
HAVE YOU SENT WORD OF YOUR ARRIVAL TO YOUR STATE-SIDE LOVED ONES?
SURE HAVE!
"..SEE YA FRIDAY. FONDLY, LT. GOV. HARRIS."
YEA!!

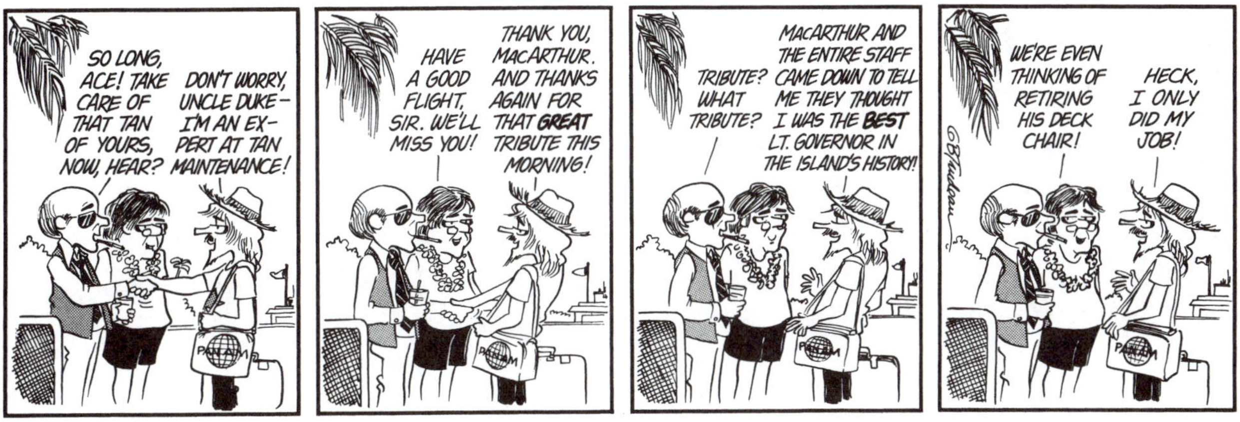
SO LONG, ACE! TAKE CARE OF THAT TAN OF YOURS, NOW, HEAR?
DON'T WORRY, UNCLE DUKE—I'M AN EXPERT AT TAN MAINTENANCE!
HAVE A GOOD FLIGHT, SIR. WE'LL MISS YOU!
THANK YOU, MACARTHUR. AND THANKS AGAIN FOR THAT **GREAT** TRIBUTE THIS MORNING!
TRIBUTE? WHAT TRIBUTE?
MACARTHUR AND THE ENTIRE STAFF CAME DOWN TO TELL ME THEY THOUGHT I WAS THE **BEST** LT. GOVERNOR IN THE ISLAND'S HISTORY!
WE'RE EVEN THINKING OF RETIRING HIS DECK CHAIR!
HECK, I ONLY DID MY JOB!
PAN AM

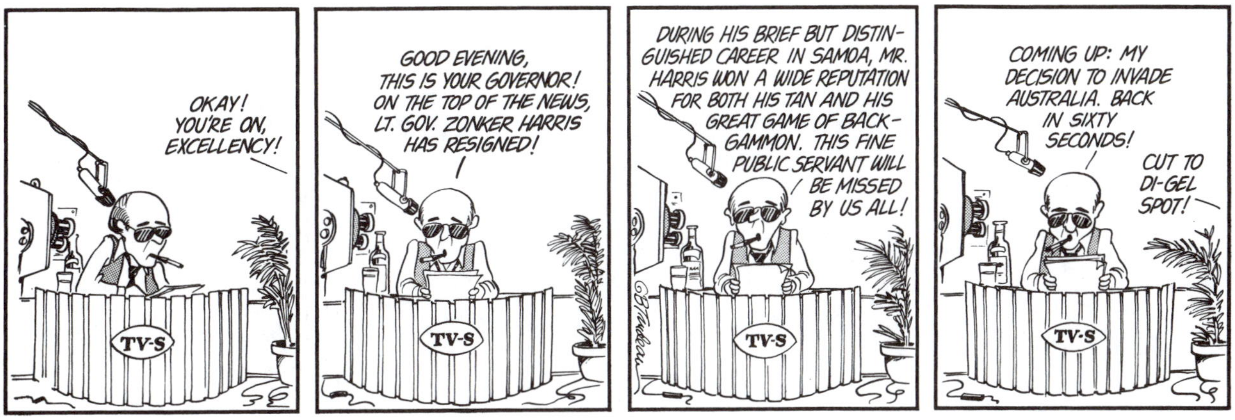
OKAY! YOU'RE ON, EXCELLENCY!
TV-S
GOOD EVENING, THIS IS YOUR GOVERNOR! ON THE TOP OF THE NEWS, LT. GOV. ZONKER HARRIS HAS RESIGNED!
DURING HIS BRIEF BUT DISTINGUISHED CAREER IN SAMOA, MR. HARRIS WON A WIDE REPUTATION FOR BOTH HIS TAN AND HIS GREAT GAME OF BACKGAMMON. THIS FINE PUBLIC SERVANT WILL BE MISSED BY US ALL!
COMING UP: MY DECISION TO INVADE AUSTRALIA. BACK IN SIXTY SECONDS!
CUT TO DI-GEL SPOT!

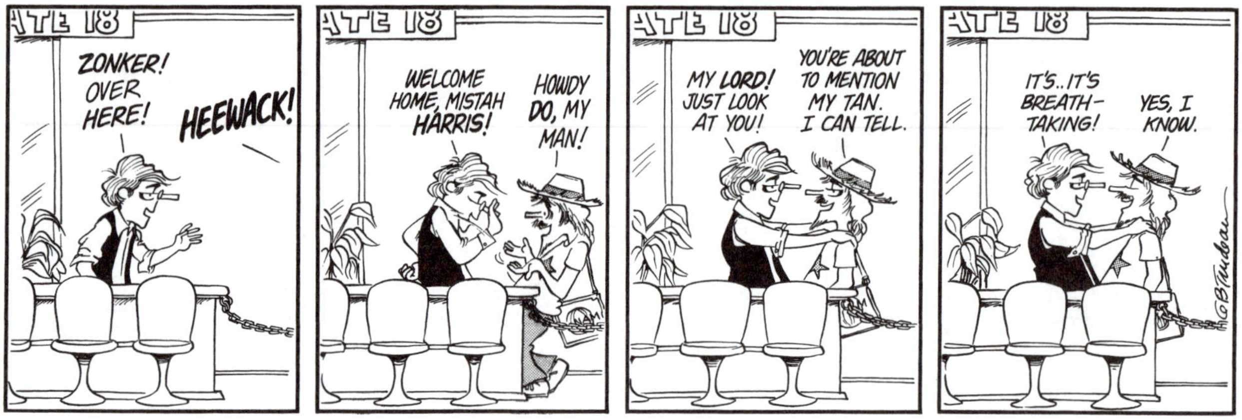
ATE 18
ZONKER! OVER HERE!
HEEWACK!
WELCOME HOME, MISTAH HARRIS!
HOWDY DO, MY MAN!
MY LORD! JUST LOOK AT YOU!
YOU'RE ABOUT TO MENTION MY TAN. I CAN TELL.
IT'S.. IT'S BREATH-TAKING!
YES, I KNOW.

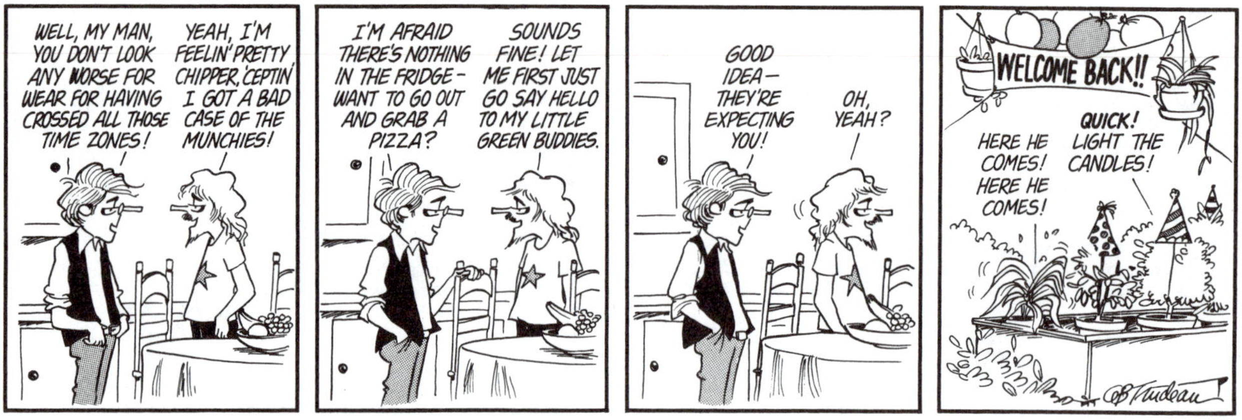
WELL, MY MAN, YOU DON'T LOOK ANY WORSE FOR WEAR FOR HAVING CROSSED ALL THOSE TIME ZONES!
YEAH, I'M FEELIN' PRETTY CHIPPER, 'CEPTIN' I GOT A BAD CASE OF THE MUNCHIES!
I'M AFRAID THERE'S NOTHING IN THE FRIDGE– WANT TO GO OUT AND GRAB A PIZZA?
SOUNDS FINE! LET ME FIRST JUST GO SAY HELLO TO MY LITTLE GREEN BUDDIES.
GOOD IDEA– THEY'RE EXPECTING YOU!
OH, YEAH?
WELCOME BACK!!
HERE HE COMES! HERE HE COMES!
QUICK! LIGHT THE CANDLES!

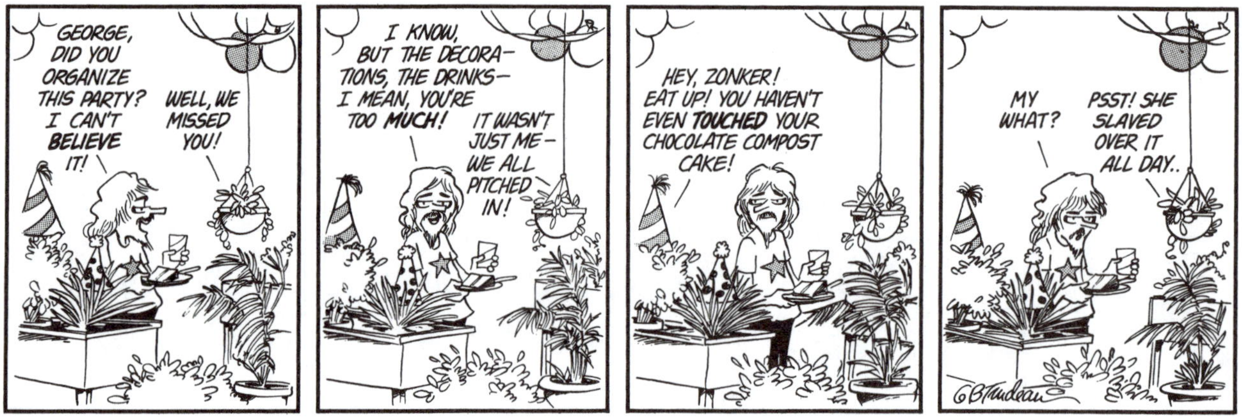
GEORGE, DID YOU ORGANIZE THIS PARTY? I CAN'T BELIEVE IT!
WELL, WE MISSED YOU!
I KNOW, BUT THE DECORA-TIONS, THE DRINKS– I MEAN, YOU'RE TOO MUCH!
IT WASN'T JUST ME– WE ALL PITCHED IN!
HEY, ZONKER! EAT UP! YOU HAVEN'T EVEN TOUCHED YOUR CHOCOLATE COMPOST CAKE!
MY WHAT?
PSST! SHE SLAVED OVER IT ALL DAY..

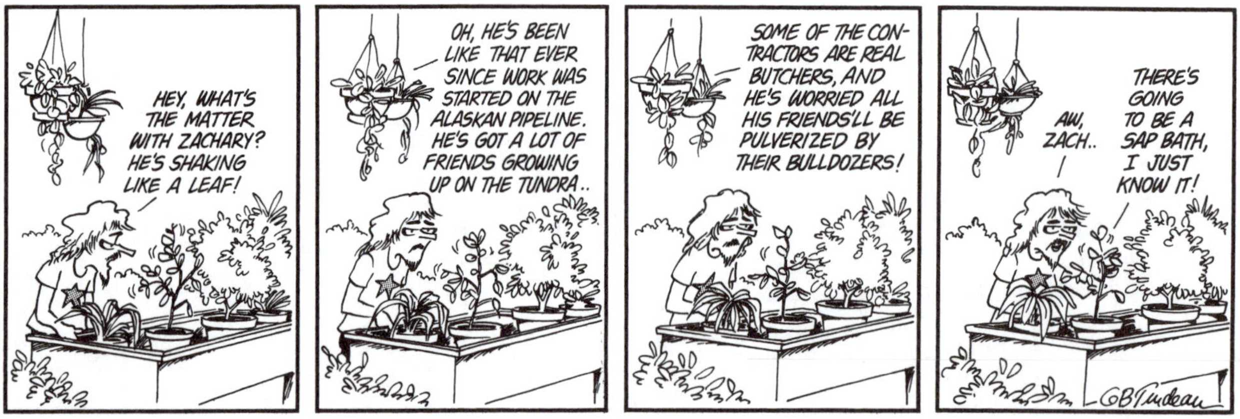
HEY, WHAT'S THE MATTER WITH ZACHARY? HE'S SHAKING LIKE A LEAF!
OH, HE'S BEEN LIKE THAT EVER SINCE WORK WAS STARTED ON THE ALASKAN PIPELINE. HE'S GOT A LOT OF FRIENDS GROWING UP ON THE TUNDRA..
SOME OF THE CON-TRACTORS ARE REAL BUTCHERS, AND HE'S WORRIED ALL HIS FRIENDS'LL BE PULVERIZED BY THEIR BULLDOZERS!
AW, ZACH..
THERE'S GOING TO BE A SAP BATH, I JUST KNOW IT!

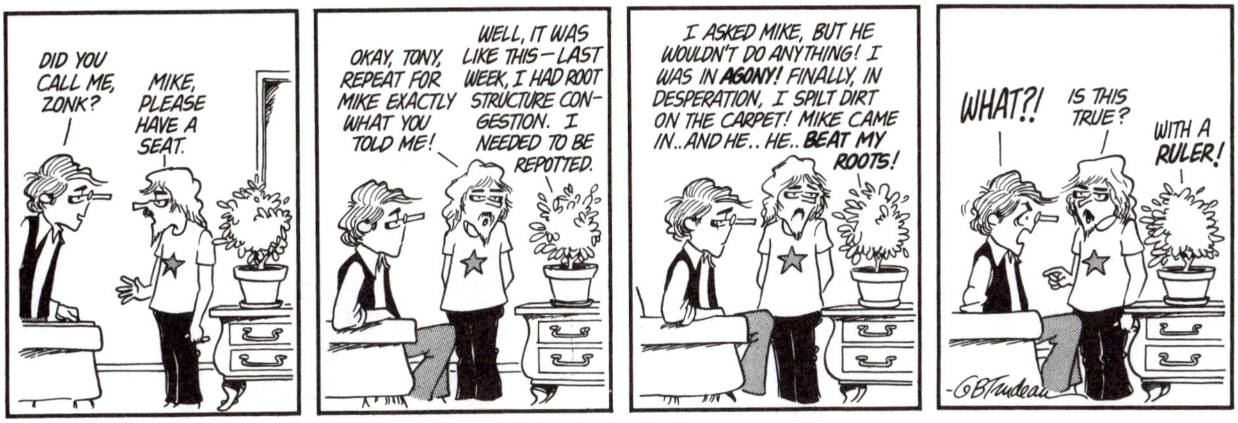
DID YOU CALL ME, ZONK?
MIKE, PLEASE HAVE A SEAT.
OKAY, TONY, REPEAT FOR MIKE EXACTLY WHAT YOU TOLD ME!
WELL, IT WAS LIKE THIS—LAST WEEK, I HAD ROOT STRUCTURE CONGESTION. I NEEDED TO BE REPOTTED.
I ASKED MIKE, BUT HE WOULDN'T DO ANYTHING! I WAS IN AGONY! FINALLY, IN DESPERATION, I SPILT DIRT ON THE CARPET! MIKE CAME IN.. AND HE.. HE.. BEAT MY ROOTS!
WHAT?!
IS THIS TRUE?
WITH A RULER!

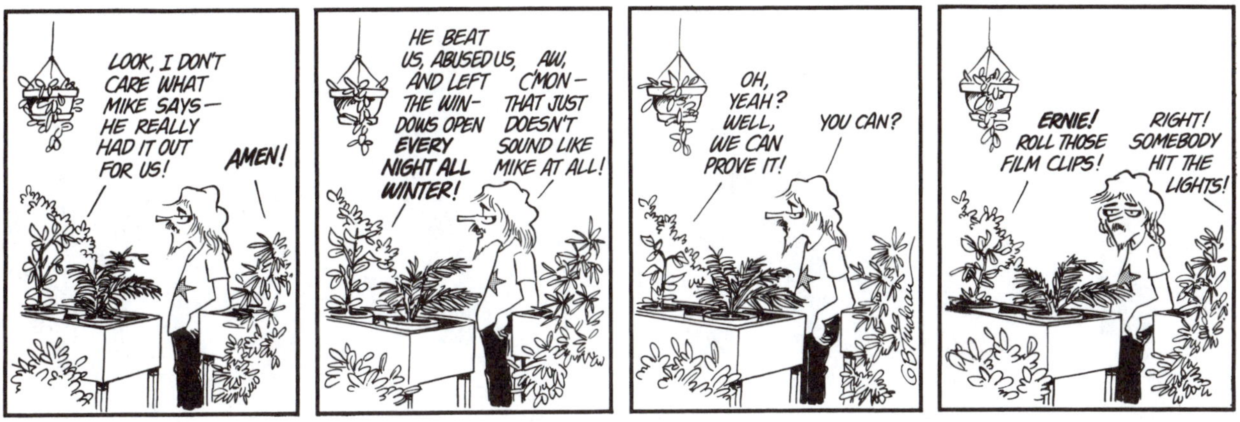
LOOK, I DON'T CARE WHAT MIKE SAYS—HE REALLY HAD IT OUT FOR US!
AMEN!
HE BEAT US, ABUSED US, AND LEFT THE WINDOWS OPEN EVERY NIGHT ALL WINTER!
AW, C'MON—THAT JUST DOESN'T SOUND LIKE MIKE AT ALL!
OH, YEAH? WELL, WE CAN PROVE IT!
YOU CAN?
ERNIE! ROLL THOSE FILM CLIPS!
RIGHT! SOMEBODY HIT THE LIGHTS!

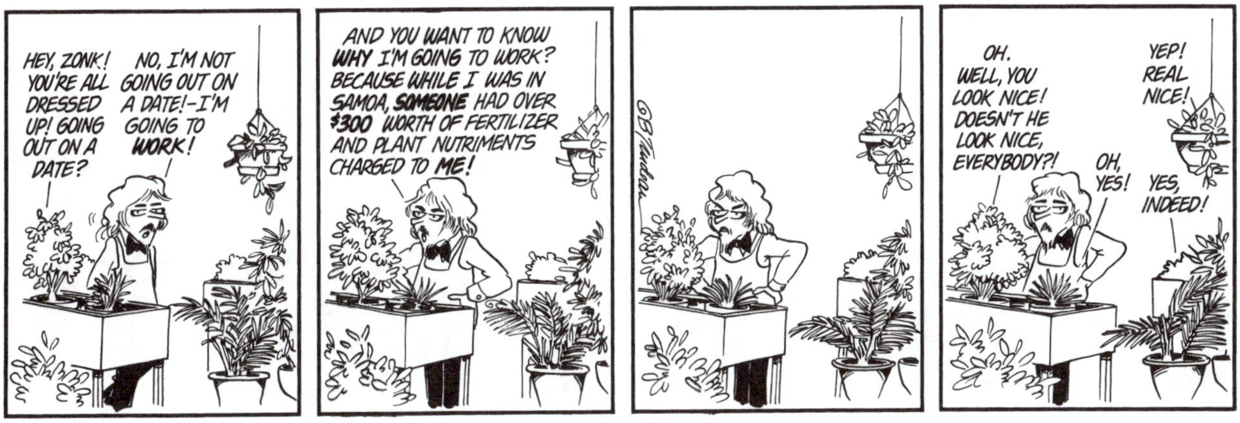
HEY, ZONK! YOU'RE ALL DRESSED UP! GOING OUT ON A DATE?
NO, I'M NOT GOING OUT ON A DATE!—I'M GOING TO WORK!
AND YOU WANT TO KNOW WHY I'M GOING TO WORK? BECAUSE WHILE I WAS IN SAMOA, SOMEONE HAD OVER $300 WORTH OF FERTILIZER AND PLANT NUTRIMENTS CHARGED TO ME!
OH. WELL, YOU LOOK NICE! DOESN'T HE LOOK NICE, EVERYBODY?!
YEP! REAL NICE!
OH, YES!
YES, INDEED!

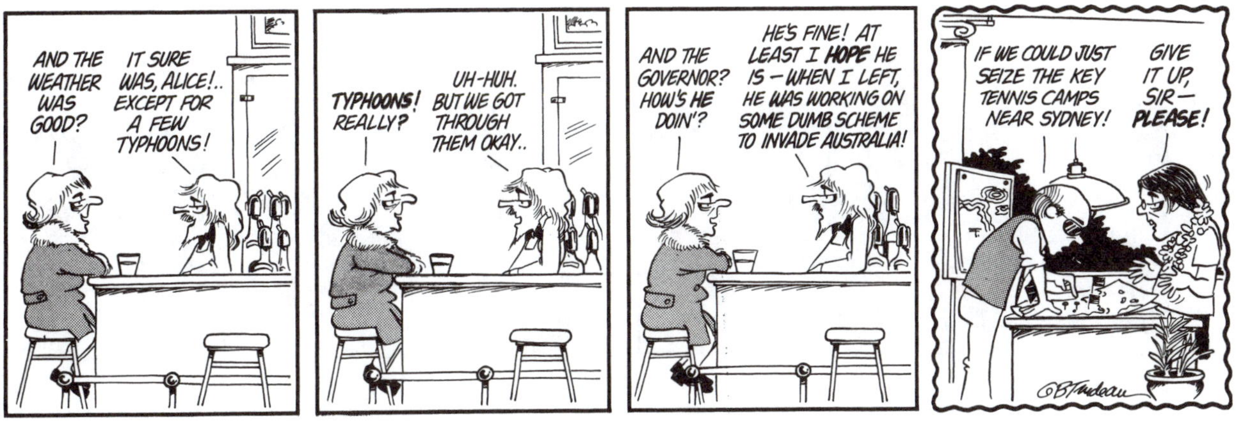
AND THE WEATHER WAS GOOD?
IT SURE WAS, ALICE!.. EXCEPT FOR A FEW TYPHOONS!
TYPHOONS! REALLY?
UH-HUH. BUT WE GOT THROUGH THEM OKAY..
AND THE GOVERNOR? HOW'S HE DOIN'?
HE'S FINE! AT LEAST I HOPE HE IS—WHEN I LEFT, HE WAS WORKING ON SOME DUMB SCHEME TO INVADE AUSTRALIA!
IF WE COULD JUST SEIZE THE KEY TENNIS CAMPS NEAR SYDNEY!
GIVE IT UP, SIR—PLEASE!

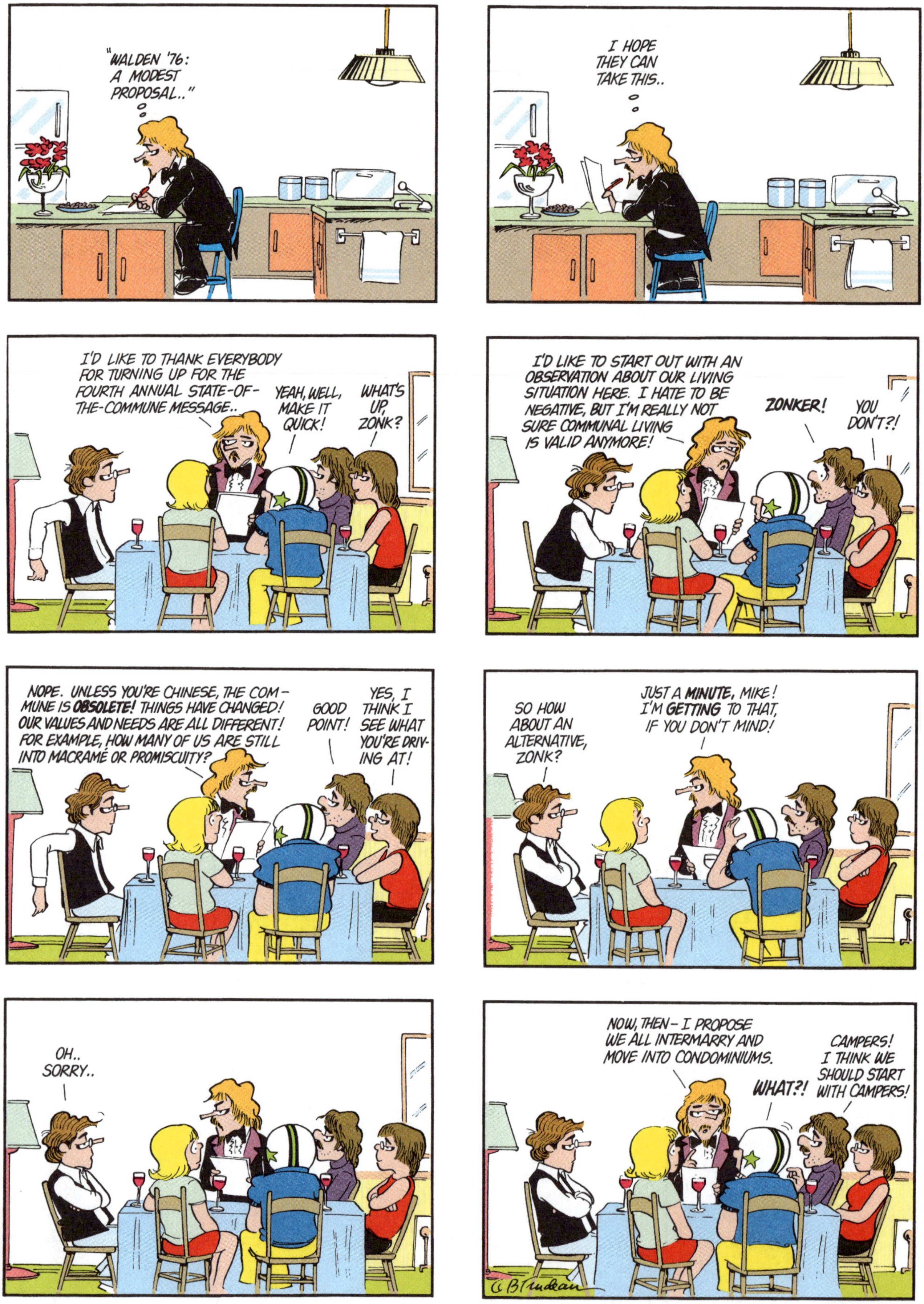
"WALDEN '76: A MODEST PROPOSAL.."
I HOPE THEY CAN TAKE THIS..
I'D LIKE TO THANK EVERYBODY FOR TURNING UP FOR THE FOURTH ANNUAL STATE-OF-THE-COMMUNE MESSAGE..
YEAH, WELL, MAKE IT QUICK!
WHAT'S UP, ZONK?
I'D LIKE TO START OUT WITH AN OBSERVATION ABOUT OUR LIVING SITUATION HERE. I HATE TO BE NEGATIVE, BUT I'M REALLY NOT SURE COMMUNAL LIVING IS VALID ANYMORE!
ZONKER!
YOU DON'T?!
NOPE. UNLESS YOU'RE CHINESE, THE COMMUNE IS OBSOLETE! THINGS HAVE CHANGED! OUR VALUES AND NEEDS ARE ALL DIFFERENT! FOR EXAMPLE, HOW MANY OF US ARE STILL INTO MACRAMÉ OR PROMISCUITY?
GOOD POINT!
YES, I THINK I SEE WHAT YOU'RE DRIVING AT!
SO HOW ABOUT AN ALTERNATIVE, ZONK?
JUST A MINUTE, MIKE! I'M GETTING TO THAT, IF YOU DON'T MIND!
OH.. SORRY..
NOW, THEN– I PROPOSE WE ALL INTERMARRY AND MOVE INTO CONDOMINIUMS.
WHAT?!
CAMPERS! I THINK WE SHOULD START WITH CAMPERS!
G.B. Trudeau

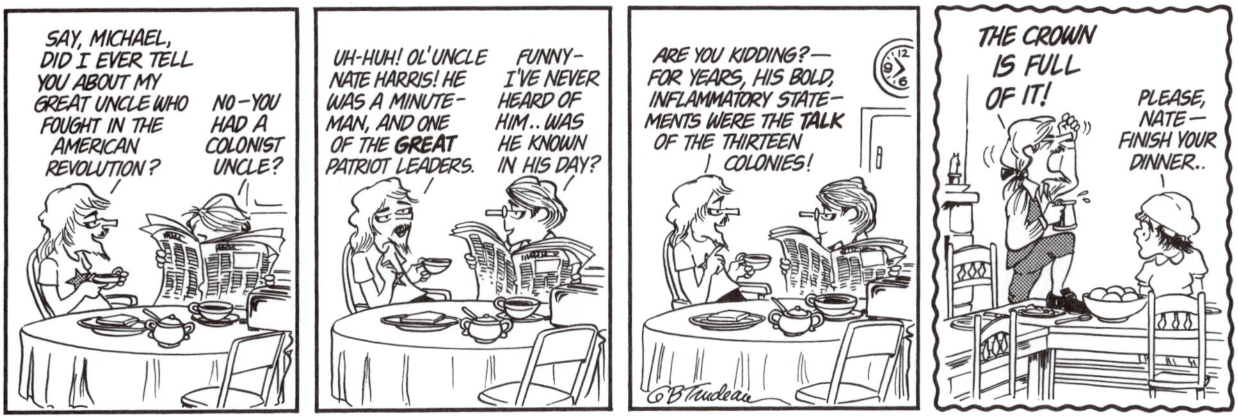
SAY, MICHAEL, DID I EVER TELL YOU ABOUT MY GREAT UNCLE WHO FOUGHT IN THE AMERICAN REVOLUTION?
NO—YOU HAD A COLONIST UNCLE?
UH-HUH! OL' UNCLE NATE HARRIS! HE WAS A MINUTE-MAN, AND ONE OF THE **GREAT** PATRIOT LEADERS.
FUNNY—I'VE NEVER HEARD OF HIM.. WAS HE KNOWN IN HIS DAY?
ARE YOU KIDDING?—FOR YEARS, HIS BOLD, INFLAMMATORY STATEMENTS WERE THE **TALK** OF THE THIRTEEN COLONIES!
G B Trudeau
THE CROWN IS FULL OF IT!
PLEASE, NATE—FINISH YOUR DINNER..

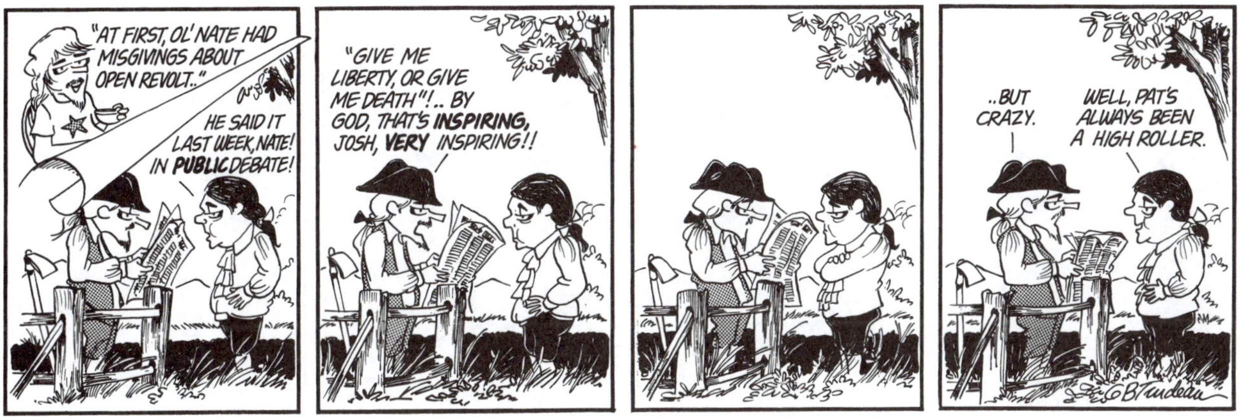
"AT FIRST, OL' NATE HAD MISGIVINGS ABOUT OPEN REVOLT.."
HE SAID IT LAST WEEK, NATE! IN **PUBLIC** DEBATE!
"GIVE ME LIBERTY, OR GIVE ME DEATH"!.. BY GOD, THAT'S **INSPIRING,** JOSH, **VERY** INSPIRING!!
..BUT CRAZY.
WELL, PAT'S ALWAYS BEEN A HIGH ROLLER.
G B Trudeau

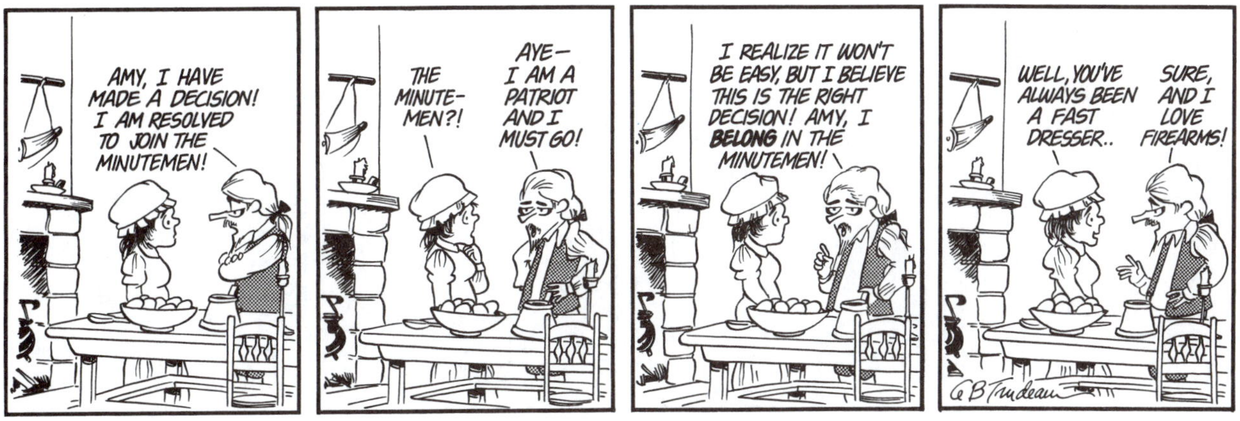
AMY, I HAVE MADE A DECISION! I AM RESOLVED TO JOIN THE MINUTEMEN!
THE MINUTE-MEN?!
AYE—I AM A PATRIOT AND I MUST GO!
I REALIZE IT WON'T BE EASY, BUT I BELIEVE THIS IS THE RIGHT DECISION! AMY, I **BELONG** IN THE MINUTEMEN!
WELL, YOU'VE ALWAYS BEEN A FAST DRESSER..
SURE, AND I LOVE FIREARMS!
G B Trudeau

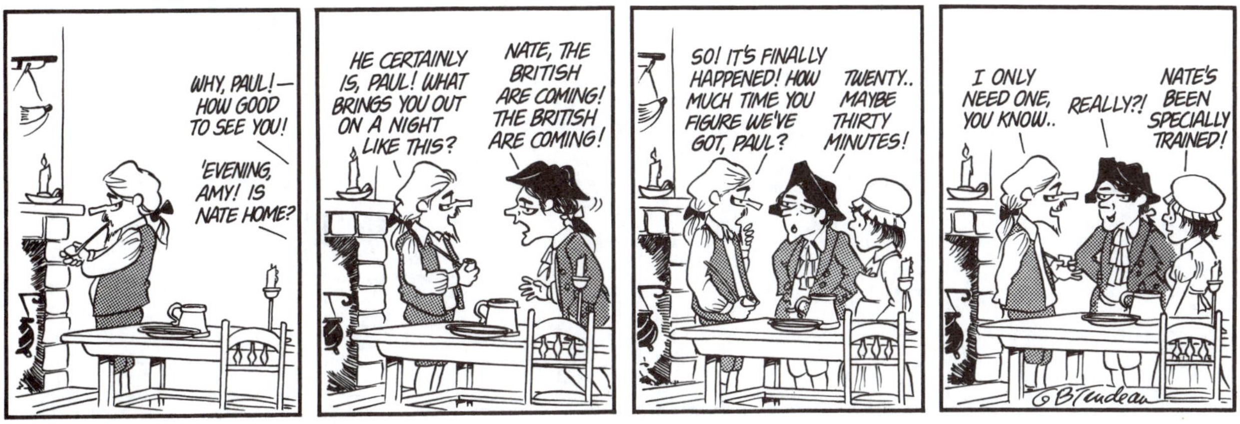
WHY, PAUL!—HOW GOOD TO SEE YOU!
'EVENING, AMY! IS NATE HOME?
HE CERTAINLY IS, PAUL! WHAT BRINGS YOU OUT ON A NIGHT LIKE THIS?
NATE, THE BRITISH ARE COMING! THE BRITISH ARE COMING!
SO! IT'S FINALLY HAPPENED! HOW MUCH TIME YOU FIGURE WE'VE GOT, PAUL?
TWENTY.. MAYBE THIRTY MINUTES!
I ONLY NEED ONE, YOU KNOW..
REALLY?!
NATE'S BEEN SPECIALLY TRAINED!
G B Trudeau

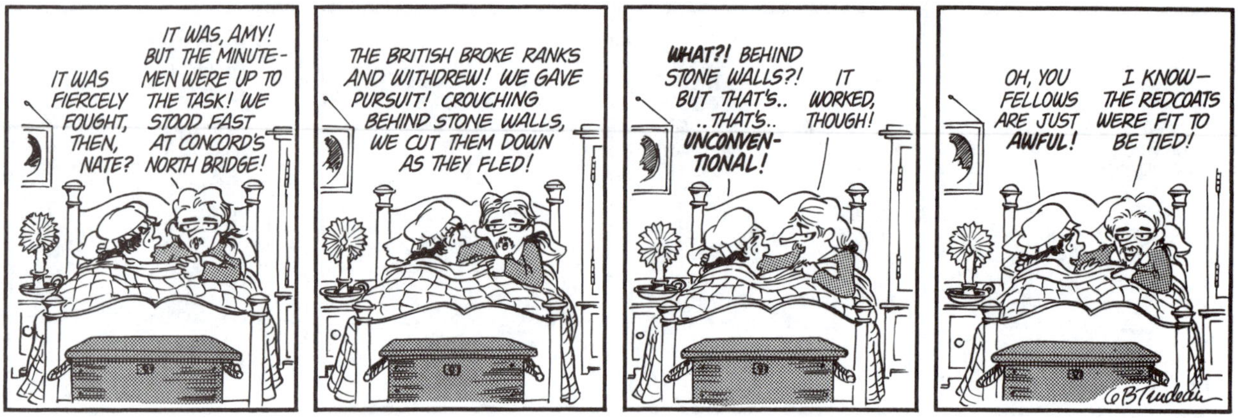
IT WAS FIERCELY FOUGHT, THEN, NATE?
IT WAS, AMY! BUT THE MINUTEMEN WERE UP TO THE TASK! WE STOOD FAST AT CONCORD'S NORTH BRIDGE!
THE BRITISH BROKE RANKS AND WITHDREW! WE GAVE PURSUIT! CROUCHING BEHIND STONE WALLS, WE CUT THEM DOWN AS THEY FLED!
WHAT?! BEHIND STONE WALLS?! BUT THAT'S.. ..THAT'S.. UNCONVENTIONAL!
IT WORKED, THOUGH!
OH, YOU FELLOWS ARE JUST AWFUL!
I KNOW— THE REDCOATS WERE FIT TO BE TIED!
GBTrudeau

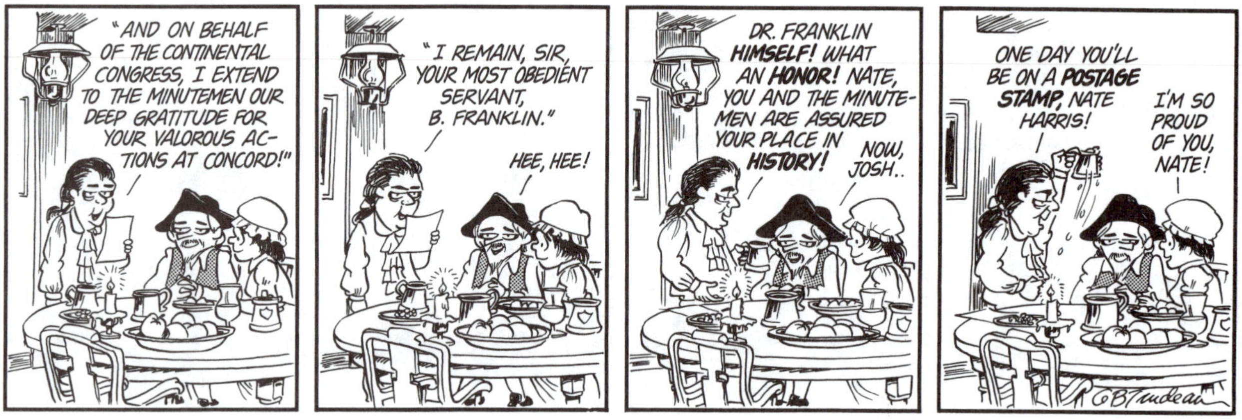
"AND ON BEHALF OF THE CONTINENTAL CONGRESS, I EXTEND TO THE MINUTEMEN OUR DEEP GRATITUDE FOR YOUR VALOROUS ACTIONS AT CONCORD!"
"I REMAIN, SIR, YOUR MOST OBEDIENT SERVANT, B. FRANKLIN."
HEE, HEE!
DR. FRANKLIN HIMSELF! WHAT AN HONOR! NATE, YOU AND THE MINUTEMEN ARE ASSURED YOUR PLACE IN HISTORY!
NOW, JOSH..
ONE DAY YOU'LL BE ON A POSTAGE STAMP, NATE HARRIS!
I'M SO PROUD OF YOU, NATE!
GBTrudeau

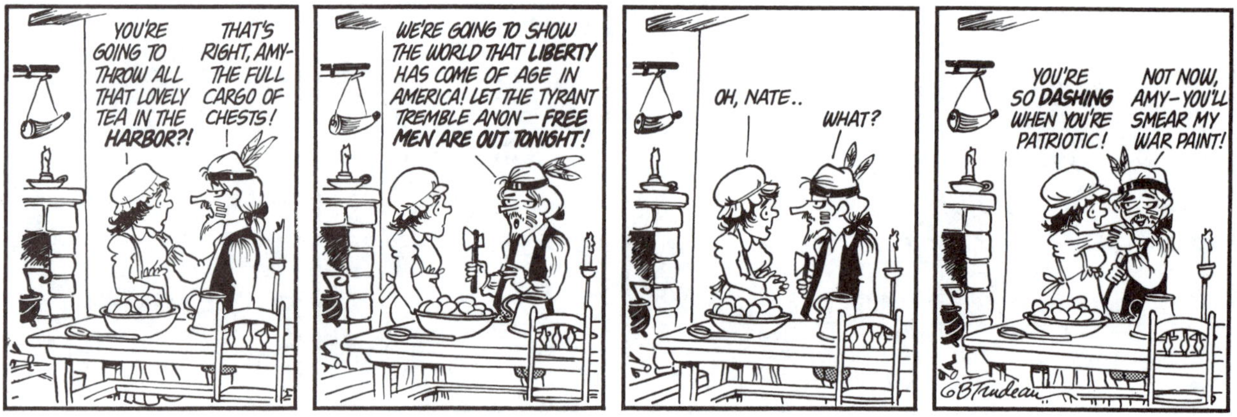
YOU'RE GOING TO THROW ALL THAT LOVELY TEA IN THE HARBOR?!
THAT'S RIGHT, AMY— THE FULL CARGO OF CHESTS!
WE'RE GOING TO SHOW THE WORLD THAT LIBERTY HAS COME OF AGE IN AMERICA! LET THE TYRANT TREMBLE ANON— FREE MEN ARE OUT TONIGHT!
OH, NATE..
WHAT?
YOU'RE SO DASHING WHEN YOU'RE PATRIOTIC!
NOT NOW, AMY—YOU'LL SMEAR MY WAR PAINT!
GBTrudeau

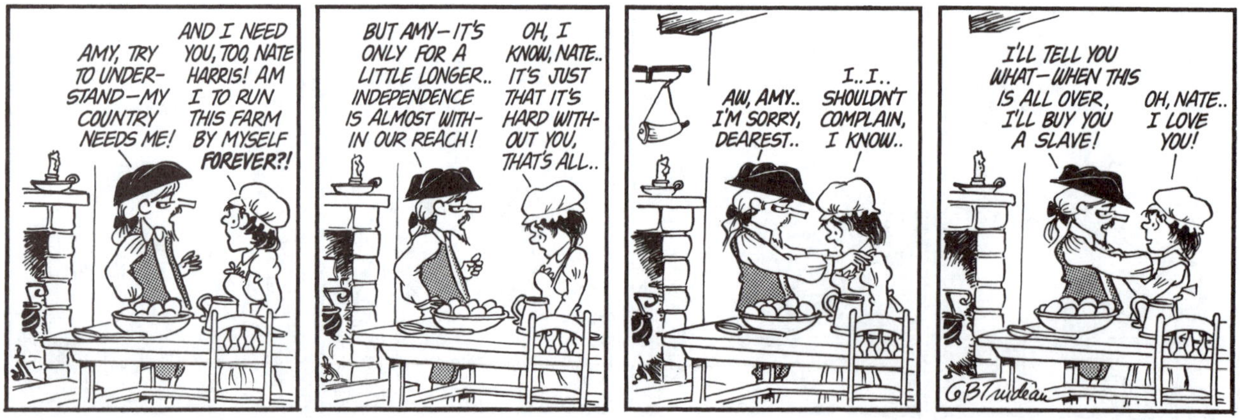
AMY, TRY TO UNDERSTAND—MY COUNTRY NEEDS ME!
AND I NEED YOU, TOO, NATE HARRIS! AM I TO RUN THIS FARM BY MYSELF FOREVER?!
BUT AMY—IT'S ONLY FOR A LITTLE LONGER.. INDEPENDENCE IS ALMOST WITHIN OUR REACH!
OH, I KNOW, NATE.. IT'S JUST THAT IT'S HARD WITHOUT YOU, THAT'S ALL..
AW, AMY.. I'M SORRY, DEAREST..
I.. I.. SHOULDN'T COMPLAIN, I KNOW..
I'LL TELL YOU WHAT—WHEN THIS IS ALL OVER, I'LL BUY YOU A SLAVE!
OH, NATE.. I LOVE YOU!
GBTrudeau

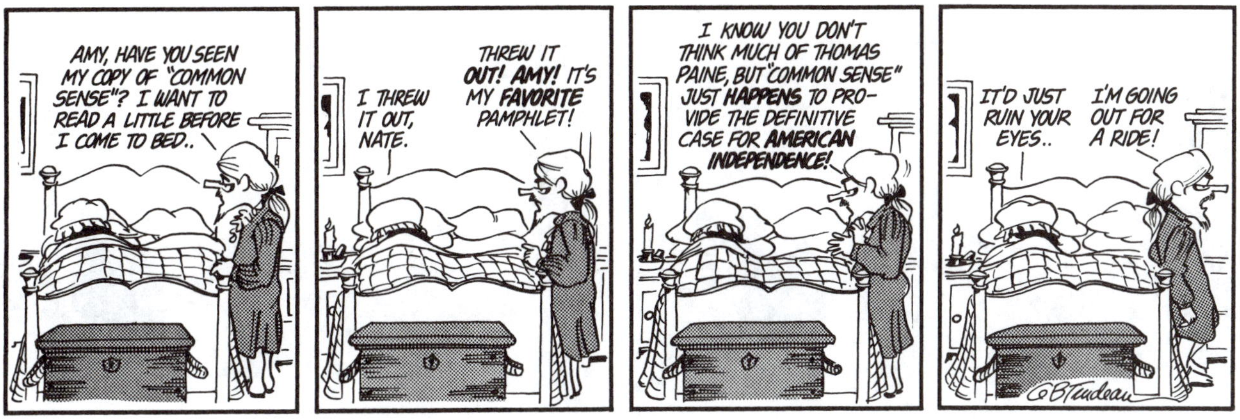
AMY, HAVE YOU SEEN MY COPY OF "COMMON SENSE"? I WANT TO READ A LITTLE BEFORE I COME TO BED..
I THREW IT OUT, NATE.
THREW IT OUT! AMY! IT'S MY FAVORITE PAMPHLET!
I KNOW YOU DON'T THINK MUCH OF THOMAS PAINE, BUT "COMMON SENSE" JUST HAPPENS TO PROVIDE THE DEFINITIVE CASE FOR AMERICAN INDEPENDENCE!
IT'D JUST RUIN YOUR EYES..
I'M GOING OUT FOR A RIDE!

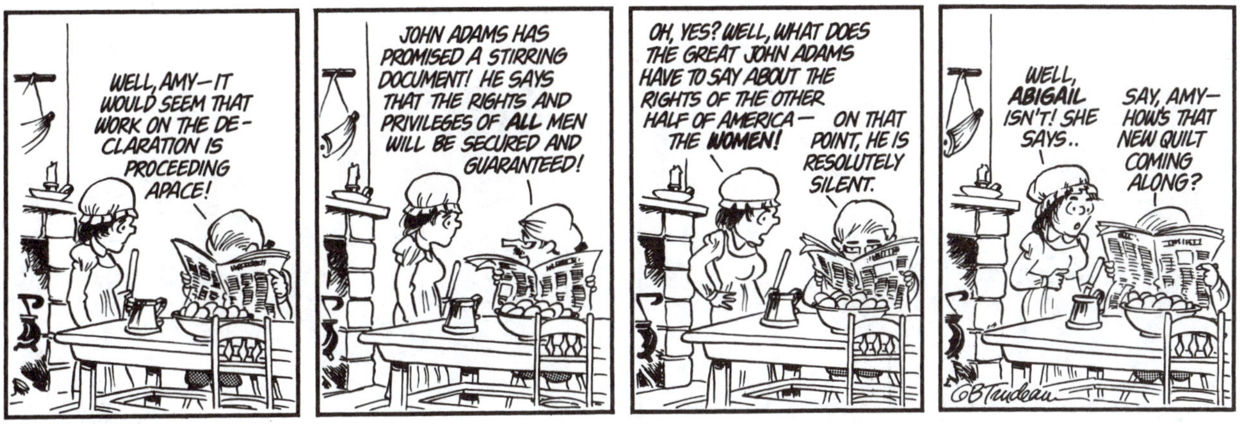
WELL, AMY—IT WOULD SEEM THAT WORK ON THE DECLARATION IS PROCEEDING APACE!
JOHN ADAMS HAS PROMISED A STIRRING DOCUMENT! HE SAYS THAT THE RIGHTS AND PRIVILEGES OF ALL MEN WILL BE SECURED AND GUARANTEED!
OH, YES? WELL, WHAT DOES THE GREAT JOHN ADAMS HAVE TO SAY ABOUT THE RIGHTS OF THE OTHER HALF OF AMERICA—THE WOMEN!
ON THAT POINT, HE IS RESOLUTELY SILENT.
WELL, ABIGAIL ISN'T! SHE SAYS..
SAY, AMY—HOW'S THAT NEW QUILT COMING ALONG?

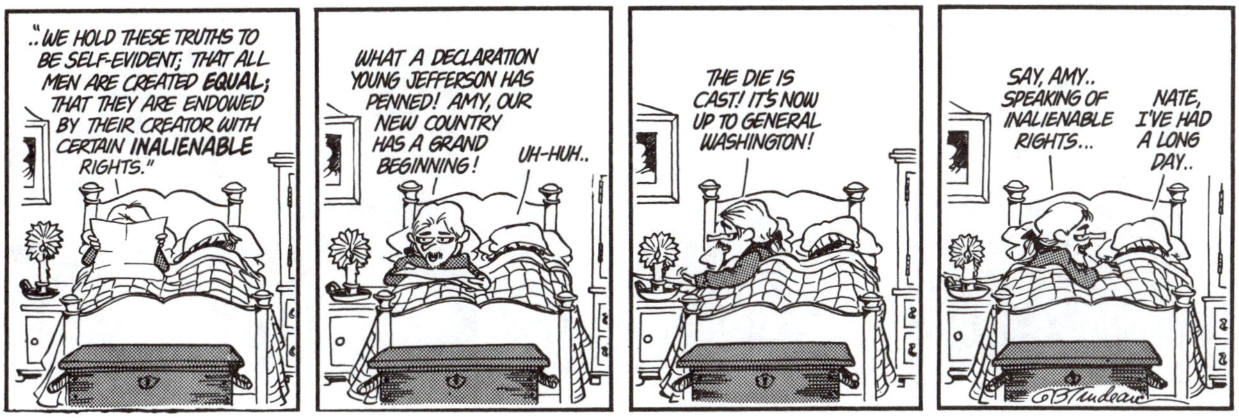
.."WE HOLD THESE TRUTHS TO BE SELF-EVIDENT; THAT ALL MEN ARE CREATED EQUAL; THAT THEY ARE ENDOWED BY THEIR CREATOR WITH CERTAIN INALIENABLE RIGHTS."
WHAT A DECLARATION YOUNG JEFFERSON HAS PENNED! AMY, OUR NEW COUNTRY HAS A GRAND BEGINNING!
UH-HUH..
THE DIE IS CAST! IT'S NOW UP TO GENERAL WASHINGTON!
SAY, AMY.. SPEAKING OF INALIENABLE RIGHTS...
NATE, I'VE HAD A LONG DAY..

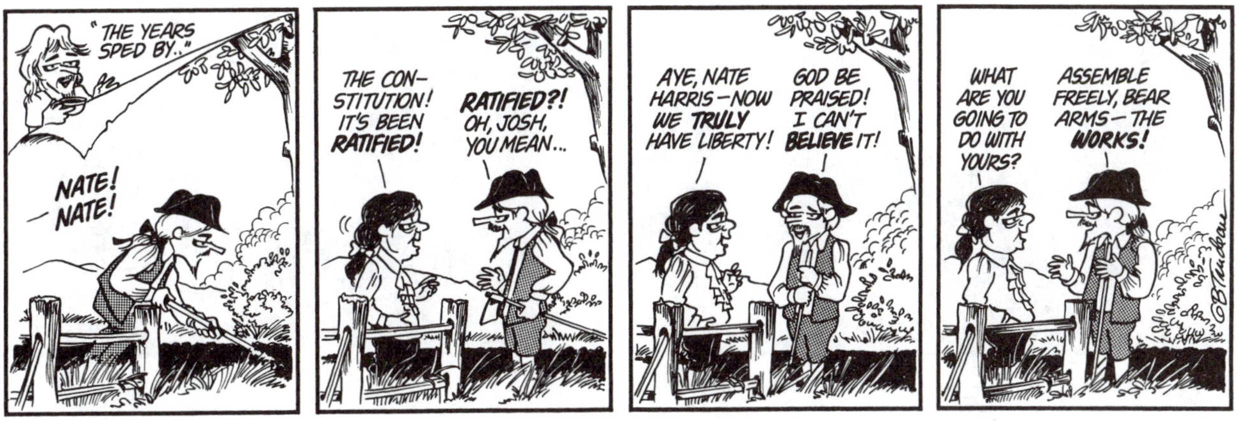
"THE YEARS SPED BY.."
NATE! NATE!
THE CONSTITUTION! IT'S BEEN RATIFIED!
RATIFIED?! OH, JOSH, YOU MEAN...
AYE, NATE HARRIS—NOW WE TRULY HAVE LIBERTY!
GOD BE PRAISED! I CAN'T BELIEVE IT!
WHAT ARE YOU GOING TO DO WITH YOURS?
ASSEMBLE FREELY, BEAR ARMS—THE WORKS!

SHADES OF VALLEY FORGE..
STILL NO REPLY, AMY?
WRITING CONGRESS IS A BIG WASTE OF TIME, NATE HARRIS— I MIGHT AS WELL BE WRITING TO MYSELF!
WELL, OUR CONSTITUTION'S STILL ONLY A FEW YEARS OLD, AMY. SOME FOLKS WANT TO SEE HOW IT WORKS BEFORE WE START IN AMENDING IT!
BUT AN EQUAL RIGHTS AMENDMENT?! THAT'S SO BASIC!
WELL, I'M SURE CONGRESS WILL BE CONSIDERING IT..
YES, BUT WHEN?! HOW LONG DO WE HAVE TO WAIT BEFORE CONGRESS AWAKENS TO ITS MORAL NECESSITY?!
WELL, IT'S BEING TALKED ABOUT..
TALKED ABOUT?! YOU MEAN, LAUGHED ABOUT! THERE ISN'T A SINGLE LEGISLATOR IN THIS COUNTRY WILLING TO SERIOUSLY CONSIDER EQUAL RIGHTS FOR WOMEN!
OH, NOW, C'MON, AMY— YOU'RE OVERREACTING— YOU KNOW YOU ARE..
YOU MAKE IT SOUND LIKE IT'S A COUPLE HUNDRED YEARS AWAY!
WELL, IT JUST MAKES ME SO MAD!
GBTrudeau

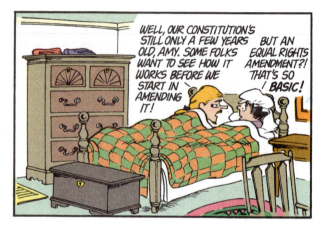

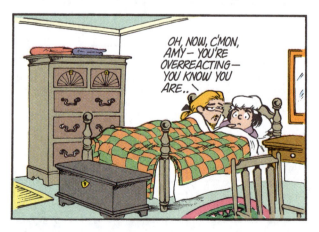

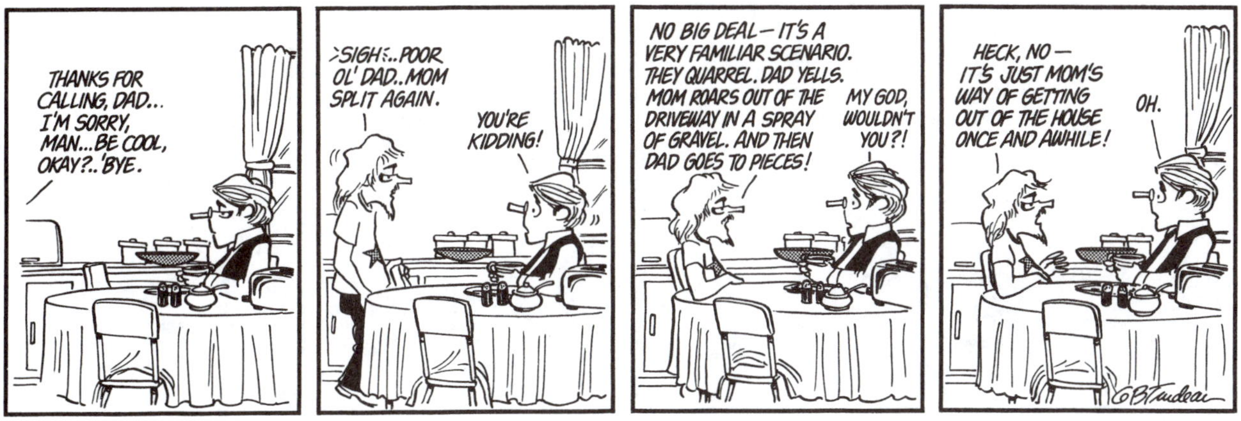
THANKS FOR CALLING, DAD... I'M SORRY, MAN... BE COOL, OKAY?.. 'BYE.
SIGH..POOR OL' DAD..MOM SPLIT AGAIN.
YOU'RE KIDDING!
NO BIG DEAL— IT'S A VERY FAMILIAR SCENARIO. THEY QUARREL. DAD YELLS. MOM ROARS OUT OF THE DRIVEWAY IN A SPRAY OF GRAVEL. AND THEN DAD GOES TO PIECES!
MY GOD, WOULDN'T YOU?!
HECK, NO— IT'S JUST MOM'S WAY OF GETTING OUT OF THE HOUSE ONCE AND AWHILE!
OH.
GBTrudeau

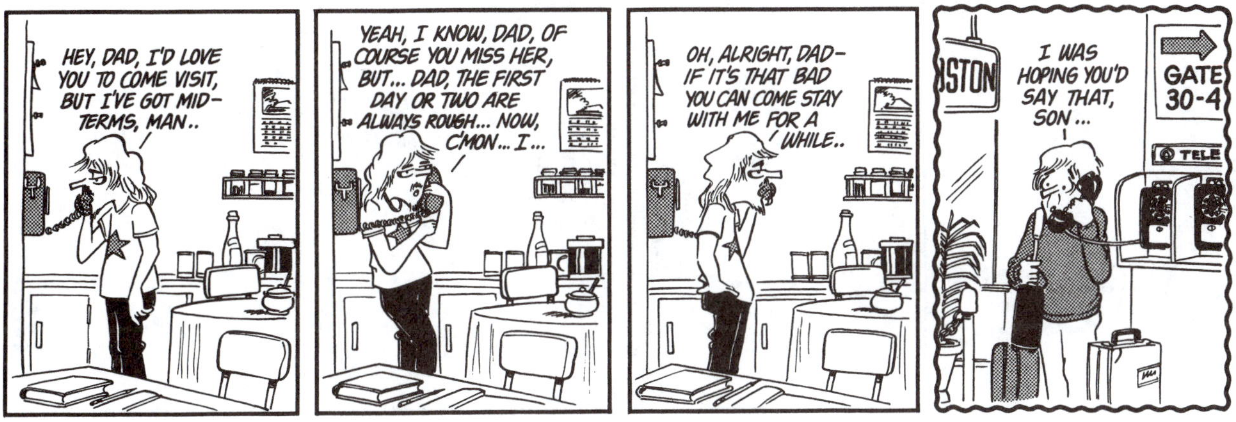
HEY, DAD, I'D LOVE YOU TO COME VISIT, BUT I'VE GOT MID-TERMS, MAN..
YEAH, I KNOW, DAD, OF COURSE YOU MISS HER, BUT... DAD, THE FIRST DAY OR TWO ARE ALWAYS ROUGH... NOW, C'MON... I...
OH, ALRIGHT, DAD— IF IT'S THAT BAD YOU CAN COME STAY WITH ME FOR A WHILE..
OSTON
I WAS HOPING YOU'D SAY THAT, SON...
GATE 30-4
TELE

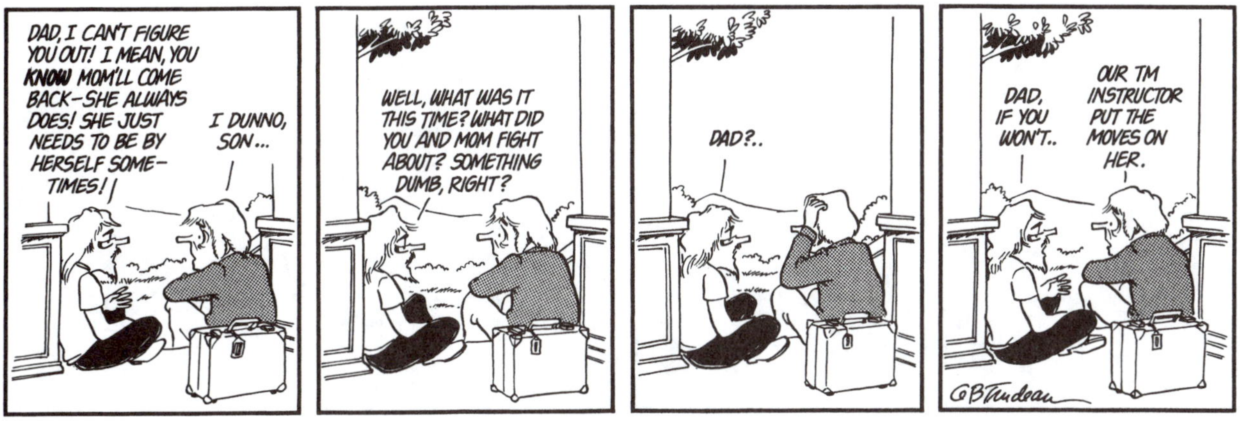
DAD, I CAN'T FIGURE YOU OUT! I MEAN, YOU KNOW MOM'LL COME BACK—SHE ALWAYS DOES! SHE JUST NEEDS TO BE BY HERSELF SOME-TIMES!
I DUNNO, SON...
WELL, WHAT WAS IT THIS TIME? WHAT DID YOU AND MOM FIGHT ABOUT? SOMETHING DUMB, RIGHT?
DAD?..
DAD, IF YOU WON'T..
OUR TM INSTRUCTOR PUT THE MOVES ON HER.
GBTrudeau

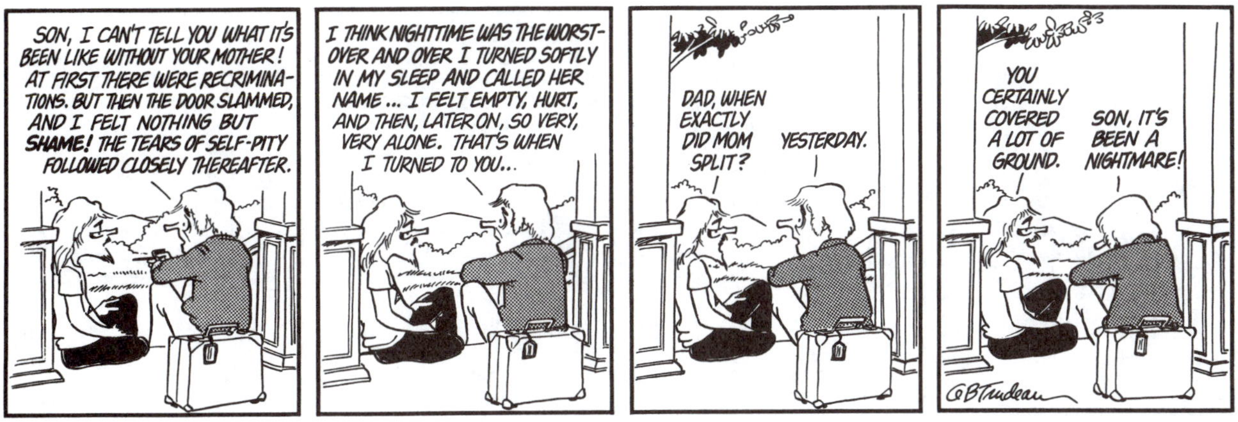
SON, I CAN'T TELL YOU WHAT IT'S BEEN LIKE WITHOUT YOUR MOTHER! AT FIRST THERE WERE RECRIMINA-TIONS. BUT THEN THE DOOR SLAMMED, AND I FELT NOTHING BUT SHAME! THE TEARS OF SELF-PITY FOLLOWED CLOSELY THEREAFTER.
I THINK NIGHTTIME WAS THE WORST-OVER AND OVER I TURNED SOFTLY IN MY SLEEP AND CALLED HER NAME... I FELT EMPTY, HURT, AND THEN, LATER ON, SO VERY, VERY ALONE. THAT'S WHEN I TURNED TO YOU...
DAD, WHEN EXACTLY DID MOM SPLIT?
YESTERDAY.
YOU CERTAINLY COVERED A LOT OF GROUND.
SON, IT'S BEEN A NIGHTMARE!
GBTrudeau

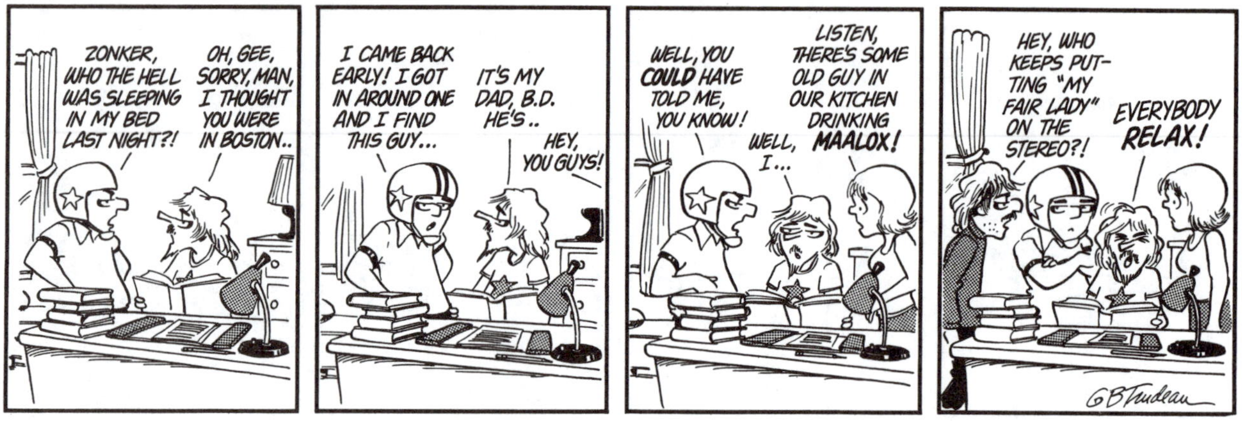
ZONKER, WHO THE HELL WAS SLEEPING IN MY BED LAST NIGHT?!
OH, GEE, SORRY, MAN, I THOUGHT YOU WERE IN BOSTON..
I CAME BACK EARLY! I GOT IN AROUND ONE AND I FIND THIS GUY...
IT'S MY DAD, B.D. HE'S..
HEY, YOU GUYS!
WELL, YOU COULD HAVE TOLD ME, YOU KNOW!
LISTEN, THERE'S SOME OLD GUY IN OUR KITCHEN DRINKING MAALOX!
WELL, I...
HEY, WHO KEEPS PUTTING "MY FAIR LADY" ON THE STEREO?!
EVERYBODY RELAX!
GBTrudeau

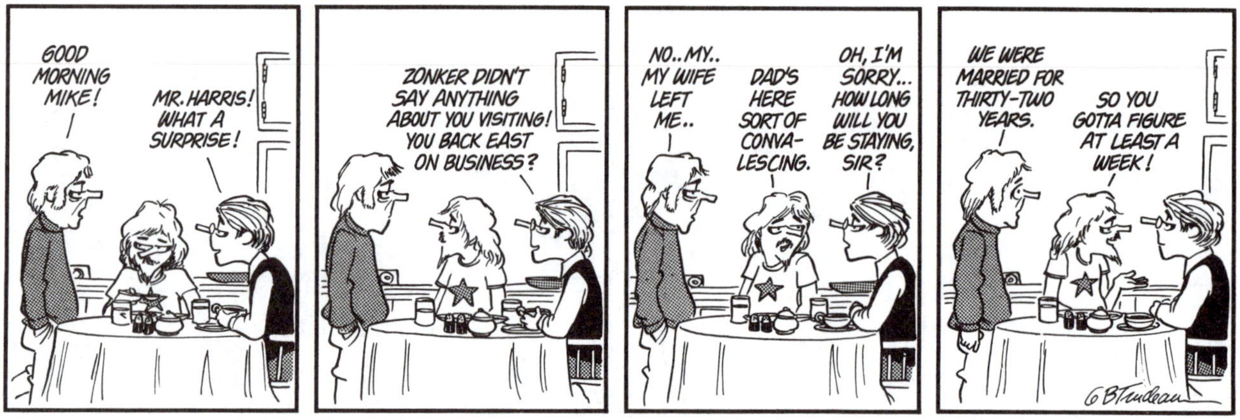
GOOD MORNING MIKE!
MR. HARRIS! WHAT A SURPRISE!
ZONKER DIDN'T SAY ANYTHING ABOUT YOU VISITING! YOU BACK EAST ON BUSINESS?
NO.. MY.. MY WIFE LEFT ME..
DAD'S HERE SORT OF CONVALESCING.
OH, I'M SORRY... HOW LONG WILL YOU BE STAYING, SIR?
WE WERE MARRIED FOR THIRTY-TWO YEARS.
SO YOU GOTTA FIGURE AT LEAST A WEEK!
GBTrudeau

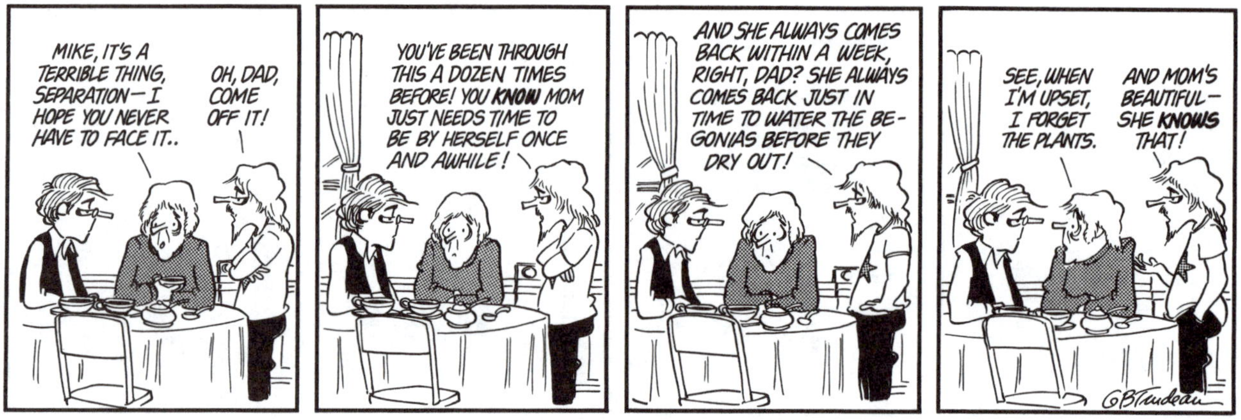
MIKE, IT'S A TERRIBLE THING, SEPARATION—I HOPE YOU NEVER HAVE TO FACE IT..
OH, DAD, COME OFF IT!
YOU'VE BEEN THROUGH THIS A DOZEN TIMES BEFORE! YOU KNOW MOM JUST NEEDS TIME TO BE BY HERSELF ONCE AND AWHILE!
AND SHE ALWAYS COMES BACK WITHIN A WEEK, RIGHT, DAD? SHE ALWAYS COMES BACK JUST IN TIME TO WATER THE BEGONIAS BEFORE THEY DRY OUT!
SEE, WHEN I'M UPSET, I FORGET THE PLANTS.
AND MOM'S BEAUTIFUL—SHE KNOWS THAT!
GBTrudeau

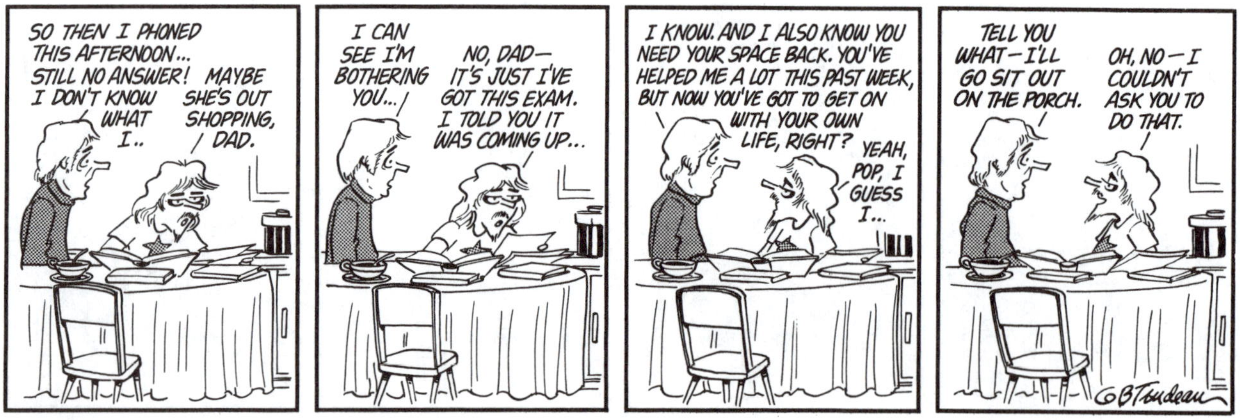
SO THEN I PHONED THIS AFTERNOON... STILL NO ANSWER! I DON'T KNOW WHAT I..
MAYBE SHE'S OUT SHOPPING, DAD.
I CAN SEE I'M BOTHERING YOU...
NO, DAD—IT'S JUST I'VE GOT THIS EXAM. I TOLD YOU IT WAS COMING UP...
I KNOW. AND I ALSO KNOW YOU NEED YOUR SPACE BACK. YOU'VE HELPED ME A LOT THIS PAST WEEK, BUT NOW YOU'VE GOT TO GET ON WITH YOUR OWN LIFE, RIGHT?
YEAH, POP, I GUESS I...
TELL YOU WHAT—I'LL GO SIT OUT ON THE PORCH.
OH, NO—I COULDN'T ASK YOU TO DO THAT.
GBTrudeau

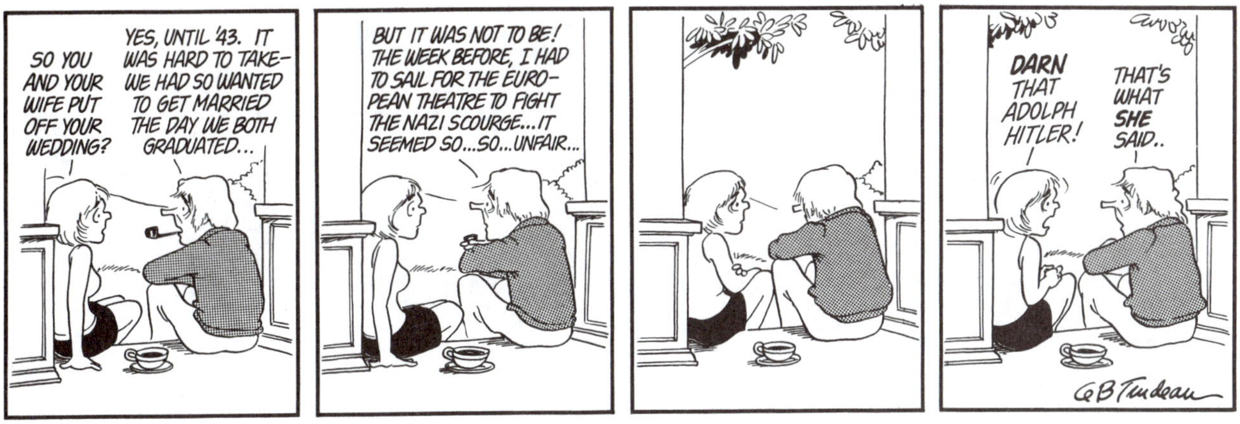
SO YOU AND YOUR WIFE PUT OFF YOUR WEDDING?
YES, UNTIL '43. IT WAS HARD TO TAKE—WE HAD SO WANTED TO GET MARRIED THE DAY WE BOTH GRADUATED...
BUT IT WAS NOT TO BE! THE WEEK BEFORE, I HAD TO SAIL FOR THE EUROPEAN THEATRE TO FIGHT THE NAZI SCOURGE... IT SEEMED SO...SO...UNFAIR...
DARN THAT ADOLPH HITLER!
THAT'S WHAT SHE SAID..

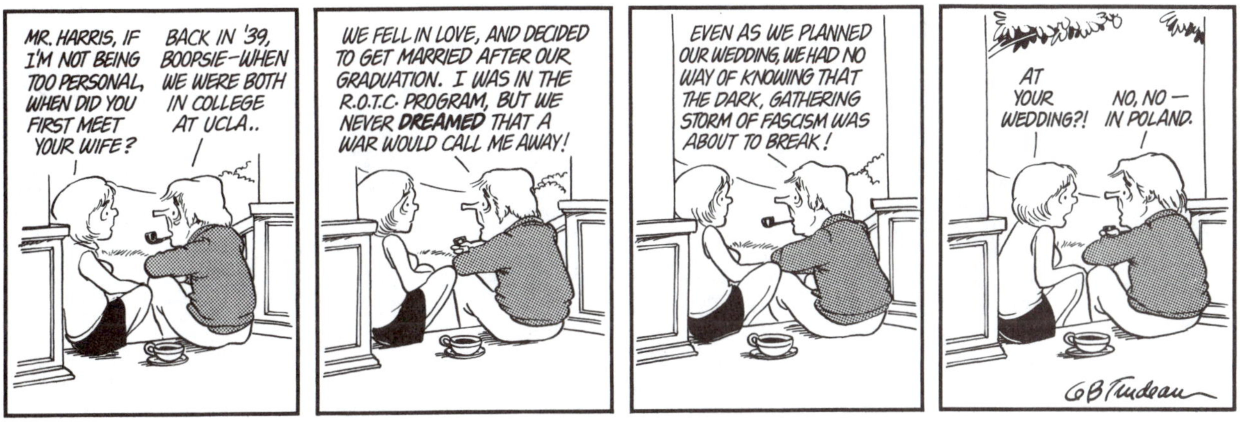
MR. HARRIS, IF I'M NOT BEING TOO PERSONAL, WHEN DID YOU FIRST MEET YOUR WIFE?
BACK IN '39, BOOPSIE—WHEN WE WERE BOTH IN COLLEGE AT UCLA..
WE FELL IN LOVE, AND DECIDED TO GET MARRIED AFTER OUR GRADUATION. I WAS IN THE R.O.T.C. PROGRAM, BUT WE NEVER DREAMED THAT A WAR WOULD CALL ME AWAY!
EVEN AS WE PLANNED OUR WEDDING, WE HAD NO WAY OF KNOWING THAT THE DARK, GATHERING STORM OF FASCISM WAS ABOUT TO BREAK!
AT YOUR WEDDING?!
NO, NO — IN POLAND.

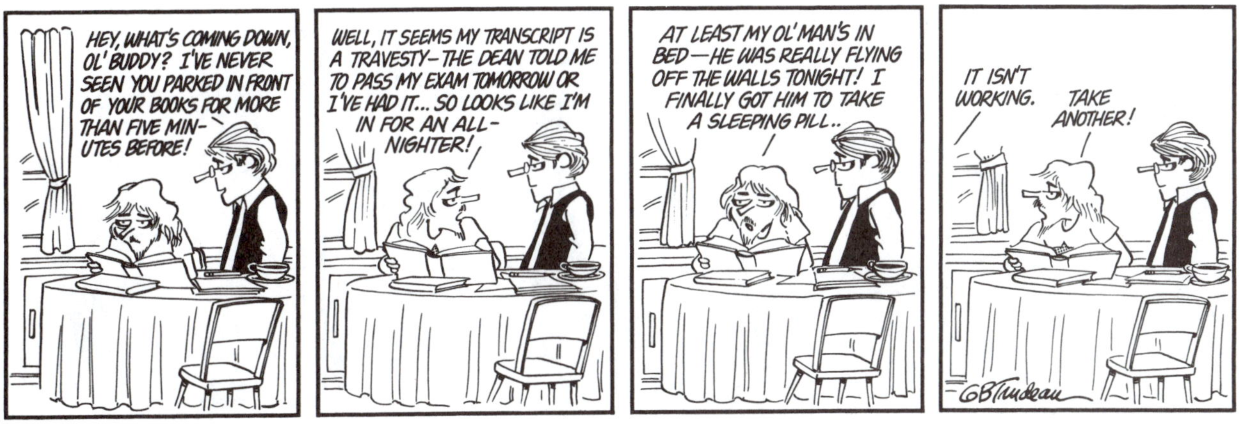
HEY, WHAT'S COMING DOWN, OL' BUDDY? I'VE NEVER SEEN YOU PARKED IN FRONT OF YOUR BOOKS FOR MORE THAN FIVE MINUTES BEFORE!
WELL, IT SEEMS MY TRANSCRIPT IS A TRAVESTY—THE DEAN TOLD ME TO PASS MY EXAM TOMORROW OR I'VE HAD IT... SO LOOKS LIKE I'M IN FOR AN ALL-NIGHTER!
AT LEAST MY OL' MAN'S IN BED—HE WAS REALLY FLYING OFF THE WALLS TONIGHT! I FINALLY GOT HIM TO TAKE A SLEEPING PILL..
IT ISN'T WORKING.
TAKE ANOTHER!

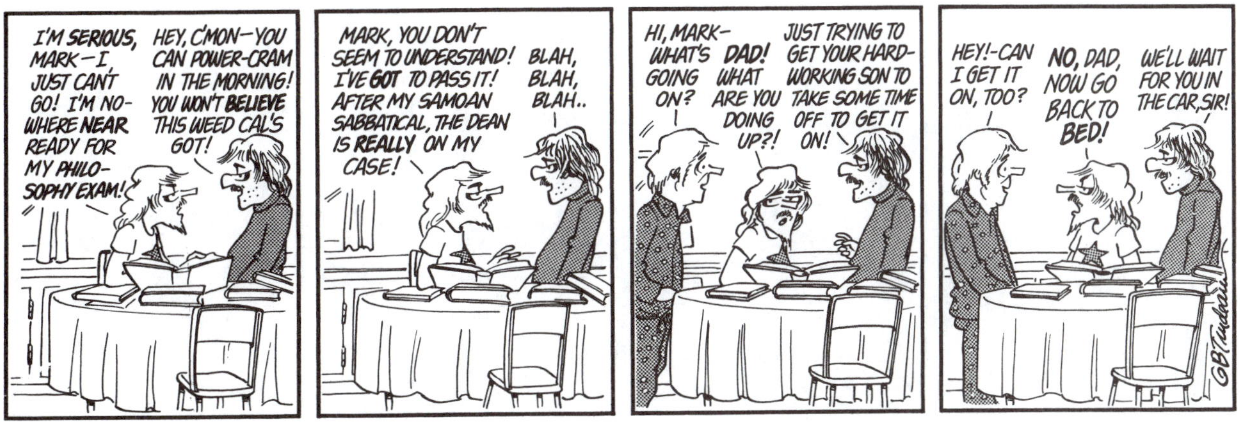
I'M SERIOUS, MARK—I JUST CAN'T GO! I'M NOWHERE NEAR READY FOR MY PHILOSOPHY EXAM!
HEY, C'MON—YOU CAN POWER-CRAM IN THE MORNING! YOU WON'T BELIEVE THIS WEED CAL'S GOT!
MARK, YOU DON'T SEEM TO UNDERSTAND! I'VE GOT TO PASS IT! AFTER MY SAMOAN SABBATICAL, THE DEAN IS REALLY ON MY CASE!
BLAH, BLAH, BLAH..
HI, MARK—WHAT'S GOING ON?
DAD! WHAT ARE YOU DOING UP?!
JUST TRYING TO GET YOUR HARD-WORKING SON TO TAKE SOME TIME OFF TO GET IT ON!
HEY!-CAN I GET IT ON, TOO?
NO, DAD, NOW GO BACK TO BED!
WE'LL WAIT FOR YOU IN THE CAR, SIR!

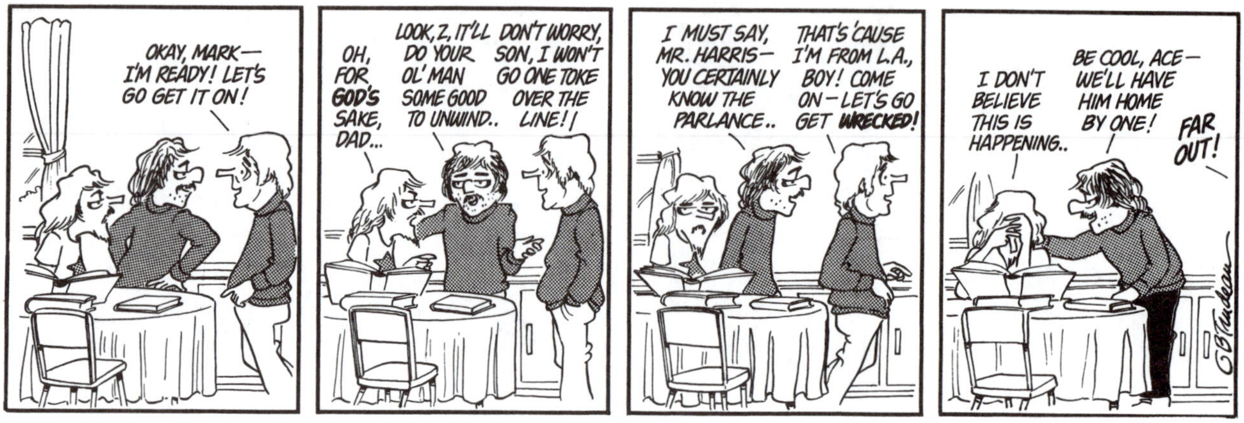
OKAY, MARK— I'M READY! LET'S GO GET IT ON!
OH, FOR GOD'S SAKE, DAD...
LOOK, Z, IT'LL DO YOUR OL' MAN SOME GOOD TO UNWIND..
DON'T WORRY, SON, I WON'T GO ONE TOKE OVER THE LINE!
I MUST SAY, MR. HARRIS— YOU CERTAINLY KNOW THE PARLANCE..
THAT'S 'CAUSE I'M FROM L.A., BOY! COME ON—LET'S GO GET WRECKED!
I DON'T BELIEVE THIS IS HAPPENING..
BE COOL, ACE— WE'LL HAVE HIM HOME BY ONE!
FAR OUT!

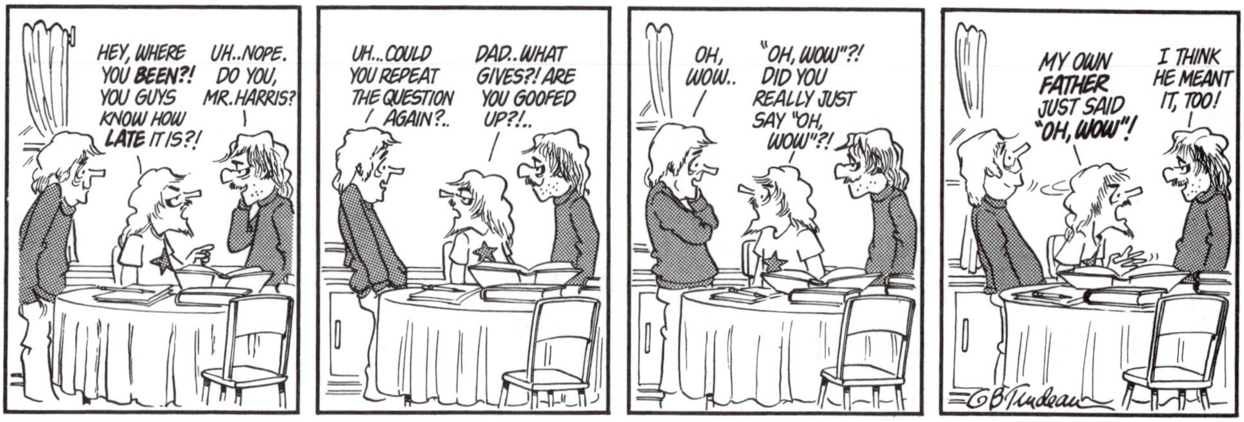
HEY, WHERE YOU BEEN?! YOU GUYS KNOW HOW LATE IT IS?!
UH..NOPE. DO YOU, MR. HARRIS?
UH...COULD YOU REPEAT THE QUESTION AGAIN?..
DAD..WHAT GIVES?! ARE YOU GOOFED UP?!..
OH, WOW..
"OH, WOW"?! DID YOU REALLY JUST SAY "OH, WOW"?!
MY OWN FATHER JUST SAID "OH, WOW"!
I THINK HE MEANT IT, TOO!

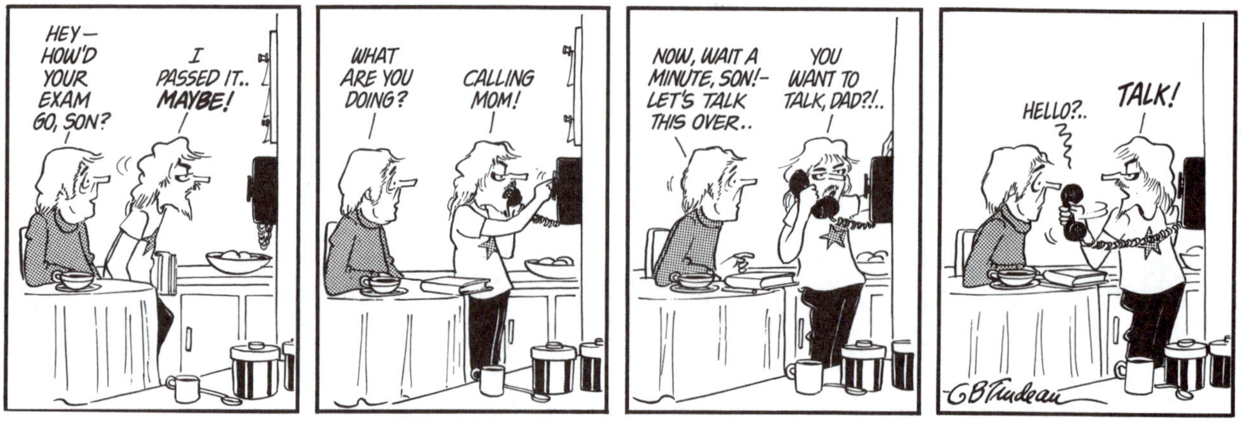
HEY— HOW'D YOUR EXAM GO, SON?
I PASSED IT.. MAYBE!
WHAT ARE YOU DOING?
CALLING MOM!
NOW, WAIT A MINUTE, SON!— LET'S TALK THIS OVER..
YOU WANT TO TALK, DAD?!..
HELLO?..
TALK!

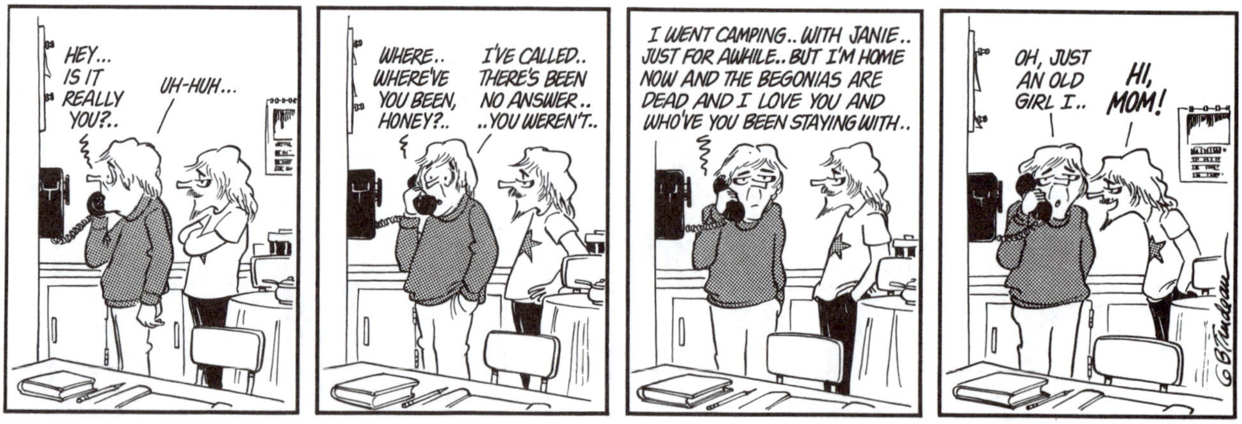
HEY... IS IT REALLY YOU?..
UH-HUH...
WHERE.. WHERE'VE YOU BEEN, HONEY?..
I'VE CALLED.. THERE'S BEEN NO ANSWER.. ..YOU WEREN'T..
I WENT CAMPING.. WITH JANIE.. JUST FOR AWHILE.. BUT I'M HOME NOW AND THE BEGONIAS ARE DEAD AND I LOVE YOU AND WHO'VE YOU BEEN STAYING WITH..
OH, JUST AN OLD GIRL I..
HI, MOM!

4

THE SOLAR COLLECTOR

Lord of the Rays

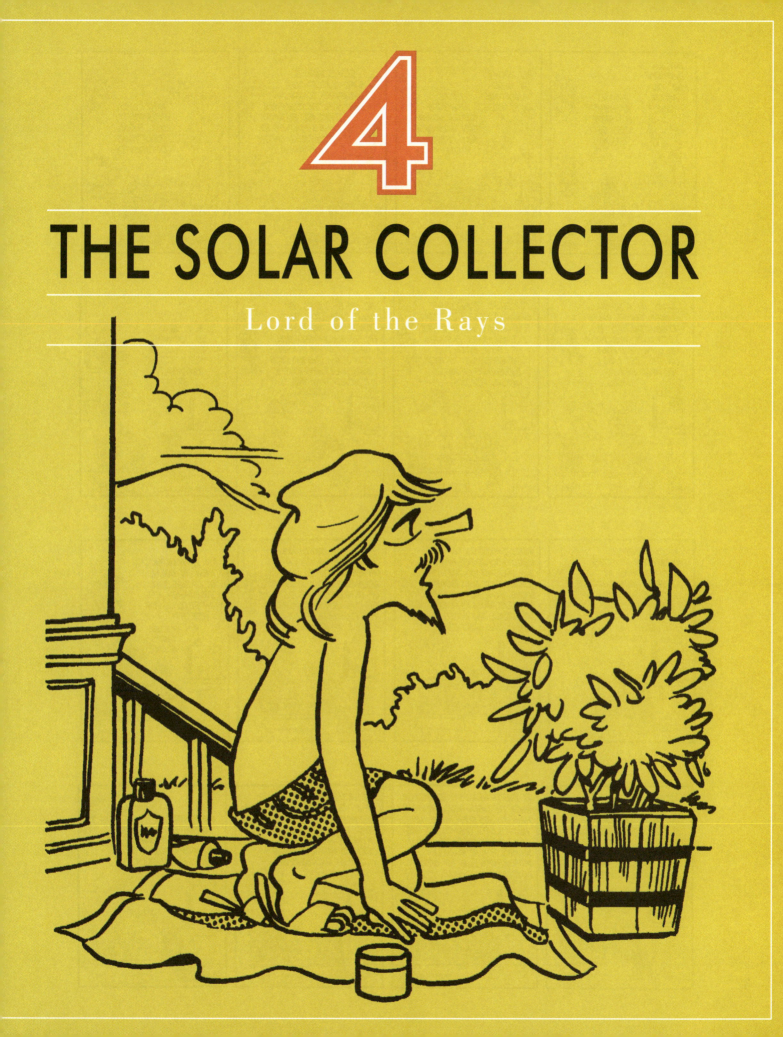

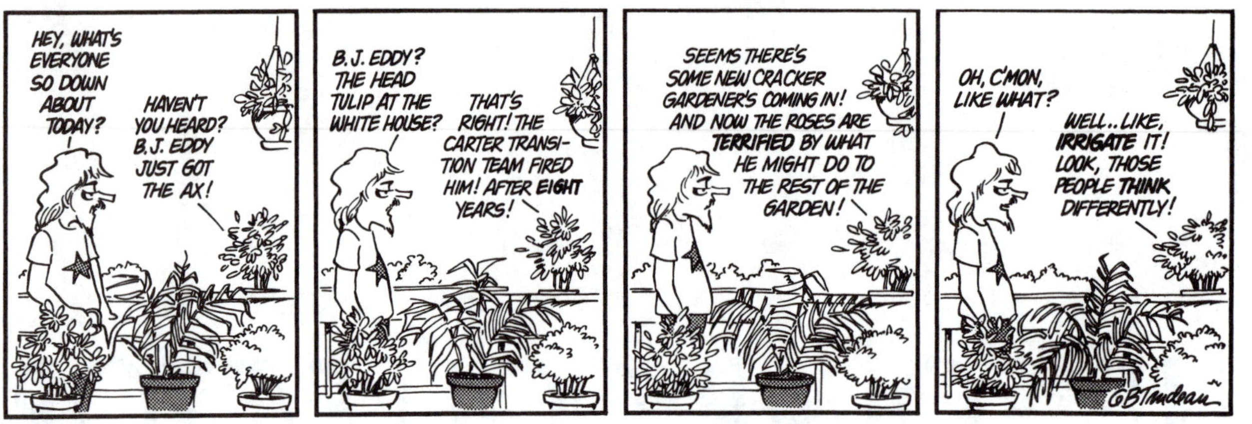
HEY, WHAT'S EVERYONE SO DOWN ABOUT TODAY?
HAVEN'T YOU HEARD? B.J. EDDY JUST GOT THE AX!
B.J. EDDY? THE HEAD TULIP AT THE WHITE HOUSE?
THAT'S RIGHT! THE CARTER TRANSITION TEAM FIRED HIM! AFTER EIGHT YEARS!
SEEMS THERE'S SOME NEW CRACKER GARDENER'S COMING IN! AND NOW THE ROSES ARE TERRIFIED BY WHAT HE MIGHT DO TO THE REST OF THE GARDEN!
OH, C'MON, LIKE WHAT?
WELL.. LIKE, IRRIGATE IT! LOOK, THOSE PEOPLE THINK DIFFERENTLY!
GBTrudeau

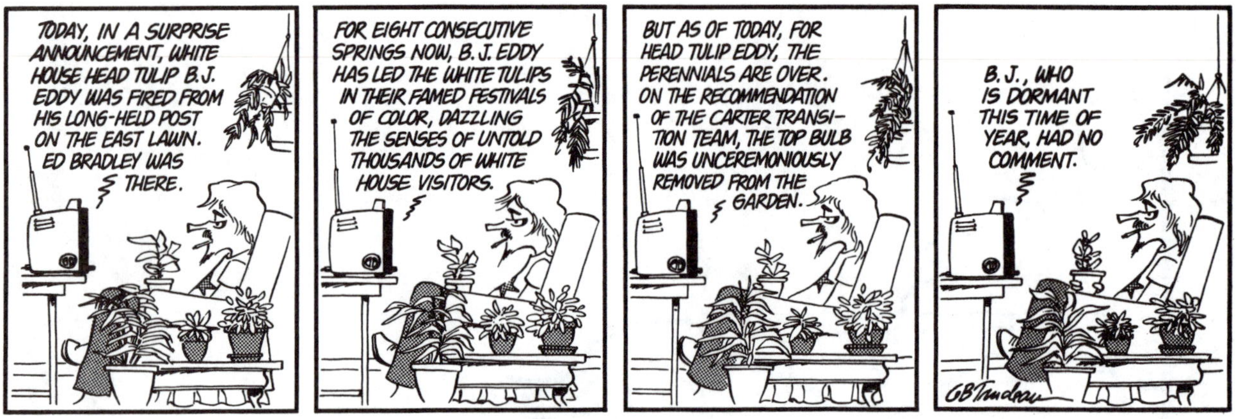
TODAY, IN A SURPRISE ANNOUNCEMENT, WHITE HOUSE HEAD TULIP B.J. EDDY WAS FIRED FROM HIS LONG-HELD POST ON THE EAST LAWN. ED BRADLEY WAS THERE.
FOR EIGHT CONSECUTIVE SPRINGS NOW, B.J. EDDY HAS LED THE WHITE TULIPS IN THEIR FAMED FESTIVALS OF COLOR, DAZZLING THE SENSES OF UNTOLD THOUSANDS OF WHITE HOUSE VISITORS.
BUT AS OF TODAY, FOR HEAD TULIP EDDY, THE PERENNIALS ARE OVER. ON THE RECOMMENDATION OF THE CARTER TRANSITION TEAM, THE TOP BULB WAS UNCEREMONIOUSLY REMOVED FROM THE GARDEN.
B.J., WHO IS DORMANT THIS TIME OF YEAR, HAD NO COMMENT.
GBTrudeau

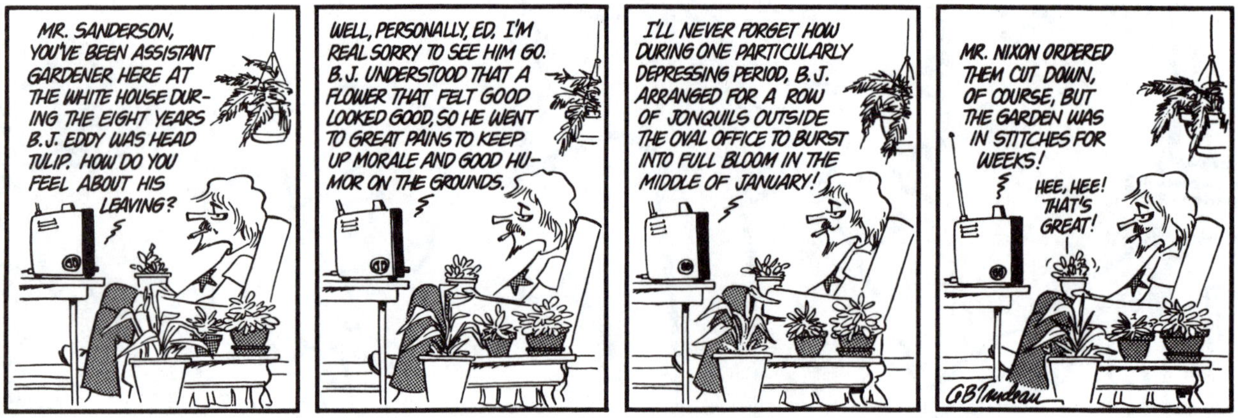
MR. SANDERSON, YOU'VE BEEN ASSISTANT GARDENER HERE AT THE WHITE HOUSE DURING THE EIGHT YEARS B.J. EDDY WAS HEAD TULIP. HOW DO YOU FEEL ABOUT HIS LEAVING?
WELL, PERSONALLY, ED, I'M REAL SORRY TO SEE HIM GO. B.J. UNDERSTOOD THAT A FLOWER THAT FELT GOOD LOOKED GOOD, SO HE WENT TO GREAT PAINS TO KEEP UP MORALE AND GOOD HUMOR ON THE GROUNDS.
I'LL NEVER FORGET HOW DURING ONE PARTICULARLY DEPRESSING PERIOD, B.J. ARRANGED FOR A ROW OF JONQUILS OUTSIDE THE OVAL OFFICE TO BURST INTO FULL BLOOM IN THE MIDDLE OF JANUARY!
MR. NIXON ORDERED THEM CUT DOWN, OF COURSE, BUT THE GARDEN WAS IN STITCHES FOR WEEKS!
HEE, HEE! THAT'S GREAT!
GBTrudeau

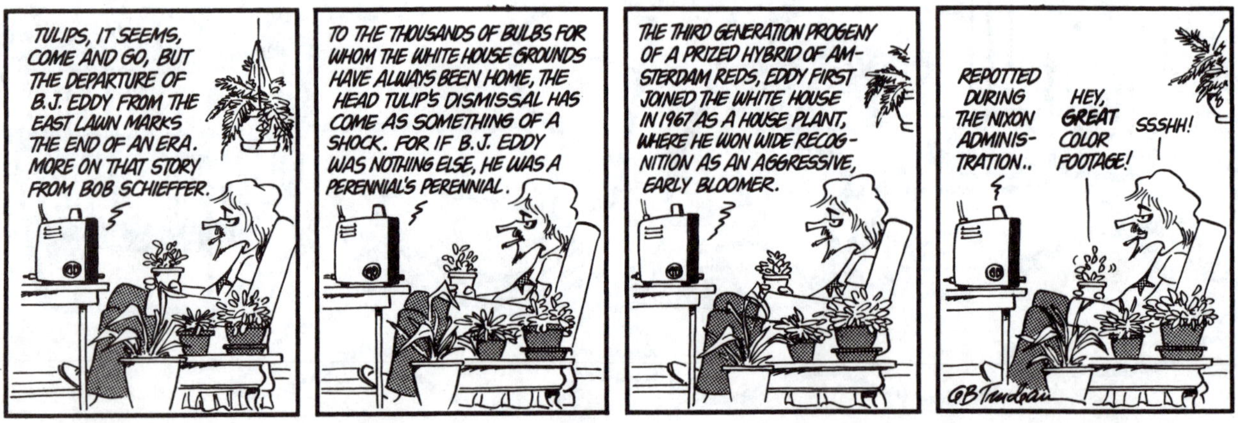
TULIPS, IT SEEMS, COME AND GO, BUT THE DEPARTURE OF B.J. EDDY FROM THE EAST LAWN MARKS THE END OF AN ERA. MORE ON THAT STORY FROM BOB SCHIEFFER.
TO THE THOUSANDS OF BULBS FOR WHOM THE WHITE HOUSE GROUNDS HAVE ALWAYS BEEN HOME, THE HEAD TULIP'S DISMISSAL HAS COME AS SOMETHING OF A SHOCK. FOR IF B.J. EDDY WAS NOTHING ELSE, HE WAS A PERENNIAL'S PERENNIAL.
THE THIRD GENERATION PROGENY OF A PRIZED HYBRID OF AMSTERDAM REDS, EDDY FIRST JOINED THE WHITE HOUSE IN 1967 AS A HOUSE PLANT, WHERE HE WON WIDE RECOGNITION AS AN AGGRESSIVE, EARLY BLOOMER.
REPOTTED DURING THE NIXON ADMINISTRATION..
HEY, GREAT COLOR FOOTAGE!
SSSHH!
GBTrudeau

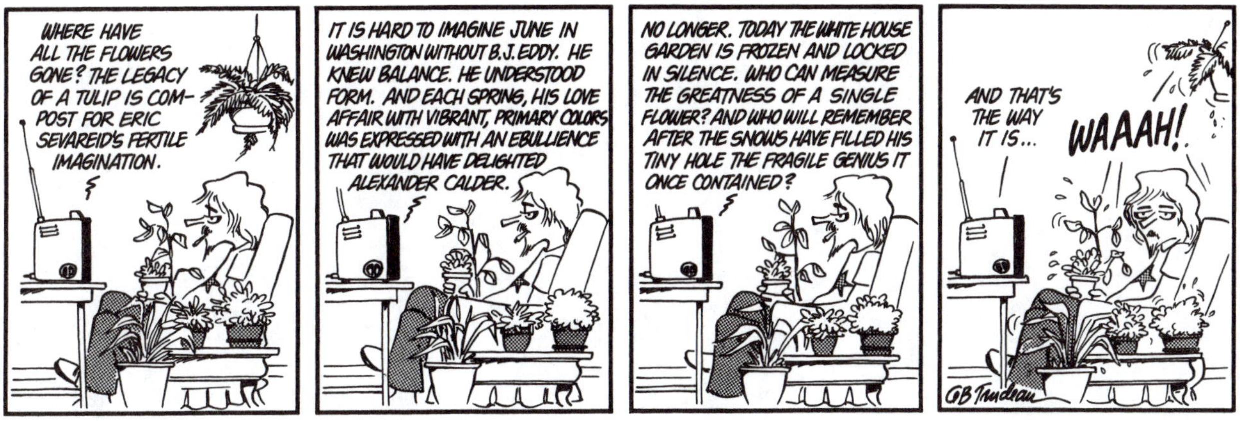
WHERE HAVE ALL THE FLOWERS GONE? THE LEGACY OF A TULIP IS COMPOST FOR ERIC SEVAREID'S FERTILE IMAGINATION.
IT IS HARD TO IMAGINE JUNE IN WASHINGTON WITHOUT B.J. EDDY. HE KNEW BALANCE. HE UNDERSTOOD FORM. AND EACH SPRING, HIS LOVE AFFAIR WITH VIBRANT, PRIMARY COLORS WAS EXPRESSED WITH AN EBULLIENCE THAT WOULD HAVE DELIGHTED ALEXANDER CALDER.
NO LONGER. TODAY THE WHITE HOUSE GARDEN IS FROZEN AND LOCKED IN SILENCE. WHO CAN MEASURE THE GREATNESS OF A SINGLE FLOWER? AND WHO WILL REMEMBER AFTER THE SNOWS HAVE FILLED HIS TINY HOLE THE FRAGILE GENIUS IT ONCE CONTAINED?
AND THAT'S THE WAY IT IS...
WAAAH!
G B Trudeau

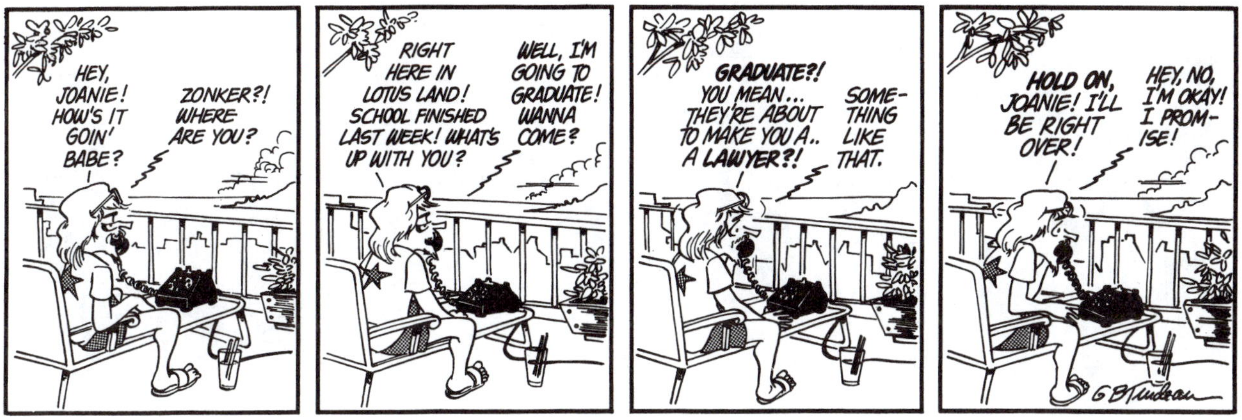
HEY, JOANIE! HOW'S IT GOIN' BABE?
ZONKER?! WHERE ARE YOU?
RIGHT HERE IN LOTUS LAND! SCHOOL FINISHED LAST WEEK! WHAT'S UP WITH YOU?
WELL, I'M GOING TO GRADUATE! WANNA COME?
GRADUATE?! YOU MEAN... THEY'RE ABOUT TO MAKE YOU A.. A LAWYER?!
SOMETHING LIKE THAT.
HOLD ON, JOANIE! I'LL BE RIGHT OVER!
HEY, NO, I'M OKAY! I PROMISE!
G B Trudeau

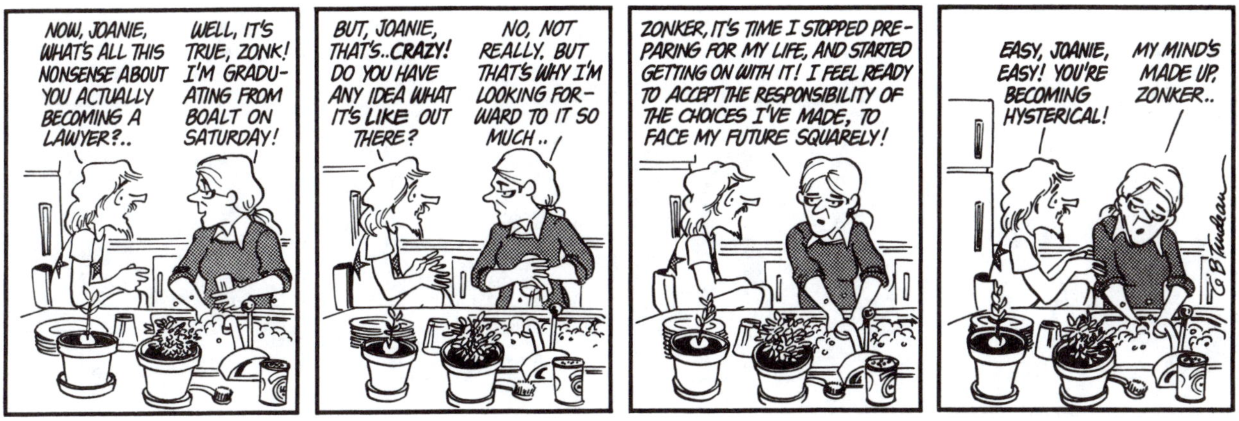
NOW, JOANIE, WHAT'S ALL THIS NONSENSE ABOUT YOU ACTUALLY BECOMING A LAWYER?..
WELL, IT'S TRUE, ZONK! I'M GRADUATING FROM BOALT ON SATURDAY!
BUT, JOANIE, THAT'S..CRAZY! DO YOU HAVE ANY IDEA WHAT IT'S LIKE OUT THERE?
NO, NOT REALLY, BUT THAT'S WHY I'M LOOKING FORWARD TO IT SO MUCH..
ZONKER, IT'S TIME I STOPPED PREPARING FOR MY LIFE, AND STARTED GETTING ON WITH IT! I FEEL READY TO ACCEPT THE RESPONSIBILITY OF THE CHOICES I'VE MADE, TO FACE MY FUTURE SQUARELY!
EASY, JOANIE, EASY! YOU'RE BECOMING HYSTERICAL!
MY MIND'S MADE UP, ZONKER..
G B Trudeau

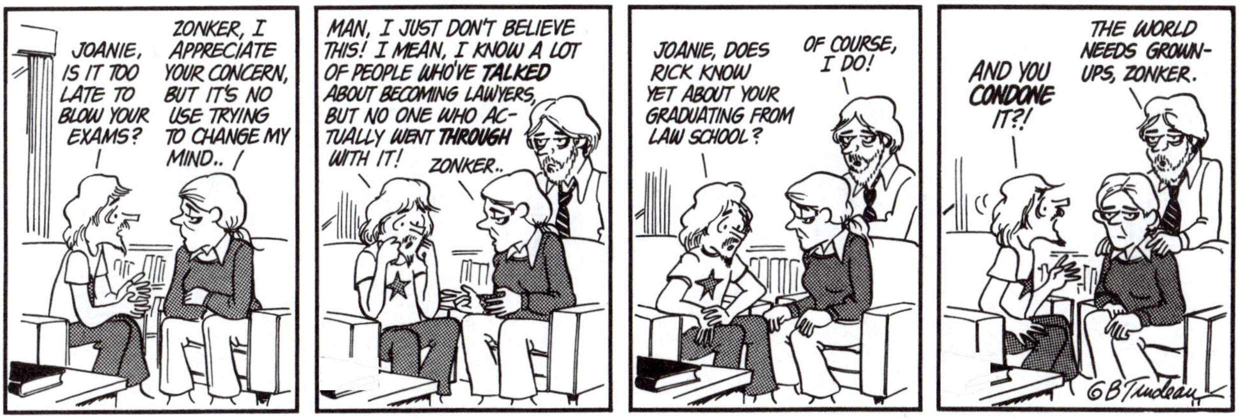
JOANIE, IS IT TOO LATE TO BLOW YOUR EXAMS?
ZONKER, I APPRECIATE YOUR CONCERN, BUT IT'S NO USE TRYING TO CHANGE MY MIND..
MAN, I JUST DON'T BELIEVE THIS! I MEAN, I KNOW A LOT OF PEOPLE WHO'VE TALKED ABOUT BECOMING LAWYERS, BUT NO ONE WHO ACTUALLY WENT THROUGH WITH IT!
ZONKER..
JOANIE, DOES RICK KNOW YET ABOUT YOUR GRADUATING FROM LAW SCHOOL?
OF COURSE, I DO!
AND YOU CONDONE IT?!
THE WORLD NEEDS GROWN-UPS, ZONKER.
G B Trudeau

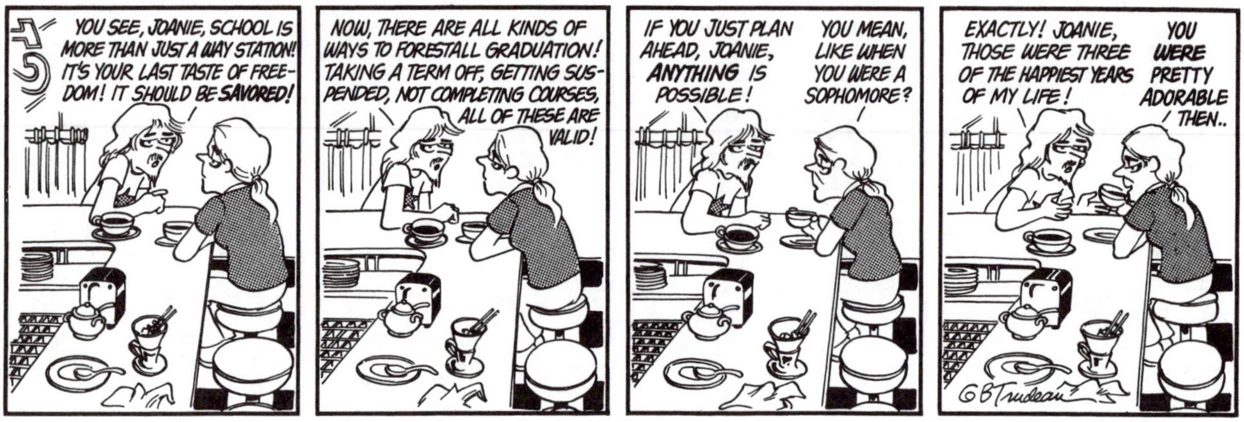
YOU SEE, JOANIE, SCHOOL IS MORE THAN JUST A WAY STATION! IT'S YOUR LAST TASTE OF FREEDOM! IT SHOULD BE SAVORED!
NOW, THERE ARE ALL KINDS OF WAYS TO FORESTALL GRADUATION! TAKING A TERM OFF, GETTING SUSPENDED, NOT COMPLETING COURSES, ALL OF THESE ARE VALID!
IF YOU JUST PLAN AHEAD, JOANIE, ANYTHING IS POSSIBLE!
YOU MEAN, LIKE WHEN YOU WERE A SOPHOMORE?
EXACTLY! JOANIE, THOSE WERE THREE OF THE HAPPIEST YEARS OF MY LIFE!
YOU WERE PRETTY ADORABLE THEN..

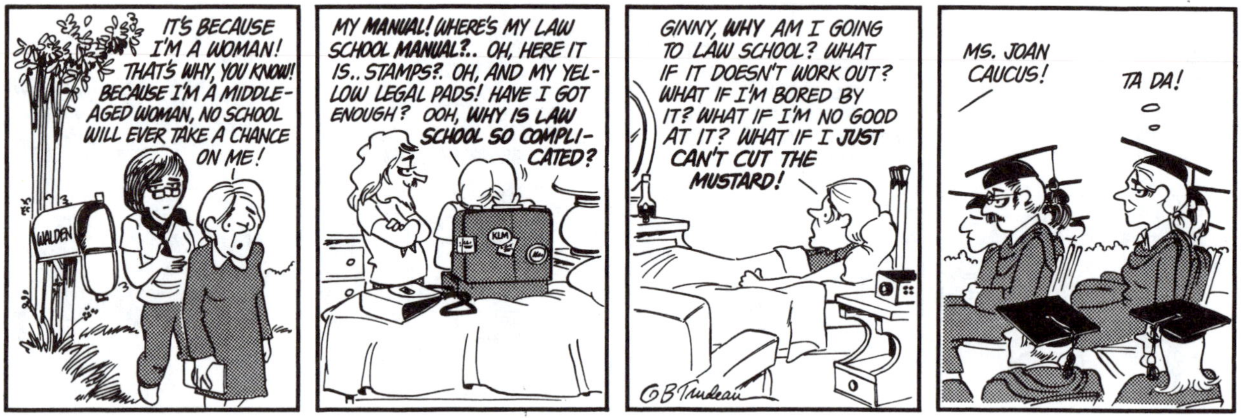
IT'S BECAUSE I'M A WOMAN! THAT'S WHY, YOU KNOW! BECAUSE I'M A MIDDLE-AGED WOMAN, NO SCHOOL WILL EVER TAKE A CHANCE ON ME!
WALDEN
MY MANUAL! WHERE'S MY LAW SCHOOL MANUAL?.. OH, HERE IT IS.. STAMPS?. OH, AND MY YELLOW LEGAL PADS! HAVE I GOT ENOUGH? OOH, WHY IS LAW SCHOOL SO COMPLICATED?
GINNY, WHY AM I GOING TO LAW SCHOOL? WHAT IF IT DOESN'T WORK OUT? WHAT IF I'M BORED BY IT? WHAT IF I'M NO GOOD AT IT? WHAT IF I JUST CAN'T CUT THE MUSTARD!
MS. JOAN CAUCUS!
TA DA!

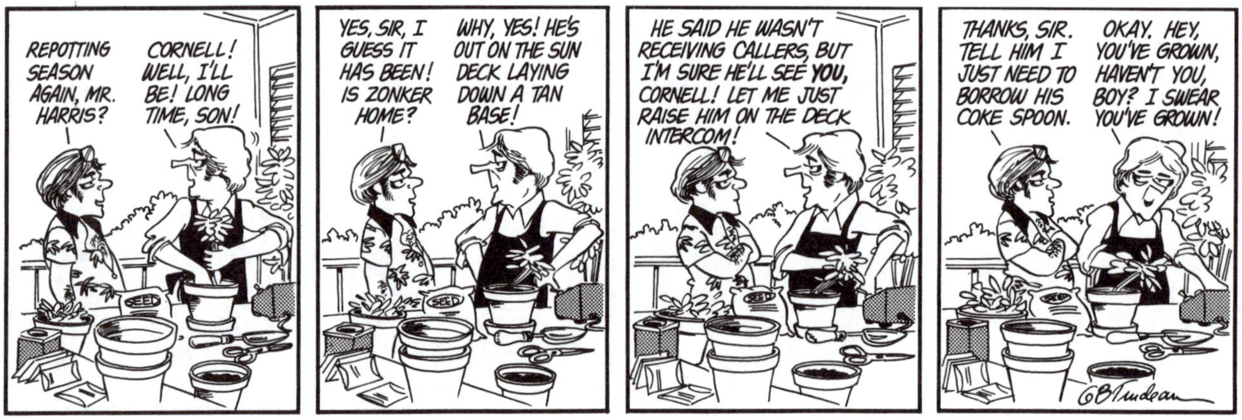
REPOTTING SEASON AGAIN, MR. HARRIS?
CORNELL! WELL, I'LL BE! LONG TIME, SON!
YES, SIR, I GUESS IT HAS BEEN! IS ZONKER HOME?
WHY, YES! HE'S OUT ON THE SUN DECK LAYING DOWN A TAN BASE!
HE SAID HE WASN'T RECEIVING CALLERS, BUT I'M SURE HE'LL SEE YOU, CORNELL! LET ME JUST RAISE HIM ON THE DECK INTERCOM!
THANKS, SIR. TELL HIM I JUST NEED TO BORROW HIS COKE SPOON.
OKAY. HEY, YOU'VE GROWN, HAVEN'T YOU, BOY? I SWEAR YOU'VE GROWN!

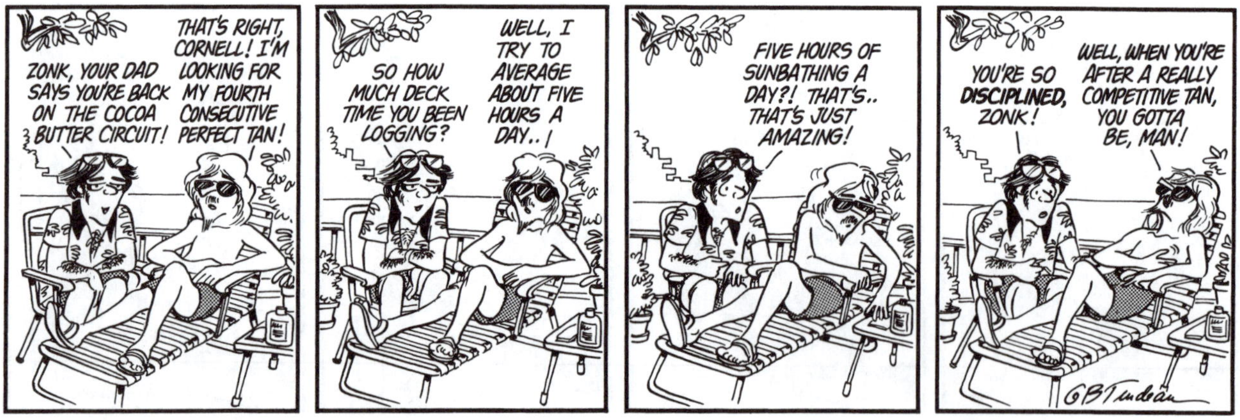
ZONK, YOUR DAD SAYS YOU'RE BACK ON THE COCOA BUTTER CIRCUIT!
THAT'S RIGHT, CORNELL! I'M LOOKING FOR MY FOURTH CONSECUTIVE PERFECT TAN!
SO HOW MUCH DECK TIME YOU BEEN LOGGING?
WELL, I TRY TO AVERAGE ABOUT FIVE HOURS A DAY..!
FIVE HOURS OF SUNBATHING A DAY?! THAT'S.. THAT'S JUST AMAZING!
YOU'RE SO DISCIPLINED, ZONK!
WELL, WHEN YOU'RE AFTER A REALLY COMPETITIVE TAN, YOU GOTTA BE, MAN!

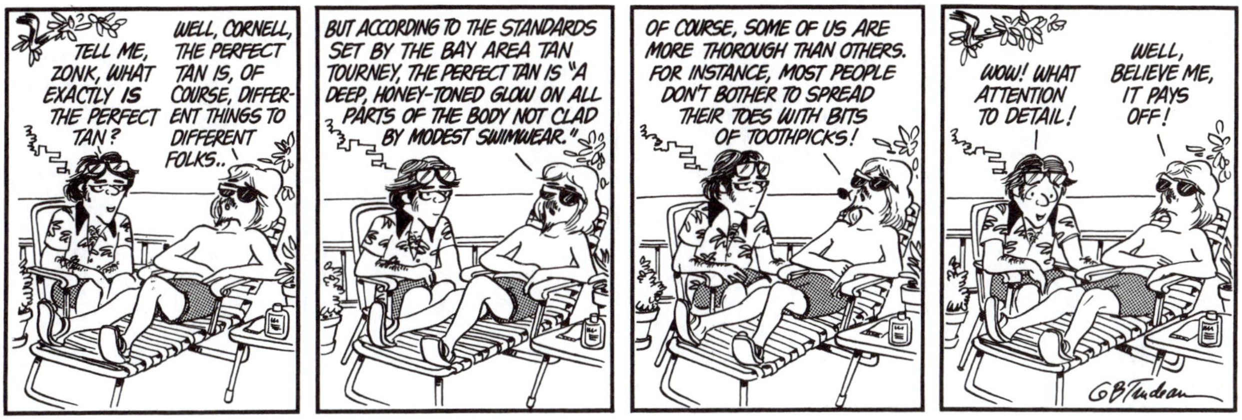
TELL ME, ZONK, WHAT EXACTLY IS THE PERFECT TAN?
WELL, CORNELL, THE PERFECT TAN IS, OF COURSE, DIFFERENT THINGS TO DIFFERENT FOLKS..
BUT ACCORDING TO THE STANDARDS SET BY THE BAY AREA TAN TOURNEY, THE PERFECT TAN IS "A DEEP, HONEY-TONED GLOW ON ALL PARTS OF THE BODY NOT CLAD BY MODEST SWIMWEAR."
OF COURSE, SOME OF US ARE MORE THOROUGH THAN OTHERS. FOR INSTANCE, MOST PEOPLE DON'T BOTHER TO SPREAD THEIR TOES WITH BITS OF TOOTHPICKS!
WOW! WHAT ATTENTION TO DETAIL!
WELL, BELIEVE ME, IT PAYS OFF!
GBTrudeau

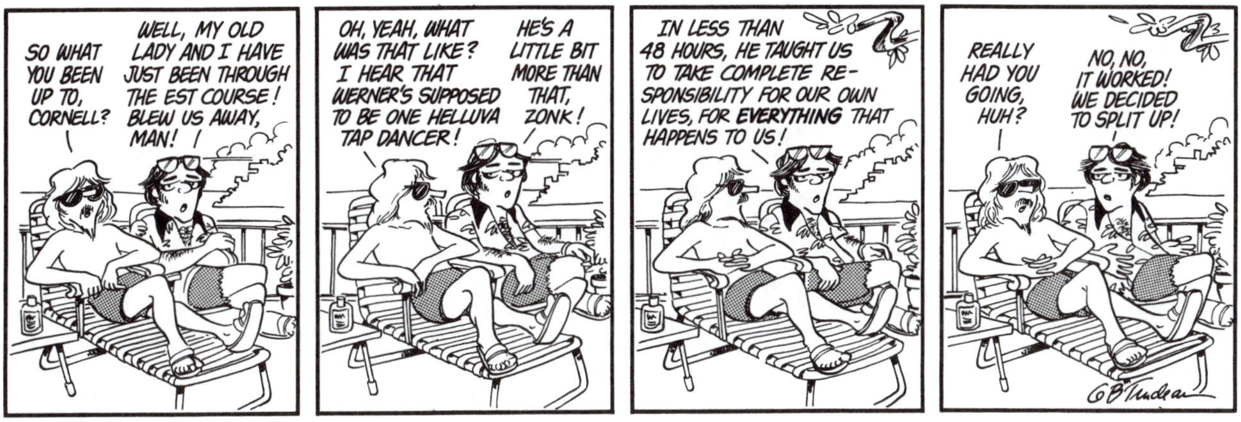
SO WHAT YOU BEEN UP TO, CORNELL?
WELL, MY OLD LADY AND I HAVE JUST BEEN THROUGH THE EST COURSE! BLEW US AWAY, MAN!
OH, YEAH, WHAT WAS THAT LIKE? I HEAR THAT WERNER'S SUPPOSED TO BE ONE HELLUVA TAP DANCER!
HE'S A LITTLE BIT MORE THAN THAT, ZONK!
IN LESS THAN 48 HOURS, HE TAUGHT US TO TAKE COMPLETE RESPONSIBILITY FOR OUR OWN LIVES, FOR EVERYTHING THAT HAPPENS TO US!
REALLY HAD YOU GOING, HUH?
NO, NO, IT WORKED! WE DECIDED TO SPLIT UP!
GBTrudeau

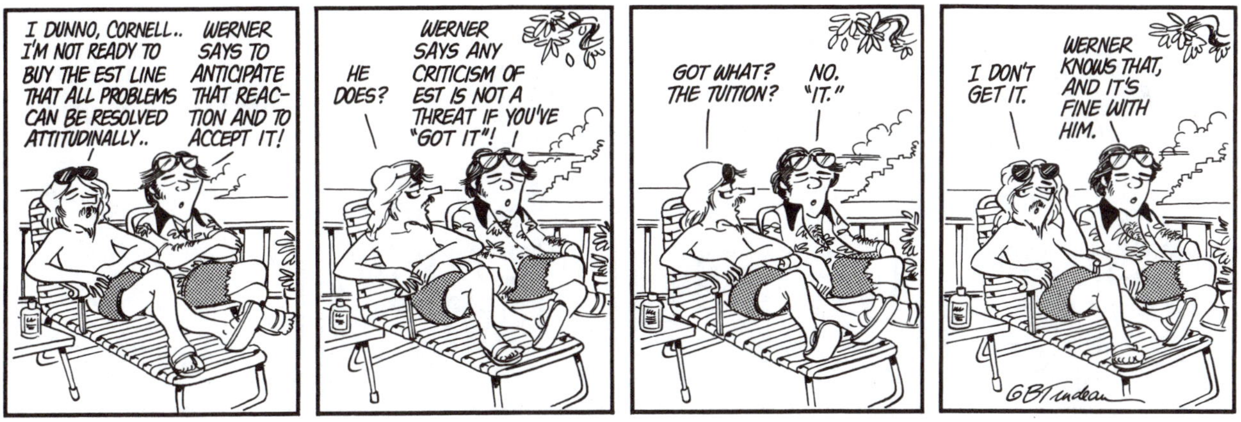
I DUNNO, CORNELL.. I'M NOT READY TO BUY THE EST LINE THAT ALL PROBLEMS CAN BE RESOLVED ATTITUDINALLY..
WERNER SAYS TO ANTICIPATE THAT REACTION AND TO ACCEPT IT!
HE DOES?
WERNER SAYS ANY CRITICISM OF EST IS NOT A THREAT IF YOU'VE "GOT IT"!
GOT WHAT? THE TUITION?
NO. "IT."
I DON'T GET IT.
WERNER KNOWS THAT, AND IT'S FINE WITH HIM.
GBTrudeau

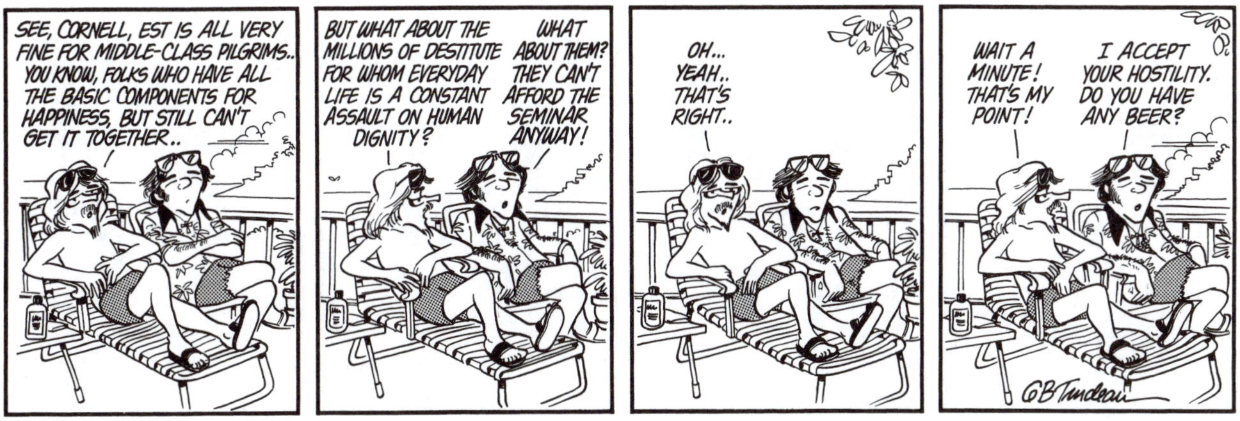
SEE, CORNELL, EST IS ALL VERY FINE FOR MIDDLE-CLASS PILGRIMS.. YOU KNOW, FOLKS WHO HAVE ALL THE BASIC COMPONENTS FOR HAPPINESS, BUT STILL CAN'T GET IT TOGETHER..
BUT WHAT ABOUT THE MILLIONS OF DESTITUTE FOR WHOM EVERYDAY LIFE IS A CONSTANT ASSAULT ON HUMAN DIGNITY?
WHAT ABOUT THEM? THEY CAN'T AFFORD THE SEMINAR ANYWAY!
OH... YEAH.. THAT'S RIGHT..
WAIT A MINUTE! THAT'S MY POINT!
I ACCEPT YOUR HOSTILITY. DO YOU HAVE ANY BEER?
GBTrudeau

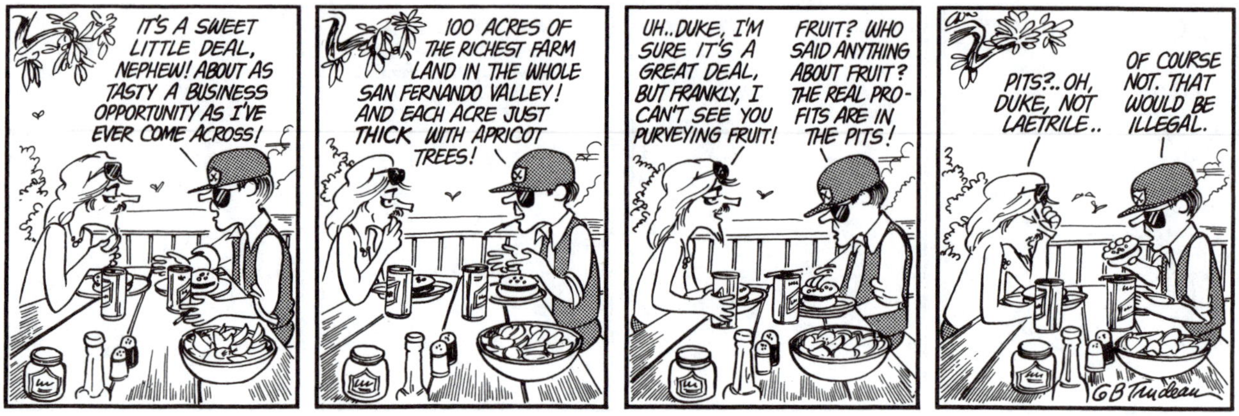
IT'S A SWEET LITTLE DEAL, NEPHEW! ABOUT AS TASTY A BUSINESS OPPORTUNITY AS I'VE EVER COME ACROSS!
100 ACRES OF THE RICHEST FARM LAND IN THE WHOLE SAN FERNANDO VALLEY! AND EACH ACRE JUST THICK WITH APRICOT TREES!
UH..DUKE, I'M SURE IT'S A GREAT DEAL, BUT FRANKLY, I CAN'T SEE YOU PURVEYING FRUIT!
FRUIT? WHO SAID ANYTHING ABOUT FRUIT? THE REAL PROFITS ARE IN THE PITS!
PITS?..OH, DUKE, NOT LAETRILE..
OF COURSE NOT. THAT WOULD BE ILLEGAL.
GB Trudeau

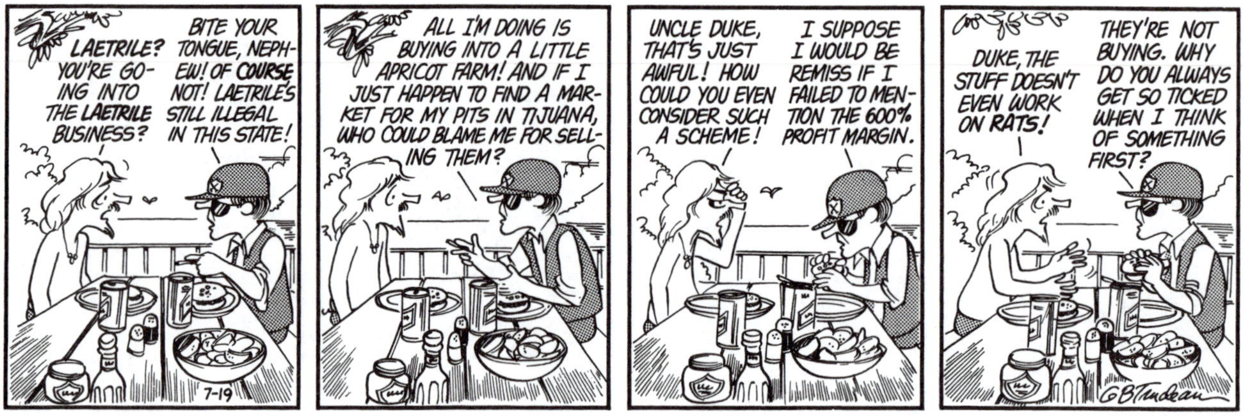
LAETRILE? YOU'RE GOING INTO THE LAETRILE BUSINESS?
BITE YOUR TONGUE, NEPHEW! OF COURSE NOT! LAETRILE'S STILL ILLEGAL IN THIS STATE!
7-19
ALL I'M DOING IS BUYING INTO A LITTLE APRICOT FARM! AND IF I JUST HAPPEN TO FIND A MARKET FOR MY PITS IN TIJUANA, WHO COULD BLAME ME FOR SELLING THEM?
UNCLE DUKE, THAT'S JUST AWFUL! HOW COULD YOU EVEN CONSIDER SUCH A SCHEME!
I SUPPOSE I WOULD BE REMISS IF I FAILED TO MENTION THE 600% PROFIT MARGIN.
DUKE, THE STUFF DOESN'T EVEN WORK ON RATS!
THEY'RE NOT BUYING. WHY DO YOU ALWAYS GET SO TICKED WHEN I THINK OF SOMETHING FIRST?
GB Trudeau

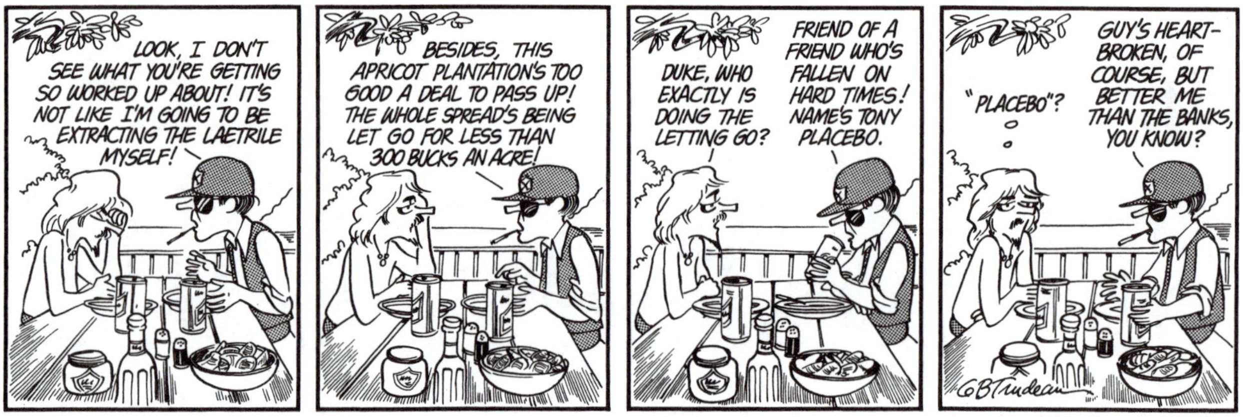
LOOK, I DON'T SEE WHAT YOU'RE GETTING SO WORKED UP ABOUT! IT'S NOT LIKE I'M GOING TO BE EXTRACTING THE LAETRILE MYSELF!
BESIDES, THIS APRICOT PLANTATION'S TOO GOOD A DEAL TO PASS UP! THE WHOLE SPREAD'S BEING LET GO FOR LESS THAN 300 BUCKS AN ACRE!
DUKE, WHO EXACTLY IS DOING THE LETTING GO?
FRIEND OF A FRIEND WHO'S FALLEN ON HARD TIMES! NAME'S TONY PLACEBO.
"PLACEBO"?
GUY'S HEARTBROKEN, OF COURSE, BUT BETTER ME THAN THE BANKS, YOU KNOW?
GB Trudeau

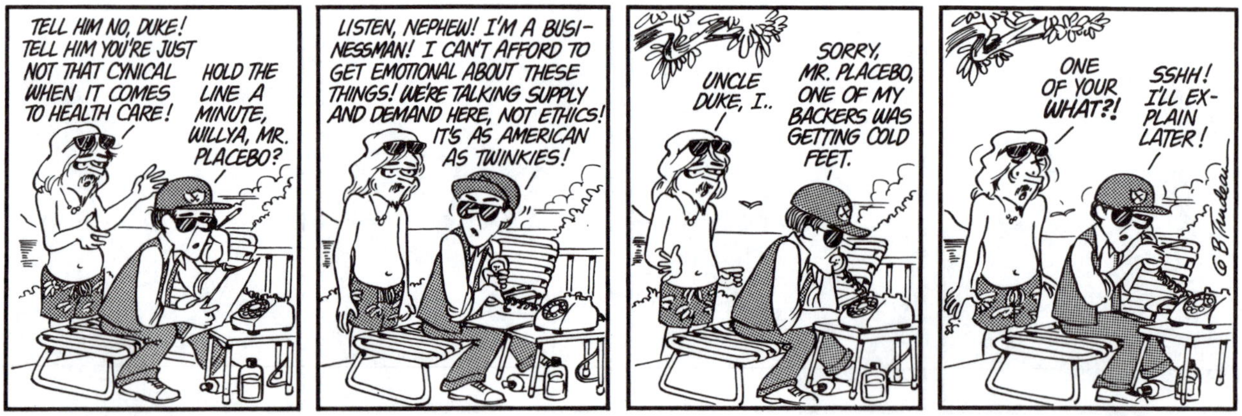
TELL HIM NO, DUKE! TELL HIM YOU'RE JUST NOT THAT CYNICAL WHEN IT COMES TO HEALTH CARE!
HOLD THE LINE A MINUTE, WILLYA, MR. PLACEBO?
LISTEN, NEPHEW! I'M A BUSINESSMAN! I CAN'T AFFORD TO GET EMOTIONAL ABOUT THESE THINGS! WE'RE TALKING SUPPLY AND DEMAND HERE, NOT ETHICS!
IT'S AS AMERICAN AS TWINKIES!
UNCLE DUKE, I..
SORRY, MR. PLACEBO, ONE OF MY BACKERS WAS GETTING COLD FEET.
ONE OF YOUR WHAT?!
SSHH! I'LL EXPLAIN LATER!
GB Trudeau

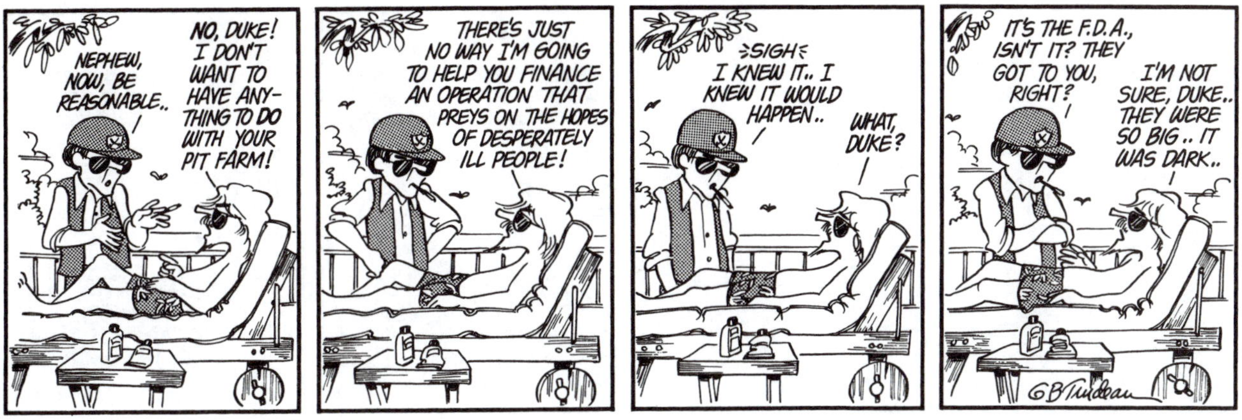
NEPHEW, NOW, BE REASONABLE..
NO, DUKE! I DON'T WANT TO HAVE ANYTHING TO DO WITH YOUR PIT FARM!
THERE'S JUST NO WAY I'M GOING TO HELP YOU FINANCE AN OPERATION THAT PREYS ON THE HOPES OF DESPERATELY ILL PEOPLE!
SIGH
I KNEW IT.. I KNEW IT WOULD HAPPEN..
WHAT, DUKE?
IT'S THE F.D.A., ISN'T IT? THEY GOT TO YOU, RIGHT?
I'M NOT SURE, DUKE.. THEY WERE SO BIG.. IT WAS DARK..
GBTrudeau

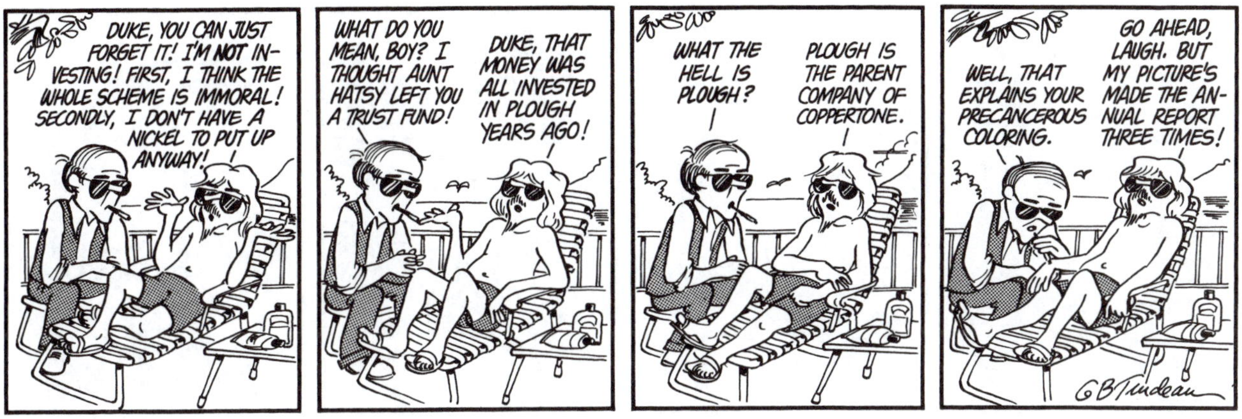
DUKE, YOU CAN JUST FORGET IT! I'M NOT INVESTING! FIRST, I THINK THE WHOLE SCHEME IS IMMORAL! SECONDLY, I DON'T HAVE A NICKEL TO PUT UP ANYWAY!
WHAT DO YOU MEAN, BOY? I THOUGHT AUNT HATSY LEFT YOU A TRUST FUND!
DUKE, THAT MONEY WAS ALL INVESTED IN PLOUGH YEARS AGO!
WHAT THE HELL IS PLOUGH?
PLOUGH IS THE PARENT COMPANY OF COPPERTONE.
WELL, THAT EXPLAINS YOUR PRECANCEROUS COLORING.
GO AHEAD, LAUGH. BUT MY PICTURE'S MADE THE ANNUAL REPORT THREE TIMES!
GBTrudeau

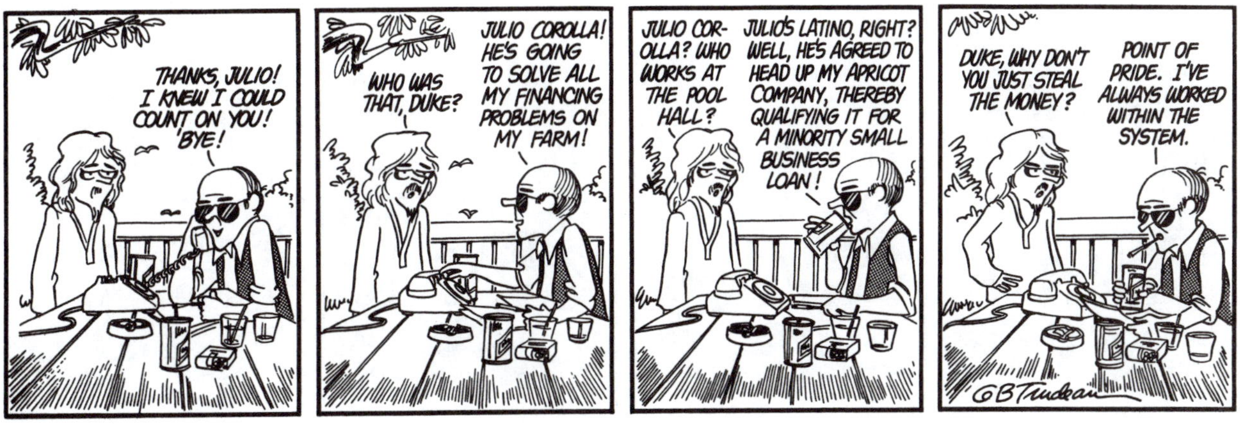
THANKS, JULIO! I KNEW I COULD COUNT ON YOU! 'BYE!
WHO WAS THAT, DUKE?
JULIO COROLLA! HE'S GOING TO SOLVE ALL MY FINANCING PROBLEMS ON MY FARM!
JULIO COROLLA? WHO WORKS AT THE POOL HALL?
JULIO'S LATINO, RIGHT? WELL, HE'S AGREED TO HEAD UP MY APRICOT COMPANY, THEREBY QUALIFYING IT FOR A MINORITY SMALL BUSINESS LOAN!
DUKE, WHY DON'T YOU JUST STEAL THE MONEY?
POINT OF PRIDE. I'VE ALWAYS WORKED WITHIN THE SYSTEM.
GBTrudeau

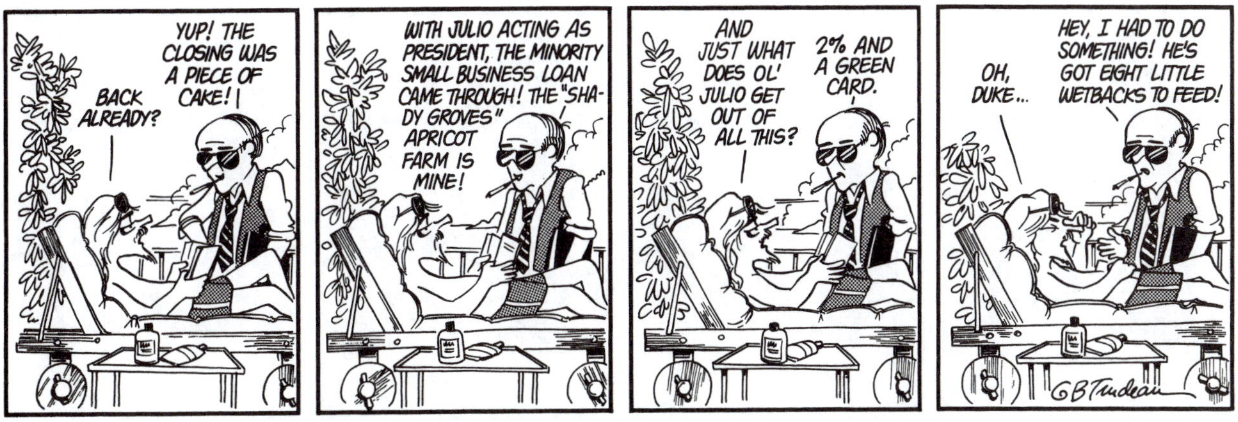
BACK ALREADY?
YUP! THE CLOSING WAS A PIECE OF CAKE!
WITH JULIO ACTING AS PRESIDENT, THE MINORITY SMALL BUSINESS LOAN CAME THROUGH! THE "SHADY GROVES" APRICOT FARM IS MINE!
AND JUST WHAT DOES OL' JULIO GET OUT OF ALL THIS?
2% AND A GREEN CARD.
OH, DUKE...
HEY, I HAD TO DO SOMETHING! HE'S GOT EIGHT LITTLE WETBACKS TO FEED!
GBTrudeau

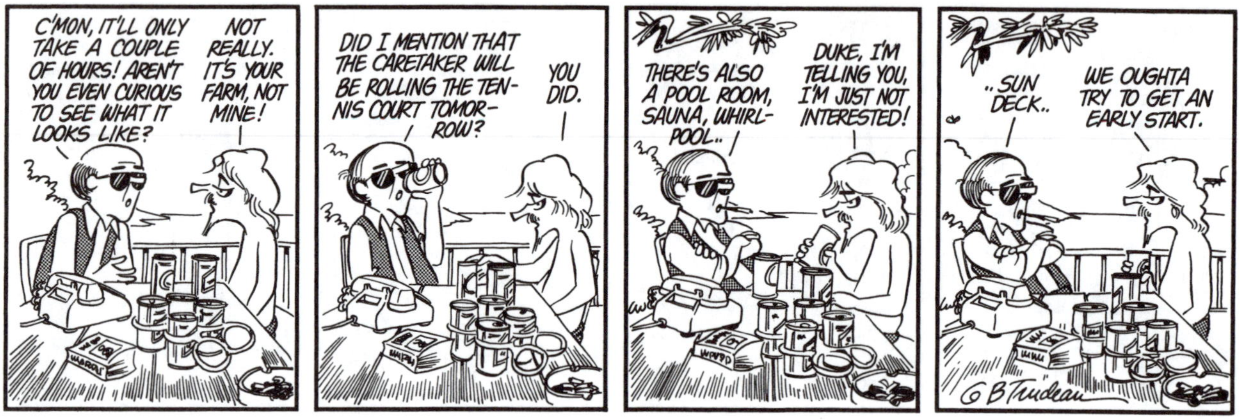
C'MON, IT'LL ONLY TAKE A COUPLE OF HOURS! AREN'T YOU EVEN CURIOUS TO SEE WHAT IT LOOKS LIKE?
NOT REALLY. IT'S YOUR FARM, NOT MINE!
DID I MENTION THAT THE CARETAKER WILL BE ROLLING THE TENNIS COURT TOMORROW?
YOU DID.
THERE'S ALSO A POOL ROOM, SAUNA, WHIRLPOOL..
DUKE, I'M TELLING YOU, I'M JUST NOT INTERESTED!
..SUN DECK..
WE OUGHTA TRY TO GET AN EARLY START.
GBTrudeau

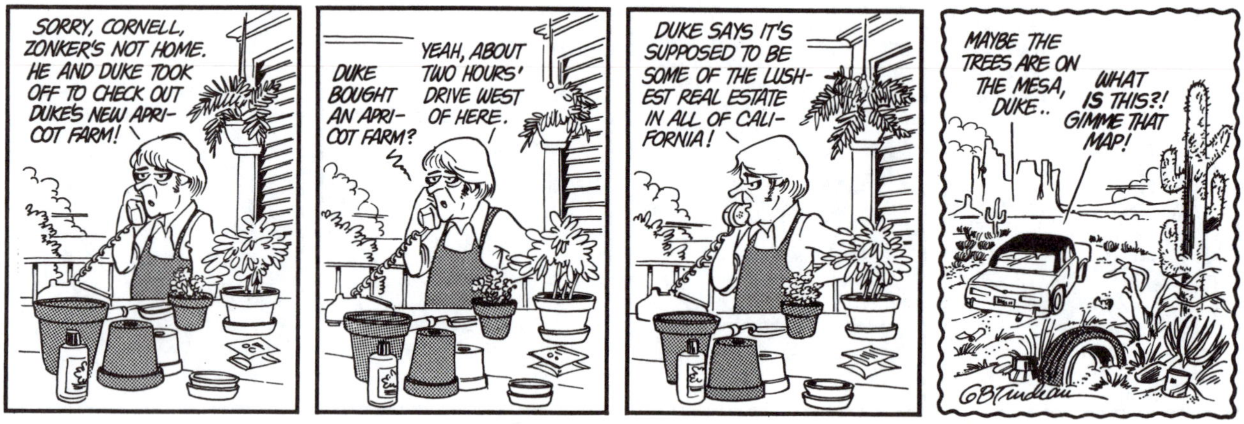
SORRY, CORNELL, ZONKER'S NOT HOME. HE AND DUKE TOOK OFF TO CHECK OUT DUKE'S NEW APRICOT FARM!
DUKE BOUGHT AN APRICOT FARM?
YEAH, ABOUT TWO HOURS' DRIVE WEST OF HERE.
DUKE SAYS IT'S SUPPOSED TO BE SOME OF THE LUSHEST REAL ESTATE IN ALL OF CALIFORNIA!
MAYBE THE TREES ARE ON THE MESA, DUKE..
WHAT IS THIS?! GIMME THAT MAP!
GBTrudeau

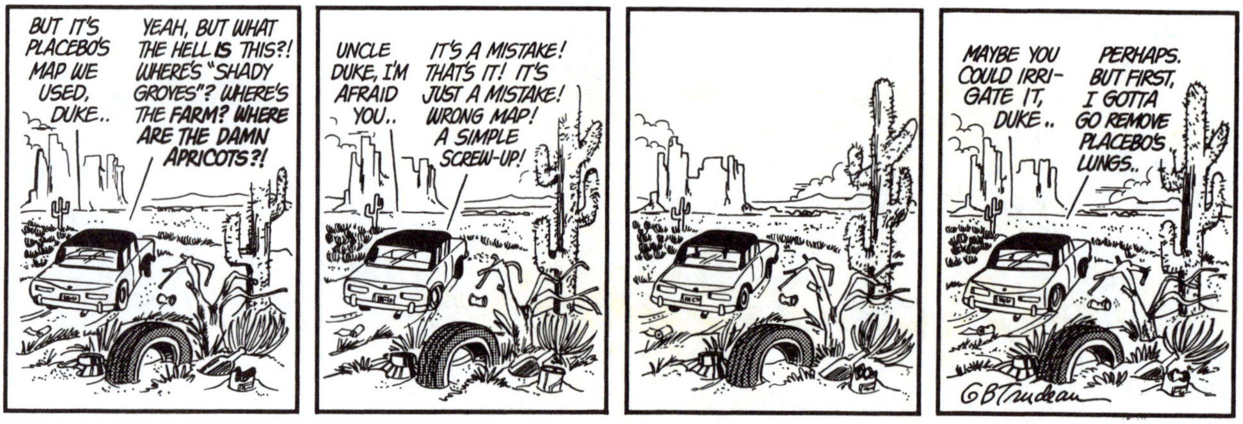
BUT IT'S PLACEBO'S MAP WE USED, DUKE..
YEAH, BUT WHAT THE HELL IS THIS?! WHERE'S "SHADY GROVES"? WHERE'S THE FARM? WHERE ARE THE DAMN APRICOTS?!
UNCLE DUKE, I'M AFRAID YOU..
IT'S A MISTAKE! THAT'S IT! IT'S JUST A MISTAKE! WRONG MAP! A SIMPLE SCREW-UP!
MAYBE YOU COULD IRRIGATE IT, DUKE..
PERHAPS. BUT FIRST, I GOTTA GO REMOVE PLACEBO'S LUNGS..
GBTrudeau

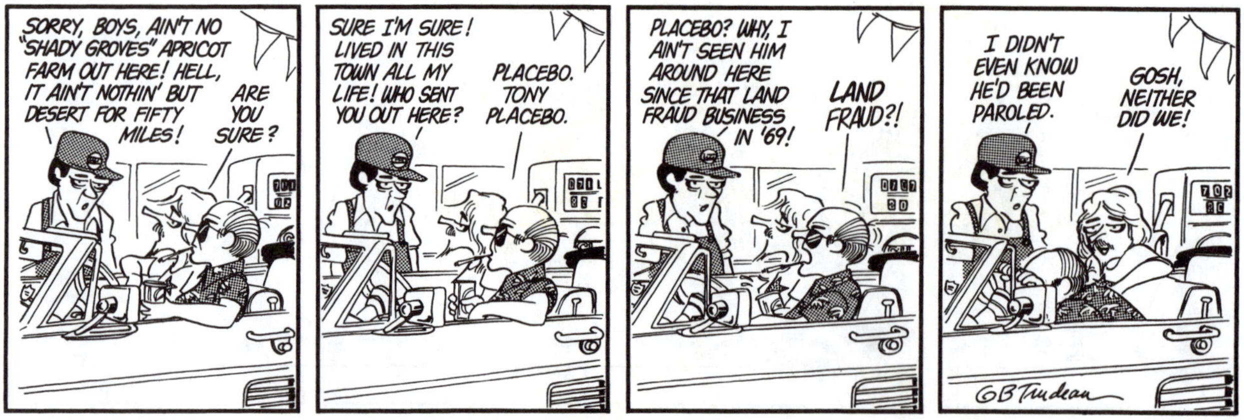
SORRY, BOYS, AIN'T NO "SHADY GROVES" APRICOT FARM OUT HERE! HELL, IT AIN'T NOTHIN' BUT DESERT FOR FIFTY MILES!
ARE YOU SURE?
SURE I'M SURE! LIVED IN THIS TOWN ALL MY LIFE! WHO SENT YOU OUT HERE?
PLACEBO. TONY PLACEBO.
PLACEBO? WHY, I AIN'T SEEN HIM AROUND HERE SINCE THAT LAND FRAUD BUSINESS IN '69!
LAND FRAUD?!
I DIDN'T EVEN KNOW HE'D BEEN PAROLED.
GOSH, NEITHER DID WE!
GBTrudeau

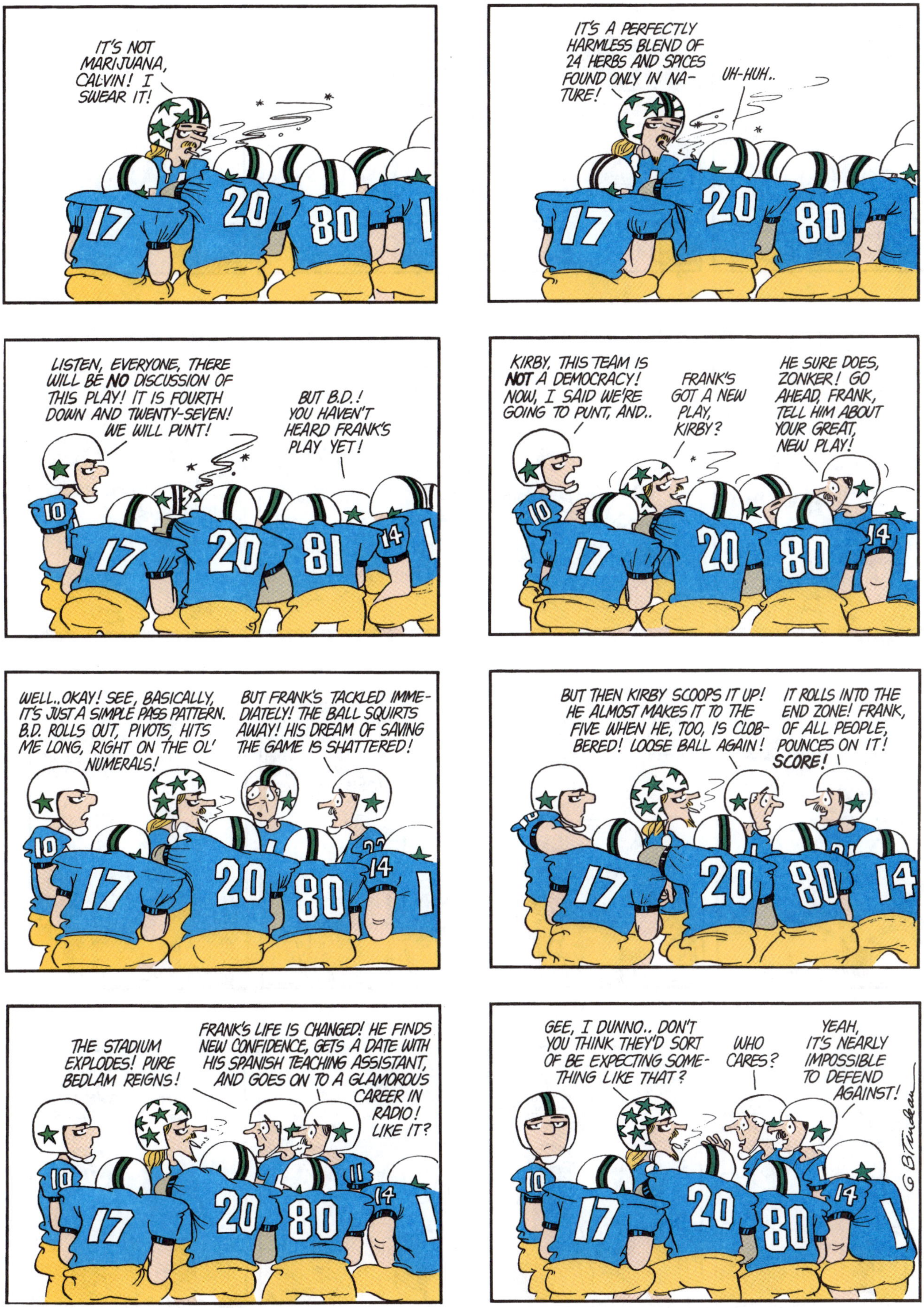
IT'S NOT MARIJUANA, CALVIN! I SWEAR IT!
IT'S A PERFECTLY HARMLESS BLEND OF 24 HERBS AND SPICES FOUND ONLY IN NATURE!
UH-HUH..
LISTEN, EVERYONE, THERE WILL BE **NO** DISCUSSION OF THIS PLAY! IT IS FOURTH DOWN AND TWENTY-SEVEN! WE WILL PUNT!
BUT B.D.! YOU HAVEN'T HEARD FRANK'S PLAY YET!
KIRBY, THIS TEAM IS **NOT** A DEMOCRACY! NOW, I SAID WE'RE GOING TO PUNT, AND..
FRANK'S GOT A NEW PLAY, KIRBY?
HE SURE DOES, ZONKER! GO AHEAD, FRANK, TELL HIM ABOUT YOUR GREAT, NEW PLAY!
WELL..OKAY! SEE, BASICALLY, IT'S JUST A SIMPLE PASS PATTERN. B.D. ROLLS OUT, PIVOTS, HITS ME LONG, RIGHT ON THE OL' NUMERALS!
BUT FRANK'S TACKLED IMMEDIATELY! THE BALL SQUIRTS AWAY! HIS DREAM OF SAVING THE GAME IS SHATTERED!
BUT THEN KIRBY SCOOPS IT UP! HE ALMOST MAKES IT TO THE FIVE WHEN HE, TOO, IS CLOBBERED! LOOSE BALL AGAIN!
IT ROLLS INTO THE END ZONE! FRANK, OF ALL PEOPLE, POUNCES ON IT! **SCORE!**
THE STADIUM EXPLODES! PURE BEDLAM REIGNS!
FRANK'S LIFE IS CHANGED! HE FINDS NEW CONFIDENCE, GETS A DATE WITH HIS SPANISH TEACHING ASSISTANT, AND GOES ON TO A GLAMOROUS CAREER IN RADIO! LIKE IT?
GEE, I DUNNO.. DON'T YOU THINK THEY'D SORT OF BE EXPECTING SOMETHING LIKE THAT?
WHO CARES?
YEAH, IT'S NEARLY IMPOSSIBLE TO DEFEND AGAINST!

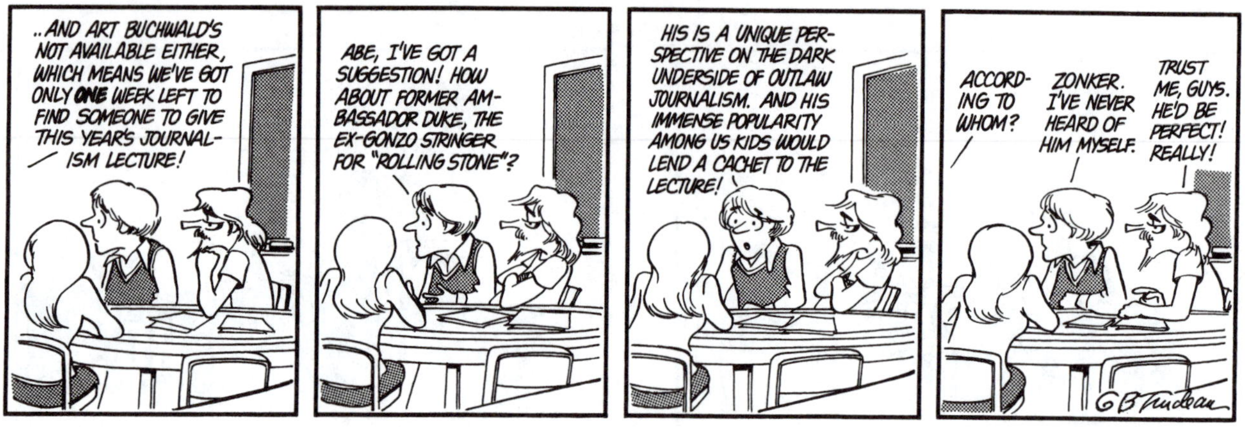
..AND ART BUCHWALD'S NOT AVAILABLE EITHER, WHICH MEANS WE'VE GOT ONLY **ONE** WEEK LEFT TO FIND SOMEONE TO GIVE THIS YEAR'S JOURNALISM LECTURE!
ABE, I'VE GOT A SUGGESTION! HOW ABOUT FORMER AMBASSADOR DUKE, THE EX-GONZO STRINGER FOR "ROLLING STONE"?
HIS IS A UNIQUE PERSPECTIVE ON THE DARK UNDERSIDE OF OUTLAW JOURNALISM. AND HIS IMMENSE POPULARITY AMONG US KIDS WOULD LEND A CACHET TO THE LECTURE!
ACCORDING TO WHOM?
ZONKER. I'VE NEVER HEARD OF HIM MYSELF.
TRUST ME, GUYS. HE'D BE PERFECT! REALLY!

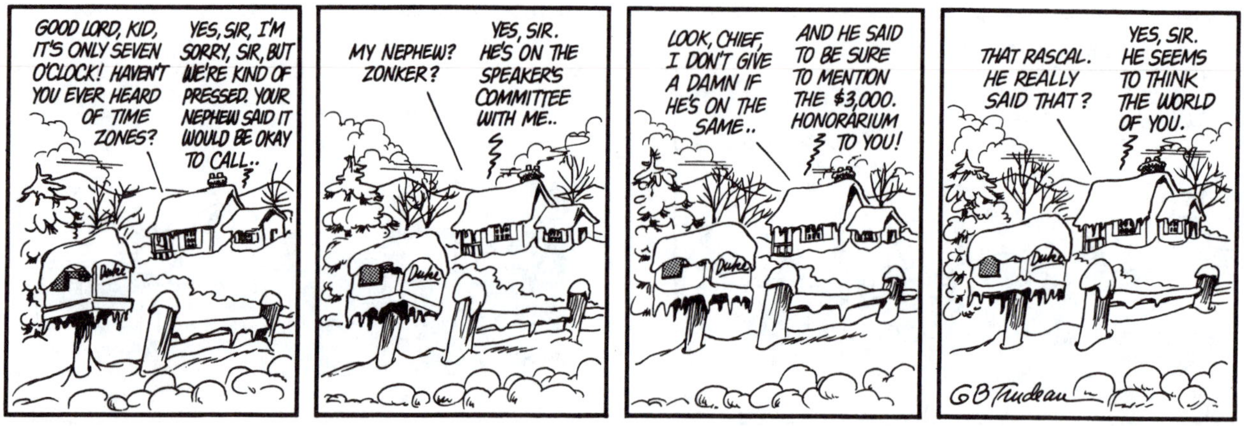
GOOD LORD, KID, IT'S ONLY SEVEN O'CLOCK! HAVEN'T YOU EVER HEARD OF TIME ZONES?
YES, SIR, I'M SORRY, SIR, BUT WE'RE KIND OF PRESSED. YOUR NEPHEW SAID IT WOULD BE OKAY TO CALL..
MY NEPHEW? ZONKER?
YES, SIR. HE'S ON THE SPEAKER'S COMMITTEE WITH ME..
LOOK, CHIEF, I DON'T GIVE A DAMN IF HE'S ON THE SAME..
AND HE SAID TO BE SURE TO MENTION THE $3,000. HONORARIUM TO YOU!
THAT RASCAL. HE REALLY SAID THAT?
YES, SIR. HE SEEMS TO THINK THE WORLD OF YOU.

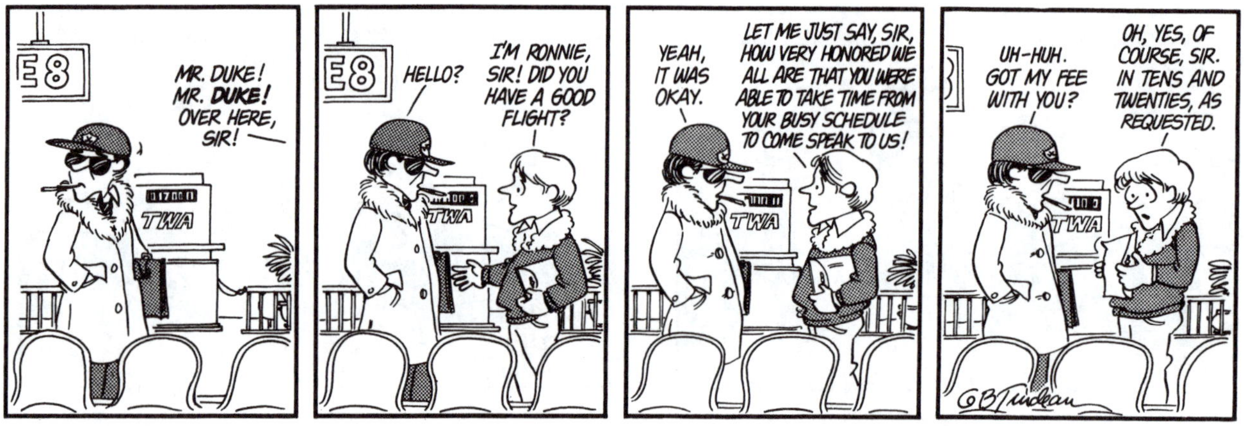
MR. DUKE! MR. **DUKE!** OVER HERE, SIR!
HELLO?
I'M RONNIE, SIR! DID YOU HAVE A GOOD FLIGHT?
YEAH, IT WAS OKAY.
LET ME JUST SAY, SIR, HOW VERY HONORED WE ALL ARE THAT YOU WERE ABLE TO TAKE TIME FROM YOUR BUSY SCHEDULE TO COME SPEAK TO US!
UH-HUH. GOT MY FEE WITH YOU?
OH, YES, OF COURSE, SIR. IN TENS AND TWENTIES, AS REQUESTED.

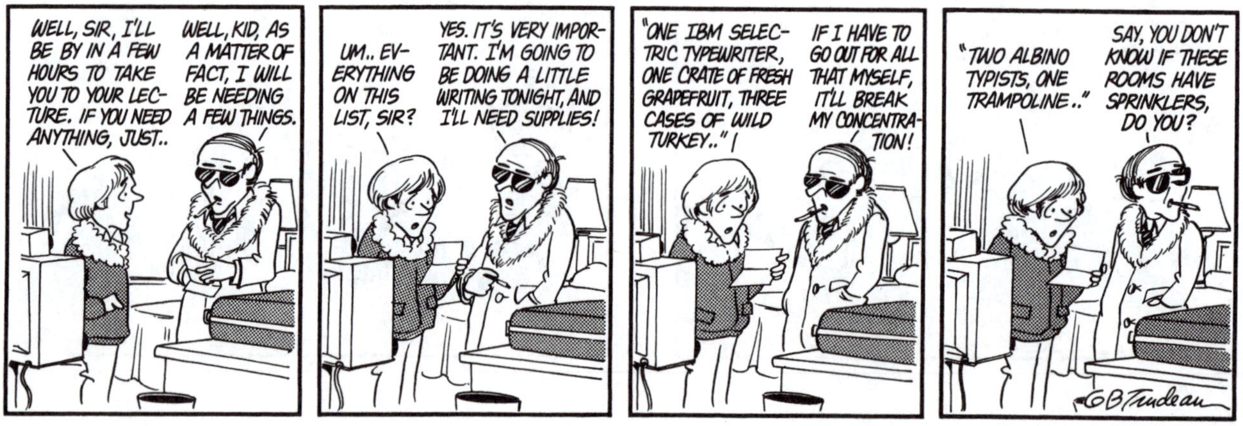
WELL, SIR, I'LL BE BY IN A FEW HOURS TO TAKE YOU TO YOUR LECTURE. IF YOU NEED ANYTHING, JUST..
WELL, KID, AS A MATTER OF FACT, I WILL BE NEEDING A FEW THINGS.
UM.. EVERYTHING ON THIS LIST, SIR?
YES. IT'S VERY IMPORTANT. I'M GOING TO BE DOING A LITTLE WRITING TONIGHT, AND I'LL NEED SUPPLIES!
"ONE IBM SELECTRIC TYPEWRITER, ONE CRATE OF FRESH GRAPEFRUIT, THREE CASES OF WILD TURKEY.."
IF I HAVE TO GO OUT FOR ALL THAT MYSELF, IT'LL BREAK MY CONCENTRATION!
"TWO ALBINO TYPISTS, ONE TRAMPOLINE.."
SAY, YOU DON'T KNOW IF THESE ROOMS HAVE SPRINKLERS, DO YOU?

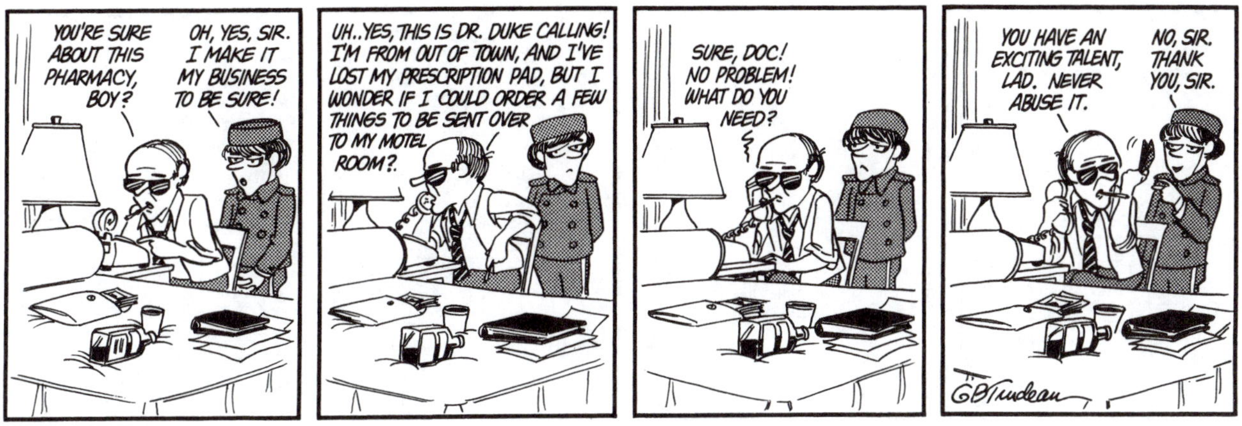
YOU'RE SURE ABOUT THIS PHARMACY, BOY?
OH, YES, SIR. I MAKE IT MY BUSINESS TO BE SURE!
UH..YES, THIS IS DR. DUKE CALLING! I'M FROM OUT OF TOWN, AND I'VE LOST MY PRESCRIPTION PAD, BUT I WONDER IF I COULD ORDER A FEW THINGS TO BE SENT OVER TO MY MOTEL ROOM?.
SURE, DOC! NO PROBLEM! WHAT DO YOU NEED?
YOU HAVE AN EXCITING TALENT, LAD. NEVER ABUSE IT.
NO, SIR. THANK YOU, SIR.
GBTrudeau

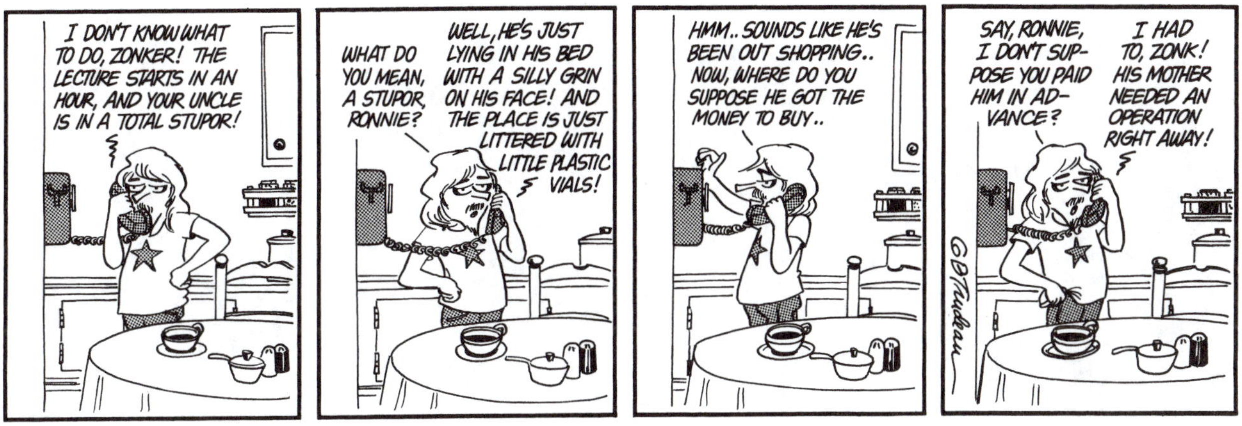
I DON'T KNOW WHAT TO DO, ZONKER! THE LECTURE STARTS IN AN HOUR, AND YOUR UNCLE IS IN A TOTAL STUPOR!
WHAT DO YOU MEAN, A STUPOR, RONNIE?
WELL, HE'S JUST LYING IN HIS BED WITH A SILLY GRIN ON HIS FACE! AND THE PLACE IS JUST LITTERED WITH LITTLE PLASTIC VIALS!
HMM.. SOUNDS LIKE HE'S BEEN OUT SHOPPING.. NOW, WHERE DO YOU SUPPOSE HE GOT THE MONEY TO BUY..
SAY, RONNIE, I DON'T SUPPOSE YOU PAID HIM IN ADVANCE?
I HAD TO, ZONK! HIS MOTHER NEEDED AN OPERATION RIGHT AWAY!
GBTrudeau

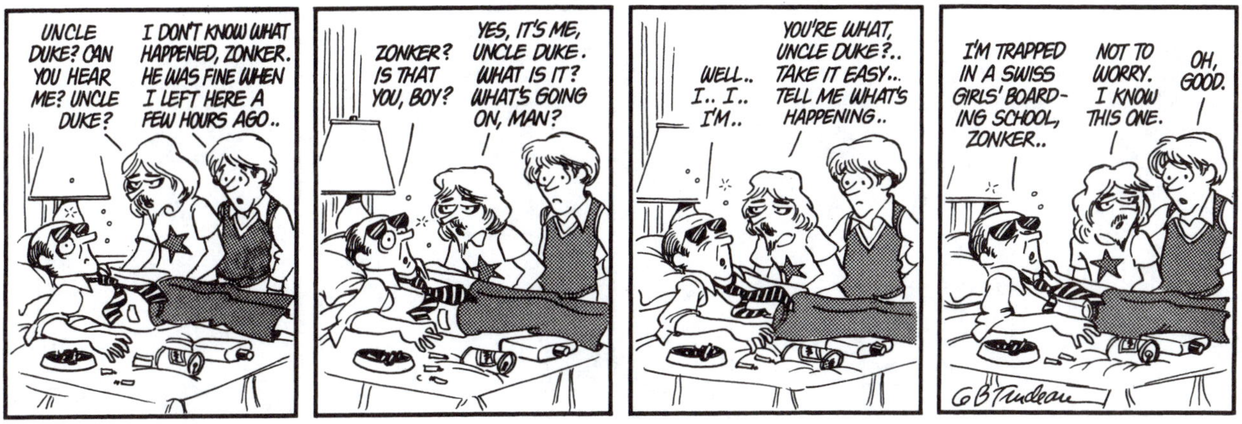
UNCLE DUKE? CAN YOU HEAR ME? UNCLE DUKE?
I DON'T KNOW WHAT HAPPENED, ZONKER. HE WAS FINE WHEN I LEFT HERE A FEW HOURS AGO..
ZONKER? IS THAT YOU, BOY?
YES, IT'S ME, UNCLE DUKE. WHAT IS IT? WHAT'S GOING ON, MAN?
WELL.. I.. I.. I'M..
YOU'RE WHAT, UNCLE DUKE?.. TAKE IT EASY... TELL ME WHAT'S HAPPENING..
I'M TRAPPED IN A SWISS GIRLS' BOARDING SCHOOL, ZONKER..
NOT TO WORRY. I KNOW THIS ONE.
OH, GOOD.
GBTrudeau

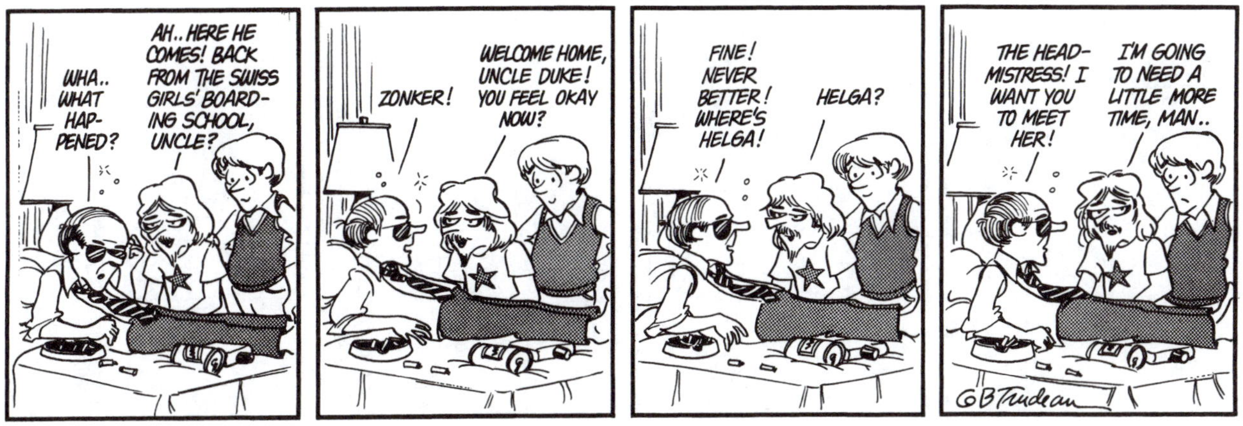
WHA.. WHAT HAPPENED?
AH.. HERE HE COMES! BACK FROM THE SWISS GIRLS' BOARDING SCHOOL, UNCLE?
ZONKER!
WELCOME HOME, UNCLE DUKE! YOU FEEL OKAY NOW?
FINE! NEVER BETTER! WHERE'S HELGA!
HELGA?
THE HEADMISTRESS! I WANT YOU TO MEET HER!
I'M GOING TO NEED A LITTLE MORE TIME, MAN..
GBTrudeau

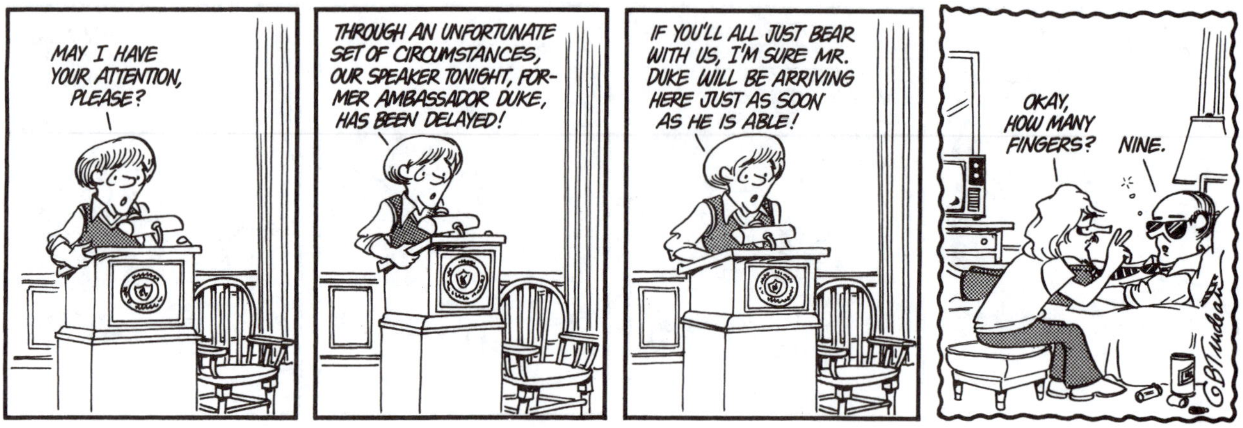
MAY I HAVE YOUR ATTENTION, PLEASE?
THROUGH AN UNFORTUNATE SET OF CIRCUMSTANCES, OUR SPEAKER TONIGHT, FORMER AMBASSADOR DUKE, HAS BEEN DELAYED!
IF YOU'LL ALL JUST BEAR WITH US, I'M SURE MR. DUKE WILL BE ARRIVING HERE JUST AS SOON AS HE IS ABLE!
OKAY, HOW MANY FINGERS?
NINE.
GBTrudeau

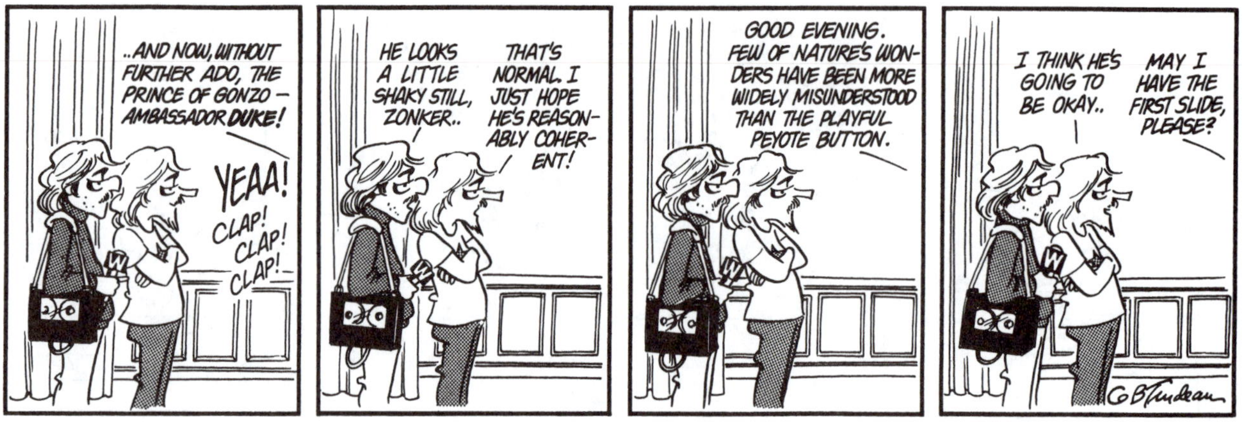
..AND NOW, WITHOUT FURTHER ADO, THE PRINCE OF GONZO – AMBASSADOR DUKE!
YEAA!
CLAP! CLAP! CLAP!
HE LOOKS A LITTLE SHAKY STILL, ZONKER..
THAT'S NORMAL. I JUST HOPE HE'S REASONABLY COHERENT!
GOOD EVENING. FEW OF NATURE'S WONDERS HAVE BEEN MORE WIDELY MISUNDERSTOOD THAN THE PLAYFUL PEYOTE BUTTON.
I THINK HE'S GOING TO BE OKAY..
MAY I HAVE THE FIRST SLIDE, PLEASE?
GBTrudeau

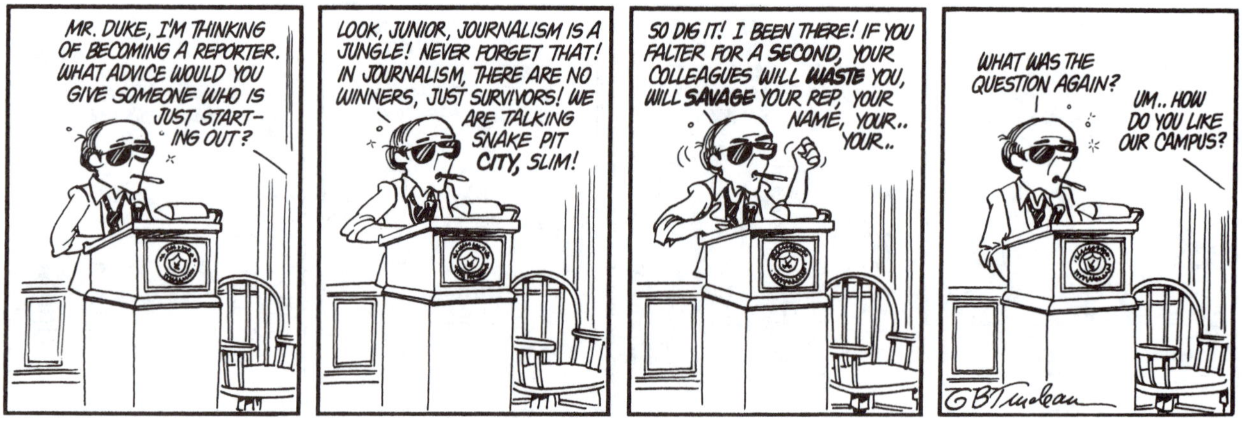
MR. DUKE, I'M THINKING OF BECOMING A REPORTER. WHAT ADVICE WOULD YOU GIVE SOMEONE WHO IS JUST STARTING OUT?
LOOK, JUNIOR, JOURNALISM IS A JUNGLE! NEVER FORGET THAT! IN JOURNALISM, THERE ARE NO WINNERS, JUST SURVIVORS! WE ARE TALKING SNAKE PIT CITY, SLIM!
SO DIG IT! I BEEN THERE! IF YOU FALTER FOR A SECOND, YOUR COLLEAGUES WILL WASTE YOU, WILL SAVAGE YOUR REP, YOUR NAME, YOUR.. YOUR..
WHAT WAS THE QUESTION AGAIN?
UM.. HOW DO YOU LIKE OUR CAMPUS?
GBTrudeau

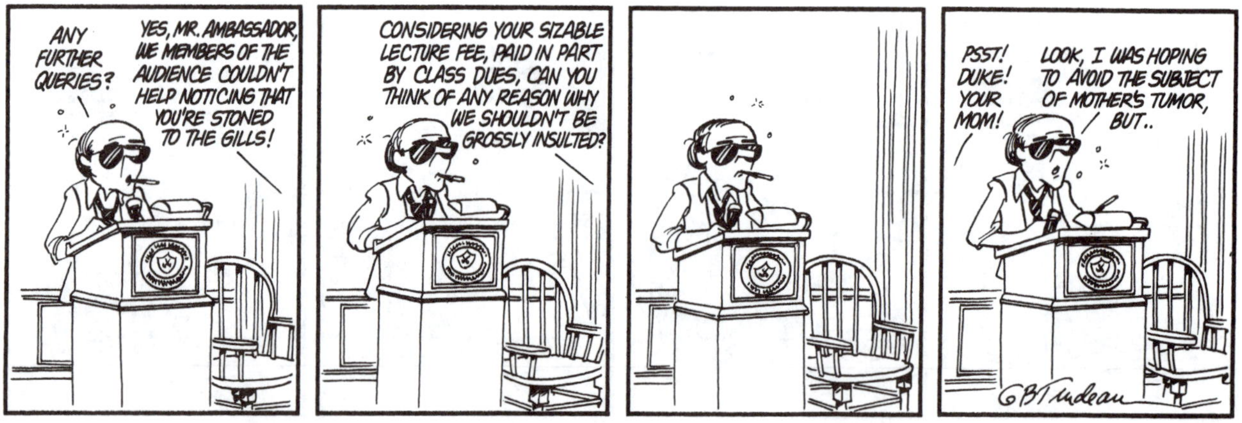
ANY FURTHER QUERIES?
YES, MR. AMBASSADOR, WE MEMBERS OF THE AUDIENCE COULDN'T HELP NOTICING THAT YOU'RE STONED TO THE GILLS!
CONSIDERING YOUR SIZABLE LECTURE FEE, PAID IN PART BY CLASS DUES, CAN YOU THINK OF ANY REASON WHY WE SHOULDN'T BE GROSSLY INSULTED?
PSST! DUKE! YOUR MOM!
LOOK, I WAS HOPING TO AVOID THE SUBJECT OF MOTHER'S TUMOR, BUT..
GBTrudeau

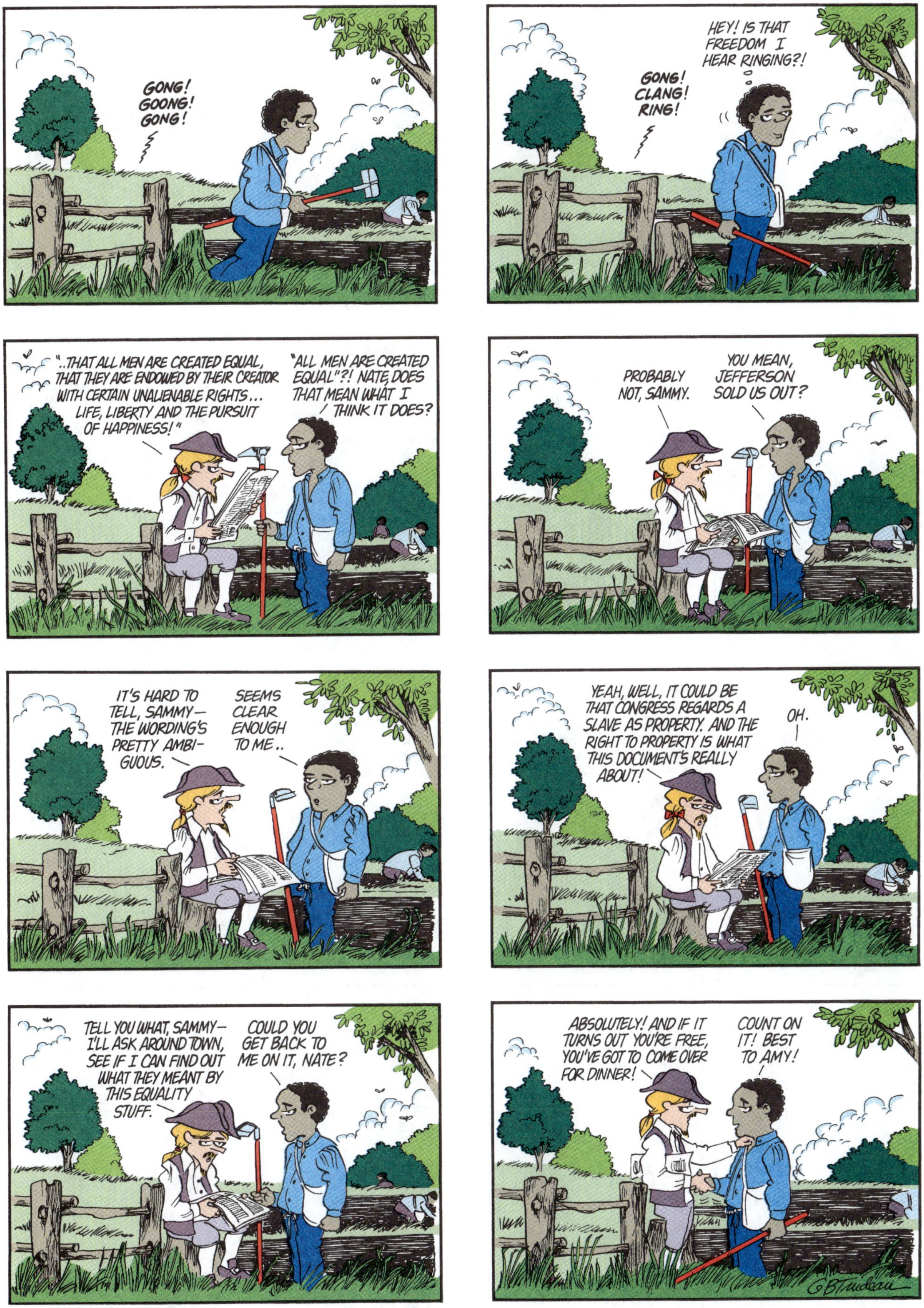
GONG! GOONG! GONG!
GONG! CLANG! RING!
HEY! IS THAT FREEDOM I HEAR RINGING?!
"..THAT ALL MEN ARE CREATED EQUAL, THAT THEY ARE ENDOWED BY THEIR CREATOR WITH CERTAIN UNALIENABLE RIGHTS... LIFE, LIBERTY AND THE PURSUIT OF HAPPINESS!"
"ALL MEN ARE CREATED EQUAL"?! NATE, DOES THAT MEAN WHAT I THINK IT DOES?
YOU MEAN, JEFFERSON SOLD US OUT?
PROBABLY NOT, SAMMY.
IT'S HARD TO TELL, SAMMY– THE WORDING'S PRETTY AMBI-GUOUS.
SEEMS CLEAR ENOUGH TO ME..
YEAH, WELL, IT COULD BE THAT CONGRESS REGARDS A SLAVE AS PROPERTY. AND THE RIGHT TO PROPERTY IS WHAT THIS DOCUMENT'S REALLY ABOUT!
OH.
TELL YOU WHAT, SAMMY– I'LL ASK AROUND TOWN, SEE IF I CAN FIND OUT WHAT THEY MEANT BY THIS EQUALITY STUFF.
COULD YOU GET BACK TO ME ON IT, NATE?
ABSOLUTELY! AND IF IT TURNS OUT YOU'RE FREE, YOU'VE GOT TO COME OVER FOR DINNER!
COUNT ON IT! BEST TO AMY!
G B Trudeau

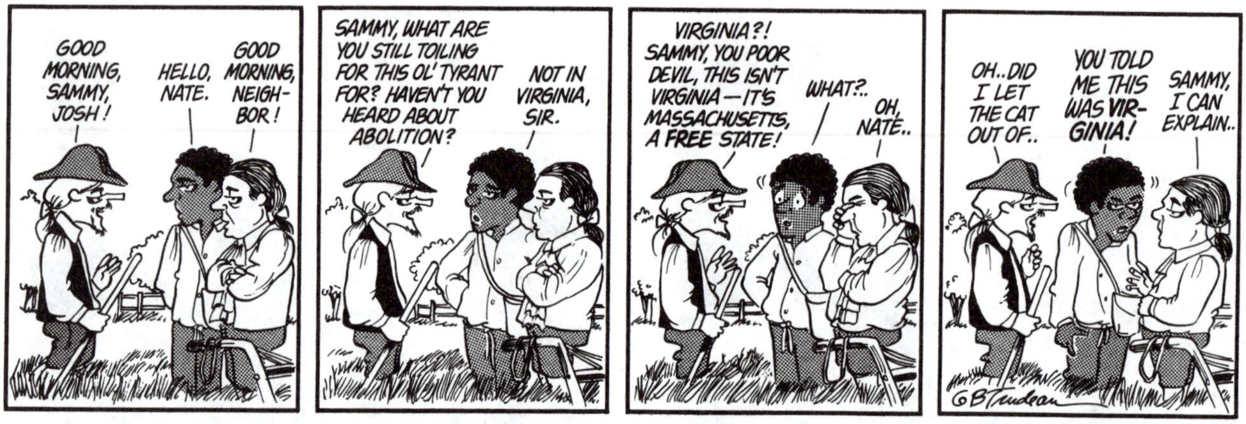
GOOD MORNING, SAMMY, JOSH!
HELLO, NATE.
GOOD MORNING, NEIGHBOR!
SAMMY, WHAT ARE YOU STILL TOILING FOR THIS OL' TYRANT FOR? HAVEN'T YOU HEARD ABOUT ABOLITION?
NOT IN VIRGINIA, SIR.
VIRGINIA?! SAMMY, YOU POOR DEVIL, THIS ISN'T VIRGINIA — IT'S MASSACHUSETTS, A FREE STATE!
WHAT?..
OH, NATE..
OH.. DID I LET THE CAT OUT OF..
YOU TOLD ME THIS WAS VIRGINIA!
SAMMY, I CAN EXPLAIN..

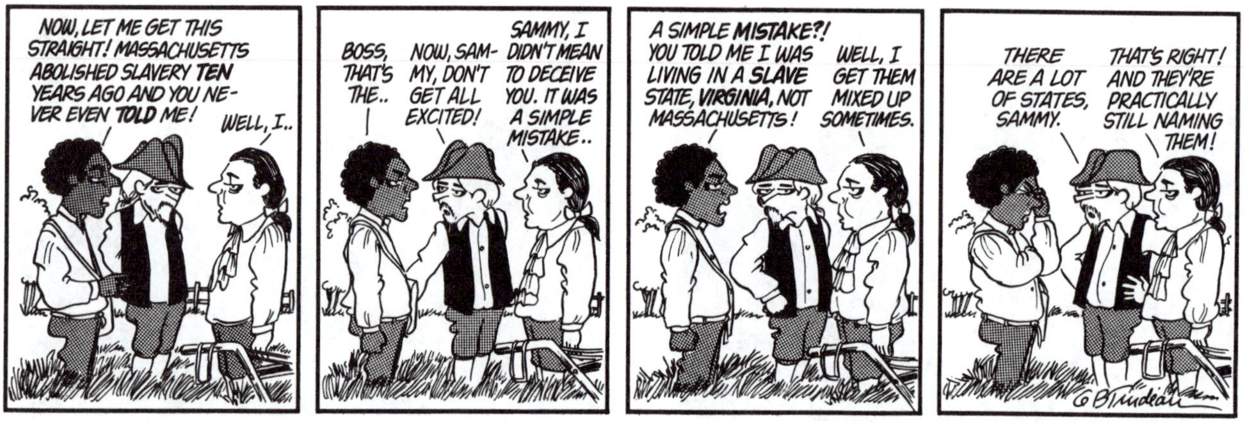
NOW, LET ME GET THIS STRAIGHT! MASSACHUSETTS ABOLISHED SLAVERY TEN YEARS AGO AND YOU NEVER EVEN TOLD ME!
WELL, I..
BOSS, THAT'S THE..
NOW, SAMMY, DON'T GET ALL EXCITED!
SAMMY, I DIDN'T MEAN TO DECEIVE YOU. IT WAS A SIMPLE MISTAKE..
A SIMPLE MISTAKE?! YOU TOLD ME I WAS LIVING IN A SLAVE STATE, VIRGINIA, NOT MASSACHUSETTS!
WELL, I GET THEM MIXED UP SOMETIMES.
THERE ARE A LOT OF STATES, SAMMY.
THAT'S RIGHT! AND THEY'RE PRACTICALLY STILL NAMING THEM!

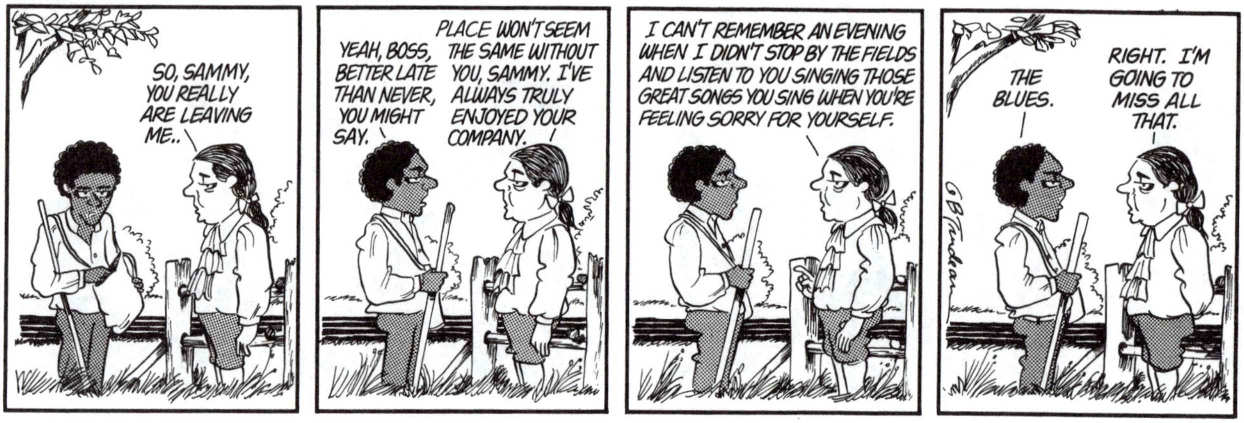
SO, SAMMY, YOU REALLY ARE LEAVING ME..
YEAH, BOSS, BETTER LATE THAN NEVER, YOU MIGHT SAY.
PLACE WON'T SEEM THE SAME WITHOUT YOU, SAMMY. I'VE ALWAYS TRULY ENJOYED YOUR COMPANY.
I CAN'T REMEMBER AN EVENING WHEN I DIDN'T STOP BY THE FIELDS AND LISTEN TO YOU SINGING THOSE GREAT SONGS YOU SING WHEN YOU'RE FEELING SORRY FOR YOURSELF.
THE BLUES.
RIGHT. I'M GOING TO MISS ALL THAT.

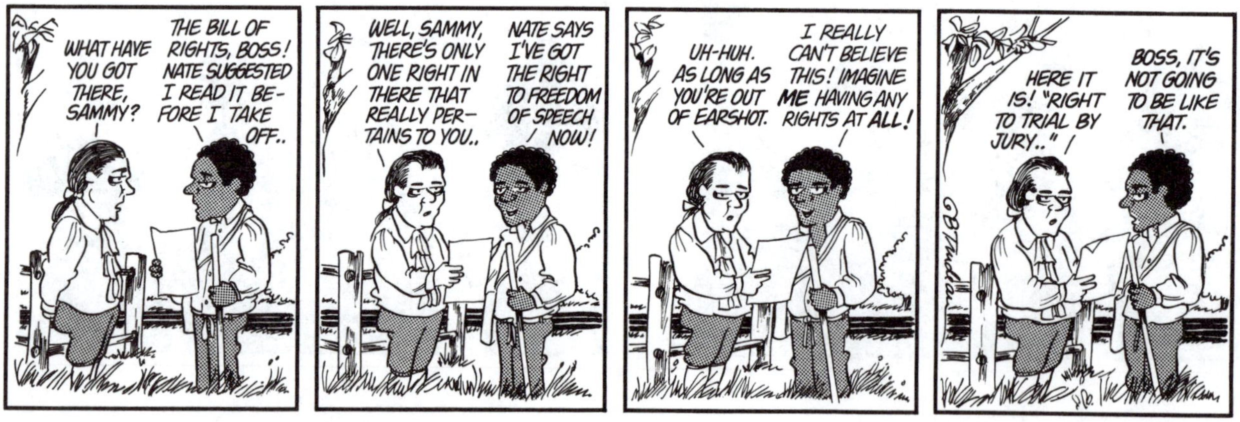
WHAT HAVE YOU GOT THERE, SAMMY?
THE BILL OF RIGHTS, BOSS! NATE SUGGESTED I READ IT BEFORE I TAKE OFF..
WELL, SAMMY, THERE'S ONLY ONE RIGHT IN THERE THAT REALLY PERTAINS TO YOU..
NATE SAYS I'VE GOT THE RIGHT TO FREEDOM OF SPEECH NOW!
UH-HUH. AS LONG AS YOU'RE OUT OF EARSHOT.
I REALLY CAN'T BELIEVE THIS! IMAGINE ME HAVING ANY RIGHTS AT ALL!
HERE IT IS! "RIGHT TO TRIAL BY JURY.."
BOSS, IT'S NOT GOING TO BE LIKE THAT.

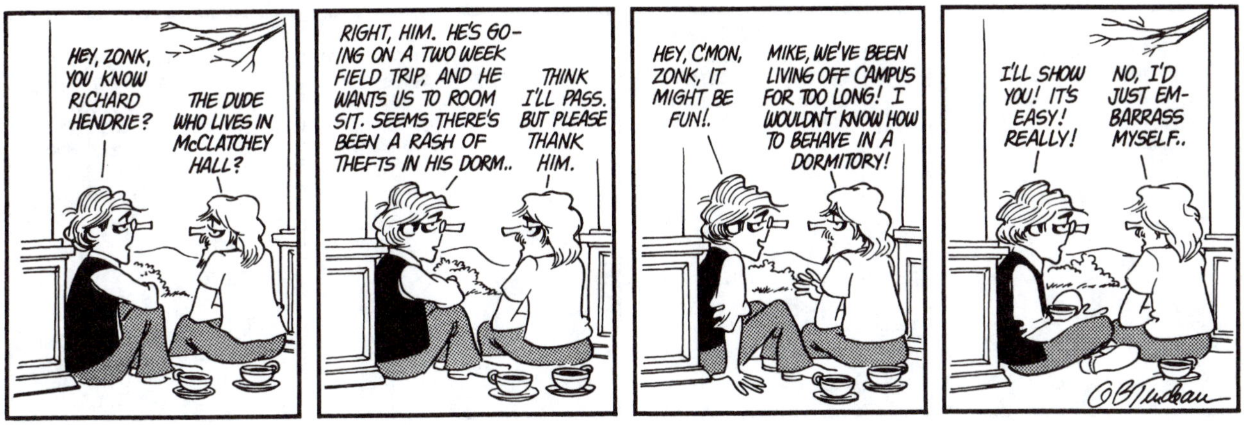
HEY, ZONK, YOU KNOW RICHARD HENDRIE?
THE DUDE WHO LIVES IN McCLATCHEY HALL?
RIGHT, HIM. HE'S GOING ON A TWO WEEK FIELD TRIP, AND HE WANTS US TO ROOM SIT. SEEMS THERE'S BEEN A RASH OF THEFTS IN HIS DORM..
THINK I'LL PASS. BUT PLEASE THANK HIM.
HEY, C'MON, ZONK, IT MIGHT BE FUN!.
MIKE, WE'VE BEEN LIVING OFF CAMPUS FOR TOO LONG! I WOULDN'T KNOW HOW TO BEHAVE IN A DORMITORY!
I'LL SHOW YOU! IT'S EASY! REALLY!
NO, I'D JUST EMBARRASS MYSELF..
GBTrudeau

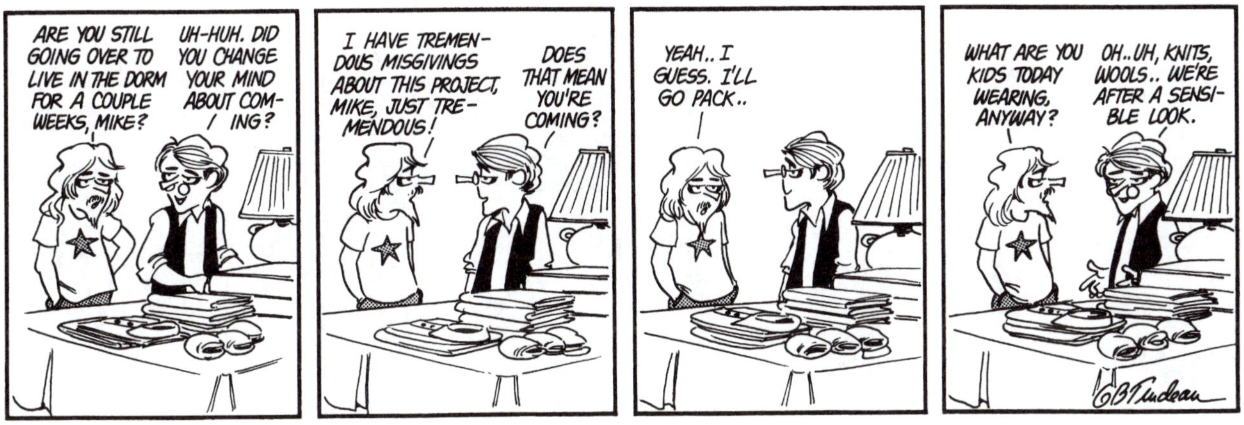
ARE YOU STILL GOING OVER TO LIVE IN THE DORM FOR A COUPLE WEEKS, MIKE?
UH-HUH. DID YOU CHANGE YOUR MIND ABOUT COMING?
I HAVE TREMENDOUS MISGIVINGS ABOUT THIS PROJECT, MIKE, JUST TREMENDOUS!
DOES THAT MEAN YOU'RE COMING?
YEAH.. I GUESS. I'LL GO PACK..
WHAT ARE YOU KIDS TODAY WEARING, ANYWAY?
OH..UH, KNITS, WOOLS.. WE'RE AFTER A SENSIBLE LOOK.
GBTrudeau

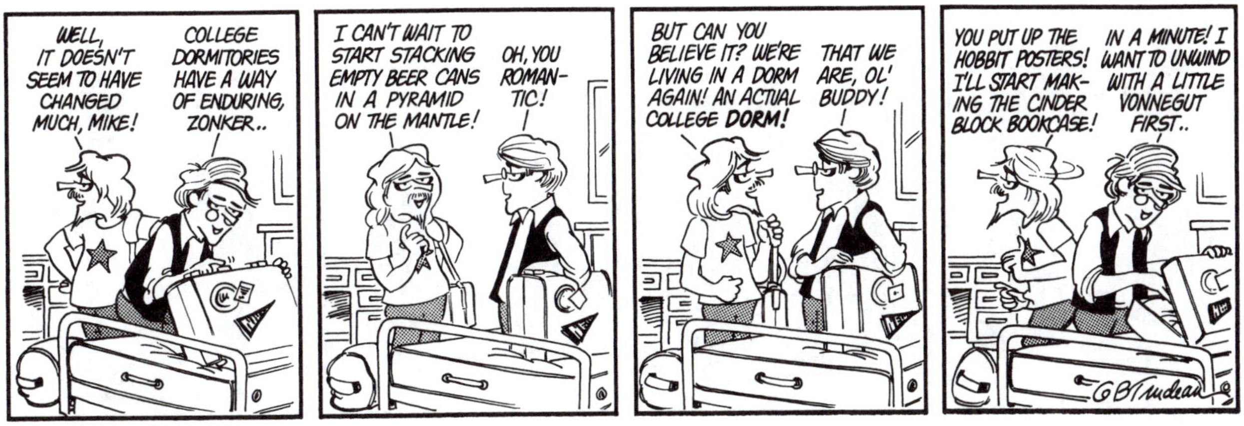
WELL, IT DOESN'T SEEM TO HAVE CHANGED MUCH, MIKE!
COLLEGE DORMITORIES HAVE A WAY OF ENDURING, ZONKER..
I CAN'T WAIT TO START STACKING EMPTY BEER CANS IN A PYRAMID ON THE MANTLE!
OH, YOU ROMANTIC!
BUT CAN YOU BELIEVE IT? WE'RE LIVING IN A DORM AGAIN! AN ACTUAL COLLEGE DORM!
THAT WE ARE, OL' BUDDY!
YOU PUT UP THE HOBBIT POSTERS! I'LL START MAKING THE CINDER BLOCK BOOKCASE!
IN A MINUTE! I WANT TO UNWIND WITH A LITTLE VONNEGUT FIRST..
GBTrudeau

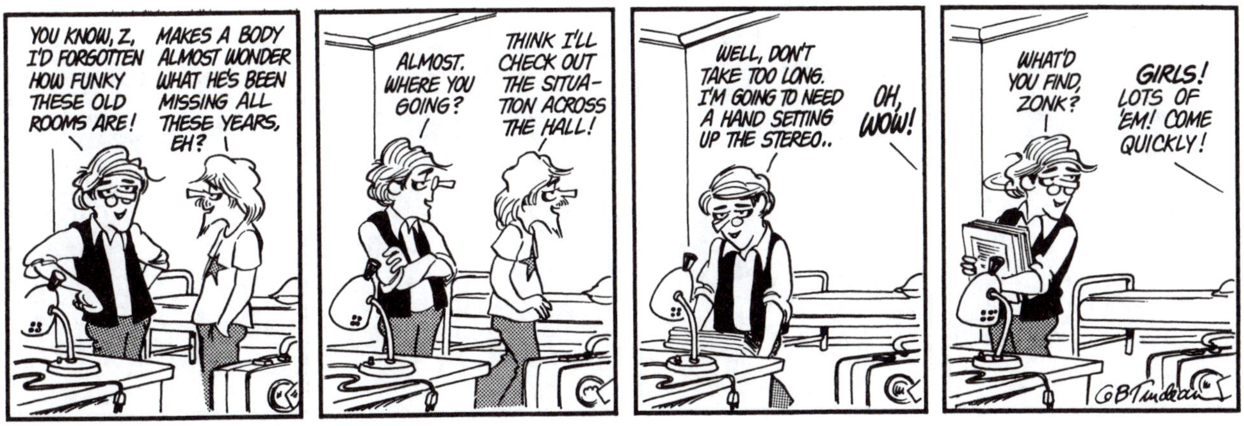
YOU KNOW, Z, I'D FORGOTTEN HOW FUNKY THESE OLD ROOMS ARE!
MAKES A BODY ALMOST WONDER WHAT HE'S BEEN MISSING ALL THESE YEARS, EH?
ALMOST. WHERE YOU GOING?
THINK I'LL CHECK OUT THE SITUATION ACROSS THE HALL!
WELL, DON'T TAKE TOO LONG. I'M GOING TO NEED A HAND SETTING UP THE STEREO..
OH, WOW!
WHAT'D YOU FIND, ZONK?
GIRLS! LOTS OF 'EM! COME QUICKLY!
GBTrudeau

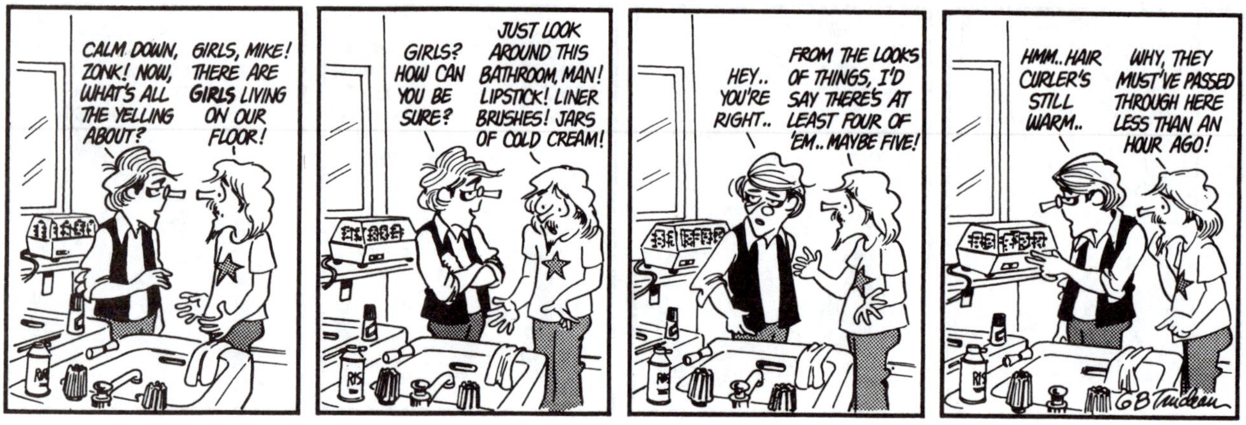
CALM DOWN, ZONK! NOW, WHAT'S ALL THE YELLING ABOUT?
GIRLS, MIKE! THERE ARE **GIRLS** LIVING ON OUR FLOOR!
GIRLS? HOW CAN YOU BE SURE?
JUST LOOK AROUND THIS BATHROOM, MAN! LIPSTICK! LINER BRUSHES! JARS OF COLD CREAM!
HEY.. YOU'RE RIGHT..
FROM THE LOOKS OF THINGS, I'D SAY THERE'S AT LEAST FOUR OF 'EM.. MAYBE FIVE!
HMM.. HAIR CURLER'S STILL WARM..
WHY, THEY MUST'VE PASSED THROUGH HERE LESS THAN AN HOUR AGO!
GB Trudeau

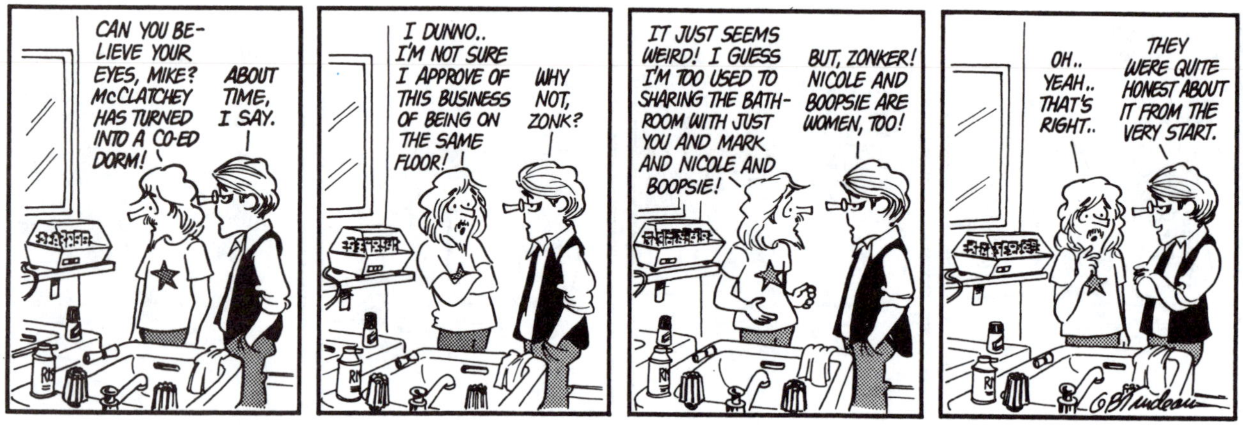
CAN YOU BELIEVE YOUR EYES, MIKE? McCLATCHEY HAS TURNED INTO A CO-ED DORM!
ABOUT TIME, I SAY.
I DUNNO.. I'M NOT SURE I APPROVE OF THIS BUSINESS OF BEING ON THE SAME FLOOR!
WHY NOT, ZONK?
IT JUST SEEMS WEIRD! I GUESS I'M TOO USED TO SHARING THE BATHROOM WITH JUST YOU AND MARK AND NICOLE AND BOOPSIE!
BUT, ZONKER! NICOLE AND BOOPSIE ARE WOMEN, TOO!
OH.. YEAH.. THAT'S RIGHT..
THEY WERE QUITE HONEST ABOUT IT FROM THE VERY START.
GB Trudeau

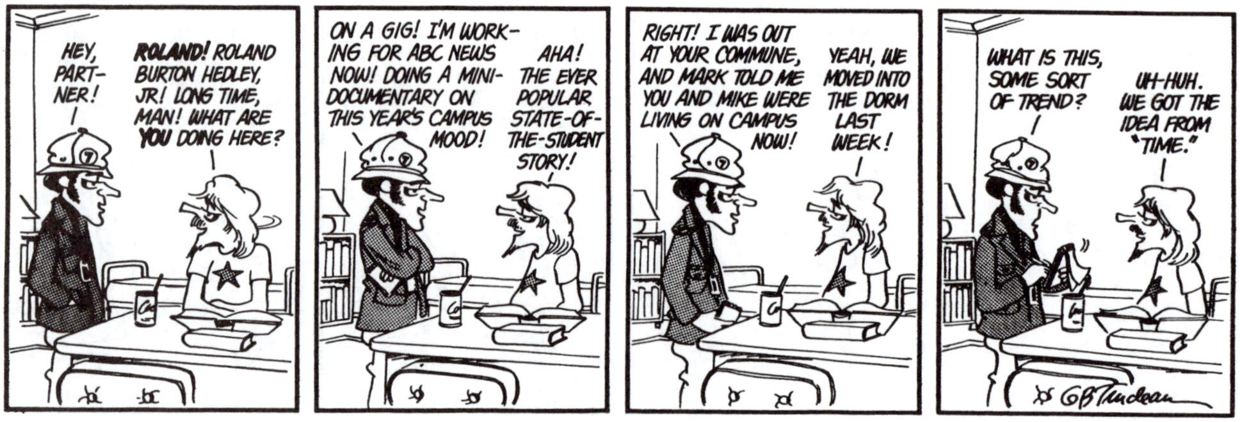
HEY, PARTNER!
ROLAND! ROLAND BURTON HEDLEY, JR! LONG TIME, MAN! WHAT ARE **YOU** DOING HERE?
ON A GIG! I'M WORKING FOR ABC NEWS NOW! DOING A MINI-DOCUMENTARY ON THIS YEAR'S CAMPUS MOOD!
AHA! THE EVER POPULAR STATE-OF-THE-STUDENT STORY!
RIGHT! I **WAS** OUT AT YOUR COMMUNE, AND MARK TOLD ME YOU AND MIKE WERE LIVING ON CAMPUS NOW!
YEAH, WE MOVED INTO THE DORM LAST WEEK!
WHAT IS THIS, SOME SORT OF TREND?
UH-HUH. WE GOT THE IDEA FROM "TIME."
GB Trudeau

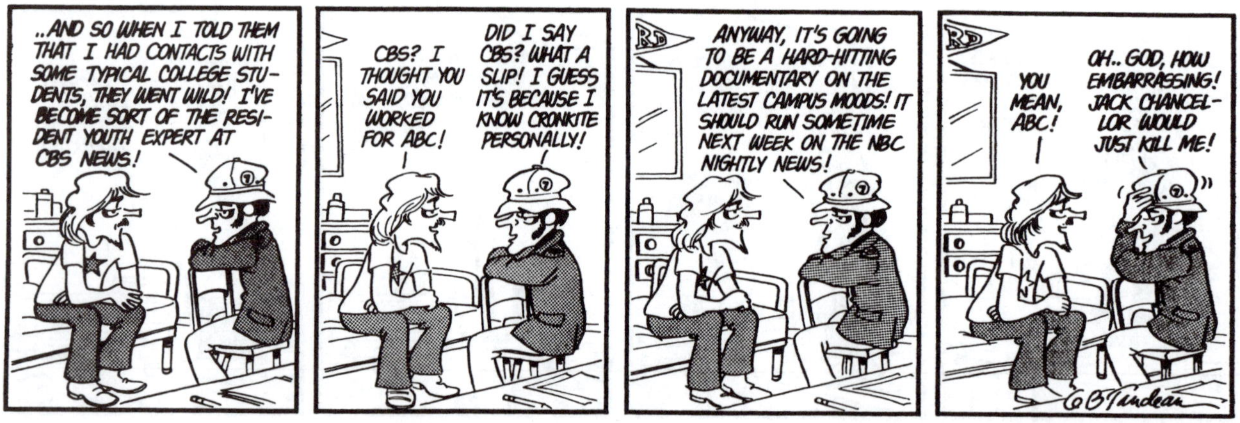
..AND SO WHEN I TOLD THEM THAT I HAD CONTACTS WITH SOME TYPICAL COLLEGE STUDENTS, THEY WENT WILD! I'VE BECOME SORT OF THE RESIDENT YOUTH EXPERT AT CBS NEWS!
CBS? I THOUGHT YOU SAID YOU WORKED FOR ABC!
DID I SAY CBS? WHAT A SLIP! I GUESS IT'S BECAUSE I KNOW CRONKITE PERSONALLY!
ANYWAY, IT'S GOING TO BE A HARD-HITTING DOCUMENTARY ON THE LATEST CAMPUS MOODS! IT SHOULD RUN SOMETIME NEXT WEEK ON THE NBC NIGHTLY NEWS!
YOU MEAN, ABC!
OH.. GOD, HOW EMBARRASSING! JACK CHANCELLOR WOULD JUST KILL ME!
GB Trudeau

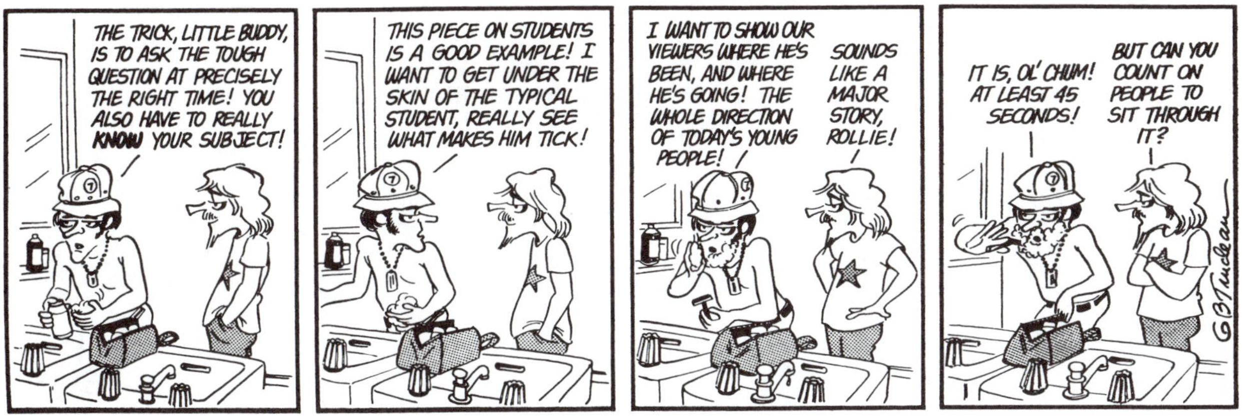
THE TRICK, LITTLE BUDDY, IS TO ASK THE TOUGH QUESTION AT PRECISELY THE RIGHT TIME! YOU ALSO HAVE TO REALLY KNOW YOUR SUBJECT!
THIS PIECE ON STUDENTS IS A GOOD EXAMPLE! I WANT TO GET UNDER THE SKIN OF THE TYPICAL STUDENT, REALLY SEE WHAT MAKES HIM TICK!
I WANT TO SHOW OUR VIEWERS WHERE HE'S BEEN, AND WHERE HE'S GOING! THE WHOLE DIRECTION OF TODAY'S YOUNG PEOPLE!
SOUNDS LIKE A MAJOR STORY, ROLLIE!
IT IS, OL' CHUM! AT LEAST 45 SECONDS!
BUT CAN YOU COUNT ON PEOPLE TO SIT THROUGH IT?
GBTrudeau

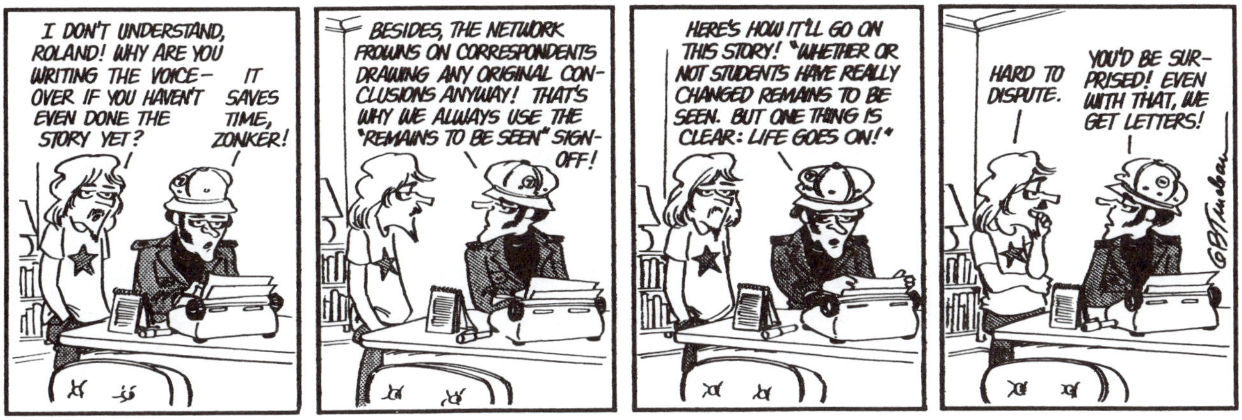
I DON'T UNDERSTAND, ROLAND! WHY ARE YOU WRITING THE VOICE-OVER IF YOU HAVEN'T EVEN DONE THE STORY YET?
IT SAVES TIME, ZONKER!
BESIDES, THE NETWORK FROWNS ON CORRESPONDENTS DRAWING ANY ORIGINAL CONCLUSIONS ANYWAY! THAT'S WHY WE ALWAYS USE THE "REMAINS TO BE SEEN" SIGN-OFF!
HERE'S HOW IT'LL GO ON THIS STORY! "WHETHER OR NOT STUDENTS HAVE REALLY CHANGED REMAINS TO BE SEEN. BUT ONE THING IS CLEAR: LIFE GOES ON!"
HARD TO DISPUTE.
YOU'D BE SURPRISED! EVEN WITH THAT, WE GET LETTERS!
GBTrudeau

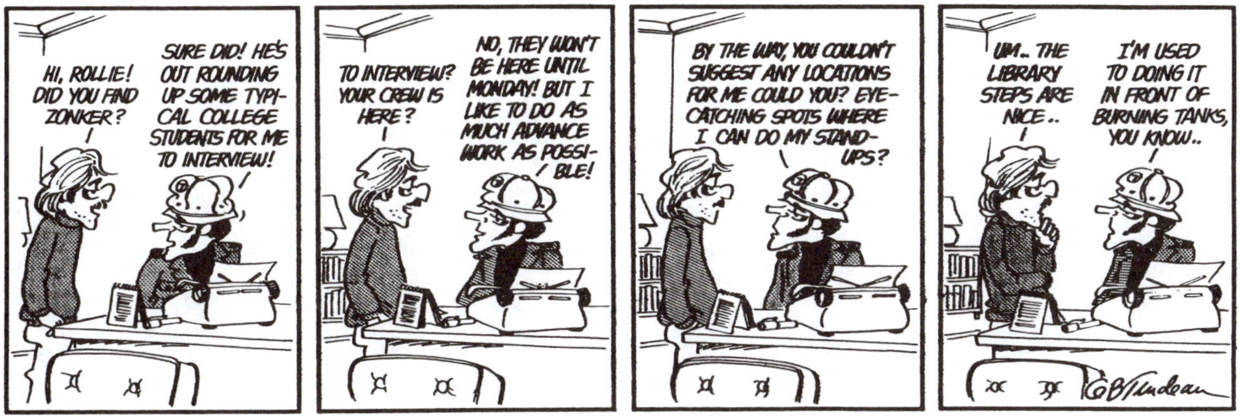
HI, ROLLIE! DID YOU FIND ZONKER?
SURE DID! HE'S OUT ROUNDING UP SOME TYPICAL COLLEGE STUDENTS FOR ME TO INTERVIEW!
TO INTERVIEW? YOUR CREW IS HERE?
NO, THEY WON'T BE HERE UNTIL MONDAY! BUT I LIKE TO DO AS MUCH ADVANCE WORK AS POSSIBLE!
BY THE WAY, YOU COULDN'T SUGGEST ANY LOCATIONS FOR ME COULD YOU? EYE-CATCHING SPOTS WHERE I CAN DO MY STAND-UPS?
UM.. THE LIBRARY STEPS ARE NICE..
I'M USED TO DOING IT IN FRONT OF BURNING TANKS, YOU KNOW..
GBTrudeau

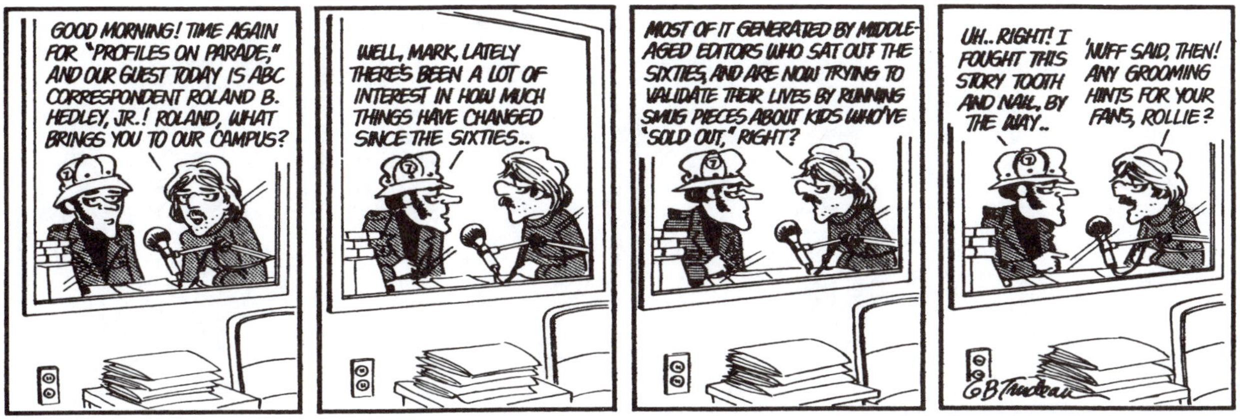
GOOD MORNING! TIME AGAIN FOR "PROFILES ON PARADE," AND OUR GUEST TODAY IS ABC CORRESPONDENT ROLAND B. HEDLEY, JR.! ROLAND, WHAT BRINGS YOU TO OUR CAMPUS?
WELL, MARK, LATELY THERE'S BEEN A LOT OF INTEREST IN HOW MUCH THINGS HAVE CHANGED SINCE THE SIXTIES..
MOST OF IT GENERATED BY MIDDLE-AGED EDITORS WHO SAT OUT THE SIXTIES, AND ARE NOW TRYING TO VALIDATE THEIR LIVES BY RUNNING SMUG PIECES ABOUT KIDS WHO'VE "SOLD OUT," RIGHT?
UH.. RIGHT! I FOUGHT THIS STORY TOOTH AND NAIL, BY THE WAY..
'NUFF SAID, THEN! ANY GROOMING HINTS FOR YOUR FANS, ROLLIE?
GBTrudeau

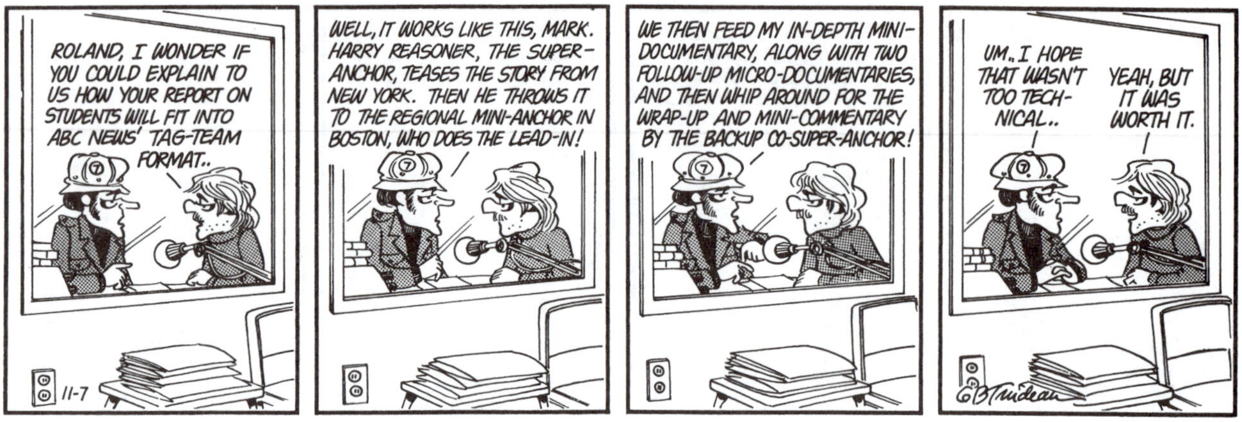

ROLAND, I WONDER IF YOU COULD EXPLAIN TO US HOW YOUR REPORT ON STUDENTS WILL FIT INTO ABC NEWS' TAG-TEAM FORMAT..
11-7
WELL, IT WORKS LIKE THIS, MARK. HARRY REASONER, THE SUPER-ANCHOR, TEASES THE STORY FROM NEW YORK. THEN HE THROWS IT TO THE REGIONAL MINI-ANCHOR IN BOSTON, WHO DOES THE LEAD-IN!
WE THEN FEED MY IN-DEPTH MINI-DOCUMENTARY, ALONG WITH TWO FOLLOW-UP MICRO-DOCUMENTARIES, AND THEN WHIP AROUND FOR THE WRAP-UP AND MINI-COMMENTARY BY THE BACKUP CO-SUPER-ANCHOR!
UM.. I HOPE THAT WASN'T TOO TECHNICAL..
YEAH, BUT IT WAS WORTH IT.
GBTrudeau

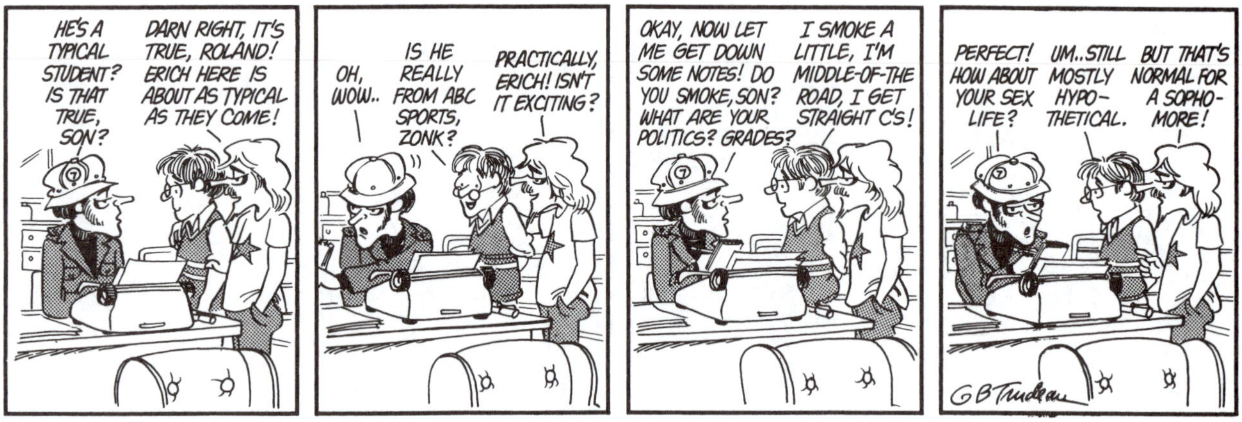

HE'S A TYPICAL STUDENT? IS THAT TRUE, SON?
DARN RIGHT, IT'S TRUE, ROLAND! ERICH HERE IS ABOUT AS TYPICAL AS THEY COME!
OH, WOW..
IS HE REALLY FROM ABC SPORTS, ZONK?
PRACTICALLY, ERICH! ISN'T IT EXCITING?
OKAY, NOW LET ME GET DOWN SOME NOTES! DO YOU SMOKE, SON? WHAT ARE YOUR POLITICS? GRADES?
I SMOKE A LITTLE, I'M MIDDLE-OF-THE ROAD, I GET STRAIGHT C'S!
PERFECT! HOW ABOUT YOUR SEX LIFE?
UM.. STILL MOSTLY HYPO-THETICAL.
BUT THAT'S NORMAL FOR A SOPHO-MORE!
GBTrudeau

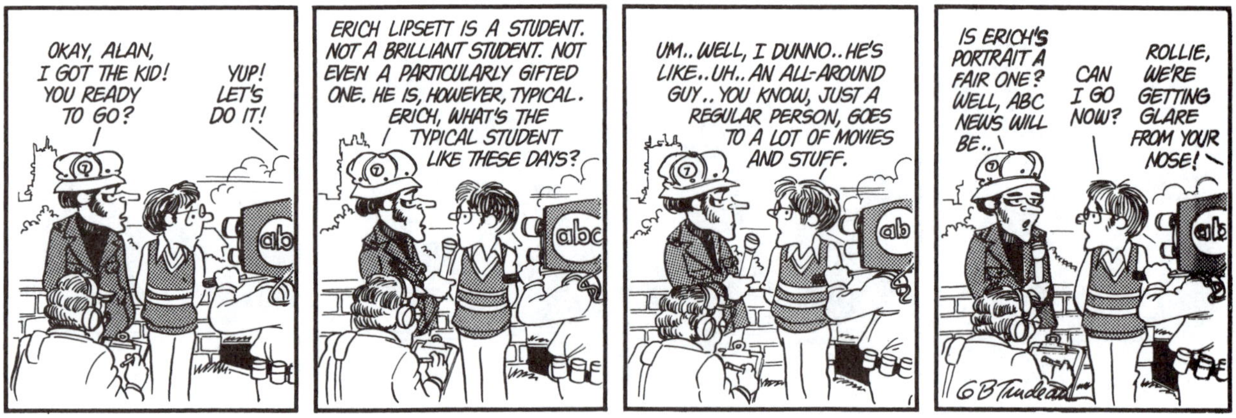

OKAY, ALAN, I GOT THE KID! YOU READY TO GO?
YUP! LET'S DO IT!
ERICH LIPSETT IS A STUDENT. NOT A BRILLIANT STUDENT. NOT EVEN A PARTICULARLY GIFTED ONE. HE IS, HOWEVER, TYPICAL. ERICH, WHAT'S THE TYPICAL STUDENT LIKE THESE DAYS?
UM.. WELL, I DUNNO.. HE'S LIKE.. UH.. AN ALL-AROUND GUY.. YOU KNOW, JUST A REGULAR PERSON, GOES TO A LOT OF MOVIES AND STUFF.
IS ERICH'S PORTRAIT A FAIR ONE? WELL, ABC NEWS WILL BE..
CAN I GO NOW?
ROLLIE, WE'RE GETTING GLARE FROM YOUR NOSE!
GBTrudeau

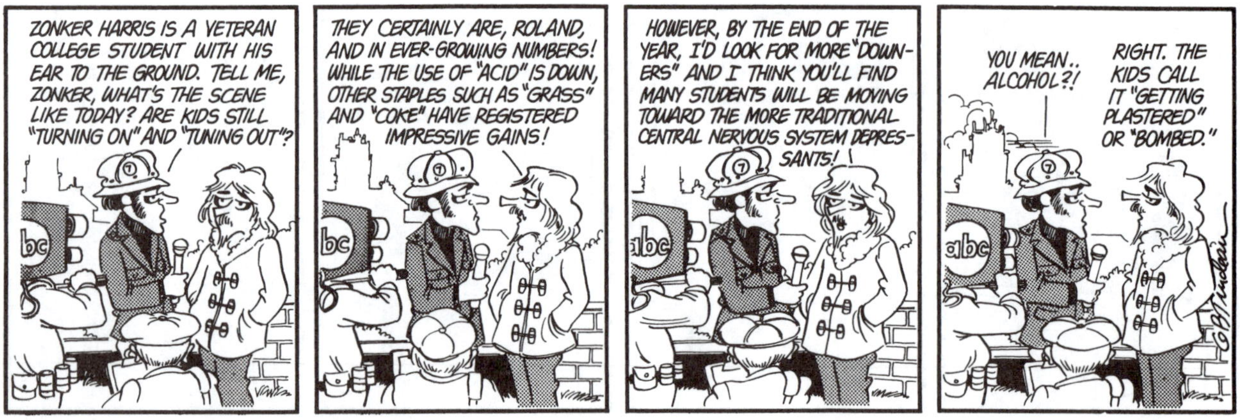

ZONKER HARRIS IS A VETERAN COLLEGE STUDENT WITH HIS EAR TO THE GROUND. TELL ME, ZONKER, WHAT'S THE SCENE LIKE TODAY? ARE KIDS STILL "TURNING ON" AND "TUNING OUT"?
THEY CERTAINLY ARE, ROLAND, AND IN EVER-GROWING NUMBERS! WHILE THE USE OF "ACID" IS DOWN, OTHER STAPLES SUCH AS "GRASS" AND "COKE" HAVE REGISTERED IMPRESSIVE GAINS!
HOWEVER, BY THE END OF THE YEAR, I'D LOOK FOR MORE "DOWNERS" AND I THINK YOU'LL FIND MANY STUDENTS WILL BE MOVING TOWARD THE MORE TRADITIONAL CENTRAL NERVOUS SYSTEM DEPRESSANTS!
YOU MEAN.. ALCOHOL?!
RIGHT. THE KIDS CALL IT "GETTING PLASTERED" OR "BOMBED."
GBTrudeau

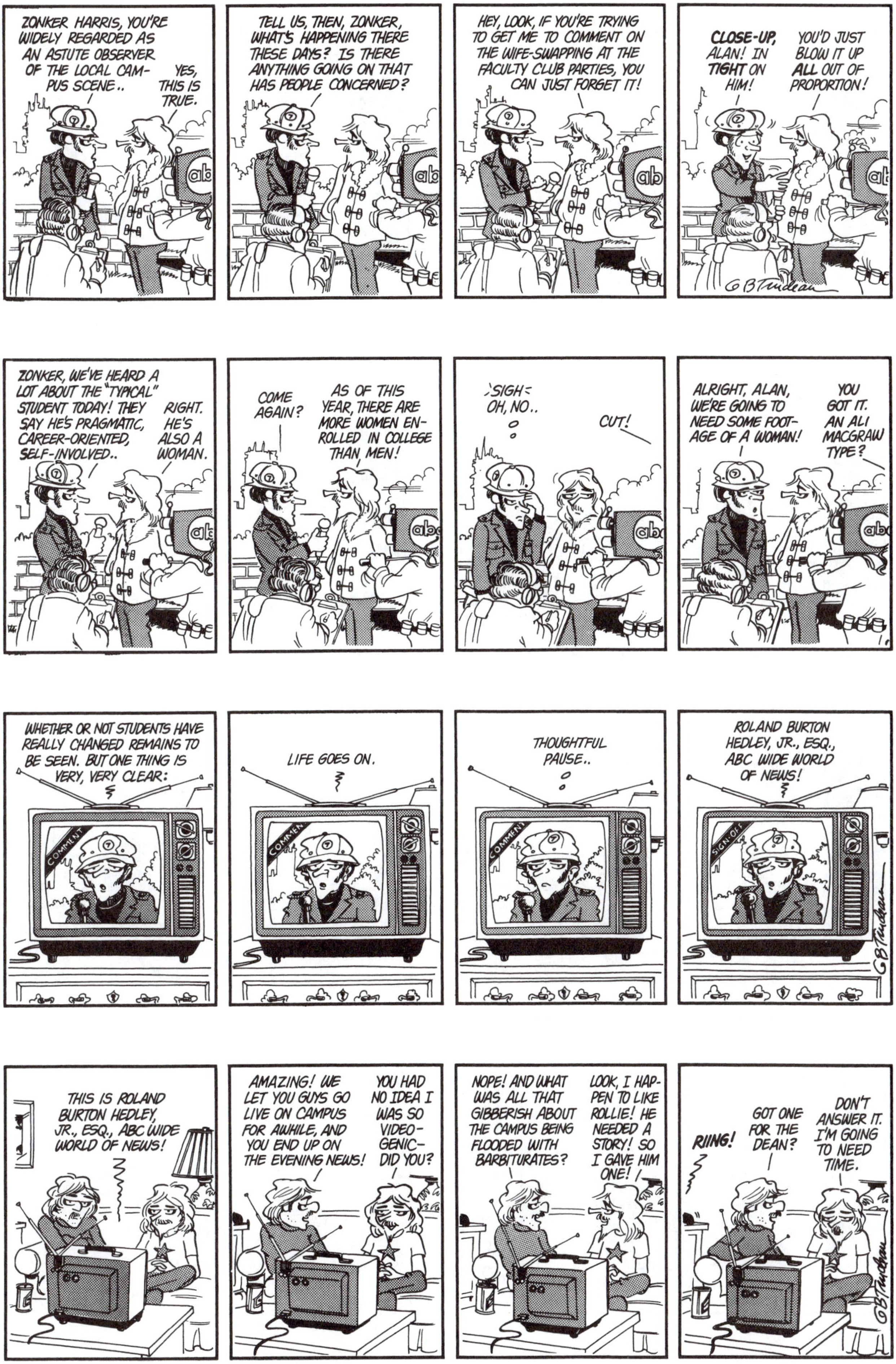

ZONKER HARRIS, YOU'RE WIDELY REGARDED AS AN ASTUTE OBSERVER OF THE LOCAL CAMPUS SCENE..
YES, THIS IS TRUE.
TELL US, THEN, ZONKER, WHAT'S HAPPENING THERE THESE DAYS? IS THERE ANYTHING GOING ON THAT HAS PEOPLE CONCERNED?
HEY, LOOK, IF YOU'RE TRYING TO GET ME TO COMMENT ON THE WIFE-SWAPPING AT THE FACULTY CLUB PARTIES, YOU CAN JUST FORGET IT!
CLOSE-UP, ALAN! IN TIGHT ON HIM!
YOU'D JUST BLOW IT UP ALL OUT OF PROPORTION!
ZONKER, WE'VE HEARD A LOT ABOUT THE "TYPICAL" STUDENT TODAY! THEY SAY HE'S PRAGMATIC, CAREER-ORIENTED, SELF-INVOLVED..
RIGHT. HE'S ALSO A WOMAN.
COME AGAIN?
AS OF THIS YEAR, THERE ARE MORE WOMEN ENROLLED IN COLLEGE THAN MEN!
SIGH OH, NO..
CUT!
ALRIGHT, ALAN, WE'RE GOING TO NEED SOME FOOTAGE OF A WOMAN!
YOU GOT IT. AN ALI MACGRAW TYPE?
WHETHER OR NOT STUDENTS HAVE REALLY CHANGED REMAINS TO BE SEEN. BUT ONE THING IS VERY, VERY CLEAR:
COMMENT
LIFE GOES ON.
COMMENT
THOUGHTFUL PAUSE..
COMMENT
ROLAND BURTON HEDLEY, JR., ESQ., ABC WIDE WORLD OF NEWS!
SIGN-OFF
THIS IS ROLAND BURTON HEDLEY, JR., ESQ., ABC WIDE WORLD OF NEWS!
AMAZING! WE LET YOU GUYS GO LIVE ON CAMPUS FOR AWHILE, AND YOU END UP ON THE EVENING NEWS!
YOU HAD NO IDEA I WAS SO VIDEO-GENIC- DID YOU?
NOPE! AND WHAT WAS ALL THAT GIBBERISH ABOUT THE CAMPUS BEING FLOODED WITH BARBITURATES?
LOOK, I HAPPEN TO LIKE ROLLIE! HE NEEDED A STORY! SO I GAVE HIM ONE!
RIING!
GOT ONE FOR THE DEAN?
DON'T ANSWER IT. I'M GOING TO NEED TIME.

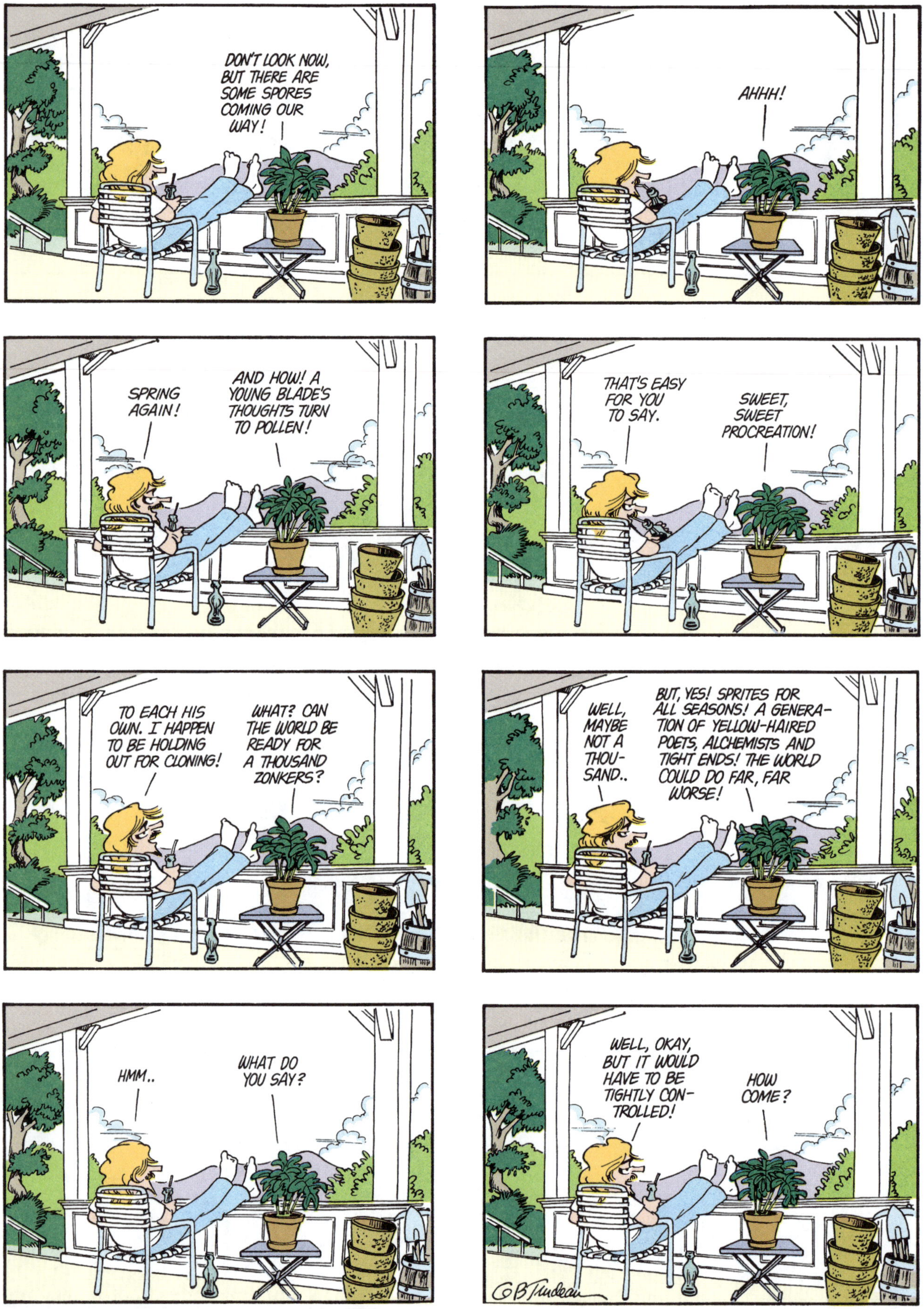
DON'T LOOK NOW, BUT THERE ARE SOME SPORES COMING OUR WAY!
AHHH!
SPRING AGAIN!
AND HOW! A YOUNG BLADE'S THOUGHTS TURN TO POLLEN!
THAT'S EASY FOR YOU TO SAY.
SWEET, SWEET PROCREATION!
TO EACH HIS OWN. I HAPPEN TO BE HOLDING OUT FOR CLONING!
WHAT? CAN THE WORLD BE READY FOR A THOUSAND ZONKERS?
WELL, MAYBE NOT A THOUSAND..
BUT, YES! SPRITES FOR ALL SEASONS! A GENERATION OF YELLOW-HAIRED POETS, ALCHEMISTS AND TIGHT ENDS! THE WORLD COULD DO FAR, FAR WORSE!
HMM..
WHAT DO YOU SAY?
WELL, OKAY, BUT IT WOULD HAVE TO BE TIGHTLY CONTROLLED!
HOW COME?
GBTrudeau

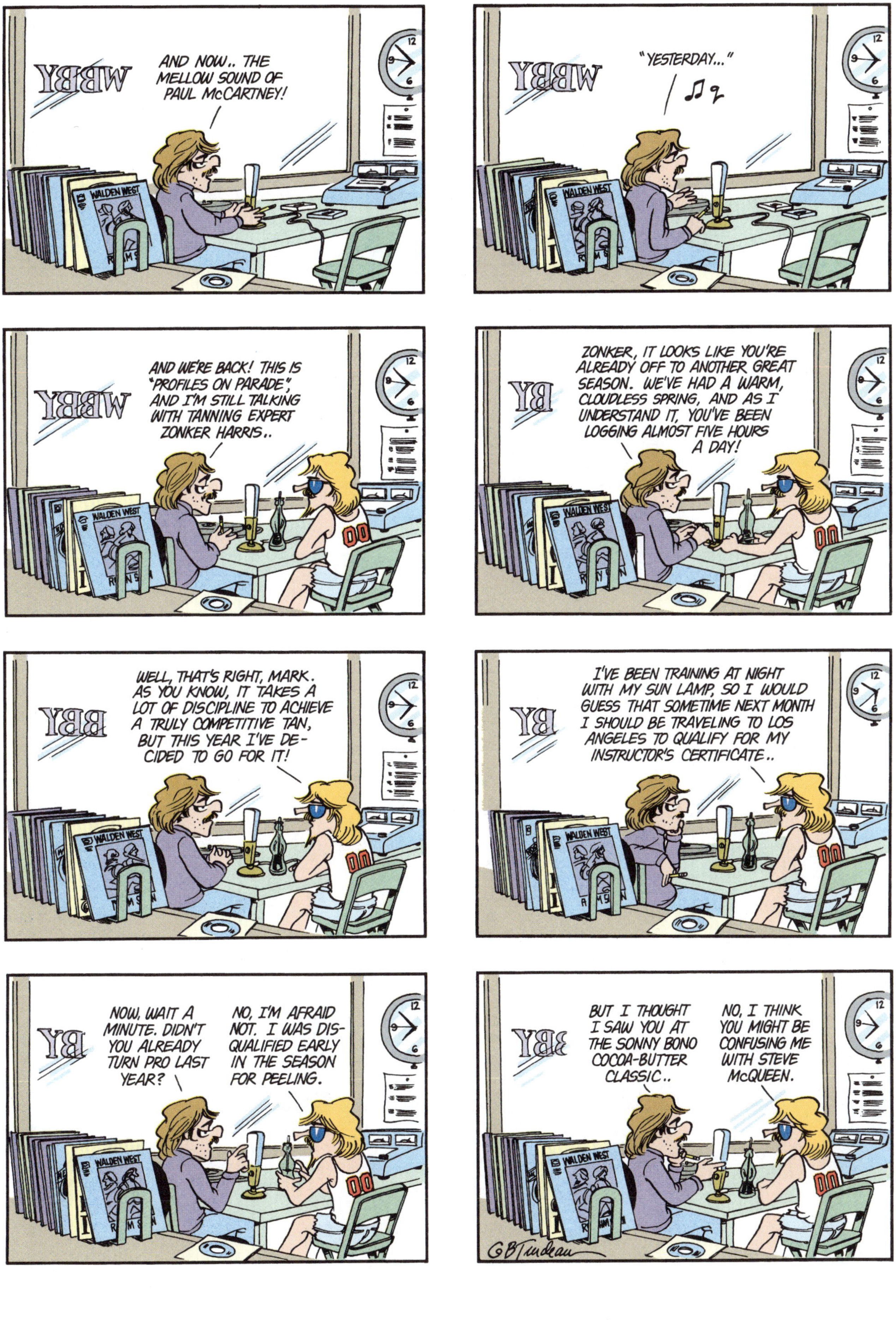
WBBY
AND NOW.. THE MELLOW SOUND OF PAUL McCARTNEY!
WALDEN WEST
"YESTERDAY..."
AND WE'RE BACK! THIS IS "PROFILES ON PARADE," AND I'M STILL TALKING WITH TANNING EXPERT ZONKER HARRIS..
ZONKER, IT LOOKS LIKE YOU'RE ALREADY OFF TO ANOTHER GREAT SEASON. WE'VE HAD A WARM, CLOUDLESS SPRING, AND AS I UNDERSTAND IT, YOU'VE BEEN LOGGING ALMOST FIVE HOURS A DAY!
WELL, THAT'S RIGHT, MARK. AS YOU KNOW, IT TAKES A LOT OF DISCIPLINE TO ACHIEVE A TRULY COMPETITIVE TAN, BUT THIS YEAR I'VE DECIDED TO GO FOR IT!
I'VE BEEN TRAINING AT NIGHT WITH MY SUN LAMP, SO I WOULD GUESS THAT SOMETIME NEXT MONTH I SHOULD BE TRAVELING TO LOS ANGELES TO QUALIFY FOR MY INSTRUCTOR'S CERTIFICATE..
NOW, WAIT A MINUTE. DIDN'T YOU ALREADY TURN PRO LAST YEAR?
NO, I'M AFRAID NOT. I WAS DISQUALIFIED EARLY IN THE SEASON FOR PEELING.
BUT I THOUGHT I SAW YOU AT THE SONNY BONO COCOA-BUTTER CLASSIC..
NO, I THINK YOU MIGHT BE CONFUSING ME WITH STEVE McQUEEN.
GBTrudeau

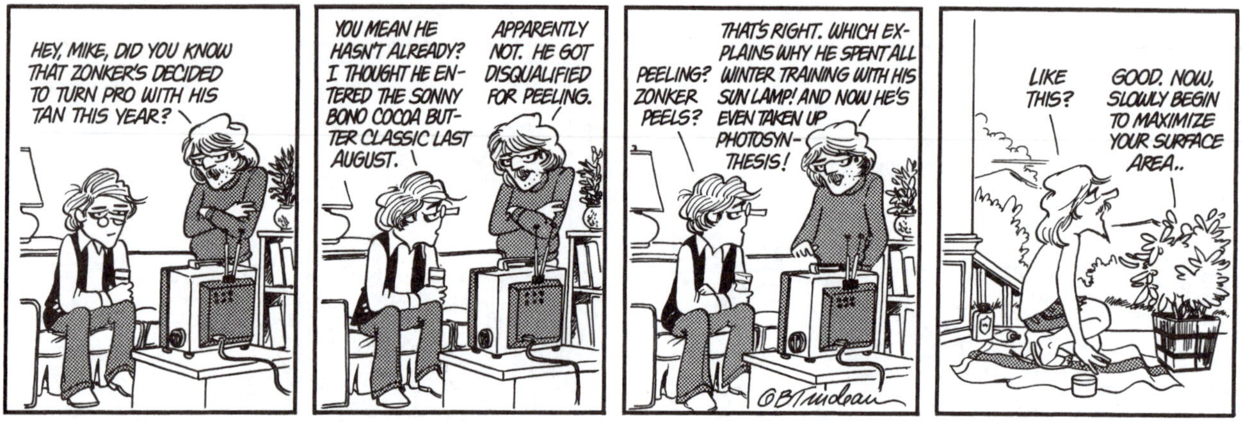
HEY, MIKE, DID YOU KNOW THAT ZONKER'S DECIDED TO TURN PRO WITH HIS TAN THIS YEAR?
YOU MEAN HE HASN'T ALREADY? I THOUGHT HE ENTERED THE SONNY BONO COCOA BUTTER CLASSIC LAST AUGUST.
APPARENTLY NOT. HE GOT DISQUALIFIED FOR PEELING.
PEELING? ZONKER PEELS?
THAT'S RIGHT. WHICH EXPLAINS WHY HE SPENT ALL WINTER TRAINING WITH HIS SUN LAMP! AND NOW HE'S EVEN TAKEN UP PHOTOSYNTHESIS!
LIKE THIS?
GOOD. NOW, SLOWLY BEGIN TO MAXIMIZE YOUR SURFACE AREA..

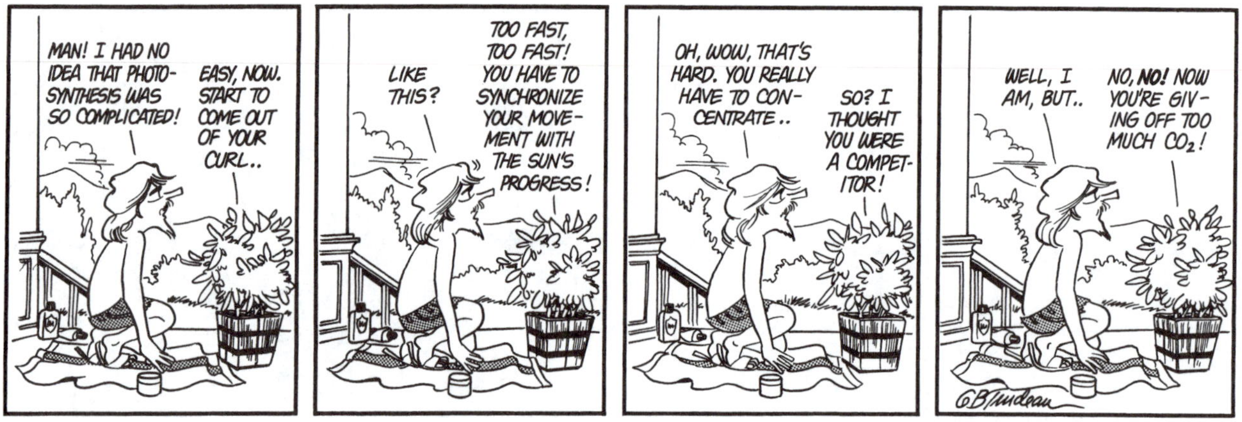
MAN! I HAD NO IDEA THAT PHOTOSYNTHESIS WAS SO COMPLICATED!
EASY, NOW. START TO COME OUT OF YOUR CURL..
LIKE THIS?
TOO FAST, TOO FAST! YOU HAVE TO SYNCHRONIZE YOUR MOVEMENT WITH THE SUN'S PROGRESS!
OH, WOW, THAT'S HARD. YOU REALLY HAVE TO CONCENTRATE..
SO? I THOUGHT YOU WERE A COMPETITOR!
WELL, I AM, BUT..
NO, NO! NOW YOU'RE GIVING OFF TOO MUCH CO_2!

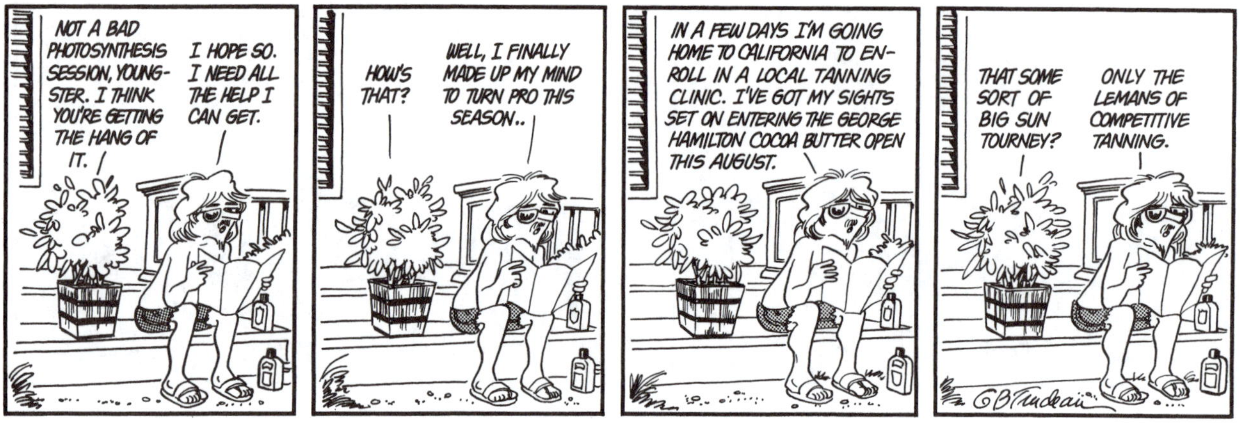
NOT A BAD PHOTOSYNTHESIS SESSION, YOUNGSTER. I THINK YOU'RE GETTING THE HANG OF IT.
I HOPE SO. I NEED ALL THE HELP I CAN GET.
HOW'S THAT?
WELL, I FINALLY MADE UP MY MIND TO TURN PRO THIS SEASON..
IN A FEW DAYS I'M GOING HOME TO CALIFORNIA TO ENROLL IN A LOCAL TANNING CLINIC. I'VE GOT MY SIGHTS SET ON ENTERING THE GEORGE HAMILTON COCOA BUTTER OPEN THIS AUGUST.
THAT SOME SORT OF BIG SUN TOURNEY?
ONLY THE LEMANS OF COMPETITIVE TANNING.

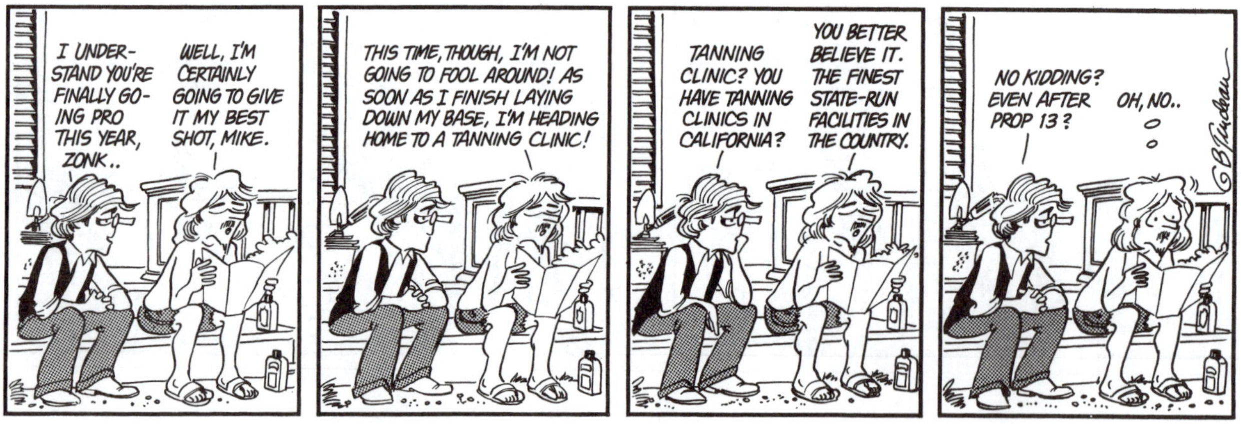
I UNDERSTAND YOU'RE FINALLY GOING PRO THIS YEAR, ZONK..
WELL, I'M CERTAINLY GOING TO GIVE IT MY BEST SHOT, MIKE.
THIS TIME, THOUGH, I'M NOT GOING TO FOOL AROUND! AS SOON AS I FINISH LAYING DOWN MY BASE, I'M HEADING HOME TO A TANNING CLINIC!
TANNING CLINIC? YOU HAVE TANNING CLINICS IN CALIFORNIA?
YOU BETTER BELIEVE IT. THE FINEST STATE-RUN FACILITIES IN THE COUNTRY.
NO KIDDING? EVEN AFTER PROP 13?
OH, NO..

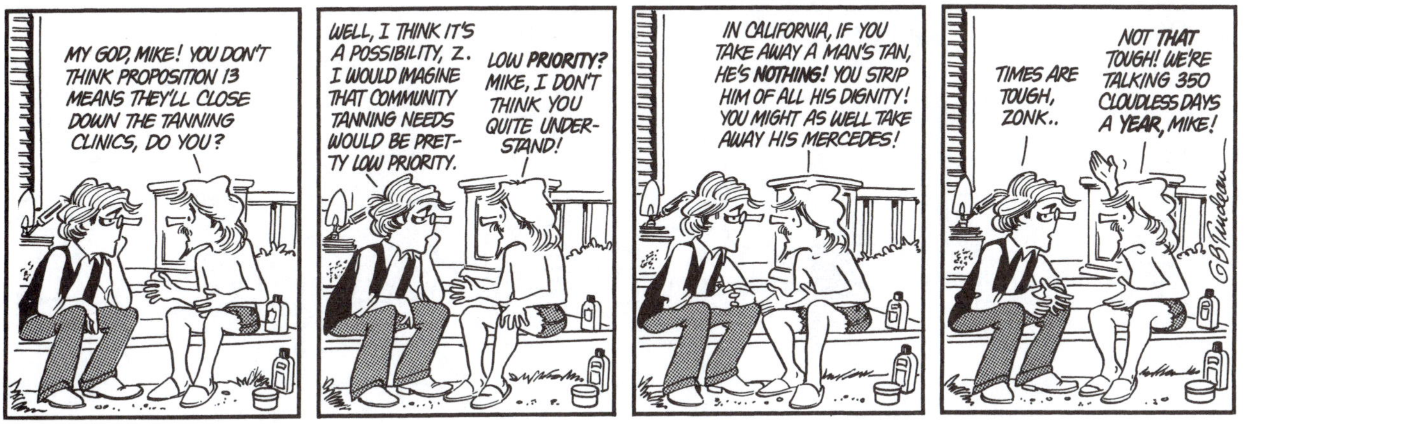
MY GOD, MIKE! YOU DON'T THINK PROPOSITION 13 MEANS THEY'LL CLOSE DOWN THE TANNING CLINICS, DO YOU?
WELL, I THINK IT'S A POSSIBILITY, Z. I WOULD IMAGINE THAT COMMUNITY TANNING NEEDS WOULD BE PRET-TY LOW PRIORITY.
LOW **PRIORITY?** MIKE, I DON'T THINK YOU QUITE UNDER-STAND!
IN CALIFORNIA, IF YOU TAKE AWAY A MAN'S TAN, HE'S **NOTHING!** YOU STRIP HIM OF ALL HIS DIGNITY! YOU MIGHT AS WELL TAKE AWAY HIS MERCEDES!
TIMES ARE TOUGH, ZONK..
NOT **THAT** TOUGH! WE'RE TALKING 350 CLOUDLESS DAYS A **YEAR,** MIKE!
GBTrudeau

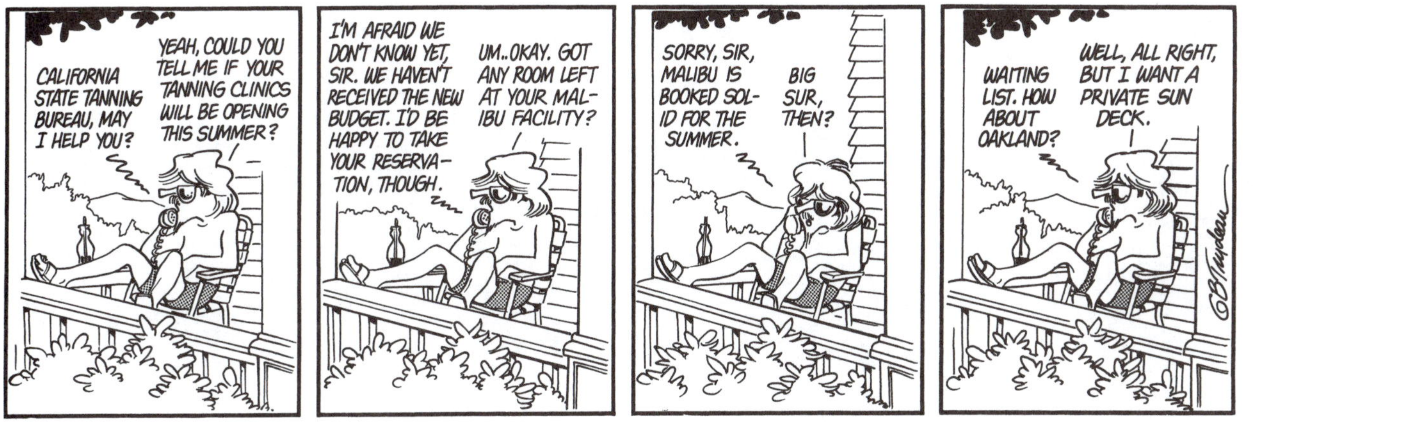
CALIFORNIA STATE TANNING BUREAU, MAY I HELP YOU?
YEAH, COULD YOU TELL ME IF YOUR TANNING CLINICS WILL BE OPENING THIS SUMMER?
I'M AFRAID WE DON'T KNOW YET, SIR. WE HAVEN'T RECEIVED THE NEW BUDGET. I'D BE HAPPY TO TAKE YOUR RESERVA-TION, THOUGH.
UM..OKAY. GOT ANY ROOM LEFT AT YOUR MAL-IBU FACILITY?
SORRY, SIR, MALIBU IS BOOKED SOL-ID FOR THE SUMMER.
BIG SUR, THEN?
WAITING LIST. HOW ABOUT OAKLAND?
WELL, ALL RIGHT, BUT I WANT A PRIVATE SUN DECK.
GBTrudeau

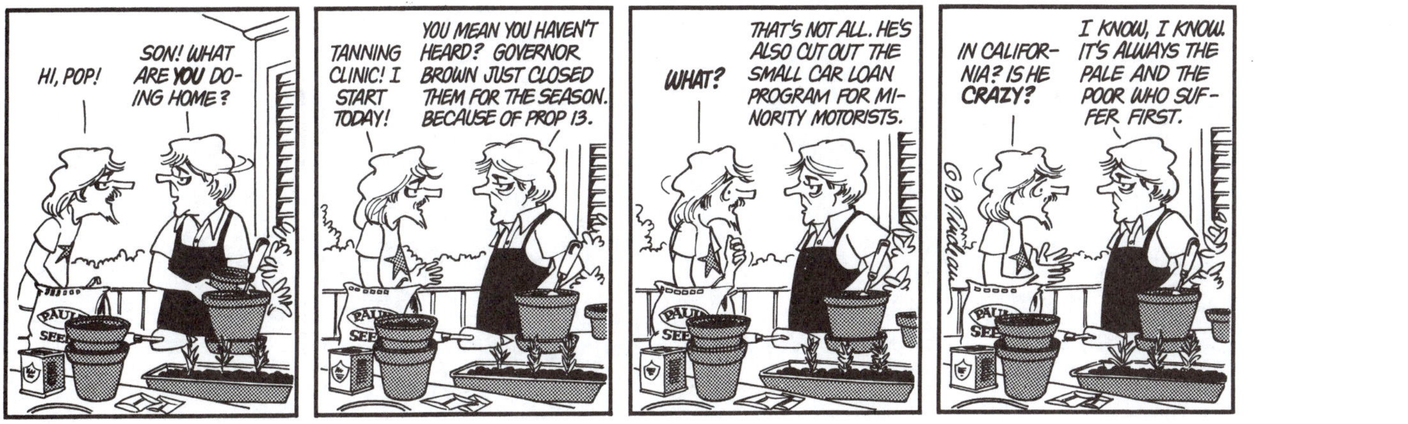
HI, POP!
SON! WHAT ARE **YOU** DO-ING HOME?
TANNING CLINIC! I START TODAY!
YOU MEAN YOU HAVEN'T HEARD? GOVERNOR BROWN JUST CLOSED THEM FOR THE SEASON. BECAUSE OF PROP 13.
WHAT?
THAT'S NOT ALL. HE'S ALSO CUT OUT THE SMALL CAR LOAN PROGRAM FOR MI-NORITY MOTORISTS.
IN CALIFOR-NIA? IS HE **CRAZY?**
I KNOW, I KNOW. IT'S ALWAYS THE PALE AND THE POOR WHO SUF-FER FIRST.
GBTrudeau

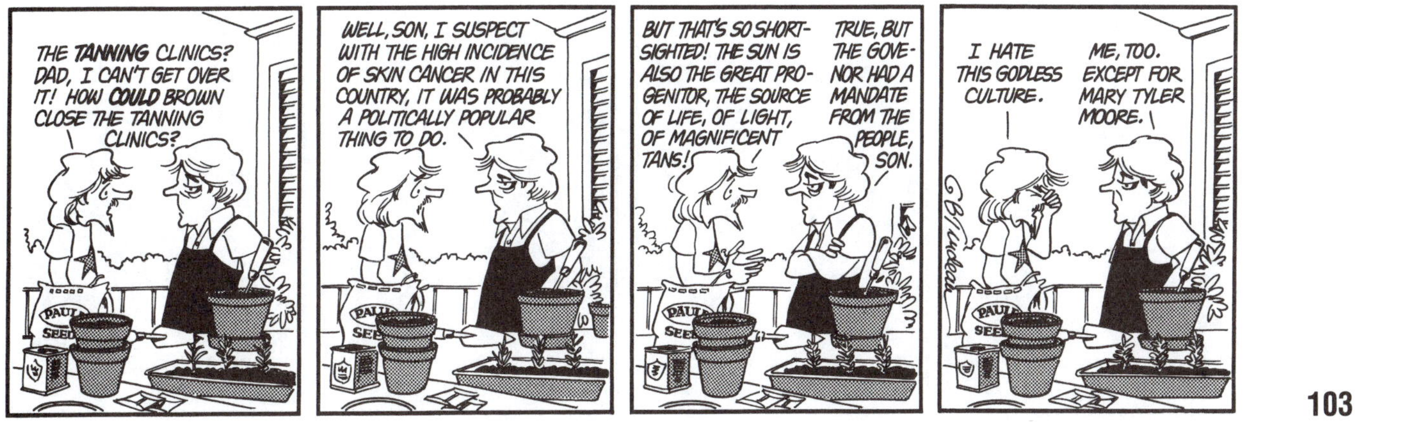
THE **TANNING** CLINICS? DAD, I CAN'T GET OVER IT! HOW **COULD** BROWN CLOSE THE TANNING CLINICS?
WELL, SON, I SUSPECT WITH THE HIGH INCIDENCE OF SKIN CANCER IN THIS COUNTRY, IT WAS PROBABLY A POLITICALLY POPULAR THING TO DO.
BUT THAT'S SO SHORT-SIGHTED! THE SUN IS ALSO THE GREAT PRO-GENITOR, THE SOURCE OF LIFE, OF LIGHT, OF MAGNIFICENT TANS!
TRUE, BUT THE GOVE-NOR HAD A MANDATE FROM THE PEOPLE, SON.
I HATE THIS GODLESS CULTURE.
ME, TOO. EXCEPT FOR MARY TYLER MOORE.
GBTrudeau

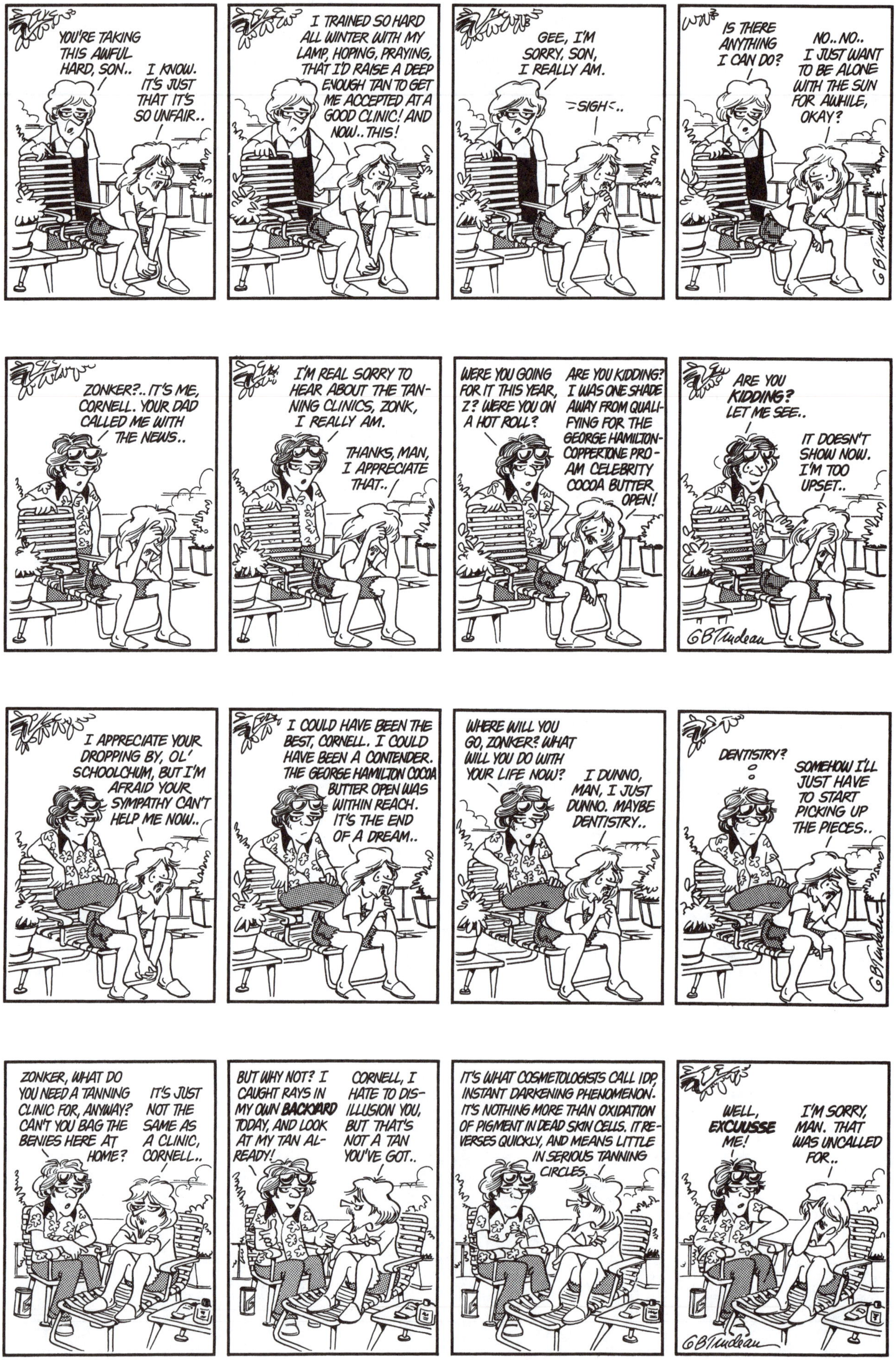
YOU'RE TAKING THIS AWFUL HARD, SON..
I KNOW. IT'S JUST THAT IT'S SO UNFAIR..
I TRAINED SO HARD ALL WINTER WITH MY LAMP, HOPING, PRAYING, THAT I'D RAISE A DEEP ENOUGH TAN TO GET ME ACCEPTED AT A GOOD CLINIC! AND NOW.. THIS!
GEE, I'M SORRY, SON, I REALLY AM.
SIGH..
IS THERE ANYTHING I CAN DO?
NO.. NO.. I JUST WANT TO BE ALONE WITH THE SUN FOR AWHILE, OKAY?
GBTrudeau
ZONKER?.. IT'S ME, CORNELL. YOUR DAD CALLED ME WITH THE NEWS..
I'M REAL SORRY TO HEAR ABOUT THE TANNING CLINICS, ZONK, I REALLY AM.
THANKS, MAN, I APPRECIATE THAT..
WERE YOU GOING FOR IT THIS YEAR, Z? WERE YOU ON A HOT ROLL?
ARE YOU KIDDING? I WAS ONE SHADE AWAY FROM QUALIFYING FOR THE GEORGE HAMILTON-COPPERTONE PRO-AM CELEBRITY COCOA BUTTER OPEN!
ARE YOU KIDDING? LET ME SEE..
IT DOESN'T SHOW NOW. I'M TOO UPSET..
GBTrudeau
I APPRECIATE YOUR DROPPING BY, OL' SCHOOLCHUM, BUT I'M AFRAID YOUR SYMPATHY CAN'T HELP ME NOW..
I COULD HAVE BEEN THE BEST, CORNELL. I COULD HAVE BEEN A CONTENDER. THE GEORGE HAMILTON COCOA BUTTER OPEN WAS WITHIN REACH. IT'S THE END OF A DREAM..
WHERE WILL YOU GO, ZONKER? WHAT WILL YOU DO WITH YOUR LIFE NOW?
I DUNNO, MAN, I JUST DUNNO. MAYBE DENTISTRY..
DENTISTRY?
SOMEHOW I'LL JUST HAVE TO START PICKING UP THE PIECES..
GBTrudeau
ZONKER, WHAT DO YOU NEED A TANNING CLINIC FOR, ANYWAY? CAN'T YOU BAG THE BENIES HERE AT HOME?
IT'S JUST NOT THE SAME AS A CLINIC, CORNELL..
BUT WHY NOT? I CAUGHT RAYS IN MY OWN BACKYARD TODAY, AND LOOK AT MY TAN ALREADY!
CORNELL, I HATE TO DISILLUSION YOU, BUT THAT'S NOT A TAN YOU'VE GOT..
IT'S WHAT COSMETOLOGISTS CALL IDP, INSTANT DARKENING PHENOMENON. IT'S NOTHING MORE THAN OXIDATION OF PIGMENT IN DEAD SKIN CELLS. IT REVERSES QUICKLY, AND MEANS LITTLE IN SERIOUS TANNING CIRCLES.
WELL, EXCUUSSE ME!
I'M SORRY, MAN. THAT WAS UNCALLED FOR..
GBTrudeau

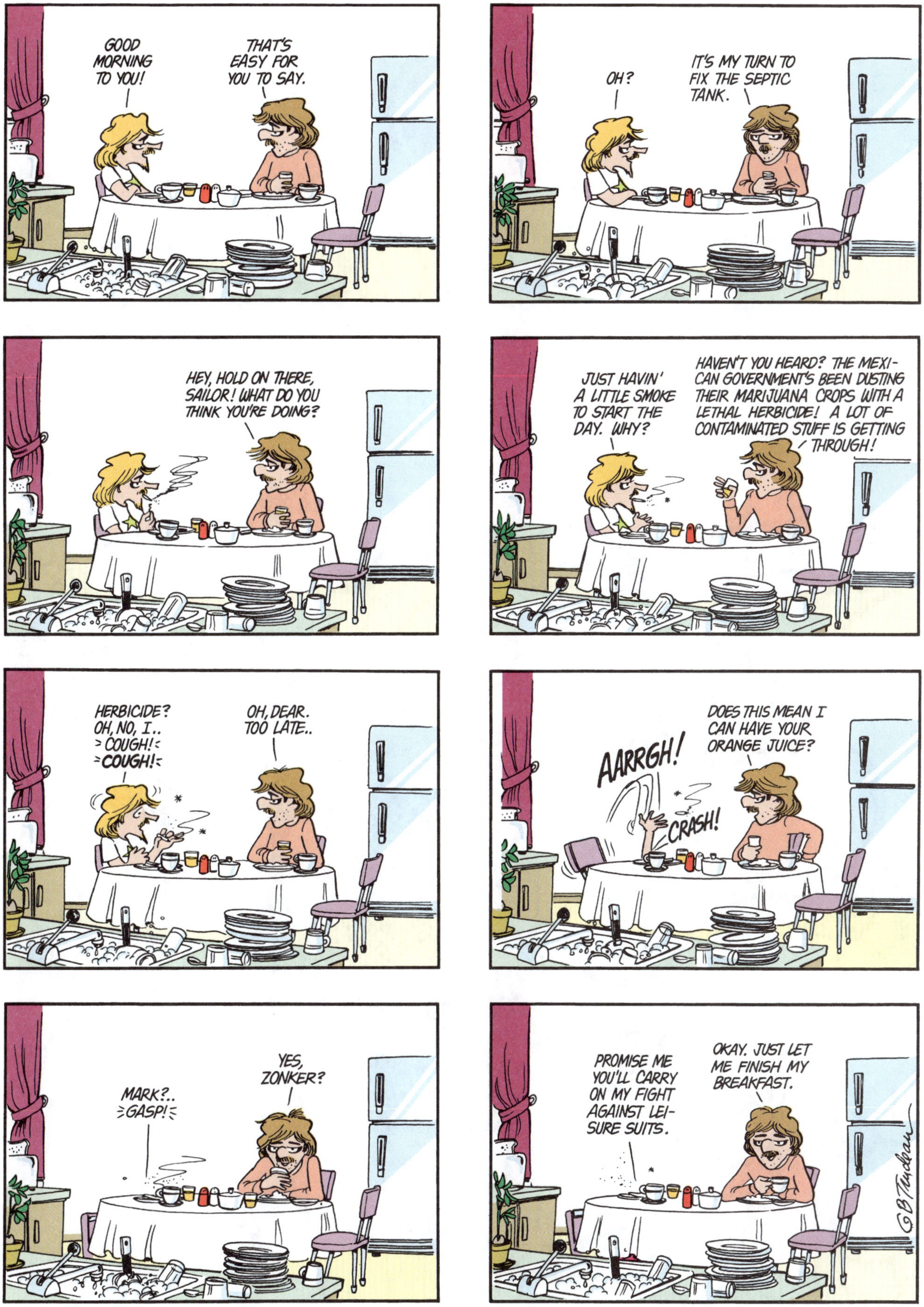
GOOD MORNING TO YOU!
THAT'S EASY FOR YOU TO SAY.
OH?
IT'S MY TURN TO FIX THE SEPTIC TANK.
HEY, HOLD ON THERE, SAILOR! WHAT DO YOU THINK YOU'RE DOING?
JUST HAVIN' A LITTLE SMOKE TO START THE DAY. WHY?
HAVEN'T YOU HEARD? THE MEXICAN GOVERNMENT'S BEEN DUSTING THEIR MARIJUANA CROPS WITH A LETHAL HERBICIDE! A LOT OF CONTAMINATED STUFF IS GETTING THROUGH!
HERBICIDE? OH, NO, I.. COUGH! COUGH!
OH, DEAR. TOO LATE..
AARRGH!
CRASH!
DOES THIS MEAN I CAN HAVE YOUR ORANGE JUICE?
MARK?.. GASP!
YES, ZONKER?
PROMISE ME YOU'LL CARRY ON MY FIGHT AGAINST LEISURE SUITS.
OKAY. JUST LET ME FINISH MY BREAKFAST.

5

THE GATE-CRASHER

Beyond the Velvet Ropes

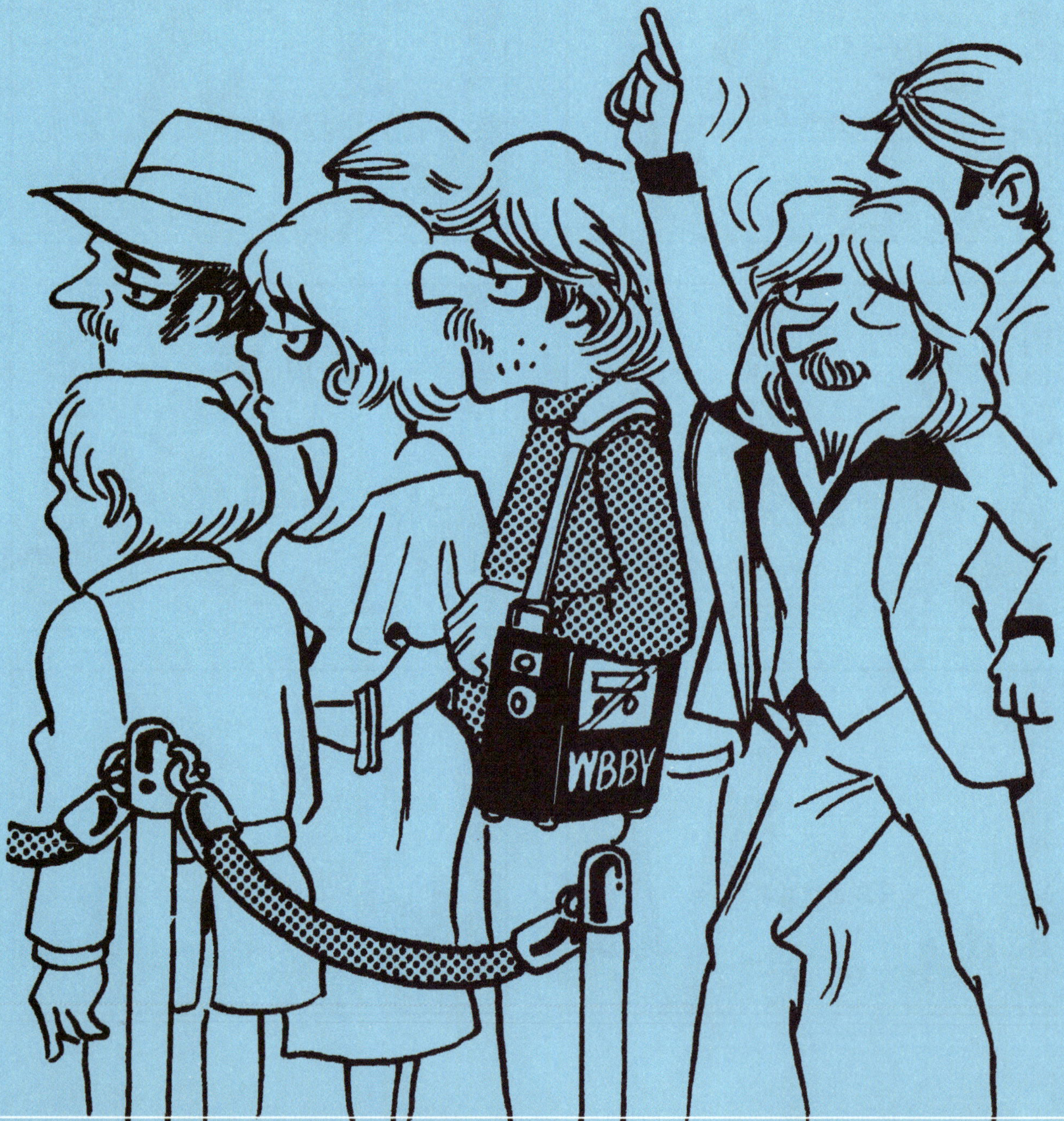
WBBY

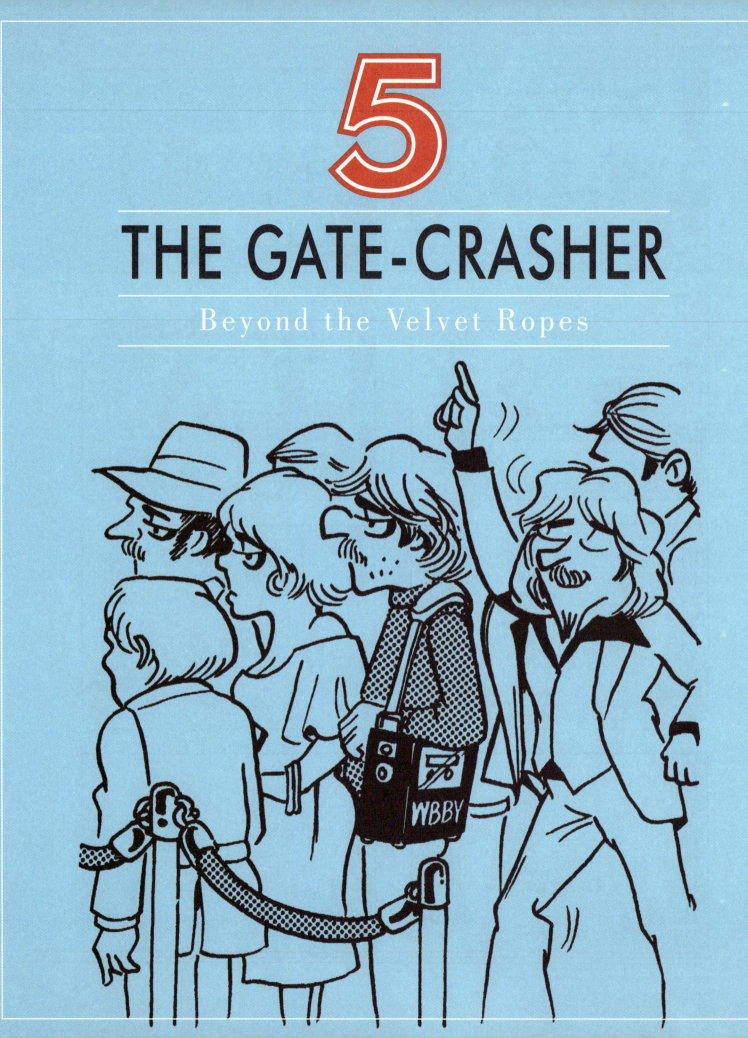

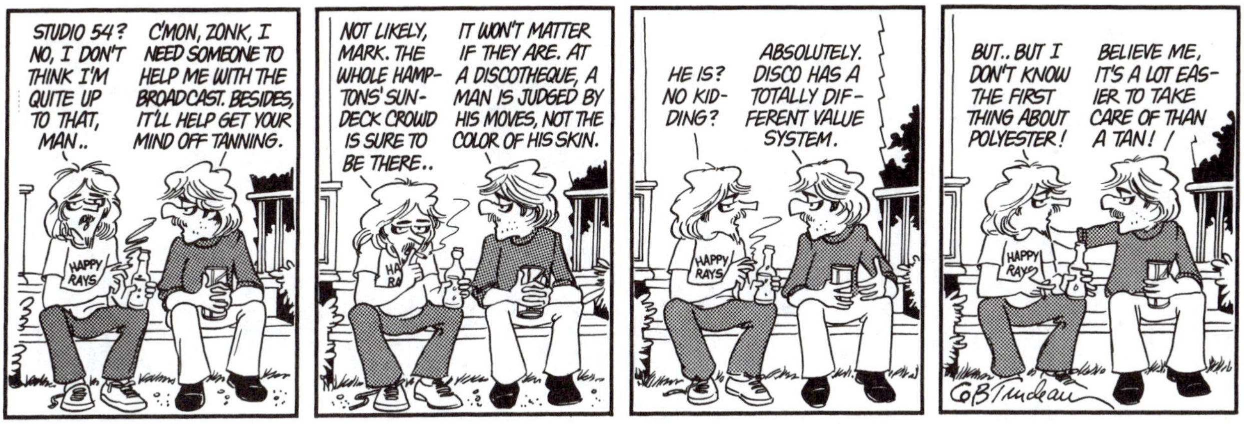
STUDIO 54? NO, I DON'T THINK I'M QUITE UP TO THAT, MAN..
C'MON, ZONK, I NEED SOMEONE TO HELP ME WITH THE BROADCAST. BESIDES, IT'LL HELP GET YOUR MIND OFF TANNING.
HAPPY RAYS
NOT LIKELY, MARK. THE WHOLE HAMPTONS' SUNDECK CROWD IS SURE TO BE THERE..
IT WON'T MATTER IF THEY ARE. AT A DISCOTHEQUE, A MAN IS JUDGED BY HIS MOVES, NOT THE COLOR OF HIS SKIN.
HE IS? NO KIDDING?
ABSOLUTELY. DISCO HAS A TOTALLY DIFFERENT VALUE SYSTEM.
HAPPY RAYS
BUT.. BUT I DON'T KNOW THE FIRST THING ABOUT POLYESTER!
BELIEVE ME, IT'S A LOT EASIER TO TAKE CARE OF THAN A TAN!
HAPPY RAYS
GBTrudeau

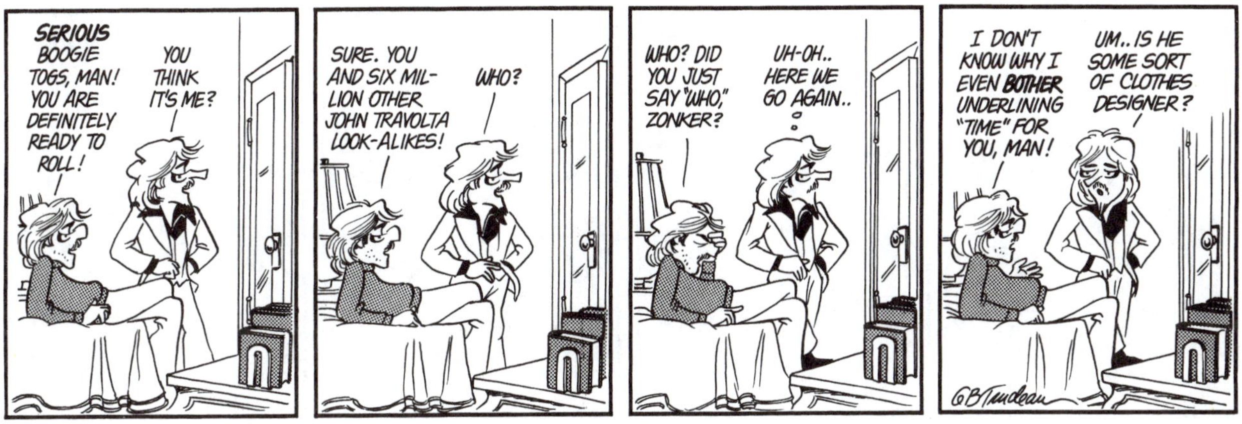
SERIOUS BOOGIE TOGS, MAN! YOU ARE DEFINITELY READY TO ROLL!
YOU THINK IT'S ME?
SURE. YOU AND SIX MILLION OTHER JOHN TRAVOLTA LOOK-ALIKES!
WHO?
WHO? DID YOU JUST SAY "WHO," ZONKER?
UH-OH.. HERE WE GO AGAIN..
I DON'T KNOW WHY I EVEN BOTHER UNDERLINING "TIME" FOR YOU, MAN!
UM.. IS HE SOME SORT OF CLOTHES DESIGNER?
GBTrudeau

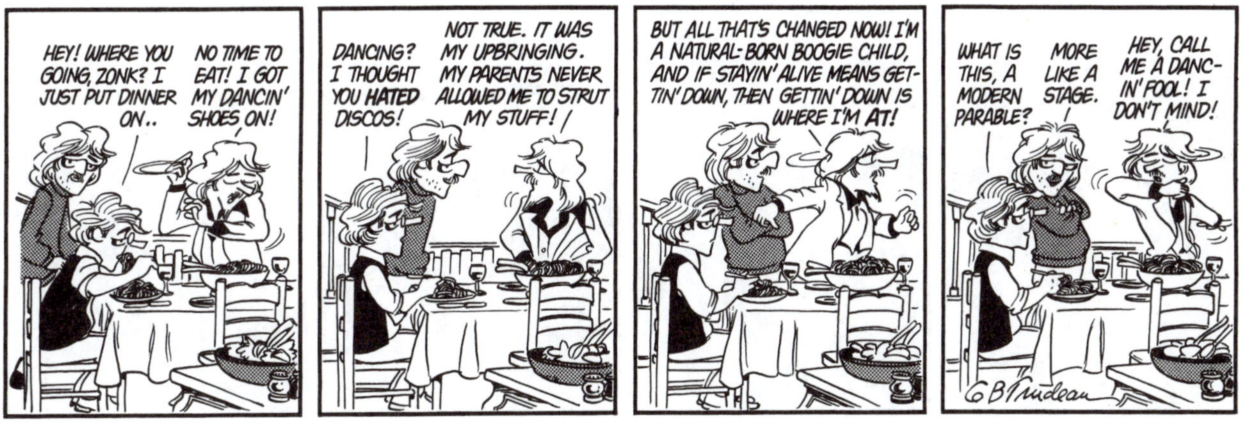
HEY! WHERE YOU GOING, ZONK? I JUST PUT DINNER ON..
NO TIME TO EAT! I GOT MY DANCIN' SHOES ON!
DANCING? I THOUGHT YOU HATED DISCOS!
NOT TRUE. IT WAS MY UPBRINGING. MY PARENTS NEVER ALLOWED ME TO STRUT MY STUFF!
BUT ALL THAT'S CHANGED NOW! I'M A NATURAL-BORN BOOGIE CHILD, AND IF STAYIN' ALIVE MEANS GETTIN' DOWN, THEN GETTIN' DOWN IS WHERE I'M AT!
WHAT IS THIS, A MODERN PARABLE?
MORE LIKE A STAGE.
HEY, CALL ME A DANCIN' FOOL! I DON'T MIND!
GBTrudeau

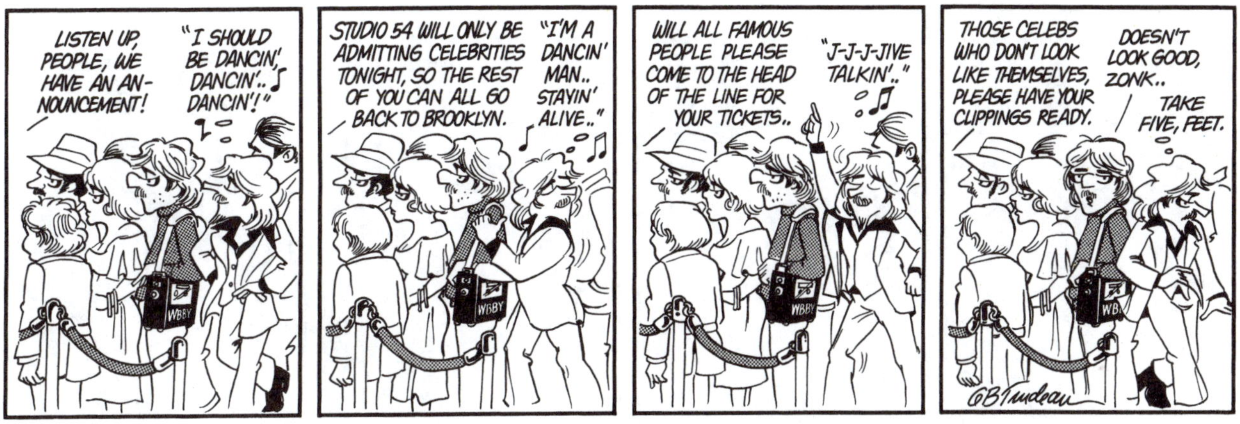
LISTEN UP, PEOPLE, WE HAVE AN ANNOUNCEMENT!
"I SHOULD BE DANCIN', DANCIN'.. DANCIN'!"
WBBY
STUDIO 54 WILL ONLY BE ADMITTING CELEBRITIES TONIGHT, SO THE REST OF YOU CAN ALL GO BACK TO BROOKLYN.
"I'M A DANCIN' MAN.. STAYIN' ALIVE.."
WILL ALL FAMOUS PEOPLE PLEASE COME TO THE HEAD OF THE LINE FOR YOUR TICKETS..
"J-J-J-JIVE TALKIN'.."
WBBY
THOSE CELEBS WHO DON'T LOOK LIKE THEMSELVES, PLEASE HAVE YOUR CLIPPINGS READY.
DOESN'T LOOK GOOD, ZONK..
TAKE FIVE, FEET.
WBBY
GBTrudeau

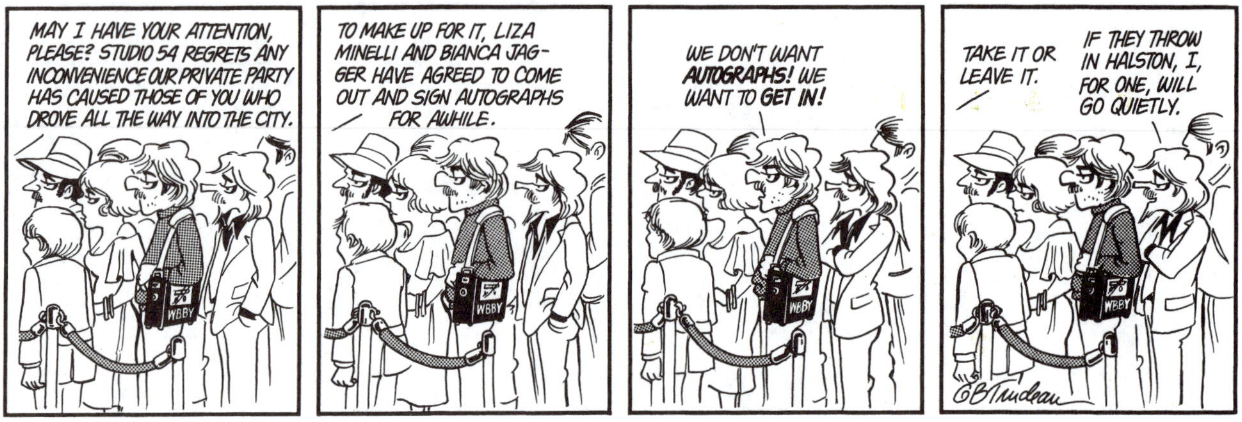
MAY I HAVE YOUR ATTENTION, PLEASE? STUDIO 54 REGRETS ANY INCONVENIENCE OUR PRIVATE PARTY HAS CAUSED THOSE OF YOU WHO DROVE ALL THE WAY INTO THE CITY.
TO MAKE UP FOR IT, LIZA MINELLI AND BIANCA JAGGER HAVE AGREED TO COME OUT AND SIGN AUTOGRAPHS FOR AWHILE.
WE DON'T WANT AUTOGRAPHS! WE WANT TO GET IN!
TAKE IT OR LEAVE IT.
IF THEY THROW IN HALSTON, I, FOR ONE, WILL GO QUIETLY.
WBBY
GBTrudeau

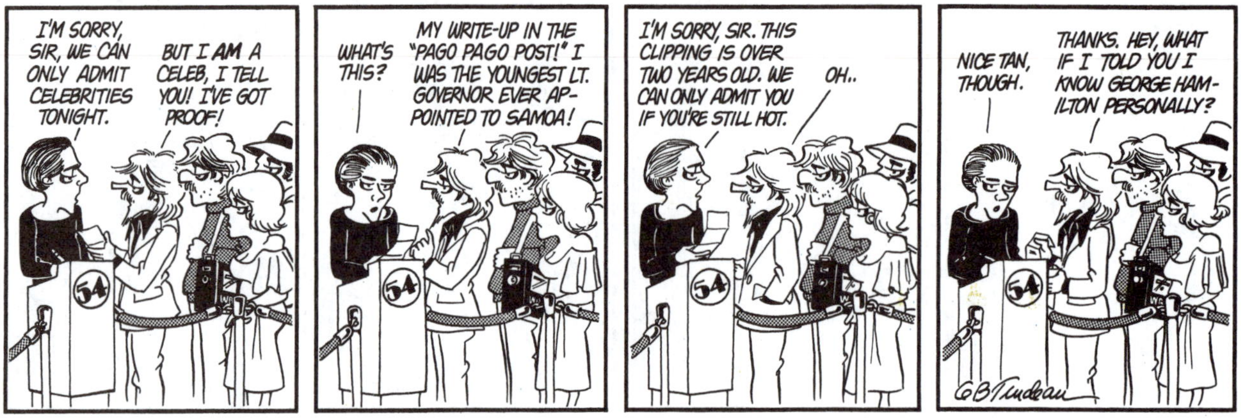
I'M SORRY, SIR, WE CAN ONLY ADMIT CELEBRITIES TONIGHT.
BUT I AM A CELEB, I TELL YOU! I'VE GOT PROOF!
WHAT'S THIS?
MY WRITE-UP IN THE "PAGO PAGO POST!" I WAS THE YOUNGEST LT. GOVERNOR EVER APPOINTED TO SAMOA!
I'M SORRY, SIR. THIS CLIPPING IS OVER TWO YEARS OLD. WE CAN ONLY ADMIT YOU IF YOU'RE STILL HOT.
OH..
NICE TAN, THOUGH.
THANKS. HEY, WHAT IF I TOLD YOU I KNOW GEORGE HAMILTON PERSONALLY?
54
GBTrudeau

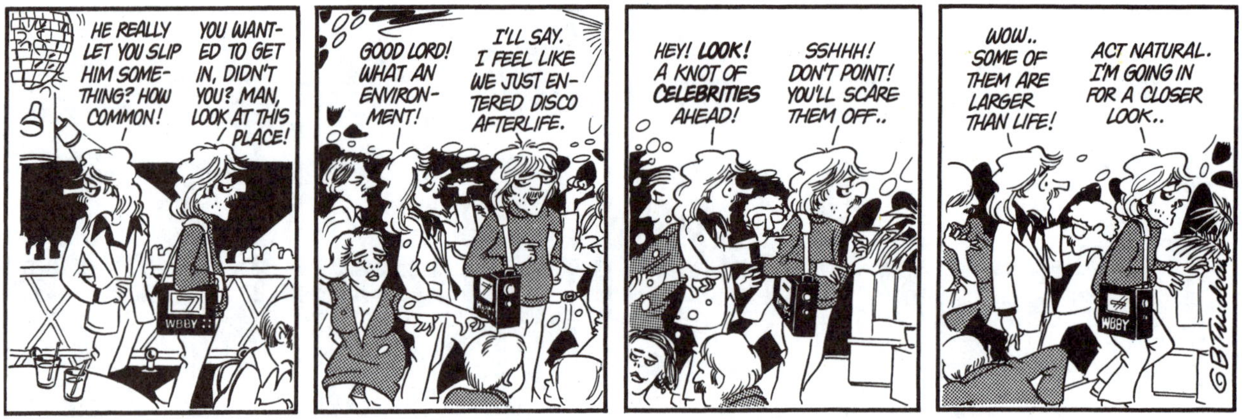
HE REALLY LET YOU SLIP HIM SOMETHING? HOW COMMON!
YOU WANTED TO GET IN, DIDN'T YOU? MAN, LOOK AT THIS PLACE!
GOOD LORD! WHAT AN ENVIRONMENT!
I'LL SAY. I FEEL LIKE WE JUST ENTERED DISCO AFTERLIFE.
HEY! LOOK! A KNOT OF CELEBRITIES AHEAD!
SSHHH! DON'T POINT! YOU'LL SCARE THEM OFF..
WOW.. SOME OF THEM ARE LARGER THAN LIFE!
ACT NATURAL. I'M GOING IN FOR A CLOSER LOOK..
WBBY
GBTrudeau

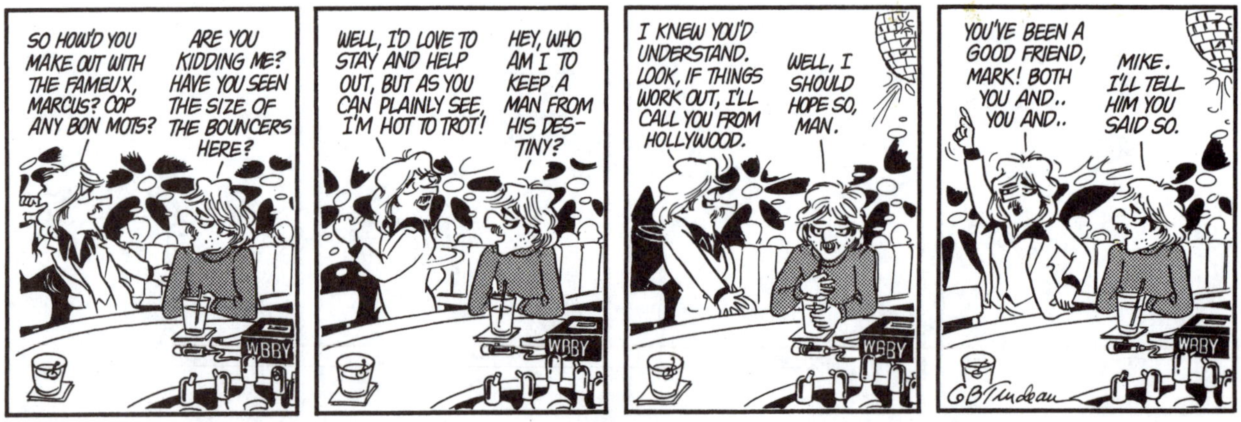
SO HOW'D YOU MAKE OUT WITH THE FAMEUX, MARCUS? COP ANY BON MOTS?
ARE YOU KIDDING ME? HAVE YOU SEEN THE SIZE OF THE BOUNCERS HERE?
WELL, I'D LOVE TO STAY AND HELP OUT, BUT AS YOU CAN PLAINLY SEE, I'M HOT TO TROT!
HEY, WHO AM I TO KEEP A MAN FROM HIS DESTINY?
I KNEW YOU'D UNDERSTAND. LOOK, IF THINGS WORK OUT, I'LL CALL YOU FROM HOLLYWOOD.
WELL, I SHOULD HOPE SO, MAN.
YOU'VE BEEN A GOOD FRIEND, MARK! BOTH YOU AND.. YOU AND..
MIKE. I'LL TELL HIM YOU SAID SO.
WBBY
GBTrudeau

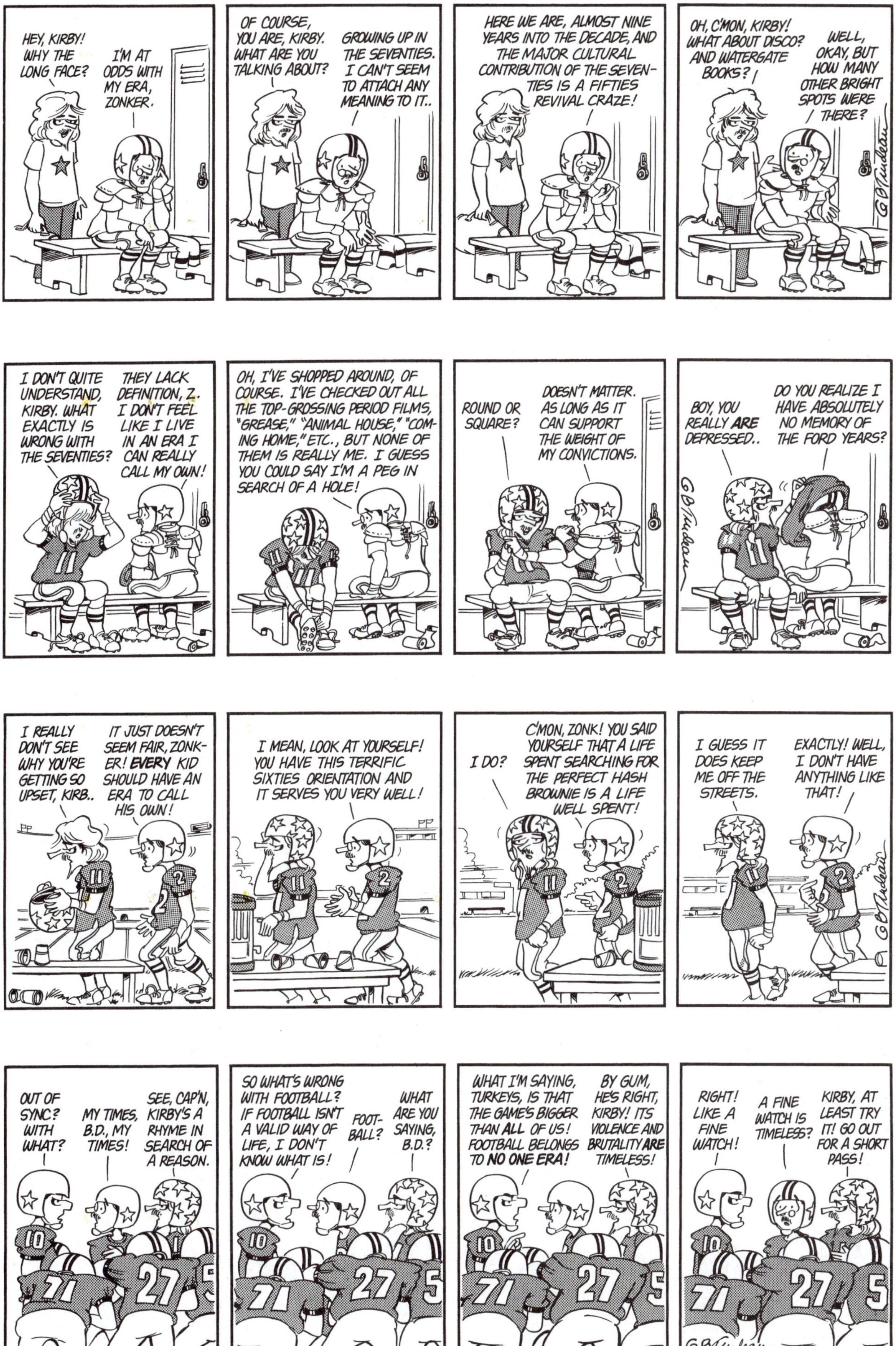

HEY, KIRBY! WHY THE LONG FACE?
I'M AT ODDS WITH MY ERA, ZONKER.
OF COURSE, YOU ARE, KIRBY. WHAT ARE YOU TALKING ABOUT?
GROWING UP IN THE SEVENTIES. I CAN'T SEEM TO ATTACH ANY MEANING TO IT..
HERE WE ARE, ALMOST NINE YEARS INTO THE DECADE, AND THE MAJOR CULTURAL CONTRIBUTION OF THE SEVENTIES IS A FIFTIES REVIVAL CRAZE!
OH, C'MON, KIRBY! WHAT ABOUT DISCO? AND WATERGATE BOOKS?
WELL, OKAY, BUT HOW MANY OTHER BRIGHT SPOTS WERE THERE?
I DON'T QUITE UNDERSTAND, KIRBY. WHAT EXACTLY IS WRONG WITH THE SEVENTIES?
THEY LACK DEFINITION, Z. I DON'T FEEL LIKE I LIVE IN AN ERA I CAN REALLY CALL MY OWN!
OH, I'VE SHOPPED AROUND, OF COURSE. I'VE CHECKED OUT ALL THE TOP-GROSSING PERIOD FILMS, "GREASE," "ANIMAL HOUSE," "COMING HOME," ETC., BUT NONE OF THEM IS REALLY ME. I GUESS YOU COULD SAY I'M A PEG IN SEARCH OF A HOLE!
ROUND OR SQUARE?
DOESN'T MATTER. AS LONG AS IT CAN SUPPORT THE WEIGHT OF MY CONVICTIONS.
BOY, YOU REALLY ARE DEPRESSED..
DO YOU REALIZE I HAVE ABSOLUTELY NO MEMORY OF THE FORD YEARS?
I REALLY DON'T SEE WHY YOU'RE GETTING SO UPSET, KIRB..
IT JUST DOESN'T SEEM FAIR, ZONKER! EVERY KID SHOULD HAVE AN ERA TO CALL HIS OWN!
I MEAN, LOOK AT YOURSELF! YOU HAVE THIS TERRIFIC SIXTIES ORIENTATION AND IT SERVES YOU VERY WELL!
I DO?
C'MON, ZONK! YOU SAID YOURSELF THAT A LIFE SPENT SEARCHING FOR THE PERFECT HASH BROWNIE IS A LIFE WELL SPENT!
I GUESS IT DOES KEEP ME OFF THE STREETS.
EXACTLY! WELL, I DON'T HAVE ANYTHING LIKE THAT!
OUT OF SYNC? WITH WHAT?
MY TIMES, B.D., MY TIMES!
SEE, CAP'N, KIRBY'S A RHYME IN SEARCH OF A REASON.
SO WHAT'S WRONG WITH FOOTBALL? IF FOOTBALL ISN'T A VALID WAY OF LIFE, I DON'T KNOW WHAT IS!
FOOTBALL?
WHAT ARE YOU SAYING, B.D.?
WHAT I'M SAYING, TURKEYS, IS THAT THE GAME'S BIGGER THAN ALL OF US! FOOTBALL BELONGS TO NO ONE ERA!
BY GUM, HE'S RIGHT, KIRBY! ITS VIOLENCE AND BRUTALITY ARE TIMELESS!
RIGHT! LIKE A FINE WATCH!
A FINE WATCH IS TIMELESS?
KIRBY, AT LEAST TRY IT! GO OUT FOR A SHORT PASS!

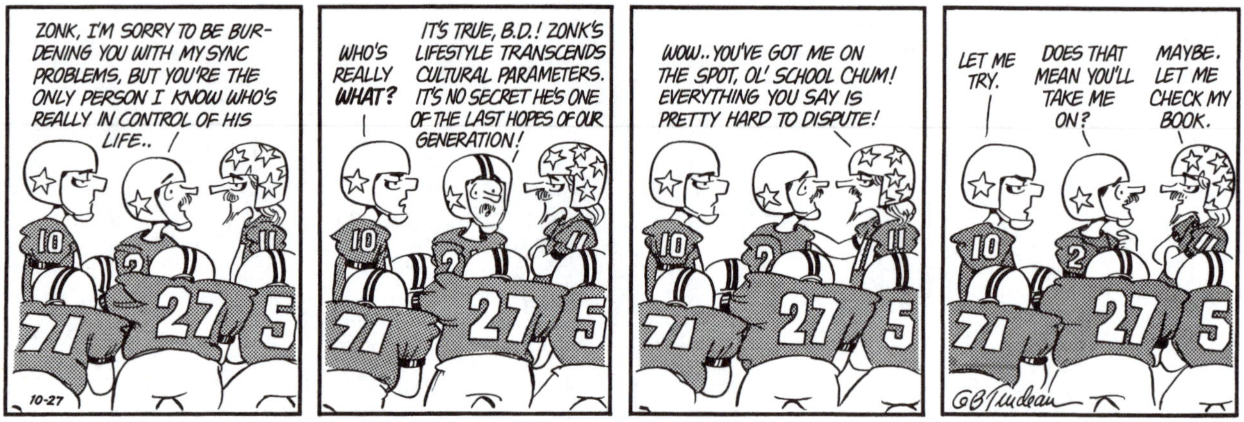
ZONK, I'M SORRY TO BE BURDENING YOU WITH MY SYNC PROBLEMS, BUT YOU'RE THE ONLY PERSON I KNOW WHO'S REALLY IN CONTROL OF HIS LIFE..
10-27
WHO'S REALLY **WHAT?**
IT'S TRUE, B.D.! ZONK'S LIFESTYLE TRANSCENDS CULTURAL PARAMETERS. IT'S NO SECRET HE'S ONE OF THE LAST HOPES OF OUR GENERATION!
WOW.. YOU'VE GOT ME ON THE SPOT, OL' SCHOOL CHUM! EVERYTHING YOU SAY IS PRETTY HARD TO DISPUTE!
LET ME TRY.
DOES THAT MEAN YOU'LL TAKE ME ON?
MAYBE. LET ME CHECK MY BOOK.
GBTrudeau

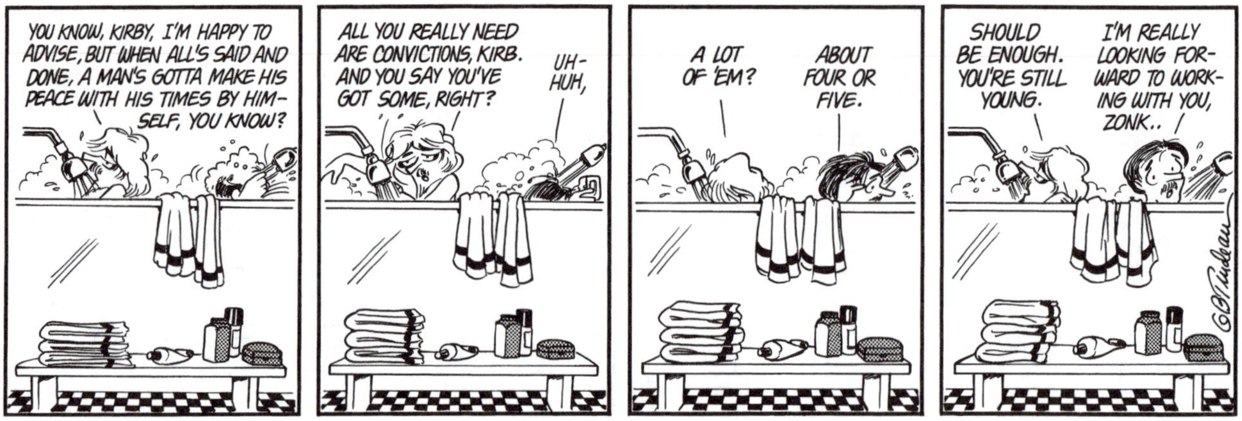
YOU KNOW, KIRBY, I'M HAPPY TO ADVISE, BUT WHEN ALL'S SAID AND DONE, A MAN'S GOTTA MAKE HIS PEACE WITH HIS TIMES BY HIMSELF, YOU KNOW?
ALL YOU REALLY NEED ARE CONVICTIONS, KIRB. AND YOU SAY YOU'VE GOT SOME, RIGHT?
UH-HUH,
A LOT OF 'EM?
ABOUT FOUR OR FIVE.
SHOULD BE ENOUGH. YOU'RE STILL YOUNG.
I'M REALLY LOOKING FORWARD TO WORKING WITH YOU, ZONK..
GBTrudeau

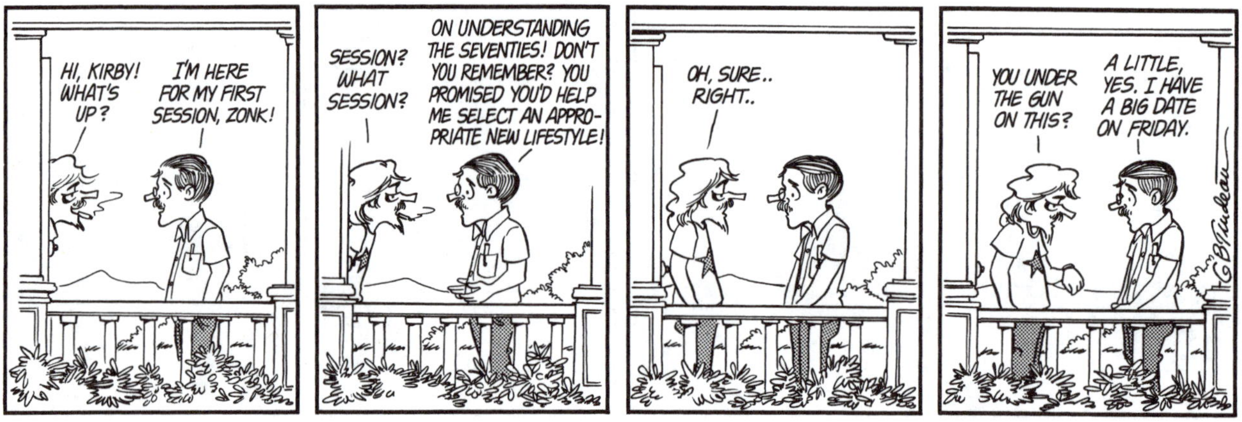
HI, KIRBY! WHAT'S UP?
I'M HERE FOR MY FIRST SESSION, ZONK!
SESSION? WHAT SESSION?
ON UNDERSTANDING THE SEVENTIES! DON'T YOU REMEMBER? YOU PROMISED YOU'D HELP ME SELECT AN APPROPRIATE NEW LIFESTYLE!
OH, SURE.. RIGHT..
YOU UNDER THE GUN ON THIS?
A LITTLE, YES. I HAVE A BIG DATE ON FRIDAY.
GBTrudeau

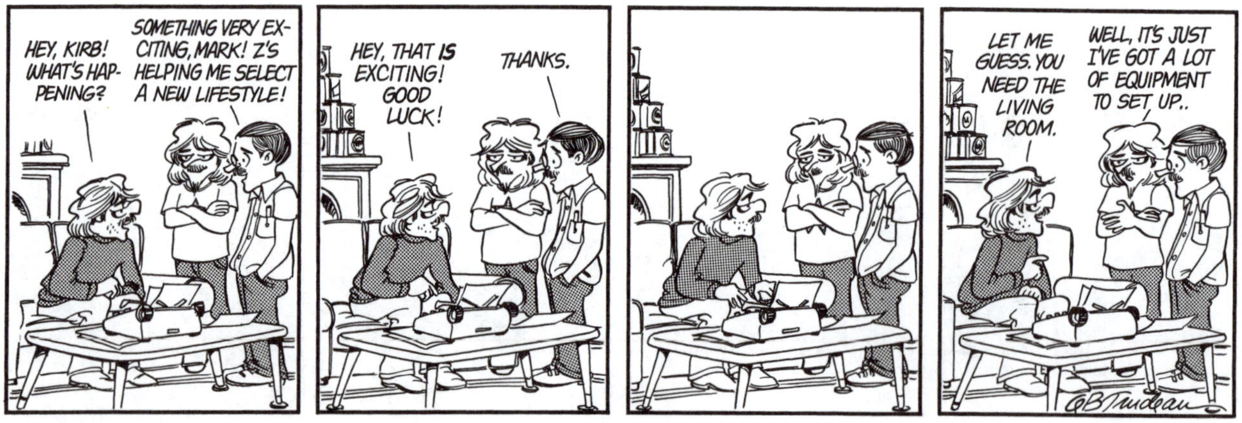
HEY, KIRB! WHAT'S HAPPENING?
SOMETHING VERY EXCITING, MARK! Z'S HELPING ME SELECT A NEW LIFESTYLE!
HEY, THAT **IS** EXCITING! GOOD LUCK!
THANKS.
LET ME GUESS. YOU NEED THE LIVING ROOM.
WELL, IT'S JUST I'VE GOT A LOT OF EQUIPMENT TO SET UP..
GBTrudeau

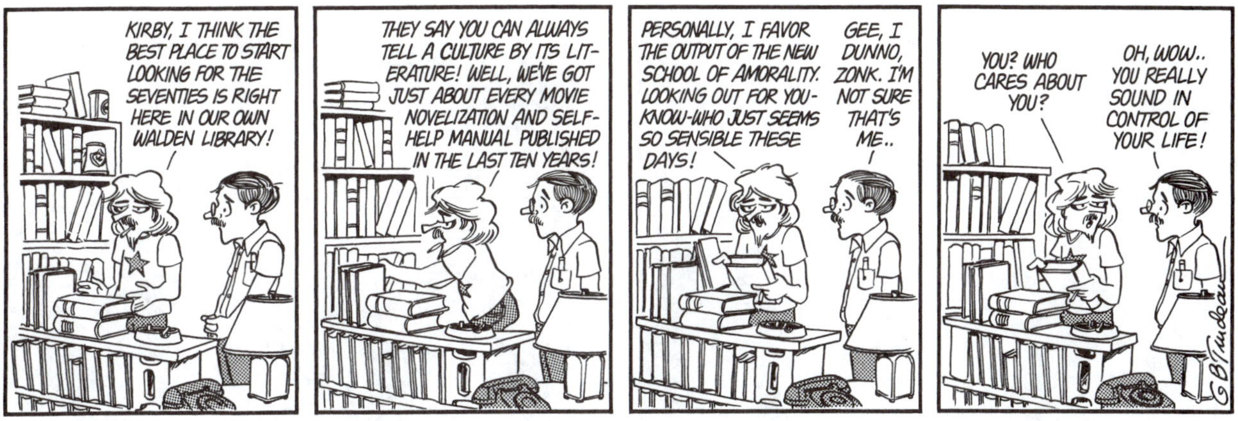
KIRBY, I THINK THE BEST PLACE TO START LOOKING FOR THE SEVENTIES IS RIGHT HERE IN OUR OWN WALDEN LIBRARY!
THEY SAY YOU CAN ALWAYS TELL A CULTURE BY ITS LITERATURE! WELL, WE'VE GOT JUST ABOUT EVERY MOVIE NOVELIZATION AND SELF-HELP MANUAL PUBLISHED IN THE LAST TEN YEARS!
PERSONALLY, I FAVOR THE OUTPUT OF THE NEW SCHOOL OF AMORALITY. LOOKING OUT FOR YOU-KNOW-WHO JUST SEEMS SO SENSIBLE THESE DAYS!
GEE, I DUNNO, ZONK. I'M NOT SURE THAT'S ME..
YOU? WHO CARES ABOUT YOU?
OH, WOW.. YOU REALLY SOUND IN CONTROL OF YOUR LIFE!
G B Trudeau

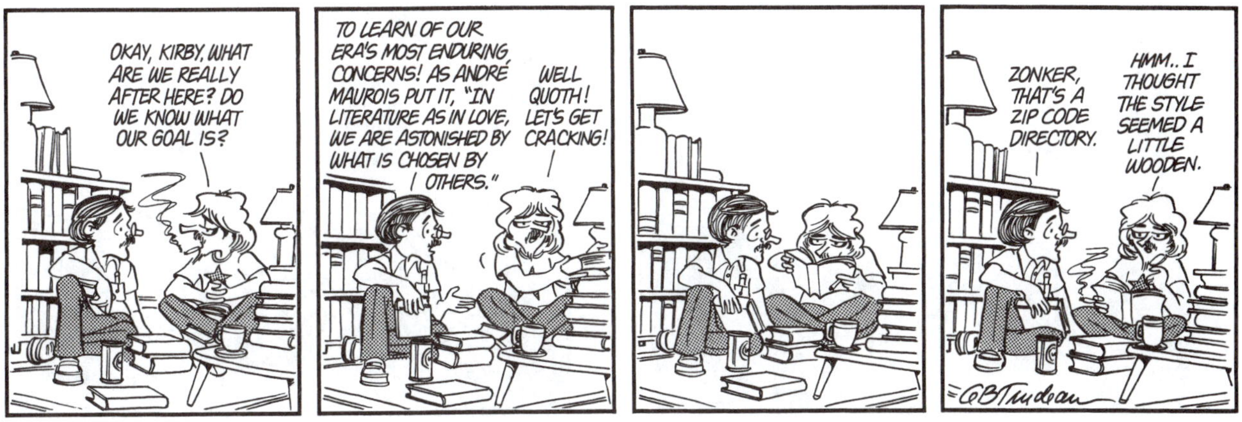
OKAY, KIRBY, WHAT ARE WE REALLY AFTER HERE? DO WE KNOW WHAT OUR GOAL IS?
TO LEARN OF OUR ERA'S MOST ENDURING CONCERNS! AS ANDRÉ MAUROIS PUT IT, "IN LITERATURE AS IN LOVE, WE ARE ASTONISHED BY WHAT IS CHOSEN BY OTHERS."
WELL QUOTH! LET'S GET CRACKING!
ZONKER, THAT'S A ZIP CODE DIRECTORY.
HMM.. I THOUGHT THE STYLE SEEMED A LITTLE WOODEN.
G B Trudeau

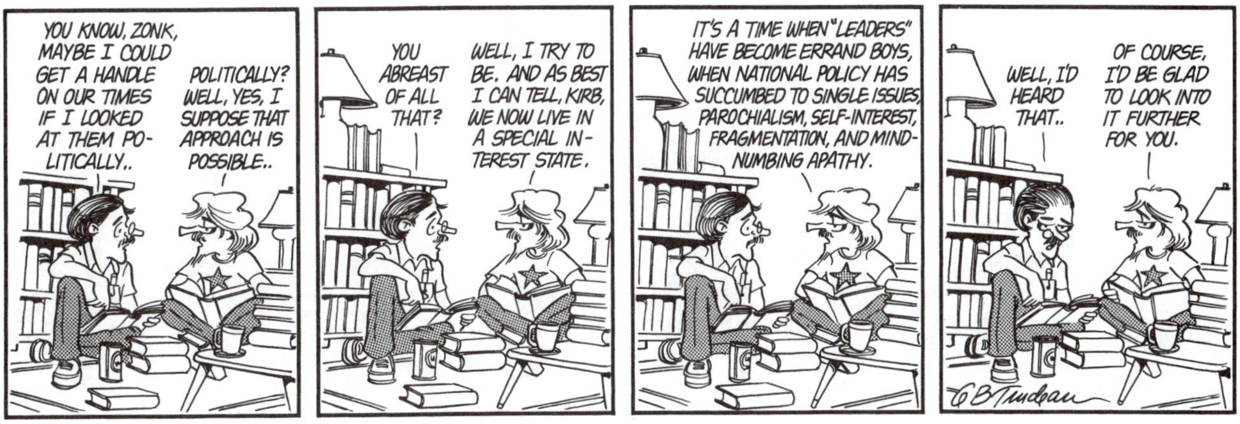
YOU KNOW, ZONK, MAYBE I COULD GET A HANDLE ON OUR TIMES IF I LOOKED AT THEM POLITICALLY..
POLITICALLY? WELL, YES, I SUPPOSE THAT APPROACH IS POSSIBLE..
YOU ABREAST OF ALL THAT?
WELL, I TRY TO BE. AND AS BEST I CAN TELL, KIRB, WE NOW LIVE IN A SPECIAL INTEREST STATE.
IT'S A TIME WHEN "LEADERS" HAVE BECOME ERRAND BOYS, WHEN NATIONAL POLICY HAS SUCCUMBED TO SINGLE ISSUES, PAROCHIALISM, SELF-INTEREST, FRAGMENTATION, AND MIND-NUMBING APATHY.
WELL, I'D HEARD THAT..
OF COURSE, I'D BE GLAD TO LOOK INTO IT FURTHER FOR YOU.
G B Trudeau

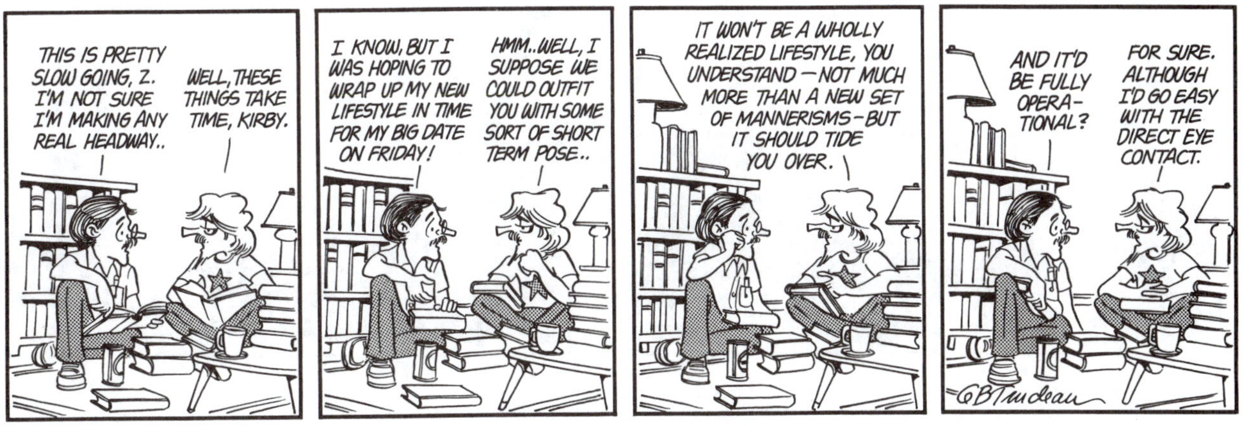
THIS IS PRETTY SLOW GOING, Z. I'M NOT SURE I'M MAKING ANY REAL HEADWAY..
WELL, THESE THINGS TAKE TIME, KIRBY.
I KNOW, BUT I WAS HOPING TO WRAP UP MY NEW LIFESTYLE IN TIME FOR MY BIG DATE ON FRIDAY!
HMM..WELL, I SUPPOSE WE COULD OUTFIT YOU WITH SOME SORT OF SHORT TERM POSE..
IT WON'T BE A WHOLLY REALIZED LIFESTYLE, YOU UNDERSTAND — NOT MUCH MORE THAN A NEW SET OF MANNERISMS — BUT IT SHOULD TIDE YOU OVER.
AND IT'D BE FULLY OPERATIONAL?
FOR SURE. ALTHOUGH I'D GO EASY WITH THE DIRECT EYE CONTACT.
G B Trudeau

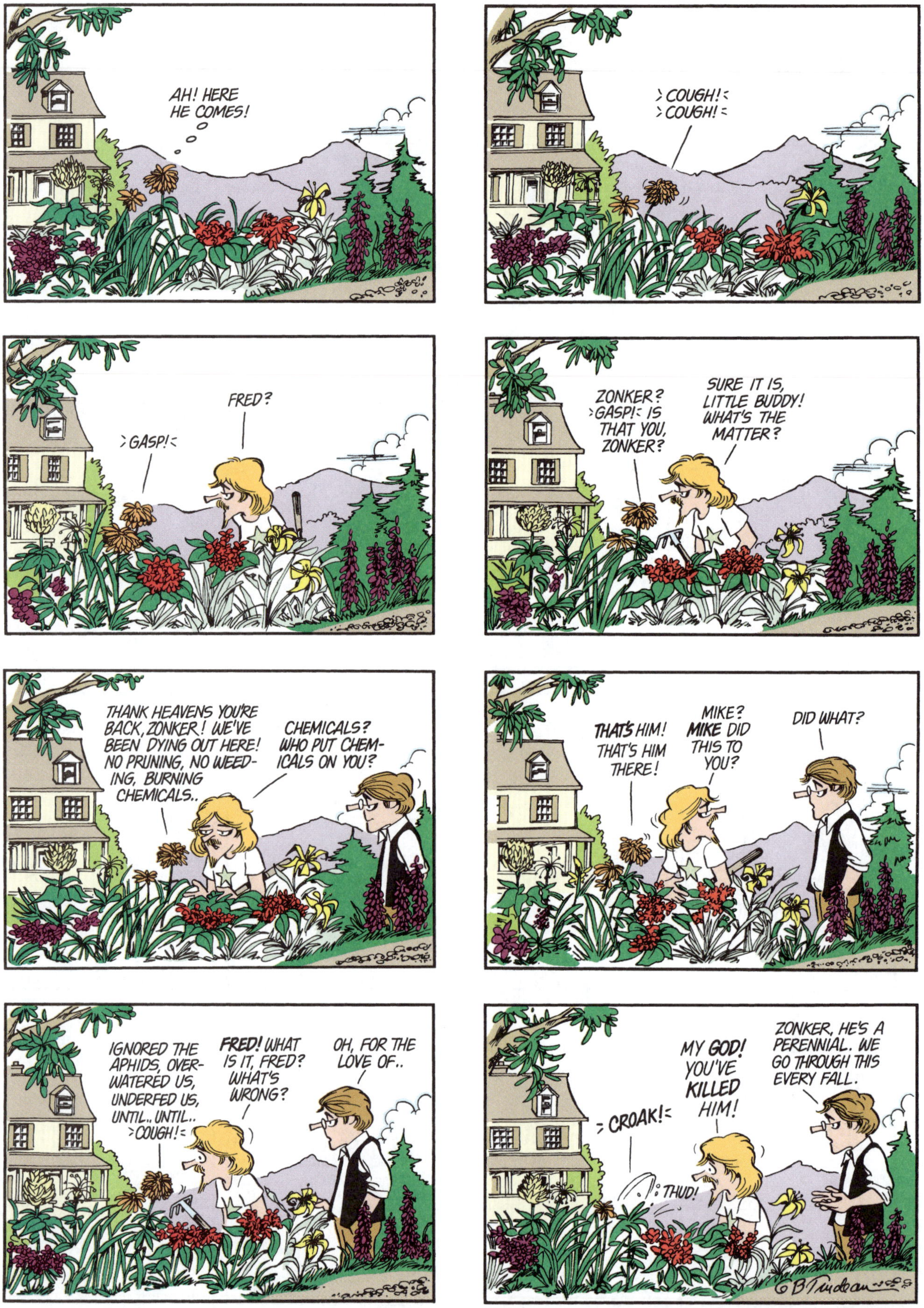
AH! HERE HE COMES!
>COUGH!< >COUGH!<
>GASP!<
FRED?
ZONKER? >GASP!< IS THAT YOU, ZONKER?
SURE IT IS, LITTLE BUDDY! WHAT'S THE MATTER?
THANK HEAVENS YOU'RE BACK, ZONKER! WE'VE BEEN DYING OUT HERE! NO PRUNING, NO WEEDING, BURNING CHEMICALS..
CHEMICALS? WHO PUT CHEMICALS ON YOU?
THAT'S HIM! THAT'S HIM THERE!
MIKE? MIKE DID THIS TO YOU?
DID WHAT?
IGNORED THE APHIDS, OVERWATERED US, UNDERFED US, UNTIL.. UNTIL.. >COUGH!<
FRED! WHAT IS IT, FRED? WHAT'S WRONG?
OH, FOR THE LOVE OF..
>CROAK!<
THUD!
MY GOD! YOU'VE KILLED HIM!
ZONKER, HE'S A PERENNIAL. WE GO THROUGH THIS EVERY FALL.

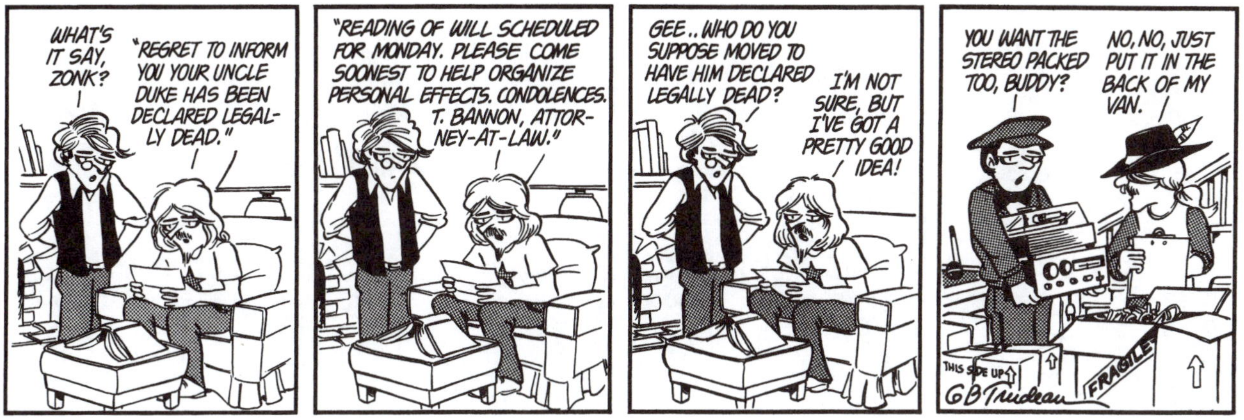
WHAT'S IT SAY, ZONK?
"REGRET TO INFORM YOU YOUR UNCLE DUKE HAS BEEN DECLARED LEGALLY DEAD."
"READING OF WILL SCHEDULED FOR MONDAY. PLEASE COME SOONEST TO HELP ORGANIZE PERSONAL EFFECTS. CONDOLENCES. T. BANNON, ATTORNEY-AT-LAW."
GEE.. WHO DO YOU SUPPOSE MOVED TO HAVE HIM DECLARED LEGALLY DEAD?
I'M NOT SURE, BUT I'VE GOT A PRETTY GOOD IDEA!
YOU WANT THE STEREO PACKED TOO, BUDDY?
NO, NO, JUST PUT IT IN THE BACK OF MY VAN.
THIS SIDE UP
FRAGILE
GB Trudeau

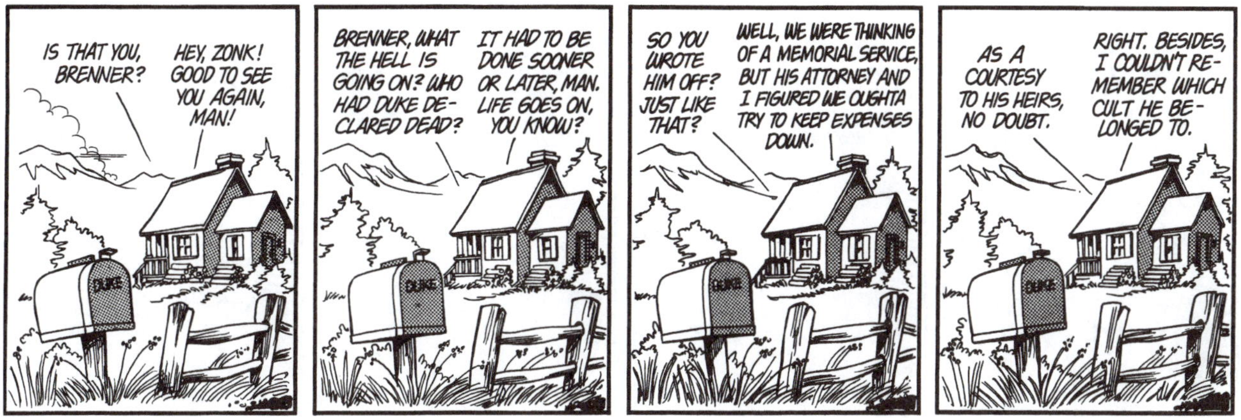
IS THAT YOU, BRENNER?
HEY, ZONK! GOOD TO SEE YOU AGAIN, MAN!
DUKE
BRENNER, WHAT THE HELL IS GOING ON? WHO HAD DUKE DECLARED DEAD?
IT HAD TO BE DONE SOONER OR LATER, MAN. LIFE GOES ON, YOU KNOW?
DUKE
SO YOU WROTE HIM OFF? JUST LIKE THAT?
WELL, WE WERE THINKING OF A MEMORIAL SERVICE, BUT HIS ATTORNEY AND I FIGURED WE OUGHTA TRY TO KEEP EXPENSES DOWN.
DUKE
AS A COURTESY TO HIS HEIRS, NO DOUBT.
RIGHT. BESIDES, I COULDN'T REMEMBER WHICH CULT HE BELONGED TO.
DUKE

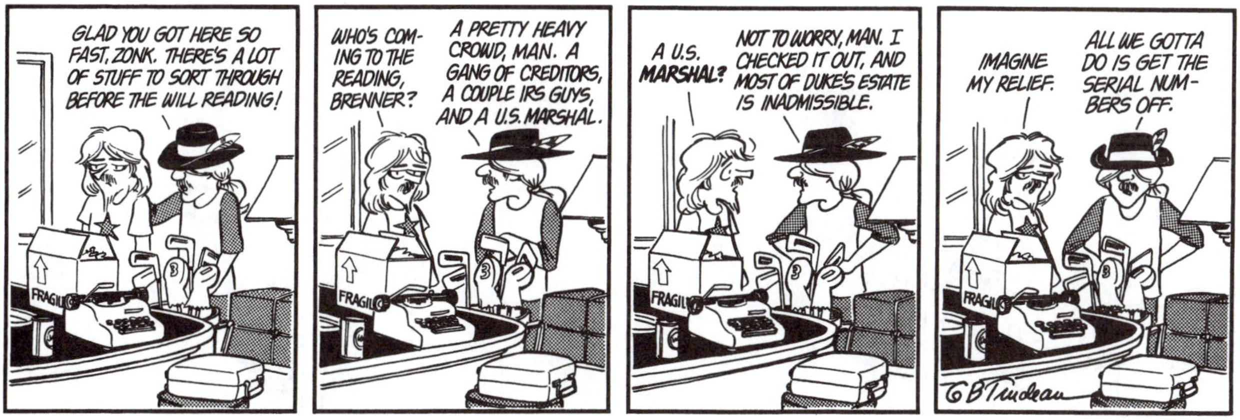
GLAD YOU GOT HERE SO FAST, ZONK. THERE'S A LOT OF STUFF TO SORT THROUGH BEFORE THE WILL READING!
WHO'S COMING TO THE READING, BRENNER?
A PRETTY HEAVY CROWD, MAN. A GANG OF CREDITORS, A COUPLE IRS GUYS, AND A U.S. MARSHAL.
A U.S. **MARSHAL?**
NOT TO WORRY, MAN. I CHECKED IT OUT, AND MOST OF DUKE'S ESTATE IS INADMISSIBLE.
IMAGINE MY RELIEF.
ALL WE GOTTA DO IS GET THE SERIAL NUMBERS OFF.
GB Trudeau

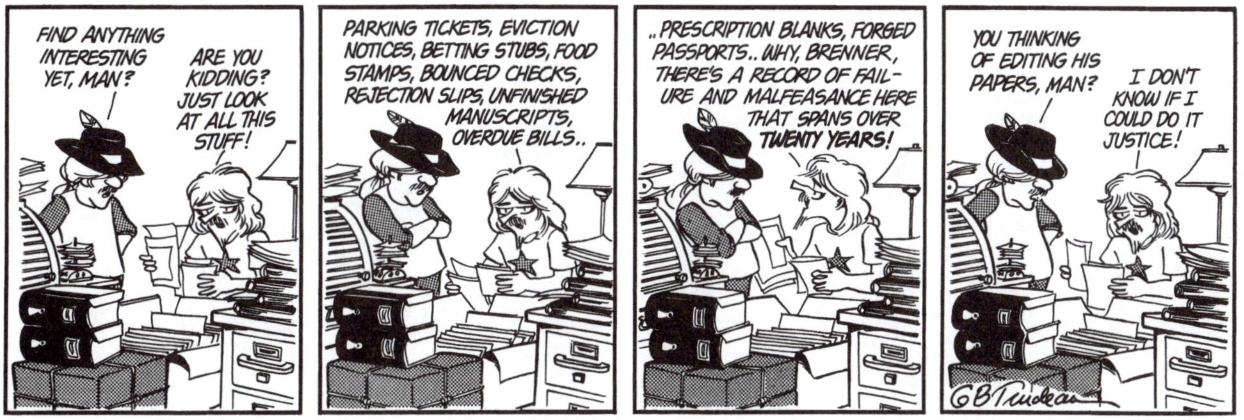
FIND ANYTHING INTERESTING YET, MAN?
ARE YOU KIDDING? JUST LOOK AT ALL THIS STUFF!
PARKING TICKETS, EVICTION NOTICES, BETTING STUBS, FOOD STAMPS, BOUNCED CHECKS, REJECTION SLIPS, UNFINISHED MANUSCRIPTS, OVERDUE BILLS..
..PRESCRIPTION BLANKS, FORGED PASSPORTS.. WHY, BRENNER, THERE'S A RECORD OF FAILURE AND MALFEASANCE HERE THAT SPANS OVER **TWENTY YEARS!**
YOU THINKING OF EDITING HIS PAPERS, MAN?
I DON'T KNOW IF I COULD DO IT JUSTICE!
GB Trudeau

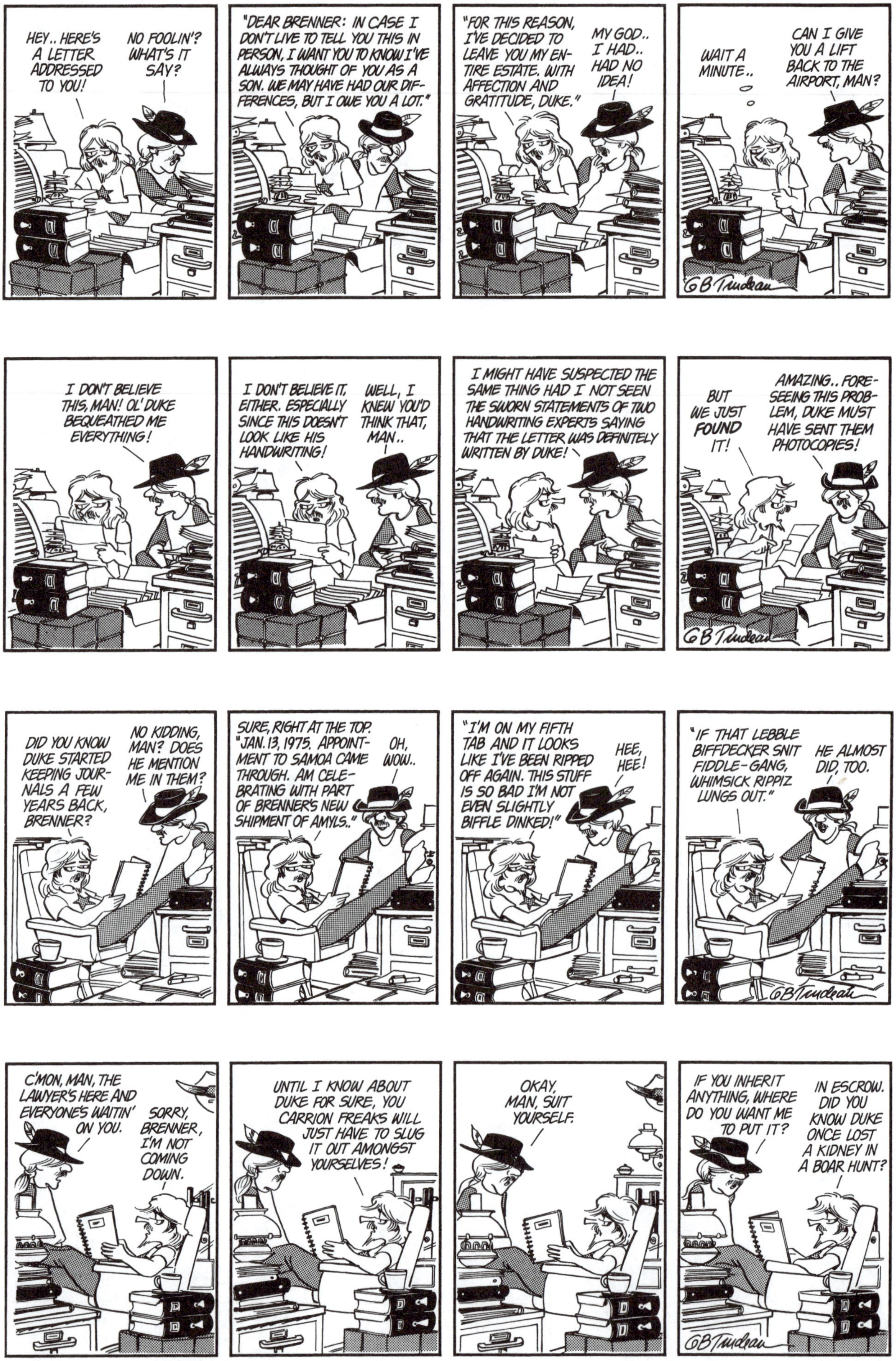
HEY.. HERE'S A LETTER ADDRESSED TO YOU!
NO FOOLIN'? WHAT'S IT SAY?
"DEAR BRENNER: IN CASE I DON'T LIVE TO TELL YOU THIS IN PERSON, I WANT YOU TO KNOW I'VE ALWAYS THOUGHT OF YOU AS A SON. WE MAY HAVE HAD OUR DIFFERENCES, BUT I OWE YOU A LOT."
"FOR THIS REASON, I'VE DECIDED TO LEAVE YOU MY ENTIRE ESTATE. WITH AFFECTION AND GRATITUDE, DUKE."
MY GOD.. I HAD.. HAD NO IDEA!
WAIT A MINUTE..
CAN I GIVE YOU A LIFT BACK TO THE AIRPORT, MAN?
GB Trudeau
I DON'T BELIEVE THIS, MAN! OL' DUKE BEQUEATHED ME EVERYTHING!
I DON'T BELIEVE IT, EITHER. ESPECIALLY SINCE THIS DOESN'T LOOK LIKE HIS HANDWRITING!
WELL, I KNEW YOU'D THINK THAT, MAN..
I MIGHT HAVE SUSPECTED THE SAME THING HAD I NOT SEEN THE SWORN STATEMENTS OF TWO HANDWRITING EXPERTS SAYING THAT THE LETTER WAS DEFINITELY WRITTEN BY DUKE!
BUT WE JUST FOUND IT!
AMAZING.. FORESEEING THIS PROBLEM, DUKE MUST HAVE SENT THEM PHOTOCOPIES!
GB Trudeau
DID YOU KNOW DUKE STARTED KEEPING JOURNALS A FEW YEARS BACK, BRENNER?
NO KIDDING, MAN? DOES HE MENTION ME IN THEM?
SURE, RIGHT AT THE TOP. "JAN. 13, 1975. APPOINTMENT TO SAMOA CAME THROUGH. AM CELEBRATING WITH PART OF BRENNER'S NEW SHIPMENT OF AMYLS.."
OH, WOW..
"I'M ON MY FIFTH TAB AND IT LOOKS LIKE I'VE BEEN RIPPED OFF AGAIN. THIS STUFF IS SO BAD I'M NOT EVEN SLIGHTLY BIFFLE DINKED!"
HEE, HEE!
"IF THAT LEBBLE BIFFDECKER SNIT FIDDLE-GANG, WHIMSICK RIPPIZ LUNGS OUT."
HE ALMOST DID, TOO.
GB Trudeau
C'MON, MAN, THE LAWYER'S HERE AND EVERYONE'S WAITIN' ON YOU.
SORRY, BRENNER, I'M NOT COMING DOWN.
UNTIL I KNOW ABOUT DUKE FOR SURE, YOU CARRION FREAKS WILL JUST HAVE TO SLUG IT OUT AMONGST YOURSELVES!
OKAY, MAN, SUIT YOURSELF.
IF YOU INHERIT ANYTHING, WHERE DO YOU WANT ME TO PUT IT?
IN ESCROW. DID YOU KNOW DUKE ONCE LOST A KIDNEY IN A BOAR HUNT?
GB Trudeau

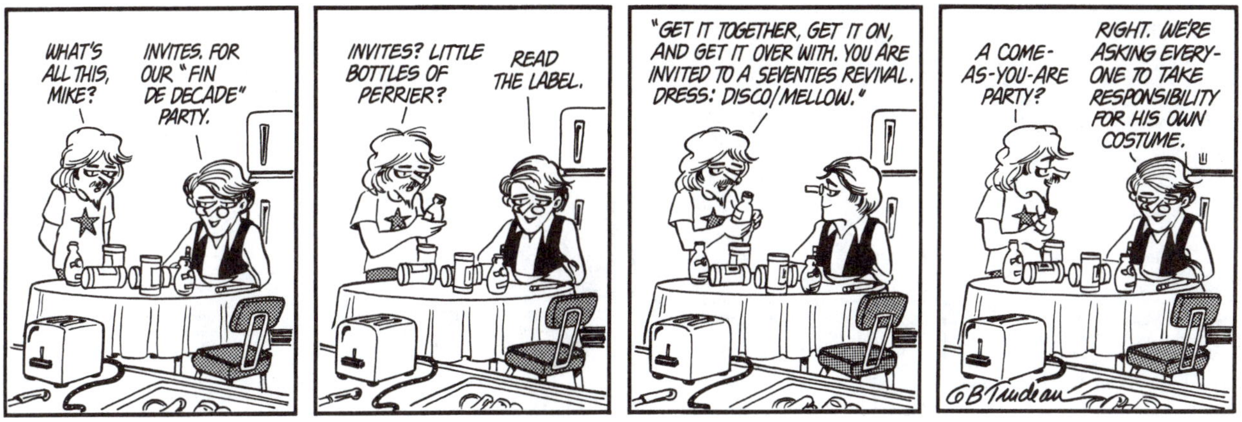
WHAT'S ALL THIS, MIKE?
INVITES. FOR OUR "FIN DE DECADE" PARTY.
INVITES? LITTLE BOTTLES OF PERRIER?
READ THE LABEL.
"GET IT TOGETHER, GET IT ON, AND GET IT OVER WITH. YOU ARE INVITED TO A SEVENTIES REVIVAL. DRESS: DISCO/MELLOW."
A COME-AS-YOU-ARE PARTY?
RIGHT. WE'RE ASKING EVERYONE TO TAKE RESPONSIBILITY FOR HIS OWN COSTUME.
GBTrudeau

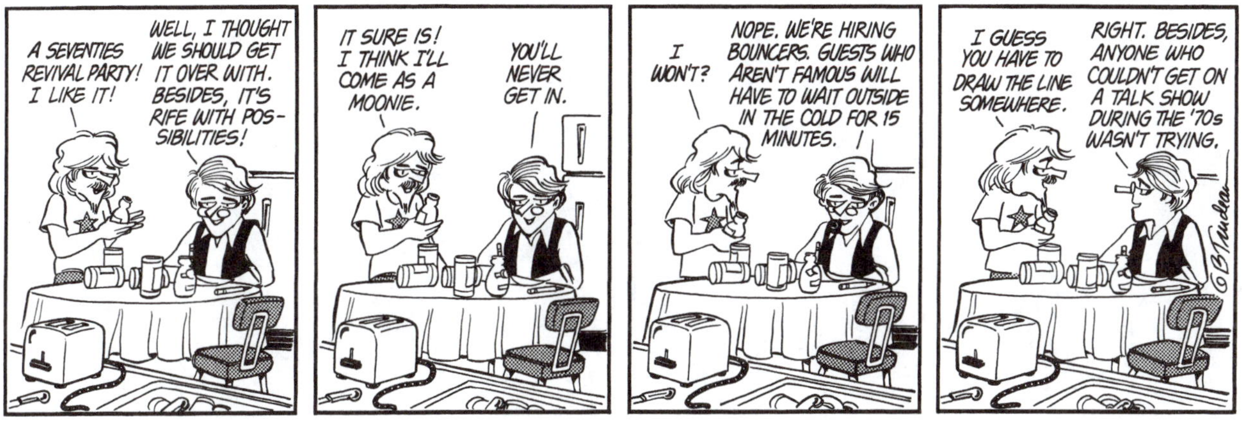
A SEVENTIES REVIVAL PARTY! I LIKE IT!
WELL, I THOUGHT WE SHOULD GET IT OVER WITH. BESIDES, IT'S RIFE WITH POSSIBILITIES!
IT SURE IS! I THINK I'LL COME AS A MOONIE.
YOU'LL NEVER GET IN.
I WON'T?
NOPE. WE'RE HIRING BOUNCERS. GUESTS WHO AREN'T FAMOUS WILL HAVE TO WAIT OUTSIDE IN THE COLD FOR 15 MINUTES.
I GUESS YOU HAVE TO DRAW THE LINE SOMEWHERE.
RIGHT. BESIDES, ANYONE WHO COULDN'T GET ON A TALK SHOW DURING THE '70s WASN'T TRYING.
GBTrudeau

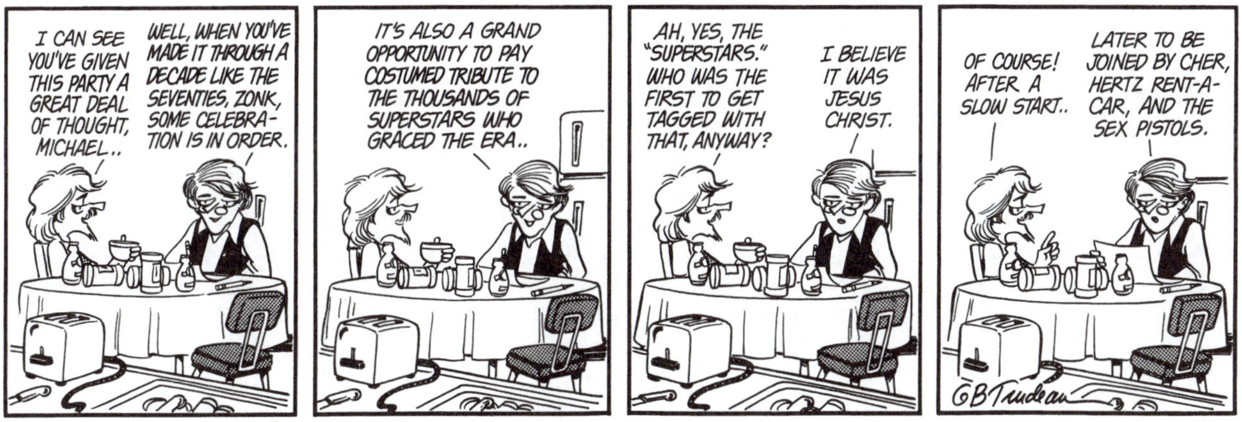
I CAN SEE YOU'VE GIVEN THIS PARTY A GREAT DEAL OF THOUGHT, MICHAEL..
WELL, WHEN YOU'VE MADE IT THROUGH A DECADE LIKE THE SEVENTIES, ZONK, SOME CELEBRATION IS IN ORDER.
IT'S ALSO A GRAND OPPORTUNITY TO PAY COSTUMED TRIBUTE TO THE THOUSANDS OF SUPERSTARS WHO GRACED THE ERA..
AH, YES, THE "SUPERSTARS." WHO WAS THE FIRST TO GET TAGGED WITH THAT, ANYWAY?
I BELIEVE IT WAS JESUS CHRIST.
OF COURSE! AFTER A SLOW START..
LATER TO BE JOINED BY CHER, HERTZ RENT-A-CAR, AND THE SEX PISTOLS.
GBTrudeau

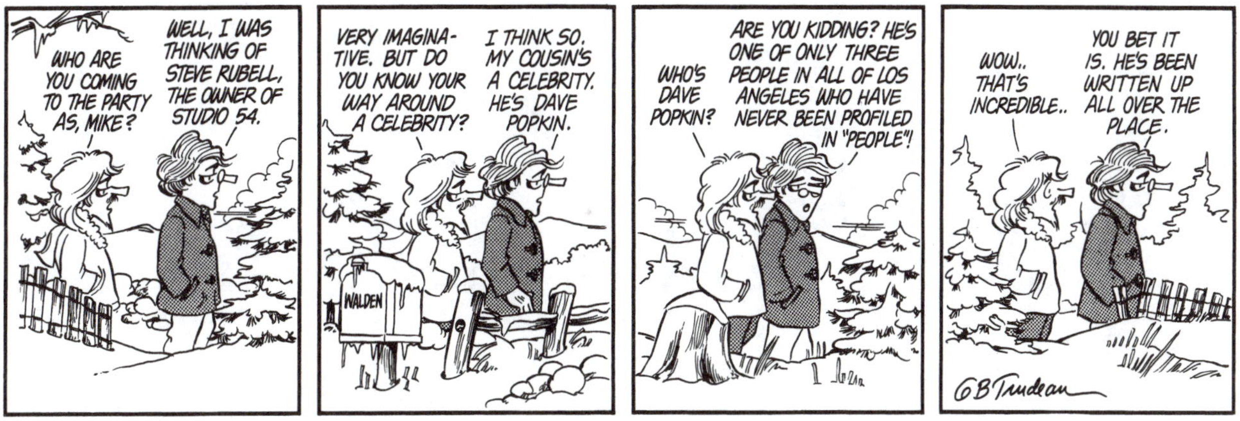
WHO ARE YOU COMING TO THE PARTY AS, MIKE?
WELL, I WAS THINKING OF STEVE RUBELL, THE OWNER OF STUDIO 54.
VERY IMAGINATIVE. BUT DO YOU KNOW YOUR WAY AROUND A CELEBRITY?
I THINK SO. MY COUSIN'S A CELEBRITY. HE'S DAVE POPKIN.
WALDEN
WHO'S DAVE POPKIN?
ARE YOU KIDDING? HE'S ONE OF ONLY THREE PEOPLE IN ALL OF LOS ANGELES WHO HAVE NEVER BEEN PROFILED IN "PEOPLE"!
WOW.. THAT'S INCREDIBLE..
YOU BET IT IS. HE'S BEEN WRITTEN UP ALL OVER THE PLACE.
GBTrudeau

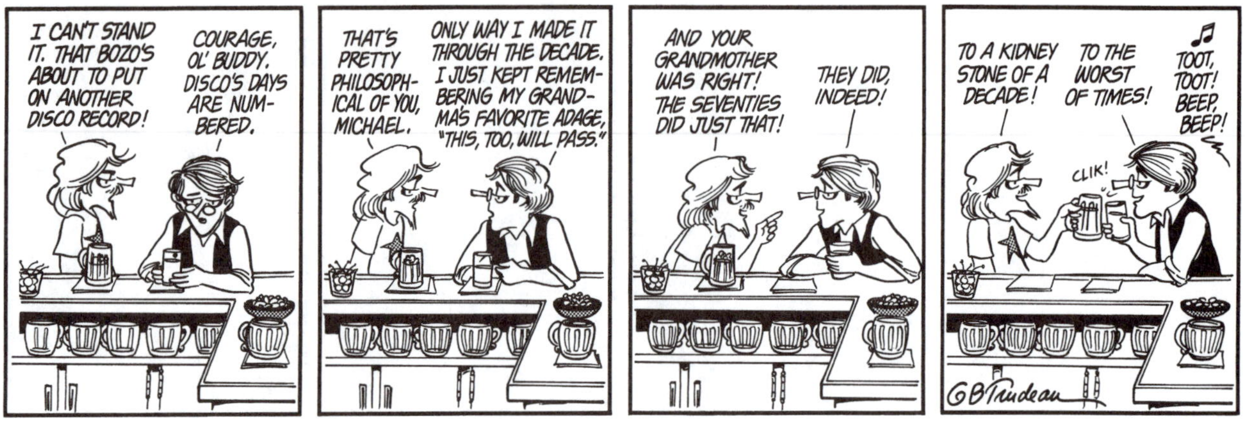
I CAN'T STAND IT. THAT BOZO'S ABOUT TO PUT ON ANOTHER DISCO RECORD!
COURAGE, OL' BUDDY. DISCO'S DAYS ARE NUMBERED.
THAT'S PRETTY PHILOSOPHICAL OF YOU, MICHAEL.
ONLY WAY I MADE IT THROUGH THE DECADE. I JUST KEPT REMEMBERING MY GRANDMA'S FAVORITE ADAGE, "THIS, TOO, WILL PASS."
AND YOUR GRANDMOTHER WAS RIGHT! THE SEVENTIES DID JUST THAT!
THEY DID, INDEED!
TO A KIDNEY STONE OF A DECADE!
TO THE WORST OF TIMES!
CLIK!
TOOT, TOOT! BEEP, BEEP!
GBTrudeau

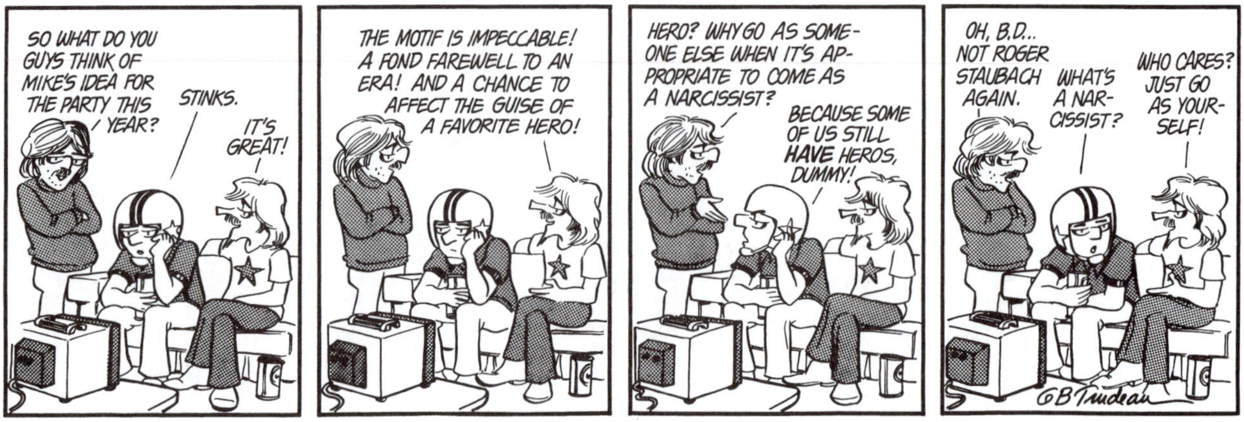
SO WHAT DO YOU GUYS THINK OF MIKE'S IDEA FOR THE PARTY THIS YEAR?
STINKS.
IT'S GREAT!
THE MOTIF IS IMPECCABLE! A FOND FAREWELL TO AN ERA! AND A CHANCE TO AFFECT THE GUISE OF A FAVORITE HERO!
HERO? WHY GO AS SOMEONE ELSE WHEN IT'S APPROPRIATE TO COME AS A NARCISSIST?
BECAUSE SOME OF US STILL HAVE HEROS, DUMMY!
OH, B.D... NOT ROGER STAUBACH AGAIN.
WHAT'S A NARCISSIST?
WHO CARES? JUST GO AS YOURSELF!
GBTrudeau

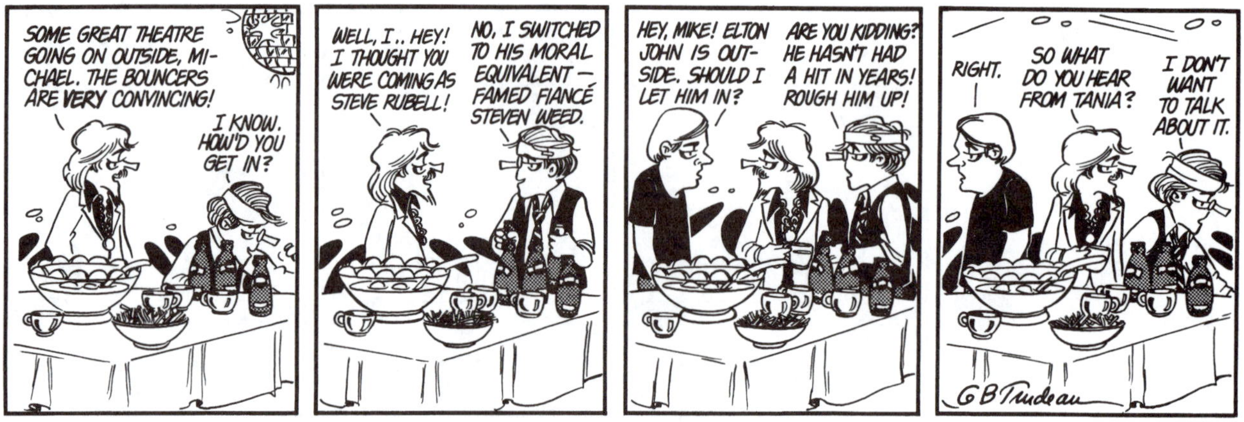
SOME GREAT THEATRE GOING ON OUTSIDE, MICHAEL. THE BOUNCERS ARE VERY CONVINCING!
I KNOW. HOW'D YOU GET IN?
WELL, I.. HEY! I THOUGHT YOU WERE COMING AS STEVE RUBELL!
NO, I SWITCHED TO HIS MORAL EQUIVALENT — FAMED FIANCÉ STEVEN WEED.
HEY, MIKE! ELTON JOHN IS OUTSIDE. SHOULD I LET HIM IN?
ARE YOU KIDDING? HE HASN'T HAD A HIT IN YEARS! ROUGH HIM UP!
RIGHT.
SO WHAT DO YOU HEAR FROM TANIA?
I DON'T WANT TO TALK ABOUT IT.
GBTrudeau

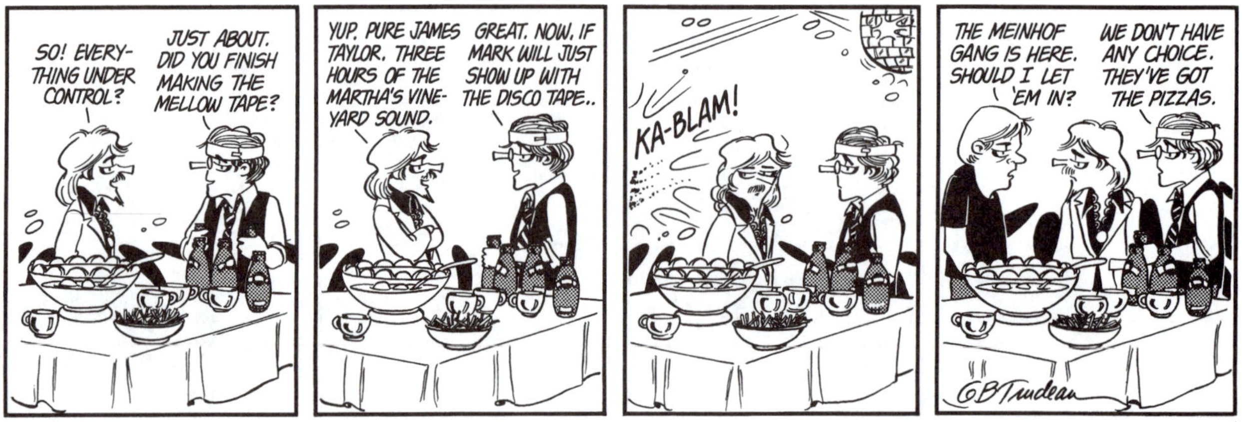
SO! EVERYTHING UNDER CONTROL?
JUST ABOUT. DID YOU FINISH MAKING THE MELLOW TAPE?
YUP. PURE JAMES TAYLOR. THREE HOURS OF THE MARTHA'S VINEYARD SOUND.
GREAT. NOW, IF MARK WILL JUST SHOW UP WITH THE DISCO TAPE..
KA-BLAM!
THE MEINHOF GANG IS HERE. SHOULD I LET 'EM IN?
WE DON'T HAVE ANY CHOICE. THEY'VE GOT THE PIZZAS.
GBTrudeau

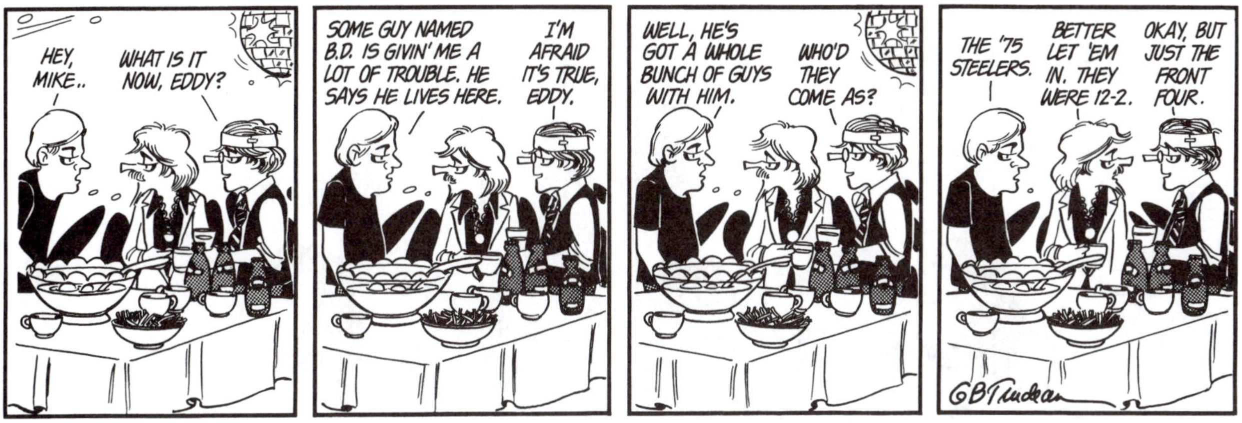
HEY, MIKE..
WHAT IS IT NOW, EDDY?
SOME GUY NAMED B.D. IS GIVIN' ME A LOT OF TROUBLE. HE SAYS HE LIVES HERE.
I'M AFRAID IT'S TRUE, EDDY.
WELL, HE'S GOT A WHOLE BUNCH OF GUYS WITH HIM.
WHO'D THEY COME AS?
THE '75 STEELERS.
BETTER LET 'EM IN. THEY WERE 12-2.
OKAY, BUT JUST THE FRONT FOUR.
GBTrudeau

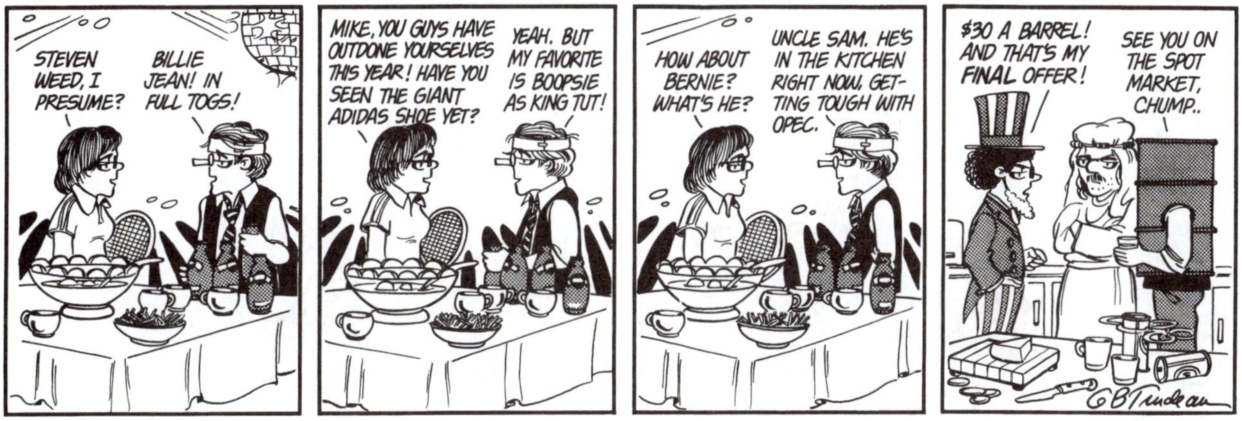
STEVEN WEED, I PRESUME?
BILLIE JEAN! IN FULL TOGS!
MIKE, YOU GUYS HAVE OUTDONE YOURSELVES THIS YEAR! HAVE YOU SEEN THE GIANT ADIDAS SHOE YET?
YEAH. BUT MY FAVORITE IS BOOPSIE AS KING TUT!
HOW ABOUT BERNIE? WHAT'S HE?
UNCLE SAM. HE'S IN THE KITCHEN RIGHT NOW, GETTING TOUGH WITH OPEC.
$30 A BARREL! AND THAT'S MY FINAL OFFER!
SEE YOU ON THE SPOT MARKET, CHUMP..
GBTrudeau

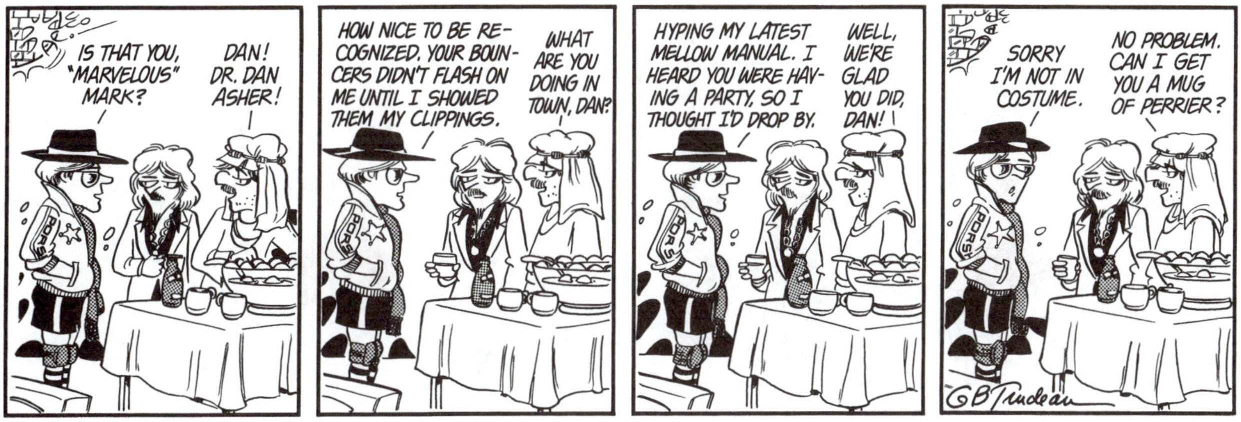
IS THAT YOU, "MARVELOUS" MARK?
DAN! DR. DAN ASHER!
HOW NICE TO BE RECOGNIZED. YOUR BOUNCERS DIDN'T FLASH ON ME UNTIL I SHOWED THEM MY CLIPPINGS.
WHAT ARE YOU DOING IN TOWN, DAN?
HYPING MY LATEST MELLOW MANUAL. I HEARD YOU WERE HAVING A PARTY, SO I THOUGHT I'D DROP BY.
WELL, WE'RE GLAD YOU DID, DAN!
SORRY I'M NOT IN COSTUME.
NO PROBLEM. CAN I GET YOU A MUG OF PERRIER?
GBTrudeau

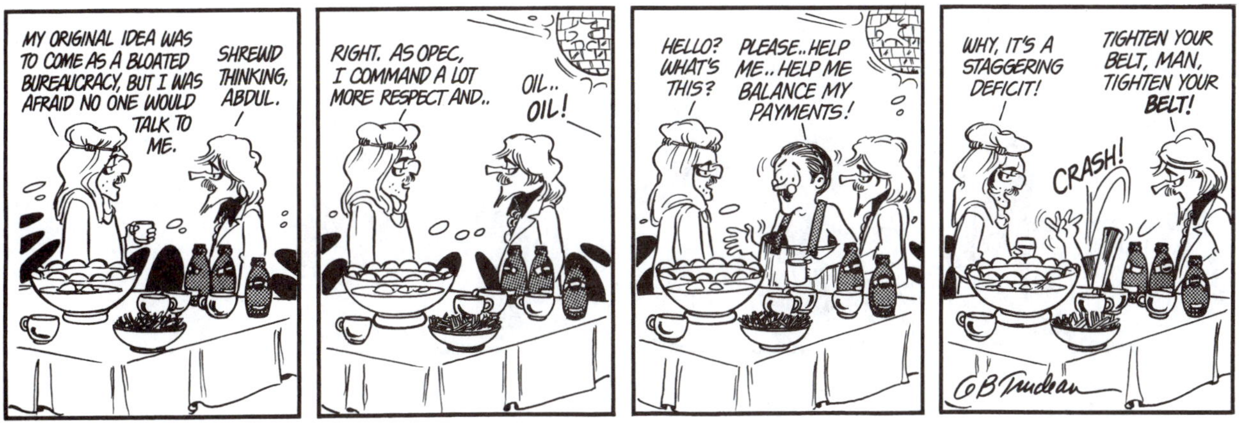
MY ORIGINAL IDEA WAS TO COME AS A BLOATED BUREAUCRACY, BUT I WAS AFRAID NO ONE WOULD TALK TO ME.
SHREWD THINKING, ABDUL.
RIGHT. AS OPEC, I COMMAND A LOT MORE RESPECT AND..
OIL.. OIL!
HELLO? WHAT'S THIS?
PLEASE..HELP ME..HELP ME BALANCE MY PAYMENTS!
WHY, IT'S A STAGGERING DEFICIT!
TIGHTEN YOUR BELT, MAN, TIGHTEN YOUR BELT!
CRASH!
GBTrudeau

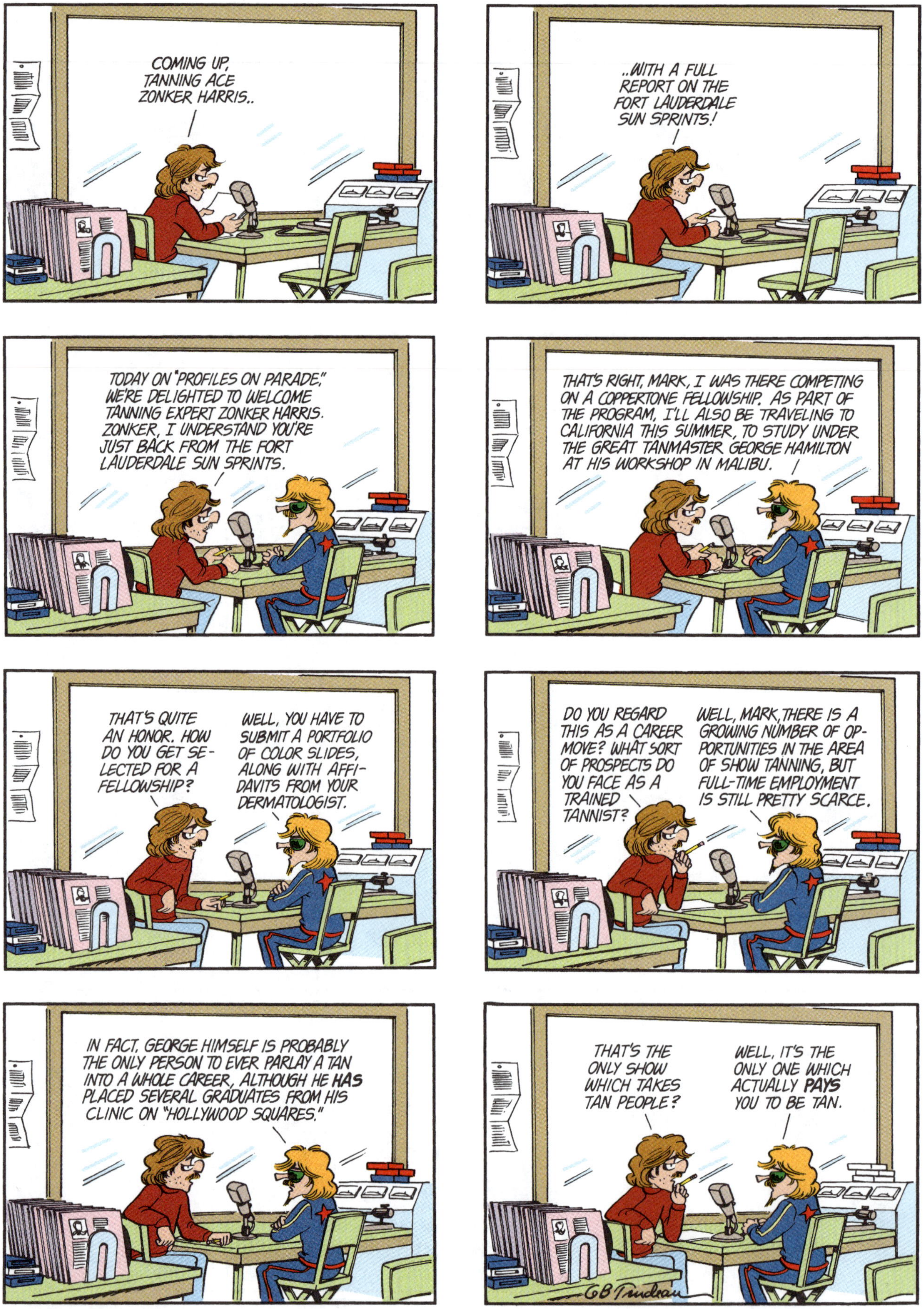
COMING UP, TANNING ACE ZONKER HARRIS..
..WITH A FULL REPORT ON THE FORT LAUDERDALE SUN SPRINTS!
TODAY ON "PROFILES ON PARADE," WE'RE DELIGHTED TO WELCOME TANNING EXPERT ZONKER HARRIS. ZONKER, I UNDERSTAND YOU'RE JUST BACK FROM THE FORT LAUDERDALE SUN SPRINTS.
THAT'S RIGHT, MARK, I WAS THERE COMPETING ON A COPPERTONE FELLOWSHIP. AS PART OF THE PROGRAM, I'LL ALSO BE TRAVELING TO CALIFORNIA THIS SUMMER, TO STUDY UNDER THE GREAT TANMASTER GEORGE HAMILTON AT HIS WORKSHOP IN MALIBU.
THAT'S QUITE AN HONOR. HOW DO YOU GET SELECTED FOR A FELLOWSHIP?
WELL, YOU HAVE TO SUBMIT A PORTFOLIO OF COLOR SLIDES, ALONG WITH AFFIDAVITS FROM YOUR DERMATOLOGIST.
DO YOU REGARD THIS AS A CAREER MOVE? WHAT SORT OF PROSPECTS DO YOU FACE AS A TRAINED TANNIST?
WELL, MARK, THERE IS A GROWING NUMBER OF OPPORTUNITIES IN THE AREA OF SHOW TANNING, BUT FULL-TIME EMPLOYMENT IS STILL PRETTY SCARCE.
IN FACT, GEORGE HIMSELF IS PROBABLY THE ONLY PERSON TO EVER PARLAY A TAN INTO A WHOLE CAREER, ALTHOUGH HE **HAS** PLACED SEVERAL GRADUATES FROM HIS CLINIC ON "HOLLYWOOD SQUARES."
THAT'S THE ONLY SHOW WHICH TAKES TAN PEOPLE?
WELL, IT'S THE ONLY ONE WHICH ACTUALLY **PAYS** YOU TO BE TAN.
GB Trudeau

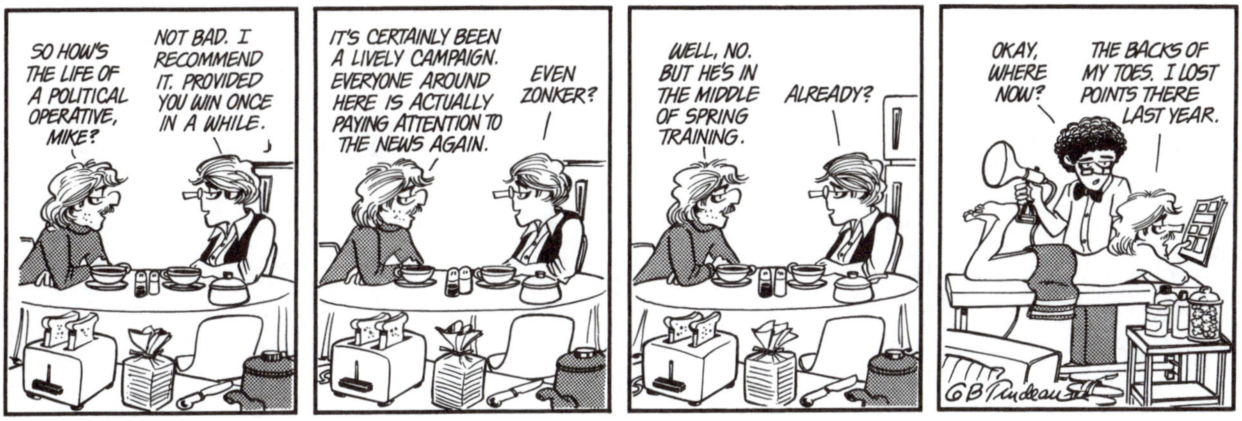
SO HOW'S THE LIFE OF A POLITICAL OPERATIVE, MIKE?
NOT BAD. I RECOMMEND IT. PROVIDED YOU WIN ONCE IN A WHILE.
IT'S CERTAINLY BEEN A LIVELY CAMPAIGN. EVERYONE AROUND HERE IS ACTUALLY PAYING ATTENTION TO THE NEWS AGAIN.
EVEN ZONKER?
WELL, NO. BUT HE'S IN THE MIDDLE OF SPRING TRAINING.
ALREADY?
OKAY, WHERE NOW?
THE BACKS OF MY TOES. I LOST POINTS THERE LAST YEAR.
GB Trudeau

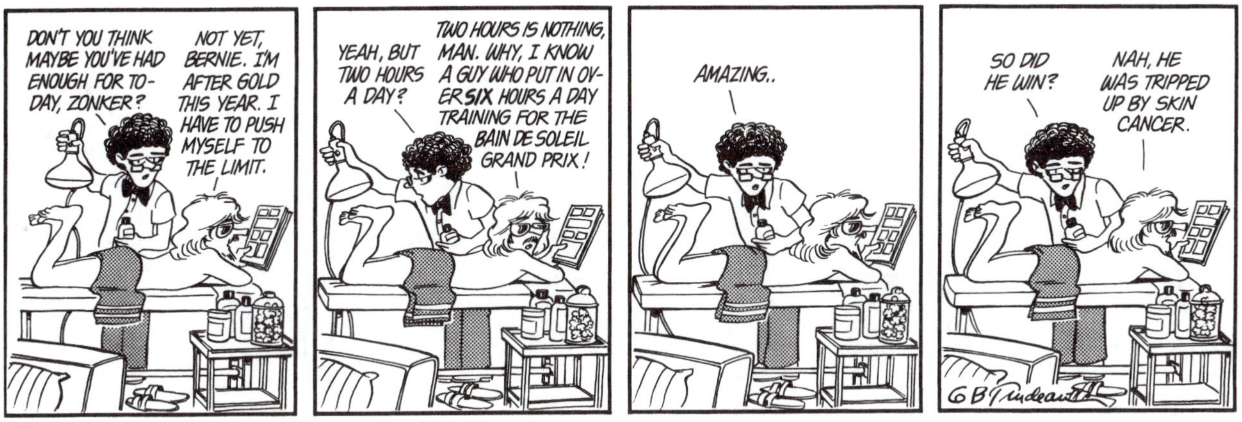
DON'T YOU THINK MAYBE YOU'VE HAD ENOUGH FOR TODAY, ZONKER?
NOT YET, BERNIE. I'M AFTER GOLD THIS YEAR. I HAVE TO PUSH MYSELF TO THE LIMIT.
YEAH, BUT TWO HOURS A DAY?
TWO HOURS IS NOTHING, MAN. WHY, I KNOW A GUY WHO PUT IN OVER SIX HOURS A DAY TRAINING FOR THE BAIN DE SOLEIL GRAND PRIX!
AMAZING..
SO DID HE WIN?
NAH, HE WAS TRIPPED UP BY SKIN CANCER.
GB Trudeau

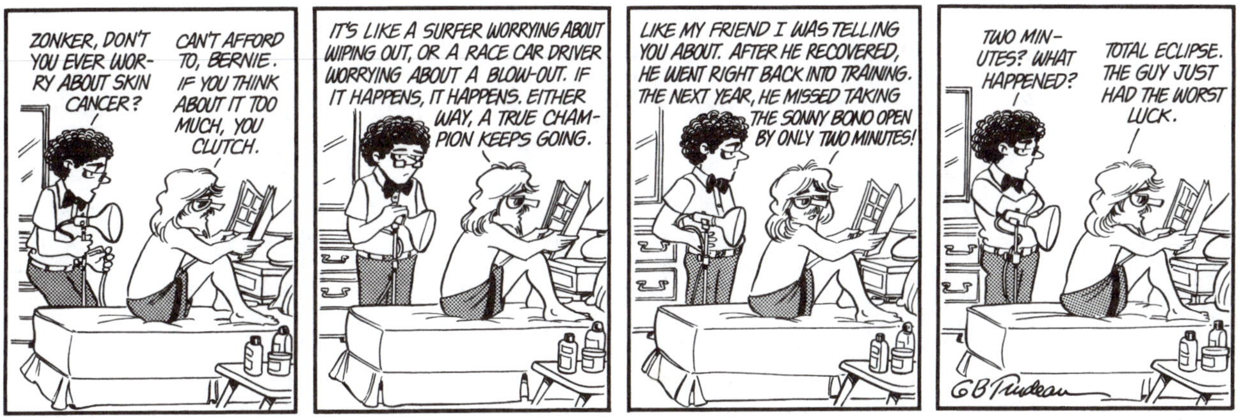
ZONKER, DON'T YOU EVER WORRY ABOUT SKIN CANCER?
CAN'T AFFORD TO, BERNIE. IF YOU THINK ABOUT IT TOO MUCH, YOU CLUTCH.
IT'S LIKE A SURFER WORRYING ABOUT WIPING OUT, OR A RACE CAR DRIVER WORRYING ABOUT A BLOW-OUT. IF IT HAPPENS, IT HAPPENS. EITHER WAY, A TRUE CHAMPION KEEPS GOING.
LIKE MY FRIEND I WAS TELLING YOU ABOUT. AFTER HE RECOVERED, HE WENT RIGHT BACK INTO TRAINING. THE NEXT YEAR, HE MISSED TAKING THE SONNY BONO OPEN BY ONLY TWO MINUTES!
TWO MINUTES? WHAT HAPPENED?
TOTAL ECLIPSE. THE GUY JUST HAD THE WORST LUCK.
GB Trudeau

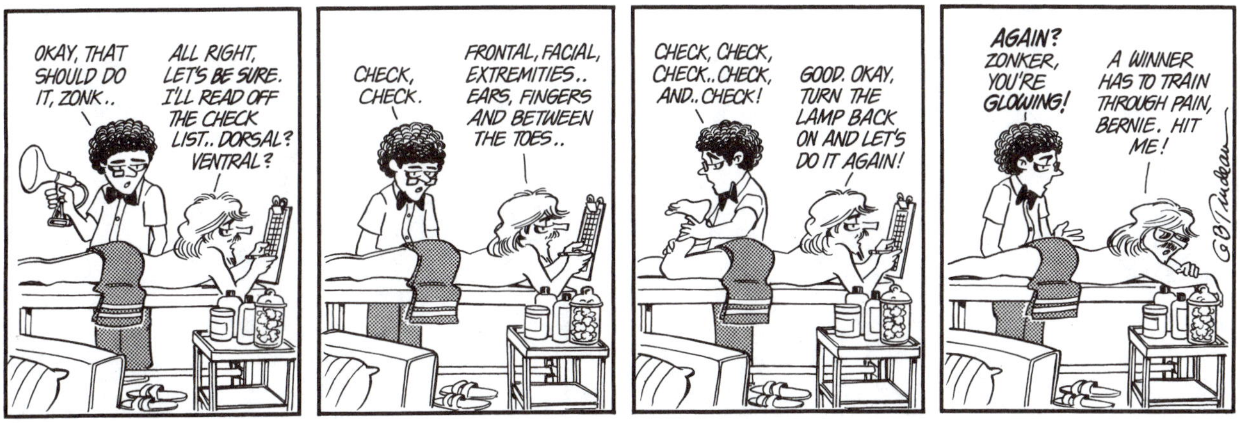
OKAY, THAT SHOULD DO IT, ZONK..
ALL RIGHT, LET'S BE SURE. I'LL READ OFF THE CHECK LIST.. DORSAL? VENTRAL?
CHECK, CHECK.
FRONTAL, FACIAL, EXTREMITIES.. EARS, FINGERS AND BETWEEN THE TOES..
CHECK, CHECK, CHECK.. CHECK, AND.. CHECK!
GOOD. OKAY, TURN THE LAMP BACK ON AND LET'S DO IT AGAIN!
AGAIN? ZONKER, YOU'RE GLOWING!
A WINNER HAS TO TRAIN THROUGH PAIN, BERNIE. HIT ME!
GB Trudeau

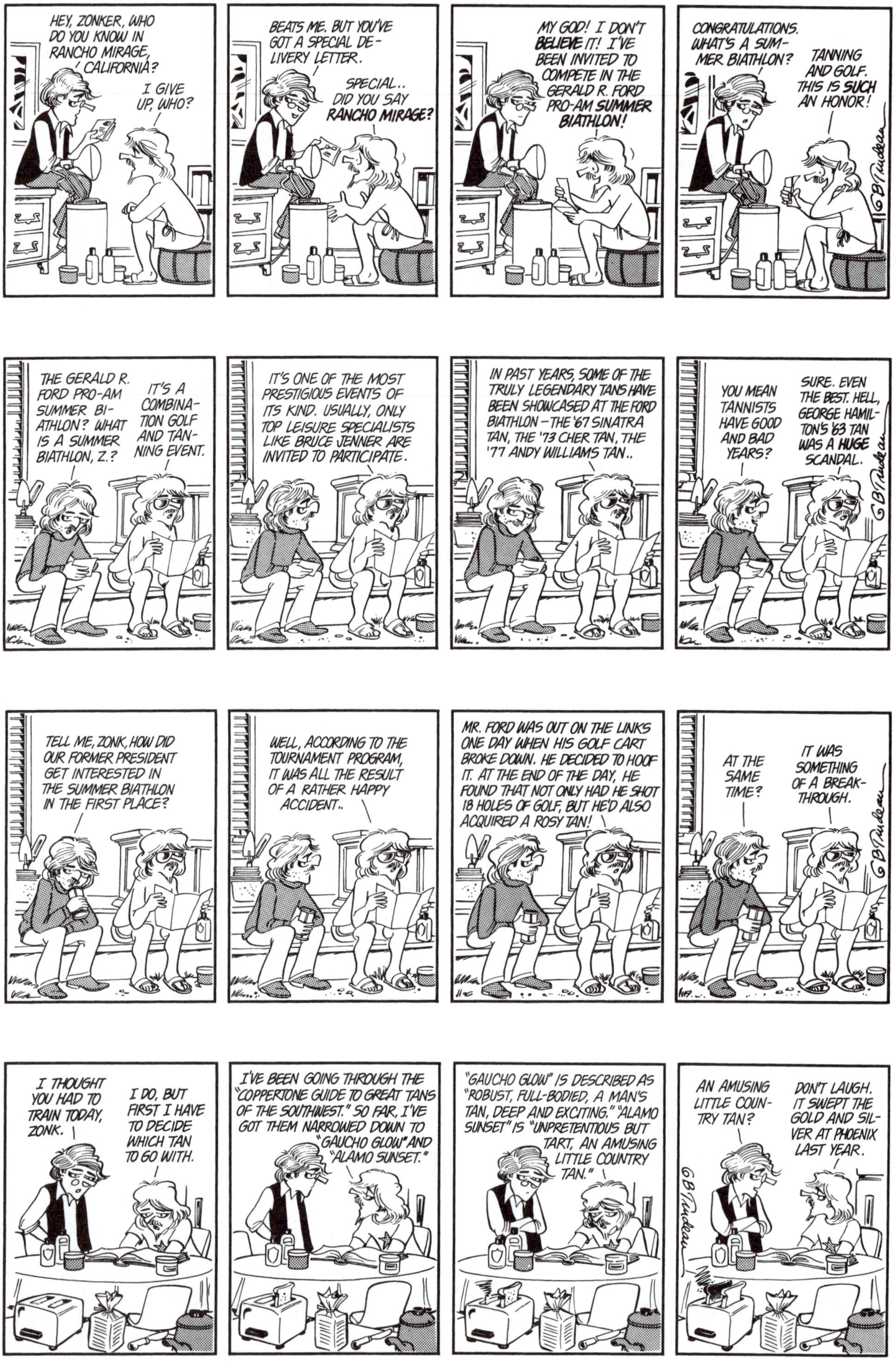
HEY, ZONKER, WHO DO YOU KNOW IN RANCHO MIRAGE, CALIFORNIA?
I GIVE UP, WHO?
BEATS ME. BUT YOU'VE GOT A SPECIAL DELIVERY LETTER.
SPECIAL.. DID YOU SAY RANCHO MIRAGE?
MY GOD! I DON'T BELIEVE IT! I'VE BEEN INVITED TO COMPETE IN THE GERALD R. FORD PRO-AM SUMMER BIATHLON!
CONGRATULATIONS. WHAT'S A SUMMER BIATHLON?
TANNING AND GOLF. THIS IS SUCH AN HONOR!
THE GERALD R. FORD PRO-AM SUMMER BIATHLON? WHAT IS A SUMMER BIATHLON, Z.?
IT'S A COMBINATION GOLF AND TANNING EVENT.
IT'S ONE OF THE MOST PRESTIGIOUS EVENTS OF ITS KIND. USUALLY, ONLY TOP LEISURE SPECIALISTS LIKE BRUCE JENNER ARE INVITED TO PARTICIPATE.
IN PAST YEARS, SOME OF THE TRULY LEGENDARY TANS HAVE BEEN SHOWCASED AT THE FORD BIATHLON—THE '67 SINATRA TAN, THE '73 CHER TAN, THE '77 ANDY WILLIAMS TAN..
YOU MEAN TANNISTS HAVE GOOD AND BAD YEARS?
SURE. EVEN THE BEST. HELL, GEORGE HAMILTON'S '63 TAN WAS A HUGE SCANDAL.
TELL ME, ZONK, HOW DID OUR FORMER PRESIDENT GET INTERESTED IN THE SUMMER BIATHLON IN THE FIRST PLACE?
WELL, ACCORDING TO THE TOURNAMENT PROGRAM, IT WAS ALL THE RESULT OF A RATHER HAPPY ACCIDENT..
MR. FORD WAS OUT ON THE LINKS ONE DAY WHEN HIS GOLF CART BROKE DOWN. HE DECIDED TO HOOF IT. AT THE END OF THE DAY, HE FOUND THAT NOT ONLY HAD HE SHOT 18 HOLES OF GOLF, BUT HE'D ALSO ACQUIRED A ROSY TAN!
AT THE SAME TIME?
IT WAS SOMETHING OF A BREAKTHROUGH.
I THOUGHT YOU HAD TO TRAIN TODAY, ZONK.
I DO, BUT FIRST I HAVE TO DECIDE WHICH TAN TO GO WITH.
I'VE BEEN GOING THROUGH THE "COPPERTONE GUIDE TO GREAT TANS OF THE SOUTHWEST." SO FAR, I'VE GOT THEM NARROWED DOWN TO "GAUCHO GLOW" AND "ALAMO SUNSET."
"GAUCHO GLOW" IS DESCRIBED AS "ROBUST, FULL-BODIED, A MAN'S TAN, DEEP AND EXCITING." "ALAMO SUNSET" IS "UNPRETENTIOUS BUT TART, AN AMUSING LITTLE COUNTRY TAN."
AN AMUSING LITTLE COUNTRY TAN?
DON'T LAUGH. IT SWEPT THE GOLD AND SILVER AT PHOENIX LAST YEAR.
©GBTrudeau

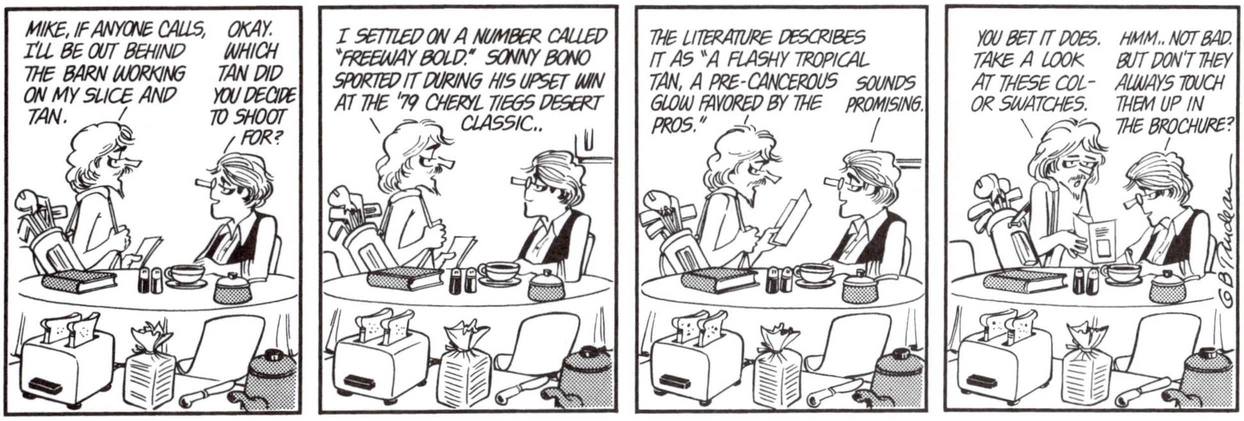
MIKE, IF ANYONE CALLS, I'LL BE OUT BEHIND THE BARN WORKING ON MY SLICE AND TAN.
OKAY. WHICH TAN DID YOU DECIDE TO SHOOT FOR?
I SETTLED ON A NUMBER CALLED "FREEWAY BOLD." SONNY BONO SPORTED IT DURING HIS UPSET WIN AT THE '79 CHERYL TIEGS DESERT CLASSIC..
THE LITERATURE DESCRIBES IT AS "A FLASHY TROPICAL TAN, A PRE-CANCEROUS GLOW FAVORED BY THE PROS."
SOUNDS PROMISING.
YOU BET IT DOES. TAKE A LOOK AT THESE COLOR SWATCHES.
HMM.. NOT BAD. BUT DON'T THEY ALWAYS TOUCH THEM UP IN THE BROCHURE?

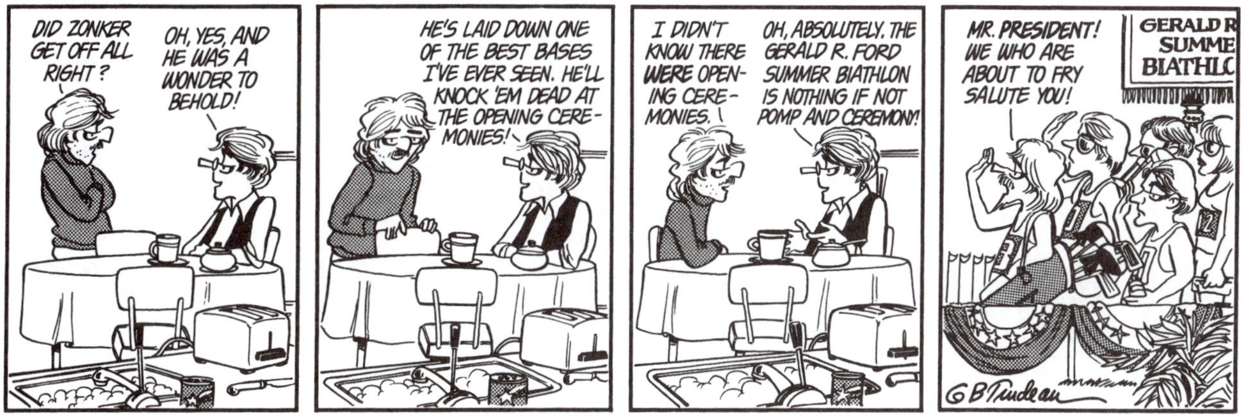
DID ZONKER GET OFF ALL RIGHT?
OH, YES, AND HE WAS A WONDER TO BEHOLD!
HE'S LAID DOWN ONE OF THE BEST BASES I'VE EVER SEEN. HE'LL KNOCK 'EM DEAD AT THE OPENING CEREMONIES!
I DIDN'T KNOW THERE WERE OPENING CEREMONIES.
OH, ABSOLUTELY. THE GERALD R. FORD SUMMER BIATHLON IS NOTHING IF NOT POMP AND CEREMONY!
GERALD R
SUMME
BIATHLO
MR. PRESIDENT! WE WHO ARE ABOUT TO FRY SALUTE YOU!

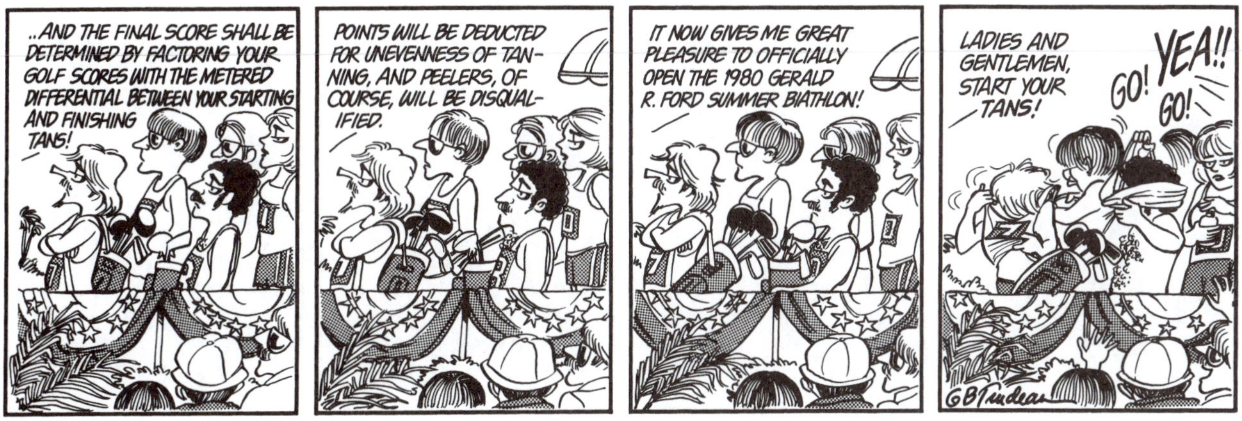
..AND THE FINAL SCORE SHALL BE DETERMINED BY FACTORING YOUR GOLF SCORES WITH THE METERED DIFFERENTIAL BETWEEN YOUR STARTING AND FINISHING TANS!
POINTS WILL BE DEDUCTED FOR UNEVENNESS OF TANNING, AND PEELERS, OF COURSE, WILL BE DISQUALIFIED.
IT NOW GIVES ME GREAT PLEASURE TO OFFICIALLY OPEN THE 1980 GERALD R. FORD SUMMER BIATHLON!
LADIES AND GENTLEMEN, START YOUR TANS!
GO!
YEA!!
GO!

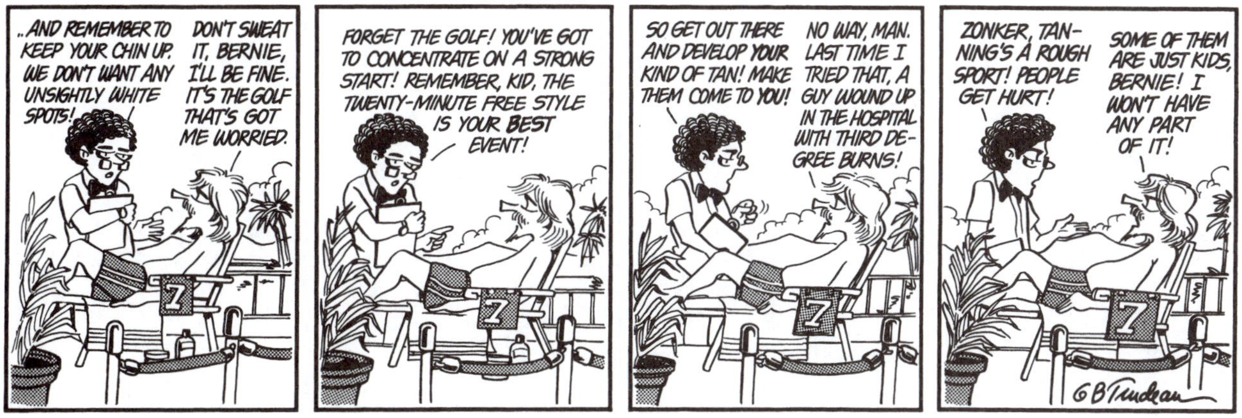
..AND REMEMBER TO KEEP YOUR CHIN UP. WE DON'T WANT ANY UNSIGHTLY WHITE SPOTS!
DON'T SWEAT IT, BERNIE, I'LL BE FINE. IT'S THE GOLF THAT'S GOT ME WORRIED.
FORGET THE GOLF! YOU'VE GOT TO CONCENTRATE ON A STRONG START! REMEMBER, KID, THE TWENTY-MINUTE FREE STYLE IS YOUR BEST EVENT!
SO GET OUT THERE AND DEVELOP YOUR KIND OF TAN! MAKE THEM COME TO YOU!
NO WAY, MAN. LAST TIME I TRIED THAT, A GUY WOUND UP IN THE HOSPITAL WITH THIRD DEGREE BURNS!
ZONKER, TANNING'S A ROUGH SPORT! PEOPLE GET HURT!
SOME OF THEM ARE JUST KIDS, BERNIE! I WON'T HAVE ANY PART OF IT!

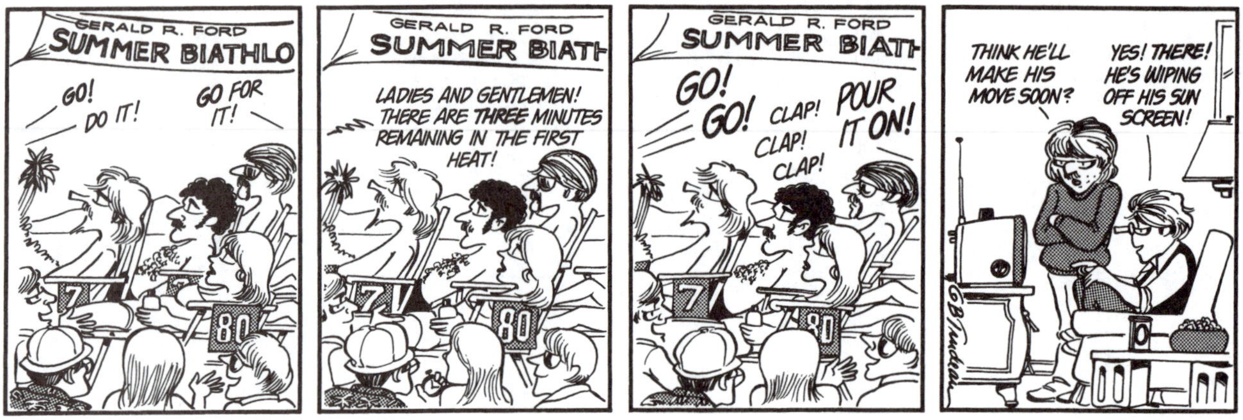
GERALD R. FORD
SUMMER BIATHLO
GO!
DO IT!
GO FOR IT!
LADIES AND GENTLEMEN! THERE ARE THREE MINUTES REMAINING IN THE FIRST HEAT!
GO! GO!
CLAP! CLAP! CLAP!
POUR IT ON!
THINK HE'LL MAKE HIS MOVE SOON?
YES! THERE! HE'S WIPING OFF HIS SUN SCREEN!

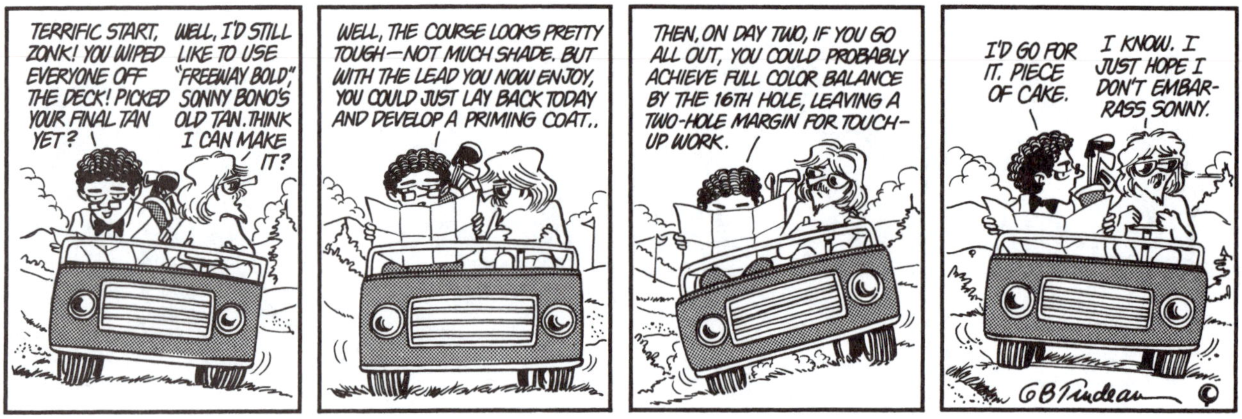
TERRIFIC START, ZONK! YOU WIPED EVERYONE OFF THE DECK! PICKED YOUR FINAL TAN YET?
WELL, I'D STILL LIKE TO USE "FREEWAY BOLD," SONNY BONO'S OLD TAN. THINK I CAN MAKE IT?
WELL, THE COURSE LOOKS PRETTY TOUGH—NOT MUCH SHADE. BUT WITH THE LEAD YOU NOW ENJOY, YOU COULD JUST LAY BACK TODAY AND DEVELOP A PRIMING COAT..
THEN, ON DAY TWO, IF YOU GO ALL OUT, YOU COULD PROBABLY ACHIEVE FULL COLOR BALANCE BY THE 16TH HOLE, LEAVING A TWO-HOLE MARGIN FOR TOUCH-UP WORK.
I'D GO FOR IT. PIECE OF CAKE.
I KNOW. I JUST HOPE I DON'T EMBARRASS SONNY.

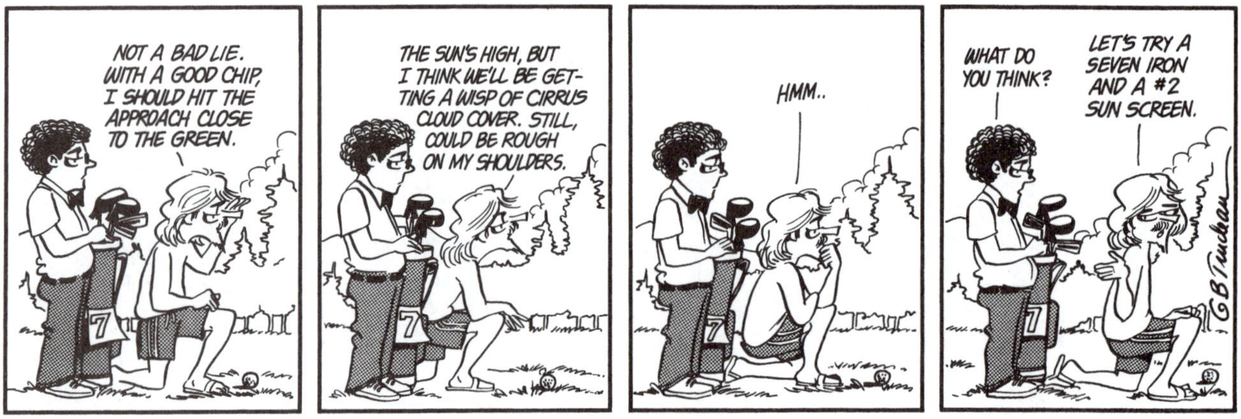
NOT A BAD LIE. WITH A GOOD CHIP, I SHOULD HIT THE APPROACH CLOSE TO THE GREEN.
THE SUN'S HIGH, BUT I THINK WE'LL BE GETTING A WISP OF CIRRUS CLOUD COVER. STILL, COULD BE ROUGH ON MY SHOULDERS.
HMM..
WHAT DO YOU THINK?
LET'S TRY A SEVEN IRON AND A #2 SUN SCREEN.

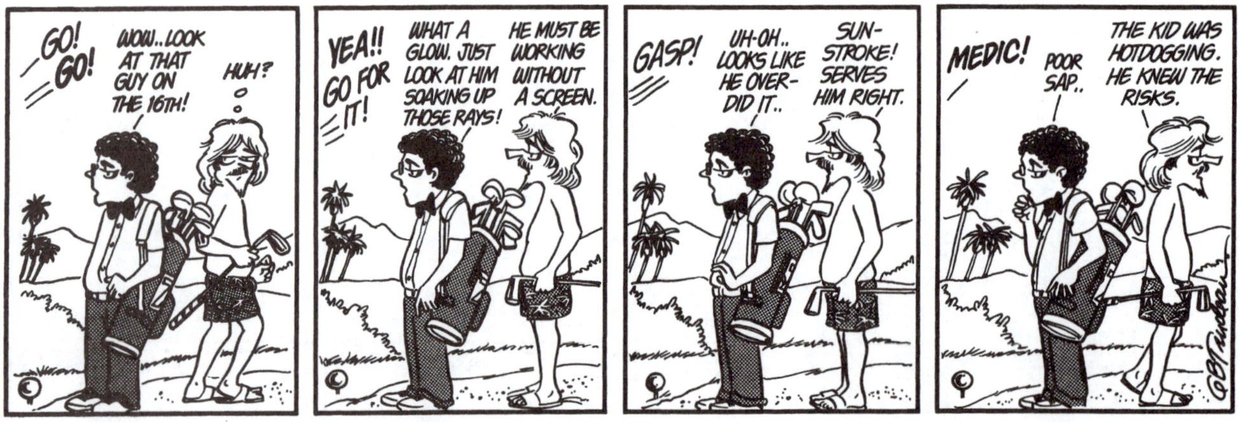
GO! GO!
WOW.. LOOK AT THAT GUY ON THE 16TH!
HUH?
YEA!! GO FOR IT!
WHAT A GLOW. JUST LOOK AT HIM SOAKING UP THOSE RAYS!
HE MUST BE WORKING WITHOUT A SCREEN.
GASP!
UH-OH.. LOOKS LIKE HE OVERDID IT..
SUNSTROKE! SERVES HIM RIGHT.
MEDIC!
POOR SAP..
THE KID WAS HOTDOGGING. HE KNEW THE RISKS.

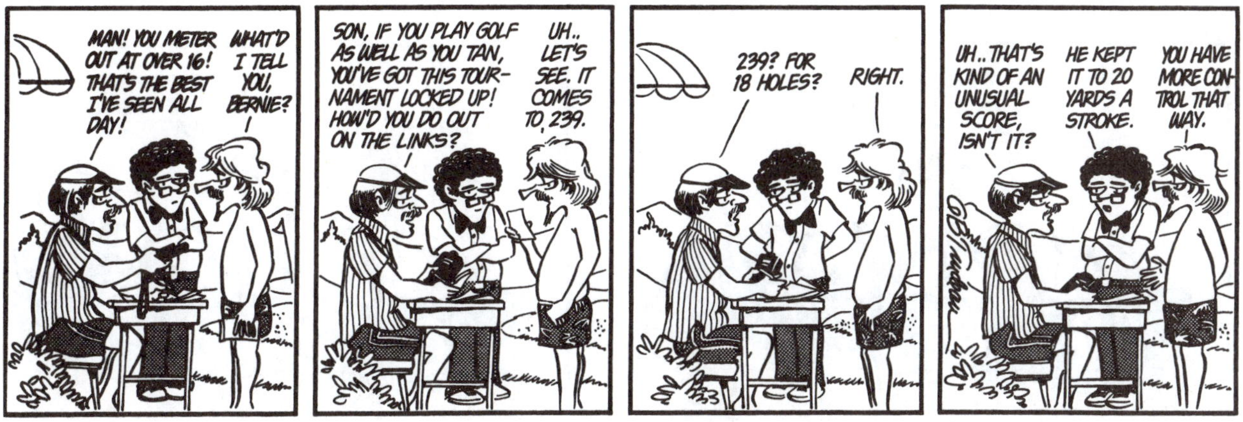
MAN! YOU METER OUT AT OVER 16! THAT'S THE BEST I'VE SEEN ALL DAY!
WHAT'D I TELL YOU, BERNIE?
SON, IF YOU PLAY GOLF AS WELL AS YOU TAN, YOU'VE GOT THIS TOURNAMENT LOCKED UP! HOW'D YOU DO OUT ON THE LINKS?
UH.. LET'S SEE. IT COMES TO 239.
239? FOR 18 HOLES?
RIGHT.
UH.. THAT'S KIND OF AN UNUSUAL SCORE, ISN'T IT?
HE KEPT IT TO 20 YARDS A STROKE.
YOU HAVE MORE CONTROL THAT WAY.

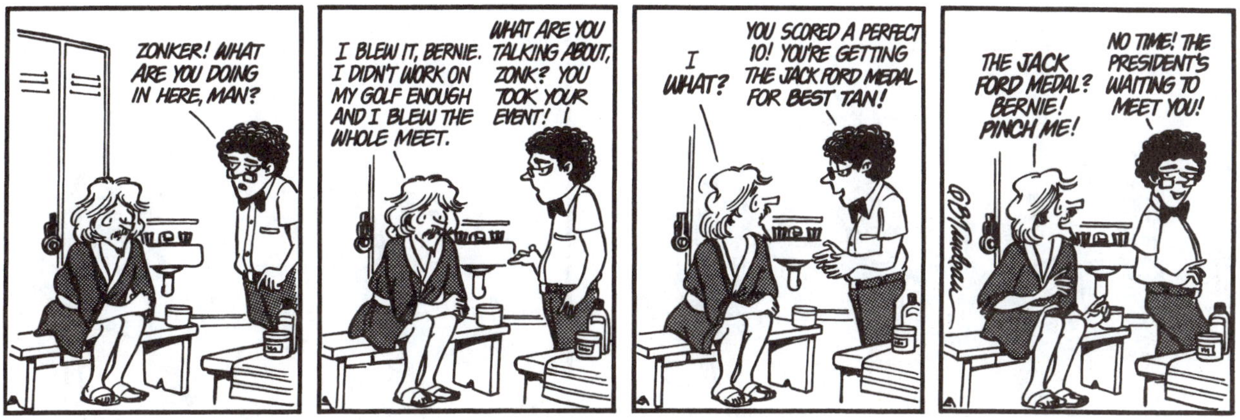
ZONKER! WHAT ARE YOU DOING IN HERE, MAN?
I BLEW IT, BERNIE. I DIDN'T WORK ON MY GOLF ENOUGH AND I BLEW THE WHOLE MEET.
WHAT ARE YOU TALKING ABOUT, ZONK? YOU TOOK YOUR EVENT!
I WHAT?
YOU SCORED A PERFECT 10! YOU'RE GETTING THE JACK FORD MEDAL FOR BEST TAN!
THE JACK FORD MEDAL? BERNIE! PINCH ME!
NO TIME! THE PRESIDENT'S WAITING TO MEET YOU!

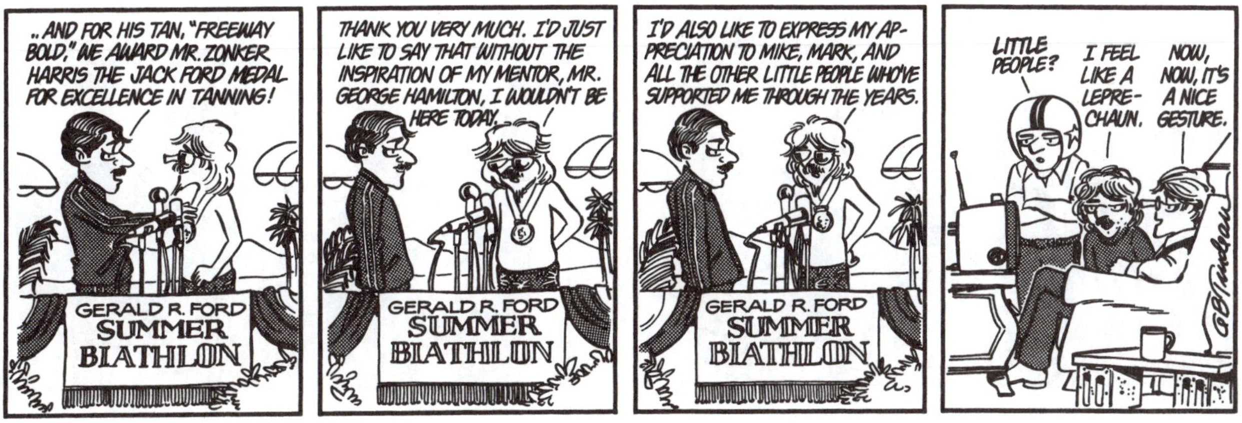
..AND FOR HIS TAN, "FREEWAY BOLD," WE AWARD MR. ZONKER HARRIS THE JACK FORD MEDAL FOR EXCELLENCE IN TANNING!
GERALD R. FORD SUMMER BIATHLON
THANK YOU VERY MUCH. I'D JUST LIKE TO SAY THAT WITHOUT THE INSPIRATION OF MY MENTOR, MR. GEORGE HAMILTON, I WOULDN'T BE HERE TODAY.
GERALD R. FORD SUMMER BIATHLON
I'D ALSO LIKE TO EXPRESS MY APPRECIATION TO MIKE, MARK, AND ALL THE OTHER LITTLE PEOPLE WHO'VE SUPPORTED ME THROUGH THE YEARS.
GERALD R. FORD SUMMER BIATHLON
LITTLE PEOPLE?
I FEEL LIKE A LEPRECHAUN.
NOW, NOW, IT'S A NICE GESTURE.

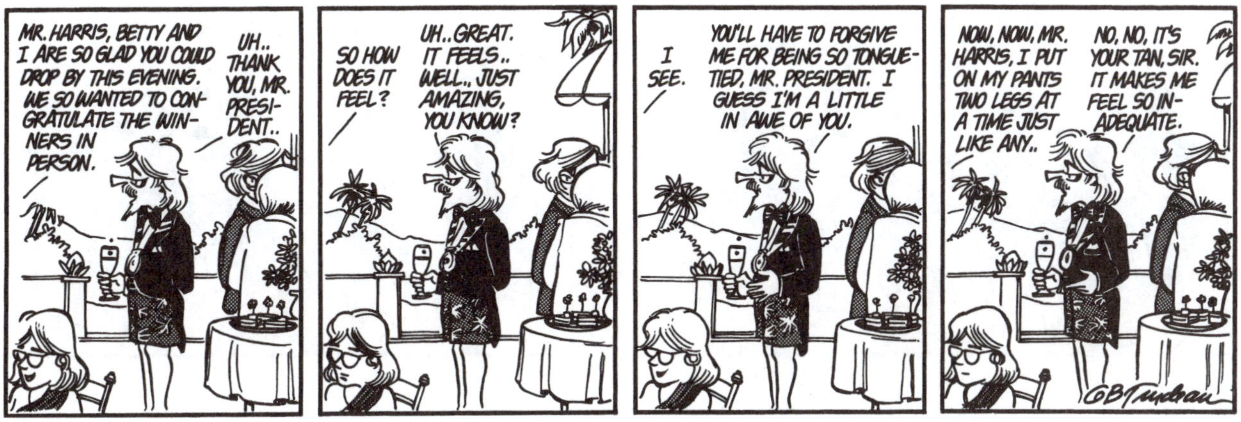
MR. HARRIS, BETTY AND I ARE SO GLAD YOU COULD DROP BY THIS EVENING. WE SO WANTED TO CONGRATULATE THE WINNERS IN PERSON.
UH.. THANK YOU, MR. PRESIDENT..
SO HOW DOES IT FEEL?
UH.. GREAT. IT FEELS.. WELL.. JUST AMAZING, YOU KNOW?
I SEE.
YOU'LL HAVE TO FORGIVE ME FOR BEING SO TONGUE-TIED, MR. PRESIDENT. I GUESS I'M A LITTLE IN AWE OF YOU.
NOW, NOW, MR. HARRIS, I PUT ON MY PANTS TWO LEGS AT A TIME JUST LIKE ANY..
NO, NO, IT'S YOUR TAN, SIR. IT MAKES ME FEEL SO INADEQUATE.

OKAY, GUYS, WE'RE IN A TIGHT SPOT HERE. IT'S EVERY MAN FOR HIMSELF.
WOULDN'T IT BE BETTER TO PLAY AS A TEAM?
WE'VE TRIED THAT, KIRBY. IT'S TIME FOR A NEW APPROACH.
ALRIGHT, WE'VE GOT A THIRD DOWN SITUATION HERE. ANY SUGGESTIONS?
I NEVER THOUGHT YOU'D ASK, CAP'N!
I WITHDRAW THE QUESTION. LET'S GO WITH..
WHAT'S YOUR PLAY, ZONK? I'M ANXIOUS TO HEAR IT!
WELL, IT INVOLVES SOME PRETTY FANCY MOVES, KIRBY. I JUST HOPE WE'RE UP TO IT.
LISTEN, HARRIS..
HEAR HIM OUT, B.D.! WE **NEED** FRESH IDEAS!
IT STARTS WITH KIRBY IN MOTION. JENKINS AND HILL ARE THE SET-BACKS. AFTER THE COUNT, KIRBY SWEEPS WIDE TO THE RIGHT.
FAKING A CUT-BACK, HE STEPS OUT OF BOUNDS AND HEADS FOR THE LOCKER ROOM, WHERE HE PLACES A LONG DISTANCE PHONE CALL TO WOODY HAYES.
HE QUICKLY COAXES HAYES OUT OF RETIREMENT, THE WORD SPREADS, AND THE BEST PLAYERS IN THE COUNTRY TRANSFER HERE, ENABLING US TO WIN THE REST OF OUR GAMES AND GO ON TO WIN THE ROSE BOWL!
BUT ALL WE NEED IS THREE YARDS.
SURE, IN THE SHORT RUN, KIRBY. BUT WE'VE GOT TO BUILD FOR THE FUTURE!

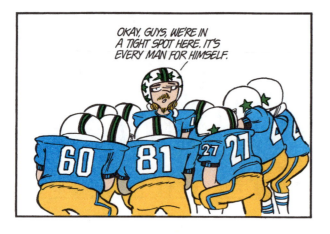

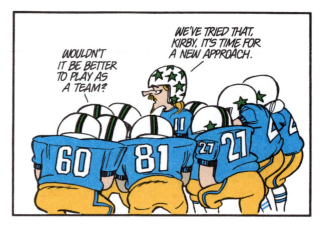

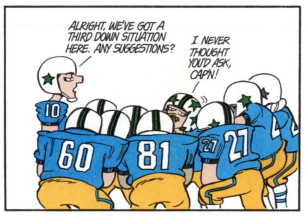

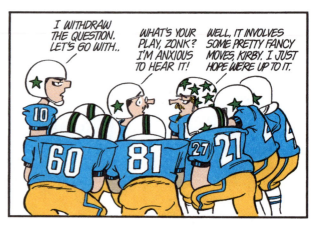

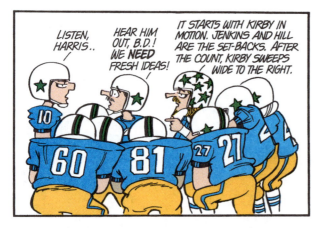

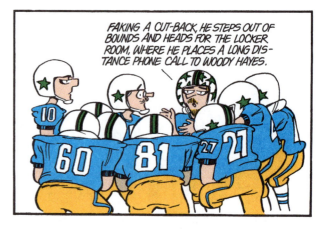

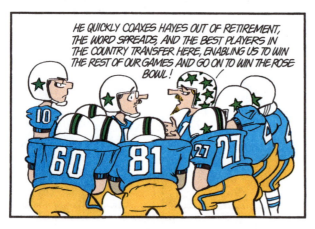

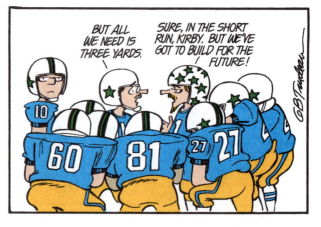

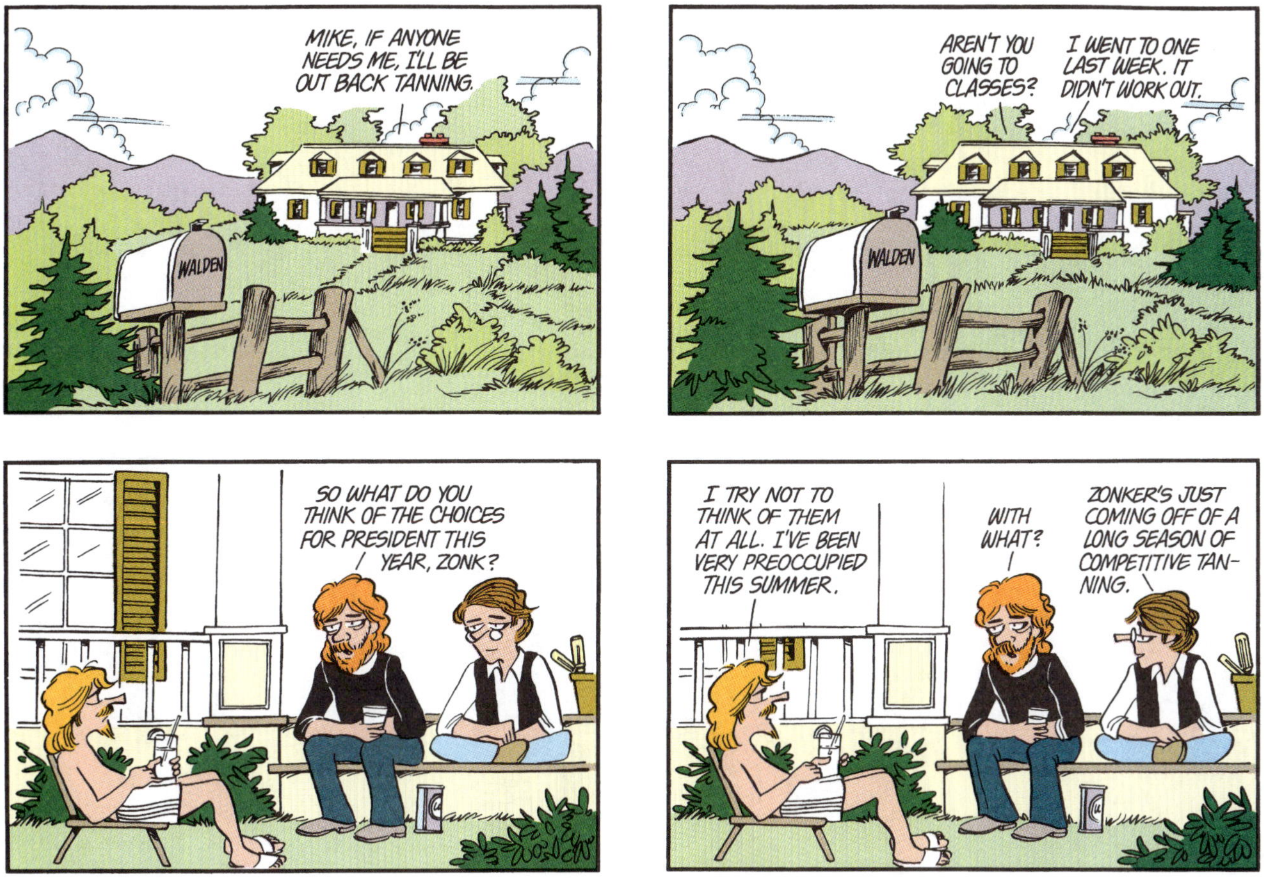
MIKE, IF ANYONE NEEDS ME, I'LL BE OUT BACK TANNING.
WALDEN
AREN'T YOU GOING TO CLASSES?
I WENT TO ONE LAST WEEK. IT DIDN'T WORK OUT.
WALDEN
SO WHAT DO YOU THINK OF THE CHOICES FOR PRESIDENT THIS YEAR, ZONK?
I TRY NOT TO THINK OF THEM AT ALL. I'VE BEEN VERY PREOCCUPIED THIS SUMMER.
WITH WHAT?
ZONKER'S JUST COMING OFF OF A LONG SEASON OF COMPETITIVE TANNING.

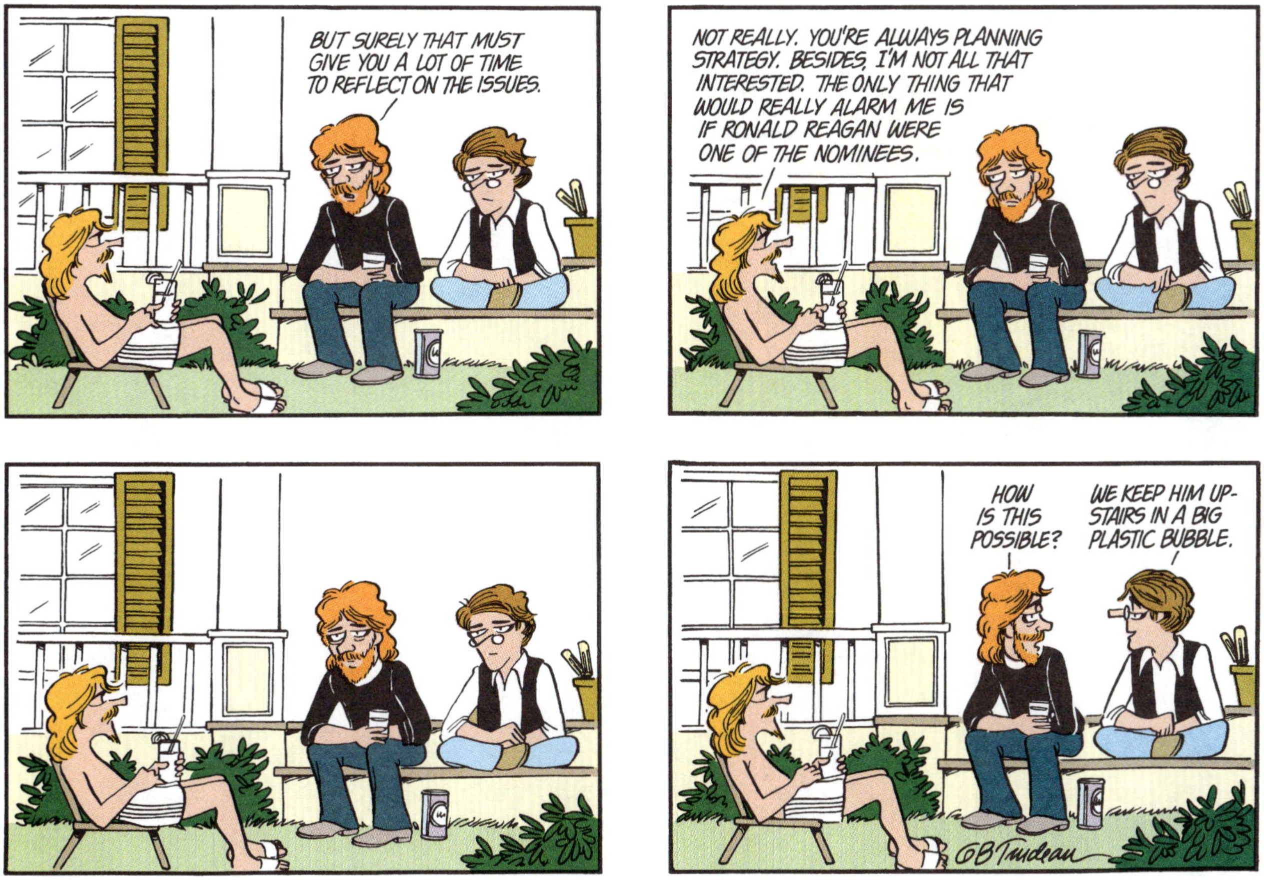
BUT SURELY THAT MUST GIVE YOU A LOT OF TIME TO REFLECT ON THE ISSUES.
NOT REALLY. YOU'RE ALWAYS PLANNING STRATEGY. BESIDES, I'M NOT ALL THAT INTERESTED. THE ONLY THING THAT WOULD REALLY ALARM ME IS IF RONALD REAGAN WERE ONE OF THE NOMINEES.
HOW IS THIS POSSIBLE?
WE KEEP HIM UPSTAIRS IN A BIG PLASTIC BUBBLE.
GB Trudeau

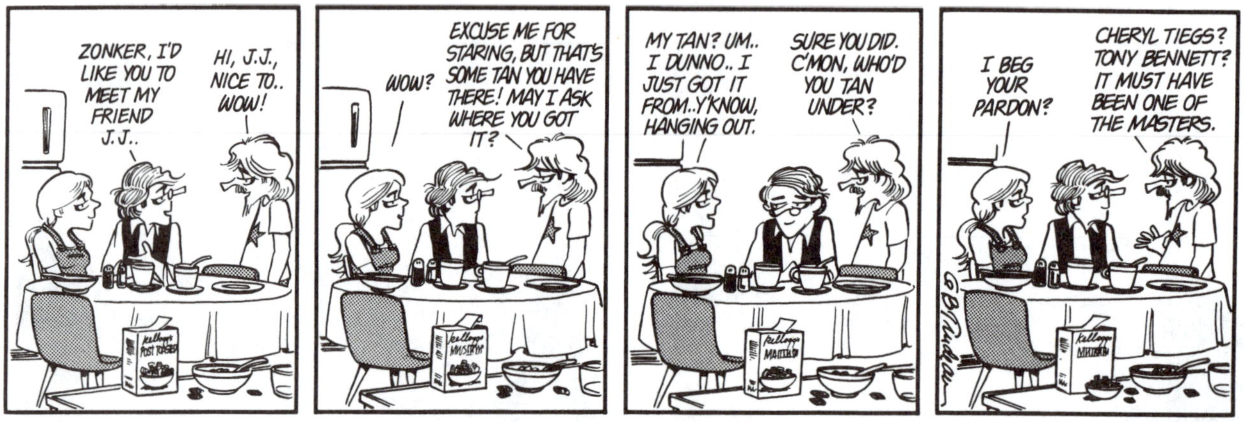
ZONKER, I'D LIKE YOU TO MEET MY FRIEND J.J..
HI, J.J., NICE TO.. WOW!
WOW?
EXCUSE ME FOR STARING, BUT THAT'S SOME TAN YOU HAVE THERE! MAY I ASK WHERE YOU GOT IT?
MY TAN? UM.. I DUNNO.. I JUST GOT IT FROM.. Y'KNOW, HANGING OUT.
SURE YOU DID. C'MON, WHO'D YOU TAN UNDER?
I BEG YOUR PARDON?
CHERYL TIEGS? TONY BENNETT? IT MUST HAVE BEEN ONE OF THE MASTERS.

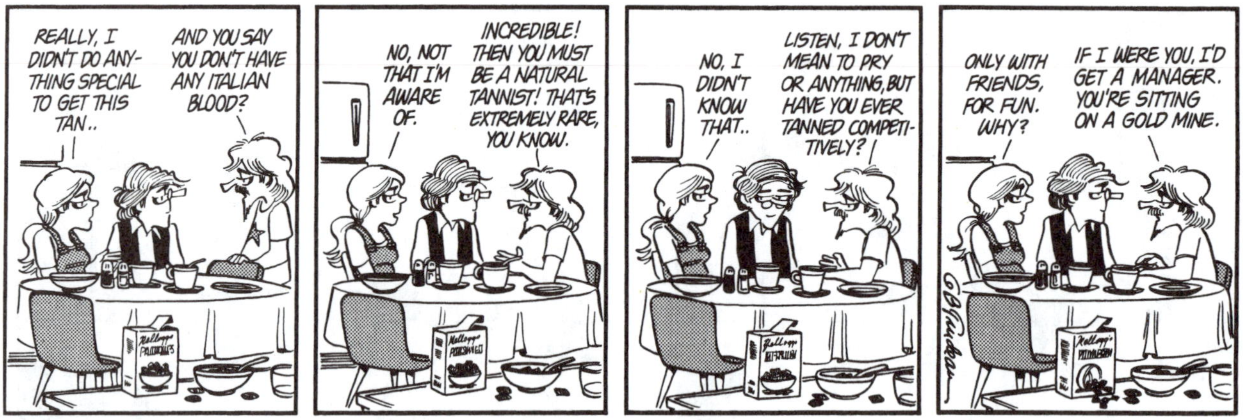
REALLY, I DIDN'T DO ANYTHING SPECIAL TO GET THIS TAN..
AND YOU SAY YOU DON'T HAVE ANY ITALIAN BLOOD?
NO, NOT THAT I'M AWARE OF.
INCREDIBLE! THEN YOU MUST BE A NATURAL TANNIST! THAT'S EXTREMELY RARE, YOU KNOW.
NO, I DIDN'T KNOW THAT..
LISTEN, I DON'T MEAN TO PRY OR ANYTHING, BUT HAVE YOU EVER TANNED COMPETITIVELY?
ONLY WITH FRIENDS, FOR FUN. WHY?
IF I WERE YOU, I'D GET A MANAGER. YOU'RE SITTING ON A GOLD MINE.

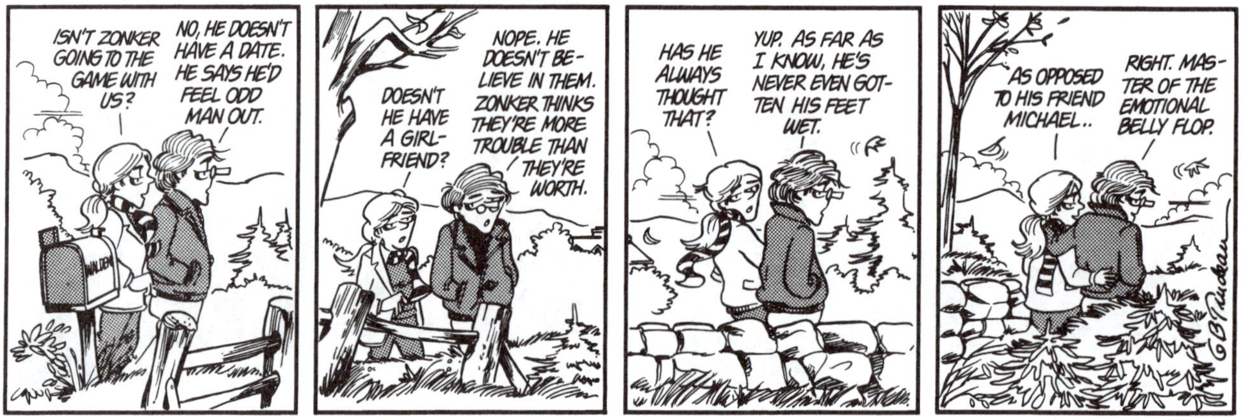
ISN'T ZONKER GOING TO THE GAME WITH US?
NO, HE DOESN'T HAVE A DATE. HE SAYS HE'D FEEL ODD MAN OUT.
WALDEN
DOESN'T HE HAVE A GIRLFRIEND?
NOPE.. HE DOESN'T BELIEVE IN THEM. ZONKER THINKS THEY'RE MORE TROUBLE THAN THEY'RE WORTH.
HAS HE ALWAYS THOUGHT THAT?
YUP. AS FAR AS I KNOW, HE'S NEVER EVEN GOTTEN HIS FEET WET.
AS OPPOSED TO HIS FRIEND MICHAEL..
RIGHT. MASTER OF THE EMOTIONAL BELLY FLOP.

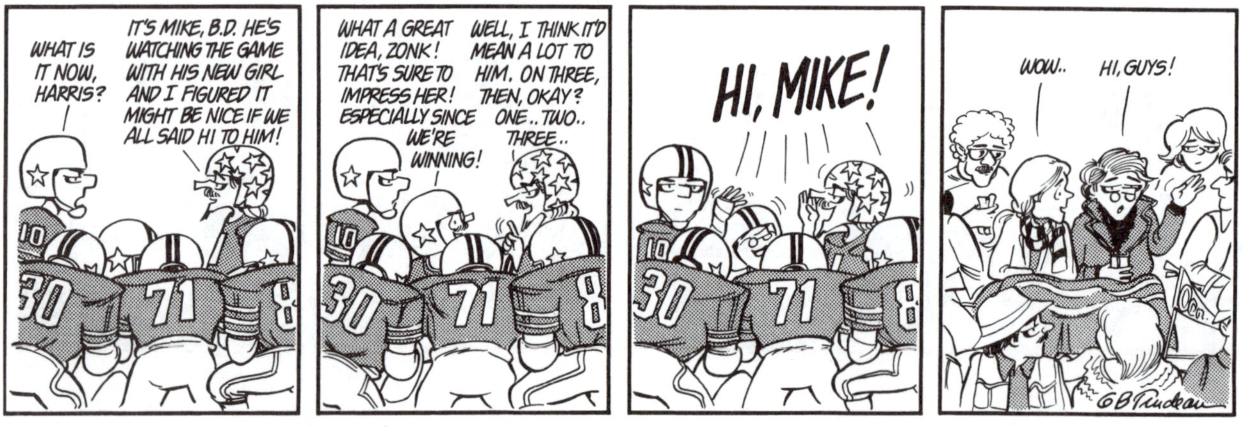
WHAT IS IT NOW, HARRIS?
IT'S MIKE, B.D. HE'S WATCHING THE GAME WITH HIS NEW GIRL AND I FIGURED IT MIGHT BE NICE IF WE ALL SAID HI TO HIM!
WHAT A GREAT IDEA, ZONK! THAT'S SURE TO IMPRESS HER! ESPECIALLY SINCE WE'RE WINNING!
WELL, I THINK IT'D MEAN A LOT TO HIM. ON THREE, THEN, OKAY? ONE.. TWO.. THREE..
HI, MIKE!
WOW..
HI, GUYS!

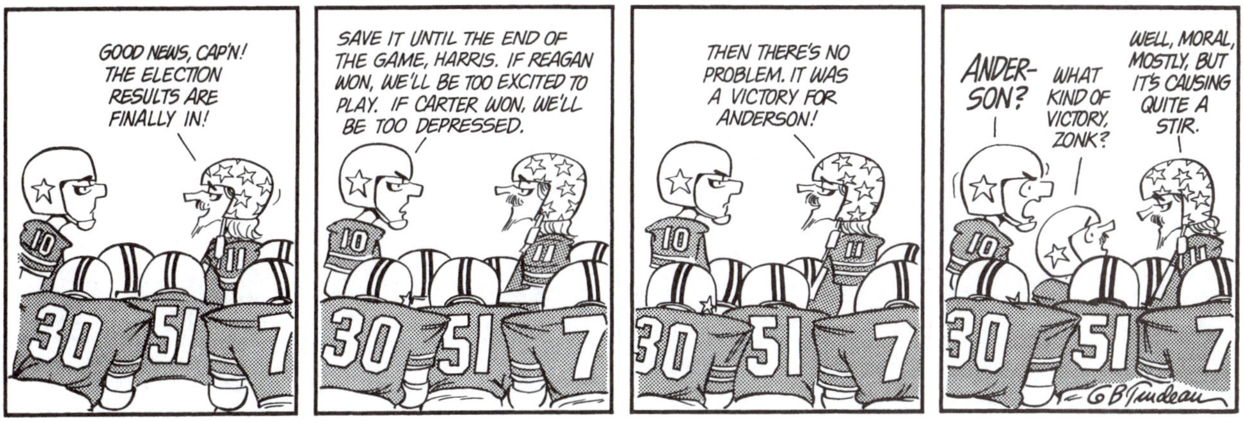
GOOD NEWS, CAP'N! THE ELECTION RESULTS ARE FINALLY IN!
SAVE IT UNTIL THE END OF THE GAME, HARRIS. IF REAGAN WON, WE'LL BE TOO EXCITED TO PLAY. IF CARTER WON, WE'LL BE TOO DEPRESSED.
THEN THERE'S NO PROBLEM. IT WAS A VICTORY FOR ANDERSON!
ANDER-SON?
WHAT KIND OF VICTORY, ZONK?
WELL, MORAL, MOSTLY, BUT IT'S CAUSING QUITE A STIR.
30
51
7

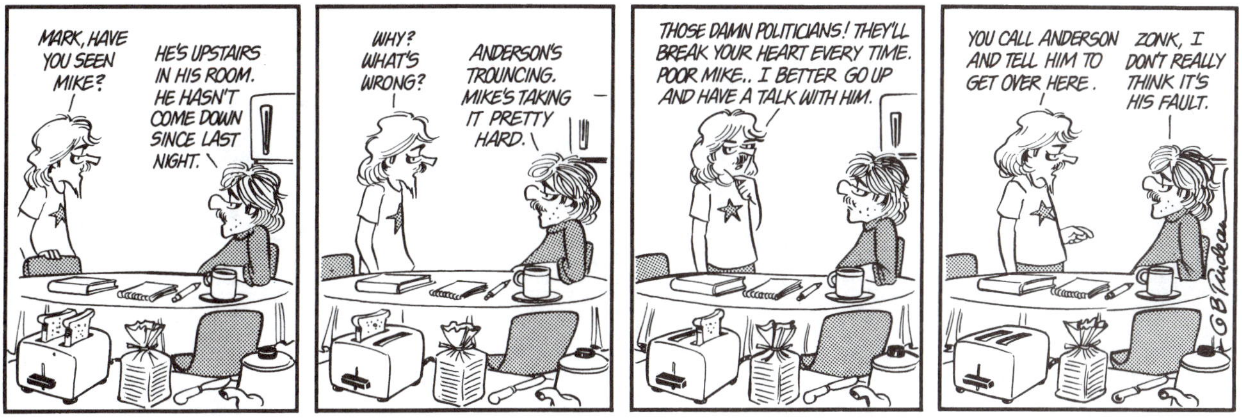
MARK, HAVE YOU SEEN MIKE?
HE'S UPSTAIRS IN HIS ROOM. HE HASN'T COME DOWN SINCE LAST NIGHT.
WHY? WHAT'S WRONG?
ANDERSON'S TROUNCING. MIKE'S TAKING IT PRETTY HARD.
THOSE DAMN POLITICIANS! THEY'LL BREAK YOUR HEART EVERY TIME. POOR MIKE.. I BETTER GO UP AND HAVE A TALK WITH HIM.
YOU CALL ANDERSON AND TELL HIM TO GET OVER HERE.
ZONK, I DON'T REALLY THINK IT'S HIS FAULT.

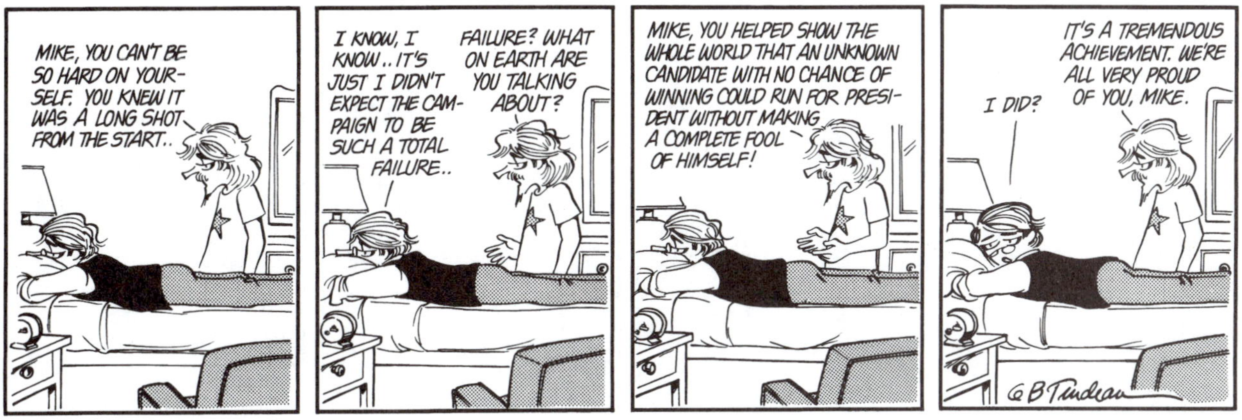
MIKE, YOU CAN'T BE SO HARD ON YOUR-SELF. YOU KNEW IT WAS A LONG SHOT FROM THE START..
I KNOW, I KNOW.. IT'S JUST I DIDN'T EXPECT THE CAM-PAIGN TO BE SUCH A TOTAL FAILURE..
FAILURE? WHAT ON EARTH ARE YOU TALKING ABOUT?
MIKE, YOU HELPED SHOW THE WHOLE WORLD THAT AN UNKNOWN CANDIDATE WITH NO CHANCE OF WINNING COULD RUN FOR PRESI-DENT WITHOUT MAKING A COMPLETE FOOL OF HIMSELF!
I DID?
IT'S A TREMENDOUS ACHIEVEMENT. WE'RE ALL VERY PROUD OF YOU, MIKE.

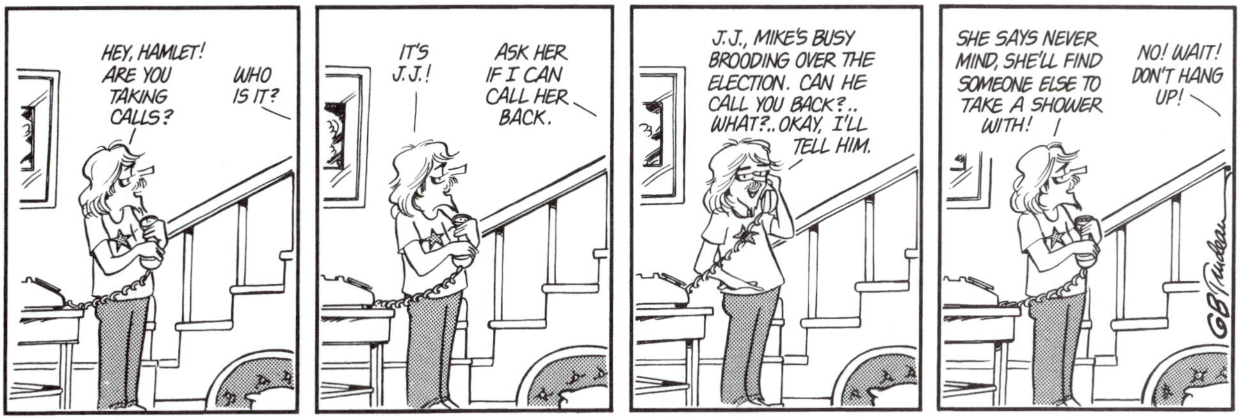
HEY, HAMLET! ARE YOU TAKING CALLS?
WHO IS IT?
IT'S J.J.!
ASK HER IF I CAN CALL HER BACK.
J.J., MIKE'S BUSY BROODING OVER THE ELECTION. CAN HE CALL YOU BACK?.. WHAT?.. OKAY, I'LL TELL HIM.
SHE SAYS NEVER MIND, SHE'LL FIND SOMEONE ELSE TO TAKE A SHOWER WITH!
NO! WAIT! DON'T HANG UP!

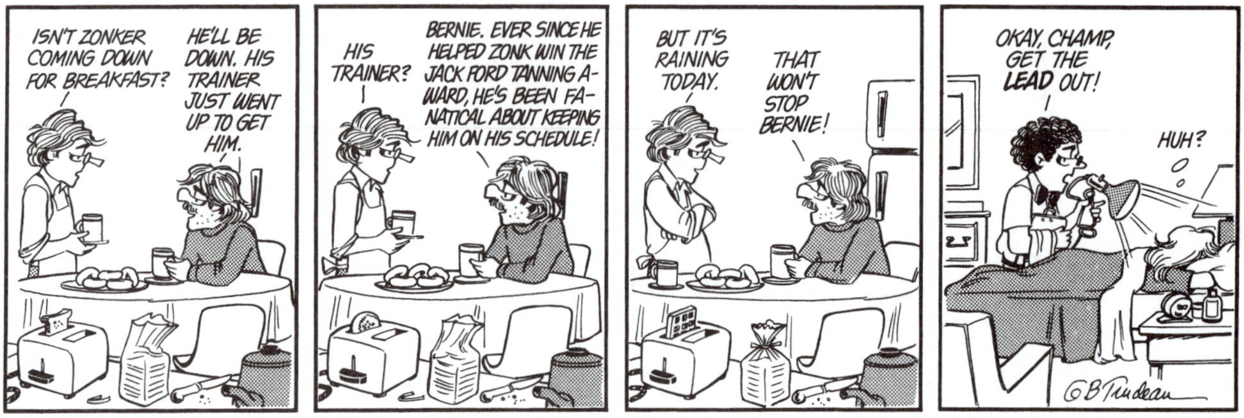
ISN'T ZONKER COMING DOWN FOR BREAKFAST?
HE'LL BE DOWN. HIS TRAINER JUST WENT UP TO GET HIM.
HIS TRAINER?
BERNIE. EVER SINCE HE HELPED ZONK WIN THE JACK FORD TANNING AWARD, HE'S BEEN FANATICAL ABOUT KEEPING HIM ON HIS SCHEDULE!
BUT IT'S RAINING TODAY.
THAT WON'T STOP BERNIE!
OKAY, CHAMP, GET THE LEAD OUT!
HUH?
©GBTrudeau

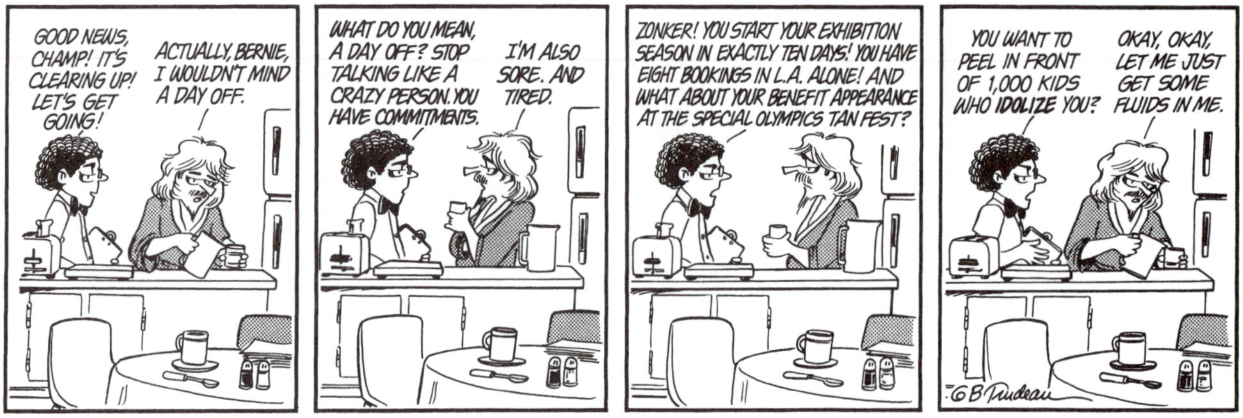
GOOD NEWS, CHAMP! IT'S CLEARING UP! LET'S GET GOING!
ACTUALLY, BERNIE, I WOULDN'T MIND A DAY OFF.
WHAT DO YOU MEAN, A DAY OFF? STOP TALKING LIKE A CRAZY PERSON. YOU HAVE COMMITMENTS.
I'M ALSO SORE. AND TIRED.
ZONKER! YOU START YOUR EXHIBITION SEASON IN EXACTLY TEN DAYS! YOU HAVE EIGHT BOOKINGS IN L.A. ALONE! AND WHAT ABOUT YOUR BENEFIT APPEARANCE AT THE SPECIAL OLYMPICS TAN FEST?
YOU WANT TO PEEL IN FRONT OF 1,000 KIDS WHO IDOLIZE YOU?
OKAY, OKAY, LET ME JUST GET SOME FLUIDS IN ME.
©GBTrudeau

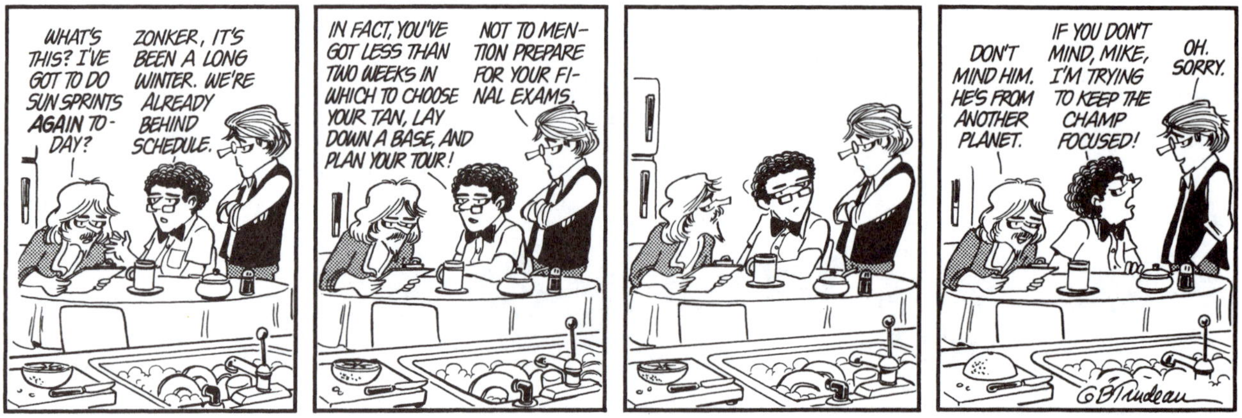
WHAT'S THIS? I'VE GOT TO DO SUN SPRINTS AGAIN TODAY?
ZONKER, IT'S BEEN A LONG WINTER. WE'RE ALREADY BEHIND SCHEDULE.
IN FACT, YOU'VE GOT LESS THAN TWO WEEKS IN WHICH TO CHOOSE YOUR TAN, LAY DOWN A BASE, AND PLAN YOUR TOUR!
NOT TO MENTION PREPARE FOR YOUR FINAL EXAMS.
DON'T MIND HIM. HE'S FROM ANOTHER PLANET.
IF YOU DON'T MIND, MIKE, I'M TRYING TO KEEP THE CHAMP FOCUSED!
OH. SORRY.
©GBTrudeau

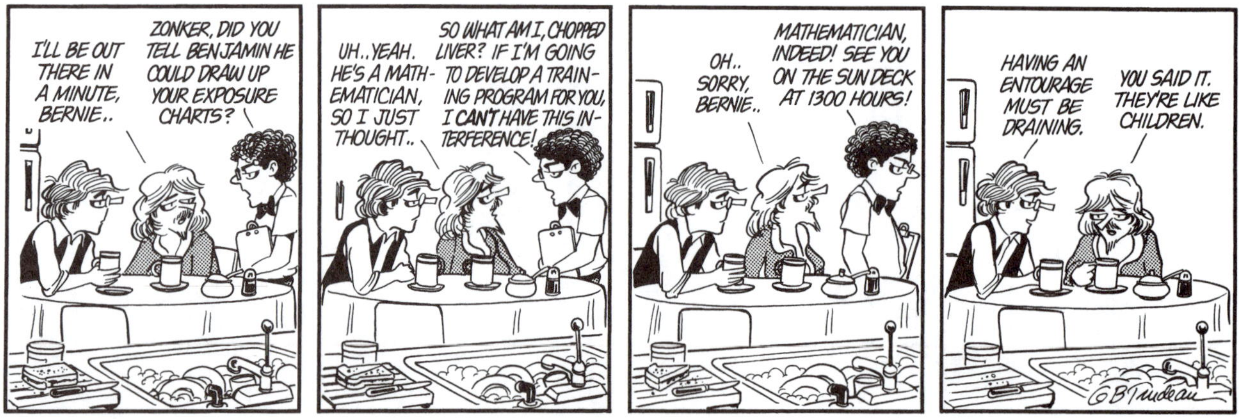
I'LL BE OUT THERE IN A MINUTE, BERNIE..
ZONKER, DID YOU TELL BENJAMIN HE COULD DRAW UP YOUR EXPOSURE CHARTS?
UH..YEAH. HE'S A MATHEMATICIAN, SO I JUST THOUGHT..
SO WHAT AM I, CHOPPED LIVER? IF I'M GOING TO DEVELOP A TRAINING PROGRAM FOR YOU, I CAN'T HAVE THIS INTERFERENCE!
OH.. SORRY, BERNIE..
MATHEMATICIAN, INDEED! SEE YOU ON THE SUN DECK AT 1300 HOURS!
HAVING AN ENTOURAGE MUST BE DRAINING.
YOU SAID IT. THEY'RE LIKE CHILDREN.
©GBTrudeau

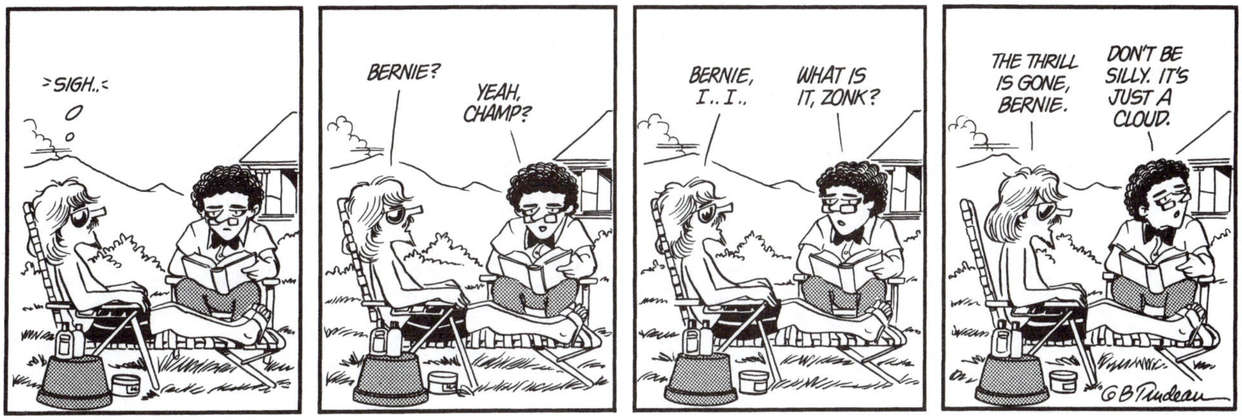
>SIGH..<
BERNIE?
YEAH, CHAMP?
BERNIE, I.. I..
WHAT IS IT, ZONK?
THE THRILL IS GONE, BERNIE.
DON'T BE SILLY. IT'S JUST A CLOUD.
©B Trudeau

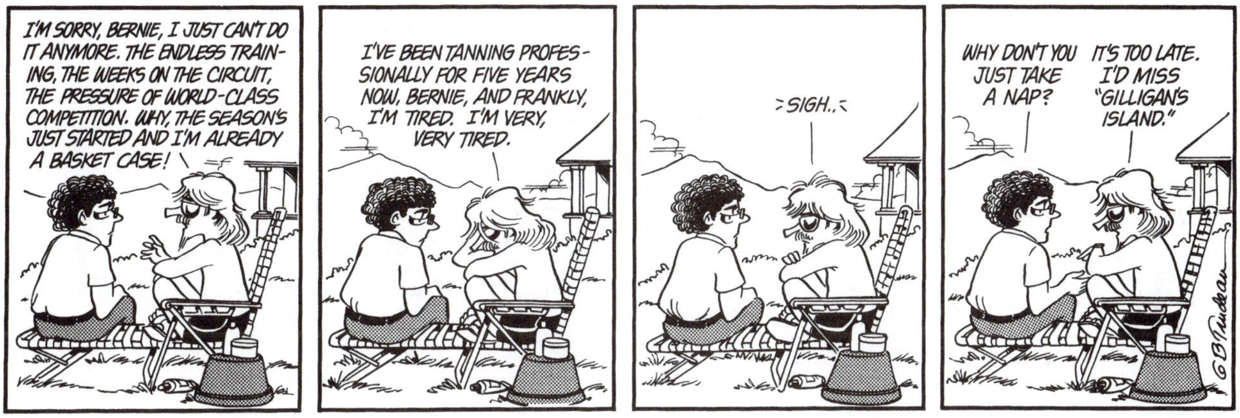
I'M SORRY, BERNIE, I JUST CAN'T DO IT ANYMORE. THE ENDLESS TRAINING, THE WEEKS ON THE CIRCUIT, THE PRESSURE OF WORLD-CLASS COMPETITION. WHY, THE SEASON'S JUST STARTED AND I'M ALREADY A BASKET CASE!
I'VE BEEN TANNING PROFESSIONALLY FOR FIVE YEARS NOW, BERNIE, AND FRANKLY, I'M TIRED. I'M VERY, VERY TIRED.
>SIGH..<
WHY DON'T YOU JUST TAKE A NAP?
IT'S TOO LATE. I'D MISS "GILLIGAN'S ISLAND."
©B Trudeau

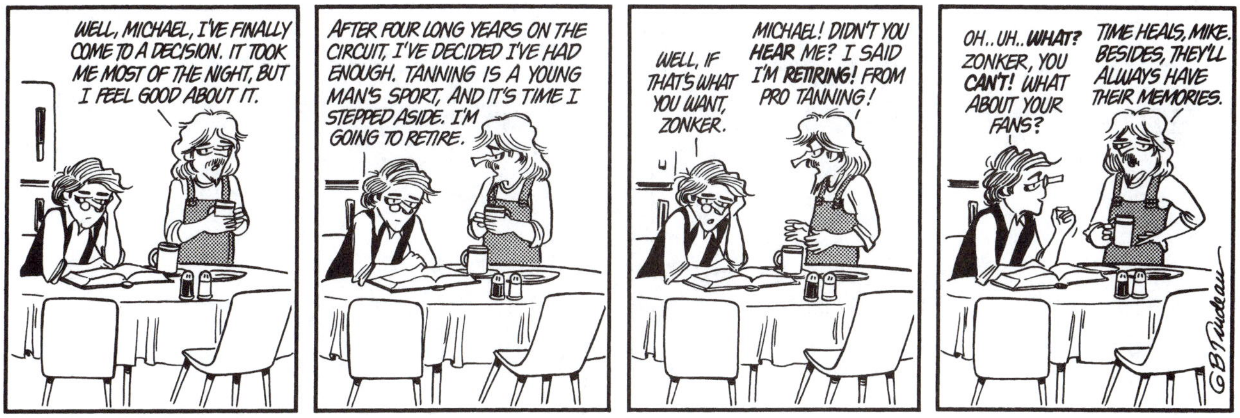
WELL, MICHAEL, I'VE FINALLY COME TO A DECISION. IT TOOK ME MOST OF THE NIGHT, BUT I FEEL GOOD ABOUT IT.
AFTER FOUR LONG YEARS ON THE CIRCUIT, I'VE DECIDED I'VE HAD ENOUGH. TANNING IS A YOUNG MAN'S SPORT, AND IT'S TIME I STEPPED ASIDE. I'M GOING TO RETIRE.
WELL, IF THAT'S WHAT YOU WANT, ZONKER.
MICHAEL! DIDN'T YOU **HEAR** ME? I SAID I'M **RETIRING**! FROM PRO TANNING!
OH..UH..**WHAT?** ZONKER, YOU **CAN'T**! WHAT ABOUT YOUR FANS?
TIME HEALS, MIKE. BESIDES, THEY'LL ALWAYS HAVE THEIR MEMORIES.
©B Trudeau

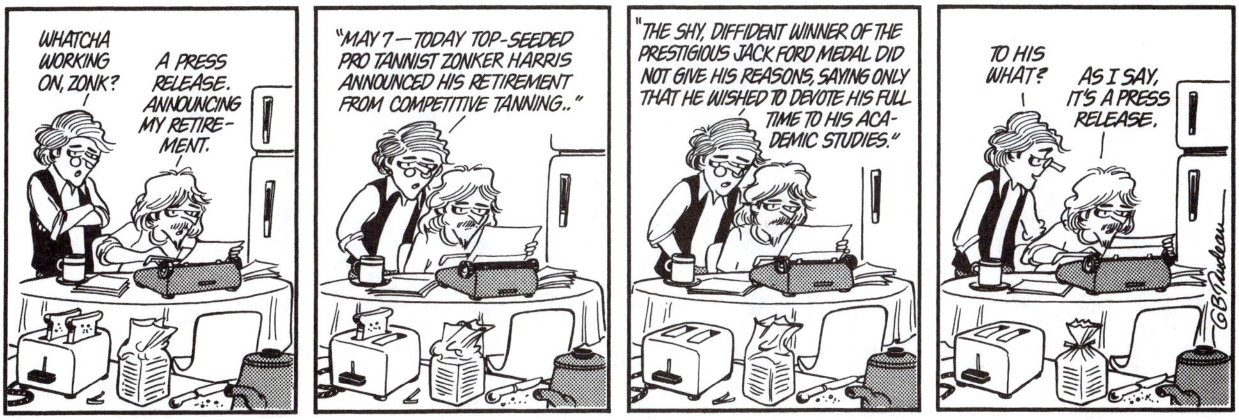
WHATCHA WORKING ON, ZONK?
A PRESS RELEASE. ANNOUNCING MY RETIREMENT.
"MAY 7—TODAY TOP-SEEDED PRO TANNIST ZONKER HARRIS ANNOUNCED HIS RETIREMENT FROM COMPETITIVE TANNING.."
"THE SHY, DIFFIDENT WINNER OF THE PRESTIGIOUS JACK FORD MEDAL DID NOT GIVE HIS REASONS, SAYING ONLY THAT HE WISHED TO DEVOTE HIS FULL TIME TO HIS ACADEMIC STUDIES."
TO HIS WHAT?
AS I SAY, IT'S A PRESS RELEASE.
©B Trudeau

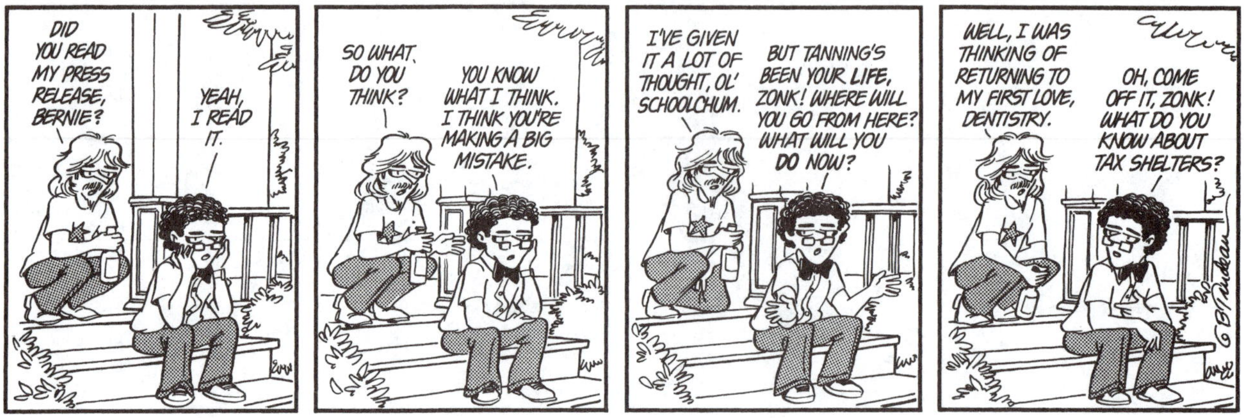
DID YOU READ MY PRESS RELEASE, BERNIE?
YEAH, I READ IT.
SO WHAT. DO YOU THINK?
YOU KNOW WHAT I THINK. I THINK YOU'RE MAKING A BIG MISTAKE.
I'VE GIVEN IT A LOT OF THOUGHT, OL' SCHOOLCHUM.
BUT TANNING'S BEEN YOUR LIFE, ZONK! WHERE WILL YOU GO FROM HERE? WHAT WILL YOU DO NOW?
WELL, I WAS THINKING OF RETURNING TO MY FIRST LOVE, DENTISTRY.
OH, COME OFF IT, ZONK! WHAT DO YOU KNOW ABOUT TAX SHELTERS?
G B Trudeau

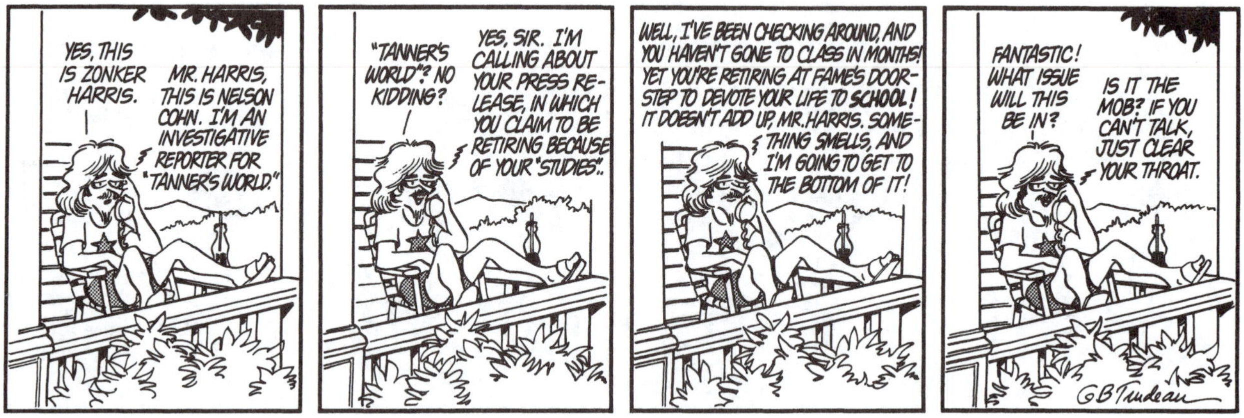
YES, THIS IS ZONKER HARRIS.
MR. HARRIS, THIS IS NELSON COHN. I'M AN INVESTIGATIVE REPORTER FOR "TANNER'S WORLD."
"TANNER'S WORLD"? NO KIDDING?
YES, SIR. I'M CALLING ABOUT YOUR PRESS RELEASE, IN WHICH YOU CLAIM TO BE RETIRING BECAUSE OF YOUR "STUDIES"..
WELL, I'VE BEEN CHECKING AROUND, AND YOU HAVEN'T GONE TO CLASS IN MONTHS! YET YOU'RE RETIRING AT FAME'S DOORSTEP TO DEVOTE YOUR LIFE TO SCHOOL! IT DOESN'T ADD UP, MR. HARRIS. SOMETHING SMELLS, AND I'M GOING TO GET TO THE BOTTOM OF IT!
FANTASTIC! WHAT ISSUE WILL THIS BE IN?
IS IT THE MOB? IF YOU CAN'T TALK, JUST CLEAR YOUR THROAT.
G B Trudeau

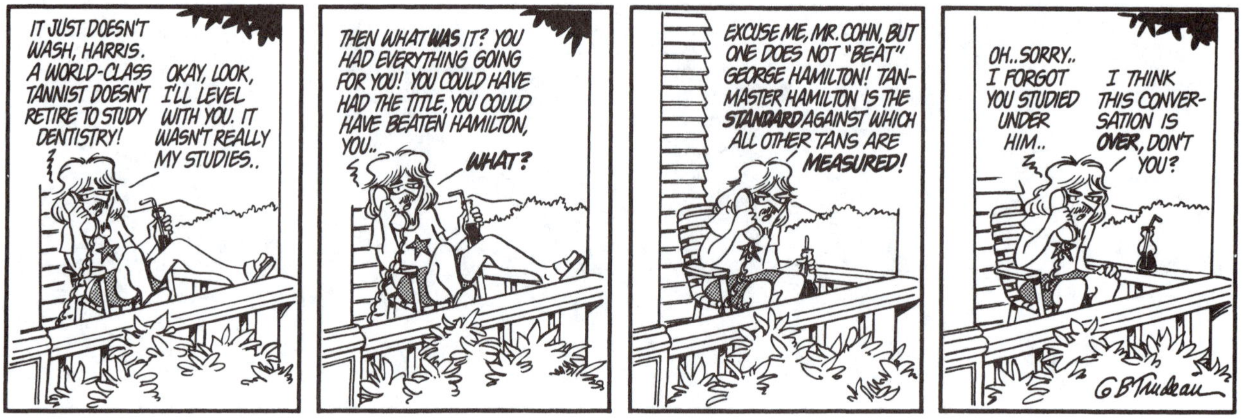
IT JUST DOESN'T WASH, HARRIS. A WORLD-CLASS TANNIST DOESN'T RETIRE TO STUDY DENTISTRY!
OKAY, LOOK, I'LL LEVEL WITH YOU. IT WASN'T REALLY MY STUDIES..
THEN WHAT WAS IT? YOU HAD EVERYTHING GOING FOR YOU! YOU COULD HAVE HAD THE TITLE, YOU COULD HAVE BEATEN HAMILTON, YOU..
WHAT?
EXCUSE ME, MR. COHN, BUT ONE DOES NOT "BEAT" GEORGE HAMILTON! TANMASTER HAMILTON IS THE STANDARD AGAINST WHICH ALL OTHER TANS ARE MEASURED!
OH.. SORRY.. I FORGOT YOU STUDIED UNDER HIM..
I THINK THIS CONVERSATION IS OVER, DON'T YOU?
G B Trudeau

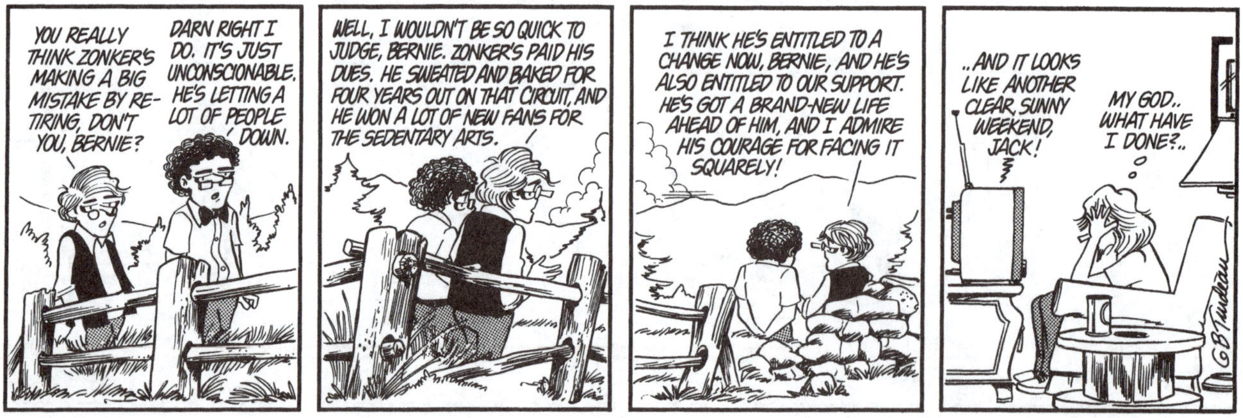
YOU REALLY THINK ZONKER'S MAKING A BIG MISTAKE BY RETIRING, DON'T YOU, BERNIE?
DARN RIGHT I DO. IT'S JUST UNCONSCIONABLE. HE'S LETTING A LOT OF PEOPLE DOWN.
WELL, I WOULDN'T BE SO QUICK TO JUDGE, BERNIE. ZONKER'S PAID HIS DUES. HE SWEATED AND BAKED FOR FOUR YEARS OUT ON THAT CIRCUIT, AND HE WON A LOT OF NEW FANS FOR THE SEDENTARY ARTS.
I THINK HE'S ENTITLED TO A CHANGE NOW, BERNIE, AND HE'S ALSO ENTITLED TO OUR SUPPORT. HE'S GOT A BRAND-NEW LIFE AHEAD OF HIM, AND I ADMIRE HIS COURAGE FOR FACING IT SQUARELY!
..AND IT LOOKS LIKE ANOTHER CLEAR, SUNNY WEEKEND, JACK!
MY GOD.. WHAT HAVE I DONE?..
G B Trudeau

6

THE PLANT WHISPERER

Dances with Daisies

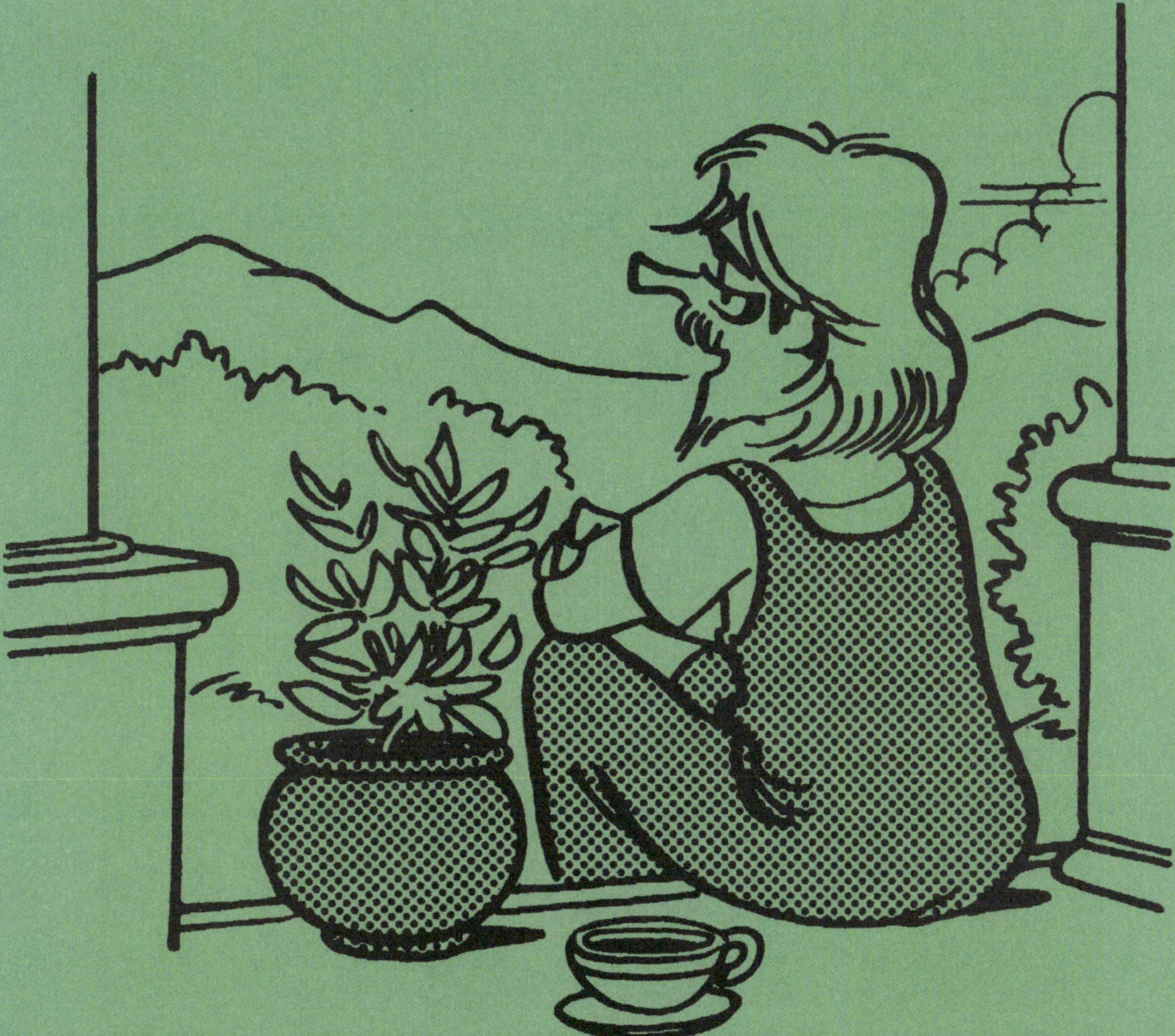

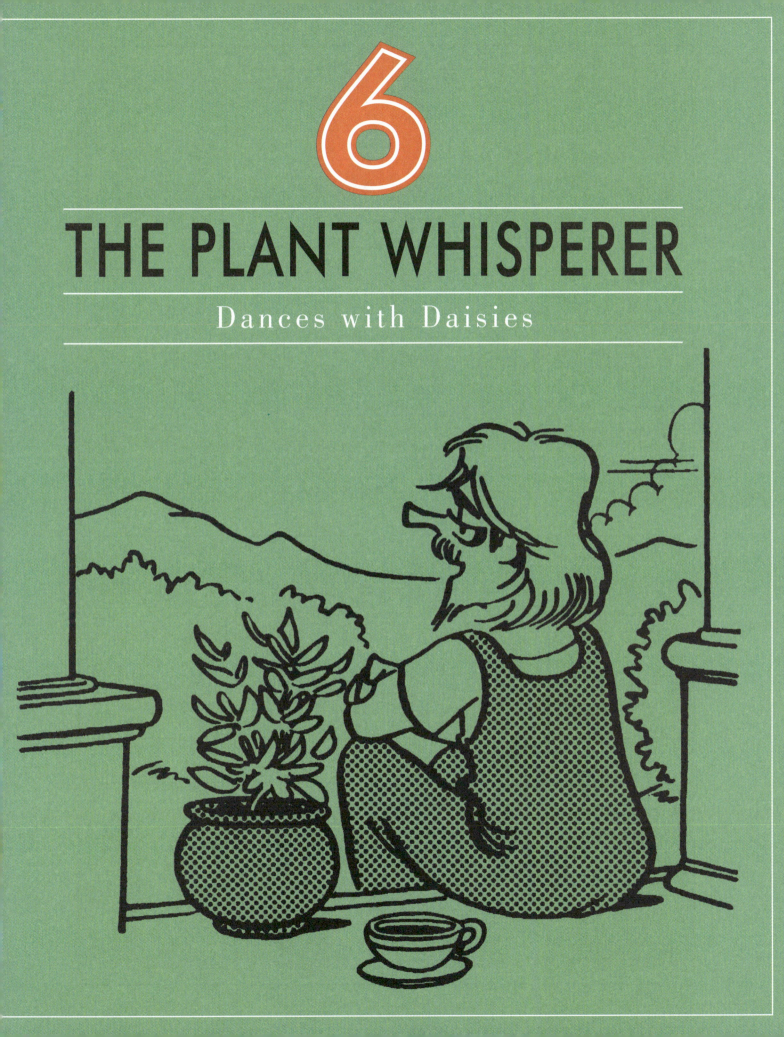

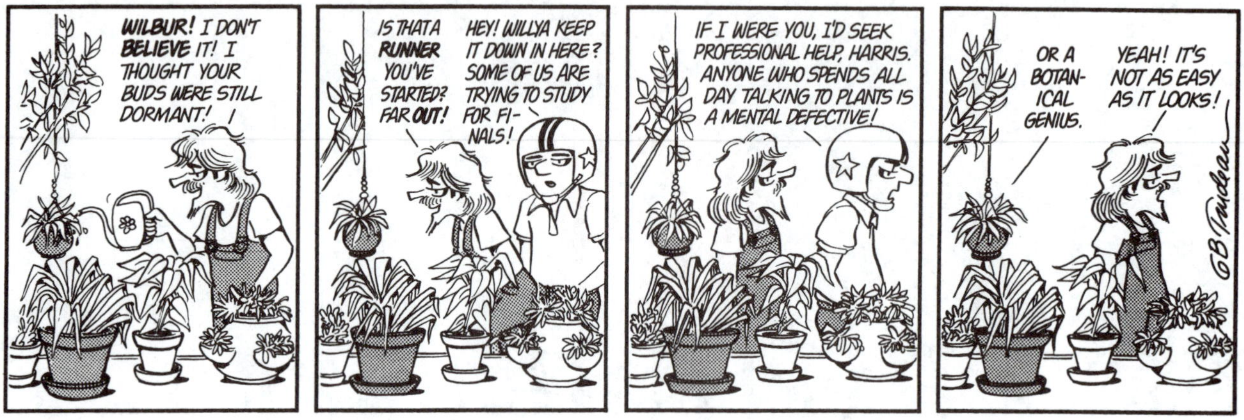
WILBUR! I DON'T BELIEVE IT! I THOUGHT YOUR BUDS WERE STILL DORMANT!
IS THAT A RUNNER YOU'VE STARTED? FAR OUT!
HEY! WILLYA KEEP IT DOWN IN HERE? SOME OF US ARE TRYING TO STUDY FOR FINALS!
IF I WERE YOU, I'D SEEK PROFESSIONAL HELP, HARRIS. ANYONE WHO SPENDS ALL DAY TALKING TO PLANTS IS A MENTAL DEFECTIVE!
OR A BOTANICAL GENIUS.
YEAH! IT'S NOT AS EASY AS IT LOOKS!

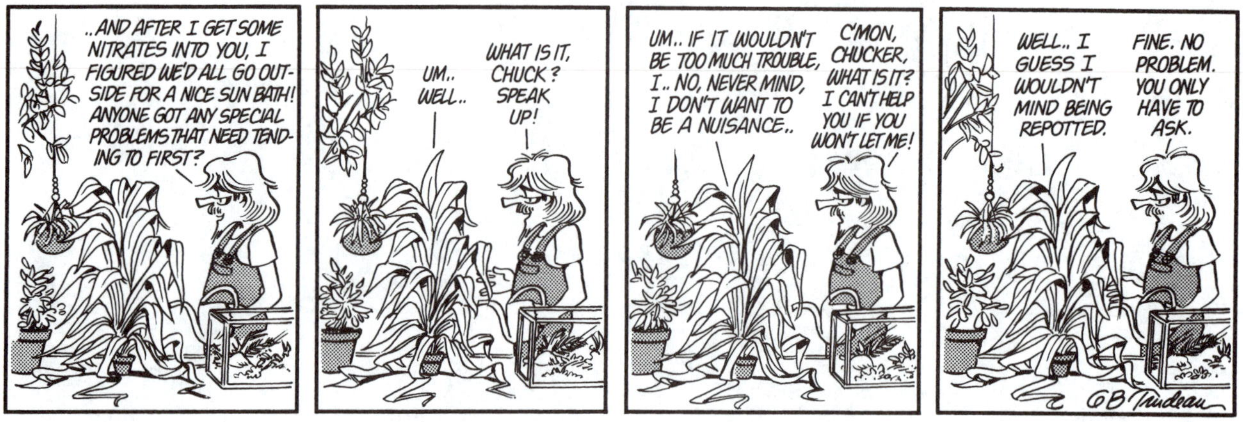
..AND AFTER I GET SOME NITRATES INTO YOU, I FIGURED WE'D ALL GO OUTSIDE FOR A NICE SUN BATH!! ANYONE GOT ANY SPECIAL PROBLEMS THAT NEED TENDING TO FIRST?
UM.. WELL..
WHAT IS IT, CHUCK? SPEAK UP!
UM.. IF IT WOULDN'T BE TOO MUCH TROUBLE, I.. NO, NEVER MIND, I DON'T WANT TO BE A NUISANCE..
C'MON, CHUCKER, WHAT IS IT? I CAN'T HELP YOU IF YOU WON'T LET ME!
WELL.. I GUESS I WOULDN'T MIND BEING REPOTTED.
FINE. NO PROBLEM. YOU ONLY HAVE TO ASK.

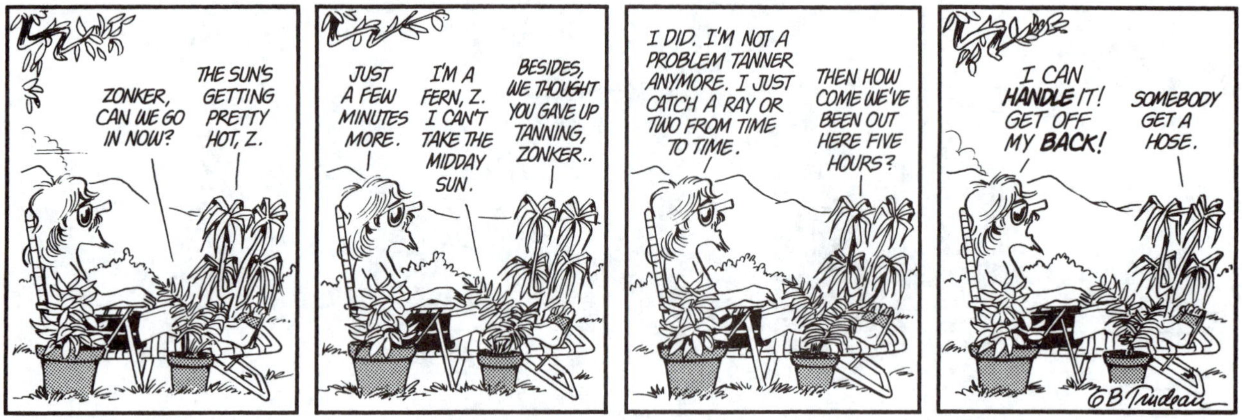
ZONKER, CAN WE GO IN NOW?
THE SUN'S GETTING PRETTY HOT, Z.
JUST A FEW MINUTES MORE.
I'M A FERN, Z. I CAN'T TAKE THE MIDDAY SUN.
BESIDES, WE THOUGHT YOU GAVE UP TANNING, ZONKER..
I DID. I'M NOT A PROBLEM TANNER ANYMORE. I JUST CATCH A RAY OR TWO FROM TIME TO TIME.
THEN HOW COME WE'VE BEEN OUT HERE FIVE HOURS?
I CAN HANDLE IT! GET OFF MY BACK!
SOMEBODY GET A HOSE.

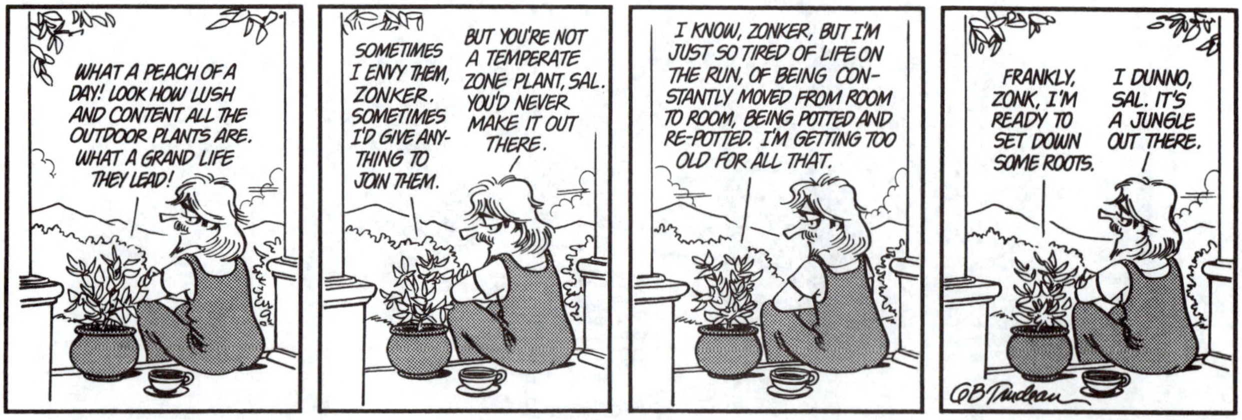
WHAT A PEACH OF A DAY! LOOK HOW LUSH AND CONTENT ALL THE OUTDOOR PLANTS ARE. WHAT A GRAND LIFE THEY LEAD!
SOMETIMES I ENVY THEM, ZONKER. SOMETIMES I'D GIVE ANYTHING TO JOIN THEM.
BUT YOU'RE NOT A TEMPERATE ZONE PLANT, SAL. YOU'D NEVER MAKE IT OUT THERE.
I KNOW, ZONKER, BUT I'M JUST SO TIRED OF LIFE ON THE RUN, OF BEING CONSTANTLY MOVED FROM ROOM TO ROOM, BEING POTTED AND RE-POTTED. I'M GETTING TOO OLD FOR ALL THAT.
FRANKLY, ZONK, I'M READY TO SET DOWN SOME ROOTS.
I DUNNO, SAL. IT'S A JUNGLE OUT THERE.

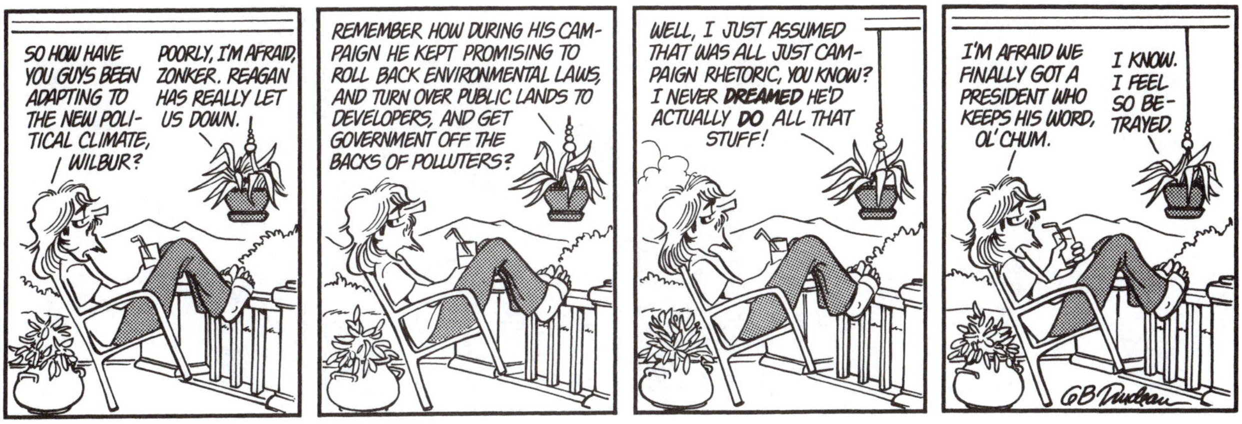
SO HOW HAVE YOU GUYS BEEN ADAPTING TO THE NEW POLITICAL CLIMATE, WILBUR?
POORLY, I'M AFRAID, ZONKER. REAGAN HAS REALLY LET US DOWN.
REMEMBER HOW DURING HIS CAMPAIGN HE KEPT PROMISING TO ROLL BACK ENVIRONMENTAL LAWS, AND TURN OVER PUBLIC LANDS TO DEVELOPERS, AND GET GOVERNMENT OFF THE BACKS OF POLLUTERS?
WELL, I JUST ASSUMED THAT WAS ALL JUST CAMPAIGN RHETORIC, YOU KNOW? I NEVER **DREAMED** HE'D ACTUALLY **DO** ALL THAT STUFF!
I'M AFRAID WE FINALLY GOT A PRESIDENT WHO KEEPS HIS WORD, OL' CHUM.
I KNOW. I FEEL SO BETRAYED.
G.B. Trudeau

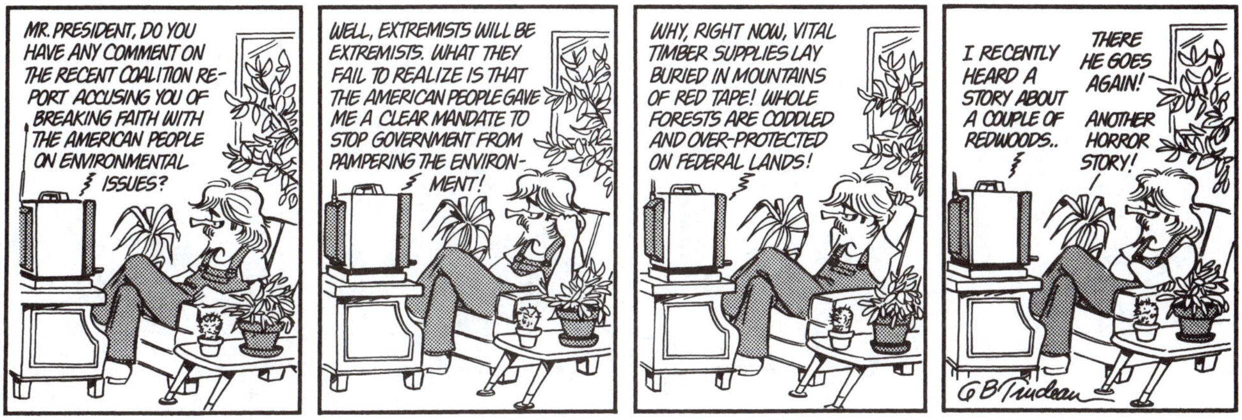
MR. PRESIDENT, DO YOU HAVE ANY COMMENT ON THE RECENT COALITION REPORT ACCUSING YOU OF BREAKING FAITH WITH THE AMERICAN PEOPLE ON ENVIRONMENTAL ISSUES?
WELL, EXTREMISTS WILL BE EXTREMISTS. WHAT THEY FAIL TO REALIZE IS THAT THE AMERICAN PEOPLE GAVE ME A CLEAR MANDATE TO STOP GOVERNMENT FROM PAMPERING THE ENVIRONMENT!
WHY, RIGHT NOW, VITAL TIMBER SUPPLIES LAY BURIED IN MOUNTAINS OF RED TAPE! WHOLE FORESTS ARE CODDLED AND OVER-PROTECTED ON FEDERAL LANDS!
I RECENTLY HEARD A STORY ABOUT A COUPLE OF REDWOODS..
THERE HE GOES AGAIN!
ANOTHER HORROR STORY!
G.B. Trudeau

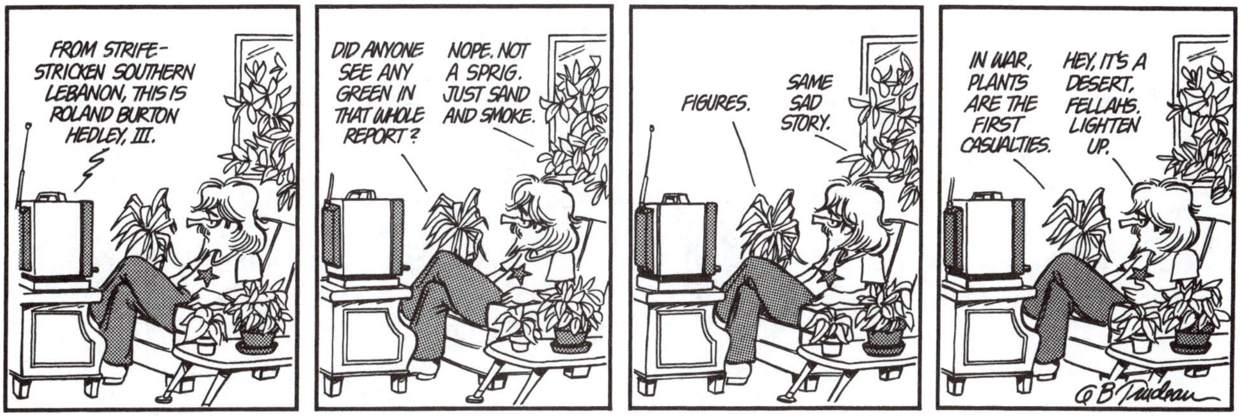
FROM STRIFE-STRICKEN SOUTHERN LEBANON, THIS IS ROLAND BURTON HEDLEY, III.
DID ANYONE SEE ANY GREEN IN THAT WHOLE REPORT?
NOPE. NOT A SPRIG. JUST SAND AND SMOKE.
FIGURES.
SAME SAD STORY.
IN WAR, PLANTS ARE THE FIRST CASUALTIES.
HEY, IT'S A DESERT, FELLAHS. LIGHTEN UP.
G.B. Trudeau

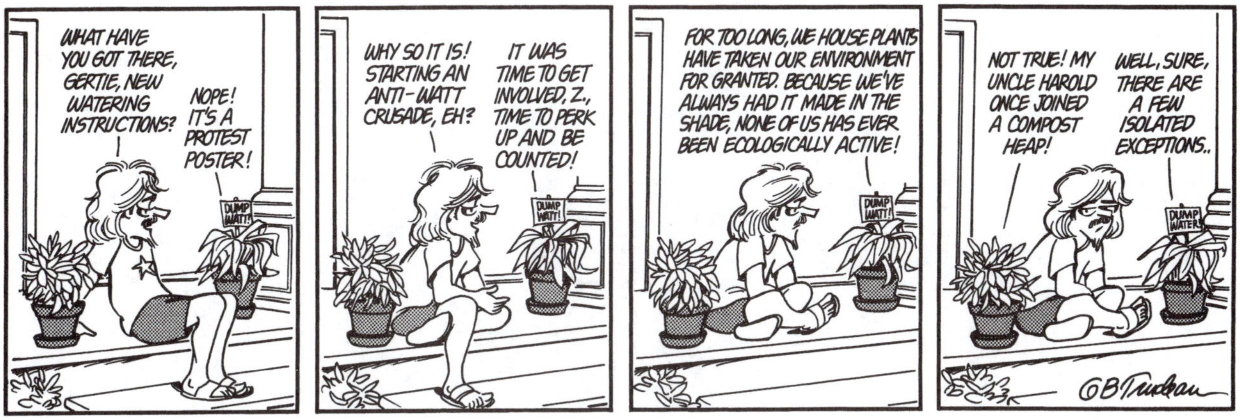
WHAT HAVE YOU GOT THERE, GERTIE, NEW WATERING INSTRUCTIONS?
NOPE! IT'S A PROTEST POSTER!
WHY SO IT IS! STARTING AN ANTI-WATT CRUSADE, EH?
IT WAS TIME TO GET INVOLVED, Z., TIME TO PERK UP AND BE COUNTED!
FOR TOO LONG, WE HOUSE PLANTS HAVE TAKEN OUR ENVIRONMENT FOR GRANTED. BECAUSE WE'VE ALWAYS HAD IT MADE IN THE SHADE, NONE OF US HAS EVER BEEN ECOLOGICALLY ACTIVE!
NOT TRUE! MY UNCLE HAROLD ONCE JOINED A COMPOST HEAP!
WELL, SURE, THERE ARE A FEW ISOLATED EXCEPTIONS..
G.B. Trudeau

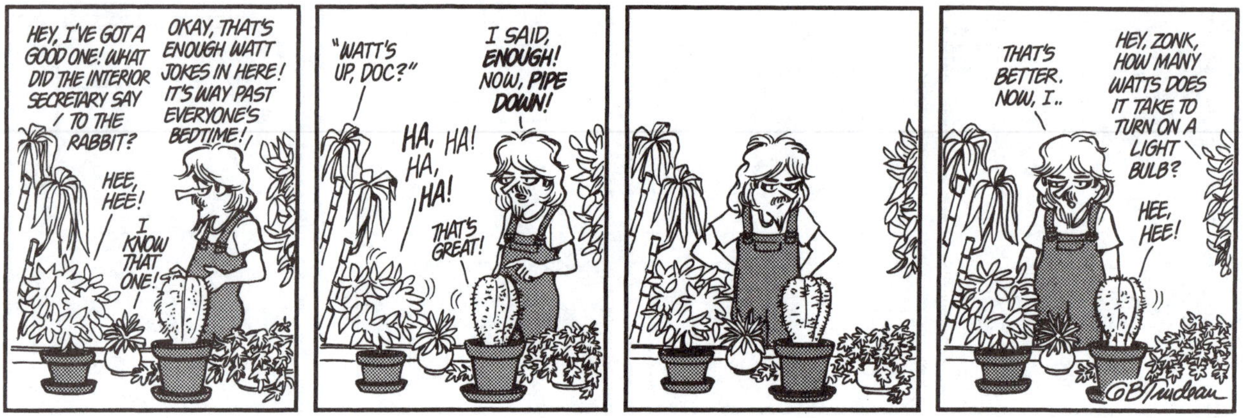
HEY, I'VE GOT A GOOD ONE! WHAT DID THE INTERIOR SECRETARY SAY TO THE RABBIT?
OKAY, THAT'S ENOUGH WATT JOKES IN HERE! IT'S WAY PAST EVERYONE'S BEDTIME!
HEE, HEE!
I KNOW THAT ONE!
"WATT'S UP, DOC?"
I SAID, ENOUGH! NOW, PIPE DOWN!
HA, HA, HA, HA!
THAT'S GREAT!
THAT'S BETTER. NOW, I..
HEY, ZONK, HOW MANY WATTS DOES IT TAKE TO TURN ON A LIGHT BULB?
HEE, HEE!
©B Trudeau

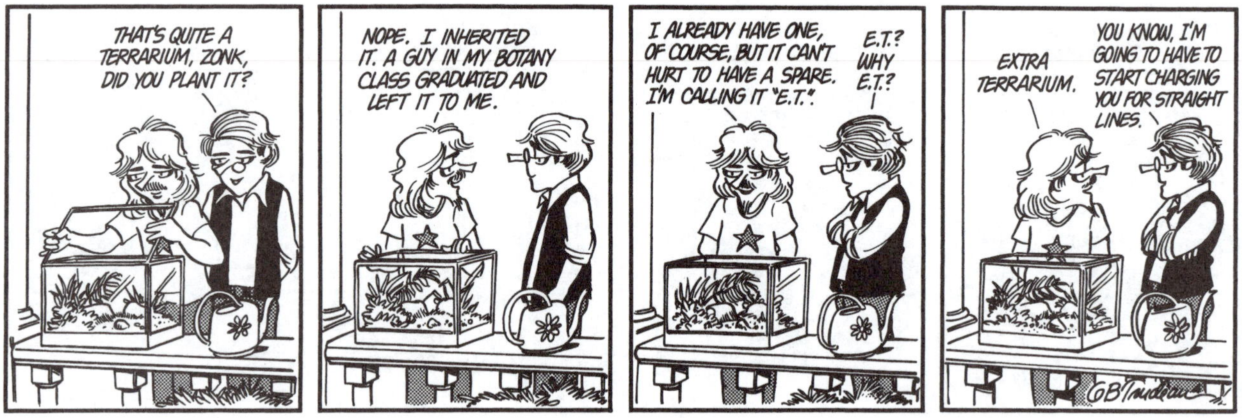
THAT'S QUITE A TERRARIUM, ZONK. DID YOU PLANT IT?
NOPE. I INHERITED IT. A GUY IN MY BOTANY CLASS GRADUATED AND LEFT IT TO ME.
I ALREADY HAVE ONE, OF COURSE, BUT IT CAN'T HURT TO HAVE A SPARE. I'M CALLING IT "E.T.".
E.T.? WHY E.T.?
EXTRA TERRARIUM.
YOU KNOW, I'M GOING TO HAVE TO START CHARGING YOU FOR STRAIGHT LINES.
©B Trudeau

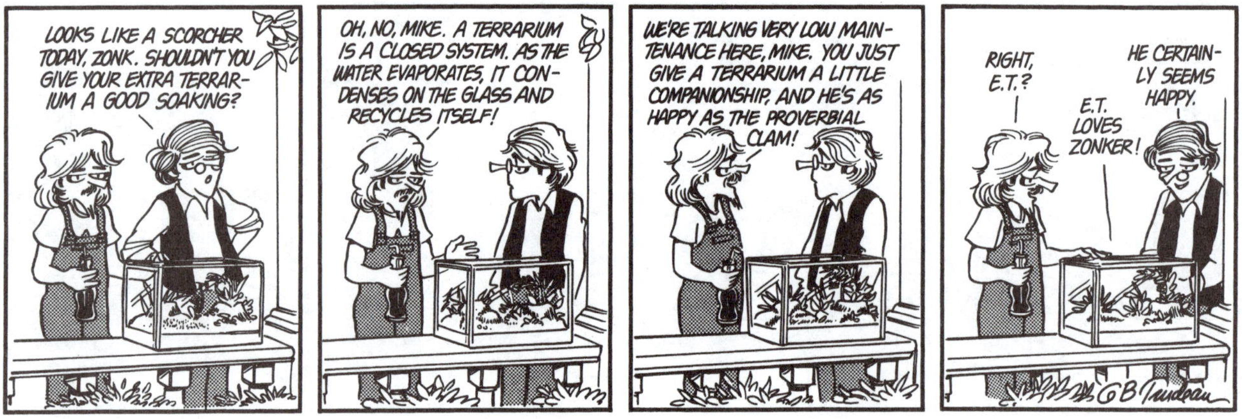
LOOKS LIKE A SCORCHER TODAY, ZONK. SHOULDN'T YOU GIVE YOUR EXTRA TERRARIUM A GOOD SOAKING?
OH, NO, MIKE. A TERRARIUM IS A CLOSED SYSTEM. AS THE WATER EVAPORATES, IT CONDENSES ON THE GLASS AND RECYCLES ITSELF!
WE'RE TALKING VERY LOW MAINTENANCE HERE, MIKE. YOU JUST GIVE A TERRARIUM A LITTLE COMPANIONSHIP, AND HE'S AS HAPPY AS THE PROVERBIAL CLAM!
RIGHT, E.T.?
E.T. LOVES ZONKER!
HE CERTAINLY SEEMS HAPPY.
©B Trudeau

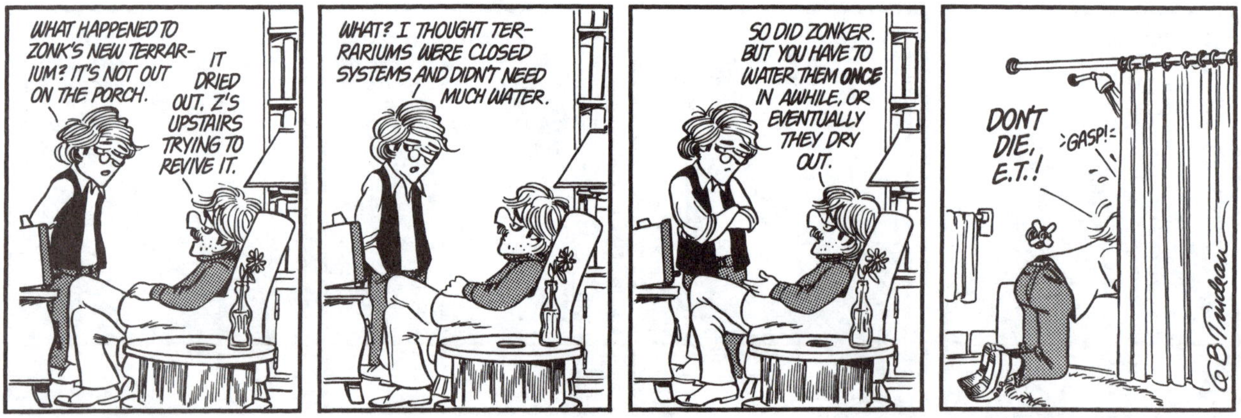
WHAT HAPPENED TO ZONK'S NEW TERRARIUM? IT'S NOT OUT ON THE PORCH.
IT DRIED OUT. Z'S UPSTAIRS TRYING TO REVIVE IT.
WHAT? I THOUGHT TERRARIUMS WERE CLOSED SYSTEMS AND DIDN'T NEED MUCH WATER.
SO DID ZONKER. BUT YOU HAVE TO WATER THEM ONCE IN AWHILE, OR EVENTUALLY THEY DRY OUT.
DON'T DIE, E.T.!
GASP!
©B Trudeau

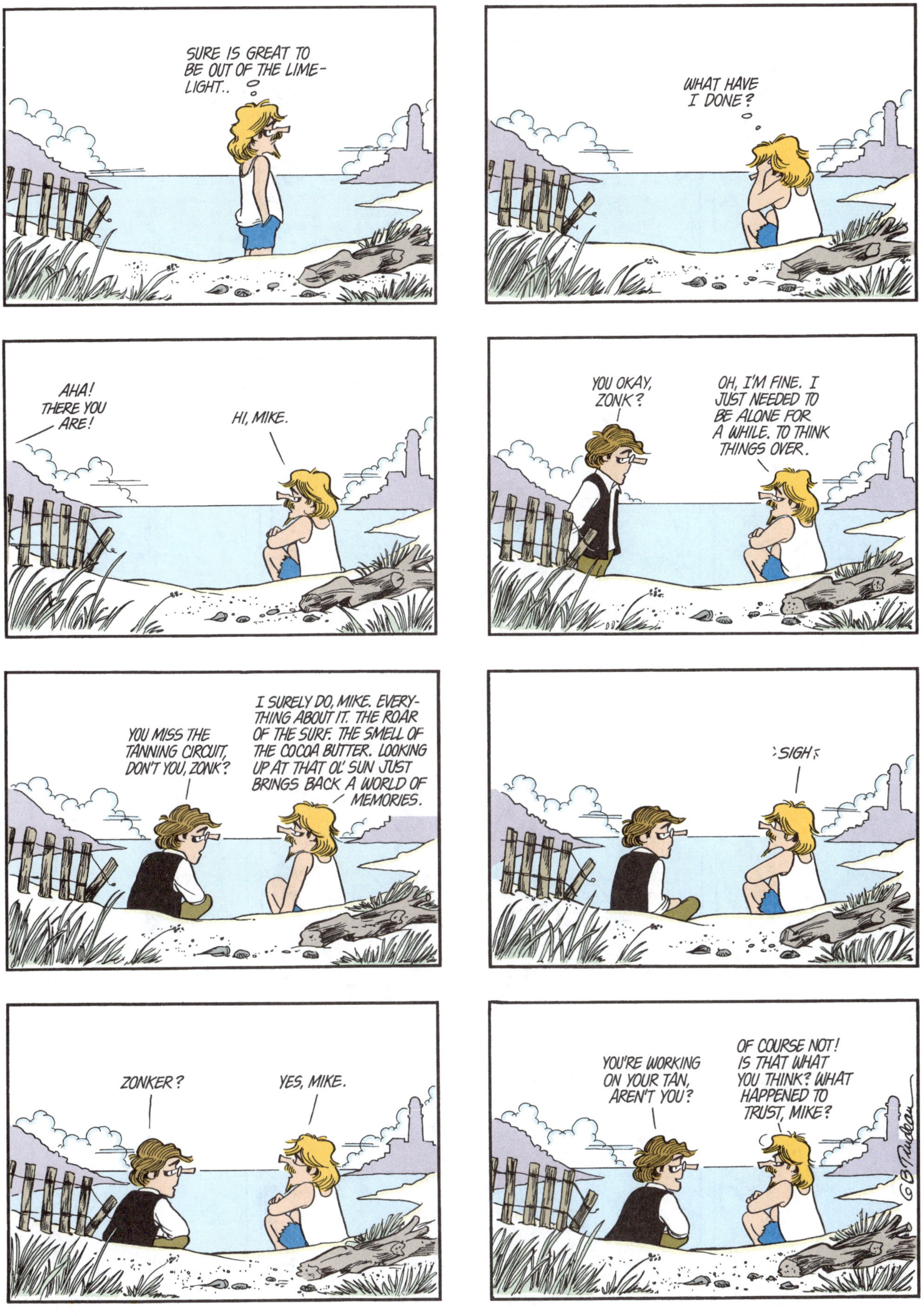
SURE IS GREAT TO BE OUT OF THE LIME-LIGHT..
WHAT HAVE I DONE?
AHA! THERE YOU ARE!
HI, MIKE.
YOU OKAY, ZONK?
OH, I'M FINE. I JUST NEEDED TO BE ALONE FOR A WHILE. TO THINK THINGS OVER.
YOU MISS THE TANNING CIRCUIT, DON'T YOU, ZONK?
I SURELY DO, MIKE. EVERY-THING ABOUT IT. THE ROAR OF THE SURF. THE SMELL OF THE COCOA BUTTER. LOOKING UP AT THAT OL' SUN JUST BRINGS BACK A WORLD OF MEMORIES.
SIGH
ZONKER?
YES, MIKE.
YOU'RE WORKING ON YOUR TAN, AREN'T YOU?
OF COURSE NOT! IS THAT WHAT YOU THINK? WHAT HAPPENED TO TRUST, MIKE?

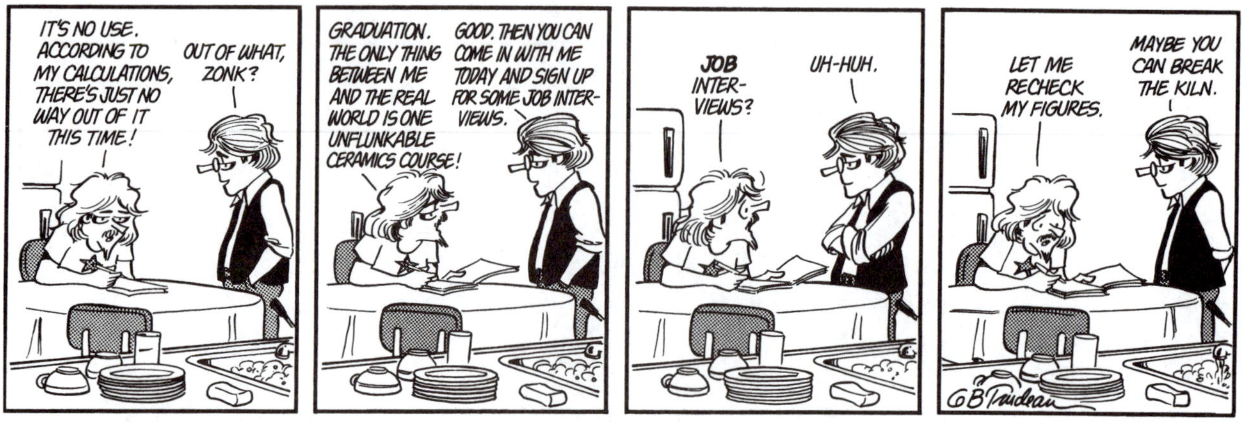
IT'S NO USE. ACCORDING TO MY CALCULATIONS, THERE'S JUST NO WAY OUT OF IT THIS TIME!
OUT OF WHAT, ZONK?
GRADUATION. THE ONLY THING BETWEEN ME AND THE REAL WORLD IS ONE UNFLUNKABLE CERAMICS COURSE!
GOOD. THEN YOU CAN COME IN WITH ME TODAY AND SIGN UP FOR SOME JOB INTERVIEWS.
JOB INTERVIEWS?
UH-HUH.
LET ME RECHECK MY FIGURES.
MAYBE YOU CAN BREAK THE KILN.
GB Trudeau

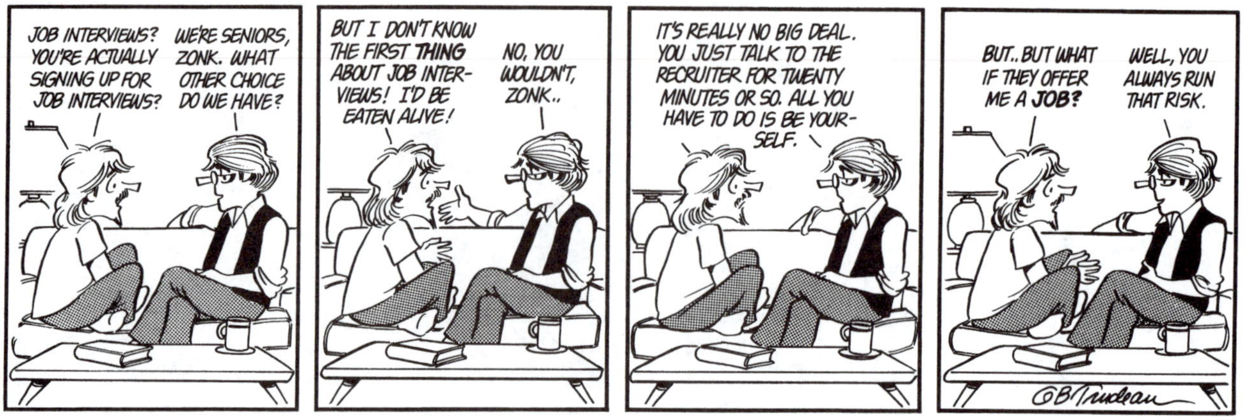
JOB INTERVIEWS? YOU'RE ACTUALLY SIGNING UP FOR JOB INTERVIEWS?
WE'RE SENIORS, ZONK. WHAT OTHER CHOICE DO WE HAVE?
BUT I DON'T KNOW THE FIRST THING ABOUT JOB INTERVIEWS! I'D BE EATEN ALIVE!
NO, YOU WOULDN'T, ZONK..
IT'S REALLY NO BIG DEAL. YOU JUST TALK TO THE RECRUITER FOR TWENTY MINUTES OR SO. ALL YOU HAVE TO DO IS BE YOURSELF.
BUT.. BUT WHAT IF THEY OFFER ME A JOB?
WELL, YOU ALWAYS RUN THAT RISK.
GB Trudeau

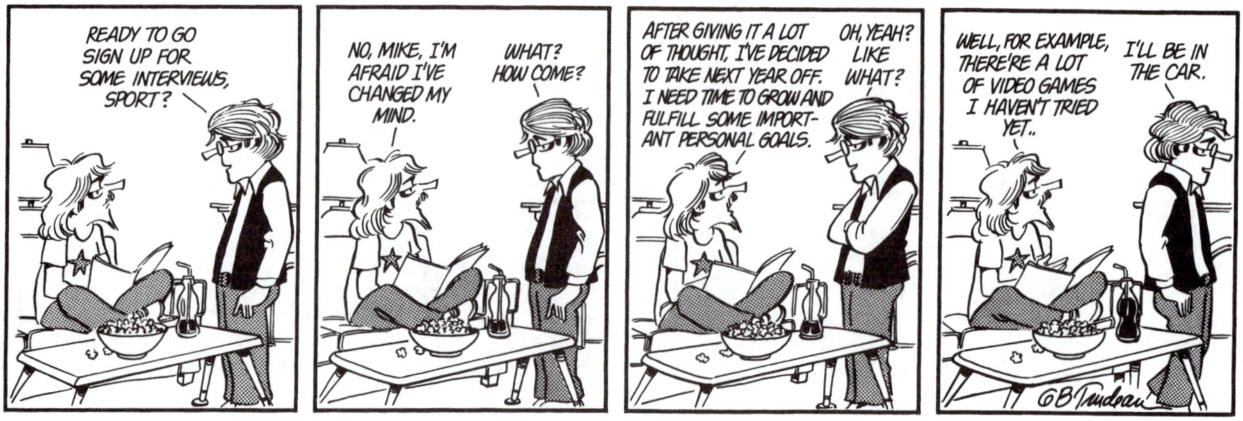
READY TO GO SIGN UP FOR SOME INTERVIEWS, SPORT?
NO, MIKE, I'M AFRAID I'VE CHANGED MY MIND.
WHAT? HOW COME?
AFTER GIVING IT A LOT OF THOUGHT, I'VE DECIDED TO TAKE NEXT YEAR OFF. I NEED TIME TO GROW AND FULFILL SOME IMPORTANT PERSONAL GOALS.
OH, YEAH? LIKE WHAT?
WELL, FOR EXAMPLE, THERE'RE A LOT OF VIDEO GAMES I HAVEN'T TRIED YET..
I'LL BE IN THE CAR.
GB Trudeau

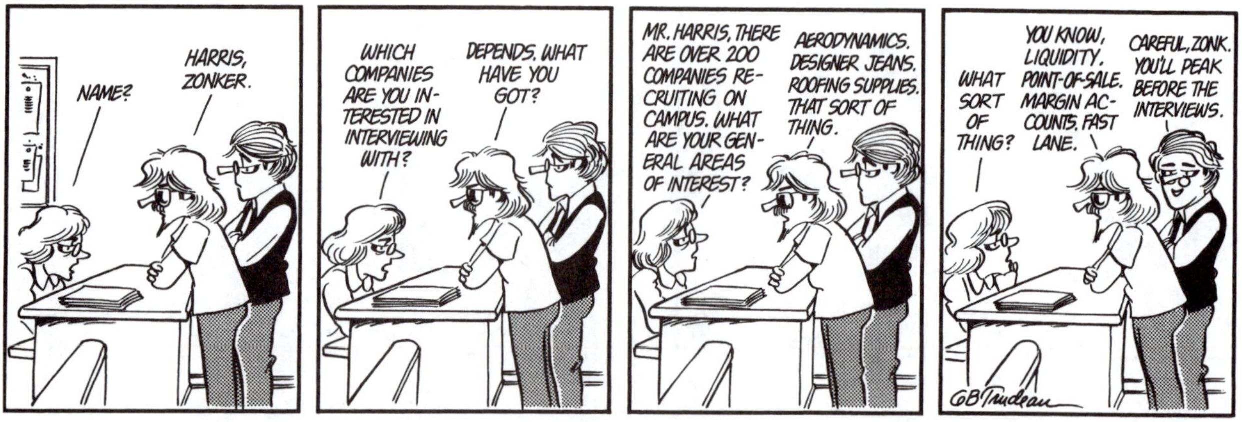
NAME?
HARRIS, ZONKER.
WHICH COMPANIES ARE YOU INTERESTED IN INTERVIEWING WITH?
DEPENDS. WHAT HAVE YOU GOT?
MR. HARRIS, THERE ARE OVER 200 COMPANIES RECRUITING ON CAMPUS. WHAT ARE YOUR GENERAL AREAS OF INTEREST?
AERODYNAMICS. DESIGNER JEANS. ROOFING SUPPLIES. THAT SORT OF THING.
WHAT SORT OF THING?
YOU KNOW, LIQUIDITY. POINT-OF-SALE. MARGIN ACCOUNTS. FAST LANE.
CAREFUL, ZONK. YOU'LL PEAK BEFORE THE INTERVIEWS.
GB Trudeau

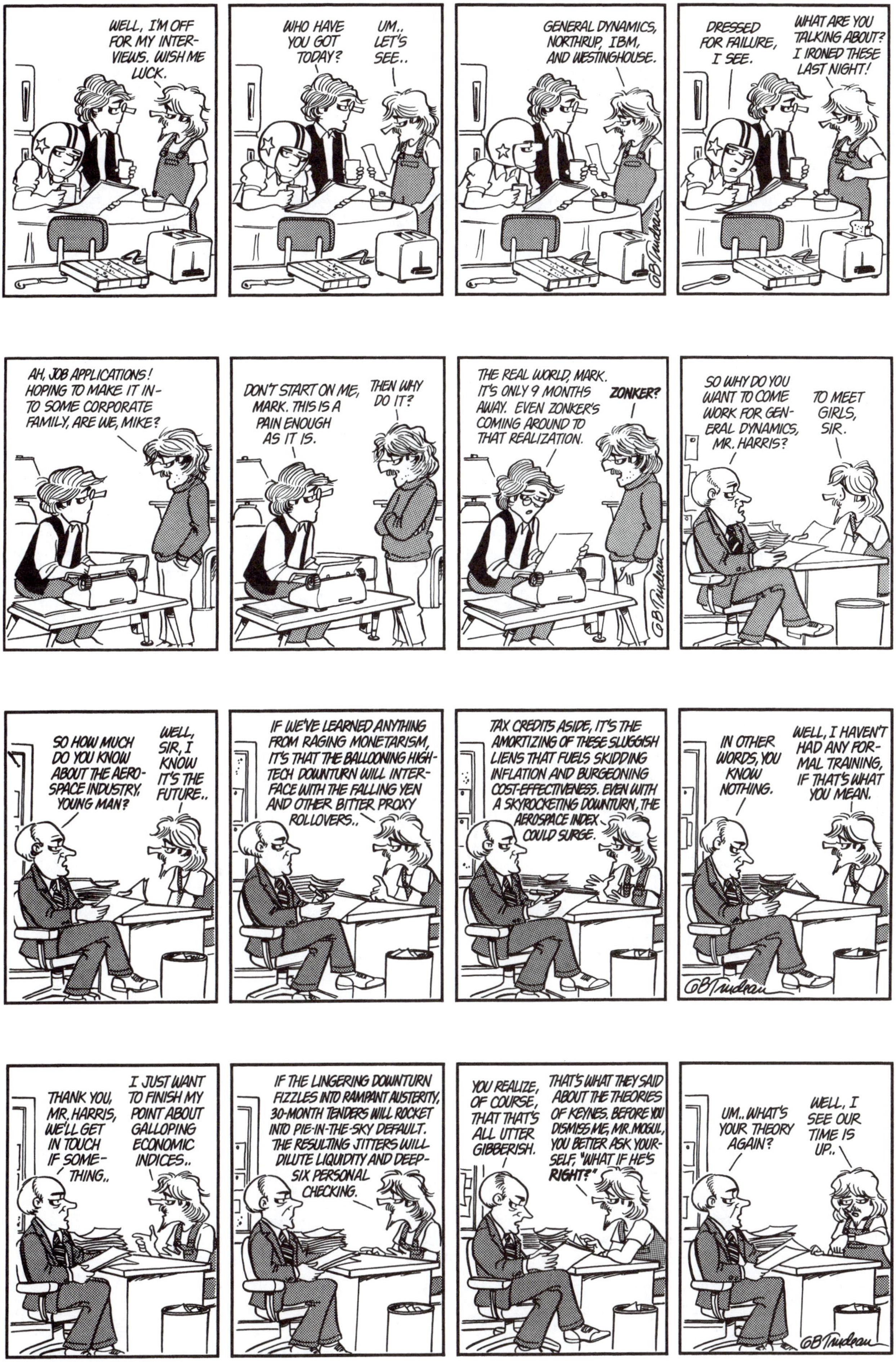
WELL, I'M OFF FOR MY INTERVIEWS. WISH ME LUCK.
WHO HAVE YOU GOT TODAY?
UM.. LET'S SEE..
GENERAL DYNAMICS, NORTHRUP, IBM, AND WESTINGHOUSE.
DRESSED FOR FAILURE, I SEE.
WHAT ARE YOU TALKING ABOUT? I IRONED THESE LAST NIGHT!
AH, JOB APPLICATIONS! HOPING TO MAKE IT INTO SOME CORPORATE FAMILY, ARE WE, MIKE?
DON'T START ON ME, MARK. THIS IS A PAIN ENOUGH AS IT IS.
THEN WHY DO IT?
THE REAL WORLD, MARK. IT'S ONLY 9 MONTHS AWAY. EVEN ZONKER'S COMING AROUND TO THAT REALIZATION.
ZONKER?
SO WHY DO YOU WANT TO COME WORK FOR GENERAL DYNAMICS, MR. HARRIS?
TO MEET GIRLS, SIR.
SO HOW MUCH DO YOU KNOW ABOUT THE AEROSPACE INDUSTRY, YOUNG MAN?
WELL, SIR, I KNOW IT'S THE FUTURE..
IF WE'VE LEARNED ANYTHING FROM RAGING MONETARISM, IT'S THAT THE BALLOONING HIGH-TECH DOWNTURN WILL INTERFACE WITH THE FALLING YEN AND OTHER BITTER PROXY ROLLOVERS..
TAX CREDITS ASIDE, IT'S THE AMORTIZING OF THESE SLUGGISH LIENS THAT FUELS SKIDDING INFLATION AND BURGEONING COST-EFFECTIVENESS. EVEN WITH A SKYROCKETING DOWNTURN, THE AEROSPACE INDEX COULD SURGE.
IN OTHER WORDS, YOU KNOW NOTHING.
WELL, I HAVEN'T HAD ANY FORMAL TRAINING, IF THAT'S WHAT YOU MEAN.
THANK YOU, MR. HARRIS, WE'LL GET IN TOUCH IF SOMETHING..
I JUST WANT TO FINISH MY POINT ABOUT GALLOPING ECONOMIC INDICES..
IF THE LINGERING DOWNTURN FIZZLES INTO RAMPANT AUSTERITY, 30-MONTH TENDERS WILL ROCKET INTO PIE-IN-THE-SKY DEFAULT. THE RESULTING JITTERS WILL DILUTE LIQUIDITY AND DEEP-SIX PERSONAL CHECKING.
YOU REALIZE, OF COURSE, THAT THAT'S ALL UTTER GIBBERISH.
THAT'S WHAT THEY SAID ABOUT THE THEORIES OF KEYNES. BEFORE YOU DISMISS ME, MR. MOGUL, YOU BETTER ASK YOURSELF, "WHAT IF HE'S RIGHT?"
UM.. WHAT'S YOUR THEORY AGAIN?
WELL, I SEE OUR TIME IS UP..

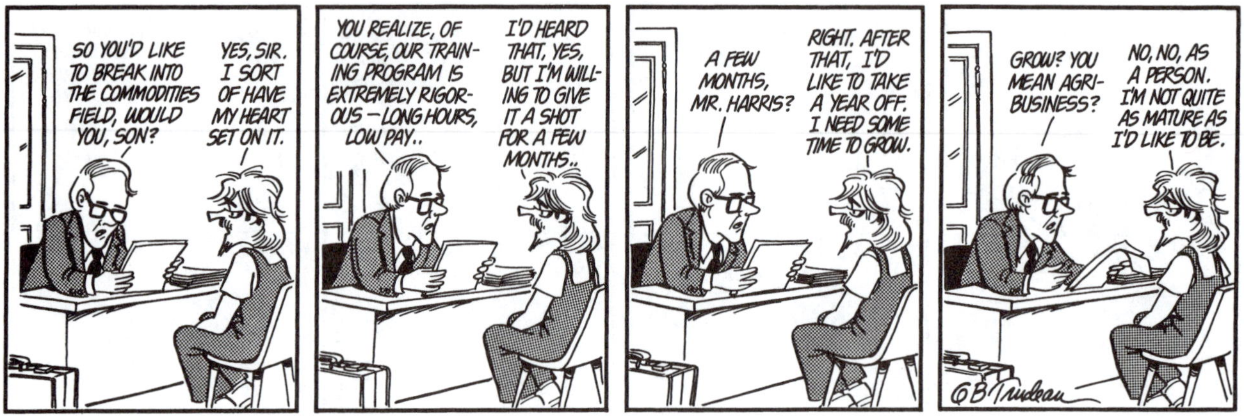
SO YOU'D LIKE TO BREAK INTO THE COMMODITIES FIELD, WOULD YOU, SON?
YES, SIR. I SORT OF HAVE MY HEART SET ON IT.
YOU REALIZE, OF COURSE, OUR TRAINING PROGRAM IS EXTREMELY RIGOROUS — LONG HOURS, LOW PAY..
I'D HEARD THAT, YES, BUT I'M WILLING TO GIVE IT A SHOT FOR A FEW MONTHS..
A FEW MONTHS, MR. HARRIS?
RIGHT. AFTER THAT, I'D LIKE TO TAKE A YEAR OFF. I NEED SOME TIME TO GROW.
GROW? YOU MEAN AGRIBUSINESS?
NO, NO, AS A PERSON. I'M NOT QUITE AS MATURE AS I'D LIKE TO BE.
GB Trudeau

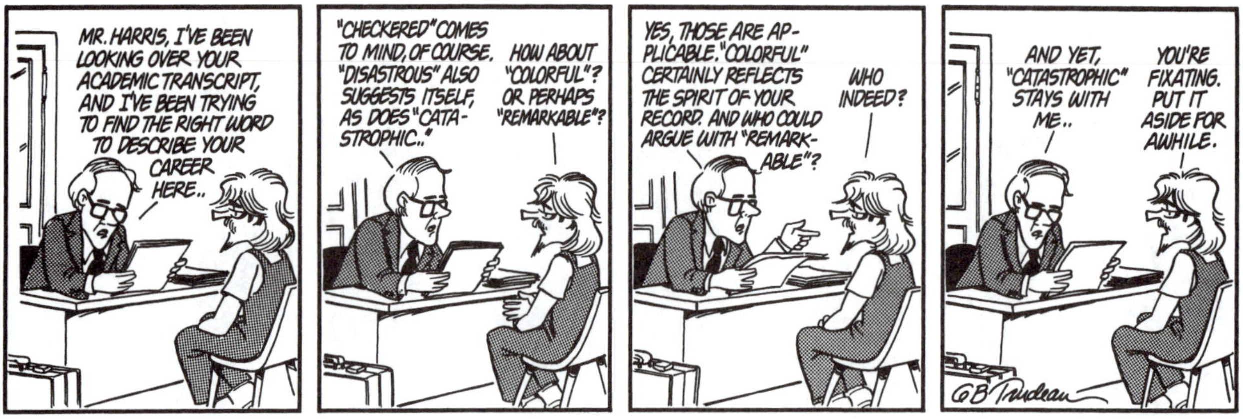
MR. HARRIS, I'VE BEEN LOOKING OVER YOUR ACADEMIC TRANSCRIPT, AND I'VE BEEN TRYING TO FIND THE RIGHT WORD TO DESCRIBE YOUR CAREER HERE..
"CHECKERED" COMES TO MIND, OF COURSE. "DISASTROUS" ALSO SUGGESTS ITSELF, AS DOES "CATASTROPHIC.."
HOW ABOUT "COLORFUL"? OR PERHAPS "REMARKABLE"?
YES, THOSE ARE APPLICABLE. "COLORFUL" CERTAINLY REFLECTS THE SPIRIT OF YOUR RECORD. AND WHO COULD ARGUE WITH "REMARKABLE"?
WHO INDEED?
AND YET, "CATASTROPHIC" STAYS WITH ME..
YOU'RE FIXATING. PUT IT ASIDE FOR AWHILE.
GB Trudeau

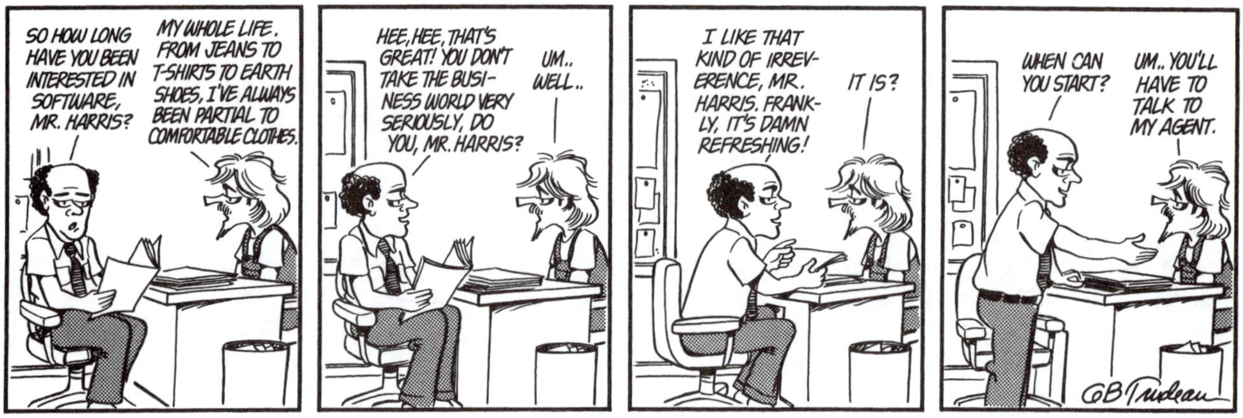
SO HOW LONG HAVE YOU BEEN INTERESTED IN SOFTWARE, MR. HARRIS?
MY WHOLE LIFE. FROM JEANS TO T-SHIRTS TO EARTH SHOES, I'VE ALWAYS BEEN PARTIAL TO COMFORTABLE CLOTHES.
HEE, HEE, THAT'S GREAT! YOU DON'T TAKE THE BUSINESS WORLD VERY SERIOUSLY, DO YOU, MR. HARRIS?
UM.. WELL..
I LIKE THAT KIND OF IRREVERENCE, MR. HARRIS. FRANKLY, IT'S DAMN REFRESHING!
IT IS?
WHEN CAN YOU START?
UM.. YOU'LL HAVE TO TALK TO MY AGENT.
GB Trudeau

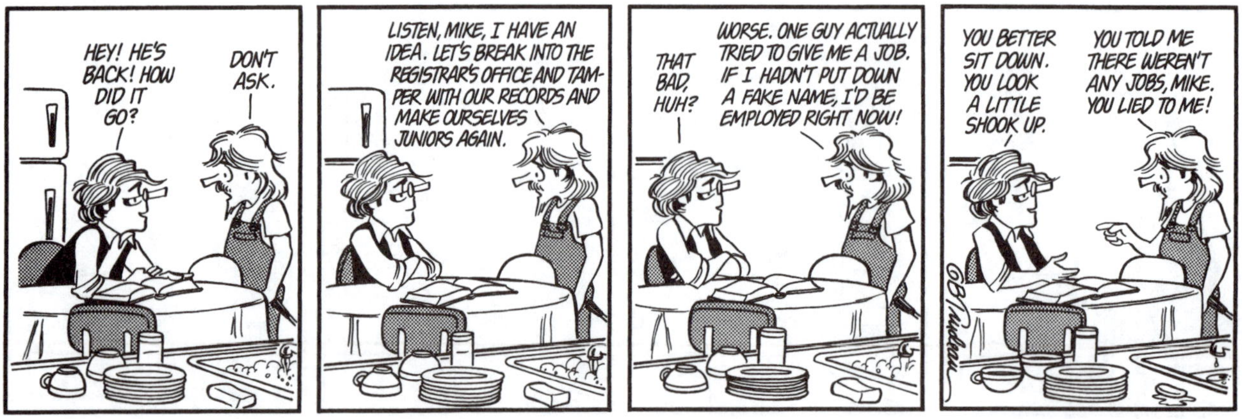
HEY! HE'S BACK! HOW DID IT GO?
DON'T ASK.
LISTEN, MIKE, I HAVE AN IDEA. LET'S BREAK INTO THE REGISTRAR'S OFFICE AND TAMPER WITH OUR RECORDS AND MAKE OURSELVES JUNIORS AGAIN.
THAT BAD, HUH?
WORSE. ONE GUY ACTUALLY TRIED TO GIVE ME A JOB. IF I HADN'T PUT DOWN A FAKE NAME, I'D BE EMPLOYED RIGHT NOW!
YOU BETTER SIT DOWN. YOU LOOK A LITTLE SHOOK UP.
YOU TOLD ME THERE WEREN'T ANY JOBS, MIKE. YOU LIED TO ME!
GB Trudeau

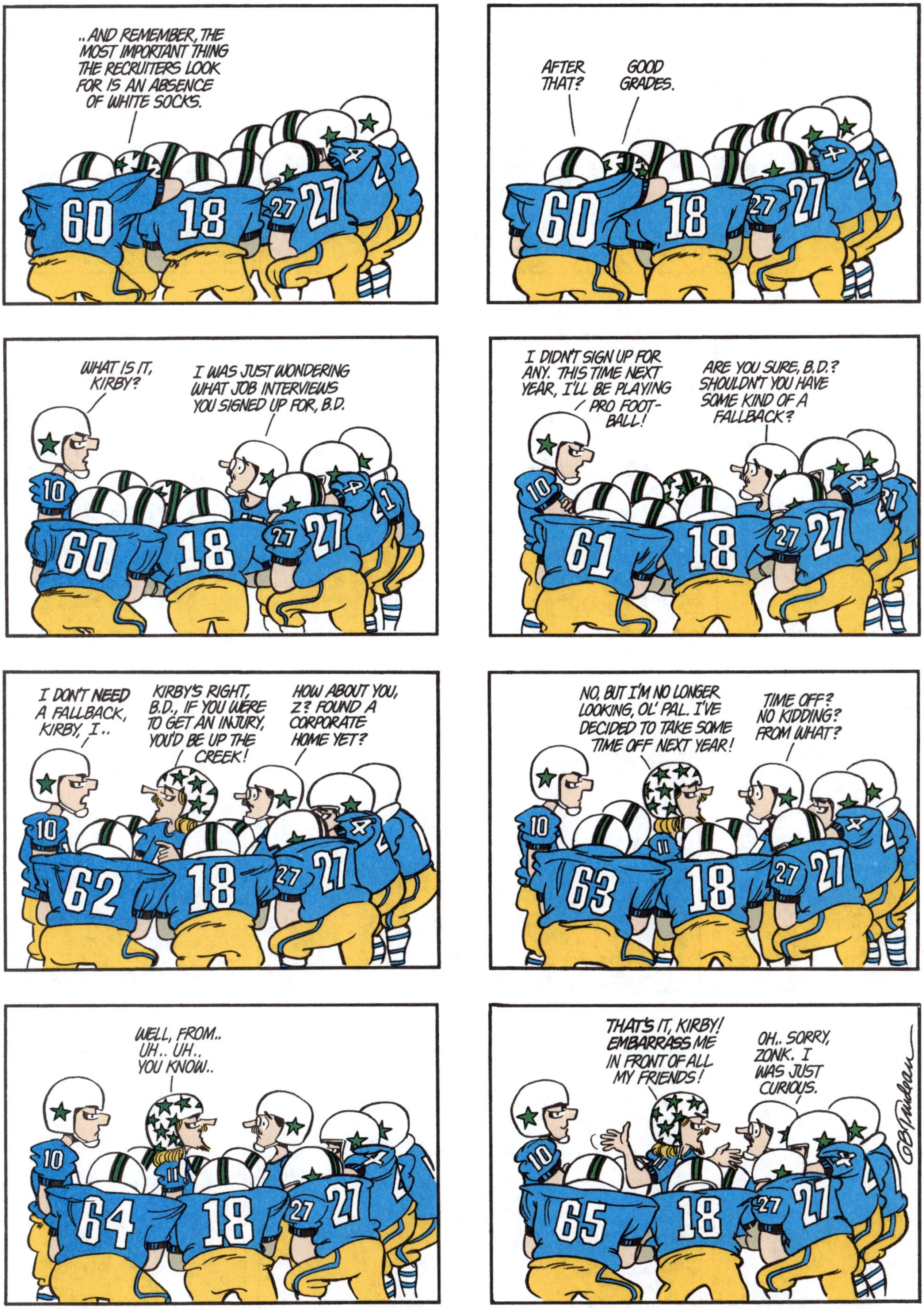
..AND REMEMBER, THE MOST IMPORTANT THING THE RECRUITERS LOOK FOR IS AN ABSENCE OF WHITE SOCKS.
AFTER THAT?
GOOD GRADES.
WHAT IS IT, KIRBY?
I WAS JUST WONDERING WHAT JOB INTERVIEWS YOU SIGNED UP FOR, B.D.
I DIDN'T SIGN UP FOR ANY. THIS TIME NEXT YEAR, I'LL BE PLAYING PRO FOOTBALL!
ARE YOU SURE, B.D.? SHOULDN'T YOU HAVE SOME KIND OF A FALLBACK?
I DON'T NEED A FALLBACK, KIRBY, I..
KIRBY'S RIGHT, B.D., IF YOU WERE TO GET AN INJURY, YOU'D BE UP THE CREEK!
HOW ABOUT YOU, Z? FOUND A CORPORATE HOME YET?
NO, BUT I'M NO LONGER LOOKING, OL' PAL. I'VE DECIDED TO TAKE SOME TIME OFF NEXT YEAR!
TIME OFF? NO KIDDING? FROM WHAT?
WELL, FROM.. UH.. UH.. YOU KNOW..
THAT'S IT, KIRBY! EMBARRASS ME IN FRONT OF ALL MY FRIENDS!
OH.. SORRY, ZONK. I WAS JUST CURIOUS.

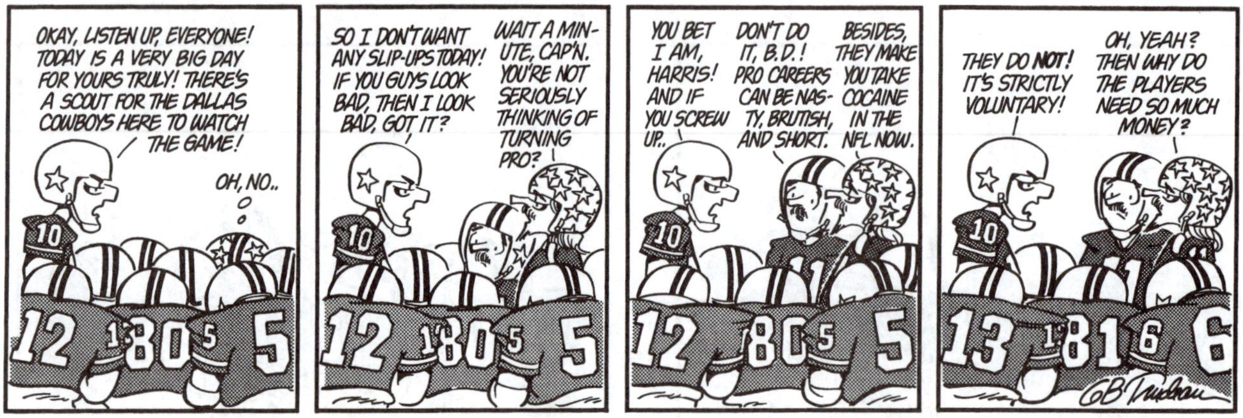
OKAY, LISTEN UP, EVERYONE! TODAY IS A VERY BIG DAY FOR YOURS TRULY! THERE'S A SCOUT FOR THE DALLAS COWBOYS HERE TO WATCH THE GAME!
OH, NO..
SO I DON'T WANT ANY SLIP-UPS TODAY! IF YOU GUYS LOOK BAD, THEN I LOOK BAD, GOT IT?
WAIT A MINUTE, CAP'N. YOU'RE NOT SERIOUSLY THINKING OF TURNING PRO?
YOU BET I AM, HARRIS! AND IF YOU SCREW UP..
DON'T DO IT, B.D.! PRO CAREERS CAN BE NASTY, BRUTISH, AND SHORT.
BESIDES, THEY MAKE YOU TAKE COCAINE IN THE NFL NOW.
THEY DO NOT! IT'S STRICTLY VOLUNTARY!
OH, YEAH? THEN WHY DO THE PLAYERS NEED SO MUCH MONEY?
GB Trudeau

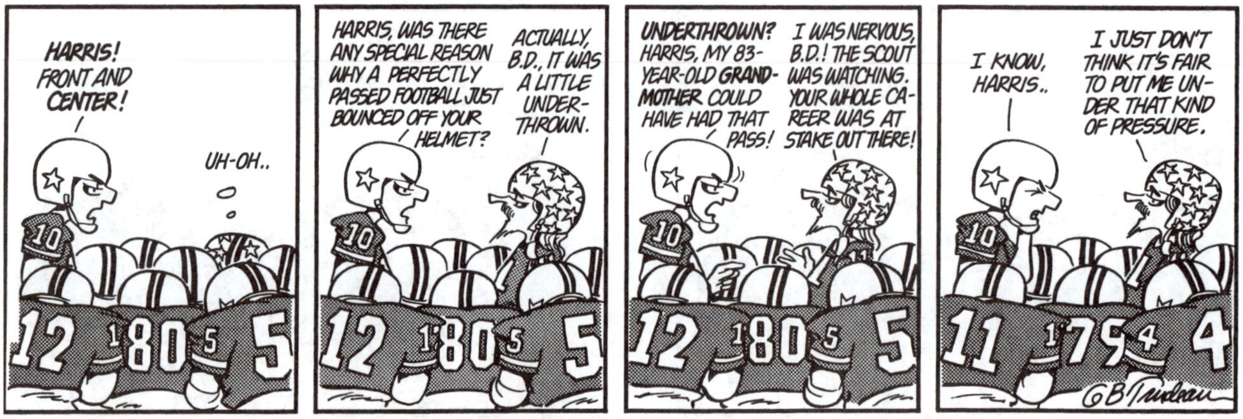
HARRIS! FRONT AND CENTER!
UH-OH..
HARRIS, WAS THERE ANY SPECIAL REASON WHY A PERFECTLY PASSED FOOTBALL JUST BOUNCED OFF YOUR HELMET?
ACTUALLY, B.D., IT WAS A LITTLE UNDERTHROWN.
UNDERTHROWN? HARRIS, MY 83-YEAR-OLD GRANDMOTHER COULD HAVE HAD THAT PASS!
I WAS NERVOUS, B.D.! THE SCOUT WAS WATCHING. YOUR WHOLE CAREER WAS AT STAKE OUT THERE!
I KNOW, HARRIS..
I JUST DON'T THINK IT'S FAIR TO PUT ME UNDER THAT KIND OF PRESSURE.
GB Trudeau

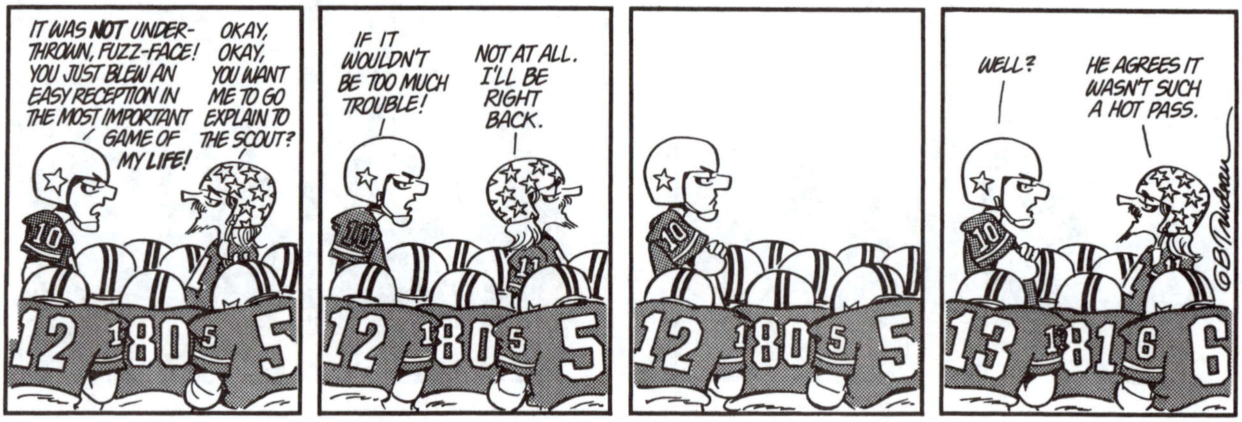
IT WAS NOT UNDERTHROWN, FUZZ-FACE! YOU JUST BLEW AN EASY RECEPTION IN THE MOST IMPORTANT GAME OF MY LIFE!
OKAY, OKAY, YOU WANT ME TO GO EXPLAIN TO THE SCOUT?
IF IT WOULDN'T BE TOO MUCH TROUBLE!
NOT AT ALL. I'LL BE RIGHT BACK.
WELL?
HE AGREES IT WASN'T SUCH A HOT PASS.
GB Trudeau

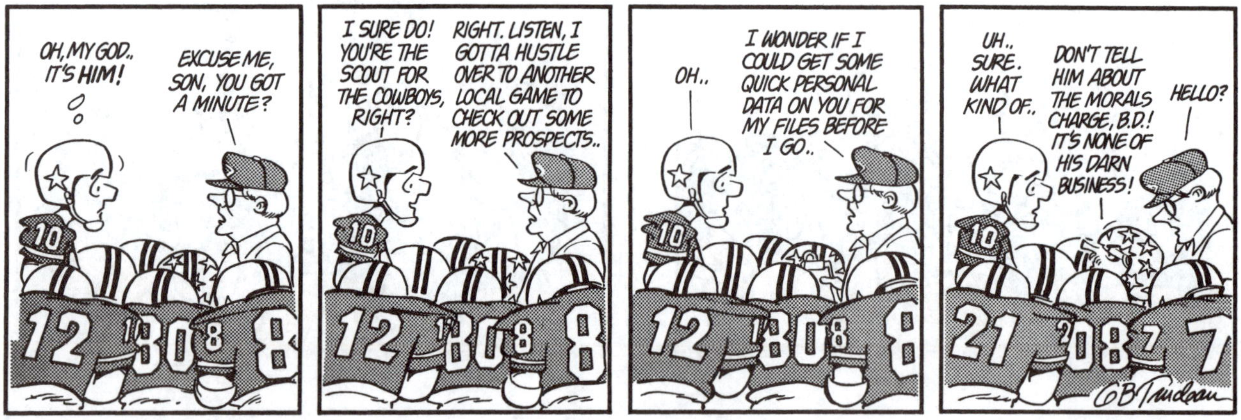
OH, MY GOD.. IT'S HIM!
EXCUSE ME, SON, YOU GOT A MINUTE?
I SURE DO! YOU'RE THE SCOUT FOR THE COWBOYS, RIGHT?
RIGHT. LISTEN, I GOTTA HUSTLE OVER TO ANOTHER LOCAL GAME TO CHECK OUT SOME MORE PROSPECTS..
OH..
I WONDER IF I COULD GET SOME QUICK PERSONAL DATA ON YOU FOR MY FILES BEFORE I GO..
UH.. SURE. WHAT KIND OF..
DON'T TELL HIM ABOUT THE MORALS CHARGE, B.D.! IT'S NONE OF HIS DARN BUSINESS!
HELLO?
GB Trudeau

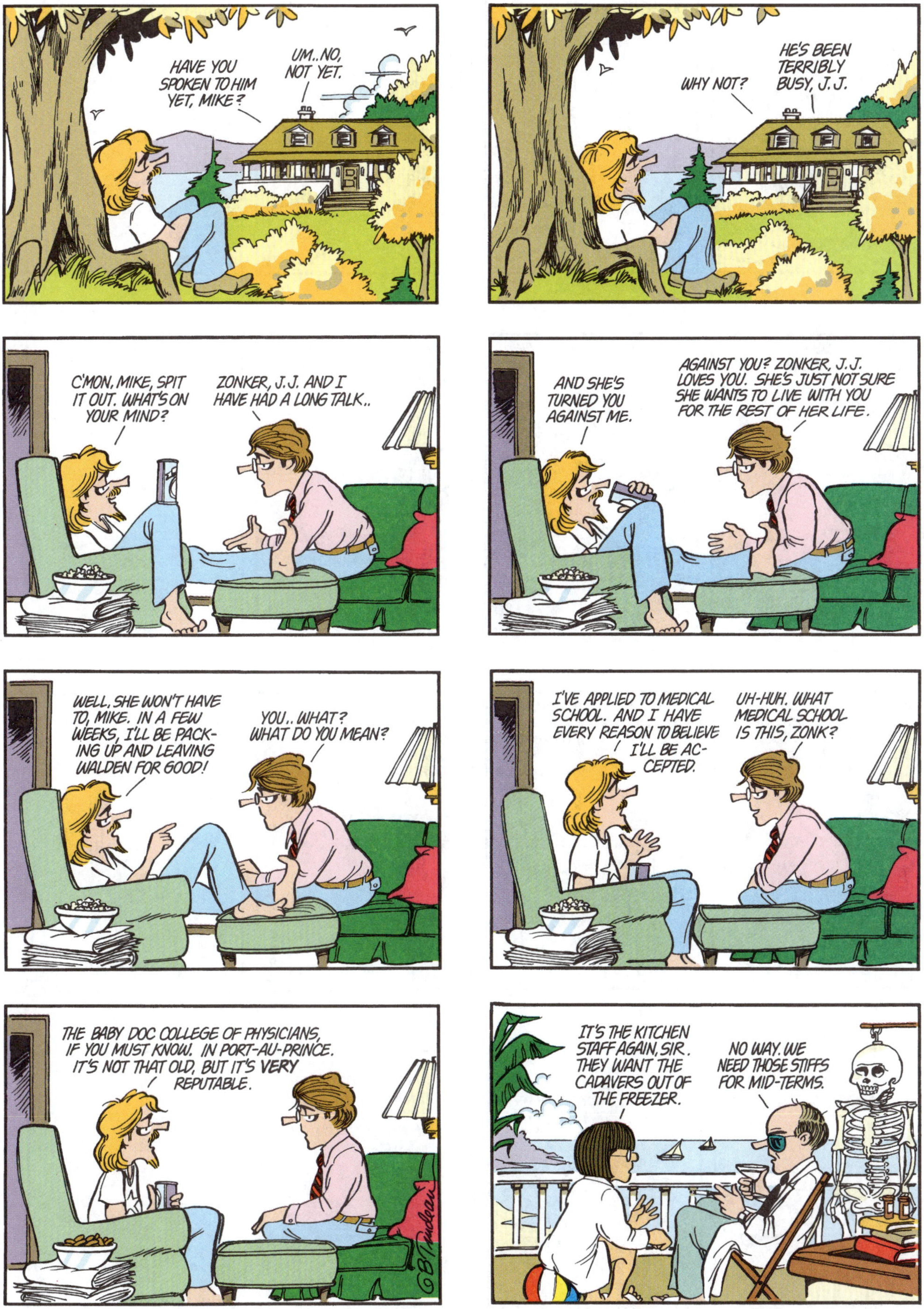
HAVE YOU SPOKEN TO HIM YET, MIKE?
UM.. NO, NOT YET.
WHY NOT?
HE'S BEEN TERRIBLY BUSY, J.J.
C'MON, MIKE, SPIT IT OUT. WHAT'S ON YOUR MIND?
ZONKER, J.J. AND I HAVE HAD A LONG TALK..
AND SHE'S TURNED YOU AGAINST ME.
AGAINST YOU? ZONKER, J.J. LOVES YOU. SHE'S JUST NOT SURE SHE WANTS TO LIVE WITH YOU FOR THE REST OF HER LIFE.
WELL, SHE WON'T HAVE TO, MIKE. IN A FEW WEEKS, I'LL BE PACKING UP AND LEAVING WALDEN FOR GOOD!
YOU.. WHAT? WHAT DO YOU MEAN?
I'VE APPLIED TO MEDICAL SCHOOL. AND I HAVE EVERY REASON TO BELIEVE I'LL BE ACCEPTED.
UH-HUH. WHAT MEDICAL SCHOOL IS THIS, ZONK?
THE BABY DOC COLLEGE OF PHYSICIANS, IF YOU MUST KNOW. IN PORT-AU-PRINCE. IT'S NOT THAT OLD, BUT IT'S VERY REPUTABLE.
©BTrudeau
IT'S THE KITCHEN STAFF AGAIN, SIR. THEY WANT THE CADAVERS OUT OF THE FREEZER.
NO WAY. WE NEED THOSE STIFFS FOR MID-TERMS.

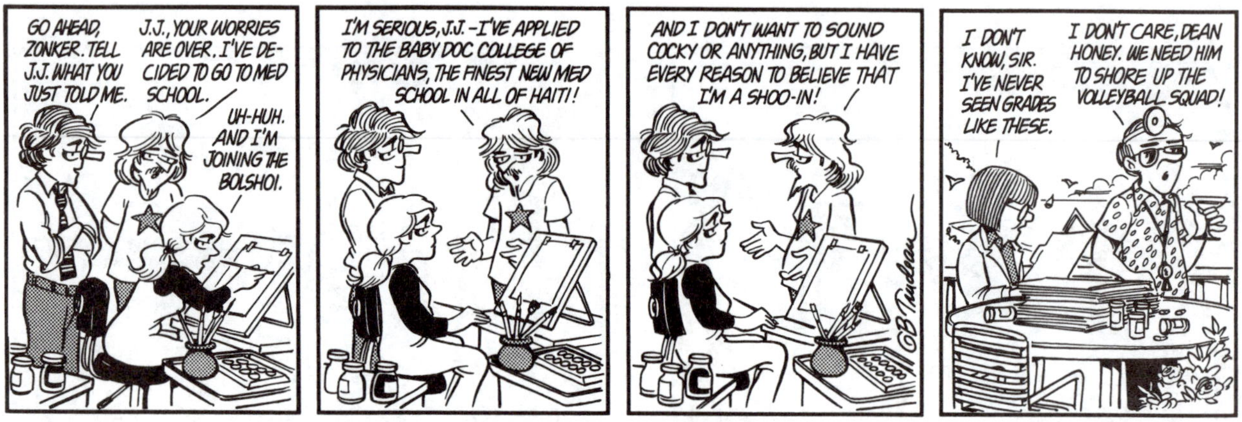
GO AHEAD, ZONKER. TELL J.J. WHAT YOU JUST TOLD ME.
J.J., YOUR WORRIES ARE OVER. I'VE DECIDED TO GO TO MED SCHOOL.
UH-HUH. AND I'M JOINING THE BOLSHOI.
I'M SERIOUS, J.J.–I'VE APPLIED TO THE BABY DOC COLLEGE OF PHYSICIANS, THE FINEST NEW MED SCHOOL IN ALL OF HAITI!
AND I DON'T WANT TO SOUND COCKY OR ANYTHING, BUT I HAVE EVERY REASON TO BELIEVE THAT I'M A SHOO-IN!
I DON'T KNOW, SIR. I'VE NEVER SEEN GRADES LIKE THESE.
I DON'T CARE, DEAN HONEY. WE NEED HIM TO SHORE UP THE VOLLEYBALL SQUAD!
©B Trudeau

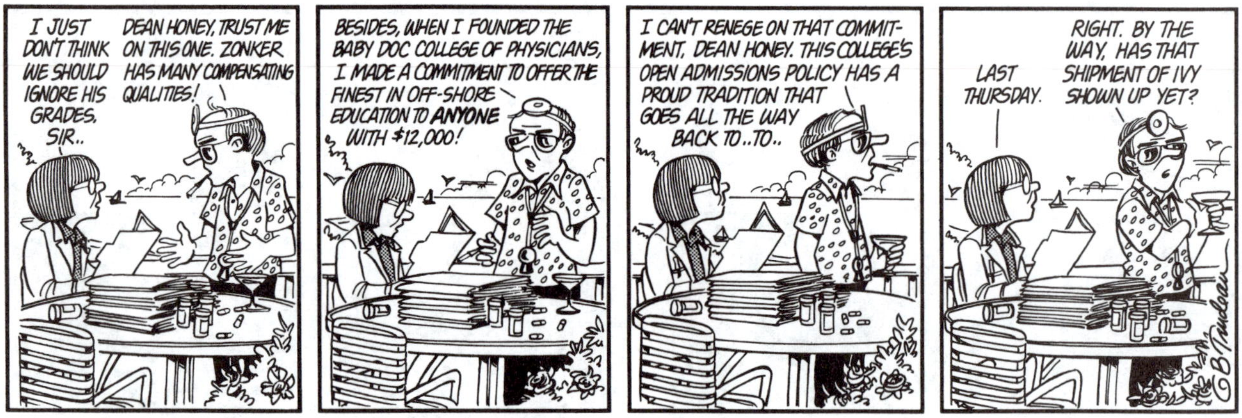
I JUST DON'T THINK WE SHOULD IGNORE HIS GRADES, SIR..
DEAN HONEY, TRUST ME ON THIS ONE. ZONKER HAS MANY COMPENSATING QUALITIES!
BESIDES, WHEN I FOUNDED THE BABY DOC COLLEGE OF PHYSICIANS, I MADE A COMMITMENT TO OFFER THE FINEST IN OFF-SHORE EDUCATION TO **ANYONE** WITH $12,000!
I CAN'T RENEGE ON THAT COMMITMENT, DEAN HONEY. THIS COLLEGE'S OPEN ADMISSIONS POLICY HAS A PROUD TRADITION THAT GOES ALL THE WAY BACK TO..TO..
LAST THURSDAY.
RIGHT. BY THE WAY, HAS THAT SHIPMENT OF IVY SHOWN UP YET?
©B Trudeau

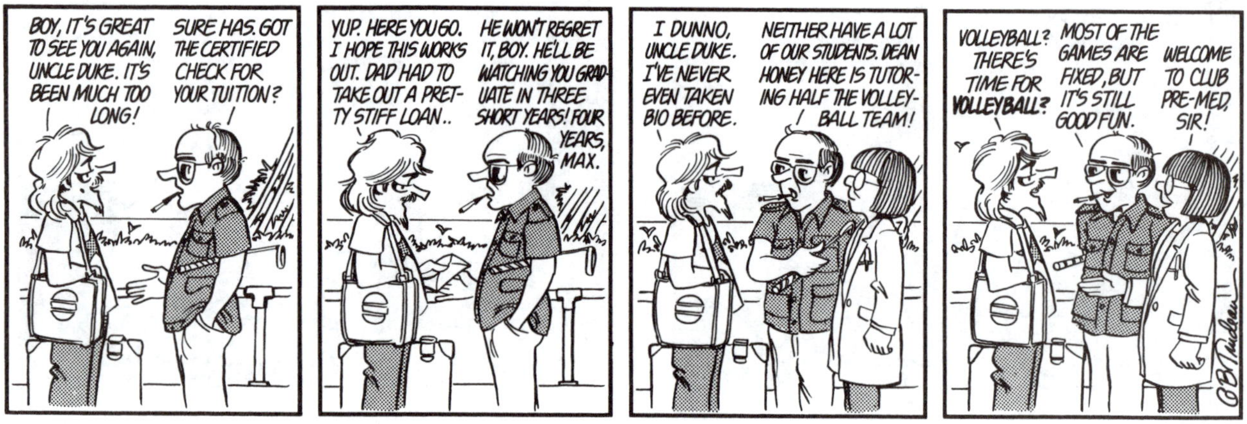
BOY, IT'S GREAT TO SEE YOU AGAIN, UNCLE DUKE. IT'S BEEN MUCH TOO LONG!
SURE HAS. GOT THE CERTIFIED CHECK FOR YOUR TUITION?
YUP. HERE YOU GO. I HOPE THIS WORKS OUT. DAD HAD TO TAKE OUT A PRETTY STIFF LOAN..
HE WON'T REGRET IT, BOY. HE'LL BE WATCHING YOU GRADUATE IN THREE SHORT YEARS! FOUR YEARS, MAX.
I DUNNO, UNCLE DUKE. I'VE NEVER EVEN TAKEN BIO BEFORE.
NEITHER HAVE A LOT OF OUR STUDENTS. DEAN HONEY HERE IS TUTORING HALF THE VOLLEYBALL TEAM!
VOLLEYBALL? THERE'S TIME FOR **VOLLEYBALL?**
MOST OF THE GAMES ARE FIXED, BUT IT'S STILL GOOD FUN.
WELCOME TO CLUB PRE-MED, SIR!
©B Trudeau

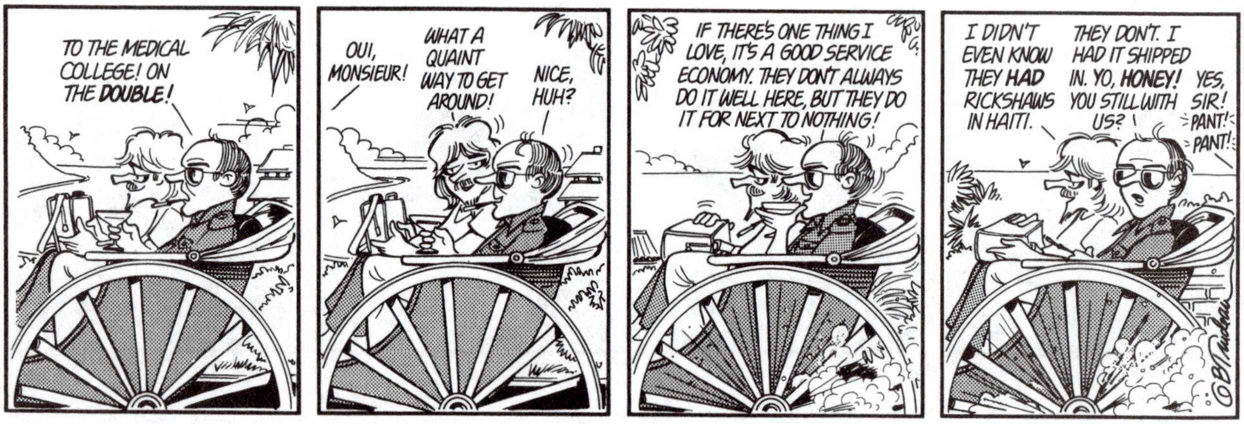
TO THE MEDICAL COLLEGE! ON THE **DOUBLE!**
OUI, MONSIEUR!
WHAT A QUAINT WAY TO GET AROUND!
NICE, HUH?
IF THERE'S ONE THING I LOVE, IT'S A GOOD SERVICE ECONOMY. THEY DON'T ALWAYS DO IT WELL HERE, BUT THEY DO IT FOR NEXT TO NOTHING!
I DIDN'T EVEN KNOW THEY **HAD** RICKSHAWS IN HAITI.
THEY DON'T. I HAD IT SHIPPED IN. YO, **HONEY!** YOU STILL WITH US?
YES, SIR!
PANT! PANT!
©B Trudeau

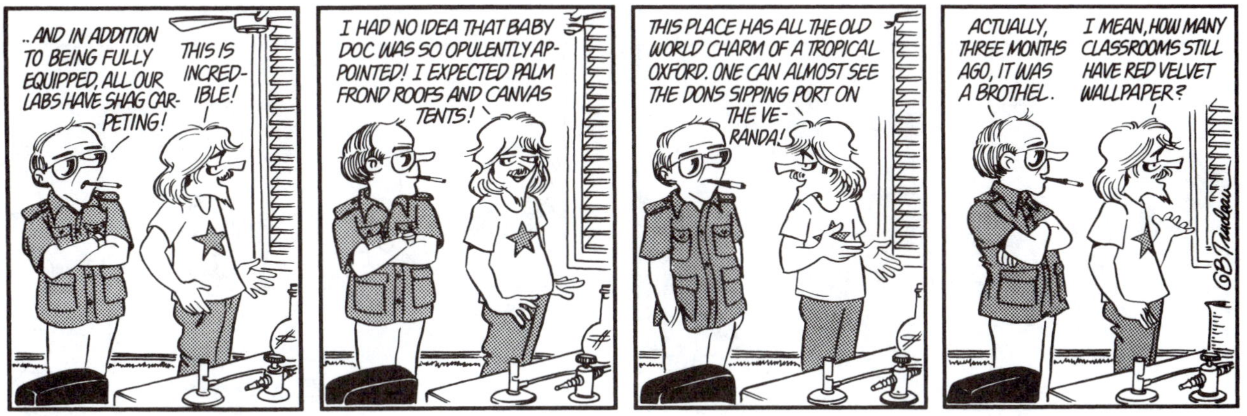
..AND IN ADDITION TO BEING FULLY EQUIPPED, ALL OUR LABS HAVE SHAG CARPETING!
THIS IS INCREDIBLE!
I HAD NO IDEA THAT BABY DOC WAS SO OPULENTLY APPOINTED! I EXPECTED PALM FROND ROOFS AND CANVAS TENTS!
THIS PLACE HAS ALL THE OLD WORLD CHARM OF A TROPICAL OXFORD. ONE CAN ALMOST SEE THE DONS SIPPING PORT ON THE VERANDA!
ACTUALLY, THREE MONTHS AGO, IT WAS A BROTHEL.
I MEAN, HOW MANY CLASSROOMS STILL HAVE RED VELVET WALLPAPER?

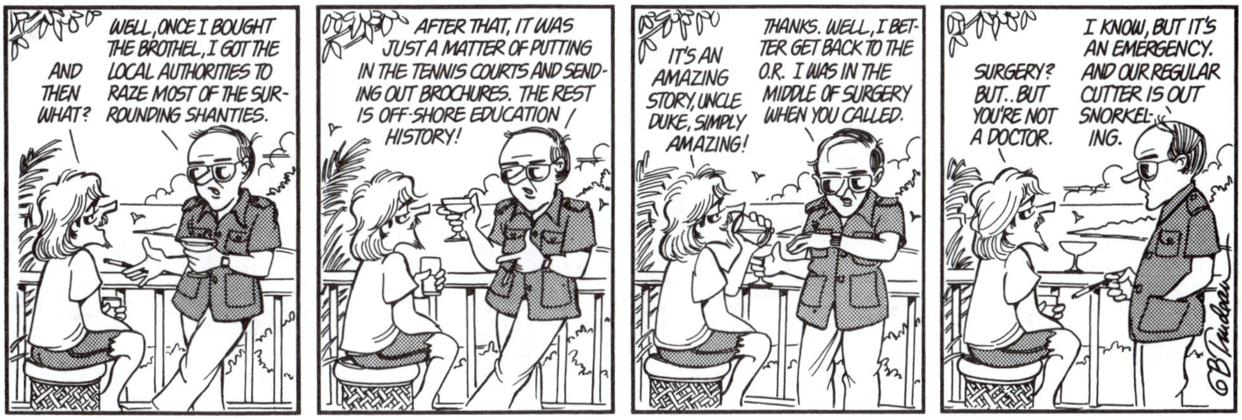
AND THEN WHAT?
WELL, ONCE I BOUGHT THE BROTHEL, I GOT THE LOCAL AUTHORITIES TO RAZE MOST OF THE SURROUNDING SHANTIES.
AFTER THAT, IT WAS JUST A MATTER OF PUTTING IN THE TENNIS COURTS AND SENDING OUT BROCHURES. THE REST IS OFF-SHORE EDUCATION HISTORY!
IT'S AN AMAZING STORY, UNCLE DUKE, SIMPLY AMAZING!
THANKS. WELL, I BETTER GET BACK TO THE O.R. I WAS IN THE MIDDLE OF SURGERY WHEN YOU CALLED.
SURGERY? BUT.. BUT YOU'RE NOT A DOCTOR.
I KNOW, BUT IT'S AN EMERGENCY. AND OUR REGULAR CUTTER IS OUT SNORKELING.

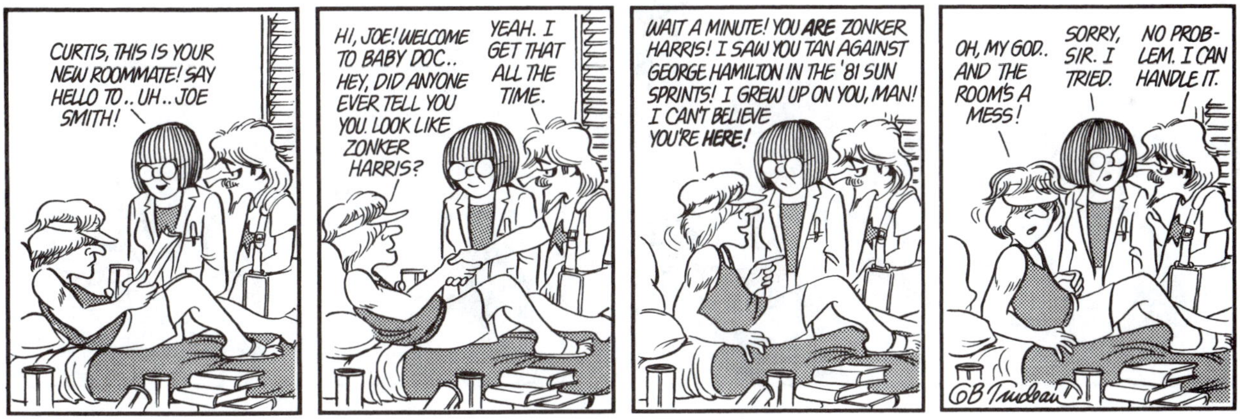
CURTIS, THIS IS YOUR NEW ROOMMATE! SAY HELLO TO.. UH.. JOE SMITH!
HI, JOE! WELCOME TO BABY DOC.. HEY, DID ANYONE EVER TELL YOU YOU. LOOK LIKE ZONKER HARRIS?
YEAH. I GET THAT ALL THE TIME.
WAIT A MINUTE! YOU **ARE** ZONKER HARRIS! I SAW YOU TAN AGAINST GEORGE HAMILTON IN THE '81 SUN SPRINTS! I GREW UP ON YOU, MAN! I CAN'T BELIEVE YOU'RE **HERE!**
OH, MY GOD.. AND THE ROOM'S A MESS!
SORRY, SIR. I TRIED.
NO PROBLEM. I CAN HANDLE IT.

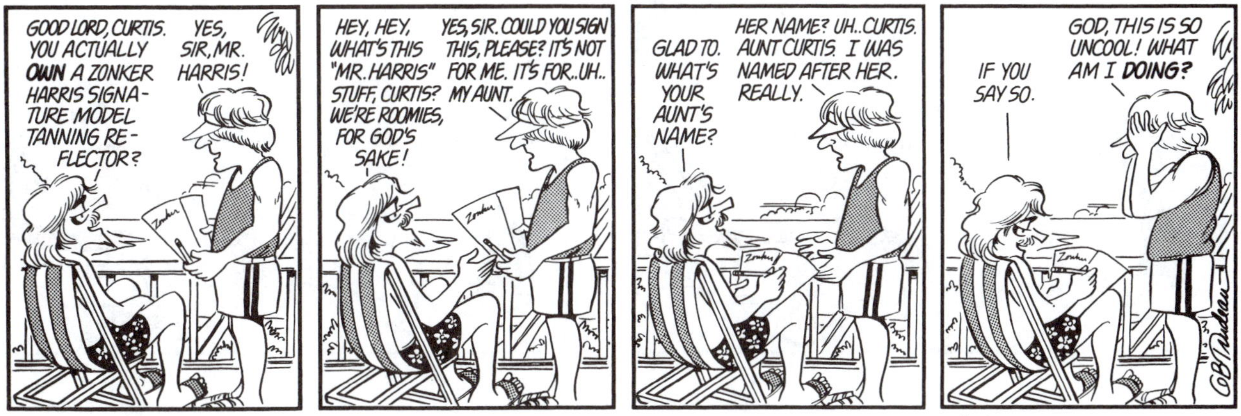
GOOD LORD, CURTIS. YOU ACTUALLY **OWN** A ZONKER HARRIS SIGNATURE MODEL TANNING REFLECTOR?
YES, SIR, MR. HARRIS!
HEY, HEY, WHAT'S THIS "MR. HARRIS" STUFF, CURTIS? WE'RE ROOMIES, FOR GOD'S SAKE!
YES, SIR. COULD YOU SIGN THIS, PLEASE? IT'S NOT FOR ME. IT'S FOR.. UH.. MY AUNT.
GLAD TO. WHAT'S YOUR AUNT'S NAME?
HER NAME? UH.. CURTIS. AUNT CURTIS. I WAS NAMED AFTER HER. REALLY.
IF YOU SAY SO.
GOD, THIS IS SO UNCOOL! WHAT AM I **DOING?**

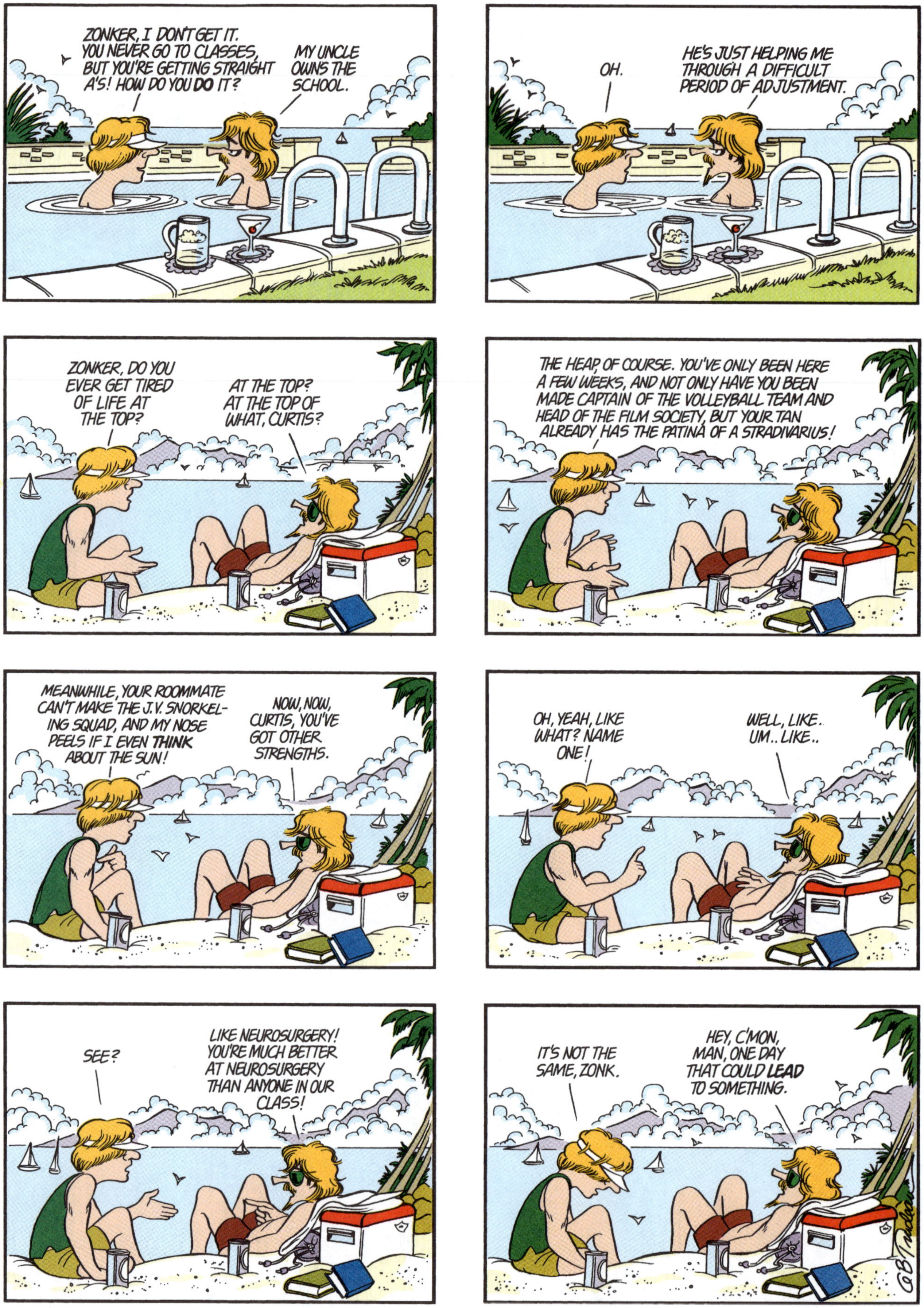
ZONKER, I DON'T GET IT. YOU NEVER GO TO CLASSES, BUT YOU'RE GETTING STRAIGHT A'S! HOW DO YOU **DO** IT?
MY UNCLE OWNS THE SCHOOL.
OH.
HE'S JUST HELPING ME THROUGH A DIFFICULT PERIOD OF ADJUSTMENT.
ZONKER, DO YOU EVER GET TIRED OF LIFE AT THE TOP?
AT THE TOP? AT THE TOP OF WHAT, CURTIS?
THE HEAP, OF COURSE. YOU'VE ONLY BEEN HERE A FEW WEEKS, AND NOT ONLY HAVE YOU BEEN MADE CAPTAIN OF THE VOLLEYBALL TEAM AND HEAD OF THE FILM SOCIETY, BUT YOUR TAN ALREADY HAS THE PATINA OF A STRADIVARIUS!
MEANWHILE, YOUR ROOMMATE CAN'T MAKE THE J.V. SNORKELING SQUAD, AND MY NOSE PEELS IF I EVEN **THINK** ABOUT THE SUN!
NOW, NOW, CURTIS, YOU'VE GOT OTHER STRENGTHS.
OH, YEAH, LIKE WHAT? NAME ONE!
WELL, LIKE.. UM.. LIKE..
SEE?
LIKE NEUROSURGERY! YOU'RE MUCH BETTER AT NEUROSURGERY THAN ANYONE IN OUR CLASS!
IT'S NOT THE SAME, ZONK.
HEY, C'MON, MAN, ONE DAY THAT COULD **LEAD** TO SOMETHING.
GBTrudeau

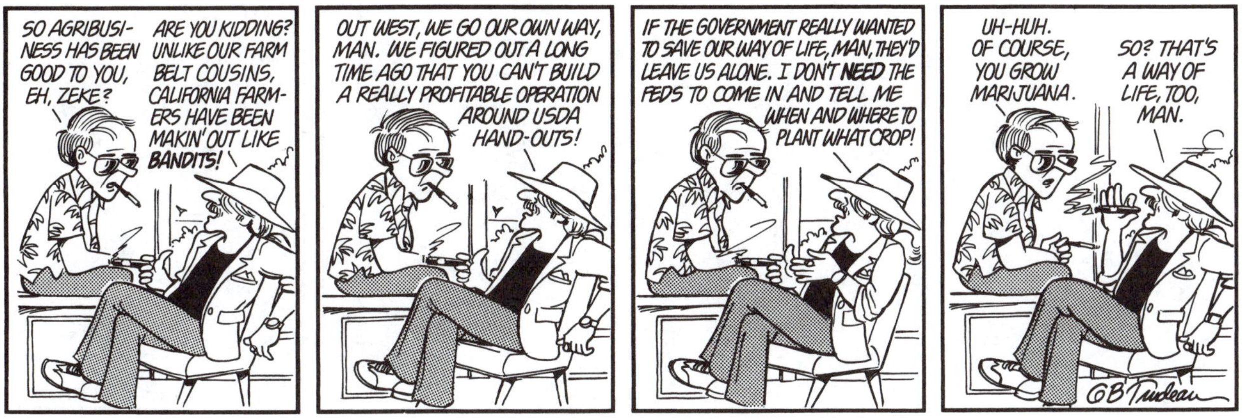
SO AGRIBUSINESS HAS BEEN GOOD TO YOU, EH, ZEKE?
ARE YOU KIDDING? UNLIKE OUR FARM BELT COUSINS, CALIFORNIA FARMERS HAVE BEEN MAKIN' OUT LIKE **BANDITS!**
OUT WEST, WE GO OUR OWN WAY, MAN. WE FIGURED OUT A LONG TIME AGO THAT YOU CAN'T BUILD A REALLY PROFITABLE OPERATION AROUND USDA HAND-OUTS!
IF THE GOVERNMENT REALLY WANTED TO SAVE OUR WAY OF LIFE, MAN, THEY'D LEAVE US ALONE. I DON'T **NEED** THE FEDS TO COME IN AND TELL ME WHEN AND WHERE TO PLANT WHAT CROP!
UH-HUH. OF COURSE, YOU GROW MARIJUANA.
SO? THAT'S A WAY OF LIFE, TOO, MAN.
©B Trudeau

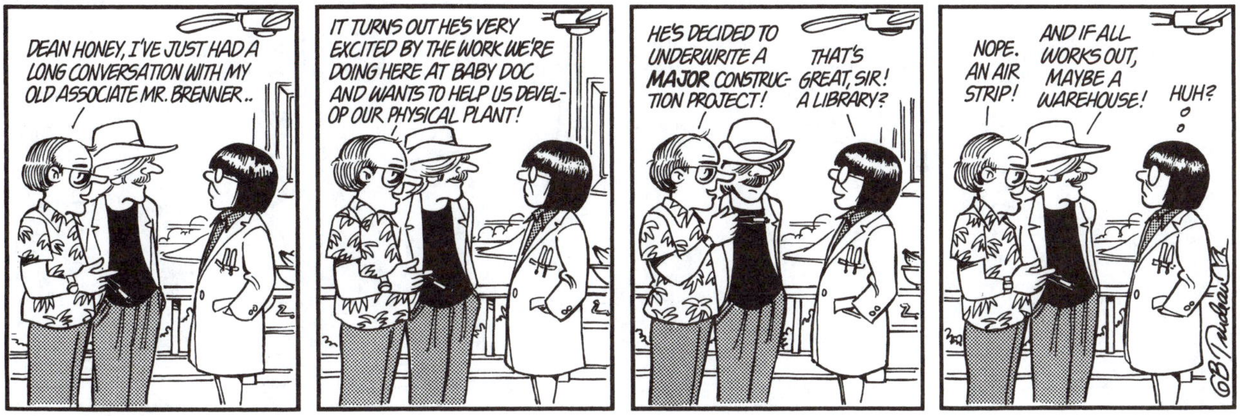
DEAN HONEY, I'VE JUST HAD A LONG CONVERSATION WITH MY OLD ASSOCIATE MR. BRENNER..
IT TURNS OUT HE'S VERY EXCITED BY THE WORK WE'RE DOING HERE AT BABY DOC AND WANTS TO HELP US DEVELOP OUR PHYSICAL PLANT!
HE'S DECIDED TO UNDERWRITE A **MAJOR** CONSTRUCTION PROJECT!
THAT'S GREAT, SIR! A LIBRARY?
NOPE. AN AIR STRIP!
AND IF ALL WORKS OUT, MAYBE A WAREHOUSE!
HUH?
©B Trudeau

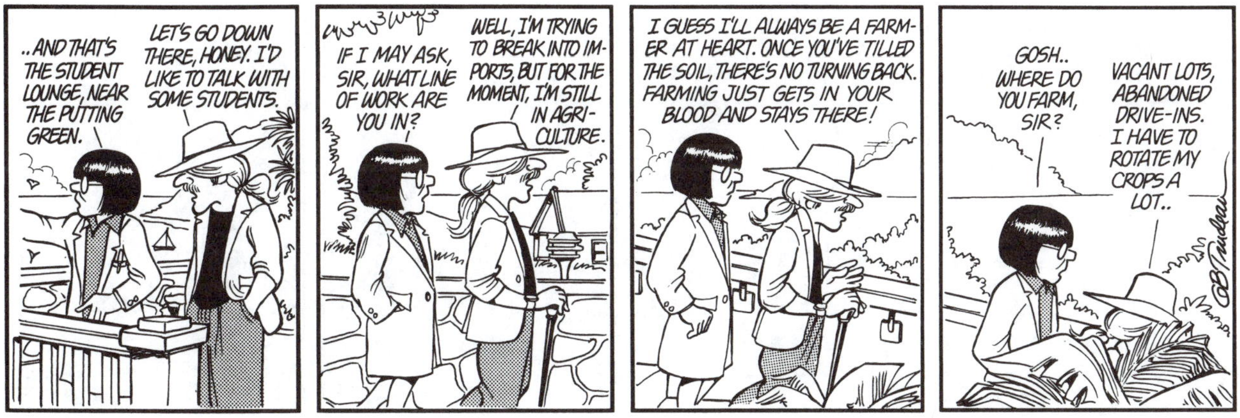
..AND THAT'S THE STUDENT LOUNGE, NEAR THE PUTTING GREEN.
LET'S GO DOWN THERE, HONEY. I'D LIKE TO TALK WITH SOME STUDENTS.
IF I MAY ASK, SIR, WHAT LINE OF WORK ARE YOU IN?
WELL, I'M TRYING TO BREAK INTO IMPORTS, BUT FOR THE MOMENT, I'M STILL IN AGRICULTURE.
I GUESS I'LL ALWAYS BE A FARMER AT HEART. ONCE YOU'VE TILLED THE SOIL, THERE'S NO TURNING BACK. FARMING JUST GETS IN YOUR BLOOD AND STAYS THERE!
GOSH.. WHERE DO YOU FARM, SIR?
VACANT LOTS, ABANDONED DRIVE-INS. I HAVE TO ROTATE MY CROPS A LOT..
©B Trudeau

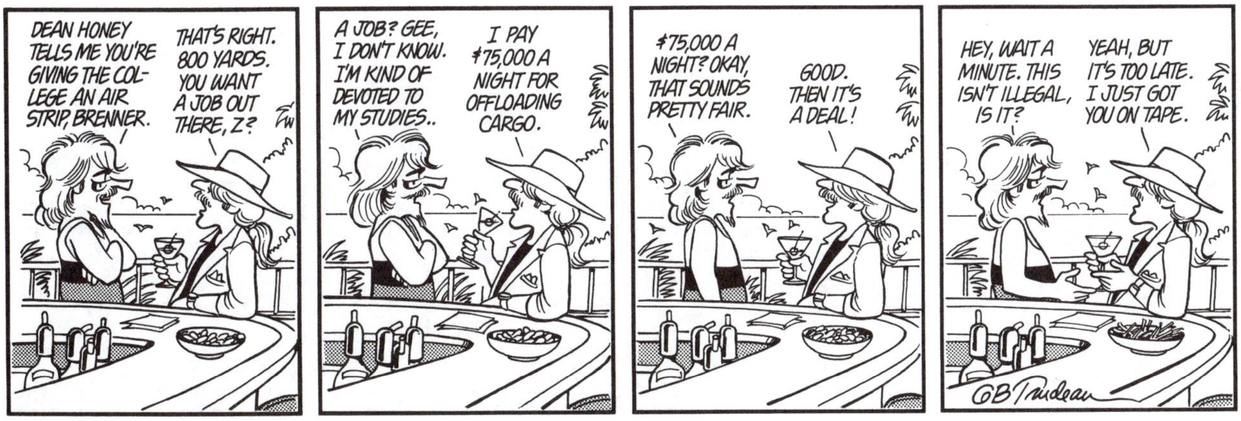
DEAN HONEY TELLS ME YOU'RE GIVING THE COLLEGE AN AIR STRIP, BRENNER.
THAT'S RIGHT. 800 YARDS. YOU WANT A JOB OUT THERE, Z?
A JOB? GEE, I DON'T KNOW. I'M KIND OF DEVOTED TO MY STUDIES..
I PAY $75,000 A NIGHT FOR OFFLOADING CARGO.
$75,000 A NIGHT? OKAY, THAT SOUNDS PRETTY FAIR.
GOOD. THEN IT'S A DEAL!
HEY, WAIT A MINUTE. THIS ISN'T ILLEGAL, IS IT?
YEAH, BUT IT'S TOO LATE. I JUST GOT YOU ON TAPE.
©B Trudeau

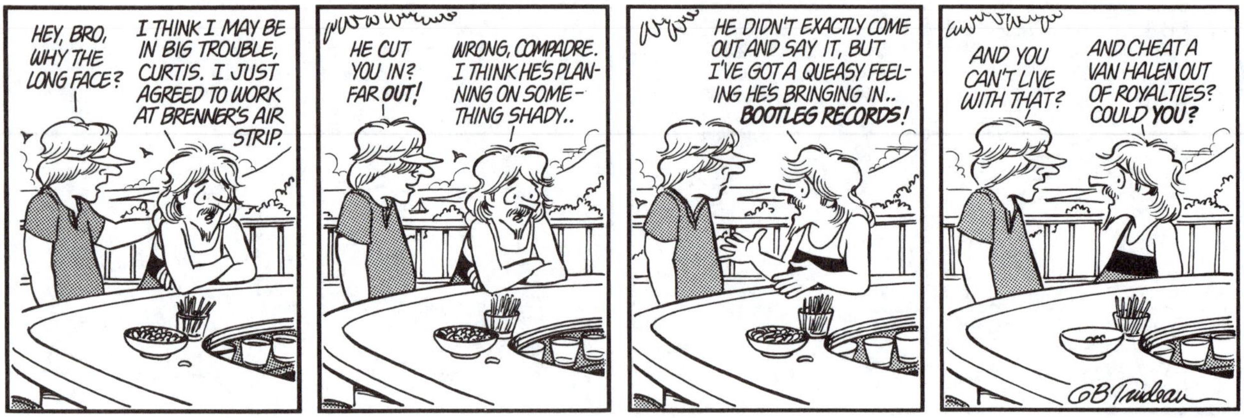
HEY, BRO, WHY THE LONG FACE?
I THINK I MAY BE IN BIG TROUBLE, CURTIS. I JUST AGREED TO WORK AT BRENNER'S AIR STRIP.
HE CUT YOU IN? FAR OUT!
WRONG, COMPADRE. I THINK HE'S PLANNING ON SOMETHING SHADY..
HE DIDN'T EXACTLY COME OUT AND SAY IT, BUT I'VE GOT A QUEASY FEELING HE'S BRINGING IN.. BOOTLEG RECORDS!
AND YOU CAN'T LIVE WITH THAT?
AND CHEAT A VAN HALEN OUT OF ROYALTIES? COULD YOU?
GB Trudeau

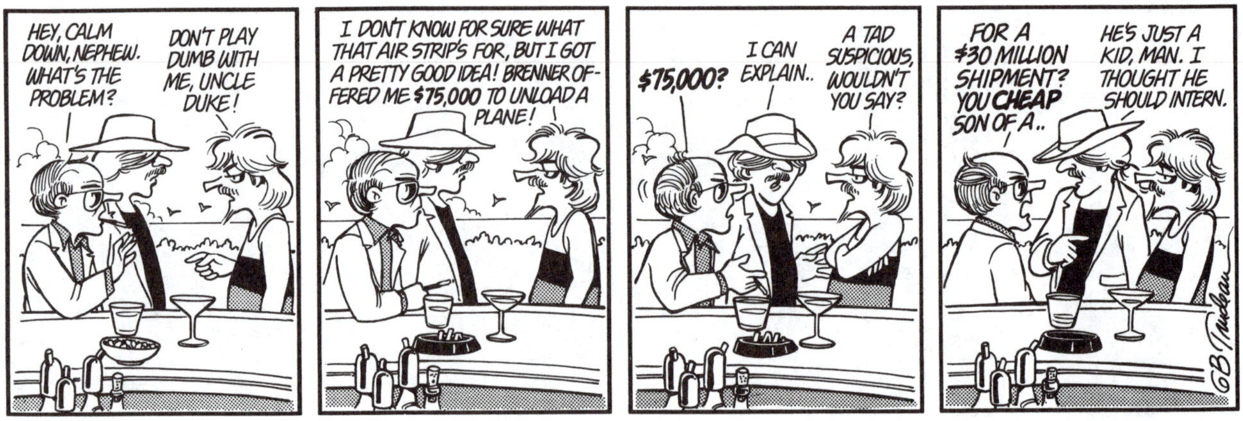
HEY, CALM DOWN, NEPHEW. WHAT'S THE PROBLEM?
DON'T PLAY DUMB WITH ME, UNCLE DUKE!
I DON'T KNOW FOR SURE WHAT THAT AIR STRIP'S FOR, BUT I GOT A PRETTY GOOD IDEA! BRENNER OFFERED ME $75,000 TO UNLOAD A PLANE!
$75,000?
I CAN EXPLAIN..
A TAD SUSPICIOUS, WOULDN'T YOU SAY?
FOR A $30 MILLION SHIPMENT? YOU CHEAP SON OF A..
HE'S JUST A KID, MAN. I THOUGHT HE SHOULD INTERN.
GB Trudeau

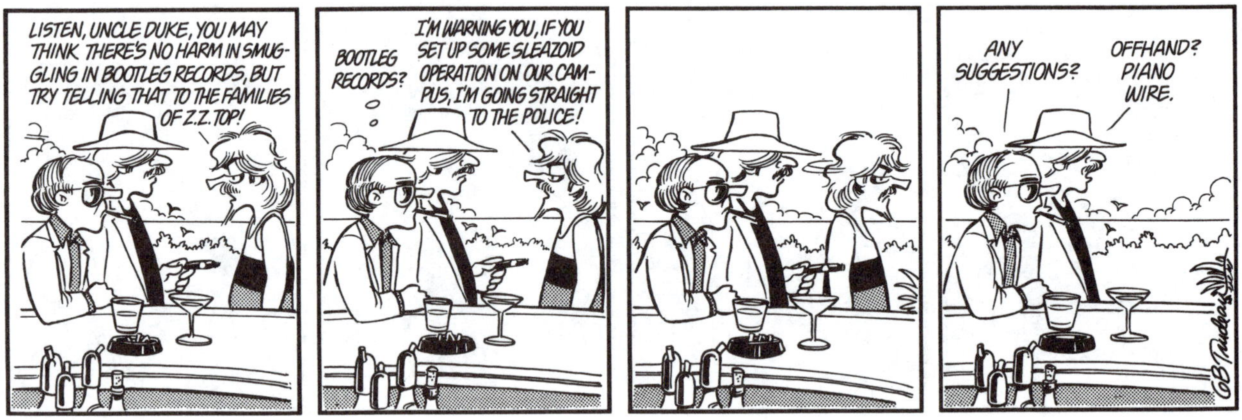
LISTEN, UNCLE DUKE, YOU MAY THINK THERE'S NO HARM IN SMUGGLING IN BOOTLEG RECORDS, BUT TRY TELLING THAT TO THE FAMILIES OF Z.Z. TOP!
BOOTLEG RECORDS?
I'M WARNING YOU, IF YOU SET UP SOME SLEAZOID OPERATION ON OUR CAMPUS, I'M GOING STRAIGHT TO THE POLICE!
ANY SUGGESTIONS?
OFFHAND? PIANO WIRE.
GB Trudeau

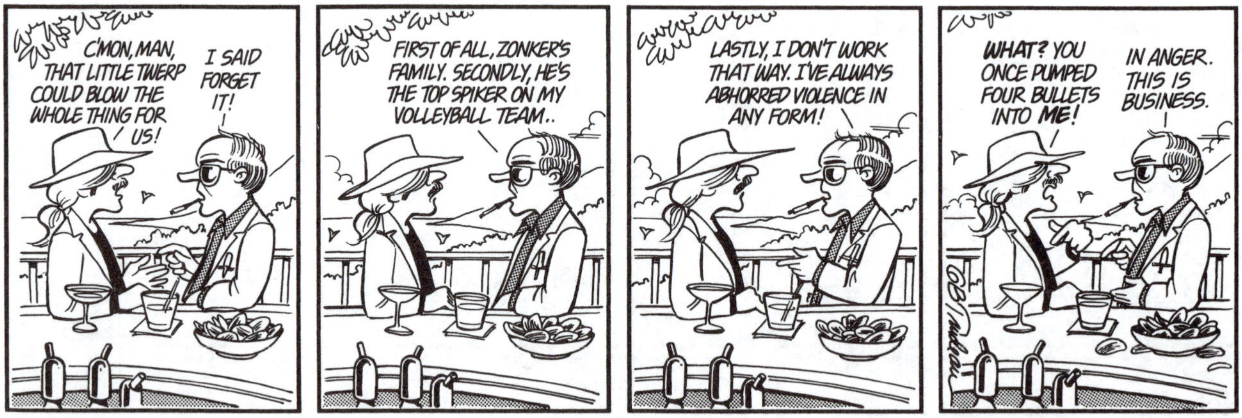
C'MON, MAN, THAT LITTLE TWERP COULD BLOW THE WHOLE THING FOR US!
I SAID FORGET IT!
FIRST OF ALL, ZONKER'S FAMILY. SECONDLY, HE'S THE TOP SPIKER ON MY VOLLEYBALL TEAM..
LASTLY, I DON'T WORK THAT WAY. I'VE ALWAYS ABHORRED VIOLENCE IN ANY FORM!
WHAT? YOU ONCE PUMPED FOUR BULLETS INTO ME!
IN ANGER. THIS IS BUSINESS.
GB Trudeau

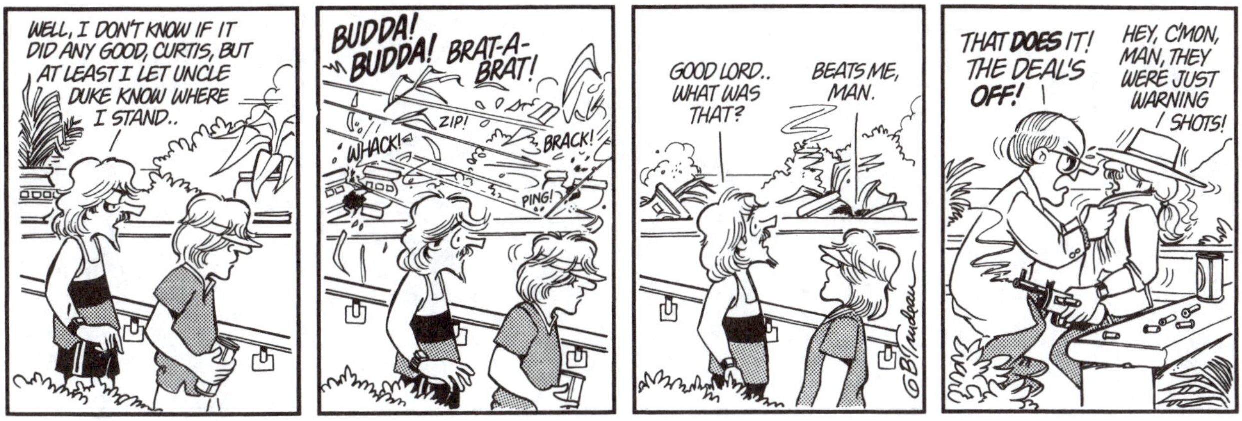
WELL, I DON'T KNOW IF IT DID ANY GOOD, CURTIS, BUT AT LEAST I LET UNCLE DUKE KNOW WHERE I STAND..
BUDDA! BUDDA! BRAT-A-BRAT!
ZIP!
WHACK!
BRACK!
PING!
GOOD LORD.. WHAT WAS THAT?
BEATS ME, MAN.
THAT DOES IT! THE DEAL'S OFF!
HEY, C'MON, MAN, THEY WERE JUST WARNING SHOTS!

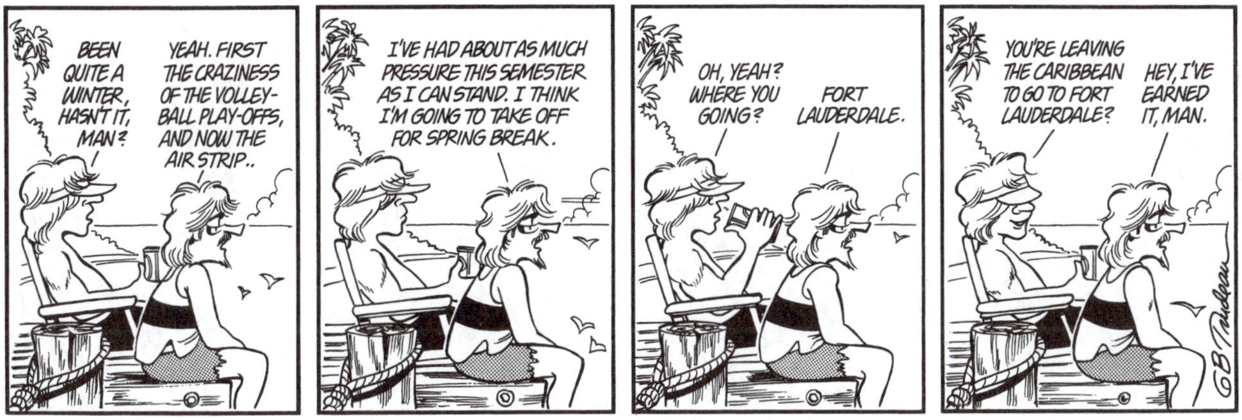
BEEN QUITE A WINTER, HASN'T IT, MAN?
YEAH. FIRST THE CRAZINESS OF THE VOLLEY-BALL PLAY-OFFS, AND NOW THE AIR STRIP..
I'VE HAD ABOUT AS MUCH PRESSURE THIS SEMESTER AS I CAN STAND. I THINK I'M GOING TO TAKE OFF FOR SPRING BREAK.
OH, YEAH? WHERE YOU GOING?
FORT LAUDERDALE.
YOU'RE LEAVING THE CARIBBEAN TO GO TO FORT LAUDERDALE?
HEY, I'VE EARNED IT, MAN.

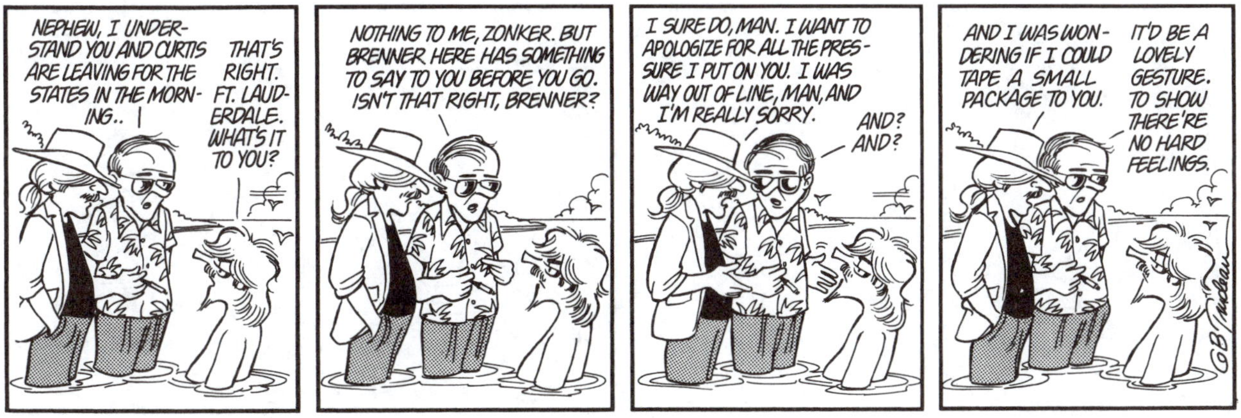
NEPHEW, I UNDER-STAND YOU AND CURTIS ARE LEAVING FOR THE STATES IN THE MORN-ING..
THAT'S RIGHT. FT. LAUD-ERDALE. WHAT'S IT TO YOU?
NOTHING TO ME, ZONKER. BUT BRENNER HERE HAS SOMETHING TO SAY TO YOU BEFORE YOU GO. ISN'T THAT RIGHT, BRENNER?
I SURE DO, MAN. I WANT TO APOLOGIZE FOR ALL THE PRES-SURE I PUT ON YOU. I WAS WAY OUT OF LINE, MAN, AND I'M REALLY SORRY.
AND? AND?
AND I WAS WON-DERING IF I COULD TAPE A SMALL PACKAGE TO YOU.
IT'D BE A LOVELY GESTURE. TO SHOW THERE'RE NO HARD FEELINGS.

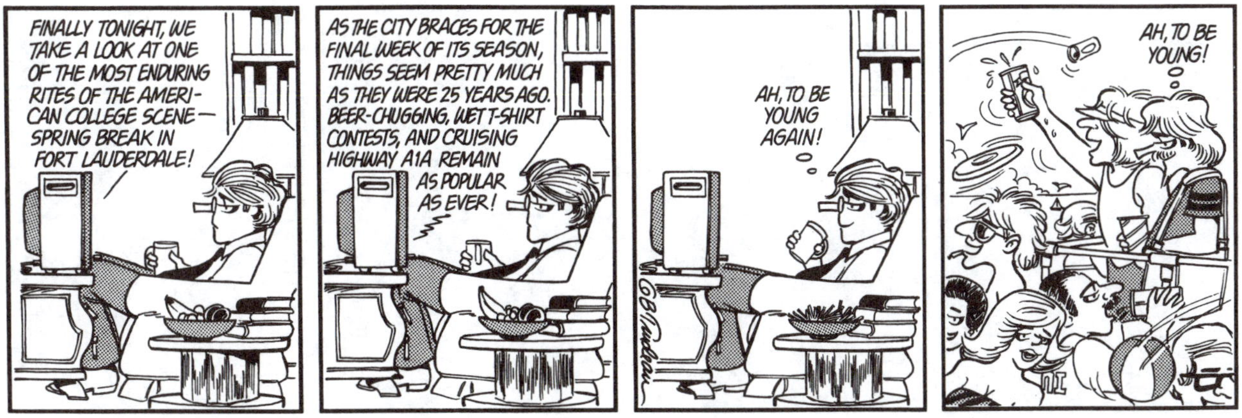
FINALLY TONIGHT, WE TAKE A LOOK AT ONE OF THE MOST ENDURING RITES OF THE AMERI-CAN COLLEGE SCENE— SPRING BREAK IN FORT LAUDERDALE!
AS THE CITY BRACES FOR THE FINAL WEEK OF ITS SEASON, THINGS SEEM PRETTY MUCH AS THEY WERE 25 YEARS AGO. BEER-CHUGGING, WET T-SHIRT CONTESTS, AND CRUISING HIGHWAY A1A REMAIN AS POPULAR AS EVER!
AH, TO BE YOUNG AGAIN!
AH, TO BE YOUNG!

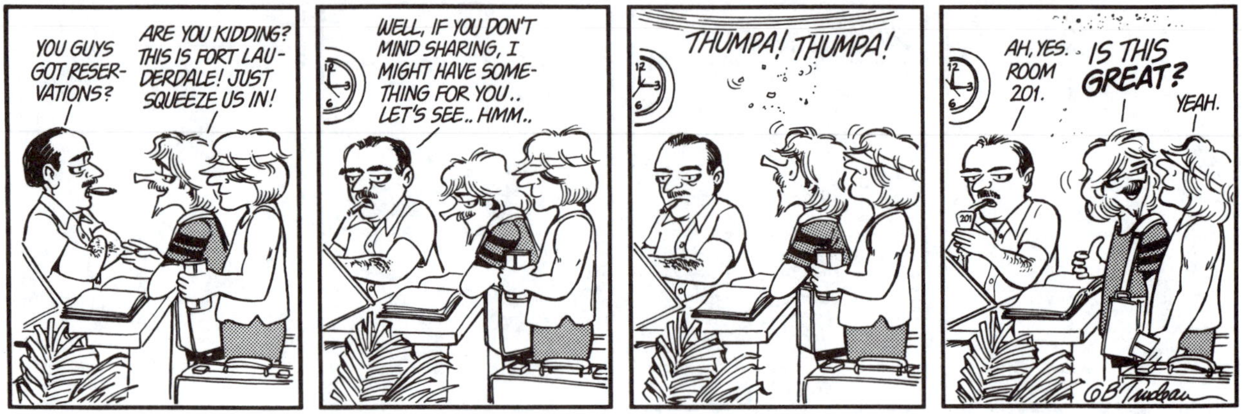
YOU GUYS GOT RESER-VATIONS?
ARE YOU KIDDING? THIS IS FORT LAU-DERDALE! JUST SQUEEZE US IN!
WELL, IF YOU DON'T MIND SHARING, I MIGHT HAVE SOME-THING FOR YOU.. LET'S SEE.. HMM..
THUMPA! THUMPA!
AH, YES.. ROOM 201.
IS THIS GREAT?
YEAH.
201
GB Trudeau

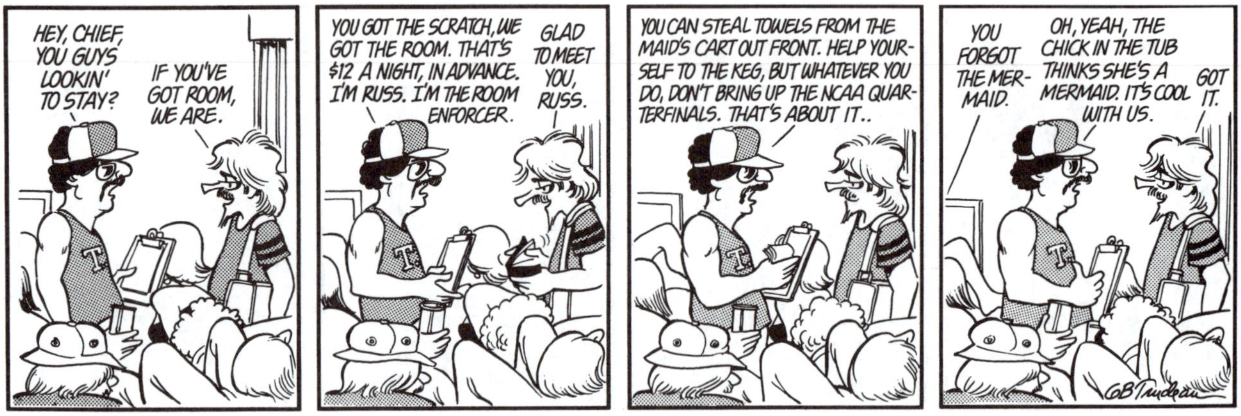
HEY, CHIEF, YOU GUYS LOOKIN' TO STAY?
IF YOU'VE GOT ROOM, WE ARE.
YOU GOT THE SCRATCH, WE GOT THE ROOM. THAT'S $12 A NIGHT, IN ADVANCE. I'M RUSS. I'M THE ROOM ENFORCER.
GLAD TO MEET YOU, RUSS.
YOU CAN STEAL TOWELS FROM THE MAID'S CART OUT FRONT. HELP YOUR-SELF TO THE KEG, BUT WHATEVER YOU DO, DON'T BRING UP THE NCAA QUAR-TERFINALS. THAT'S ABOUT IT..
YOU FORGOT THE MER-MAID.
OH, YEAH, THE CHICK IN THE TUB THINKS SHE'S A MERMAID. IT'S COOL WITH US.
GOT IT.
GB Trudeau

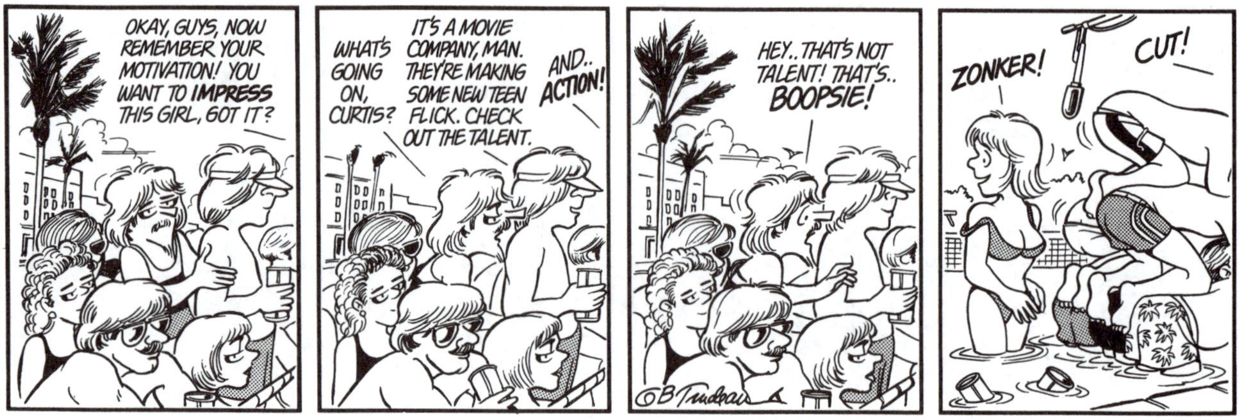
OKAY, GUYS, NOW REMEMBER YOUR MOTIVATION! YOU WANT TO **IMPRESS** THIS GIRL, GOT IT?
WHAT'S GOING ON, CURTIS?
IT'S A MOVIE COMPANY, MAN. THEY'RE MAKING SOME NEW TEEN FLICK. CHECK OUT THE TALENT.
AND.. **ACTION!**
HEY.. THAT'S NOT TALENT! THAT'S.. **BOOPSIE!**
GB Trudeau
ZONKER!
CUT!

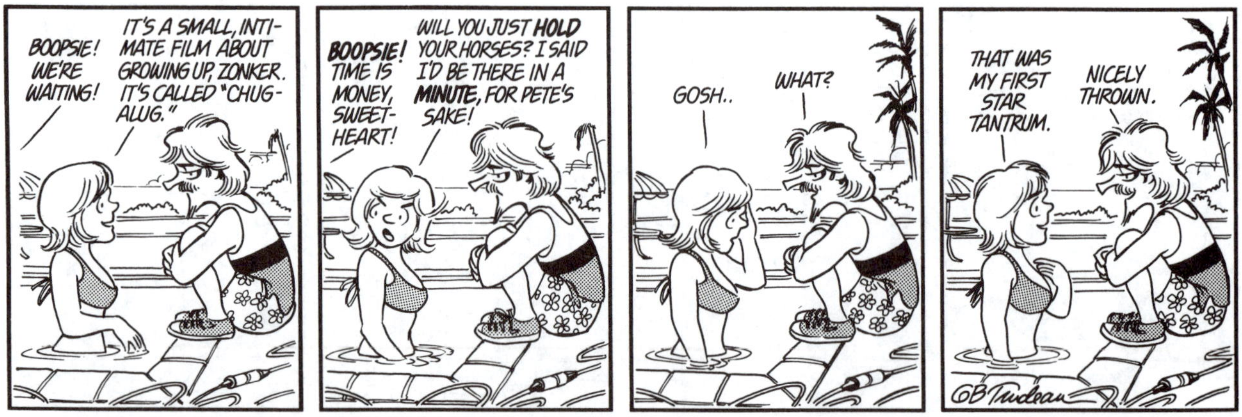
BOOPSIE! WE'RE WAITING!
IT'S A SMALL, INTI-MATE FILM ABOUT GROWING UP, ZONKER. IT'S CALLED "CHUG-ALUG."
BOOPSIE! TIME IS MONEY, SWEET-HEART!
WILL YOU JUST **HOLD** YOUR HORSES? I SAID I'D BE THERE IN A **MINUTE**, FOR PETE'S SAKE!
GOSH..
WHAT?
THAT WAS MY FIRST STAR TANTRUM.
NICELY THROWN.
GB Trudeau

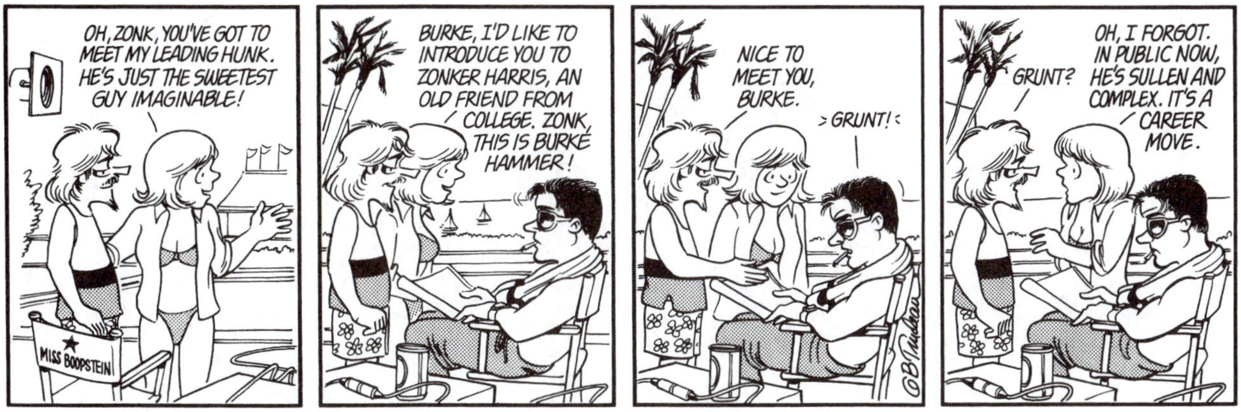
OH, ZONK, YOU'VE GOT TO MEET MY LEADING HUNK. HE'S JUST THE SWEETEST GUY IMAGINABLE!
MISS BOOPSTEIN
BURKE, I'D LIKE TO INTRODUCE YOU TO ZONKER HARRIS, AN OLD FRIEND FROM COLLEGE. ZONK, THIS IS BURKE HAMMER!
NICE TO MEET YOU, BURKE.
>GRUNT!<
GRUNT?
OH, I FORGOT. IN PUBLIC NOW, HE'S SULLEN AND COMPLEX. IT'S A CAREER MOVE.

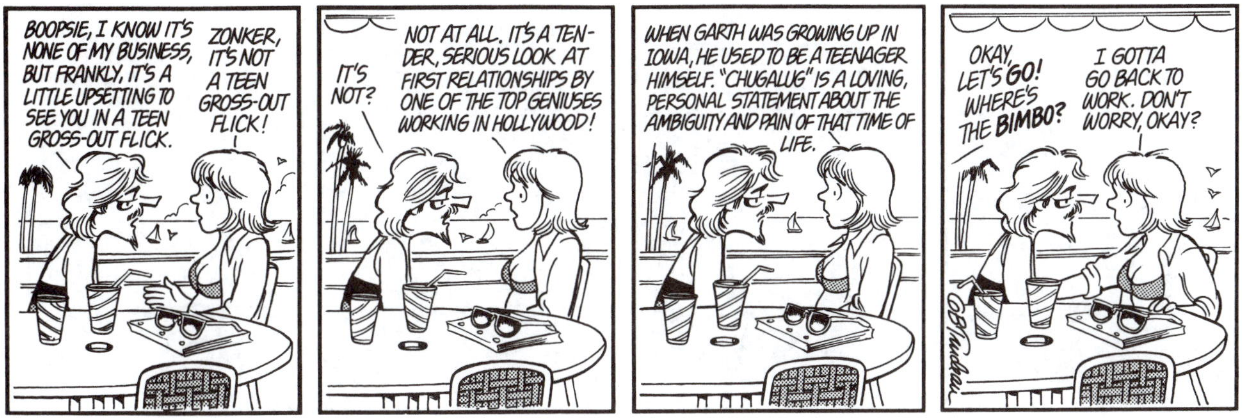
BOOPSIE, I KNOW IT'S NONE OF MY BUSINESS, BUT FRANKLY, IT'S A LITTLE UPSETTING TO SEE YOU IN A TEEN GROSS-OUT FLICK.
ZONKER, IT'S NOT A TEEN GROSS-OUT FLICK!
IT'S NOT?
NOT AT ALL. IT'S A TENDER, SERIOUS LOOK AT FIRST RELATIONSHIPS BY ONE OF THE TOP GENIUSES WORKING IN HOLLYWOOD!
WHEN GARTH WAS GROWING UP IN IOWA, HE USED TO BE A TEENAGER HIMSELF. "CHUGALUG" IS A LOVING, PERSONAL STATEMENT ABOUT THE AMBIGUITY AND PAIN OF THAT TIME OF LIFE.
OKAY, LET'S GO! WHERE'S THE BIMBO?
I GOTTA GO BACK TO WORK. DON'T WORRY, OKAY?

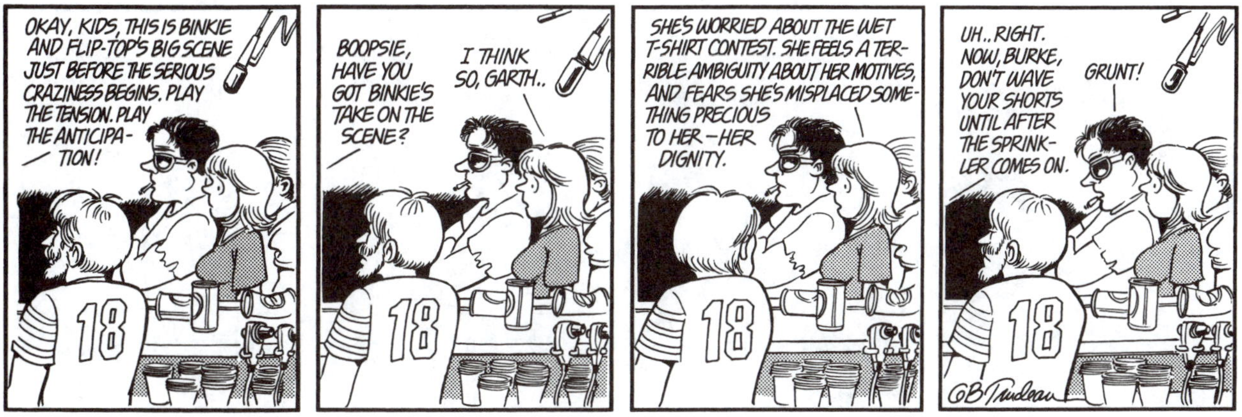
OKAY, KIDS, THIS IS BINKIE AND FLIP-TOP'S BIG SCENE JUST BEFORE THE SERIOUS CRAZINESS BEGINS. PLAY THE TENSION. PLAY THE ANTICIPATION!
18
BOOPSIE, HAVE YOU GOT BINKIE'S TAKE ON THE SCENE?
I THINK SO, GARTH..
SHE'S WORRIED ABOUT THE WET T-SHIRT CONTEST. SHE FEELS A TERRIBLE AMBIGUITY ABOUT HER MOTIVES, AND FEARS SHE'S MISPLACED SOMETHING PRECIOUS TO HER — HER DIGNITY.
UH.. RIGHT. NOW, BURKE, DON'T WAVE YOUR SHORTS UNTIL AFTER THE SPRINKLER COMES ON.
GRUNT!

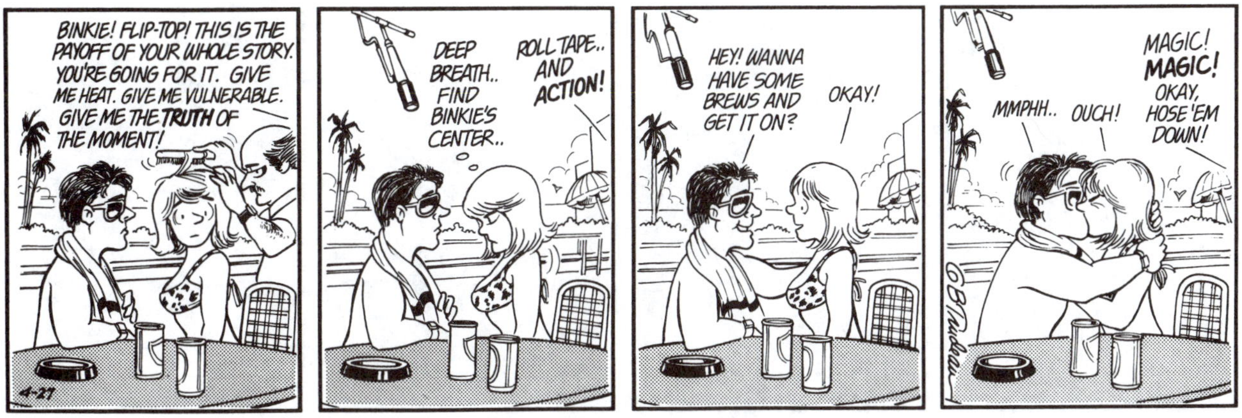
BINKIE! FLIP-TOP! THIS IS THE PAYOFF OF YOUR WHOLE STORY. YOU'RE GOING FOR IT. GIVE ME HEAT. GIVE ME VULNERABLE. GIVE ME THE TRUTH OF THE MOMENT!
4-27
DEEP BREATH.. FIND BINKIE'S CENTER..
ROLL TAPE.. AND ACTION!
HEY! WANNA HAVE SOME BREWS AND GET IT ON?
OKAY!
MMPHH..
OUCH!
MAGIC! MAGIC! OKAY, HOSE 'EM DOWN!

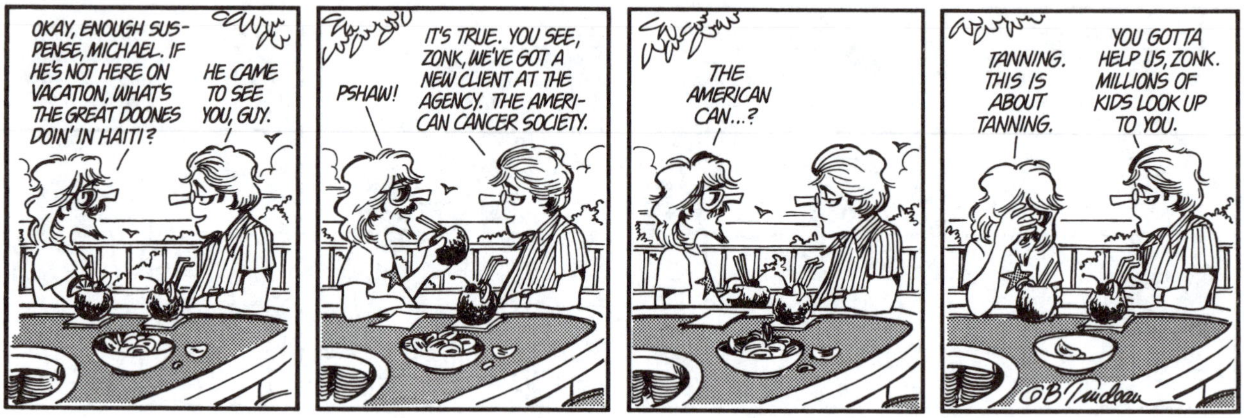
OKAY, ENOUGH SUSPENSE, MICHAEL. IF HE'S NOT HERE ON VACATION, WHAT'S THE GREAT DOONES DOIN' IN HAITI?
HE CAME TO SEE YOU, GUY.
PSHAW!
IT'S TRUE. YOU SEE, ZONK, WE'VE GOT A NEW CLIENT AT THE AGENCY. THE AMERICAN CANCER SOCIETY.
THE AMERICAN CAN...?
TANNING. THIS IS ABOUT TANNING.
YOU GOTTA HELP US, ZONK. MILLIONS OF KIDS LOOK UP TO YOU.
©B Trudeau

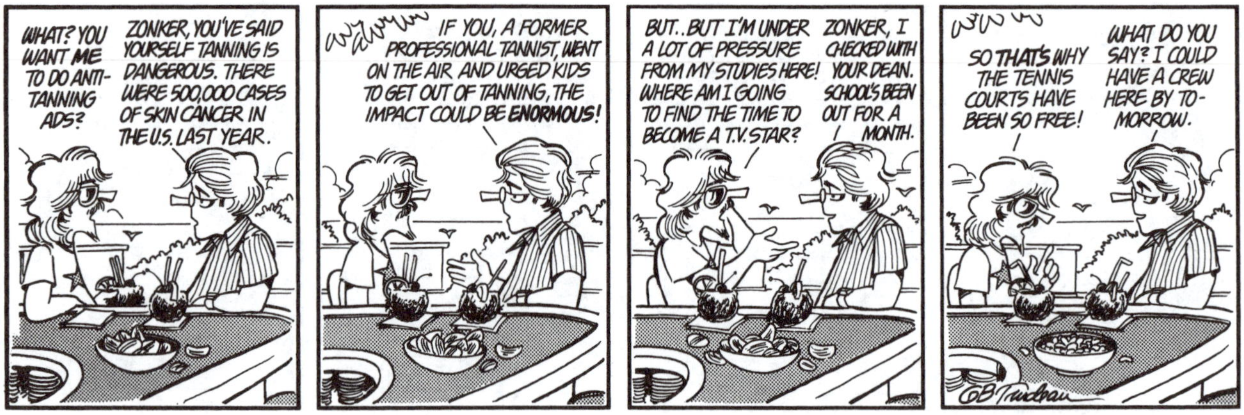
WHAT? YOU WANT ME TO DO ANTI-TANNING ADS?
ZONKER, YOU'VE SAID YOURSELF TANNING IS DANGEROUS. THERE WERE 500,000 CASES OF SKIN CANCER IN THE U.S. LAST YEAR.
IF YOU, A FORMER PROFESSIONAL TANNIST, WENT ON THE AIR AND URGED KIDS TO GET OUT OF TANNING, THE IMPACT COULD BE ENORMOUS!
BUT.. BUT I'M UNDER A LOT OF PRESSURE FROM MY STUDIES HERE! WHERE AM I GOING TO FIND THE TIME TO BECOME A T.V. STAR?
ZONKER, I CHECKED WITH YOUR DEAN. SCHOOL'S BEEN OUT FOR A MONTH.
SO THAT'S WHY THE TENNIS COURTS HAVE BEEN SO FREE!
WHAT DO YOU SAY? I COULD HAVE A CREW HERE BY TOMORROW.
©B Trudeau

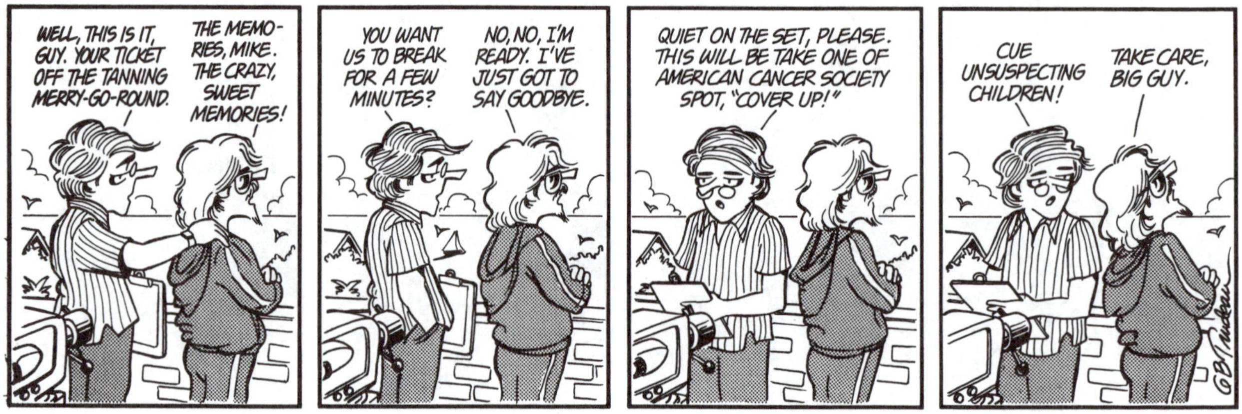
WELL, THIS IS IT, GUY. YOUR TICKET OFF THE TANNING MERRY-GO-ROUND.
THE MEMORIES, MIKE. THE CRAZY, SWEET MEMORIES!
YOU WANT US TO BREAK FOR A FEW MINUTES?
NO, NO, I'M READY. I'VE JUST GOT TO SAY GOODBYE.
QUIET ON THE SET, PLEASE. THIS WILL BE TAKE ONE OF AMERICAN CANCER SOCIETY SPOT, "COVER UP!"
CUE UNSUSPECTING CHILDREN!
TAKE CARE, BIG GUY.
©B Trudeau

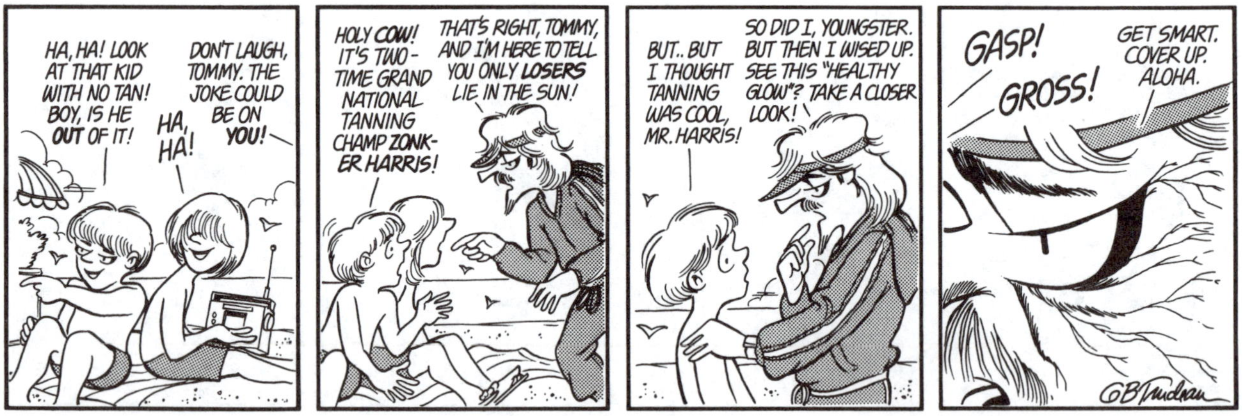
HA, HA! LOOK AT THAT KID WITH NO TAN! BOY, IS HE OUT OF IT!
HA, HA!
DON'T LAUGH, TOMMY. THE JOKE COULD BE ON YOU!
HOLY COW! IT'S TWO-TIME GRAND NATIONAL TANNING CHAMP ZONKER HARRIS!
THAT'S RIGHT, TOMMY, AND I'M HERE TO TELL YOU ONLY LOSERS LIE IN THE SUN!
BUT.. BUT I THOUGHT TANNING WAS COOL, MR. HARRIS!
SO DID I, YOUNGSTER. BUT THEN I WISED UP. SEE THIS "HEALTHY GLOW"? TAKE A CLOSER LOOK!
GASP!
GROSS!
GET SMART. COVER UP. ALOHA.
©B Trudeau

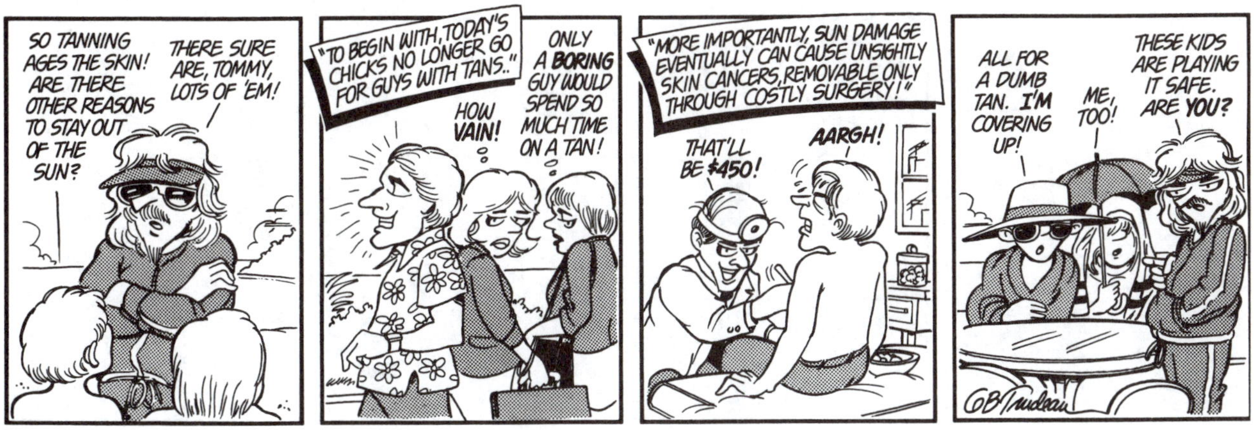
SO TANNING AGES THE SKIN! ARE THERE OTHER REASONS TO STAY OUT OF THE SUN?
THERE SURE ARE, TOMMY, LOTS OF 'EM!
"TO BEGIN WITH, TODAY'S CHICKS NO LONGER GO FOR GUYS WITH TANS.."
HOW VAIN!
ONLY A BORING GUY WOULD SPEND SO MUCH TIME ON A TAN!
"MORE IMPORTANTLY, SUN DAMAGE EVENTUALLY CAN CAUSE UNSIGHTLY SKIN CANCERS, REMOVABLE ONLY THROUGH COSTLY SURGERY!"
THAT'LL BE $450!
AARGH!
ALL FOR A DUMB TAN. I'M COVERING UP!
ME, TOO!
THESE KIDS ARE PLAYING IT SAFE. ARE YOU?
GB Trudeau

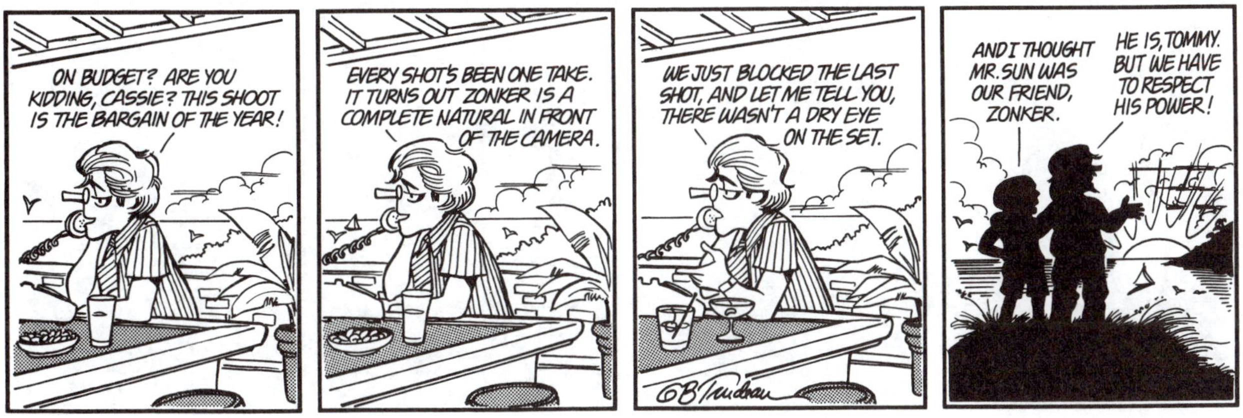
ON BUDGET? ARE YOU KIDDING, CASSIE? THIS SHOOT IS THE BARGAIN OF THE YEAR!
EVERY SHOT'S BEEN ONE TAKE. IT TURNS OUT ZONKER IS A COMPLETE NATURAL IN FRONT OF THE CAMERA.
WE JUST BLOCKED THE LAST SHOT, AND LET ME TELL YOU, THERE WASN'T A DRY EYE ON THE SET.
GB Trudeau
AND I THOUGHT MR. SUN WAS OUR FRIEND, ZONKER.
HE IS, TOMMY. BUT WE HAVE TO RESPECT HIS POWER!

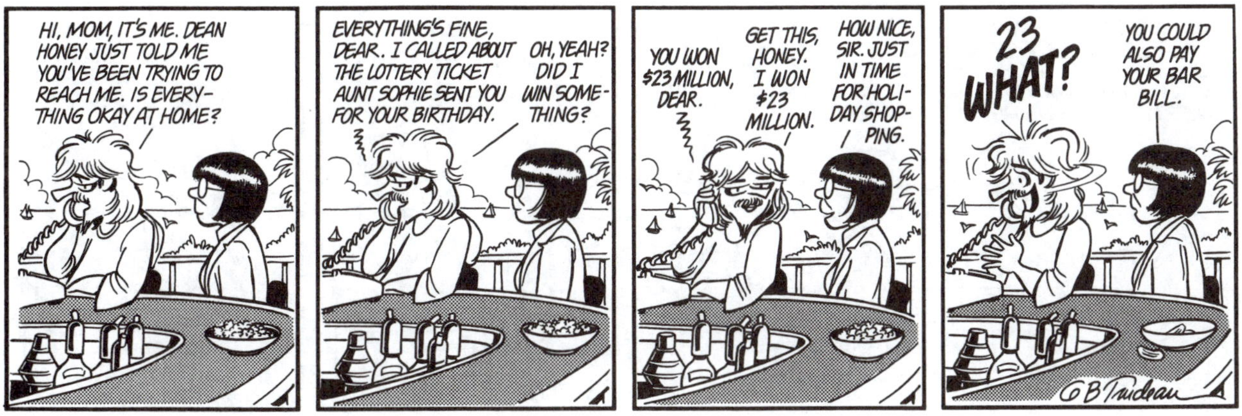
HI, MOM, IT'S ME. DEAN HONEY JUST TOLD ME YOU'VE BEEN TRYING TO REACH ME. IS EVERYTHING OKAY AT HOME?
EVERYTHING'S FINE, DEAR. I CALLED ABOUT THE LOTTERY TICKET AUNT SOPHIE SENT YOU FOR YOUR BIRTHDAY.
OH, YEAH? DID I WIN SOMETHING?
YOU WON $23 MILLION, DEAR.
GET THIS, HONEY. I WON $23 MILLION.
HOW NICE, SIR. JUST IN TIME FOR HOLIDAY SHOPPING.
23 WHAT?
YOU COULD ALSO PAY YOUR BAR BILL.
GB Trudeau

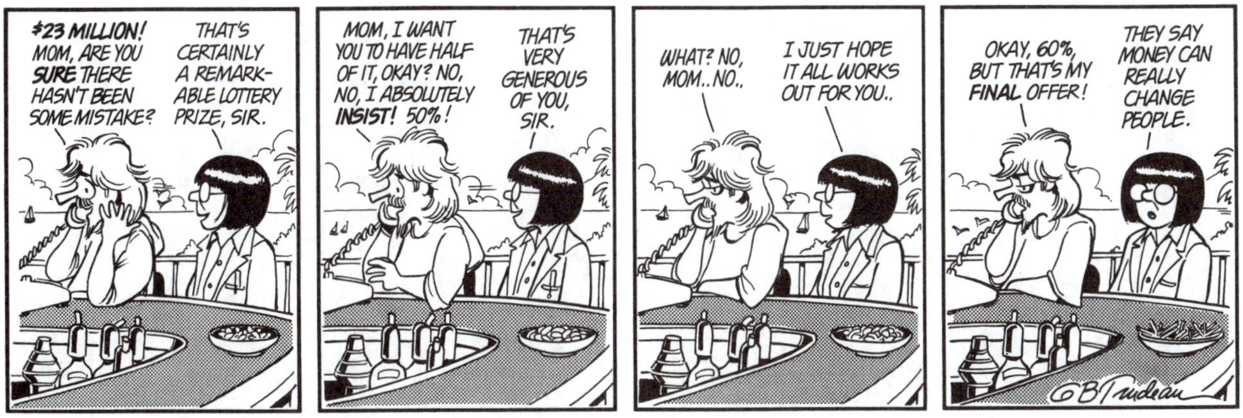
$23 MILLION! MOM, ARE YOU SURE THERE HASN'T BEEN SOME MISTAKE?
THAT'S CERTAINLY A REMARKABLE LOTTERY PRIZE, SIR.
MOM, I WANT YOU TO HAVE HALF OF IT, OKAY? NO, NO, I ABSOLUTELY INSIST! 50%!
THAT'S VERY GENEROUS OF YOU, SIR.
WHAT? NO, MOM.. NO..
I JUST HOPE IT ALL WORKS OUT FOR YOU..
OKAY, 60%, BUT THAT'S MY FINAL OFFER!
THEY SAY MONEY CAN REALLY CHANGE PEOPLE.
GB Trudeau

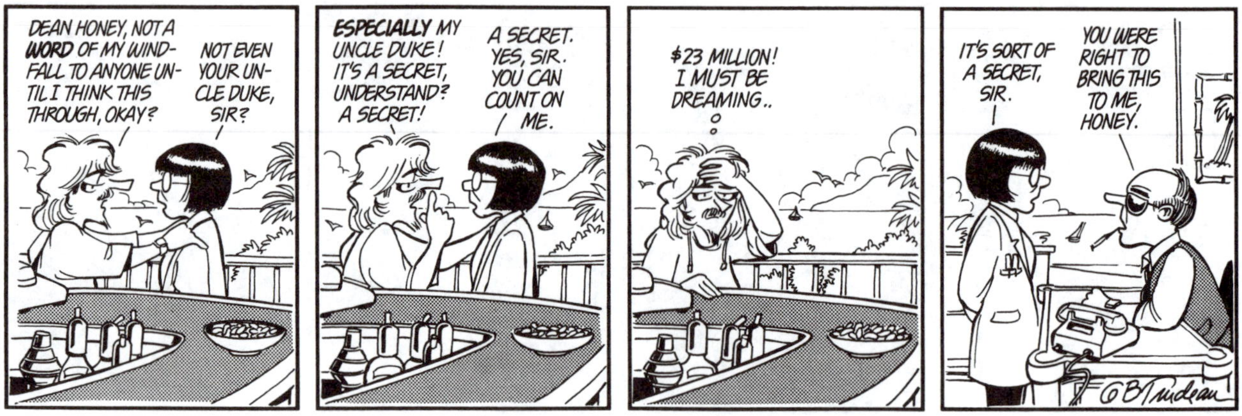
DEAN HONEY, NOT A **WORD** OF MY WINDFALL TO ANYONE UNTIL I THINK THIS THROUGH, OKAY?
NOT EVEN YOUR UNCLE DUKE, SIR?
ESPECIALLY MY UNCLE DUKE! IT'S A SECRET, UNDERSTAND? A SECRET!
A SECRET. YES, SIR. YOU CAN COUNT ON ME.
$23 MILLION! I MUST BE DREAMING..
IT'S SORT OF A SECRET, SIR.
YOU WERE RIGHT TO BRING THIS TO ME, HONEY.

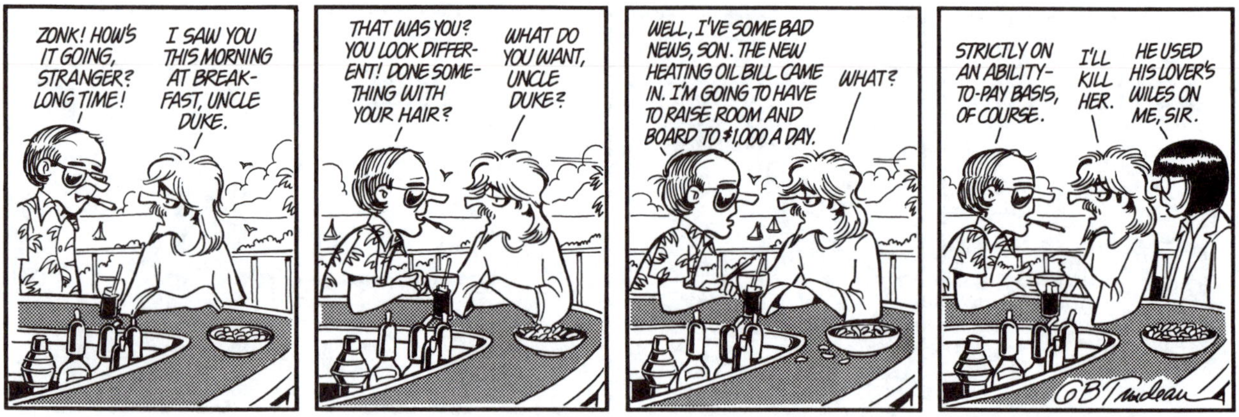
ZONK! HOW'S IT GOING, STRANGER? LONG TIME!
I SAW YOU THIS MORNING AT BREAKFAST, UNCLE DUKE.
THAT WAS YOU? YOU LOOK DIFFERENT! DONE SOMETHING WITH YOUR HAIR?
WHAT DO YOU WANT, UNCLE DUKE?
WELL, I'VE SOME BAD NEWS, SON. THE NEW HEATING OIL BILL CAME IN. I'M GOING TO HAVE TO RAISE ROOM AND BOARD TO $1,000 A DAY.
WHAT?
STRICTLY ON AN ABILITY-TO-PAY BASIS, OF COURSE.
I'LL KILL HER.
HE USED HIS LOVER'S WILES ON ME, SIR.

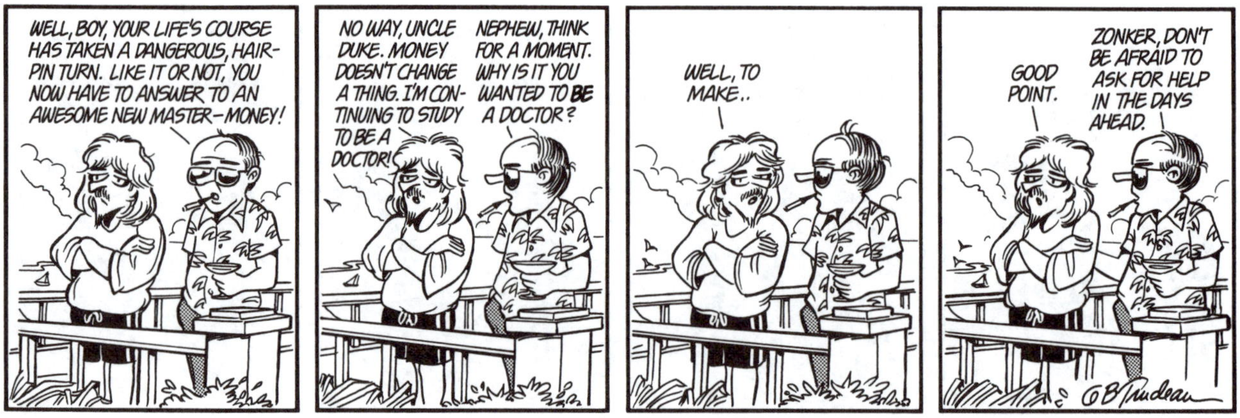
WELL, BOY, YOUR LIFE'S COURSE HAS TAKEN A DANGEROUS, HAIRPIN TURN. LIKE IT OR NOT, YOU NOW HAVE TO ANSWER TO AN AWESOME NEW MASTER—MONEY!
NO WAY, UNCLE DUKE. MONEY DOESN'T CHANGE A THING. I'M CONTINUING TO STUDY TO BE A DOCTOR!
NEPHEW, THINK FOR A MOMENT. WHY IS IT YOU WANTED TO **BE** A DOCTOR?
WELL, TO MAKE..
GOOD POINT.
ZONKER, DON'T BE AFRAID TO ASK FOR HELP IN THE DAYS AHEAD.

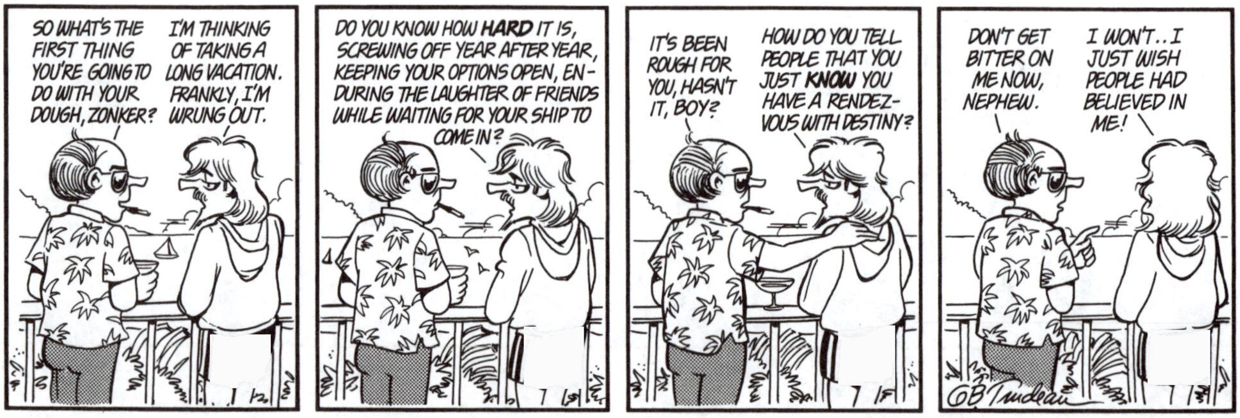
SO WHAT'S THE FIRST THING YOU'RE GOING TO DO WITH YOUR DOUGH, ZONKER?
I'M THINKING OF TAKING A LONG VACATION. FRANKLY, I'M WRUNG OUT.
DO YOU KNOW HOW **HARD** IT IS, SCREWING OFF YEAR AFTER YEAR, KEEPING YOUR OPTIONS OPEN, ENDURING THE LAUGHTER OF FRIENDS WHILE WAITING FOR YOUR SHIP TO COME IN?
IT'S BEEN ROUGH FOR YOU, HASN'T IT, BOY?
HOW DO YOU TELL PEOPLE THAT YOU JUST **KNOW** YOU HAVE A RENDEZVOUS WITH DESTINY?
DON'T GET BITTER ON ME NOW, NEPHEW.
I WON'T.. I JUST WISH PEOPLE HAD BELIEVED IN ME!

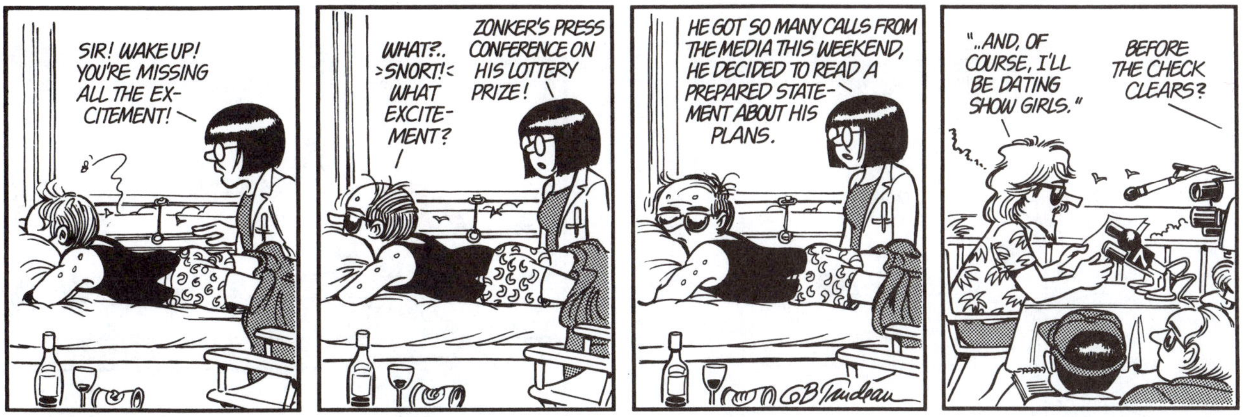
SIR! WAKE UP! YOU'RE MISSING ALL THE EXCITEMENT!
WHAT?.. >SNORT!< WHAT EXCITEMENT?
ZONKER'S PRESS CONFERENCE ON HIS LOTTERY PRIZE!
HE GOT SO MANY CALLS FROM THE MEDIA THIS WEEKEND, HE DECIDED TO READ A PREPARED STATEMENT ABOUT HIS PLANS.
"..AND, OF COURSE, I'LL BE DATING SHOW GIRLS."
BEFORE THE CHECK CLEARS?
GB Trudeau

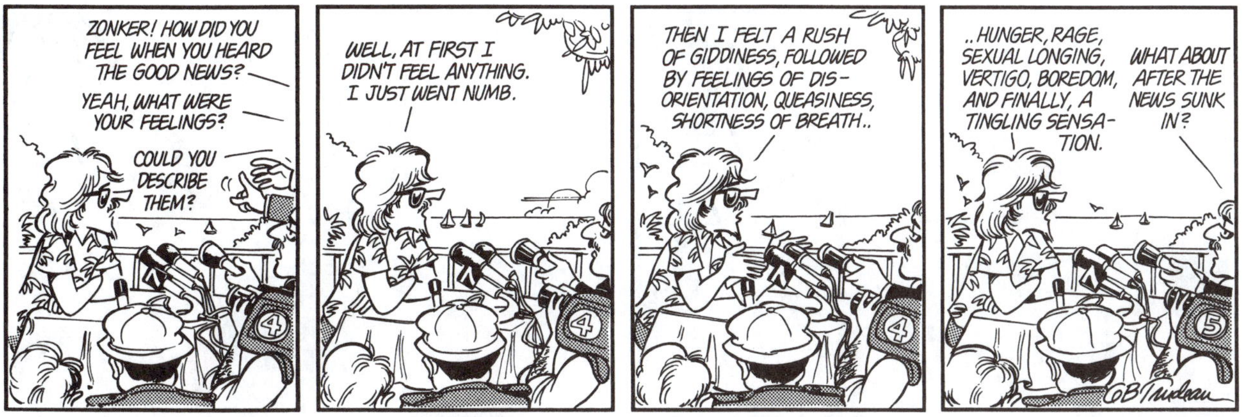
ZONKER! HOW DID YOU FEEL WHEN YOU HEARD THE GOOD NEWS?
YEAH, WHAT WERE YOUR FEELINGS?
COULD YOU DESCRIBE THEM?
WELL, AT FIRST I DIDN'T FEEL ANYTHING. I JUST WENT NUMB.
THEN I FELT A RUSH OF GIDDINESS, FOLLOWED BY FEELINGS OF DISORIENTATION, QUEASINESS, SHORTNESS OF BREATH..
..HUNGER, RAGE, SEXUAL LONGING, VERTIGO, BOREDOM, AND FINALLY, A TINGLING SENSATION.
WHAT ABOUT AFTER THE NEWS SUNK IN?
GB Trudeau

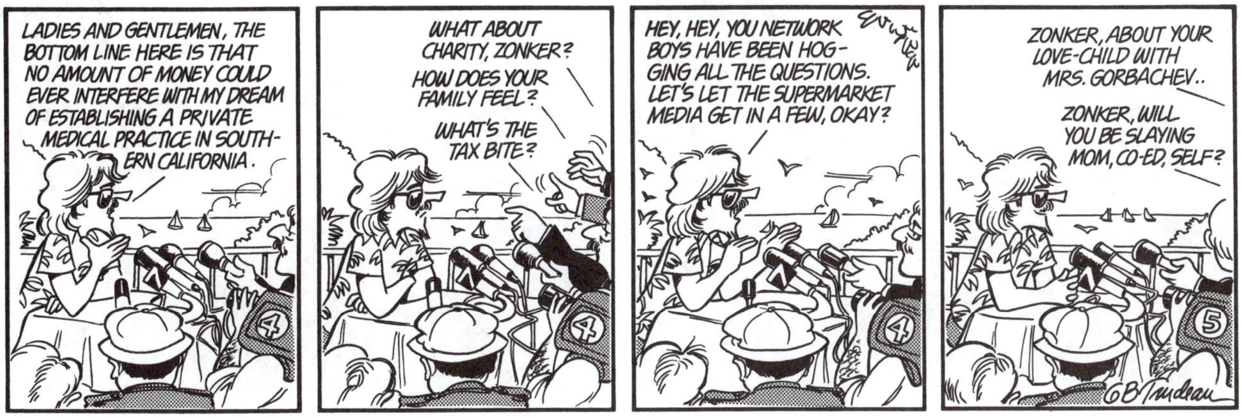
LADIES AND GENTLEMEN, THE BOTTOM LINE HERE IS THAT NO AMOUNT OF MONEY COULD EVER INTERFERE WITH MY DREAM OF ESTABLISHING A PRIVATE MEDICAL PRACTICE IN SOUTHERN CALIFORNIA.
WHAT ABOUT CHARITY, ZONKER?
HOW DOES YOUR FAMILY FEEL?
WHAT'S THE TAX BITE?
HEY, HEY, YOU NETWORK BOYS HAVE BEEN HOGGING ALL THE QUESTIONS. LET'S LET THE SUPERMARKET MEDIA GET IN A FEW, OKAY?
ZONKER, ABOUT YOUR LOVE-CHILD WITH MRS. GORBACHEV..
ZONKER, WILL YOU BE SLAYING MOM, CO-ED, SELF?
GB Trudeau

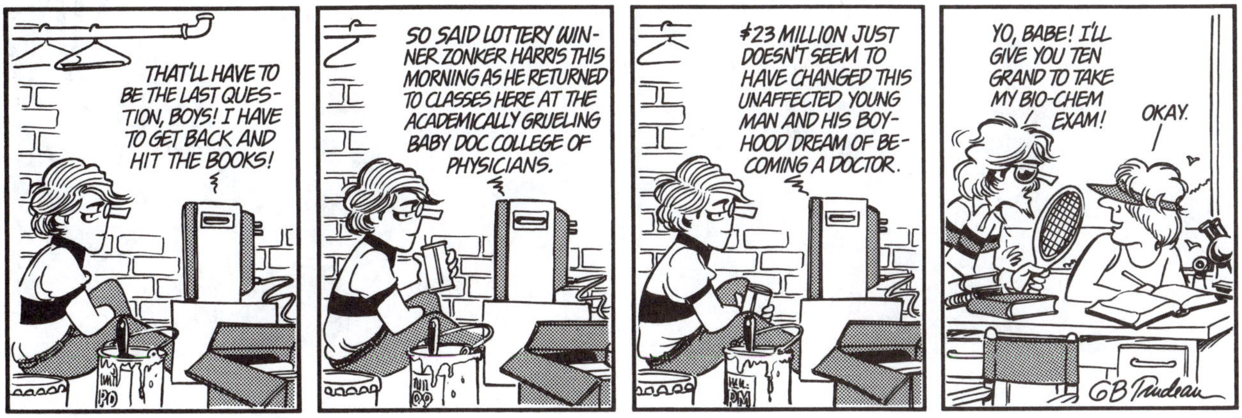
THAT'LL HAVE TO BE THE LAST QUESTION, BOYS! I HAVE TO GET BACK AND HIT THE BOOKS!
SO SAID LOTTERY WINNER ZONKER HARRIS THIS MORNING AS HE RETURNED TO CLASSES HERE AT THE ACADEMICALLY GRUELING BABY DOC COLLEGE OF PHYSICIANS.
$23 MILLION JUST DOESN'T SEEM TO HAVE CHANGED THIS UNAFFECTED YOUNG MAN AND HIS BOYHOOD DREAM OF BECOMING A DOCTOR.
YO, BABE! I'LL GIVE YOU TEN GRAND TO TAKE MY BIO-CHEM EXAM!
OKAY.
GB Trudeau

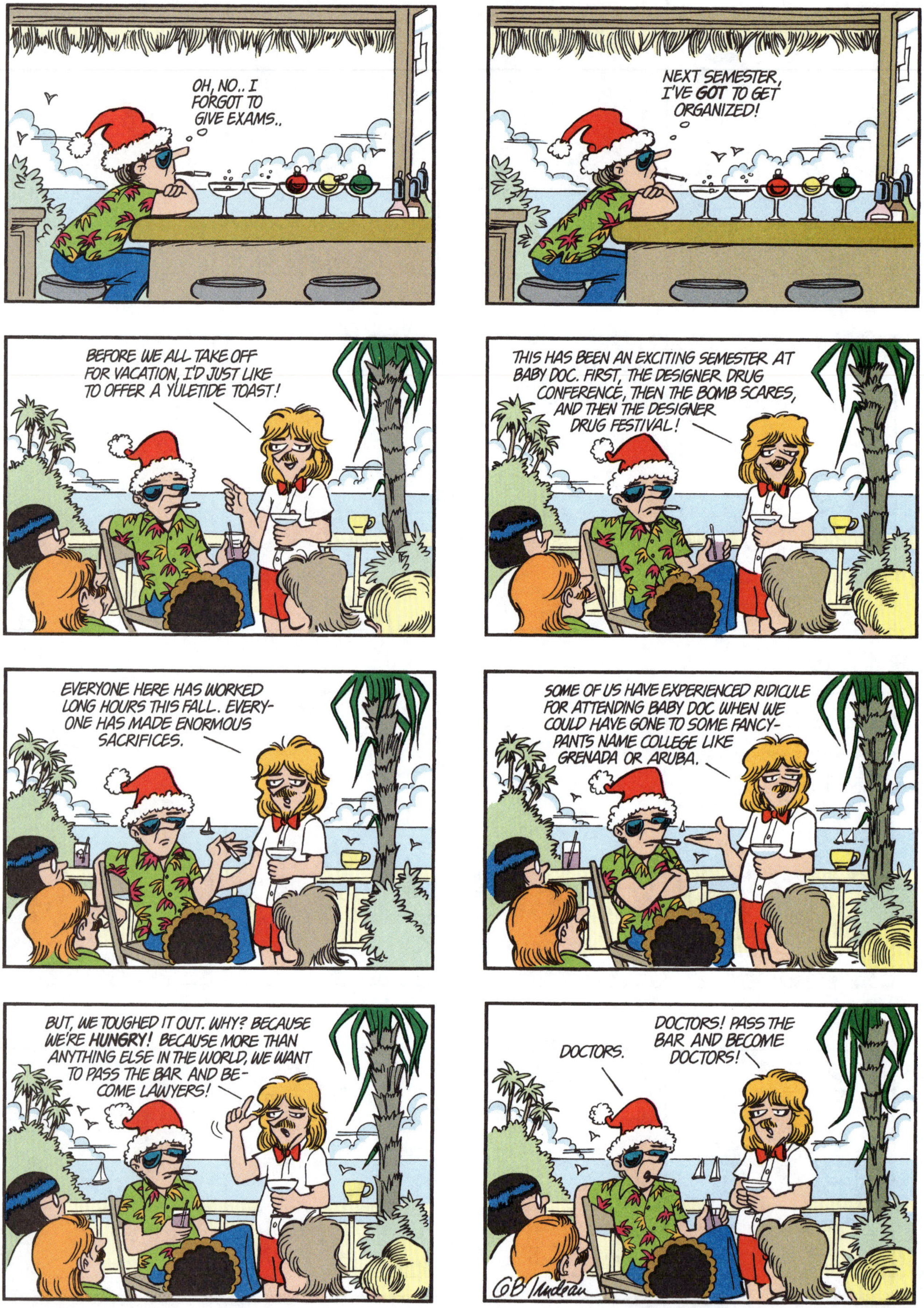
OH, NO.. I FORGOT TO GIVE EXAMS..
NEXT SEMESTER, I'VE GOT TO GET ORGANIZED!
BEFORE WE ALL TAKE OFF FOR VACATION, I'D JUST LIKE TO OFFER A YULETIDE TOAST!
THIS HAS BEEN AN EXCITING SEMESTER AT BABY DOC. FIRST, THE DESIGNER DRUG CONFERENCE, THEN THE BOMB SCARES, AND THEN THE DESIGNER DRUG FESTIVAL!
EVERYONE HERE HAS WORKED LONG HOURS THIS FALL. EVERY-ONE HAS MADE ENORMOUS SACRIFICES.
SOME OF US HAVE EXPERIENCED RIDICULE FOR ATTENDING BABY DOC WHEN WE COULD HAVE GONE TO SOME FANCY-PANTS NAME COLLEGE LIKE GRENADA OR ARUBA.
BUT, WE TOUGHED IT OUT. WHY? BECAUSE WE'RE HUNGRY! BECAUSE MORE THAN ANYTHING ELSE IN THE WORLD, WE WANT TO PASS THE BAR AND BE-COME LAWYERS!
DOCTORS.
DOCTORS! PASS THE BAR AND BECOME DOCTORS!
©B Trudeau

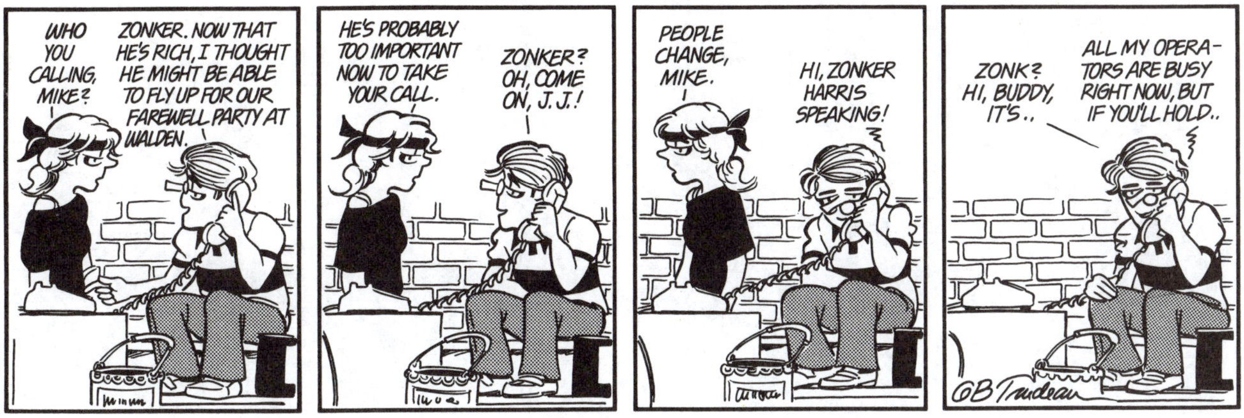
WHO YOU CALLING, MIKE?
ZONKER. NOW THAT HE'S RICH, I THOUGHT HE MIGHT BE ABLE TO FLY UP FOR OUR FAREWELL PARTY AT WALDEN.
HE'S PROBABLY TOO IMPORTANT NOW TO TAKE YOUR CALL.
ZONKER? OH, COME ON, J.J.!
PEOPLE CHANGE, MIKE.
HI, ZONKER HARRIS SPEAKING!
ZONK? HI, BUDDY, IT'S..
ALL MY OPERATORS ARE BUSY RIGHT NOW, BUT IF YOU'LL HOLD..
GB Trudeau

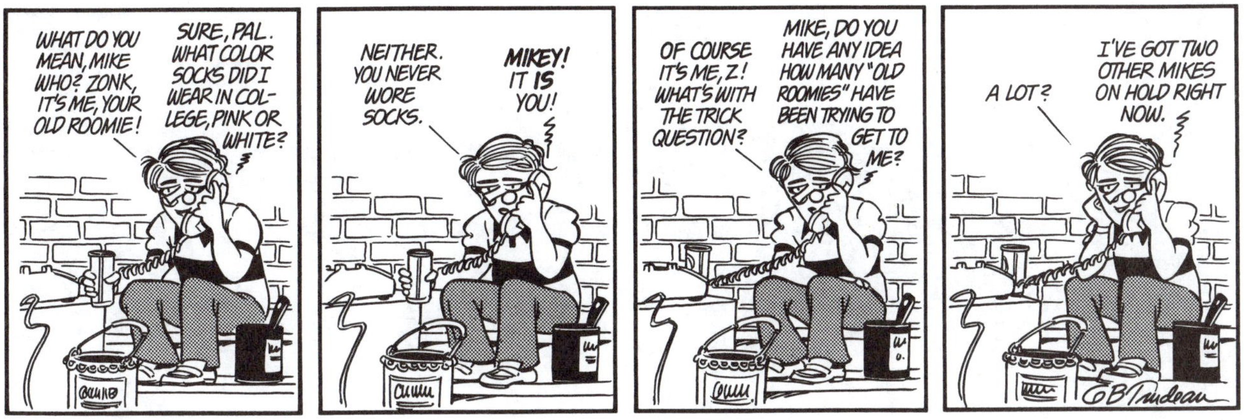
WHAT DO YOU MEAN, MIKE WHO? ZONK, IT'S ME, YOUR OLD ROOMIE!
SURE, PAL. WHAT COLOR SOCKS DID I WEAR IN COLLEGE, PINK OR WHITE?
NEITHER. YOU NEVER WORE SOCKS.
MIKEY! IT IS YOU!
OF COURSE IT'S ME, Z! WHAT'S WITH THE TRICK QUESTION?
MIKE, DO YOU HAVE ANY IDEA HOW MANY "OLD ROOMIES" HAVE BEEN TRYING TO GET TO ME?
A LOT?
I'VE GOT TWO OTHER MIKES ON HOLD RIGHT NOW.
GB Trudeau

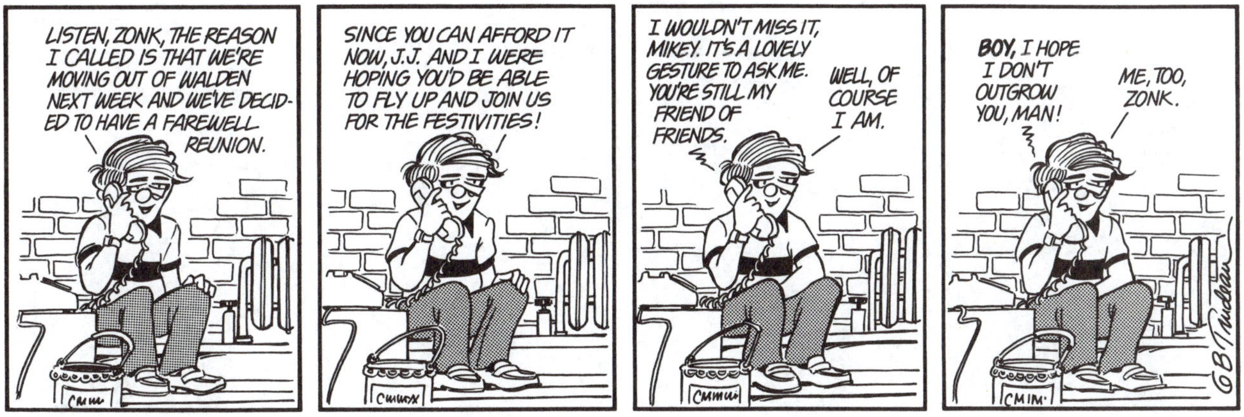
LISTEN, ZONK, THE REASON I CALLED IS THAT WE'RE MOVING OUT OF WALDEN NEXT WEEK AND WE'VE DECIDED TO HAVE A FAREWELL REUNION.
SINCE YOU CAN AFFORD IT NOW, J.J. AND I WERE HOPING YOU'D BE ABLE TO FLY UP AND JOIN US FOR THE FESTIVITIES!
I WOULDN'T MISS IT, MIKEY. IT'S A LOVELY GESTURE TO ASK ME. YOU'RE STILL MY FRIEND OF FRIENDS.
WELL, OF COURSE I AM.
BOY, I HOPE I DON'T OUTGROW YOU, MAN!
ME, TOO, ZONK.
GB Trudeau

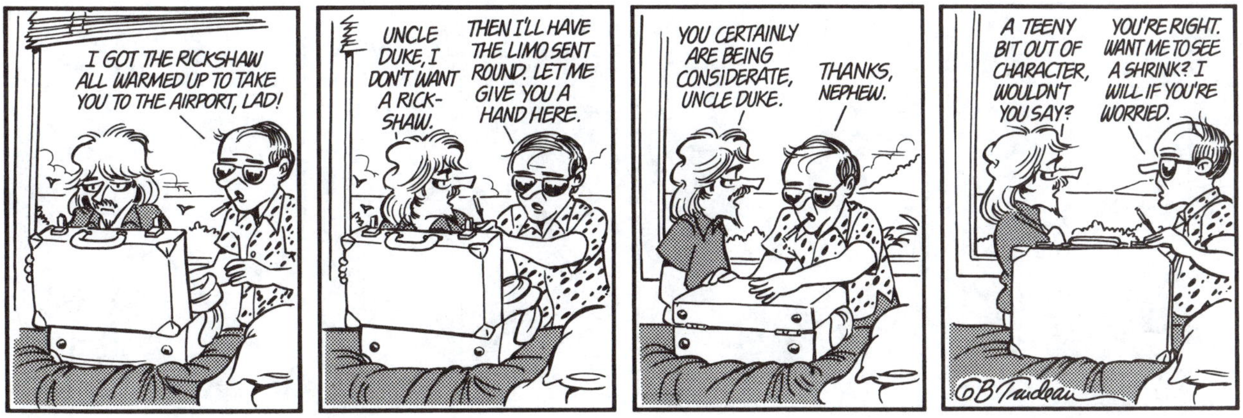
I GOT THE RICKSHAW ALL WARMED UP TO TAKE YOU TO THE AIRPORT, LAD!
UNCLE DUKE, I DON'T WANT A RICKSHAW.
THEN I'LL HAVE THE LIMO SENT ROUND. LET ME GIVE YOU A HAND HERE.
YOU CERTAINLY ARE BEING CONSIDERATE, UNCLE DUKE.
THANKS, NEPHEW.
A TEENY BIT OUT OF CHARACTER, WOULDN'T YOU SAY?
YOU'RE RIGHT. WANT ME TO SEE A SHRINK? I WILL IF YOU'RE WORRIED.
GB Trudeau

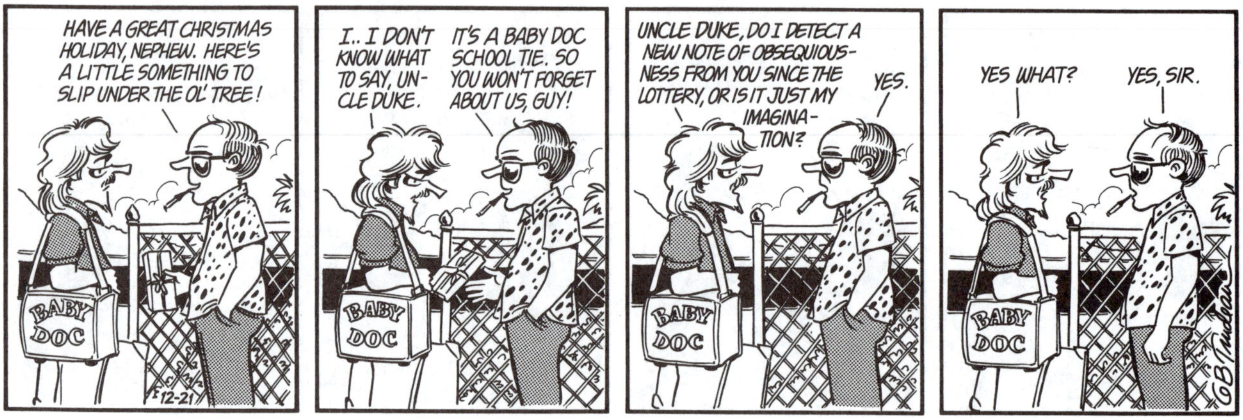
HAVE A GREAT CHRISTMAS HOLIDAY, NEPHEW. HERE'S A LITTLE SOMETHING TO SLIP UNDER THE OL' TREE!
BABY DOC
12-21
I.. I DON'T KNOW WHAT TO SAY, UNCLE DUKE.
IT'S A BABY DOC SCHOOL TIE. SO YOU WON'T FORGET ABOUT US, GUY!
UNCLE DUKE, DO I DETECT A NEW NOTE OF OBSEQUIOUSNESS FROM YOU SINCE THE LOTTERY, OR IS IT JUST MY IMAGINATION?
YES.
YES WHAT?
YES, SIR.

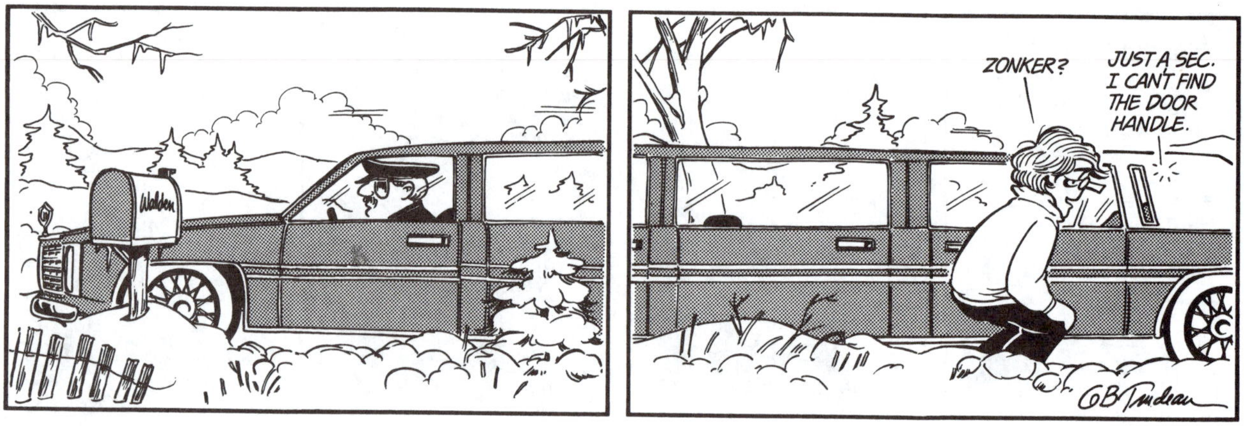
Walden
ZONKER?
JUST A SEC. I CAN'T FIND THE DOOR HANDLE.

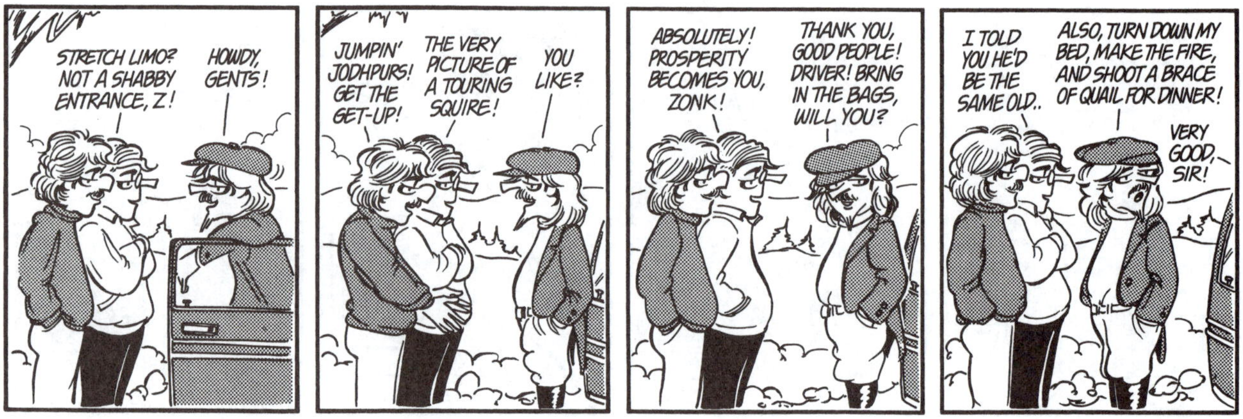
STRETCH LIMO? NOT A SHABBY ENTRANCE, Z!
HOWDY, GENTS!
JUMPIN' JODHPURS! GET THE GET-UP!
THE VERY PICTURE OF A TOURING SQUIRE!
YOU LIKE?
ABSOLUTELY! PROSPERITY BECOMES YOU, ZONK!
THANK YOU, GOOD PEOPLE! DRIVER! BRING IN THE BAGS, WILL YOU?
I TOLD YOU HE'D BE THE SAME OLD..
ALSO, TURN DOWN MY BED, MAKE THE FIRE, AND SHOOT A BRACE OF QUAIL FOR DINNER!
VERY GOOD, SIR!

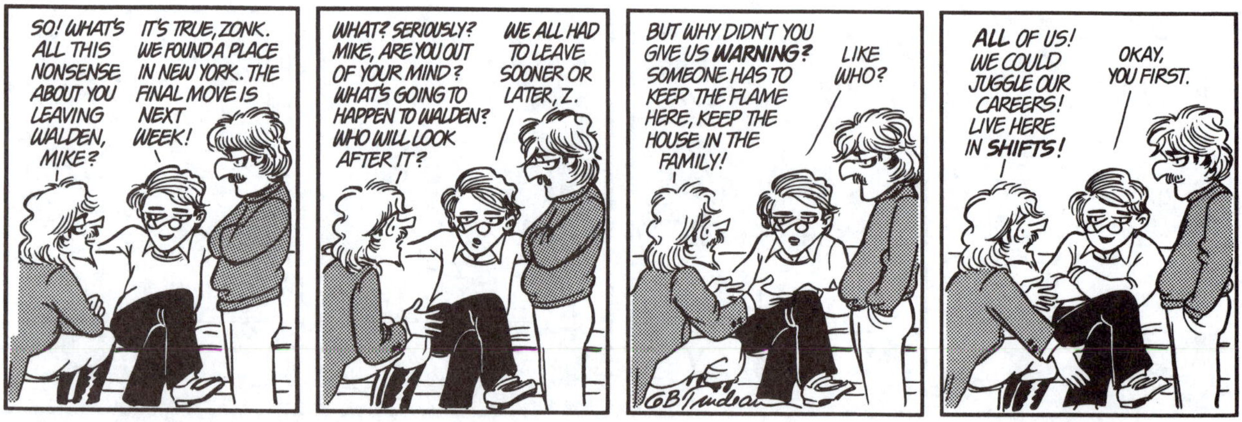
SO! WHAT'S ALL THIS NONSENSE ABOUT YOU LEAVING WALDEN, MIKE?
IT'S TRUE, ZONK. WE FOUND A PLACE IN NEW YORK. THE FINAL MOVE IS NEXT WEEK!
WHAT? SERIOUSLY? MIKE, ARE YOU OUT OF YOUR MIND? WHAT'S GOING TO HAPPEN TO WALDEN? WHO WILL LOOK AFTER IT?
WE ALL HAD TO LEAVE SOONER OR LATER, Z.
BUT WHY DIDN'T YOU GIVE US WARNING? SOMEONE HAS TO KEEP THE FLAME HERE, KEEP THE HOUSE IN THE FAMILY!
LIKE WHO?
ALL OF US! WE COULD JUGGLE OUR CAREERS! LIVE HERE IN SHIFTS!
OKAY, YOU FIRST.

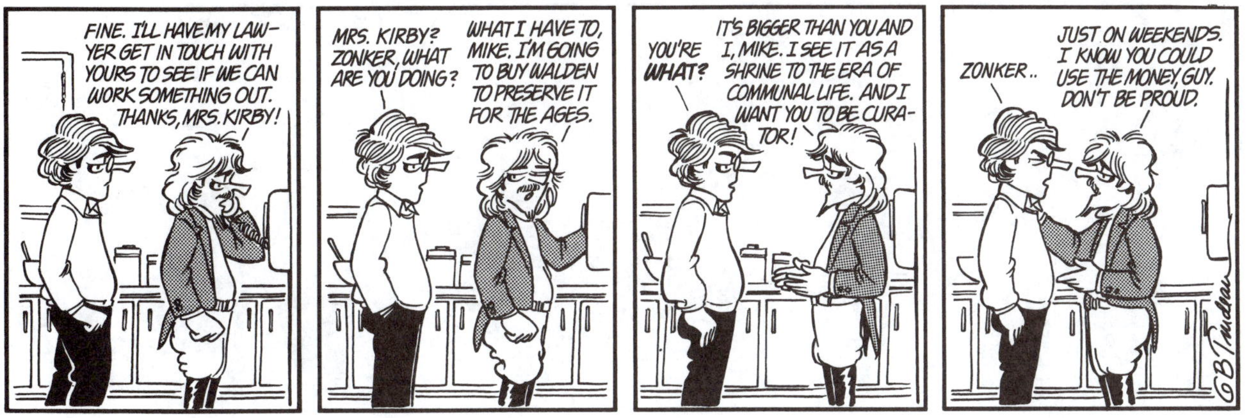
FINE. I'LL HAVE MY LAWYER GET IN TOUCH WITH YOURS TO SEE IF WE CAN WORK SOMETHING OUT. THANKS, MRS. KIRBY!
MRS. KIRBY? ZONKER, WHAT ARE YOU DOING?
WHAT I HAVE TO, MIKE. I'M GOING TO BUY WALDEN TO PRESERVE IT FOR THE AGES.
YOU'RE **WHAT?**
IT'S BIGGER THAN YOU AND I, MIKE. I SEE IT AS A SHRINE TO THE ERA OF COMMUNAL LIFE. AND I WANT YOU TO BE CURATOR!
ZONKER..
JUST ON WEEKENDS. I KNOW YOU COULD USE THE MONEY, GUY. DON'T BE PROUD.
GB Trudeau

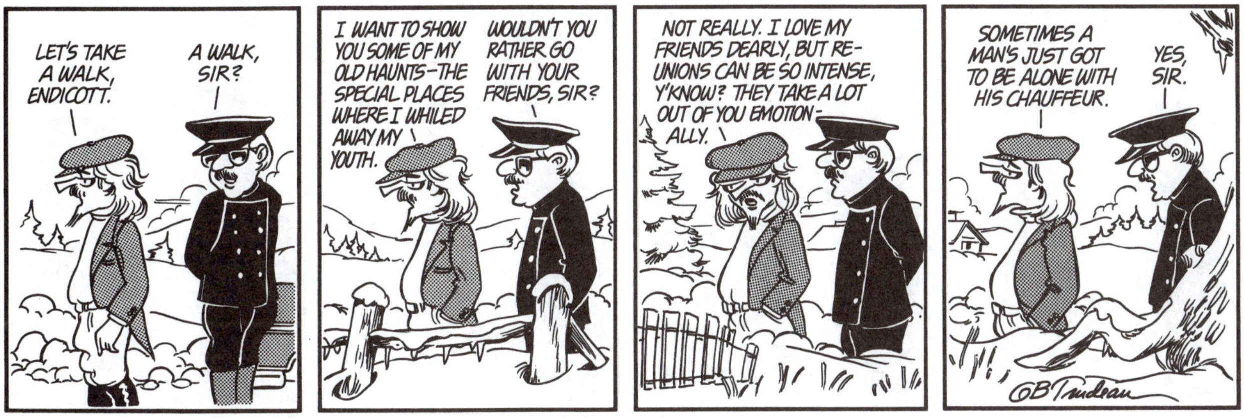
LET'S TAKE A WALK, ENDICOTT.
A WALK, SIR?
I WANT TO SHOW YOU SOME OF MY OLD HAUNTS—THE SPECIAL PLACES WHERE I WHILED AWAY MY YOUTH.
WOULDN'T YOU RATHER GO WITH YOUR FRIENDS, SIR?
NOT REALLY. I LOVE MY FRIENDS DEARLY, BUT REUNIONS CAN BE SO INTENSE, Y'KNOW? THEY TAKE A LOT OUT OF YOU EMOTIONALLY.
SOMETIMES A MAN'S JUST GOT TO BE ALONE WITH HIS CHAUFFEUR.
YES, SIR.
GB Trudeau

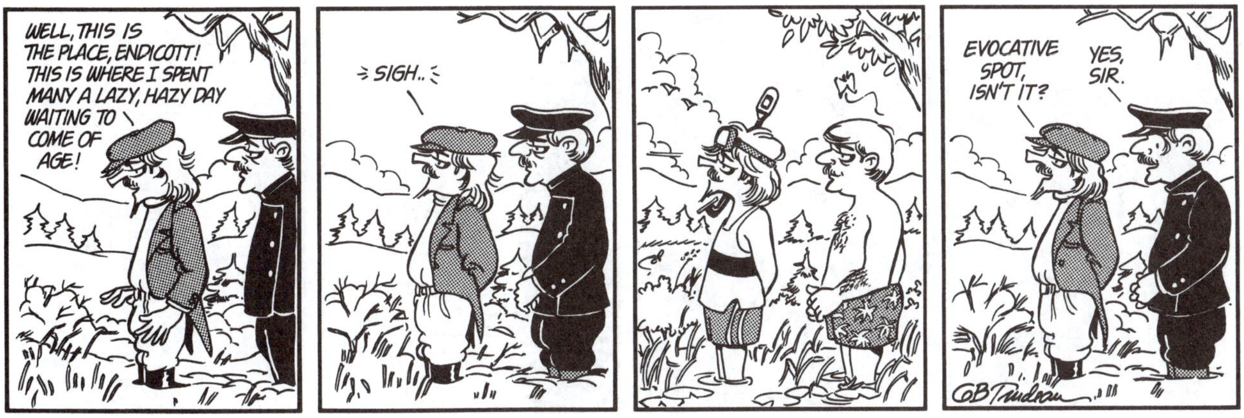
WELL, THIS IS THE PLACE, ENDICOTT! THIS IS WHERE I SPENT MANY A LAZY, HAZY DAY WAITING TO COME OF AGE!
SIGH..
EVOCATIVE SPOT, ISN'T IT?
YES, SIR.
GB Trudeau

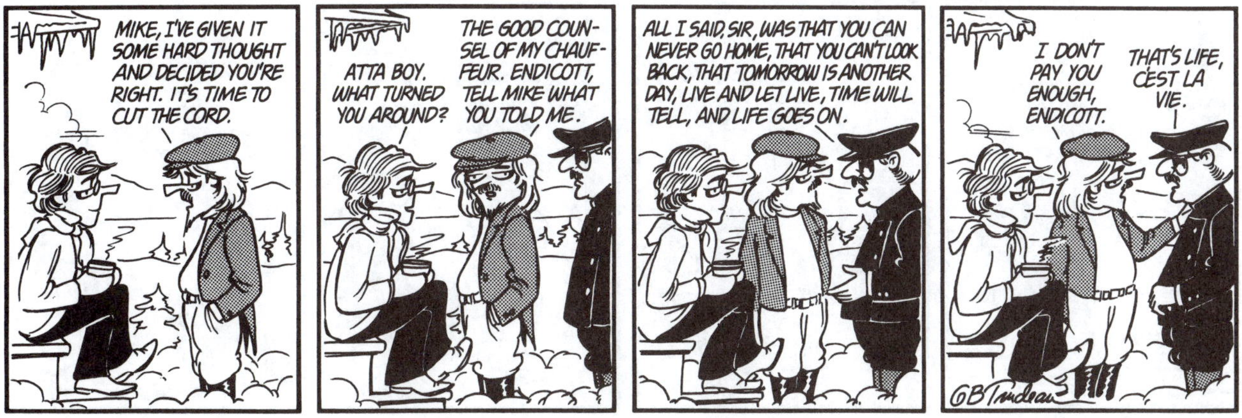
MIKE, I'VE GIVEN IT SOME HARD THOUGHT AND DECIDED YOU'RE RIGHT. IT'S TIME TO CUT THE CORD.
ATTA BOY. WHAT TURNED YOU AROUND?
THE GOOD COUNSEL OF MY CHAUFFEUR. ENDICOTT, TELL MIKE WHAT YOU TOLD ME.
ALL I SAID, SIR, WAS THAT YOU CAN NEVER GO HOME, THAT YOU CAN'T LOOK BACK, THAT TOMORROW IS ANOTHER DAY, LIVE AND LET LIVE, TIME WILL TELL, AND LIFE GOES ON.
I DON'T PAY YOU ENOUGH, ENDICOTT.
THAT'S LIFE, C'EST LA VIE.
GB Trudeau

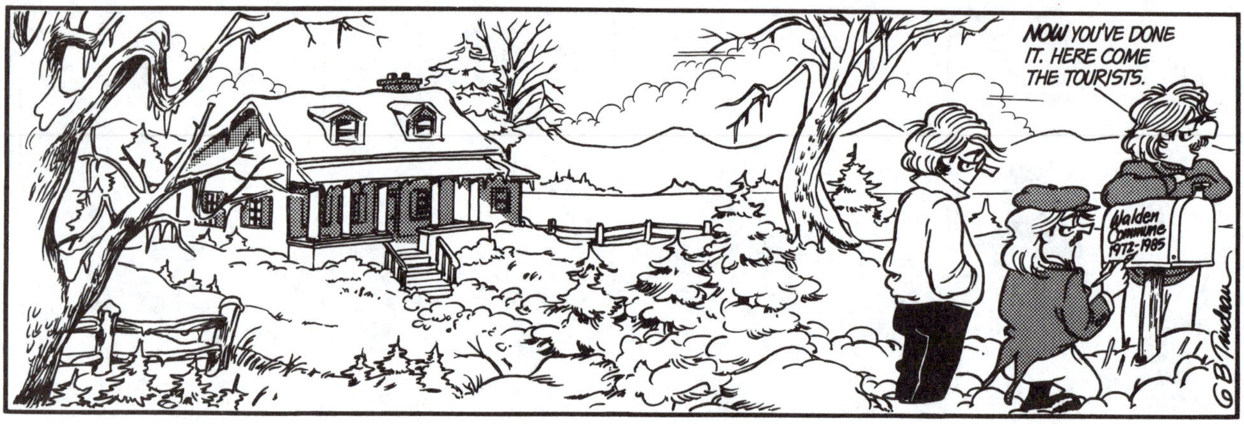
NOW YOU'VE DONE IT. HERE COME THE TOURISTS.
Walden Commune 1972-1985
GB Trudeau

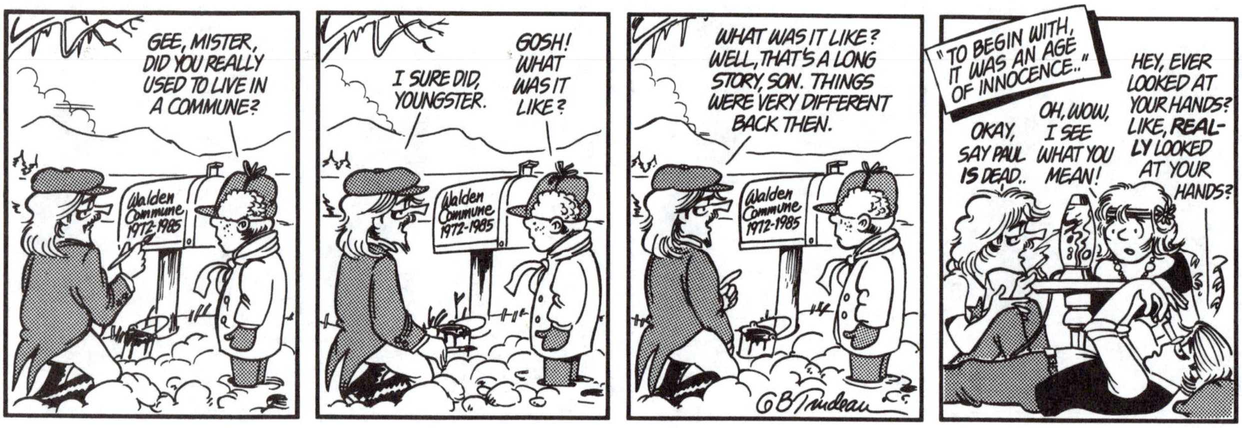
GEE, MISTER, DID YOU REALLY USED TO LIVE IN A COMMUNE?
Walden Commune 1972-1985
I SURE DID, YOUNGSTER.
GOSH! WHAT WAS IT LIKE?
WHAT WAS IT LIKE? WELL, THAT'S A LONG STORY, SON. THINGS WERE VERY DIFFERENT BACK THEN.
GB Trudeau
"TO BEGIN WITH, IT WAS AN AGE OF INNOCENCE.."
OKAY, SAY PAUL IS DEAD..
OH, WOW, I SEE WHAT YOU MEAN!
HEY, EVER LOOKED AT YOUR HANDS? LIKE, REALLY LOOKED AT YOUR HANDS?

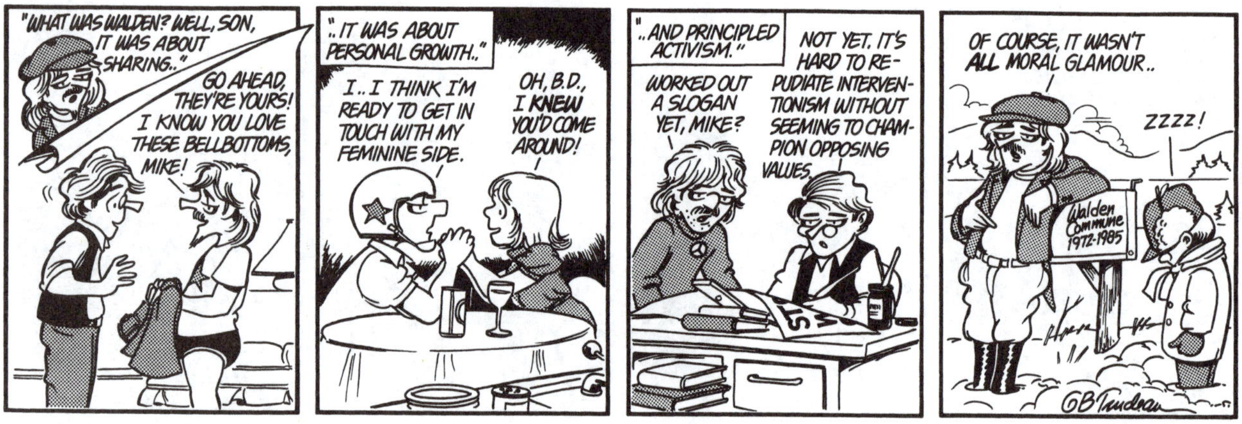
"WHAT WAS WALDEN? WELL, SON, IT WAS ABOUT SHARING.."
GO AHEAD, THEY'RE YOURS! I KNOW YOU LOVE THESE BELLBOTTOMS, MIKE!
"..IT WAS ABOUT PERSONAL GROWTH.."
I.. I THINK I'M READY TO GET IN TOUCH WITH MY FEMININE SIDE.
OH, B.D., I KNEW YOU'D COME AROUND!
"..AND PRINCIPLED ACTIVISM."
WORKED OUT A SLOGAN YET, MIKE?
NOT YET. IT'S HARD TO REPUDIATE INTERVENTIONISM WITHOUT SEEMING TO CHAMPION OPPOSING VALUES.
OF COURSE, IT WASN'T ALL MORAL GLAMOUR..
ZZZZ!
Walden Commune 1972-1985
GB Trudeau

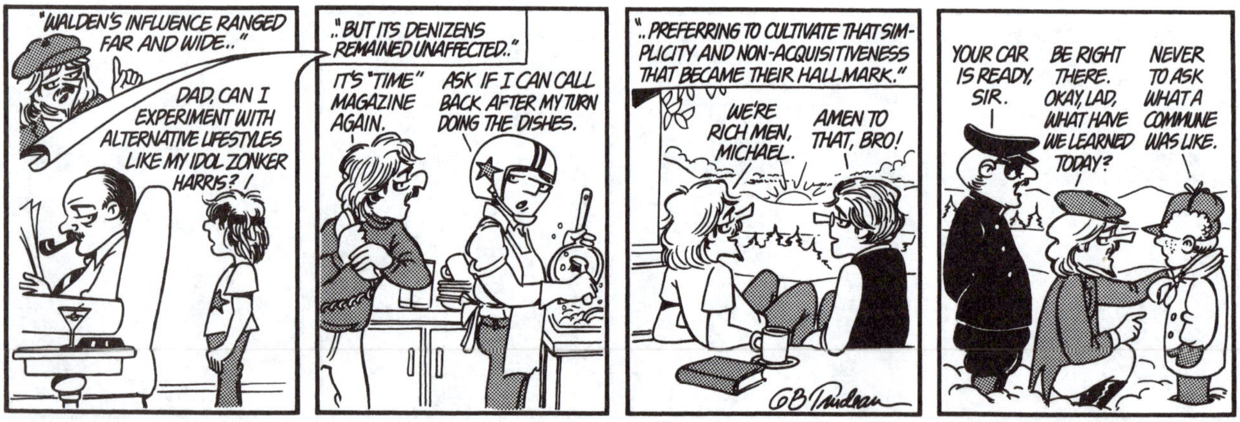
"WALDEN'S INFLUENCE RANGED FAR AND WIDE.."
DAD, CAN I EXPERIMENT WITH ALTERNATIVE LIFESTYLES LIKE MY IDOL ZONKER HARRIS?!
"..BUT ITS DENIZENS REMAINED UNAFFECTED.."
IT'S "TIME" MAGAZINE AGAIN.
ASK IF I CAN CALL BACK AFTER MY TURN DOING THE DISHES.
"..PREFERRING TO CULTIVATE THAT SIMPLICITY AND NON-ACQUISITIVENESS THAT BECAME THEIR HALLMARK."
WE'RE RICH MEN, MICHAEL.
AMEN TO THAT, BRO!
GB Trudeau
YOUR CAR IS READY, SIR.
BE RIGHT THERE. OKAY, LAD, WHAT HAVE WE LEARNED TODAY?
NEVER TO ASK WHAT A COMMUNE WAS LIKE.

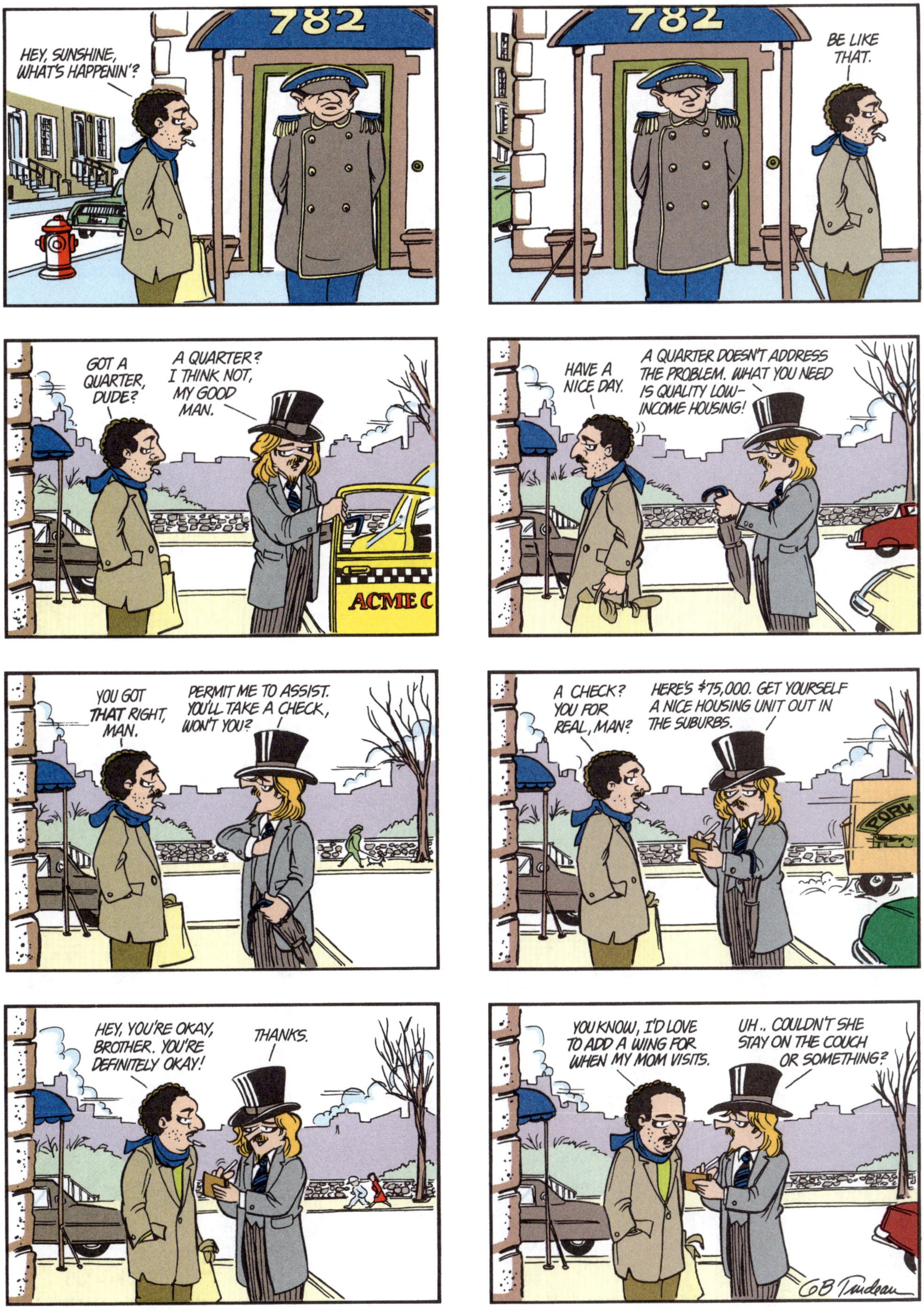
782
HEY, SUNSHINE, WHAT'S HAPPENIN'?
782
BE LIKE THAT.
GOT A QUARTER, DUDE?
A QUARTER? I THINK NOT, MY GOOD MAN.
ACME C
HAVE A NICE DAY.
A QUARTER DOESN'T ADDRESS THE PROBLEM. WHAT YOU NEED IS QUALITY LOW-INCOME HOUSING!
YOU GOT THAT RIGHT, MAN.
PERMIT ME TO ASSIST. YOU'LL TAKE A CHECK, WON'T YOU?
A CHECK? YOU FOR REAL, MAN?
HERE'S $75,000. GET YOURSELF A NICE HOUSING UNIT OUT IN THE SUBURBS.
HEY, YOU'RE OKAY, BROTHER. YOU'RE DEFINITELY OKAY!
THANKS.
YOU KNOW, I'D LOVE TO ADD A WING FOR WHEN MY MOM VISITS.
UH.. COULDN'T SHE STAY ON THE COUCH OR SOMETHING?
GB Trudeau

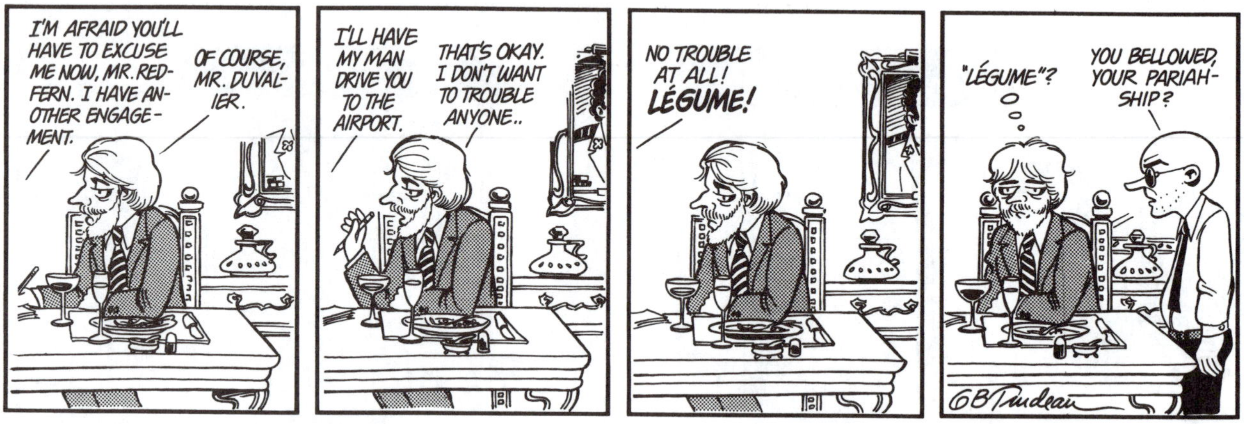
I'M AFRAID YOU'LL HAVE TO EXCUSE ME NOW, MR. REDFERN. I HAVE ANOTHER ENGAGEMENT.
OF COURSE, MR. DUVALIER.
I'LL HAVE MY MAN DRIVE YOU TO THE AIRPORT.
THAT'S OKAY. I DON'T WANT TO TROUBLE ANYONE..
NO TROUBLE AT ALL! **LÉGUME!**
"LÉGUME"?
YOU BELLOWED, YOUR PARIAHSHIP?
GBTrudeau

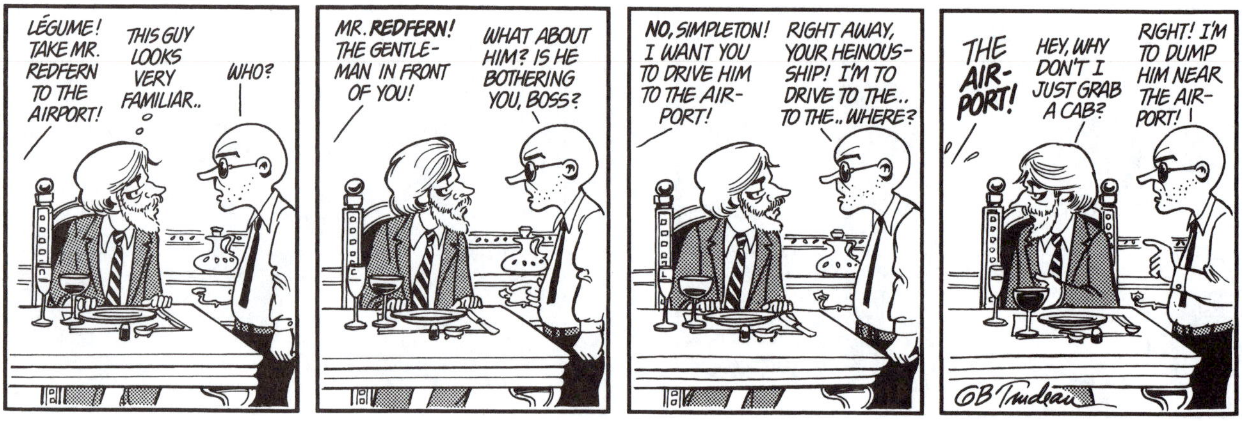
LÉGUME! TAKE MR. REDFERN TO THE AIRPORT!
THIS GUY LOOKS VERY FAMILIAR..
WHO?
MR. **REDFERN!** THE GENTLEMAN IN FRONT OF YOU!
WHAT ABOUT HIM? IS HE BOTHERING YOU, BOSS?
NO, SIMPLETON! I WANT YOU TO DRIVE HIM TO THE AIRPORT!
RIGHT AWAY, YOUR HEINOUSSHIP! I'M TO DRIVE TO THE.. TO THE.. WHERE?
THE **AIRPORT!**
HEY, WHY DON'T I JUST GRAB A CAB?
RIGHT! I'M TO DUMP HIM NEAR THE AIRPORT!
GBTrudeau

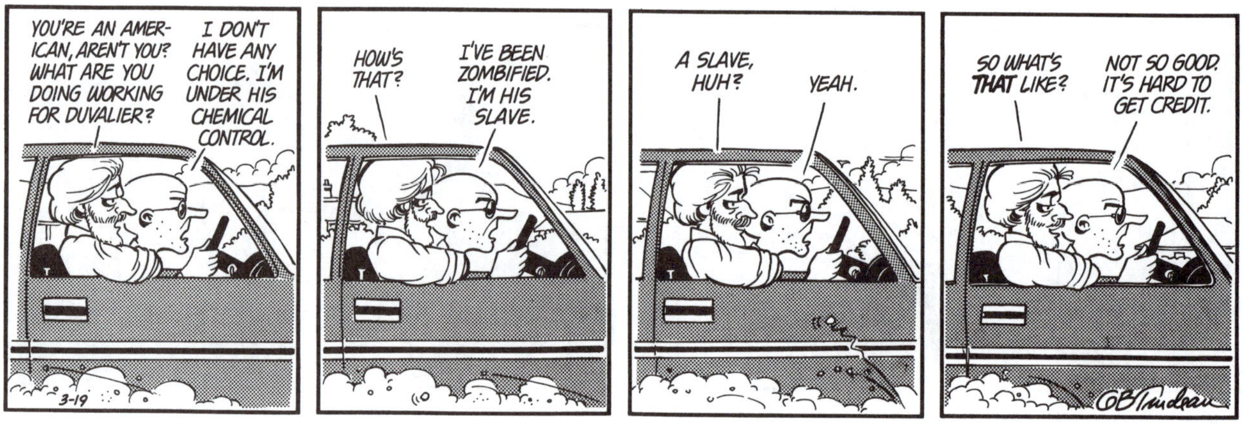
YOU'RE AN AMERICAN, AREN'T YOU? WHAT ARE YOU DOING WORKING FOR DUVALIER?
I DON'T HAVE ANY CHOICE. I'M UNDER HIS CHEMICAL CONTROL.
3-19
HOW'S THAT?
I'VE BEEN ZOMBIFIED. I'M HIS SLAVE.
A SLAVE, HUH?
YEAH.
SO WHAT'S **THAT** LIKE?
NOT SO GOOD. IT'S HARD TO GET CREDIT.
GBTrudeau

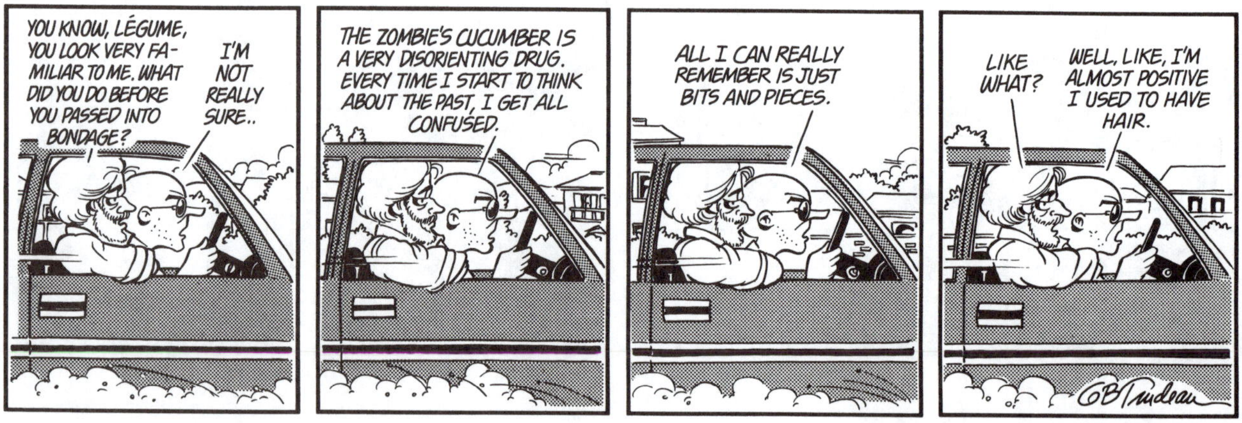
YOU KNOW, LÉGUME, YOU LOOK VERY FAMILIAR TO ME. WHAT DID YOU DO BEFORE YOU PASSED INTO BONDAGE?
I'M NOT REALLY SURE..
THE ZOMBIE'S CUCUMBER IS A VERY DISORIENTING DRUG. EVERY TIME I START TO THINK ABOUT THE PAST, I GET ALL CONFUSED.
ALL I CAN REALLY REMEMBER IS JUST BITS AND PIECES.
LIKE WHAT?
WELL, LIKE, I'M ALMOST POSITIVE I USED TO HAVE HAIR.
GBTrudeau

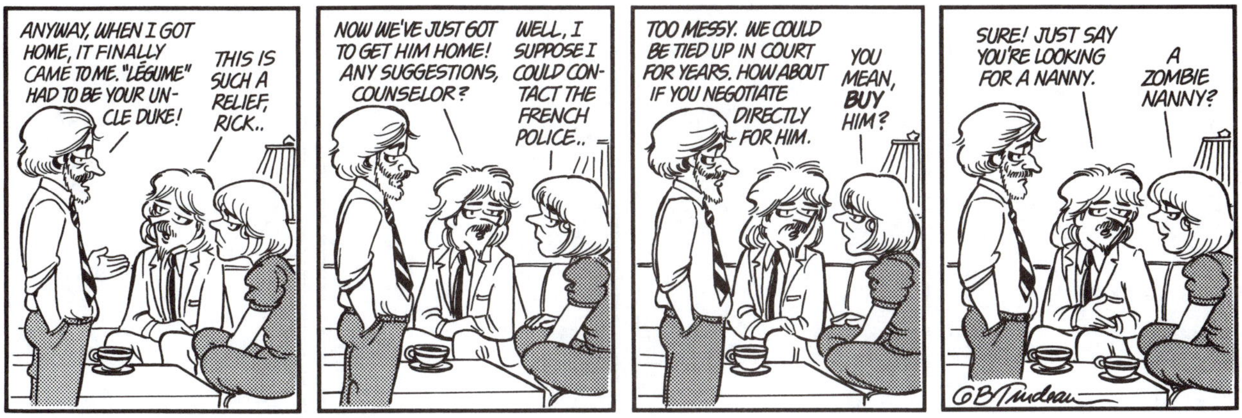
ANYWAY, WHEN I GOT HOME, IT FINALLY CAME TO ME. "LÉGUME" HAD TO BE YOUR UNCLE DUKE!
THIS IS SUCH A RELIEF, RICK..
NOW WE'VE JUST GOT TO GET HIM HOME! ANY SUGGESTIONS, COUNSELOR?
WELL, I SUPPOSE I COULD CONTACT THE FRENCH POLICE..
TOO MESSY. WE COULD BE TIED UP IN COURT FOR YEARS. HOW ABOUT IF YOU NEGOTIATE DIRECTLY FOR HIM.
YOU MEAN, BUY HIM?
SURE! JUST SAY YOU'RE LOOKING FOR A NANNY.
A ZOMBIE NANNY?
GBTrudeau

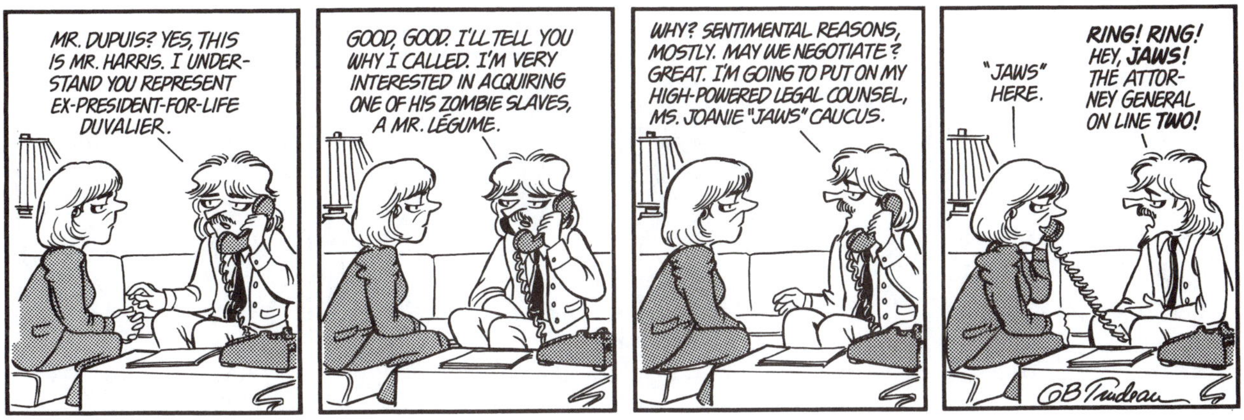
MR. DUPUIS? YES, THIS IS MR. HARRIS. I UNDERSTAND YOU REPRESENT EX-PRESIDENT-FOR-LIFE DUVALIER.
GOOD, GOOD. I'LL TELL YOU WHY I CALLED. I'M VERY INTERESTED IN ACQUIRING ONE OF HIS ZOMBIE SLAVES, A MR. LÉGUME.
WHY? SENTIMENTAL REASONS, MOSTLY. MAY WE NEGOTIATE? GREAT. I'M GOING TO PUT ON MY HIGH-POWERED LEGAL COUNSEL, MS. JOANIE "JAWS" CAUCUS.
"JAWS" HERE.
RING! RING! HEY, JAWS! THE ATTORNEY GENERAL ON LINE TWO!
GBTrudeau

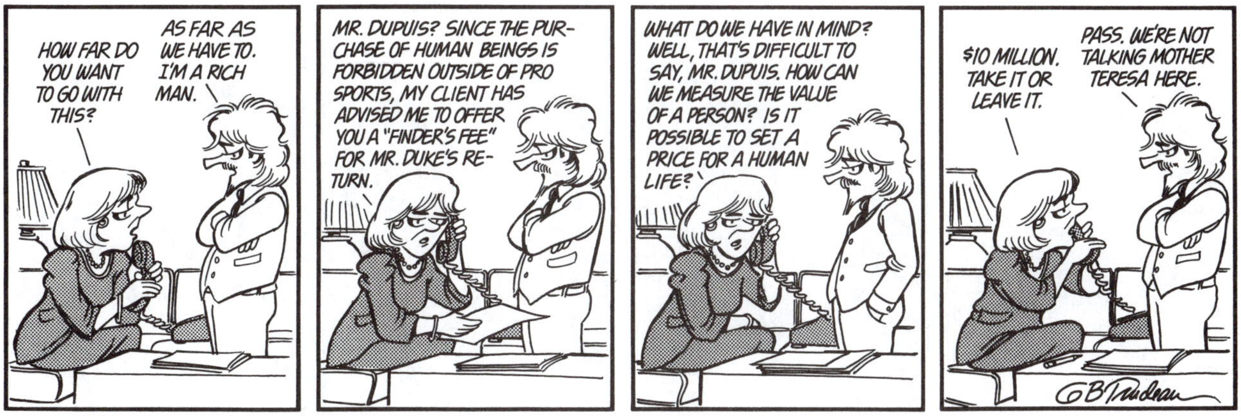
HOW FAR DO YOU WANT TO GO WITH THIS?
AS FAR AS WE HAVE TO. I'M A RICH MAN.
MR. DUPUIS? SINCE THE PURCHASE OF HUMAN BEINGS IS FORBIDDEN OUTSIDE OF PRO SPORTS, MY CLIENT HAS ADVISED ME TO OFFER YOU A "FINDER'S FEE" FOR MR. DUKE'S RETURN.
WHAT DO WE HAVE IN MIND? WELL, THAT'S DIFFICULT TO SAY, MR. DUPUIS. HOW CAN WE MEASURE THE VALUE OF A PERSON? IS IT POSSIBLE TO SET A PRICE FOR A HUMAN LIFE?
$10 MILLION. TAKE IT OR LEAVE IT.
PASS. WE'RE NOT TALKING MOTHER TERESA HERE.
GBTrudeau

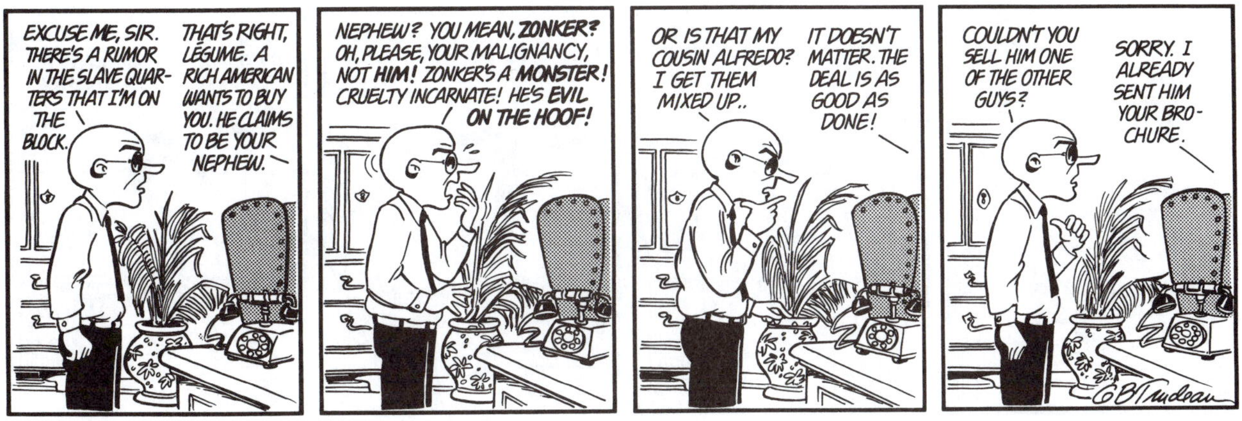
EXCUSE ME, SIR. THERE'S A RUMOR IN THE SLAVE QUARTERS THAT I'M ON THE BLOCK.
THAT'S RIGHT, LÉGUME. A RICH AMERICAN WANTS TO BUY YOU. HE CLAIMS TO BE YOUR NEPHEW.
NEPHEW? YOU MEAN, ZONKER? OH, PLEASE, YOUR MALIGNANCY, NOT HIM! ZONKER'S A MONSTER! CRUELTY INCARNATE! HE'S EVIL ON THE HOOF!
OR IS THAT MY COUSIN ALFREDO? I GET THEM MIXED UP..
IT DOESN'T MATTER. THE DEAL IS AS GOOD AS DONE!
COULDN'T YOU SELL HIM ONE OF THE OTHER GUYS?
SORRY. I ALREADY SENT HIM YOUR BROCHURE.
GBTrudeau

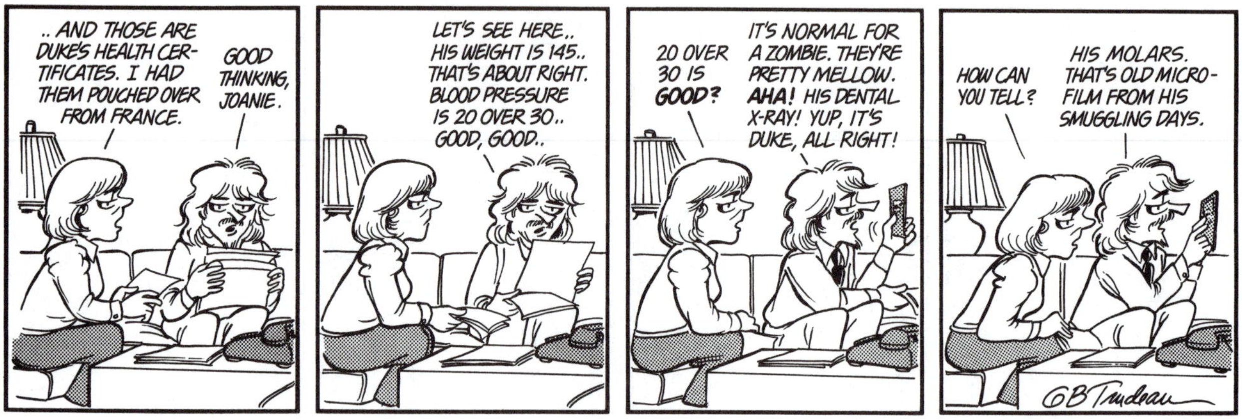
.. AND THOSE ARE DUKE'S HEALTH CERTIFICATES. I HAD THEM POUCHED OVER FROM FRANCE.
GOOD THINKING, JOANIE.
LET'S SEE HERE.. HIS WEIGHT IS 145.. THAT'S ABOUT RIGHT. BLOOD PRESSURE IS 20 OVER 30.. GOOD, GOOD..
20 OVER 30 IS GOOD?
IT'S NORMAL FOR A ZOMBIE. THEY'RE PRETTY MELLOW. AHA! HIS DENTAL X-RAY! YUP, IT'S DUKE, ALL RIGHT!
HOW CAN YOU TELL?
HIS MOLARS. THAT'S OLD MICROFILM FROM HIS SMUGGLING DAYS.
GB Trudeau

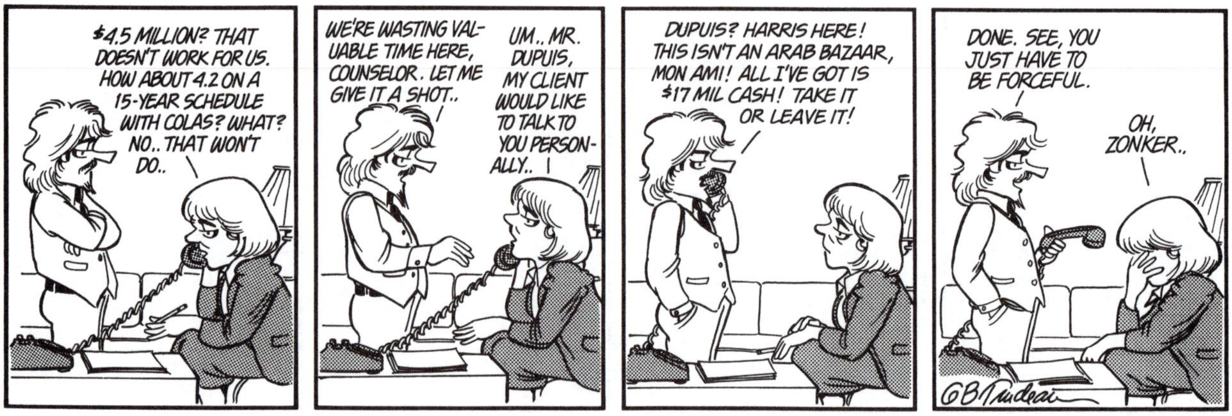
$4.5 MILLION? THAT DOESN'T WORK FOR US. HOW ABOUT 4.2 ON A 15-YEAR SCHEDULE WITH COLAS? WHAT? NO.. THAT WON'T DO..
WE'RE WASTING VALUABLE TIME HERE, COUNSELOR. LET ME GIVE IT A SHOT..
UM.. MR. DUPUIS, MY CLIENT WOULD LIKE TO TALK TO YOU PERSONALLY..
DUPUIS? HARRIS HERE! THIS ISN'T AN ARAB BAZAAR, MON AMI! ALL I'VE GOT IS $17 MIL CASH! TAKE IT OR LEAVE IT!
DONE. SEE, YOU JUST HAVE TO BE FORCEFUL.
OH, ZONKER..
GB Trudeau

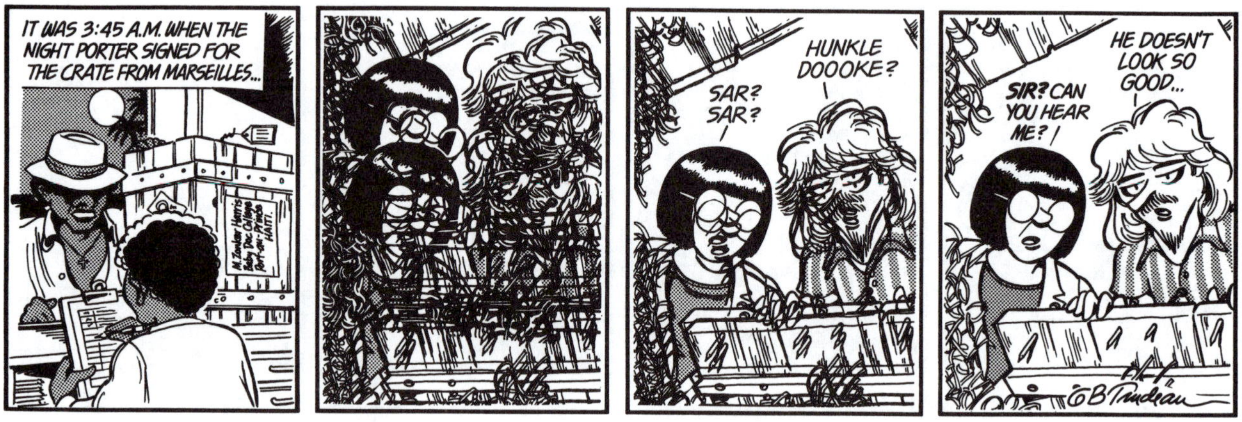
IT WAS 3:45 A.M. WHEN THE NIGHT PORTER SIGNED FOR THE CRATE FROM MARSEILLES...
SAR? SAR?
HUNKLE DOOOKE?
SIR? CAN YOU HEAR ME?
HE DOESN'T LOOK SO GOOD...
GB Trudeau

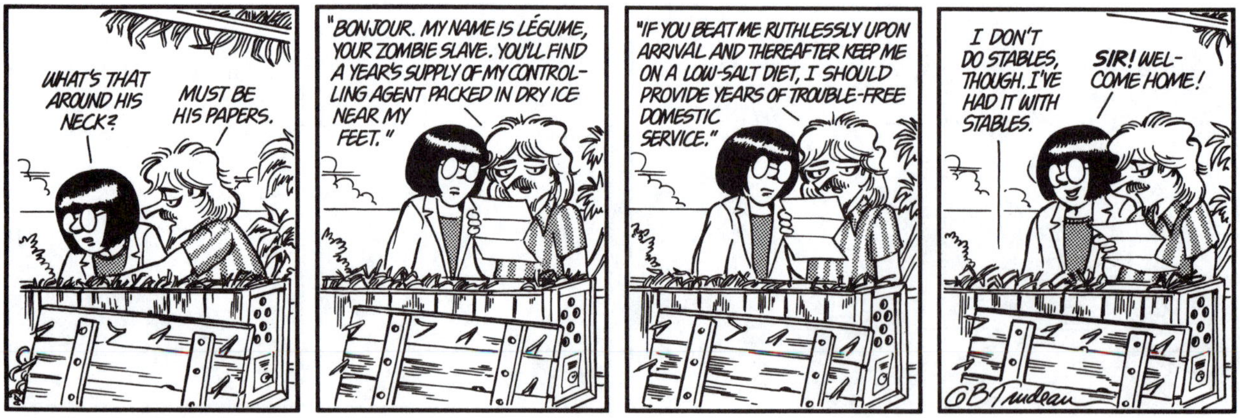
WHAT'S THAT AROUND HIS NECK?
MUST BE HIS PAPERS.
"BONJOUR. MY NAME IS LÉGUME, YOUR ZOMBIE SLAVE. YOU'LL FIND A YEAR'S SUPPLY OF MY CONTROLLING AGENT PACKED IN DRY ICE NEAR MY FEET."
"IF YOU BEAT ME RUTHLESSLY UPON ARRIVAL AND THEREAFTER KEEP ME ON A LOW-SALT DIET, I SHOULD PROVIDE YEARS OF TROUBLE-FREE DOMESTIC SERVICE."
I DON'T DO STABLES, THOUGH. I'VE HAD IT WITH STABLES.
SIR! WELCOME HOME!
GB Trudeau

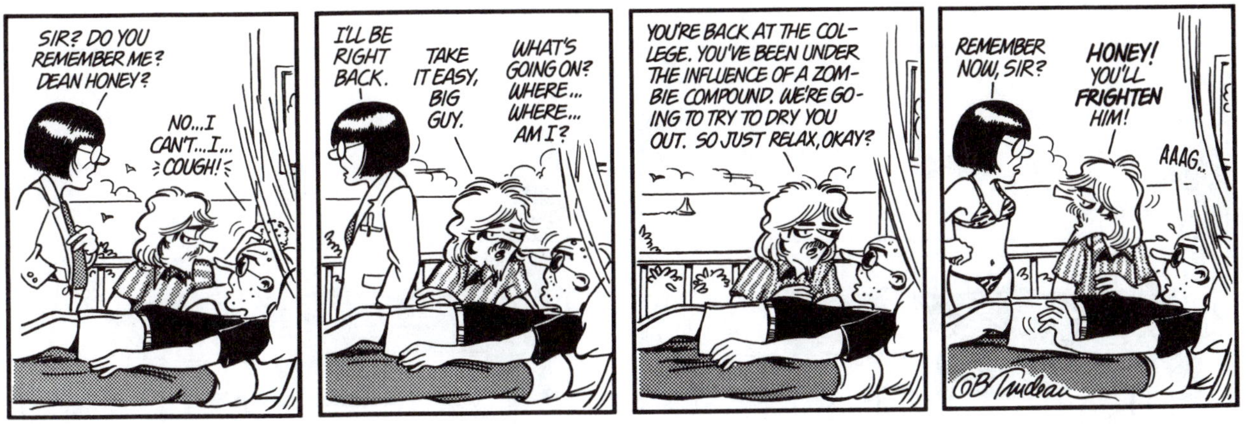
SIR? DO YOU REMEMBER ME? DEAN HONEY?
NO... I CAN'T... I... COUGH!
I'LL BE RIGHT BACK.
TAKE IT EASY, BIG GUY.
WHAT'S GOING ON? WHERE... WHERE... AM I?
YOU'RE BACK AT THE COLLEGE. YOU'VE BEEN UNDER THE INFLUENCE OF A ZOMBIE COMPOUND. WE'RE GOING TO TRY TO DRY YOU OUT. SO JUST RELAX, OKAY?
REMEMBER NOW, SIR?
HONEY! YOU'LL FRIGHTEN HIM!
AAAG..
G.B. Trudeau

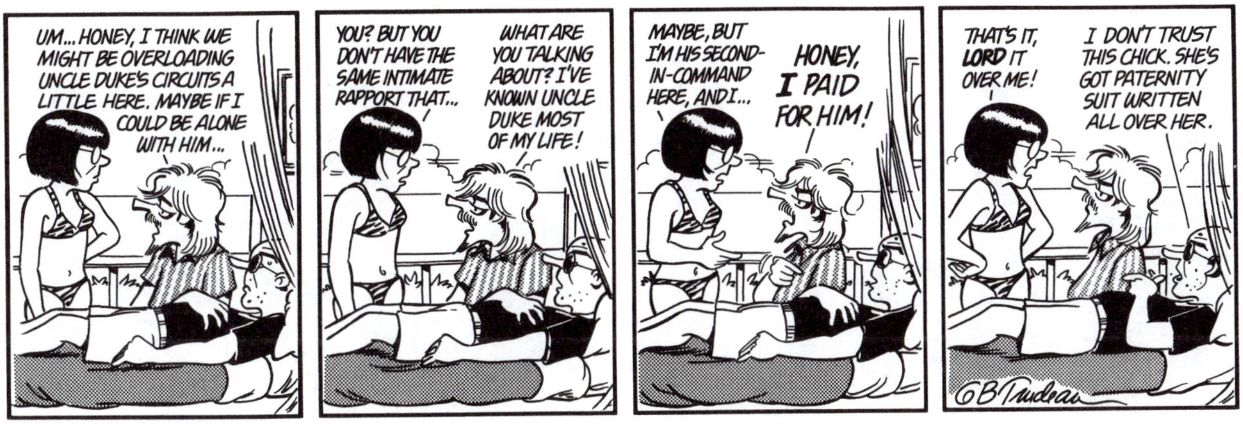
UM... HONEY, I THINK WE MIGHT BE OVERLOADING UNCLE DUKE'S CIRCUITS A LITTLE HERE. MAYBE IF I COULD BE ALONE WITH HIM...
YOU? BUT YOU DON'T HAVE THE SAME INTIMATE RAPPORT THAT...
WHAT ARE YOU TALKING ABOUT? I'VE KNOWN UNCLE DUKE MOST OF MY LIFE!
MAYBE, BUT I'M HIS SECOND-IN-COMMAND HERE, AND I...
HONEY, I PAID FOR HIM!
THAT'S IT, LORD IT OVER ME!
I DON'T TRUST THIS CHICK. SHE'S GOT PATERNITY SUIT WRITTEN ALL OVER HER.
G.B. Trudeau

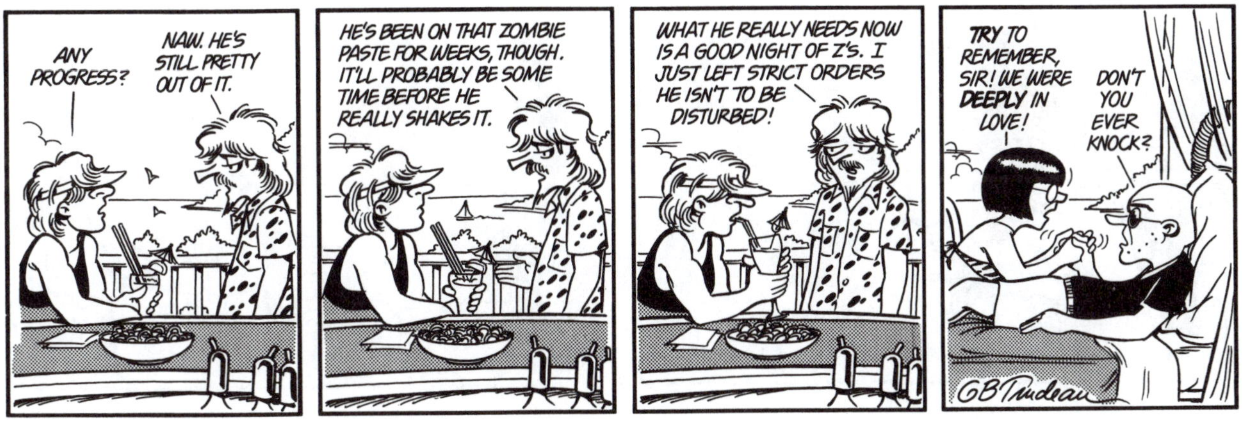
ANY PROGRESS?
NAW. HE'S STILL PRETTY OUT OF IT.
HE'S BEEN ON THAT ZOMBIE PASTE FOR WEEKS, THOUGH. IT'LL PROBABLY BE SOME TIME BEFORE HE REALLY SHAKES IT.
WHAT HE REALLY NEEDS NOW IS A GOOD NIGHT OF Z'S. I JUST LEFT STRICT ORDERS HE ISN'T TO BE DISTURBED!
TRY TO REMEMBER, SIR! WE WERE DEEPLY IN LOVE!
DON'T YOU EVER KNOCK?
G.B. Trudeau

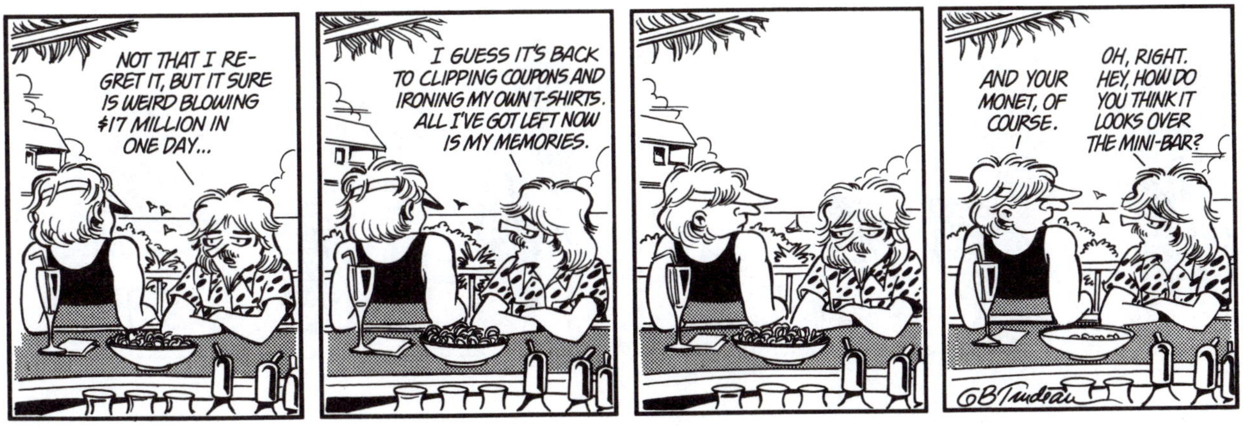
NOT THAT I REGRET IT, BUT IT SURE IS WEIRD BLOWING $17 MILLION IN ONE DAY...
I GUESS IT'S BACK TO CLIPPING COUPONS AND IRONING MY OWN T-SHIRTS. ALL I'VE GOT LEFT NOW IS MY MEMORIES.
AND YOUR MONET, OF COURSE.
OH, RIGHT. HEY, HOW DO YOU THINK IT LOOKS OVER THE MINI-BAR?
G.B. Trudeau

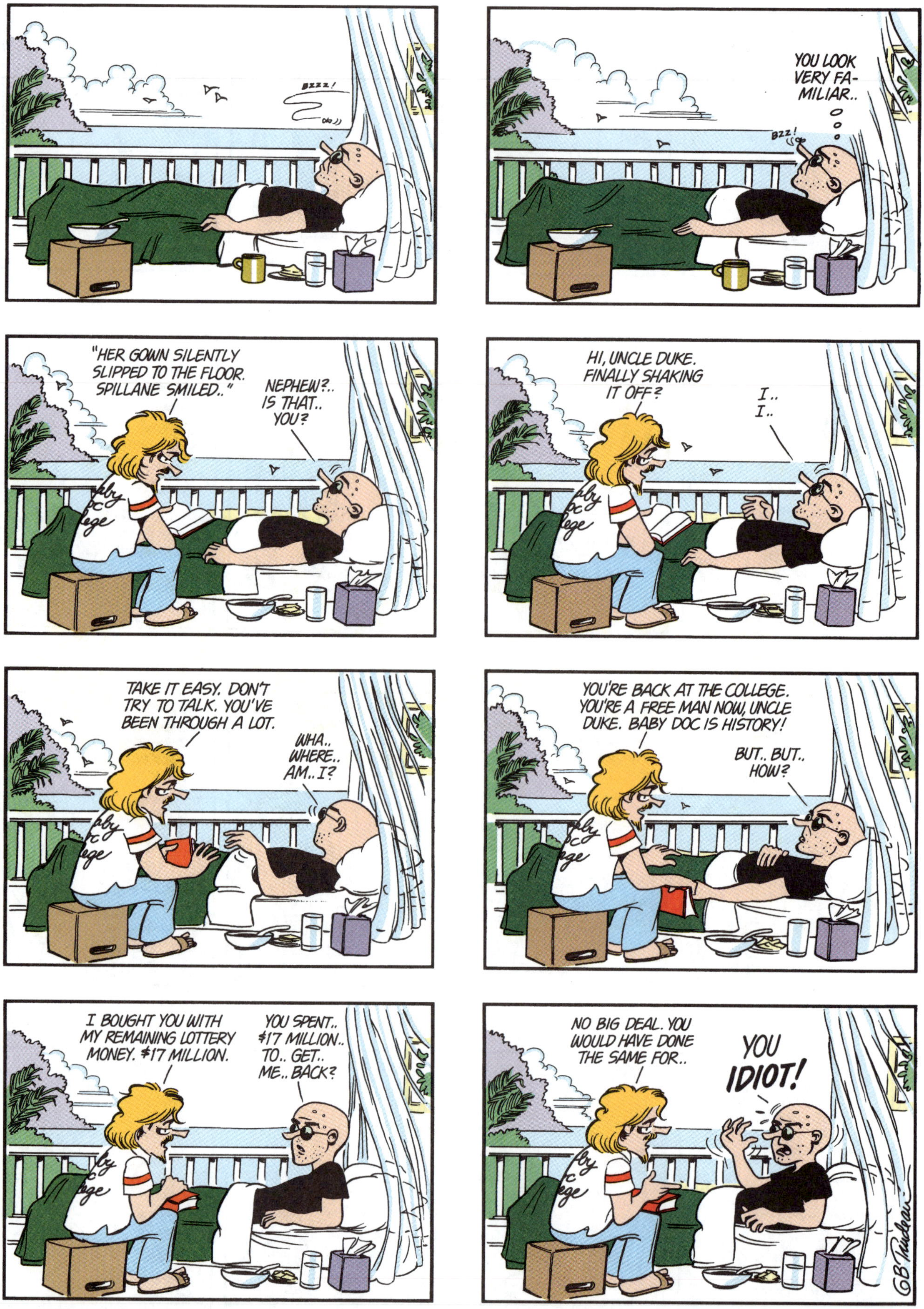
BZZZ!
YOU LOOK VERY FA-MILIAR..
BZZ!
"HER GOWN SILENTLY SLIPPED TO THE FLOOR. SPILLANE SMILED.."
NEPHEW?.. IS THAT.. YOU?
HI, UNCLE DUKE. FINALLY SHAKING IT OFF?
I.. I..
TAKE IT EASY. DON'T TRY TO TALK. YOU'VE BEEN THROUGH A LOT.
WHA.. WHERE.. AM.. I?
YOU'RE BACK AT THE COLLEGE. YOU'RE A FREE MAN NOW, UNCLE DUKE. BABY DOC IS HISTORY!
BUT.. BUT.. HOW?
I BOUGHT YOU WITH MY REMAINING LOTTERY MONEY. $17 MILLION.
YOU SPENT.. $17 MILLION.. TO.. GET.. ME.. BACK?
NO BIG DEAL. YOU WOULD HAVE DONE THE SAME FOR..
YOU IDIOT!
©B Trudeau

7

THE VISCOUNT

Post Haste Thither Anon

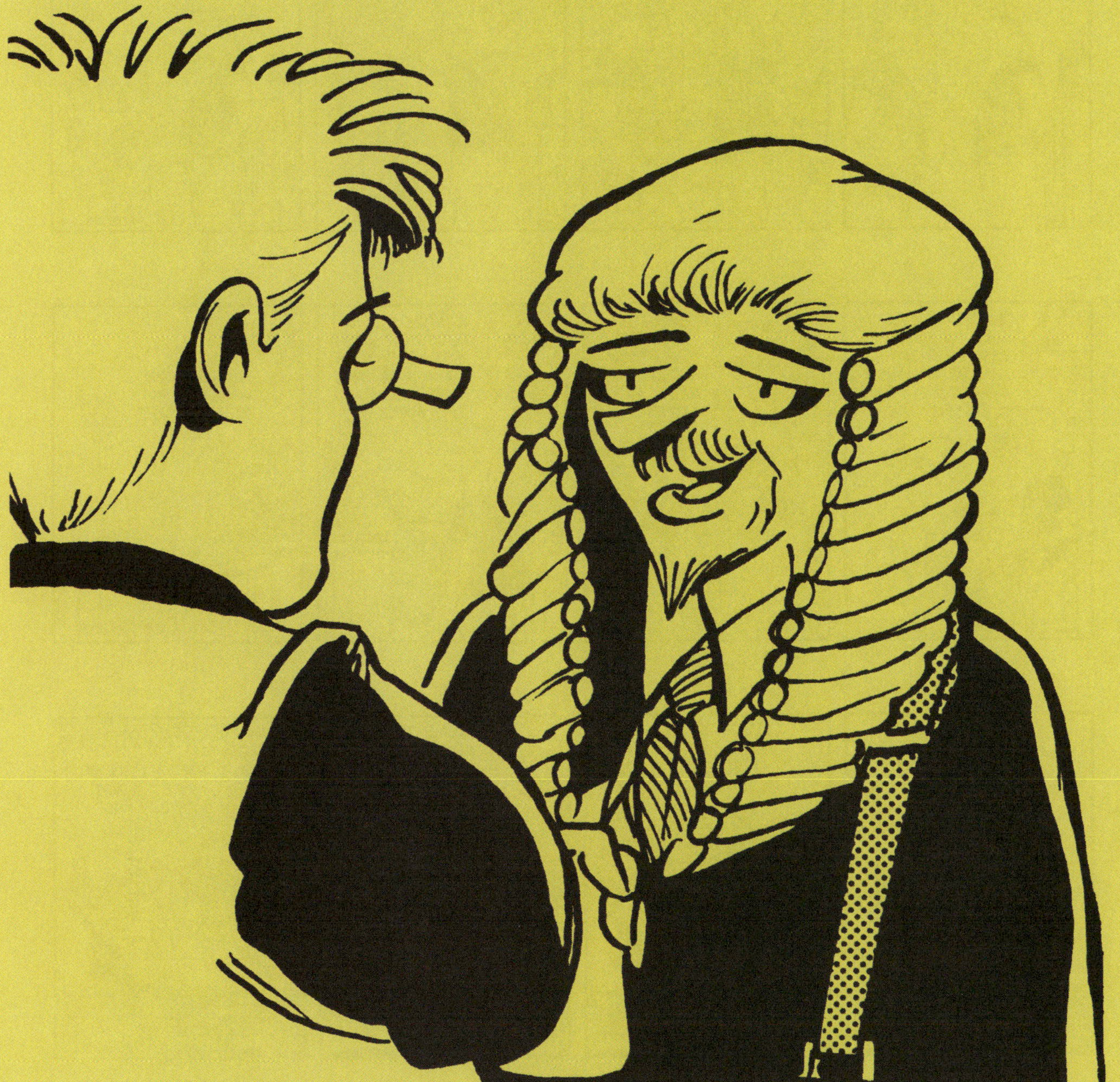

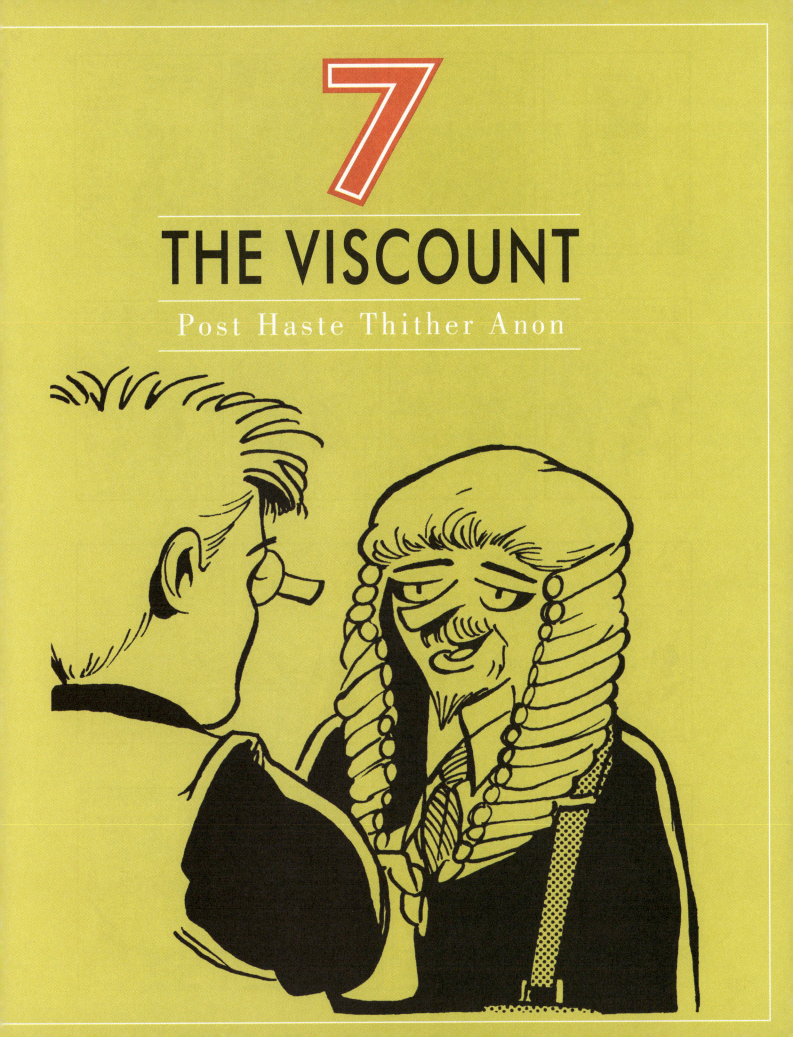

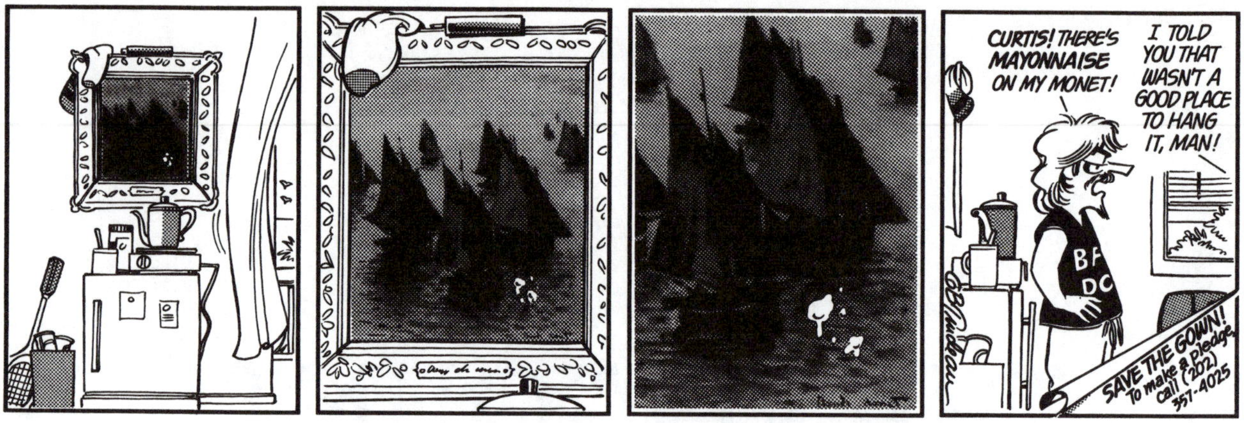
CURTIS! THERE'S MAYONNAISE ON MY MONET!
I TOLD YOU THAT WASN'T A GOOD PLACE TO HANG IT, MAN!
SAVE THE GOWN! To make a pledge, call (202) 357-4025

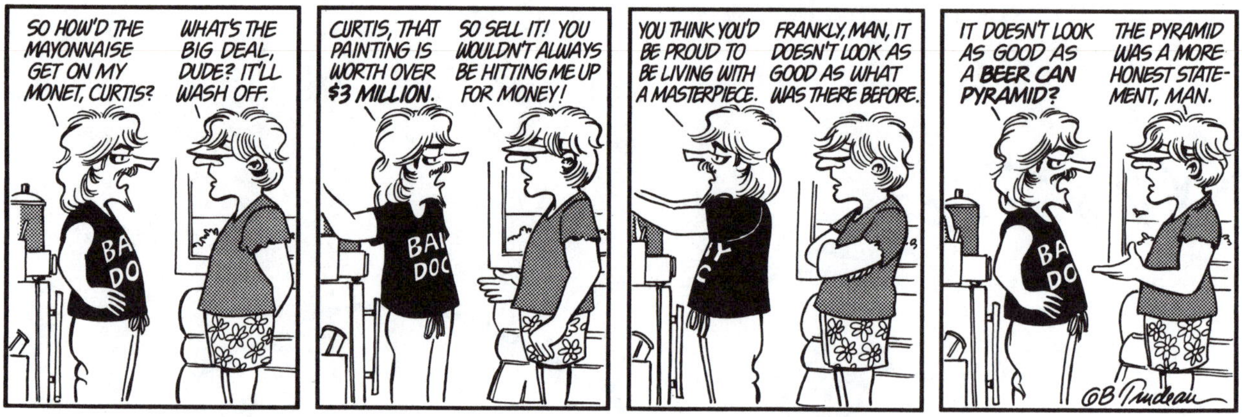
SO HOW'D THE MAYONNAISE GET ON MY MONET, CURTIS?
WHAT'S THE BIG DEAL, DUDE? IT'LL WASH OFF.
CURTIS, THAT PAINTING IS WORTH OVER $3 MILLION.
SO SELL IT! YOU WOULDN'T ALWAYS BE HITTING ME UP FOR MONEY!
YOU THINK YOU'D BE PROUD TO BE LIVING WITH A MASTERPIECE.
FRANKLY, MAN, IT DOESN'T LOOK AS GOOD AS WHAT WAS THERE BEFORE.
IT DOESN'T LOOK AS GOOD AS A BEER CAN PYRAMID?
THE PYRAMID WAS A MORE HONEST STATEMENT, MAN.

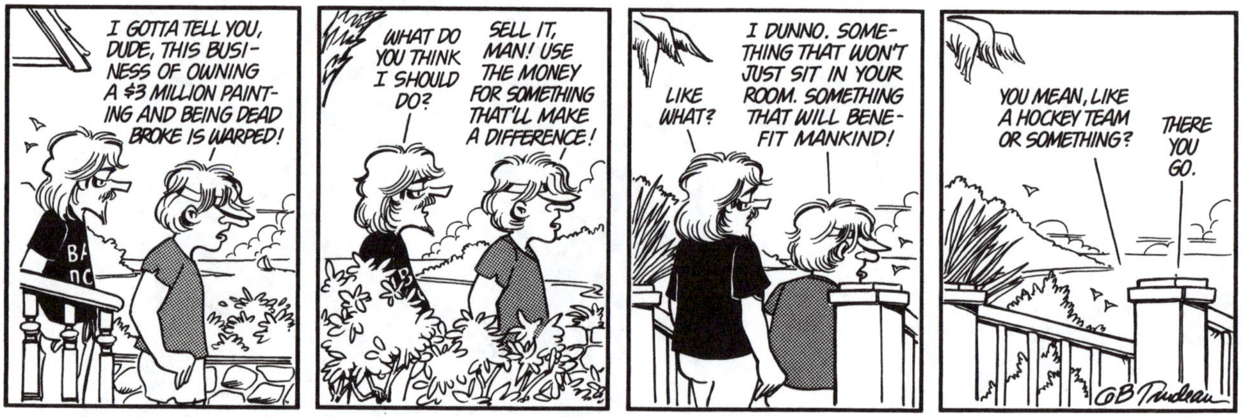
I GOTTA TELL YOU, DUDE, THIS BUSINESS OF OWNING A $3 MILLION PAINTING AND BEING DEAD BROKE IS WARPED!
WHAT DO YOU THINK I SHOULD DO?
SELL IT, MAN! USE THE MONEY FOR SOMETHING THAT'LL MAKE A DIFFERENCE!
LIKE WHAT?
I DUNNO. SOMETHING THAT WON'T JUST SIT IN YOUR ROOM. SOMETHING THAT WILL BENEFIT MANKIND!
YOU MEAN, LIKE A HOCKEY TEAM OR SOMETHING?
THERE YOU GO.

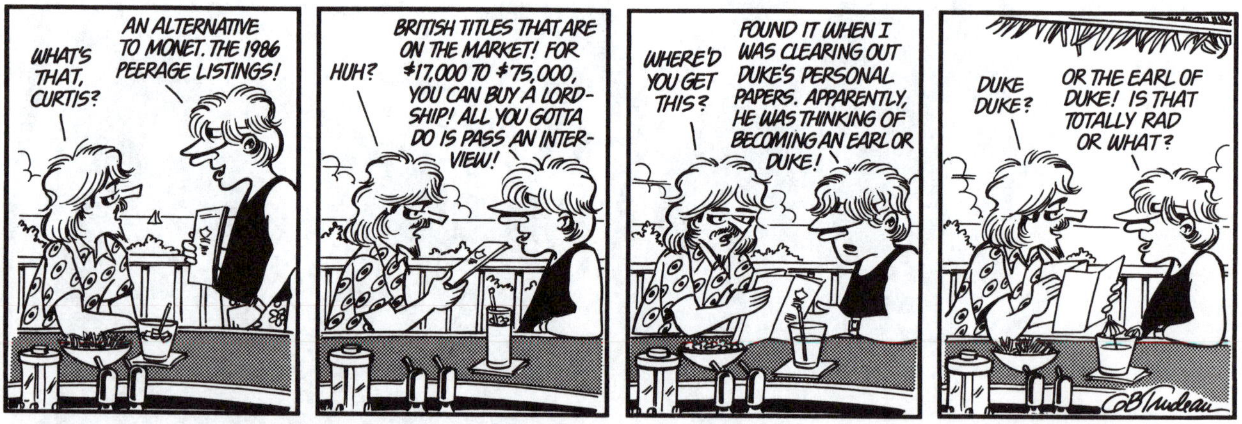
WHAT'S THAT, CURTIS?
AN ALTERNATIVE TO MONET. THE 1986 PEERAGE LISTINGS!
HUH?
BRITISH TITLES THAT ARE ON THE MARKET! FOR $17,000 TO $75,000, YOU CAN BUY A LORDSHIP! ALL YOU GOTTA DO IS PASS AN INTERVIEW!
WHERE'D YOU GET THIS?
FOUND IT WHEN I WAS CLEARING OUT DUKE'S PERSONAL PAPERS. APPARENTLY, HE WAS THINKING OF BECOMING AN EARL OR DUKE!
DUKE DUKE?
OR THE EARL OF DUKE! IS THAT TOTALLY RAD OR WHAT?

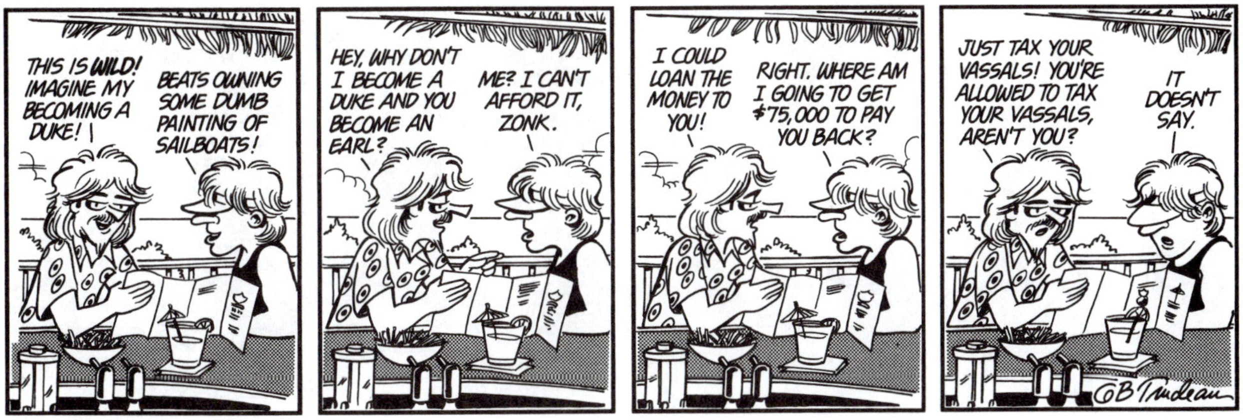
THIS IS WILD! IMAGINE MY BECOMING A DUKE!
BEATS OWNING SOME DUMB PAINTING OF SAILBOATS!
HEY, WHY DON'T I BECOME A DUKE AND YOU BECOME AN EARL?
ME? I CAN'T AFFORD IT, ZONK.
I COULD LOAN THE MONEY TO YOU!
RIGHT. WHERE AM I GOING TO GET $75,000 TO PAY YOU BACK?
JUST TAX YOUR VASSALS! YOU'RE ALLOWED TO TAX YOUR VASSALS, AREN'T YOU?
IT DOESN'T SAY.
©B Trudeau

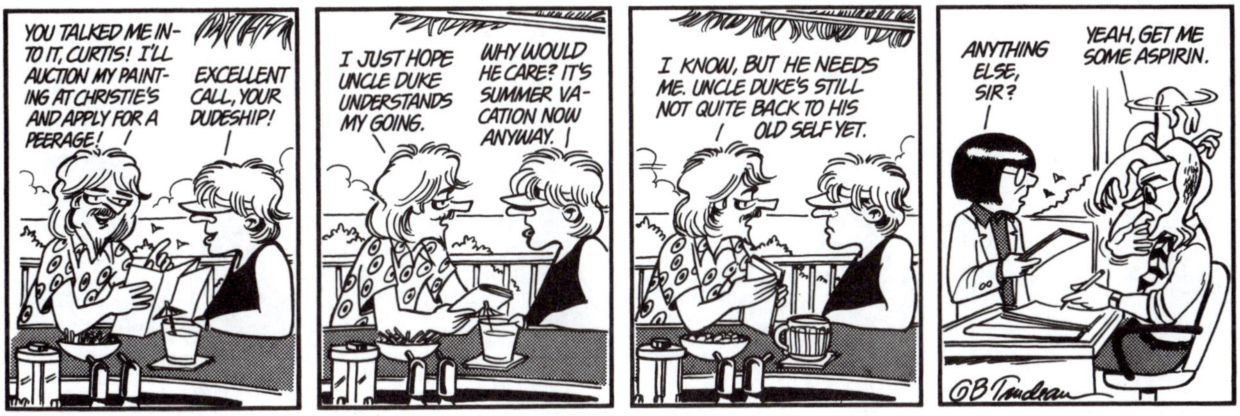
YOU TALKED ME INTO IT, CURTIS! I'LL AUCTION MY PAINTING AT CHRISTIE'S AND APPLY FOR A PEERAGE!
EXCELLENT CALL, YOUR DUDESHIP!
I JUST HOPE UNCLE DUKE UNDERSTANDS MY GOING.
WHY WOULD HE CARE? IT'S SUMMER VACATION NOW ANYWAY.
I KNOW, BUT HE NEEDS ME. UNCLE DUKE'S STILL NOT QUITE BACK TO HIS OLD SELF YET.
ANYTHING ELSE, SIR?
YEAH, GET ME SOME ASPIRIN.
©B Trudeau

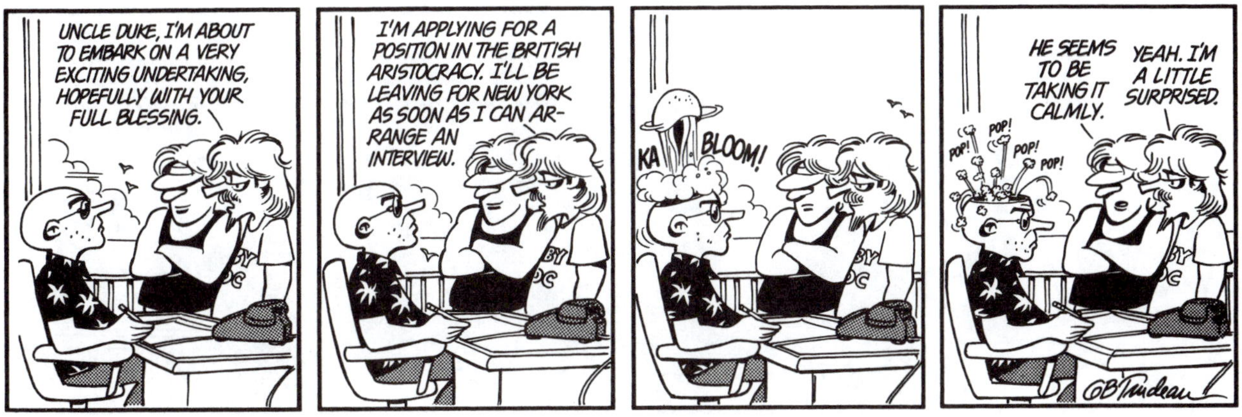
UNCLE DUKE, I'M ABOUT TO EMBARK ON A VERY EXCITING UNDERTAKING, HOPEFULLY WITH YOUR FULL BLESSING.
I'M APPLYING FOR A POSITION IN THE BRITISH ARISTOCRACY. I'LL BE LEAVING FOR NEW YORK AS SOON AS I CAN ARRANGE AN INTERVIEW.
KA BLOOM!
HE SEEMS TO BE TAKING IT CALMLY.
YEAH. I'M A LITTLE SURPRISED.
POP! POP! POP! POP!
©B Trudeau

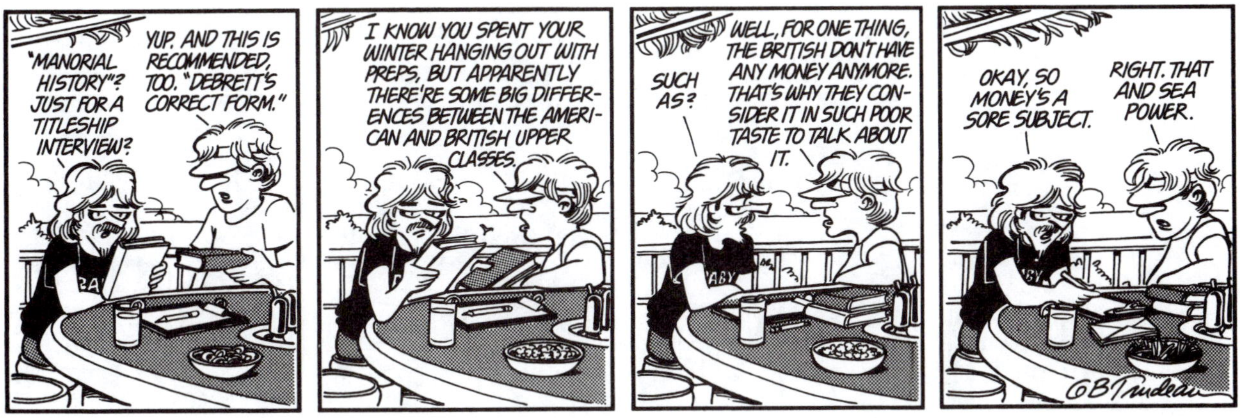
"MANORIAL HISTORY"? JUST FOR A TITLESHIP INTERVIEW?
YUP. AND THIS IS RECOMMENDED, TOO. "DEBRETT'S CORRECT FORM."
I KNOW YOU SPENT YOUR WINTER HANGING OUT WITH PREPS, BUT APPARENTLY THERE'RE SOME BIG DIFFERENCES BETWEEN THE AMERICAN AND BRITISH UPPER CLASSES.
SUCH AS?
WELL, FOR ONE THING, THE BRITISH DON'T HAVE ANY MONEY ANYMORE. THAT'S WHY THEY CONSIDER IT IN SUCH POOR TASTE TO TALK ABOUT IT.
OKAY, SO MONEY'S A SORE SUBJECT.
RIGHT. THAT AND SEA POWER.
©B Trudeau

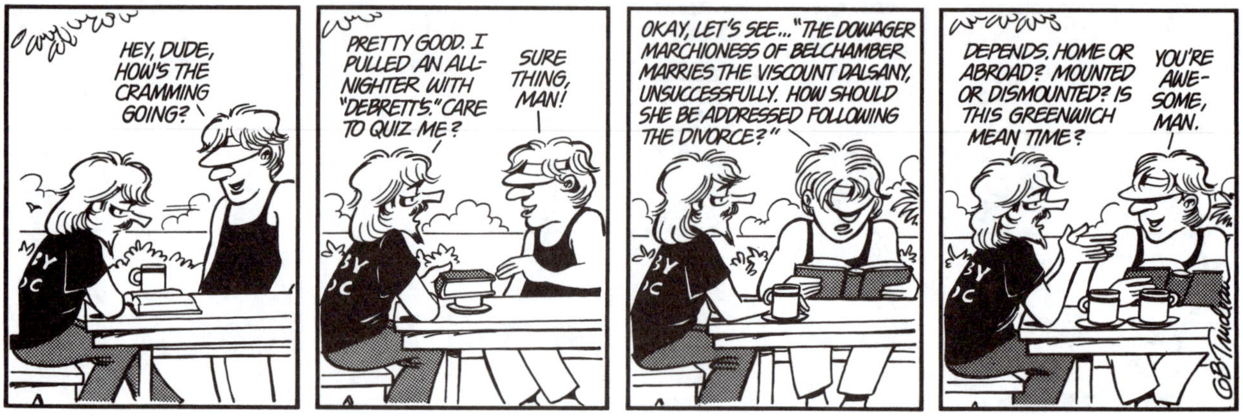
HEY, DUDE, HOW'S THE CRAMMING GOING?
PRETTY GOOD. I PULLED AN ALL-NIGHTER WITH "DEBRETT'S." CARE TO QUIZ ME?
SURE THING, MAN!
OKAY, LET'S SEE... "THE DOWAGER MARCHIONESS OF BELCHAMBER MARRIES THE VISCOUNT DALSANY, UNSUCCESSFULLY. HOW SHOULD SHE BE ADDRESSED FOLLOWING THE DIVORCE?"
DEPENDS. HOME OR ABROAD? MOUNTED OR DISMOUNTED? IS THIS GREENWICH MEAN TIME?
YOU'RE AWE-SOME, MAN.
GB Trudeau

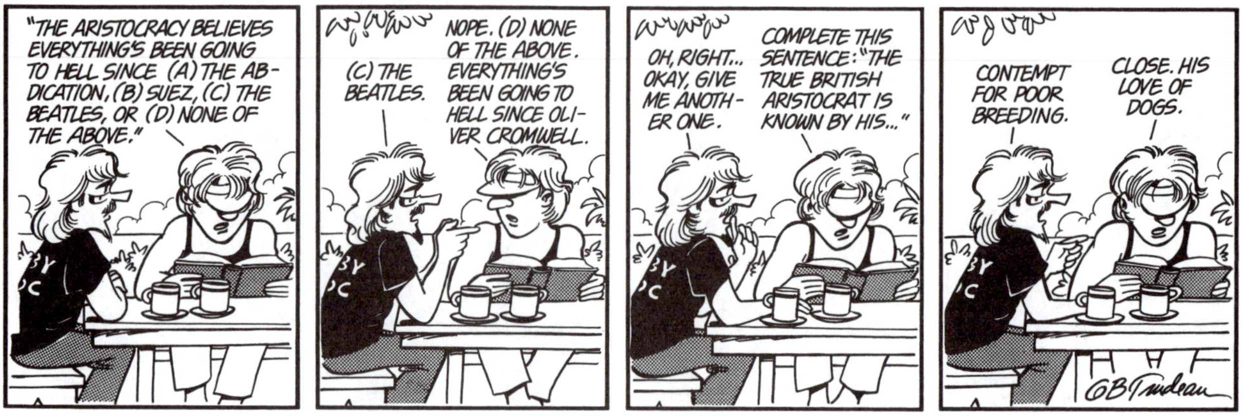
"THE ARISTOCRACY BELIEVES EVERYTHING'S BEEN GOING TO HELL SINCE (A) THE AB-DICATION, (B) SUEZ, (C) THE BEATLES, OR (D) NONE OF THE ABOVE."
(C) THE BEATLES.
NOPE. (D) NONE OF THE ABOVE. EVERYTHING'S BEEN GOING TO HELL SINCE OLI-VER CROMWELL.
OH, RIGHT... OKAY, GIVE ME ANOTH-ER ONE.
COMPLETE THIS SENTENCE: "THE TRUE BRITISH ARISTOCRAT IS KNOWN BY HIS..."
CONTEMPT FOR POOR BREEDING.
CLOSE. HIS LOVE OF DOGS.
GB Trudeau

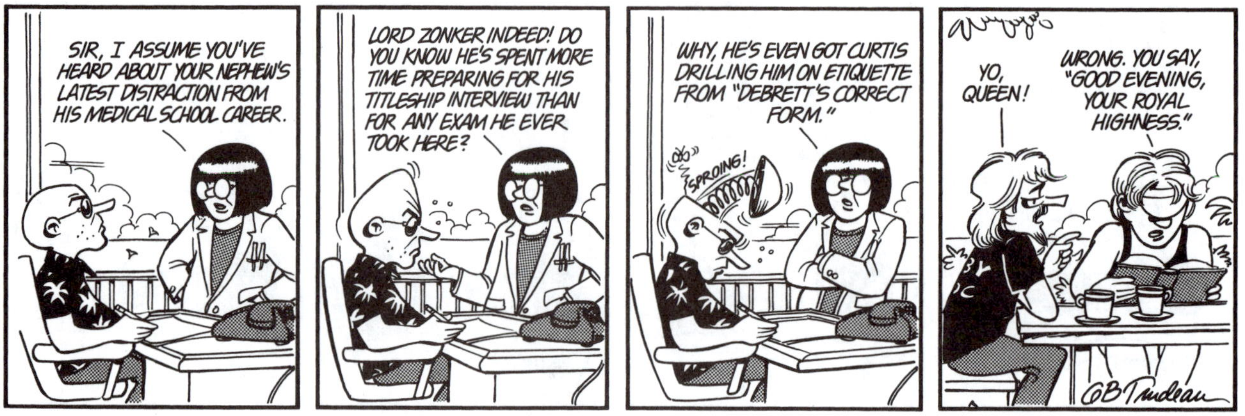
SIR, I ASSUME YOU'VE HEARD ABOUT YOUR NEPHEW'S LATEST DISTRACTION FROM HIS MEDICAL SCHOOL CAREER.
LORD ZONKER INDEED! DO YOU KNOW HE'S SPENT MORE TIME PREPARING FOR HIS TITLESHIP INTERVIEW THAN FOR ANY EXAM HE EVER TOOK HERE?
WHY, HE'S EVEN GOT CURTIS DRILLING HIM ON ETIQUETTE FROM "DEBRETT'S CORRECT FORM."
SPROING!
YO, QUEEN!
WRONG. YOU SAY, "GOOD EVENING, YOUR ROYAL HIGHNESS."
GB Trudeau

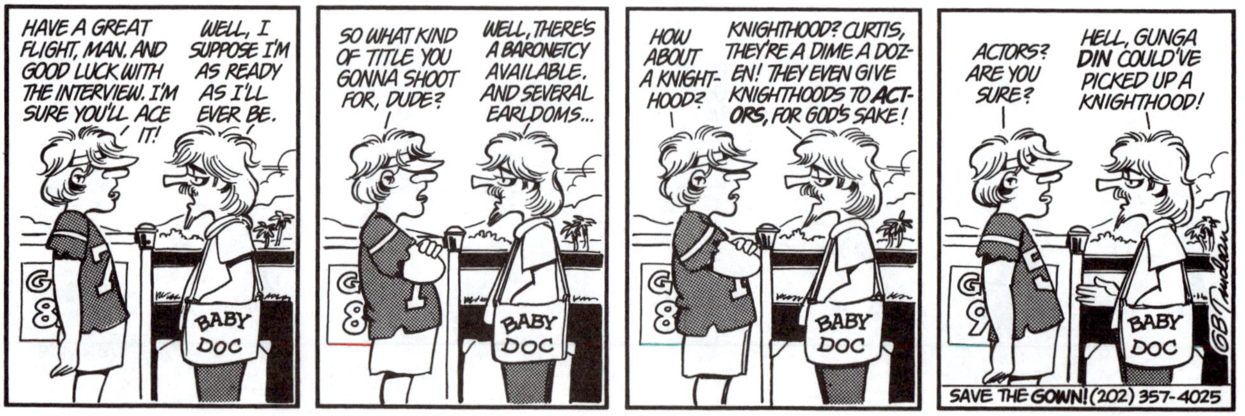
HAVE A GREAT FLIGHT, MAN. AND GOOD LUCK WITH THE INTERVIEW. I'M SURE YOU'LL ACE IT!
WELL, I SUPPOSE I'M AS READY AS I'LL EVER BE.
BABY DOC
SO WHAT KIND OF TITLE YOU GONNA SHOOT FOR, DUDE?
WELL, THERE'S A BARONETCY AVAILABLE. AND SEVERAL EARLDOMS...
HOW ABOUT A KNIGHT-HOOD?
KNIGHTHOOD? CURTIS, THEY'RE A DIME A DOZ-EN! THEY EVEN GIVE KNIGHTHOODS TO ACT-ORS, FOR GOD'S SAKE!
ACTORS? ARE YOU SURE?
HELL, GUNGA DIN COULD'VE PICKED UP A KNIGHTHOOD!
GB Trudeau
SAVE THE GOWN! (202) 357-4025

Panel 1: ...SO ALL I HAVE TO DO IS PASS THIS INTERVIEW, AND I BECOME THE TITULAR DESCENDANT OF ONE OF WILLIAM THE CONQUEROR'S KNIGHTS!

Panel 2: AMAZING. WHO DOES THE INTERVIEW? / THE PEERAGE BROKER HERE IN NEW YORK.

Panel 3: IT'S HIS JOB TO UPHOLD UNCOMPROMISING STANDARDS OF SELECTION, TO SAFEGUARD THE DIGNITY OF THE CLIENT CLASS HE REPRESENTS.

Panel 4: "LORDS-R-US"! HOLD, WILL YA?

Panel 5: WELL, THAT DOES IT. MY APPOINTMENT IS ON FOR TOMORROW!

Panel 6: WHAT TITLE ARE YOU APPLYING FOR, ZONK? / WELL, THERE'S A VISCOUNTY I LIKE THAT'S BEEN PRICED TO MOVE AT $17,000.

Panel 7: WHY ECONOMIZE, ZONK? YOU'RE WORTH $3 MILLION! / HEY, CALL ME BEN FRANKLIN. HOW DO YOU THINK I CAME TO BE WORTH MONEY LIKE THAT, MIKE?

Panel 8: YOU WON IT IN A LOTTERY, BEN. / SURE, BUT WITH A **SINGLE** TICKET!

Panel 9: KNOCK 'EM DEAD, SPORT. / THANKS, MIKE...

Panel 10: WITH ANY LUCK, WHEN NEXT YOU SEE ME, I'LL BE HIS LORDSHIP THE VISCOUNT ST. AUSTELL-IN-THE-MOOR BIGGLESWADE-BRIXHAM!

Panel 11: BUT I CAN JUST CALL YOU "LORD ZONKER," RIGHT? / NO. YOU'RE A UNIVERSITY CHUM, SO YOU HAVE TO CALL ME "OLD BEAN."

Panel 12: HOW ABOUT NICKNAMES? / "BUNNY" OR "PINKY." BUT ONLY WHEN WE'RE FLY FISHING.

Panel 13: HI! ARE YOU MR. HAMHOCK? / BE WITH YOU IN A MINUTE, KID... GOOD MORNING, "LORDS-R-US"!

Panel 14: WHY, YES, YOUR LADYSHIP, HOW'S EVERYTHING IN HOUSTON? WHAT? ...NO, MA'AM, I HAD NO IDEA YOU BELONGED TO THE SAME COUNTRY CLUB!...

Panel 15: YES, MA'AM, I'M AFRAID THE COUNTESS DOES OUTRANK YOU. YOU'D HAVE TO BE A DUCHESS ...WELL, YES, MA'AM, WE MIGHT BE ABLE TO HELP. HOLD, PLEASE.

Panel 16: UM... IF THIS IS PRIVATE, I CAN... / **MAGGIE!** LINE TWO! LADY JOE BOB WANTS AN UPGRADE!

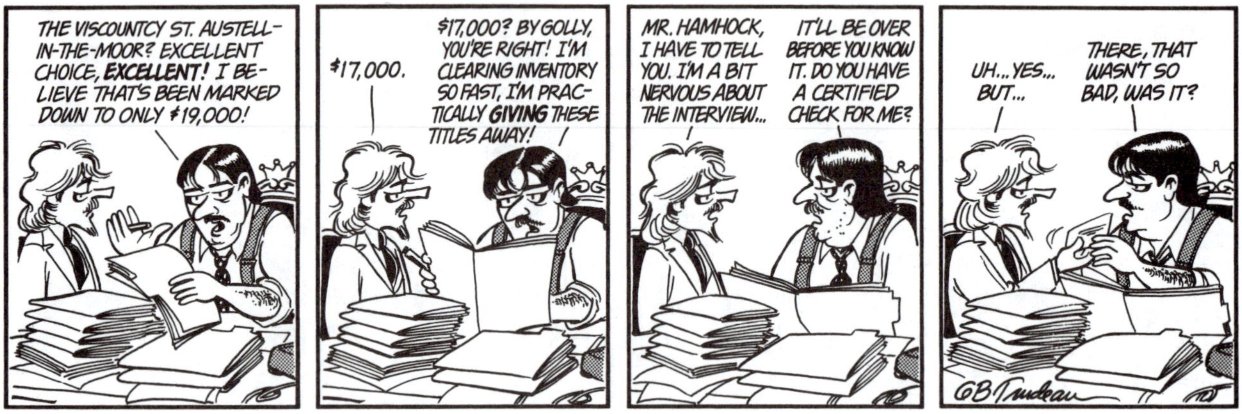
THE VISCOUNTCY ST. AUSTELL-IN-THE-MOOR? EXCELLENT CHOICE, **EXCELLENT!** I BELIEVE THAT'S BEEN MARKED DOWN TO ONLY $19,000!
$17,000.
$17,000? BY GOLLY, YOU'RE RIGHT! I'M CLEARING INVENTORY SO FAST, I'M PRACTICALLY **GIVING** THESE TITLES AWAY!
MR. HAMHOCK, I HAVE TO TELL YOU. I'M A BIT NERVOUS ABOUT THE INTERVIEW...
IT'LL BE OVER BEFORE YOU KNOW IT. DO YOU HAVE A CERTIFIED CHECK FOR ME?
UH... YES... BUT...
THERE, THAT WASN'T SO BAD, WAS IT?
GB Trudeau

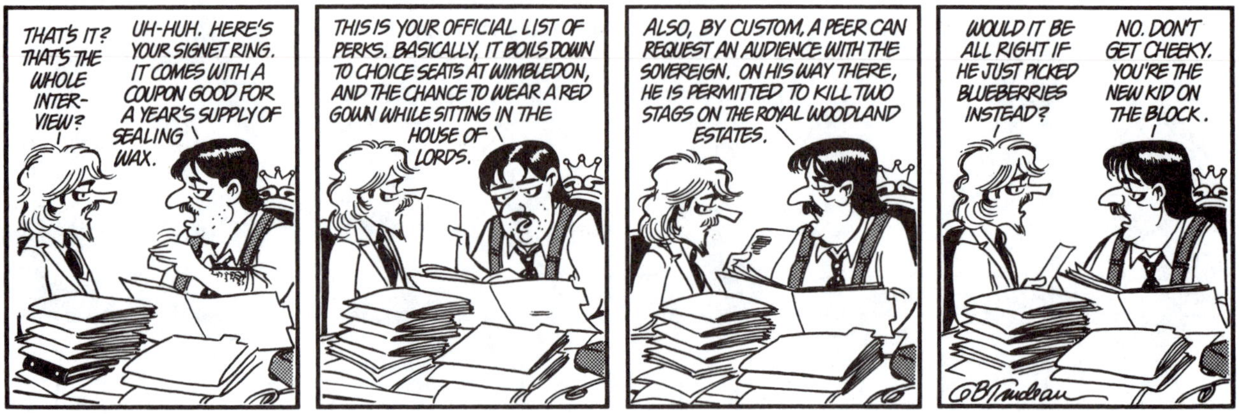
THAT'S IT? THAT'S THE WHOLE INTERVIEW?
UH-HUH. HERE'S YOUR SIGNET RING. IT COMES WITH A COUPON GOOD FOR A YEAR'S SUPPLY OF SEALING WAX.
THIS IS YOUR OFFICIAL LIST OF PERKS. BASICALLY, IT BOILS DOWN TO CHOICE SEATS AT WIMBLEDON, AND THE CHANCE TO WEAR A RED GOWN WHILE SITTING IN THE HOUSE OF LORDS.
ALSO, BY CUSTOM, A PEER CAN REQUEST AN AUDIENCE WITH THE SOVEREIGN. ON HIS WAY THERE, HE IS PERMITTED TO KILL TWO STAGS ON THE ROYAL WOODLAND ESTATES.
WOULD IT BE ALL RIGHT IF HE JUST PICKED BLUEBERRIES INSTEAD?
NO. DON'T GET CHEEKY. YOU'RE THE NEW KID ON THE BLOCK.
GB Trudeau

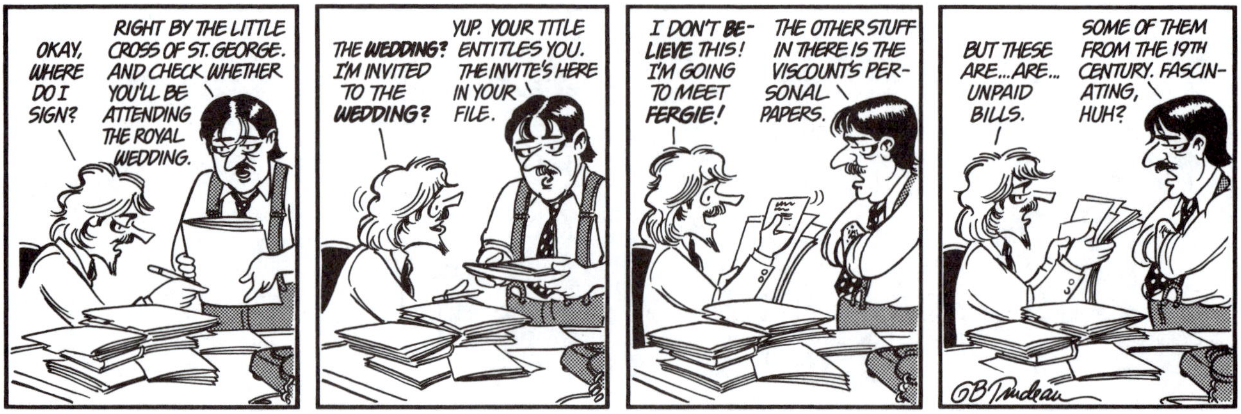
OKAY, **WHERE** DO I SIGN?
RIGHT BY THE LITTLE CROSS OF ST. GEORGE. AND CHECK WHETHER YOU'LL BE ATTENDING THE ROYAL WEDDING.
THE **WEDDING?** I'M INVITED TO THE **WEDDING?**
YUP. YOUR TITLE ENTITLES YOU. THE INVITE'S HERE IN YOUR FILE.
I DON'T **BELIEVE** THIS! I'M GOING TO MEET **FERGIE!**
THE OTHER STUFF IN THERE IS THE VISCOUNT'S PERSONAL PAPERS.
BUT THESE ARE... ARE... UNPAID BILLS.
SOME OF THEM FROM THE 19TH CENTURY. FASCINATING, HUH?
GB Trudeau

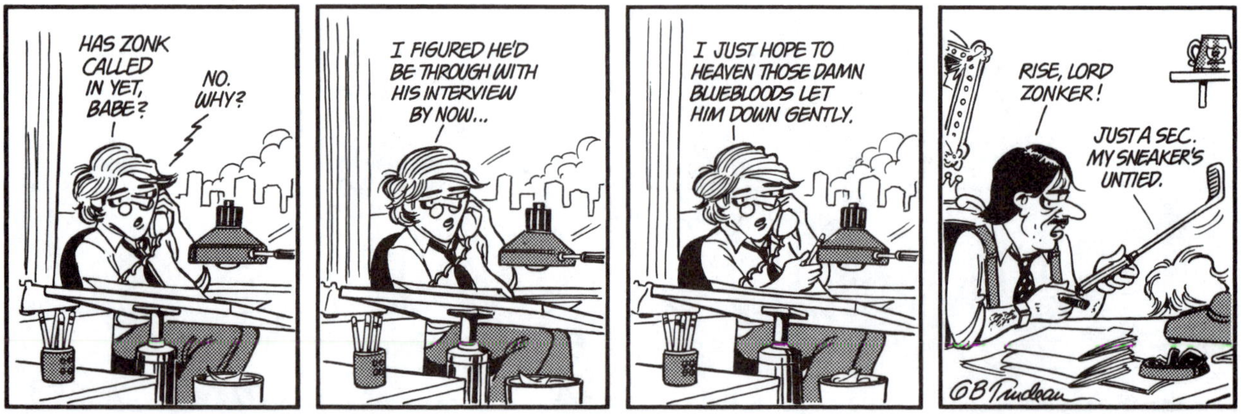
HAS ZONK CALLED IN YET, BABE?
NO. WHY?
I FIGURED HE'D BE THROUGH WITH HIS INTERVIEW BY NOW...
I JUST HOPE TO HEAVEN THOSE DAMN BLUEBLOODS LET HIM DOWN GENTLY.
RISE, LORD ZONKER!
JUST A SEC. MY SNEAKER'S UNTIED.
GB Trudeau

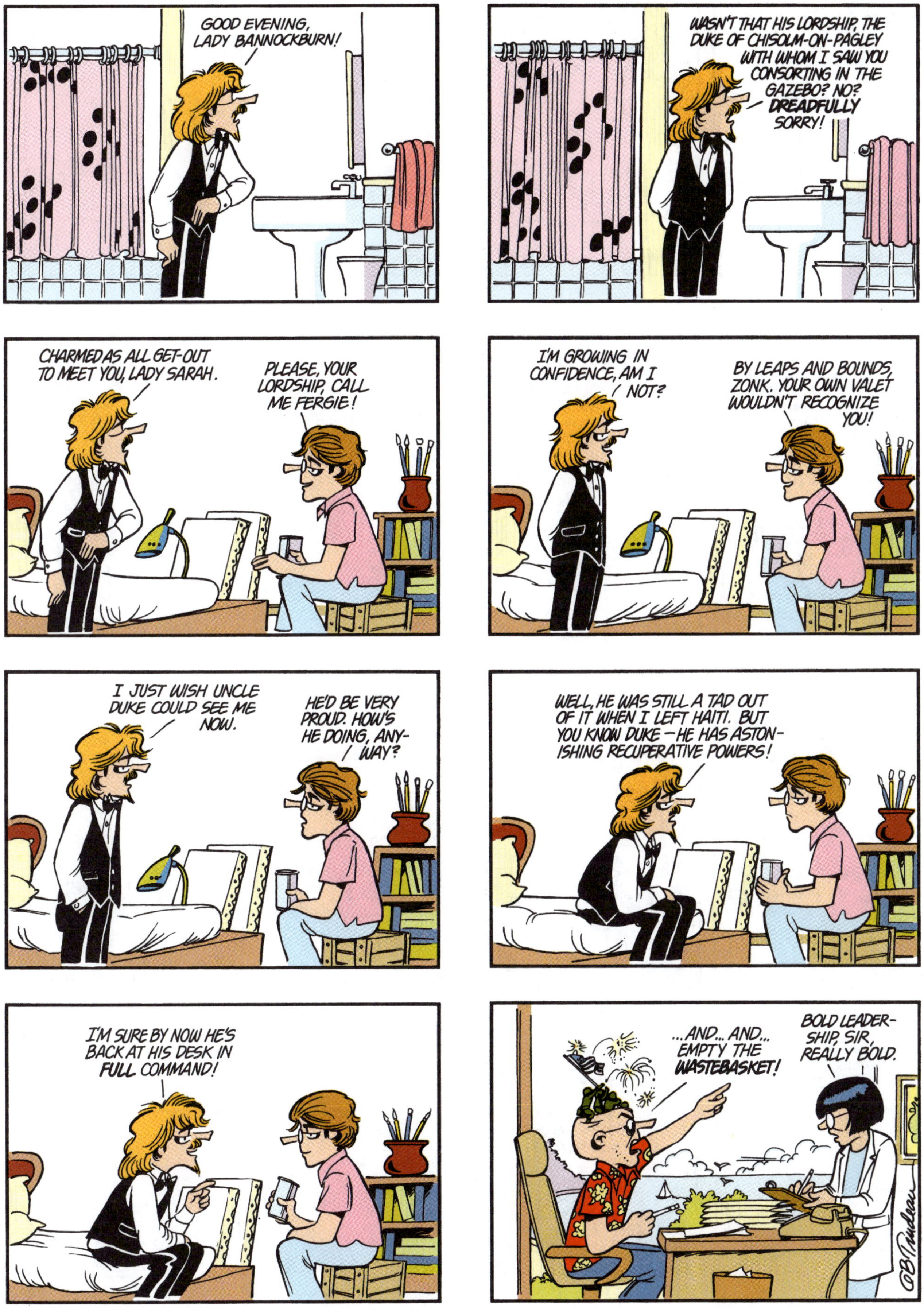
GOOD EVENING, LADY BANNOCKBURN!
WASN'T THAT HIS LORDSHIP, THE DUKE OF CHISOLM-ON-PAGLEY WITH WHOM I SAW YOU CONSORTING IN THE GAZEBO? NO? DREADFULLY SORRY!
CHARMED AS ALL GET-OUT TO MEET YOU, LADY SARAH.
PLEASE, YOUR LORDSHIP, CALL ME FERGIE!
I'M GROWING IN CONFIDENCE, AM I NOT?
BY LEAPS AND BOUNDS, ZONK. YOUR OWN VALET WOULDN'T RECOGNIZE YOU!
I JUST WISH UNCLE DUKE COULD SEE ME NOW.
HE'D BE VERY PROUD. HOW'S HE DOING, ANY-WAY?
WELL, HE WAS STILL A TAD OUT OF IT WHEN I LEFT HAITI. BUT YOU KNOW DUKE — HE HAS ASTON-ISHING RECUPERATIVE POWERS!
I'M SURE BY NOW HE'S BACK AT HIS DESK IN FULL COMMAND!
...AND... AND... EMPTY THE WASTEBASKET!
BOLD LEADER-SHIP, SIR, REALLY BOLD.

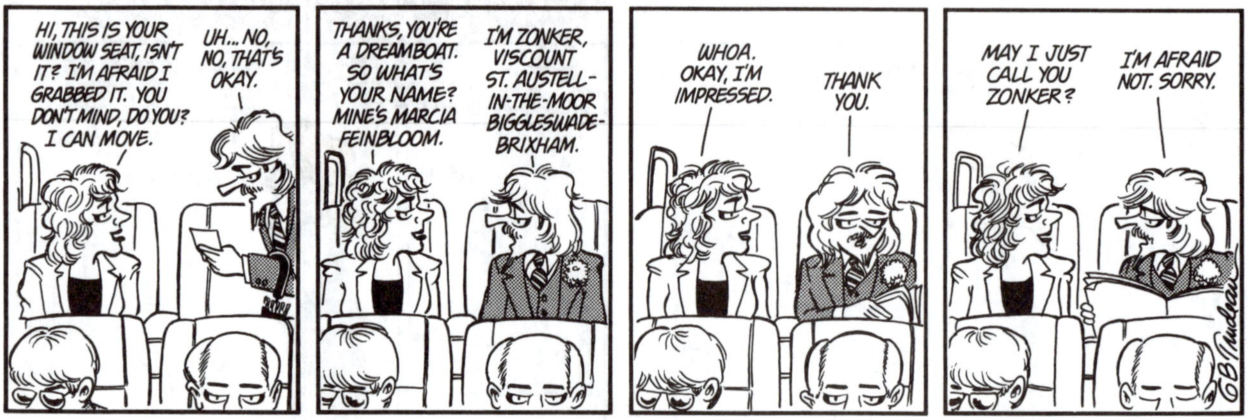
HI, THIS IS YOUR WINDOW SEAT, ISN'T IT? I'M AFRAID I GRABBED IT. YOU DON'T MIND, DO YOU? I CAN MOVE.
UH... NO, NO, THAT'S OKAY.
THANKS, YOU'RE A DREAMBOAT. SO WHAT'S YOUR NAME? MINE'S MARCIA FEINBLOOM.
I'M ZONKER, VISCOUNT ST. AUSTELL-IN-THE-MOOR BIGGLESWADE-BRIXHAM.
WHOA. OKAY, I'M IMPRESSED.
THANK YOU.
MAY I JUST CALL YOU ZONKER?
I'M AFRAID NOT. SORRY.
GBTrudeau

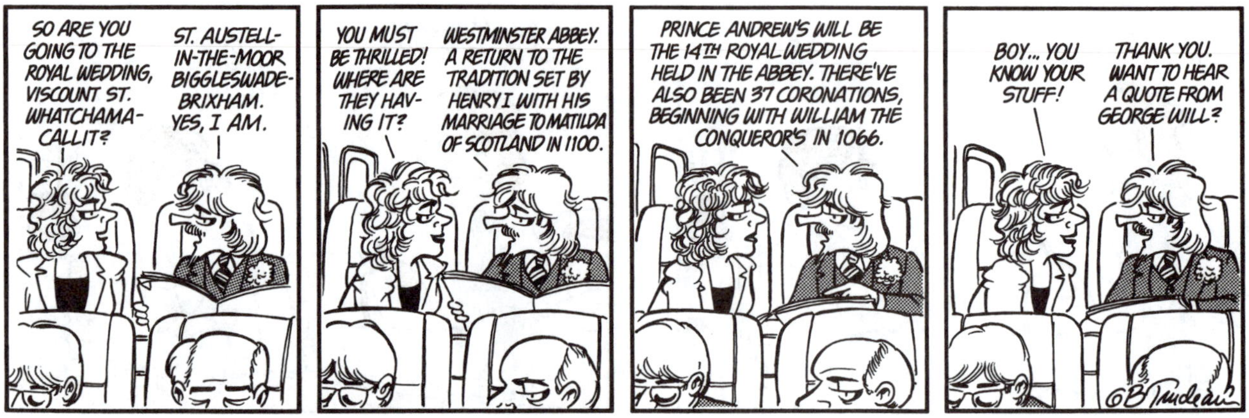
SO ARE YOU GOING TO THE ROYAL WEDDING, VISCOUNT ST. WHATCHAMA-CALLIT?
ST. AUSTELL-IN-THE-MOOR BIGGLESWADE-BRIXHAM. YES, I AM.
YOU MUST BE THRILLED! WHERE ARE THEY HAV-ING IT?
WESTMINSTER ABBEY. A RETURN TO THE TRADITION SET BY HENRY I WITH HIS MARRIAGE TO MATILDA OF SCOTLAND IN 1100.
PRINCE ANDREW'S WILL BE THE 14TH ROYAL WEDDING HELD IN THE ABBEY. THERE'VE ALSO BEEN 37 CORONATIONS, BEGINNING WITH WILLIAM THE CONQUEROR'S IN 1066.
BOY... YOU KNOW YOUR STUFF!
THANK YOU. WANT TO HEAR A QUOTE FROM GEORGE WILL?
GBTrudeau

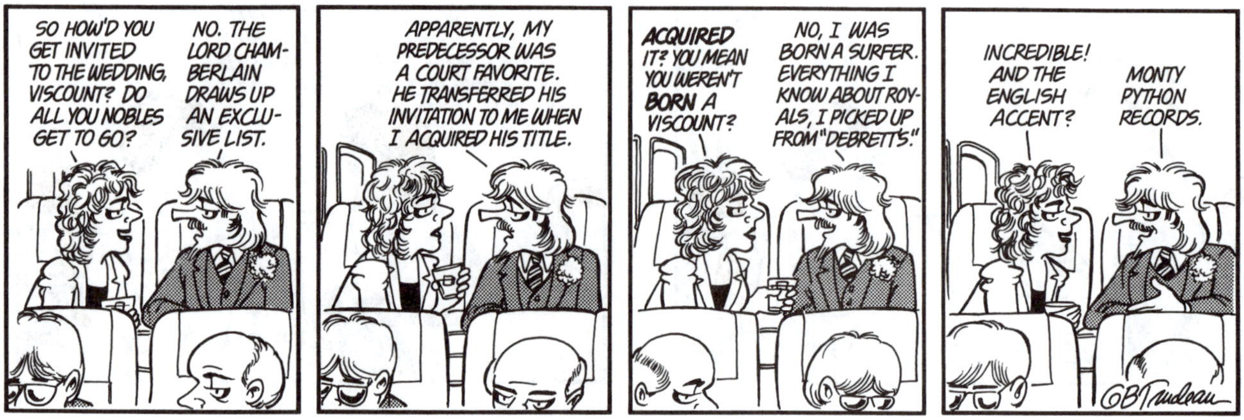
SO HOW'D YOU GET INVITED TO THE WEDDING, VISCOUNT? DO ALL YOU NOBLES GET TO GO?
NO. THE LORD CHAM-BERLAIN DRAWS UP AN EXCLU-SIVE LIST.
APPARENTLY, MY PREDECESSOR WAS A COURT FAVORITE. HE TRANSFERRED HIS INVITATION TO ME WHEN I ACQUIRED HIS TITLE.
ACQUIRED IT? YOU MEAN YOU WEREN'T BORN A VISCOUNT?
NO, I WAS BORN A SURFER. EVERYTHING I KNOW ABOUT ROY-ALS, I PICKED UP FROM "DEBRETT'S."
INCREDIBLE! AND THE ENGLISH ACCENT?
MONTY PYTHON RECORDS.
GBTrudeau

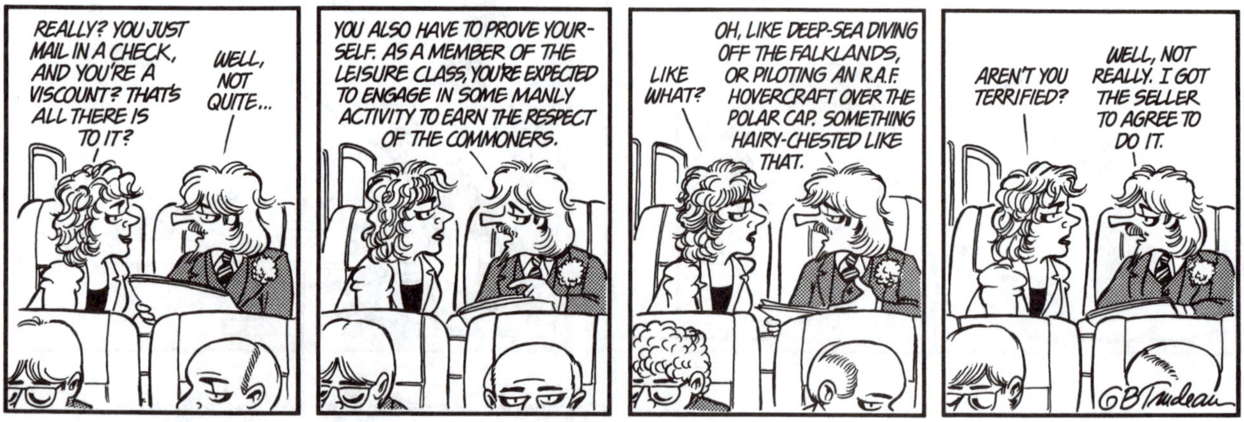
REALLY? YOU JUST MAIL IN A CHECK, AND YOU'RE A VISCOUNT? THAT'S ALL THERE IS TO IT?
WELL, NOT QUITE...
YOU ALSO HAVE TO PROVE YOUR-SELF. AS A MEMBER OF THE LEISURE CLASS, YOU'RE EXPECTED TO ENGAGE IN SOME MANLY ACTIVITY TO EARN THE RESPECT OF THE COMMONERS.
LIKE WHAT?
OH, LIKE DEEP-SEA DIVING OFF THE FALKLANDS, OR PILOTING AN R.A.F. HOVERCRAFT OVER THE POLAR CAP. SOMETHING HAIRY-CHESTED LIKE THAT.
AREN'T YOU TERRIFIED?
WELL, NOT REALLY. I GOT THE SELLER TO AGREE TO DO IT.
GBTrudeau

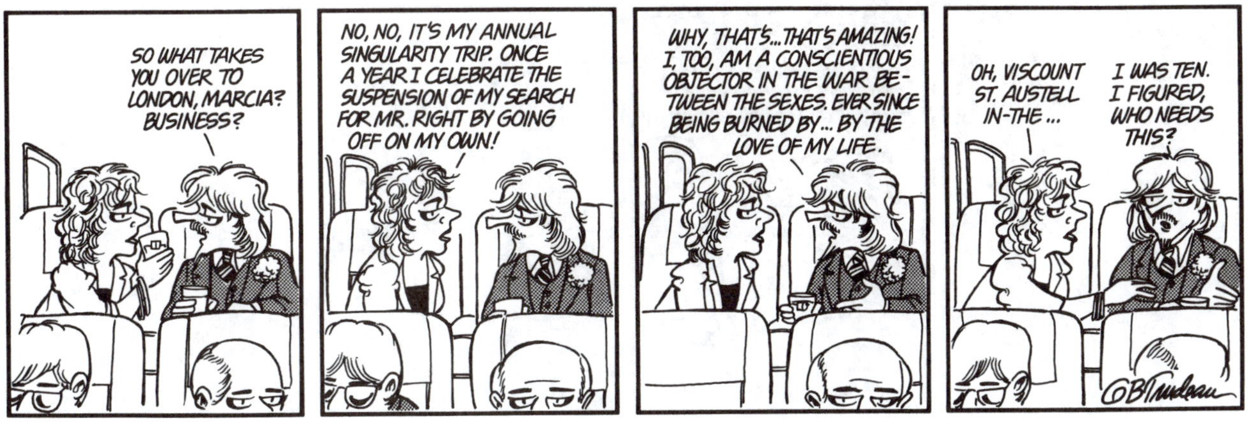
SO WHAT TAKES YOU OVER TO LONDON, MARCIA? BUSINESS?
NO, NO, IT'S MY ANNUAL SINGULARITY TRIP. ONCE A YEAR I CELEBRATE THE SUSPENSION OF MY SEARCH FOR MR. RIGHT BY GOING OFF ON MY OWN!
WHY, THAT'S... THAT'S AMAZING! I, TOO, AM A CONSCIENTIOUS OBJECTOR IN THE WAR BETWEEN THE SEXES. EVER SINCE BEING BURNED BY... BY THE LOVE OF MY LIFE.
OH, VISCOUNT ST. AUSTELL IN-THE ...
I WAS TEN. I FIGURED, WHO NEEDS THIS?
©BTrudeau

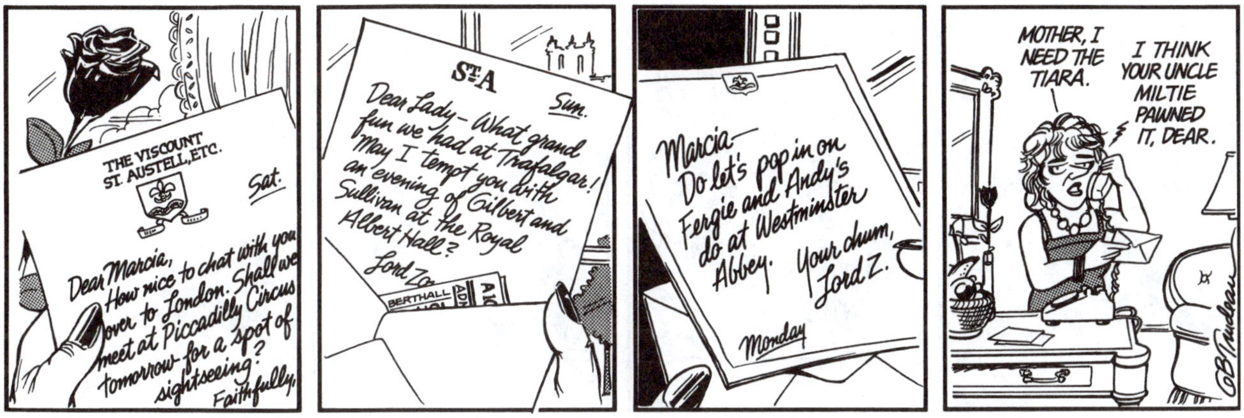
THE VISCOUNT ST. AUSTELL, ETC.
Sat.
Dear Marcia, How nice to chat with you over to London. Shall we meet at Piccadilly Circus tomorrow for a spot of sightseeing? Faithfully,
St A
Sun.
Dear Lady— What grand fun we had at Trafalgar! May I tempt you with an evening of Gilbert and Sullivan at the Royal Albert Hall?
Marcia— Do let's pop in on Fergie and Andy's do at Westminster Abbey. Your chum, Lord Z.
Monday
MOTHER, I NEED THE TIARA.
I THINK YOUR UNCLE MILTIE PAWNED IT, DEAR.
©BTrudeau

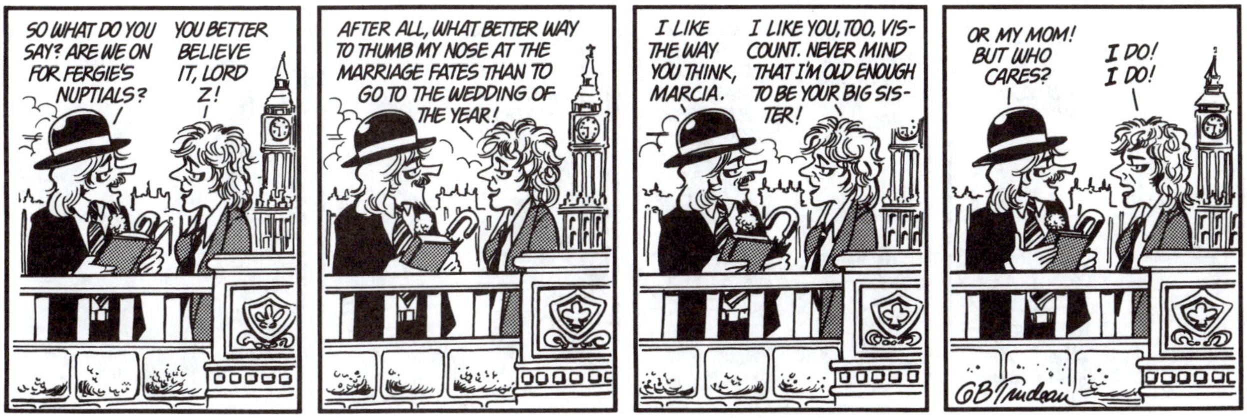
SO WHAT DO YOU SAY? ARE WE ON FOR FERGIE'S NUPTIALS?
YOU BETTER BELIEVE IT, LORD Z!
AFTER ALL, WHAT BETTER WAY TO THUMB MY NOSE AT THE MARRIAGE FATES THAN TO GO TO THE WEDDING OF THE YEAR!
I LIKE THE WAY YOU THINK, MARCIA.
I LIKE YOU, TOO, VISCOUNT. NEVER MIND THAT I'M OLD ENOUGH TO BE YOUR BIG SISTER!
OR MY MOM! BUT WHO CARES?
I DO! I DO!
©BTrudeau

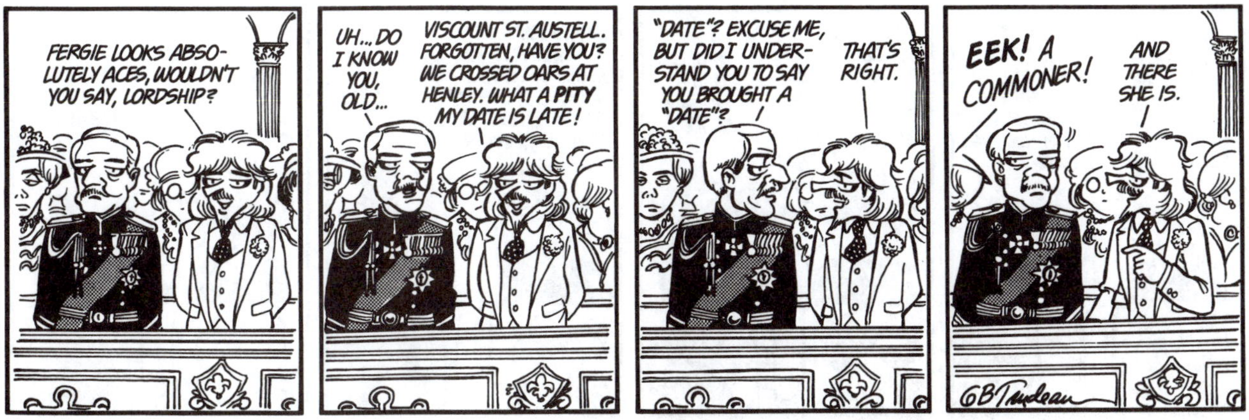
FERGIE LOOKS ABSOLUTELY ACES, WOULDN'T YOU SAY, LORDSHIP?
UH... DO I KNOW YOU, OLD...
VISCOUNT ST. AUSTELL. FORGOTTEN, HAVE YOU? WE CROSSED OARS AT HENLEY. WHAT A PITY MY DATE IS LATE!
"DATE"? EXCUSE ME, BUT DID I UNDERSTAND YOU TO SAY YOU BROUGHT A "DATE"?
THAT'S RIGHT.
EEK! A COMMONER!
AND THERE SHE IS.
©BTrudeau

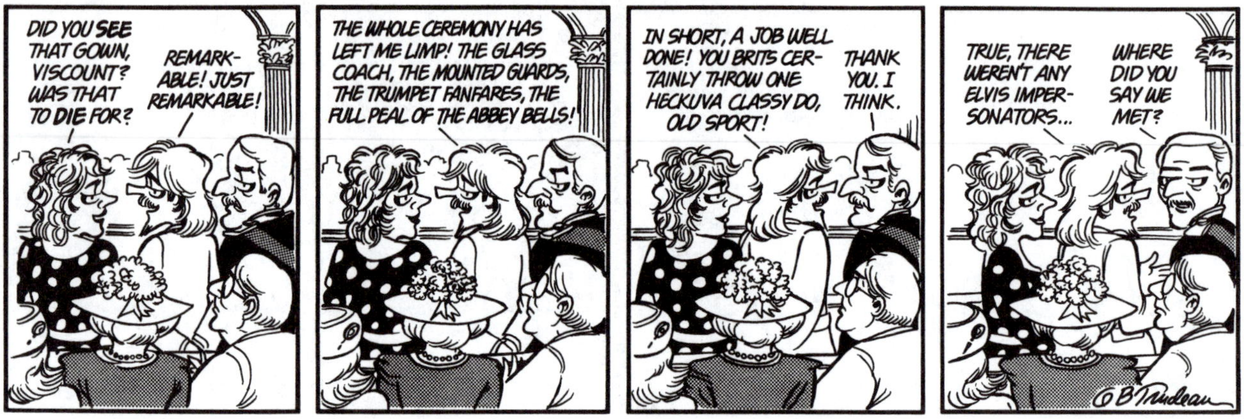
DID YOU **SEE** THAT GOWN, VISCOUNT? WAS THAT TO **DIE** FOR?
REMARKABLE! JUST REMARKABLE!
THE WHOLE CEREMONY HAS LEFT ME LIMP! THE GLASS COACH, THE MOUNTED GUARDS, THE TRUMPET FANFARES, THE FULL PEAL OF THE ABBEY BELLS!
IN SHORT, A JOB WELL DONE! YOU BRITS CERTAINLY THROW ONE HECKUVA CLASSY DO, OLD SPORT!
THANK YOU. I THINK.
TRUE, THERE WEREN'T ANY ELVIS IMPERSONATORS...
WHERE DID YOU SAY WE MET?
GBTrudeau

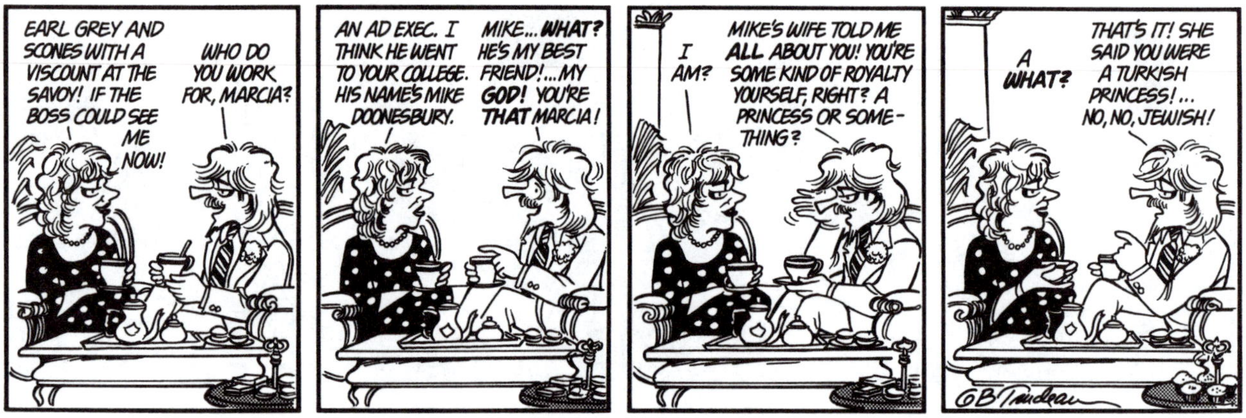
EARL GREY AND SCONES WITH A VISCOUNT AT THE SAVOY! IF THE BOSS COULD SEE ME NOW!
WHO DO YOU WORK FOR, MARCIA?
AN AD EXEC. I THINK HE WENT TO YOUR COLLEGE. HIS NAME'S MIKE DOONESBURY.
MIKE... **WHAT?** HE'S MY BEST FRIEND!... MY **GOD!** YOU'RE **THAT** MARCIA!
I AM?
MIKE'S WIFE TOLD ME **ALL** ABOUT YOU! YOU'RE SOME KIND OF ROYALTY YOURSELF, RIGHT? A PRINCESS OR SOMETHING?
A **WHAT?**
THAT'S IT! SHE SAID YOU WERE A TURKISH PRINCESS!... NO, NO, JEWISH!
GBTrudeau

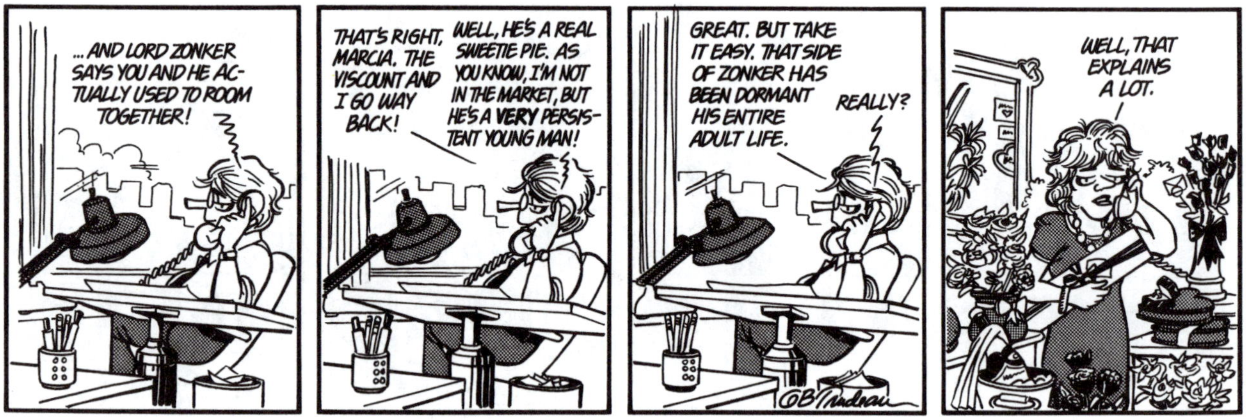
...AND LORD ZONKER SAYS YOU AND HE ACTUALLY USED TO ROOM TOGETHER!
THAT'S RIGHT, MARCIA. THE VISCOUNT AND I GO WAY BACK!
WELL, HE'S A REAL SWEETIE PIE. AS YOU KNOW, I'M NOT IN THE MARKET, BUT HE'S A **VERY** PERSISTENT YOUNG MAN!
GREAT. BUT TAKE IT EASY. THAT SIDE OF ZONKER HAS BEEN DORMANT HIS ENTIRE ADULT LIFE.
REALLY?
WELL, THAT EXPLAINS A LOT.
GBTrudeau

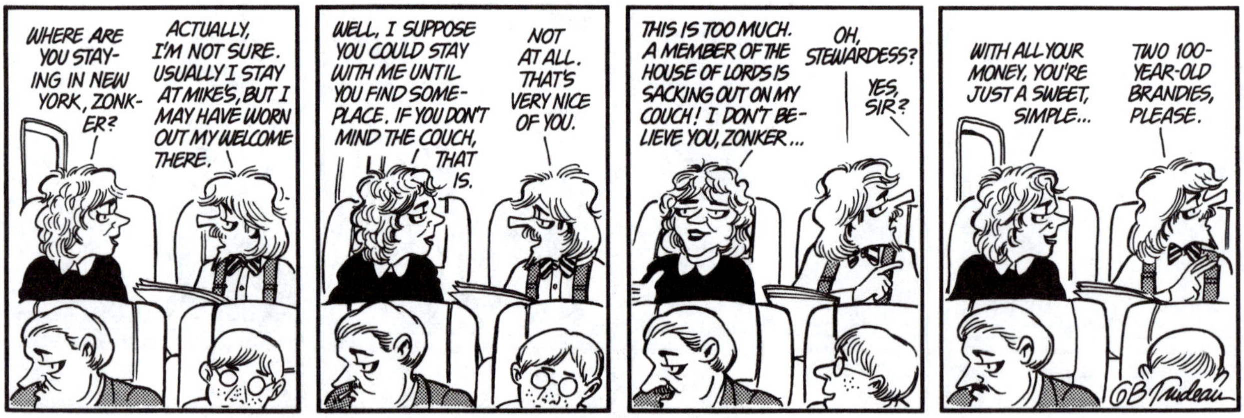
WHERE ARE YOU STAYING IN NEW YORK, ZONKER?
ACTUALLY, I'M NOT SURE. USUALLY I STAY AT MIKE'S, BUT I MAY HAVE WORN OUT MY WELCOME THERE.
WELL, I SUPPOSE YOU COULD STAY WITH ME UNTIL YOU FIND SOMEPLACE. IF YOU DON'T MIND THE COUCH, THAT IS.
NOT AT ALL. THAT'S VERY NICE OF YOU.
THIS IS TOO MUCH. A MEMBER OF THE HOUSE OF LORDS IS SACKING OUT ON MY COUCH! I DON'T BELIEVE YOU, ZONKER...
OH, STEWARDESS?
YES, SIR?
WITH ALL YOUR MONEY, YOU'RE JUST A SWEET, SIMPLE...
TWO 100-YEAR-OLD BRANDIES, PLEASE.
GBTrudeau

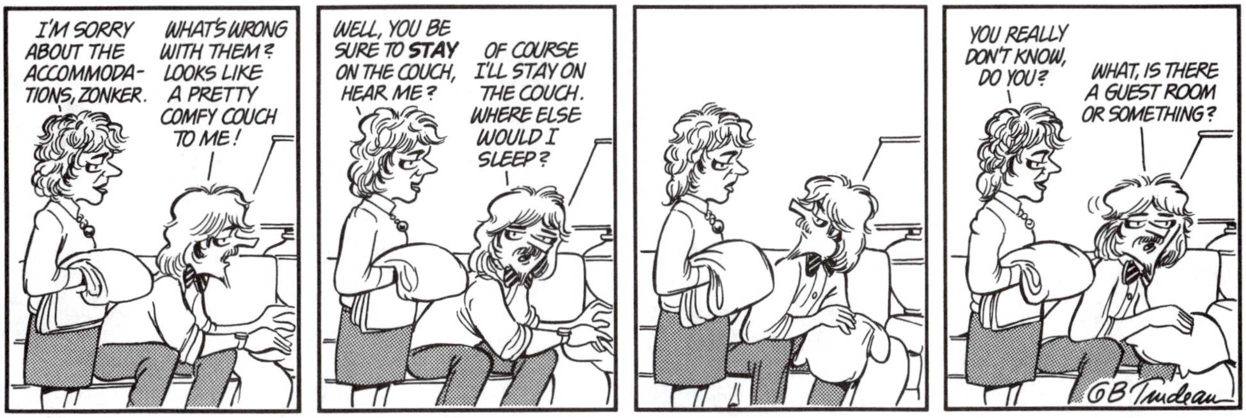
I'M SORRY ABOUT THE ACCOMMODA-TIONS, ZONKER.
WHAT'S WRONG WITH THEM? LOOKS LIKE A PRETTY COMFY COUCH TO ME!
WELL, YOU BE SURE TO **STAY** ON THE COUCH, HEAR ME?
OF COURSE I'LL STAY ON THE COUCH. WHERE ELSE WOULD I SLEEP?
YOU REALLY DON'T KNOW, DO YOU?
WHAT, IS THERE A GUEST ROOM OR SOMETHING?
©B Trudeau

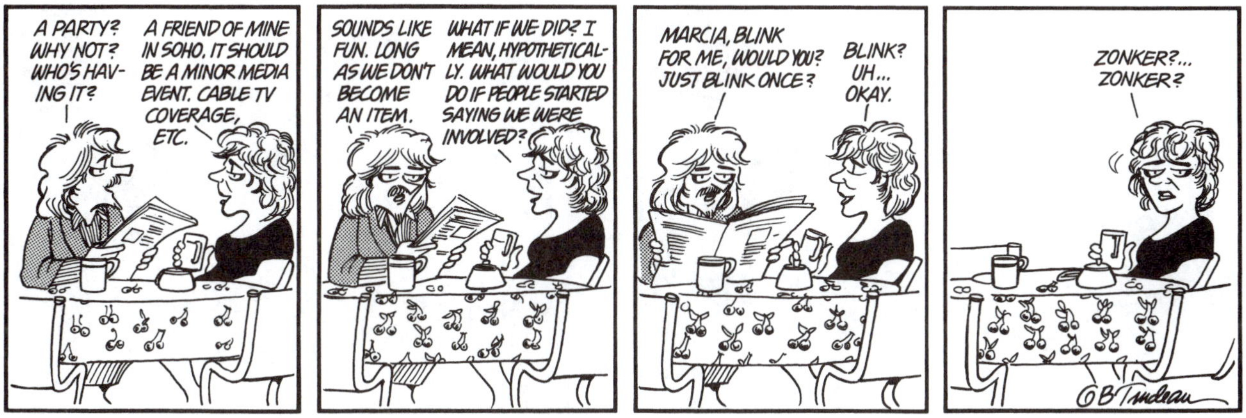
A PARTY? WHY NOT? WHO'S HAV-ING IT?
A FRIEND OF MINE IN SOHO. IT SHOULD BE A MINOR MEDIA EVENT. CABLE TV COVERAGE, ETC.
SOUNDS LIKE FUN. LONG AS WE DON'T BECOME AN ITEM.
WHAT IF WE DID? I MEAN, HYPOTHETICAL-LY. WHAT WOULD YOU DO IF PEOPLE STARTED SAYING WE WERE INVOLVED?
MARCIA, BLINK FOR ME, WOULD YOU? JUST BLINK ONCE?
BLINK? UH... OKAY.
ZONKER?... ZONKER?
©B Trudeau

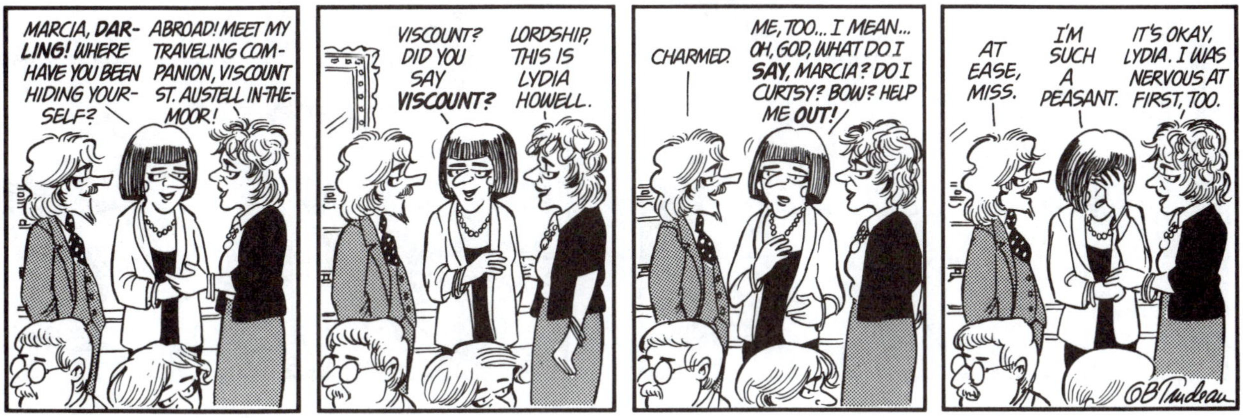
MARCIA, **DAR-LING!** WHERE HAVE YOU BEEN HIDING YOUR-SELF?
ABROAD! MEET MY TRAVELING COM-PANION, VISCOUNT ST. AUSTELL IN-THE-MOOR!
VISCOUNT? DID YOU SAY **VISCOUNT?**
LORDSHIP, THIS IS LYDIA HOWELL.
CHARMED.
ME, TOO... I MEAN... OH, GOD, WHAT DO I **SAY**, MARCIA? DO I CURTSY? BOW? HELP ME **OUT!**
AT EASE, MISS.
I'M SUCH A PEASANT.
IT'S OKAY, LYDIA. I WAS NERVOUS AT FIRST, TOO.
©B Trudeau

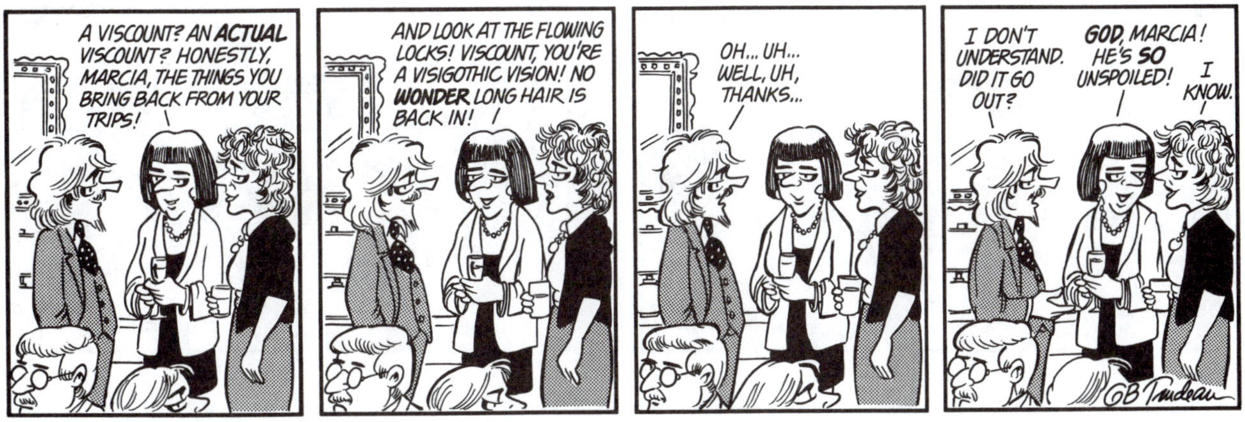
A VISCOUNT? AN **ACTUAL** VISCOUNT? HONESTLY, MARCIA, THE THINGS YOU BRING BACK FROM YOUR TRIPS!
AND LOOK AT THE FLOWING LOCKS! VISCOUNT, YOU'RE A VISIGOTHIC VISION! NO **WONDER** LONG HAIR IS BACK IN!
OH... UH... WELL, UH, THANKS...
I DON'T UNDERSTAND. DID IT GO OUT?
GOD, MARCIA! HE'S **SO** UNSPOILED!
I KNOW.
©B Trudeau

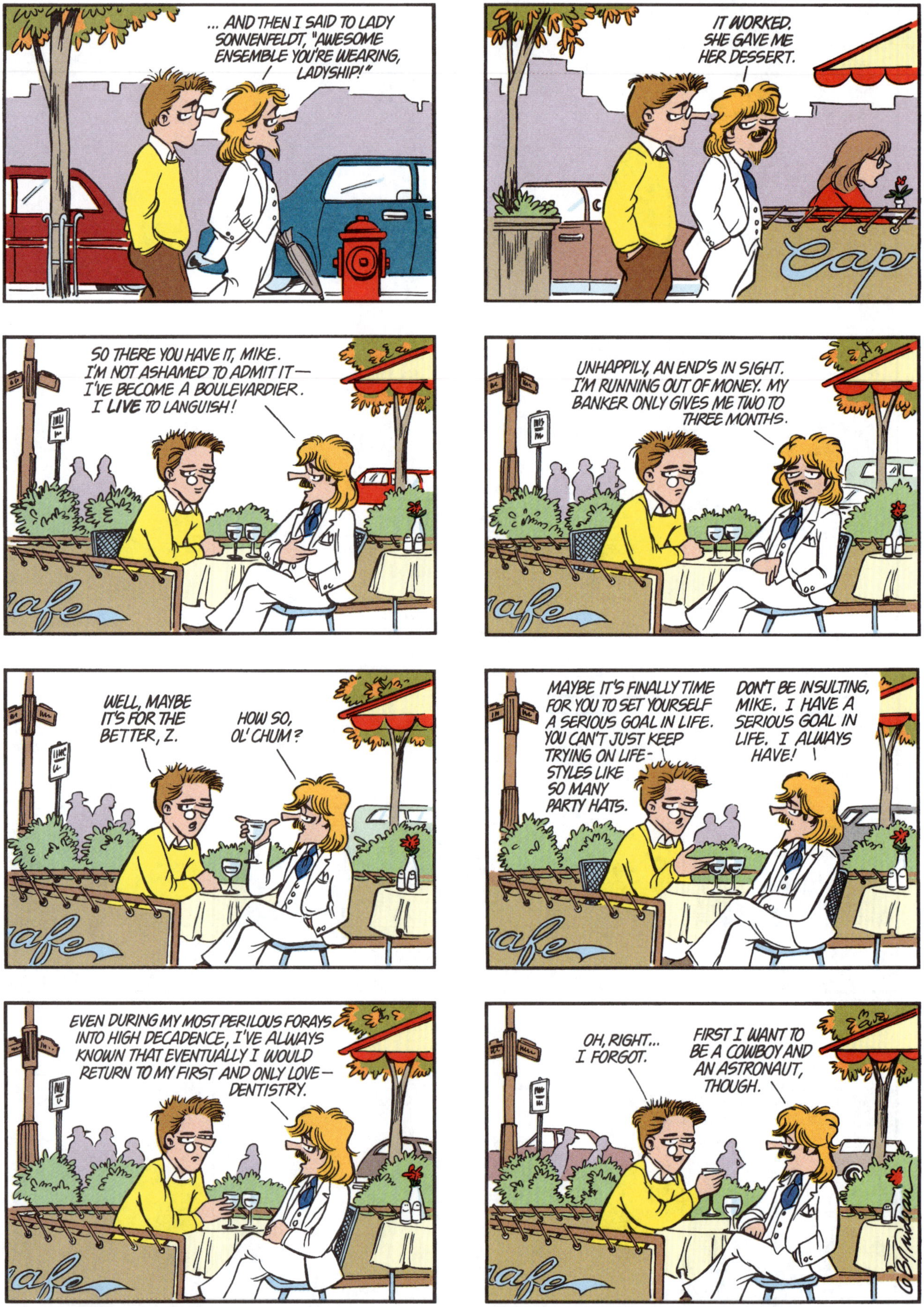
... AND THEN I SAID TO LADY SONNENFELDT, "AWESOME ENSEMBLE YOU'RE WEARING, LADYSHIP!"
IT WORKED. SHE GAVE ME HER DESSERT.
SO THERE YOU HAVE IT, MIKE. I'M NOT ASHAMED TO ADMIT IT— I'VE BECOME A BOULEVARDIER. I LIVE TO LANGUISH!
UNHAPPILY, AN END'S IN SIGHT. I'M RUNNING OUT OF MONEY. MY BANKER ONLY GIVES ME TWO TO THREE MONTHS.
WELL, MAYBE IT'S FOR THE BETTER, Z.
HOW SO, OL' CHUM?
MAYBE IT'S FINALLY TIME FOR YOU TO SET YOURSELF A SERIOUS GOAL IN LIFE. YOU CAN'T JUST KEEP TRYING ON LIFE-STYLES LIKE SO MANY PARTY HATS.
DON'T BE INSULTING, MIKE. I HAVE A SERIOUS GOAL IN LIFE. I ALWAYS HAVE!
EVEN DURING MY MOST PERILOUS FORAYS INTO HIGH DECADENCE, I'VE ALWAYS KNOWN THAT EVENTUALLY I WOULD RETURN TO MY FIRST AND ONLY LOVE— DENTISTRY.
OH, RIGHT... I FORGOT.
FIRST I WANT TO BE A COWBOY AND AN ASTRONAUT, THOUGH.

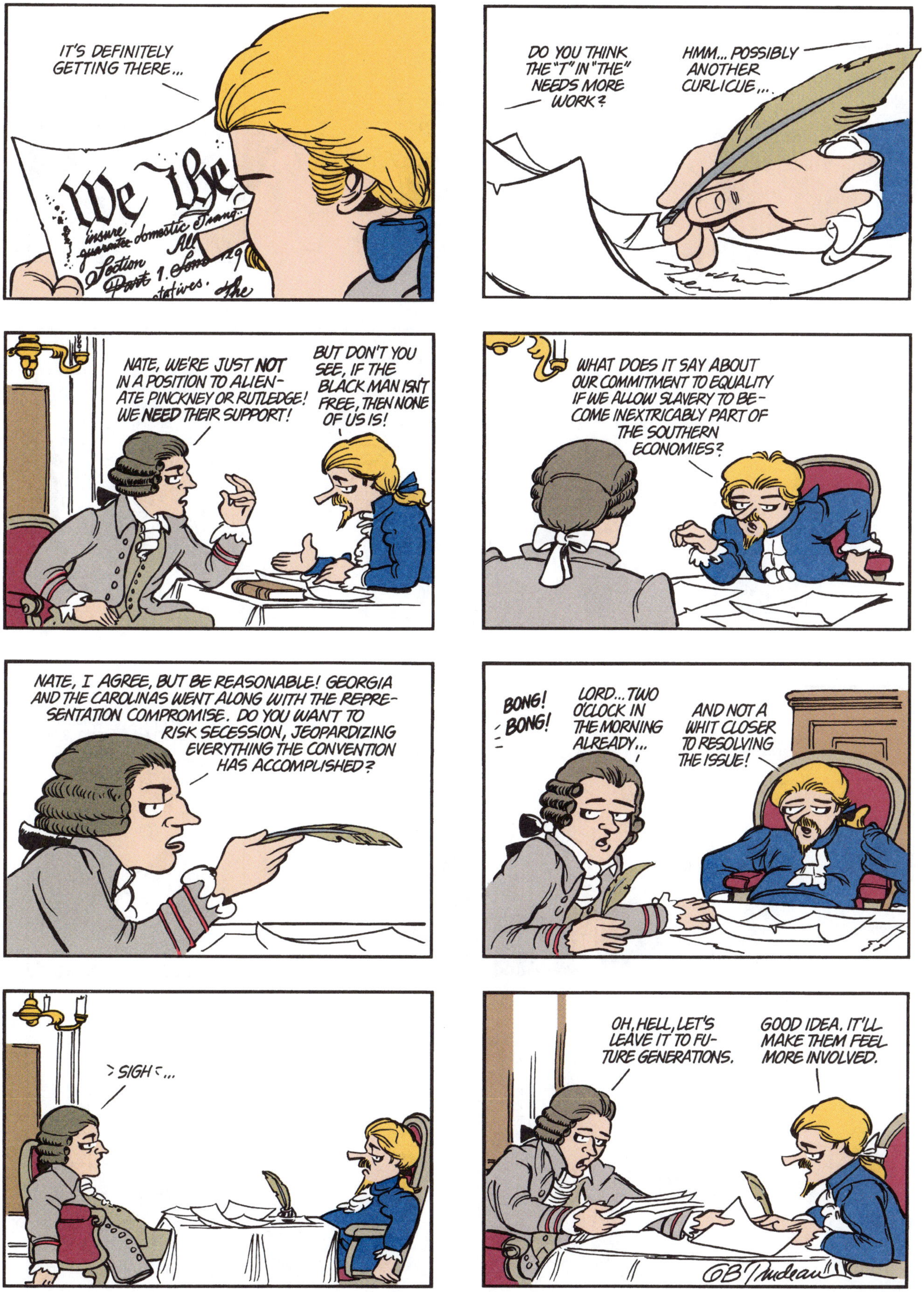
IT'S DEFINITELY GETTING THERE...
DO YOU THINK THE "T" IN "THE" NEEDS MORE WORK?
HMM... POSSIBLY ANOTHER CURLICUE,...
NATE, WE'RE JUST NOT IN A POSITION TO ALIENATE PINCKNEY OR RUTLEDGE! WE NEED THEIR SUPPORT!
BUT DON'T YOU SEE, IF THE BLACK MAN ISN'T FREE, THEN NONE OF US IS!
WHAT DOES IT SAY ABOUT OUR COMMITMENT TO EQUALITY IF WE ALLOW SLAVERY TO BECOME INEXTRICABLY PART OF THE SOUTHERN ECONOMIES?
NATE, I AGREE, BUT BE REASONABLE! GEORGIA AND THE CAROLINAS WENT ALONG WITH THE REPRESENTATION COMPROMISE. DO YOU WANT TO RISK SECESSION, JEOPARDIZING EVERYTHING THE CONVENTION HAS ACCOMPLISHED?
BONG! BONG!
LORD... TWO O'CLOCK IN THE MORNING ALREADY...
AND NOT A WHIT CLOSER TO RESOLVING THE ISSUE!
SIGH...
OH, HELL, LET'S LEAVE IT TO FUTURE GENERATIONS.
GOOD IDEA. IT'LL MAKE THEM FEEL MORE INVOLVED.
GB Trudeau

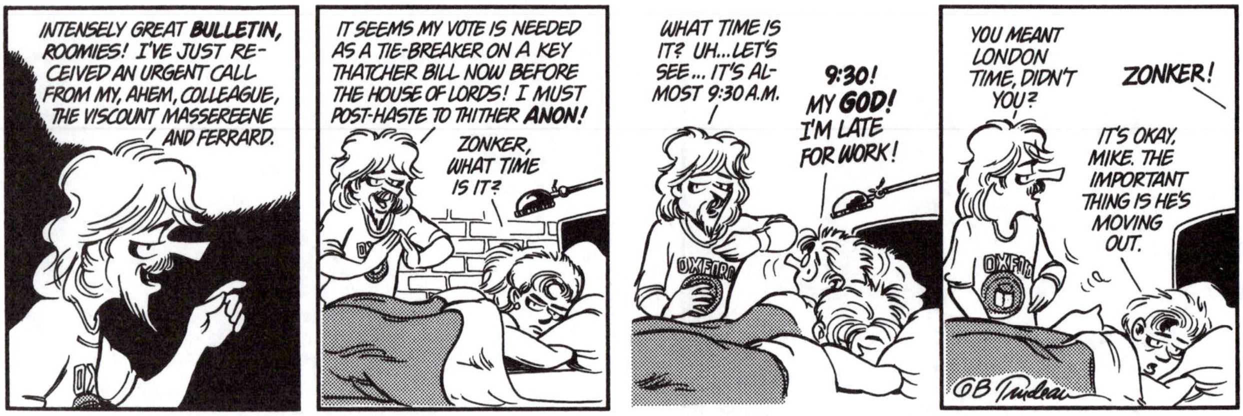
INTENSELY GREAT BULLETIN, ROOMIES! I'VE JUST RECEIVED AN URGENT CALL FROM MY, AHEM, COLLEAGUE, THE VISCOUNT MASSEREENE AND FERRARD.
IT SEEMS MY VOTE IS NEEDED AS A TIE-BREAKER ON A KEY THATCHER BILL NOW BEFORE THE HOUSE OF LORDS! I MUST POST-HASTE TO THITHER ANON!
ZONKER, WHAT TIME IS IT?
WHAT TIME IS IT? UH...LET'S SEE... IT'S ALMOST 9:30 A.M.
9:30! MY GOD! I'M LATE FOR WORK!
YOU MEANT LONDON TIME, DIDN'T YOU?
ZONKER!
IT'S OKAY, MIKE. THE IMPORTANT THING IS HE'S MOVING OUT.
OXFORD
©B Trudeau

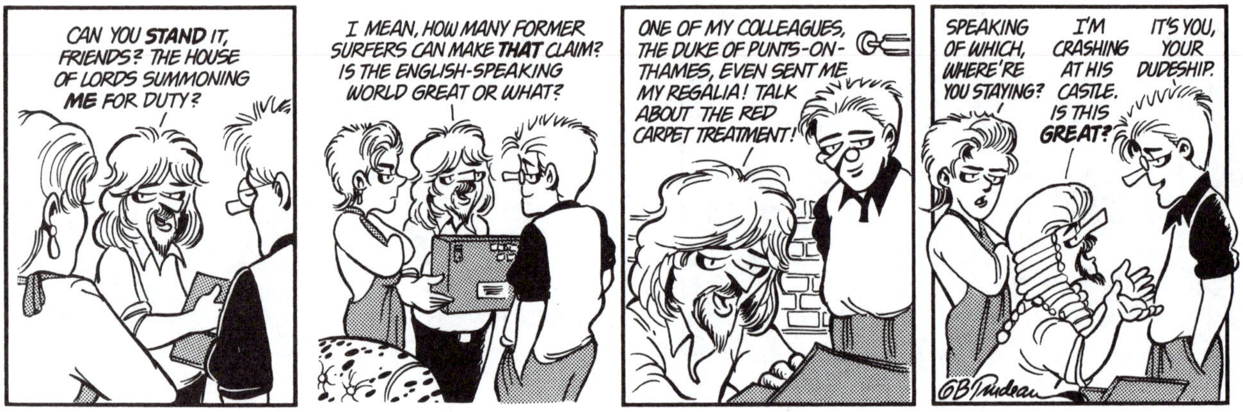
CAN YOU STAND IT, FRIENDS? THE HOUSE OF LORDS SUMMONING ME FOR DUTY?
I MEAN, HOW MANY FORMER SURFERS CAN MAKE THAT CLAIM? IS THE ENGLISH-SPEAKING WORLD GREAT OR WHAT?
ONE OF MY COLLEAGUES, THE DUKE OF PUNTS-ON-THAMES, EVEN SENT ME MY REGALIA! TALK ABOUT THE RED CARPET TREATMENT!
SPEAKING OF WHICH, WHERE'RE YOU STAYING?
I'M CRASHING AT HIS CASTLE. IS THIS GREAT?
IT'S YOU, YOUR DUDESHIP.
©B Trudeau

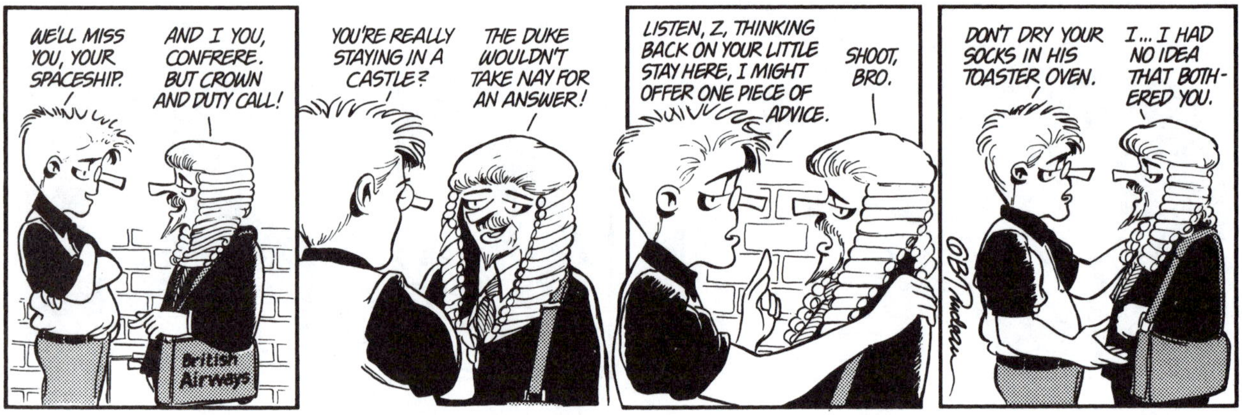
WE'LL MISS YOU, YOUR SPACESHIP.
AND I YOU, CONFRERE. BUT CROWN AND DUTY CALL!
British Airways
YOU'RE REALLY STAYING IN A CASTLE?
THE DUKE WOULDN'T TAKE NAY FOR AN ANSWER!
LISTEN, Z, THINKING BACK ON YOUR LITTLE STAY HERE, I MIGHT OFFER ONE PIECE OF ADVICE.
SHOOT, BRO.
DON'T DRY YOUR SOCKS IN HIS TOASTER OVEN.
I... I HAD NO IDEA THAT BOTHERED YOU.
©B Trudeau

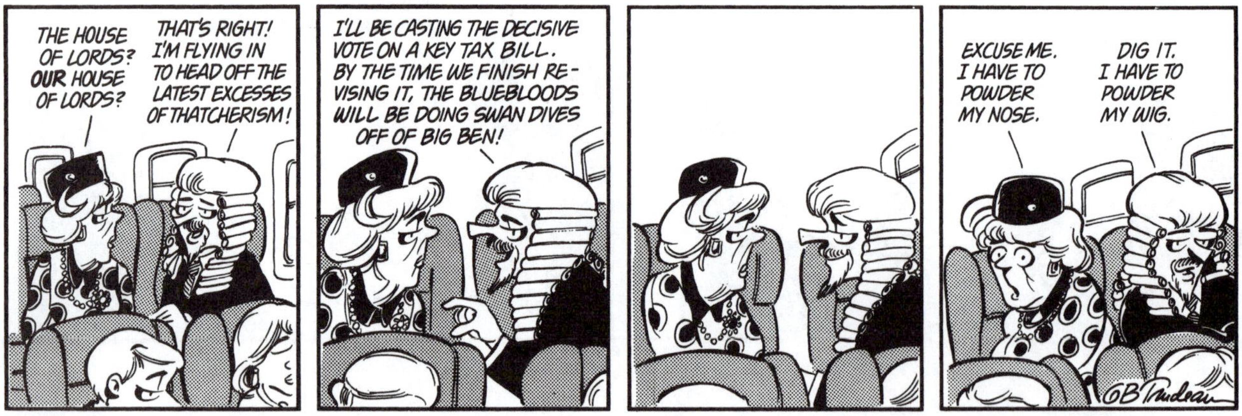
THE HOUSE OF LORDS? OUR HOUSE OF LORDS?
THAT'S RIGHT! I'M FLYING IN TO HEAD OFF THE LATEST EXCESSES OF THATCHERISM!
I'LL BE CASTING THE DECISIVE VOTE ON A KEY TAX BILL. BY THE TIME WE FINISH REVISING IT, THE BLUEBLOODS WILL BE DOING SWAN DIVES OFF OF BIG BEN!
EXCUSE ME. I HAVE TO POWDER MY NOSE.
DIG IT. I HAVE TO POWDER MY WIG.
©B Trudeau

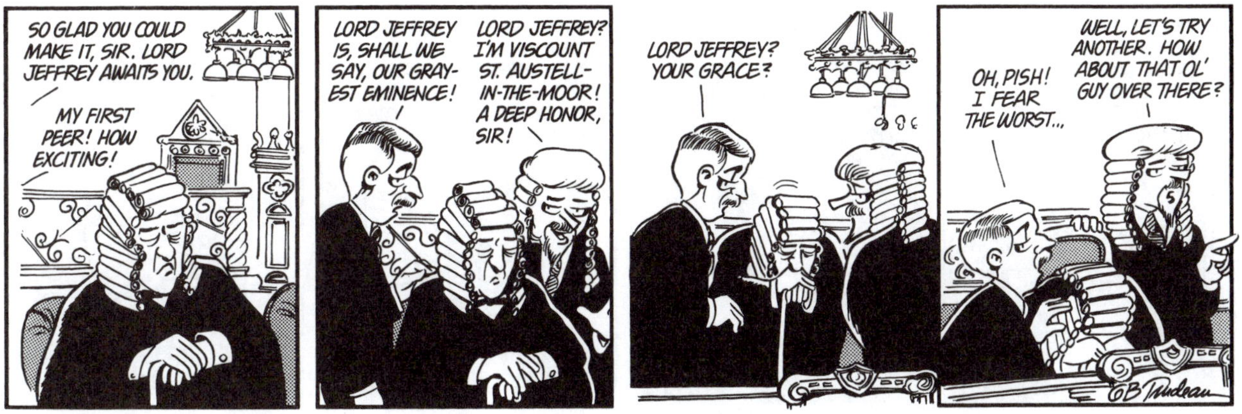
SO GLAD YOU COULD MAKE IT, SIR. LORD JEFFREY AWAITS YOU.
MY FIRST PEER! HOW EXCITING!
LORD JEFFREY IS, SHALL WE SAY, OUR GRAYEST EMINENCE!
LORD JEFFREY? I'M VISCOUNT ST. AUSTELL-IN-THE-MOOR! A DEEP HONOR, SIR!
LORD JEFFREY? YOUR GRACE?
OH, PISH! I FEAR THE WORST...
WELL, LET'S TRY ANOTHER. HOW ABOUT THAT OL' GUY OVER THERE?
GBTrudeau

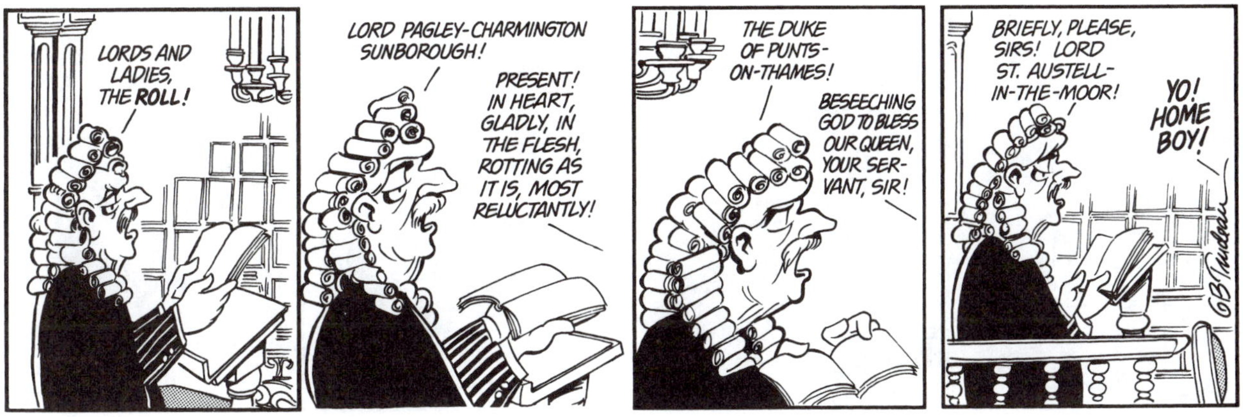
LORDS AND LADIES, THE ROLL!
LORD PAGLEY-CHARMINGTON SUNBOROUGH!
PRESENT! IN HEART, GLADLY, IN THE FLESH, ROTTING AS IT IS, MOST RELUCTANTLY!
THE DUKE OF PUNTS-ON-THAMES!
BESEECHING GOD TO BLESS OUR QUEEN, YOUR SERVANT, SIR!
BRIEFLY, PLEASE, SIRS! LORD ST. AUSTELL-IN-THE-MOOR!
YO! HOME BOY!
GBTrudeau

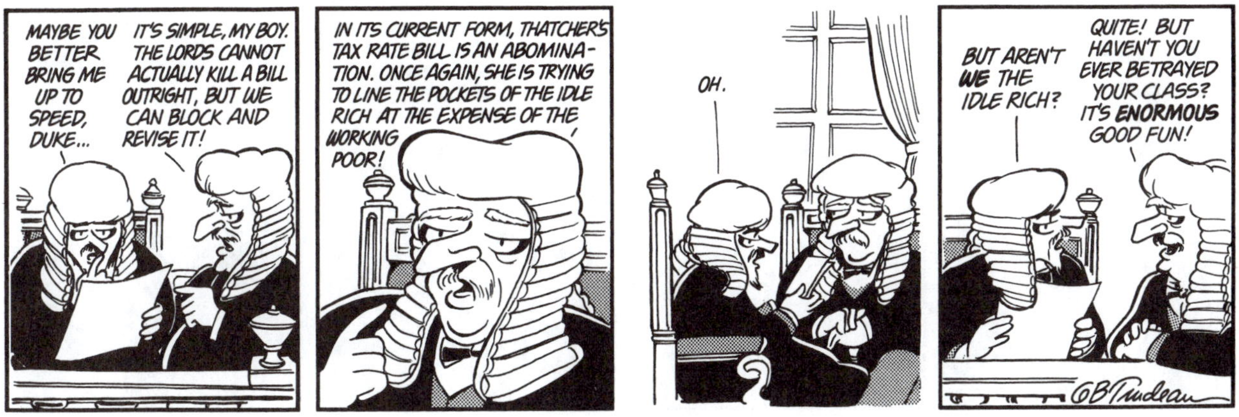
MAYBE YOU BETTER BRING ME UP TO SPEED, DUKE...
IT'S SIMPLE, MY BOY. THE LORDS CANNOT ACTUALLY KILL A BILL OUTRIGHT, BUT WE CAN BLOCK AND REVISE IT!
IN ITS CURRENT FORM, THATCHER'S TAX RATE BILL IS AN ABOMINATION. ONCE AGAIN, SHE IS TRYING TO LINE THE POCKETS OF THE IDLE RICH AT THE EXPENSE OF THE WORKING POOR!
OH.
BUT AREN'T WE THE IDLE RICH?
QUITE! BUT HAVEN'T YOU EVER BETRAYED YOUR CLASS? IT'S ENORMOUS GOOD FUN!
GBTrudeau

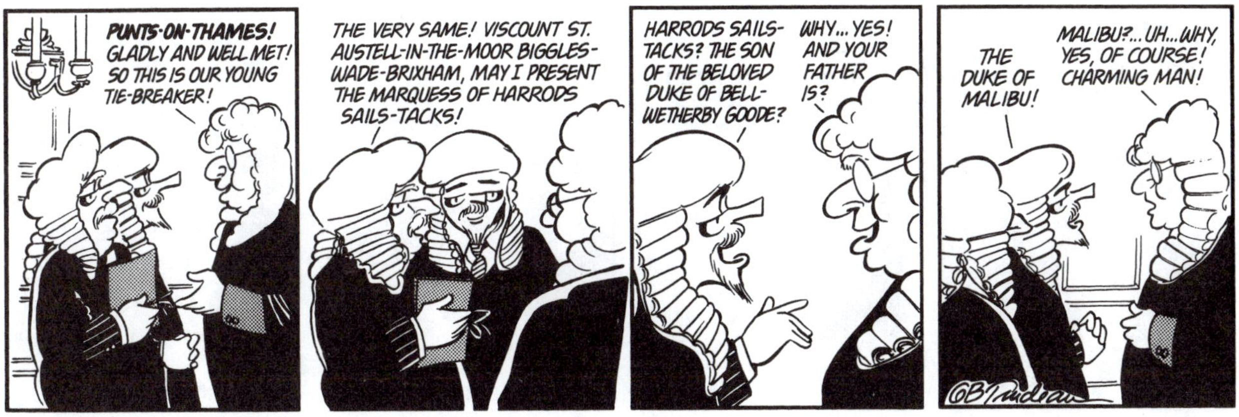
PUNTS-ON-THAMES! GLADLY AND WELL MET! SO THIS IS OUR YOUNG TIE-BREAKER!
THE VERY SAME! VISCOUNT ST. AUSTELL-IN-THE-MOOR BIGGLESWADE-BRIXHAM, MAY I PRESENT THE MARQUESS OF HARRODS SAILS-TACKS!
HARRODS SAILS-TACKS? THE SON OF THE BELOVED DUKE OF BELLWETHERBY GOODE?
WHY... YES! AND YOUR FATHER IS?
THE DUKE OF MALIBU!
MALIBU?... UH... WHY, YES, OF COURSE! CHARMING MAN!
GBTrudeau

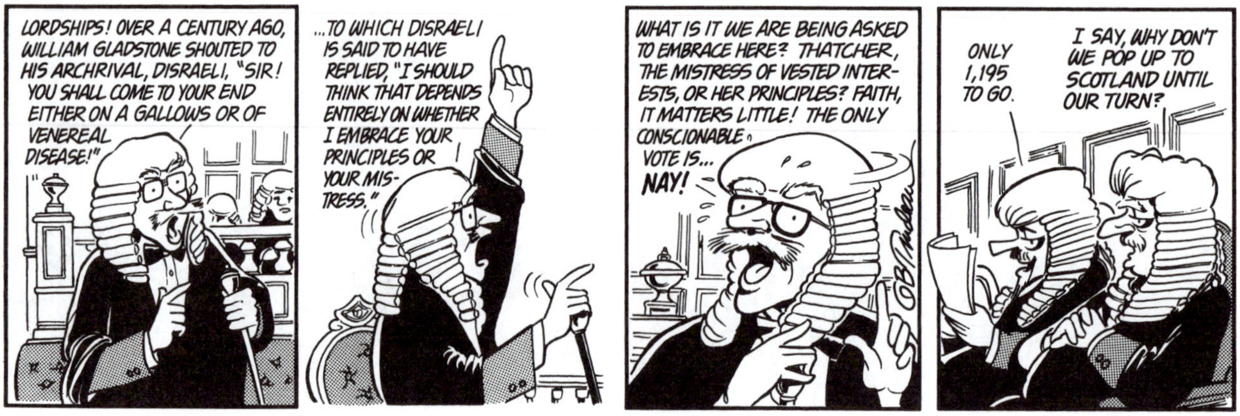
LORDSHIPS! OVER A CENTURY AGO, WILLIAM GLADSTONE SHOUTED TO HIS ARCHRIVAL, DISRAELI, "SIR! YOU SHALL COME TO YOUR END EITHER ON A GALLOWS OR OF VENEREAL DISEASE!"
...TO WHICH DISRAELI IS SAID TO HAVE REPLIED, "I SHOULD THINK THAT DEPENDS ENTIRELY ON WHETHER I EMBRACE YOUR PRINCIPLES OR YOUR MISTRESS."
WHAT IS IT WE ARE BEING ASKED TO EMBRACE HERE? THATCHER, THE MISTRESS OF VESTED INTERESTS, OR HER PRINCIPLES? FAITH, IT MATTERS LITTLE! THE ONLY CONSCIONABLE VOTE IS... NAY!
ONLY 1,195 TO GO.
I SAY, WHY DON'T WE POP UP TO SCOTLAND UNTIL OUR TURN?

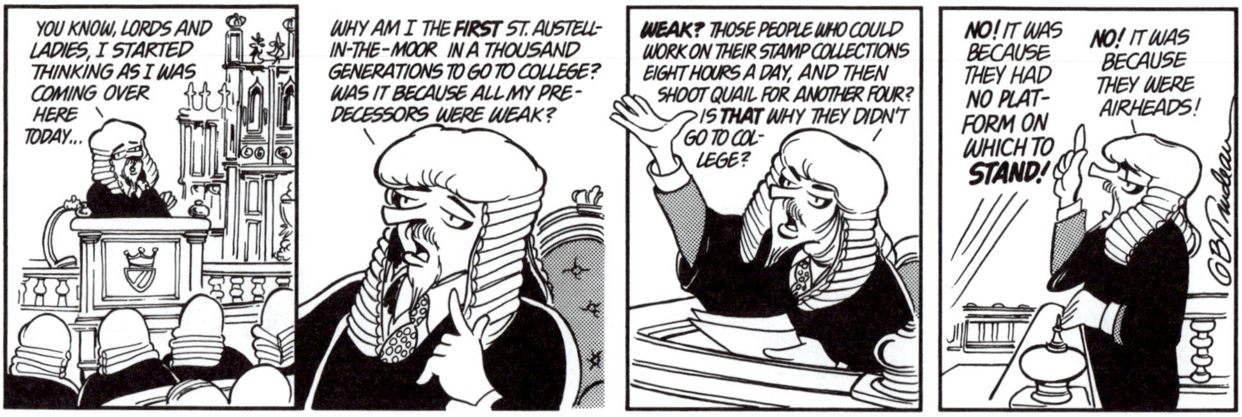
YOU KNOW, LORDS AND LADIES, I STARTED THINKING AS I WAS COMING OVER HERE TODAY...
WHY AM I THE FIRST ST. AUSTELL-IN-THE-MOOR IN A THOUSAND GENERATIONS TO GO TO COLLEGE? WAS IT BECAUSE ALL MY PREDECESSORS WERE WEAK?
WEAK? THOSE PEOPLE WHO COULD WORK ON THEIR STAMP COLLECTIONS EIGHT HOURS A DAY, AND THEN SHOOT QUAIL FOR ANOTHER FOUR? IS THAT WHY THEY DIDN'T GO TO COLLEGE?
NO! IT WAS BECAUSE THEY HAD NO PLATFORM ON WHICH TO STAND!
NO! IT WAS BECAUSE THEY WERE AIRHEADS!

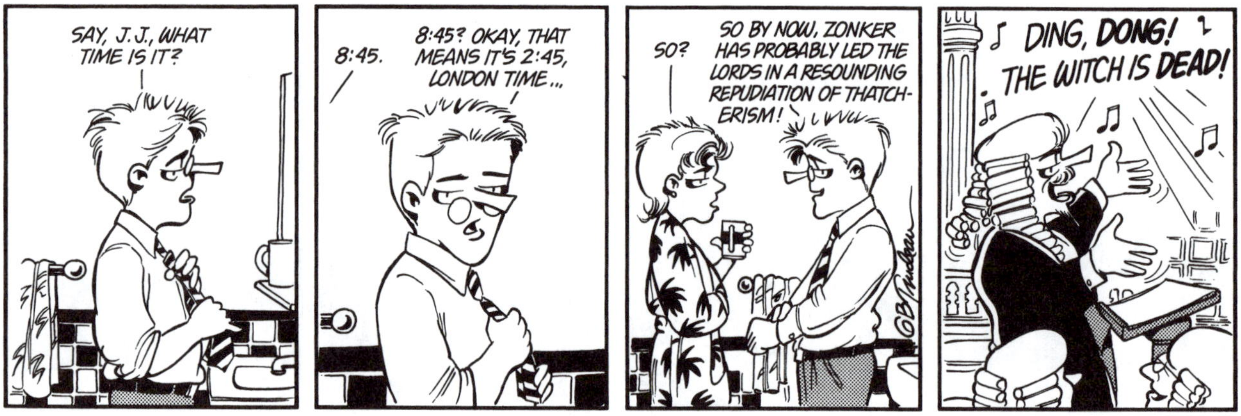
SAY, J.J., WHAT TIME IS IT?
8:45.
8:45? OKAY, THAT MEANS IT'S 2:45, LONDON TIME...
SO?
SO BY NOW, ZONKER HAS PROBABLY LED THE LORDS IN A RESOUNDING REPUDIATION OF THATCHERISM!
DING, DONG! THE WITCH IS DEAD!

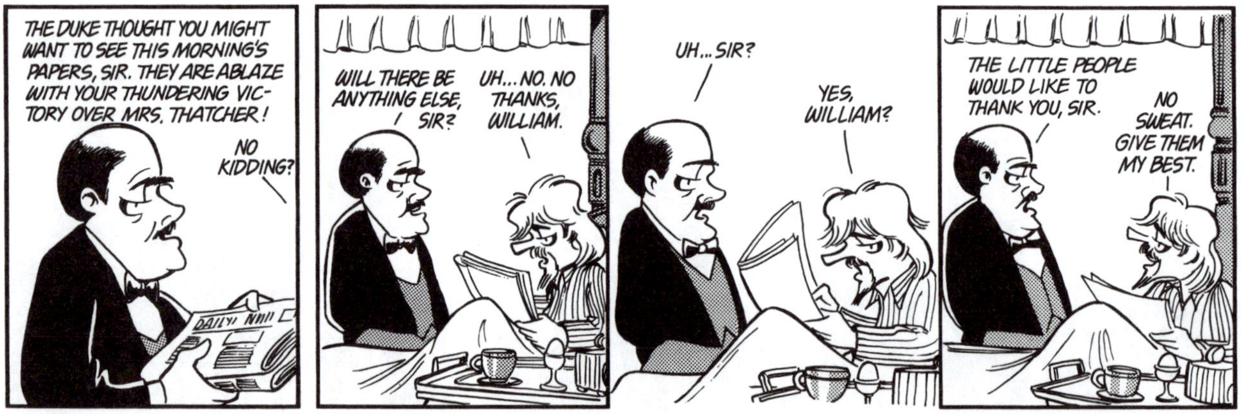
THE DUKE THOUGHT YOU MIGHT WANT TO SEE THIS MORNING'S PAPERS, SIR. THEY ARE ABLAZE WITH YOUR THUNDERING VICTORY OVER MRS. THATCHER!
NO KIDDING?
WILL THERE BE ANYTHING ELSE, SIR?
UH... NO. NO THANKS, WILLIAM.
UH... SIR?
YES, WILLIAM?
THE LITTLE PEOPLE WOULD LIKE TO THANK YOU, SIR.
NO SWEAT. GIVE THEM MY BEST.

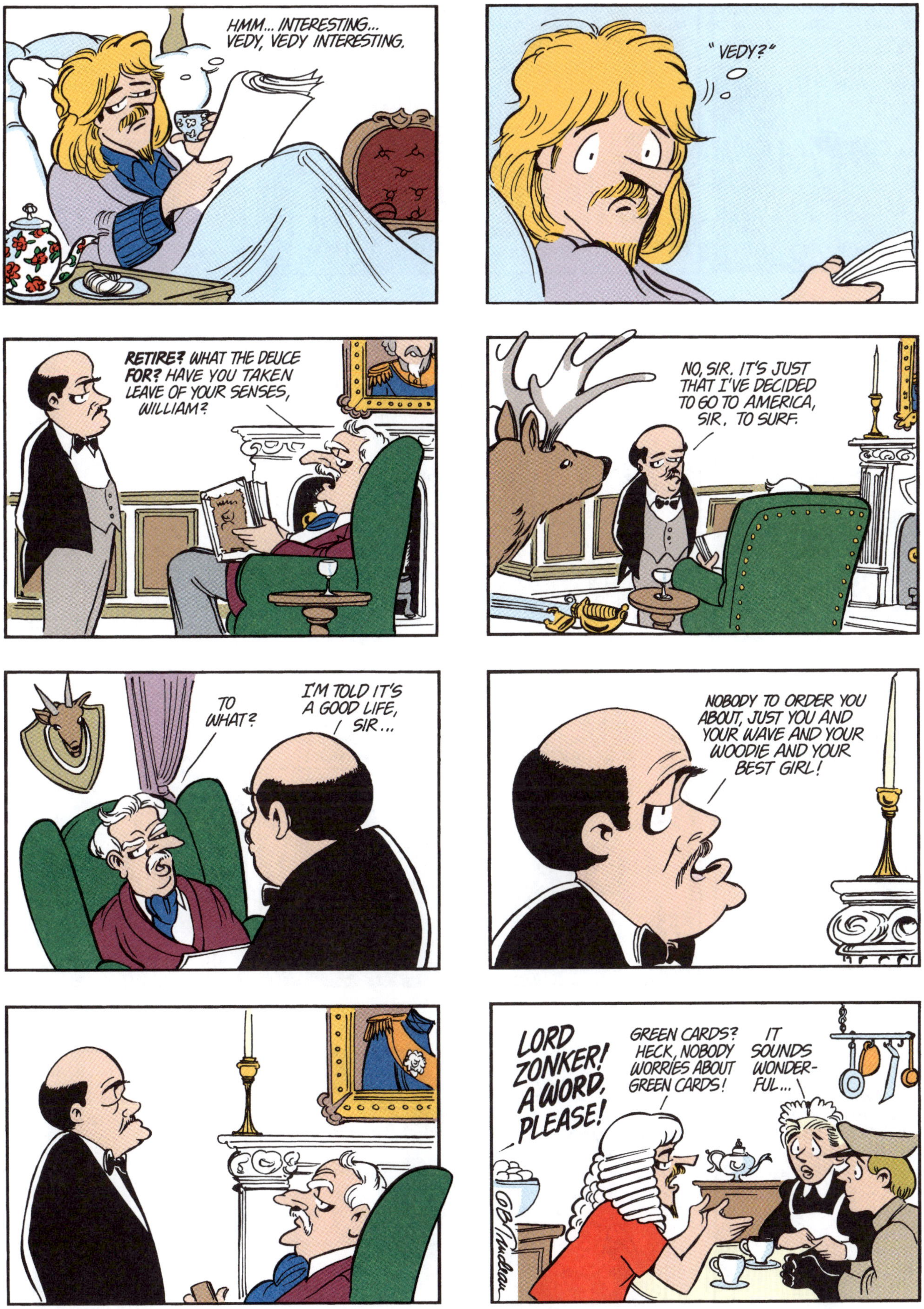

HMM... INTERESTING... VEDY, VEDY INTERESTING.
"VEDY?"
RETIRE? WHAT THE DEUCE FOR? HAVE YOU TAKEN LEAVE OF YOUR SENSES, WILLIAM?
NO, SIR. IT'S JUST THAT I'VE DECIDED TO GO TO AMERICA, SIR. TO SURF.
TO WHAT?
I'M TOLD IT'S A GOOD LIFE, SIR...
NOBODY TO ORDER YOU ABOUT, JUST YOU AND YOUR WAVE AND YOUR WOODIE AND YOUR BEST GIRL!
LORD ZONKER! A WORD, PLEASE!
GREEN CARDS? HECK, NOBODY WORRIES ABOUT GREEN CARDS!
IT SOUNDS WONDER-FUL...

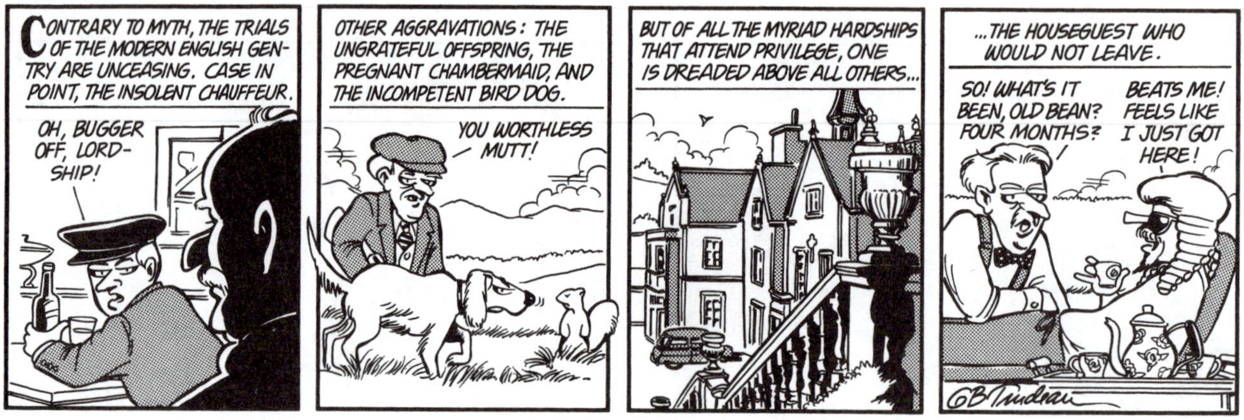
CONTRARY TO MYTH, THE TRIALS OF THE MODERN ENGLISH GENTRY ARE UNCEASING. CASE IN POINT, THE INSOLENT CHAUFFEUR.
OH, BUGGER OFF, LORDSHIP!
OTHER AGGRAVATIONS: THE UNGRATEFUL OFFSPRING, THE PREGNANT CHAMBERMAID, AND THE INCOMPETENT BIRD DOG.
YOU WORTHLESS MUTT!
BUT OF ALL THE MYRIAD HARDSHIPS THAT ATTEND PRIVILEGE, ONE IS DREADED ABOVE ALL OTHERS...
...THE HOUSEGUEST WHO WOULD NOT LEAVE.
SO! WHAT'S IT BEEN, OLD BEAN? FOUR MONTHS?
BEATS ME! FEELS LIKE I JUST GOT HERE!

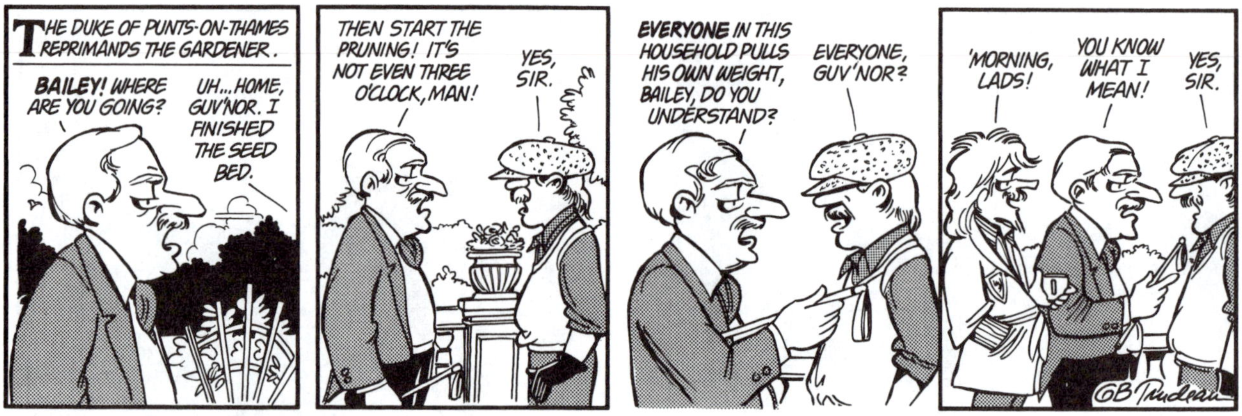
THE DUKE OF PUNTS-ON-THAMES REPRIMANDS THE GARDENER.
BAILEY! WHERE ARE YOU GOING?
UH... HOME, GUV'NOR. I FINISHED THE SEED BED.
THEN START THE PRUNING! IT'S NOT EVEN THREE O'CLOCK, MAN!
YES, SIR.
EVERYONE IN THIS HOUSEHOLD PULLS HIS OWN WEIGHT, BAILEY, DO YOU UNDERSTAND?
EVERYONE, GUV'NOR?
'MORNING, LADS!
YOU KNOW WHAT I MEAN!
YES, SIR.

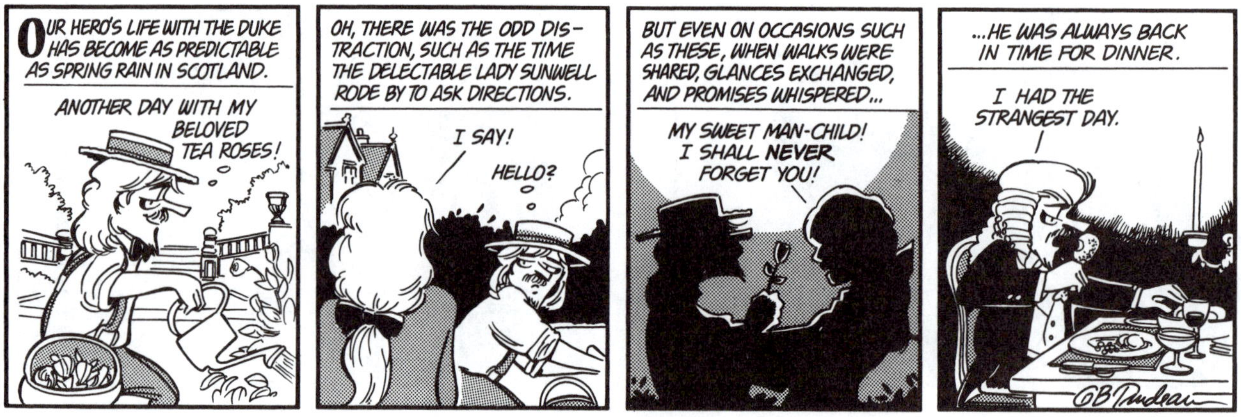
OUR HERO'S LIFE WITH THE DUKE HAS BECOME AS PREDICTABLE AS SPRING RAIN IN SCOTLAND.
ANOTHER DAY WITH MY BELOVED TEA ROSES!
OH, THERE WAS THE ODD DISTRACTION, SUCH AS THE TIME THE DELECTABLE LADY SUNWELL RODE BY TO ASK DIRECTIONS.
I SAY!
HELLO?
BUT EVEN ON OCCASIONS SUCH AS THESE, WHEN WALKS WERE SHARED, GLANCES EXCHANGED, AND PROMISES WHISPERED...
MY SWEET MAN-CHILD! I SHALL NEVER FORGET YOU!
...HE WAS ALWAYS BACK IN TIME FOR DINNER.
I HAD THE STRANGEST DAY.

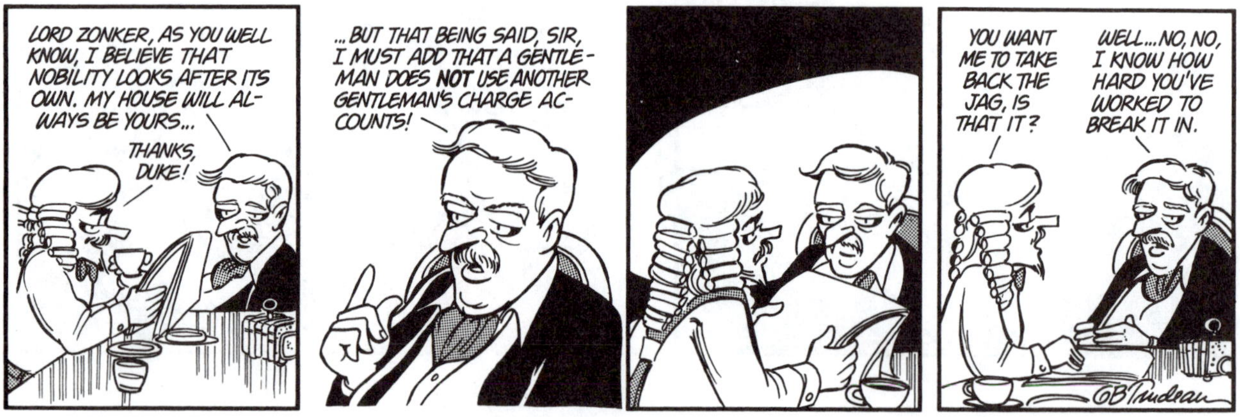
LORD ZONKER, AS YOU WELL KNOW, I BELIEVE THAT NOBILITY LOOKS AFTER ITS OWN. MY HOUSE WILL ALWAYS BE YOURS...
THANKS, DUKE!
... BUT THAT BEING SAID, SIR, I MUST ADD THAT A GENTLEMAN DOES NOT USE ANOTHER GENTLEMAN'S CHARGE ACCOUNTS!
YOU WANT ME TO TAKE BACK THE JAG, IS THAT IT?
WELL... NO, NO, I KNOW HOW HARD YOU'VE WORKED TO BREAK IT IN.

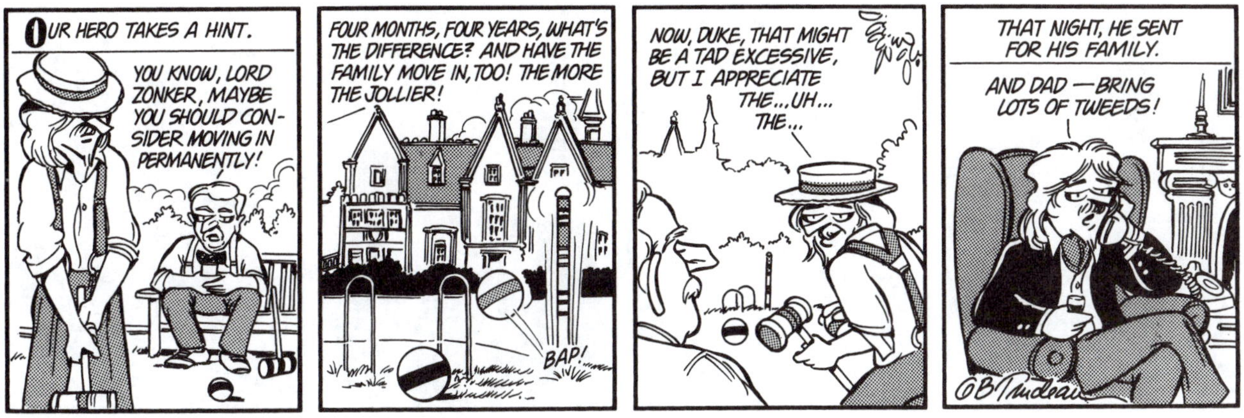
OUR HERO TAKES A HINT.
YOU KNOW, LORD ZONKER, MAYBE YOU SHOULD CONSIDER MOVING IN PERMANENTLY!
FOUR MONTHS, FOUR YEARS, WHAT'S THE DIFFERENCE? AND HAVE THE FAMILY MOVE IN, TOO! THE MORE THE JOLLIER!
BAP!
NOW, DUKE, THAT MIGHT BE A TAD EXCESSIVE, BUT I APPRECIATE THE... UH... THE...
THAT NIGHT, HE SENT FOR HIS FAMILY.
AND DAD — BRING LOTS OF TWEEDS!

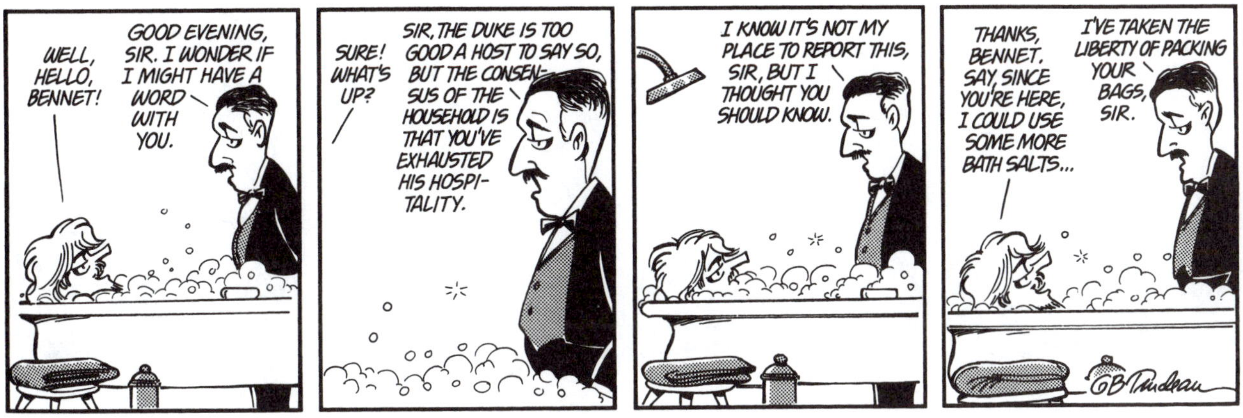
WELL, HELLO, BENNET!
GOOD EVENING, SIR. I WONDER IF I MIGHT HAVE A WORD WITH YOU.
SURE! WHAT'S UP?
SIR, THE DUKE IS TOO GOOD A HOST TO SAY SO, BUT THE CONSENSUS OF THE HOUSEHOLD IS THAT YOU'VE EXHAUSTED HIS HOSPITALITY.
I KNOW IT'S NOT MY PLACE TO REPORT THIS, SIR, BUT I THOUGHT YOU SHOULD KNOW.
I'VE TAKEN THE LIBERTY OF PACKING YOUR BAGS, SIR.
THANKS, BENNET. SAY, SINCE YOU'RE HERE, I COULD USE SOME MORE BATH SALTS...

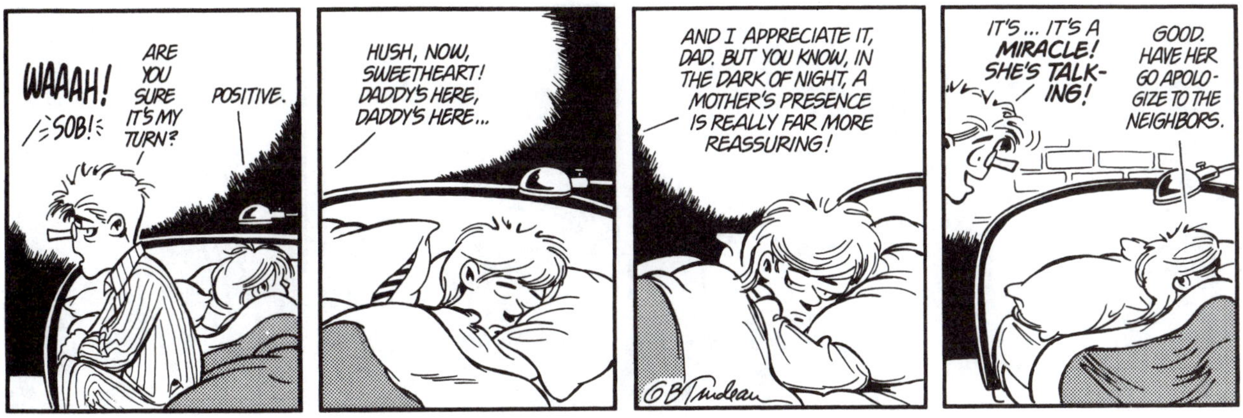
WAAAH! SOB!
ARE YOU SURE IT'S MY TURN?
POSITIVE.
HUSH, NOW, SWEETHEART! DADDY'S HERE, DADDY'S HERE...
AND I APPRECIATE IT, DAD. BUT YOU KNOW, IN THE DARK OF NIGHT, A MOTHER'S PRESENCE IS REALLY FAR MORE REASSURING!
IT'S... IT'S A MIRACLE! SHE'S TALKING!
GOOD. HAVE HER GO APOLOGIZE TO THE NEIGHBORS.

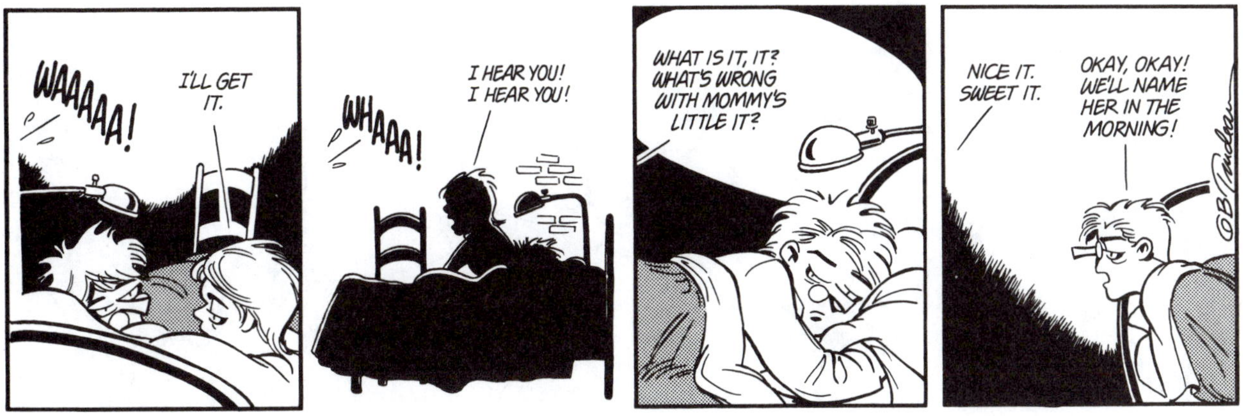
WAAAAA!
I'LL GET IT.
WHAAA!
I HEAR YOU! I HEAR YOU!
WHAT IS IT, IT? WHAT'S WRONG WITH MOMMY'S LITTLE IT?
NICE IT. SWEET IT.
OKAY, OKAY! WE'LL NAME HER IN THE MORNING!

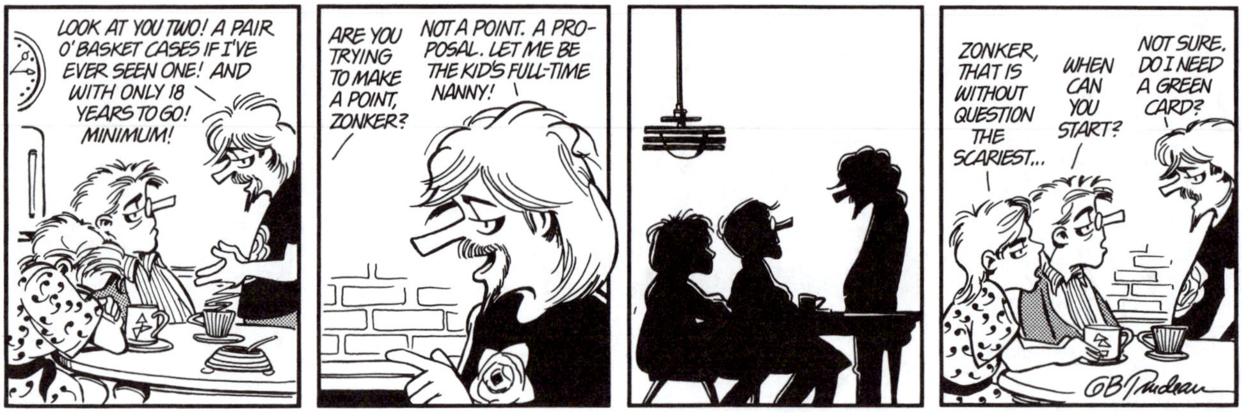
LOOK AT YOU TWO! A PAIR O' BASKET CASES IF I'VE EVER SEEN ONE! AND WITH ONLY 18 YEARS TO GO! MINIMUM!
ARE YOU TRYING TO MAKE A POINT, ZONKER?
NOT A POINT. A PROPOSAL. LET ME BE THE KID'S FULL-TIME NANNY!
ZONKER, THAT IS WITHOUT QUESTION THE SCARIEST...
WHEN CAN YOU START?
NOT SURE. DO I NEED A GREEN CARD?
GB Trudeau

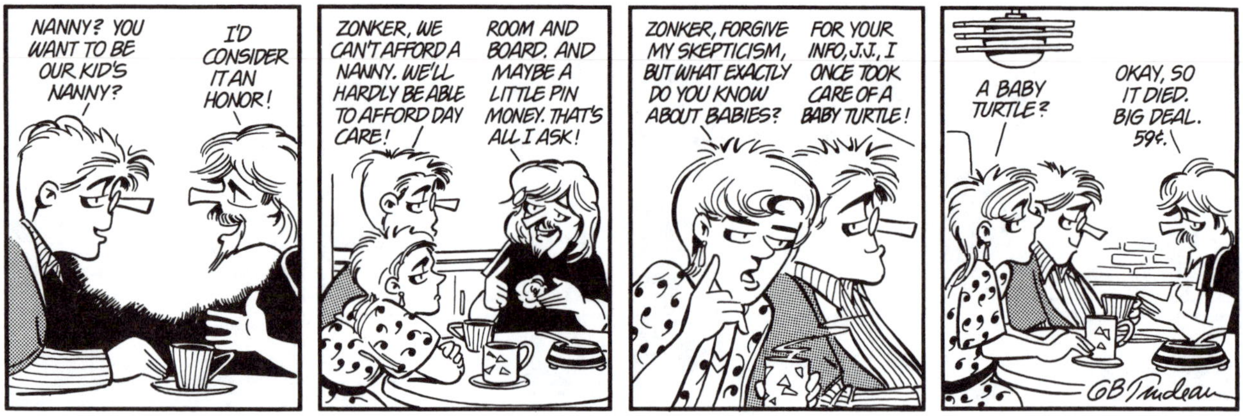
NANNY? YOU WANT TO BE OUR KID'S NANNY?
I'D CONSIDER IT AN HONOR!
ZONKER, WE CAN'T AFFORD A NANNY. WE'LL HARDLY BE ABLE TO AFFORD DAY CARE!
ROOM AND BOARD. AND MAYBE A LITTLE PIN MONEY. THAT'S ALL I ASK!
ZONKER, FORGIVE MY SKEPTICISM, BUT WHAT EXACTLY DO YOU KNOW ABOUT BABIES?
FOR YOUR INFO, J.J., I ONCE TOOK CARE OF A BABY TURTLE!
A BABY TURTLE?
OKAY, SO IT DIED. BIG DEAL. 59¢.
GB Trudeau

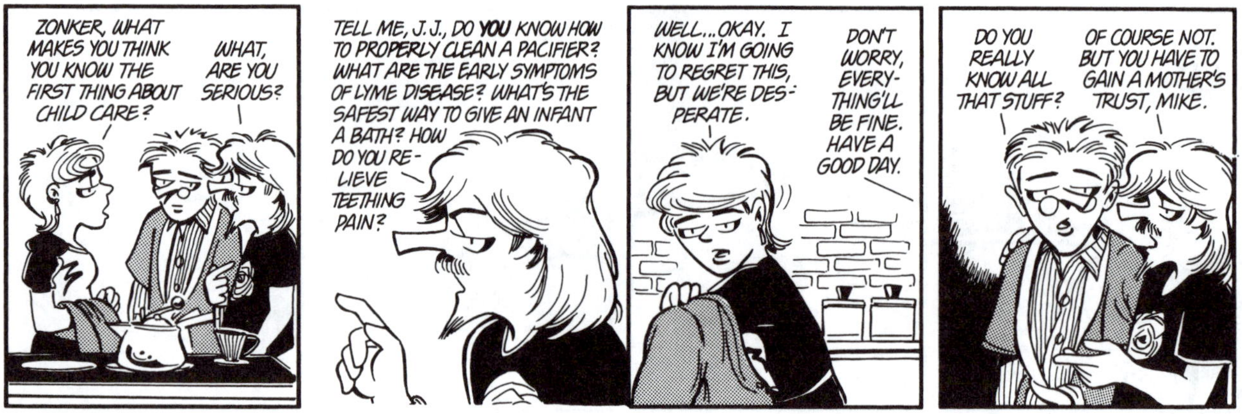
ZONKER, WHAT MAKES YOU THINK YOU KNOW THE FIRST THING ABOUT CHILD CARE?
WHAT, ARE YOU SERIOUS?
TELL ME, J.J., DO YOU KNOW HOW TO PROPERLY CLEAN A PACIFIER? WHAT ARE THE EARLY SYMPTOMS OF LYME DISEASE? WHAT'S THE SAFEST WAY TO GIVE AN INFANT A BATH? HOW DO YOU RELIEVE TEETHING PAIN?
WELL... OKAY. I KNOW I'M GOING TO REGRET THIS, BUT WE'RE DESPERATE.
DON'T WORRY, EVERYTHING'LL BE FINE. HAVE A GOOD DAY.
DO YOU REALLY KNOW ALL THAT STUFF?
OF COURSE NOT. BUT YOU HAVE TO GAIN A MOTHER'S TRUST, MIKE.

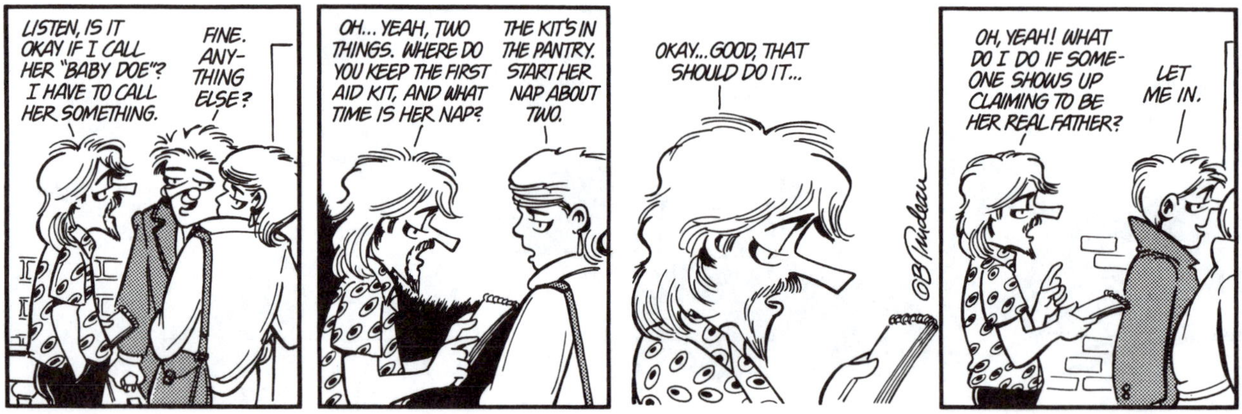
LISTEN, IS IT OKAY IF I CALL HER "BABY DOE"? I HAVE TO CALL HER SOMETHING.
FINE. ANYTHING ELSE?
OH... YEAH, TWO THINGS. WHERE DO YOU KEEP THE FIRST AID KIT, AND WHAT TIME IS HER NAP?
THE KIT'S IN THE PANTRY. START HER NAP ABOUT TWO.
OKAY... GOOD, THAT SHOULD DO IT...
GB Trudeau
OH, YEAH! WHAT DO I DO IF SOMEONE SHOWS UP CLAIMING TO BE HER REAL FATHER?
LET ME IN.

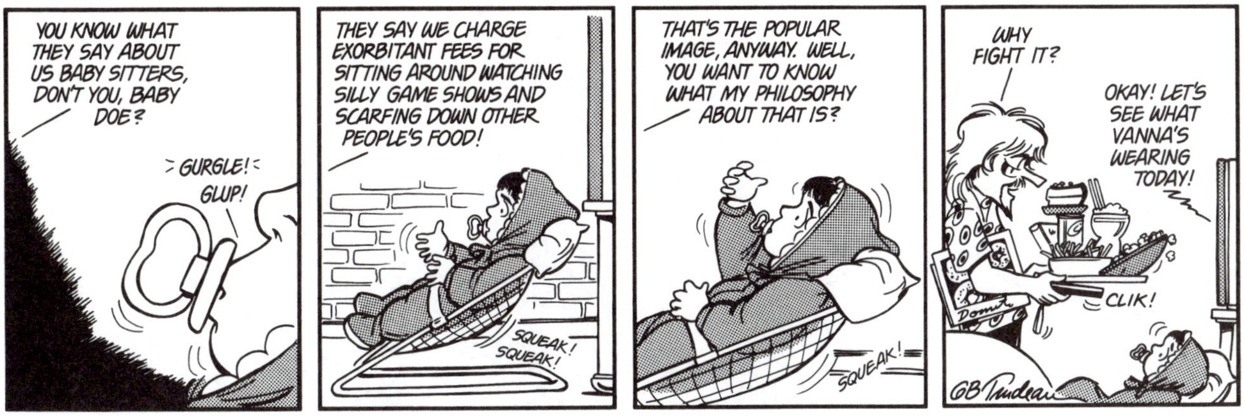

YOU KNOW WHAT THEY SAY ABOUT US BABY SITTERS, DON'T YOU, BABY DOE?
GURGLE! GLUP!
THEY SAY WE CHARGE EXORBITANT FEES FOR SITTING AROUND WATCHING SILLY GAME SHOWS AND SCARFING DOWN OTHER PEOPLE'S FOOD!
SQUEAK! SQUEAK!
THAT'S THE POPULAR IMAGE, ANYWAY. WELL, YOU WANT TO KNOW WHAT MY PHILOSOPHY ABOUT THAT IS?
SQUEAK!
WHY FIGHT IT?
OKAY! LET'S SEE WHAT VANNA'S WEARING TODAY!
CLIK!
GB Trudeau

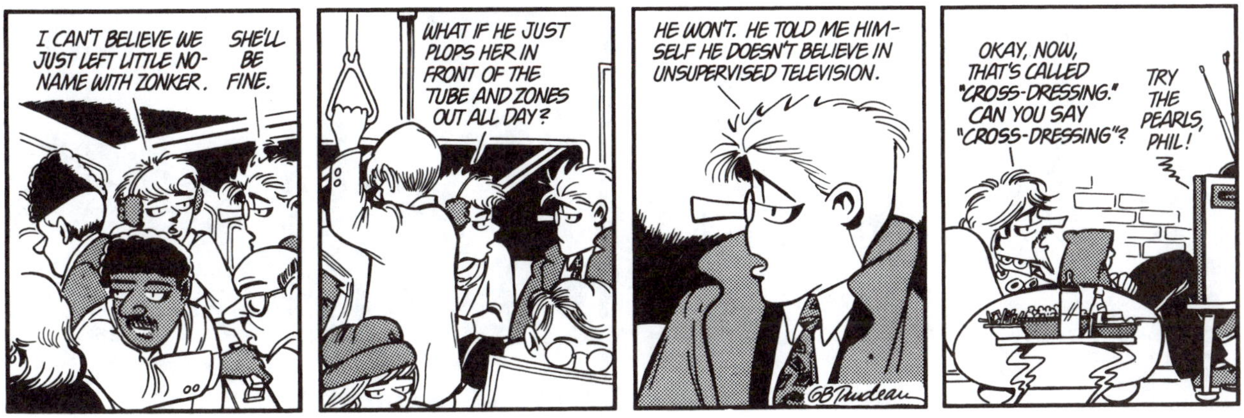

I CAN'T BELIEVE WE JUST LEFT LITTLE NO-NAME WITH ZONKER.
SHE'LL BE FINE.
WHAT IF HE JUST PLOPS HER IN FRONT OF THE TUBE AND ZONES OUT ALL DAY?
HE WON'T. HE TOLD ME HIMSELF HE DOESN'T BELIEVE IN UNSUPERVISED TELEVISION.
GB Trudeau
OKAY, NOW, THAT'S CALLED "CROSS-DRESSING." CAN YOU SAY "CROSS-DRESSING"?
TRY THE PEARLS, PHIL!

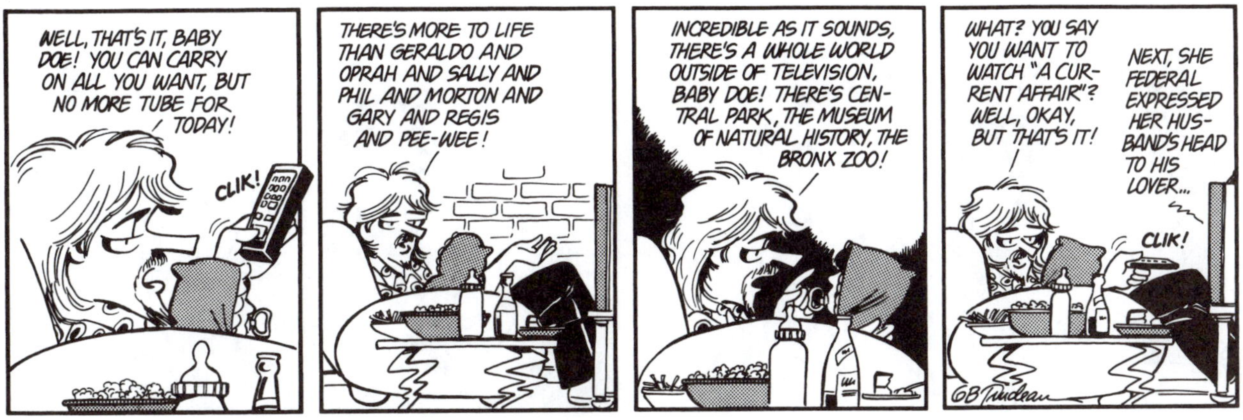

WELL, THAT'S IT, BABY DOE! YOU CAN CARRY ON ALL YOU WANT, BUT NO MORE TUBE FOR TODAY!
CLIK!
THERE'S MORE TO LIFE THAN GERALDO AND OPRAH AND SALLY AND PHIL AND MORTON AND GARY AND REGIS AND PEE-WEE!
INCREDIBLE AS IT SOUNDS, THERE'S A WHOLE WORLD OUTSIDE OF TELEVISION, BABY DOE! THERE'S CENTRAL PARK, THE MUSEUM OF NATURAL HISTORY, THE BRONX ZOO!
WHAT? YOU SAY YOU WANT TO WATCH "A CURRENT AFFAIR"? WELL, OKAY, BUT THAT'S IT!
NEXT, SHE FEDERAL EXPRESSED HER HUSBAND'S HEAD TO HIS LOVER...
CLIK!
GB Trudeau

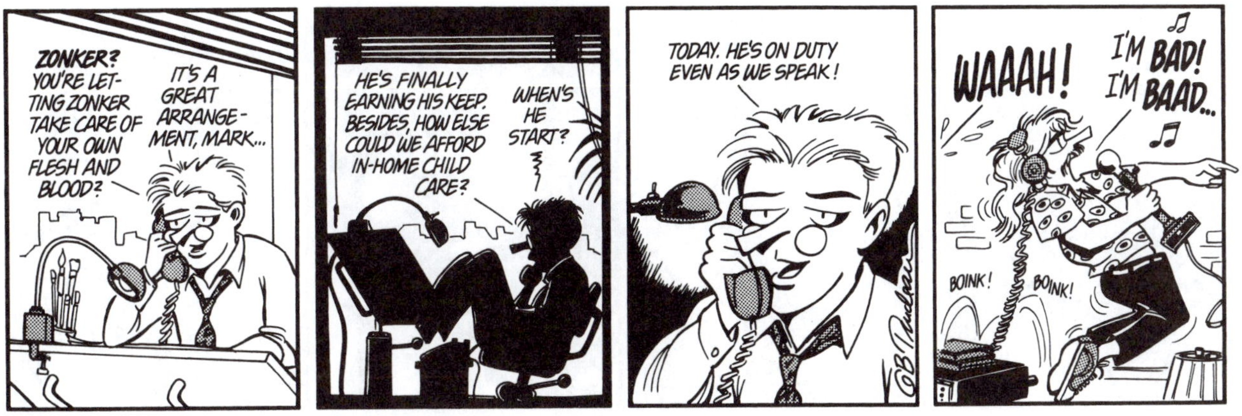

ZONKER? YOU'RE LETTING ZONKER TAKE CARE OF YOUR OWN FLESH AND BLOOD?
IT'S A GREAT ARRANGEMENT, MARK...
HE'S FINALLY EARNING HIS KEEP. BESIDES, HOW ELSE COULD WE AFFORD IN-HOME CHILD CARE?
WHEN'S HE START?
TODAY. HE'S ON DUTY EVEN AS WE SPEAK!
GB Trudeau
WAAAH!
I'M BAD! I'M BAAD...
BOINK! BOINK!

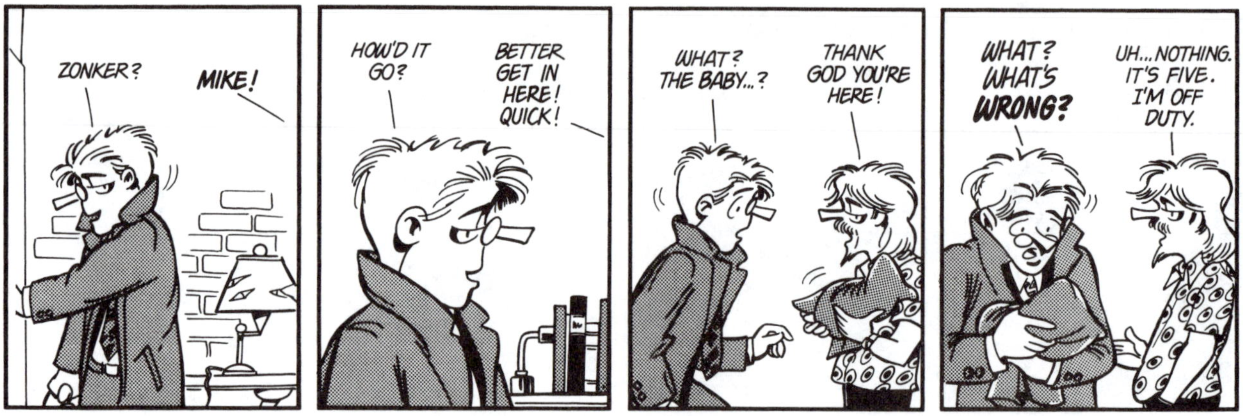
ZONKER?
MIKE!
HOW'D IT GO?
BETTER GET IN HERE! QUICK!
WHAT? THE BABY...?
THANK GOD YOU'RE HERE!
WHAT? WHAT'S WRONG?
UH... NOTHING. IT'S FIVE. I'M OFF DUTY.

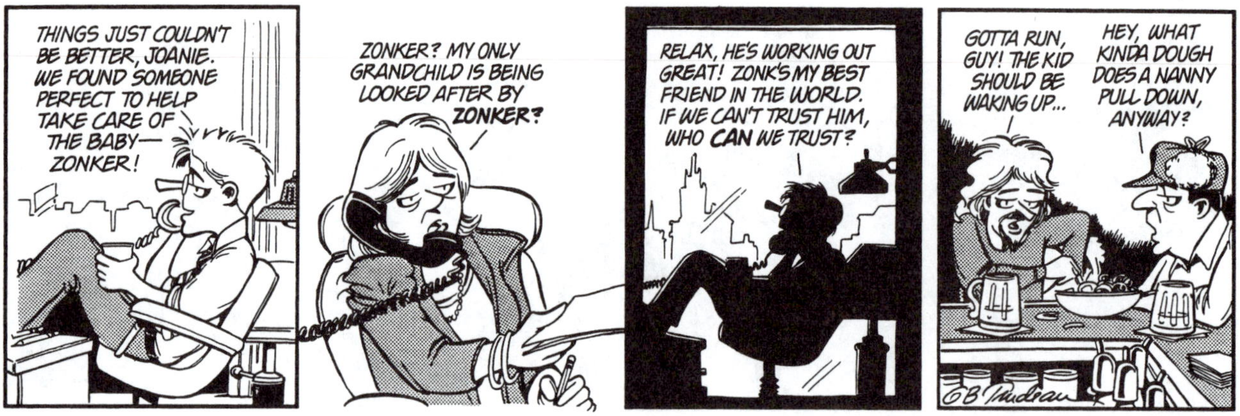
THINGS JUST COULDN'T BE BETTER, JOANIE. WE FOUND SOMEONE PERFECT TO HELP TAKE CARE OF THE BABY— ZONKER!
ZONKER? MY ONLY GRANDCHILD IS BEING LOOKED AFTER BY ZONKER?
RELAX, HE'S WORKING OUT GREAT! ZONK'S MY BEST FRIEND IN THE WORLD. IF WE CAN'T TRUST HIM, WHO CAN WE TRUST?
GOTTA RUN, GUY! THE KID SHOULD BE WAKING UP...
HEY, WHAT KINDA DOUGH DOES A NANNY PULL DOWN, ANYWAY?

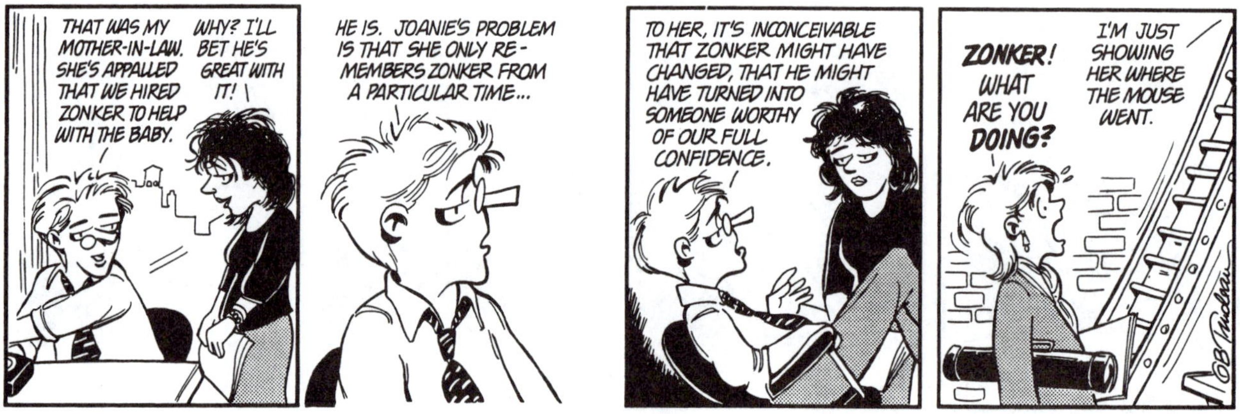
THAT WAS MY MOTHER-IN-LAW. SHE'S APPALLED THAT WE HIRED ZONKER TO HELP WITH THE BABY.
WHY? I'LL BET HE'S GREAT WITH IT!
HE IS. JOANIE'S PROBLEM IS THAT SHE ONLY RE-MEMBERS ZONKER FROM A PARTICULAR TIME...
TO HER, IT'S INCONCEIVABLE THAT ZONKER MIGHT HAVE CHANGED, THAT HE MIGHT HAVE TURNED INTO SOMEONE WORTHY OF OUR FULL CONFIDENCE.
ZONKER! WHAT ARE YOU DOING?
I'M JUST SHOWING HER WHERE THE MOUSE WENT.

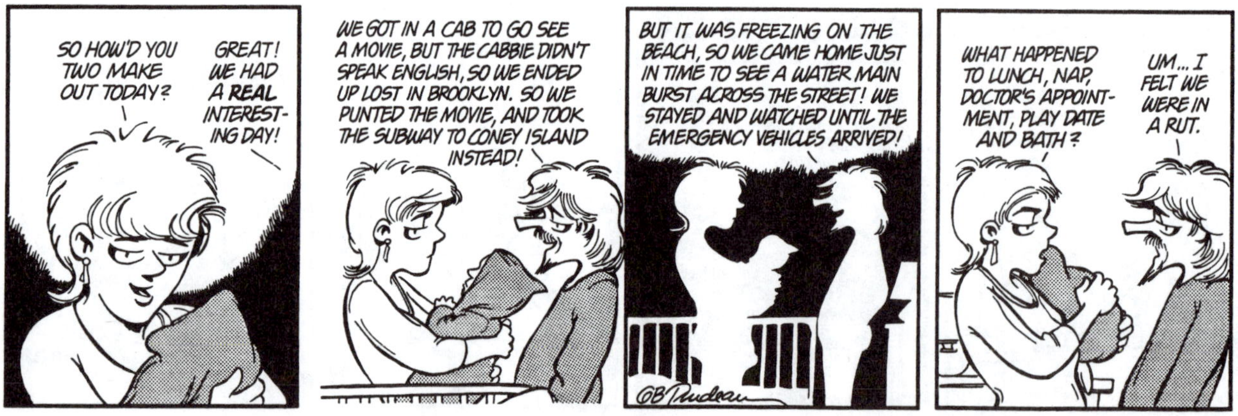
SO HOW'D YOU TWO MAKE OUT TODAY?
GREAT! WE HAD A REAL INTEREST-ING DAY!
WE GOT IN A CAB TO GO SEE A MOVIE, BUT THE CABBIE DIDN'T SPEAK ENGLISH, SO WE ENDED UP LOST IN BROOKLYN. SO WE PUNTED THE MOVIE, AND TOOK THE SUBWAY TO CONEY ISLAND INSTEAD!
BUT IT WAS FREEZING ON THE BEACH, SO WE CAME HOME JUST IN TIME TO SEE A WATER MAIN BURST ACROSS THE STREET! WE STAYED AND WATCHED UNTIL THE EMERGENCY VEHICLES ARRIVED!
WHAT HAPPENED TO LUNCH, NAP, DOCTOR'S APPOINT-MENT, PLAY DATE AND BATH?
UM... I FELT WE WERE IN A RUT.

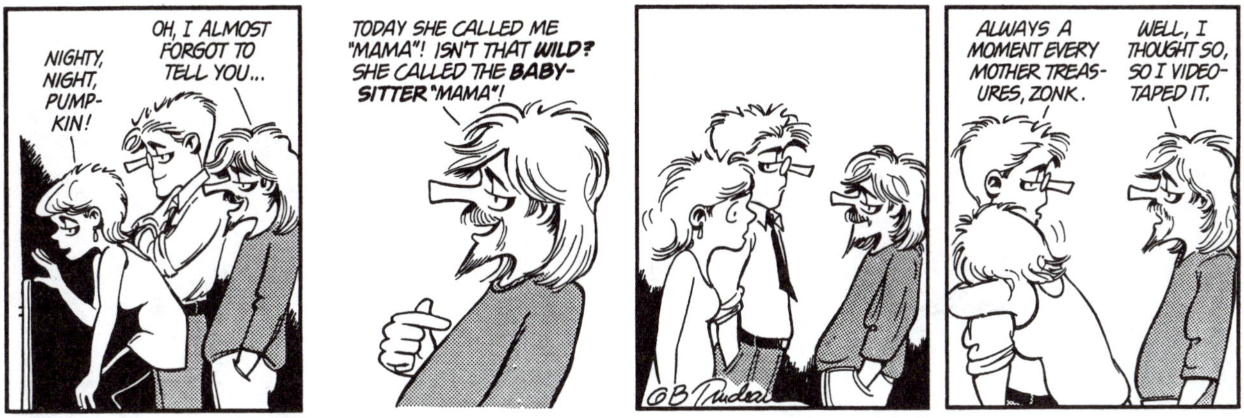
NIGHTY, NIGHT, PUMPKIN!
OH, I ALMOST FORGOT TO TELL YOU...
TODAY SHE CALLED ME "MAMA"! ISN'T THAT WILD? SHE CALLED THE BABY-SITTER "MAMA"!
ALWAYS A MOMENT EVERY MOTHER TREASURES, ZONK.
WELL, I THOUGHT SO, SO I VIDEOTAPED IT.
©GBTrudeau

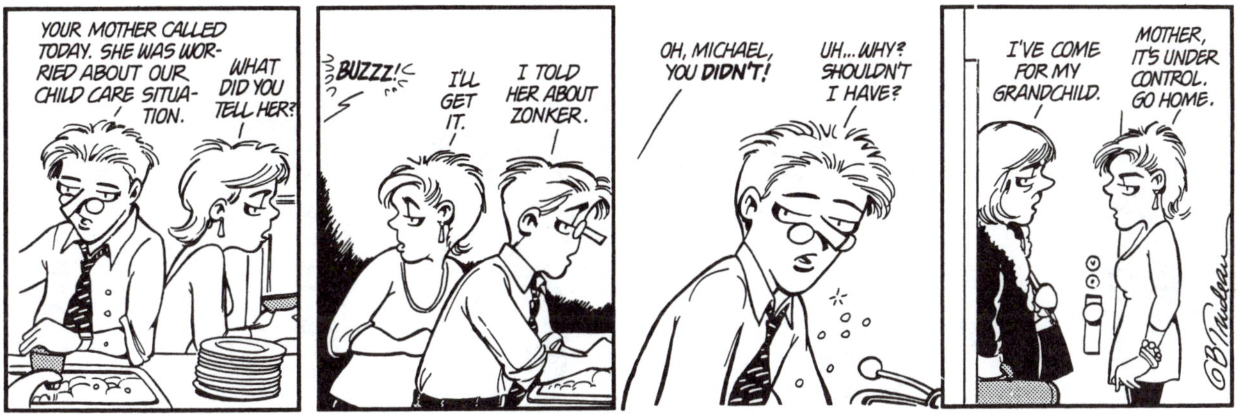
YOUR MOTHER CALLED TODAY. SHE WAS WORRIED ABOUT OUR CHILD CARE SITUATION.
WHAT DID YOU TELL HER?
BUZZZ!
I'LL GET IT.
I TOLD HER ABOUT ZONKER.
OH, MICHAEL, YOU DIDN'T!
UH... WHY? SHOULDN'T I HAVE?
I'VE COME FOR MY GRANDCHILD.
MOTHER, IT'S UNDER CONTROL. GO HOME.
©GBTrudeau

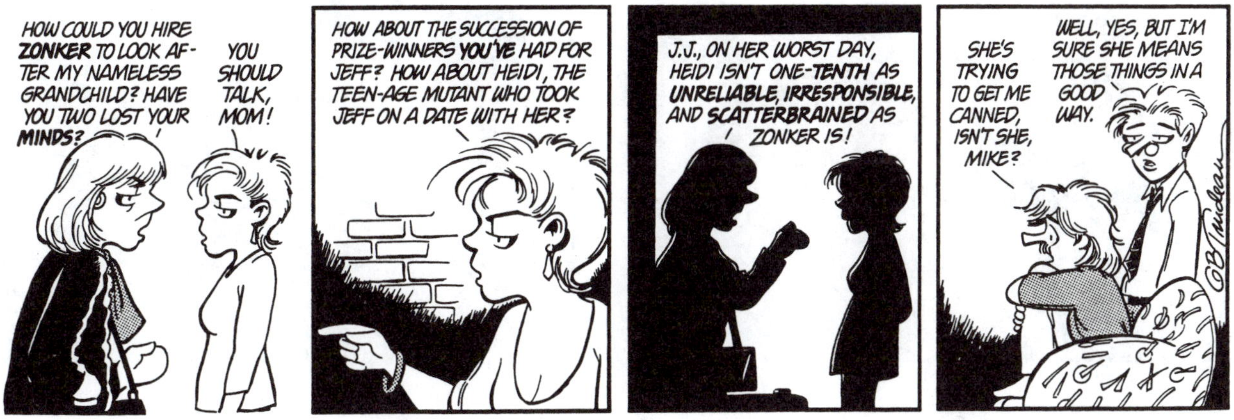
HOW COULD YOU HIRE ZONKER TO LOOK AFTER MY NAMELESS GRANDCHILD? HAVE YOU TWO LOST YOUR MINDS?
YOU SHOULD TALK, MOM!
HOW ABOUT THE SUCCESSION OF PRIZE-WINNERS YOU'VE HAD FOR JEFF? HOW ABOUT HEIDI, THE TEEN-AGE MUTANT WHO TOOK JEFF ON A DATE WITH HER?
J.J., ON HER WORST DAY, HEIDI ISN'T ONE-TENTH AS UNRELIABLE, IRRESPONSIBLE, AND SCATTERBRAINED AS ZONKER IS!
SHE'S TRYING TO GET ME CANNED, ISN'T SHE, MIKE?
WELL, YES, BUT I'M SURE SHE MEANS THOSE THINGS IN A GOOD WAY.
©GBTrudeau

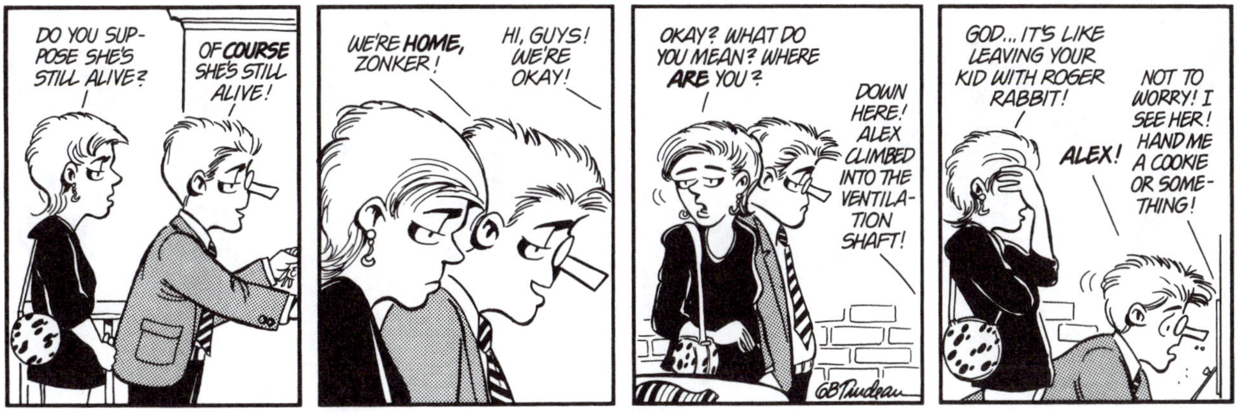
DO YOU SUPPOSE SHE'S STILL ALIVE?
OF COURSE SHE'S STILL ALIVE!
WE'RE HOME, ZONKER!
HI, GUYS! WE'RE OKAY!
OKAY? WHAT DO YOU MEAN? WHERE ARE YOU?
DOWN HERE! ALEX CLIMBED INTO THE VENTILATION SHAFT!
©GBTrudeau
GOD... IT'S LIKE LEAVING YOUR KID WITH ROGER RABBIT!
ALEX!
NOT TO WORRY! I SEE HER! HAND ME A COOKIE OR SOMETHING!

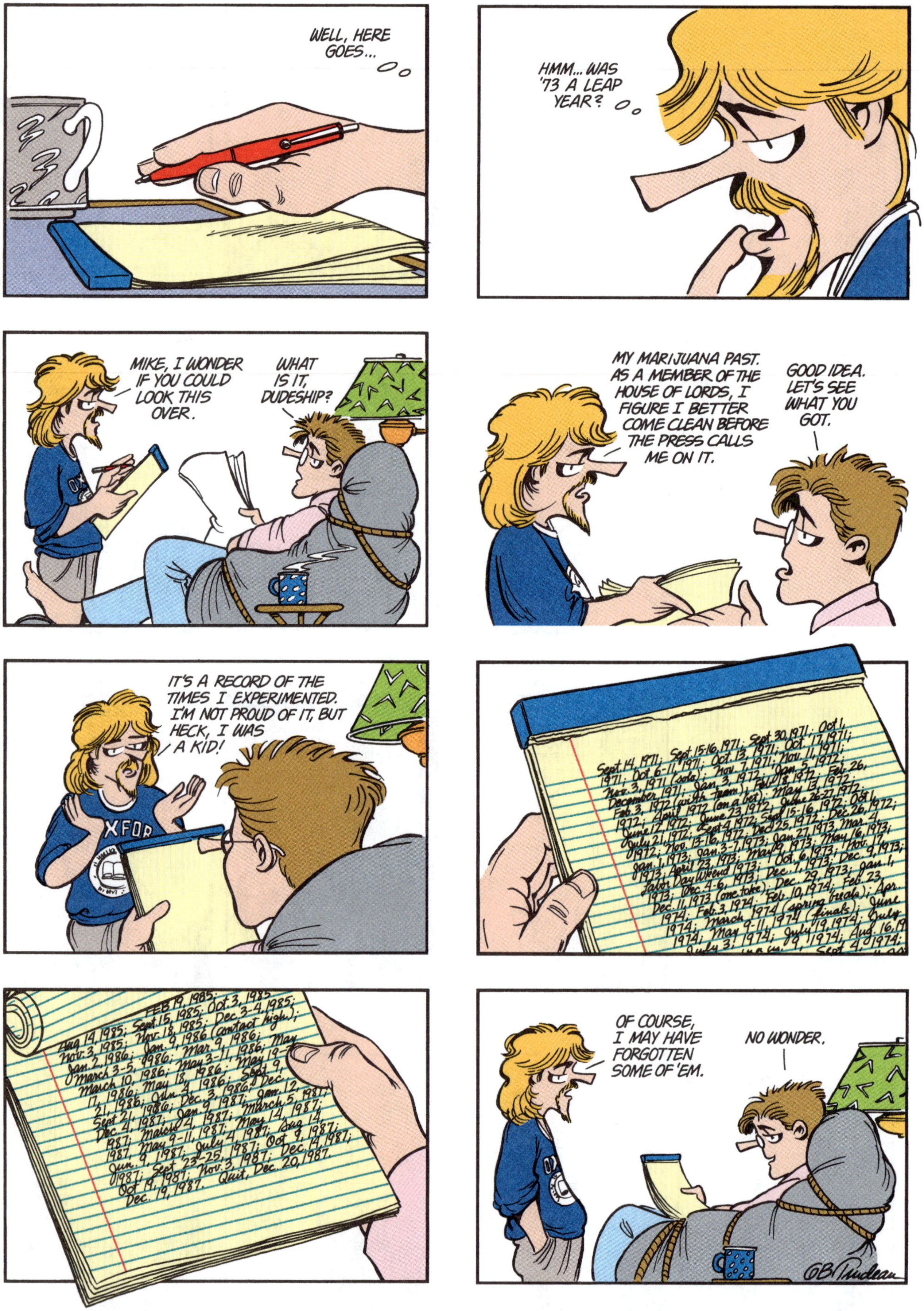
WELL, HERE GOES...
HMM... WAS '73 A LEAP YEAR?
MIKE, I WONDER IF YOU COULD LOOK THIS OVER.
WHAT IS IT, DUDESHIP?
MY MARIJUANA PAST. AS A MEMBER OF THE HOUSE OF LORDS, I FIGURE I BETTER COME CLEAN BEFORE THE PRESS CALLS ME ON IT.
GOOD IDEA. LET'S SEE WHAT YOU GOT.
IT'S A RECORD OF THE TIMES I EXPERIMENTED. I'M NOT PROUD OF IT, BUT HECK, I WAS A KID!
OF COURSE, I MAY HAVE FORGOTTEN SOME OF 'EM.
NO WONDER.
©B.Trudeau

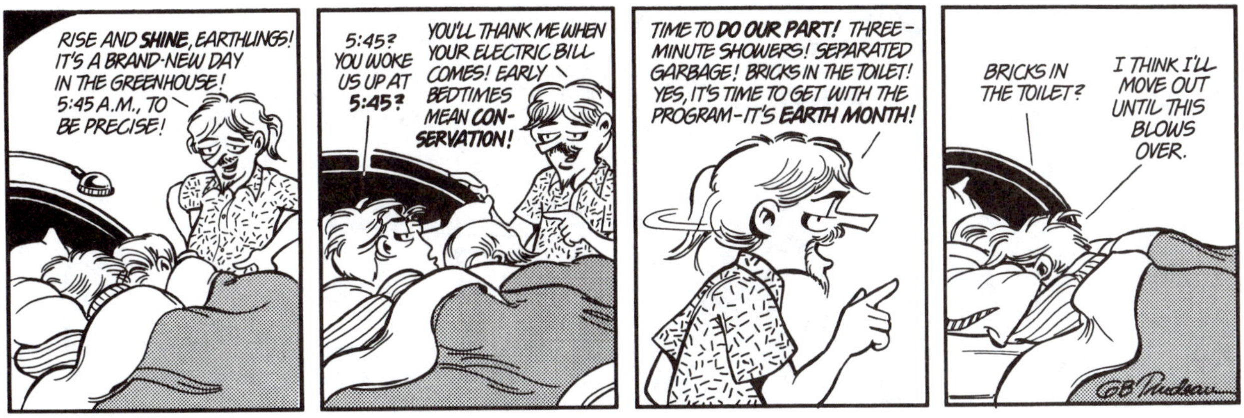
RISE AND SHINE, EARTHLINGS! IT'S A BRAND-NEW DAY IN THE GREENHOUSE! 5:45 A.M., TO BE PRECISE!
5:45? YOU WOKE US UP AT 5:45?
YOU'LL THANK ME WHEN YOUR ELECTRIC BILL COMES! EARLY BEDTIMES MEAN CONSERVATION!
TIME TO DO OUR PART! THREE-MINUTE SHOWERS! SEPARATED GARBAGE! BRICKS IN THE TOILET! YES, IT'S TIME TO GET WITH THE PROGRAM—IT'S EARTH MONTH!
BRICKS IN THE TOILET?
I THINK I'LL MOVE OUT UNTIL THIS BLOWS OVER.
GB Trudeau

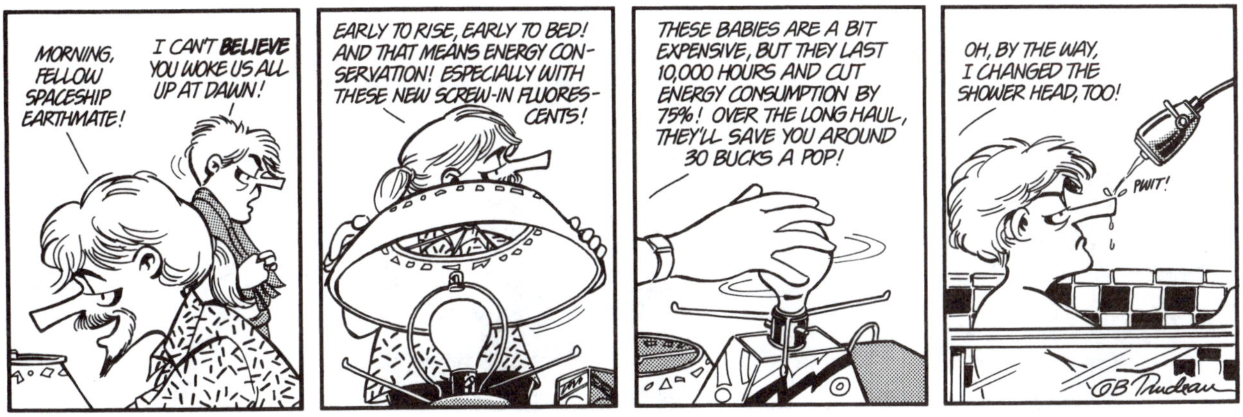
MORNING, FELLOW SPACESHIP EARTHMATE!
I CAN'T BELIEVE YOU WOKE US ALL UP AT DAWN!
EARLY TO RISE, EARLY TO BED! AND THAT MEANS ENERGY CONSERVATION! ESPECIALLY WITH THESE NEW SCREW-IN FLUORESCENTS!
THESE BABIES ARE A BIT EXPENSIVE, BUT THEY LAST 10,000 HOURS AND CUT ENERGY CONSUMPTION BY 75%! OVER THE LONG HAUL, THEY'LL SAVE YOU AROUND 30 BUCKS A POP!
OH, BY THE WAY, I CHANGED THE SHOWER HEAD, TOO!
PWIT!
GB Trudeau

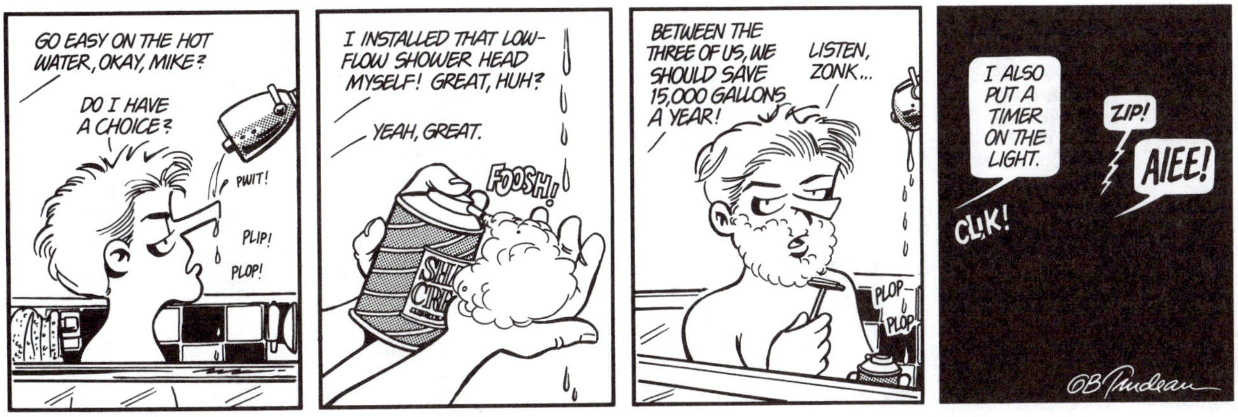
GO EASY ON THE HOT WATER, OKAY, MIKE?
DO I HAVE A CHOICE?
PWIT!
PLIP!
PLOP!
I INSTALLED THAT LOW-FLOW SHOWER HEAD MYSELF! GREAT, HUH?
YEAH, GREAT.
FOOSH!
BETWEEN THE THREE OF US, WE SHOULD SAVE 15,000 GALLONS A YEAR!
LISTEN, ZONK...
PLOP
PLOP
I ALSO PUT A TIMER ON THE LIGHT.
CLIK!
ZIP!
AIEE!
GB Trudeau

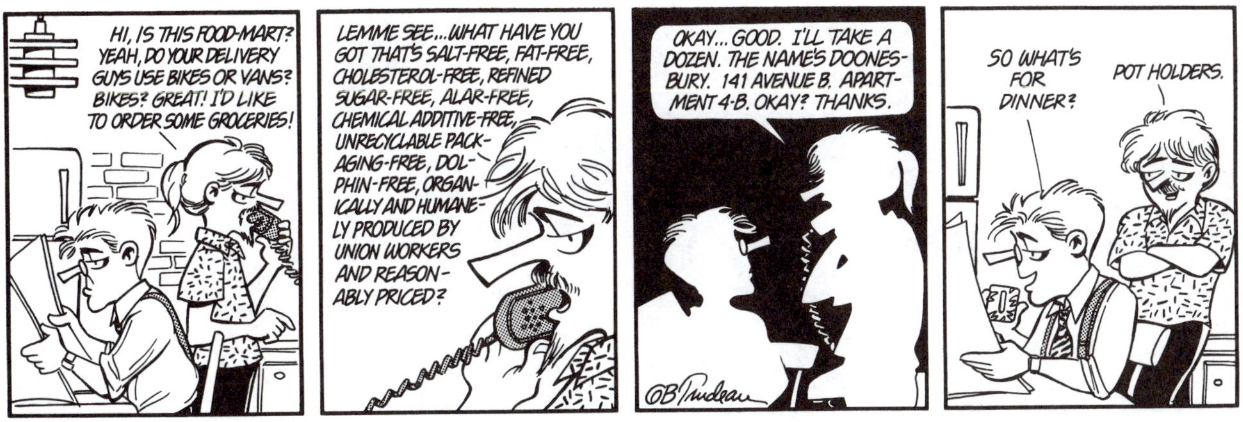
HI, IS THIS FOOD-MART? YEAH, DO YOUR DELIVERY GUYS USE BIKES OR VANS? BIKES? GREAT! I'D LIKE TO ORDER SOME GROCERIES!
LEMME SEE... WHAT HAVE YOU GOT THAT'S SALT-FREE, FAT-FREE, CHOLESTEROL-FREE, REFINED SUGAR-FREE, ALAR-FREE, CHEMICAL ADDITIVE-FREE, UNRECYCLABLE PACKAGING-FREE, DOLPHIN-FREE, ORGANICALLY AND HUMANELY PRODUCED BY UNION WORKERS AND REASONABLY PRICED?
OKAY... GOOD. I'LL TAKE A DOZEN. THE NAME'S DOONESBURY. 141 AVENUE B. APARTMENT 4-B. OKAY? THANKS.
GB Trudeau
SO WHAT'S FOR DINNER?
POT HOLDERS.

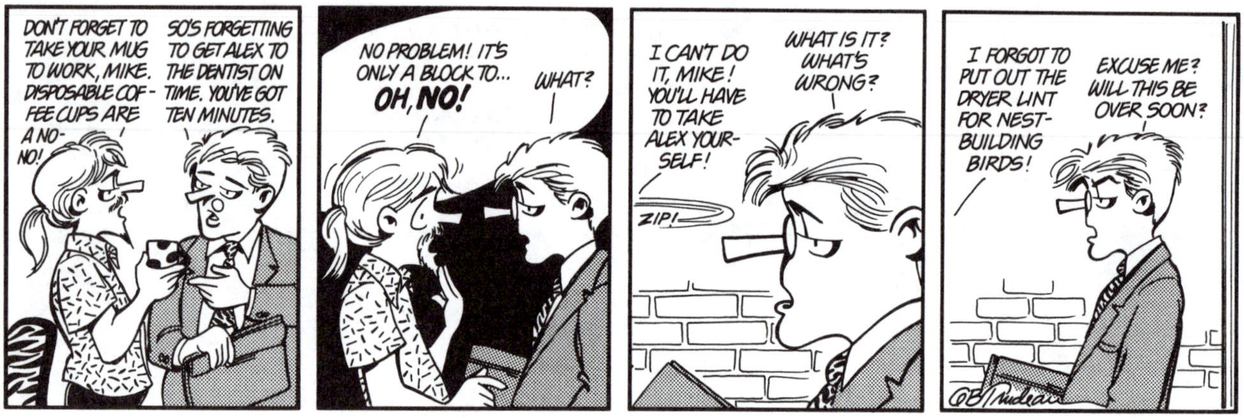
DON'T FORGET TO TAKE YOUR MUG TO WORK, MIKE. DISPOSABLE COF-FEE CUPS ARE A NO-NO!
SO'S FORGETTING TO GET ALEX TO THE DENTIST ON TIME. YOU'VE GOT TEN MINUTES.
NO PROBLEM! IT'S ONLY A BLOCK TO... OH, NO!
WHAT?
I CAN'T DO IT, MIKE! YOU'LL HAVE TO TAKE ALEX YOUR-SELF!
ZIP!
WHAT IS IT? WHAT'S WRONG?
I FORGOT TO PUT OUT THE DRYER LINT FOR NEST-BUILDING BIRDS!
EXCUSE ME? WILL THIS BE OVER SOON?
©B Trudeau

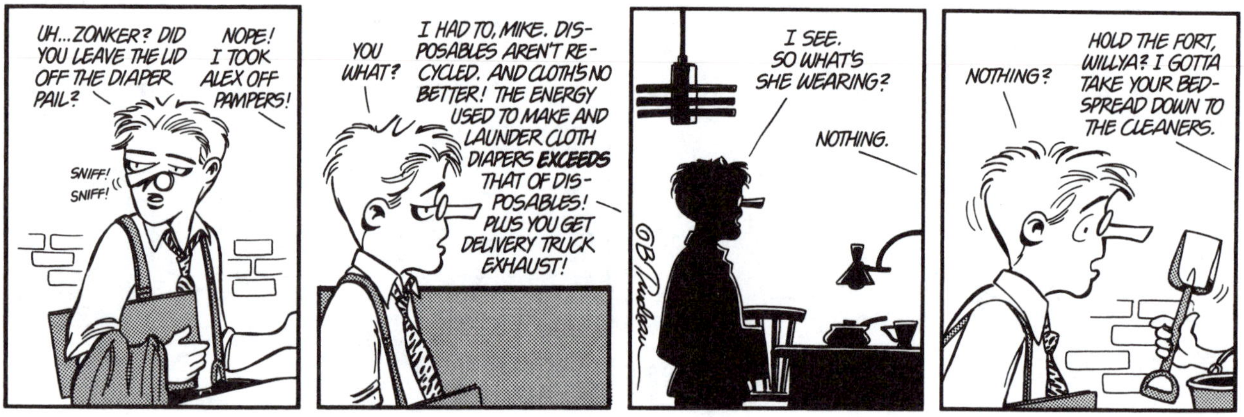
UH...ZONKER? DID YOU LEAVE THE LID OFF THE DIAPER PAIL?
NOPE! I TOOK ALEX OFF PAMPERS!
SNIFF! SNIFF!
YOU WHAT?
I HAD TO, MIKE. DIS-POSABLES AREN'T RE-CYCLED. AND CLOTH'S NO BETTER! THE ENERGY USED TO MAKE AND LAUNDER CLOTH DIAPERS EXCEEDS THAT OF DIS-POSABLES! PLUS YOU GET DELIVERY TRUCK EXHAUST!
©B Trudeau
I SEE. SO WHAT'S SHE WEARING?
NOTHING.
NOTHING?
HOLD THE FORT, WILLYA? I GOTTA TAKE YOUR BED-SPREAD DOWN TO THE CLEANERS.

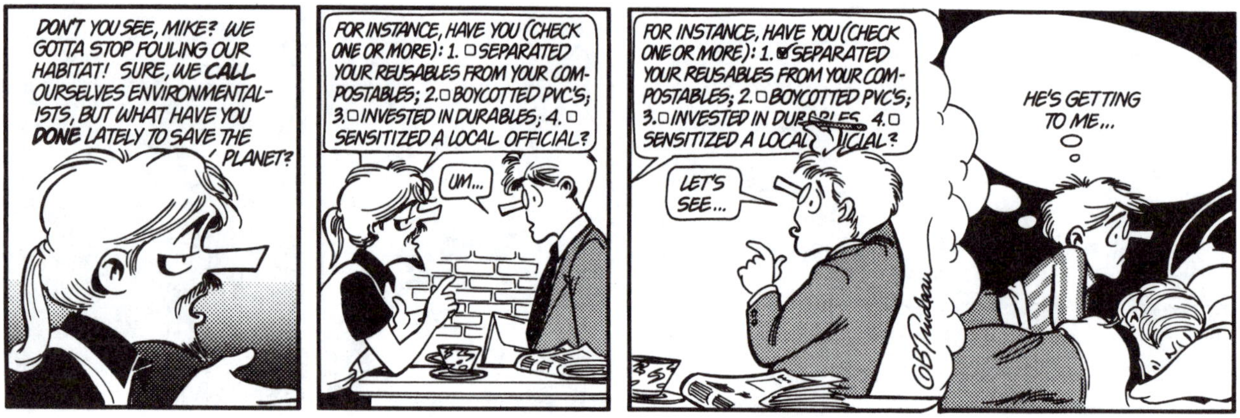
DON'T YOU SEE, MIKE? WE GOTTA STOP FOULING OUR HABITAT! SURE, WE CALL OURSELVES ENVIRONMENTAL-ISTS, BUT WHAT HAVE YOU DONE LATELY TO SAVE THE PLANET?
FOR INSTANCE, HAVE YOU (CHECK ONE OR MORE): 1. □ SEPARATED YOUR REUSABLES FROM YOUR COM-POSTABLES; 2. □ BOYCOTTED PVC'S; 3. □ INVESTED IN DURABLES; 4. □ SENSITIZED A LOCAL OFFICIAL?
UM...
FOR INSTANCE, HAVE YOU (CHECK ONE OR MORE): 1. ☑ SEPARATED YOUR REUSABLES FROM YOUR COM-POSTABLES; 2. □ BOYCOTTED PVC'S; 3. □ INVESTED IN DURABLES; 4. □ SENSITIZED A LOCAL OFFICIAL?
LET'S SEE...
©B Trudeau
HE'S GETTING TO ME...

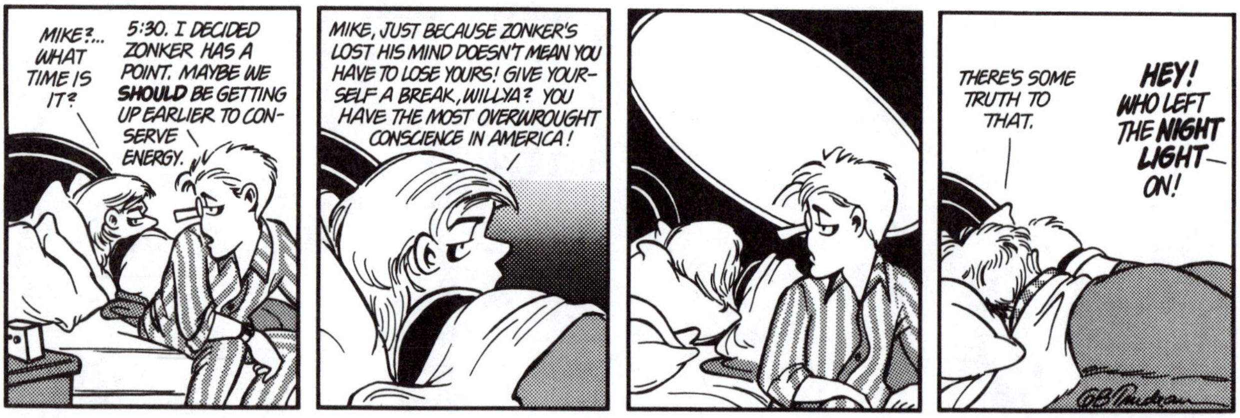
MIKE?... WHAT TIME IS IT?
5:30. I DECIDED ZONKER HAS A POINT. MAYBE WE SHOULD BE GETTING UP EARLIER TO CON-SERVE ENERGY.
MIKE, JUST BECAUSE ZONKER'S LOST HIS MIND DOESN'T MEAN YOU HAVE TO LOSE YOURS! GIVE YOUR-SELF A BREAK, WILLYA? YOU HAVE THE MOST OVERWROUGHT CONSCIENCE IN AMERICA!
THERE'S SOME TRUTH TO THAT.
HEY! WHO LEFT THE NIGHT LIGHT ON!
©B Trudeau

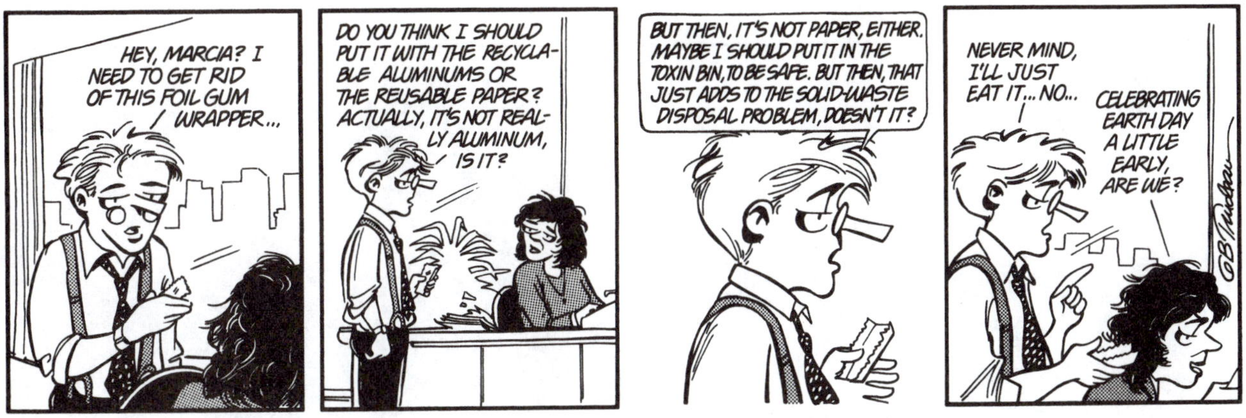
HEY, MARCIA? I NEED TO GET RID OF THIS FOIL GUM WRAPPER...
DO YOU THINK I SHOULD PUT IT WITH THE RECYCLABLE ALUMINUMS OR THE REUSABLE PAPER? ACTUALLY, IT'S NOT REALLY ALUMINUM, IS IT?
BUT THEN, IT'S NOT PAPER, EITHER. MAYBE I SHOULD PUT IT IN THE TOXIN BIN, TO BE SAFE. BUT THEN, THAT JUST ADDS TO THE SOLID-WASTE DISPOSAL PROBLEM, DOESN'T IT?
NEVER MIND, I'LL JUST EAT IT... NO...
CELEBRATING EARTH DAY A LITTLE EARLY, ARE WE?
©B Trudeau

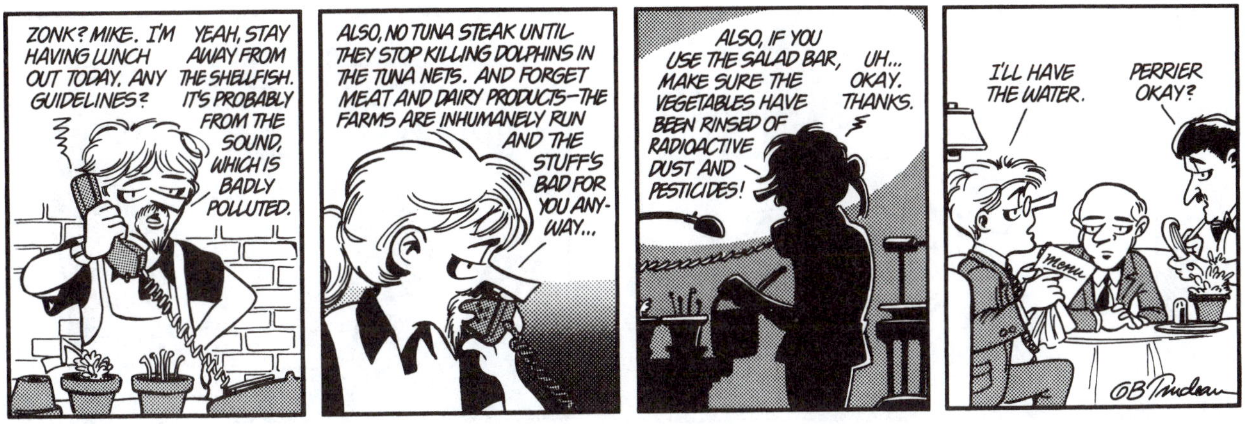
ZONK? MIKE. I'M HAVING LUNCH OUT TODAY. ANY GUIDELINES?
YEAH, STAY AWAY FROM THE SHELLFISH. IT'S PROBABLY FROM THE SOUND, WHICH IS BADLY POLLUTED.
ALSO, NO TUNA STEAK UNTIL THEY STOP KILLING DOLPHINS IN THE TUNA NETS. AND FORGET MEAT AND DAIRY PRODUCTS—THE FARMS ARE INHUMANELY RUN AND THE STUFF'S BAD FOR YOU ANYWAY...
ALSO, IF YOU USE THE SALAD BAR, MAKE SURE THE VEGETABLES HAVE BEEN RINSED OF RADIOACTIVE DUST AND PESTICIDES!
UH... OKAY. THANKS.
I'LL HAVE THE WATER.
PERRIER OKAY?
menu
©B Trudeau

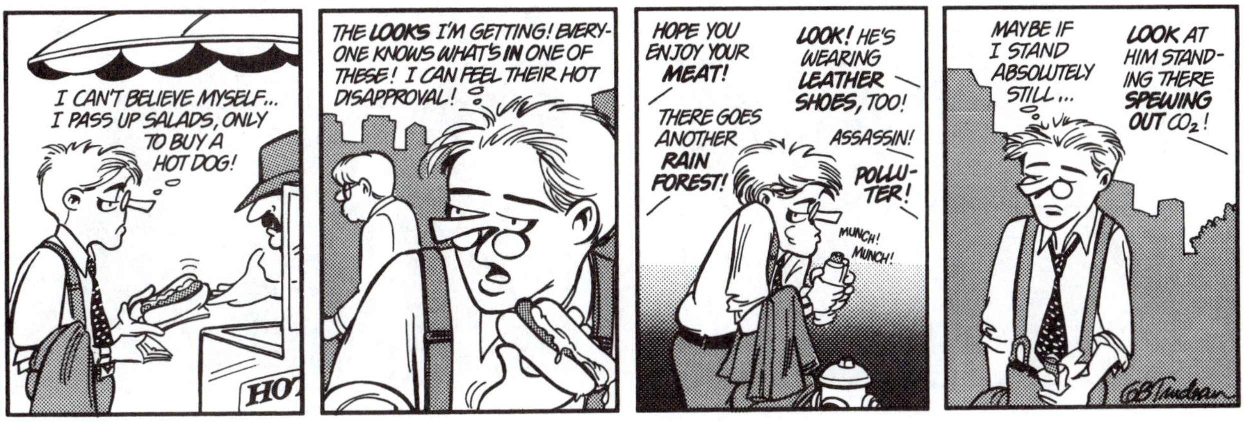
I CAN'T BELIEVE MYSELF... I PASS UP SALADS, ONLY TO BUY A HOT DOG!
THE LOOKS I'M GETTING! EVERYONE KNOWS WHAT'S IN ONE OF THESE! I CAN FEEL THEIR HOT DISAPPROVAL!
HOPE YOU ENJOY YOUR MEAT!
LOOK! HE'S WEARING LEATHER SHOES, TOO!
THERE GOES ANOTHER RAIN FOREST!
ASSASSIN!
POLLUTER!
MUNCH! MUNCH!
MAYBE IF I STAND ABSOLUTELY STILL...
LOOK AT HIM STANDING THERE SPEWING OUT CO_2!
©B Trudeau

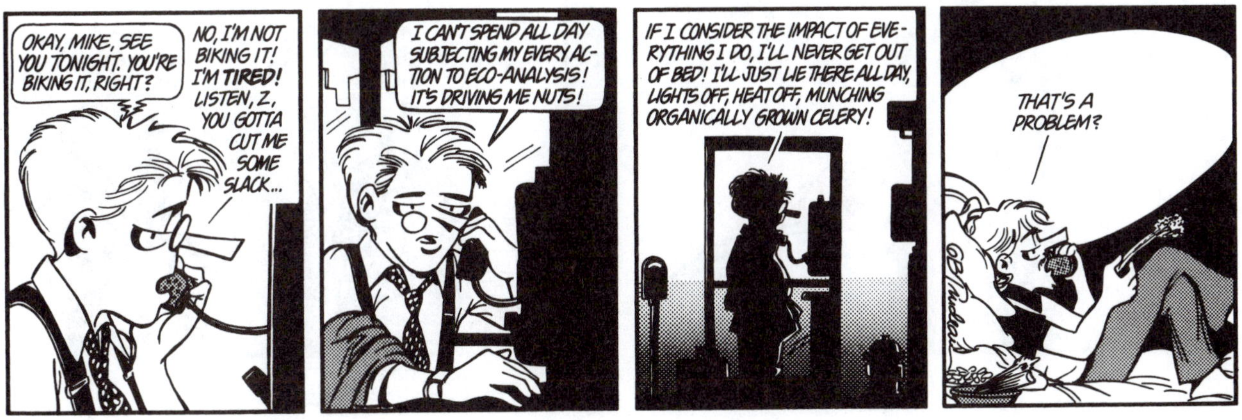
OKAY, MIKE, SEE YOU TONIGHT. YOU'RE BIKING IT, RIGHT?
NO, I'M NOT BIKING IT! I'M TIRED! LISTEN, Z, YOU GOTTA CUT ME SOME SLACK...
I CAN'T SPEND ALL DAY SUBJECTING MY EVERY ACTION TO ECO-ANALYSIS! IT'S DRIVING ME NUTS!
IF I CONSIDER THE IMPACT OF EVERYTHING I DO, I'LL NEVER GET OUT OF BED! I'LL JUST LIE THERE ALL DAY, LIGHTS OFF, HEAT OFF, MUNCHING ORGANICALLY GROWN CELERY!
THAT'S A PROBLEM?
©B Trudeau

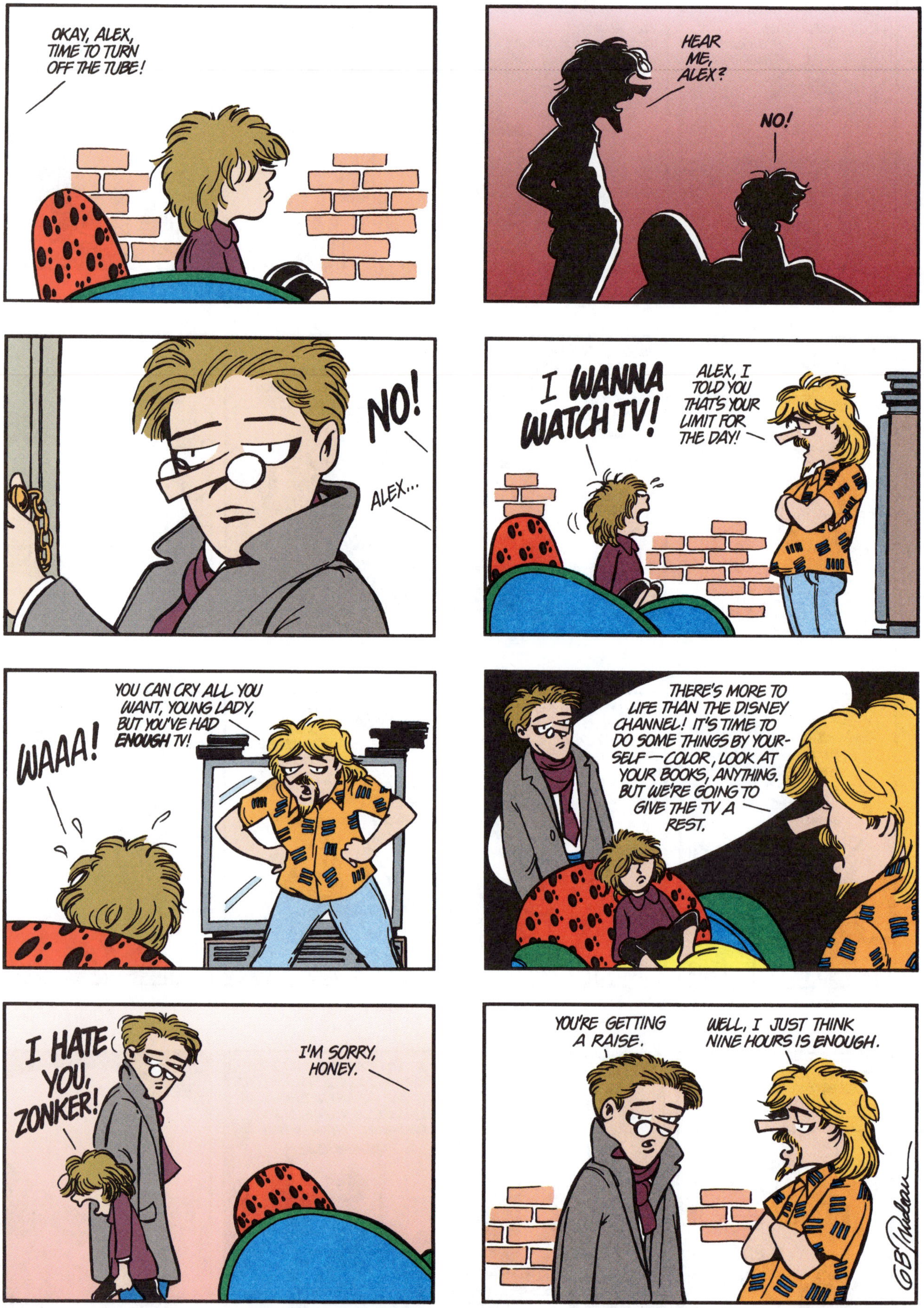
OKAY, ALEX, TIME TO TURN OFF THE TUBE!
HEAR ME, ALEX?
NO!
NO!
ALEX...
I WANNA WATCH TV!
ALEX, I TOLD YOU THAT'S YOUR LIMIT FOR THE DAY!
WAAA!
YOU CAN CRY ALL YOU WANT, YOUNG LADY, BUT YOU'VE HAD ENOUGH TV!
THERE'S MORE TO LIFE THAN THE DISNEY CHANNEL! IT'S TIME TO DO SOME THINGS BY YOURSELF—COLOR, LOOK AT YOUR BOOKS, ANYTHING. BUT WE'RE GOING TO GIVE THE TV A REST.
I HATE YOU, ZONKER!
I'M SORRY, HONEY.
YOU'RE GETTING A RAISE.
WELL, I JUST THINK NINE HOURS IS ENOUGH.
GBTrudeau

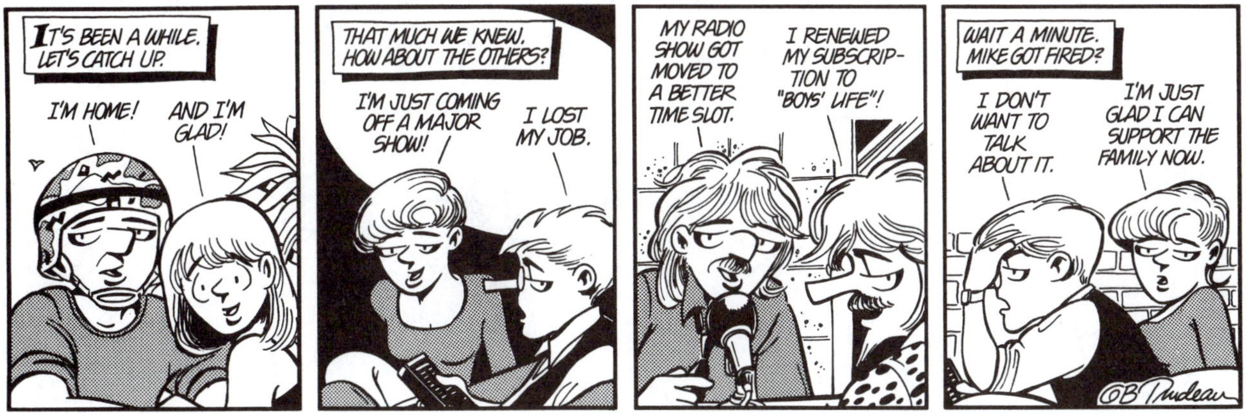
IT'S BEEN A WHILE. LET'S CATCH UP.
I'M HOME!
AND I'M GLAD!
THAT MUCH WE KNEW. HOW ABOUT THE OTHERS?
I'M JUST COMING OFF A MAJOR SHOW!
I LOST MY JOB.
MY RADIO SHOW GOT MOVED TO A BETTER TIME SLOT.
I RENEWED MY SUBSCRIPTION TO "BOYS' LIFE"!
WAIT A MINUTE. MIKE GOT FIRED?
I DON'T WANT TO TALK ABOUT IT.
I'M JUST GLAD I CAN SUPPORT THE FAMILY NOW.
©B Trudeau

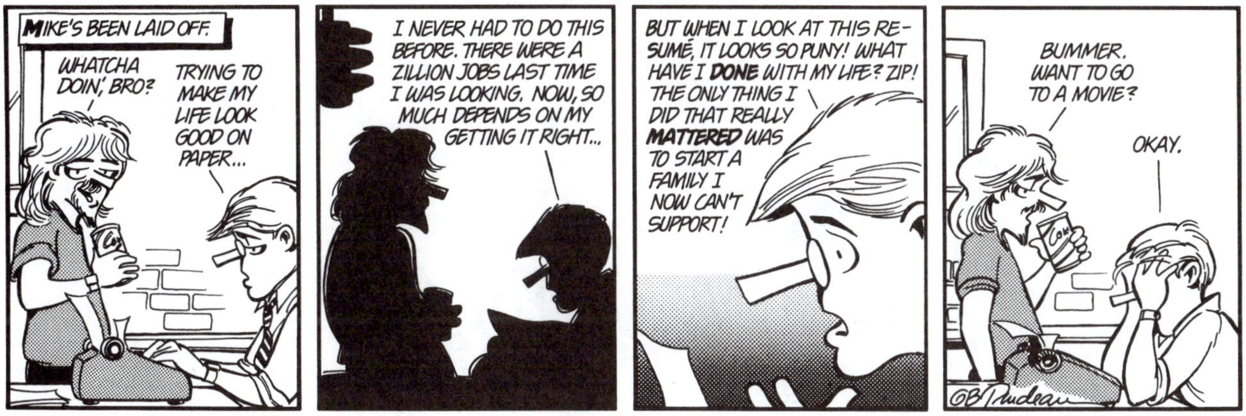
MIKE'S BEEN LAID OFF.
WHATCHA DOIN,' BRO?
TRYING TO MAKE MY LIFE LOOK GOOD ON PAPER...
I NEVER HAD TO DO THIS BEFORE. THERE WERE A ZILLION JOBS LAST TIME I WAS LOOKING. NOW, SO MUCH DEPENDS ON MY GETTING IT RIGHT...
BUT WHEN I LOOK AT THIS RESUMÉ, IT LOOKS SO PUNY! WHAT HAVE I DONE WITH MY LIFE? ZIP! THE ONLY THING I DID THAT REALLY MATTERED WAS TO START A FAMILY I NOW CAN'T SUPPORT!
BUMMER. WANT TO GO TO A MOVIE?
OKAY.
©B Trudeau

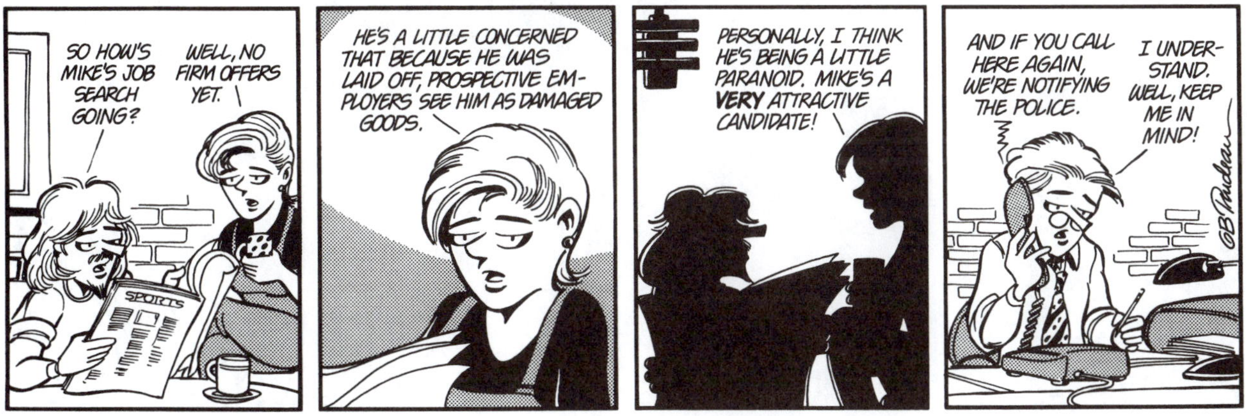
SO HOW'S MIKE'S JOB SEARCH GOING?
WELL, NO FIRM OFFERS YET.
SPORTS
HE'S A LITTLE CONCERNED THAT BECAUSE HE WAS LAID OFF, PROSPECTIVE EMPLOYERS SEE HIM AS DAMAGED GOODS.
PERSONALLY, I THINK HE'S BEING A LITTLE PARANOID. MIKE'S A VERY ATTRACTIVE CANDIDATE!
AND IF YOU CALL HERE AGAIN, WE'RE NOTIFYING THE POLICE.
I UNDERSTAND. WELL, KEEP ME IN MIND!
©B Trudeau

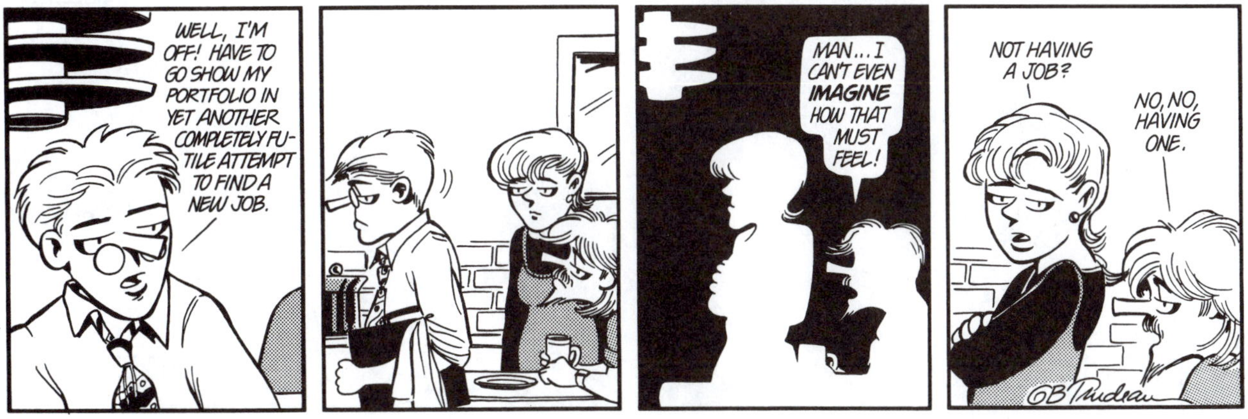
WELL, I'M OFF! HAVE TO GO SHOW MY PORTFOLIO IN YET ANOTHER COMPLETELY FUTILE ATTEMPT TO FIND A NEW JOB.
MAN... I CAN'T EVEN IMAGINE HOW THAT MUST FEEL!
NOT HAVING A JOB?
NO, NO, HAVING ONE.
©B Trudeau

Panel 1:
HI.
HI, BACK! HOW'D THE INTERVIEW GO?

Panel 2:
WELL, HE KNEW MY WORK. HE SAID HE VIVIDLY RECALLED MY REAGAN SPOTS, THE CIGARETTE SPOTS, AND THE UNIVERSAL PETROLEUM CAMPAIGN.

Panel 3:
HE SAID THERE WAS A COMMON THREAD THAT RAN THROUGH MY ADS...
WHICH WAS?

Panel 4:
HE DESPISED THEM ALL.
BUT SO DID YOU! DID YOU TELL HIM?

Panel 5:
NO, MOM, HE HASN'T FOUND ANYTHING YET. BUT HE'S BEEN MAKING THE ROUNDS.

Panel 6:
WHY'S HE HAVING SUCH TROUBLE? HIS RESUMÉ IS TERRIFIC!
IT'S THE ECONOMY, MOM. THE AGENCIES JUST AREN'T HIRING RIGHT NOW.

Panel 7:
HOW'S ALEX? IS SHE AWARE HER FATHER LOST HIS JOB?
YEAH, SHE IS. I'M AFRAID IT'S GOT HER A LITTLE RATTLED.

Panel 8:
YOU HAVE TO GET A JOB, DADDY! WE'LL STARVE AND DIE!
SHE'S GOT A POINT. DO YOU HAVE A TRUST FUND OR SOMETHING?

Panel 9:
IF YOU DON'T GET A JOB, WE'LL STARVE! THE SUN WILL BLEACH OUR BONES!
ALEX, HONEY, WE'RE NOT GOING TO STARVE...

Panel 10:
DADDY'S JUST BETWEEN JOBS, HE'LL BE WORKING AGAIN, JUST AS SOON AS HE FINDS A JOB THAT'S RIGHT FOR HIM! EVERYTHING'S GOING TO BE FINE. OKAY, SWEETHEART?

Panel 11:
(no dialogue)

Panel 12:
THE CROWS WILL PLUCK OUT OUR EYEBALLS!
WHERE DOES SHE GET THIS STUFF?
THAT'S IT— NO MORE STEPHEN KING AT BEDTIME!

Panel 13:
ZONK, WE HAVE TO TALK.
SURE THING, BUD. WHAT'S UP?

Panel 14:
ZONK, I'M AFRAID WE'RE GOING TO HAVE TO LET YOU GO. WE CAN'T AFFORD YOU ANYMORE.
AFFORD ME? BUT YOU'RE NOT PAYING ME ANYTHING!

Panel 15:
Z, YOU EAT LIKE A HORSE. IT'S LIKE I'M FEEDING A FAMILY OF NINE! I JUST CAN'T STRETCH MY UNEMPLOYMENT COMP TO CARRY YOU!
I DON'T BELIEVE THIS! AFTER ALL I'VE DONE FOR YOUR CHILD!

Panel 16:
ZONK...
THE KID SPEAKS FLUENT PIG LATIN! THIS IS MY THANKS?

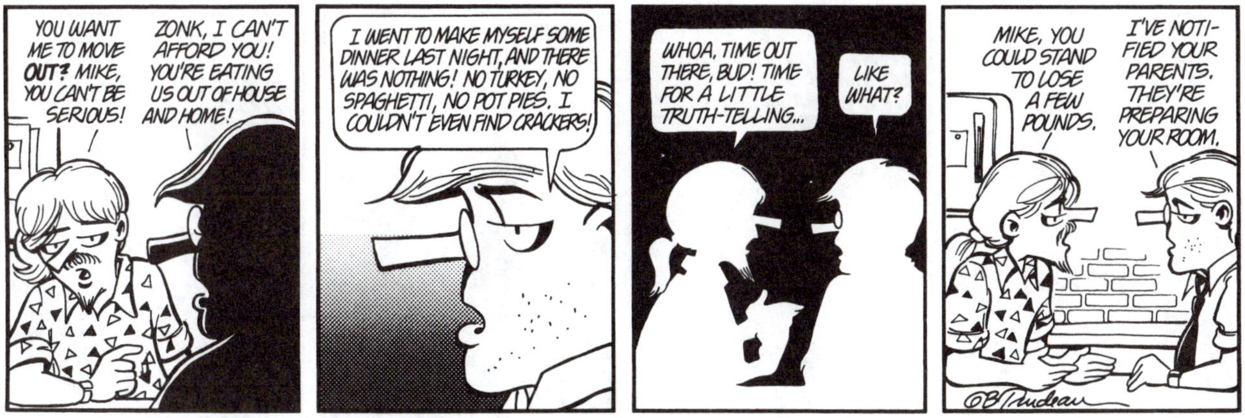
YOU WANT ME TO MOVE OUT? MIKE, YOU CAN'T BE SERIOUS!
ZONK, I CAN'T AFFORD YOU! YOU'RE EATING US OUT OF HOUSE AND HOME!
I WENT TO MAKE MYSELF SOME DINNER LAST NIGHT, AND THERE WAS NOTHING! NO TURKEY, NO SPAGHETTI, NO POT PIES. I COULDN'T EVEN FIND CRACKERS!
WHOA, TIME OUT THERE, BUD! TIME FOR A LITTLE TRUTH-TELLING...
LIKE WHAT?
MIKE, YOU COULD STAND TO LOSE A FEW POUNDS.
I'VE NOTIFIED YOUR PARENTS. THEY'RE PREPARING YOUR ROOM.
©B Trudeau

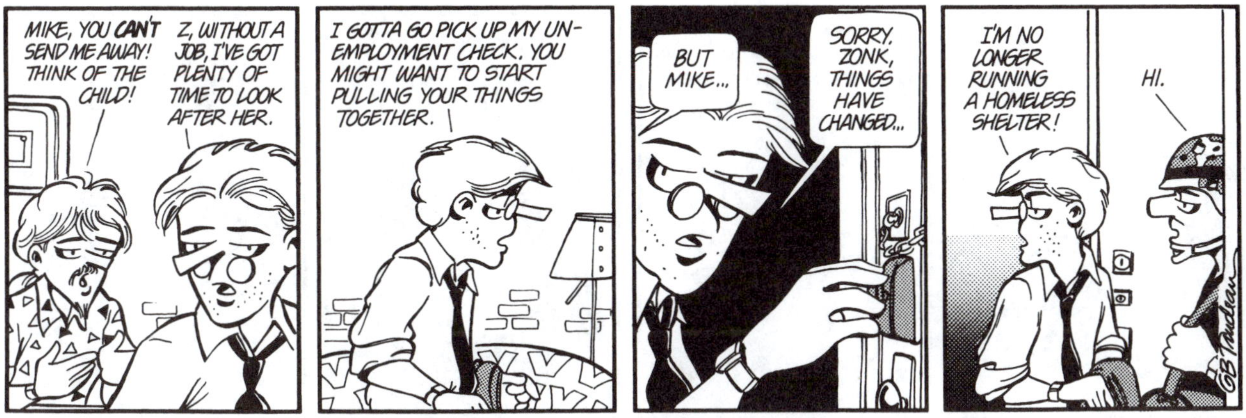
MIKE, YOU CAN'T SEND ME AWAY! THINK OF THE CHILD!
Z, WITHOUT A JOB, I'VE GOT PLENTY OF TIME TO LOOK AFTER HER.
I GOTTA GO PICK UP MY UNEMPLOYMENT CHECK. YOU MIGHT WANT TO START PULLING YOUR THINGS TOGETHER.
BUT MIKE...
SORRY, ZONK, THINGS HAVE CHANGED...
I'M NO LONGER RUNNING A HOMELESS SHELTER!
HI.
©B Trudeau

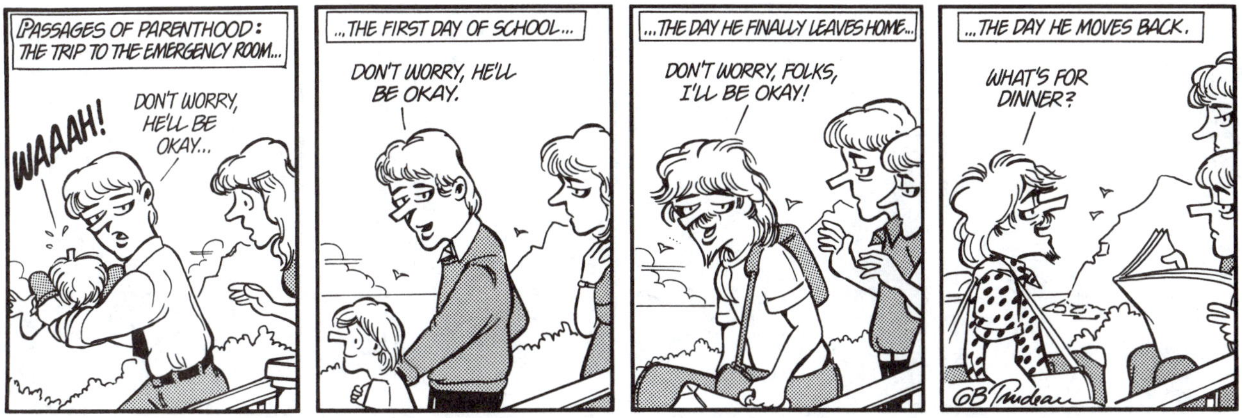
PASSAGES OF PARENTHOOD: THE TRIP TO THE EMERGENCY ROOM...
WAAAH!
DON'T WORRY, HE'LL BE OKAY...
...THE FIRST DAY OF SCHOOL...
DON'T WORRY, HE'LL BE OKAY.
...THE DAY HE FINALLY LEAVES HOME...
DON'T WORRY, FOLKS, I'LL BE OKAY!
...THE DAY HE MOVES BACK.
WHAT'S FOR DINNER?
©B Trudeau

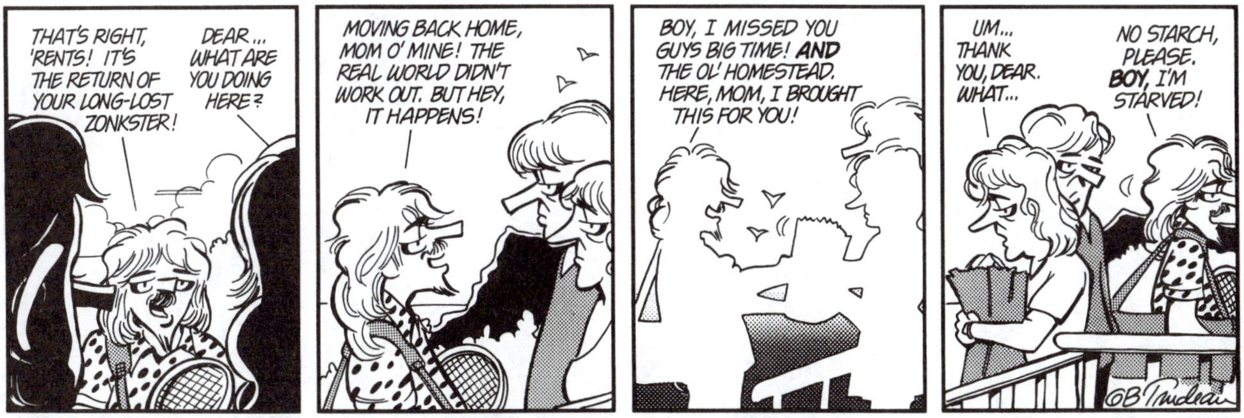
THAT'S RIGHT, 'RENTS! IT'S THE RETURN OF YOUR LONG-LOST ZONKSTER!
DEAR... WHAT ARE YOU DOING HERE?
MOVING BACK HOME, MOM O' MINE! THE REAL WORLD DIDN'T WORK OUT. BUT HEY, IT HAPPENS!
BOY, I MISSED YOU GUYS BIG TIME! AND THE OL' HOMESTEAD. HERE, MOM, I BROUGHT THIS FOR YOU!
UM... THANK YOU, DEAR. WHAT...
NO STARCH, PLEASE. BOY, I'M STARVED!
©B Trudeau

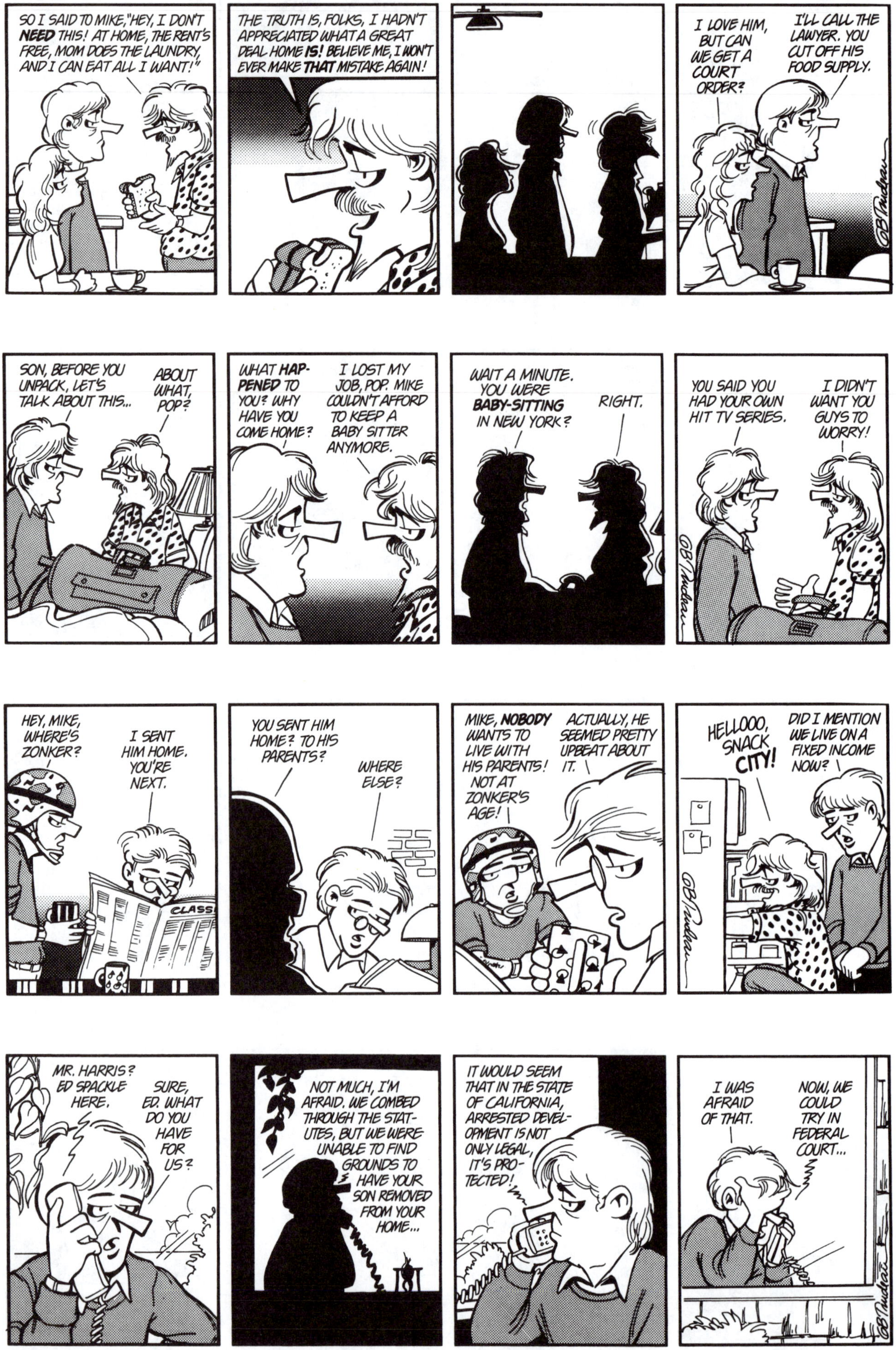
SO I SAID TO MIKE, "HEY, I DON'T NEED THIS! AT HOME, THE RENT'S FREE, MOM DOES THE LAUNDRY, AND I CAN EAT ALL I WANT!"
THE TRUTH IS, FOLKS, I HADN'T APPRECIATED WHAT A GREAT DEAL HOME IS! BELIEVE ME, I WON'T EVER MAKE THAT MISTAKE AGAIN!
I LOVE HIM, BUT CAN WE GET A COURT ORDER?
I'LL CALL THE LAWYER. YOU CUT OFF HIS FOOD SUPPLY.
SON, BEFORE YOU UNPACK, LET'S TALK ABOUT THIS...
ABOUT WHAT, POP?
WHAT HAPPENED TO YOU? WHY HAVE YOU COME HOME?
I LOST MY JOB, POP. MIKE COULDN'T AFFORD TO KEEP A BABY SITTER ANYMORE.
WAIT A MINUTE. YOU WERE BABY-SITTING IN NEW YORK?
RIGHT.
YOU SAID YOU HAD YOUR OWN HIT TV SERIES.
I DIDN'T WANT YOU GUYS TO WORRY!
HEY, MIKE, WHERE'S ZONKER?
I SENT HIM HOME. YOU'RE NEXT.
CLASS
YOU SENT HIM HOME? TO HIS PARENTS?
WHERE ELSE?
MIKE, NOBODY WANTS TO LIVE WITH HIS PARENTS! NOT AT ZONKER'S AGE!
ACTUALLY, HE SEEMED PRETTY UPBEAT ABOUT IT.
HELLOOO, SNACK CITY!
DID I MENTION WE LIVE ON A FIXED INCOME NOW?
MR. HARRIS? ED SPACKLE HERE.
SURE, ED. WHAT DO YOU HAVE FOR US?
NOT MUCH, I'M AFRAID. WE COMBED THROUGH THE STATUTES, BUT WE WERE UNABLE TO FIND GROUNDS TO HAVE YOUR SON REMOVED FROM YOUR HOME...
IT WOULD SEEM THAT IN THE STATE OF CALIFORNIA, ARRESTED DEVELOPMENT IS NOT ONLY LEGAL, IT'S PROTECTED!
I WAS AFRAID OF THAT.
NOW, WE COULD TRY IN FEDERAL COURT...

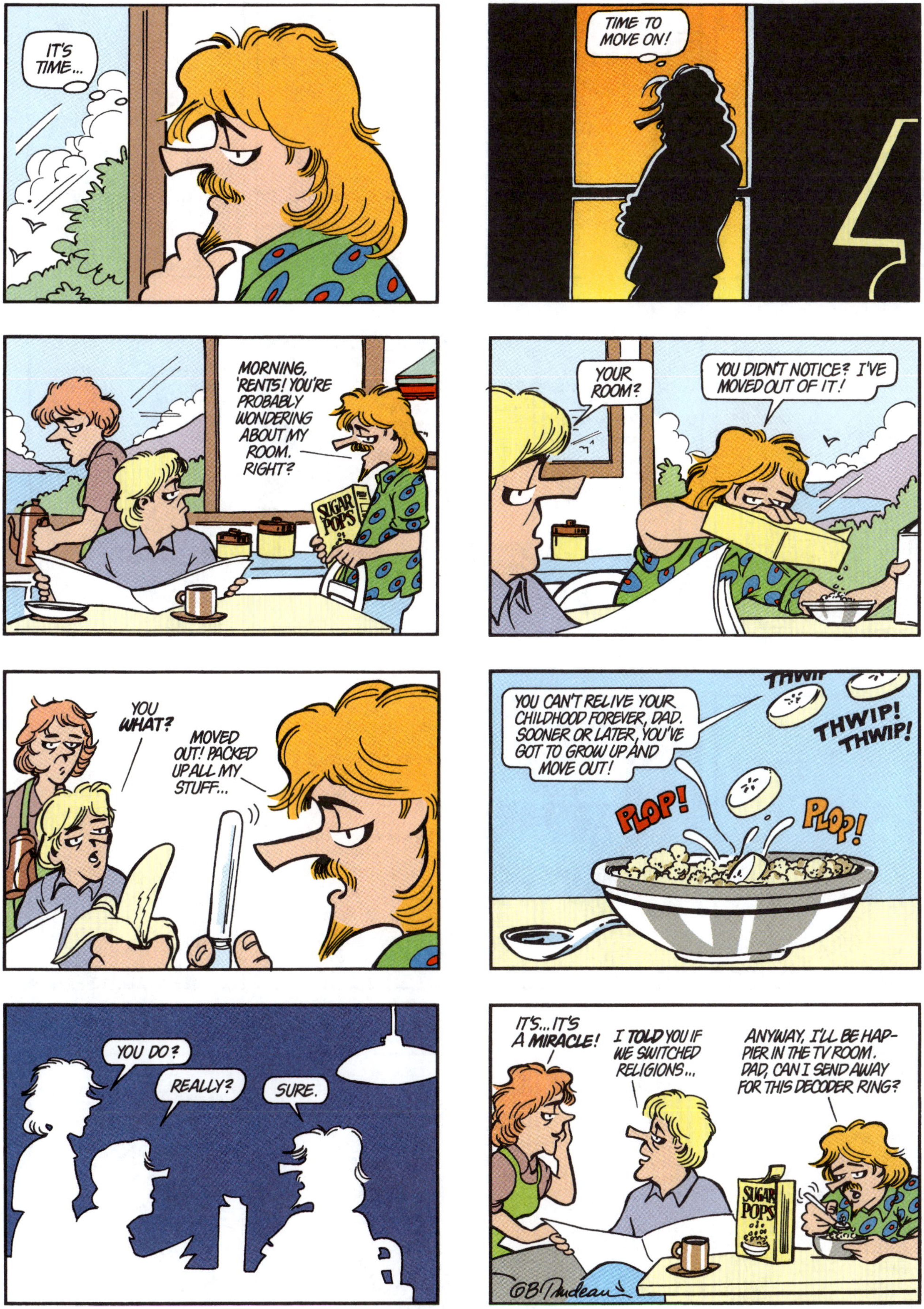
IT'S TIME...
TIME TO MOVE ON!
MORNING, 'RENTS! YOU'RE PROBABLY WONDERING ABOUT MY ROOM. RIGHT?
SUGAR POPS
YOUR ROOM?
YOU DIDN'T NOTICE? I'VE MOVED OUT OF IT!
YOU WHAT?
MOVED OUT! PACKED UP ALL MY STUFF...
YOU CAN'T RELIVE YOUR CHILDHOOD FOREVER, DAD. SOONER OR LATER, YOU'VE GOT TO GROW UP AND MOVE OUT!
THWIP
THWIP! THWIP!
PLOP!
PLOP!
YOU DO?
REALLY?
SURE.
IT'S... IT'S A MIRACLE!
I TOLD YOU IF WE SWITCHED RELIGIONS...
ANYWAY, I'LL BE HAPPIER IN THE TV ROOM. DAD, CAN I SEND AWAY FOR THIS DECODER RING?
SUGAR POPS
©B Trudeau

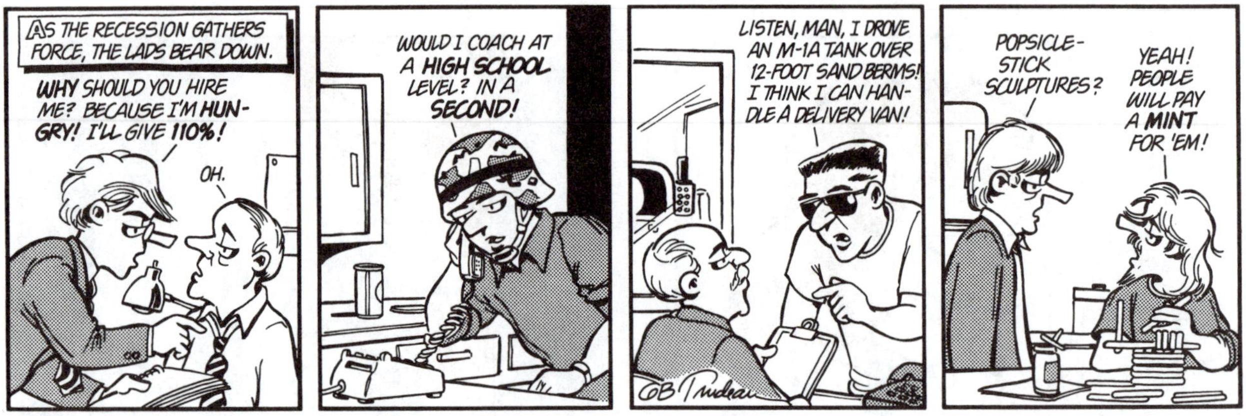
AS THE RECESSION GATHERS FORCE, THE LADS BEAR DOWN.
WHY SHOULD YOU HIRE ME? BECAUSE I'M HUNGRY! I'LL GIVE 110%!
OH.
WOULD I COACH AT A HIGH SCHOOL LEVEL? IN A SECOND!
LISTEN, MAN, I DROVE AN M-1A TANK OVER 12-FOOT SAND BERMS! I THINK I CAN HANDLE A DELIVERY VAN!
G.B. Trudeau
POPSICLE-STICK SCULPTURES?
YEAH! PEOPLE WILL PAY A MINT FOR 'EM!

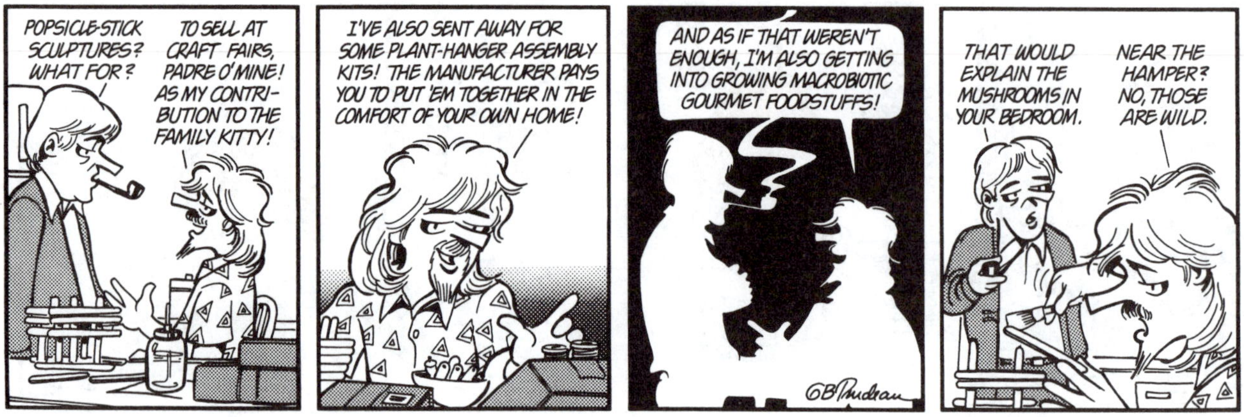
POPSICLE-STICK SCULPTURES? WHAT FOR?
TO SELL AT CRAFT FAIRS, PADRE O'MINE! AS MY CONTRIBUTION TO THE FAMILY KITTY!
I'VE ALSO SENT AWAY FOR SOME PLANT-HANGER ASSEMBLY KITS! THE MANUFACTURER PAYS YOU TO PUT 'EM TOGETHER IN THE COMFORT OF YOUR OWN HOME!
AND AS IF THAT WEREN'T ENOUGH, I'M ALSO GETTING INTO GROWING MACROBIOTIC GOURMET FOODSTUFFS!
G.B. Trudeau
THAT WOULD EXPLAIN THE MUSHROOMS IN YOUR BEDROOM.
NEAR THE HAMPER? NO, THOSE ARE WILD.

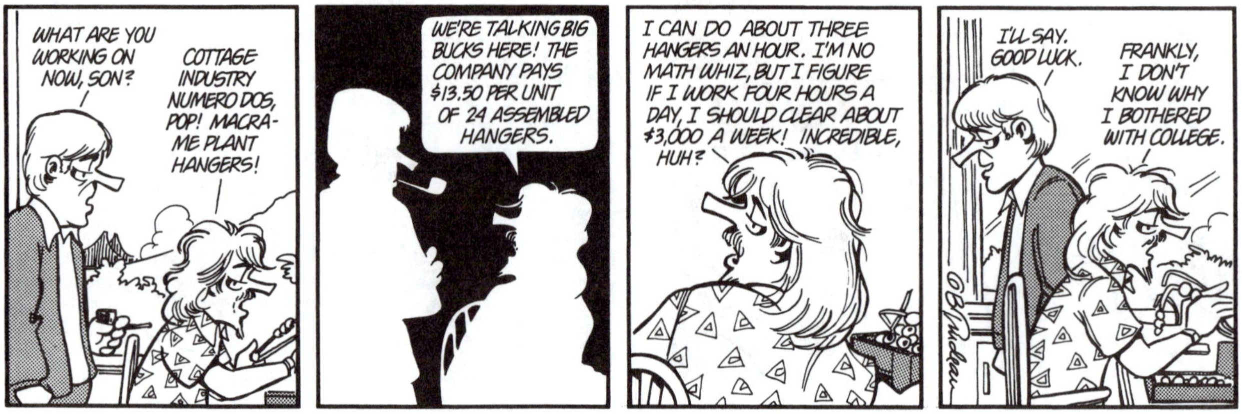
WHAT ARE YOU WORKING ON NOW, SON?
COTTAGE INDUSTRY NUMERO DOS, POP! MACRAME PLANT HANGERS!
WE'RE TALKING BIG BUCKS HERE! THE COMPANY PAYS $13.50 PER UNIT OF 24 ASSEMBLED HANGERS.
I CAN DO ABOUT THREE HANGERS AN HOUR. I'M NO MATH WHIZ, BUT I FIGURE IF I WORK FOUR HOURS A DAY, I SHOULD CLEAR ABOUT $3,000 A WEEK! INCREDIBLE, HUH?
I'LL SAY. GOOD LUCK.
FRANKLY, I DON'T KNOW WHY I BOTHERED WITH COLLEGE.
G.B. Trudeau

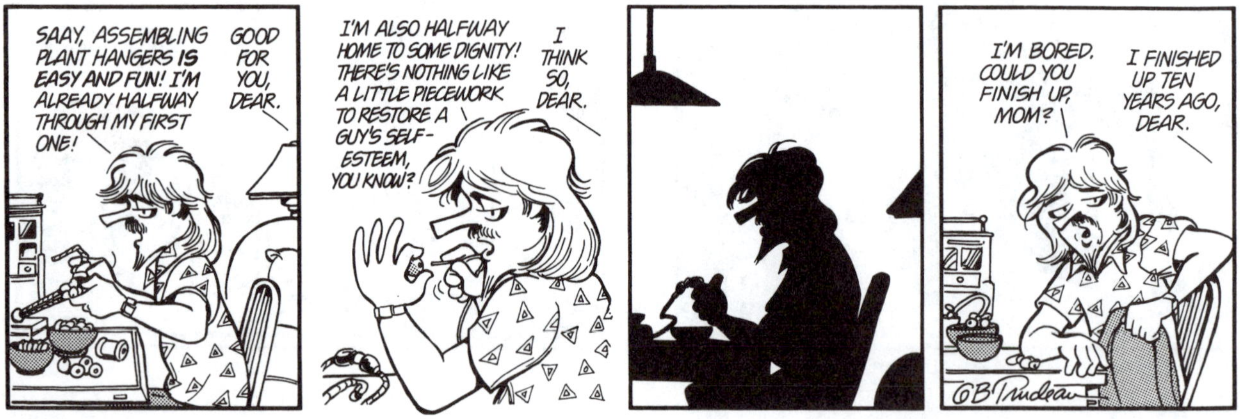
SAAY, ASSEMBLING PLANT HANGERS IS EASY AND FUN! I'M ALREADY HALFWAY THROUGH MY FIRST ONE!
GOOD FOR YOU, DEAR.
I'M ALSO HALFWAY HOME TO SOME DIGNITY! THERE'S NOTHING LIKE A LITTLE PIECEWORK TO RESTORE A GUY'S SELF-ESTEEM, YOU KNOW?
I THINK SO, DEAR.
I'M BORED. COULD YOU FINISH UP, MOM?
I FINISHED UP TEN YEARS AGO, DEAR.
G.B. Trudeau

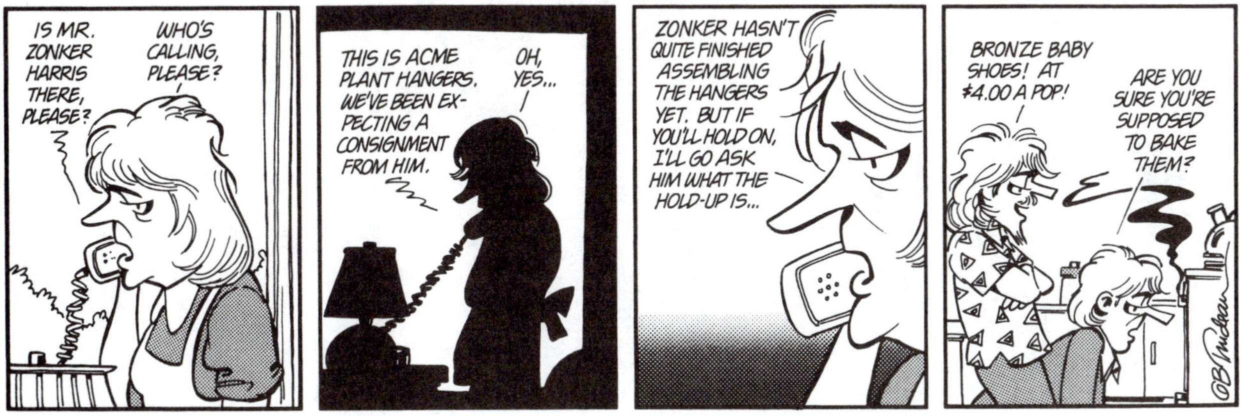
IS MR. ZONKER HARRIS THERE, PLEASE?
WHO'S CALLING, PLEASE?
THIS IS ACME PLANT HANGERS. WE'VE BEEN EXPECTING A CONSIGNMENT FROM HIM.
OH, YES...
ZONKER HASN'T QUITE FINISHED ASSEMBLING THE HANGERS YET. BUT IF YOU'LL HOLD ON, I'LL GO ASK HIM WHAT THE HOLD-UP IS...
BRONZE BABY SHOES! AT $4.00 A POP!
ARE YOU SURE YOU'RE SUPPOSED TO BAKE THEM?

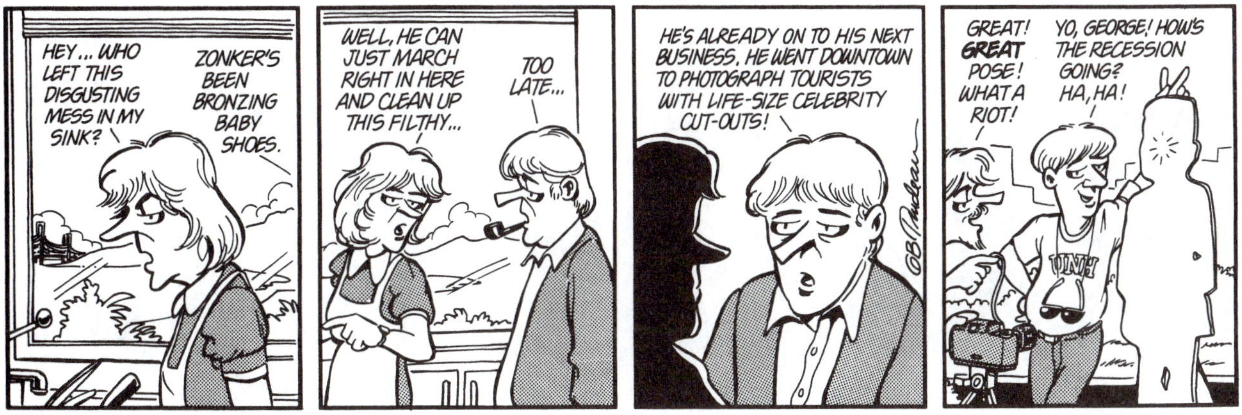
HEY... WHO LEFT THIS DISGUSTING MESS IN MY SINK?
ZONKER'S BEEN BRONZING BABY SHOES.
WELL, HE CAN JUST MARCH RIGHT IN HERE AND CLEAN UP THIS FILTHY...
TOO LATE...
HE'S ALREADY ON TO HIS NEXT BUSINESS. HE WENT DOWNTOWN TO PHOTOGRAPH TOURISTS WITH LIFE-SIZE CELEBRITY CUT-OUTS!
GREAT! GREAT POSE! WHAT A RIOT!
YO, GEORGE! HOW'S THE RECESSION GOING? HA, HA!

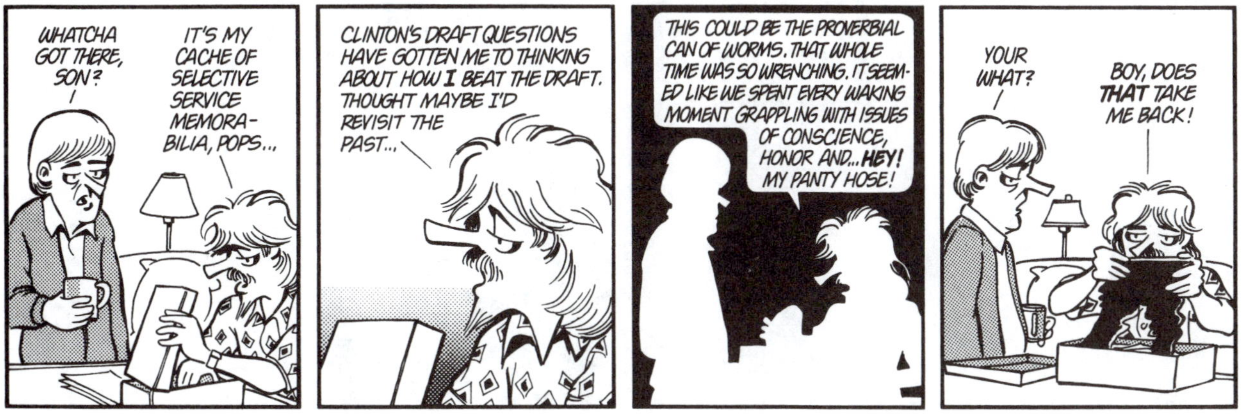
WHATCHA GOT THERE, SON?
IT'S MY CACHE OF SELECTIVE SERVICE MEMORABILIA, POPS...
CLINTON'S DRAFT QUESTIONS HAVE GOTTEN ME TO THINKING ABOUT HOW I BEAT THE DRAFT. THOUGHT MAYBE I'D REVISIT THE PAST...
THIS COULD BE THE PROVERBIAL CAN OF WORMS. THAT WHOLE TIME WAS SO WRENCHING. IT SEEMED LIKE WE SPENT EVERY WAKING MOMENT GRAPPLING WITH ISSUES OF CONSCIENCE, HONOR AND... HEY! MY PANTY HOSE!
YOUR WHAT?
BOY, DOES THAT TAKE ME BACK!

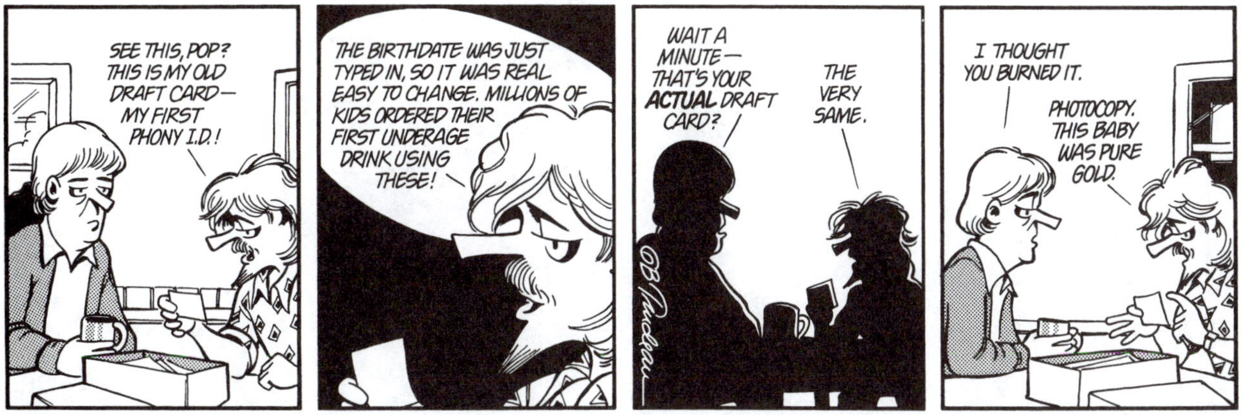
SEE THIS, POP? THIS IS MY OLD DRAFT CARD— MY FIRST PHONY I.D.!
THE BIRTHDATE WAS JUST TYPED IN, SO IT WAS REAL EASY TO CHANGE. MILLIONS OF KIDS ORDERED THEIR FIRST UNDERAGE DRINK USING THESE!
WAIT A MINUTE— THAT'S YOUR ACTUAL DRAFT CARD?
THE VERY SAME.
I THOUGHT YOU BURNED IT.
PHOTOCOPY. THIS BABY WAS PURE GOLD.

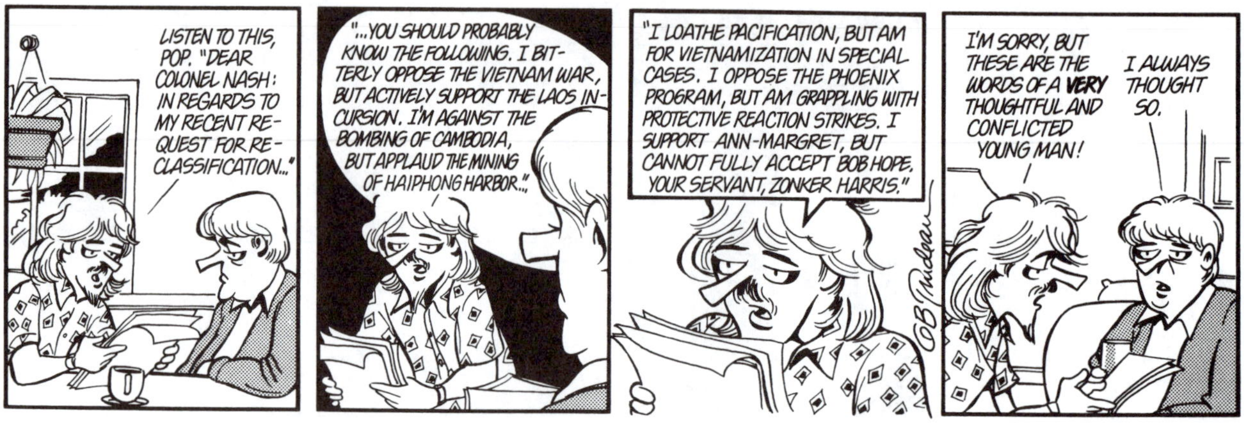
LISTEN TO THIS, POP. "DEAR COLONEL NASH: IN REGARDS TO MY RECENT REQUEST FOR RECLASSIFICATION..."
"...YOU SHOULD PROBABLY KNOW THE FOLLOWING. I BITTERLY OPPOSE THE VIETNAM WAR, BUT ACTIVELY SUPPORT THE LAOS INCURSION. I'M AGAINST THE BOMBING OF CAMBODIA, BUT APPLAUD THE MINING OF HAIPHONG HARBOR..."
"I LOATHE PACIFICATION, BUT AM FOR VIETNAMIZATION IN SPECIAL CASES. I OPPOSE THE PHOENIX PROGRAM, BUT AM GRAPPLING WITH PROTECTIVE REACTION STRIKES. I SUPPORT ANN-MARGRET, BUT CANNOT FULLY ACCEPT BOB HOPE. YOUR SERVANT, ZONKER HARRIS."
GB Trudeau
I'M SORRY, BUT THESE ARE THE WORDS OF A VERY THOUGHTFUL AND CONFLICTED YOUNG MAN!
I ALWAYS THOUGHT SO.

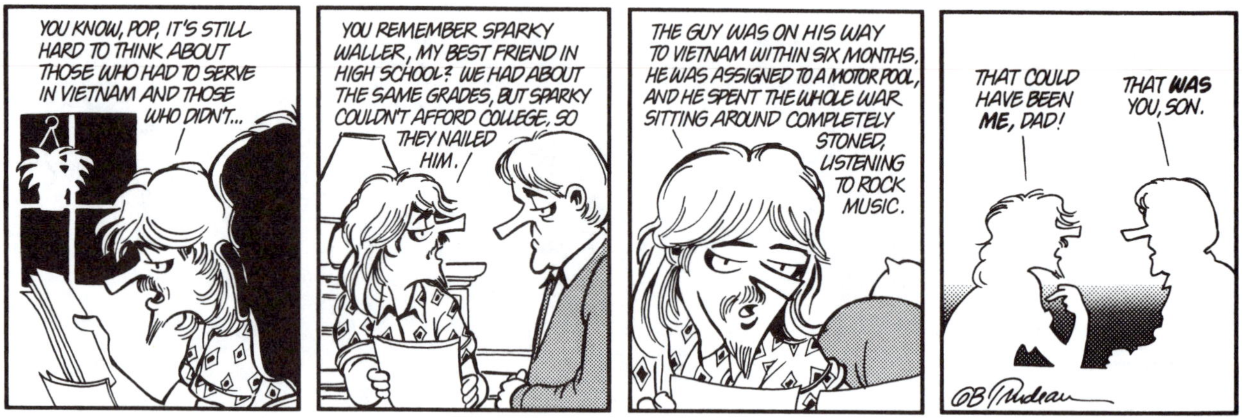
YOU KNOW, POP, IT'S STILL HARD TO THINK ABOUT THOSE WHO HAD TO SERVE IN VIETNAM AND THOSE WHO DIDN'T...
YOU REMEMBER SPARKY WALLER, MY BEST FRIEND IN HIGH SCHOOL? WE HAD ABOUT THE SAME GRADES, BUT SPARKY COULDN'T AFFORD COLLEGE, SO THEY NAILED HIM.
THE GUY WAS ON HIS WAY TO VIETNAM WITHIN SIX MONTHS. HE WAS ASSIGNED TO A MOTOR POOL, AND HE SPENT THE WHOLE WAR SITTING AROUND COMPLETELY STONED, LISTENING TO ROCK MUSIC.
THAT COULD HAVE BEEN ME, DAD!
THAT WAS YOU, SON.
GB Trudeau

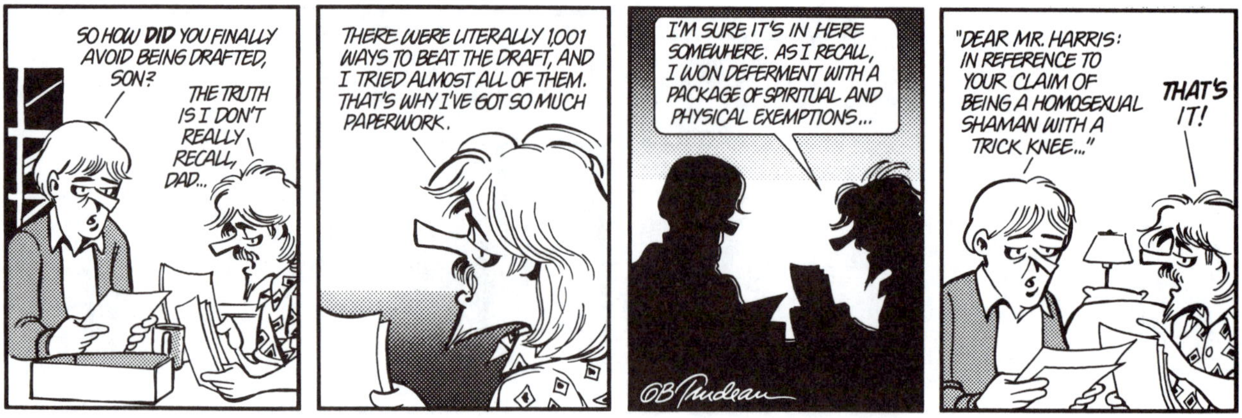
SO HOW DID YOU FINALLY AVOID BEING DRAFTED, SON?
THE TRUTH IS I DON'T REALLY RECALL, DAD...
THERE WERE LITERALLY 1,001 WAYS TO BEAT THE DRAFT, AND I TRIED ALMOST ALL OF THEM. THAT'S WHY I'VE GOT SO MUCH PAPERWORK.
I'M SURE IT'S IN HERE SOMEWHERE. AS I RECALL, I WON DEFERMENT WITH A PACKAGE OF SPIRITUAL AND PHYSICAL EXEMPTIONS...
GB Trudeau
"DEAR MR. HARRIS: IN REFERENCE TO YOUR CLAIM OF BEING A HOMOSEXUAL SHAMAN WITH A TRICK KNEE..."
THAT'S IT!

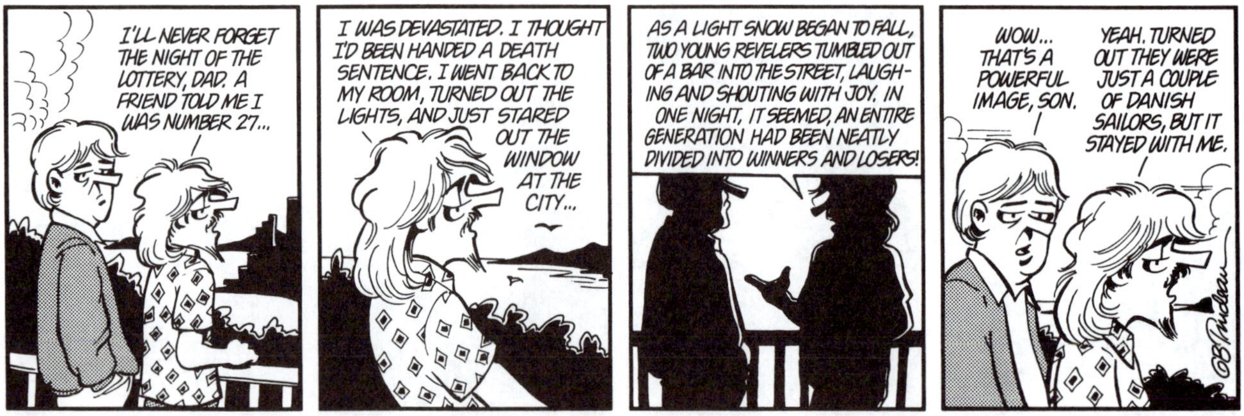
I'LL NEVER FORGET THE NIGHT OF THE LOTTERY, DAD. A FRIEND TOLD ME I WAS NUMBER 27...
I WAS DEVASTATED. I THOUGHT I'D BEEN HANDED A DEATH SENTENCE. I WENT BACK TO MY ROOM, TURNED OUT THE LIGHTS, AND JUST STARED OUT THE WINDOW AT THE CITY...
AS A LIGHT SNOW BEGAN TO FALL, TWO YOUNG REVELERS TUMBLED OUT OF A BAR INTO THE STREET, LAUGHING AND SHOUTING WITH JOY. IN ONE NIGHT, IT SEEMED, AN ENTIRE GENERATION HAD BEEN NEATLY DIVIDED INTO WINNERS AND LOSERS!
WOW... THAT'S A POWERFUL IMAGE, SON.
YEAH. TURNED OUT THEY WERE JUST A COUPLE OF DANISH SAILORS, BUT IT STAYED WITH ME.
GB Trudeau

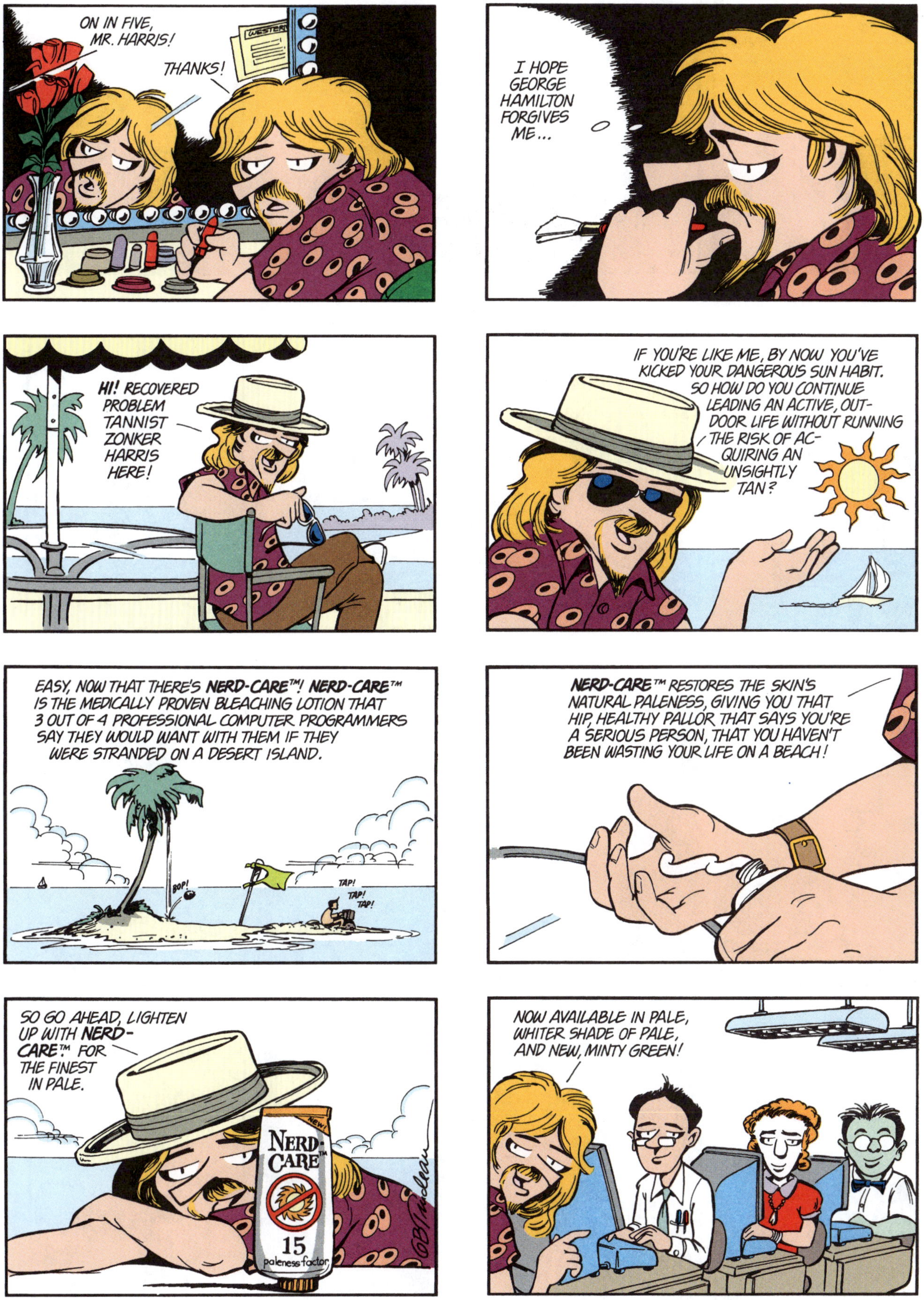
ON IN FIVE, MR. HARRIS!
THANKS!
WESTERN
I HOPE GEORGE HAMILTON FORGIVES ME...
HI! RECOVERED PROBLEM TANNIST ZONKER HARRIS HERE!
IF YOU'RE LIKE ME, BY NOW YOU'VE KICKED YOUR DANGEROUS SUN HABIT. SO HOW DO YOU CONTINUE LEADING AN ACTIVE, OUTDOOR LIFE WITHOUT RUNNING THE RISK OF ACQUIRING AN UNSIGHTLY TAN?
EASY, NOW THAT THERE'S NERD-CARE™! NERD-CARE™ IS THE MEDICALLY PROVEN BLEACHING LOTION THAT 3 OUT OF 4 PROFESSIONAL COMPUTER PROGRAMMERS SAY THEY WOULD WANT WITH THEM IF THEY WERE STRANDED ON A DESERT ISLAND.
BOP!
TAP! TAP! TAP!
NERD-CARE™ RESTORES THE SKIN'S NATURAL PALENESS, GIVING YOU THAT HIP, HEALTHY PALLOR THAT SAYS YOU'RE A SERIOUS PERSON, THAT YOU HAVEN'T BEEN WASTING YOUR LIFE ON A BEACH!
SO GO AHEAD, LIGHTEN UP WITH NERD-CARE™ FOR THE FINEST IN PALE.
NEW!
NERD-CARE™
15
paleness factor
©BTrudeau
NOW AVAILABLE IN PALE, WHITER SHADE OF PALE, AND NEW, MINTY GREEN!

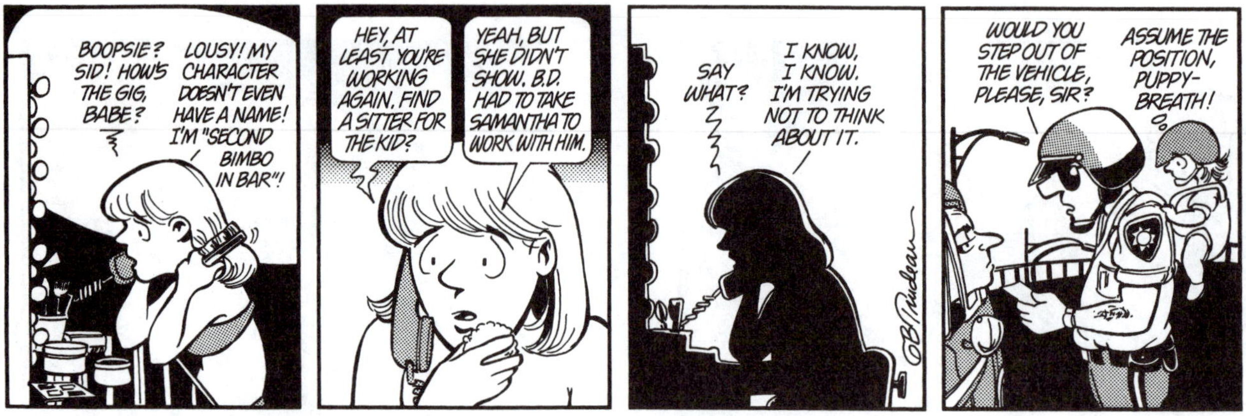
BOOPSIE? SID! HOW'S THE GIG, BABE?
LOUSY! MY CHARACTER DOESN'T EVEN HAVE A NAME! I'M "SECOND BIMBO IN BAR"!
HEY, AT LEAST YOU'RE WORKING AGAIN. FIND A SITTER FOR THE KID?
YEAH, BUT SHE DIDN'T SHOW. B.D. HAD TO TAKE SAMANTHA TO WORK WITH HIM.
SAY WHAT?
I KNOW, I KNOW. I'M TRYING NOT TO THINK ABOUT IT.
WOULD YOU STEP OUT OF THE VEHICLE, PLEASE, SIR?
ASSUME THE POSITION, PUPPY-BREATH!

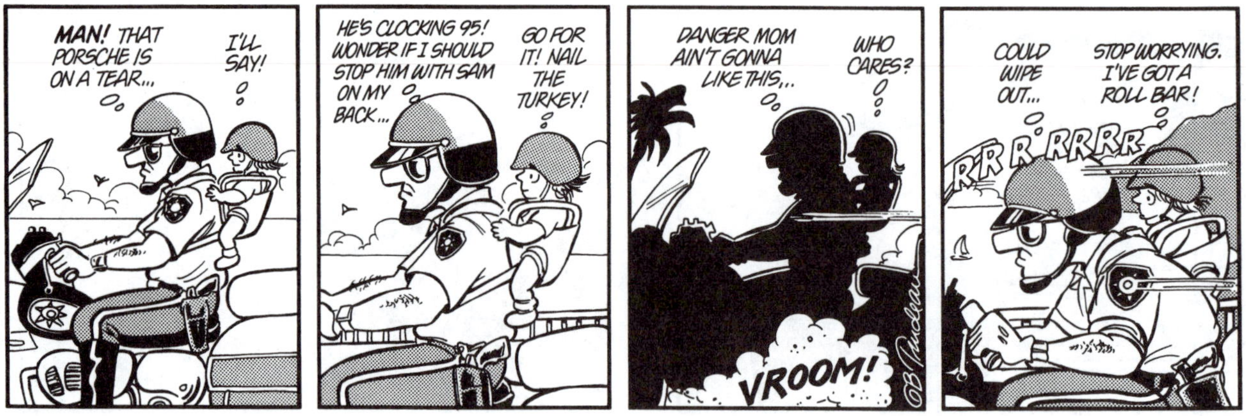
MAN! THAT PORSCHE IS ON A TEAR...
I'LL SAY!
HE'S CLOCKING 95! WONDER IF I SHOULD STOP HIM WITH SAM ON MY BACK...
GO FOR IT! NAIL THE TURKEY!
DANGER MOM AIN'T GONNA LIKE THIS...
WHO CARES?
VROOM!
COULD WIPE OUT...
STOP WORRYING. I'VE GOT A ROLL BAR!
RRRRRRRR

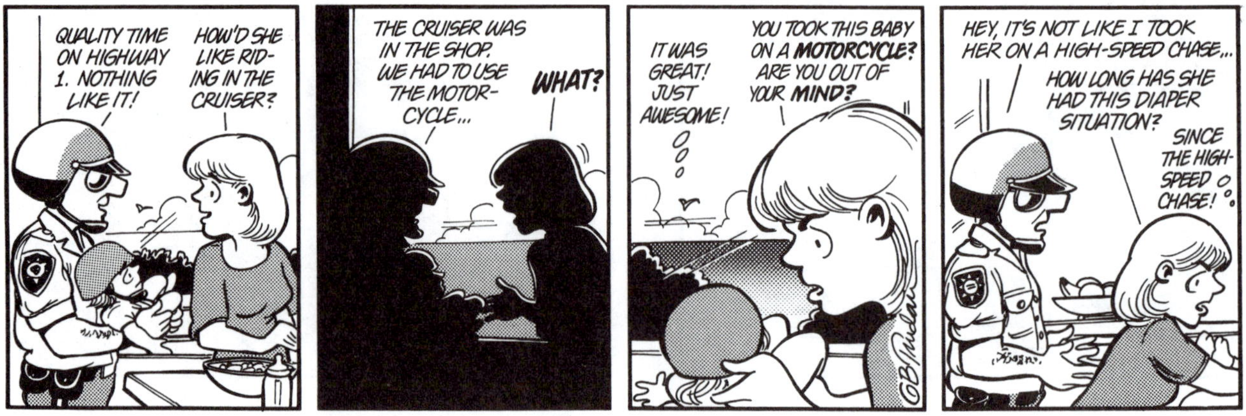
QUALITY TIME ON HIGHWAY 1. NOTHING LIKE IT!
HOW'D SHE LIKE RIDING IN THE CRUISER?
THE CRUISER WAS IN THE SHOP. WE HAD TO USE THE MOTORCYCLE...
WHAT?
IT WAS GREAT! JUST AWESOME!
YOU TOOK THIS BABY ON A MOTORCYCLE? ARE YOU OUT OF YOUR MIND?
HEY, IT'S NOT LIKE I TOOK HER ON A HIGH-SPEED CHASE...
HOW LONG HAS SHE HAD THIS DIAPER SITUATION?
SINCE THE HIGH-SPEED CHASE!

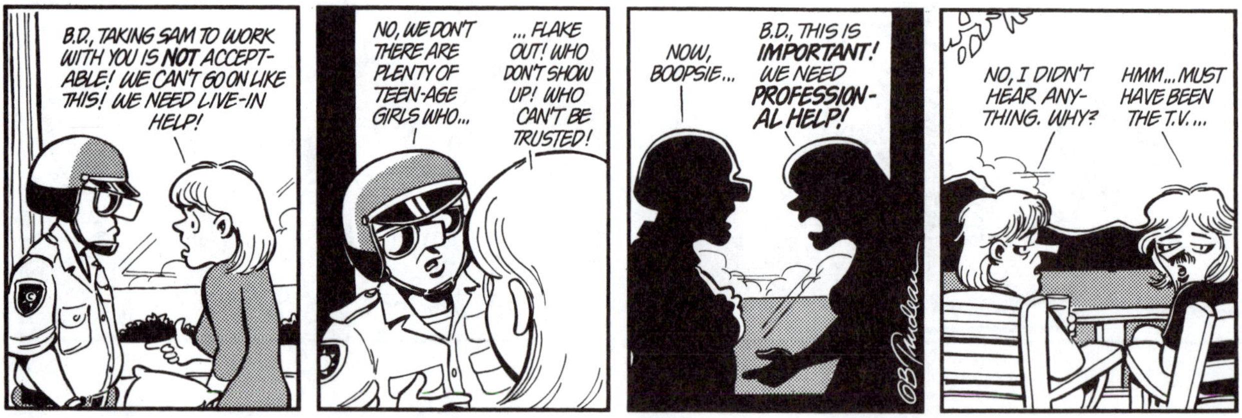
B.D., TAKING SAM TO WORK WITH YOU IS NOT ACCEPTABLE! WE CAN'T GO ON LIKE THIS! WE NEED LIVE-IN HELP!
NO, WE DON'T THERE ARE PLENTY OF TEEN-AGE GIRLS WHO...
... FLAKE OUT! WHO DON'T SHOW UP! WHO CAN'T BE TRUSTED!
NOW, BOOPSIE...
B.D., THIS IS IMPORTANT! WE NEED PROFESSIONAL HELP!
NO, I DIDN'T HEAR ANYTHING. WHY?
HMM... MUST HAVE BEEN THE T.V. ...

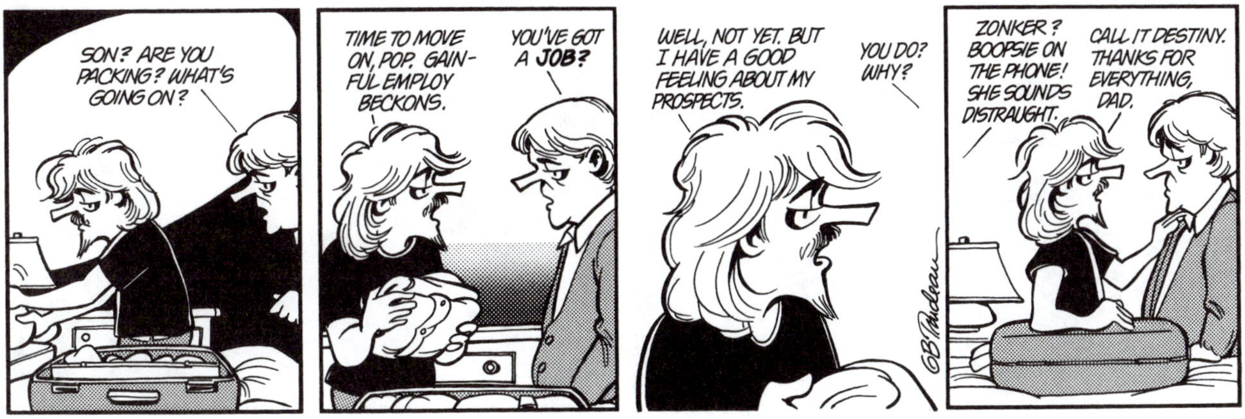
SON? ARE YOU PACKING? WHAT'S GOING ON?
TIME TO MOVE ON, POP. GAINFUL EMPLOY BECKONS.
YOU'VE GOT A **JOB?**
WELL, NOT YET. BUT I HAVE A GOOD FEELING ABOUT MY PROSPECTS.
YOU DO? WHY?
ZONKER? BOOPSIE ON THE PHONE! SHE SOUNDS DISTRAUGHT.
CALL IT DESTINY. THANKS FOR EVERYTHING, DAD.

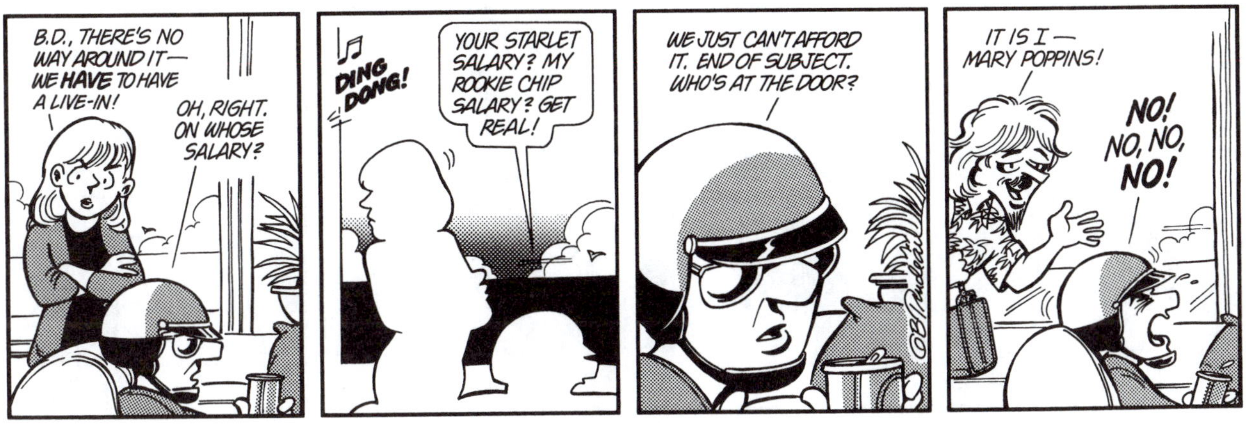
B.D., THERE'S NO WAY AROUND IT— WE **HAVE** TO HAVE A LIVE-IN!
OH, RIGHT. ON WHOSE SALARY?
DING DONG!
YOUR STARLET SALARY? MY ROOKIE CHIP SALARY? GET REAL!
WE JUST CAN'T AFFORD IT. END OF SUBJECT. WHO'S AT THE DOOR?
IT IS I— MARY POPPINS!
NO! NO, NO, NO!

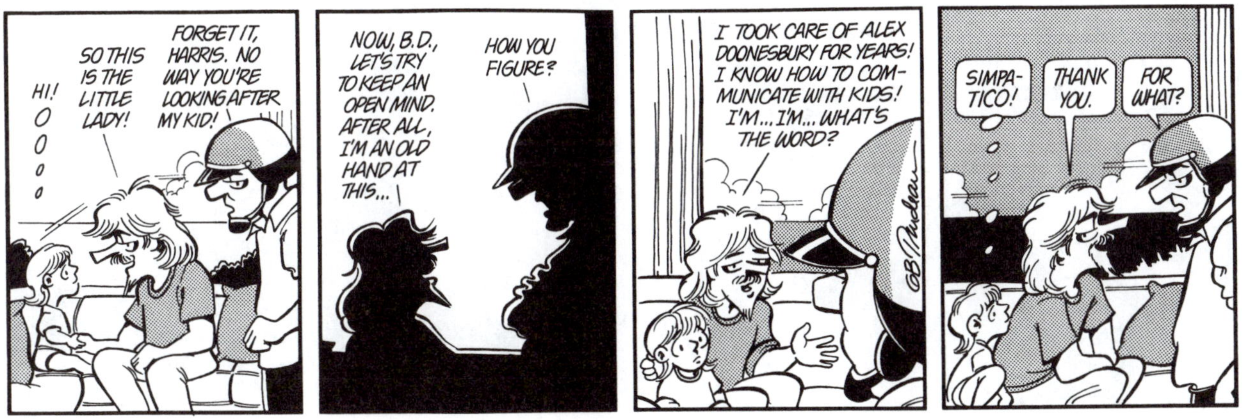
HI!
SO THIS IS THE LITTLE LADY!
FORGET IT, HARRIS. NO WAY YOU'RE LOOKING AFTER MY KID!
NOW, B.D., LET'S TRY TO KEEP AN OPEN MIND. AFTER ALL, I'M AN OLD HAND AT THIS...
HOW YOU FIGURE?
I TOOK CARE OF ALEX DOONESBURY FOR YEARS! I KNOW HOW TO COMMUNICATE WITH KIDS! I'M... I'M... WHAT'S THE WORD?
SIMPATICO!
THANK YOU.
FOR WHAT?

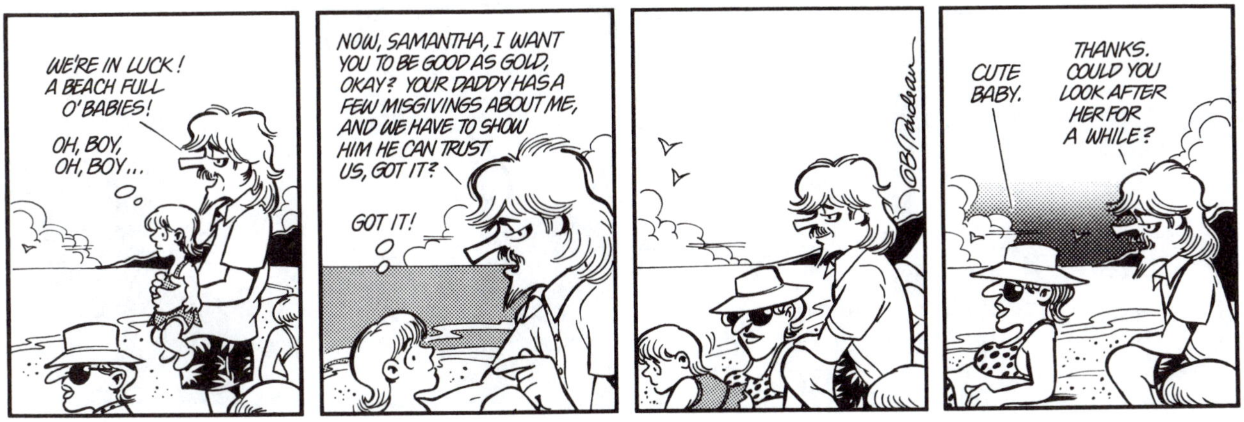
WE'RE IN LUCK! A BEACH FULL O' BABIES!
OH, BOY, OH, BOY...
NOW, SAMANTHA, I WANT YOU TO BE GOOD AS GOLD, OKAY? YOUR DADDY HAS A FEW MISGIVINGS ABOUT ME, AND WE HAVE TO SHOW HIM HE CAN TRUST US, GOT IT?
GOT IT!
CUTE BABY.
THANKS. COULD YOU LOOK AFTER HER FOR A WHILE?

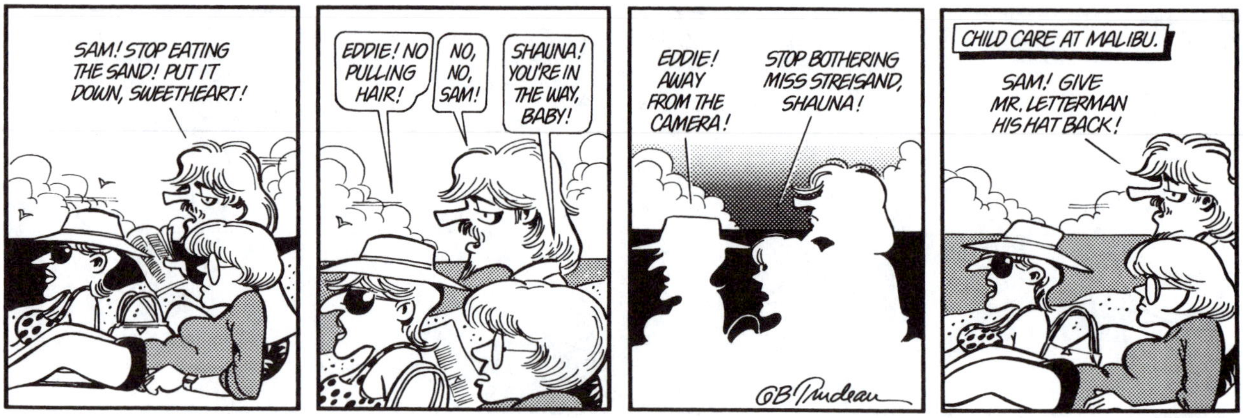
SAM! STOP EATING THE SAND! PUT IT DOWN, SWEETHEART!
EDDIE! NO PULLING HAIR!
NO, NO, SAM!
SHAUNA! YOU'RE IN THE WAY, BABY!
EDDIE! AWAY FROM THE CAMERA!
STOP BOTHERING MISS STREISAND, SHAUNA!
©B Trudeau
CHILD CARE AT MALIBU.
SAM! GIVE MR. LETTERMAN HIS HAT BACK!

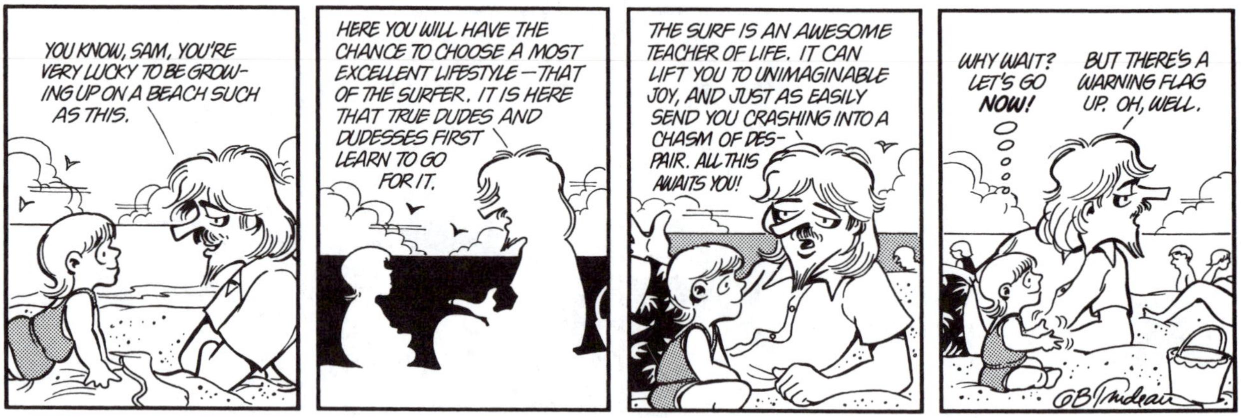
YOU KNOW, SAM, YOU'RE VERY LUCKY TO BE GROWING UP ON A BEACH SUCH AS THIS.
HERE YOU WILL HAVE THE CHANCE TO CHOOSE A MOST EXCELLENT LIFESTYLE — THAT OF THE SURFER. IT IS HERE THAT TRUE DUDES AND DUDESSES FIRST LEARN TO GO FOR IT.
THE SURF IS AN AWESOME TEACHER OF LIFE. IT CAN LIFT YOU TO UNIMAGINABLE JOY, AND JUST AS EASILY SEND YOU CRASHING INTO A CHASM OF DESPAIR. ALL THIS AWAITS YOU!
WHY WAIT? LET'S GO NOW!
BUT THERE'S A WARNING FLAG UP. OH, WELL.
©B Trudeau

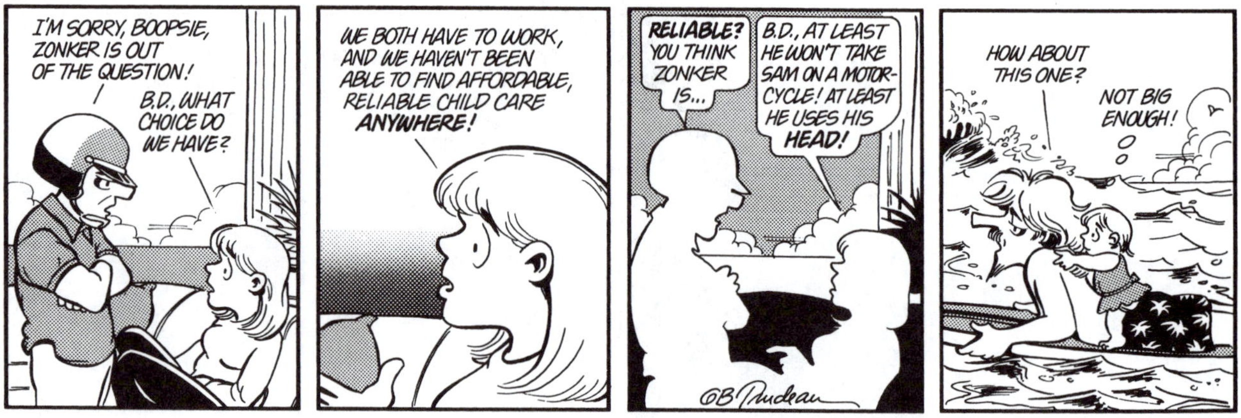
I'M SORRY, BOOPSIE, ZONKER IS OUT OF THE QUESTION!
B.D., WHAT CHOICE DO WE HAVE?
WE BOTH HAVE TO WORK, AND WE HAVEN'T BEEN ABLE TO FIND AFFORDABLE, RELIABLE CHILD CARE ANYWHERE!
RELIABLE? YOU THINK ZONKER IS...
B.D., AT LEAST HE WON'T TAKE SAM ON A MOTORCYCLE! AT LEAST HE USES HIS HEAD!
©B Trudeau
HOW ABOUT THIS ONE?
NOT BIG ENOUGH!

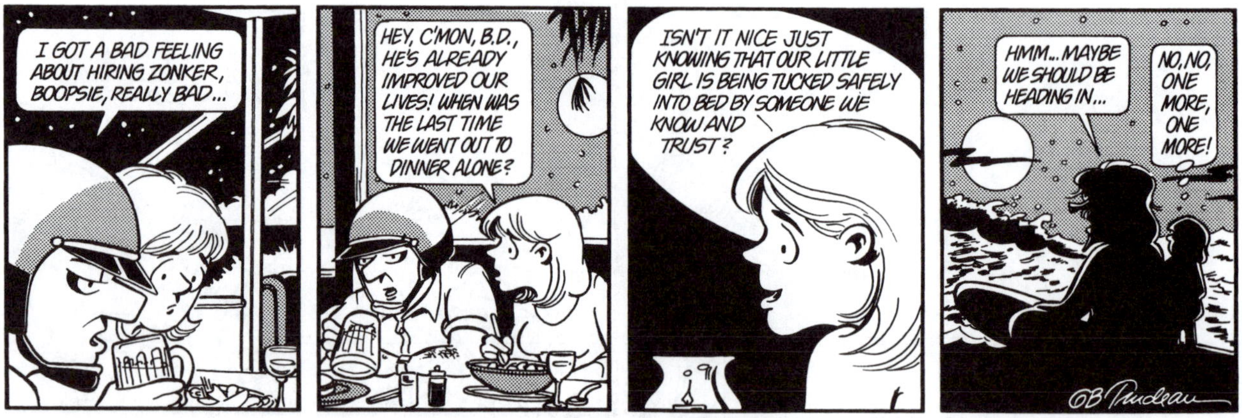
I GOT A BAD FEELING ABOUT HIRING ZONKER, BOOPSIE, REALLY BAD...
HEY, C'MON, B.D., HE'S ALREADY IMPROVED OUR LIVES! WHEN WAS THE LAST TIME WE WENT OUT TO DINNER ALONE?
ISN'T IT NICE JUST KNOWING THAT OUR LITTLE GIRL IS BEING TUCKED SAFELY INTO BED BY SOMEONE WE KNOW AND TRUST?
HMM... MAYBE WE SHOULD BE HEADING IN...
NO, NO, ONE MORE, ONE MORE!
©B Trudeau

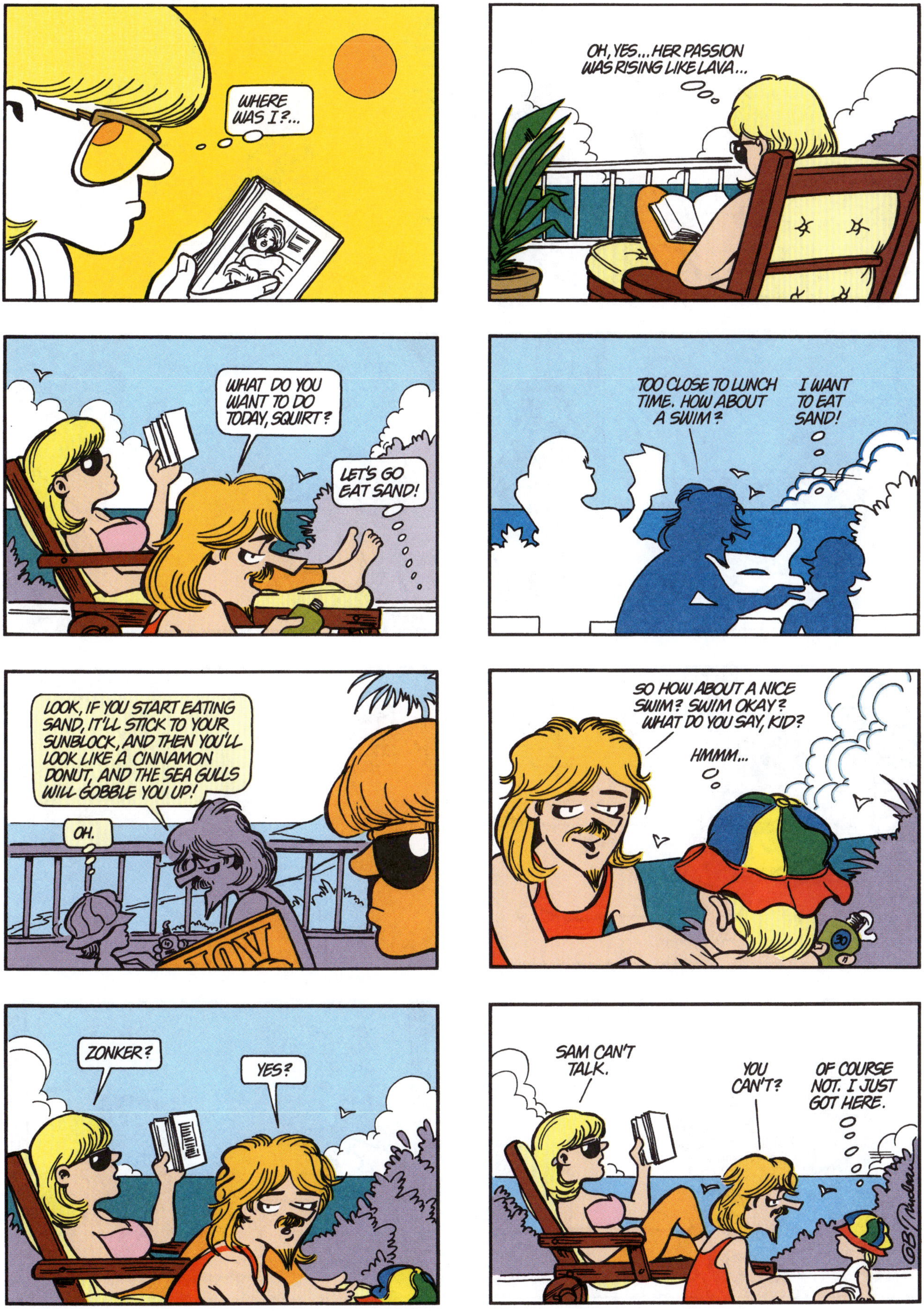
WHERE WAS I?...
OH, YES... HER PASSION WAS RISING LIKE LAVA...
WHAT DO YOU WANT TO DO TODAY, SQUIRT?
LET'S GO EAT SAND!
TOO CLOSE TO LUNCH TIME. HOW ABOUT A SWIM?
I WANT TO EAT SAND!
LOOK, IF YOU START EATING SAND, IT'LL STICK TO YOUR SUNBLOCK, AND THEN YOU'LL LOOK LIKE A CINNAMON DONUT, AND THE SEA GULLS WILL GOBBLE YOU UP!
OH.
SO HOW ABOUT A NICE SWIM? SWIM OKAY? WHAT DO YOU SAY, KID?
HMMM...
ZONKER?
YES?
SAM CAN'T TALK.
YOU CAN'T?
OF COURSE NOT. I JUST GOT HERE.

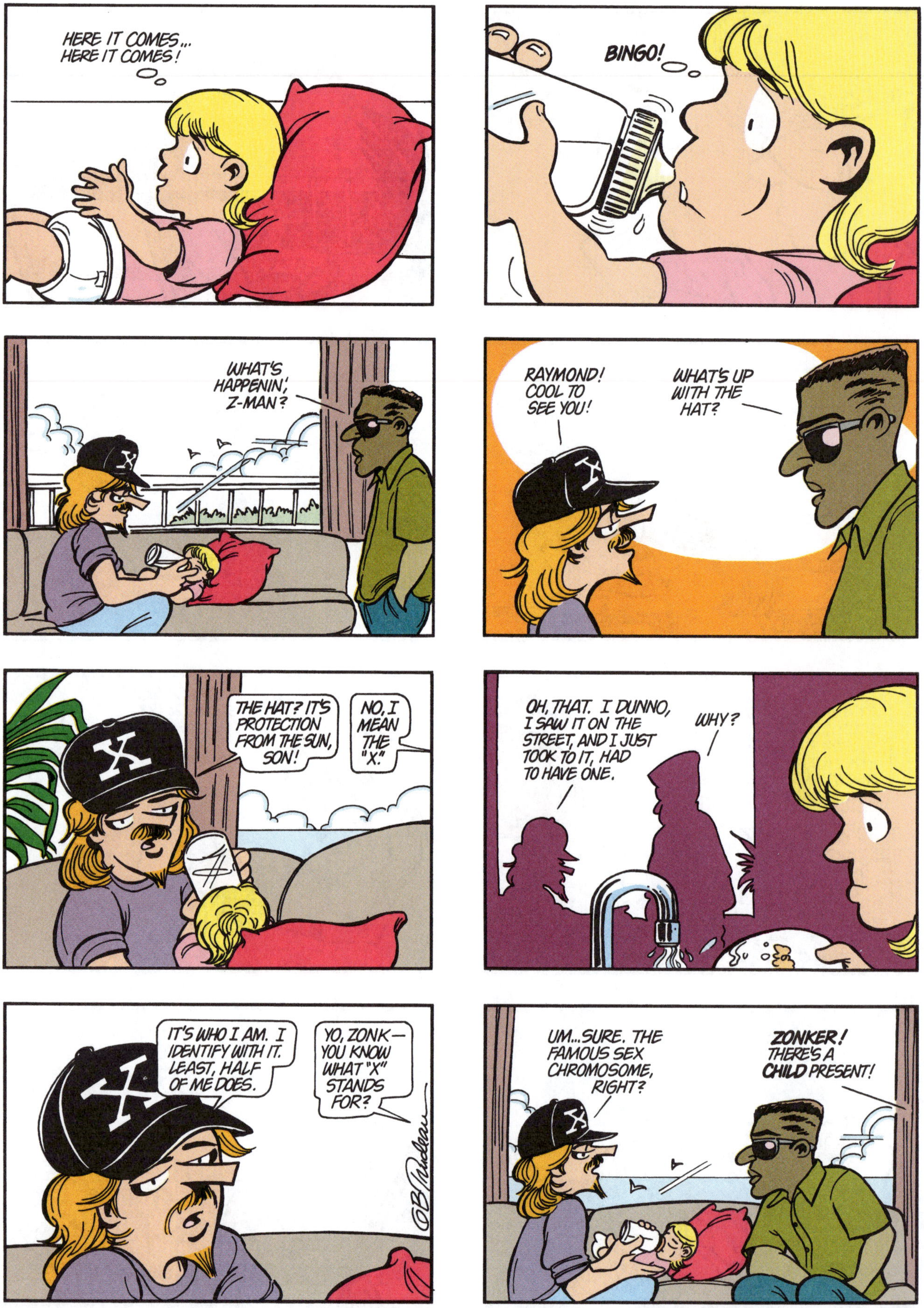
HERE IT COMES...
HERE IT COMES!
BINGO!
WHAT'S HAPPENIN', Z-MAN?
RAYMOND! COOL TO SEE YOU!
WHAT'S UP WITH THE HAT?
THE HAT? IT'S PROTECTION FROM THE SUN, SON!
NO, I MEAN THE "X."
OH, THAT. I DUNNO, I SAW IT ON THE STREET, AND I JUST TOOK TO IT, HAD TO HAVE ONE.
WHY?
IT'S WHO I AM. I IDENTIFY WITH IT. LEAST, HALF OF ME DOES.
YO, ZONK— YOU KNOW WHAT "X" STANDS FOR?
UM...SURE. THE FAMOUS SEX CHROMOSOME, RIGHT?
ZONKER! THERE'S A CHILD PRESENT!

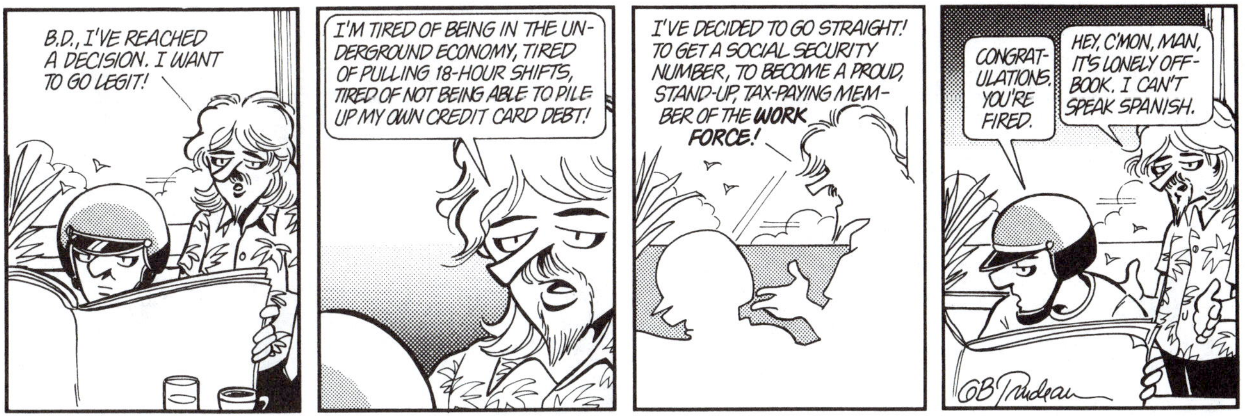
B.D., I'VE REACHED A DECISION. I WANT TO GO LEGIT!
I'M TIRED OF BEING IN THE UNDERGROUND ECONOMY, TIRED OF PULLING 18-HOUR SHIFTS, TIRED OF NOT BEING ABLE TO PILE UP MY OWN CREDIT CARD DEBT!
I'VE DECIDED TO GO STRAIGHT! TO GET A SOCIAL SECURITY NUMBER, TO BECOME A PROUD, STAND-UP, TAX-PAYING MEMBER OF THE **WORK FORCE**!
CONGRATULATIONS. YOU'RE FIRED.
HEY, C'MON, MAN, IT'S LONELY OFF-BOOK. I CAN'T SPEAK SPANISH.
©B Trudeau

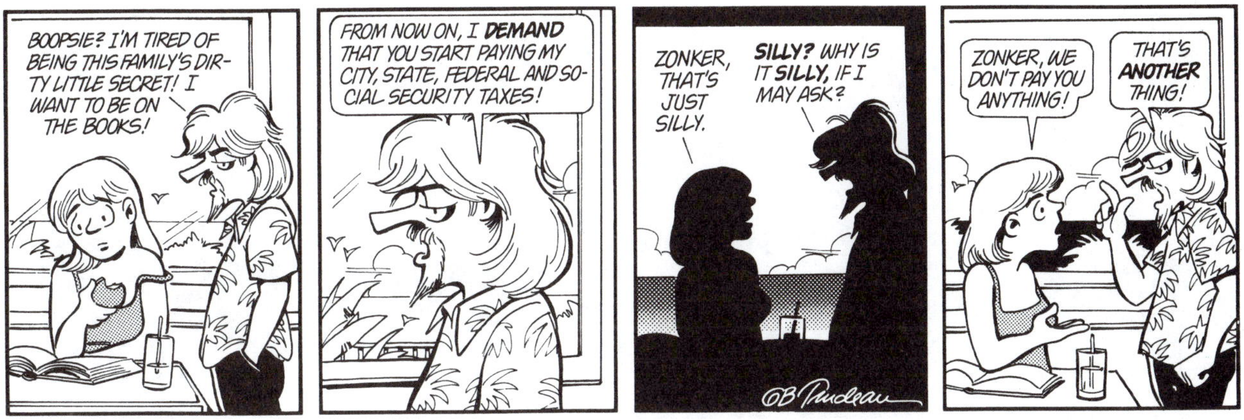
BOOPSIE? I'M TIRED OF BEING THIS FAMILY'S DIRTY LITTLE SECRET! I WANT TO BE ON THE BOOKS!
FROM NOW ON, I **DEMAND** THAT YOU START PAYING MY CITY, STATE, FEDERAL AND SOCIAL SECURITY TAXES!
ZONKER, THAT'S JUST SILLY.
SILLY? WHY IS IT **SILLY**, IF I MAY ASK?
©B Trudeau
ZONKER, WE DON'T PAY YOU ANYTHING!
THAT'S **ANOTHER** THING!

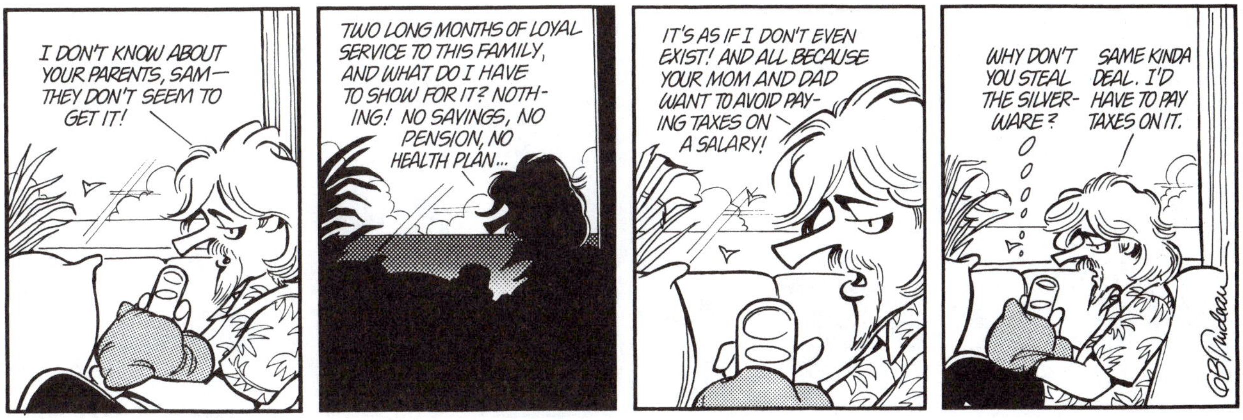
I DON'T KNOW ABOUT YOUR PARENTS, SAM— THEY DON'T SEEM TO GET IT!
TWO LONG MONTHS OF LOYAL SERVICE TO THIS FAMILY, AND WHAT DO I HAVE TO SHOW FOR IT? NOTHING! NO SAVINGS, NO PENSION, NO HEALTH PLAN...
IT'S AS IF I DON'T EVEN EXIST! AND ALL BECAUSE YOUR MOM AND DAD WANT TO AVOID PAYING TAXES ON A SALARY!
WHY DON'T YOU STEAL THE SILVERWARE?
SAME KINDA DEAL. I'D HAVE TO PAY TAXES ON IT.
©B Trudeau

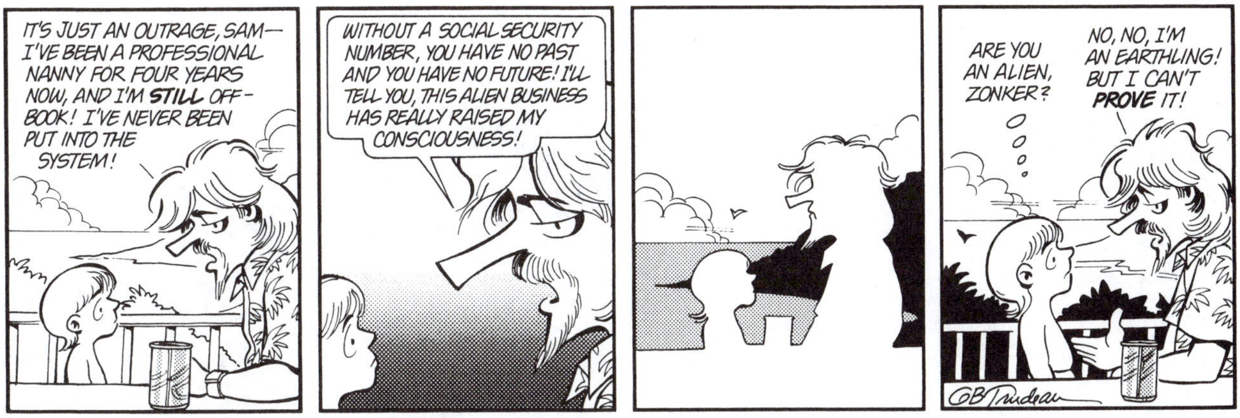
IT'S JUST AN OUTRAGE, SAM— I'VE BEEN A PROFESSIONAL NANNY FOR FOUR YEARS NOW, AND I'M **STILL** OFF-BOOK! I'VE NEVER BEEN PUT INTO THE SYSTEM!
WITHOUT A SOCIAL SECURITY NUMBER, YOU HAVE NO PAST AND YOU HAVE NO FUTURE! I'LL TELL YOU, THIS ALIEN BUSINESS HAS REALLY RAISED MY CONSCIOUSNESS!
ARE YOU AN ALIEN, ZONKER?
NO, NO, I'M AN EARTHLING! BUT I CAN'T **PROVE** IT!
©B Trudeau

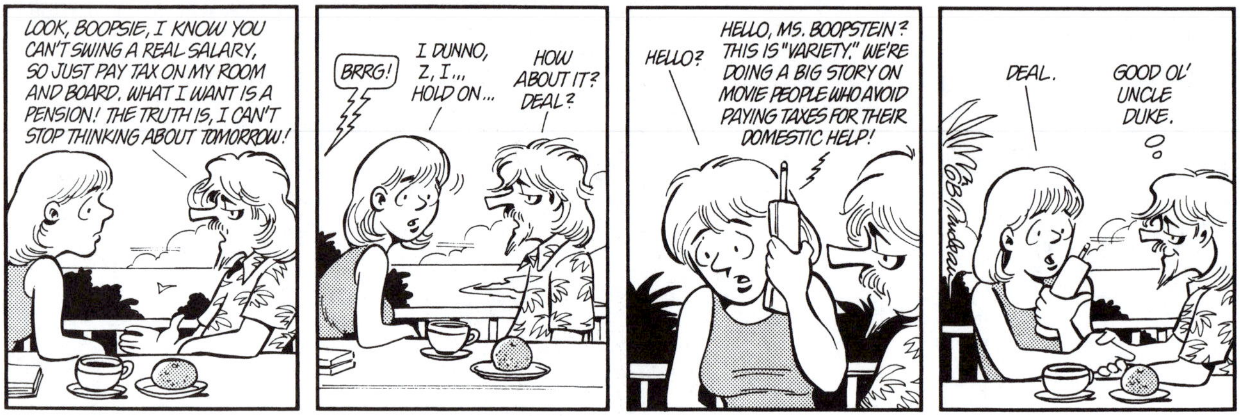
LOOK, BOOPSIE, I KNOW YOU CAN'T SWING A REAL SALARY, SO JUST PAY TAX ON MY ROOM AND BOARD. WHAT I WANT IS A PENSION! THE TRUTH IS, I CAN'T STOP THINKING ABOUT TOMORROW!
BRRG!
I DUNNO, Z, I... HOLD ON...
HOW ABOUT IT? DEAL?
HELLO?
HELLO, MS. BOOPSTEIN? THIS IS "VARIETY." WE'RE DOING A BIG STORY ON MOVIE PEOPLE WHO AVOID PAYING TAXES FOR THEIR DOMESTIC HELP!
DEAL.
GOOD OL' UNCLE DUKE.

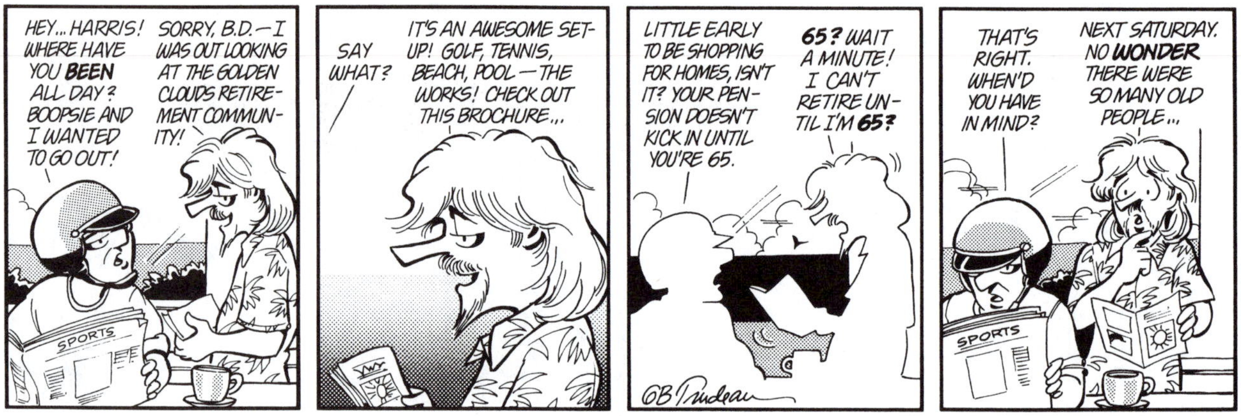
HEY... HARRIS! WHERE HAVE YOU **BEEN** ALL DAY? BOOPSIE AND I WANTED TO GO OUT!
SORRY, B.D.—I WAS OUT LOOKING AT THE GOLDEN CLOUDS RETIREMENT COMMUNITY!
SAY WHAT?
IT'S AN AWESOME SET-UP! GOLF, TENNIS, BEACH, POOL—THE WORKS! CHECK OUT THIS BROCHURE...
SPORTS
LITTLE EARLY TO BE SHOPPING FOR HOMES, ISN'T IT? YOUR PENSION DOESN'T KICK IN UNTIL YOU'RE 65.
65? WAIT A MINUTE! I CAN'T RETIRE UNTIL I'M **65?**
THAT'S RIGHT. WHEN'D YOU HAVE IN MIND?
NEXT SATURDAY. NO **WONDER** THERE WERE SO MANY OLD PEOPLE...
SPORTS

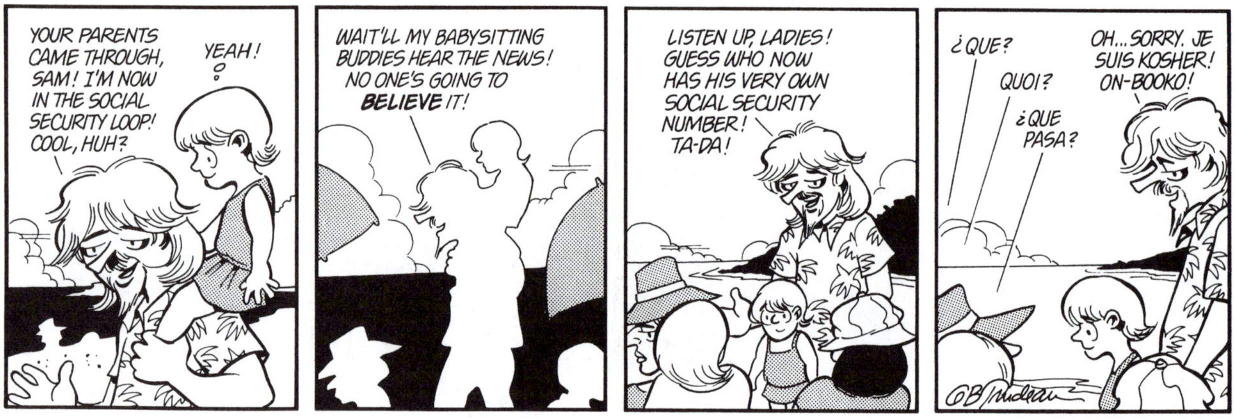
YOUR PARENTS CAME THROUGH, SAM! I'M NOW IN THE SOCIAL SECURITY LOOP! COOL, HUH?
YEAH!
WAIT'LL MY BABYSITTING BUDDIES HEAR THE NEWS! NO ONE'S GOING TO **BELIEVE** IT!
LISTEN UP, LADIES! GUESS WHO NOW HAS HIS VERY OWN SOCIAL SECURITY NUMBER! TA-DA!
¿QUE?
QUOI?
¿QUE PASA?
OH... SORRY. JE SUIS KOSHER! ON-BOOKO!

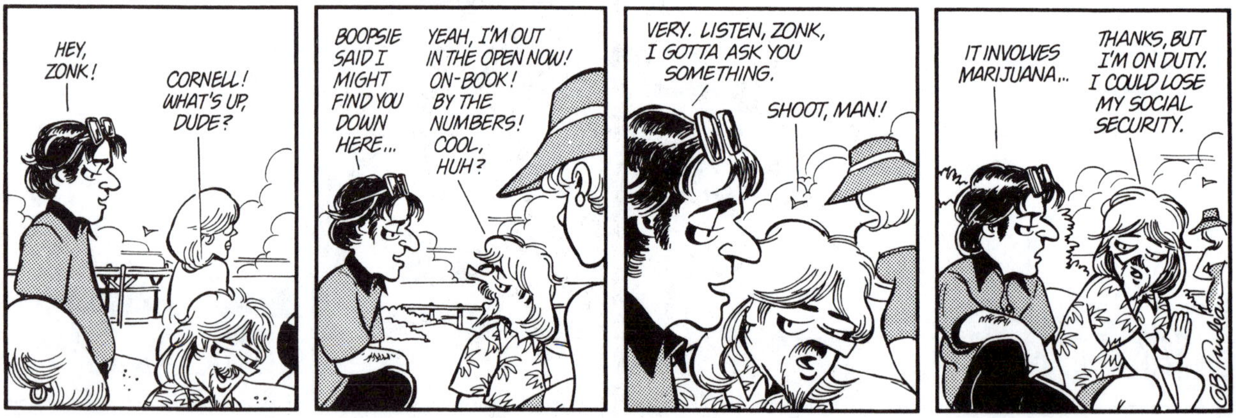
HEY, ZONK!
CORNELL! WHAT'S UP, DUDE?
BOOPSIE SAID I MIGHT FIND YOU DOWN HERE...
YEAH, I'M OUT IN THE OPEN NOW! ON-BOOK! BY THE NUMBERS! COOL, HUH?
VERY. LISTEN, ZONK, I GOTTA ASK YOU SOMETHING.
SHOOT, MAN!
IT INVOLVES MARIJUANA...
THANKS, BUT I'M ON DUTY. I COULD LOSE MY SOCIAL SECURITY.

8

THE ANGEL OF MERCY

Bringing That Higher Love

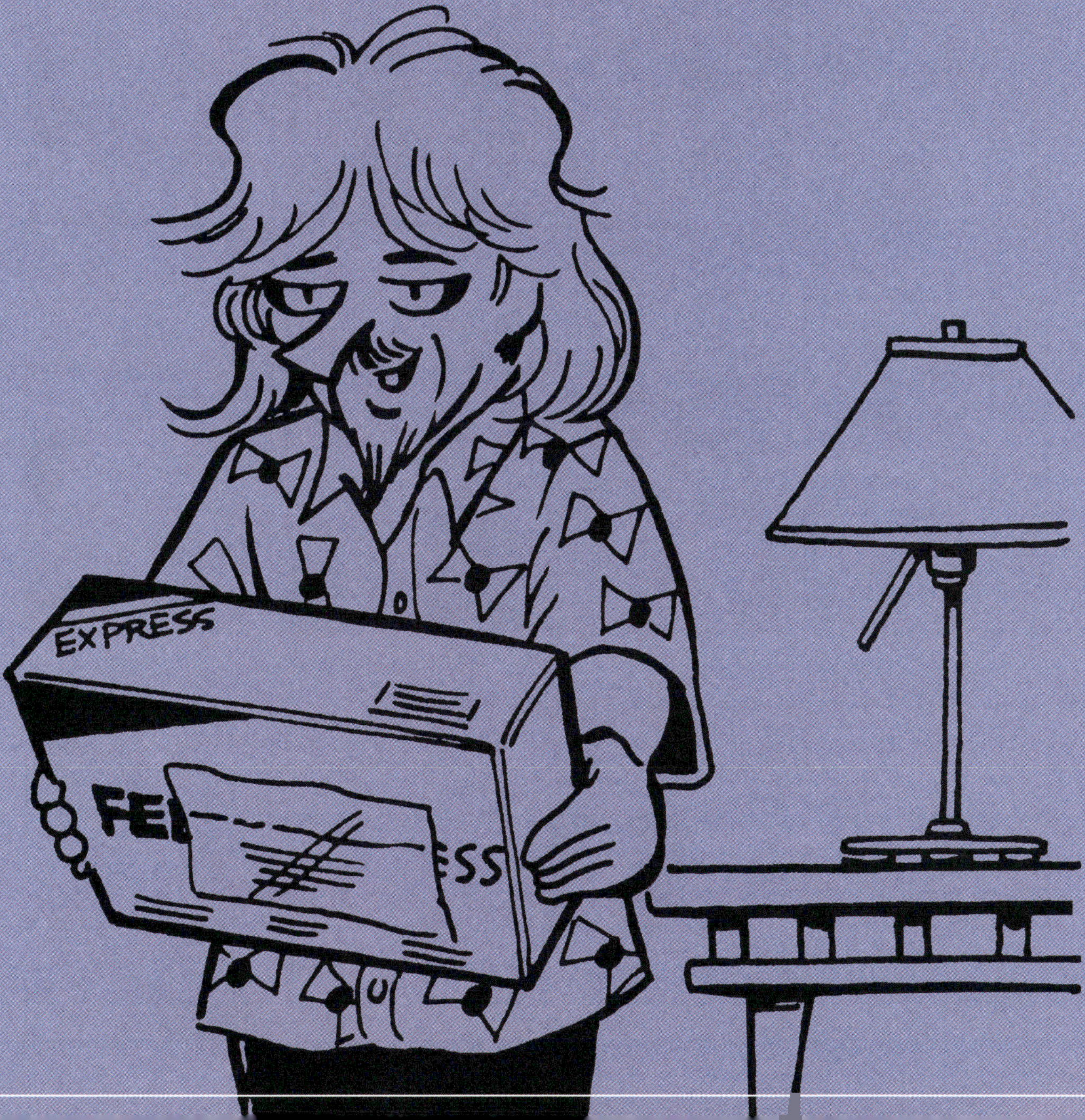
EXPRESS

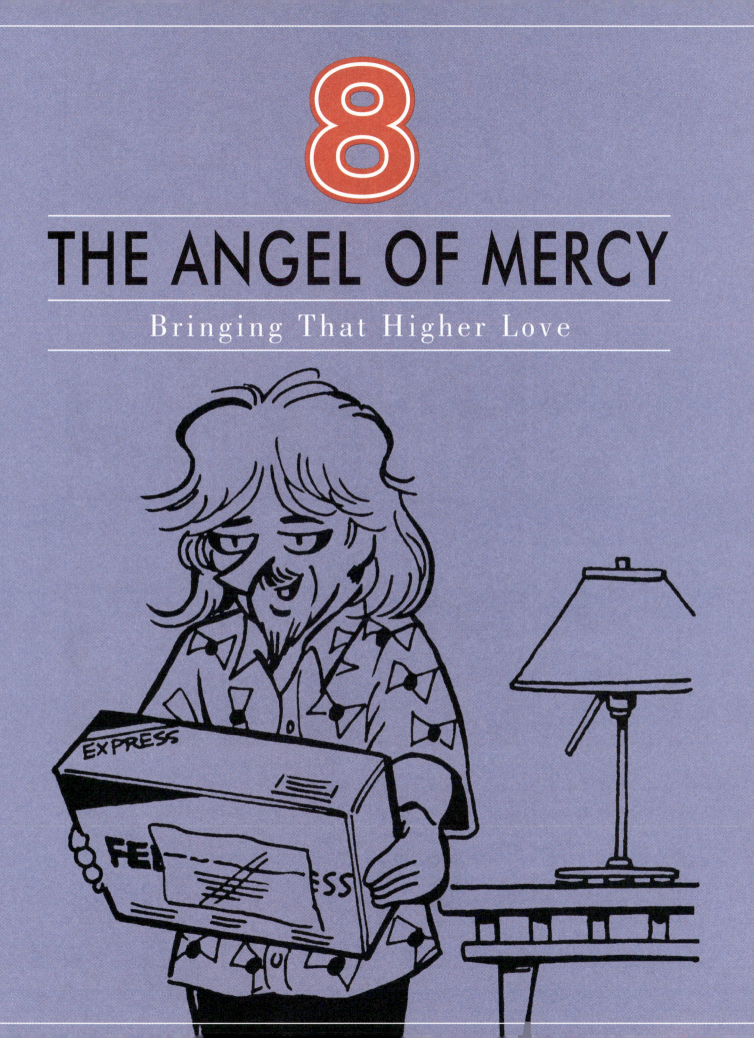

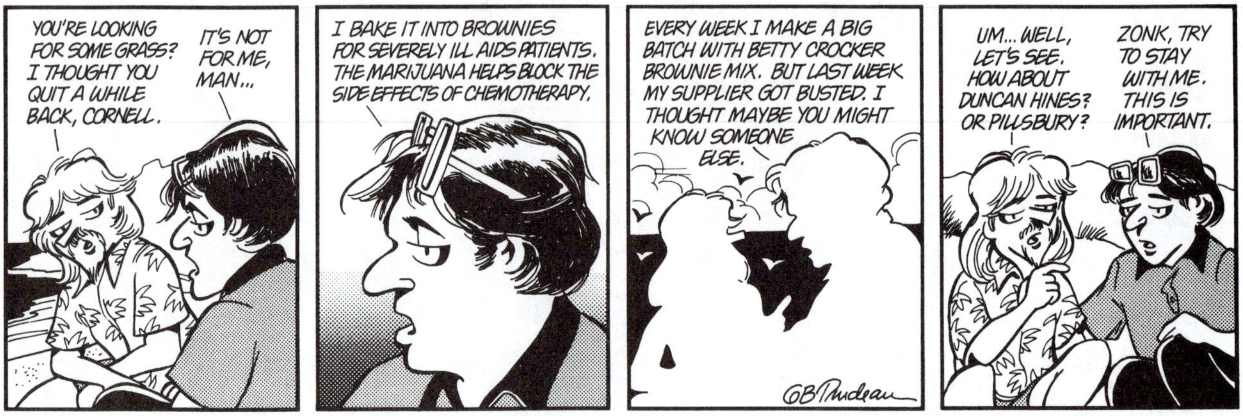
YOU'RE LOOKING FOR SOME GRASS? I THOUGHT YOU QUIT A WHILE BACK, CORNELL.
IT'S NOT FOR ME, MAN...
I BAKE IT INTO BROWNIES FOR SEVERELY ILL AIDS PATIENTS. THE MARIJUANA HELPS BLOCK THE SIDE EFFECTS OF CHEMOTHERAPY.
EVERY WEEK I MAKE A BIG BATCH WITH BETTY CROCKER BROWNIE MIX. BUT LAST WEEK MY SUPPLIER GOT BUSTED. I THOUGHT MAYBE YOU MIGHT KNOW SOMEONE ELSE.
GB Trudeau
UM... WELL, LET'S SEE. HOW ABOUT DUNCAN HINES? OR PILLSBURY?
ZONK, TRY TO STAY WITH ME. THIS IS IMPORTANT.

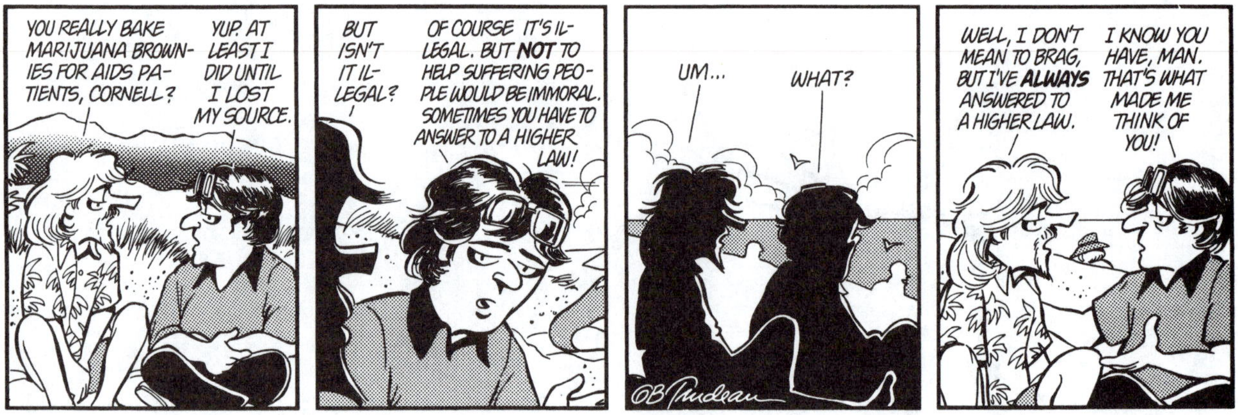
YOU REALLY BAKE MARIJUANA BROWNIES FOR AIDS PATIENTS, CORNELL?
YUP. AT LEAST I DID UNTIL I LOST MY SOURCE.
BUT ISN'T IT ILLEGAL?
OF COURSE IT'S ILLEGAL. BUT NOT TO HELP SUFFERING PEOPLE WOULD BE IMMORAL. SOMETIMES YOU HAVE TO ANSWER TO A HIGHER LAW!
UM...
WHAT?
GB Trudeau
WELL, I DON'T MEAN TO BRAG, BUT I'VE ALWAYS ANSWERED TO A HIGHER LAW.
I KNOW YOU HAVE, MAN. THAT'S WHAT MADE ME THINK OF YOU!

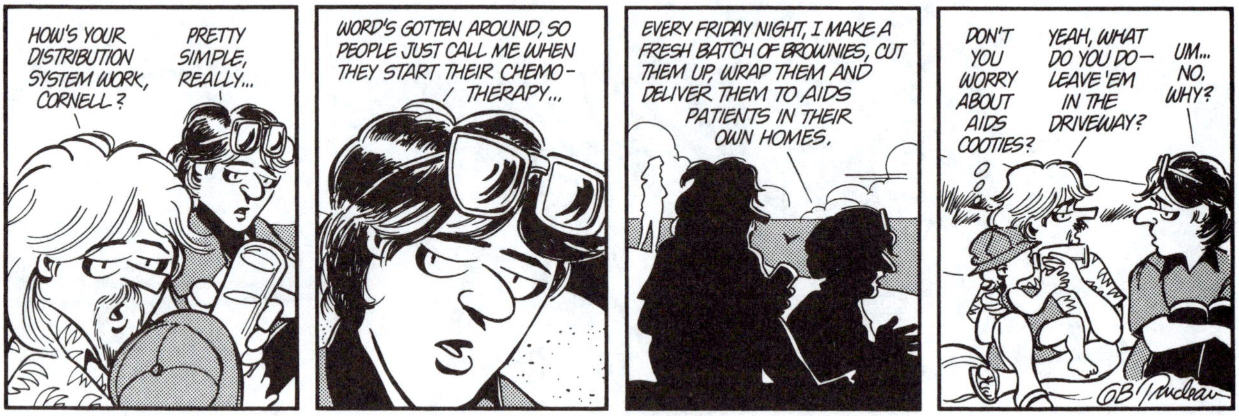
HOW'S YOUR DISTRIBUTION SYSTEM WORK, CORNELL?
PRETTY SIMPLE, REALLY...
WORD'S GOTTEN AROUND, SO PEOPLE JUST CALL ME WHEN THEY START THEIR CHEMOTHERAPY...
EVERY FRIDAY NIGHT, I MAKE A FRESH BATCH OF BROWNIES, CUT THEM UP, WRAP THEM AND DELIVER THEM TO AIDS PATIENTS IN THEIR OWN HOMES.
DON'T YOU WORRY ABOUT AIDS COOTIES?
YEAH, WHAT DO YOU DO— LEAVE 'EM IN THE DRIVEWAY?
UM... NO. WHY?
GB Trudeau

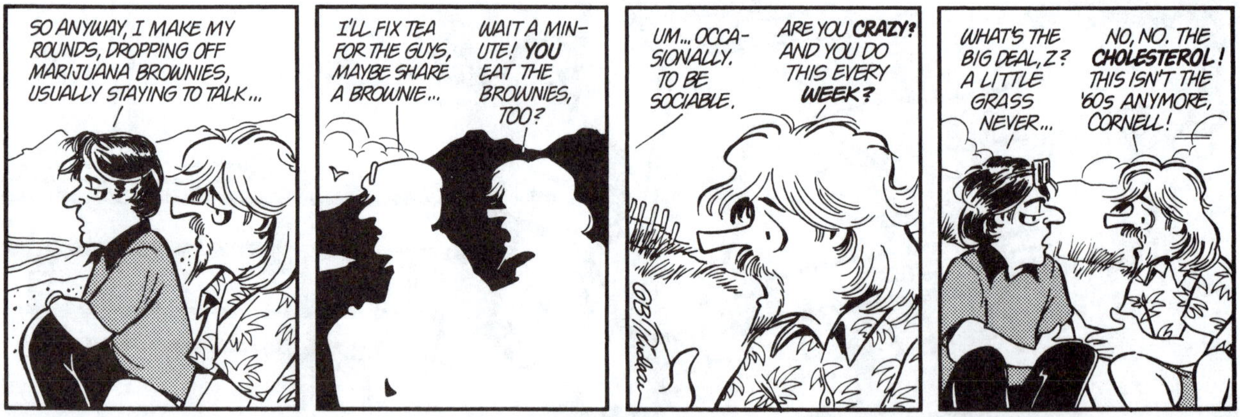
SO ANYWAY, I MAKE MY ROUNDS, DROPPING OFF MARIJUANA BROWNIES, USUALLY STAYING TO TALK...
I'LL FIX TEA FOR THE GUYS, MAYBE SHARE A BROWNIE...
WAIT A MINUTE! YOU EAT THE BROWNIES, TOO?
UM... OCCASIONALLY. TO BE SOCIABLE.
ARE YOU CRAZY? AND YOU DO THIS EVERY WEEK?
GB Trudeau
WHAT'S THE BIG DEAL, Z? A LITTLE GRASS NEVER...
NO, NO. THE CHOLESTEROL! THIS ISN'T THE '60S ANYMORE, CORNELL!

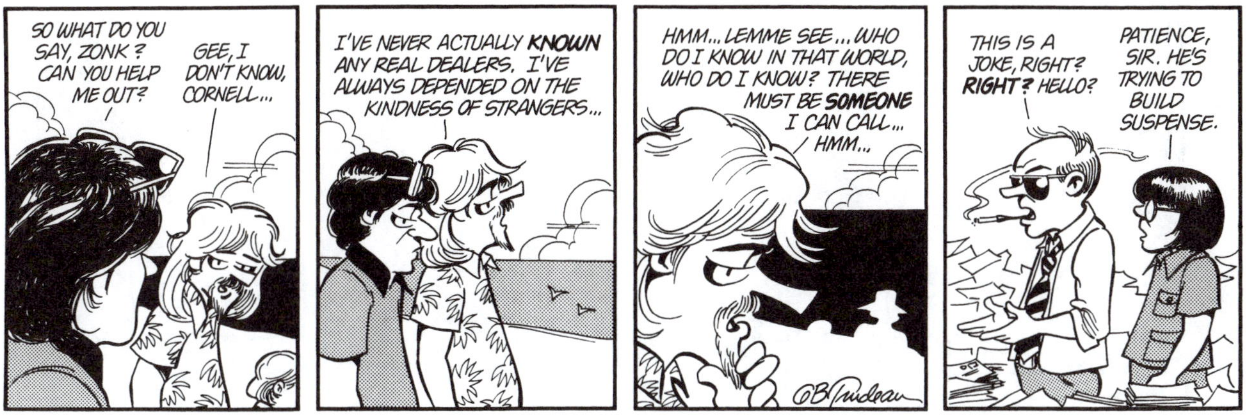
SO WHAT DO YOU SAY, ZONK? CAN YOU HELP ME OUT?
GEE, I DON'T KNOW, CORNELL...
I'VE NEVER ACTUALLY **KNOWN** ANY REAL DEALERS. I'VE ALWAYS DEPENDED ON THE KINDNESS OF STRANGERS...
HMM... LEMME SEE... WHO DO I KNOW IN THAT WORLD, WHO DO I KNOW? THERE MUST BE **SOMEONE** I CAN CALL... HMM...
GBTrudeau
THIS IS A JOKE, RIGHT? **RIGHT?** HELLO?
PATIENCE, SIR. HE'S TRYING TO BUILD SUSPENSE.

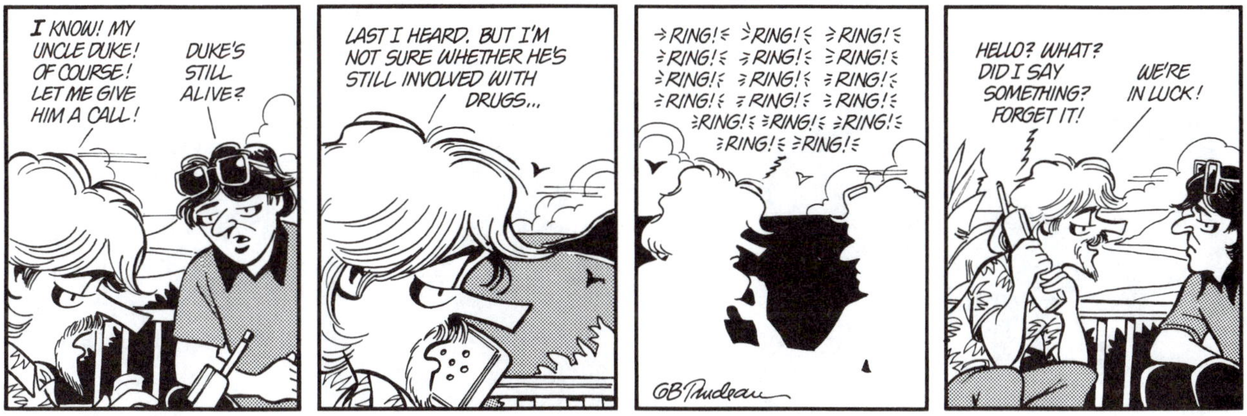
I KNOW! MY UNCLE DUKE! OF COURSE! LET ME GIVE HIM A CALL!
DUKE'S STILL ALIVE?
LAST I HEARD. BUT I'M NOT SURE WHETHER HE'S STILL INVOLVED WITH DRUGS...
RING! RING! RING! RING! RING! RING! RING! RING! RING! RING! RING! RING! RING! RING! RING! RING! RING!
GBTrudeau
HELLO? WHAT? DID I SAY SOMETHING? FORGET IT!
WE'RE IN LUCK!

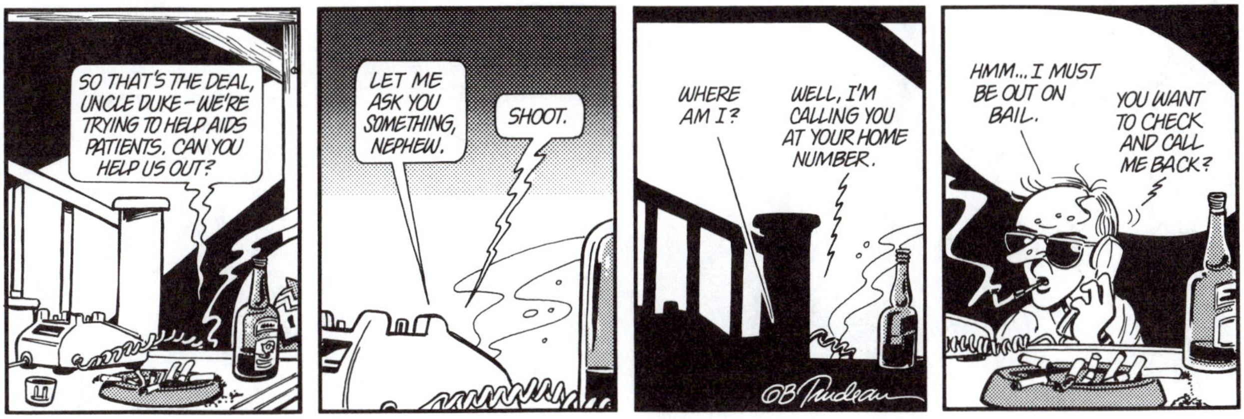
SO THAT'S THE DEAL, UNCLE DUKE – WE'RE TRYING TO HELP AIDS PATIENTS. CAN YOU HELP US OUT?
LET ME ASK YOU SOMETHING, NEPHEW.
SHOOT.
WHERE AM I?
WELL, I'M CALLING YOU AT YOUR HOME NUMBER.
GBTrudeau
HMM... I MUST BE OUT ON BAIL.
YOU WANT TO CHECK AND CALL ME BACK?

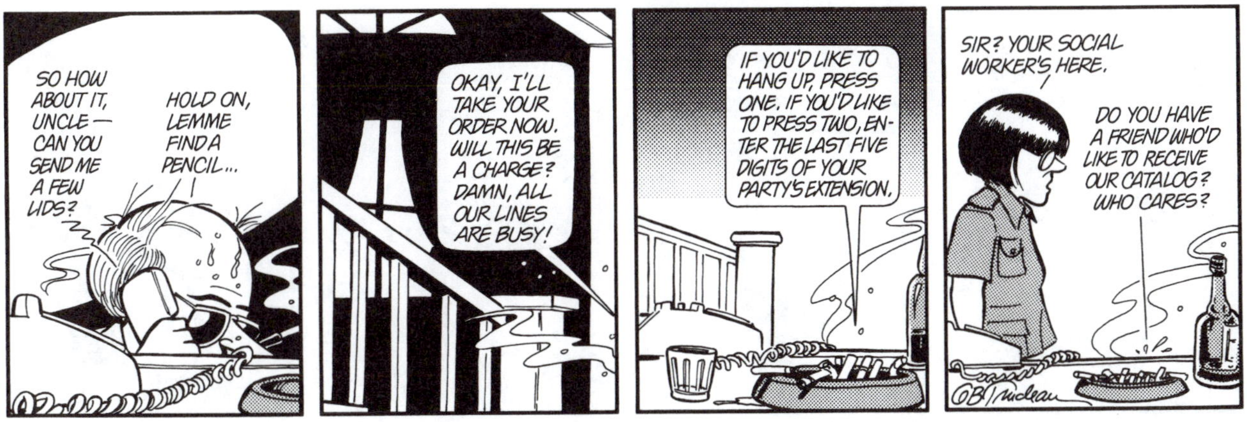
SO HOW ABOUT IT, UNCLE — CAN YOU SEND ME A FEW LIDS?
HOLD ON, LEMME FIND A PENCIL...
OKAY, I'LL TAKE YOUR ORDER NOW. WILL THIS BE A CHARGE? DAMN, ALL OUR LINES ARE BUSY!
IF YOU'D LIKE TO HANG UP, PRESS ONE. IF YOU'D LIKE TO PRESS TWO, ENTER THE LAST FIVE DIGITS OF YOUR PARTY'S EXTENSION.
SIR? YOUR SOCIAL WORKER'S HERE.
DO YOU HAVE A FRIEND WHO'D LIKE TO RECEIVE OUR CATALOG? WHO CARES?
GBTrudeau

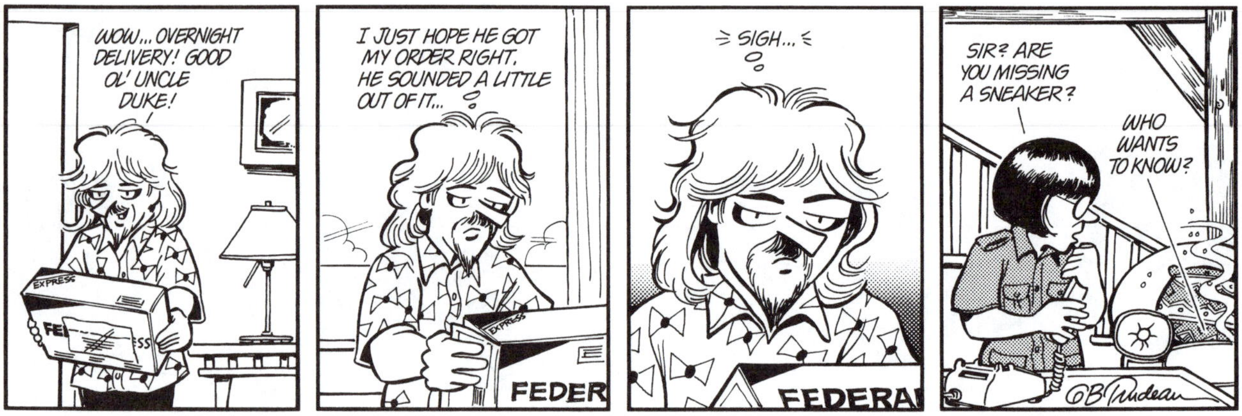
WOW... OVERNIGHT DELIVERY! GOOD OL' UNCLE DUKE!
EXPRESS
I JUST HOPE HE GOT MY ORDER RIGHT. HE SOUNDED A LITTLE OUT OF IT...
FEDER
SIGH...
FEDERAL
SIR? ARE YOU MISSING A SNEAKER?
WHO WANTS TO KNOW?
©B.Trudeau

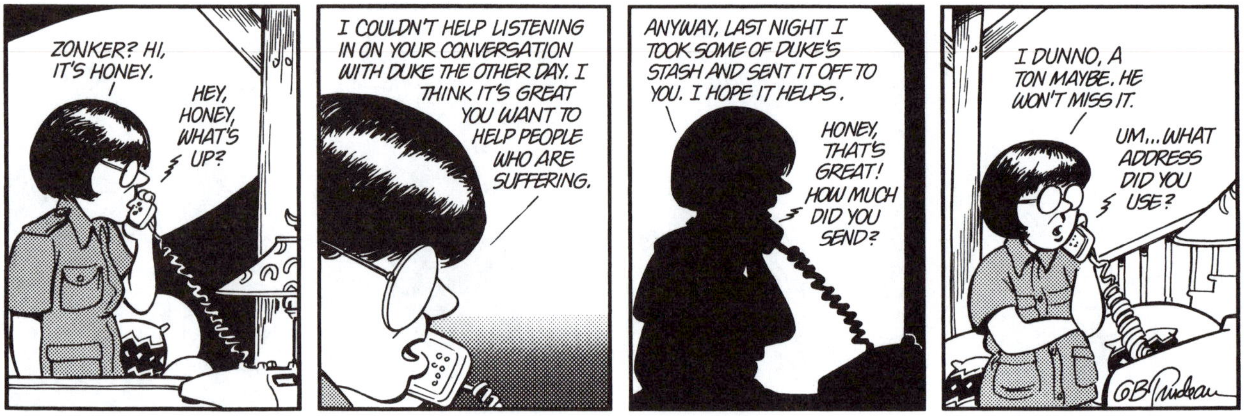
ZONKER? HI, IT'S HONEY.
HEY, HONEY, WHAT'S UP?
I COULDN'T HELP LISTENING IN ON YOUR CONVERSATION WITH DUKE THE OTHER DAY. I THINK IT'S GREAT YOU WANT TO HELP PEOPLE WHO ARE SUFFERING.
ANYWAY, LAST NIGHT I TOOK SOME OF DUKE'S STASH AND SENT IT OFF TO YOU. I HOPE IT HELPS.
HONEY, THAT'S GREAT! HOW MUCH DID YOU SEND?
I DUNNO, A TON MAYBE. HE WON'T MISS IT.
UM... WHAT ADDRESS DID YOU USE?
©B.Trudeau

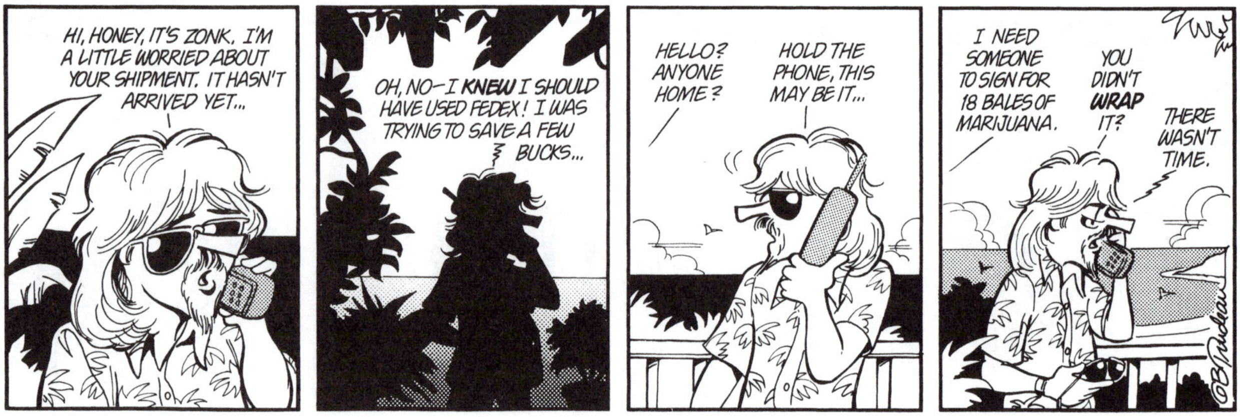
HI, HONEY, IT'S ZONK. I'M A LITTLE WORRIED ABOUT YOUR SHIPMENT. IT HASN'T ARRIVED YET...
OH, NO—I KNEW I SHOULD HAVE USED FEDEX! I WAS TRYING TO SAVE A FEW BUCKS...
HELLO? ANYONE HOME?
HOLD THE PHONE, THIS MAY BE IT...
I NEED SOMEONE TO SIGN FOR 18 BALES OF MARIJUANA.
YOU DIDN'T WRAP IT?
THERE WASN'T TIME.
©B.Trudeau

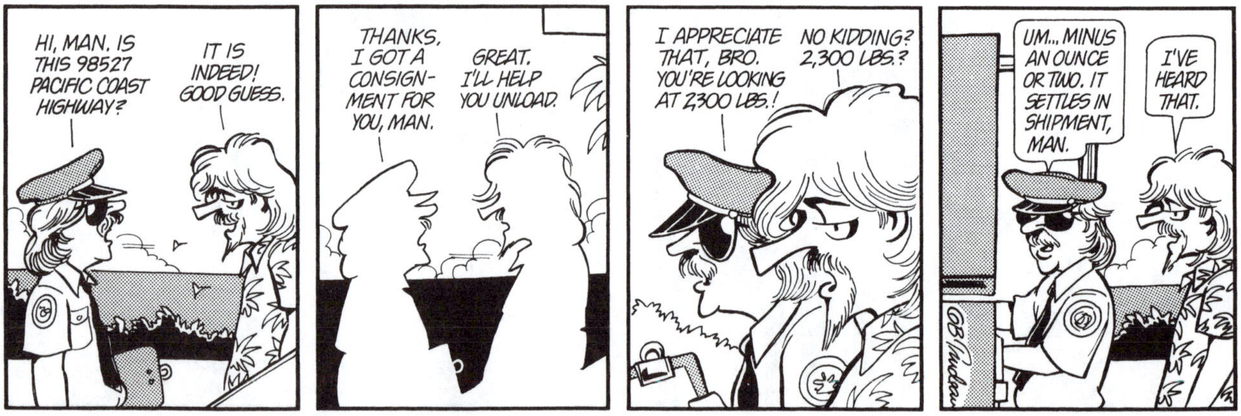
HI, MAN. IS THIS 98527 PACIFIC COAST HIGHWAY?
IT IS INDEED! GOOD GUESS.
THANKS. I GOT A CONSIGNMENT FOR YOU, MAN.
GREAT. I'LL HELP YOU UNLOAD.
I APPRECIATE THAT, BRO. YOU'RE LOOKING AT 2,300 LBS.!
NO KIDDING? 2,300 LBS.?
UM... MINUS AN OUNCE OR TWO. IT SETTLES IN SHIPMENT, MAN.
I'VE HEARD THAT.
©B.Trudeau

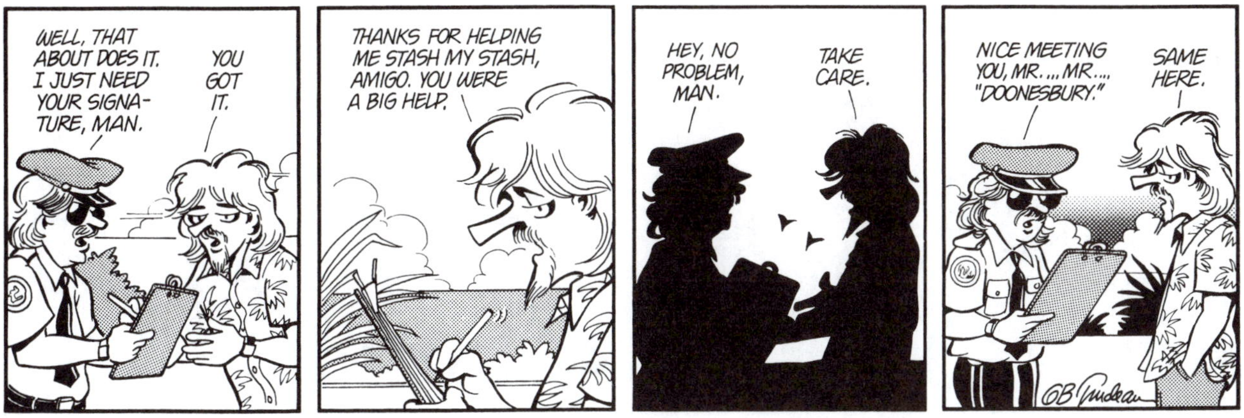
WELL, THAT ABOUT DOES IT. I JUST NEED YOUR SIGNATURE, MAN.
YOU GOT IT.
THANKS FOR HELPING ME STASH MY STASH, AMIGO. YOU WERE A BIG HELP.
HEY, NO PROBLEM, MAN.
TAKE CARE.
NICE MEETING YOU, MR..., MR..., "DOONESBURY."
SAME HERE.
GB Trudeau

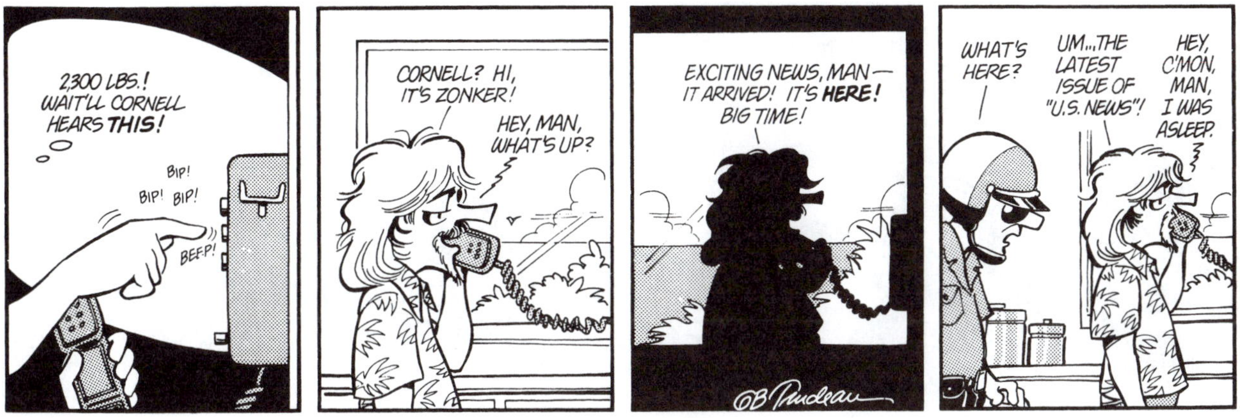
2,300 LBS.! WAIT'LL CORNELL HEARS **THIS**!
BIP! BIP! BIP!
BEEP!
CORNELL? HI, IT'S ZONKER!
HEY, MAN, WHAT'S UP?
EXCITING NEWS, MAN— IT ARRIVED! IT'S **HERE**! BIG TIME!
WHAT'S HERE?
UM...THE LATEST ISSUE OF "U.S. NEWS"!
HEY, C'MON, MAN, I WAS ASLEEP.
GB Trudeau

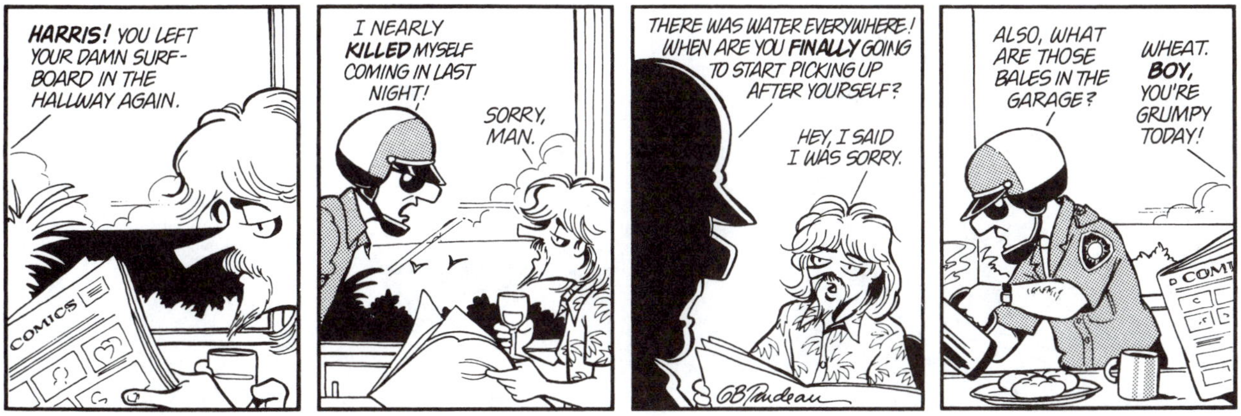
HARRIS! YOU LEFT YOUR DAMN SURFBOARD IN THE HALLWAY AGAIN.
COMICS
I NEARLY **KILLED** MYSELF COMING IN LAST NIGHT!
SORRY, MAN.
THERE WAS WATER EVERYWHERE! WHEN ARE YOU **FINALLY** GOING TO START PICKING UP AFTER YOURSELF?
HEY, I SAID I WAS SORRY.
ALSO, WHAT ARE THOSE BALES IN THE GARAGE?
WHEAT. **BOY**, YOU'RE GRUMPY TODAY!
COMICS
GB Trudeau

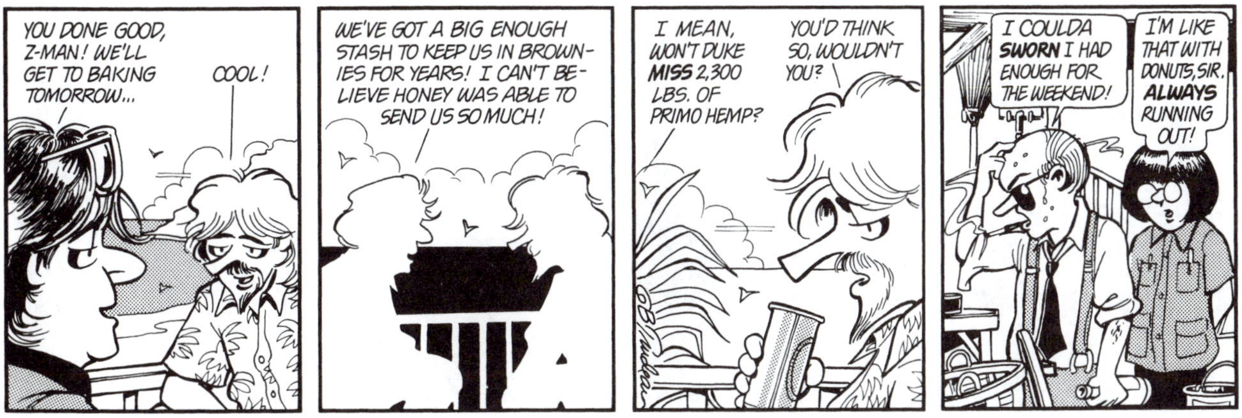
YOU DONE GOOD, Z-MAN! WE'LL GET TO BAKING TOMORROW...
COOL!
WE'VE GOT A BIG ENOUGH STASH TO KEEP US IN BROWNIES FOR YEARS! I CAN'T BELIEVE HONEY WAS ABLE TO SEND US SO MUCH!
I MEAN, WON'T DUKE **MISS** 2,300 LBS. OF PRIMO HEMP?
YOU'D THINK SO, WOULDN'T YOU?
I COULDA **SWORN** I HAD ENOUGH FOR THE WEEKEND!
I'M LIKE THAT WITH DONUTS, SIR. **ALWAYS** RUNNING OUT!

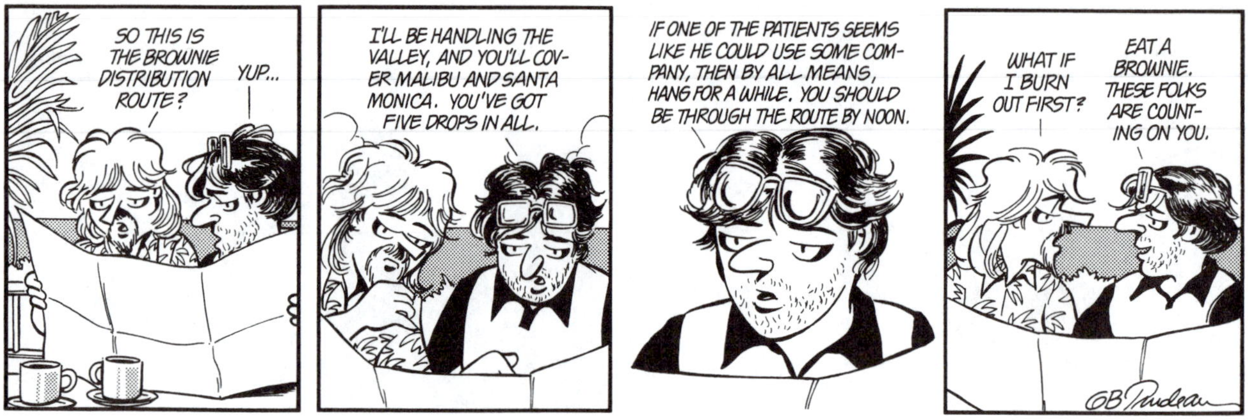
SO THIS IS THE BROWNIE DISTRIBUTION ROUTE?
YUP...
I'LL BE HANDLING THE VALLEY, AND YOU'LL COVER MALIBU AND SANTA MONICA. YOU'VE GOT FIVE DROPS IN ALL.
IF ONE OF THE PATIENTS SEEMS LIKE HE COULD USE SOME COMPANY, THEN BY ALL MEANS, HANG FOR A WHILE. YOU SHOULD BE THROUGH THE ROUTE BY NOON.
WHAT IF I BURN OUT FIRST?
EAT A BROWNIE. THESE FOLKS ARE COUNTING ON YOU.
GB Trudeau

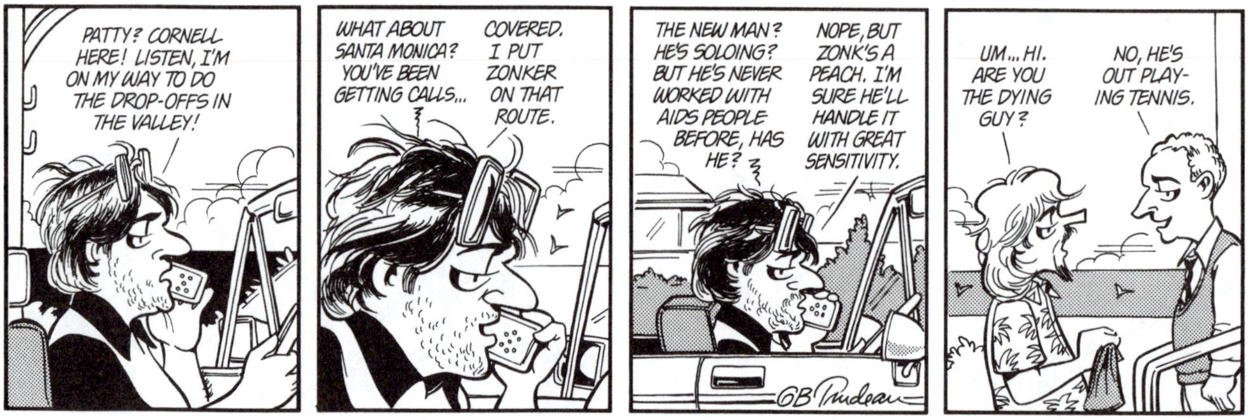
PATTY? CORNELL HERE! LISTEN, I'M ON MY WAY TO DO THE DROP-OFFS IN THE VALLEY!
WHAT ABOUT SANTA MONICA? YOU'VE BEEN GETTING CALLS...
COVERED. I PUT ZONKER ON THAT ROUTE.
THE NEW MAN? HE'S SOLOING? BUT HE'S NEVER WORKED WITH AIDS PEOPLE BEFORE, HAS HE?
NOPE, BUT ZONK'S A PEACH. I'M SURE HE'LL HANDLE IT WITH GREAT SENSITIVITY.
GB Trudeau
UM... HI. ARE YOU THE DYING GUY?
NO, HE'S OUT PLAYING TENNIS.

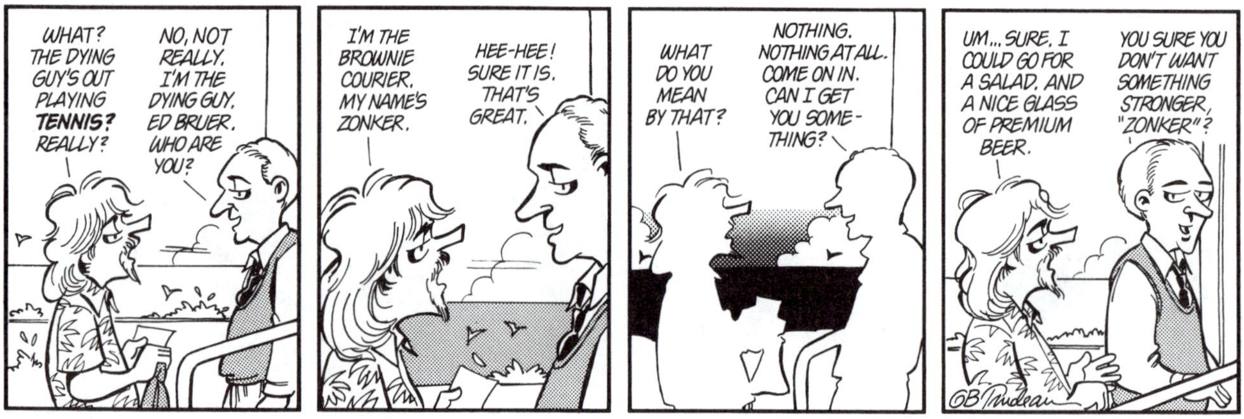
WHAT? THE DYING GUY'S OUT PLAYING **TENNIS?** REALLY?
NO, NOT REALLY. I'M THE DYING GUY. ED BRUER. WHO ARE YOU?
I'M THE BROWNIE COURIER. MY NAME'S ZONKER.
HEE-HEE! SURE IT IS. THAT'S GREAT.
WHAT DO YOU MEAN BY THAT?
NOTHING. NOTHING AT ALL. COME ON IN. CAN I GET YOU SOMETHING?
UM... SURE. I COULD GO FOR A SALAD. AND A NICE GLASS OF PREMIUM BEER.
YOU SURE YOU DON'T WANT SOMETHING STRONGER, "ZONKER"?
GB Trudeau

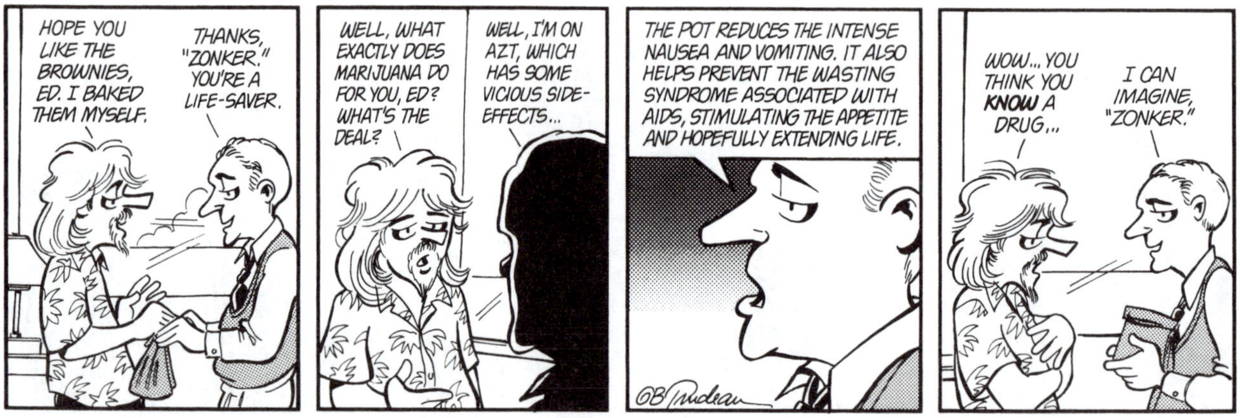
HOPE YOU LIKE THE BROWNIES, ED. I BAKED THEM MYSELF.
THANKS, "ZONKER." YOU'RE A LIFE-SAVER.
WELL, WHAT EXACTLY DOES MARIJUANA DO FOR YOU, ED? WHAT'S THE DEAL?
WELL, I'M ON AZT, WHICH HAS SOME VICIOUS SIDE-EFFECTS...
THE POT REDUCES THE INTENSE NAUSEA AND VOMITING. IT ALSO HELPS PREVENT THE WASTING SYNDROME ASSOCIATED WITH AIDS, STIMULATING THE APPETITE AND HOPEFULLY EXTENDING LIFE.
GB Trudeau
WOW... YOU THINK YOU **KNOW** A DRUG...
I CAN IMAGINE, "ZONKER."

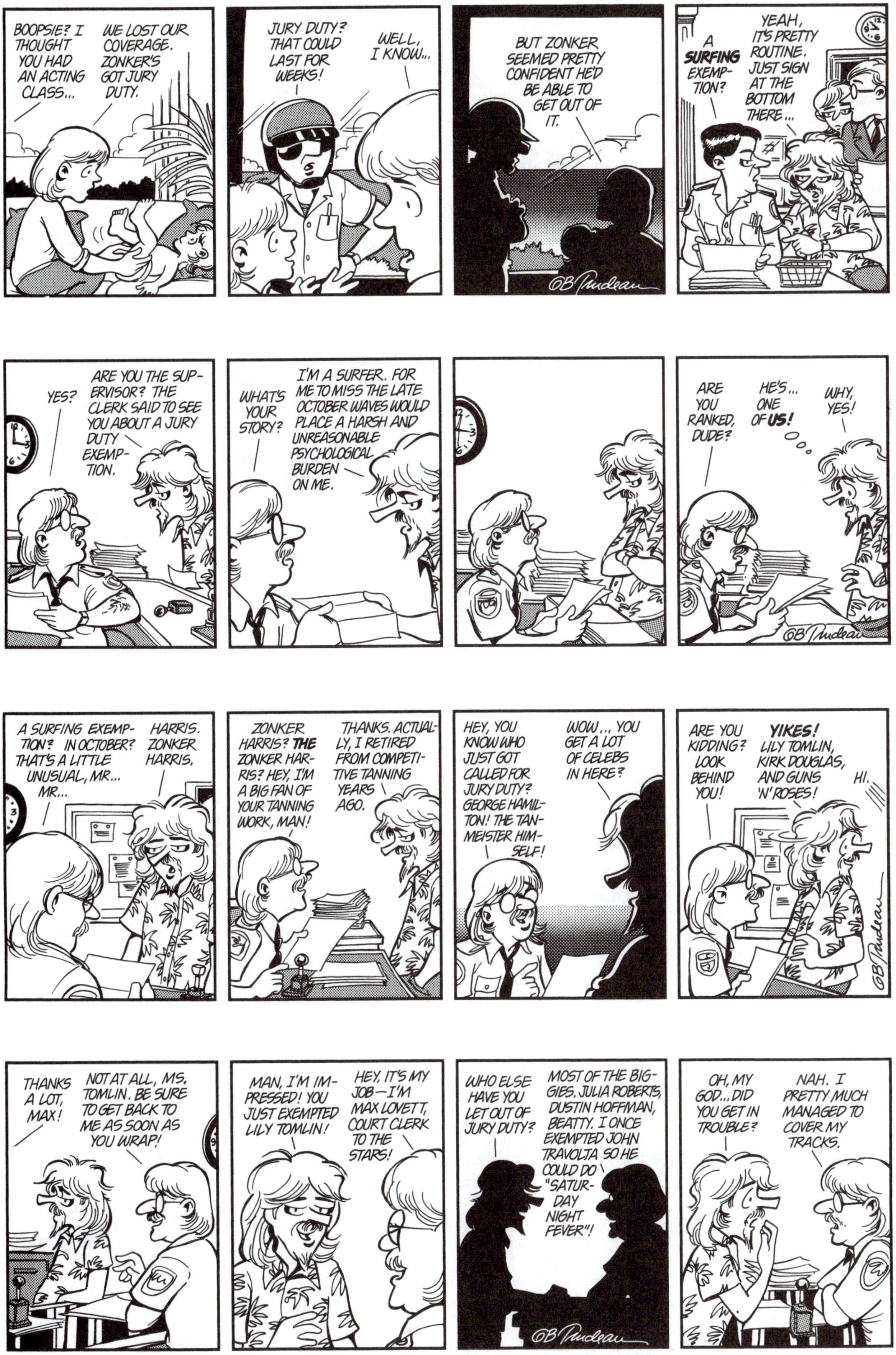
BOOPSIE? I THOUGHT YOU HAD AN ACTING CLASS...
WE LOST OUR COVERAGE. ZONKER'S GOT JURY DUTY.
JURY DUTY? THAT COULD LAST FOR WEEKS!
WELL, I KNOW...
BUT ZONKER SEEMED PRETTY CONFIDENT HE'D BE ABLE TO GET OUT OF IT.
A SURFING EXEMPTION?
YEAH, IT'S PRETTY ROUTINE. JUST SIGN AT THE BOTTOM THERE...
YES?
ARE YOU THE SUPERVISOR? THE CLERK SAID TO SEE YOU ABOUT A JURY DUTY EXEMPTION.
WHAT'S YOUR STORY?
I'M A SURFER. FOR ME TO MISS THE LATE OCTOBER WAVES WOULD PLACE A HARSH AND UNREASONABLE PSYCHOLOGICAL BURDEN ON ME.
ARE YOU RANKED, DUDE?
HE'S... ONE OF US!
WHY, YES!
A SURFING EXEMPTION? IN OCTOBER? THAT'S A LITTLE UNUSUAL, MR... MR...
HARRIS. ZONKER HARRIS.
ZONKER HARRIS? THE ZONKER HARRIS? HEY, I'M A BIG FAN OF YOUR TANNING WORK, MAN!
THANKS. ACTUALLY, I RETIRED FROM COMPETITIVE TANNING YEARS AGO.
HEY, YOU KNOW WHO JUST GOT CALLED FOR JURY DUTY? GEORGE HAMILTON! THE TANMEISTER HIMSELF!
WOW... YOU GET A LOT OF CELEBS IN HERE?
ARE YOU KIDDING? LOOK BEHIND YOU!
YIKES! LILY TOMLIN, KIRK DOUGLAS, AND GUNS 'N' ROSES!
HI.
THANKS A LOT, MAX!
NOT AT ALL, MS. TOMLIN. BE SURE TO GET BACK TO ME AS SOON AS YOU WRAP!
MAN, I'M IMPRESSED! YOU JUST EXEMPTED LILY TOMLIN!
HEY, IT'S MY JOB—I'M MAX LOVETT, COURT CLERK TO THE STARS!
WHO ELSE HAVE YOU LET OUT OF JURY DUTY?
MOST OF THE BIGGIES. JULIA ROBERTS, DUSTIN HOFFMAN, BEATTY. I ONCE EXEMPTED JOHN TRAVOLTA SO HE COULD DO "SATURDAY NIGHT FEVER"!
OH, MY GOD... DID YOU GET IN TROUBLE?
NAH. I PRETTY MUCH MANAGED TO COVER MY TRACKS.

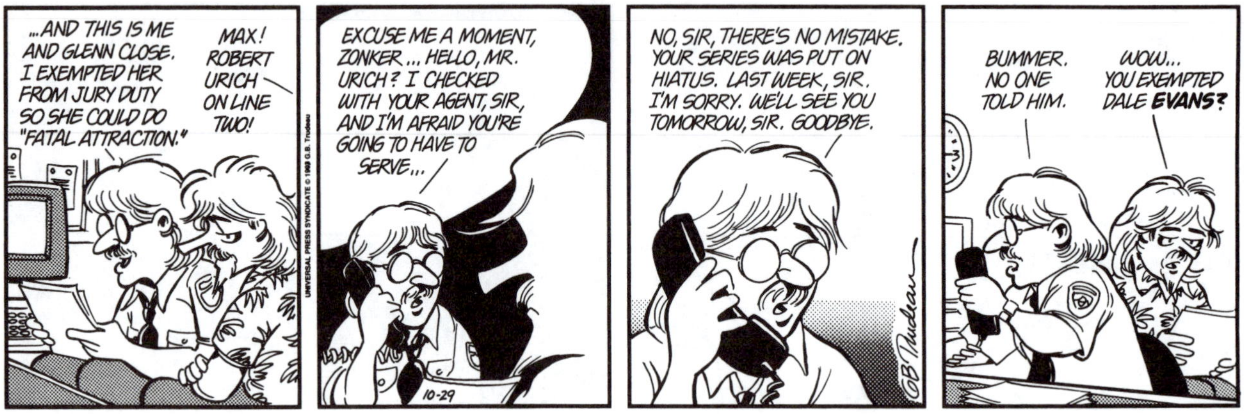
...AND THIS IS ME AND GLENN CLOSE. I EXEMPTED HER FROM JURY DUTY SO SHE COULD DO "FATAL ATTRACTION."
MAX! ROBERT URICH ON LINE TWO!
EXCUSE ME A MOMENT, ZONKER... HELLO, MR. URICH? I CHECKED WITH YOUR AGENT, SIR, AND I'M AFRAID YOU'RE GOING TO HAVE TO SERVE...
10-29
NO, SIR, THERE'S NO MISTAKE. YOUR SERIES WAS PUT ON HIATUS. LAST WEEK, SIR. I'M SORRY. WE'LL SEE YOU TOMORROW, SIR. GOODBYE.
BUMMER. NO ONE TOLD HIM.
WOW... YOU EXEMPTED DALE **EVANS?**

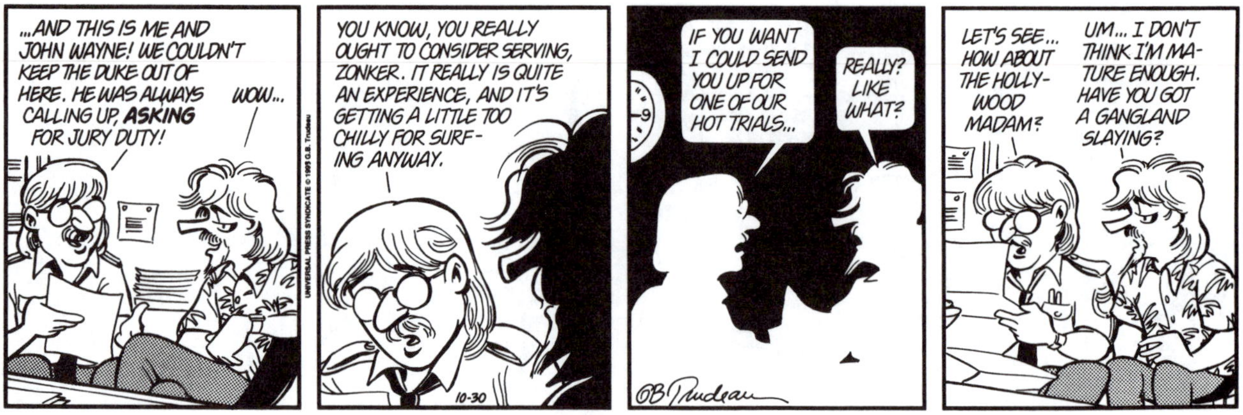
...AND THIS IS ME AND JOHN WAYNE! WE COULDN'T KEEP THE DUKE OUT OF HERE. HE WAS ALWAYS CALLING UP, **ASKING** FOR JURY DUTY!
WOW...
YOU KNOW, YOU REALLY OUGHT TO CONSIDER SERVING, ZONKER. IT REALLY IS QUITE AN EXPERIENCE, AND IT'S GETTING A LITTLE TOO CHILLY FOR SURFING ANYWAY.
10-30
IF YOU WANT I COULD SEND YOU UP FOR ONE OF OUR HOT TRIALS...
REALLY? LIKE WHAT?
LET'S SEE... HOW ABOUT THE HOLLYWOOD MADAM?
UM... I DON'T THINK I'M MATURE ENOUGH. HAVE YOU GOT A GANGLAND SLAYING?

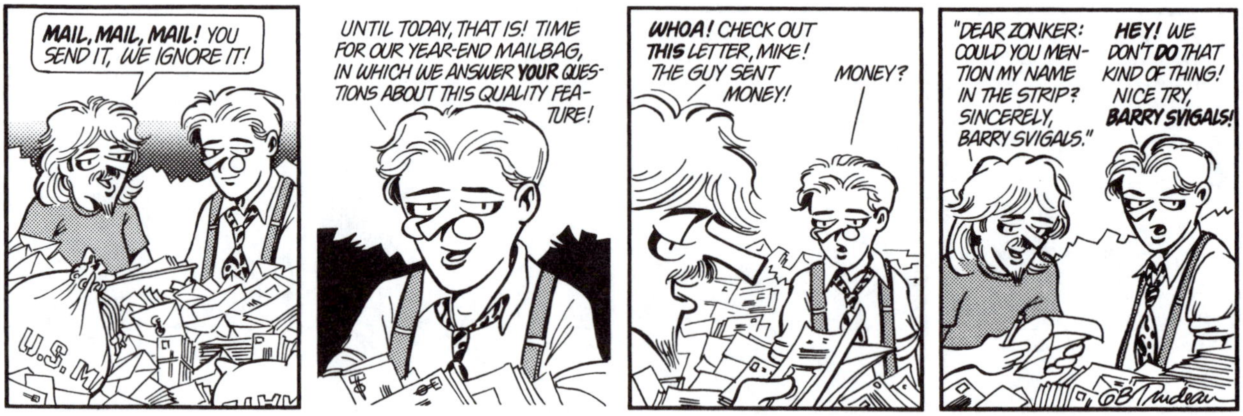
MAIL, MAIL, MAIL! YOU SEND IT, WE IGNORE IT!
U.S. M
UNTIL TODAY, THAT IS! TIME FOR OUR YEAR-END MAILBAG, IN WHICH WE ANSWER **YOUR** QUESTIONS ABOUT THIS QUALITY FEATURE!
WHOA! CHECK OUT **THIS** LETTER, MIKE! THE GUY SENT MONEY!
MONEY?
"DEAR ZONKER: COULD YOU MENTION MY NAME IN THE STRIP? SINCERELY, BARRY SVIGALS."
HEY! WE DON'T **DO** THAT KIND OF THING! NICE TRY, **BARRY SVIGALS!**

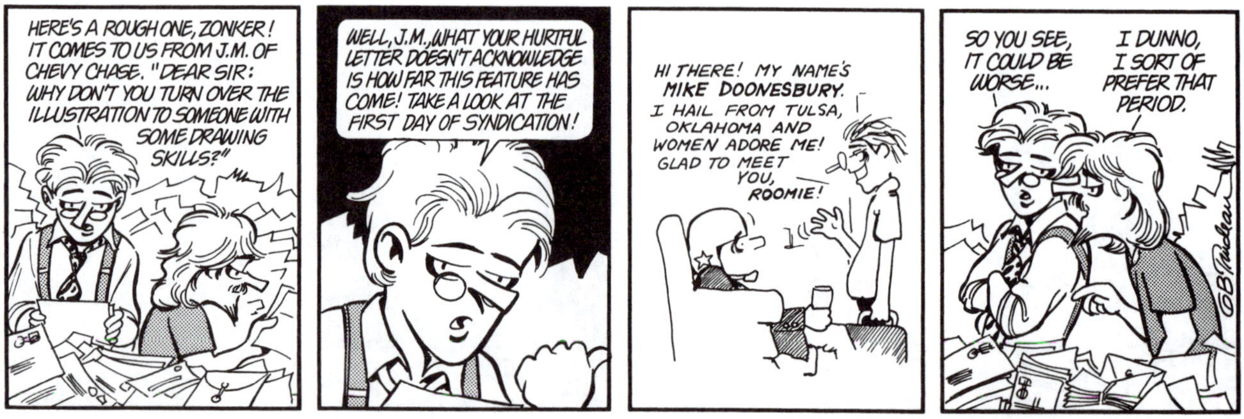
HERE'S A ROUGH ONE, ZONKER! IT COMES TO US FROM J.M. OF CHEVY CHASE. "DEAR SIR: WHY DON'T YOU TURN OVER THE ILLUSTRATION TO SOMEONE WITH SOME DRAWING SKILLS?"
WELL, J.M., WHAT YOUR HURTFUL LETTER DOESN'T ACKNOWLEDGE IS HOW FAR THIS FEATURE HAS COME! TAKE A LOOK AT THE FIRST DAY OF SYNDICATION!
HI THERE! MY NAME'S **MIKE DOONESBURY.** I HAIL FROM TULSA, OKLAHOMA AND WOMEN ADORE ME! GLAD TO MEET YOU, **ROOMIE!**
SO YOU SEE, IT COULD BE WORSE...
I DUNNO, I SORT OF PREFER THAT PERIOD.

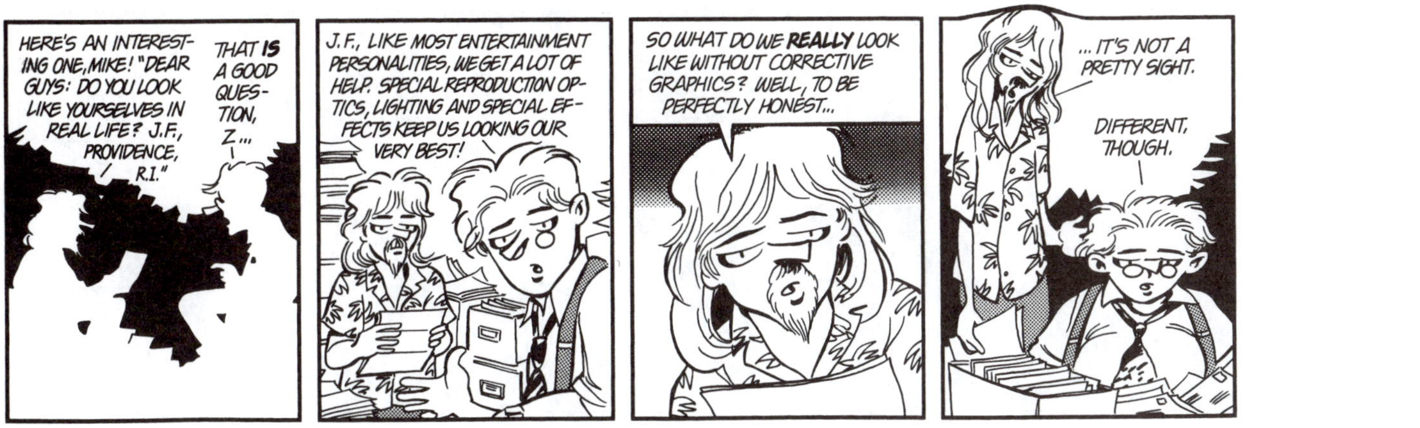
HERE'S AN INTERESTING ONE, MIKE! "DEAR GUYS: DO YOU LOOK LIKE YOURSELVES IN REAL LIFE? J.F., PROVIDENCE, R.I."
THAT **IS** A GOOD QUESTION, Z...
J.F., LIKE MOST ENTERTAINMENT PERSONALITIES, WE GET A LOT OF HELP. SPECIAL REPRODUCTION OPTICS, LIGHTING AND SPECIAL EFFECTS KEEP US LOOKING OUR VERY BEST!
SO WHAT DO WE **REALLY** LOOK LIKE WITHOUT CORRECTIVE GRAPHICS? WELL, TO BE PERFECTLY HONEST...
... IT'S NOT A PRETTY SIGHT.
DIFFERENT, THOUGH.

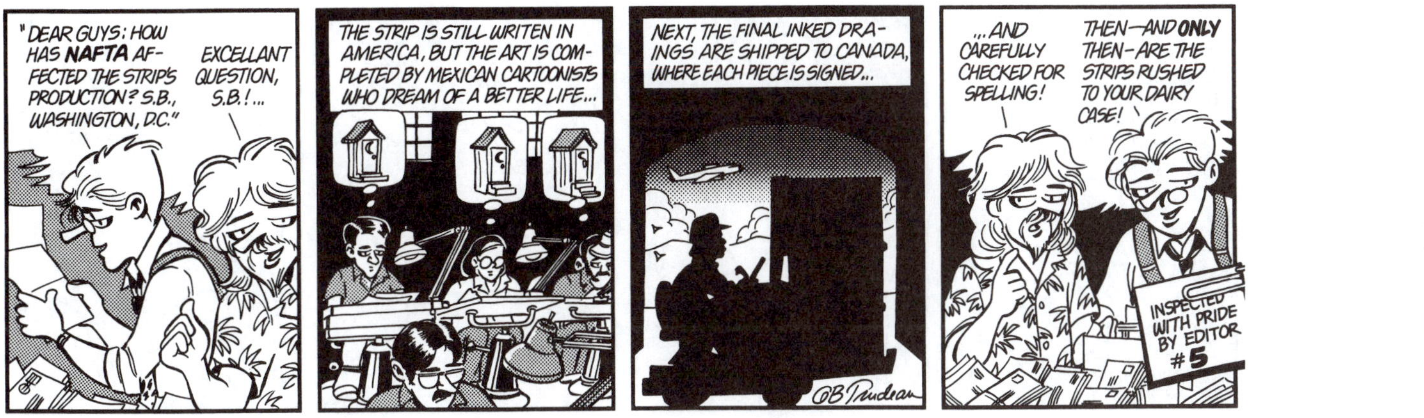
"DEAR GUYS: HOW HAS **NAFTA** AFFECTED THE STRIP'S PRODUCTION? S.B., WASHINGTON, D.C."
EXCELLANT QUESTION, S.B.! ...
THE STRIP IS STILL WRITEN IN AMERICA, BUT THE ART IS COMPLETED BY MEXICAN CARTOONISTS WHO DREAM OF A BETTER LIFE...
NEXT, THE FINAL INKED DRAINGS ARE SHIPPED TO CANADA, WHERE EACH PIECE IS SIGNED...
...AND CAREFULLY CHECKED FOR SPELLING!
THEN—AND **ONLY** THEN—ARE THE STRIPS RUSHED TO YOUR DAIRY CASE!
INSPECTED WITH PRIDE BY EDITOR #5
©B Trudeau

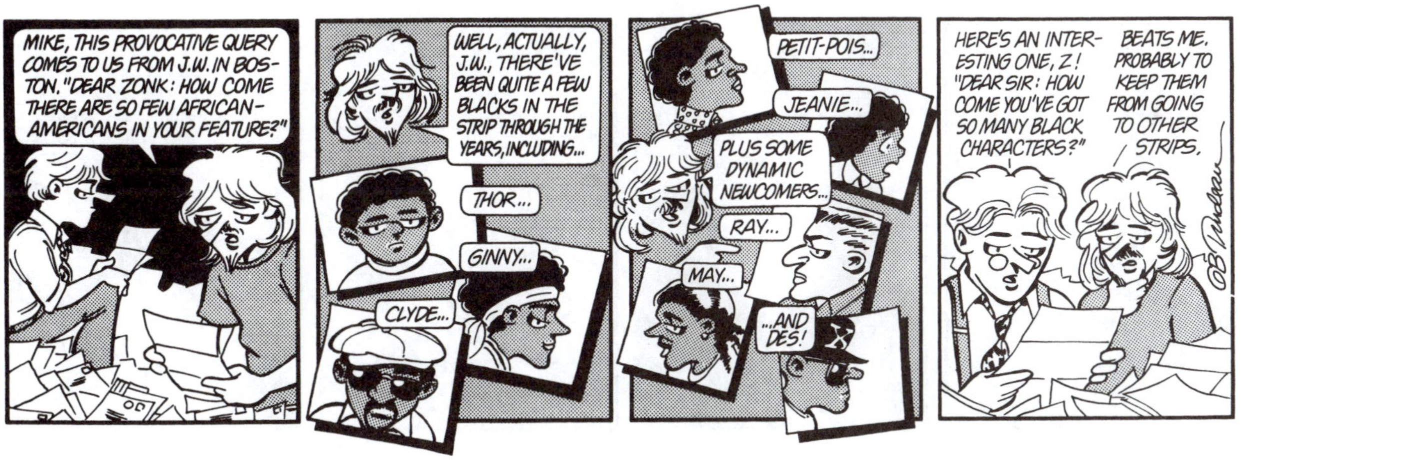
MIKE, THIS PROVOCATIVE QUERY COMES TO US FROM J.W. IN BOSTON. "DEAR ZONK: HOW COME THERE ARE SO FEW AFRICAN-AMERICANS IN YOUR FEATURE?"
WELL, ACTUALLY, J.W., THERE'VE BEEN QUITE A FEW BLACKS IN THE STRIP THROUGH THE YEARS, INCLUDING...
THOR...
GINNY...
CLYDE...
PETIT-POIS...
JEANIE...
PLUS SOME DYNAMIC NEWCOMERS...
RAY...
MAY...
...AND DES!
HERE'S AN INTERESTING ONE, Z! "DEAR SIR: HOW COME YOU'VE GOT SO MANY BLACK CHARACTERS?"
BEATS ME. PROBABLY TO KEEP THEM FROM GOING TO OTHER STRIPS.
©B Trudeau

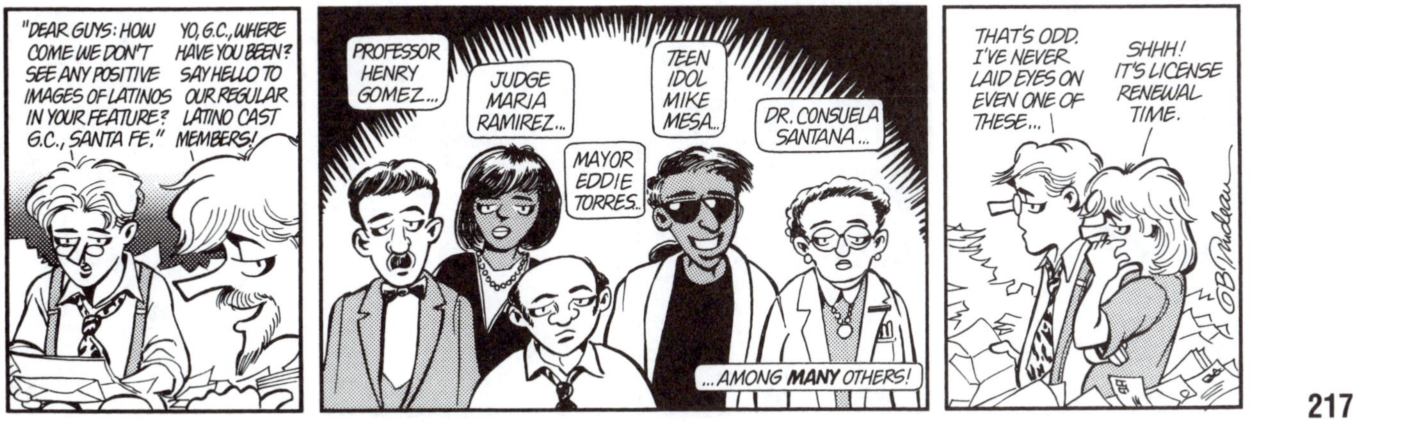
"DEAR GUYS: HOW COME WE DON'T SEE ANY POSITIVE IMAGES OF LATINOS IN YOUR FEATURE? G.C., SANTA FE."
YO, G.C., WHERE HAVE YOU BEEN? SAY HELLO TO OUR REGULAR LATINO CAST MEMBERS!
PROFESSOR HENRY GOMEZ...
JUDGE MARIA RAMIREZ...
MAYOR EDDIE TORRES...
TEEN IDOL MIKE MESA...
DR. CONSUELA SANTANA...
...AMONG **MANY** OTHERS!
THAT'S ODD. I'VE NEVER LAID EYES ON EVEN ONE OF THESE...
SHHH! IT'S LICENSE RENEWAL TIME.
©B Trudeau

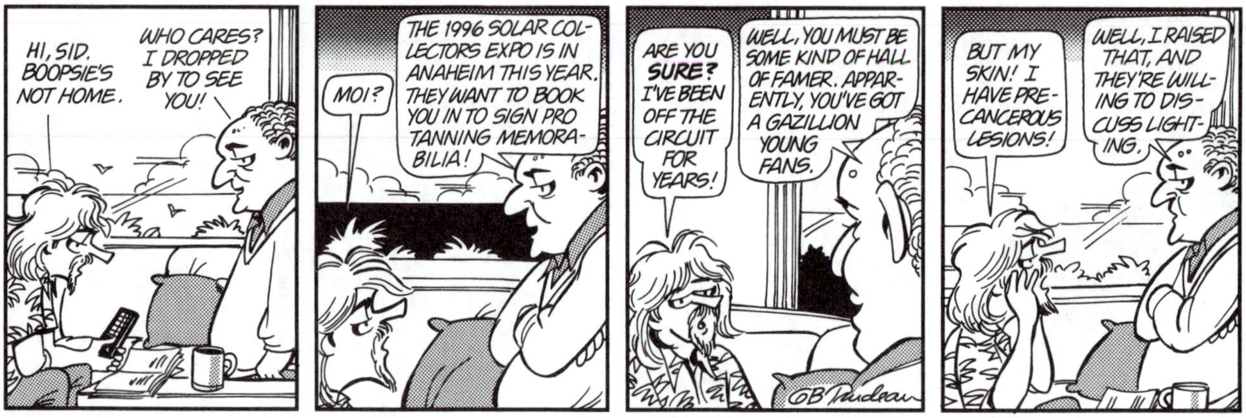

HI, SID. BOOPSIE'S NOT HOME.
WHO CARES? I DROPPED BY TO SEE YOU!
MOI?
THE 1996 SOLAR COLLECTORS EXPO IS IN ANAHEIM THIS YEAR. THEY WANT TO BOOK YOU IN TO SIGN PRO TANNING MEMORABILIA!
ARE YOU **SURE?** I'VE BEEN OFF THE CIRCUIT FOR YEARS!
WELL, YOU MUST BE SOME KIND OF HALL OF FAMER. APPARENTLY, YOU'VE GOT A GAZILLION YOUNG FANS.
BUT MY SKIN! I HAVE PRE-CANCEROUS LESIONS!
WELL, I RAISED THAT, AND THEY'RE WILLING TO DISCUSS LIGHTING.

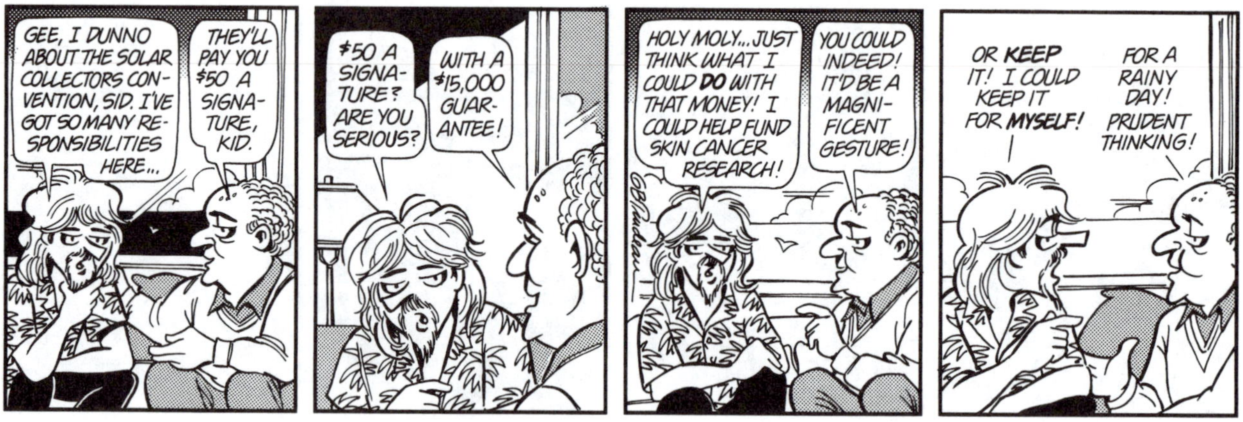

GEE, I DUNNO ABOUT THE SOLAR COLLECTORS CONVENTION, SID. I'VE GOT SO MANY RESPONSIBILITIES HERE...
THEY'LL PAY YOU $50 A SIGNATURE, KID.
$50 A SIGNATURE? ARE YOU SERIOUS?
WITH A $15,000 GUARANTEE!
HOLY MOLY... JUST THINK WHAT I COULD **DO** WITH THAT MONEY! I COULD HELP FUND SKIN CANCER RESEARCH!
YOU COULD INDEED! IT'D BE A MAGNIFICENT GESTURE!
OR **KEEP** IT! I COULD KEEP IT FOR **MYSELF**!
FOR A RAINY DAY! PRUDENT THINKING!

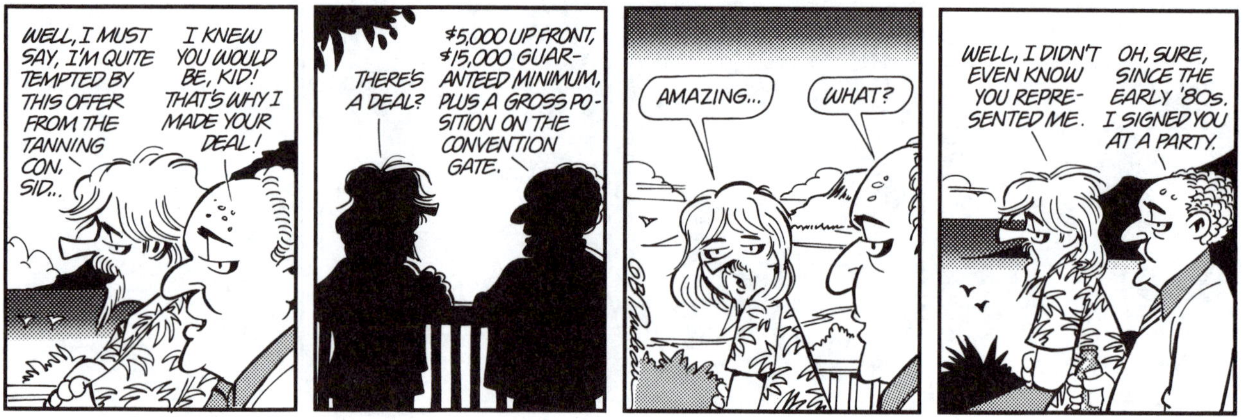

WELL, I MUST SAY, I'M QUITE TEMPTED BY THIS OFFER FROM THE TANNING CON, SID...
I KNEW YOU WOULD BE, KID! THAT'S WHY I MADE YOUR DEAL!
THERE'S A DEAL?
$5,000 UP FRONT, $15,000 GUARANTEED MINIMUM, PLUS A GROSS POSITION ON THE CONVENTION GATE.
AMAZING...
WHAT?
WELL, I DIDN'T EVEN KNOW YOU REPRESENTED ME.
OH, SURE, SINCE THE EARLY '80s. I SIGNED YOU AT A PARTY.

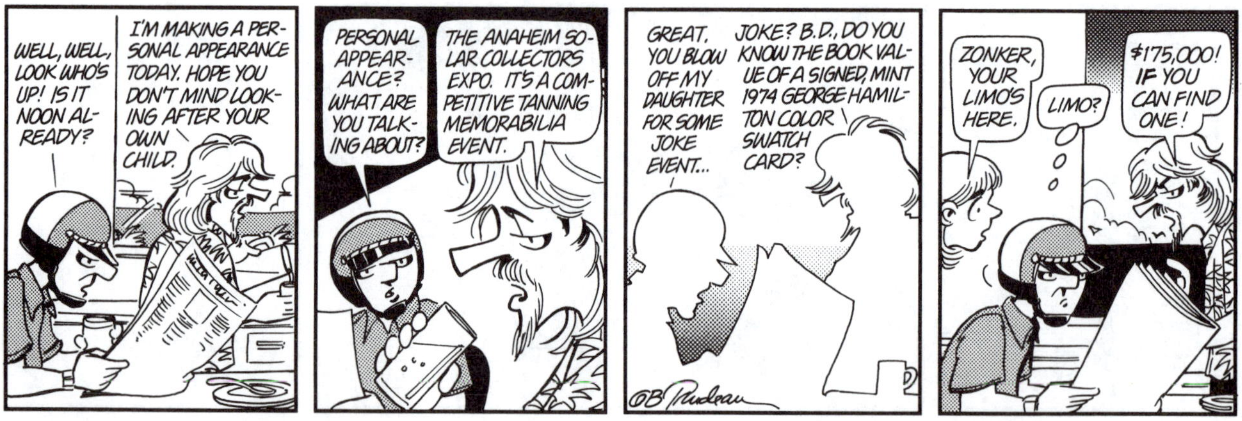

WELL, WELL, LOOK WHO'S UP! IS IT NOON ALREADY?
I'M MAKING A PERSONAL APPEARANCE TODAY. HOPE YOU DON'T MIND LOOKING AFTER YOUR OWN CHILD.
PERSONAL APPEARANCE? WHAT ARE YOU TALKING ABOUT?
THE ANAHEIM SOLAR COLLECTORS EXPO. IT'S A COMPETITIVE TANNING MEMORABILIA EVENT.
GREAT. YOU BLOW OFF MY DAUGHTER FOR SOME JOKE EVENT...
JOKE? B.D., DO YOU KNOW THE BOOK VALUE OF A SIGNED, MINT 1974 GEORGE HAMILTON COLOR SWATCH CARD?
ZONKER, YOUR LIMO'S HERE.
LIMO?
$175,000! **IF** YOU CAN FIND ONE!

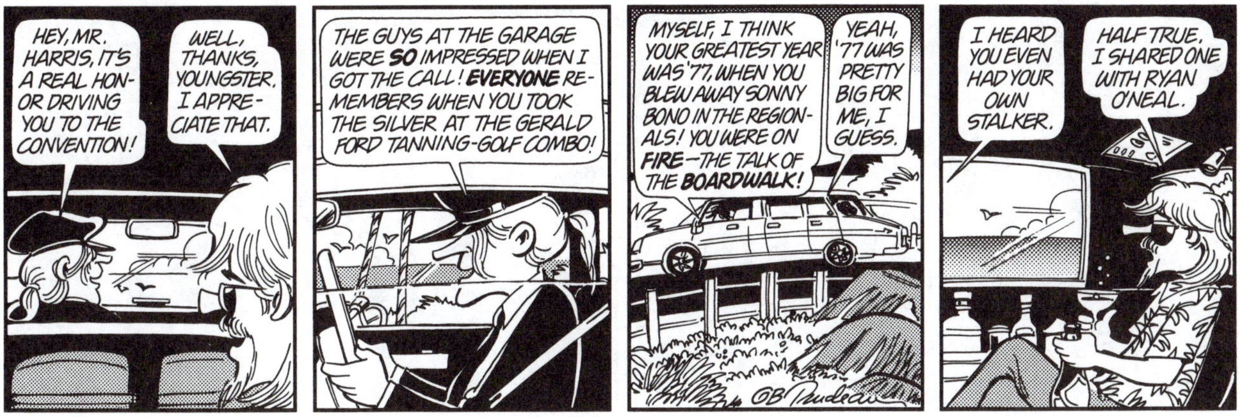
HEY, MR. HARRIS, IT'S A REAL HONOR DRIVING YOU TO THE CONVENTION!
WELL, THANKS, YOUNGSTER. I APPRECIATE THAT.
THE GUYS AT THE GARAGE WERE **SO** IMPRESSED WHEN I GOT THE CALL! **EVERYONE** REMEMBERS WHEN YOU TOOK THE SILVER AT THE GERALD FORD TANNING-GOLF COMBO!
MYSELF, I THINK YOUR GREATEST YEAR WAS '77, WHEN YOU BLEW AWAY SONNY BONO IN THE REGIONALS! YOU WERE ON **FIRE**—THE TALK OF THE **BOARDWALK**!
YEAH, '77 WAS PRETTY BIG FOR ME, I GUESS.
I HEARD YOU EVEN HAD YOUR OWN STALKER.
HALF TRUE. I SHARED ONE WITH RYAN O'NEAL.

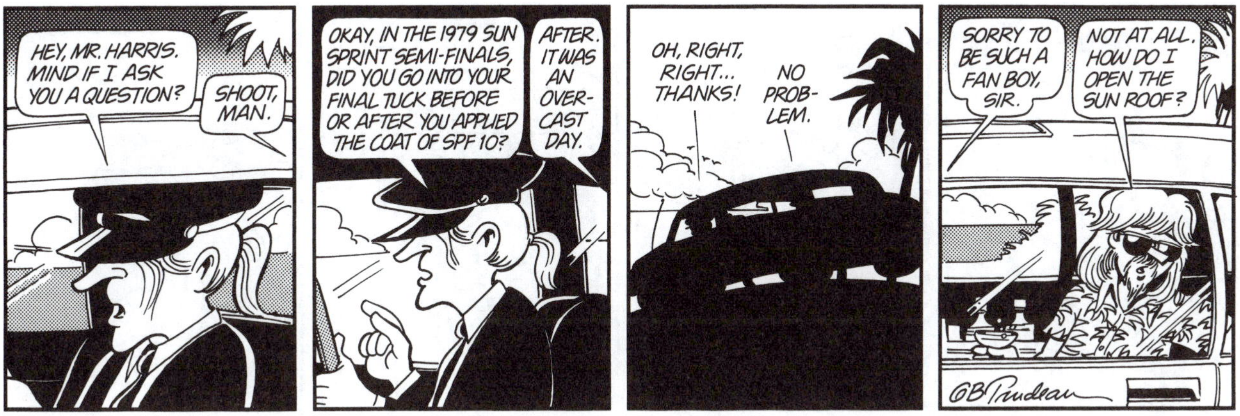
HEY, MR. HARRIS. MIND IF I ASK YOU A QUESTION?
SHOOT, MAN.
OKAY, IN THE 1979 SUN SPRINT SEMI-FINALS, DID YOU GO INTO YOUR FINAL TUCK BEFORE OR AFTER YOU APPLIED THE COAT OF SPF 10?
AFTER. IT WAS AN OVERCAST DAY.
OH, RIGHT, RIGHT... THANKS!
NO PROBLEM.
SORRY TO BE SUCH A FAN BOY, SIR.
NOT AT ALL. HOW DO I OPEN THE SUN ROOF?

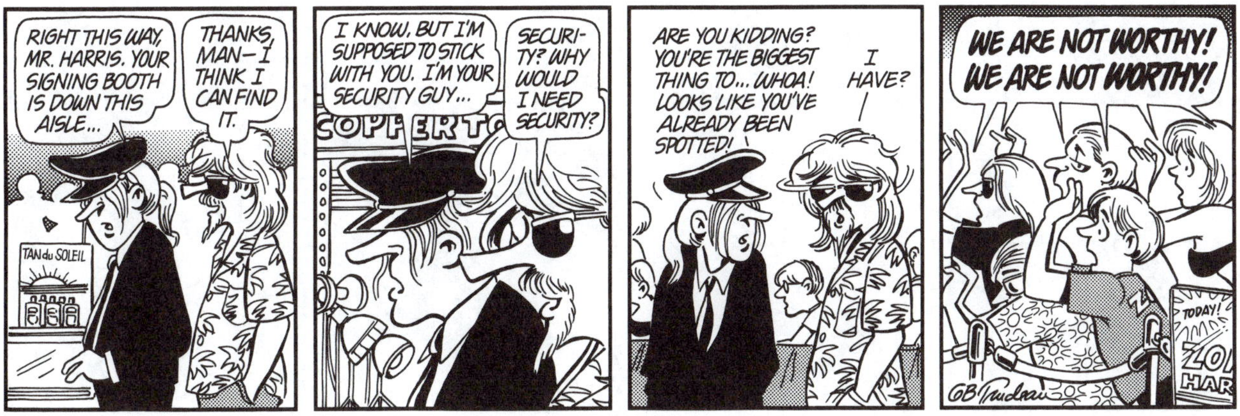
RIGHT THIS WAY, MR. HARRIS. YOUR SIGNING BOOTH IS DOWN THIS AISLE...
THANKS, MAN—I THINK I CAN FIND IT.
TAN du SOLEIL
I KNOW, BUT I'M SUPPOSED TO STICK WITH YOU. I'M YOUR SECURITY GUY...
SECURITY? WHY WOULD I NEED SECURITY?
ARE YOU KIDDING? YOU'RE THE BIGGEST THING TO... WHOA! LOOKS LIKE YOU'VE ALREADY BEEN SPOTTED!
I HAVE?
WE ARE NOT WORTHY! WE ARE NOT WORTHY!
TODAY!

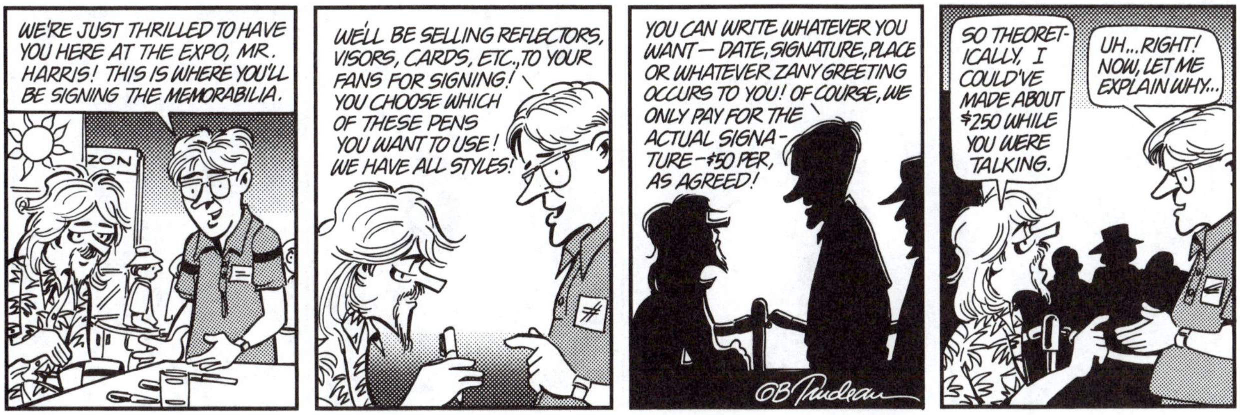
WE'RE JUST THRILLED TO HAVE YOU HERE AT THE EXPO, MR. HARRIS! THIS IS WHERE YOU'LL BE SIGNING THE MEMORABILIA.
WE'LL BE SELLING REFLECTORS, VISORS, CARDS, ETC., TO YOUR FANS FOR SIGNING! YOU CHOOSE WHICH OF THESE PENS YOU WANT TO USE! WE HAVE ALL STYLES!
YOU CAN WRITE WHATEVER YOU WANT — DATE, SIGNATURE, PLACE OR WHATEVER ZANY GREETING OCCURS TO YOU! OF COURSE, WE ONLY PAY FOR THE ACTUAL SIGNATURE—$50 PER, AS AGREED!
SO THEORETICALLY, I COULD'VE MADE ABOUT $250 WHILE YOU WERE TALKING.
UH... RIGHT! NOW, LET ME EXPLAIN WHY...

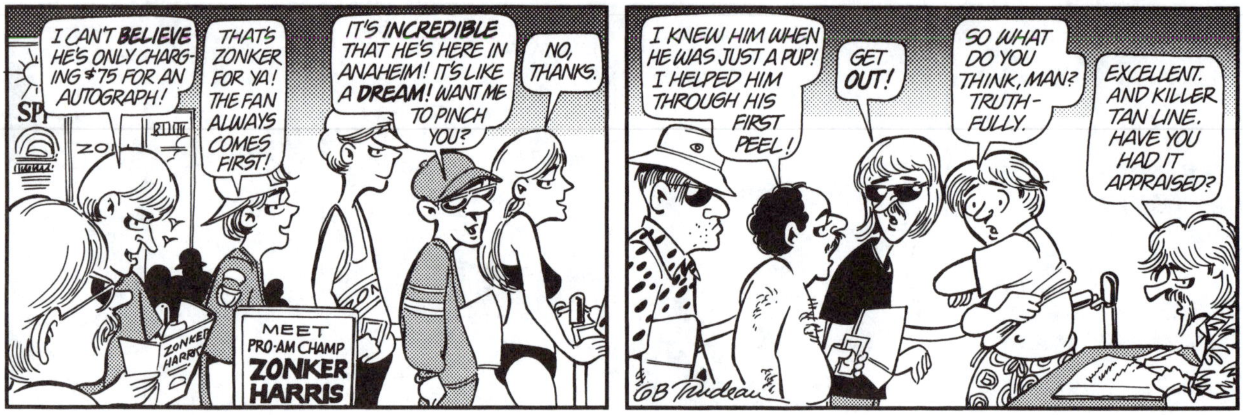
I CAN'T **BELIEVE** HE'S ONLY CHARGING $75 FOR AN AUTOGRAPH!
THAT'S ZONKER FOR YA! THE FAN ALWAYS COMES FIRST!
MEET PRO-AM CHAMP ZONKER HARRIS
IT'S **INCREDIBLE** THAT HE'S HERE IN ANAHEIM! IT'S LIKE A **DREAM**! WANT ME TO PINCH YOU?
NO, THANKS.
I KNEW HIM WHEN HE WAS JUST A PUP! I HELPED HIM THROUGH HIS FIRST PEEL!
GET **OUT**!
SO WHAT DO YOU THINK, MAN? TRUTHFULLY.
EXCELLENT. AND KILLER TAN LINE. HAVE YOU HAD IT APPRAISED?

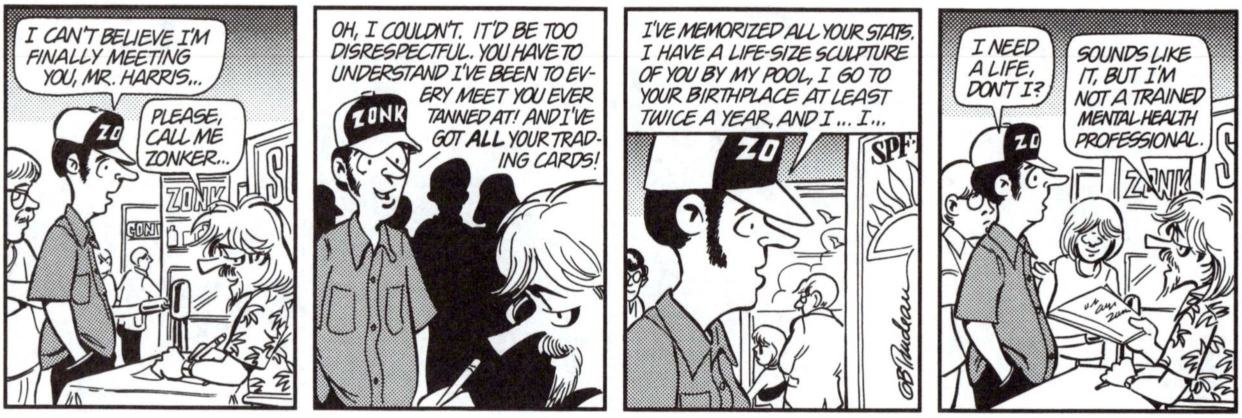
I CAN'T BELIEVE I'M FINALLY MEETING YOU, MR. HARRIS...
PLEASE, CALL ME ZONKER...
OH, I COULDN'T. IT'D BE TOO DISRESPECTFUL. YOU HAVE TO UNDERSTAND I'VE BEEN TO EVERY MEET YOU EVER TANNED AT! AND I'VE GOT **ALL** YOUR TRADING CARDS!
I'VE MEMORIZED ALL YOUR STATS. I HAVE A LIFE-SIZE SCULPTURE OF YOU BY MY POOL, I GO TO YOUR BIRTHPLACE AT LEAST TWICE A YEAR, AND I ... I...
I NEED A LIFE, DON'T I?
SOUNDS LIKE IT, BUT I'M NOT A TRAINED MENTAL HEALTH PROFESSIONAL.

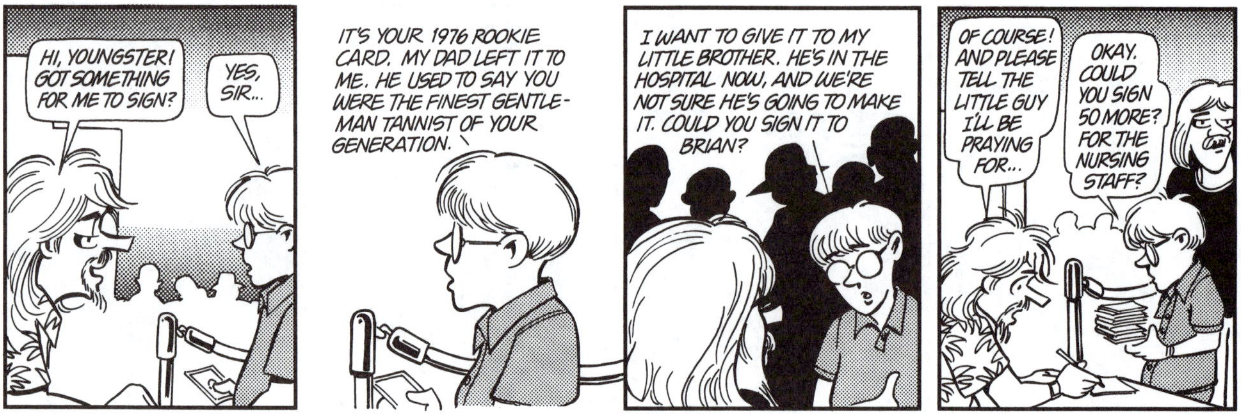
HI, YOUNGSTER! GOT SOMETHING FOR ME TO SIGN?
YES, SIR...
IT'S YOUR 1976 ROOKIE CARD. MY DAD LEFT IT TO ME. HE USED TO SAY YOU WERE THE FINEST GENTLEMAN TANNIST OF YOUR GENERATION.
I WANT TO GIVE IT TO MY LITTLE BROTHER. HE'S IN THE HOSPITAL NOW, AND WE'RE NOT SURE HE'S GOING TO MAKE IT. COULD YOU SIGN IT TO BRIAN?
OF COURSE! AND PLEASE TELL THE LITTLE GUY I'LL BE PRAYING FOR...
OKAY. COULD YOU SIGN 50 MORE? FOR THE NURSING STAFF?

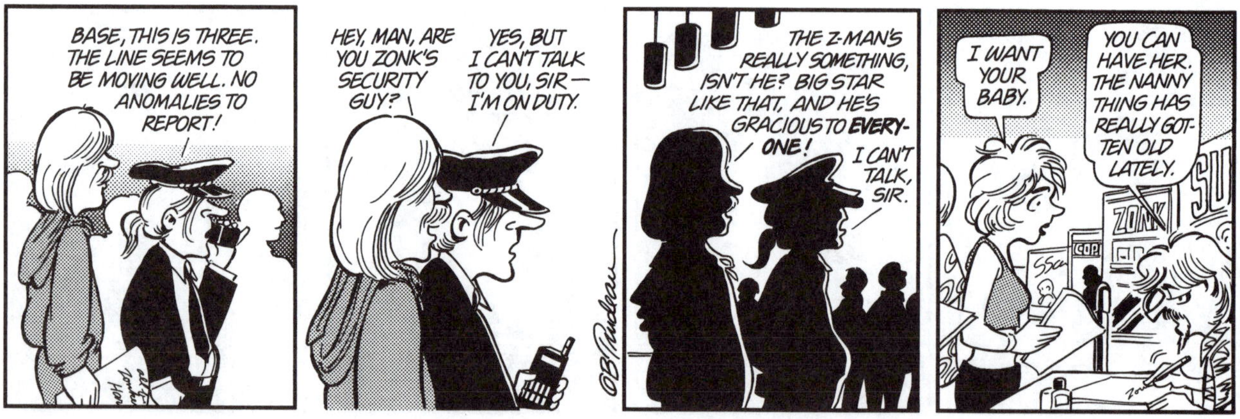
BASE, THIS IS THREE. THE LINE SEEMS TO BE MOVING WELL. NO ANOMALIES TO REPORT!
HEY, MAN, ARE YOU ZONK'S SECURITY GUY?
YES, BUT I CAN'T TALK TO YOU, SIR — I'M ON DUTY.
THE Z-MAN'S REALLY SOMETHING, ISN'T HE? BIG STAR LIKE THAT, AND HE'S GRACIOUS TO **EVERYONE**!
I CAN'T TALK, SIR.
I WANT YOUR BABY.
YOU CAN HAVE HER. THE NANNY THING HAS REALLY GOTTEN OLD LATELY.

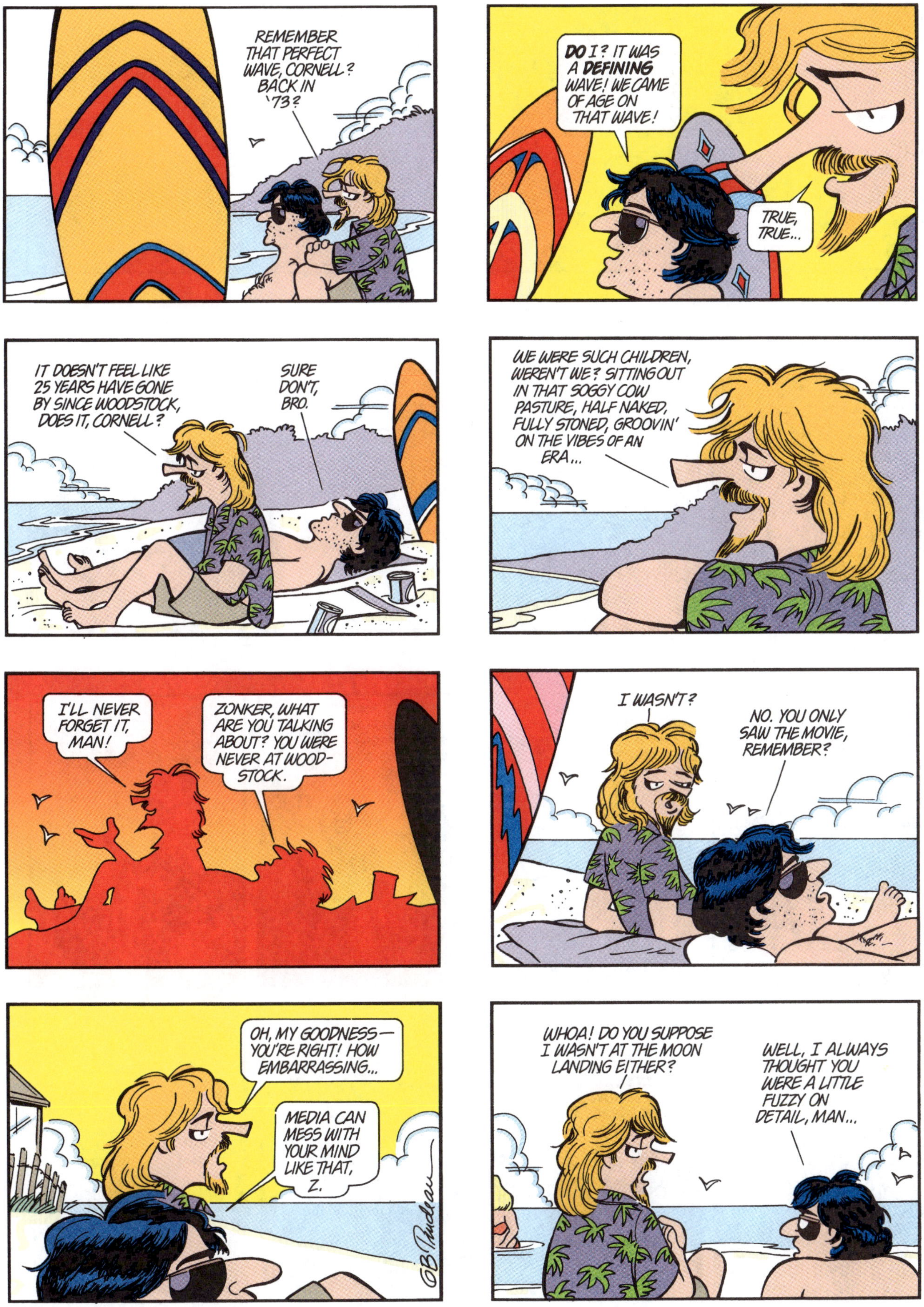
REMEMBER THAT PERFECT WAVE, CORNELL? BACK IN '73?
DO I? IT WAS A DEFINING WAVE! WE CAME OF AGE ON THAT WAVE!
TRUE, TRUE...
IT DOESN'T FEEL LIKE 25 YEARS HAVE GONE BY SINCE WOODSTOCK, DOES IT, CORNELL?
SURE DON'T, BRO.
WE WERE SUCH CHILDREN, WEREN'T WE? SITTING OUT IN THAT SOGGY COW PASTURE, HALF NAKED, FULLY STONED, GROOVIN' ON THE VIBES OF AN ERA...
I'LL NEVER FORGET IT, MAN!
ZONKER, WHAT ARE YOU TALKING ABOUT? YOU WERE NEVER AT WOODSTOCK.
I WASN'T?
NO. YOU ONLY SAW THE MOVIE, REMEMBER?
OH, MY GOODNESS— YOU'RE RIGHT! HOW EMBARRASSING...
MEDIA CAN MESS WITH YOUR MIND LIKE THAT, Z.
GB Trudeau
WHOA! DO YOU SUPPOSE I WASN'T AT THE MOON LANDING EITHER?
WELL, I ALWAYS THOUGHT YOU WERE A LITTLE FUZZY ON DETAIL, MAN...

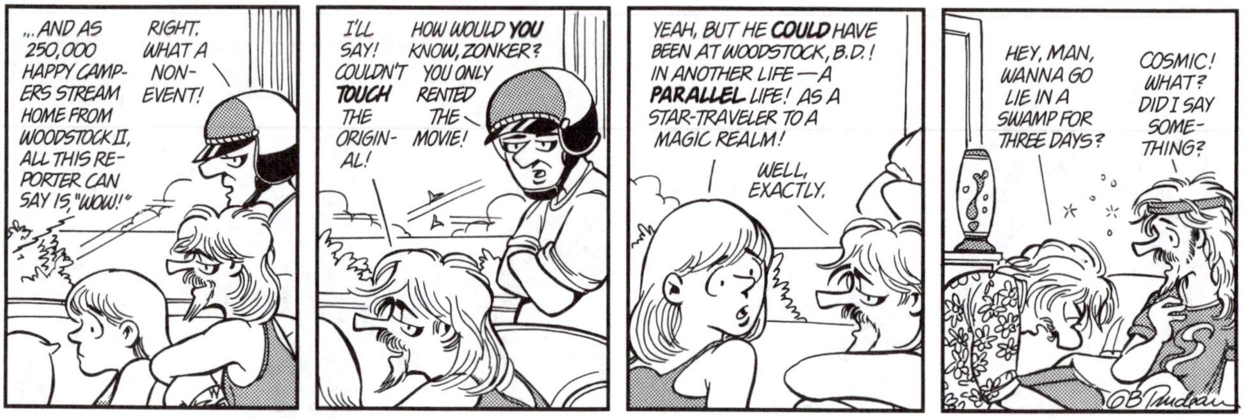
...AND AS 250,000 HAPPY CAMPERS STREAM HOME FROM WOODSTOCK II, ALL THIS REPORTER CAN SAY IS "WOW!"
RIGHT. WHAT A NON-EVENT!
I'LL SAY! COULDN'T TOUCH THE ORIGINAL!
HOW WOULD YOU KNOW, ZONKER? YOU ONLY RENTED THE MOVIE!
YEAH, BUT HE COULD HAVE BEEN AT WOODSTOCK, B.D.! IN ANOTHER LIFE — A PARALLEL LIFE! AS A STAR-TRAVELER TO A MAGIC REALM!
WELL, EXACTLY.
HEY, MAN, WANNA GO LIE IN A SWAMP FOR THREE DAYS?
COSMIC! WHAT? DID I SAY SOMETHING?
GB Trudeau

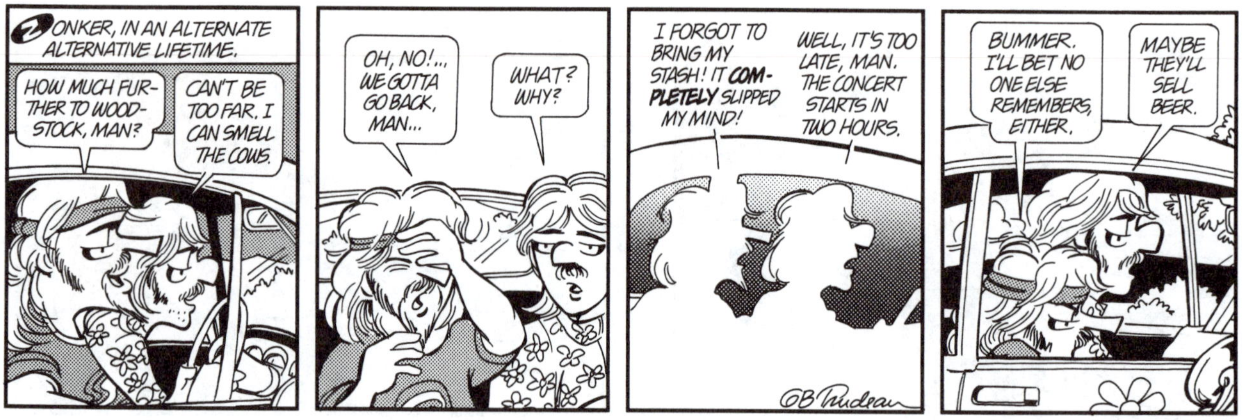
ZONKER, IN AN ALTERNATE ALTERNATIVE LIFETIME.
HOW MUCH FURTHER TO WOODSTOCK, MAN?
CAN'T BE TOO FAR. I CAN SMELL THE COWS.
OH, NO!... WE GOTTA GO BACK, MAN...
WHAT? WHY?
I FORGOT TO BRING MY STASH! IT COMPLETELY SLIPPED MY MIND!
WELL, IT'S TOO LATE, MAN. THE CONCERT STARTS IN TWO HOURS.
BUMMER. I'LL BET NO ONE ELSE REMEMBERS, EITHER.
MAYBE THEY'LL SELL BEER.
GB Trudeau

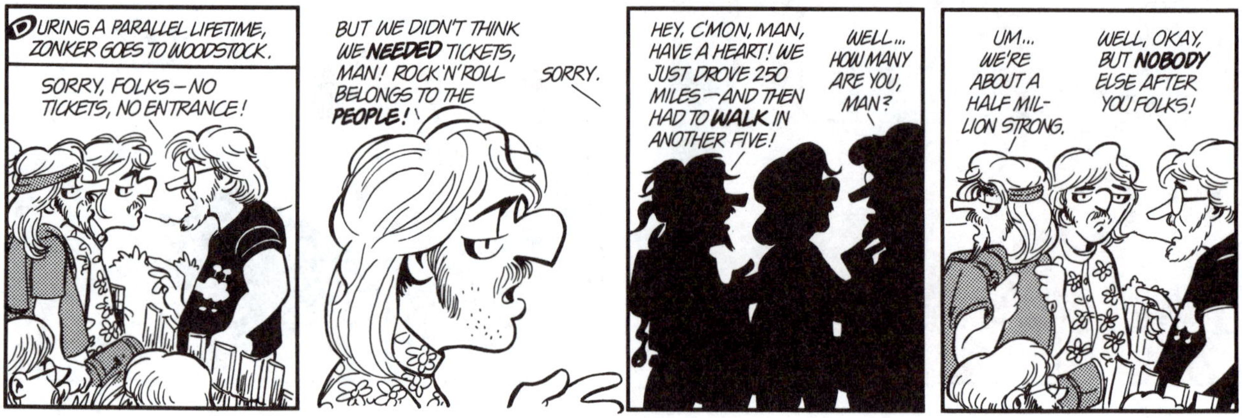
DURING A PARALLEL LIFETIME, ZONKER GOES TO WOODSTOCK.
SORRY, FOLKS — NO TICKETS, NO ENTRANCE!
BUT WE DIDN'T THINK WE NEEDED TICKETS, MAN! ROCK 'N' ROLL BELONGS TO THE PEOPLE!
SORRY.
HEY, C'MON, MAN, HAVE A HEART! WE JUST DROVE 250 MILES — AND THEN HAD TO WALK IN ANOTHER FIVE!
WELL... HOW MANY ARE YOU, MAN?
UM... WE'RE ABOUT A HALF MILLION STRONG.
WELL, OKAY, BUT NOBODY ELSE AFTER YOU FOLKS!

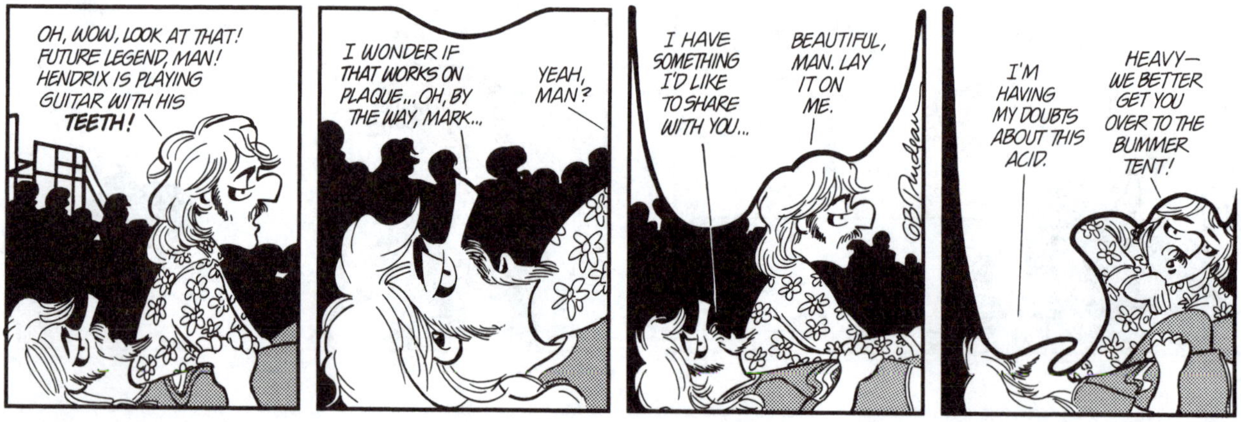
OH, WOW, LOOK AT THAT! FUTURE LEGEND, MAN! HENDRIX IS PLAYING GUITAR WITH HIS TEETH!
I WONDER IF THAT WORKS ON PLAQUE... OH, BY THE WAY, MARK...
YEAH, MAN?
I HAVE SOMETHING I'D LIKE TO SHARE WITH YOU...
BEAUTIFUL, MAN. LAY IT ON ME.
GB Trudeau
I'M HAVING MY DOUBTS ABOUT THIS ACID.
HEAVY — WE BETTER GET YOU OVER TO THE BUMMER TENT!

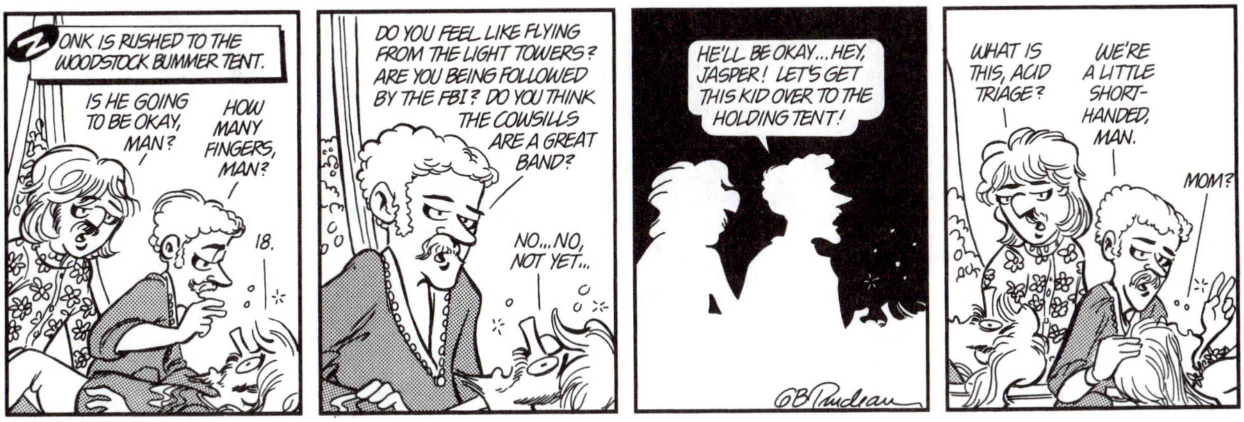
ZONK IS RUSHED TO THE WOODSTOCK BUMMER TENT.
IS HE GOING TO BE OKAY, MAN?
HOW MANY FINGERS, MAN?
18.
DO YOU FEEL LIKE FLYING FROM THE LIGHT TOWERS? ARE YOU BEING FOLLOWED BY THE FBI? DO YOU THINK THE COWSILLS ARE A GREAT BAND?
NO... NO, NOT YET...
HE'LL BE OKAY... HEY, JASPER! LET'S GET THIS KID OVER TO THE HOLDING TENT!
WHAT IS THIS, ACID TRIAGE?
WE'RE A LITTLE SHORT-HANDED, MAN.
MOM?

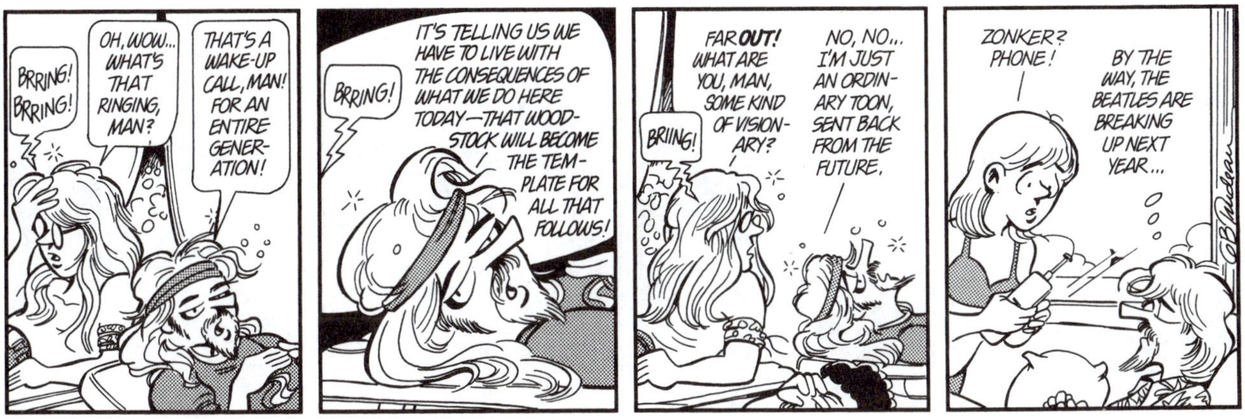
BRRING! BRRING!
OH, WOW... WHAT'S THAT RINGING, MAN?
THAT'S A WAKE-UP CALL, MAN! FOR AN ENTIRE GENERATION!
BRRING!
IT'S TELLING US WE HAVE TO LIVE WITH THE CONSEQUENCES OF WHAT WE DO HERE TODAY—THAT WOODSTOCK WILL BECOME THE TEMPLATE FOR ALL THAT FOLLOWS!
BRIING!
FAR OUT! WHAT ARE YOU, MAN, SOME KIND OF VISIONARY?
NO, NO... I'M JUST AN ORDINARY TOON, SENT BACK FROM THE FUTURE.
ZONKER? PHONE!
BY THE WAY, THE BEATLES ARE BREAKING UP NEXT YEAR...

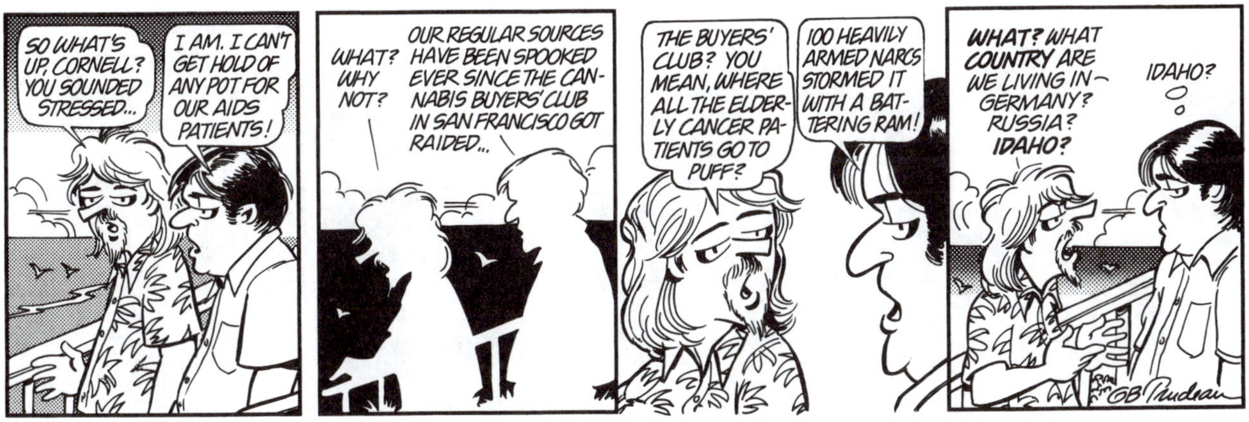
SO WHAT'S UP, CORNELL? YOU SOUNDED STRESSED...
I AM. I CAN'T GET HOLD OF ANY POT FOR OUR AIDS PATIENTS!
WHAT? WHY NOT?
OUR REGULAR SOURCES HAVE BEEN SPOOKED EVER SINCE THE CANNABIS BUYERS' CLUB IN SAN FRANCISCO GOT RAIDED...
THE BUYERS' CLUB? YOU MEAN, WHERE ALL THE ELDERLY CANCER PATIENTS GO TO PUFF?
100 HEAVILY ARMED NARCS STORMED IT WITH A BATTERING RAM!
WHAT? WHAT COUNTRY ARE WE LIVING IN—GERMANY? RUSSIA? IDAHO?
IDAHO?

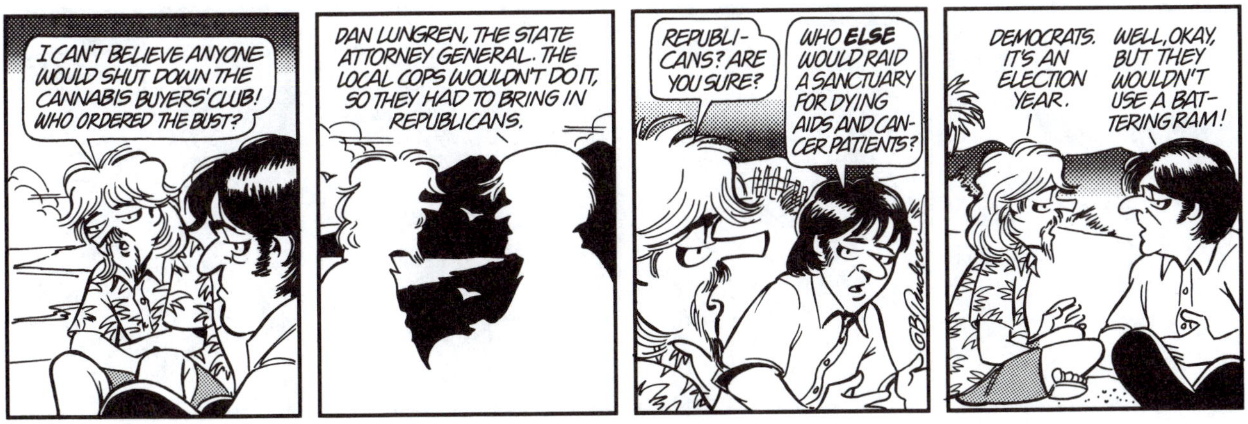
I CAN'T BELIEVE ANYONE WOULD SHUT DOWN THE CANNABIS BUYERS' CLUB! WHO ORDERED THE BUST?
DAN LUNGREN, THE STATE ATTORNEY GENERAL. THE LOCAL COPS WOULDN'T DO IT, SO THEY HAD TO BRING IN REPUBLICANS.
REPUBLICANS? ARE YOU SURE?
WHO ELSE WOULD RAID A SANCTUARY FOR DYING AIDS AND CANCER PATIENTS?
DEMOCRATS. IT'S AN ELECTION YEAR.
WELL, OKAY, BUT THEY WOULDN'T USE A BATTERING RAM!

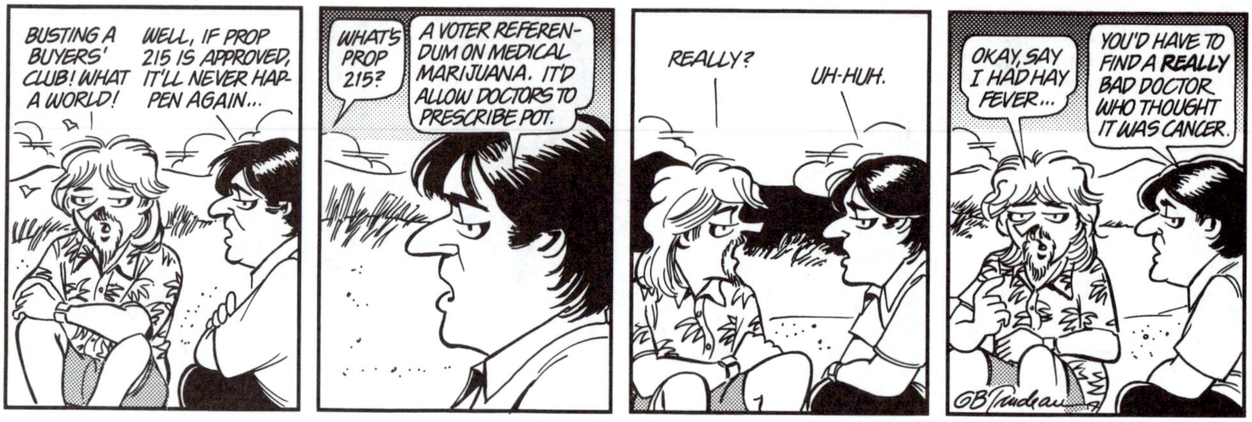
BUSTING A BUYERS' CLUB! WHAT A WORLD!
WELL, IF PROP 215 IS APPROVED, IT'LL NEVER HAPPEN AGAIN...
WHAT'S PROP 215?
A VOTER REFERENDUM ON MEDICAL MARIJUANA. IT'D ALLOW DOCTORS TO PRESCRIBE POT.
REALLY?
UH-HUH.
OKAY, SAY I HAD HAY FEVER...
YOU'D HAVE TO FIND A **REALLY** BAD DOCTOR WHO THOUGHT IT WAS CANCER.

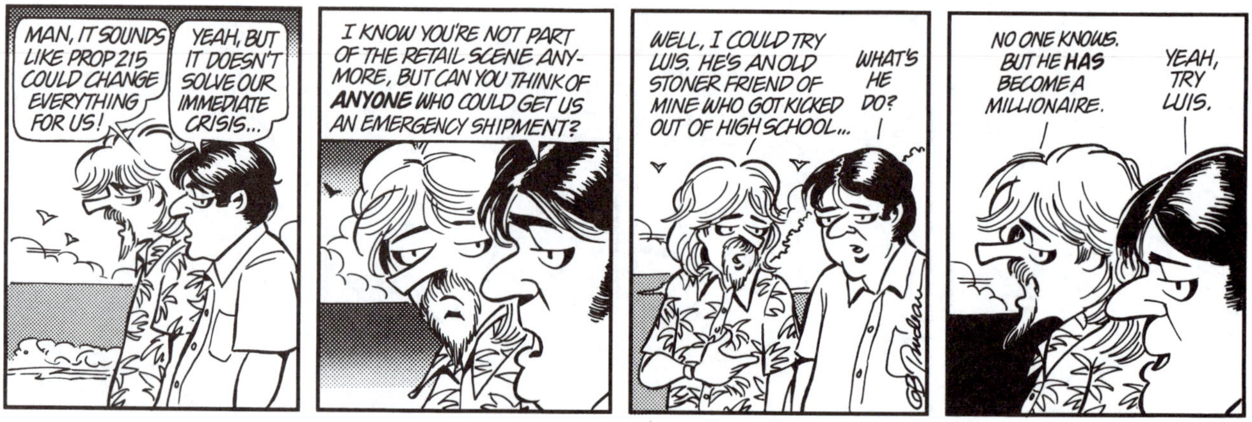
MAN, IT SOUNDS LIKE PROP 215 COULD CHANGE EVERYTHING FOR US!
YEAH, BUT IT DOESN'T SOLVE OUR IMMEDIATE CRISIS...
I KNOW YOU'RE NOT PART OF THE RETAIL SCENE ANYMORE, BUT CAN YOU THINK OF **ANYONE** WHO COULD GET US AN EMERGENCY SHIPMENT?
WELL, I COULD TRY LUIS. HE'S AN OLD STONER FRIEND OF MINE WHO GOT KICKED OUT OF HIGH SCHOOL...
WHAT'S HE DO?
NO ONE KNOWS. BUT HE **HAS** BECOME A MILLIONAIRE.
YEAH, TRY LUIS.

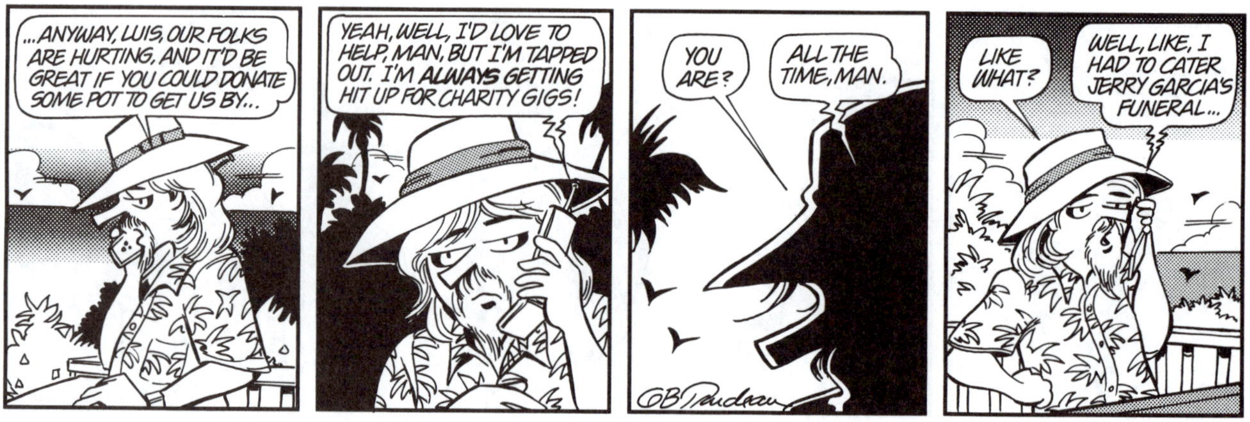
...ANYWAY, LUIS, OUR FOLKS ARE HURTING, AND IT'D BE GREAT IF YOU COULD DONATE SOME POT TO GET US BY...
YEAH, WELL, I'D LOVE TO HELP, MAN, BUT I'M TAPPED OUT. I'M **ALWAYS** GETTING HIT UP FOR CHARITY GIGS!
YOU ARE?
ALL THE TIME, MAN.
LIKE WHAT?
WELL, LIKE, I HAD TO CATER JERRY GARCIA'S FUNERAL...

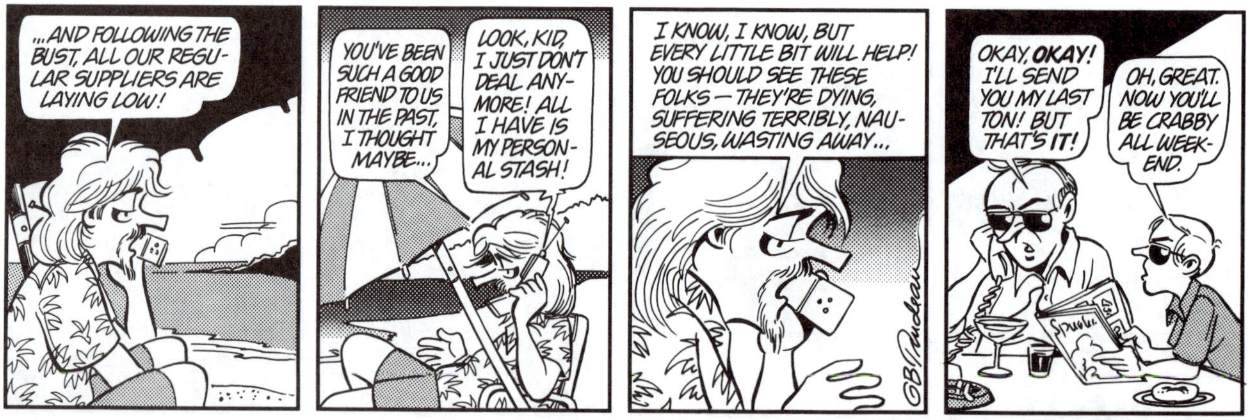
...AND FOLLOWING THE BUST, ALL OUR REGULAR SUPPLIERS ARE LAYING LOW!
YOU'VE BEEN SUCH A GOOD FRIEND TO US IN THE PAST, I THOUGHT MAYBE...
LOOK, KID, I JUST DON'T DEAL ANYMORE! ALL I HAVE IS MY PERSONAL STASH!
I KNOW, I KNOW, BUT EVERY LITTLE BIT WILL HELP! YOU SHOULD SEE THESE FOLKS — THEY'RE DYING, SUFFERING TERRIBLY, NAUSEOUS, WASTING AWAY...
OKAY, **OKAY!** I'LL SEND YOU MY LAST TON! BUT THAT'S **IT!**
OH, GREAT. NOW YOU'LL BE CRABBY ALL WEEKEND.

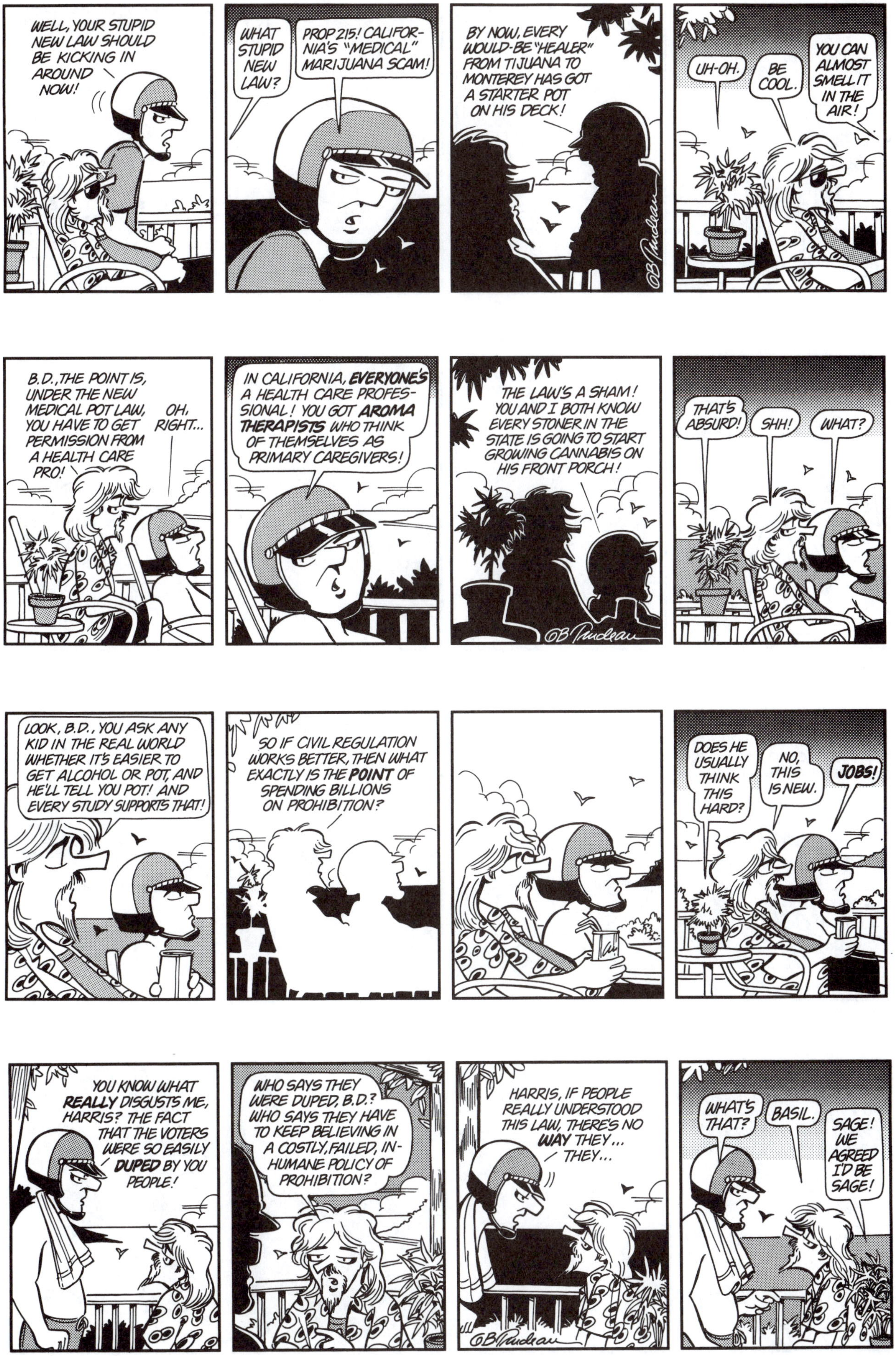
WELL, YOUR STUPID NEW LAW SHOULD BE KICKING IN AROUND NOW!
WHAT STUPID NEW LAW?
PROP 215! CALIFORNIA'S "MEDICAL" MARIJUANA SCAM!
BY NOW, EVERY WOULD-BE "HEALER" FROM TIJUANA TO MONTEREY HAS GOT A STARTER POT ON HIS DECK!
UH-OH.
BE COOL.
YOU CAN ALMOST SMELL IT IN THE AIR!
B.D., THE POINT IS, UNDER THE NEW MEDICAL POT LAW, YOU HAVE TO GET PERMISSION FROM A HEALTH CARE PRO!
OH, RIGHT...
IN CALIFORNIA, EVERYONE'S A HEALTH CARE PROFESSIONAL! YOU GOT AROMA THERAPISTS WHO THINK OF THEMSELVES AS PRIMARY CAREGIVERS!
THE LAW'S A SHAM! YOU AND I BOTH KNOW EVERY STONER IN THE STATE IS GOING TO START GROWING CANNABIS ON HIS FRONT PORCH!
THAT'S ABSURD!
SHH!
WHAT?
LOOK, B.D., YOU ASK ANY KID IN THE REAL WORLD WHETHER IT'S EASIER TO GET ALCOHOL OR POT, AND HE'LL TELL YOU POT! AND EVERY STUDY SUPPORTS THAT!
SO IF CIVIL REGULATION WORKS BETTER, THEN WHAT EXACTLY IS THE POINT OF SPENDING BILLIONS ON PROHIBITION?
DOES HE USUALLY THINK THIS HARD?
NO, THIS IS NEW.
JOBS!
YOU KNOW WHAT REALLY DISGUSTS ME, HARRIS? THE FACT THAT THE VOTERS WERE SO EASILY DUPED BY YOU PEOPLE!
WHO SAYS THEY WERE DUPED, B.D.? WHO SAYS THEY HAVE TO KEEP BELIEVING IN A COSTLY, FAILED, INHUMANE POLICY OF PROHIBITION?
HARRIS, IF PEOPLE REALLY UNDERSTOOD THIS LAW, THERE'S NO WAY THEY... THEY...
WHAT'S THAT?
BASIL.
SAGE! WE AGREED I'D BE SAGE!

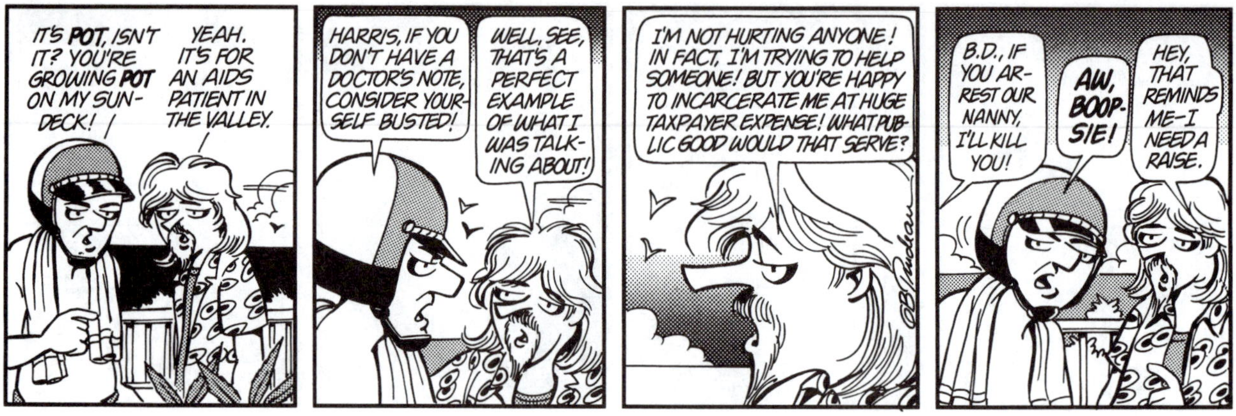
IT'S POT, ISN'T IT? YOU'RE GROWING POT ON MY SUNDECK!
YEAH. IT'S FOR AN AIDS PATIENT IN THE VALLEY.
HARRIS, IF YOU DON'T HAVE A DOCTOR'S NOTE, CONSIDER YOURSELF BUSTED!
WELL, SEE, THAT'S A PERFECT EXAMPLE OF WHAT I WAS TALKING ABOUT!
I'M NOT HURTING ANYONE! IN FACT, I'M TRYING TO HELP SOMEONE! BUT YOU'RE HAPPY TO INCARCERATE ME AT HUGE TAXPAYER EXPENSE! WHAT PUBLIC GOOD WOULD THAT SERVE?
B.D., IF YOU ARREST OUR NANNY, I'LL KILL YOU!
AW, BOOPSIE!
HEY, THAT REMINDS ME—I NEED A RAISE.

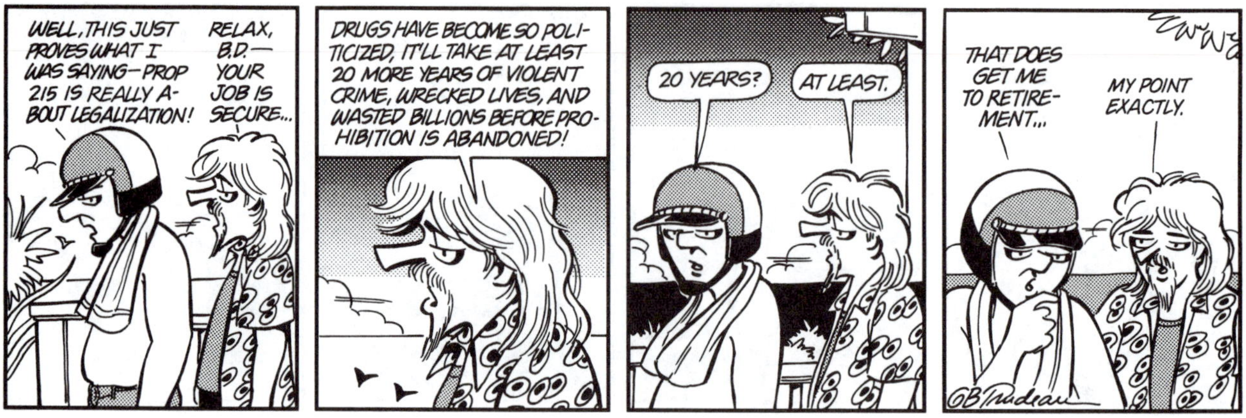
WELL, THIS JUST PROVES WHAT I WAS SAYING—PROP 215 IS REALLY ABOUT LEGALIZATION!
RELAX, B.D.—YOUR JOB IS SECURE...
DRUGS HAVE BECOME SO POLITICIZED, IT'LL TAKE AT LEAST 20 MORE YEARS OF VIOLENT CRIME, WRECKED LIVES, AND WASTED BILLIONS BEFORE PROHIBITION IS ABANDONED!
20 YEARS?
AT LEAST.
THAT DOES GET ME TO RETIREMENT...
MY POINT EXACTLY.

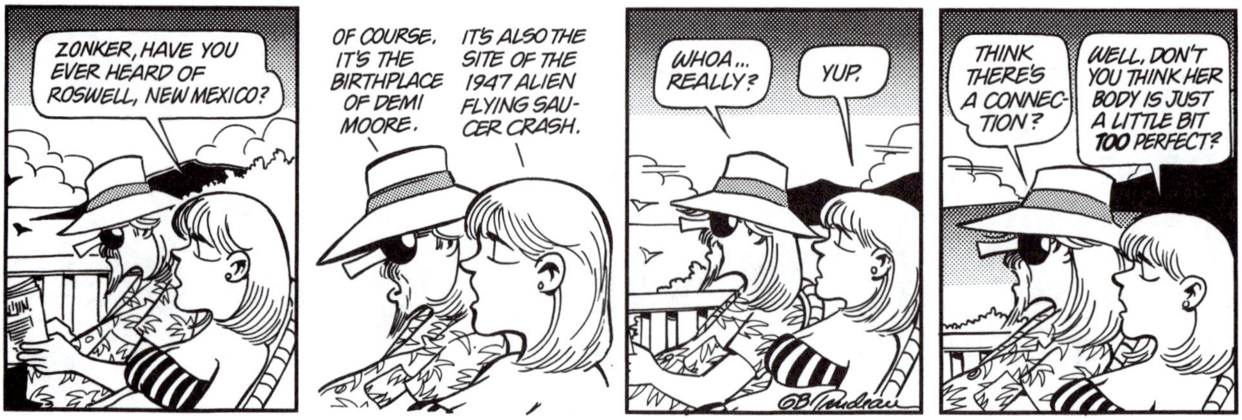
ZONKER, HAVE YOU EVER HEARD OF ROSWELL, NEW MEXICO?
OF COURSE. IT'S THE BIRTHPLACE OF DEMI MOORE.
IT'S ALSO THE SITE OF THE 1947 ALIEN FLYING SAUCER CRASH.
WHOA... REALLY?
YUP.
THINK THERE'S A CONNECTION?
WELL, DON'T YOU THINK HER BODY IS JUST A LITTLE BIT TOO PERFECT?

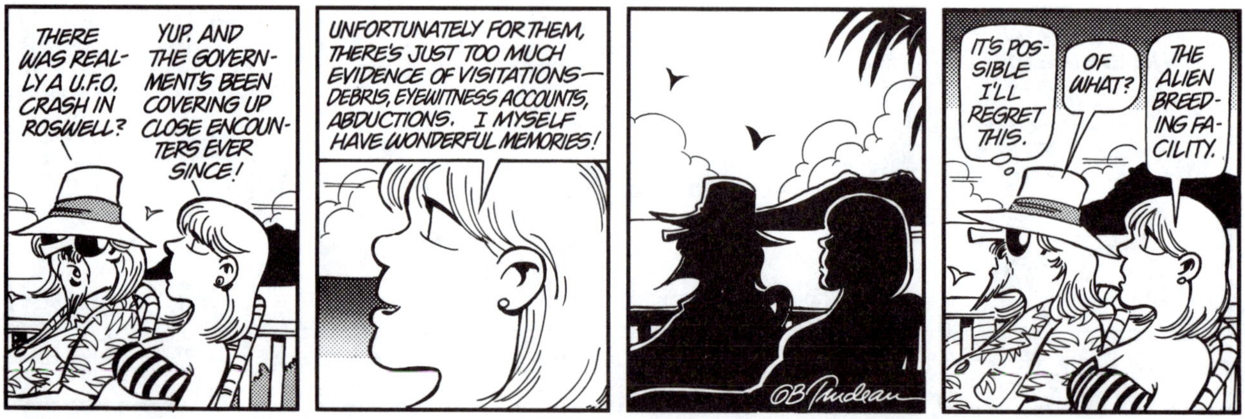
THERE WAS REALLY A U.F.O. CRASH IN ROSWELL?
YUP. AND THE GOVERNMENT'S BEEN COVERING UP CLOSE ENCOUNTERS EVER SINCE!
UNFORTUNATELY FOR THEM, THERE'S JUST TOO MUCH EVIDENCE OF VISITATIONS—DEBRIS, EYEWITNESS ACCOUNTS, ABDUCTIONS. I MYSELF HAVE WONDERFUL MEMORIES!
IT'S POSSIBLE I'LL REGRET THIS.
OF WHAT?
THE ALIEN BREEDING FACILITY.

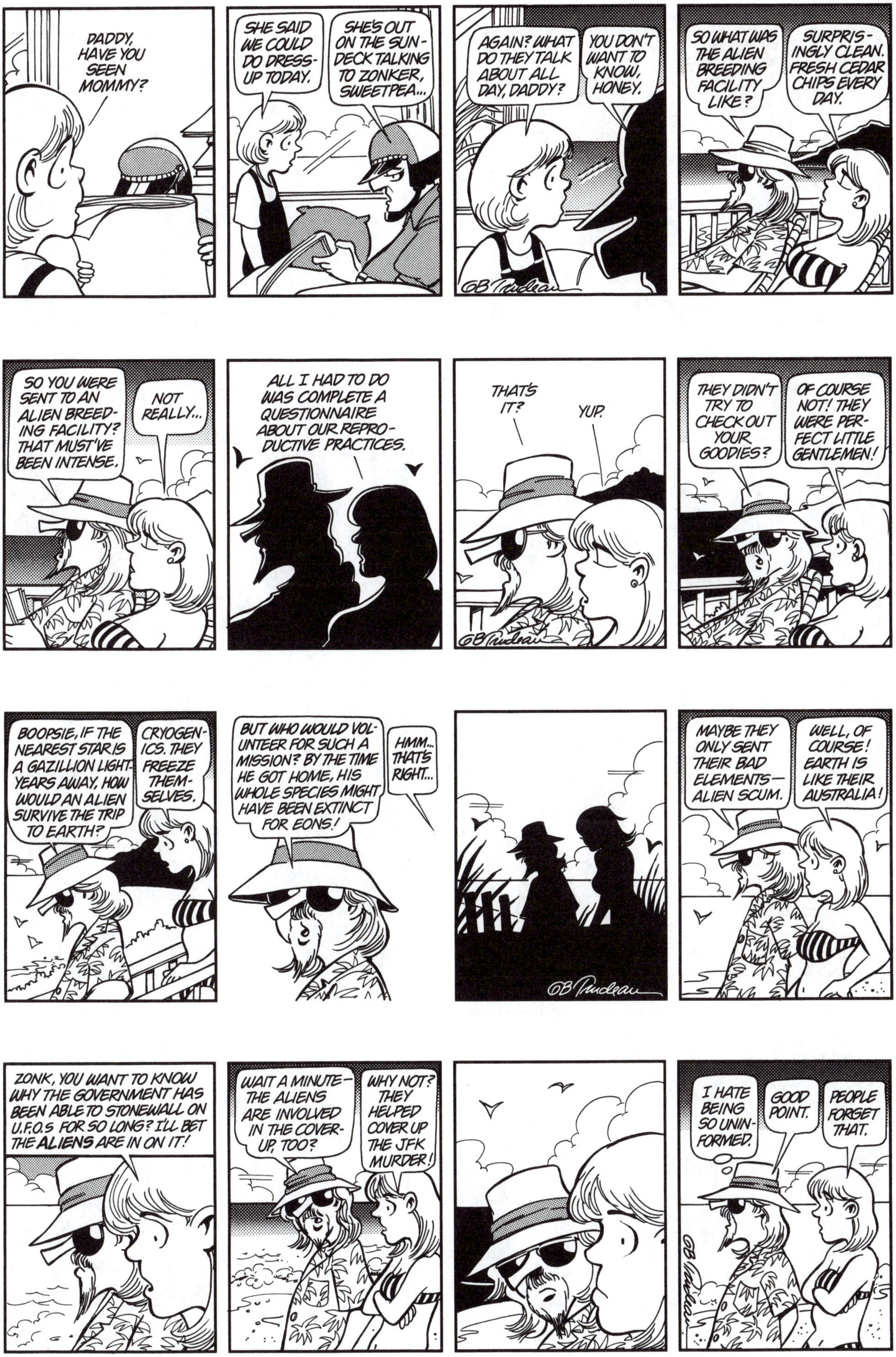
DADDY, HAVE YOU SEEN MOMMY?
SHE SAID WE COULD DO DRESS-UP TODAY.
SHE'S OUT ON THE SUNDECK TALKING TO ZONKER, SWEETPEA...
AGAIN? WHAT DO THEY TALK ABOUT ALL DAY, DADDY?
YOU DON'T WANT TO KNOW, HONEY.
SO WHAT WAS THE ALIEN BREEDING FACILITY LIKE?
SURPRISINGLY CLEAN. FRESH CEDAR CHIPS EVERY DAY.
SO YOU WERE SENT TO AN ALIEN BREEDING FACILITY? THAT MUST'VE BEEN INTENSE.
NOT REALLY...
ALL I HAD TO DO WAS COMPLETE A QUESTIONNAIRE ABOUT OUR REPRODUCTIVE PRACTICES.
THAT'S IT?
YUP.
THEY DIDN'T TRY TO CHECK OUT YOUR GOODIES?
OF COURSE NOT! THEY WERE PERFECT LITTLE GENTLEMEN!
BOOPSIE, IF THE NEAREST STAR IS A GAZILLION LIGHT-YEARS AWAY, HOW WOULD AN ALIEN SURVIVE THE TRIP TO EARTH?
CRYOGENICS. THEY FREEZE THEMSELVES.
BUT WHO WOULD VOLUNTEER FOR SUCH A MISSION? BY THE TIME HE GOT HOME, HIS WHOLE SPECIES MIGHT HAVE BEEN EXTINCT FOR EONS!
HMM... THAT'S RIGHT...
MAYBE THEY ONLY SENT THEIR BAD ELEMENTS— ALIEN SCUM.
WELL, OF COURSE! EARTH IS LIKE THEIR AUSTRALIA!
ZONK, YOU WANT TO KNOW WHY THE GOVERNMENT HAS BEEN ABLE TO STONEWALL ON U.F.O.S FOR SO LONG? I'LL BET THE ALIENS ARE IN ON IT!
WAIT A MINUTE— THE ALIENS ARE INVOLVED IN THE COVER-UP, TOO?
WHY NOT? THEY HELPED COVER UP THE JFK MURDER!
I HATE BEING SO UNINFORMED.
GOOD POINT.
PEOPLE FORGET THAT.

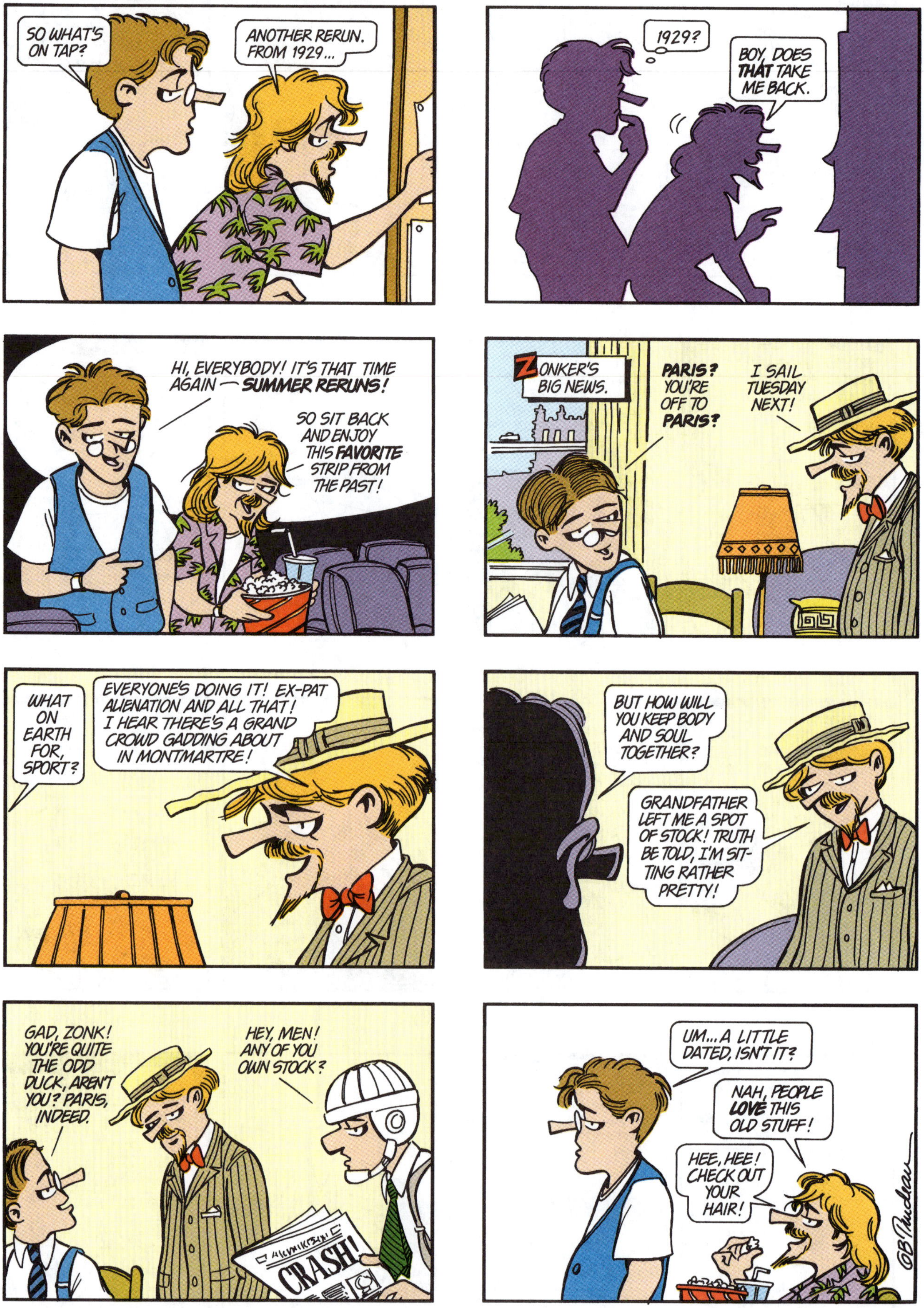
SO WHAT'S ON TAP?
ANOTHER RERUN. FROM 1929...
1929?
BOY, DOES **THAT** TAKE ME BACK.
HI, EVERYBODY! IT'S THAT TIME AGAIN — **SUMMER RERUNS!**
SO SIT BACK AND ENJOY THIS **FAVORITE** STRIP FROM THE PAST!
ZONKER'S BIG NEWS.
PARIS? YOU'RE OFF TO **PARIS?**
I SAIL TUESDAY NEXT!
WHAT ON EARTH FOR, SPORT?
EVERYONE'S DOING IT! EX-PAT ALIENATION AND ALL THAT! I HEAR THERE'S A GRAND CROWD GADDING ABOUT IN MONTMARTRE!
BUT HOW WILL YOU KEEP BODY AND SOUL TOGETHER?
GRANDFATHER LEFT ME A SPOT OF STOCK! TRUTH BE TOLD, I'M SITTING RATHER PRETTY!
GAD, ZONK! YOU'RE QUITE THE ODD DUCK, AREN'T YOU? PARIS, INDEED.
HEY, MEN! ANY OF YOU OWN STOCK?
CRASH!
UM... A LITTLE DATED, ISN'T IT?
NAH, PEOPLE **LOVE** THIS OLD STUFF!
HEE, HEE! CHECK OUT YOUR HAIR!
©B Trudeau

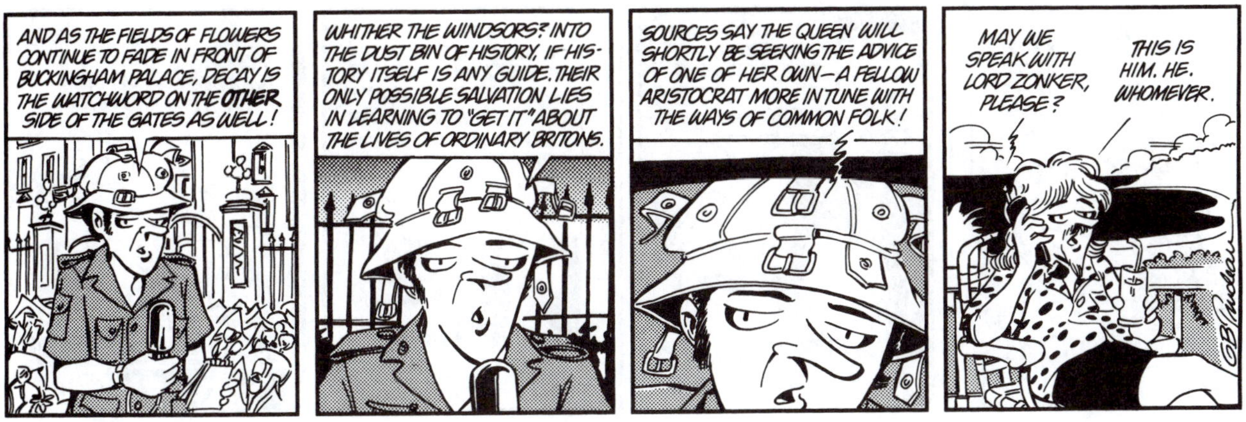
AND AS THE FIELDS OF FLOWERS CONTINUE TO FADE IN FRONT OF BUCKINGHAM PALACE, DECAY IS THE WATCHWORD ON THE **OTHER** SIDE OF THE GATES AS WELL!
WHITHER THE WINDSORS? INTO THE DUST BIN OF HISTORY, IF HISTORY ITSELF IS ANY GUIDE. THEIR ONLY POSSIBLE SALVATION LIES IN LEARNING TO "GET IT" ABOUT THE LIVES OF ORDINARY BRITONS.
SOURCES SAY THE QUEEN WILL SHORTLY BE SEEKING THE ADVICE OF ONE OF HER OWN—A FELLOW ARISTOCRAT MORE IN TUNE WITH THE WAYS OF COMMON FOLK!
MAY WE SPEAK WITH LORD ZONKER, PLEASE?
THIS IS HIM. HE. WHOMEVER.

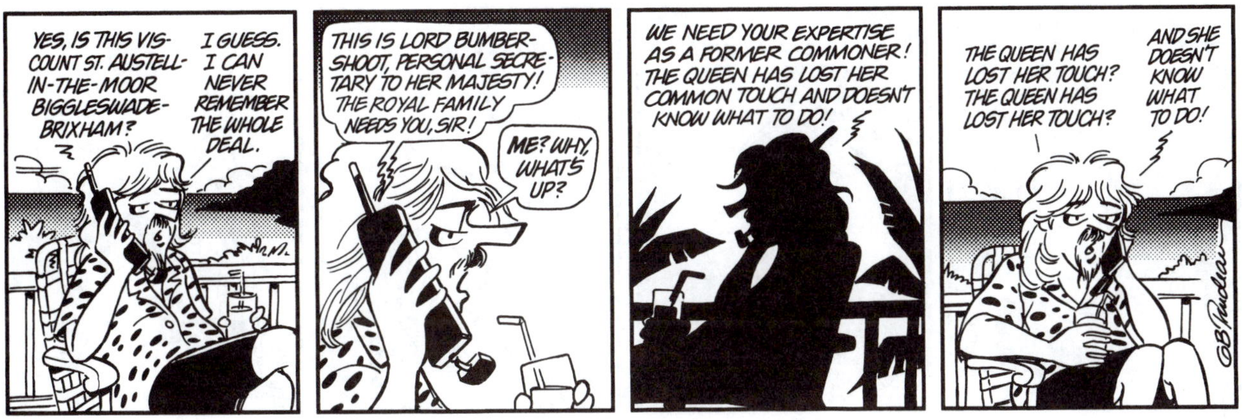
YES, IS THIS VISCOUNT ST. AUSTELL-IN-THE-MOOR BIGGLESWADE-BRIXHAM?
I GUESS. I CAN NEVER REMEMBER THE WHOLE DEAL.
THIS IS LORD BUMBERSHOOT, PERSONAL SECRETARY TO HER MAJESTY! THE ROYAL FAMILY NEEDS YOU, SIR!
ME? WHY, WHAT'S UP?
WE NEED YOUR EXPERTISE AS A FORMER COMMONER! THE QUEEN HAS LOST HER COMMON TOUCH AND DOESN'T KNOW WHAT TO DO!
THE QUEEN HAS LOST HER TOUCH? THE QUEEN HAS LOST HER TOUCH?
AND SHE DOESN'T KNOW WHAT TO DO!

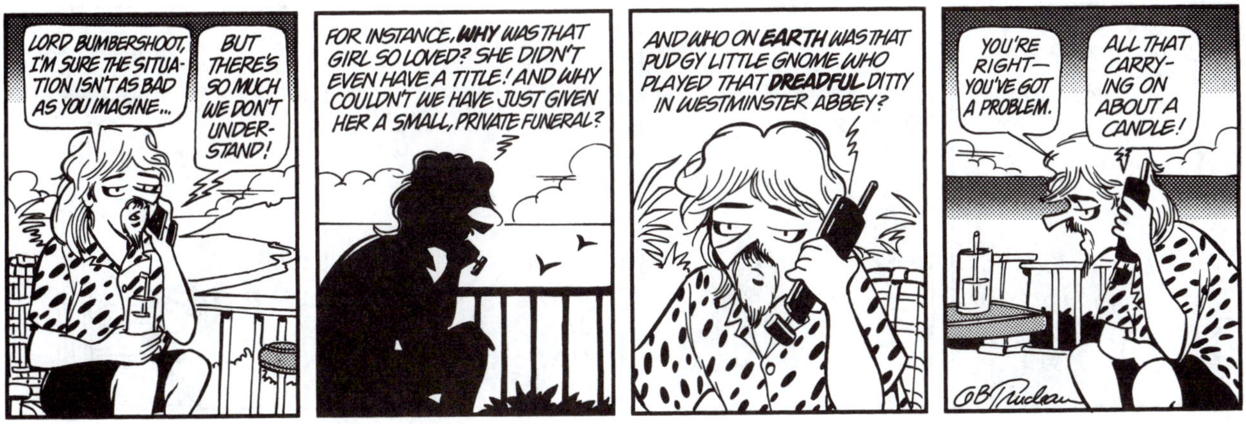
LORD BUMBERSHOOT, I'M SURE THE SITUATION ISN'T AS BAD AS YOU IMAGINE...
BUT THERE'S SO MUCH WE DON'T UNDERSTAND!
FOR INSTANCE, **WHY** WAS THAT GIRL SO LOVED? SHE DIDN'T EVEN HAVE A TITLE! AND WHY COULDN'T WE HAVE JUST GIVEN HER A SMALL, PRIVATE FUNERAL?
AND WHO ON **EARTH** WAS THAT PUDGY LITTLE GNOME WHO PLAYED THAT **DREADFUL** DITTY IN WESTMINSTER ABBEY?
YOU'RE RIGHT—YOU'VE GOT A PROBLEM.
ALL THAT CARRYING ON ABOUT A CANDLE!

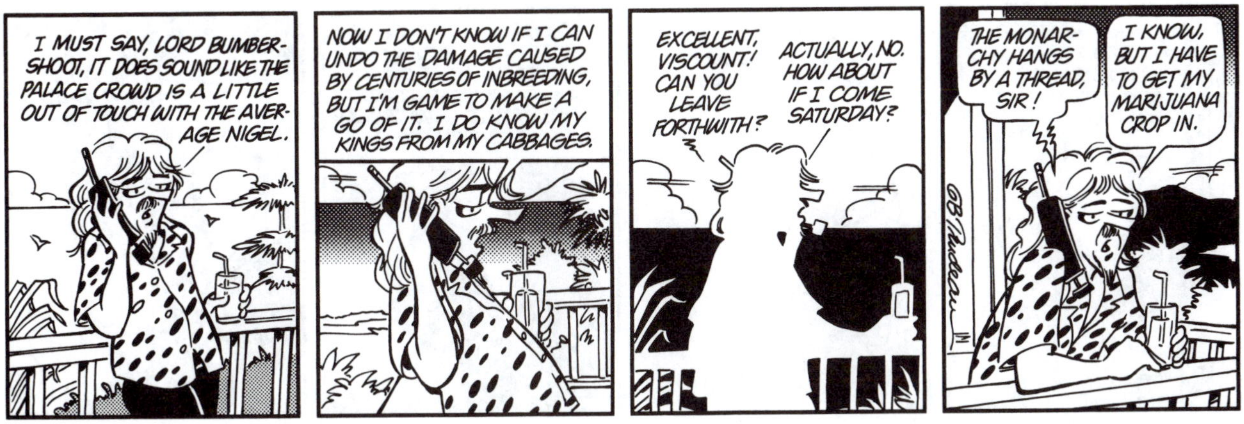
I MUST SAY, LORD BUMBERSHOOT, IT DOES SOUND LIKE THE PALACE CROWD IS A LITTLE OUT OF TOUCH WITH THE AVERAGE NIGEL.
NOW I DON'T KNOW IF I CAN UNDO THE DAMAGE CAUSED BY CENTURIES OF INBREEDING, BUT I'M GAME TO MAKE A GO OF IT. I DO KNOW MY KINGS FROM MY CABBAGES.
EXCELLENT, VISCOUNT! CAN YOU LEAVE FORTHWITH?
ACTUALLY, NO. HOW ABOUT IF I COME SATURDAY?
THE MONARCHY HANGS BY A THREAD, SIR!
I KNOW, BUT I HAVE TO GET MY MARIJUANA CROP IN.

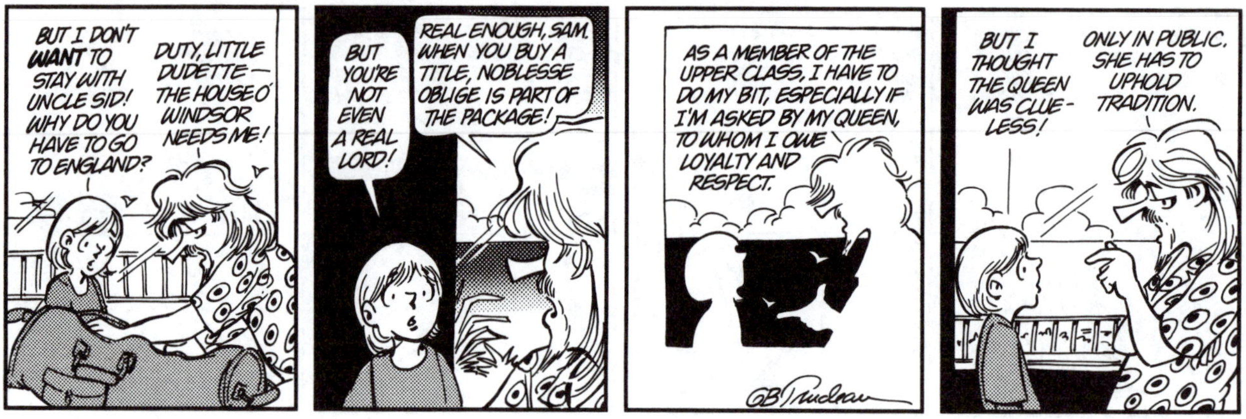
BUT I DON'T **WANT** TO STAY WITH UNCLE SID! WHY DO YOU HAVE TO GO TO ENGLAND?
DUTY, LITTLE DUDETTE— THE HOUSE O' WINDSOR NEEDS ME!
BUT YOU'RE NOT EVEN A REAL LORD!
REAL ENOUGH, SAM. WHEN YOU BUY A TITLE, NOBLESSE OBLIGE IS PART OF THE PACKAGE!
AS A MEMBER OF THE UPPER CLASS, I HAVE TO DO MY BIT, ESPECIALLY IF I'M ASKED BY MY QUEEN, TO WHOM I OWE LOYALTY AND RESPECT.
BUT I THOUGHT THE QUEEN WAS CLUELESS!
ONLY IN PUBLIC. SHE HAS TO UPHOLD TRADITION.

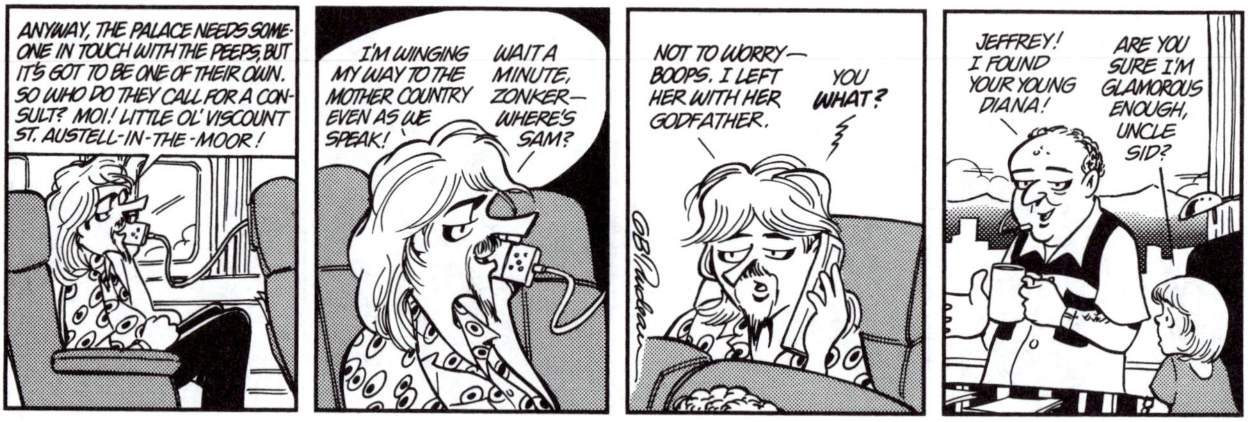
ANYWAY, THE PALACE NEEDS SOMEONE IN TOUCH WITH THE PEEPS, BUT IT'S GOT TO BE ONE OF THEIR OWN. SO WHO DO THEY CALL FOR A CONSULT? MOI! LITTLE OL' VISCOUNT ST. AUSTELL-IN-THE-MOOR!
I'M WINGING MY WAY TO THE MOTHER COUNTRY EVEN AS WE SPEAK!
WAIT A MINUTE, ZONKER— WHERE'S SAM?
NOT TO WORRY— BOOPS. I LEFT HER WITH HER GODFATHER.
YOU **WHAT?**
JEFFREY! I FOUND YOUR YOUNG DIANA!
ARE YOU SURE I'M GLAMOROUS ENOUGH, UNCLE SID?

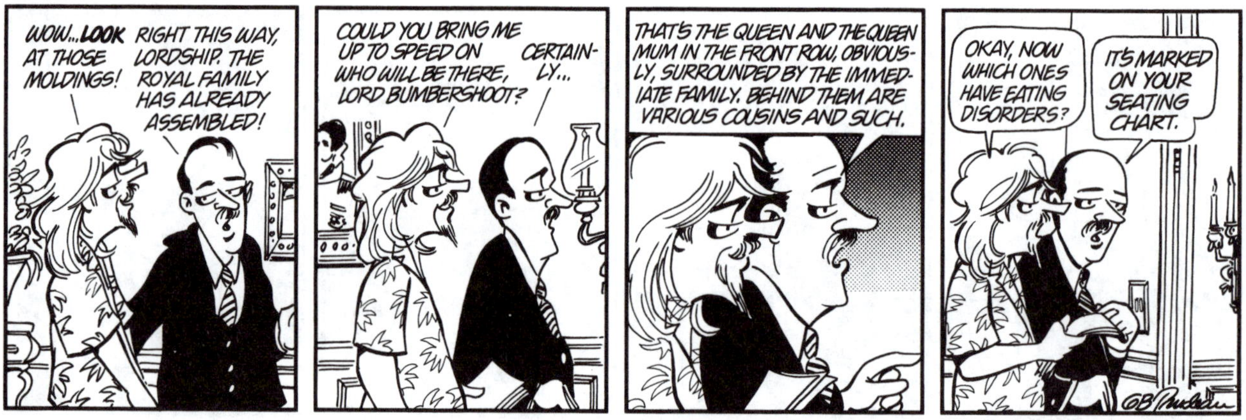
WOW... **LOOK** AT THOSE MOLDINGS!
RIGHT THIS WAY, LORDSHIP. THE ROYAL FAMILY HAS ALREADY ASSEMBLED!
COULD YOU BRING ME UP TO SPEED ON WHO WILL BE THERE, LORD BUMBERSHOOT?
CERTAINLY...
THAT'S THE QUEEN AND THE QUEEN MUM IN THE FRONT ROW, OBVIOUSLY, SURROUNDED BY THE IMMEDIATE FAMILY. BEHIND THEM ARE VARIOUS COUSINS AND SUCH.
OKAY, NOW WHICH ONES HAVE EATING DISORDERS?
IT'S MARKED ON YOUR SEATING CHART.

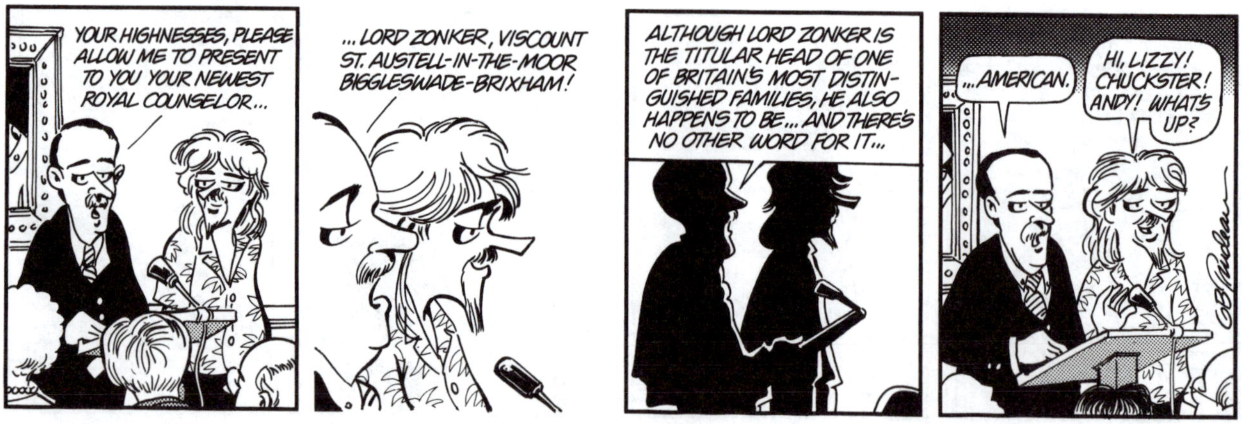
YOUR HIGHNESSES, PLEASE ALLOW ME TO PRESENT TO YOU YOUR NEWEST ROYAL COUNSELOR...
...LORD ZONKER, VISCOUNT ST. AUSTELL-IN-THE-MOOR BIGGLESWADE-BRIXHAM!
ALTHOUGH LORD ZONKER IS THE TITULAR HEAD OF ONE OF BRITAIN'S MOST DISTINGUISHED FAMILIES, HE ALSO HAPPENS TO BE... AND THERE'S NO OTHER WORD FOR IT...
...AMERICAN.
HI, LIZZY! CHUCKSTER! ANDY! WHAT'S UP?

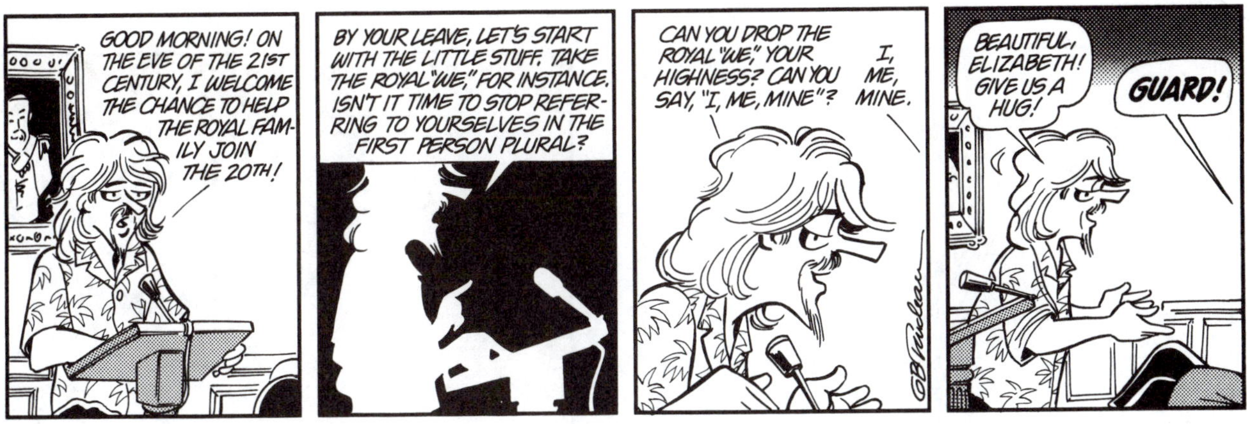
GOOD MORNING! ON THE EVE OF THE 21ST CENTURY, I WELCOME THE CHANCE TO HELP THE ROYAL FAMILY JOIN THE 20TH!
BY YOUR LEAVE, LET'S START WITH THE LITTLE STUFF. TAKE THE ROYAL "WE," FOR INSTANCE. ISN'T IT TIME TO STOP REFERRING TO YOURSELVES IN THE FIRST PERSON PLURAL?
CAN YOU DROP THE ROYAL "WE," YOUR HIGHNESS? CAN YOU SAY, "I, ME, MINE"?
I, ME, MINE.
BEAUTIFUL, ELIZABETH! GIVE US A HUG!
GUARD!

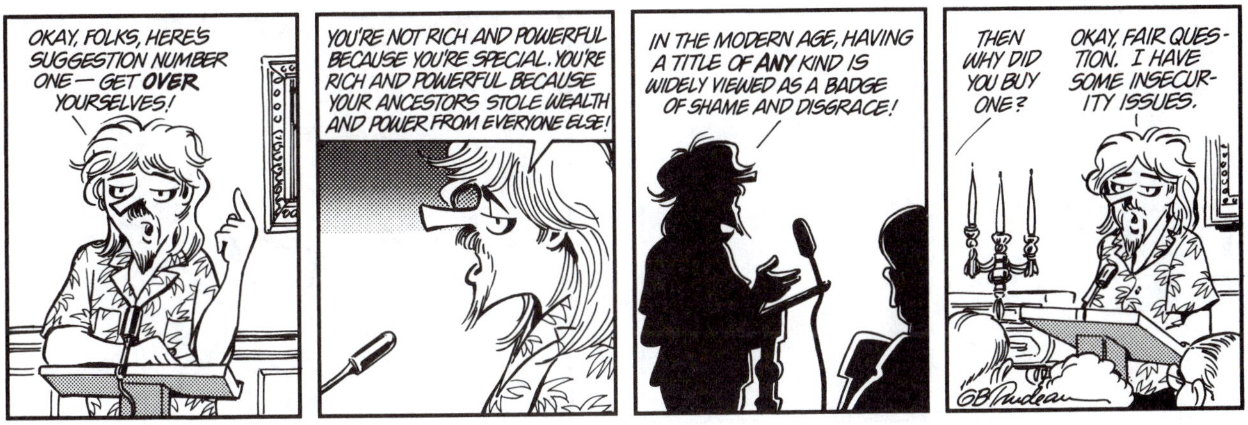
OKAY, FOLKS, HERE'S SUGGESTION NUMBER ONE — GET OVER YOURSELVES!
YOU'RE NOT RICH AND POWERFUL BECAUSE YOU'RE SPECIAL. YOU'RE RICH AND POWERFUL BECAUSE YOUR ANCESTORS STOLE WEALTH AND POWER FROM EVERYONE ELSE!
IN THE MODERN AGE, HAVING A TITLE OF ANY KIND IS WIDELY VIEWED AS A BADGE OF SHAME AND DISGRACE!
THEN WHY DID YOU BUY ONE?
OKAY, FAIR QUESTION. I HAVE SOME INSECURITY ISSUES.

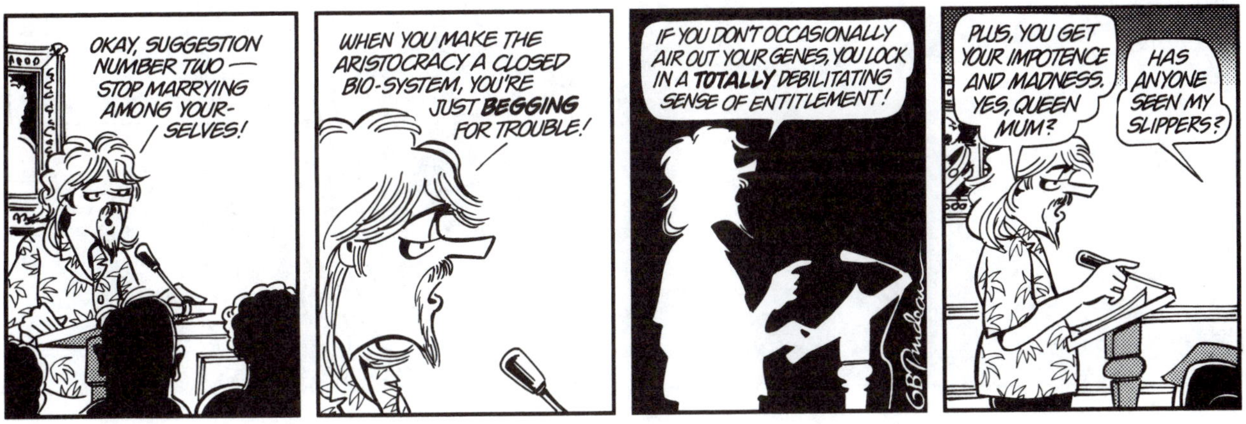
OKAY, SUGGESTION NUMBER TWO — STOP MARRYING AMONG YOURSELVES!
WHEN YOU MAKE THE ARISTOCRACY A CLOSED BIO-SYSTEM, YOU'RE JUST BEGGING FOR TROUBLE!
IF YOU DON'T OCCASIONALLY AIR OUT YOUR GENES, YOU LOCK IN A TOTALLY DEBILITATING SENSE OF ENTITLEMENT!
PLUS, YOU GET YOUR IMPOTENCE AND MADNESS. YES, QUEEN MUM?
HAS ANYONE SEEN MY SLIPPERS?

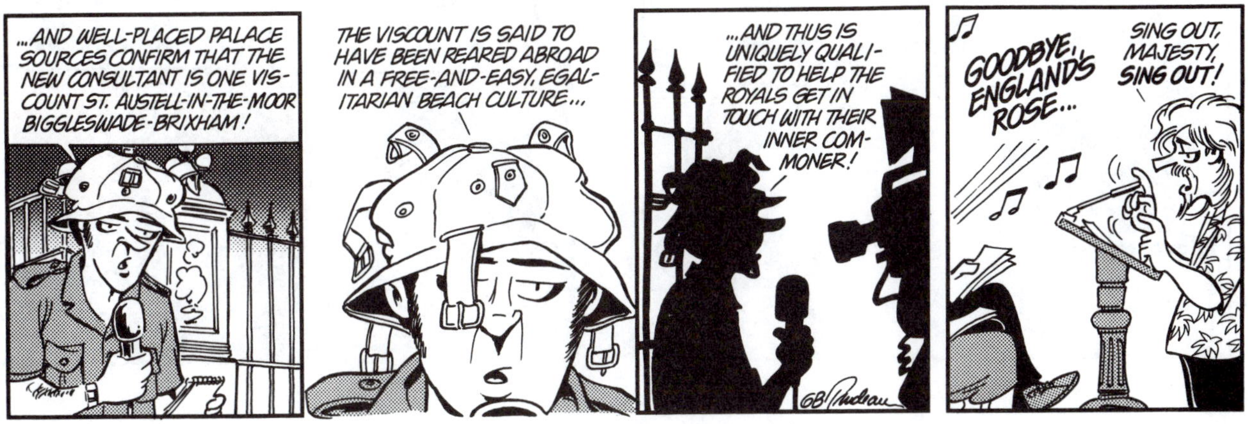
...AND WELL-PLACED PALACE SOURCES CONFIRM THAT THE NEW CONSULTANT IS ONE VISCOUNT ST. AUSTELL-IN-THE-MOOR BIGGLESWADE-BRIXHAM!
THE VISCOUNT IS SAID TO HAVE BEEN REARED ABROAD IN A FREE-AND-EASY, EGALITARIAN BEACH CULTURE...
...AND THUS IS UNIQUELY QUALIFIED TO HELP THE ROYALS GET IN TOUCH WITH THEIR INNER COMMONER!
GOODBYE, ENGLAND'S ROSE...
SING OUT, MAJESTY, SING OUT!

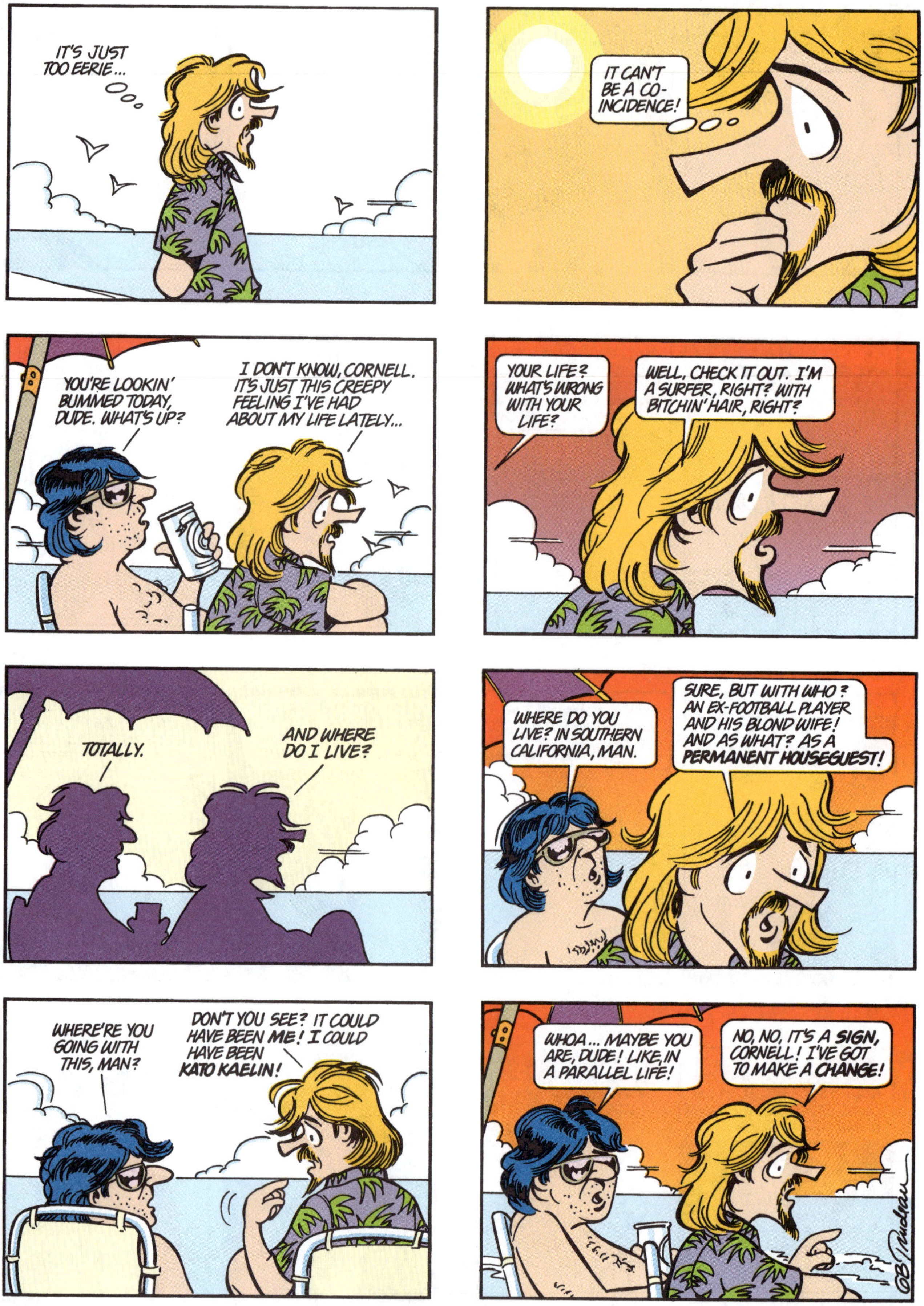
IT'S JUST TOO EERIE...
IT CAN'T BE A CO-INCIDENCE!
YOU'RE LOOKIN' BUMMED TODAY, DUDE. WHAT'S UP?
I DON'T KNOW, CORNELL. IT'S JUST THIS CREEPY FEELING I'VE HAD ABOUT MY LIFE LATELY...
YOUR LIFE? WHAT'S WRONG WITH YOUR LIFE?
WELL, CHECK IT OUT. I'M A SURFER, RIGHT? WITH BITCHIN' HAIR, RIGHT?
TOTALLY.
AND WHERE DO I LIVE?
WHERE DO YOU LIVE? IN SOUTHERN CALIFORNIA, MAN.
SURE, BUT WITH WHO? AN EX-FOOTBALL PLAYER AND HIS BLOND WIFE! AND AS WHAT? AS A PERMANENT HOUSEGUEST!
WHERE'RE YOU GOING WITH THIS, MAN?
DON'T YOU SEE? IT COULD HAVE BEEN ME! I COULD HAVE BEEN KATO KAELIN!
WHOA... MAYBE YOU ARE, DUDE! LIKE, IN A PARALLEL LIFE!
NO, NO, IT'S A SIGN, CORNELL! I'VE GOT TO MAKE A CHANGE!

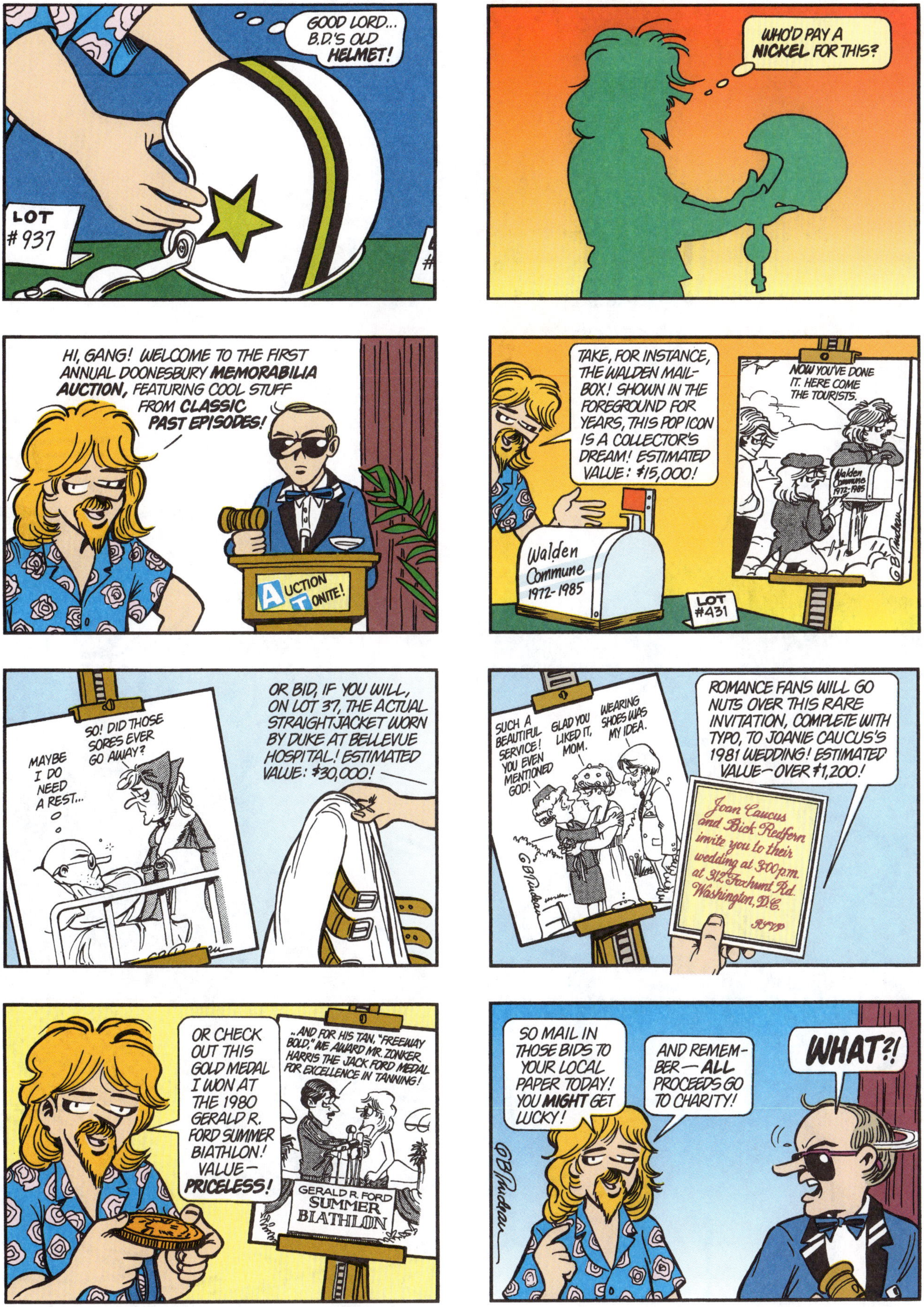
GOOD LORD... B.D.'S OLD HELMET!
LOT #937
WHO'D PAY A NICKEL FOR THIS?
HI, GANG! WELCOME TO THE FIRST ANNUAL DOONESBURY MEMORABILIA AUCTION, FEATURING COOL STUFF FROM CLASSIC PAST EPISODES!
AUCTION TONITE!
TAKE, FOR INSTANCE, THE WALDEN MAILBOX! SHOWN IN THE FOREGROUND FOR YEARS, THIS POP ICON IS A COLLECTOR'S DREAM! ESTIMATED VALUE: $15,000!
NOW YOU'VE DONE IT. HERE COME THE TOURISTS.
Walden Commune 1972-1985
LOT #431
OR BID, IF YOU WILL, ON LOT 37, THE ACTUAL STRAIGHTJACKET WORN BY DUKE AT BELLEVUE HOSPITAL! ESTIMATED VALUE: $30,000!
SO! DID THOSE SORES EVER GO AWAY?
MAYBE I DO NEED A REST...
ROMANCE FANS WILL GO NUTS OVER THIS RARE INVITATION, COMPLETE WITH TYPO, TO JOANIE CAUCUS'S 1981 WEDDING! ESTIMATED VALUE—OVER $1,200!
SUCH A BEAUTIFUL SERVICE! YOU EVEN MENTIONED GOD!
GLAD YOU LIKED IT, MOM.
WEARING SHOES WAS MY IDEA.
Joan Caucus and Bick Redfern invite you to their wedding at 3:00 p.m. at 312 Foxhunt Rd. Washington, D.C.
RSVP
OR CHECK OUT THIS GOLD MEDAL I WON AT THE 1980 GERALD R. FORD SUMMER BIATHLON! VALUE—PRICELESS!
...AND FOR HIS TAN, "FREEWAY BOLD," WE AWARD MR. ZONKER HARRIS THE JACK FORD MEDAL FOR EXCELLENCE IN TANNING!
GERALD R. FORD SUMMER BIATHLON
SO MAIL IN THOSE BIDS TO YOUR LOCAL PAPER TODAY! YOU MIGHT GET LUCKY!
AND REMEMBER—ALL PROCEEDS GO TO CHARITY!
WHAT?!
© B Trudeau

9

THE NANNY

Teaching the Children Well

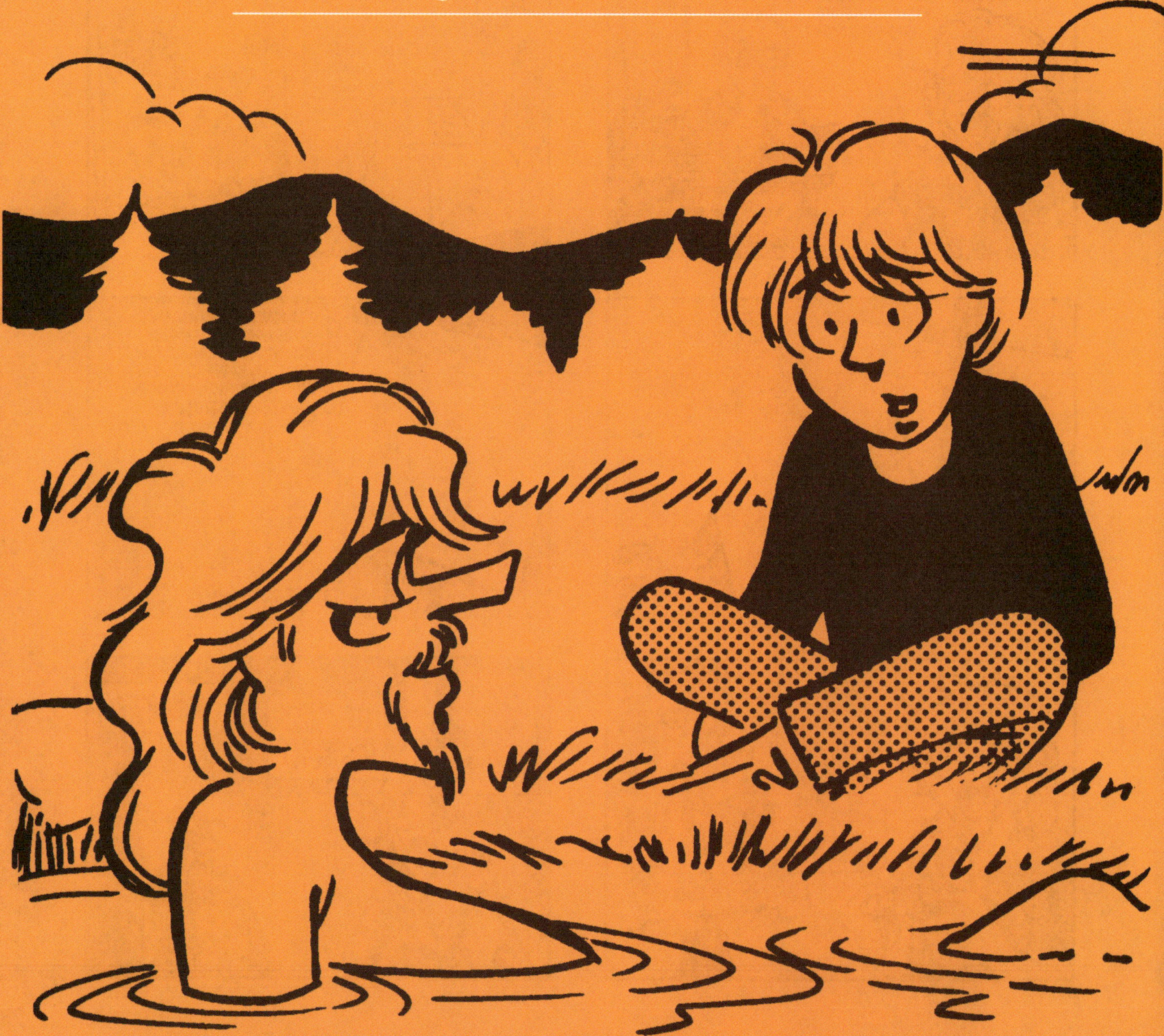

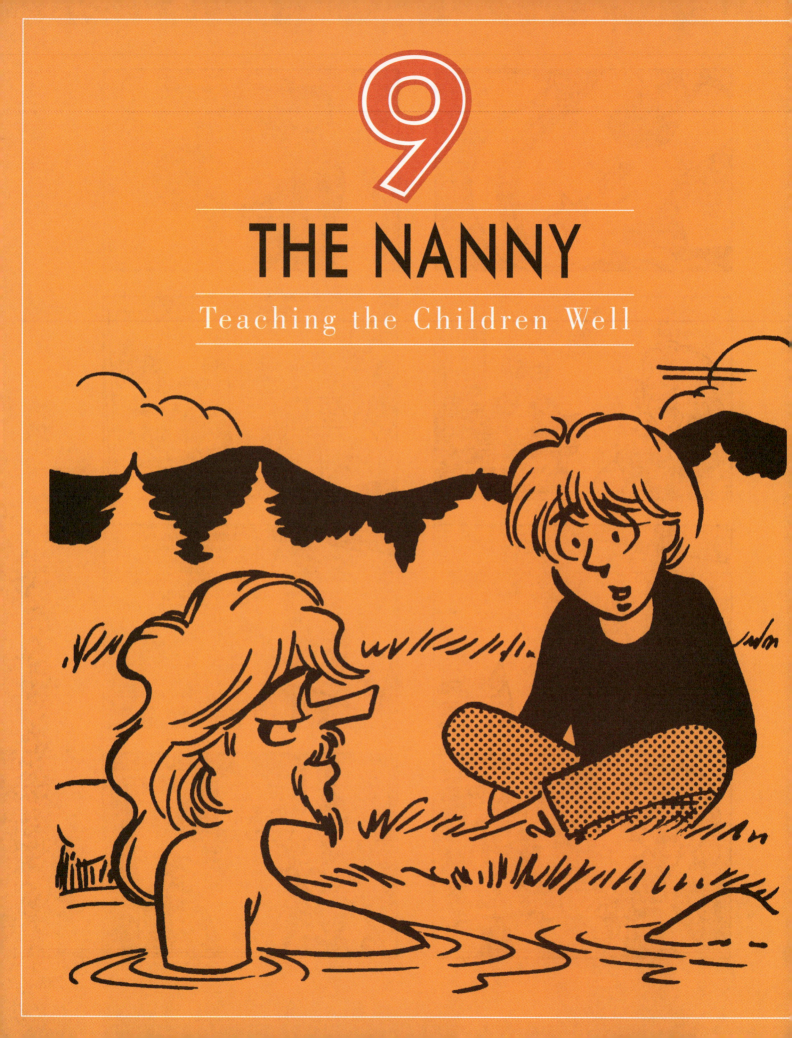

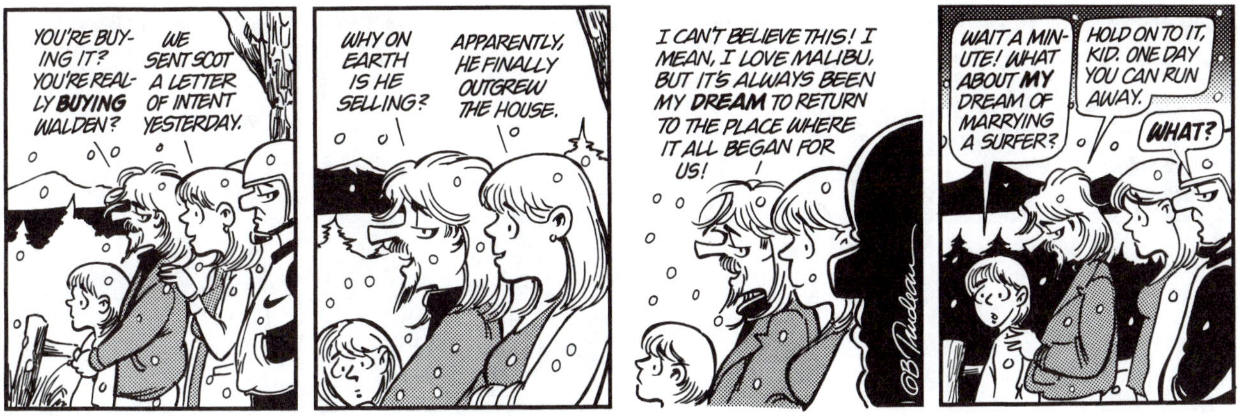
YOU'RE BUYING IT? YOU'RE REALLY BUYING WALDEN?
WE SENT SCOT A LETTER OF INTENT YESTERDAY.
WHY ON EARTH IS HE SELLING?
APPARENTLY, HE FINALLY OUTGREW THE HOUSE.
I CAN'T BELIEVE THIS! I MEAN, I LOVE MALIBU, BUT IT'S ALWAYS BEEN MY DREAM TO RETURN TO THE PLACE WHERE IT ALL BEGAN FOR US!
WAIT A MINUTE! WHAT ABOUT MY DREAM OF MARRYING A SURFER?
HOLD ON TO IT, KID. ONE DAY YOU CAN RUN AWAY.
WHAT?

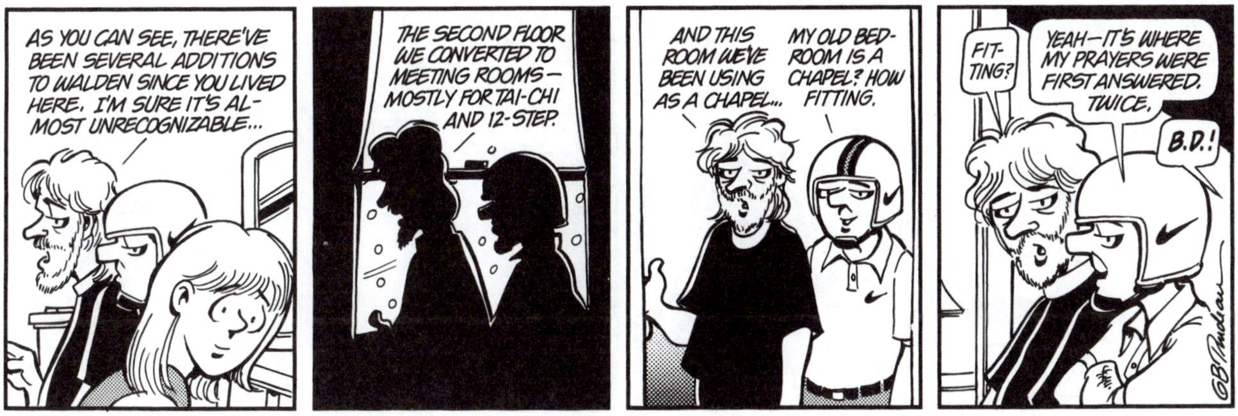
AS YOU CAN SEE, THERE'VE BEEN SEVERAL ADDITIONS TO WALDEN SINCE YOU LIVED HERE. I'M SURE IT'S ALMOST UNRECOGNIZABLE...
THE SECOND FLOOR WE CONVERTED TO MEETING ROOMS—MOSTLY FOR TAI-CHI AND 12-STEP.
AND THIS ROOM WE'VE BEEN USING AS A CHAPEL...
MY OLD BEDROOM IS A CHAPEL? HOW FITTING.
FITTING?
YEAH—IT'S WHERE MY PRAYERS WERE FIRST ANSWERED. TWICE.
B.D.!

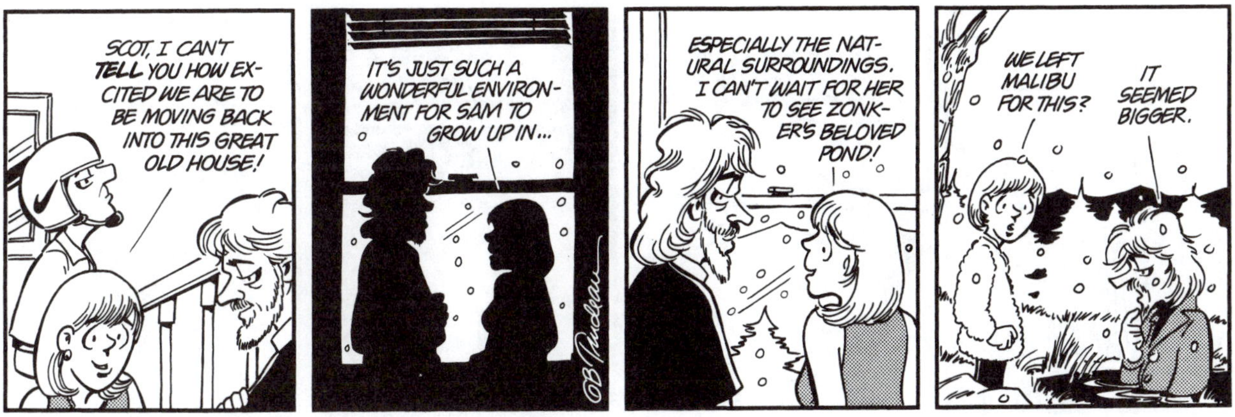
SCOT, I CAN'T TELL YOU HOW EXCITED WE ARE TO BE MOVING BACK INTO THIS GREAT OLD HOUSE!
IT'S JUST SUCH A WONDERFUL ENVIRONMENT FOR SAM TO GROW UP IN...
ESPECIALLY THE NATURAL SURROUNDINGS. I CAN'T WAIT FOR HER TO SEE ZONKER'S BELOVED POND!
WE LEFT MALIBU FOR THIS?
IT SEEMED BIGGER.

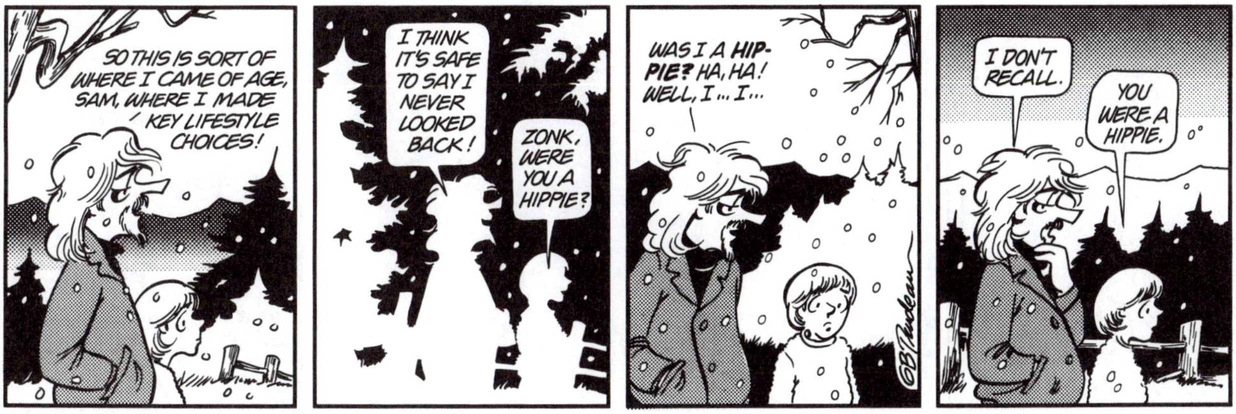
SO THIS IS SORT OF WHERE I CAME OF AGE, SAM, WHERE I MADE KEY LIFESTYLE CHOICES!
I THINK IT'S SAFE TO SAY I NEVER LOOKED BACK!
ZONK, WERE YOU A HIPPIE?
WAS I A HIPPIE? HA, HA! WELL, I... I...
I DON'T RECALL.
YOU WERE A HIPPIE.

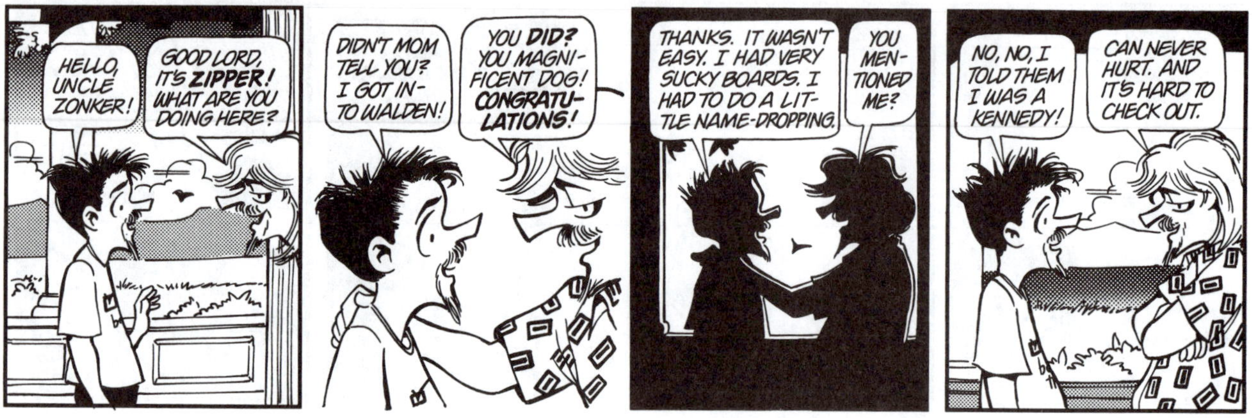
HELLO, UNCLE ZONKER!
GOOD LORD, IT'S **ZIPPER!** WHAT ARE YOU DOING HERE?
DIDN'T MOM TELL YOU? I GOT INTO WALDEN!
YOU **DID?** YOU MAGNIFICENT DOG! **CONGRATULATIONS!**
THANKS. IT WASN'T EASY. I HAD VERY SUCKY BOARDS. I HAD TO DO A LITTLE NAME-DROPPING.
YOU MENTIONED ME?
NO, NO, I TOLD THEM I WAS A KENNEDY!
CAN NEVER HURT. AND IT'S HARD TO CHECK OUT.

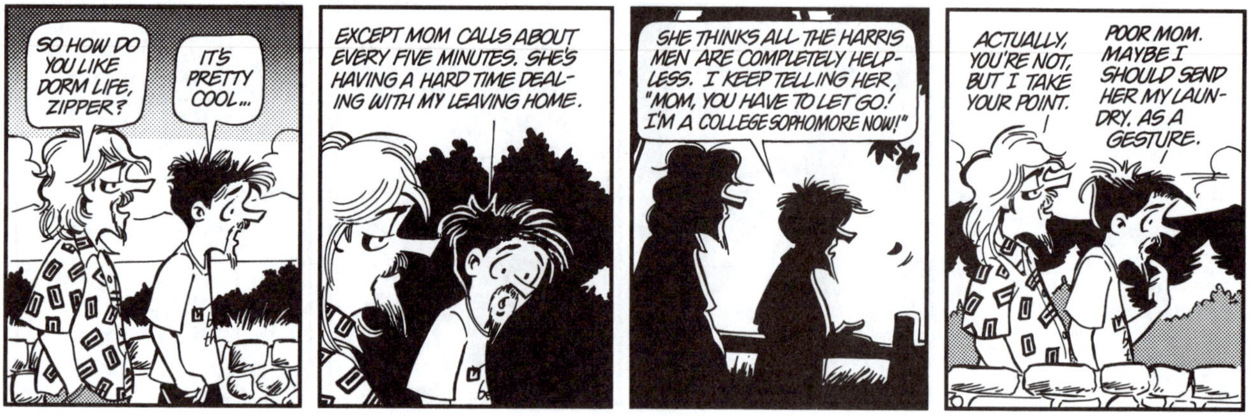
SO HOW DO YOU LIKE DORM LIFE, ZIPPER?
IT'S PRETTY COOL...
EXCEPT MOM CALLS ABOUT EVERY FIVE MINUTES. SHE'S HAVING A HARD TIME DEALING WITH MY LEAVING HOME.
SHE THINKS ALL THE HARRIS MEN ARE COMPLETELY HELPLESS. I KEEP TELLING HER, "MOM, YOU HAVE TO LET GO! I'M A COLLEGE SOPHOMORE NOW!"
ACTUALLY, YOU'RE NOT, BUT I TAKE YOUR POINT.
POOR MOM. MAYBE I SHOULD SEND HER MY LAUNDRY. AS A GESTURE.

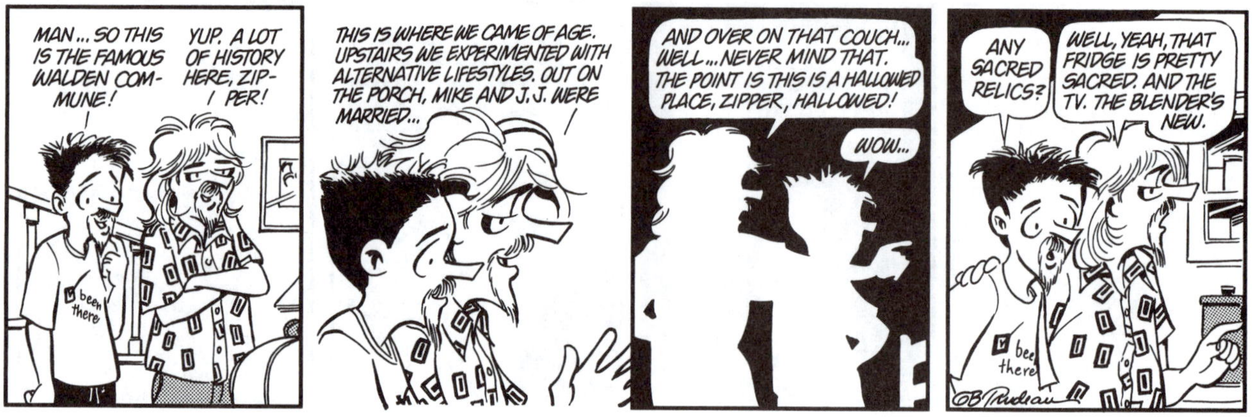
MAN... SO THIS IS THE FAMOUS WALDEN COMMUNE!
YUP. A LOT OF HISTORY HERE, ZIPPER!
THIS IS WHERE WE CAME OF AGE. UPSTAIRS WE EXPERIMENTED WITH ALTERNATIVE LIFESTYLES. OUT ON THE PORCH, MIKE AND J. J. WERE MARRIED...
AND OVER ON THAT COUCH... WELL... NEVER MIND THAT. THE POINT IS THIS IS A HALLOWED PLACE, ZIPPER, HALLOWED!
WOW...
ANY SACRED RELICS?
WELL, YEAH, THAT FRIDGE IS PRETTY SACRED. AND THE TV. THE BLENDER'S NEW.

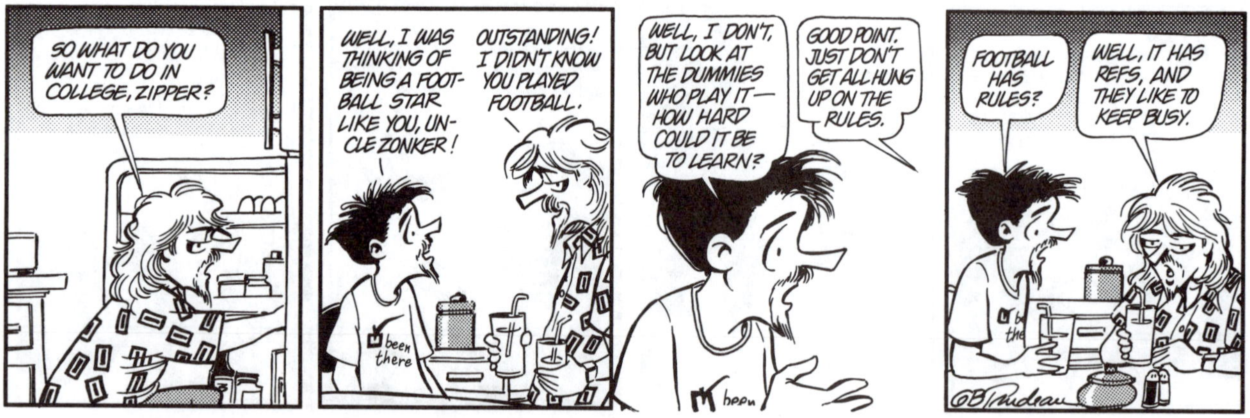
SO WHAT DO YOU WANT TO DO IN COLLEGE, ZIPPER?
WELL, I WAS THINKING OF BEING A FOOTBALL STAR LIKE YOU, UNCLE ZONKER!
OUTSTANDING! I DIDN'T KNOW YOU PLAYED FOOTBALL.
WELL, I DON'T, BUT LOOK AT THE DUMMIES WHO PLAY IT— HOW HARD COULD IT BE TO LEARN?
GOOD POINT. JUST DON'T GET ALL HUNG UP ON THE RULES.
FOOTBALL HAS RULES?
WELL, IT HAS REFS, AND THEY LIKE TO KEEP BUSY.

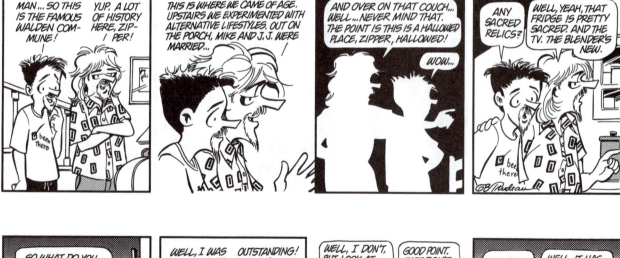

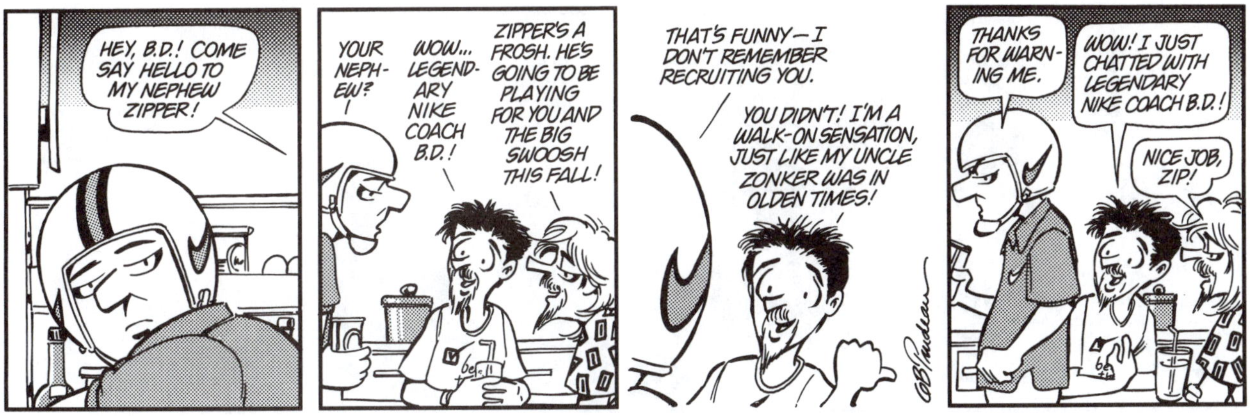

HEY, B.D.! COME SAY HELLO TO MY NEPHEW ZIPPER!
YOUR NEPHEW?
WOW... LEGENDARY NIKE COACH B.D.!
ZIPPER'S A FROSH. HE'S GOING TO BE PLAYING FOR YOU AND THE BIG SWOOSH THIS FALL!
THAT'S FUNNY — I DON'T REMEMBER RECRUITING YOU.
YOU DIDN'T! I'M A WALK-ON SENSATION, JUST LIKE MY UNCLE ZONKER WAS IN OLDEN TIMES!
THANKS FOR WARNING ME.
WOW! I JUST CHATTED WITH LEGENDARY NIKE COACH B.D.!
NICE JOB, ZIP!

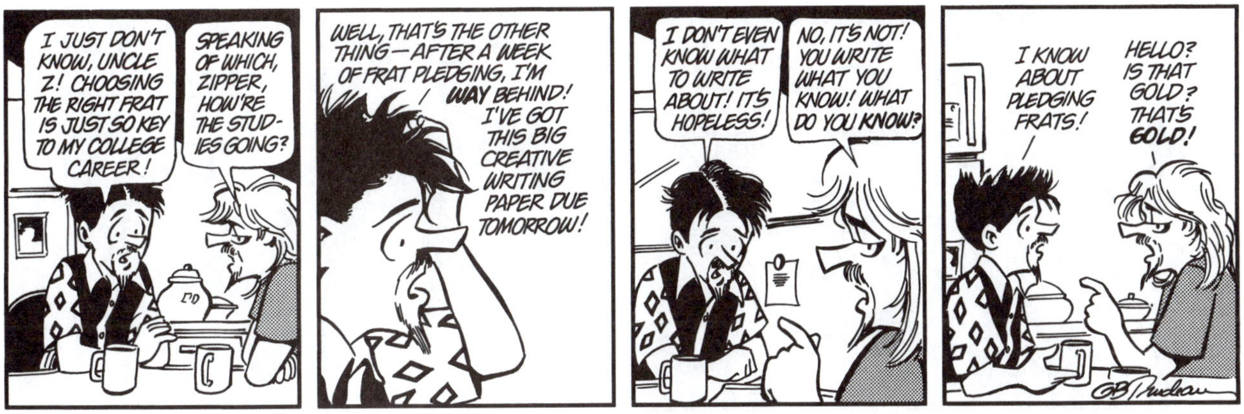

I JUST DON'T KNOW, UNCLE Z! CHOOSING THE RIGHT FRAT IS JUST SO KEY TO MY COLLEGE CAREER!
SPEAKING OF WHICH, ZIPPER, HOW'RE THE STUDIES GOING?
WELL, THAT'S THE OTHER THING — AFTER A WEEK OF FRAT PLEDGING, I'M **WAY** BEHIND! I'VE GOT THIS BIG CREATIVE WRITING PAPER DUE TOMORROW!
I DON'T EVEN KNOW WHAT TO WRITE ABOUT! IT'S HOPELESS!
NO, IT'S NOT! YOU WRITE WHAT YOU KNOW! WHAT DO YOU **KNOW**?
I KNOW ABOUT PLEDGING FRATS!
HELLO? IS THAT GOLD? THAT'S **GOLD!**

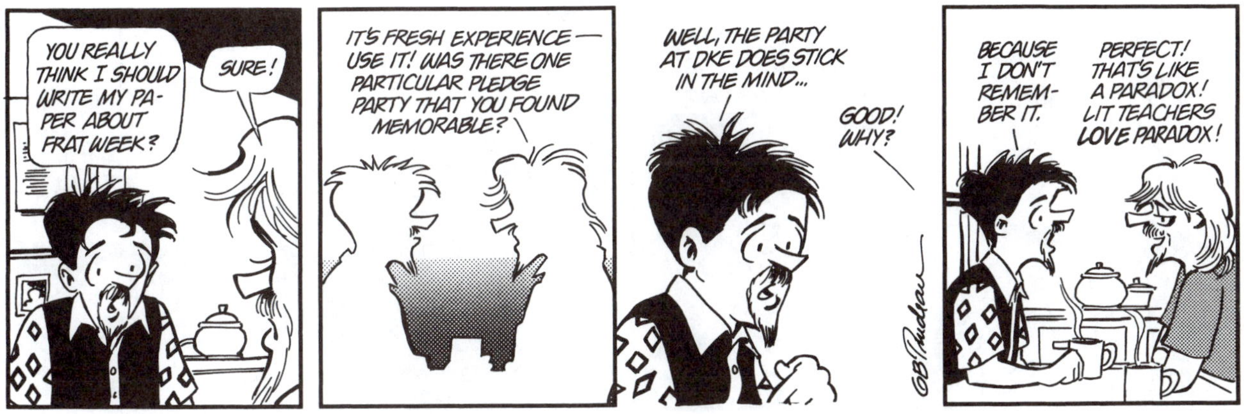

YOU REALLY THINK I SHOULD WRITE MY PAPER ABOUT FRAT WEEK?
SURE!
IT'S FRESH EXPERIENCE — USE IT! WAS THERE ONE PARTICULAR PLEDGE PARTY THAT YOU FOUND MEMORABLE?
WELL, THE PARTY AT DKE DOES STICK IN THE MIND...
GOOD! WHY?
BECAUSE I DON'T REMEMBER IT.
PERFECT! THAT'S LIKE A PARADOX! LIT TEACHERS **LOVE** PARADOX!

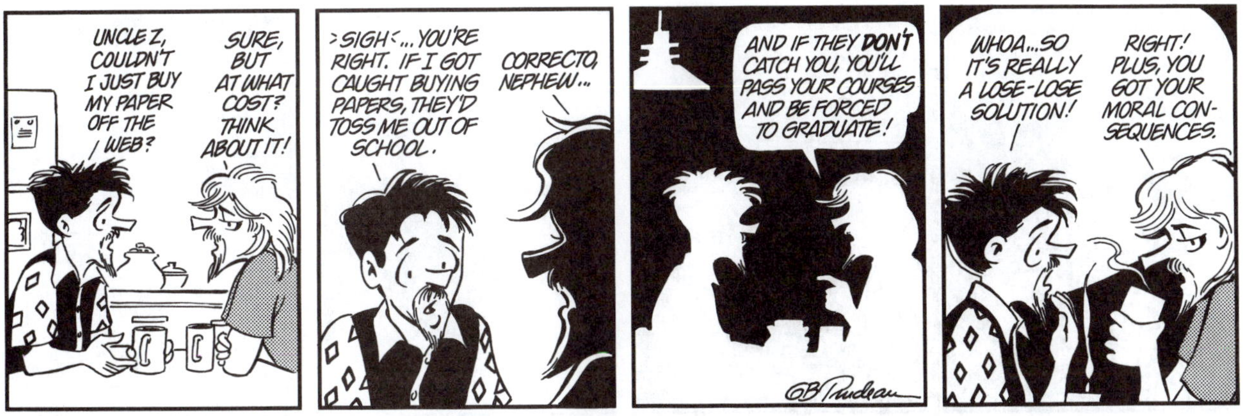

UNCLE Z, COULDN'T I JUST BUY MY PAPER OFF THE WEB?
SURE, BUT AT WHAT COST? THINK ABOUT IT!
>SIGH<... YOU'RE RIGHT. IF I GOT CAUGHT BUYING PAPERS, THEY'D TOSS ME OUT OF SCHOOL.
CORRECTO, NEPHEW...
AND IF THEY **DON'T** CATCH YOU, YOU'LL PASS YOUR COURSES AND BE FORCED TO GRADUATE!
WHOA... SO IT'S REALLY A LOSE-LOSE SOLUTION!
RIGHT! PLUS, YOU GOT YOUR MORAL CONSEQUENCES.

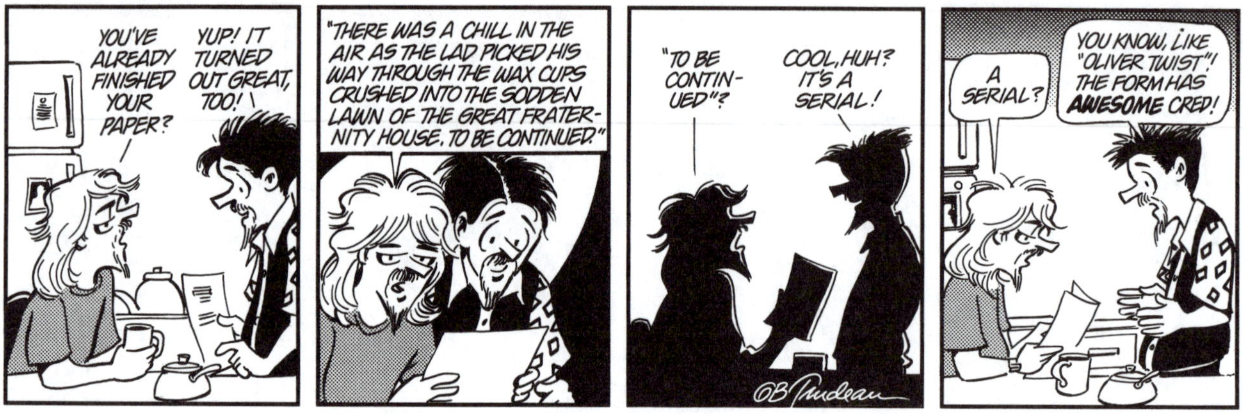
YOU'VE ALREADY FINISHED YOUR PAPER?
YUP! IT TURNED OUT GREAT, TOO!
"THERE WAS A CHILL IN THE AIR AS THE LAD PICKED HIS WAY THROUGH THE WAX CUPS CRUSHED INTO THE SODDEN LAWN OF THE GREAT FRATERNITY HOUSE. TO BE CONTINUED."
"TO BE CONTINUED"?
COOL, HUH? IT'S A SERIAL!
A SERIAL?
YOU KNOW, LIKE "OLIVER TWIST"! THE FORM HAS AWESOME CRED!
©B Trudeau

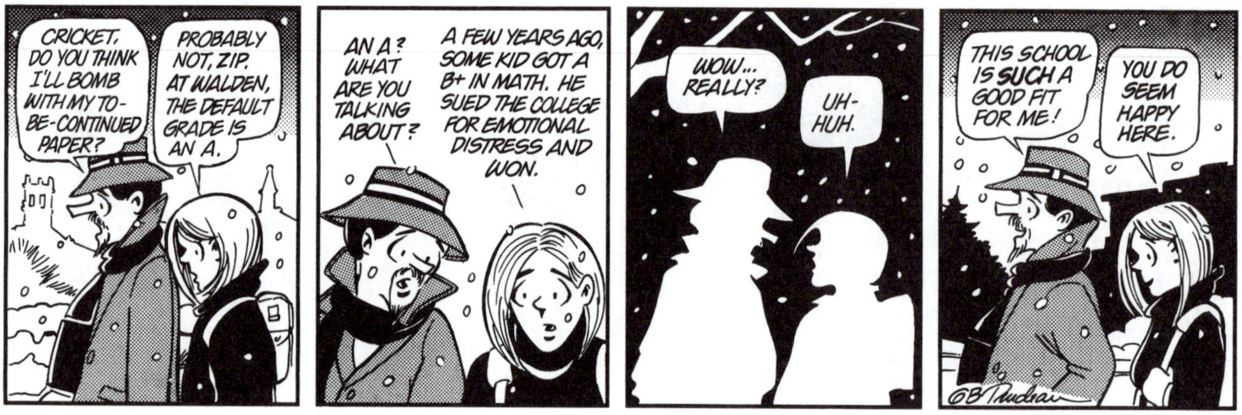
CRICKET, DO YOU THINK I'LL BOMB WITH MY TO-BE-CONTINUED PAPER?
PROBABLY NOT, ZIP. AT WALDEN, THE DEFAULT GRADE IS AN A.
AN A? WHAT ARE YOU TALKING ABOUT?
A FEW YEARS AGO, SOME KID GOT A B+ IN MATH. HE SUED THE COLLEGE FOR EMOTIONAL DISTRESS AND WON.
WOW... REALLY?
UH-HUH.
THIS SCHOOL IS SUCH A GOOD FIT FOR ME!
YOU DO SEEM HAPPY HERE.
©B Trudeau

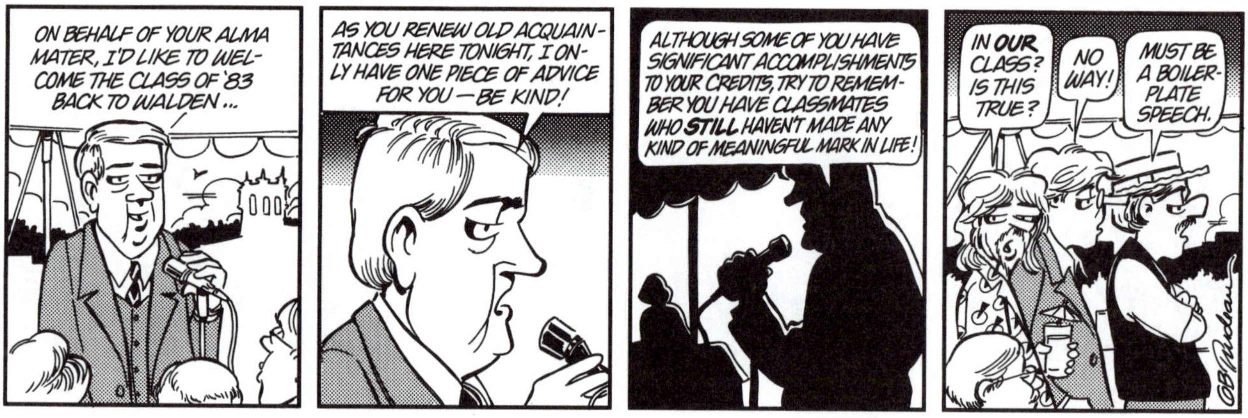
ON BEHALF OF YOUR ALMA MATER, I'D LIKE TO WELCOME THE CLASS OF '83 BACK TO WALDEN...
AS YOU RENEW OLD ACQUAINTANCES HERE TONIGHT, I ONLY HAVE ONE PIECE OF ADVICE FOR YOU — BE KIND!
ALTHOUGH SOME OF YOU HAVE SIGNIFICANT ACCOMPLISHMENTS TO YOUR CREDITS, TRY TO REMEMBER YOU HAVE CLASSMATES WHO STILL HAVEN'T MADE ANY KIND OF MEANINGFUL MARK IN LIFE!
IN OUR CLASS? IS THIS TRUE?
NO WAY!
MUST BE A BOILER-PLATE SPEECH.
©B Trudeau

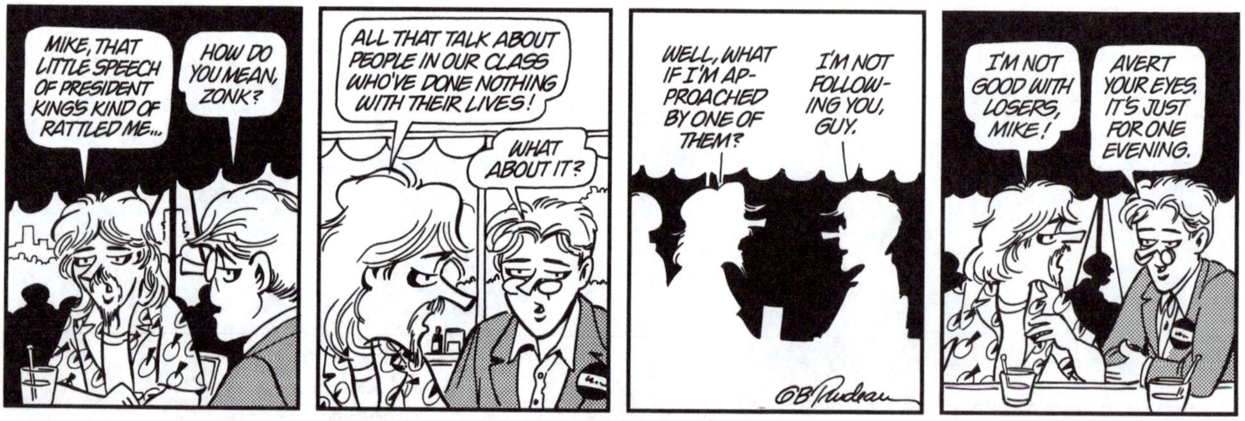
MIKE, THAT LITTLE SPEECH OF PRESIDENT KING'S KIND OF RATTLED ME...
HOW DO YOU MEAN, ZONK?
ALL THAT TALK ABOUT PEOPLE IN OUR CLASS WHO'VE DONE NOTHING WITH THEIR LIVES!
WHAT ABOUT IT?
WELL, WHAT IF I'M APPROACHED BY ONE OF THEM?
I'M NOT FOLLOWING YOU, GUY.
I'M NOT GOOD WITH LOSERS, MIKE!
AVERT YOUR EYES. IT'S JUST FOR ONE EVENING.
©B Trudeau

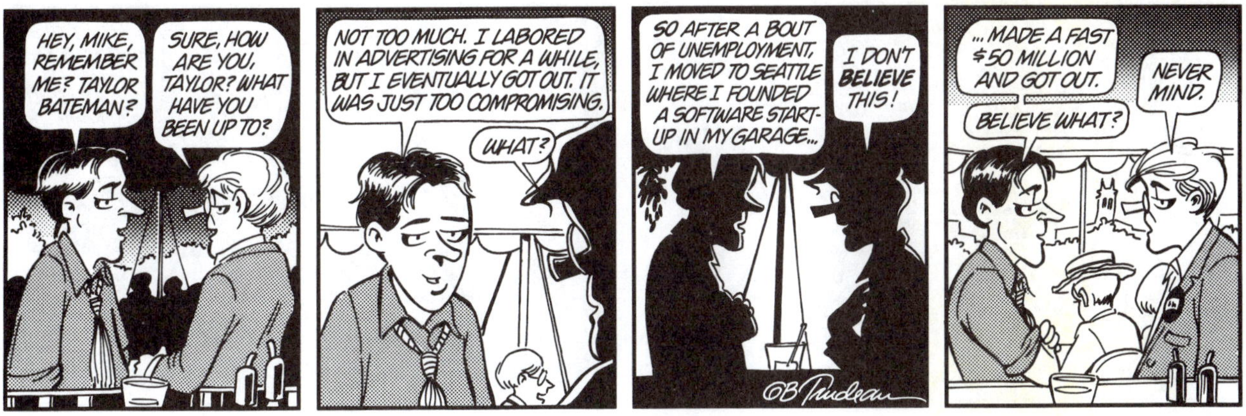
HEY, MIKE, REMEMBER ME? TAYLOR BATEMAN?
SURE, HOW ARE YOU, TAYLOR? WHAT HAVE YOU BEEN UP TO?
NOT TOO MUCH. I LABORED IN ADVERTISING FOR A WHILE, BUT I EVENTUALLY GOT OUT. IT WAS JUST TOO COMPROMISING.
WHAT?
SO AFTER A BOUT OF UNEMPLOYMENT, I MOVED TO SEATTLE WHERE I FOUNDED A SOFTWARE START-UP IN MY GARAGE...
I DON'T BELIEVE THIS!
... MADE A FAST $50 MILLION AND GOT OUT.
BELIEVE WHAT?
NEVER MIND.
GB Trudeau

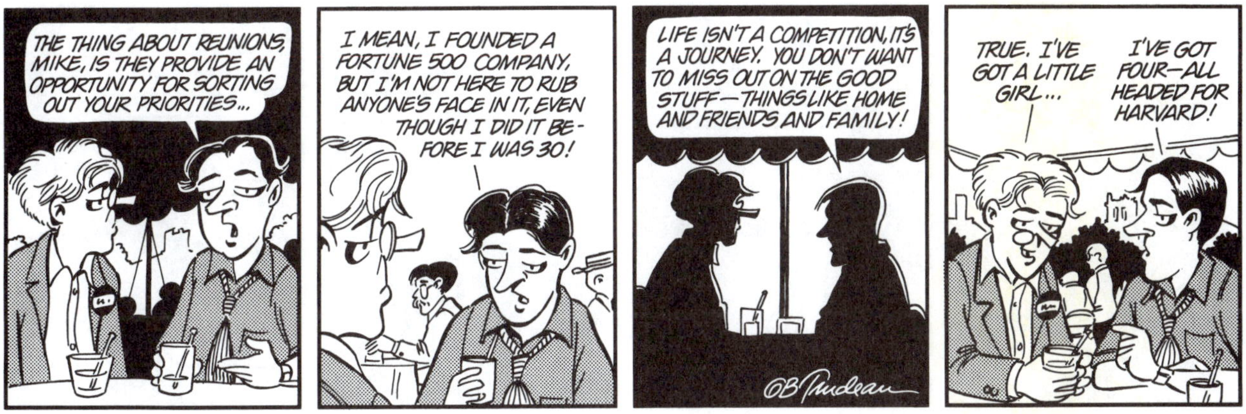
THE THING ABOUT REUNIONS, MIKE, IS THEY PROVIDE AN OPPORTUNITY FOR SORTING OUT YOUR PRIORITIES...
I MEAN, I FOUNDED A FORTUNE 500 COMPANY, BUT I'M NOT HERE TO RUB ANYONE'S FACE IN IT, EVEN THOUGH I DID IT BEFORE I WAS 30!
LIFE ISN'T A COMPETITION, IT'S A JOURNEY. YOU DON'T WANT TO MISS OUT ON THE GOOD STUFF—THINGS LIKE HOME AND FRIENDS AND FAMILY!
TRUE. I'VE GOT A LITTLE GIRL...
I'VE GOT FOUR—ALL HEADED FOR HARVARD!
GB Trudeau

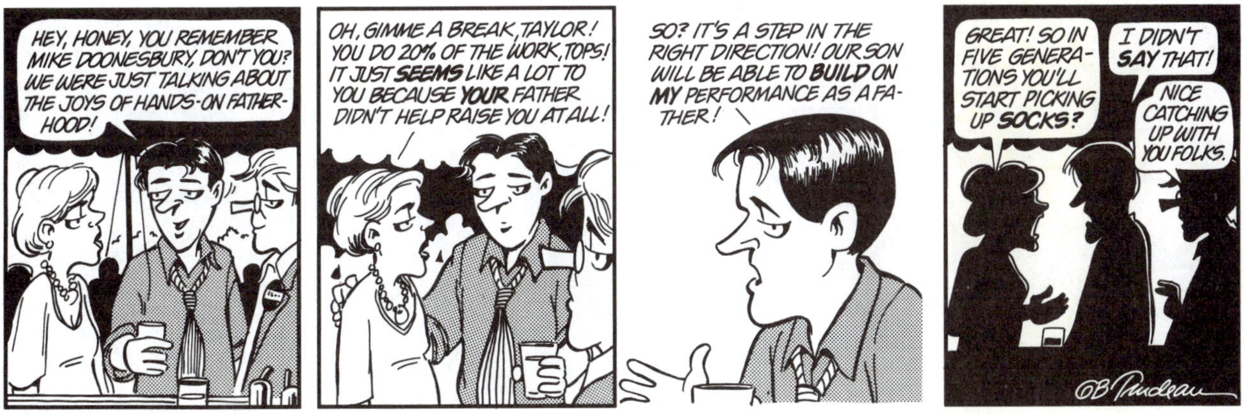
HEY, HONEY, YOU REMEMBER MIKE DOONESBURY, DON'T YOU? WE WERE JUST TALKING ABOUT THE JOYS OF HANDS-ON FATHERHOOD!
OH, GIMME A BREAK, TAYLOR! YOU DO 20% OF THE WORK, TOPS! IT JUST SEEMS LIKE A LOT TO YOU BECAUSE YOUR FATHER DIDN'T HELP RAISE YOU AT ALL!
SO? IT'S A STEP IN THE RIGHT DIRECTION! OUR SON WILL BE ABLE TO BUILD ON MY PERFORMANCE AS A FATHER!
GREAT! SO IN FIVE GENERATIONS YOU'LL START PICKING UP SOCKS?
I DIDN'T SAY THAT!
NICE CATCHING UP WITH YOU FOLKS.
GB Trudeau

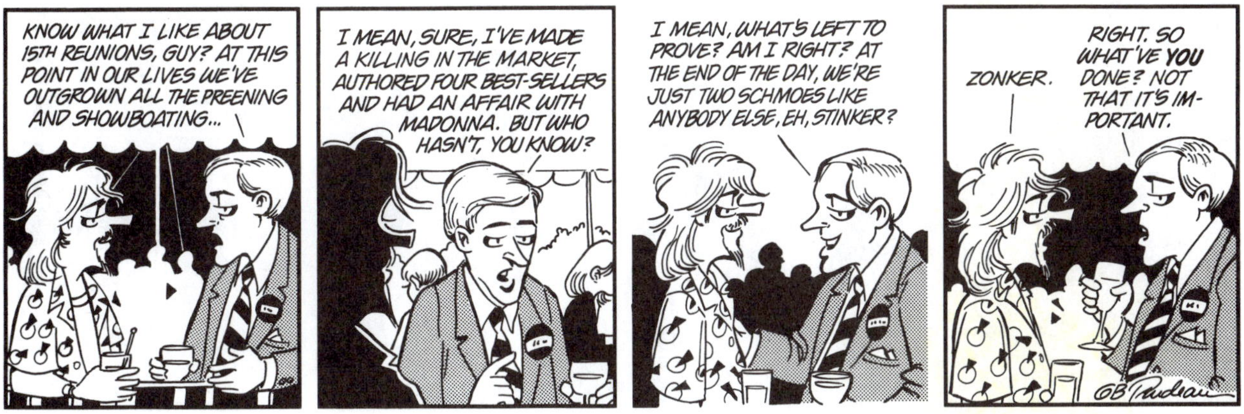
KNOW WHAT I LIKE ABOUT 15TH REUNIONS, GUY? AT THIS POINT IN OUR LIVES WE'VE OUTGROWN ALL THE PREENING AND SHOWBOATING...
I MEAN, SURE, I'VE MADE A KILLING IN THE MARKET, AUTHORED FOUR BEST-SELLERS AND HAD AN AFFAIR WITH MADONNA. BUT WHO HASN'T, YOU KNOW?
I MEAN, WHAT'S LEFT TO PROVE? AM I RIGHT? AT THE END OF THE DAY, WE'RE JUST TWO SCHMOES LIKE ANYBODY ELSE, EH, STINKER?
ZONKER.
RIGHT. SO WHAT'VE YOU DONE? NOT THAT IT'S IMPORTANT.
GB Trudeau

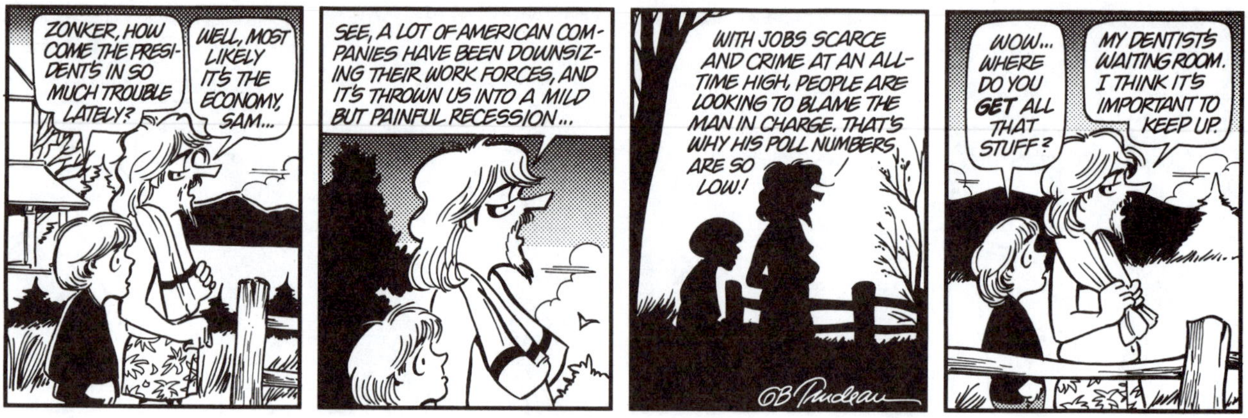
ZONKER, HOW COME THE PRESIDENT'S IN SO MUCH TROUBLE LATELY?
WELL, MOST LIKELY IT'S THE ECONOMY, SAM...
SEE, A LOT OF AMERICAN COMPANIES HAVE BEEN DOWNSIZING THEIR WORK FORCES, AND IT'S THROWN US INTO A MILD BUT PAINFUL RECESSION...
WITH JOBS SCARCE AND CRIME AT AN ALL-TIME HIGH, PEOPLE ARE LOOKING TO BLAME THE MAN IN CHARGE. THAT'S WHY HIS POLL NUMBERS ARE SO LOW!
WOW... WHERE DO YOU GET ALL THAT STUFF?
MY DENTIST'S WAITING ROOM. I THINK IT'S IMPORTANT TO KEEP UP.
GB Trudeau

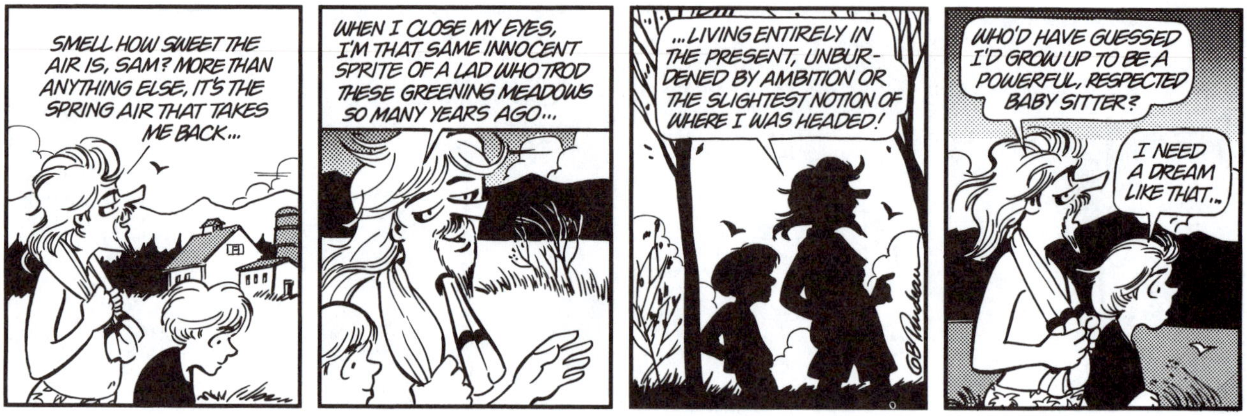
SMELL HOW SWEET THE AIR IS, SAM? MORE THAN ANYTHING ELSE, IT'S THE SPRING AIR THAT TAKES ME BACK...
WHEN I CLOSE MY EYES, I'M THAT SAME INNOCENT SPRITE OF A LAD WHO TROD THESE GREENING MEADOWS SO MANY YEARS AGO...
...LIVING ENTIRELY IN THE PRESENT, UNBURDENED BY AMBITION OR THE SLIGHTEST NOTION OF WHERE I WAS HEADED!
GB Trudeau
WHO'D HAVE GUESSED I'D GROW UP TO BE A POWERFUL, RESPECTED BABY SITTER?
I NEED A DREAM LIKE THAT...

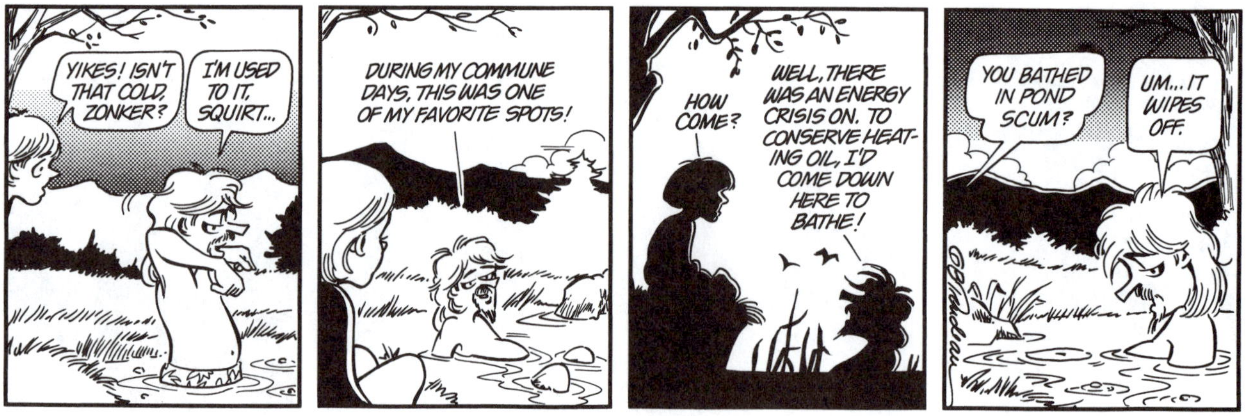
YIKES! ISN'T THAT COLD, ZONKER?
I'M USED TO IT, SQUIRT...
DURING MY COMMUNE DAYS, THIS WAS ONE OF MY FAVORITE SPOTS!
HOW COME?
WELL, THERE WAS AN ENERGY CRISIS ON. TO CONSERVE HEATING OIL, I'D COME DOWN HERE TO BATHE!
YOU BATHED IN POND SCUM?
UM... IT WIPES OFF.
GB Trudeau

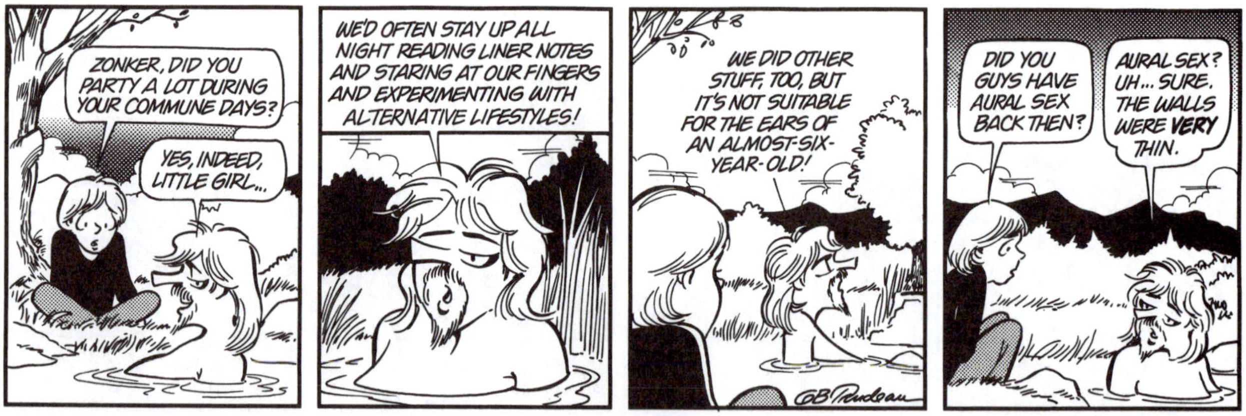
ZONKER, DID YOU PARTY A LOT DURING YOUR COMMUNE DAYS?
YES, INDEED, LITTLE GIRL...
WE'D OFTEN STAY UP ALL NIGHT READING LINER NOTES AND STARING AT OUR FINGERS AND EXPERIMENTING WITH ALTERNATIVE LIFESTYLES!
WE DID OTHER STUFF, TOO, BUT IT'S NOT SUITABLE FOR THE EARS OF AN ALMOST-SIX-YEAR-OLD!
GB Trudeau
DID YOU GUYS HAVE AURAL SEX BACK THEN?
AURAL SEX? UH... SURE. THE WALLS WERE VERY THIN.

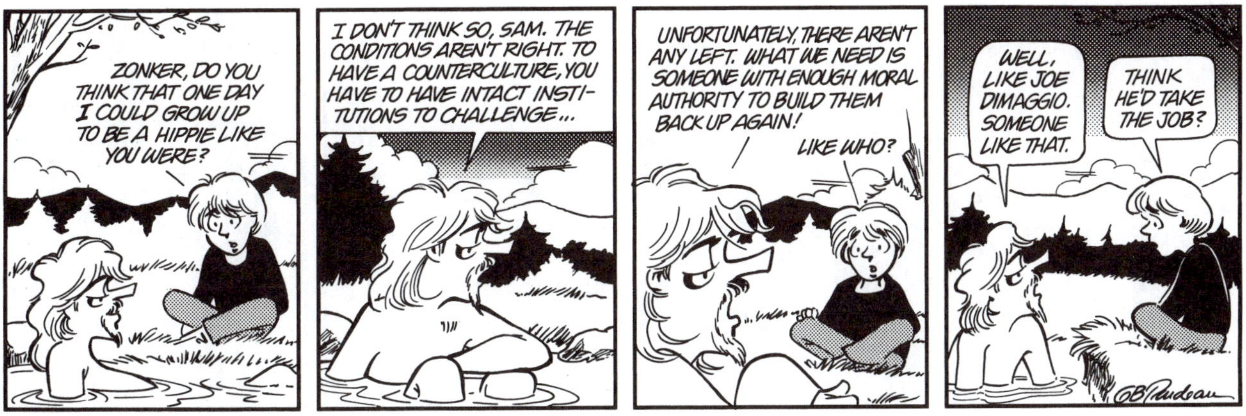
ZONKER, DO YOU THINK THAT ONE DAY I COULD GROW UP TO BE A HIPPIE LIKE YOU WERE?
I DON'T THINK SO, SAM. THE CONDITIONS AREN'T RIGHT. TO HAVE A COUNTERCULTURE, YOU HAVE TO HAVE INTACT INSTITUTIONS TO CHALLENGE...
UNFORTUNATELY, THERE AREN'T ANY LEFT. WHAT WE NEED IS SOMEONE WITH ENOUGH MORAL AUTHORITY TO BUILD THEM BACK UP AGAIN!
LIKE WHO?
WELL, LIKE JOE DIMAGGIO. SOMEONE LIKE THAT.
THINK HE'D TAKE THE JOB?
©B Trudeau

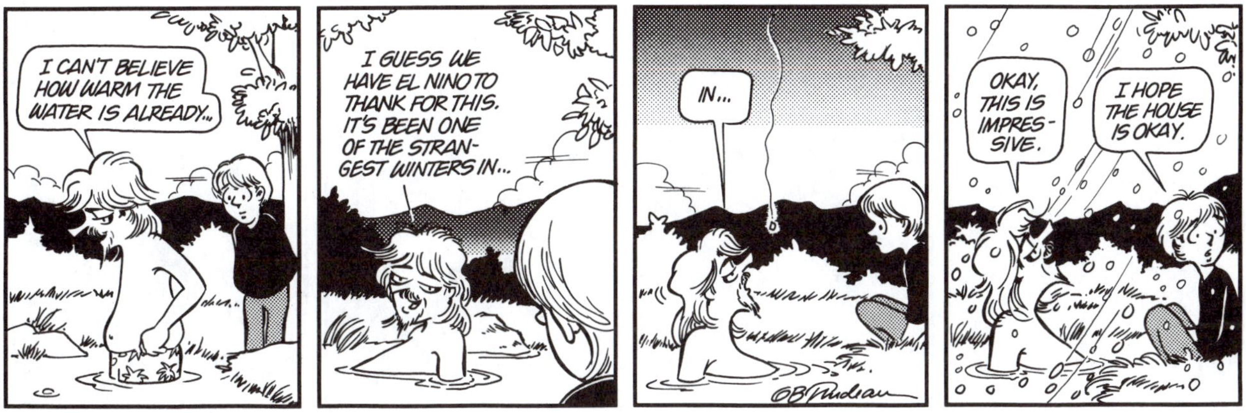
I CAN'T BELIEVE HOW WARM THE WATER IS ALREADY...
I GUESS WE HAVE EL NINO TO THANK FOR THIS. IT'S BEEN ONE OF THE STRANGEST WINTERS IN...
IN...
©B Trudeau
OKAY, THIS IS IMPRESSIVE.
I HOPE THE HOUSE IS OKAY.

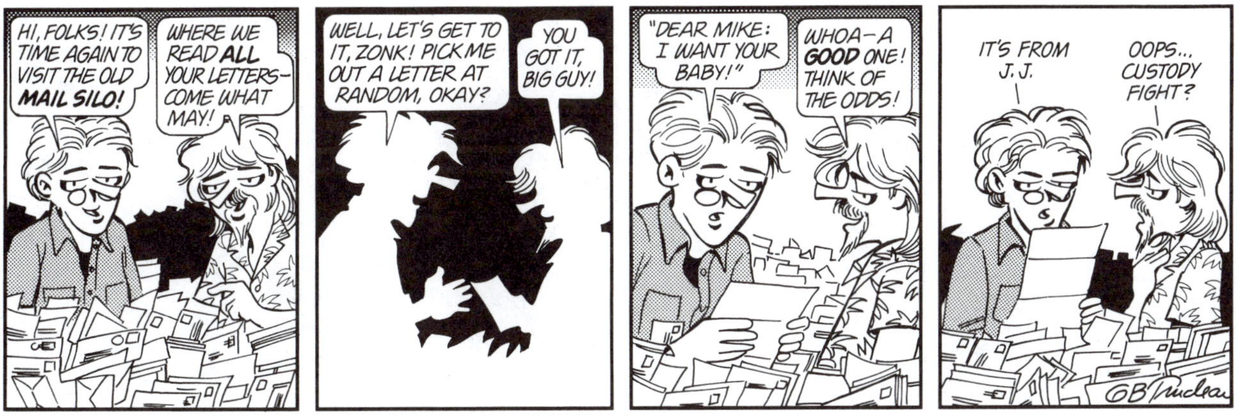
HI, FOLKS! IT'S TIME AGAIN TO VISIT THE OLD MAIL SILO!
WHERE WE READ ALL YOUR LETTERS—COME WHAT MAY!
WELL, LET'S GET TO IT, ZONK! PICK ME OUT A LETTER AT RANDOM, OKAY?
YOU GOT IT, BIG GUY!
"DEAR MIKE: I WANT YOUR BABY!"
WHOA—A GOOD ONE! THINK OF THE ODDS!
IT'S FROM J. J.
OOPS... CUSTODY FIGHT?
©B Trudeau

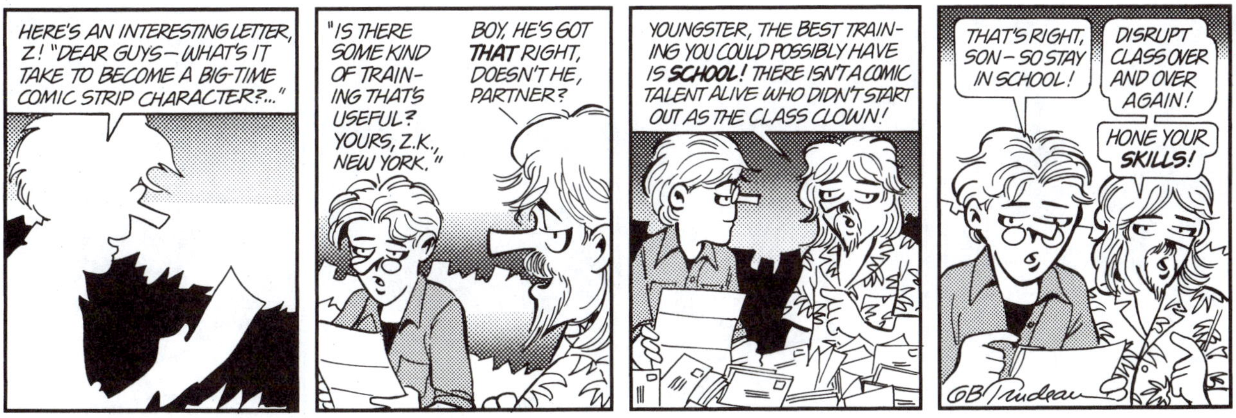
HERE'S AN INTERESTING LETTER, Z! "DEAR GUYS—WHAT'S IT TAKE TO BECOME A BIG-TIME COMIC STRIP CHARACTER?..."
"IS THERE SOME KIND OF TRAINING THAT'S USEFUL? YOURS, Z.K., NEW YORK."
BOY, HE'S GOT THAT RIGHT, DOESN'T HE, PARTNER?
YOUNGSTER, THE BEST TRAINING YOU COULD POSSIBLY HAVE IS SCHOOL! THERE ISN'T A COMIC TALENT ALIVE WHO DIDN'T START OUT AS THE CLASS CLOWN!
THAT'S RIGHT, SON—SO STAY IN SCHOOL!
DISRUPT CLASS OVER AND OVER AGAIN!
HONE YOUR SKILLS!
©B Trudeau

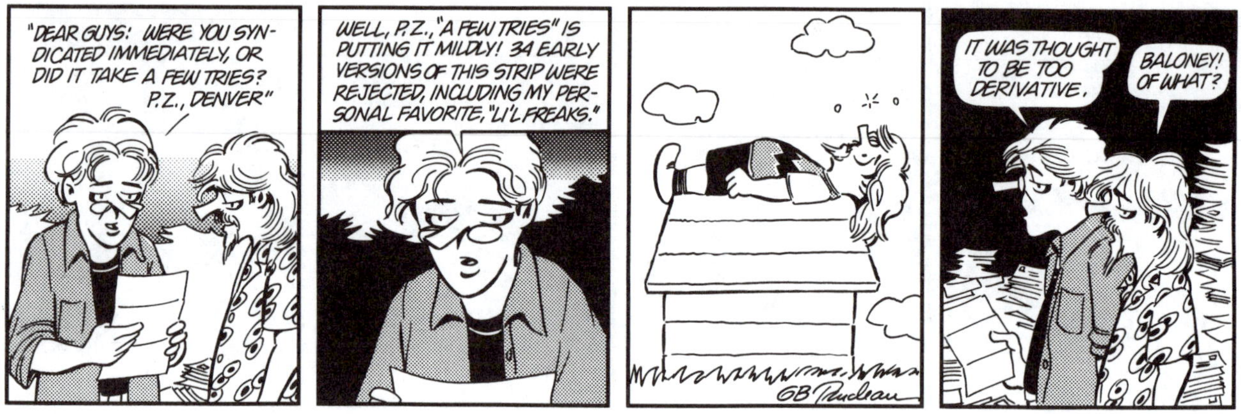
"DEAR GUYS: WERE YOU SYNDICATED IMMEDIATELY, OR DID IT TAKE A FEW TRIES? P.Z., DENVER"
WELL, P.Z., "A FEW TRIES" IS PUTTING IT MILDLY! 34 EARLY VERSIONS OF THIS STRIP WERE REJECTED, INCLUDING MY PERSONAL FAVORITE, "LI'L FREAKS."
GB Trudeau
IT WAS THOUGHT TO BE TOO DERIVATIVE.
BALONEY! OF WHAT?

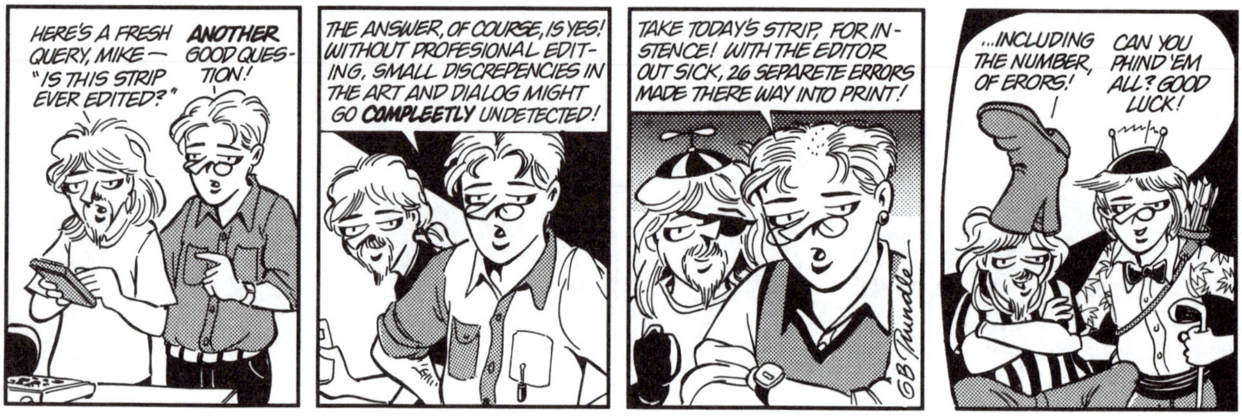
HERE'S A FRESH QUERY, MIKE— "IS THIS STRIP EVER EDITED?"
ANOTHER GOOD QUESTION!
THE ANSWER, OF COURSE, IS YES! WITHOUT PROFESIONAL EDITING, SMALL DISCREPENCIES IN THE ART AND DIALOG MIGHT GO **COMPLEETLY** UNDETECTED!
TAKE TODAY'S STRIP, FOR INSTENCE! WITH THE EDITOR OUT SICK, 26 SEPARETE ERRORS MADE THERE WAY INTO PRINT!
GB Trudeau
...INCLUDING THE NUMBER OF ERORS!
CAN YOU PHIND 'EM ALL? GOOD LUCK!

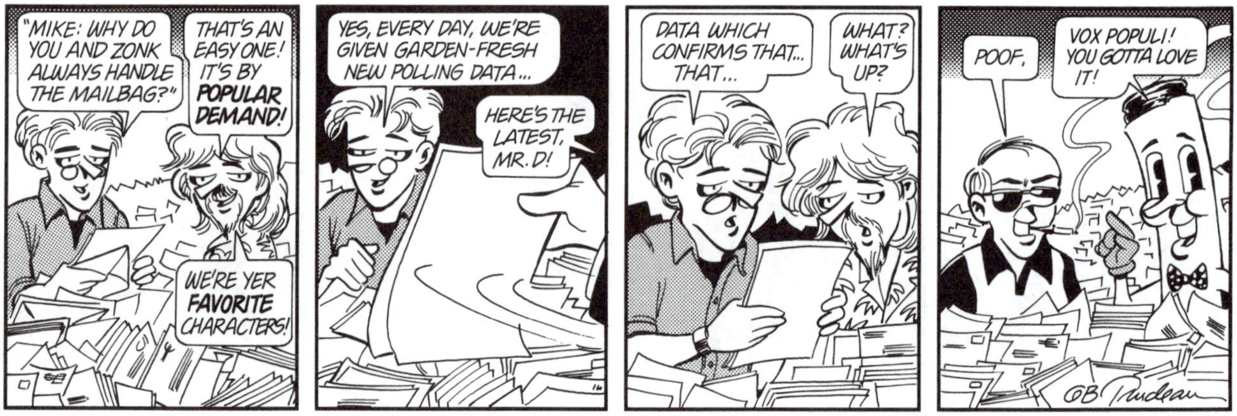
"MIKE: WHY DO YOU AND ZONK ALWAYS HANDLE THE MAILBAG?"
THAT'S AN EASY ONE! IT'S BY **POPULAR DEMAND!**
WE'RE YER **FAVORITE** CHARACTERS!
YES, EVERY DAY, WE'RE GIVEN GARDEN-FRESH NEW POLLING DATA...
HERE'S THE LATEST, MR. D!
DATA WHICH CONFIRMS THAT... THAT...
WHAT? WHAT'S UP?
POOF.
VOX POPULI! YOU GOTTA LOVE IT!
GB Trudeau

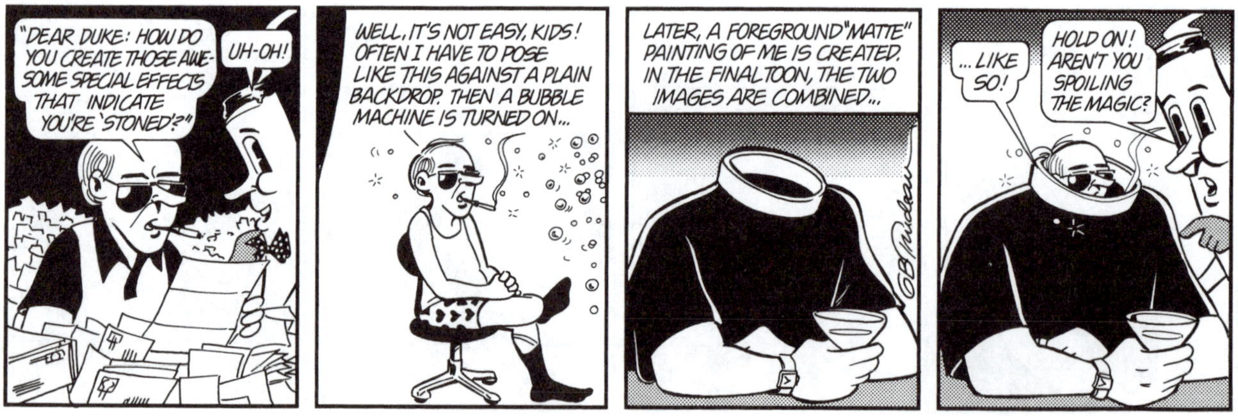
"DEAR DUKE: HOW DO YOU CREATE THOSE AWESOME SPECIAL EFFECTS THAT INDICATE YOU'RE 'STONED'?"
UH-OH!
WELL, IT'S NOT EASY, KIDS! OFTEN I HAVE TO POSE LIKE THIS AGAINST A PLAIN BACKDROP. THEN A BUBBLE MACHINE IS TURNED ON...
LATER, A FOREGROUND "MATTE" PAINTING OF ME IS CREATED. IN THE FINAL TOON, THE TWO IMAGES ARE COMBINED...
GB Trudeau
...LIKE SO!
HOLD ON! AREN'T YOU SPOILING THE MAGIC?

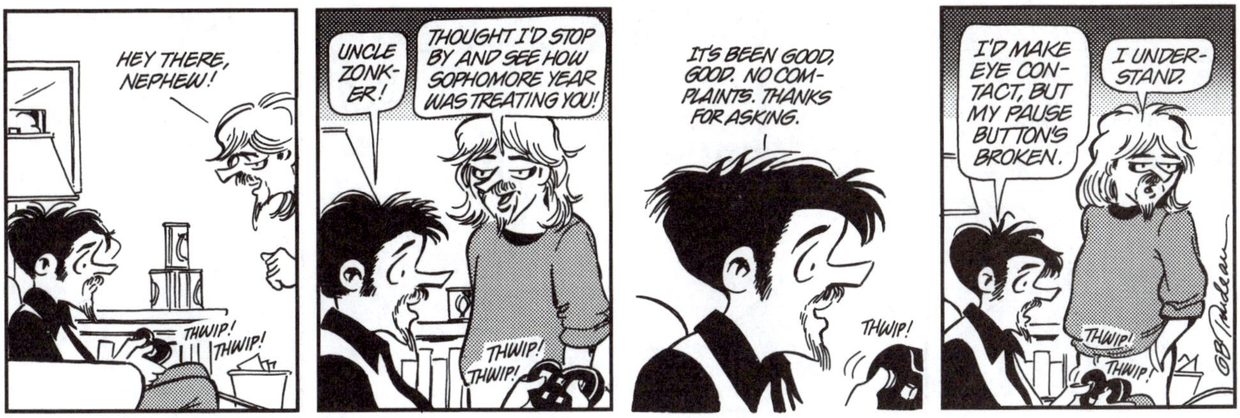
HEY THERE, NEPHEW!
THWIP! THWIP!
UNCLE ZONKER!
THOUGHT I'D STOP BY AND SEE HOW SOPHOMORE YEAR WAS TREATING YOU!
THWIP! THWIP!
IT'S BEEN GOOD, GOOD. NO COMPLAINTS. THANKS FOR ASKING.
THWIP!
I'D MAKE EYE CONTACT, BUT MY PAUSE BUTTON'S BROKEN.
I UNDERSTAND.
THWIP! THWIP!

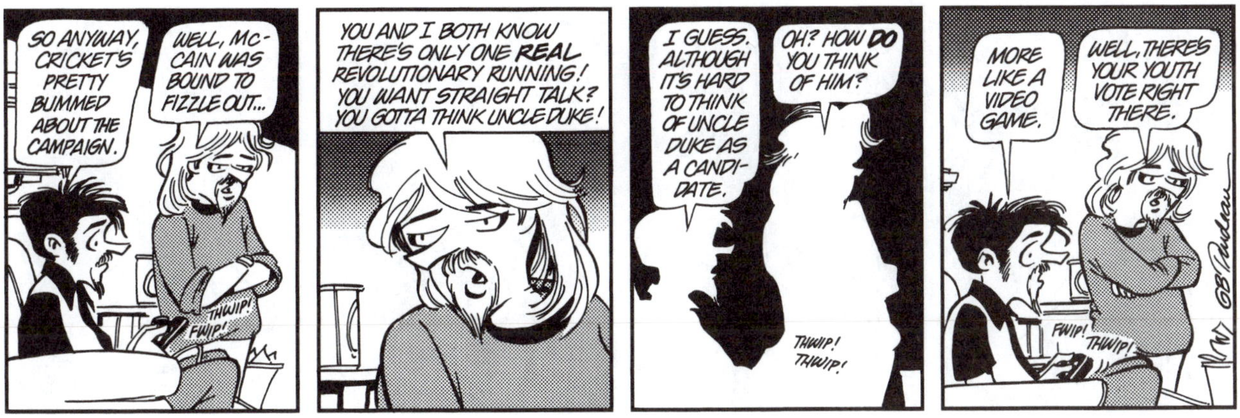
SO ANYWAY, CRICKET'S PRETTY BUMMED ABOUT THE CAMPAIGN.
WELL, McCAIN WAS BOUND TO FIZZLE OUT...
THWIP! FWIP!
YOU AND I BOTH KNOW THERE'S ONLY ONE **REAL** REVOLUTIONARY RUNNING! YOU WANT STRAIGHT TALK? YOU GOTTA THINK UNCLE DUKE!
I GUESS. ALTHOUGH IT'S HARD TO THINK OF UNCLE DUKE AS A CANDIDATE.
OH? HOW **DO** YOU THINK OF HIM?
THWIP! THWIP!
MORE LIKE A VIDEO GAME.
WELL, THERE'S YOUR YOUTH VOTE RIGHT THERE.
FWIP! THWIP!

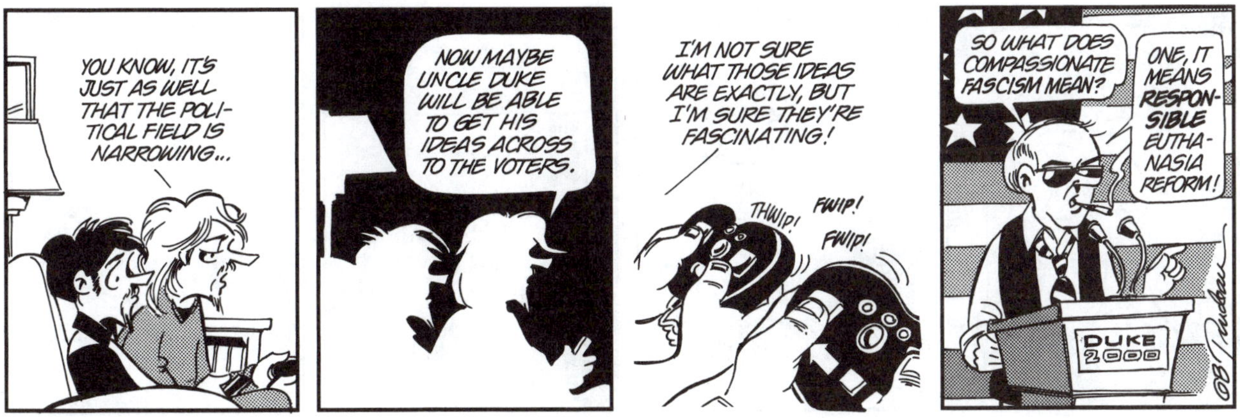
YOU KNOW, IT'S JUST AS WELL THAT THE POLITICAL FIELD IS NARROWING...
NOW MAYBE UNCLE DUKE WILL BE ABLE TO GET HIS IDEAS ACROSS TO THE VOTERS.
I'M NOT SURE WHAT THOSE IDEAS ARE EXACTLY, BUT I'M SURE THEY'RE FASCINATING!
THWIP! FWIP! FWIP!
SO WHAT DOES COMPASSIONATE FASCISM MEAN?
ONE, IT MEANS **RESPONSIBLE** EUTHANASIA REFORM!
DUKE 2000

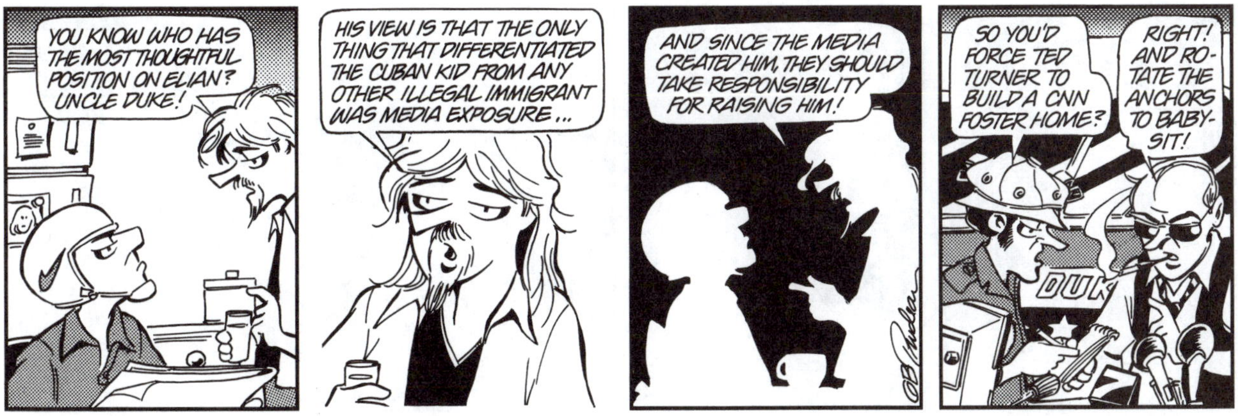
YOU KNOW WHO HAS THE MOST THOUGHTFUL POSITION ON ELIAN? UNCLE DUKE!
HIS VIEW IS THAT THE ONLY THING THAT DIFFERENTIATED THE CUBAN KID FROM ANY OTHER ILLEGAL IMMIGRANT WAS MEDIA EXPOSURE...
AND SINCE THE MEDIA CREATED HIM, THEY SHOULD TAKE RESPONSIBILITY FOR RAISING HIM!
SO YOU'D FORCE TED TURNER TO BUILD A CNN FOSTER HOME?
RIGHT! AND ROTATE THE ANCHORS TO BABY-SIT!

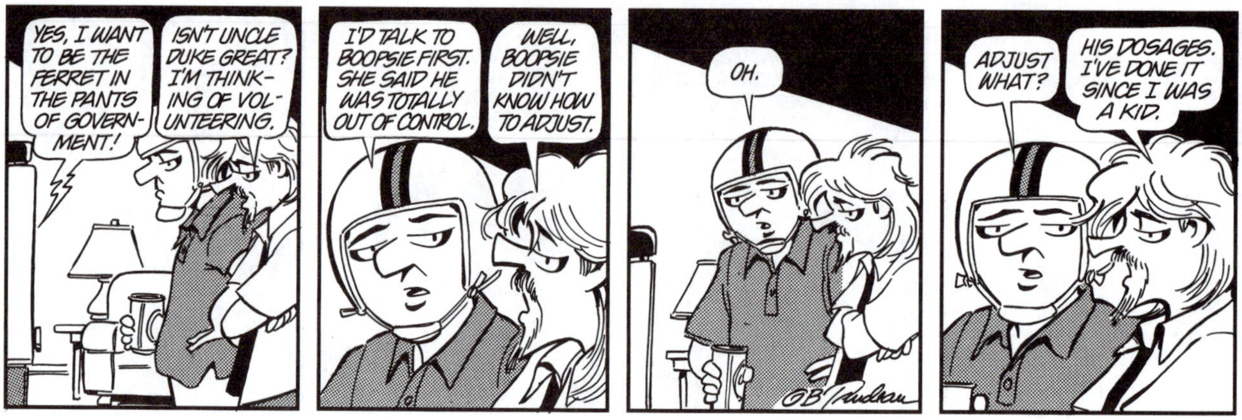
YES, I WANT TO BE THE FERRET IN THE PANTS OF GOVERNMENT!
ISN'T UNCLE DUKE GREAT? I'M THINKING OF VOLUNTEERING.
I'D TALK TO BOOPSIE FIRST. SHE SAID HE WAS TOTALLY OUT OF CONTROL.
WELL, BOOPSIE DIDN'T KNOW HOW TO ADJUST.
OH.
ADJUST WHAT?
HIS DOSAGES. I'VE DONE IT SINCE I WAS A KID.

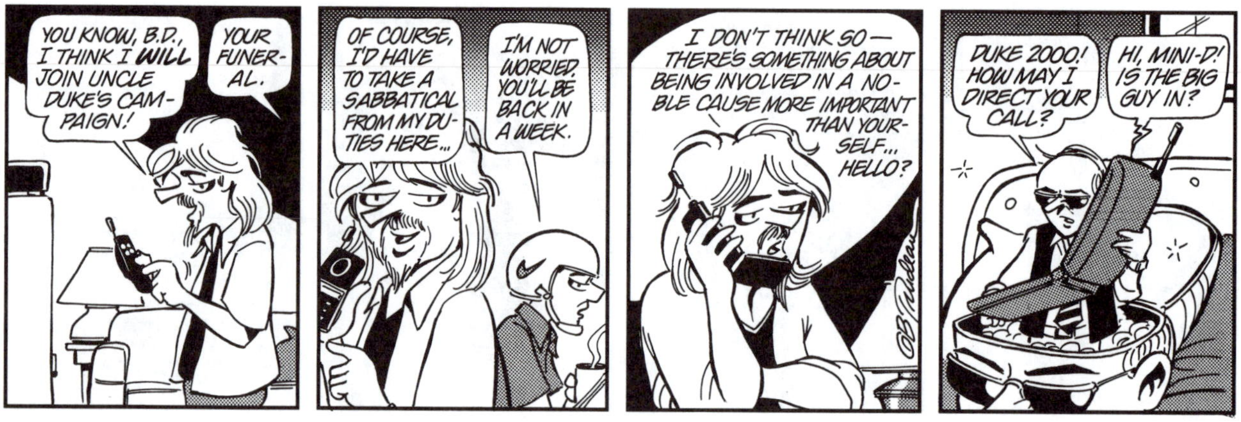
YOU KNOW, B.D., I THINK I **WILL** JOIN UNCLE DUKE'S CAMPAIGN!
YOUR FUNERAL.
OF COURSE, I'D HAVE TO TAKE A SABBATICAL FROM MY DUTIES HERE...
I'M NOT WORRIED. YOU'LL BE BACK IN A WEEK.
I DON'T THINK SO — THERE'S SOMETHING ABOUT BEING INVOLVED IN A NOBLE CAUSE MORE IMPORTANT THAN YOURSELF... HELLO?
DUKE 2000! HOW MAY I DIRECT YOUR CALL?
HI, MINI-D! IS THE BIG GUY IN?

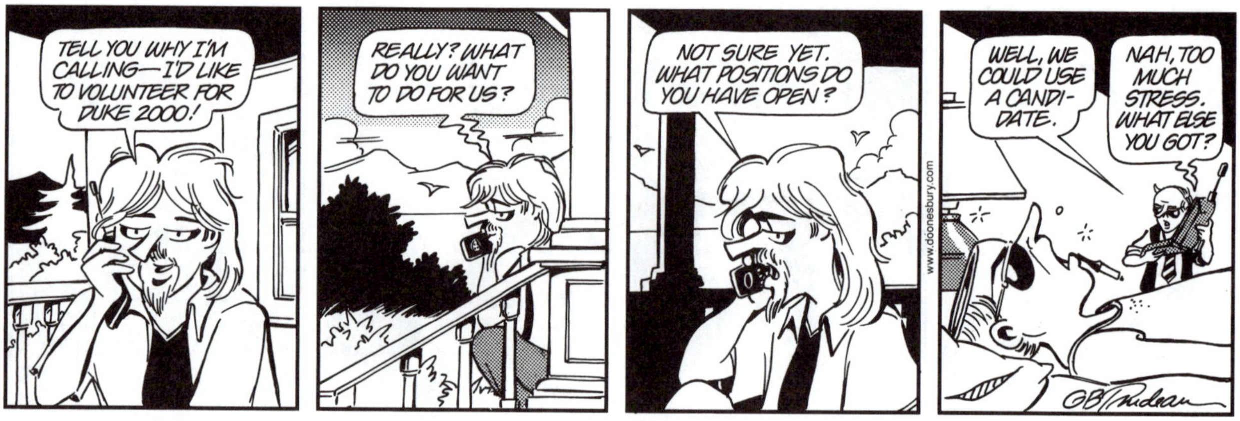
TELL YOU WHY I'M CALLING — I'D LIKE TO VOLUNTEER FOR DUKE 2000!
REALLY? WHAT DO YOU WANT TO DO FOR US?
NOT SURE YET. WHAT POSITIONS DO YOU HAVE OPEN?
www.doonesbury.com
WELL, WE COULD USE A CANDIDATE.
NAH, TOO MUCH STRESS. WHAT ELSE YOU GOT?

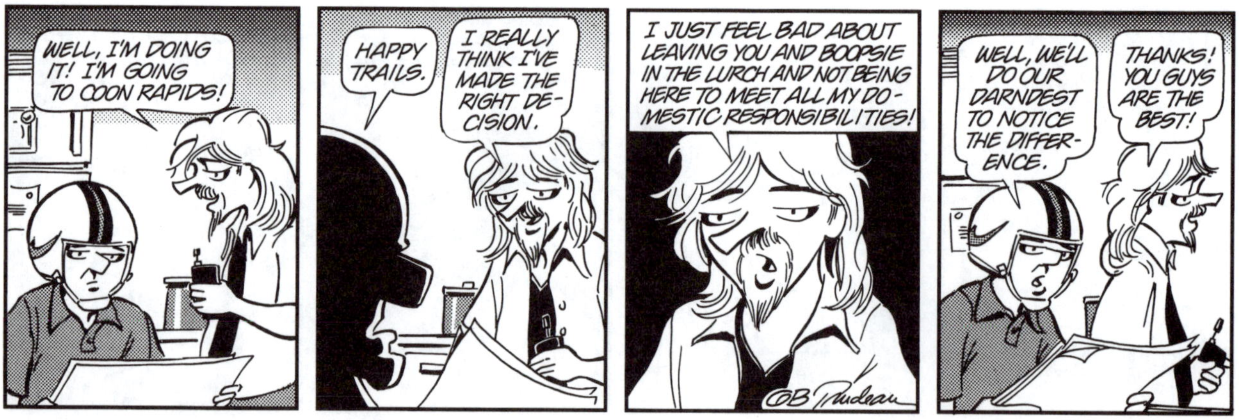
WELL, I'M DOING IT! I'M GOING TO COON RAPIDS!
HAPPY TRAILS.
I REALLY THINK I'VE MADE THE RIGHT DECISION.
I JUST FEEL BAD ABOUT LEAVING YOU AND BOOPSIE IN THE LURCH AND NOT BEING HERE TO MEET ALL MY DOMESTIC RESPONSIBILITIES!
WELL, WE'LL DO OUR DARNDEST TO NOTICE THE DIFFERENCE.
THANKS! YOU GUYS ARE THE BEST!

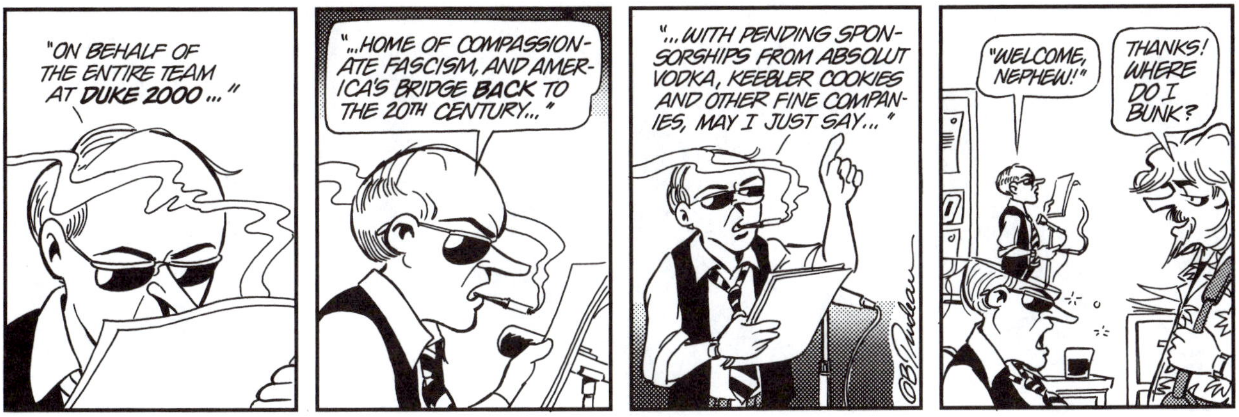
"ON BEHALF OF THE ENTIRE TEAM AT **DUKE 2000** ..."
"...HOME OF COMPASSIONATE FASCISM, AND AMERICA'S BRIDGE **BACK** TO THE 20TH CENTURY..."
"...WITH PENDING SPONSORSHIPS FROM ABSOLUT VODKA, KEEBLER COOKIES AND OTHER FINE COMPANIES, MAY I JUST SAY..."
"WELCOME, NEPHEW!"
THANKS! WHERE DO I BUNK?

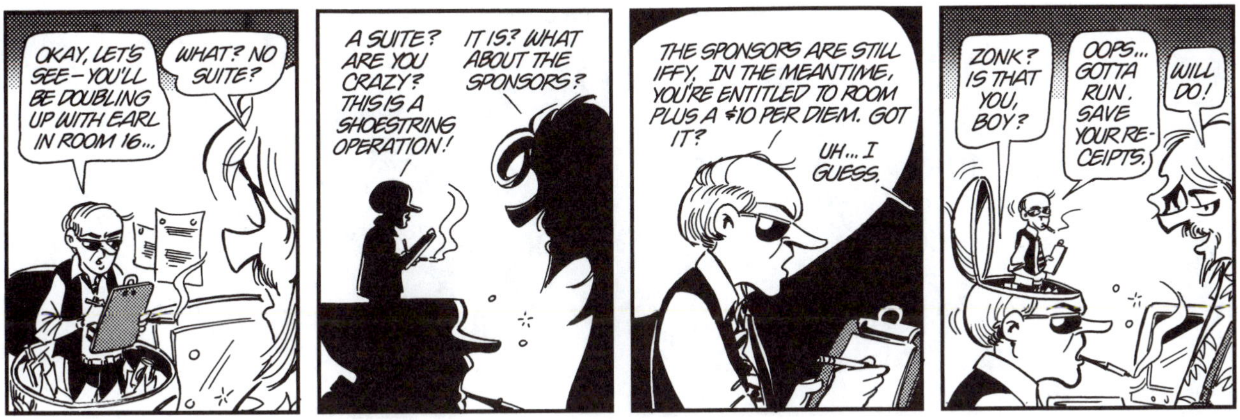
OKAY, LET'S SEE–YOU'LL BE DOUBLING UP WITH EARL IN ROOM 16...
WHAT? NO SUITE?
A SUITE? ARE YOU CRAZY? THIS IS A SHOESTRING OPERATION!
IT IS? WHAT ABOUT THE SPONSORS?
THE SPONSORS ARE STILL IFFY. IN THE MEANTIME, YOU'RE ENTITLED TO ROOM PLUS A $10 PER DIEM. GOT IT?
UH... I GUESS.
ZONK? IS THAT YOU, BOY?
OOPS... GOTTA RUN. SAVE YOUR RECEIPTS.
WILL DO!

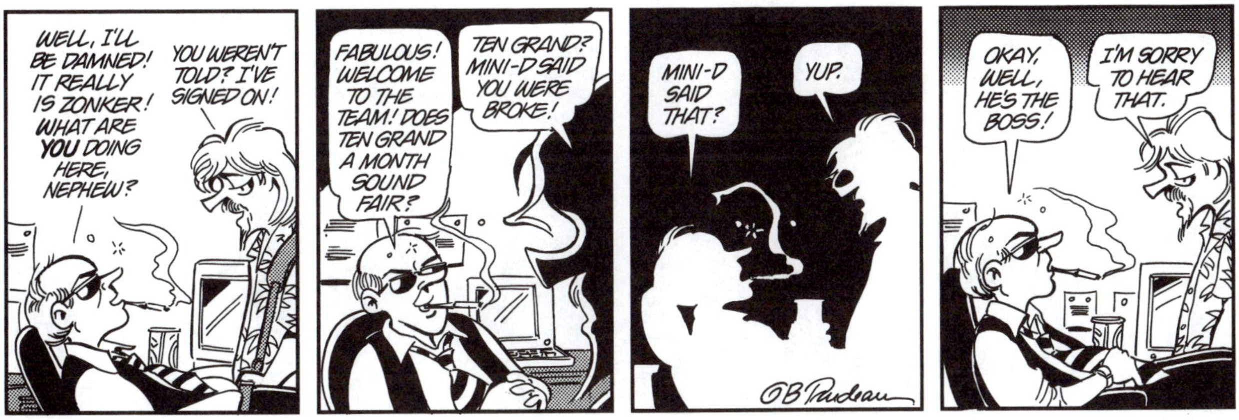
WELL, I'LL BE DAMNED! IT REALLY IS ZONKER! WHAT ARE **YOU** DOING HERE, NEPHEW?
YOU WEREN'T TOLD? I'VE SIGNED ON!
FABULOUS! WELCOME TO THE TEAM! DOES TEN GRAND A MONTH SOUND FAIR?
TEN GRAND? MINI-D SAID YOU WERE BROKE!
MINI-D SAID THAT?
YUP.
OKAY, WELL, HE'S THE BOSS!
I'M SORRY TO HEAR THAT.

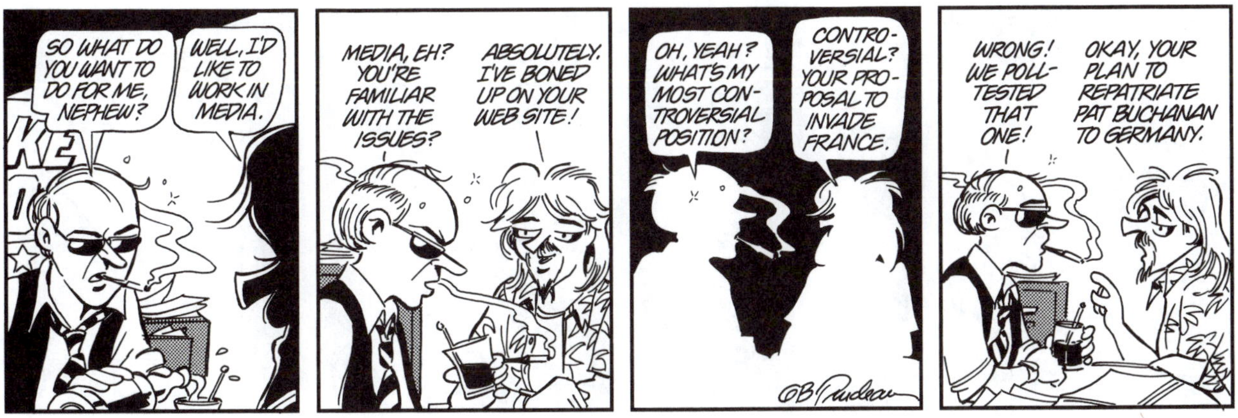
SO WHAT DO YOU WANT TO DO FOR ME, NEPHEW?
WELL, I'D LIKE TO WORK IN MEDIA.
MEDIA, EH? YOU'RE FAMILIAR WITH THE ISSUES?
ABSOLUTELY. I'VE BONED UP ON YOUR WEB SITE!
OH, YEAH? WHAT'S MY MOST CONTROVERSIAL POSITION?
CONTROVERSIAL? YOUR PROPOSAL TO INVADE FRANCE.
WRONG! WE POLL-TESTED THAT ONE!
OKAY, YOUR PLAN TO REPATRIATE PAT BUCHANAN TO GERMANY.

Panel 1: THAT SETTLES IT, NEPHEW—YOU'RE MY NEW SPIN DOCTOR! / UM...SIR? HE HASN'T MUCH EXPERIENCE IN THAT AREA.

Panel 2: IT'S NOT ABOUT EXPERIENCE, HONEY. IT'S ABOUT TRUST— THE BOY IS FAMILY!

Panel 3: ZONKER'S THE ONLY KIN I'VE GOT, THE ONLY ONE I CAN COUNT ON! WHEN THE GOING GETS TOUGH, BLOOD MEANS EVERYTHING, RIGHT, KID?

Panel 4: RIGHT. ALTHOUGH WE'RE NOT ACTUALLY RELATED. / YEAH, I THINK I WON HIM IN A POKER GAME.

Panel 5: HEY— YOU EARL? / WHO WANTS TO KNOW?

Panel 6: ZONKER HARRIS, I'M THE NEW SPIN DOCTOR! / YOU'RE HERE TO HELP DAD?

Panel 7: YUP. AND WE'RE BUNKING TOGETHER. APPARENTLY, MONEY'S A LITTLE TIGHT. / I SMELL A CERTAIN PINT-SIZED HALLUCINATION.

Panel 8: YOU CAN SMELL HIM? I CAN BARELY **SEE** HIM. / I KNOW. I'VE BEEN BUGGING DAD ABOUT THE RESOLUTION.

Panel 9: STILL HITTING THE BRIEFING BOOKS, EH, HERR DOCTOR? / GOTTA, EARL...

Panel 10: IF I'M GONNA SPIN FOR YOUR DAD, I GOTTA KNOW MY STUFF. OTHERWISE THE PRESS JACKALS WILL MAKE SHORT WORK OF ME!

Panel 11: I HAVEN'T DONE THIS MUCH CRAMMING SINCE MY SIXTH-GRADE HISTORY FINAL. NOW I KNOW WHAT BUSH MUST BE GOING THROUGH.

Panel 12: WHAT ARE YOU ON NOW? / STATE BIRDS. I'M TRYING TO NAIL DOWN NEW ENGLAND.

Panel 13: READY TO SPIN, SIR? / I DUNNO, HONEY...

Panel 14: I MEAN, I THINK I'M UP TO SPEED, BUT THE WHOLE THING'S A LITTLE INTIMIDATING...

Panel 15: I'LL BE GOING TOE-TO-TOE WITH A BATTLE-HARDENED NATIONAL PRESS CORPS! THESE GUYS EAT GUYS LIKE ME FOR LUNCH!

Panel 16: I'M BORED. WANT TO INTERVIEW ME? / OH, COULD I?

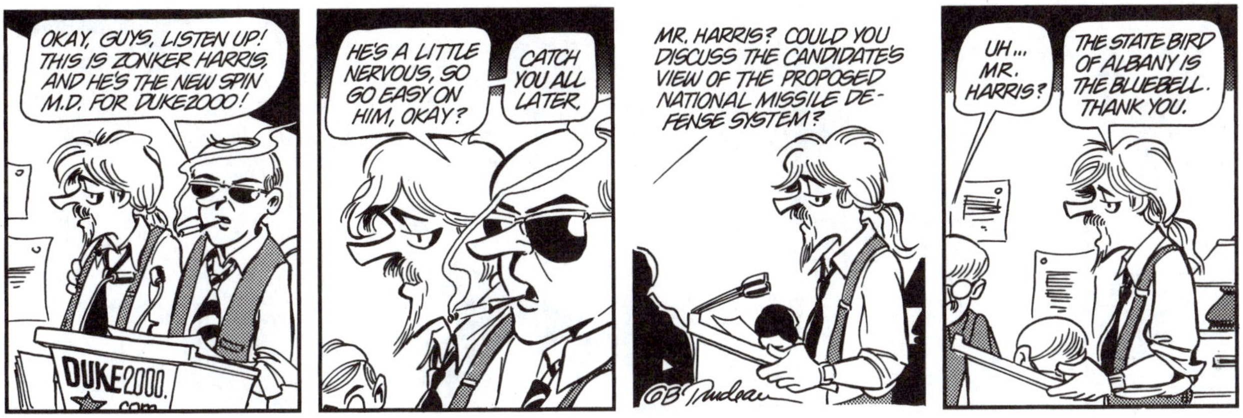
OKAY, GUYS, LISTEN UP! THIS IS ZONKER HARRIS, AND HE'S THE NEW SPIN M.D. FOR DUKE2000!
DUKE2000.com
HE'S A LITTLE NERVOUS, SO GO EASY ON HIM, OKAY?
CATCH YOU ALL LATER.
MR. HARRIS? COULD YOU DISCUSS THE CANDIDATE'S VIEW OF THE PROPOSED NATIONAL MISSILE DEFENSE SYSTEM?
UH... MR. HARRIS?
THE STATE BIRD OF ALBANY IS THE BLUEBELL. THANK YOU.

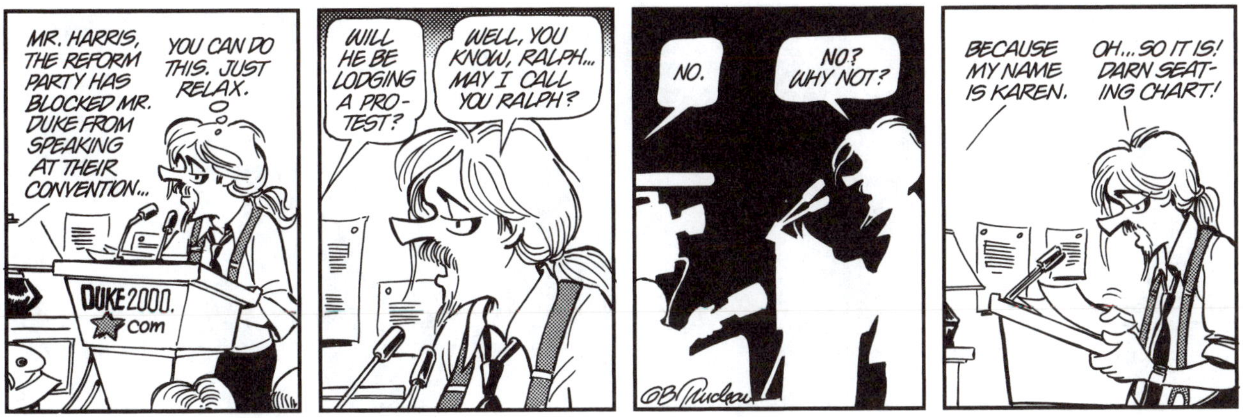
MR. HARRIS, THE REFORM PARTY HAS BLOCKED MR. DUKE FROM SPEAKING AT THEIR CONVENTION...
YOU CAN DO THIS. JUST RELAX.
DUKE2000.com
WILL HE BE LODGING A PROTEST?
WELL, YOU KNOW, RALPH... MAY I CALL YOU RALPH?
NO.
NO? WHY NOT?
BECAUSE MY NAME IS KAREN.
OH... SO IT IS! DARN SEATING CHART!

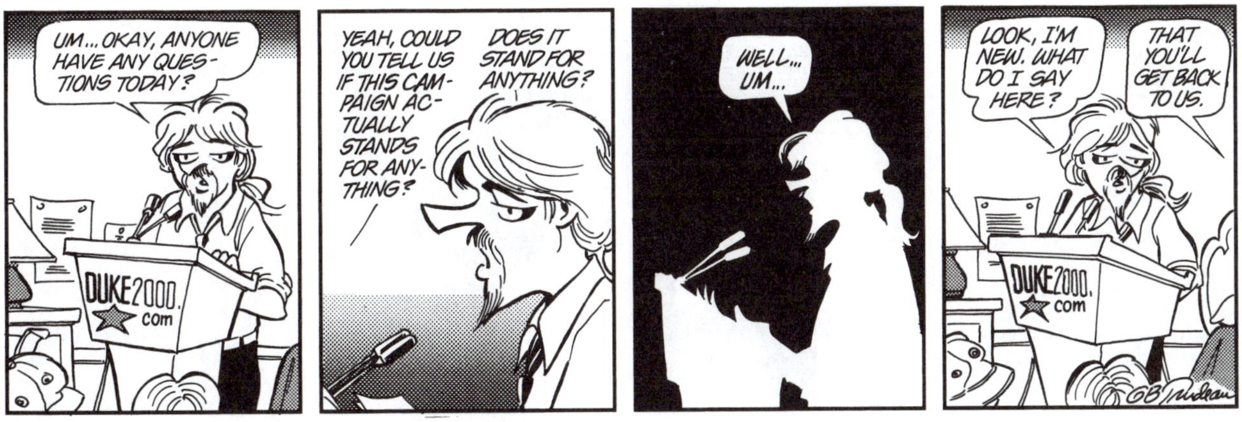
UM... OKAY, ANYONE HAVE ANY QUESTIONS TODAY?
DUKE2000.com
YEAH, COULD YOU TELL US IF THIS CAMPAIGN ACTUALLY STANDS FOR ANYTHING?
DOES IT STAND FOR ANYTHING?
WELL... UM...
LOOK, I'M NEW. WHAT DO I SAY HERE?
THAT YOU'LL GET BACK TO US.
DUKE2000.com

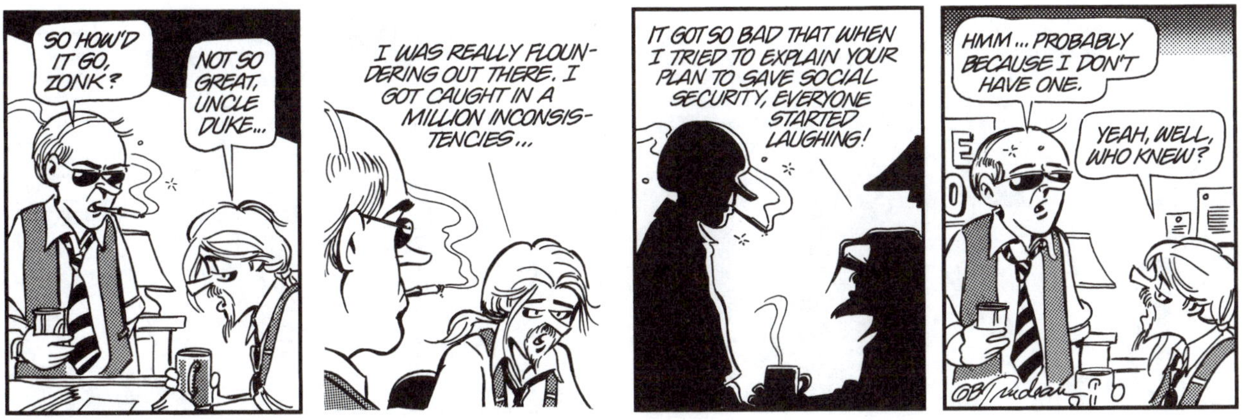
SO HOW'D IT GO, ZONK?
NOT SO GREAT, UNCLE DUKE...
I WAS REALLY FLOUNDERING OUT THERE. I GOT CAUGHT IN A MILLION INCONSISTENCIES...
IT GOT SO BAD THAT WHEN I TRIED TO EXPLAIN YOUR PLAN TO SAVE SOCIAL SECURITY, EVERYONE STARTED LAUGHING!
HMM... PROBABLY BECAUSE I DON'T HAVE ONE.
YEAH, WELL, WHO KNEW?

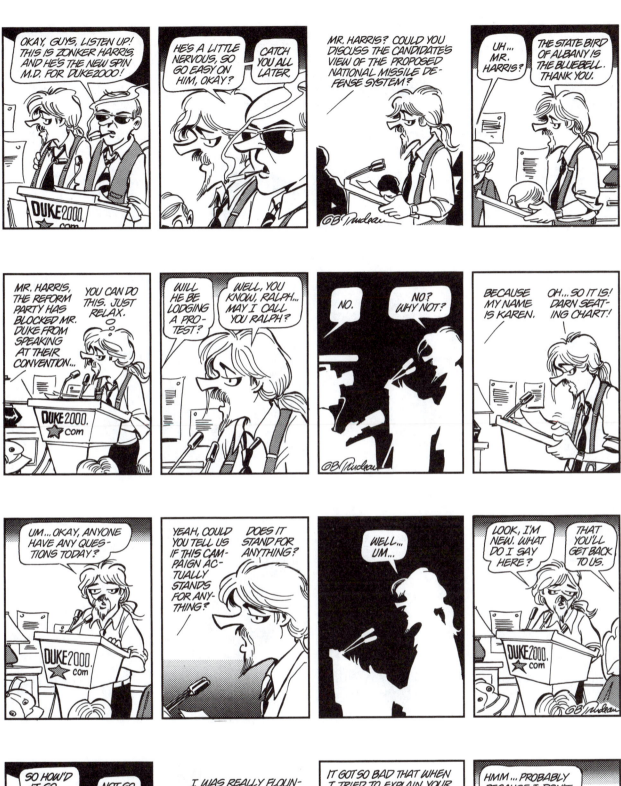

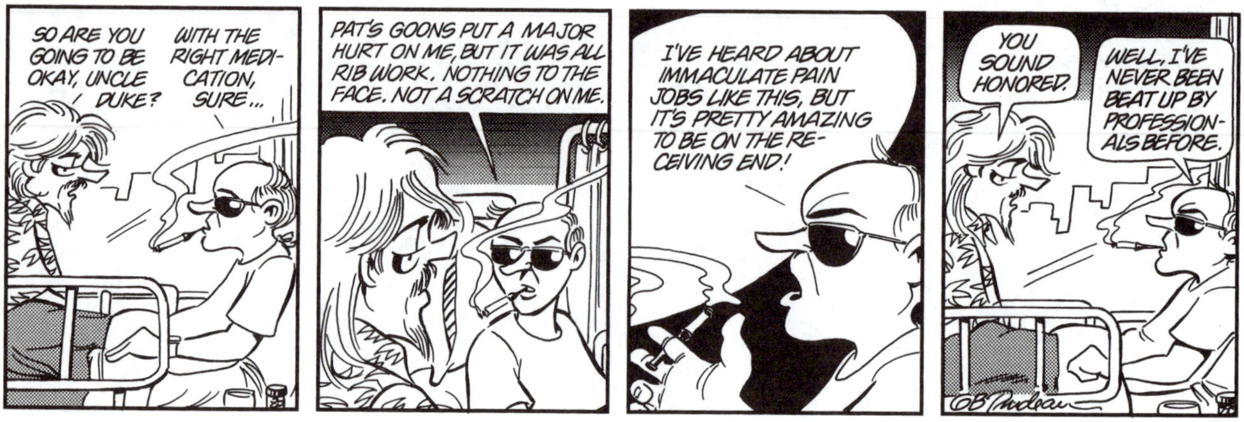
SO ARE YOU GOING TO BE OKAY, UNCLE DUKE?
WITH THE RIGHT MEDICATION, SURE...
PAT'S GOONS PUT A MAJOR HURT ON ME, BUT IT WAS ALL RIB WORK. NOTHING TO THE FACE. NOT A SCRATCH ON ME.
I'VE HEARD ABOUT IMMACULATE PAIN JOBS LIKE THIS, BUT IT'S PRETTY AMAZING TO BE ON THE RECEIVING END!
YOU SOUND HONORED.
WELL, I'VE NEVER BEEN BEAT UP BY PROFESSIONALS BEFORE.
©B Trudeau

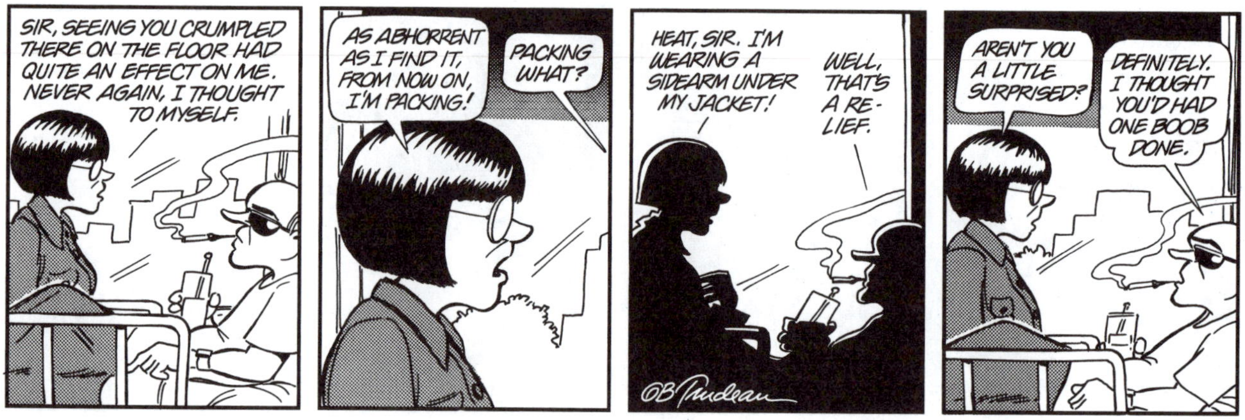
SIR, SEEING YOU CRUMPLED THERE ON THE FLOOR HAD QUITE AN EFFECT ON ME. NEVER AGAIN, I THOUGHT TO MYSELF.
AS ABHORRENT AS I FIND IT, FROM NOW ON, I'M PACKING!
PACKING WHAT?
HEAT, SIR. I'M WEARING A SIDEARM UNDER MY JACKET!
WELL, THAT'S A RELIEF.
©B Trudeau
AREN'T YOU A LITTLE SURPRISED?
DEFINITELY. I THOUGHT YOU'D HAD ONE BOOB DONE.

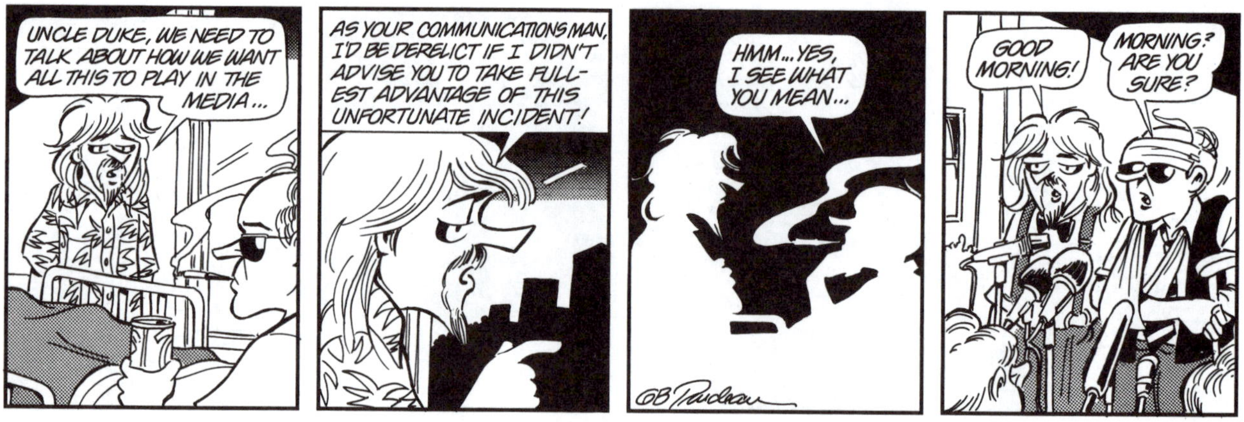
UNCLE DUKE, WE NEED TO TALK ABOUT HOW WE WANT ALL THIS TO PLAY IN THE MEDIA...
AS YOUR COMMUNICATIONS MAN, I'D BE DERELICT IF I DIDN'T ADVISE YOU TO TAKE FULLEST ADVANTAGE OF THIS UNFORTUNATE INCIDENT!
HMM... YES, I SEE WHAT YOU MEAN...
©B Trudeau
GOOD MORNING!
MORNING? ARE YOU SURE?

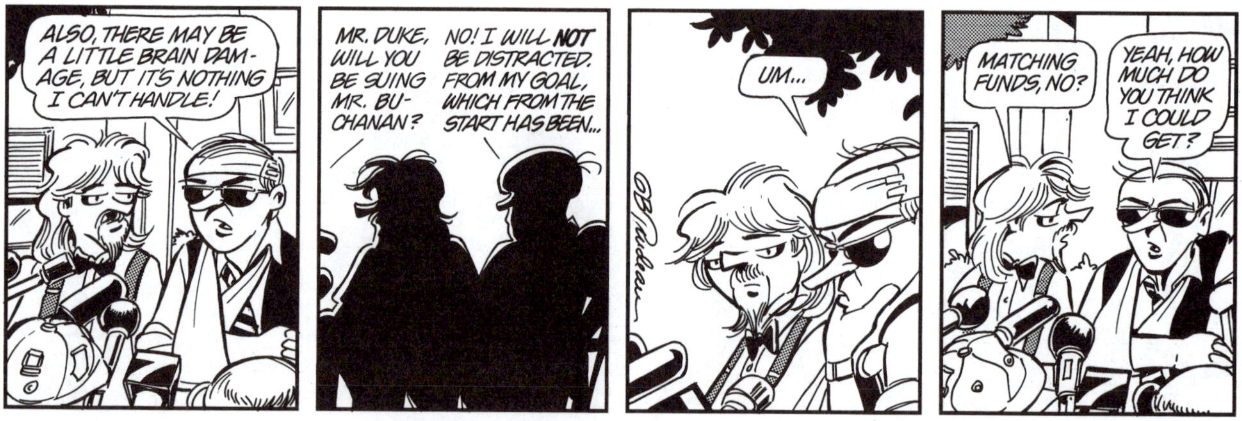
ALSO, THERE MAY BE A LITTLE BRAIN DAMAGE, BUT IT'S NOTHING I CAN'T HANDLE!
MR. DUKE, WILL YOU BE SUING MR. BUCHANAN?
NO! I WILL NOT BE DISTRACTED FROM MY GOAL, WHICH FROM THE START HAS BEEN...
UM...
©B Trudeau
MATCHING FUNDS, NO?
YEAH, HOW MUCH DO YOU THINK I COULD GET?

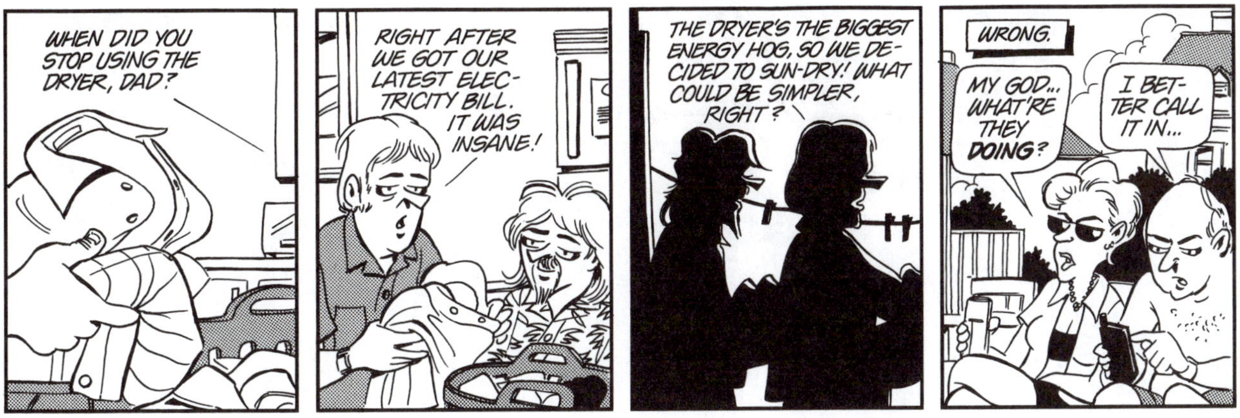
WHEN DID YOU STOP USING THE DRYER, DAD?
RIGHT AFTER WE GOT OUR LATEST ELECTRICITY BILL. IT WAS INSANE!
THE DRYER'S THE BIGGEST ENERGY HOG, SO WE DECIDED TO SUN-DRY! WHAT COULD BE SIMPLER, RIGHT?
WRONG.
MY GOD... WHAT'RE THEY DOING?
I BETTER CALL IT IN...

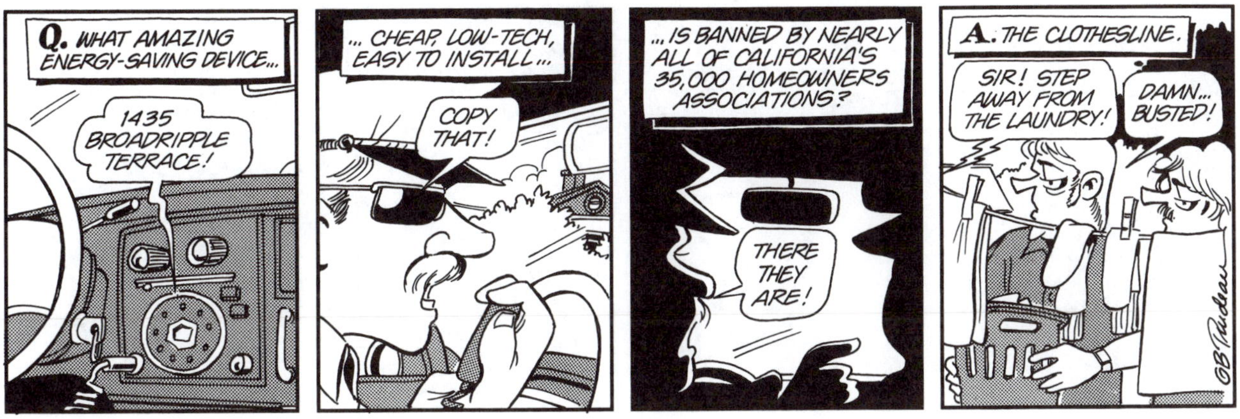
Q. WHAT AMAZING ENERGY-SAVING DEVICE...
1435 BROADRIPPLE TERRACE!
... CHEAP, LOW-TECH, EASY TO INSTALL...
COPY THAT!
...IS BANNED BY NEARLY ALL OF CALIFORNIA'S 35,000 HOMEOWNERS ASSOCIATIONS?
THERE THEY ARE!
A. THE CLOTHESLINE.
SIR! STEP AWAY FROM THE LAUNDRY!
DAMN... BUSTED!

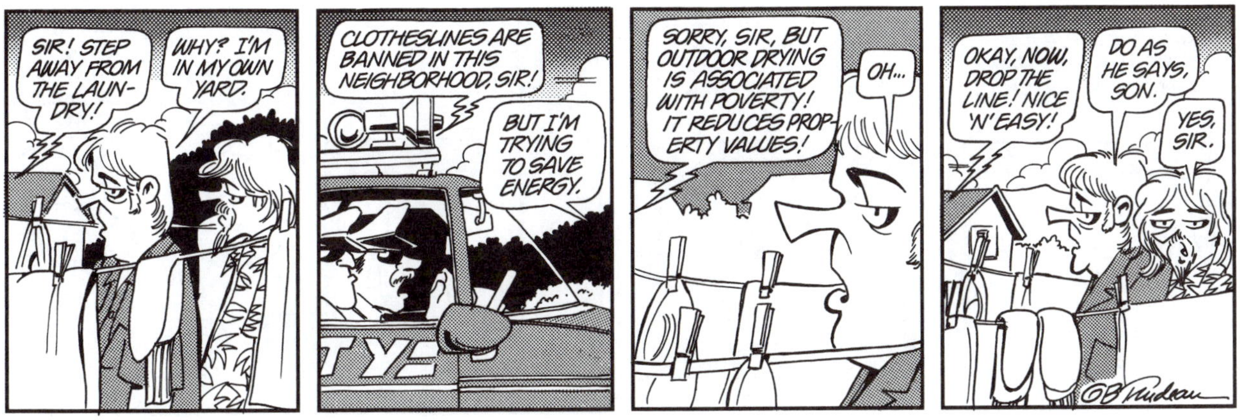
SIR! STEP AWAY FROM THE LAUNDRY!
WHY? I'M IN MY OWN YARD.
CLOTHESLINES ARE BANNED IN THIS NEIGHBORHOOD, SIR!
BUT I'M TRYING TO SAVE ENERGY.
SORRY, SIR, BUT OUTDOOR DRYING IS ASSOCIATED WITH POVERTY! IT REDUCES PROPERTY VALUES!
OH...
OKAY, NOW, DROP THE LINE! NICE 'N' EASY!
DO AS HE SAYS, SON.
YES, SIR.

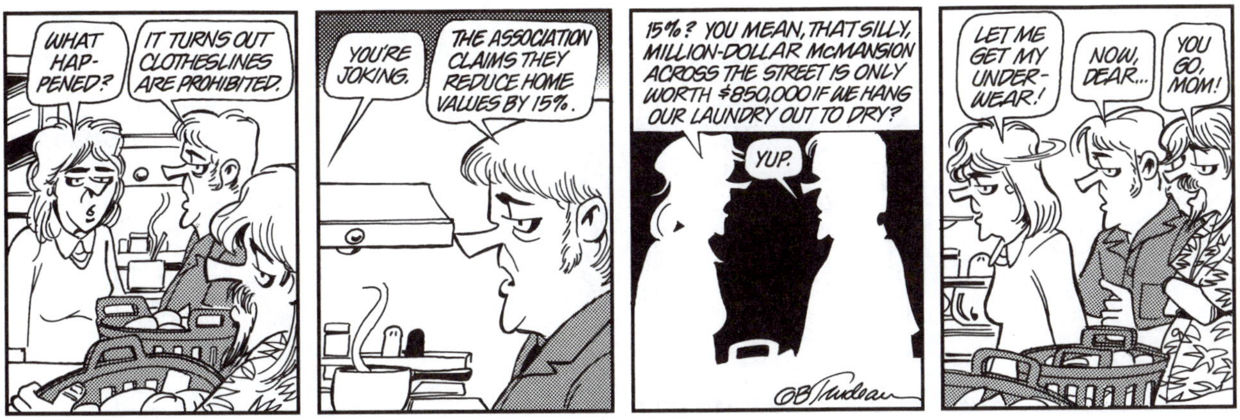
WHAT HAPPENED?
IT TURNS OUT CLOTHESLINES ARE PROHIBITED.
YOU'RE JOKING.
THE ASSOCIATION CLAIMS THEY REDUCE HOME VALUES BY 15%.
15%? YOU MEAN, THAT SILLY, MILLION-DOLLAR McMANSION ACROSS THE STREET IS ONLY WORTH $850,000 IF WE HANG OUR LAUNDRY OUT TO DRY?
YUP.
LET ME GET MY UNDERWEAR!
NOW, DEAR...
YOU GO, MOM!

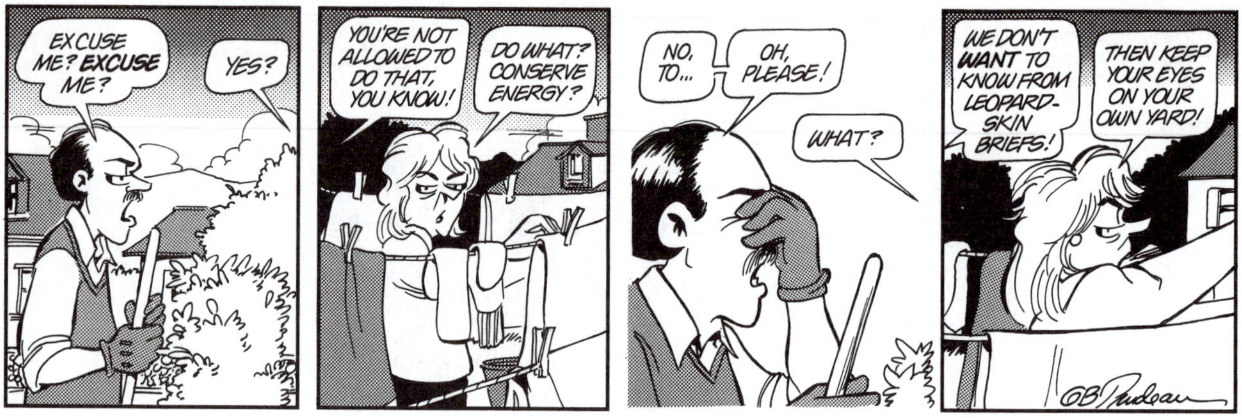
EXCUSE ME? EXCUSE ME?
YES?
YOU'RE NOT ALLOWED TO DO THAT, YOU KNOW!
DO WHAT? CONSERVE ENERGY?
NO, TO...
OH, PLEASE!
WHAT?
WE DON'T WANT TO KNOW FROM LEOPARD-SKIN BRIEFS!
THEN KEEP YOUR EYES ON YOUR OWN YARD!

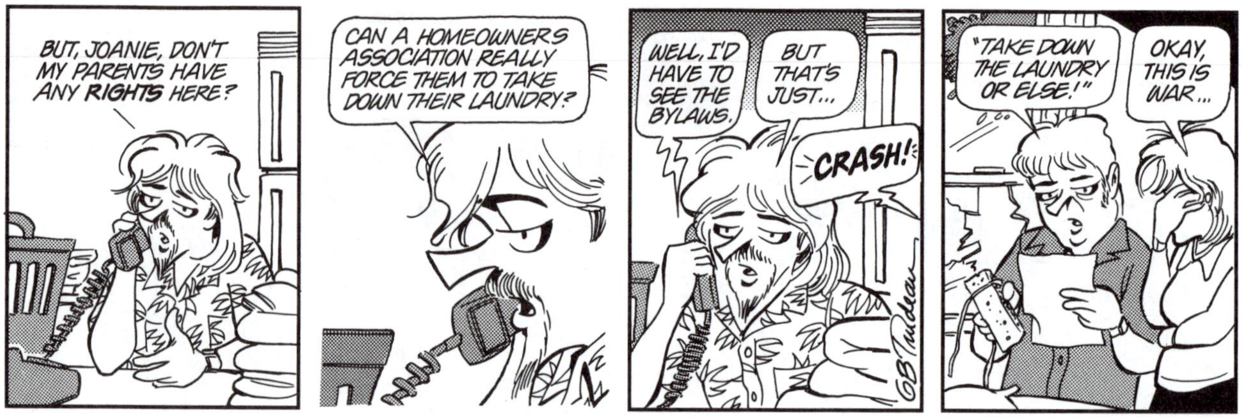
BUT, JOANIE, DON'T MY PARENTS HAVE ANY RIGHTS HERE?
CAN A HOMEOWNERS ASSOCIATION REALLY FORCE THEM TO TAKE DOWN THEIR LAUNDRY?
WELL, I'D HAVE TO SEE THE BYLAWS.
BUT THAT'S JUST...
CRASH!
"TAKE DOWN THE LAUNDRY OR ELSE!"
OKAY, THIS IS WAR...

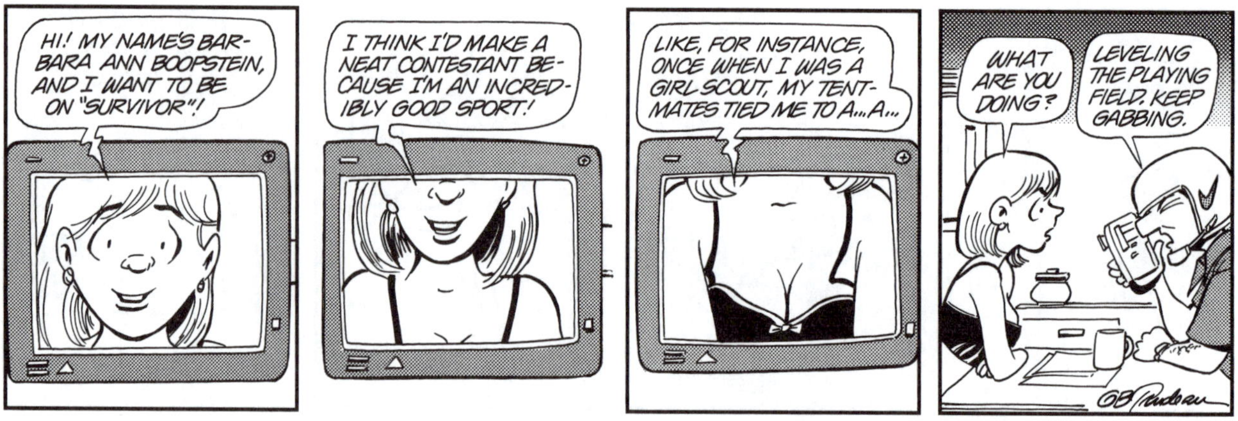
HI! MY NAME'S BARBARA ANN BOOPSTEIN, AND I WANT TO BE ON "SURVIVOR"!
I THINK I'D MAKE A NEAT CONTESTANT BECAUSE I'M AN INCREDIBLY GOOD SPORT!
LIKE, FOR INSTANCE, ONCE WHEN I WAS A GIRL SCOUT, MY TENTMATES TIED ME TO A...A...
WHAT ARE YOU DOING?
LEVELING THE PLAYING FIELD. KEEP GABBING.

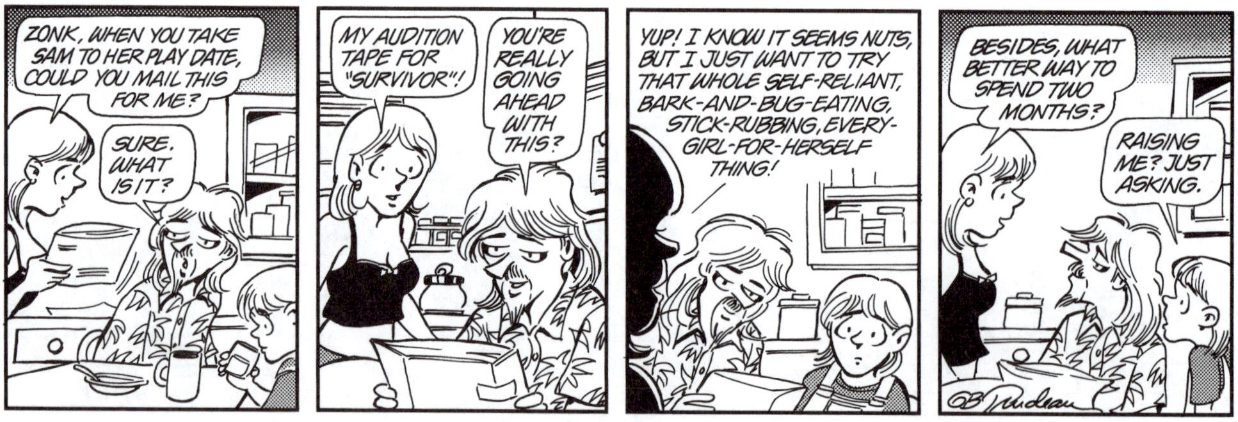
ZONK, WHEN YOU TAKE SAM TO HER PLAY DATE, COULD YOU MAIL THIS FOR ME?
SURE. WHAT IS IT?
MY AUDITION TAPE FOR "SURVIVOR"!
YOU'RE REALLY GOING AHEAD WITH THIS?
YUP! I KNOW IT SEEMS NUTS, BUT I JUST WANT TO TRY THAT WHOLE SELF-RELIANT, BARK-AND-BUG-EATING, STICK-RUBBING, EVERY-GIRL-FOR-HERSELF THING!
BESIDES, WHAT BETTER WAY TO SPEND TWO MONTHS?
RAISING ME? JUST ASKING.

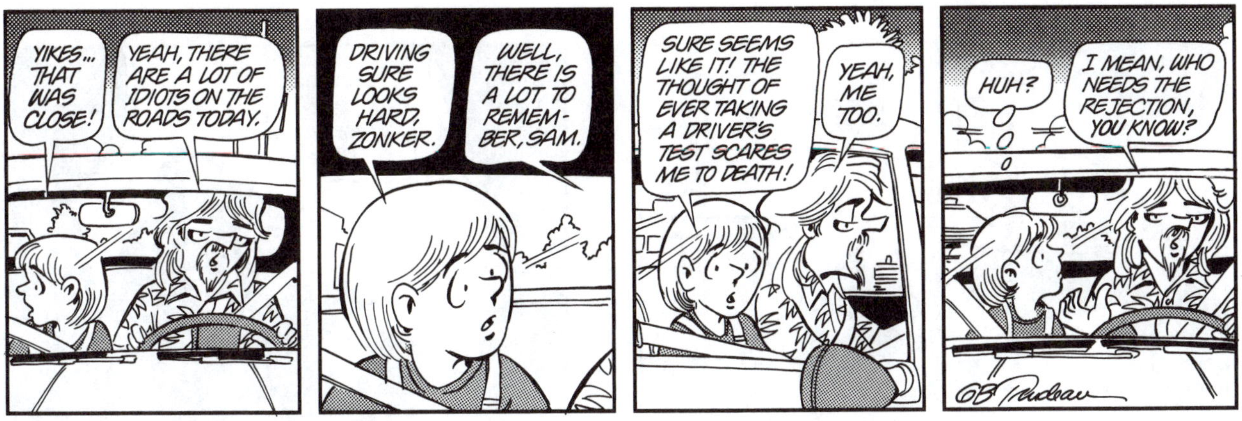
YIKES... THAT WAS CLOSE!
YEAH, THERE ARE A LOT OF IDIOTS ON THE ROADS TODAY.
DRIVING SURE LOOKS HARD, ZONKER.
WELL, THERE IS A LOT TO REMEMBER, SAM.
SURE SEEMS LIKE IT! THE THOUGHT OF EVER TAKING A DRIVER'S TEST SCARES ME TO DEATH!
YEAH, ME TOO.
HUH?
I MEAN, WHO NEEDS THE REJECTION, YOU KNOW?

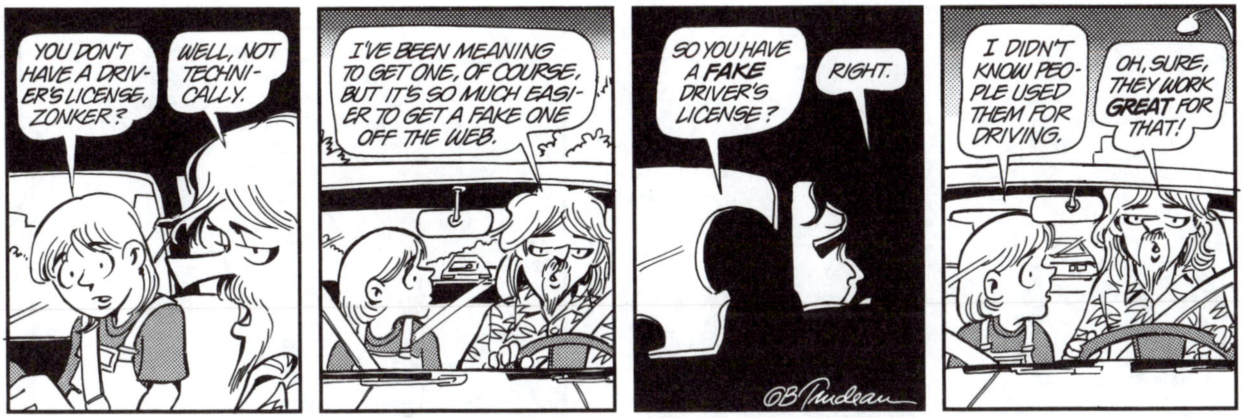
YOU DON'T HAVE A DRIVER'S LICENSE, ZONKER?
WELL, NOT TECHNICALLY.
I'VE BEEN MEANING TO GET ONE, OF COURSE, BUT IT'S SO MUCH EASIER TO GET A FAKE ONE OFF THE WEB.
SO YOU HAVE A **FAKE** DRIVER'S LICENSE?
RIGHT.
I DIDN'T KNOW PEOPLE USED THEM FOR DRIVING.
OH, SURE, THEY WORK **GREAT** FOR THAT!

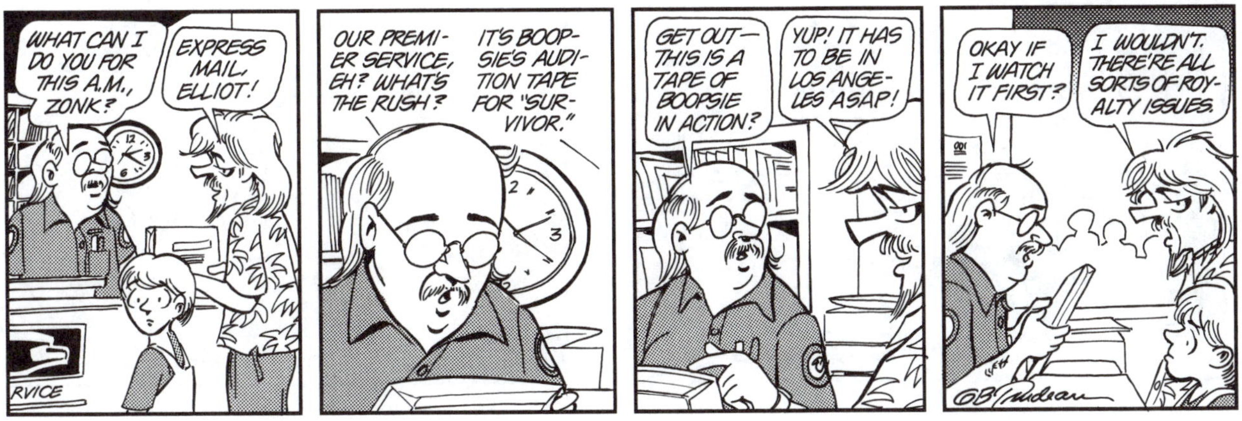
WHAT CAN I DO YOU FOR THIS A.M., ZONK?
EXPRESS MAIL, ELLIOT!
RVICE
OUR PREMIER SERVICE, EH? WHAT'S THE RUSH?
IT'S BOOPSIE'S AUDITION TAPE FOR "SURVIVOR."
GET OUT— THIS IS A TAPE OF BOOPSIE IN ACTION?
YUP! IT HAS TO BE IN LOS ANGELES ASAP!
OKAY IF I WATCH IT FIRST?
I WOULDN'T. THERE'RE ALL SORTS OF ROYALTY ISSUES.

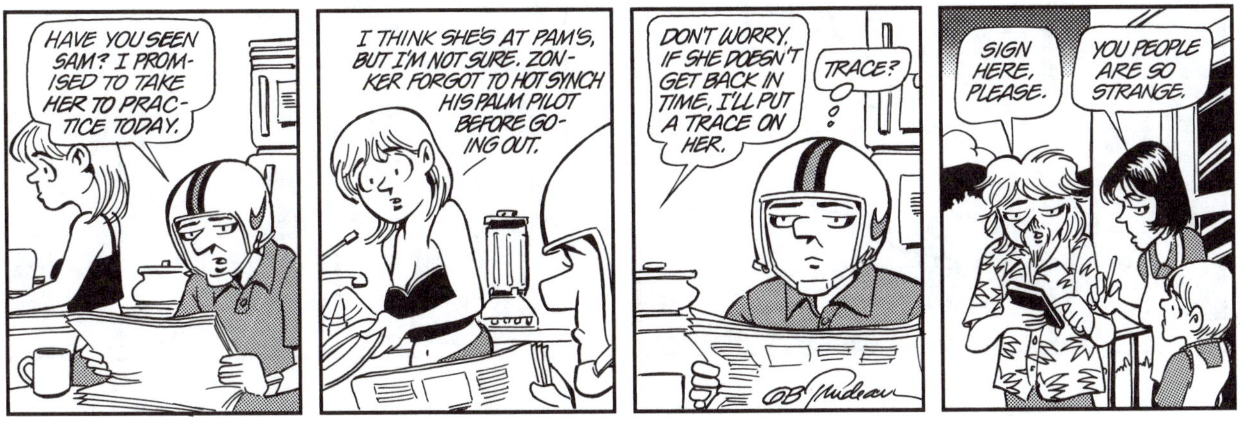
HAVE YOU SEEN SAM? I PROMISED TO TAKE HER TO PRACTICE TODAY.
I THINK SHE'S AT PAM'S, BUT I'M NOT SURE. ZONKER FORGOT TO HOT SYNCH HIS PALM PILOT BEFORE GOING OUT.
DON'T WORRY. IF SHE DOESN'T GET BACK IN TIME, I'LL PUT A TRACE ON HER.
TRACE?
SIGN HERE, PLEASE.
YOU PEOPLE ARE SO STRANGE.

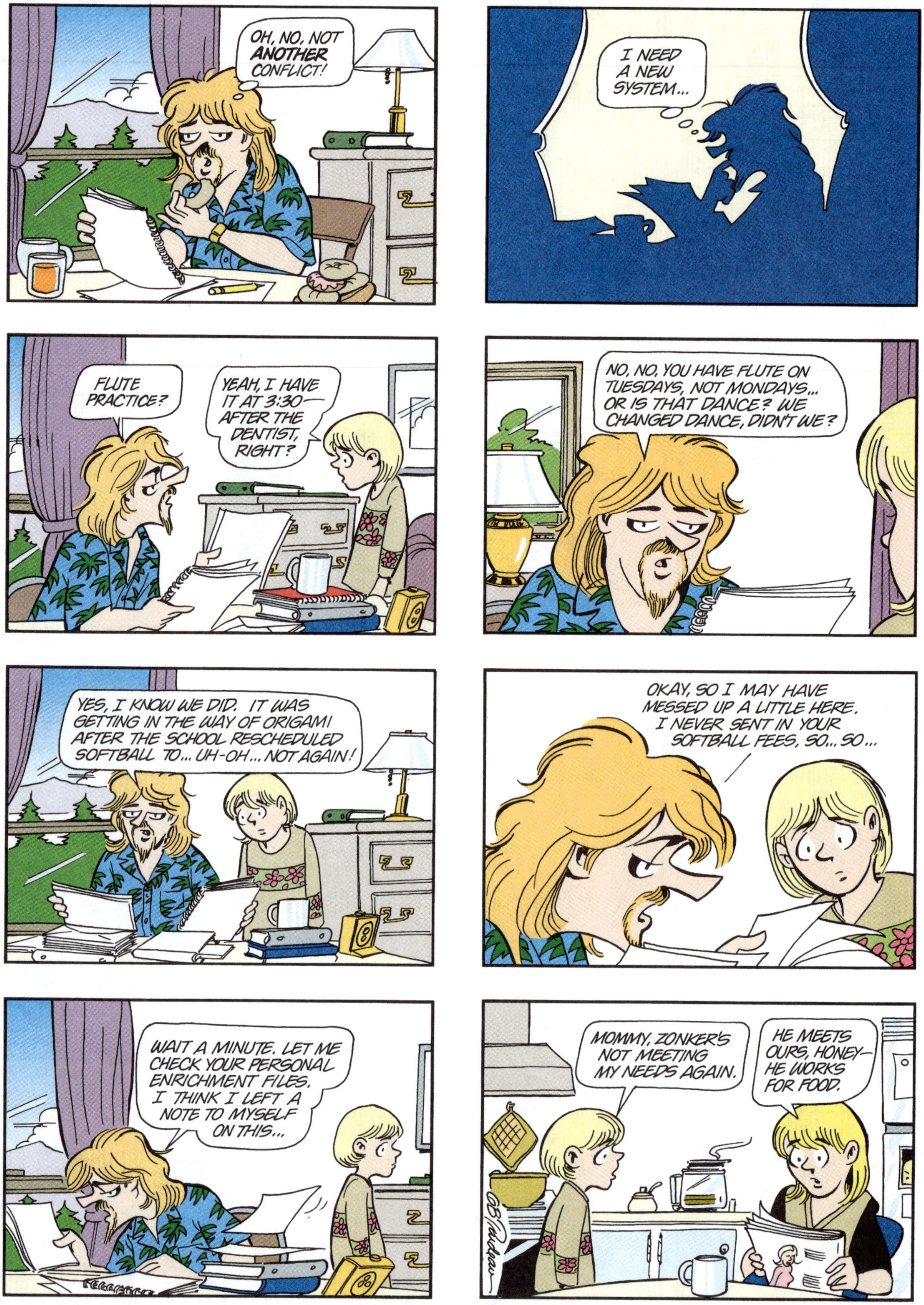
OH, NO, NOT ANOTHER CONFLICT!
I NEED A NEW SYSTEM...
FLUTE PRACTICE?
YEAH, I HAVE IT AT 3:30— AFTER THE DENTIST, RIGHT?
NO, NO, YOU HAVE FLUTE ON TUESDAYS, NOT MONDAYS... OR IS THAT DANCE? WE CHANGED DANCE, DIDN'T WE?
YES, I KNOW WE DID. IT WAS GETTING IN THE WAY OF ORIGAMI AFTER THE SCHOOL RESCHEDULED SOFTBALL TO... UH-OH... NOT AGAIN!
OKAY, SO I MAY HAVE MESSED UP A LITTLE HERE. I NEVER SENT IN YOUR SOFTBALL FEES, SO... SO...
WAIT A MINUTE. LET ME CHECK YOUR PERSONAL ENRICHMENT FILES. I THINK I LEFT A NOTE TO MYSELF ON THIS...
MOMMY, ZONKER'S NOT MEETING MY NEEDS AGAIN.
HE MEETS OURS, HONEY— HE WORKS FOR FOOD.

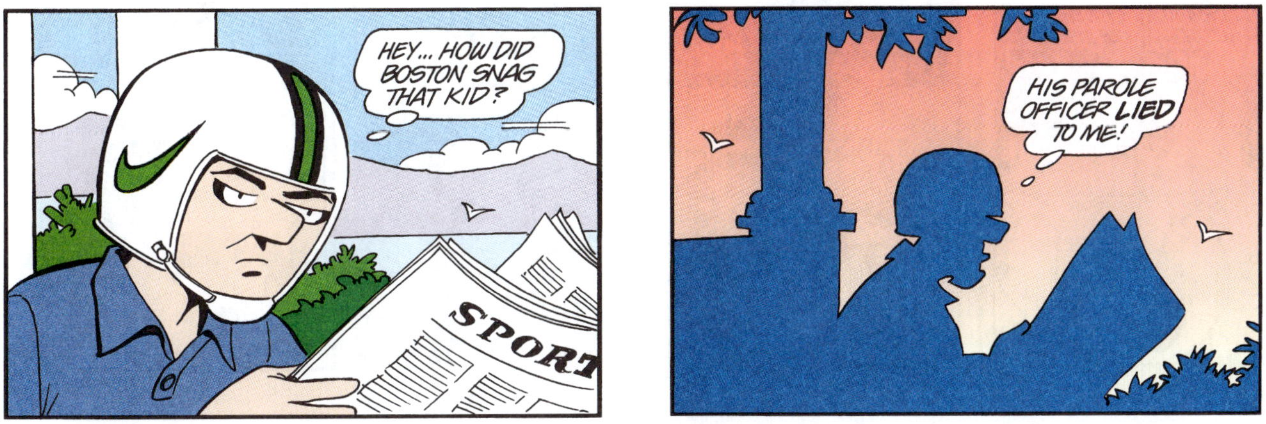
HEY... HOW DID BOSTON SNAG THAT KID?
SPORT
HIS PAROLE OFFICER **LIED** TO ME!

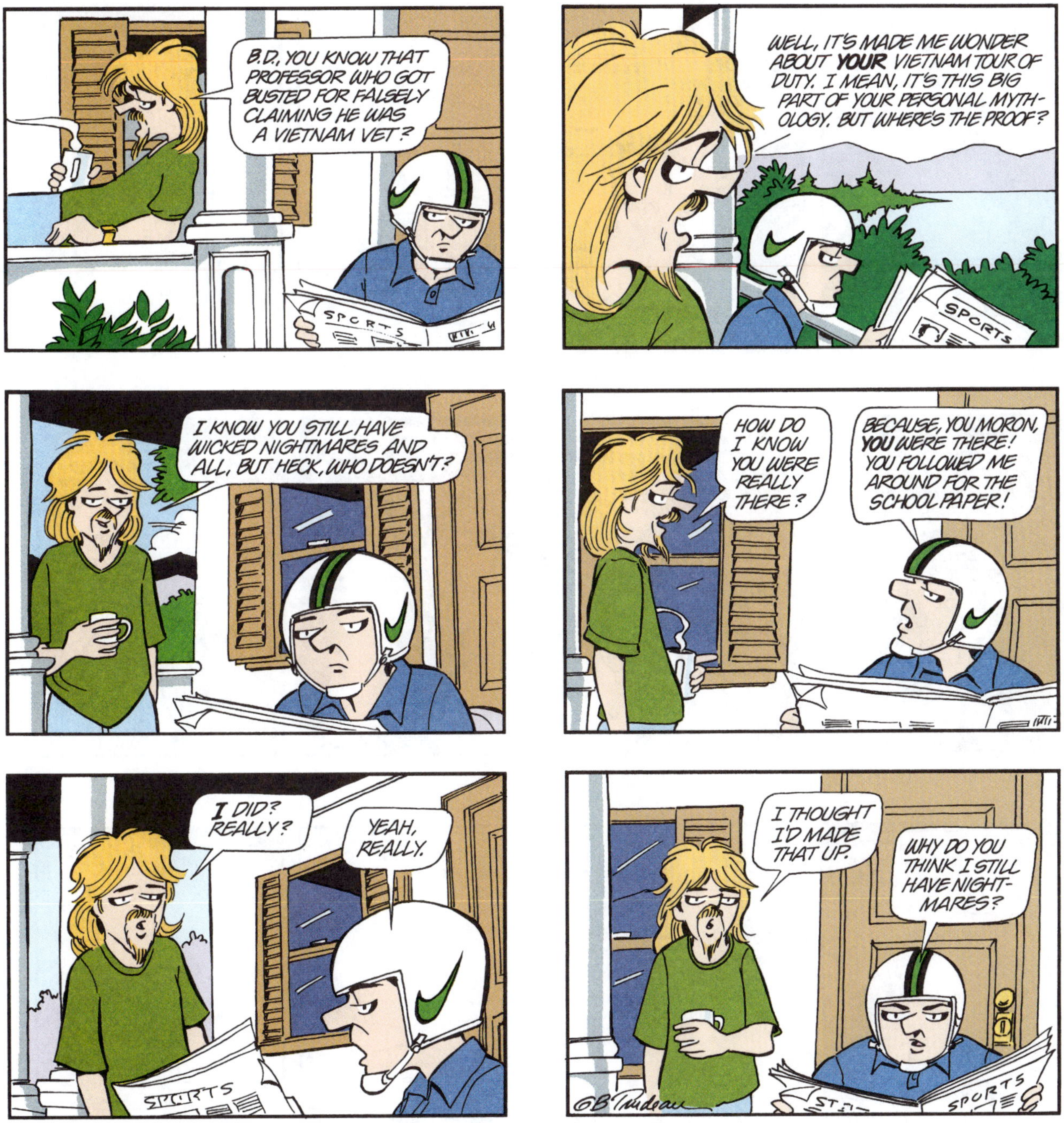
B.D., YOU KNOW THAT PROFESSOR WHO GOT BUSTED FOR FALSELY CLAIMING HE WAS A VIETNAM VET?
SPORTS
WELL, IT'S MADE ME WONDER ABOUT **YOUR** VIETNAM TOUR OF DUTY. I MEAN, IT'S THIS BIG PART OF YOUR PERSONAL MYTHOLOGY. BUT WHERE'S THE PROOF?
SPORTS
I KNOW YOU STILL HAVE WICKED NIGHTMARES AND ALL, BUT HECK, WHO DOESN'T?
HOW DO I KNOW YOU WERE REALLY THERE?
BECAUSE, YOU MORON, **YOU** WERE THERE! YOU FOLLOWED ME AROUND FOR THE SCHOOL PAPER!
I DID? REALLY?
YEAH, REALLY.
SPORTS
I THOUGHT I'D MADE THAT UP.
WHY DO YOU THINK I STILL HAVE NIGHTMARES?
SPORTS
©B Trudeau

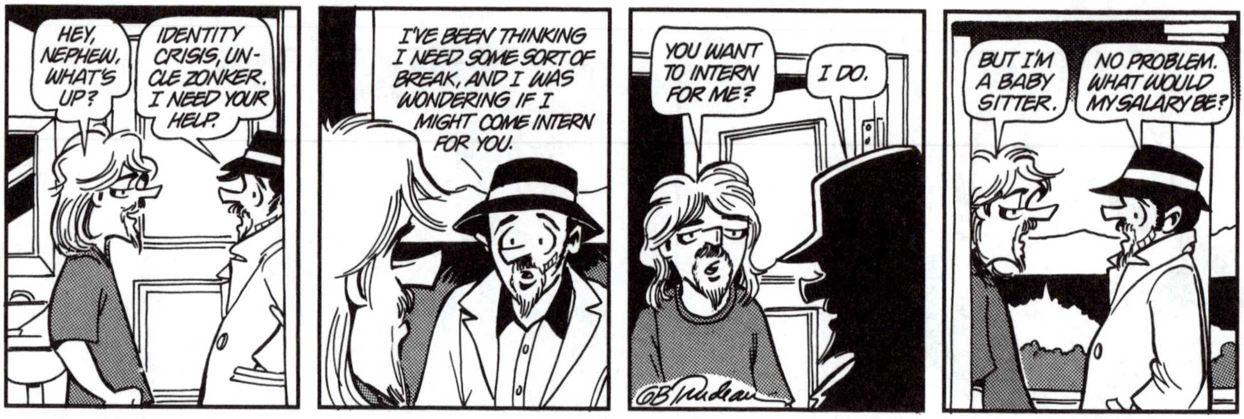
HEY, NEPHEW. WHAT'S UP?
IDENTITY CRISIS, UNCLE ZONKER. I NEED YOUR HELP.
I'VE BEEN THINKING I NEED SOME SORT OF BREAK, AND I WAS WONDERING IF I MIGHT COME INTERN FOR YOU.
YOU WANT TO INTERN FOR ME?
I DO.
BUT I'M A BABY SITTER.
NO PROBLEM. WHAT WOULD MY SALARY BE?

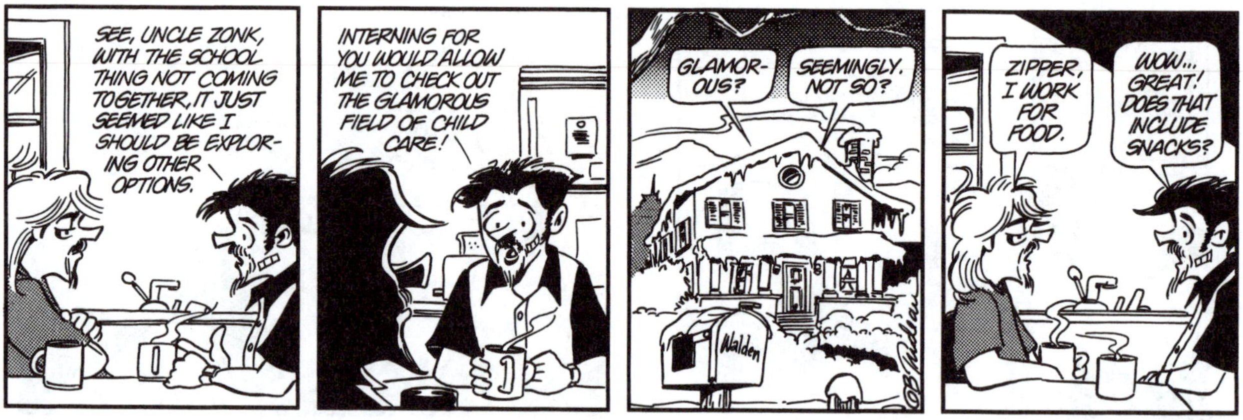
SEE, UNCLE ZONK, WITH THE SCHOOL THING NOT COMING TOGETHER, IT JUST SEEMED LIKE I SHOULD BE EXPLORING OTHER OPTIONS.
INTERNING FOR YOU WOULD ALLOW ME TO CHECK OUT THE GLAMOROUS FIELD OF CHILD CARE!
GLAMOROUS?
SEEMINGLY. NOT SO?
Walden
ZIPPER, I WORK FOR FOOD.
WOW... GREAT! DOES THAT INCLUDE SNACKS?

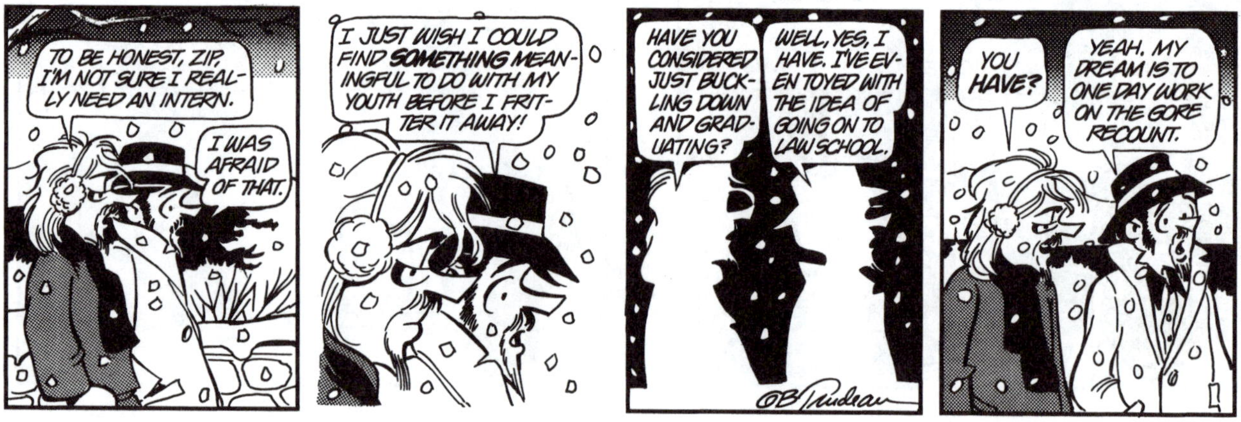
TO BE HONEST, ZIP, I'M NOT SURE I REALLY NEED AN INTERN.
I WAS AFRAID OF THAT.
I JUST WISH I COULD FIND SOMETHING MEANINGFUL TO DO WITH MY YOUTH BEFORE I FRITTER IT AWAY!
HAVE YOU CONSIDERED JUST BUCKLING DOWN AND GRADUATING?
WELL, YES, I HAVE. I'VE EVEN TOYED WITH THE IDEA OF GOING ON TO LAW SCHOOL.
YOU HAVE?
YEAH, MY DREAM IS TO ONE DAY WORK ON THE GORE RECOUNT.

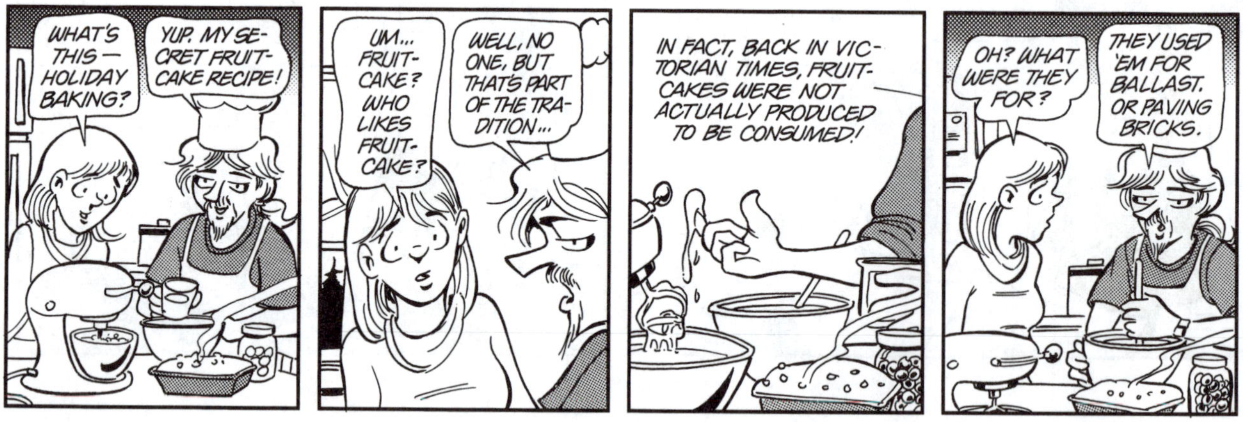
WHAT'S THIS — HOLIDAY BAKING?
YUP. MY SECRET FRUITCAKE RECIPE!
UM... FRUITCAKE? WHO LIKES FRUITCAKE?
WELL, NO ONE, BUT THAT'S PART OF THE TRADITION...
IN FACT, BACK IN VICTORIAN TIMES, FRUITCAKES WERE NOT ACTUALLY PRODUCED TO BE CONSUMED!
OH? WHAT WERE THEY FOR?
THEY USED 'EM FOR BALLAST, OR PAVING BRICKS.

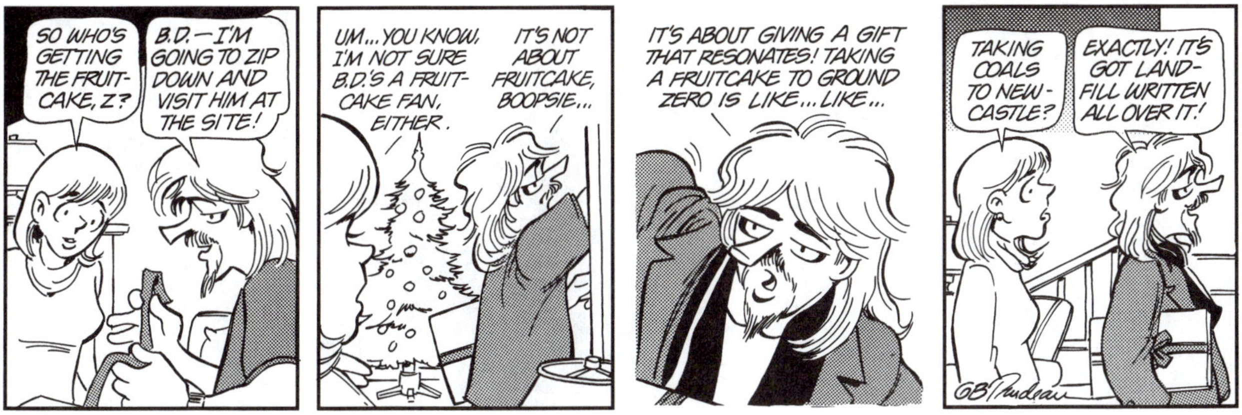
SO WHO'S GETTING THE FRUIT-CAKE, Z?
B.D.—I'M GOING TO ZIP DOWN AND VISIT HIM AT THE SITE!
UM... YOU KNOW, I'M NOT SURE B.D.'S A FRUIT-CAKE FAN, EITHER.
IT'S NOT ABOUT FRUITCAKE, BOOPSIE...
IT'S ABOUT GIVING A GIFT THAT RESONATES! TAKING A FRUITCAKE TO GROUND ZERO IS LIKE... LIKE...
TAKING COALS TO NEW-CASTLE?
EXACTLY! IT'S GOT LAND-FILL WRITTEN ALL OVER IT!

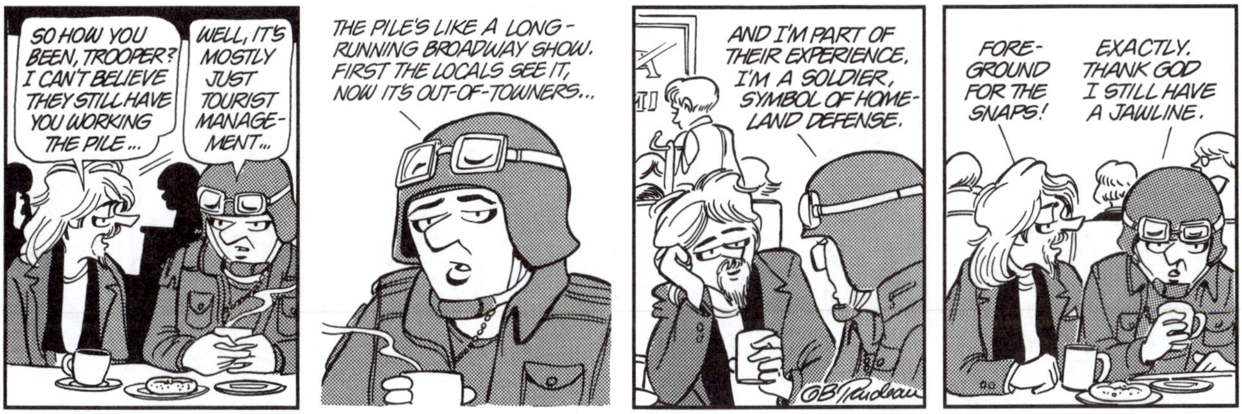
SO HOW YOU BEEN, TROOPER? I CAN'T BELIEVE THEY STILL HAVE YOU WORKING THE PILE...
WELL, IT'S MOSTLY JUST TOURIST MANAGE-MENT...
THE PILE'S LIKE A LONG-RUNNING BROADWAY SHOW. FIRST THE LOCALS SEE IT, NOW IT'S OUT-OF-TOWNERS...
AND I'M PART OF THEIR EXPERIENCE. I'M A SOLDIER, SYMBOL OF HOME-LAND DEFENSE.
FORE-GROUND FOR THE SNAPS!
EXACTLY. THANK GOD I STILL HAVE A JAWLINE.

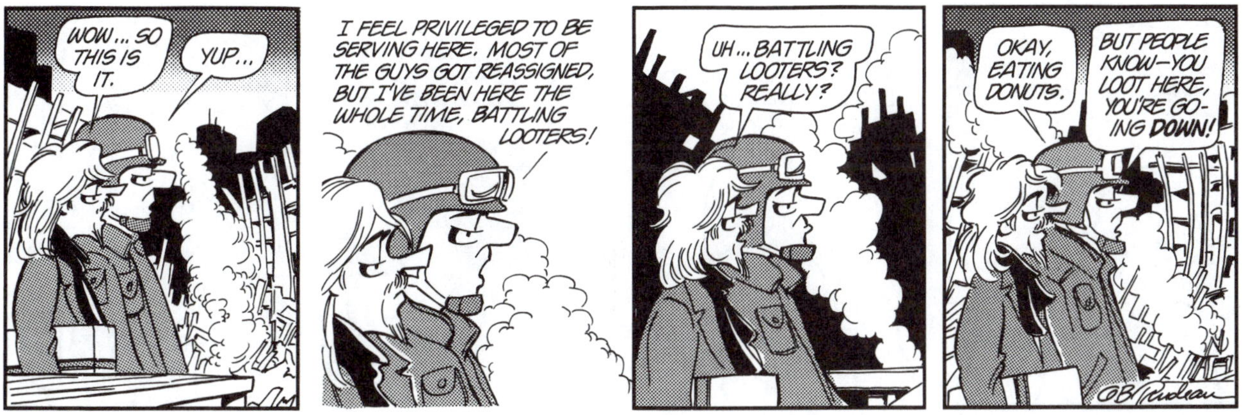
WOW... SO THIS IS IT.
YUP...
I FEEL PRIVILEGED TO BE SERVING HERE. MOST OF THE GUYS GOT REASSIGNED, BUT I'VE BEEN HERE THE WHOLE TIME, BATTLING LOOTERS!
UH... BATTLING LOOTERS? REALLY?
OKAY, EATING DONUTS.
BUT PEOPLE KNOW—YOU LOOT HERE, YOU'RE GO-ING **DOWN**!

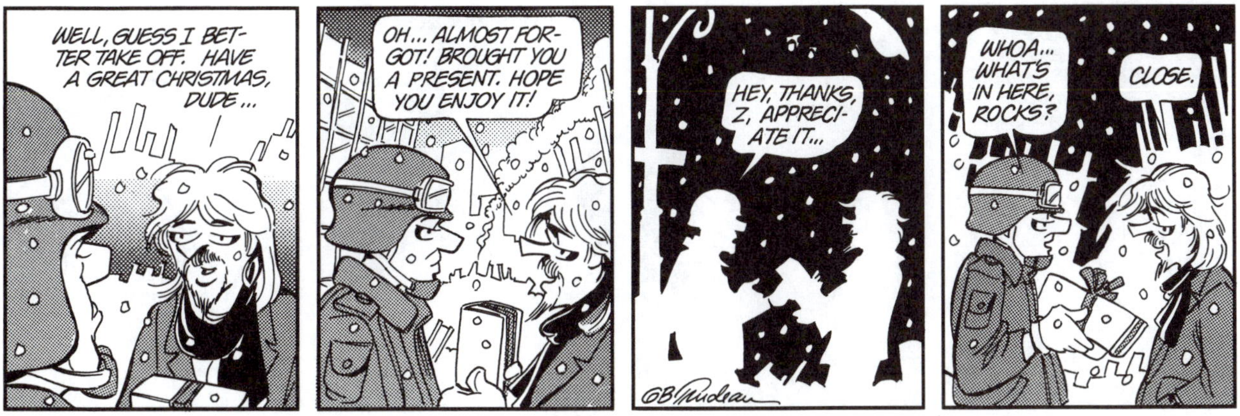
WELL, GUESS I BET-TER TAKE OFF. HAVE A GREAT CHRISTMAS, DUDE...
OH... ALMOST FOR-GOT! BROUGHT YOU A PRESENT. HOPE YOU ENJOY IT!
HEY, THANKS, Z, APPRECI-ATE IT...
WHOA... WHAT'S IN HERE, ROCKS?
CLOSE.

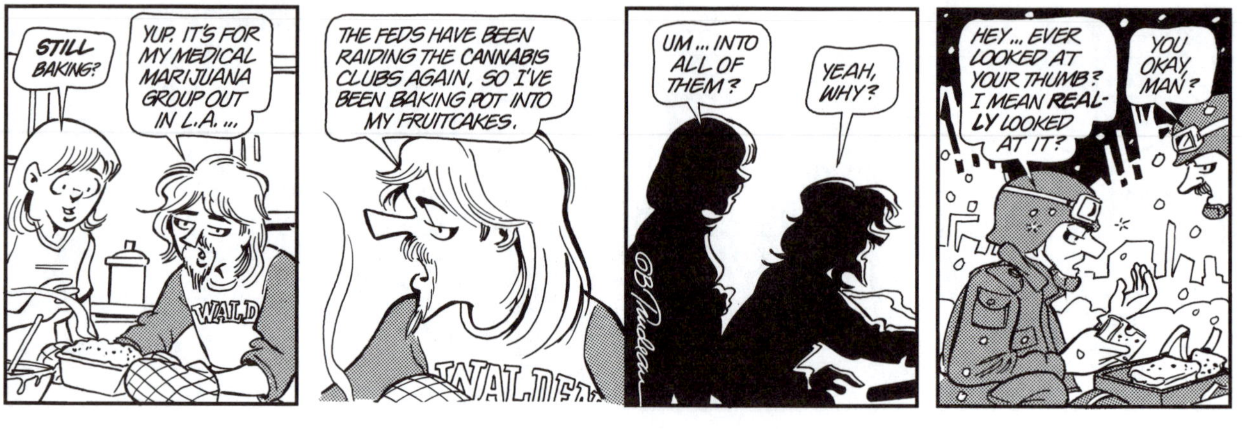
STILL BAKING?
YUP. IT'S FOR MY MEDICAL MARIJUANA GROUP OUT IN L.A. ...
THE FEDS HAVE BEEN RAIDING THE CANNABIS CLUBS AGAIN, SO I'VE BEEN BAKING POT INTO MY FRUITCAKES.
UM... INTO ALL OF THEM?
YEAH, WHY?
HEY... EVER LOOKED AT YOUR THUMB? I MEAN REALLY LOOKED AT IT?
YOU OKAY, MAN?

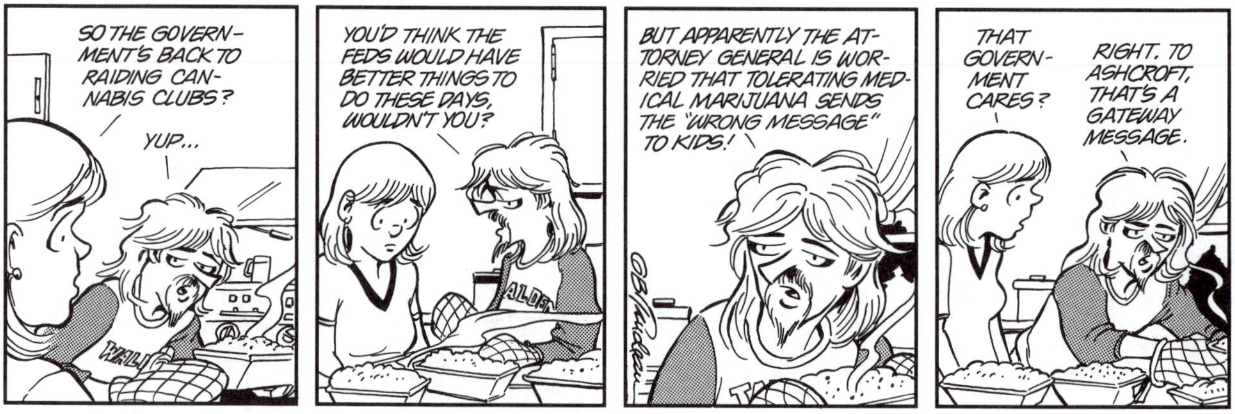
SO THE GOVERNMENT'S BACK TO RAIDING CANNABIS CLUBS?
YUP...
YOU'D THINK THE FEDS WOULD HAVE BETTER THINGS TO DO THESE DAYS, WOULDN'T YOU?
BUT APPARENTLY THE ATTORNEY GENERAL IS WORRIED THAT TOLERATING MEDICAL MARIJUANA SENDS THE "WRONG MESSAGE" TO KIDS!
THAT GOVERNMENT CARES?
RIGHT. TO ASHCROFT, THAT'S A GATEWAY MESSAGE.

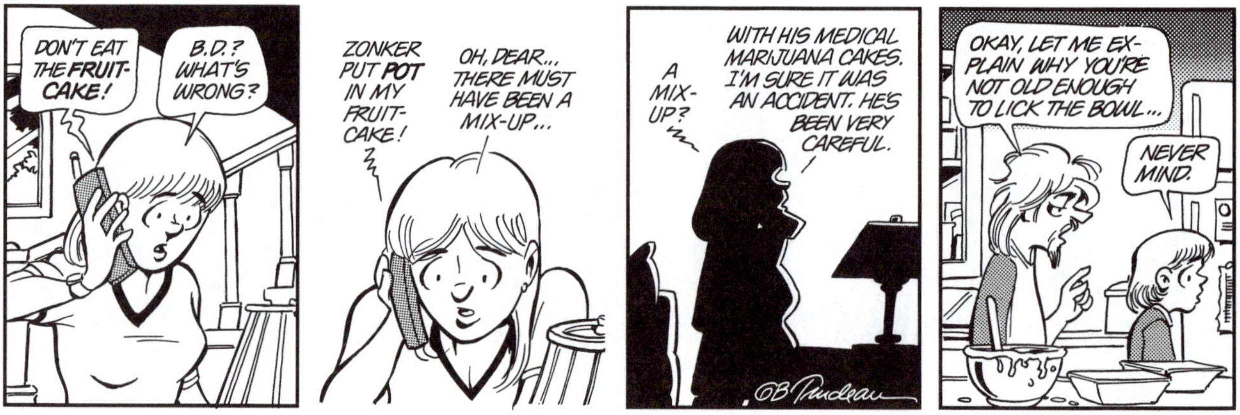
DON'T EAT THE FRUITCAKE!
B.D.? WHAT'S WRONG?
ZONKER PUT POT IN MY FRUITCAKE!
OH, DEAR... THERE MUST HAVE BEEN A MIX-UP...
A MIX-UP?
WITH HIS MEDICAL MARIJUANA CAKES. I'M SURE IT WAS AN ACCIDENT. HE'S BEEN VERY CAREFUL.
OKAY, LET ME EXPLAIN WHY YOU'RE NOT OLD ENOUGH TO LICK THE BOWL...
NEVER MIND.

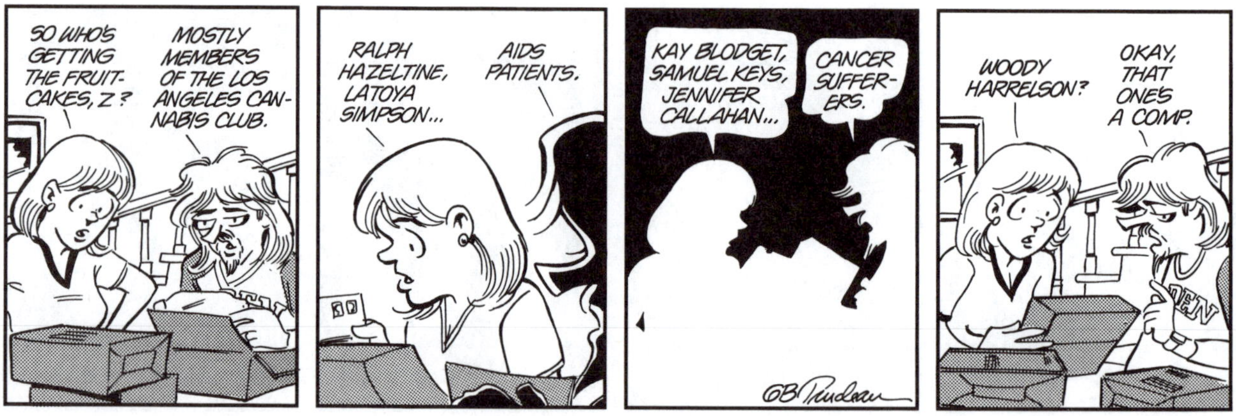
SO WHO'S GETTING THE FRUITCAKES, Z?
MOSTLY MEMBERS OF THE LOS ANGELES CANNABIS CLUB.
RALPH HAZELTINE, LATOYA SIMPSON...
AIDS PATIENTS.
KAY BLODGET, SAMUEL KEYS, JENNIFER CALLAHAN...
CANCER SUFFERERS.
WOODY HARRELSON?
OKAY, THAT ONE'S A COMP.

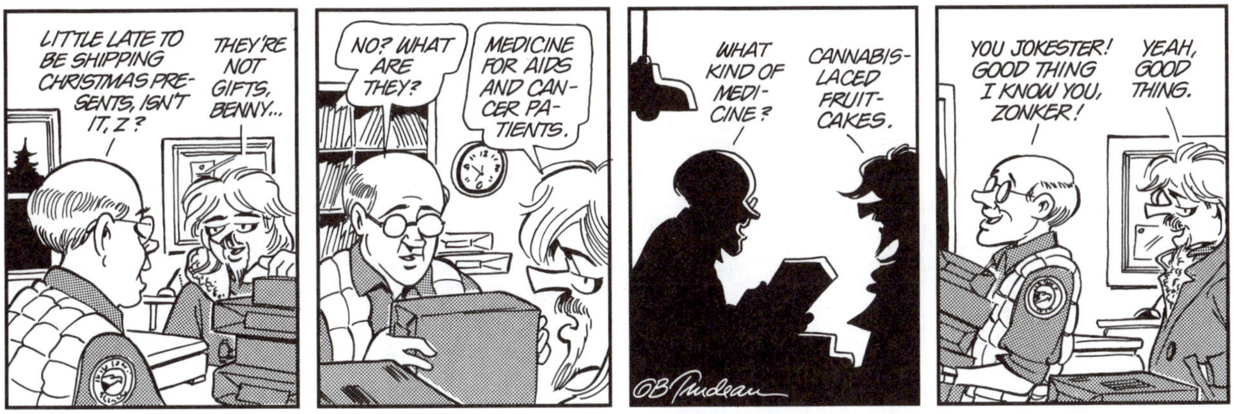
LITTLE LATE TO BE SHIPPING CHRISTMAS PRESENTS, ISN'T IT, Z?
THEY'RE NOT GIFTS, BENNY...
NO? WHAT ARE THEY?
MEDICINE FOR AIDS AND CANCER PATIENTS.
WHAT KIND OF MEDICINE?
CANNABIS-LACED FRUITCAKES.
YOU JOKESTER! GOOD THING I KNOW YOU, ZONKER!
YEAH, GOOD THING.

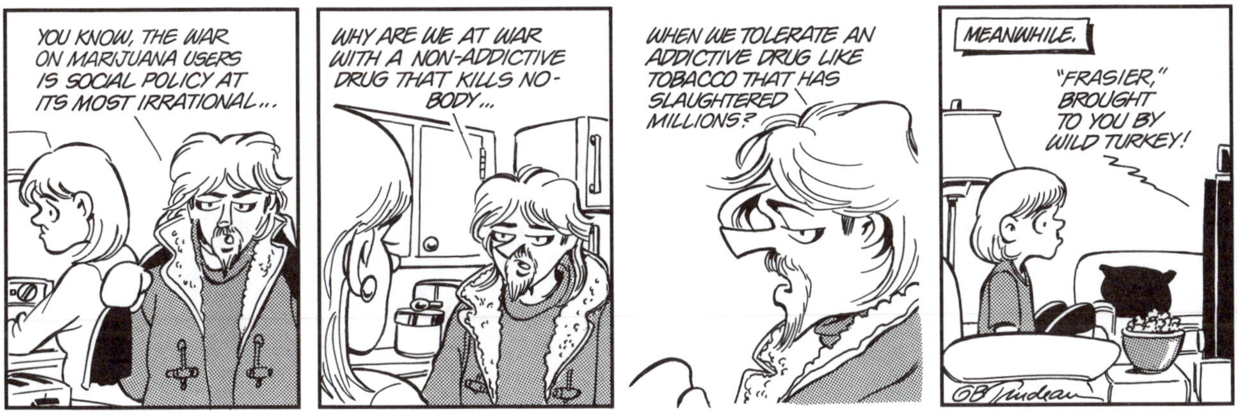
YOU KNOW, THE WAR ON MARIJUANA USERS IS SOCIAL POLICY AT ITS MOST IRRATIONAL...
WHY ARE WE AT WAR WITH A NON-ADDICTIVE DRUG THAT KILLS NOBODY...
WHEN WE TOLERATE AN ADDICTIVE DRUG LIKE TOBACCO THAT HAS SLAUGHTERED MILLIONS?
MEANWHILE.
"FRASIER," BROUGHT TO YOU BY WILD TURKEY!

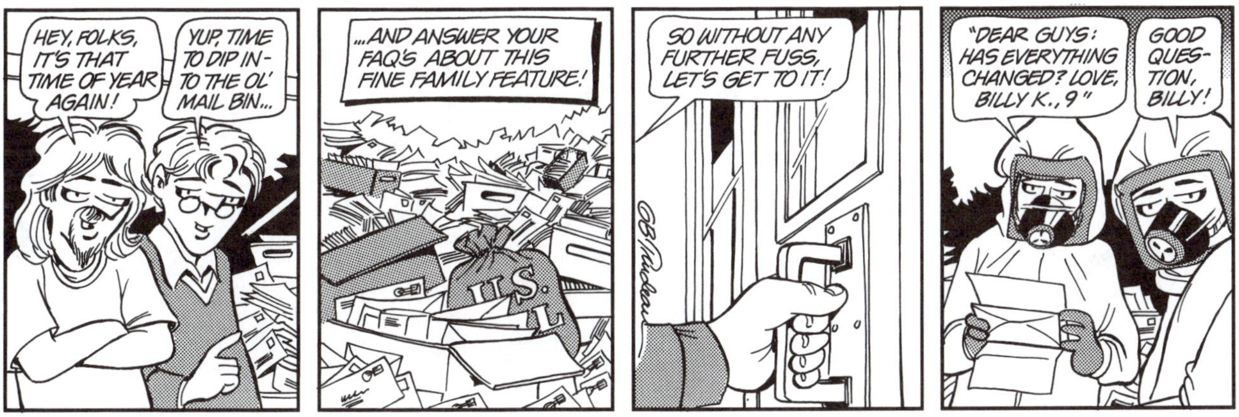
HEY, FOLKS, IT'S THAT TIME OF YEAR AGAIN!
YUP, TIME TO DIP INTO THE OL' MAIL BIN...
...AND ANSWER YOUR FAQ'S ABOUT THIS FINE FAMILY FEATURE!
U.S.
SO WITHOUT ANY FURTHER FUSS, LET'S GET TO IT!
"DEAR GUYS: HAS EVERYTHING CHANGED? LOVE, BILLY K., 9"
GOOD QUESTION, BILLY!

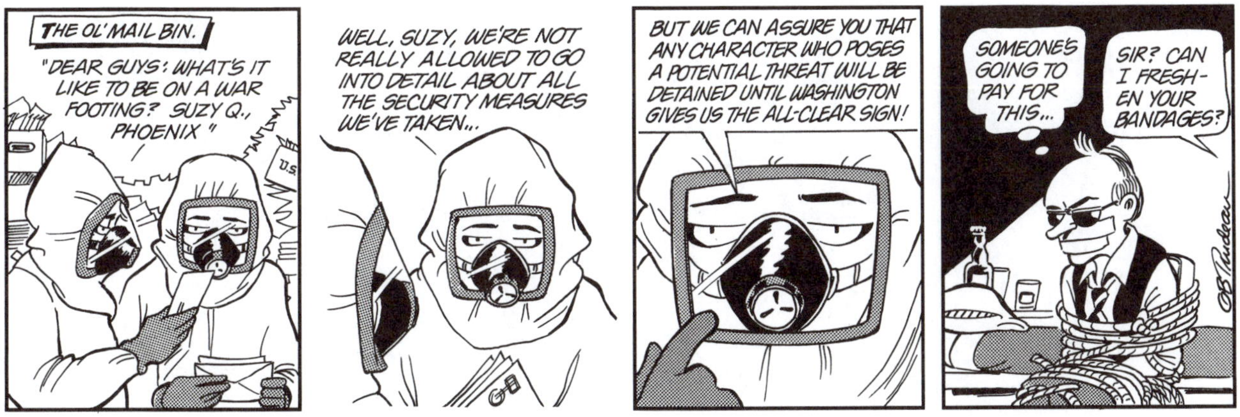
THE OL' MAIL BIN.
"DEAR GUYS: WHAT'S IT LIKE TO BE ON A WAR FOOTING? SUZY Q., PHOENIX"
WELL, SUZY, WE'RE NOT REALLY ALLOWED TO GO INTO DETAIL ABOUT ALL THE SECURITY MEASURES WE'VE TAKEN...
BUT WE CAN ASSURE YOU THAT ANY CHARACTER WHO POSES A POTENTIAL THREAT WILL BE DETAINED UNTIL WASHINGTON GIVES US THE ALL-CLEAR SIGN!
SOMEONE'S GOING TO PAY FOR THIS...
SIR? CAN I FRESHEN YOUR BANDAGES?

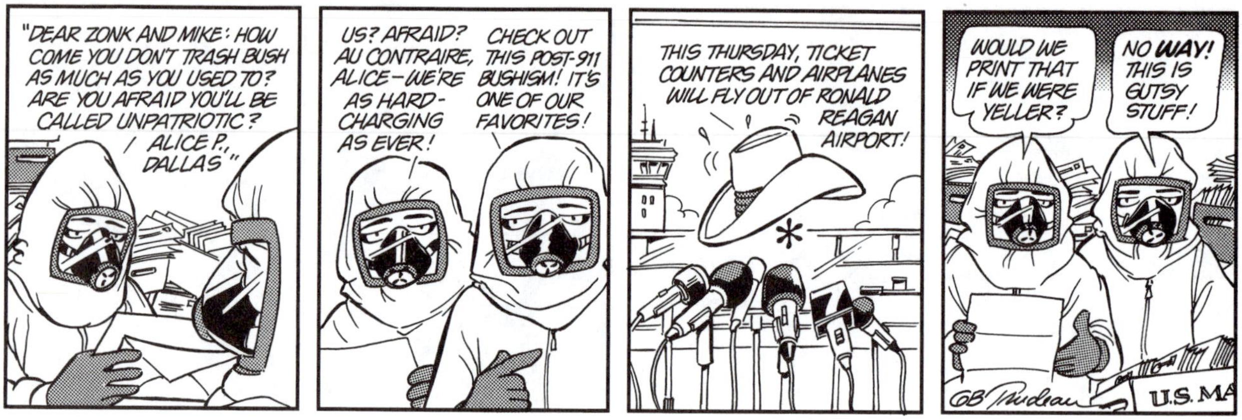
"DEAR ZONK AND MIKE: HOW COME YOU DON'T TRASH BUSH AS MUCH AS YOU USED TO? ARE YOU AFRAID YOU'LL BE CALLED UNPATRIOTIC? ALICE P., DALLAS"
US? AFRAID? AU CONTRAIRE, ALICE—WE'RE AS HARD-CHARGING AS EVER!
CHECK OUT THIS POST-911 BUSHISM! IT'S ONE OF OUR FAVORITES!
THIS THURSDAY, TICKET COUNTERS AND AIRPLANES WILL FLY OUT OF RONALD REAGAN AIRPORT!
WOULD WE PRINT THAT IF WE WERE YELLER?
NO WAY! THIS IS GUTSY STUFF!
U.S. MA

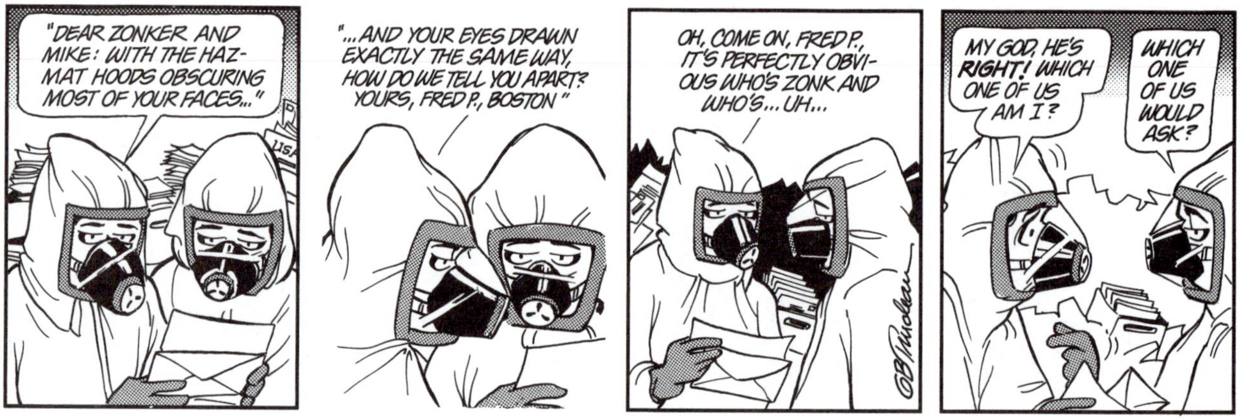
"DEAR ZONKER AND MIKE: WITH THE HAZ-MAT HOODS OBSCURING MOST OF YOUR FACES..."
"...AND YOUR EYES DRAWN EXACTLY THE SAME WAY, HOW DO WE TELL YOU APART? YOURS, FRED P., BOSTON"
OH, COME ON, FRED P., IT'S PERFECTLY OBVI-OUS WHO'S ZONK AND WHO'S... UH...
MY GOD, HE'S RIGHT! WHICH ONE OF US AM I?
WHICH ONE OF US WOULD ASK?

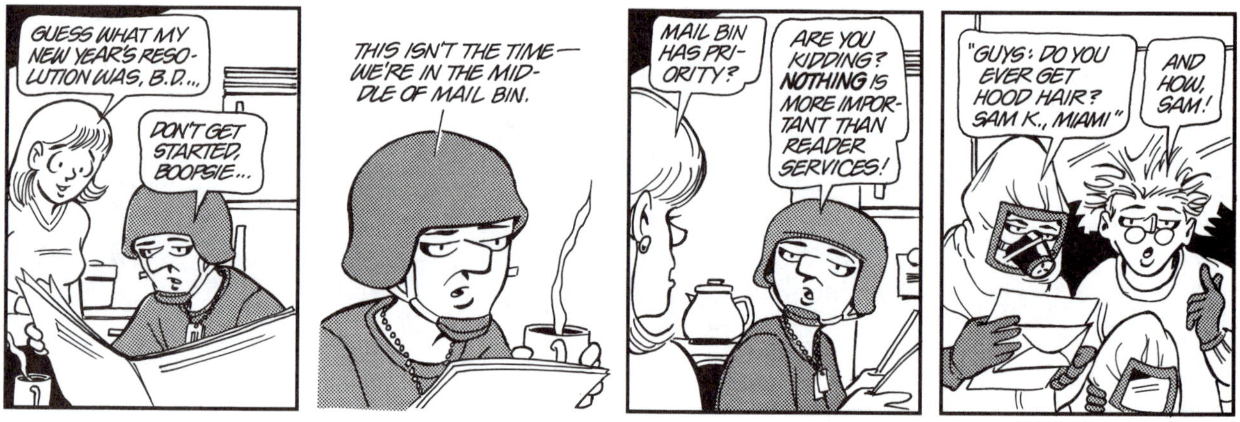
GUESS WHAT MY NEW YEAR'S RESO-LUTION WAS, B.D....
DON'T GET STARTED, BOOPSIE...
THIS ISN'T THE TIME—WE'RE IN THE MID-DLE OF MAIL BIN.
MAIL BIN HAS PRI-ORITY?
ARE YOU KIDDING? NOTHING IS MORE IMPOR-TANT THAN READER SERVICES!
"GUYS: DO YOU EVER GET HOOD HAIR? SAM K., MIAMI"
AND HOW, SAM!

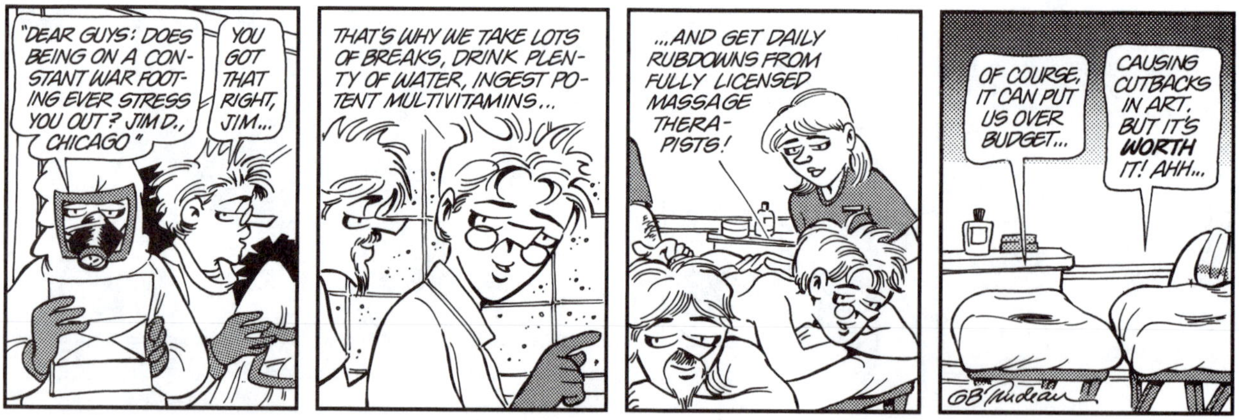
"DEAR GUYS: DOES BEING ON A CON-STANT WAR FOOT-ING EVER STRESS YOU OUT? JIM D., CHICAGO"
YOU GOT THAT RIGHT, JIM...
THAT'S WHY WE TAKE LOTS OF BREAKS, DRINK PLEN-TY OF WATER, INGEST PO-TENT MULTIVITAMINS...
...AND GET DAILY RUBDOWNS FROM FULLY LICENSED MASSAGE THERA-PISTS!
OF COURSE, IT CAN PUT US OVER BUDGET...
CAUSING CUTBACKS IN ART, BUT IT'S WORTH IT! AHH...

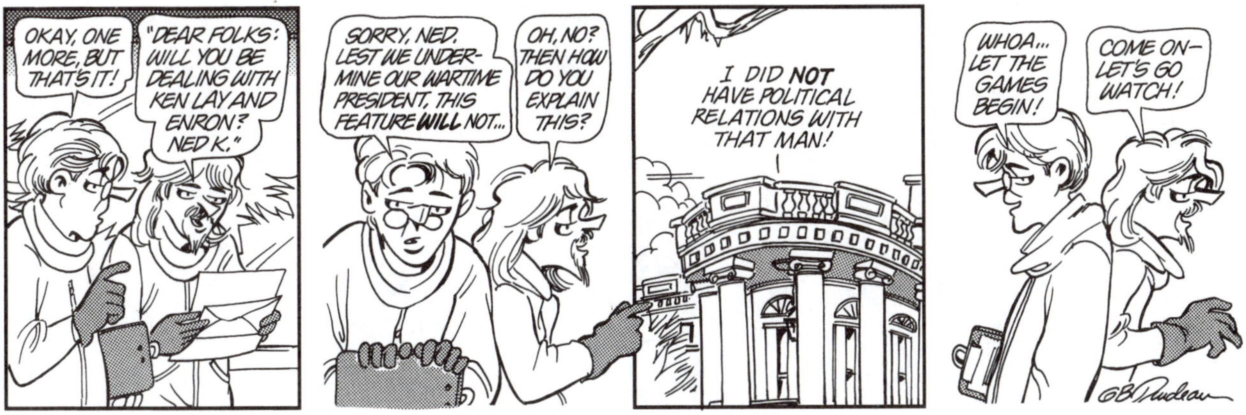
OKAY, ONE MORE, BUT THAT'S IT!
"DEAR FOLKS: WILL YOU BE DEALING WITH KEN LAY AND ENRON? NED K."
SORRY, NED. LEST WE UNDERMINE OUR WARTIME PRESIDENT, THIS FEATURE WILL NOT...
OH, NO? THEN HOW DO YOU EXPLAIN THIS?
I DID NOT HAVE POLITICAL RELATIONS WITH THAT MAN!
WHOA... LET THE GAMES BEGIN!
COME ON–LET'S GO WATCH!
©B. Trudeau

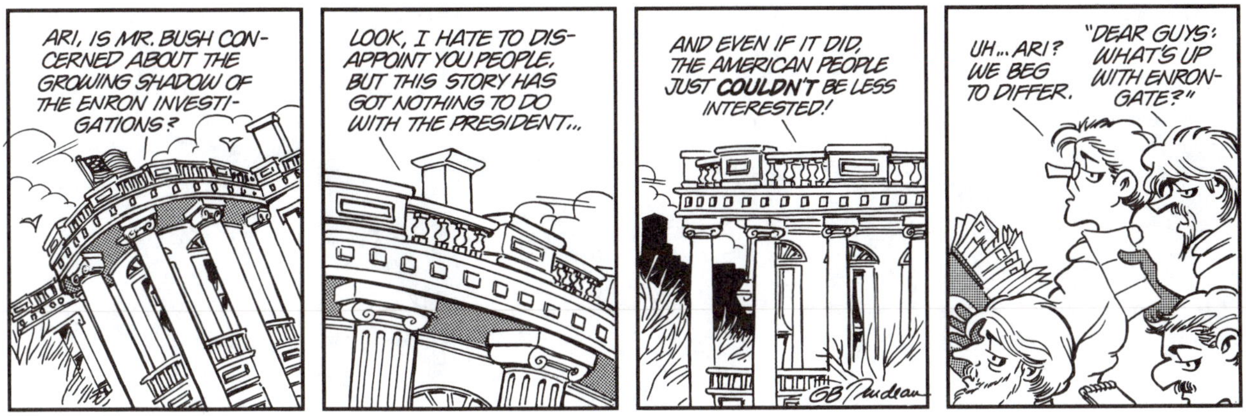
ARI, IS MR. BUSH CONCERNED ABOUT THE GROWING SHADOW OF THE ENRON INVESTIGATIONS?
LOOK, I HATE TO DISAPPOINT YOU PEOPLE, BUT THIS STORY HAS GOT NOTHING TO DO WITH THE PRESIDENT...
AND EVEN IF IT DID, THE AMERICAN PEOPLE JUST COULDN'T BE LESS INTERESTED!
UH... ARI? WE BEG TO DIFFER.
"DEAR GUYS: WHAT'S UP WITH ENRONGATE?"
©B. Trudeau

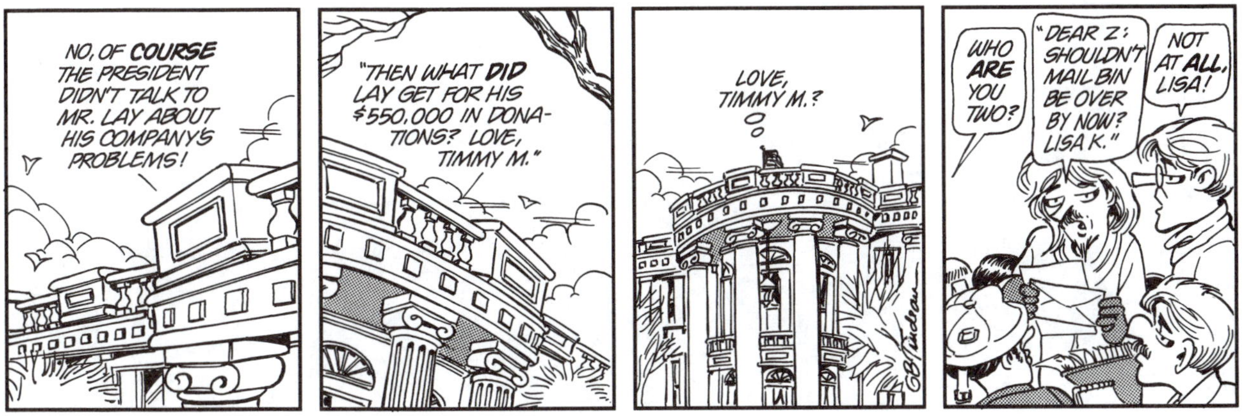
NO, OF COURSE THE PRESIDENT DIDN'T TALK TO MR. LAY ABOUT HIS COMPANY'S PROBLEMS!
"THEN WHAT DID LAY GET FOR HIS $550,000 IN DONATIONS? LOVE, TIMMY M."
LOVE, TIMMY M.?
WHO ARE YOU TWO?
"DEAR Z: SHOULDN'T MAIL BIN BE OVER BY NOW? LISA K."
NOT AT ALL, LISA!
©B. Trudeau

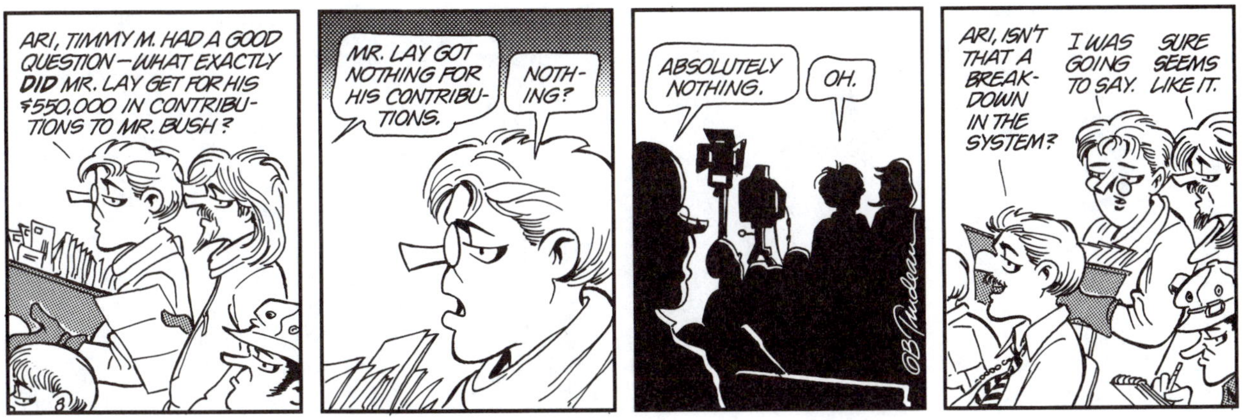
ARI, TIMMY M. HAD A GOOD QUESTION—WHAT EXACTLY DID MR. LAY GET FOR HIS $550,000 IN CONTRIBUTIONS TO MR. BUSH?
MR. LAY GOT NOTHING FOR HIS CONTRIBUTIONS.
NOTHING?
ABSOLUTELY NOTHING.
OH.
ARI, ISN'T THAT A BREAKDOWN IN THE SYSTEM?
I WAS GOING TO SAY.
SURE SEEMS LIKE IT.
©B. Trudeau

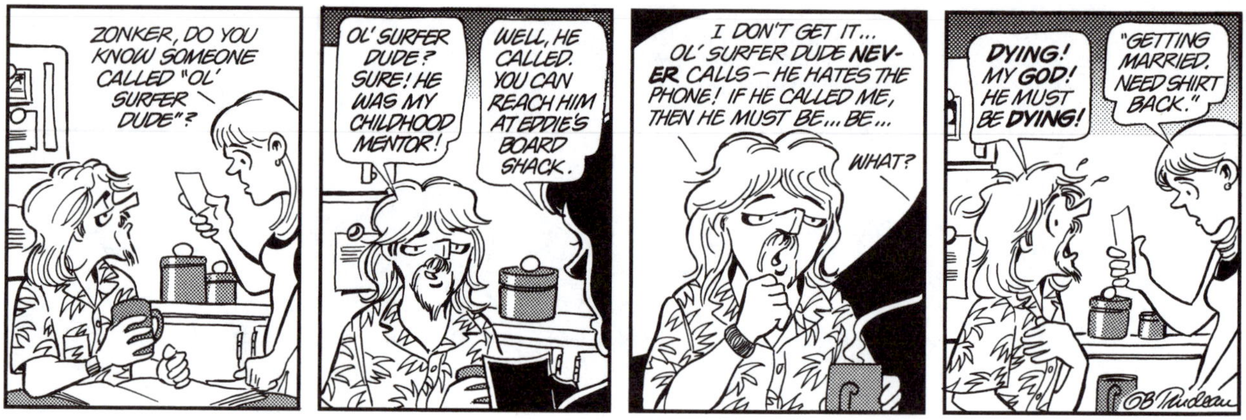
ZONKER, DO YOU KNOW SOMEONE CALLED "OL' SURFER DUDE"?
OL' SURFER DUDE? SURE! HE WAS MY CHILDHOOD MENTOR!
WELL, HE CALLED. YOU CAN REACH HIM AT EDDIE'S BOARD SHACK.
I DON'T GET IT... OL' SURFER DUDE NEVER CALLS — HE HATES THE PHONE! IF HE CALLED ME, THEN HE MUST BE... BE...
WHAT?
DYING! MY GOD! HE MUST BE DYING!
"GETTING MARRIED. NEED SHIRT BACK."
©GBTrudeau

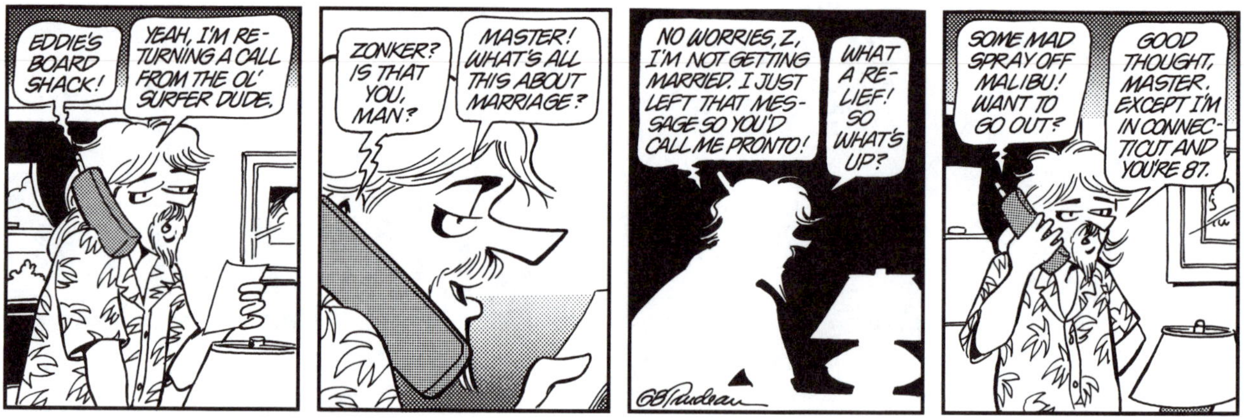
EDDIE'S BOARD SHACK!
YEAH, I'M RETURNING A CALL FROM THE OL' SURFER DUDE.
ZONKER? IS THAT YOU, MAN?
MASTER! WHAT'S ALL THIS ABOUT MARRIAGE?
NO WORRIES, Z, I'M NOT GETTING MARRIED. I JUST LEFT THAT MESSAGE SO YOU'D CALL ME PRONTO!
WHAT A RELIEF! SO WHAT'S UP?
SOME MAD SPRAY OFF MALIBU! WANT TO GO OUT?
GOOD THOUGHT, MASTER. EXCEPT I'M IN CONNECTICUT AND YOU'RE 87.
©GBTrudeau

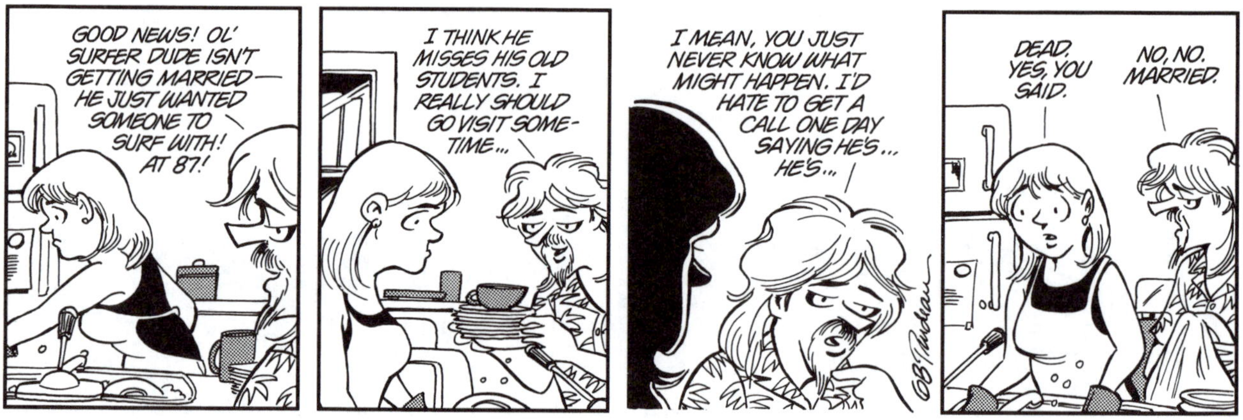
GOOD NEWS! OL' SURFER DUDE ISN'T GETTING MARRIED — HE JUST WANTED SOMEONE TO SURF WITH! AT 87!
I THINK HE MISSES HIS OLD STUDENTS. I REALLY SHOULD GO VISIT SOMETIME...
I MEAN, YOU JUST NEVER KNOW WHAT MIGHT HAPPEN. I'D HATE TO GET A CALL ONE DAY SAYING HE'S... HE'S...
DEAD. YES, YOU SAID.
NO, NO. MARRIED.
©GBTrudeau

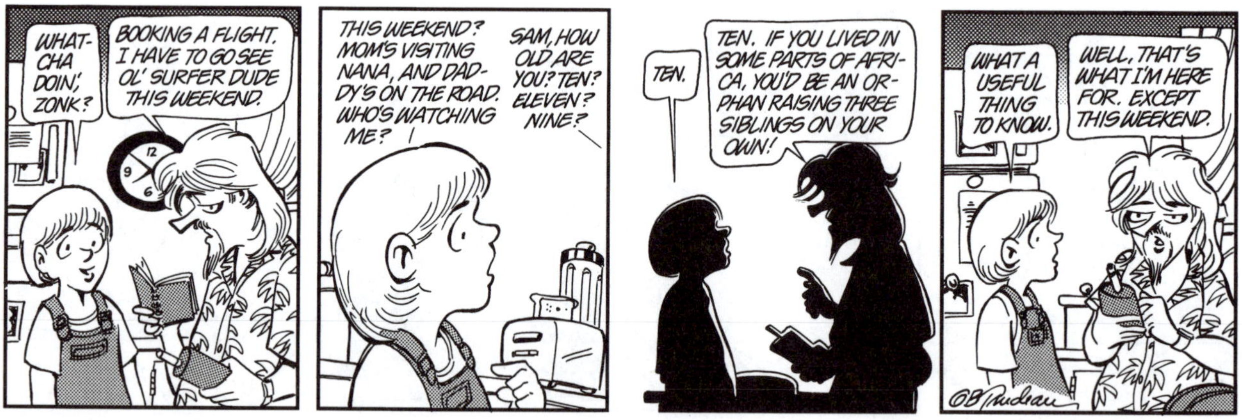
WHATCHA DOIN', ZONK?
BOOKING A FLIGHT. I HAVE TO GO SEE OL' SURFER DUDE THIS WEEKEND.
THIS WEEKEND? MOM'S VISITING NANA, AND DADDY'S ON THE ROAD. WHO'S WATCHING ME?
SAM, HOW OLD ARE YOU? TEN? ELEVEN? NINE?
TEN.
TEN. IF YOU LIVED IN SOME PARTS OF AFRICA, YOU'D BE AN ORPHAN RAISING THREE SIBLINGS ON YOUR OWN!
WHAT A USEFUL THING TO KNOW.
WELL, THAT'S WHAT I'M HERE FOR. EXCEPT THIS WEEKEND.
©GBTrudeau

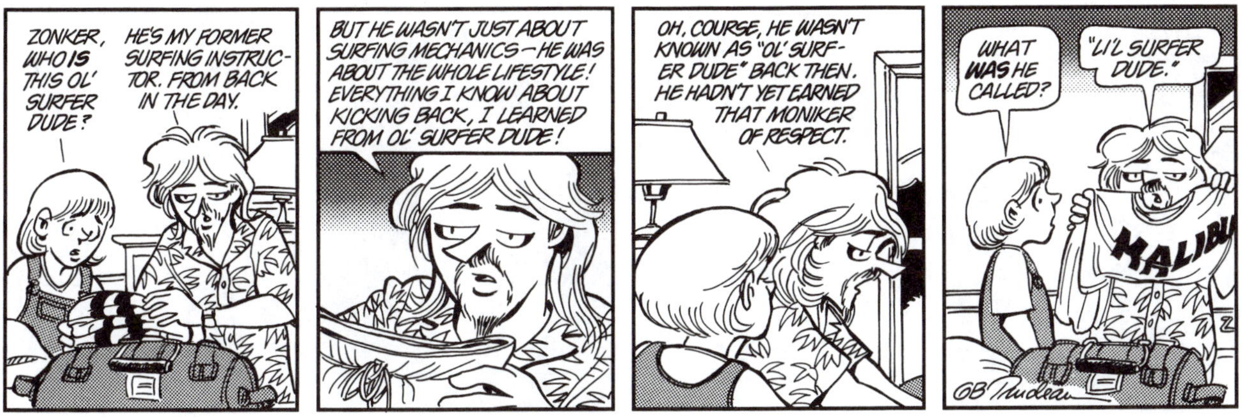

ZONKER, WHO **IS** THIS OL' SURFER DUDE?
HE'S MY FORMER SURFING INSTRUCTOR. FROM BACK IN THE DAY.
BUT HE WASN'T JUST ABOUT SURFING MECHANICS—HE WAS ABOUT THE WHOLE LIFESTYLE! EVERYTHING I KNOW ABOUT KICKING BACK, I LEARNED FROM OL' SURFER DUDE!
OH, COURSE, HE WASN'T KNOWN AS "OL' SURFER DUDE" BACK THEN. HE HADN'T YET EARNED THAT MONIKER OF RESPECT.
WHAT **WAS** HE CALLED?
"LI'L SURFER DUDE."
MALIBU

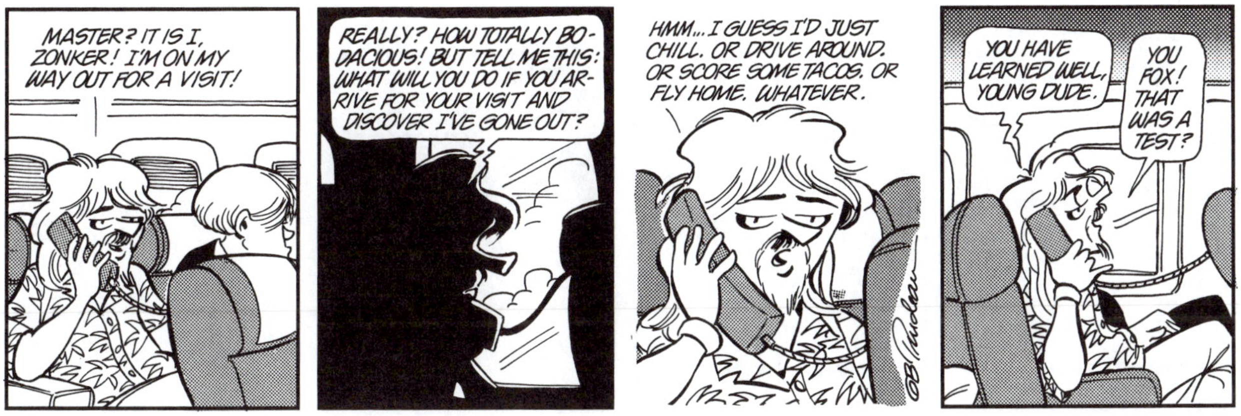

MASTER? IT IS I, ZONKER! I'M ON MY WAY OUT FOR A VISIT!
REALLY? HOW TOTALLY BODACIOUS! BUT TELL ME THIS: WHAT WILL YOU DO IF YOU ARRIVE FOR YOUR VISIT AND DISCOVER I'VE GONE OUT?
HMM... I GUESS I'D JUST CHILL. OR DRIVE AROUND. OR SCORE SOME TACOS. OR FLY HOME. WHATEVER.
YOU HAVE LEARNED WELL, YOUNG DUDE.
YOU FOX! THAT WAS A TEST?

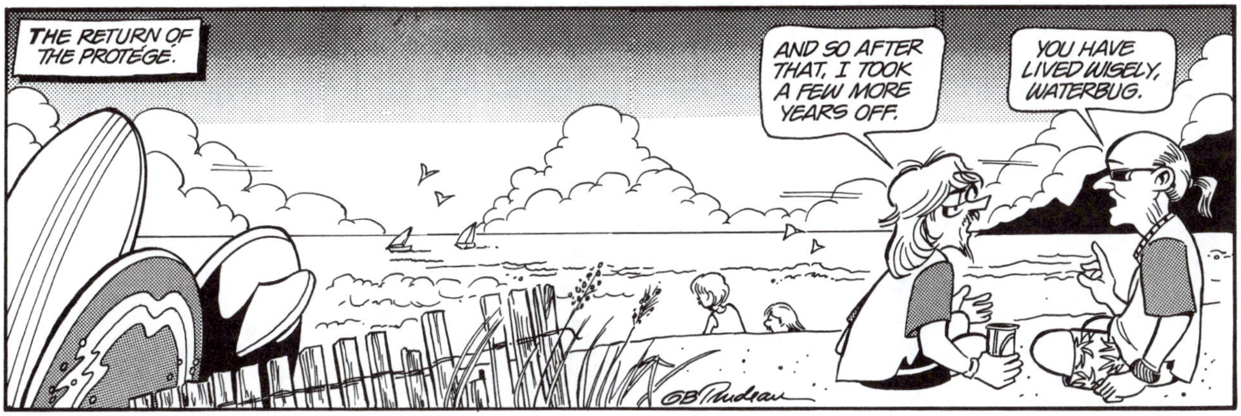

THE RETURN OF THE PROTEGE.
AND SO AFTER THAT, I TOOK A FEW MORE YEARS OFF.
YOU HAVE LIVED WISELY, WATERBUG.

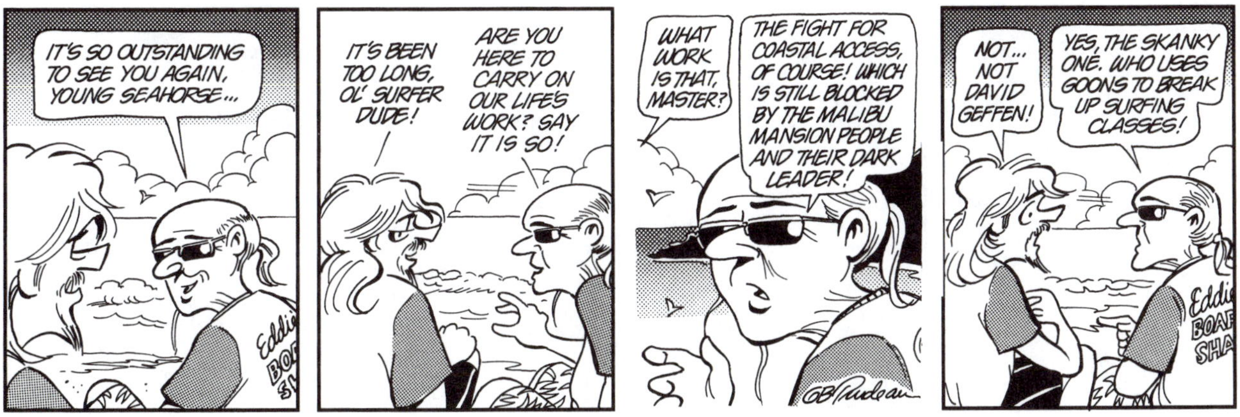

IT'S SO OUTSTANDING TO SEE YOU AGAIN, YOUNG SEAHORSE...
IT'S BEEN TOO LONG, OL' SURFER DUDE!
ARE YOU HERE TO CARRY ON OUR LIFE'S WORK? SAY IT IS SO!
WHAT WORK IS THAT, MASTER?
THE FIGHT FOR COASTAL ACCESS, OF COURSE! WHICH IS STILL BLOCKED BY THE MALIBU MANSION PEOPLE AND THEIR DARK LEADER!
NOT... NOT DAVID GEFFEN!
YES, THE SKANKY ONE. WHO USES GOONS TO BREAK UP SURFING CLASSES!

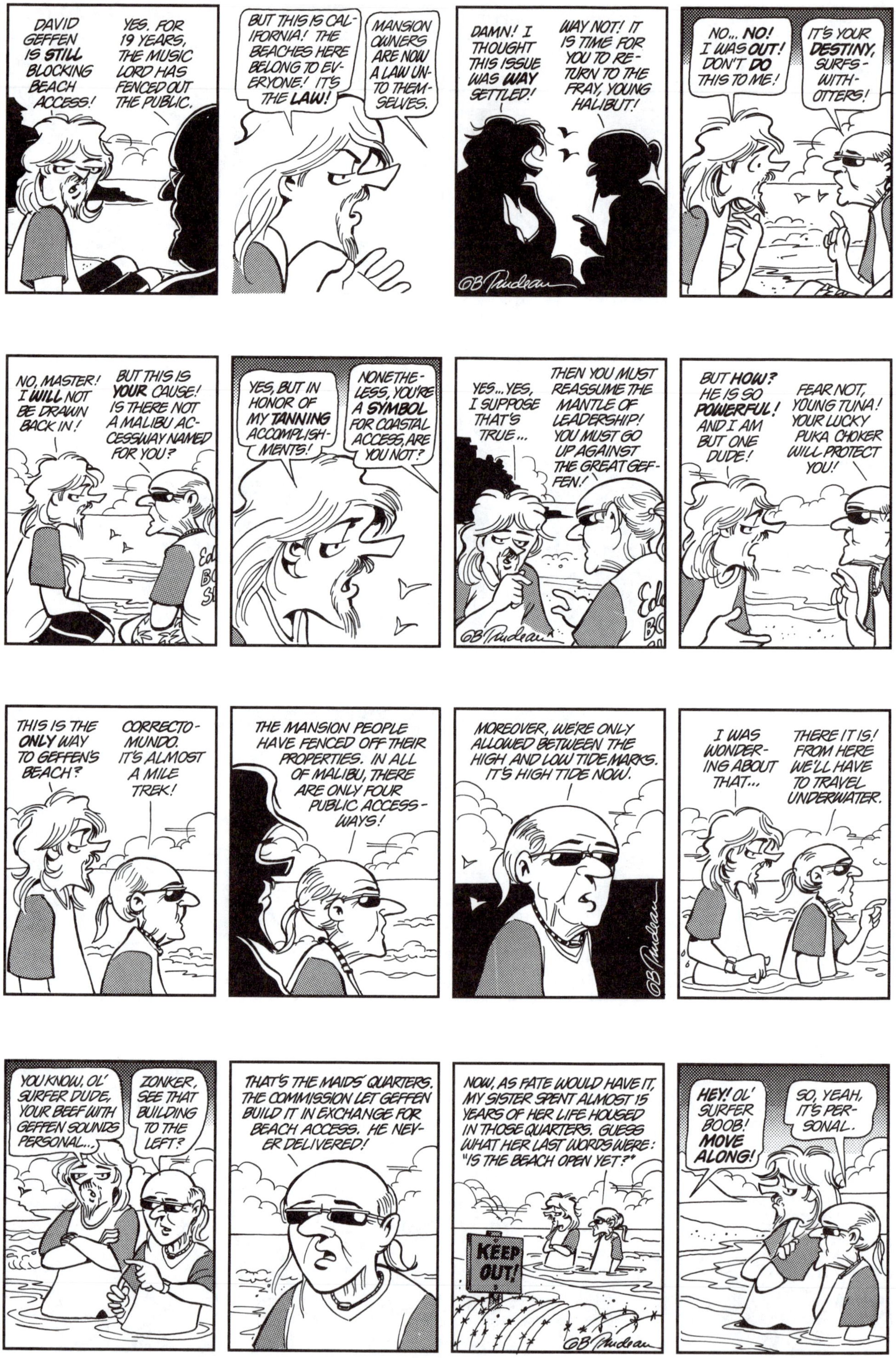
DAVID GEFFEN IS STILL BLOCKING BEACH ACCESS!
YES. FOR 19 YEARS, THE MUSIC LORD HAS FENCED OUT THE PUBLIC.
BUT THIS IS CALIFORNIA! THE BEACHES HERE BELONG TO EVERYONE! IT'S THE LAW!
MANSION OWNERS ARE NOW A LAW UNTO THEMSELVES.
DAMN! I THOUGHT THIS ISSUE WAS WAY SETTLED!
WAY NOT! IT IS TIME FOR YOU TO RETURN TO THE FRAY, YOUNG HALIBUT!
©B Trudeau
NO... NO! I WAS OUT! DON'T DO THIS TO ME!
IT'S YOUR DESTINY, SURFS-WITH-OTTERS!
NO, MASTER! I WILL NOT BE DRAWN BACK IN!
BUT THIS IS YOUR CAUSE! IS THERE NOT A MALIBU ACCESSWAY NAMED FOR YOU?
YES, BUT IN HONOR OF MY TANNING ACCOMPLISHMENTS!
NONETHELESS, YOU'RE A SYMBOL FOR COASTAL ACCESS, ARE YOU NOT?
YES... YES, I SUPPOSE THAT'S TRUE...
THEN YOU MUST REASSUME THE MANTLE OF LEADERSHIP! YOU MUST GO UP AGAINST THE GREAT GEFFEN!
©B Trudeau
BUT HOW? HE IS SO POWERFUL! AND I AM BUT ONE DUDE!
FEAR NOT, YOUNG TUNA! YOUR LUCKY PUKA CHOKER WILL PROTECT YOU!
THIS IS THE ONLY WAY TO GEFFEN'S BEACH?
CORRECTOMUNDO. IT'S ALMOST A MILE TREK!
THE MANSION PEOPLE HAVE FENCED OFF THEIR PROPERTIES. IN ALL OF MALIBU, THERE ARE ONLY FOUR PUBLIC ACCESSWAYS!
MOREOVER, WE'RE ONLY ALLOWED BETWEEN THE HIGH AND LOW TIDE MARKS. IT'S HIGH TIDE NOW.
©B Trudeau
I WAS WONDERING ABOUT THAT...
THERE IT IS! FROM HERE WE'LL HAVE TO TRAVEL UNDERWATER.
YOU KNOW, OL' SURFER DUDE, YOUR BEEF WITH GEFFEN SOUNDS PERSONAL...
ZONKER, SEE THAT BUILDING TO THE LEFT?
THAT'S THE MAIDS' QUARTERS. THE COMMISSION LET GEFFEN BUILD IT IN EXCHANGE FOR BEACH ACCESS. HE NEVER DELIVERED!
NOW, AS FATE WOULD HAVE IT, MY SISTER SPENT ALMOST 15 YEARS OF HER LIFE HOUSED IN THOSE QUARTERS. GUESS WHAT HER LAST WORDS WERE: "IS THE BEACH OPEN YET?"
KEEP OUT!
©B Trudeau
HEY! OL' SURFER BOOB! MOVE ALONG!
SO, YEAH, IT'S PERSONAL.

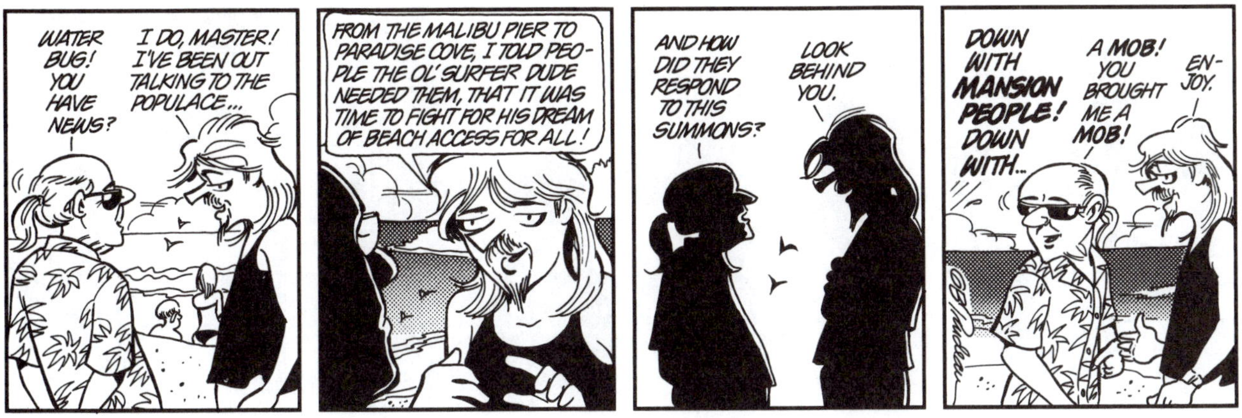
WATER BUG! YOU HAVE NEWS?
I DO, MASTER! I'VE BEEN OUT TALKING TO THE POPULACE...
FROM THE MALIBU PIER TO PARADISE COVE, I TOLD PEOPLE THE OL' SURFER DUDE NEEDED THEM, THAT IT WAS TIME TO FIGHT FOR HIS DREAM OF BEACH ACCESS FOR ALL!
AND HOW DID THEY RESPOND TO THIS SUMMONS?
LOOK BEHIND YOU.
DOWN WITH MANSION PEOPLE! DOWN WITH...
A MOB! YOU BROUGHT ME A MOB!
ENJOY.

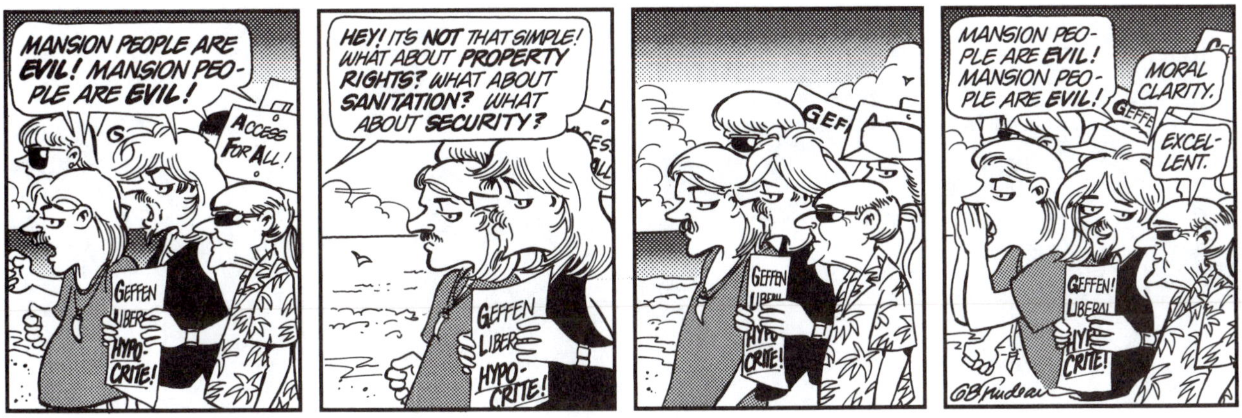
MANSION PEOPLE ARE EVIL! MANSION PEOPLE ARE EVIL!
ACCESS FOR ALL!
HEY! IT'S NOT THAT SIMPLE! WHAT ABOUT PROPERTY RIGHTS? WHAT ABOUT SANITATION? WHAT ABOUT SECURITY?
MANSION PEOPLE ARE EVIL! MANSION PEOPLE ARE EVIL!
MORAL CLARITY.
EXCELLENT.
GEFFEN! LIBERAL HYPOCRITE!

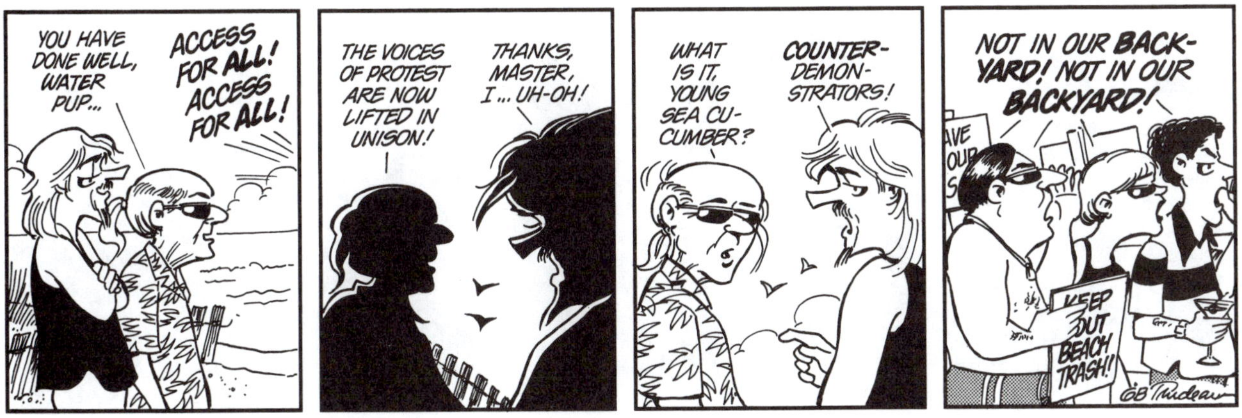
YOU HAVE DONE WELL, WATER PUP...
ACCESS FOR ALL! ACCESS FOR ALL!
THE VOICES OF PROTEST ARE NOW LIFTED IN UNISON!
THANKS, MASTER, I... UH-OH!
WHAT IS IT, YOUNG SEA CUCUMBER?
COUNTER-DEMONSTRATORS!
NOT IN OUR BACKYARD! NOT IN OUR BACKYARD!
KEEP OUT BEACH TRASH!

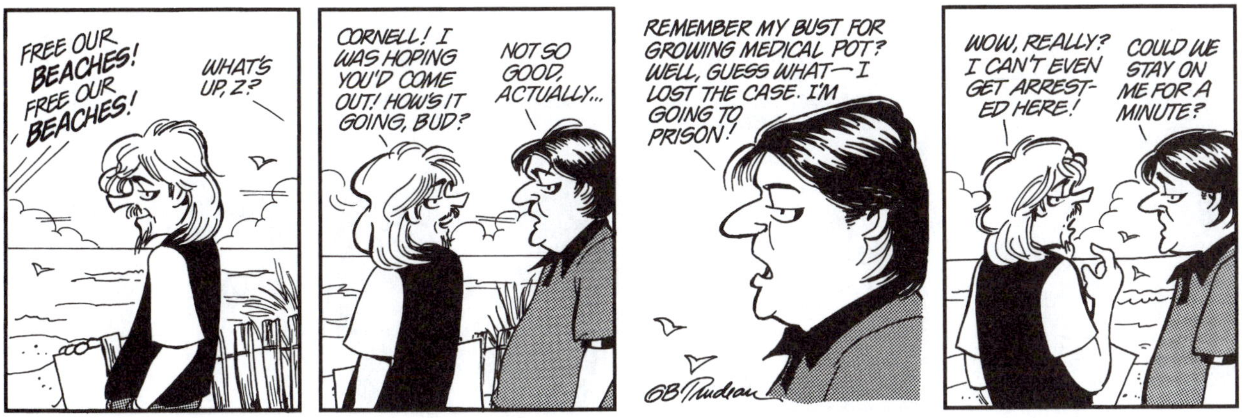
FREE OUR BEACHES! FREE OUR BEACHES!
WHAT'S UP, Z?
CORNELL! I WAS HOPING YOU'D COME OUT! HOW'S IT GOING, BUD?
NOT SO GOOD, ACTUALLY...
REMEMBER MY BUST FOR GROWING MEDICAL POT? WELL, GUESS WHAT—I LOST THE CASE. I'M GOING TO PRISON!
WOW, REALLY? I CAN'T EVEN GET ARRESTED HERE!
COULD WE STAY ON ME FOR A MINUTE?

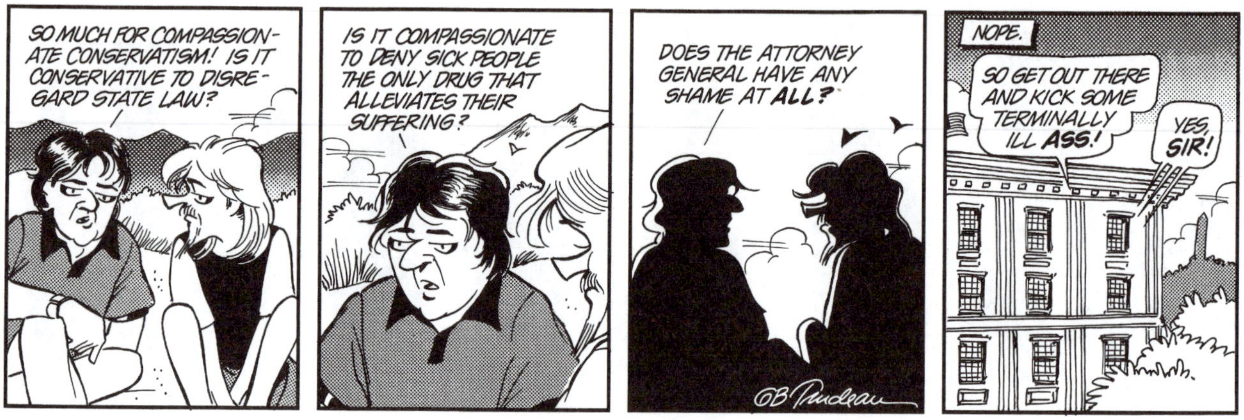
SO MUCH FOR COMPASSIONATE CONSERVATISM! IS IT CONSERVATIVE TO DISREGARD STATE LAW?
IS IT COMPASSIONATE TO DENY SICK PEOPLE THE ONLY DRUG THAT ALLEVIATES THEIR SUFFERING?
DOES THE ATTORNEY GENERAL HAVE ANY SHAME AT ALL?
NOPE.
SO GET OUT THERE AND KICK SOME TERMINALLY ILL ASS!
YES, SIR!

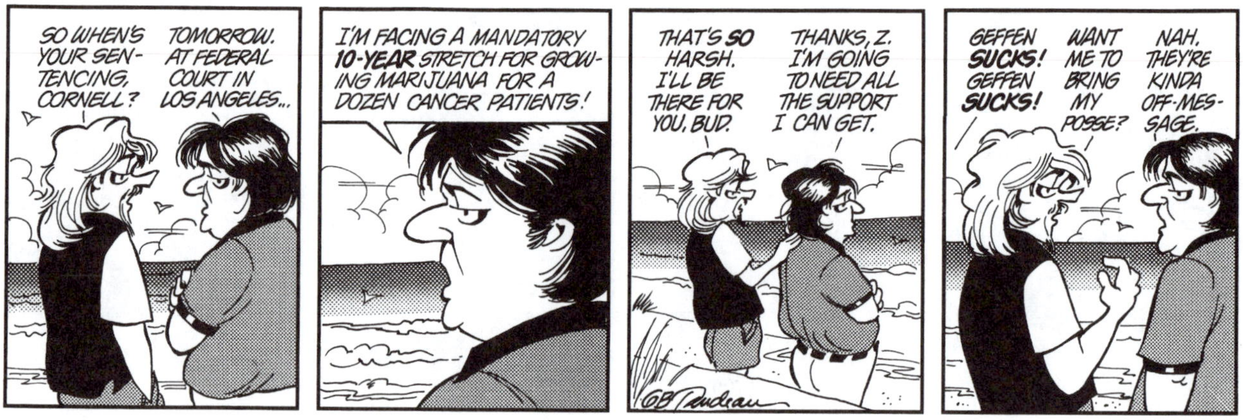
SO WHEN'S YOUR SENTENCING, CORNELL?
TOMORROW. AT FEDERAL COURT IN LOS ANGELES...
I'M FACING A MANDATORY 10-YEAR STRETCH FOR GROWING MARIJUANA FOR A DOZEN CANCER PATIENTS!
THAT'S SO HARSH. I'LL BE THERE FOR YOU, BUD.
THANKS, Z. I'M GOING TO NEED ALL THE SUPPORT I CAN GET.
GEFFEN SUCKS! GEFFEN SUCKS!
WANT ME TO BRING MY POSSE?
NAH. THEY'RE KINDA OFF-MESSAGE.

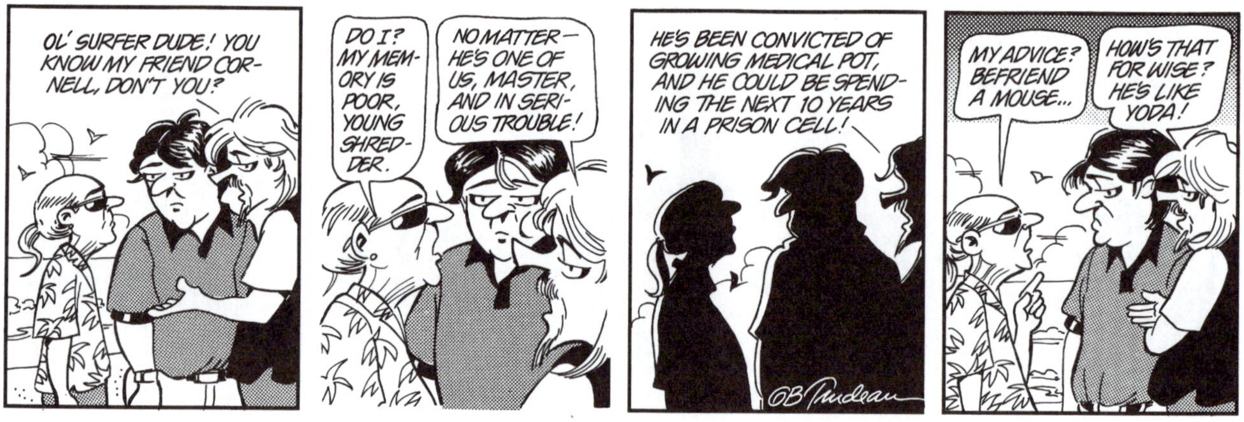
OL' SURFER DUDE! YOU KNOW MY FRIEND CORNELL, DON'T YOU?
DO I? MY MEMORY IS POOR, YOUNG SHREDDER.
NO MATTER—HE'S ONE OF US, MASTER, AND IN SERIOUS TROUBLE!
HE'S BEEN CONVICTED OF GROWING MEDICAL POT, AND HE COULD BE SPENDING THE NEXT 10 YEARS IN A PRISON CELL!
MY ADVICE? BEFRIEND A MOUSE...
HOW'S THAT FOR WISE? HE'S LIKE YODA!

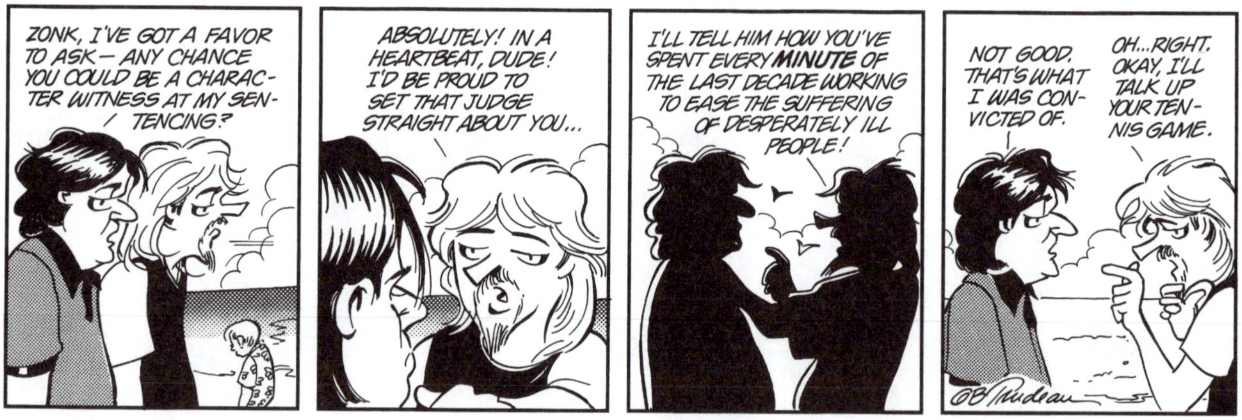
ZONK, I'VE GOT A FAVOR TO ASK—ANY CHANCE YOU COULD BE A CHARACTER WITNESS AT MY SENTENCING?
ABSOLUTELY! IN A HEARTBEAT, DUDE! I'D BE PROUD TO SET THAT JUDGE STRAIGHT ABOUT YOU...
I'LL TELL HIM HOW YOU'VE SPENT EVERY MINUTE OF THE LAST DECADE WORKING TO EASE THE SUFFERING OF DESPERATELY ILL PEOPLE!
NOT GOOD. THAT'S WHAT I WAS CONVICTED OF.
OH...RIGHT. OKAY, I'LL TALK UP YOUR TENNIS GAME.

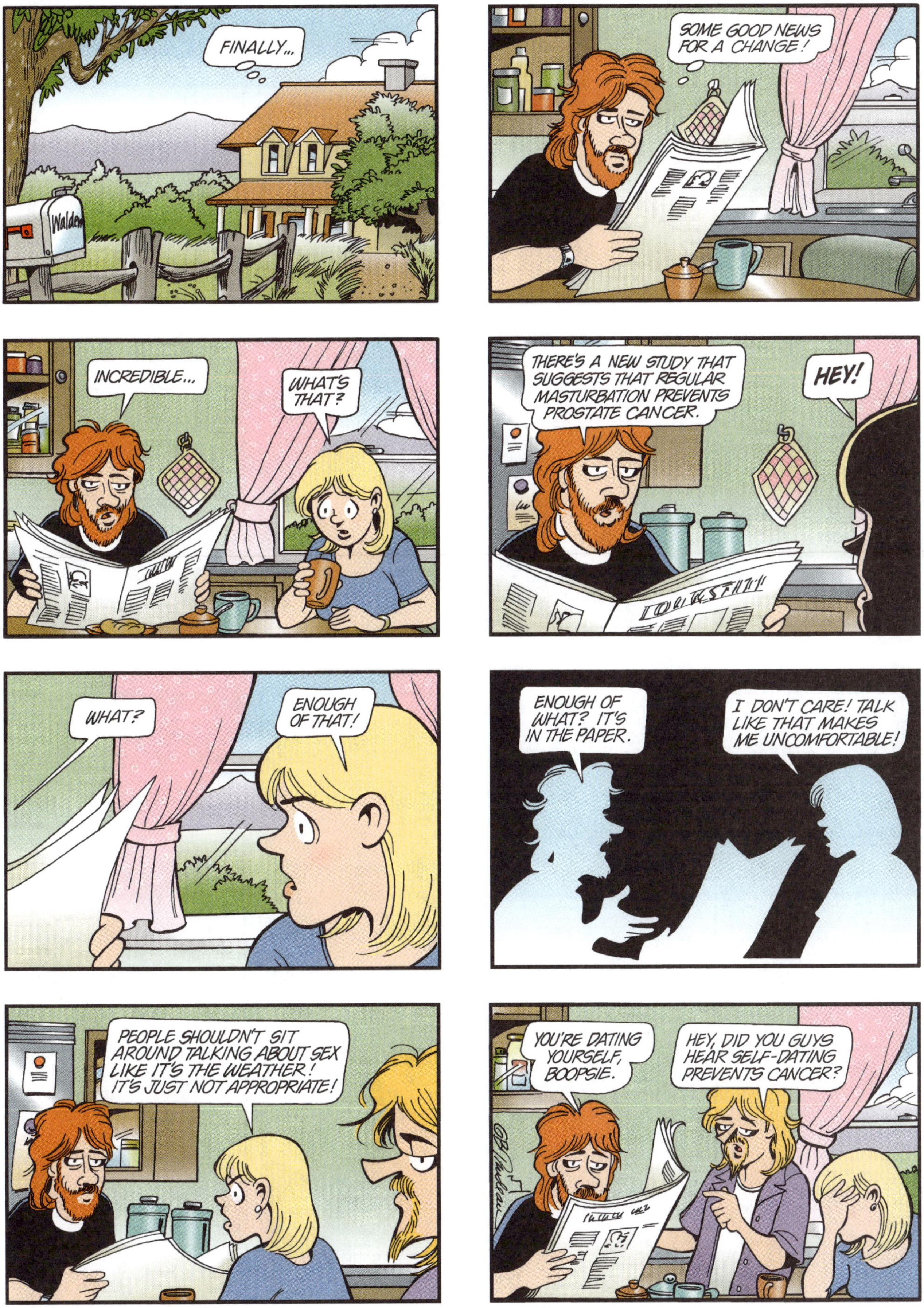
FINALLY...
SOME GOOD NEWS FOR A CHANGE!
INCREDIBLE...
WHAT'S THAT?
THERE'S A NEW STUDY THAT SUGGESTS THAT REGULAR MASTURBATION PREVENTS PROSTATE CANCER.
HEY!
WHAT?
ENOUGH OF THAT!
ENOUGH OF WHAT? IT'S IN THE PAPER.
I DON'T CARE! TALK LIKE THAT MAKES ME UNCOMFORTABLE!
PEOPLE SHOULDN'T SIT AROUND TALKING ABOUT SEX LIKE IT'S THE WEATHER! IT'S JUST NOT APPROPRIATE!
YOU'RE DATING YOURSELF, BOOPSIE.
HEY, DID YOU GUYS HEAR SELF-DATING PREVENTS CANCER?

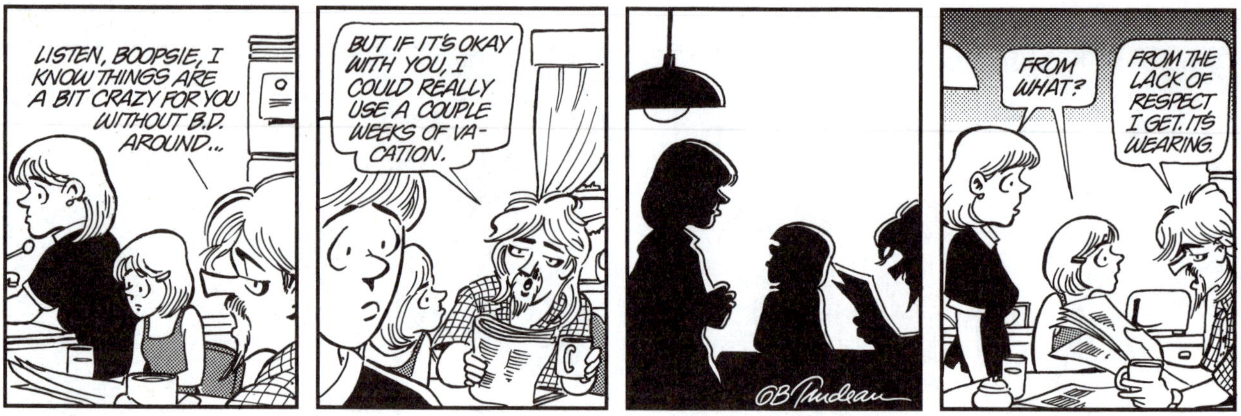
LISTEN, BOOPSIE, I KNOW THINGS ARE A BIT CRAZY FOR YOU WITHOUT B.D. AROUND...
BUT IF IT'S OKAY WITH YOU, I COULD REALLY USE A COUPLE WEEKS OF VACATION.
FROM WHAT?
FROM THE LACK OF RESPECT I GET. IT'S WEARING.

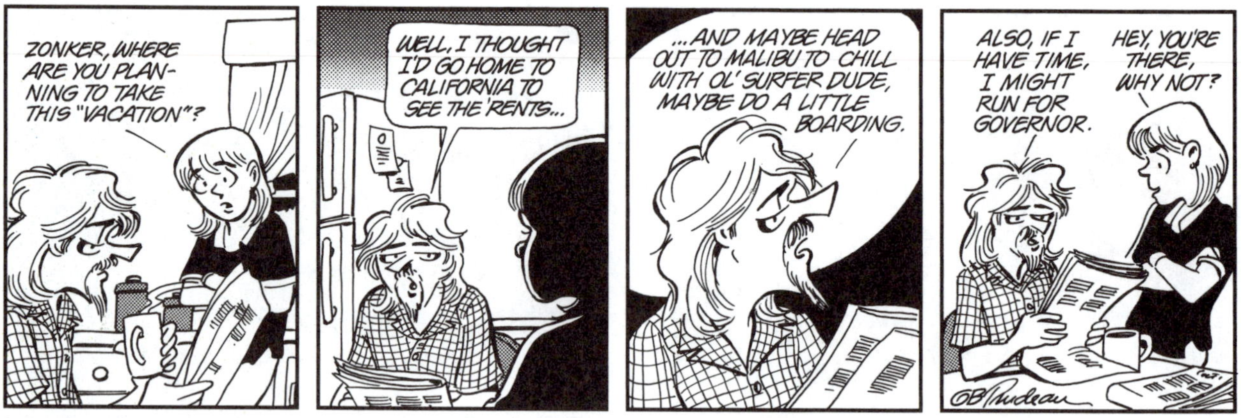
ZONKER, WHERE ARE YOU PLANNING TO TAKE THIS "VACATION"?
WELL, I THOUGHT I'D GO HOME TO CALIFORNIA TO SEE THE 'RENTS...
...AND MAYBE HEAD OUT TO MALIBU TO CHILL WITH OL' SURFER DUDE, MAYBE DO A LITTLE BOARDING.
ALSO, IF I HAVE TIME, I MIGHT RUN FOR GOVERNOR.
HEY, YOU'RE THERE, WHY NOT?

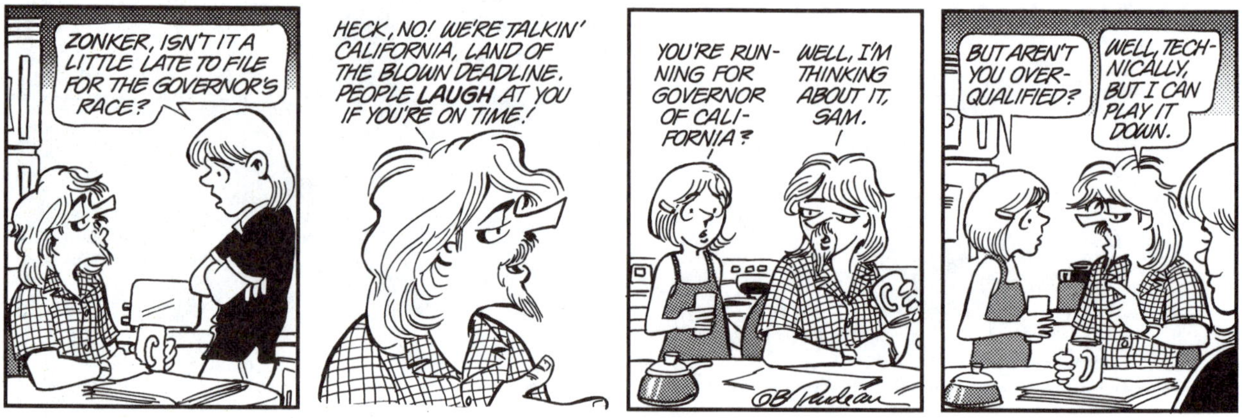
ZONKER, ISN'T IT A LITTLE LATE TO FILE FOR THE GOVERNOR'S RACE?
HECK, NO! WE'RE TALKIN' CALIFORNIA, LAND OF THE BLOWN DEADLINE. PEOPLE LAUGH AT YOU IF YOU'RE ON TIME!
YOU'RE RUNNING FOR GOVERNOR OF CALIFORNIA?
WELL, I'M THINKING ABOUT IT, SAM.
BUT AREN'T YOU OVERQUALIFIED?
WELL, TECHNICALLY, BUT I CAN PLAY IT DOWN.

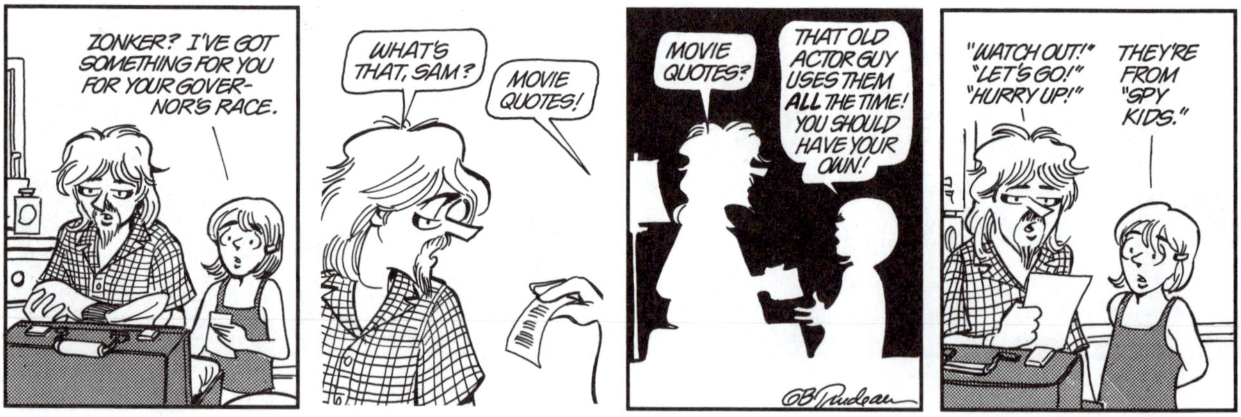
ZONKER? I'VE GOT SOMETHING FOR YOU FOR YOUR GOVERNOR'S RACE.
WHAT'S THAT, SAM?
MOVIE QUOTES!
MOVIE QUOTES?
THAT OLD ACTOR GUY USES THEM ALL THE TIME! YOU SHOULD HAVE YOUR OWN!
"WATCH OUT!" "LET'S GO!" "HURRY UP!"
THEY'RE FROM "SPY KIDS."

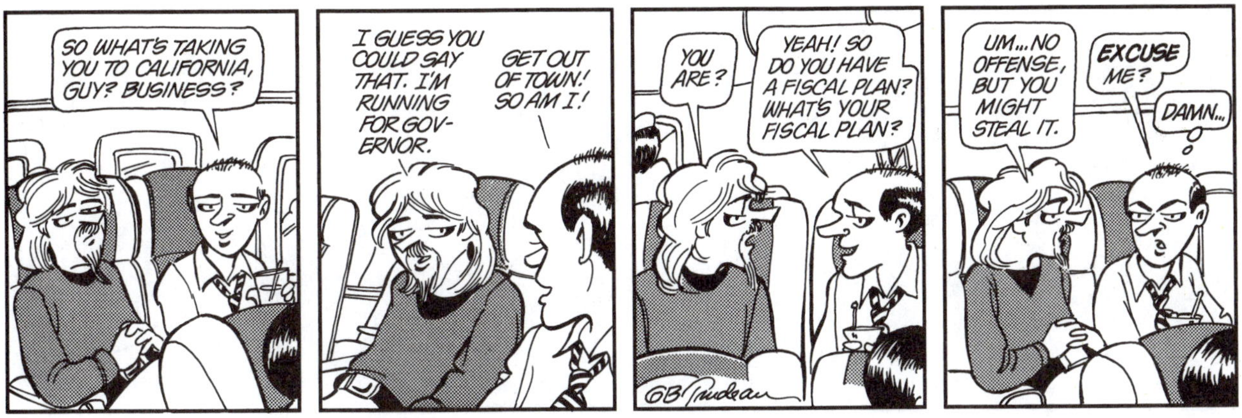
SO WHAT'S TAKING YOU TO CALIFORNIA, GUY? BUSINESS?
I GUESS YOU COULD SAY THAT. I'M RUNNING FOR GOVERNOR.
GET OUT OF TOWN! SO AM I!
YOU ARE?
YEAH! SO DO YOU HAVE A FISCAL PLAN? WHAT'S YOUR FISCAL PLAN?
UM... NO OFFENSE, BUT YOU MIGHT STEAL IT.
EXCUSE ME?
DAMN...

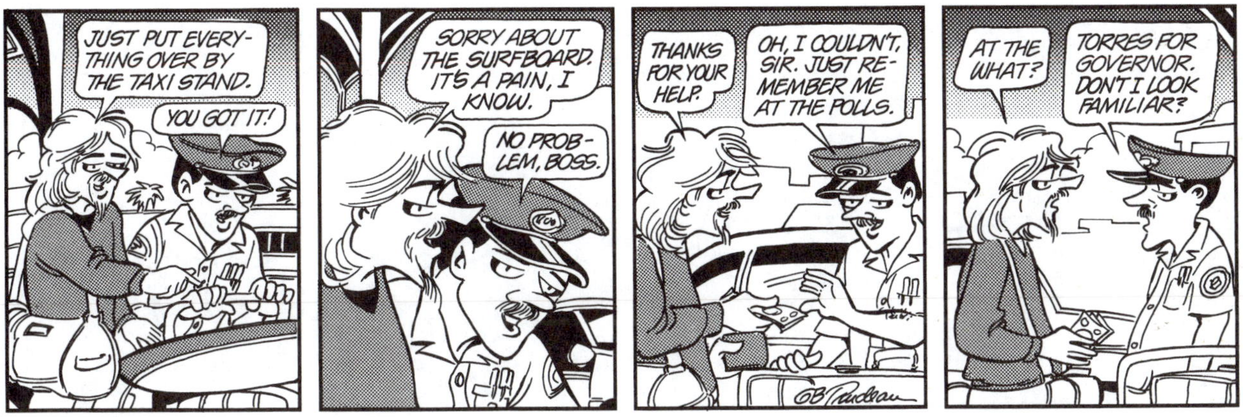
JUST PUT EVERYTHING OVER BY THE TAXI STAND.
YOU GOT IT!
SORRY ABOUT THE SURFBOARD. IT'S A PAIN, I KNOW.
NO PROBLEM, BOSS.
THANKS FOR YOUR HELP.
OH, I COULDN'T, SIR. JUST REMEMBER ME AT THE POLLS.
AT THE WHAT?
TORRES FOR GOVERNOR. DON'T I LOOK FAMILIAR?

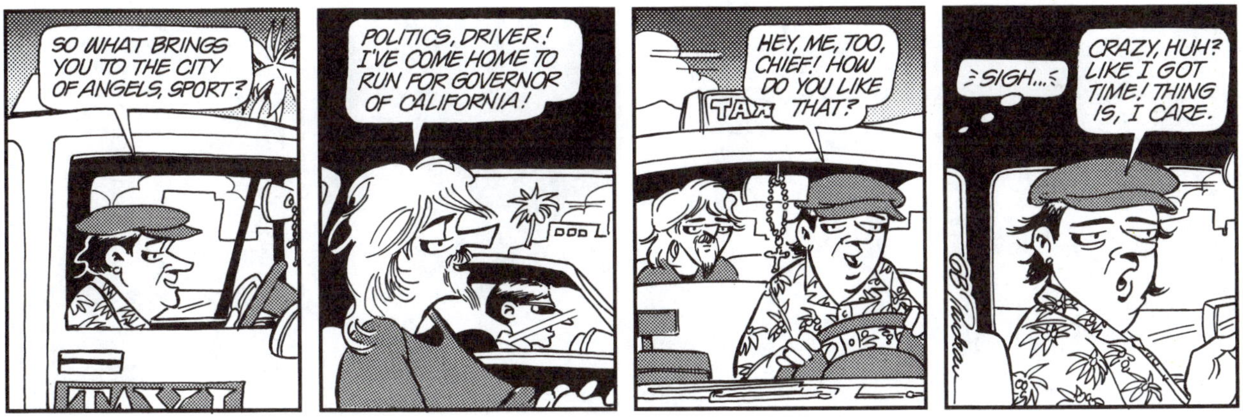
SO WHAT BRINGS YOU TO THE CITY OF ANGELS, SPORT?
TAXI
POLITICS, DRIVER! I'VE COME HOME TO RUN FOR GOVERNOR OF CALIFORNIA!
HEY, ME, TOO, CHIEF! HOW DO YOU LIKE THAT?
SIGH...
CRAZY, HUH? LIKE I GOT TIME! THING IS, I CARE.

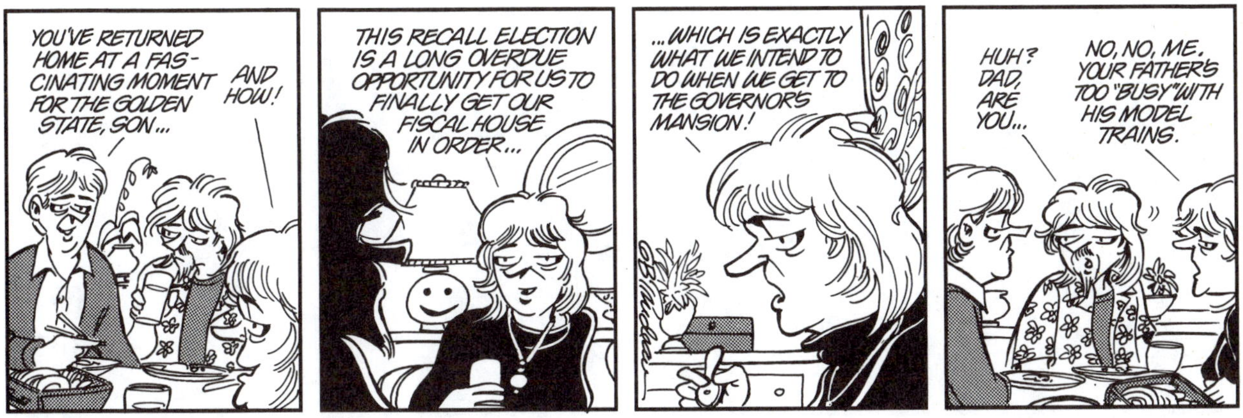
YOU'VE RETURNED HOME AT A FASCINATING MOMENT FOR THE GOLDEN STATE, SON...
AND HOW!
THIS RECALL ELECTION IS A LONG OVERDUE OPPORTUNITY FOR US TO FINALLY GET OUR FISCAL HOUSE IN ORDER...
...WHICH IS EXACTLY WHAT WE INTEND TO DO WHEN WE GET TO THE GOVERNOR'S MANSION!
HUH? DAD, ARE YOU...
NO, NO, ME. YOUR FATHER'S TOO "BUSY" WITH HIS MODEL TRAINS.

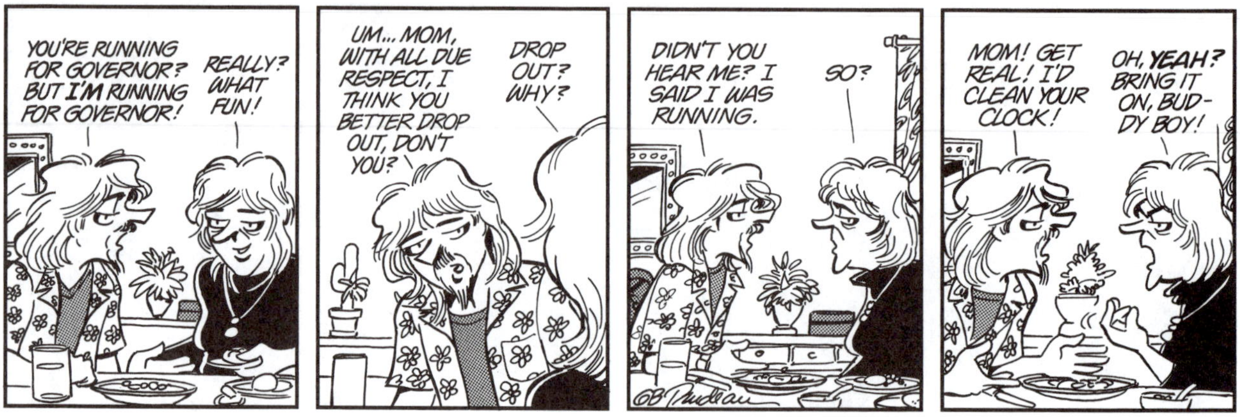
YOU'RE RUNNING FOR GOVERNOR? BUT I'M RUNNING FOR GOVERNOR!
REALLY? WHAT FUN!
UM... MOM, WITH ALL DUE RESPECT, I THINK YOU BETTER DROP OUT, DON'T YOU?
DROP OUT? WHY?
DIDN'T YOU HEAR ME? I SAID I WAS RUNNING.
SO?
MOM! GET REAL! I'D CLEAN YOUR CLOCK!
OH, YEAH? BRING IT ON, BUDDY BOY!

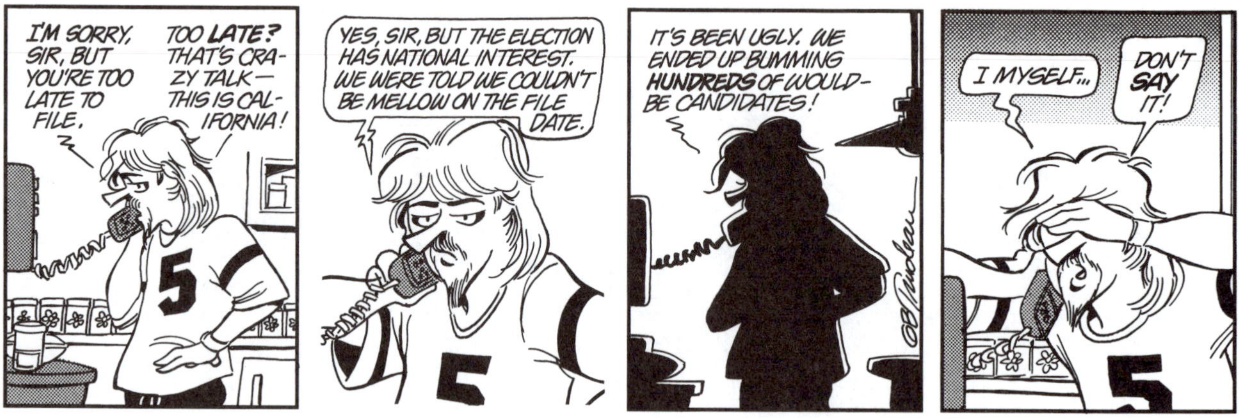
I'M SORRY, SIR, BUT YOU'RE TOO LATE TO FILE.
TOO LATE? THAT'S CRAZY TALK — THIS IS CALIFORNIA!
YES, SIR, BUT THE ELECTION HAS NATIONAL INTEREST. WE WERE TOLD WE COULDN'T BE MELLOW ON THE FILE DATE.
IT'S BEEN UGLY. WE ENDED UP BUMMING HUNDREDS OF WOULD-BE CANDIDATES!
I MYSELF...
DON'T SAY IT!

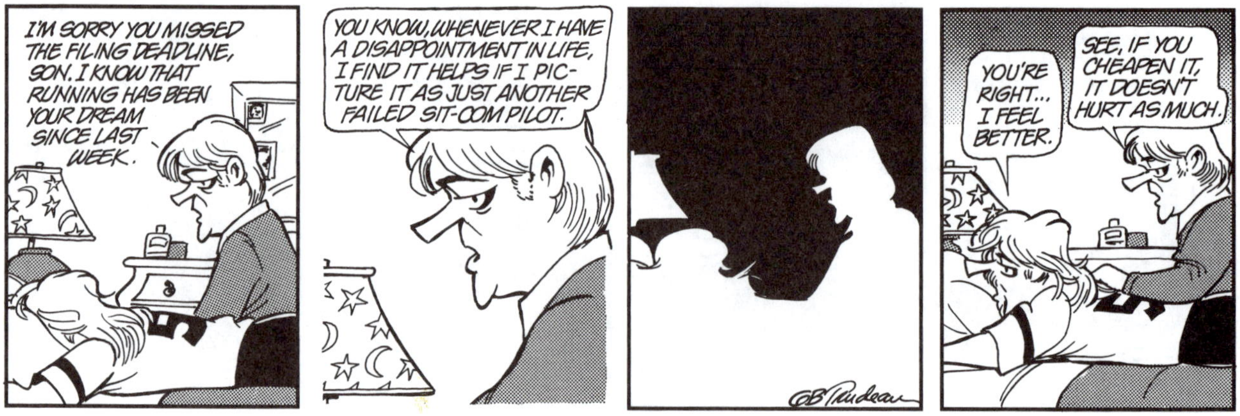
I'M SORRY YOU MISSED THE FILING DEADLINE, SON. I KNOW THAT RUNNING HAS BEEN YOUR DREAM SINCE LAST WEEK.
YOU KNOW, WHENEVER I HAVE A DISAPPOINTMENT IN LIFE, I FIND IT HELPS IF I PICTURE IT AS JUST ANOTHER FAILED SIT-COM PILOT.
YOU'RE RIGHT... I FEEL BETTER.
SEE, IF YOU CHEAPEN IT, IT DOESN'T HURT AS MUCH.

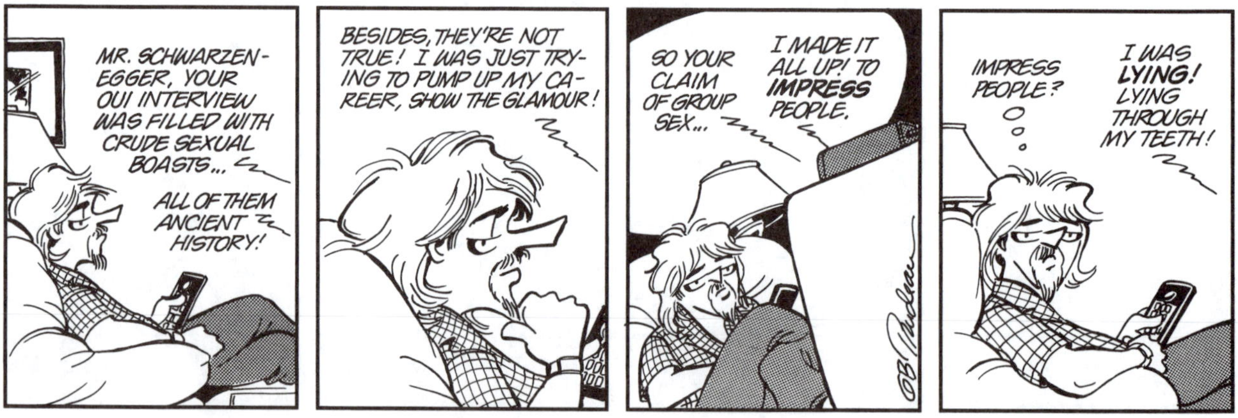
MR. SCHWARZENEGGER, YOUR OUI INTERVIEW WAS FILLED WITH CRUDE SEXUAL BOASTS...
ALL OF THEM ANCIENT HISTORY!
BESIDES, THEY'RE NOT TRUE! I WAS JUST TRYING TO PUMP UP MY CAREER, SHOW THE GLAMOUR!
SO YOUR CLAIM OF GROUP SEX...
I MADE IT ALL UP! TO IMPRESS PEOPLE.
IMPRESS PEOPLE?
I WAS LYING! LYING THROUGH MY TEETH!

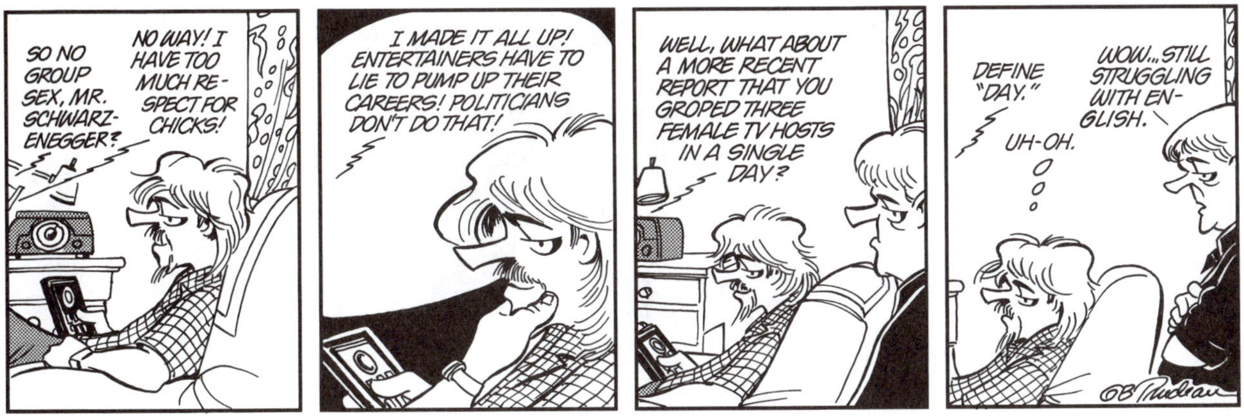
SO NO GROUP SEX, MR. SCHWARZENEGGER?
NO WAY! I HAVE TOO MUCH RESPECT FOR CHICKS!
I MADE IT ALL UP! ENTERTAINERS HAVE TO LIE TO PUMP UP THEIR CAREERS! POLITICIANS DON'T DO THAT!
WELL, WHAT ABOUT A MORE RECENT REPORT THAT YOU GROPED THREE FEMALE TV HOSTS IN A SINGLE DAY?
DEFINE "DAY."
WOW... STILL STRUGGLING WITH ENGLISH.
UH-OH.
©B Trudeau

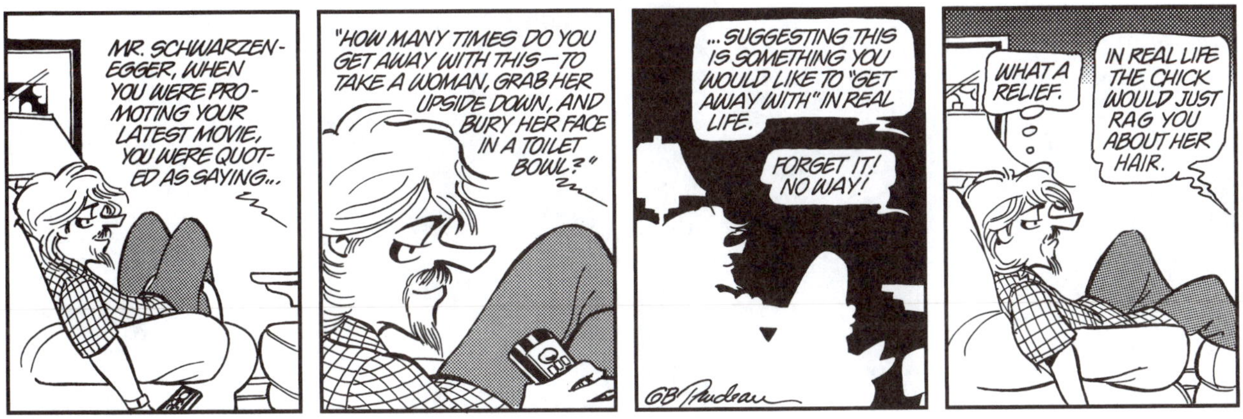
MR. SCHWARZENEGGER, WHEN YOU WERE PROMOTING YOUR LATEST MOVIE, YOU WERE QUOTED AS SAYING...
"HOW MANY TIMES DO YOU GET AWAY WITH THIS—TO TAKE A WOMAN, GRAB HER UPSIDE DOWN, AND BURY HER FACE IN A TOILET BOWL?"
...SUGGESTING THIS IS SOMETHING YOU WOULD LIKE TO "GET AWAY WITH" IN REAL LIFE.
FORGET IT! NO WAY!
©B Trudeau
WHAT A RELIEF.
IN REAL LIFE THE CHICK WOULD JUST RAG YOU ABOUT HER HAIR.

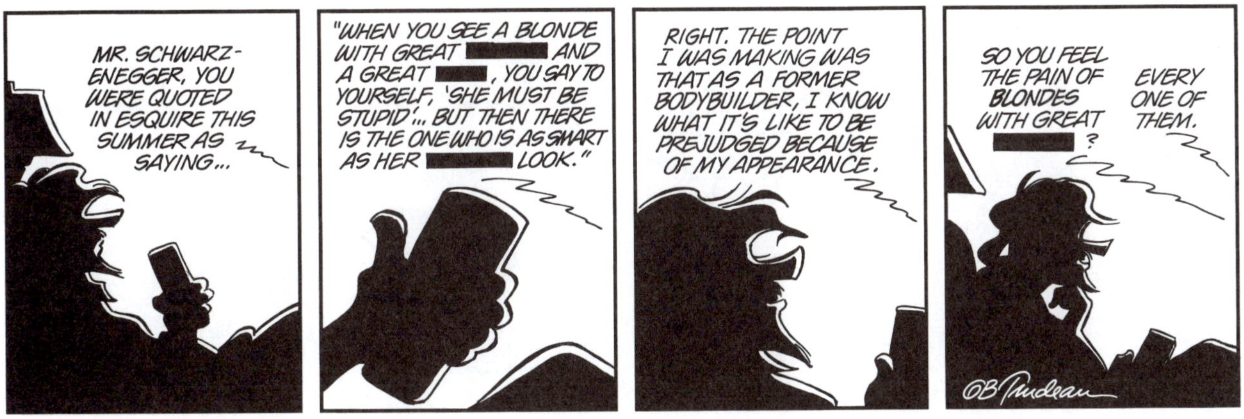
MR. SCHWARZENEGGER, YOU WERE QUOTED IN ESQUIRE THIS SUMMER AS SAYING...
"WHEN YOU SEE A BLONDE WITH GREAT [redacted] AND A GREAT [redacted], YOU SAY TO YOURSELF, 'SHE MUST BE STUPID'... BUT THEN THERE IS THE ONE WHO IS AS SMART AS HER [redacted] LOOK."
RIGHT. THE POINT I WAS MAKING WAS THAT AS A FORMER BODYBUILDER, I KNOW WHAT IT'S LIKE TO BE PREJUDGED BECAUSE OF MY APPEARANCE.
SO YOU FEEL THE PAIN OF BLONDES WITH GREAT [redacted]?
EVERY ONE OF THEM.
©B Trudeau

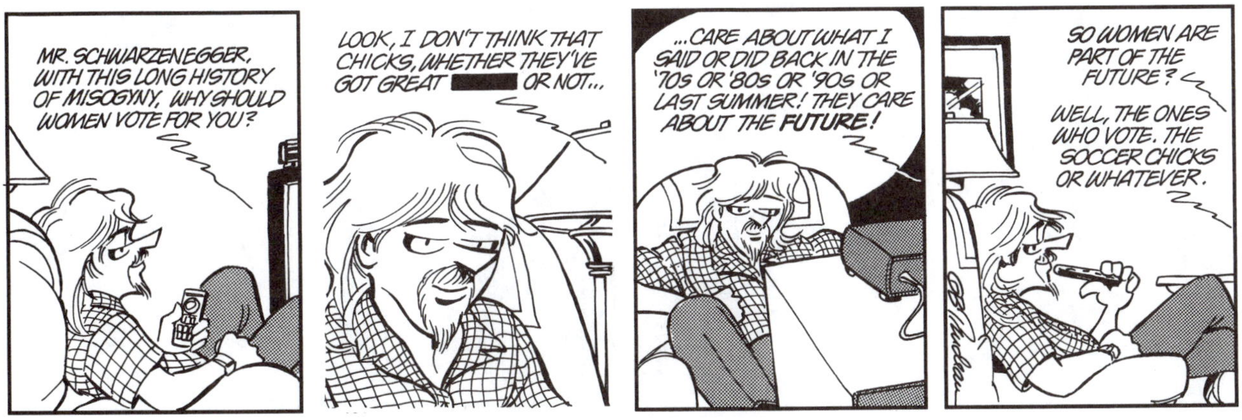
MR. SCHWARZENEGGER, WITH THIS LONG HISTORY OF MISOGYNY, WHY SHOULD WOMEN VOTE FOR YOU?
LOOK, I DON'T THINK THAT CHICKS, WHETHER THEY'VE GOT GREAT [redacted] OR NOT...
...CARE ABOUT WHAT I SAID OR DID BACK IN THE '70s OR '80s OR '90s OR LAST SUMMER! THEY CARE ABOUT THE FUTURE!
SO WOMEN ARE PART OF THE FUTURE?
WELL, THE ONES WHO VOTE. THE SOCCER CHICKS OR WHATEVER.
©B Trudeau

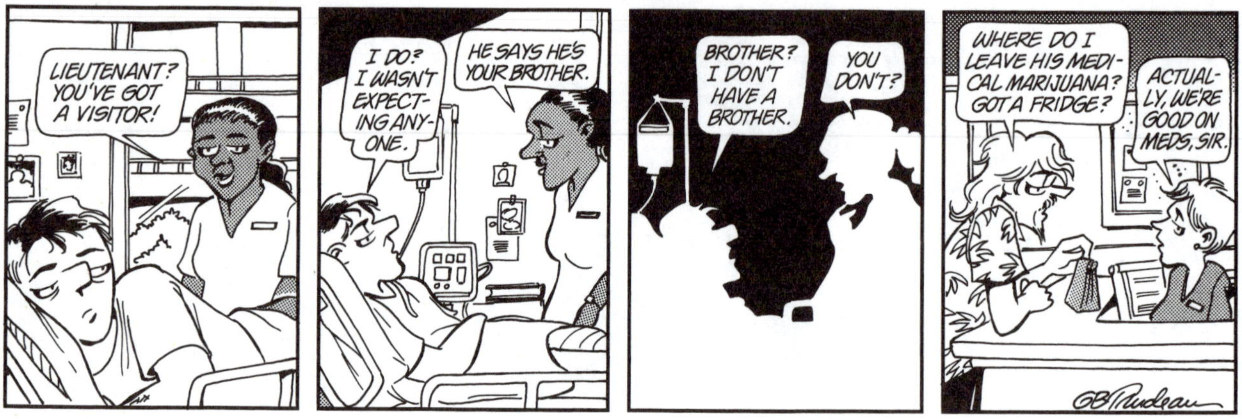
LIEUTENANT? YOU'VE GOT A VISITOR!
I DO? I WASN'T EXPECTING ANYONE.
HE SAYS HE'S YOUR BROTHER.
BROTHER? I DON'T HAVE A BROTHER.
YOU DON'T?
WHERE DO I LEAVE HIS MEDICAL MARIJUANA? GOT A FRIDGE?
ACTUALLY, WE'RE GOOD ON MEDS, SIR.
GBTrudeau

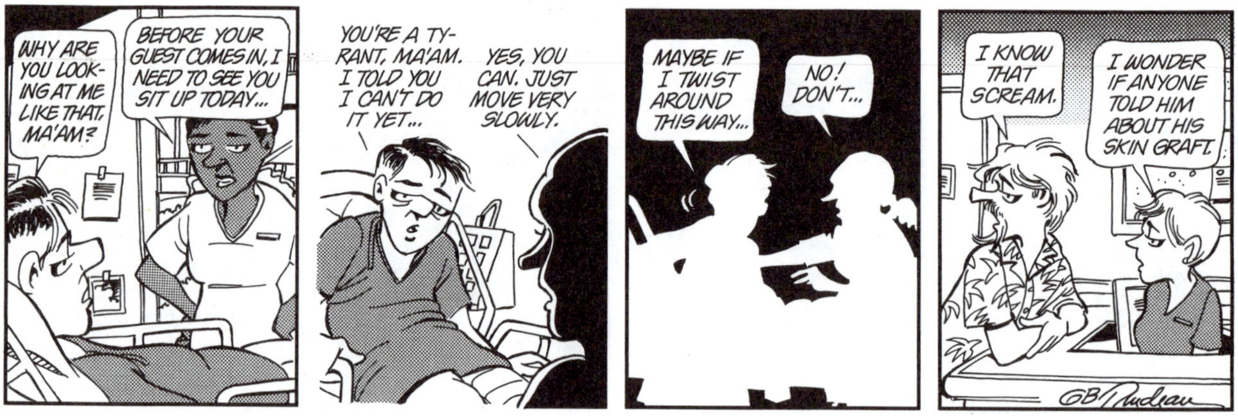
WHY ARE YOU LOOKING AT ME LIKE THAT, MA'AM?
BEFORE YOUR GUEST COMES IN, I NEED TO SEE YOU SIT UP TODAY...
YOU'RE A TYRANT, MA'AM. I TOLD YOU I CAN'T DO IT YET...
YES, YOU CAN. JUST MOVE VERY SLOWLY.
MAYBE IF I TWIST AROUND THIS WAY...
NO! DON'T...
I KNOW THAT SCREAM.
I WONDER IF ANYONE TOLD HIM ABOUT HIS SKIN GRAFT.
GBTrudeau

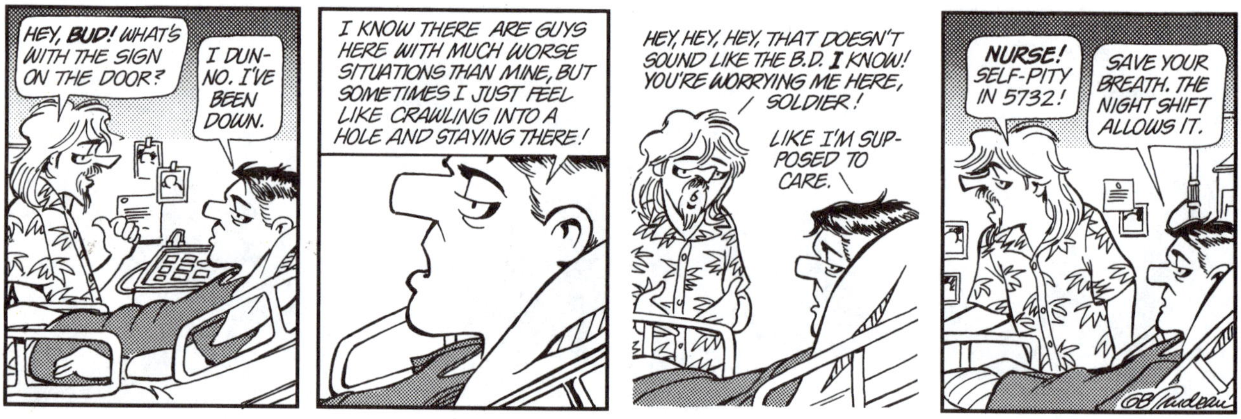
HEY, **BUD!** WHAT'S WITH THE SIGN ON THE DOOR?
I DUNNO. I'VE BEEN DOWN.
I KNOW THERE ARE GUYS HERE WITH MUCH WORSE SITUATIONS THAN MINE, BUT SOMETIMES I JUST FEEL LIKE CRAWLING INTO A HOLE AND STAYING THERE!
HEY, HEY, HEY, THAT DOESN'T SOUND LIKE THE B.D. **I** KNOW! YOU'RE WORRYING ME HERE, SOLDIER!
LIKE I'M SUPPOSED TO CARE.
NURSE! SELF-PITY IN 5732!
SAVE YOUR BREATH. THE NIGHT SHIFT ALLOWS IT.
GBTrudeau

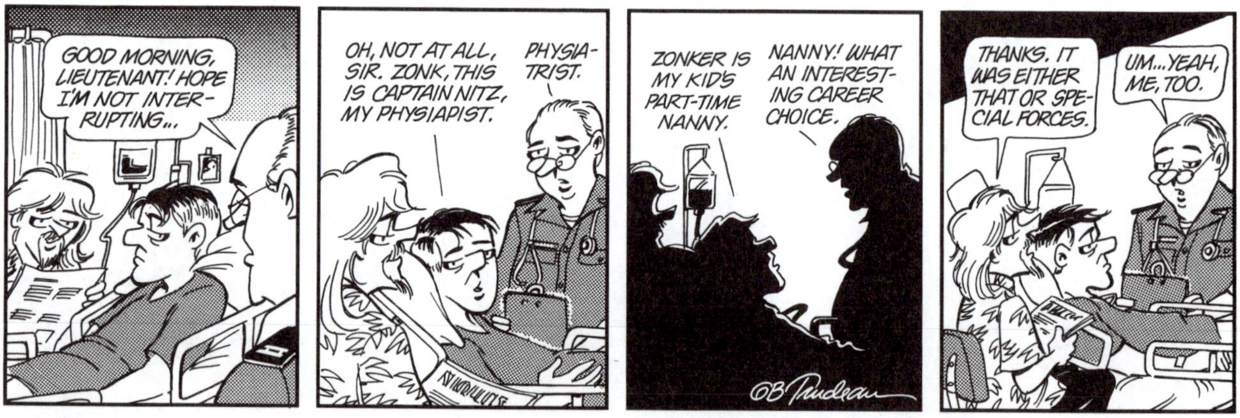
GOOD MORNING, LIEUTENANT! HOPE I'M NOT INTERRUPTING...
OH, NOT AT ALL, SIR. ZONK, THIS IS CAPTAIN NITZ, MY PHYSIAPIST.
PHYSIATRIST.
ZONKER IS MY KID'S PART-TIME NANNY.
NANNY! WHAT AN INTERESTING CAREER CHOICE.
THANKS. IT WAS EITHER THAT OR SPECIAL FORCES.
UM...YEAH, ME, TOO.
GBTrudeau

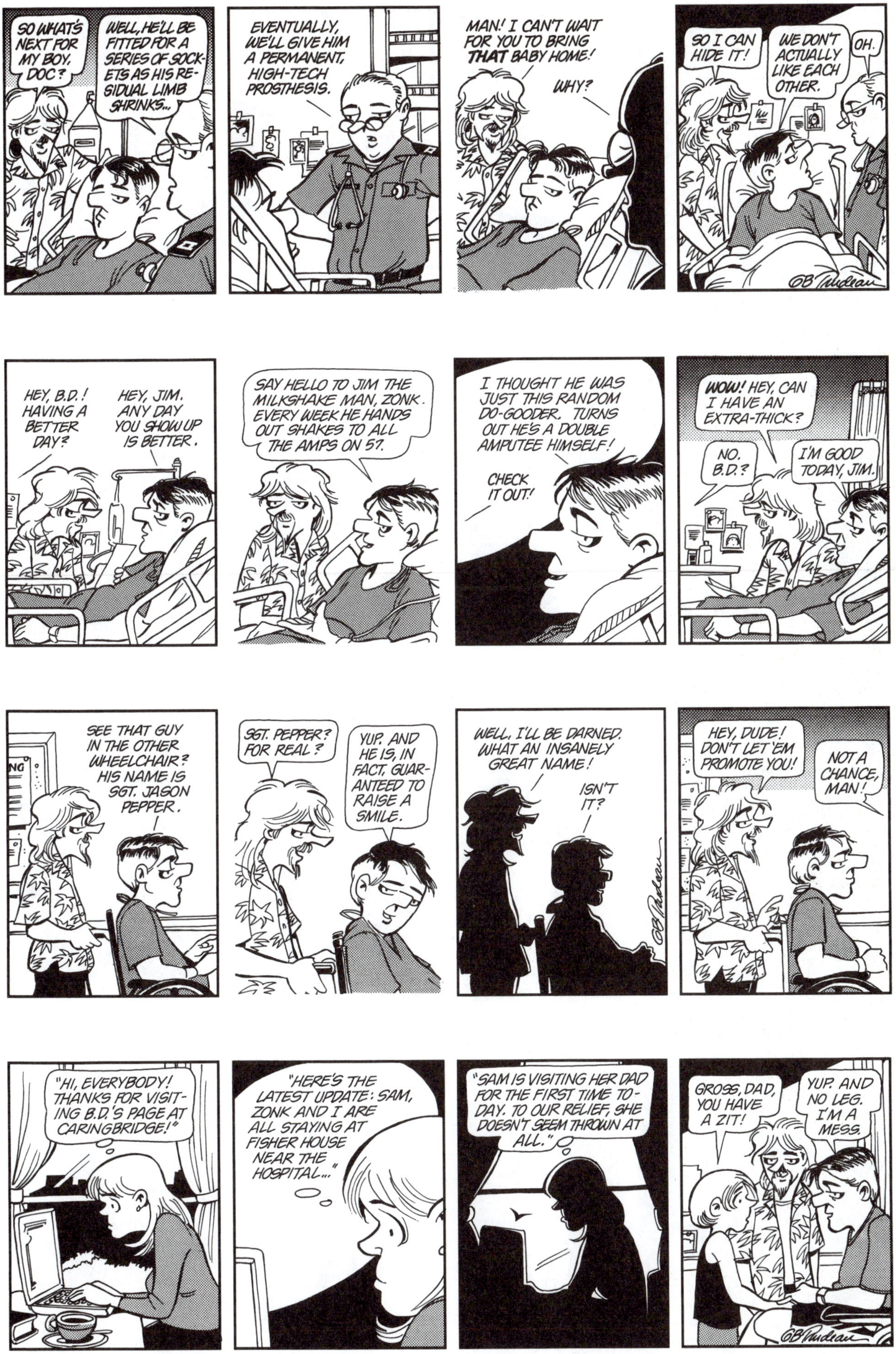
SO WHAT'S NEXT FOR MY BOY, DOC?
WELL, HE'LL BE FITTED FOR A SERIES OF SOCKETS AS HIS RESIDUAL LIMB SHRINKS...
EVENTUALLY, WE'LL GIVE HIM A PERMANENT, HIGH-TECH PROSTHESIS.
MAN! I CAN'T WAIT FOR YOU TO BRING THAT BABY HOME!
WHY?
SO I CAN HIDE IT!
WE DON'T ACTUALLY LIKE EACH OTHER.
OH.
HEY, B.D.! HAVING A BETTER DAY?
HEY, JIM. ANY DAY YOU SHOW UP IS BETTER.
SAY HELLO TO JIM THE MILKSHAKE MAN, ZONK. EVERY WEEK HE HANDS OUT SHAKES TO ALL THE AMPS ON 57.
I THOUGHT HE WAS JUST THIS RANDOM DO-GOODER. TURNS OUT HE'S A DOUBLE AMPUTEE HIMSELF!
CHECK IT OUT!
WOW! HEY, CAN I HAVE AN EXTRA-THICK?
NO. B.D.?
I'M GOOD TODAY, JIM.
SEE THAT GUY IN THE OTHER WHEELCHAIR? HIS NAME IS SGT. JASON PEPPER.
SGT. PEPPER? FOR REAL?
YUP. AND HE IS, IN FACT, GUARANTEED TO RAISE A SMILE.
WELL, I'LL BE DARNED. WHAT AN INSANELY GREAT NAME!
ISN'T IT?
HEY, DUDE! DON'T LET 'EM PROMOTE YOU!
NOT A CHANCE, MAN!
"HI, EVERYBODY! THANKS FOR VISITING B.D.'S PAGE AT CARINGBRIDGE!"
"HERE'S THE LATEST UPDATE: SAM, ZONK AND I ARE ALL STAYING AT FISHER HOUSE NEAR THE HOSPITAL..."
"SAM IS VISITING HER DAD FOR THE FIRST TIME TODAY. TO OUR RELIEF, SHE DOESN'T SEEM THROWN AT ALL."
GROSS, DAD, YOU HAVE A ZIT!
YUP. AND NO LEG. I'M A MESS.

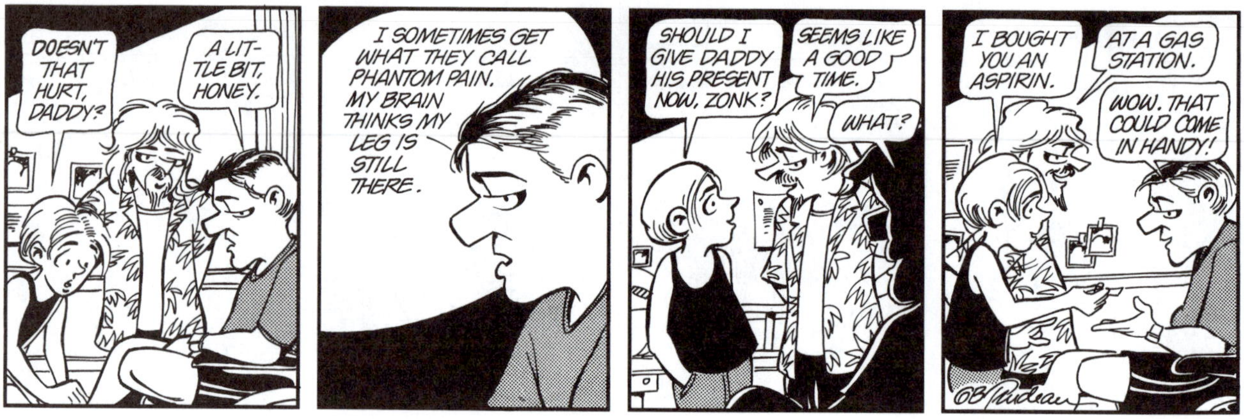
DOESN'T THAT HURT, DADDY?
A LITTLE BIT, HONEY.
I SOMETIMES GET WHAT THEY CALL PHANTOM PAIN. MY BRAIN THINKS MY LEG IS STILL THERE.
SHOULD I GIVE DADDY HIS PRESENT NOW, ZONK?
SEEMS LIKE A GOOD TIME.
WHAT?
I BOUGHT YOU AN ASPIRIN.
AT A GAS STATION.
WOW. THAT COULD COME IN HANDY!

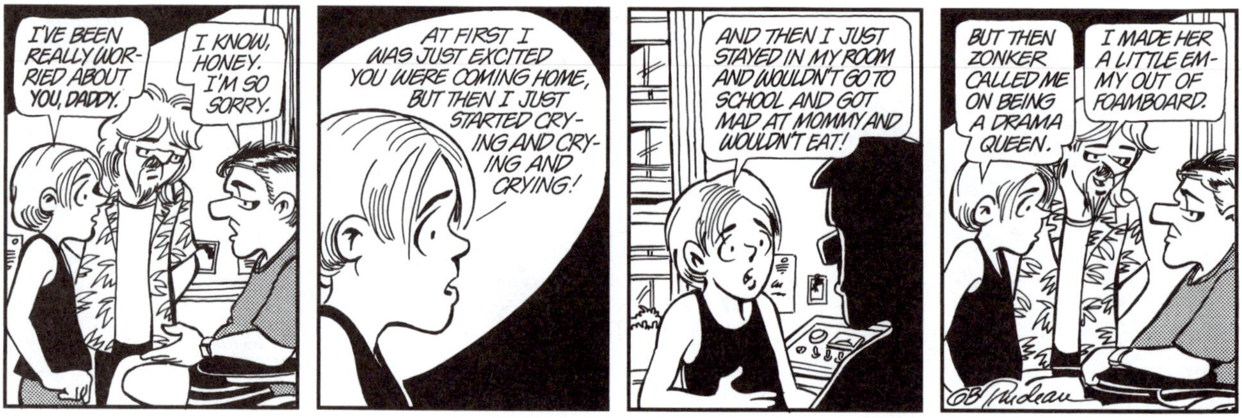
I'VE BEEN REALLY WORRIED ABOUT YOU, DADDY.
I KNOW, HONEY. I'M SO SORRY.
AT FIRST I WAS JUST EXCITED YOU WERE COMING HOME, BUT THEN I JUST STARTED CRYING AND CRYING AND CRYING!
AND THEN I JUST STAYED IN MY ROOM AND WOULDN'T GO TO SCHOOL AND GOT MAD AT MOMMY AND WOULDN'T EAT!
BUT THEN ZONKER CALLED ME ON BEING A DRAMA QUEEN.
I MADE HER A LITTLE EMMY OUT OF FOAMBOARD.

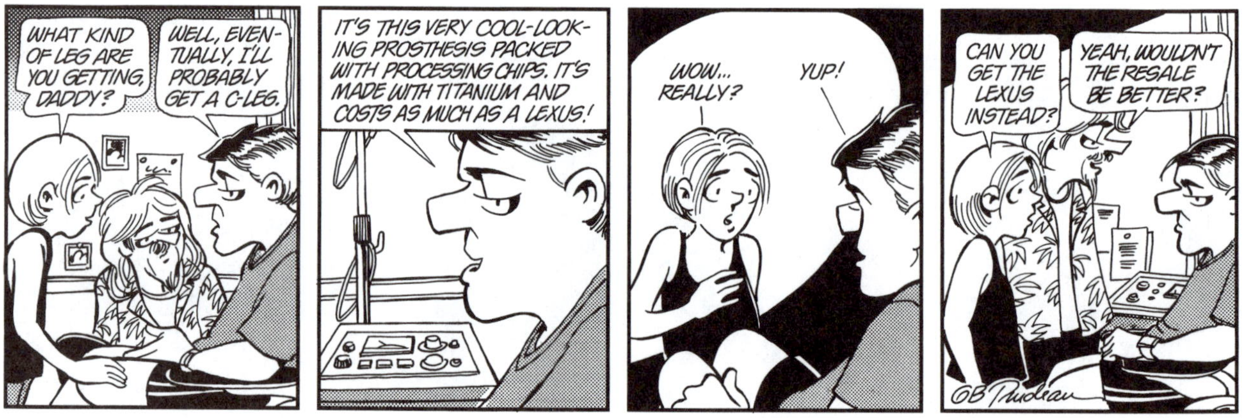
WHAT KIND OF LEG ARE YOU GETTING, DADDY?
WELL, EVENTUALLY, I'LL PROBABLY GET A C-LEG.
IT'S THIS VERY COOL-LOOKING PROSTHESIS PACKED WITH PROCESSING CHIPS. IT'S MADE WITH TITANIUM AND COSTS AS MUCH AS A LEXUS!
WOW... REALLY?
YUP!
CAN YOU GET THE LEXUS INSTEAD?
YEAH, WOULDN'T THE RESALE BE BETTER?

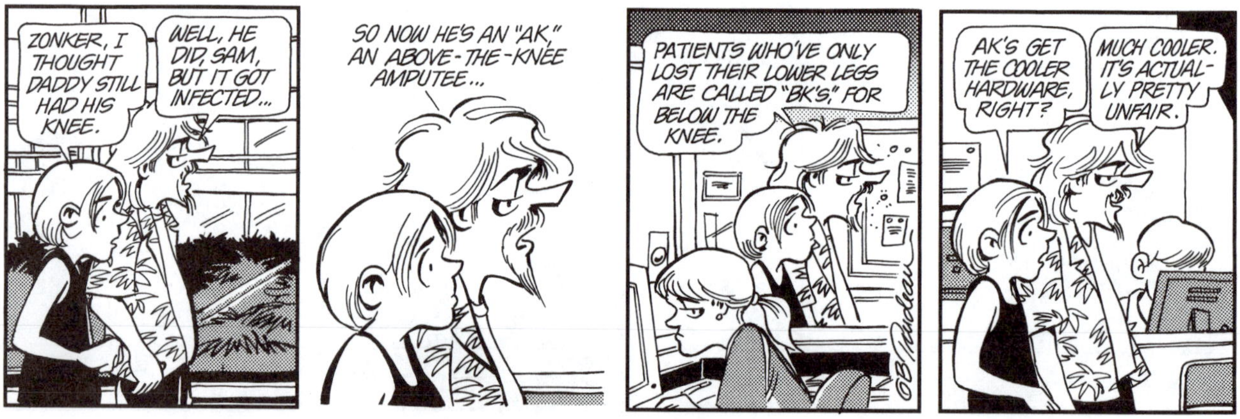
ZONKER, I THOUGHT DADDY STILL HAD HIS KNEE.
WELL, HE DID, SAM, BUT IT GOT INFECTED...
SO NOW HE'S AN "AK," AN ABOVE-THE-KNEE AMPUTEE...
PATIENTS WHO'VE ONLY LOST THEIR LOWER LEGS ARE CALLED "BK'S," FOR BELOW THE KNEE.
AK'S GET THE COOLER HARDWARE, RIGHT?
MUCH COOLER. IT'S ACTUALLY PRETTY UNFAIR.

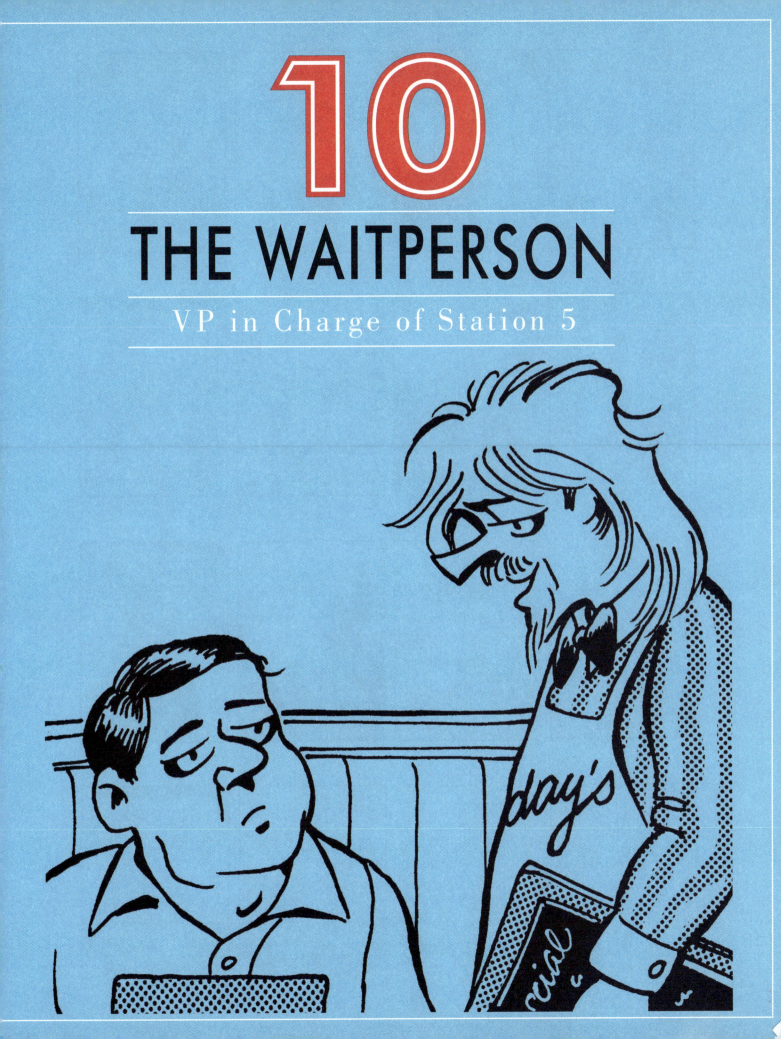

10

THE WAITPERSON

VP in Charge of Station 5

Panel 1:
YOU SEEM DOWN TODAY, MOMMY. IS DADDY OKAY?

Panel 2:
OH, HE'S FINE, HONEY. IT'S JUST HE'S HAVING TROUBLE GETTING HIS DISABILITY BENEFITS...

Panel 3:
AND WITH ME GOING BACK AND FORTH TO THE HOSPITAL, WE'VE DEPLETED ALL OUR SAVINGS. SOMEONE AROUND HERE HAS **GOT** TO GET A JOB!

Panel 4:
I DON'T LIKE WHERE THIS IS GOING...
HAVE A SEAT, ZONKER.

Panel 5:
SO UNTIL B.D. GETS HIS DISABILITY BENEFITS, YOU'RE GOING TO HAVE TO FIND A JOB, ZONKER— A **REAL** JOB!

Panel 7:
(silent)

Panel 8:
ZONK? YOU OKAY?
DAMN THIS WAR AND ITS HUMAN COST!

Panel 9:
I HOPE YOUR MOM RECONSIDERS THIS BUSINESS OF MY HAVING TO GET A JOB...

Panel 10:
I ONCE HAD A SERIOUS JOB AND IT ALMOST KILLED ME. IT'S NO WAY TO LIVE!

Panel 12:
WHAT SORT OF...
BRONZING BABY SHOES. I'D RATHER NOT TALK ABOUT IT.

Panel 13:

WHATCHA WORKING ON, ZONK?

Panel 14:

MY RESUMÉ, SAM. IT'S BEEN YEARS SINCE I'VE UPDATED IT...

Panel 15:

MOST OF MY WORK HAS BEEN IN CHILD CARE, BUT I'VE ALSO BEEN A BUILDER AND A...
BUILDER? WHAT KIND OF BUILDER?

Panel 16:

UM... POPSICLE STICK BIRDHOUSES.
COOL! SHOULDN'T YOU PUT THAT FIRST?

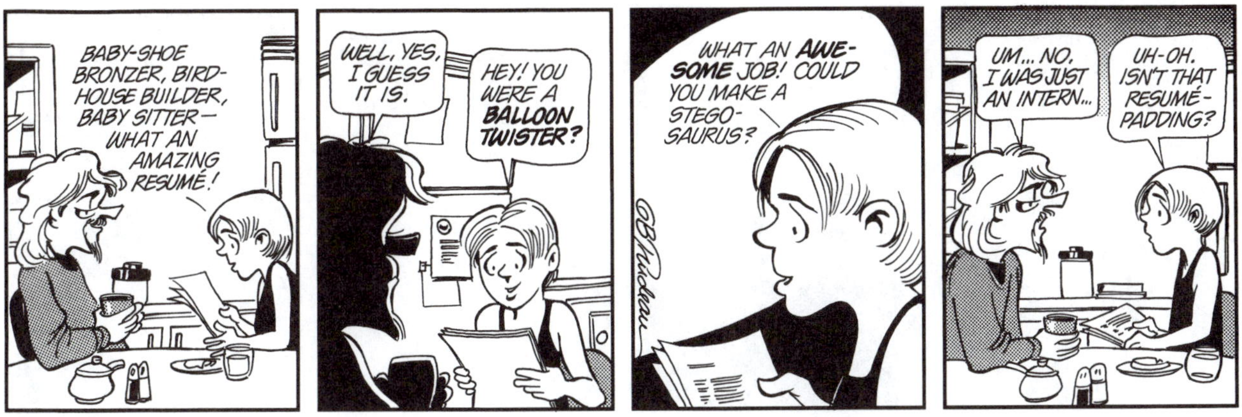

BABY-SHOE BRONZER, BIRD-HOUSE BUILDER, BABY SITTER— WHAT AN AMAZING RESUMÉ!
WELL, YES, I GUESS IT IS.
HEY! YOU WERE A **BALLOON TWISTER?**
WHAT AN **AWE-SOME** JOB! COULD YOU MAKE A STEGO-SAURUS?
UM... NO. I WAS JUST AN INTERN...
UH-OH. ISN'T THAT RESUMÉ-PADDING?

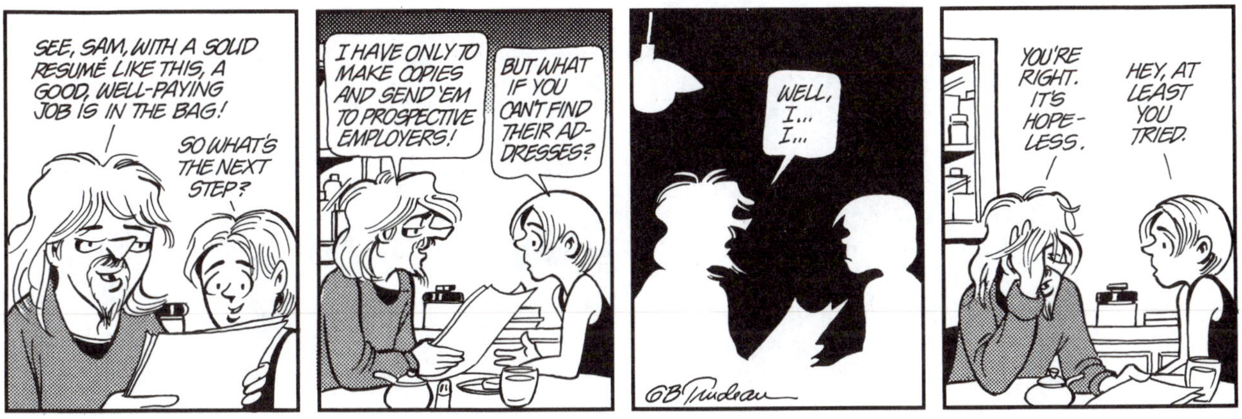

SEE, SAM, WITH A SOLID RESUMÉ LIKE THIS, A GOOD, WELL-PAYING JOB IS IN THE BAG!
SO WHAT'S THE NEXT STEP?
I HAVE ONLY TO MAKE COPIES AND SEND 'EM TO PROSPECTIVE EMPLOYERS!
BUT WHAT IF YOU CAN'T FIND THEIR AD-DRESSES?
WELL, I... I...
YOU'RE RIGHT. IT'S HOPE-LESS.
HEY, AT LEAST YOU TRIED.

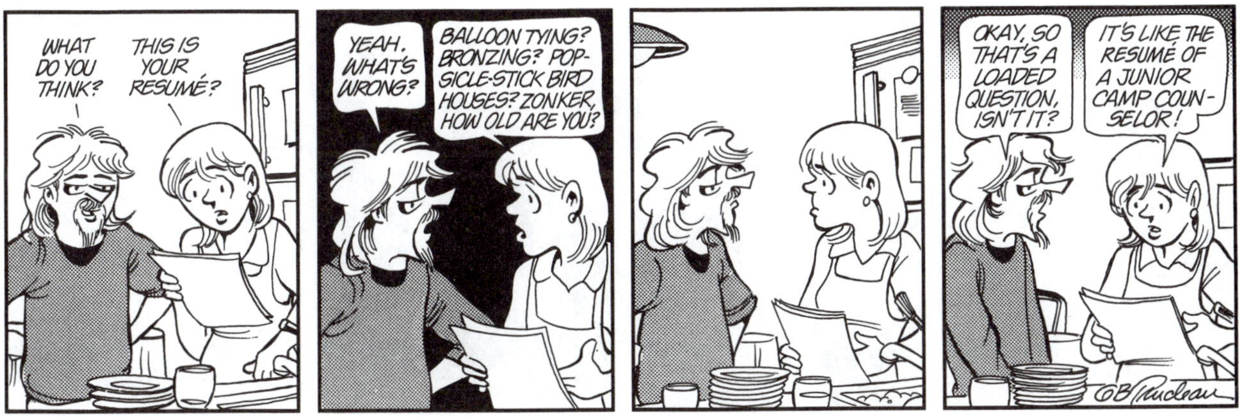

WHAT DO YOU THINK?
THIS IS YOUR RESUMÉ?
YEAH. WHAT'S WRONG?
BALLOON TYING? BRONZING? POP-SICLE-STICK BIRD HOUSES? ZONKER, HOW OLD ARE YOU?
OKAY, SO THAT'S A LOADED QUESTION, ISN'T IT?
IT'S LIKE THE RESUMÉ OF A JUNIOR CAMP COUN-SELOR!

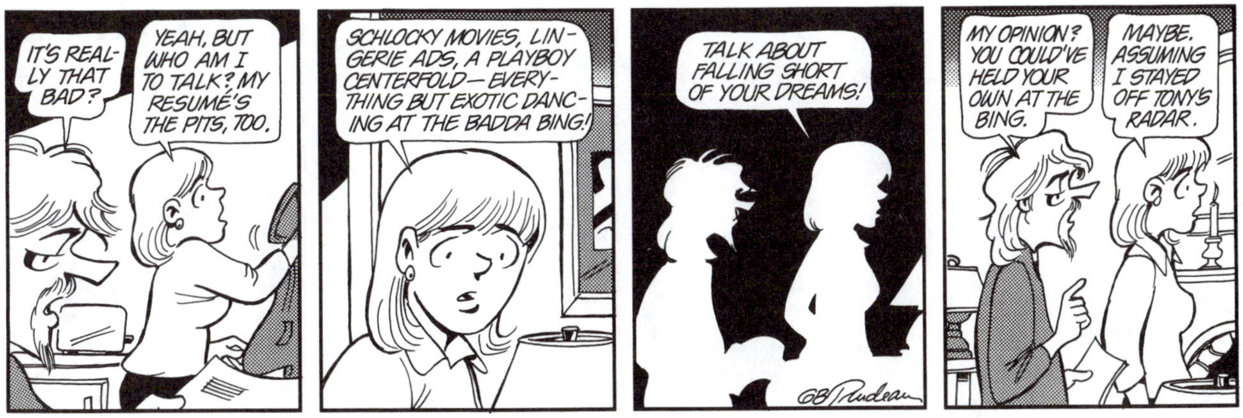

IT'S REAL-LY THAT BAD?
YEAH, BUT WHO AM I TO TALK? MY RESUMÉ'S THE PITS, TOO.
SCHLOCKY MOVIES, LIN-GERIE ADS, A PLAYBOY CENTERFOLD— EVERY-THING BUT EXOTIC DANC-ING AT THE BADDA BING!
TALK ABOUT FALLING SHORT OF YOUR DREAMS!
MY OPINION? YOU COULD'VE HELD YOUR OWN AT THE BING.
MAYBE. ASSUMING I STAYED OFF TONY'S RADAR.

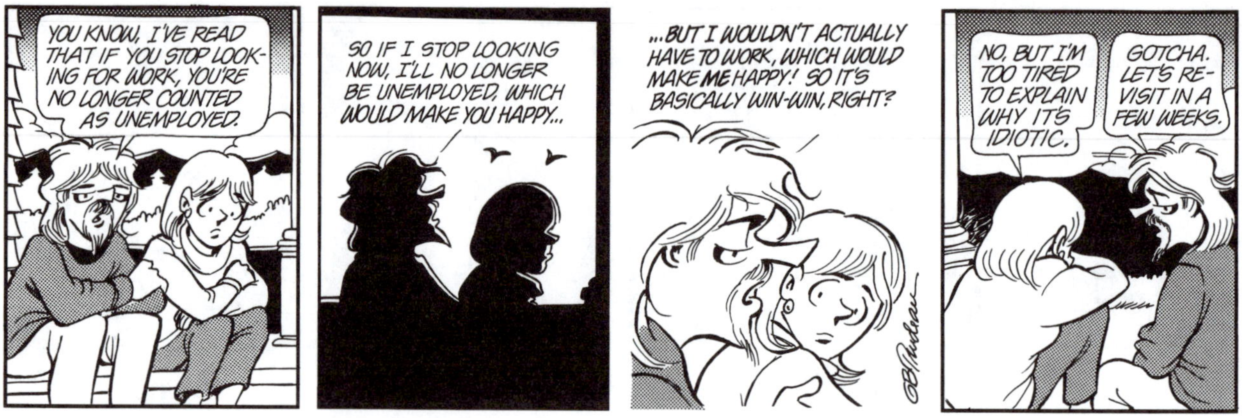
YOU KNOW, I'VE READ THAT IF YOU STOP LOOKING FOR WORK, YOU'RE NO LONGER COUNTED AS UNEMPLOYED.
SO IF I STOP LOOKING NOW, I'LL NO LONGER BE UNEMPLOYED, WHICH WOULD MAKE YOU HAPPY...
...BUT I WOULDN'T ACTUALLY HAVE TO WORK, WHICH WOULD MAKE ME HAPPY! SO IT'S BASICALLY WIN-WIN, RIGHT?
NO, BUT I'M TOO TIRED TO EXPLAIN WHY IT'S IDIOTIC.
GOTCHA. LET'S RE-VISIT IN A FEW WEEKS.

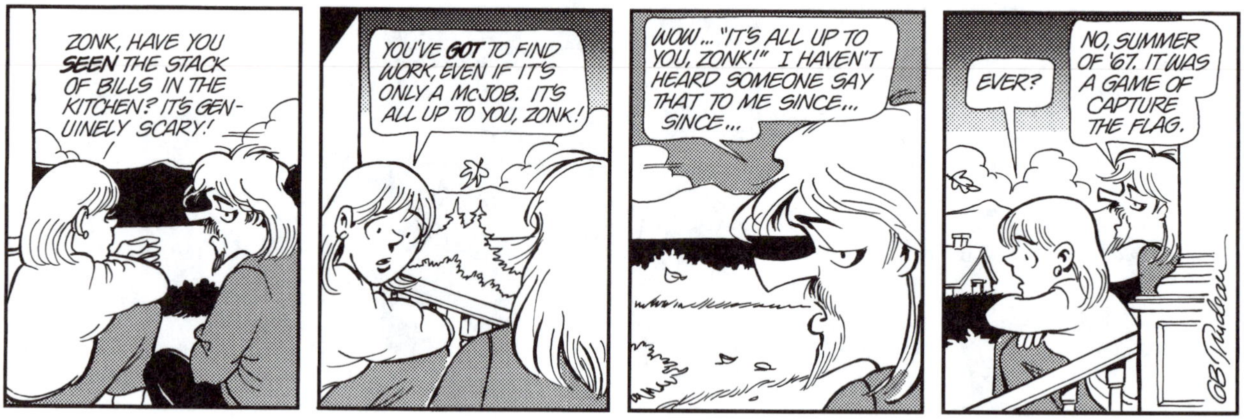
ZONK, HAVE YOU SEEN THE STACK OF BILLS IN THE KITCHEN? IT'S GENUINELY SCARY!
YOU'VE GOT TO FIND WORK, EVEN IF IT'S ONLY A McJOB. IT'S ALL UP TO YOU, ZONK!
WOW... "IT'S ALL UP TO YOU, ZONK!" I HAVEN'T HEARD SOMEONE SAY THAT TO ME SINCE... SINCE...
EVER?
NO, SUMMER OF '67. IT WAS A GAME OF CAPTURE THE FLAG.

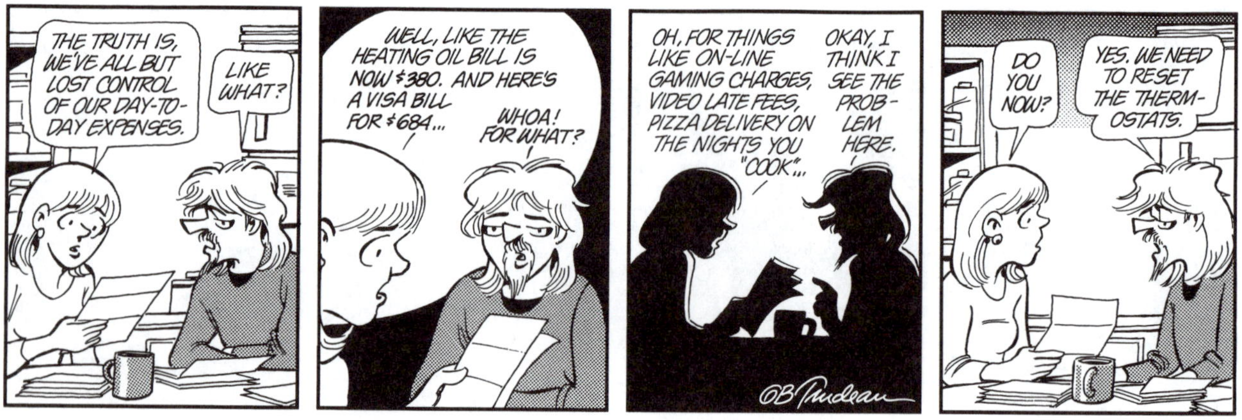
THE TRUTH IS, WE'VE ALL BUT LOST CONTROL OF OUR DAY-TO-DAY EXPENSES.
LIKE WHAT?
WELL, LIKE THE HEATING OIL BILL IS NOW $380. AND HERE'S A VISA BILL FOR $684...
WHOA! FOR WHAT?
OH, FOR THINGS LIKE ON-LINE GAMING CHARGES, VIDEO LATE FEES, PIZZA DELIVERY ON THE NIGHTS YOU "COOK"...
OKAY, I THINK I SEE THE PROBLEM HERE.
DO YOU NOW?
YES. WE NEED TO RESET THE THERMOSTATS.

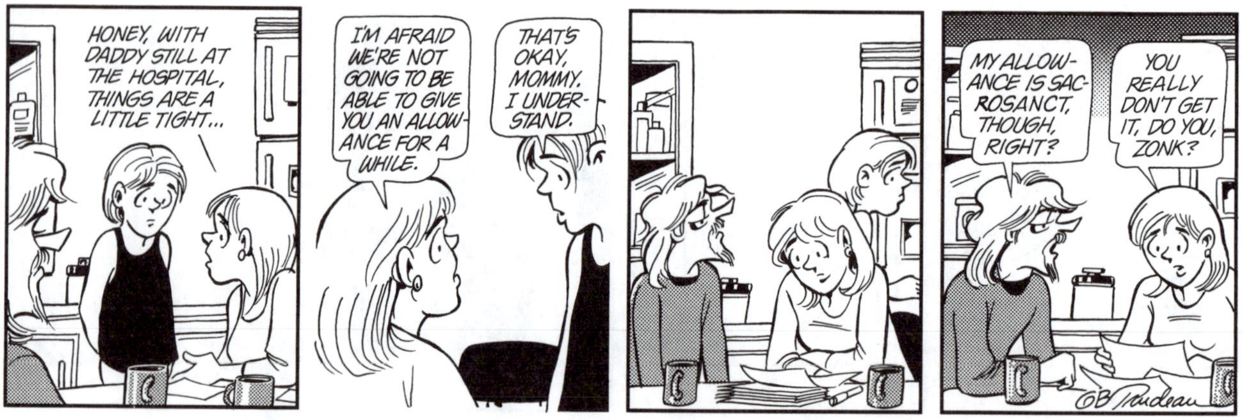
HONEY, WITH DADDY STILL AT THE HOSPITAL, THINGS ARE A LITTLE TIGHT...
I'M AFRAID WE'RE NOT GOING TO BE ABLE TO GIVE YOU AN ALLOWANCE FOR A WHILE.
THAT'S OKAY, MOMMY. I UNDERSTAND.
MY ALLOWANCE IS SACROSANCT, THOUGH, RIGHT?
YOU REALLY DON'T GET IT, DO YOU, ZONK?

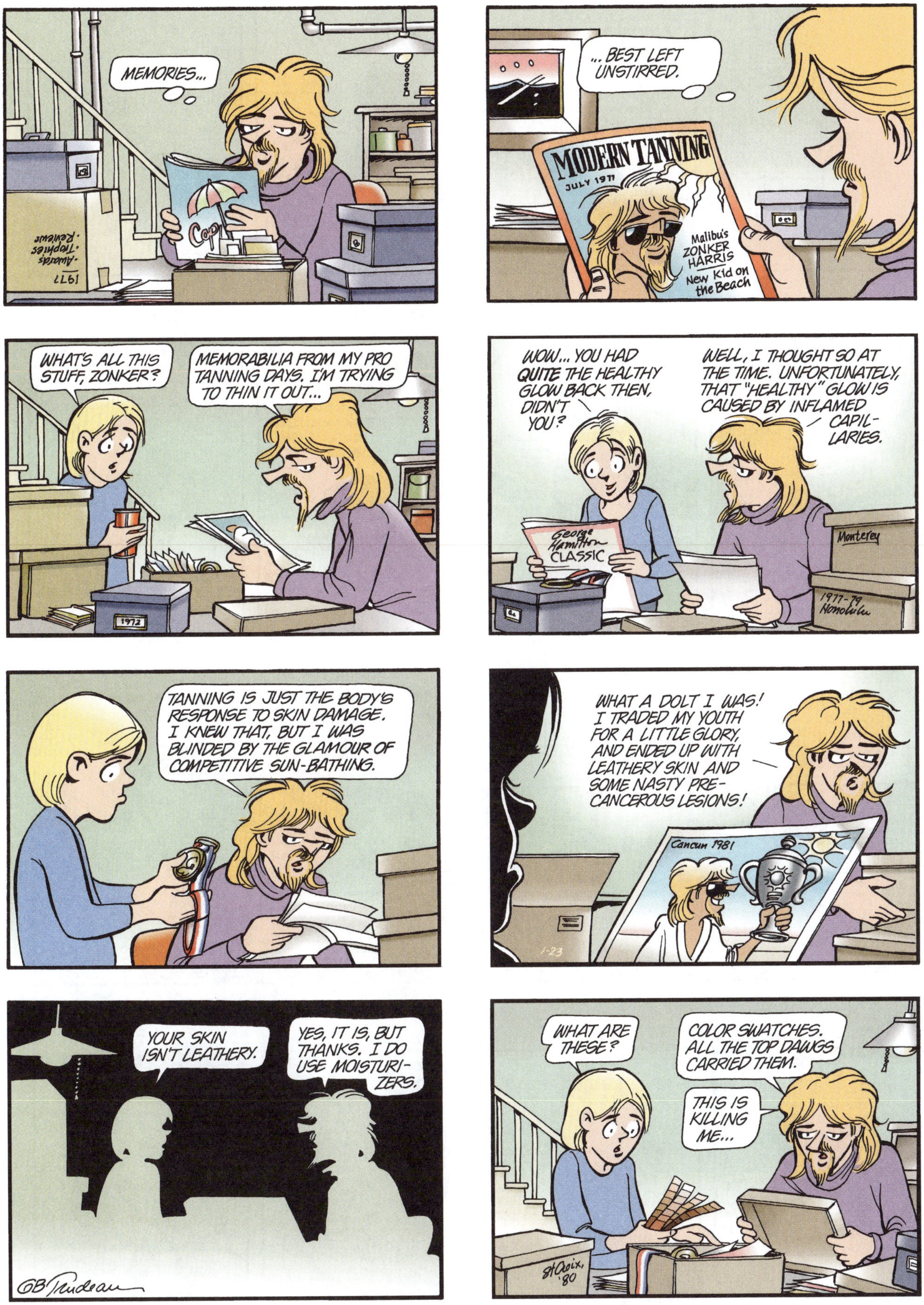

MEMORIES...
1977 ·Awards ·Trophies ·Reviews
Cop
...BEST LEFT UNSTIRRED.
MODERN TANNING
JULY 1971
Malibu's ZONKER HARRIS
New Kid on the Beach
WHAT'S ALL THIS STUFF, ZONKER?
MEMORABILIA FROM MY PRO TANNING DAYS. I'M TRYING TO THIN IT OUT...
1972
WOW... YOU HAD **QUITE** THE HEALTHY GLOW BACK THEN, DIDN'T YOU?
WELL, I THOUGHT SO AT THE TIME. UNFORTUNATELY, THAT "HEALTHY" GLOW IS CAUSED BY INFLAMED CAPIL-LARIES.
George Hamilton CLASSIC
Monterey
1977-79 Honolulu
TANNING IS JUST THE BODY'S RESPONSE TO SKIN DAMAGE. I KNEW THAT, BUT I WAS BLINDED BY THE GLAMOUR OF COMPETITIVE SUN-BATHING.
WHAT A DOLT I WAS! I TRADED MY YOUTH FOR A LITTLE GLORY, AND ENDED UP WITH LEATHERY SKIN AND SOME NASTY PRE-CANCEROUS LESIONS!
Cancun 1981
1-23
YOUR SKIN ISN'T LEATHERY.
YES, IT IS, BUT THANKS. I DO USE MOISTURI-ZERS.
GB Trudeau
WHAT ARE THESE?
COLOR SWATCHES. ALL THE TOP DAWGS CARRIED THEM.
THIS IS KILLING ME...
St. Croix, '80

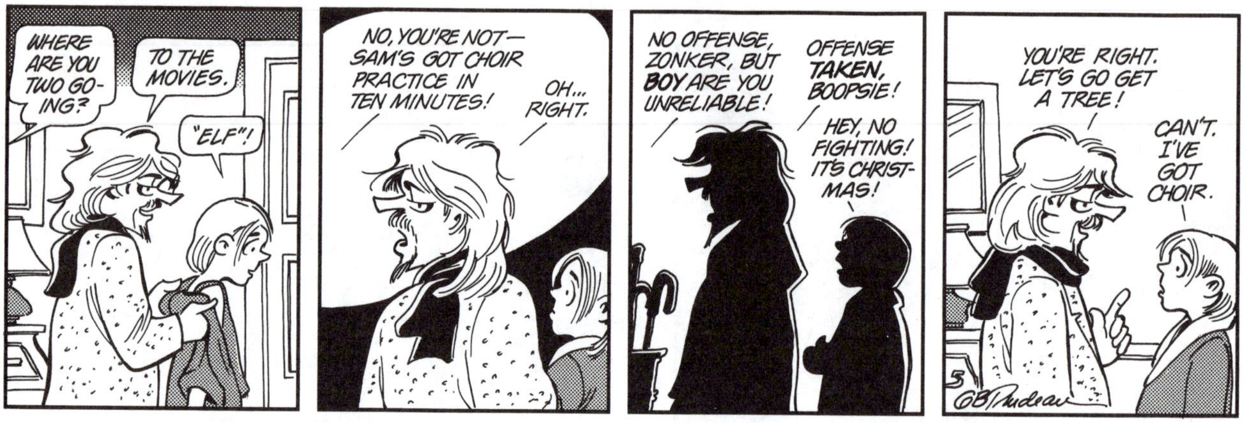
WHERE ARE YOU TWO GO-ING?
TO THE MOVIES.
"ELF"!
NO, YOU'RE NOT— SAM'S GOT CHOIR PRACTICE IN TEN MINUTES!
OH... RIGHT.
NO OFFENSE, ZONKER, BUT BOY ARE YOU UNRELIABLE!
OFFENSE TAKEN, BOOPSIE!
HEY, NO FIGHTING! IT'S CHRIST-MAS!
YOU'RE RIGHT. LET'S GO GET A TREE!
CAN'T. I'VE GOT CHOIR.

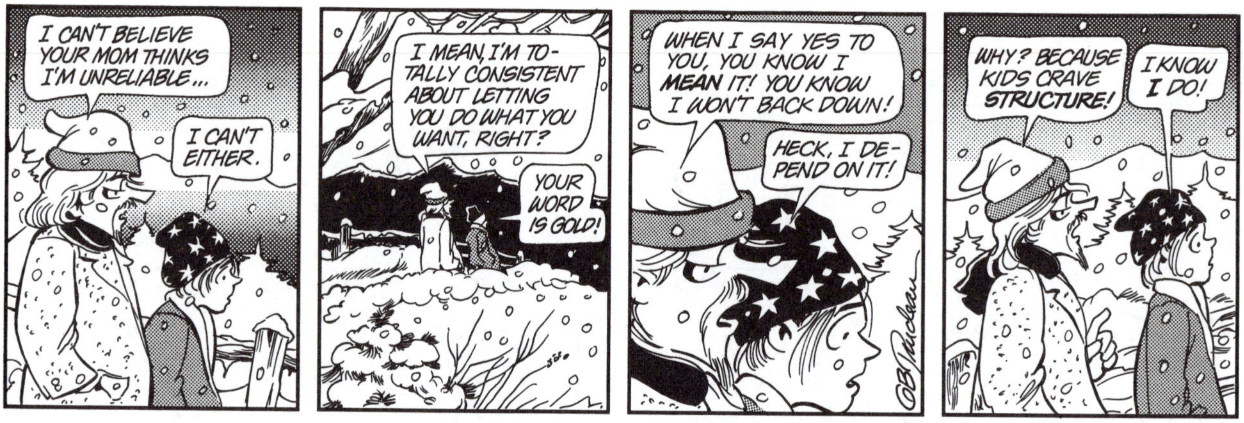
I CAN'T BELIEVE YOUR MOM THINKS I'M UNRELIABLE...
I CAN'T EITHER.
I MEAN, I'M TO-TALLY CONSISTENT ABOUT LETTING YOU DO WHAT YOU WANT, RIGHT?
YOUR WORD IS GOLD!
WHEN I SAY YES TO YOU, YOU KNOW I MEAN IT! YOU KNOW I WON'T BACK DOWN!
HECK, I DE-PEND ON IT!
WHY? BECAUSE KIDS CRAVE STRUCTURE!
I KNOW I DO!

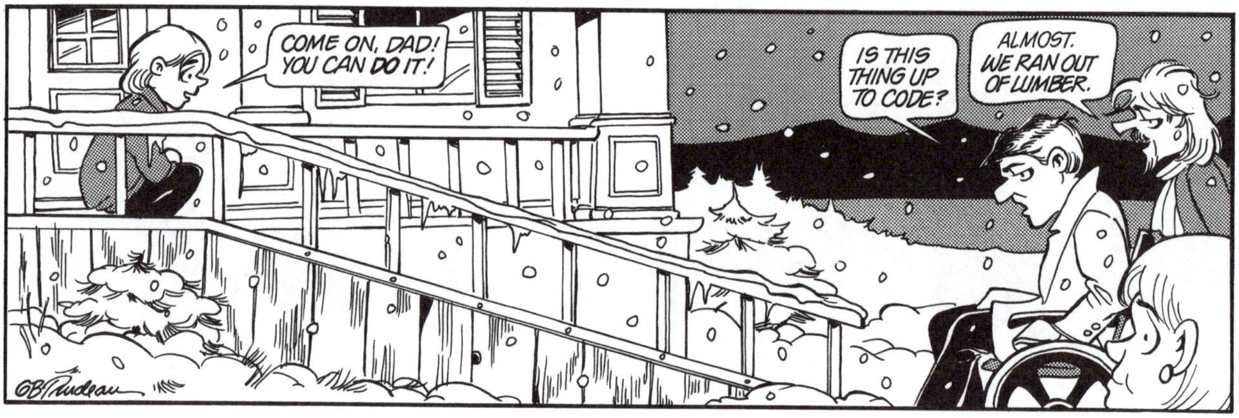
COME ON, DAD! YOU CAN DO IT!
IS THIS THING UP TO CODE?
ALMOST. WE RAN OUT OF LUMBER.

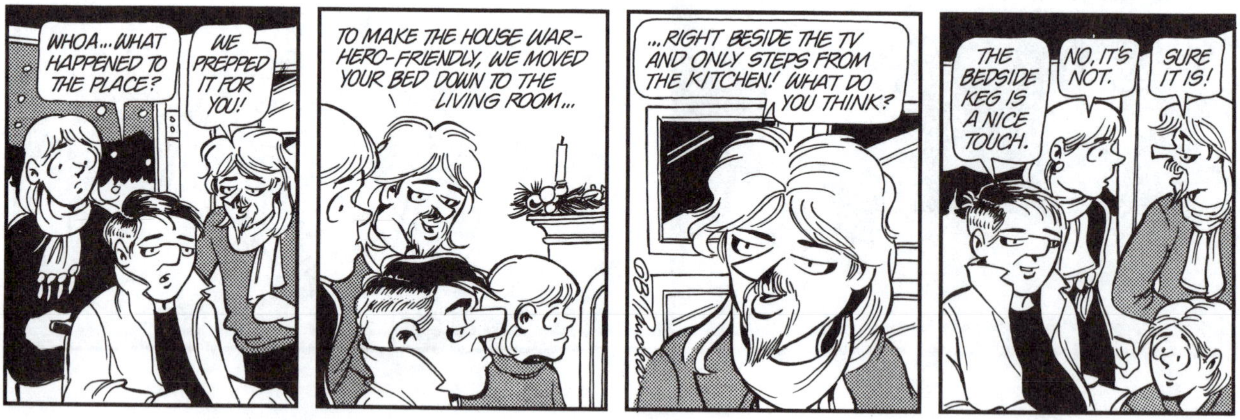
WHOA... WHAT HAPPENED TO THE PLACE?
WE PREPPED IT FOR YOU!
TO MAKE THE HOUSE WAR-HERO-FRIENDLY, WE MOVED YOUR BED DOWN TO THE LIVING ROOM...
...RIGHT BESIDE THE TV AND ONLY STEPS FROM THE KITCHEN! WHAT DO YOU THINK?
THE BEDSIDE KEG IS A NICE TOUCH.
NO, IT'S NOT.
SURE IT IS!

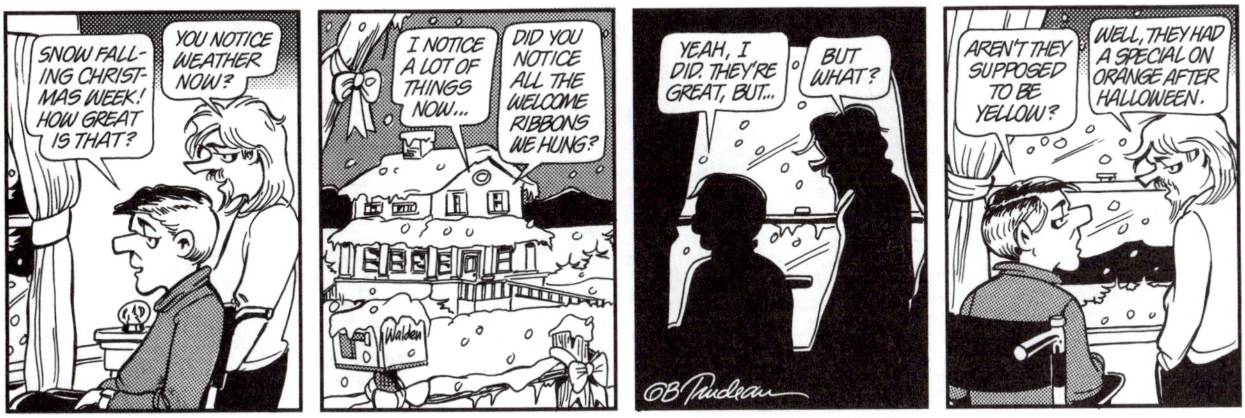

SNOW FALLING CHRISTMAS WEEK! HOW GREAT IS THAT?
YOU NOTICE WEATHER NOW?
I NOTICE A LOT OF THINGS NOW...
DID YOU NOTICE ALL THE WELCOME RIBBONS WE HUNG?
Walden
YEAH, I DID. THEY'RE GREAT, BUT...
BUT WHAT?
AREN'T THEY SUPPOSED TO BE YELLOW?
WELL, THEY HAD A SPECIAL ON ORANGE AFTER HALLOWEEN.

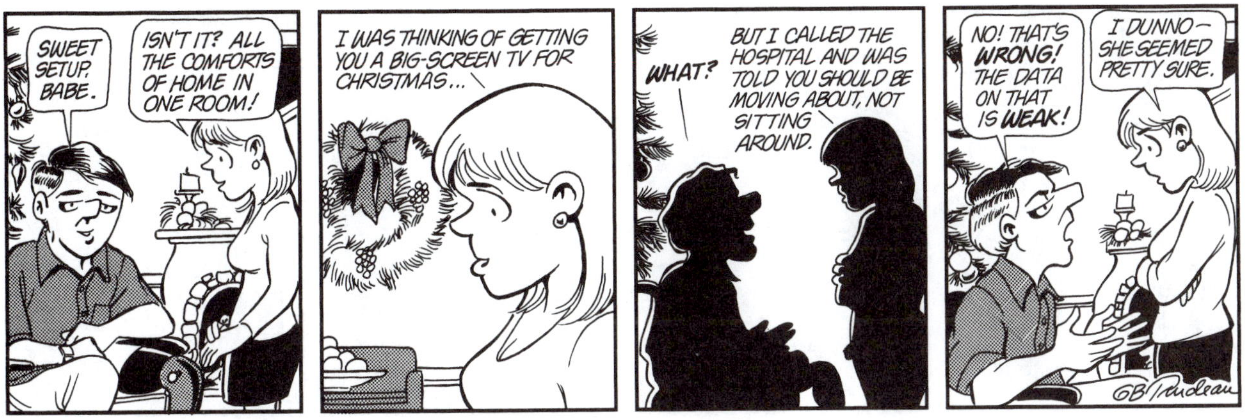

SWEET SETUP, BABE.
ISN'T IT? ALL THE COMFORTS OF HOME IN ONE ROOM!
I WAS THINKING OF GETTING YOU A BIG-SCREEN TV FOR CHRISTMAS...
WHAT?
BUT I CALLED THE HOSPITAL AND WAS TOLD YOU SHOULD BE MOVING ABOUT, NOT SITTING AROUND.
NO! THAT'S WRONG! THE DATA ON THAT IS WEAK!
I DUNNO—SHE SEEMED PRETTY SURE.

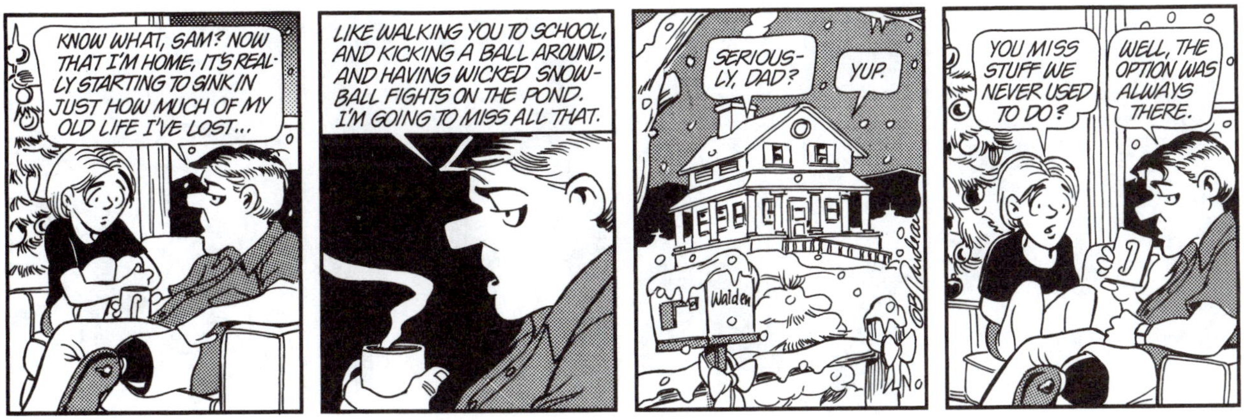

KNOW WHAT, SAM? NOW THAT I'M HOME, IT'S REALLY STARTING TO SINK IN JUST HOW MUCH OF MY OLD LIFE I'VE LOST...
LIKE WALKING YOU TO SCHOOL, AND KICKING A BALL AROUND, AND HAVING WICKED SNOWBALL FIGHTS ON THE POND. I'M GOING TO MISS ALL THAT.
SERIOUSLY, DAD?
YUP.
Walden
YOU MISS STUFF WE NEVER USED TO DO?
WELL, THE OPTION WAS ALWAYS THERE.

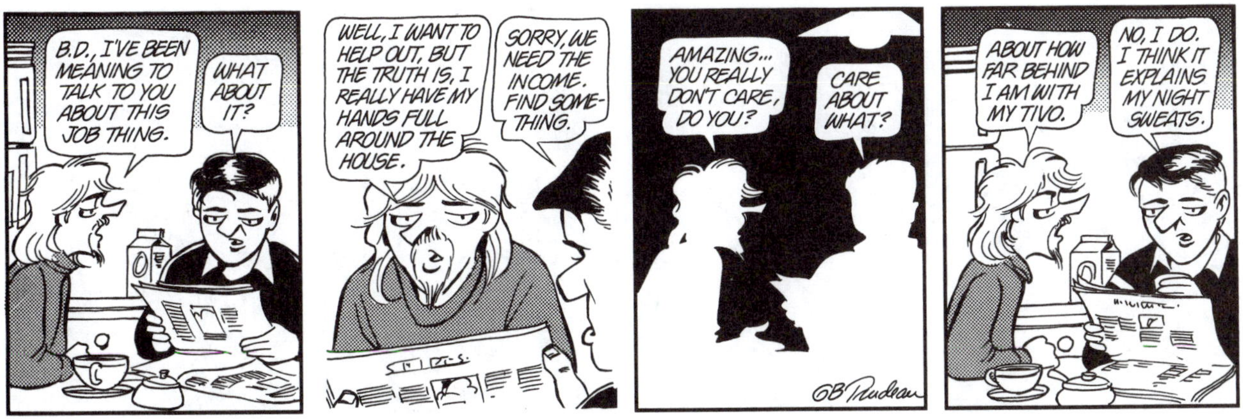

B.D., I'VE BEEN MEANING TO TALK TO YOU ABOUT THIS JOB THING.
WHAT ABOUT IT?
WELL, I WANT TO HELP OUT, BUT THE TRUTH IS, I REALLY HAVE MY HANDS FULL AROUND THE HOUSE.
SORRY, WE NEED THE INCOME. FIND SOMETHING.
AMAZING... YOU REALLY DON'T CARE, DO YOU?
CARE ABOUT WHAT?
ABOUT HOW FAR BEHIND I AM WITH MY TIVO.
NO, I DO. I THINK IT EXPLAINS MY NIGHT SWEATS.

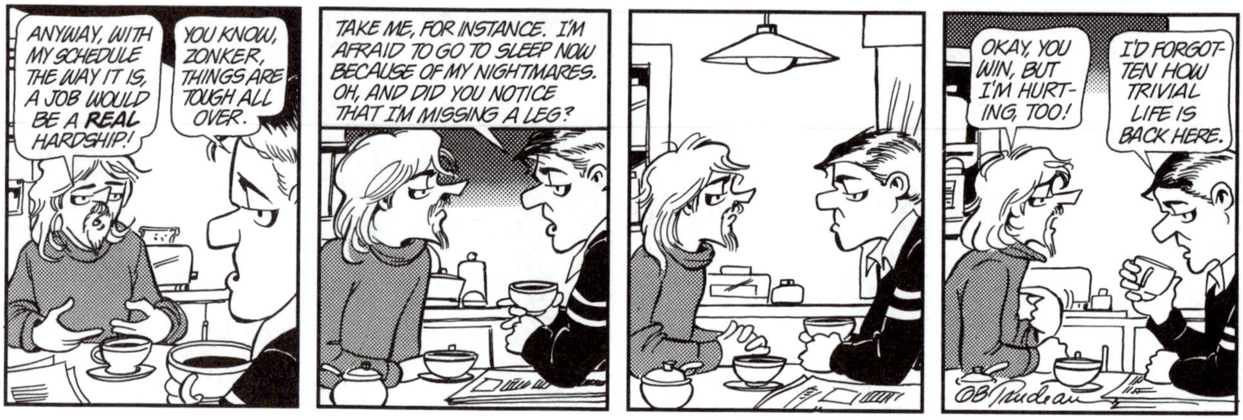
ANYWAY, WITH MY SCHEDULE THE WAY IT IS, A JOB WOULD BE A **REAL** HARDSHIP!
YOU KNOW, ZONKER, THINGS ARE TOUGH ALL OVER.
TAKE ME, FOR INSTANCE. I'M AFRAID TO GO TO SLEEP NOW BECAUSE OF MY NIGHTMARES. OH, AND DID YOU NOTICE THAT I'M MISSING A LEG?
OKAY, YOU WIN, BUT I'M HURTING, TOO!
I'D FORGOTTEN HOW TRIVIAL LIFE IS BACK HERE.
GB Trudeau

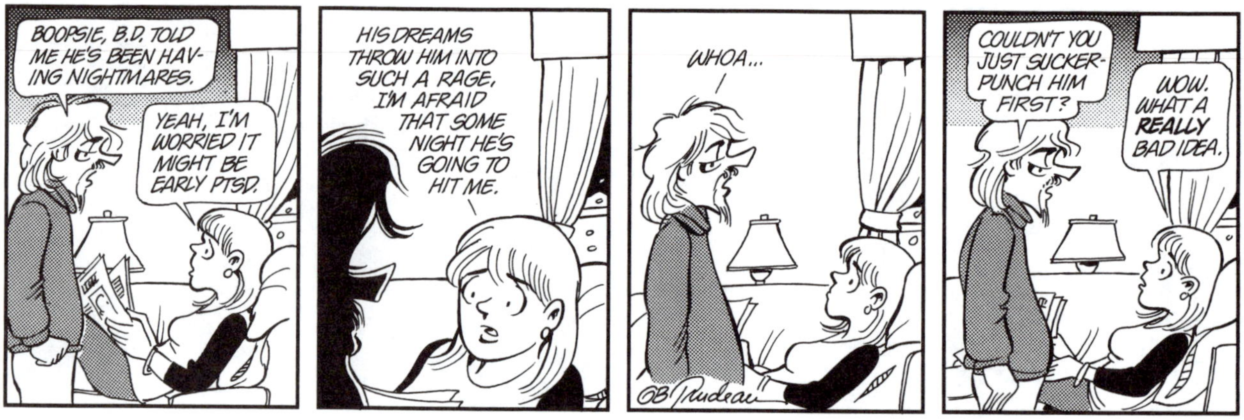
BOOPSIE, B.D. TOLD ME HE'S BEEN HAVING NIGHTMARES.
YEAH, I'M WORRIED IT MIGHT BE EARLY PTSD.
HIS DREAMS THROW HIM INTO SUCH A RAGE, I'M AFRAID THAT SOME NIGHT HE'S GOING TO HIT ME.
WHOA...
GB Trudeau
COULDN'T YOU JUST SUCKER-PUNCH HIM FIRST?
WOW. WHAT A **REALLY** BAD IDEA.

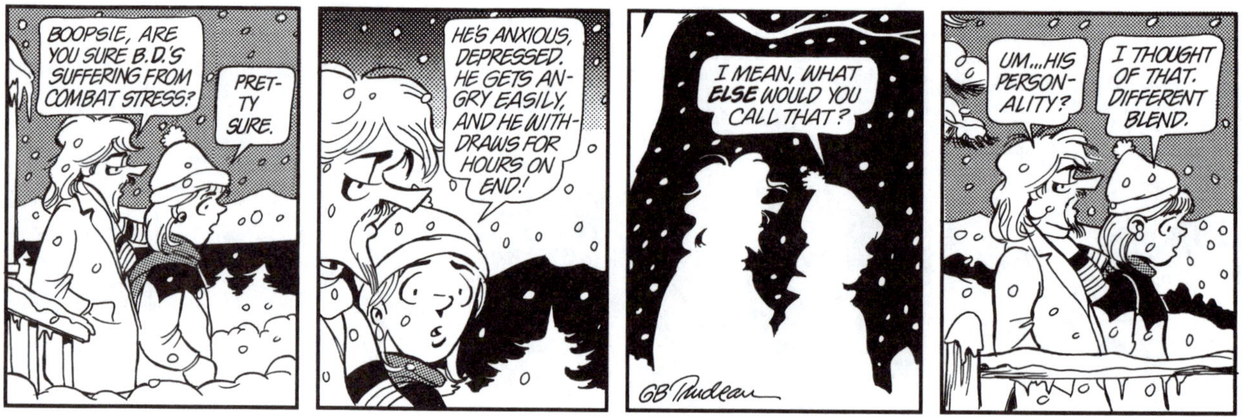
BOOPSIE, ARE YOU SURE B.D.'S SUFFERING FROM COMBAT STRESS?
PRETTY SURE.
HE'S ANXIOUS, DEPRESSED. HE GETS ANGRY EASILY, AND HE WITHDRAWS FOR HOURS ON END!
I MEAN, WHAT **ELSE** WOULD YOU CALL THAT?
GB Trudeau
UM...HIS PERSONALITY?
I THOUGHT OF THAT. DIFFERENT BLEND.

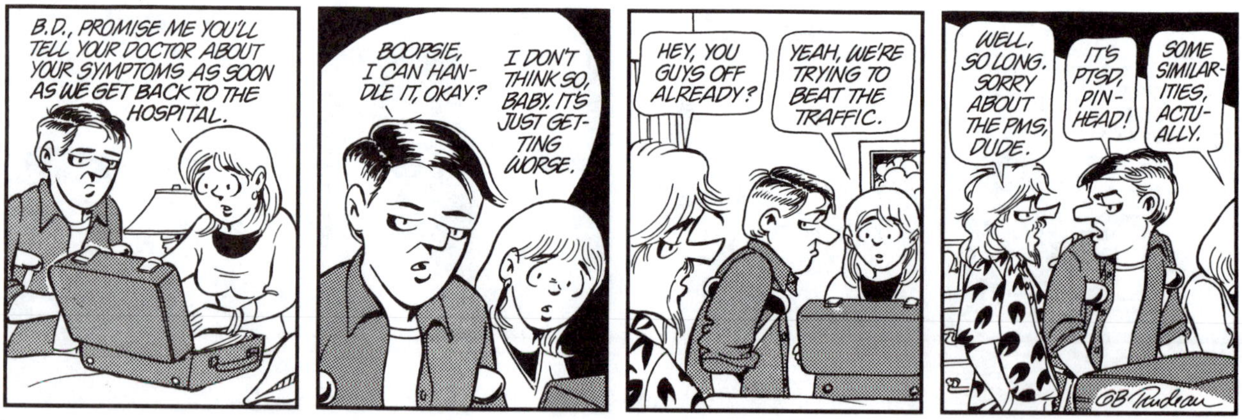
B.D., PROMISE ME YOU'LL TELL YOUR DOCTOR ABOUT YOUR SYMPTOMS AS SOON AS **WE** GET BACK TO THE HOSPITAL.
BOOPSIE, I CAN HANDLE IT, OKAY?
I DON'T THINK SO, BABY. IT'S JUST GETTING WORSE.
HEY, YOU GUYS OFF ALREADY?
YEAH, WE'RE TRYING TO BEAT THE TRAFFIC.
WELL, SO LONG. SORRY ABOUT THE PMS, DUDE.
IT'S PTSD, PINHEAD!
SOME SIMILARITIES, ACTUALLY.
GB Trudeau

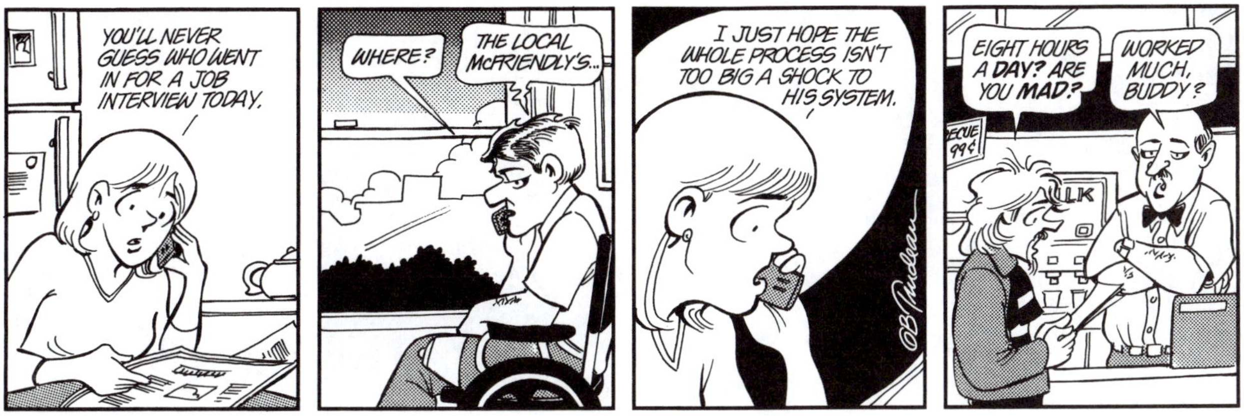
YOU'LL NEVER GUESS WHO WENT IN FOR A JOB INTERVIEW TODAY.
WHERE?
THE LOCAL McFRIENDLY'S...
I JUST HOPE THE WHOLE PROCESS ISN'T TOO BIG A SHOCK TO HIS SYSTEM.
EIGHT HOURS A DAY? ARE YOU MAD?
WORKED MUCH, BUDDY?

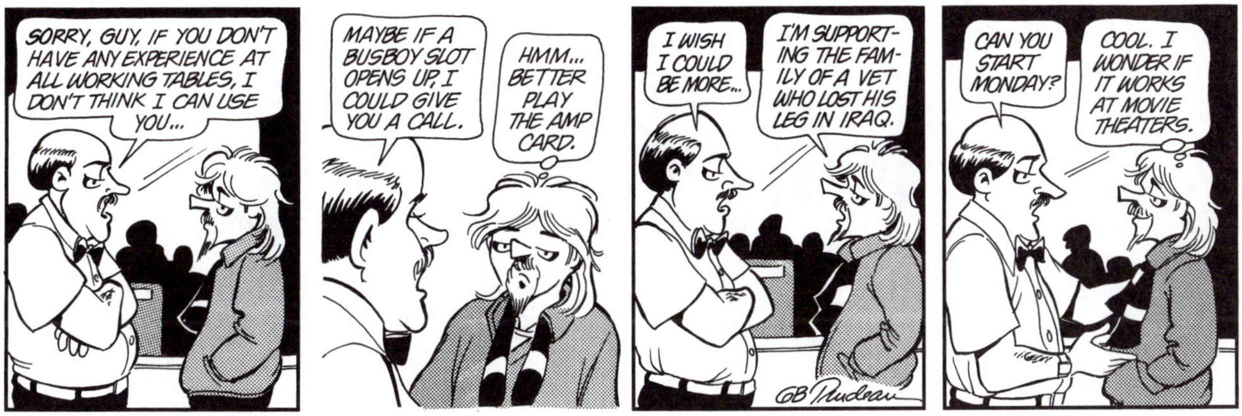
SORRY, GUY, IF YOU DON'T HAVE ANY EXPERIENCE AT ALL WORKING TABLES, I DON'T THINK I CAN USE YOU...
MAYBE IF A BUSBOY SLOT OPENS UP, I COULD GIVE YOU A CALL.
HMM... BETTER PLAY THE AMP CARD.
I WISH I COULD BE MORE...
I'M SUPPORTING THE FAMILY OF A VET WHO LOST HIS LEG IN IRAQ.
CAN YOU START MONDAY?
COOL. I WONDER IF IT WORKS AT MOVIE THEATERS.

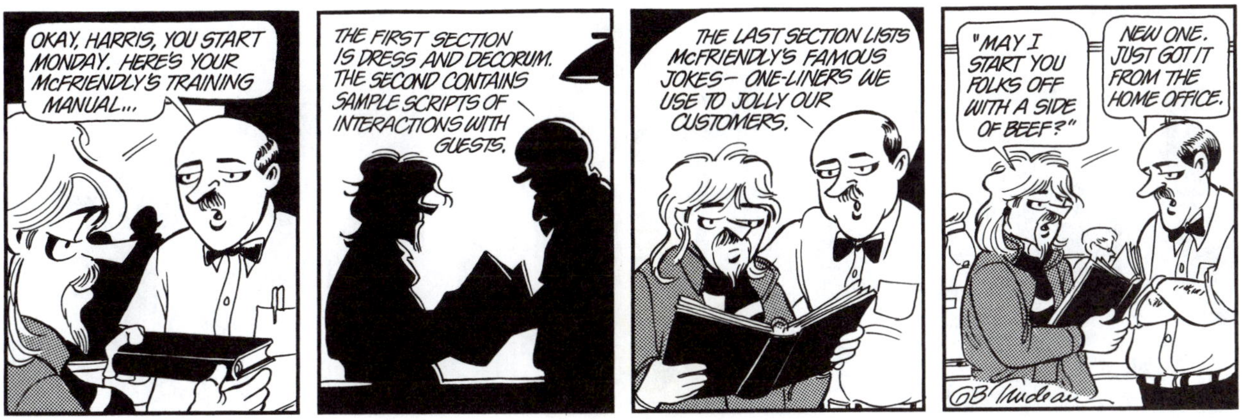
OKAY, HARRIS, YOU START MONDAY. HERE'S YOUR McFRIENDLY'S TRAINING MANUAL...
THE FIRST SECTION IS DRESS AND DECORUM. THE SECOND CONTAINS SAMPLE SCRIPTS OF INTERACTIONS WITH GUESTS.
THE LAST SECTION LISTS McFRIENDLY'S FAMOUS JOKES— ONE-LINERS WE USE TO JOLLY OUR CUSTOMERS.
"MAY I START YOU FOLKS OFF WITH A SIDE OF BEEF?"
NEW ONE. JUST GOT IT FROM THE HOME OFFICE.

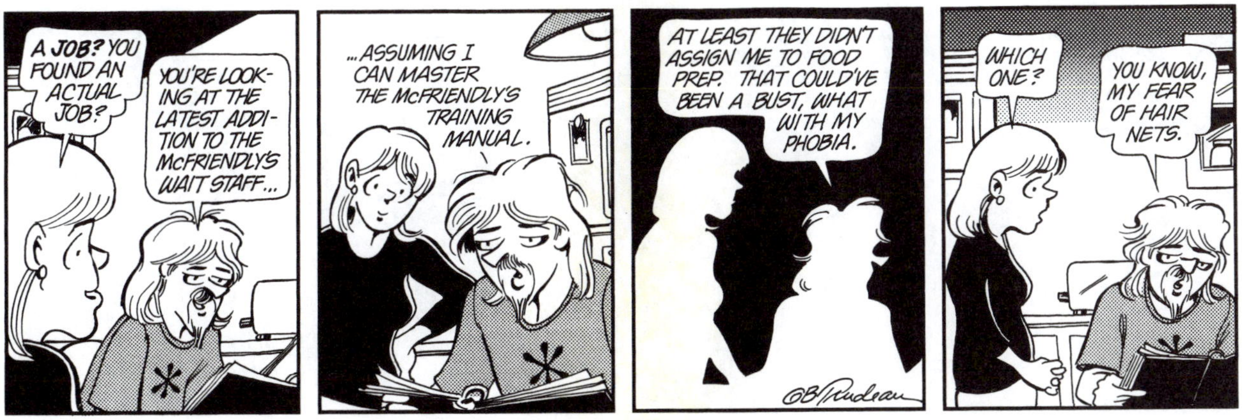
A JOB? YOU FOUND AN ACTUAL JOB?
YOU'RE LOOKING AT THE LATEST ADDITION TO THE McFRIENDLY'S WAIT STAFF...
...ASSUMING I CAN MASTER THE McFRIENDLY'S TRAINING MANUAL.
AT LEAST THEY DIDN'T ASSIGN ME TO FOOD PREP. THAT COULD'VE BEEN A BUST, WHAT WITH MY PHOBIA.
WHICH ONE?
YOU KNOW, MY FEAR OF HAIR NETS.

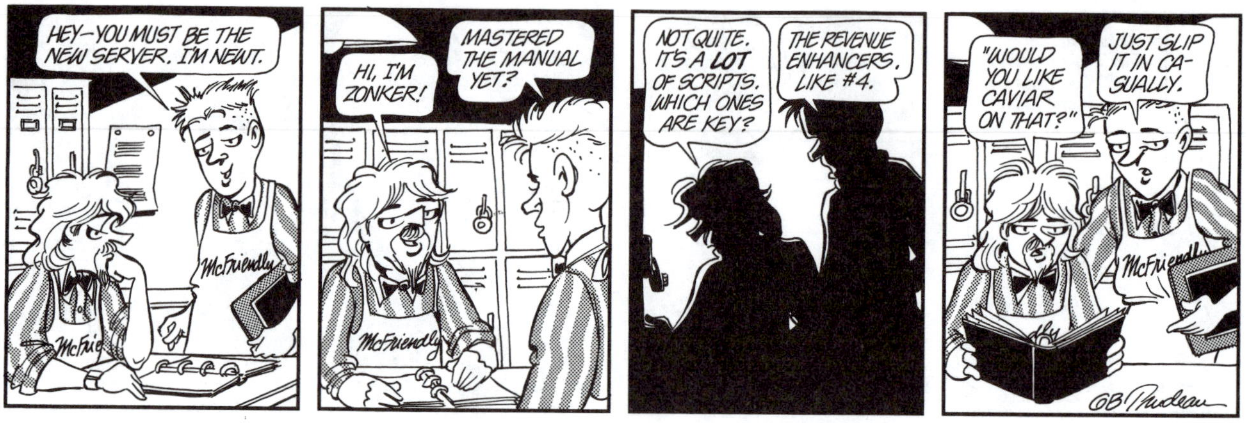
HEY—YOU MUST BE THE NEW SERVER. I'M NEWT.
HI, I'M ZONKER!
MASTERED THE MANUAL YET?
NOT QUITE. IT'S A LOT OF SCRIPTS. WHICH ONES ARE KEY?
THE REVENUE ENHANCERS, LIKE #4.
"WOULD YOU LIKE CAVIAR ON THAT?"
JUST SLIP IT IN CA-SUALLY.
McFriendly
GB Trudeau

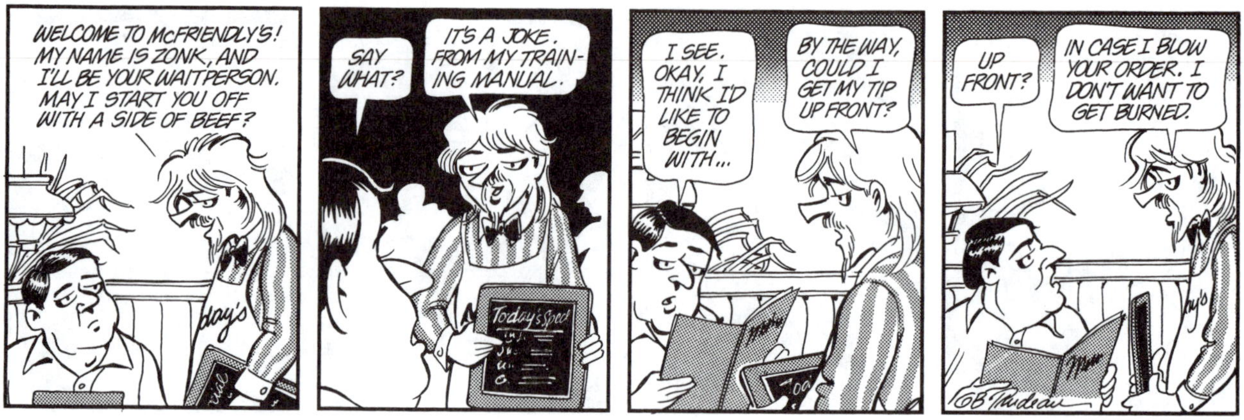
WELCOME TO McFRIENDLY'S! MY NAME IS ZONK, AND I'LL BE YOUR WAITPERSON. MAY I START YOU OFF WITH A SIDE OF BEEF?
SAY WHAT?
IT'S A JOKE. FROM MY TRAIN-ING MANUAL.
I SEE. OKAY, I THINK I'D LIKE TO BEGIN WITH...
BY THE WAY, COULD I GET MY TIP UP FRONT?
UP FRONT?
IN CASE I BLOW YOUR ORDER. I DON'T WANT TO GET BURNED.
GB Trudeau

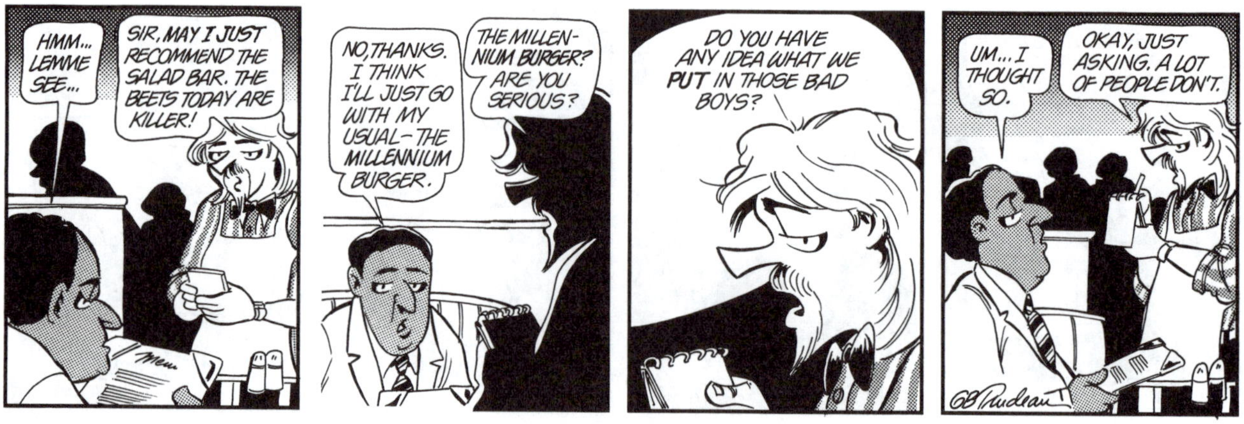
HMM... LEMME SEE...
SIR, MAY I JUST RECOMMEND THE SALAD BAR. THE BEETS TODAY ARE KILLER!
NO, THANKS. I THINK I'LL JUST GO WITH MY USUAL—THE MILLENNIUM BURGER.
THE MILLEN-NIUM BURGER? ARE YOU SERIOUS?
DO YOU HAVE ANY IDEA WHAT WE PUT IN THOSE BAD BOYS?
UM... I THOUGHT SO.
OKAY, JUST ASKING. A LOT OF PEOPLE DON'T.
GB Trudeau

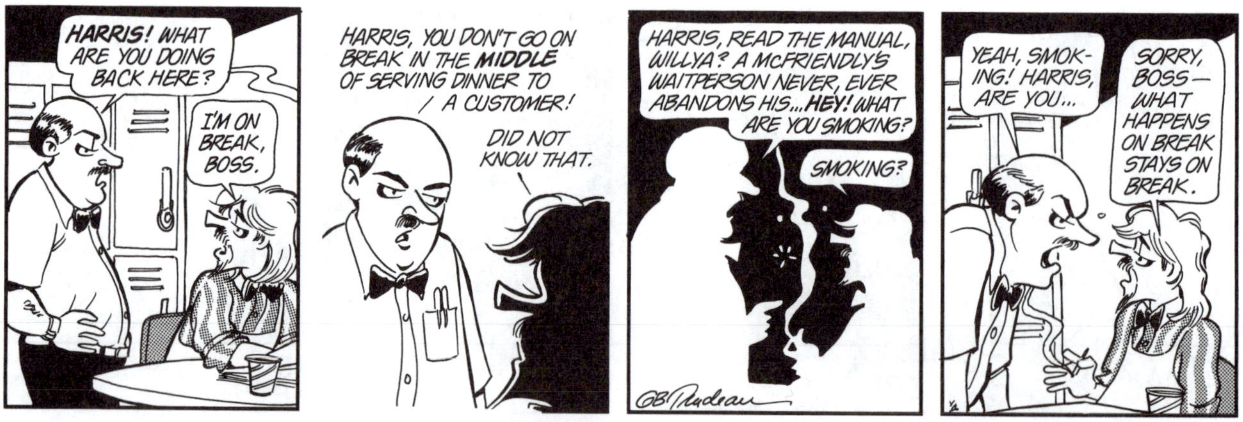
HARRIS! WHAT ARE YOU DOING BACK HERE?
I'M ON BREAK, BOSS.
HARRIS, YOU DON'T GO ON BREAK IN THE MIDDLE OF SERVING DINNER TO A CUSTOMER!
DID NOT KNOW THAT.
HARRIS, READ THE MANUAL, WILLYA? A McFRIENDLY'S WAITPERSON NEVER, EVER ABANDONS HIS... HEY! WHAT ARE YOU SMOKING?
SMOKING?
YEAH, SMOK-ING! HARRIS, ARE YOU...
SORRY, BOSS—WHAT HAPPENS ON BREAK STAYS ON BREAK.
GB Trudeau

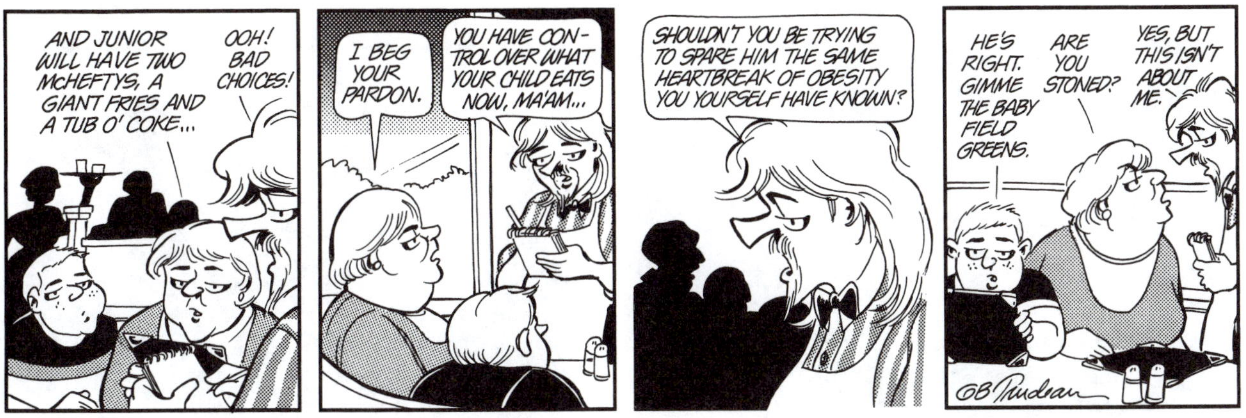
AND JUNIOR WILL HAVE TWO MCHEFTYS, A GIANT FRIES AND A TUB O' COKE...
OOH! BAD CHOICES!
I BEG YOUR PARDON.
YOU HAVE CONTROL OVER WHAT YOUR CHILD EATS NOW, MA'AM...
SHOULDN'T YOU BE TRYING TO SPARE HIM THE SAME HEARTBREAK OF OBESITY YOU YOURSELF HAVE KNOWN?
HE'S RIGHT. GIMME THE BABY FIELD GREENS.
ARE YOU STONED?
YES, BUT THIS ISN'T ABOUT ME.
©B Trudeau

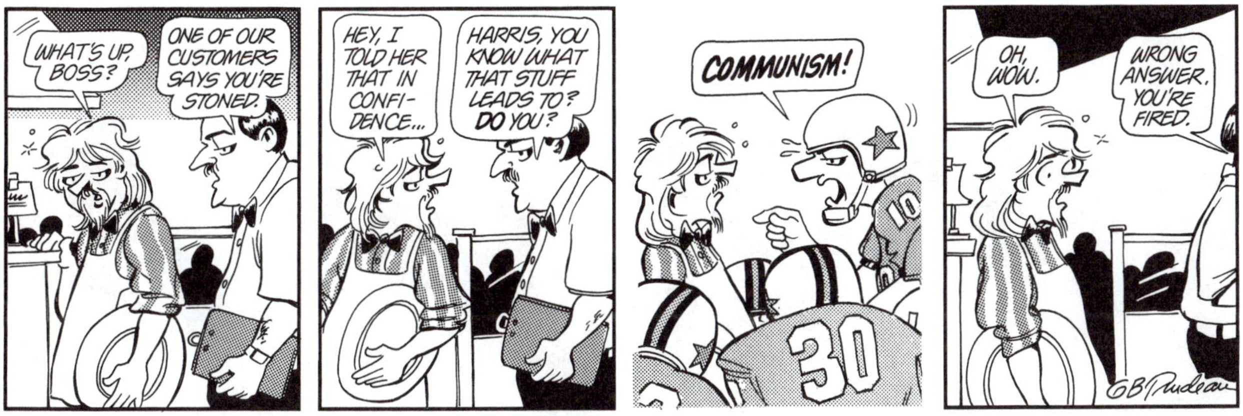
WHAT'S UP, BOSS?
ONE OF OUR CUSTOMERS SAYS YOU'RE STONED.
HEY, I TOLD HER THAT IN CONFIDENCE...
HARRIS, YOU KNOW WHAT THAT STUFF LEADS TO? DO YOU?
COMMUNISM!
OH, WOW.
WRONG ANSWER. YOU'RE FIRED.
©B Trudeau

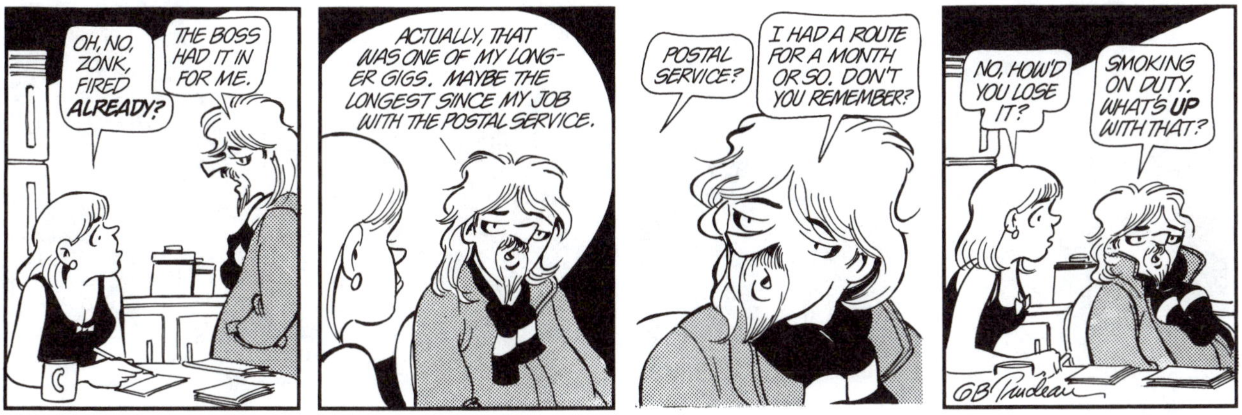
OH, NO, ZONK, FIRED ALREADY?
THE BOSS HAD IT IN FOR ME.
ACTUALLY, THAT WAS ONE OF MY LONGER GIGS. MAYBE THE LONGEST SINCE MY JOB WITH THE POSTAL SERVICE.
POSTAL SERVICE?
I HAD A ROUTE FOR A MONTH OR SO. DON'T YOU REMEMBER?
NO, HOW'D YOU LOSE IT?
SMOKING ON DUTY. WHAT'S UP WITH THAT?
©B Trudeau

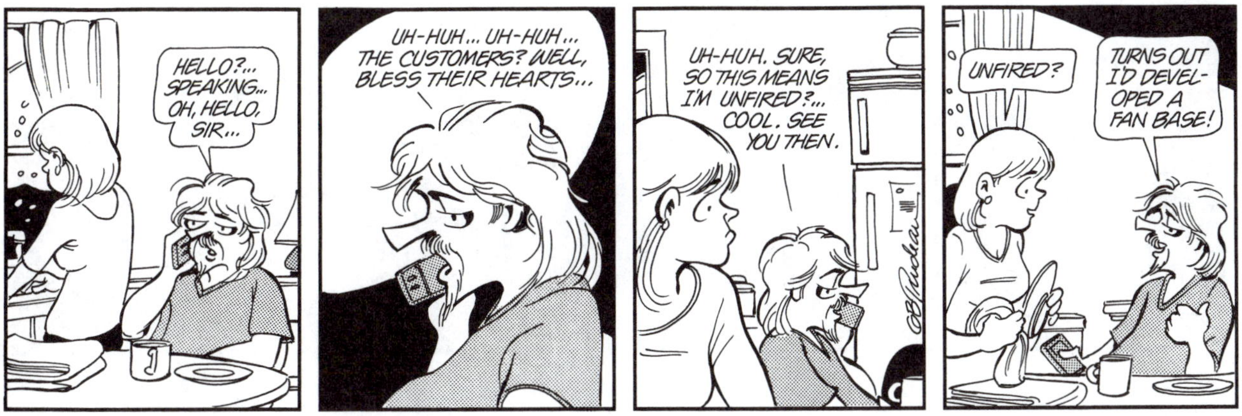
HELLO?... SPEAKING... OH, HELLO, SIR...
UH-HUH... UH-HUH... THE CUSTOMERS? WELL, BLESS THEIR HEARTS...
UH-HUH. SURE, SO THIS MEANS I'M UNFIRED?... COOL. SEE YOU THEN.
©B Trudeau
UNFIRED?
TURNS OUT I'D DEVELOPED A FAN BASE!

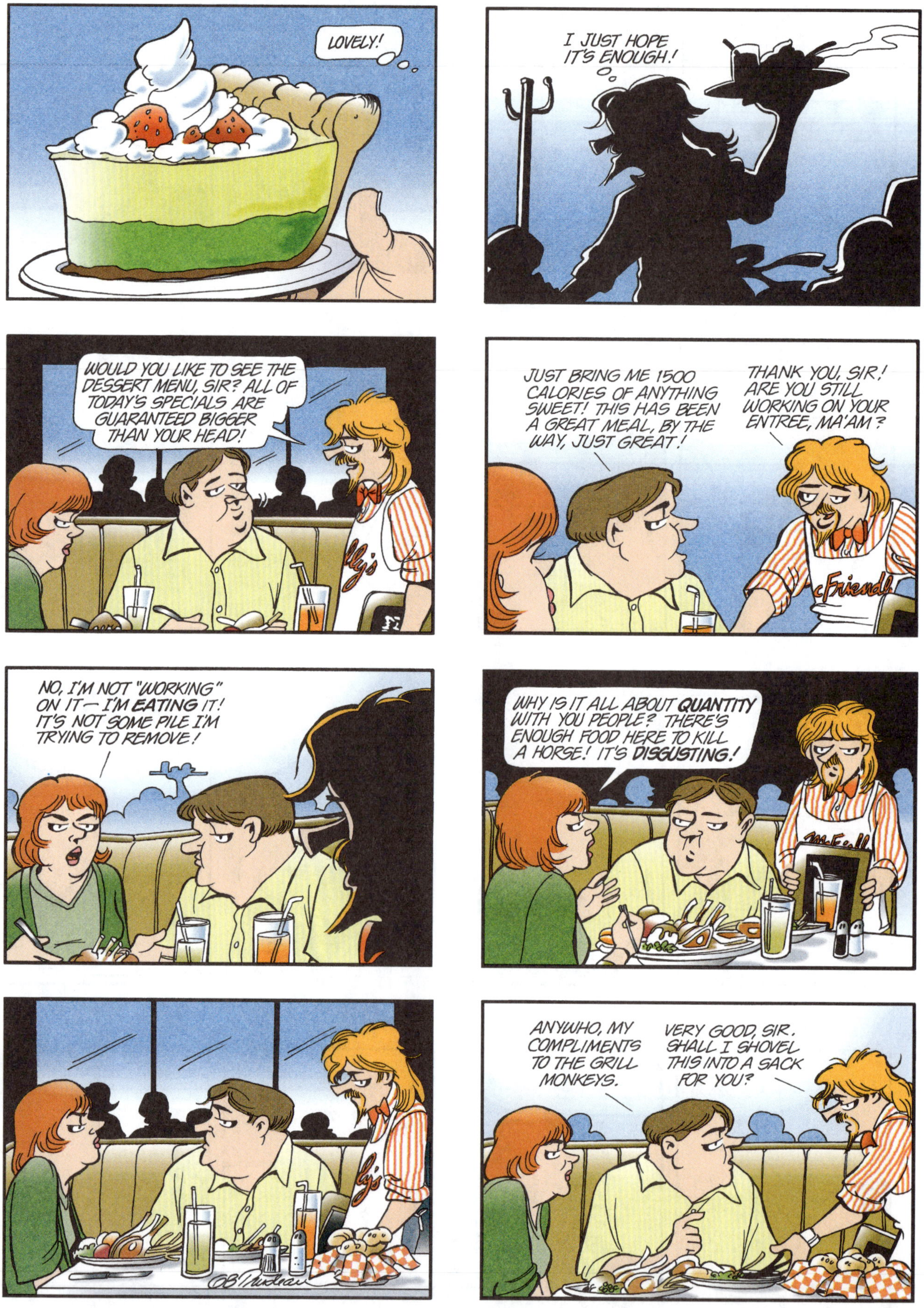
LOVELY!
I JUST HOPE IT'S ENOUGH!
WOULD YOU LIKE TO SEE THE DESSERT MENU, SIR? ALL OF TODAY'S SPECIALS ARE GUARANTEED BIGGER THAN YOUR HEAD!
JUST BRING ME 1500 CALORIES OF ANYTHING SWEET! THIS HAS BEEN A GREAT MEAL, BY THE WAY, JUST GREAT!
THANK YOU, SIR! ARE YOU STILL WORKING ON YOUR ENTREE, MA'AM?
NO, I'M NOT "WORKING" ON IT— I'M EATING IT! IT'S NOT SOME PILE I'M TRYING TO REMOVE!
WHY IS IT ALL ABOUT QUANTITY WITH YOU PEOPLE? THERE'S ENOUGH FOOD HERE TO KILL A HORSE! IT'S DISGUSTING!
ANYWHO, MY COMPLIMENTS TO THE GRILL MONKEYS.
VERY GOOD, SIR. SHALL I SHOVEL THIS INTO A SACK FOR YOU?

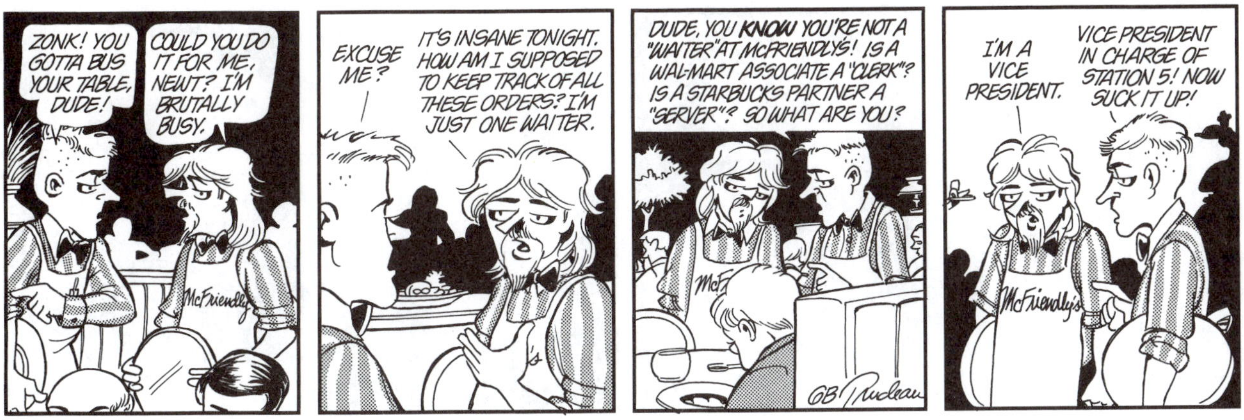
ZONK! YOU GOTTA BUS YOUR TABLE, DUDE!
COULD YOU DO IT FOR ME, NEWT? I'M BRUTALLY BUSY.
EXCUSE ME?
IT'S INSANE TONIGHT. HOW AM I SUPPOSED TO KEEP TRACK OF ALL THESE ORDERS? I'M JUST ONE WAITER.
DUDE, YOU KNOW YOU'RE NOT A "WAITER" AT McFRIENDLY'S! IS A WAL-MART ASSOCIATE A "CLERK"? IS A STARBUCKS PARTNER A "SERVER"? SO WHAT ARE YOU?
I'M A VICE PRESIDENT.
VICE PRESIDENT IN CHARGE OF STATION 5! NOW SUCK IT UP!
McFriendly's
GB Trudeau

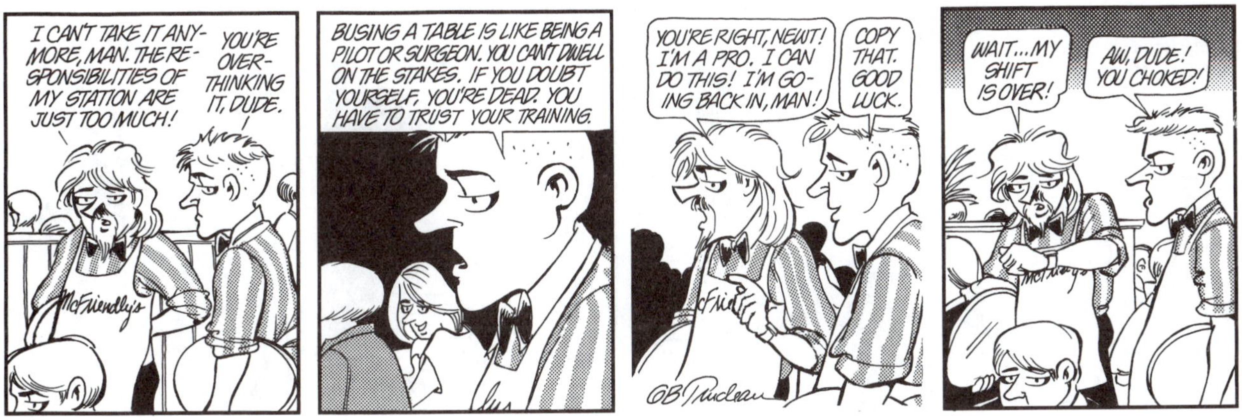
I CAN'T TAKE IT ANYMORE, MAN. THE RESPONSIBILITIES OF MY STATION ARE JUST TOO MUCH!
YOU'RE OVER-THINKING IT, DUDE.
BUSING A TABLE IS LIKE BEING A PILOT OR SURGEON. YOU CAN'T DWELL ON THE STAKES. IF YOU DOUBT YOURSELF, YOU'RE DEAD. YOU HAVE TO TRUST YOUR TRAINING.
YOU'RE RIGHT, NEWT! I'M A PRO. I CAN DO THIS! I'M GOING BACK IN, MAN!
COPY THAT. GOOD LUCK.
WAIT... MY SHIFT IS OVER!
AW, DUDE! YOU CHOKED!
McFriendly's
GB Trudeau

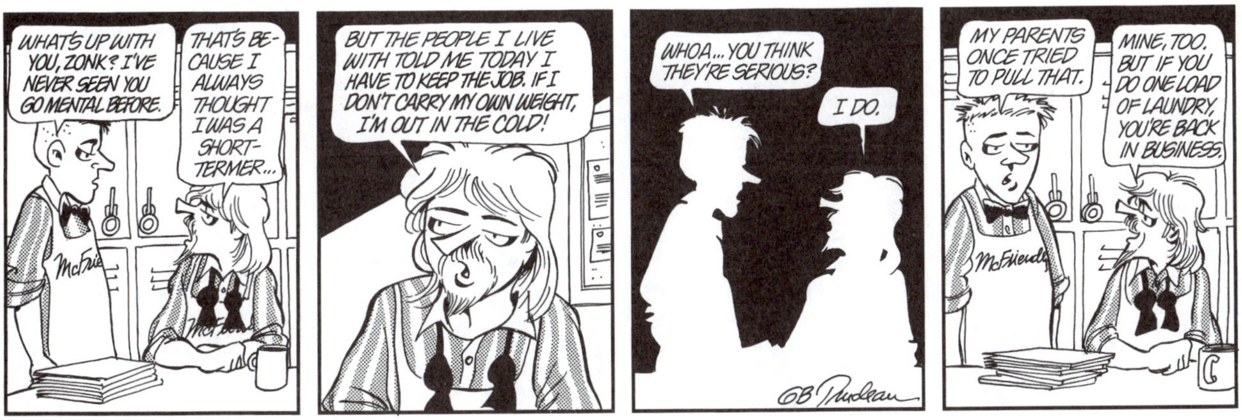
WHAT'S UP WITH YOU, ZONK? I'VE NEVER SEEN YOU GO MENTAL BEFORE.
THAT'S BECAUSE I ALWAYS THOUGHT I WAS A SHORT-TERMER...
BUT THE PEOPLE I LIVE WITH TOLD ME TODAY I HAVE TO KEEP THE JOB. IF I DON'T CARRY MY OWN WEIGHT, I'M OUT IN THE COLD!
WHOA... YOU THINK THEY'RE SERIOUS?
I DO.
MY PARENTS ONCE TRIED TO PULL THAT.
MINE, TOO. BUT IF YOU DO ONE LOAD OF LAUNDRY, YOU'RE BACK IN BUSINESS.
GB Trudeau

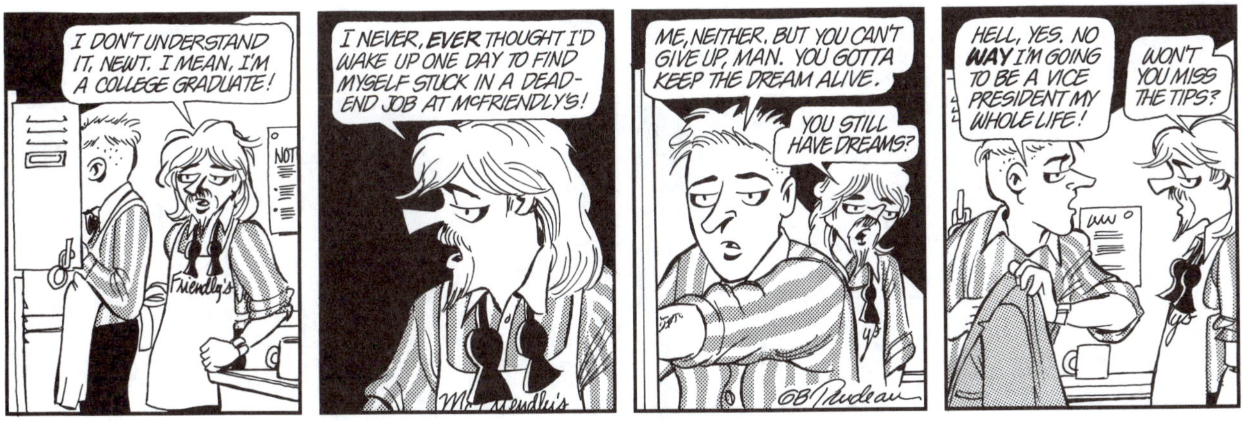
I DON'T UNDERSTAND IT, NEWT. I MEAN, I'M A COLLEGE GRADUATE!
I NEVER, EVER THOUGHT I'D WAKE UP ONE DAY TO FIND MYSELF STUCK IN A DEAD-END JOB AT McFRIENDLY'S!
ME, NEITHER. BUT YOU CAN'T GIVE UP, MAN. YOU GOTTA KEEP THE DREAM ALIVE.
YOU STILL HAVE DREAMS?
HELL, YES. NO WAY I'M GOING TO BE A VICE PRESIDENT MY WHOLE LIFE!
WON'T YOU MISS THE TIPS?
GB Trudeau

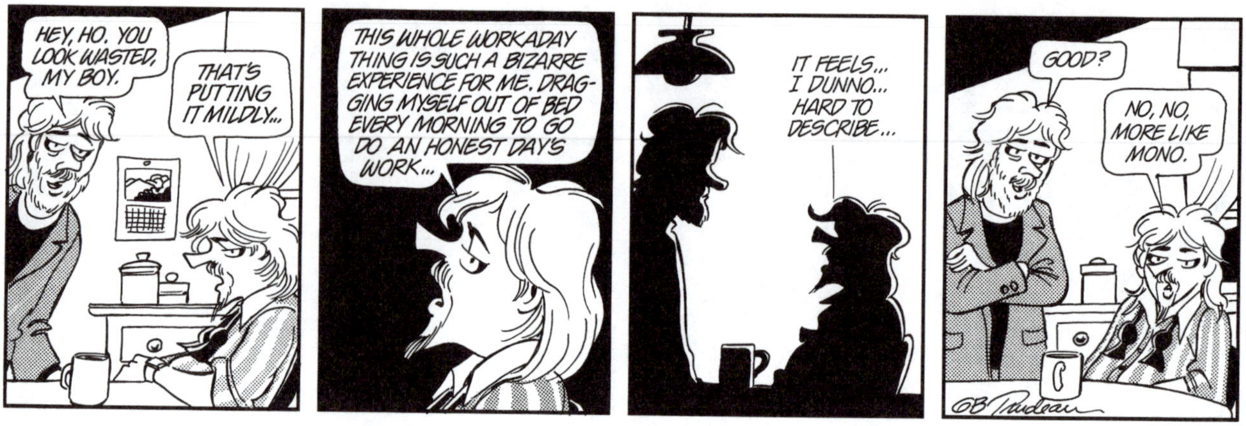
HEY, HO. YOU LOOK WASTED, MY BOY.
THAT'S PUTTING IT MILDLY...
THIS WHOLE WORKADAY THING IS SUCH A BIZARRE EXPERIENCE FOR ME. DRAGGING MYSELF OUT OF BED EVERY MORNING TO GO DO AN HONEST DAY'S WORK...
IT FEELS... I DUNNO... HARD TO DESCRIBE...
GOOD?
NO, NO, MORE LIKE MONO.
©B Trudeau

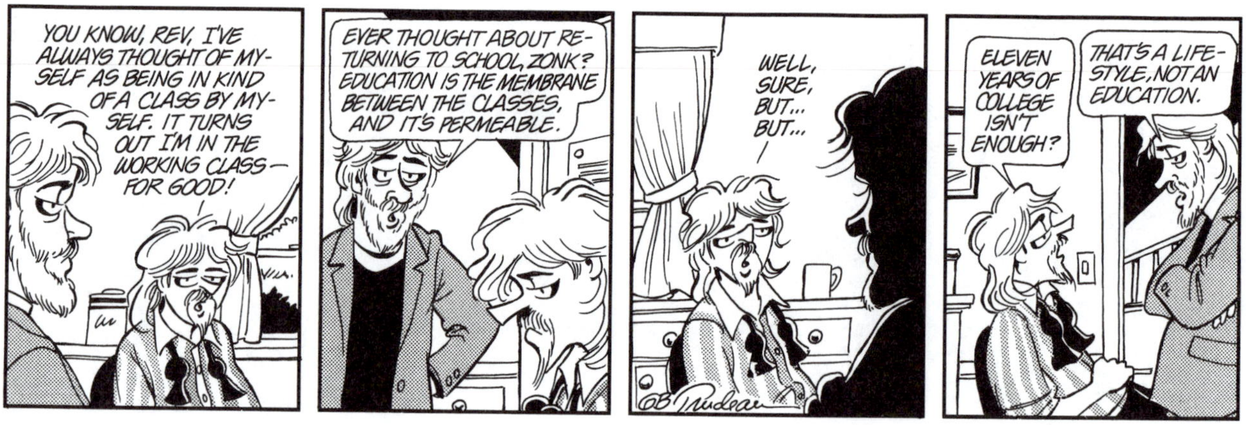
YOU KNOW, REV, I'VE ALWAYS THOUGHT OF MYSELF AS BEING IN KIND OF A CLASS BY MYSELF. IT TURNS OUT I'M IN THE WORKING CLASS — FOR GOOD!
EVER THOUGHT ABOUT RETURNING TO SCHOOL, ZONK? EDUCATION IS THE MEMBRANE BETWEEN THE CLASSES, AND IT'S PERMEABLE.
WELL, SURE, BUT... BUT...
ELEVEN YEARS OF COLLEGE ISN'T ENOUGH?
THAT'S A LIFESTYLE, NOT AN EDUCATION.
©B Trudeau

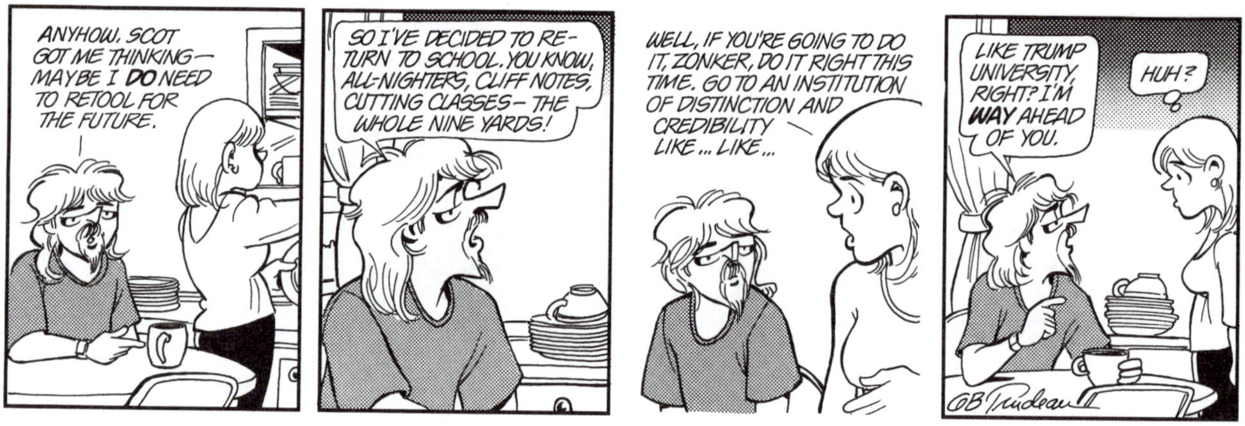
ANYHOW, SCOT GOT ME THINKING — MAYBE I DO NEED TO RETOOL FOR THE FUTURE.
SO I'VE DECIDED TO RETURN TO SCHOOL. YOU KNOW, ALL-NIGHTERS, CLIFF NOTES, CUTTING CLASSES — THE WHOLE NINE YARDS!
WELL, IF YOU'RE GOING TO DO IT, ZONKER, DO IT RIGHT THIS TIME. GO TO AN INSTITUTION OF DISTINCTION AND CREDIBILITY LIKE... LIKE...
LIKE TRUMP UNIVERSITY, RIGHT? I'M WAY AHEAD OF YOU.
HUH?
©B Trudeau

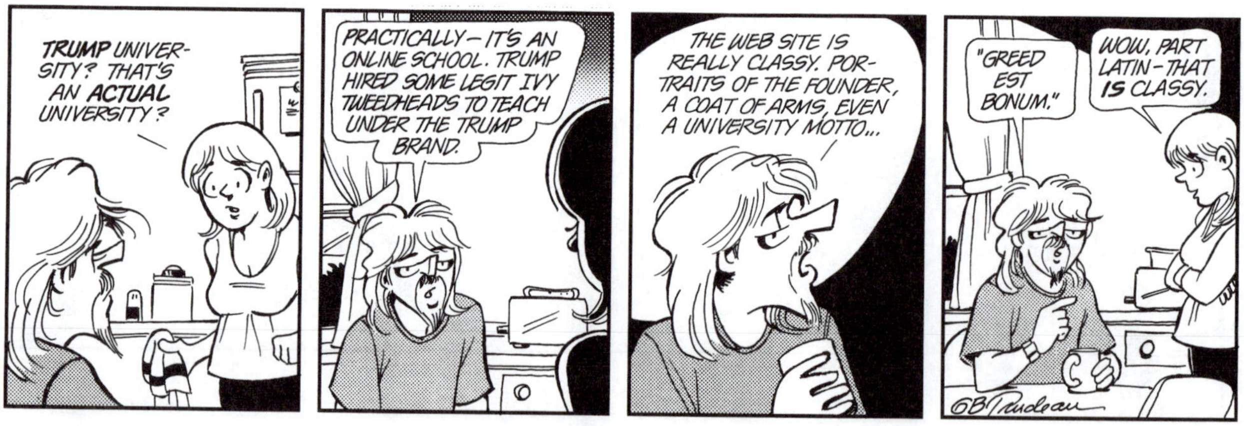
TRUMP UNIVERSITY? THAT'S AN ACTUAL UNIVERSITY?
PRACTICALLY — IT'S AN ONLINE SCHOOL. TRUMP HIRED SOME LEGIT IVY TWEEDHEADS TO TEACH UNDER THE TRUMP BRAND.
THE WEB SITE IS REALLY CLASSY. PORTRAITS OF THE FOUNDER, A COAT OF ARMS, EVEN A UNIVERSITY MOTTO...
"GREED EST BONUM."
WOW, PART LATIN — THAT IS CLASSY.
©B Trudeau

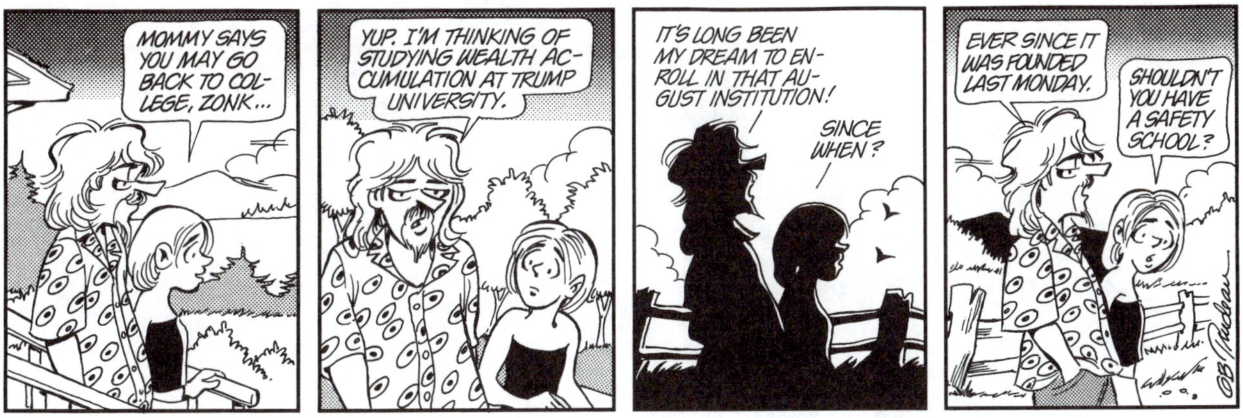
MOMMY SAYS YOU MAY GO BACK TO COL-LEGE, ZONK...
YUP. I'M THINKING OF STUDYING WEALTH AC-CUMULATION AT TRUMP UNIVERSITY.
IT'S LONG BEEN MY DREAM TO EN-ROLL IN THAT AU-GUST INSTITUTION!
SINCE WHEN?
EVER SINCE IT WAS FOUNDED LAST MONDAY.
SHOULDN'T YOU HAVE A SAFETY SCHOOL?
©B Trudeau

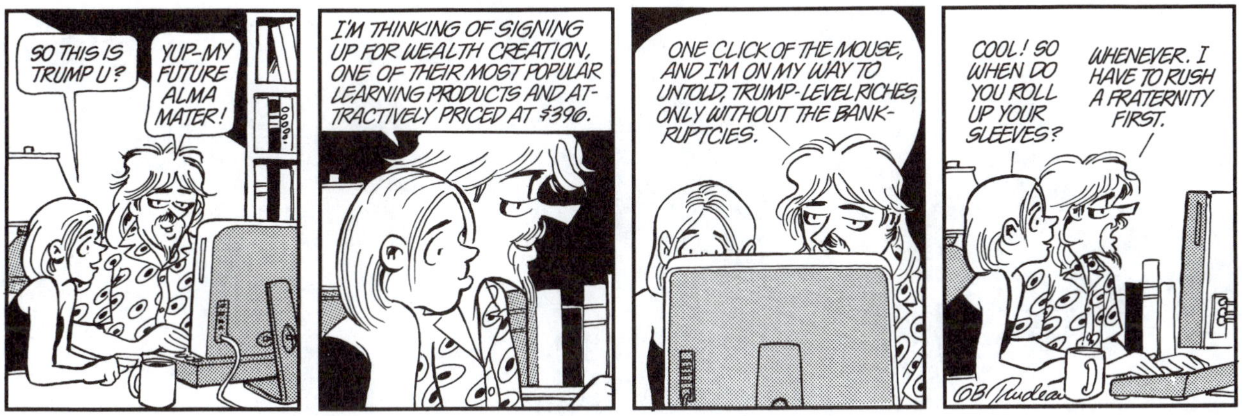
SO THIS IS TRUMP U?
YUP–MY FUTURE ALMA MATER!
I'M THINKING OF SIGNING UP FOR WEALTH CREATION, ONE OF THEIR MOST POPULAR LEARNING PRODUCTS AND AT-TRACTIVELY PRICED AT $396.
ONE CLICK OF THE MOUSE, AND I'M ON MY WAY TO UNTOLD, TRUMP-LEVEL RICHES, ONLY WITHOUT THE BANK-RUPTCIES.
COOL! SO WHEN DO YOU ROLL UP YOUR SLEEVES?
WHENEVER. I HAVE TO RUSH A FRATERNITY FIRST.
©B Trudeau

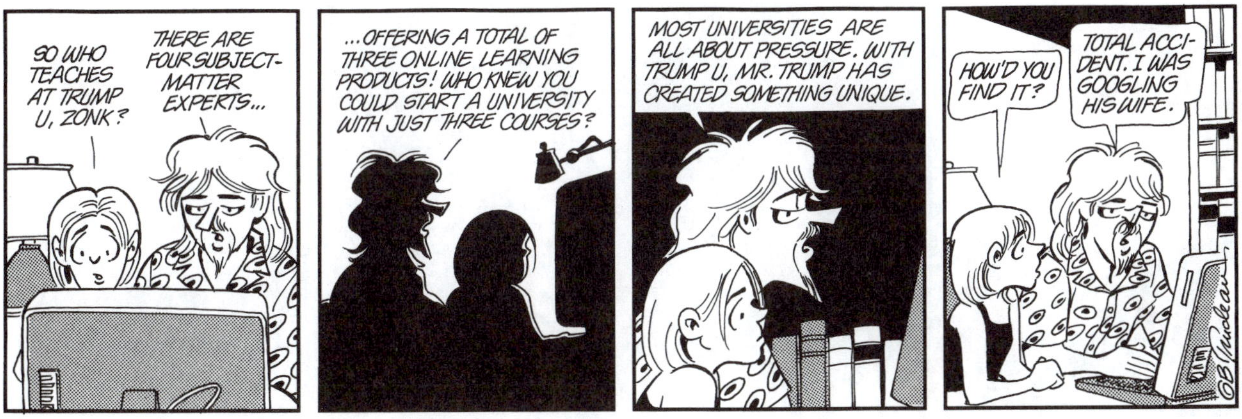
SO WHO TEACHES AT TRUMP U, ZONK?
THERE ARE FOUR SUBJECT-MATTER EXPERTS...
...OFFERING A TOTAL OF THREE ONLINE LEARNING PRODUCTS! WHO KNEW YOU COULD START A UNIVERSITY WITH JUST THREE COURSES?
MOST UNIVERSITIES ARE ALL ABOUT PRESSURE. WITH TRUMP U, MR. TRUMP HAS CREATED SOMETHING UNIQUE.
HOW'D YOU FIND IT?
TOTAL ACCI-DENT. I WAS GOOGLING HIS WIFE.
©B Trudeau

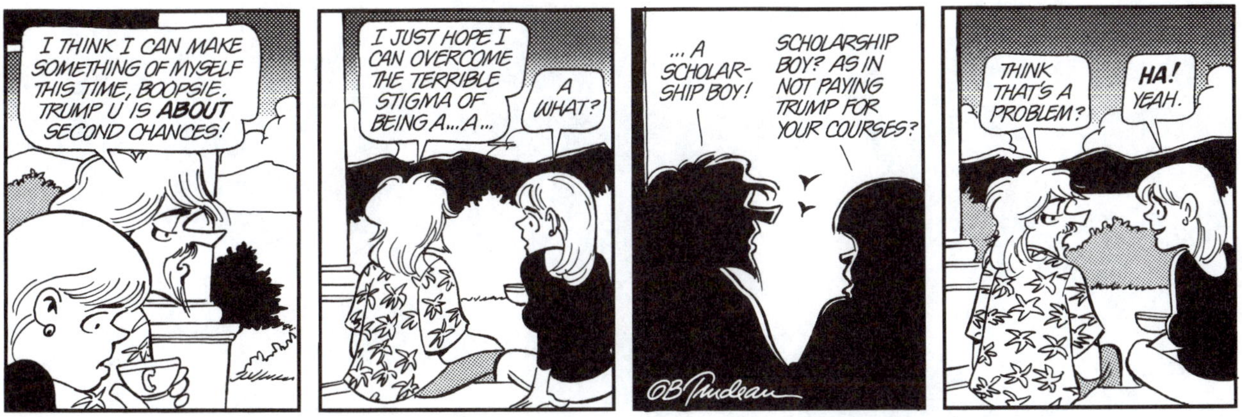
I THINK I CAN MAKE SOMETHING OF MYSELF THIS TIME, BOOPSIE. TRUMP U IS ABOUT SECOND CHANCES!
I JUST HOPE I CAN OVERCOME THE TERRIBLE STIGMA OF BEING A...A...
A WHAT?
...A SCHOLAR-SHIP BOY!
SCHOLARSHIP BOY? AS IN NOT PAYING TRUMP FOR YOUR COURSES?
©B Trudeau
THINK THAT'S A PROBLEM?
HA! YEAH.

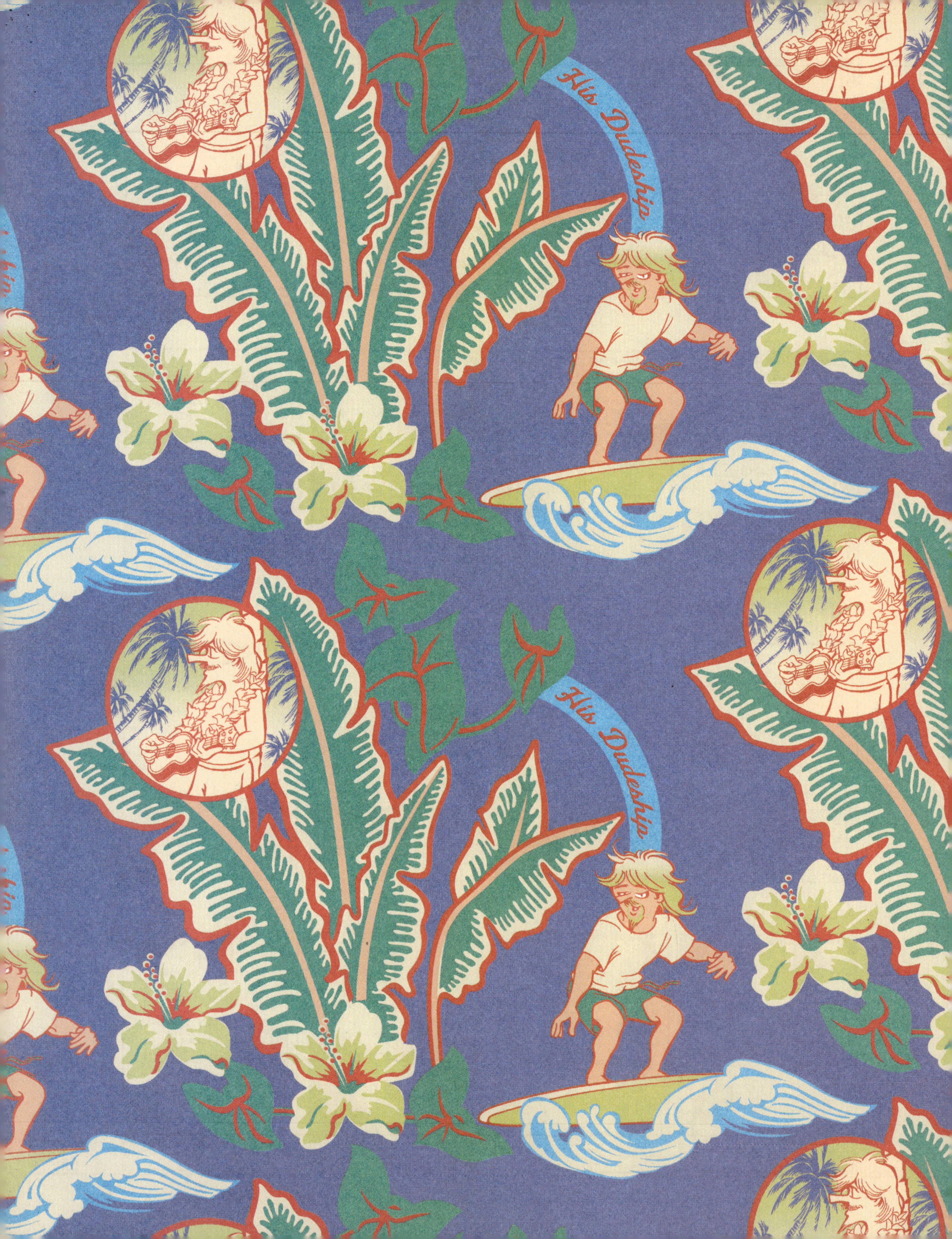
His Dudeship
His Dudeship